STRUCTURED PRODUCTS VOLUME 1

Exotic Options; Interest Rates & Currency

The Swaps & Financial Derivatives Library

Third Edition Revised

STRUCTURED PRODUCTS VOLUME 1

Exotic Options; Interest Rates & Currency

The Swaps & Financial Derivatives Library

Third Edition Revised

Satyajit Das

John Wiley & Sons (Asia) Pte Ltd

Published in 2006 by John Wiley & Sons (Asia) Pte Ltd
2 Clementi Loop, #02-01, Singapore 129809

Other Wiley Editorial Offices

John Wiley & Sons, Inc., 111 River Street, Hoboken, NJ 07030, USA
John Wiley & Sons Ltd, The Atrium, Southern Gate, Chichester P019 8SQ, England
John Wiley & Sons (Canada) Ltd, 22 Worcester Road, Rexdale, Ontario M9W 1L1, Canada
John Wiley & Sons Australia Ltd, 33 Park Road (PO Box 1226), Milton, Queensland 4064, Australia
Wiley-VCH, Pappelallee 3, 69469 Weinheim, Germany

Library of Congress Cataloging-in-Publication Data
ISBN-13   978-0-470-82166-4
ISBN-10   0-470-82166-3

Typeset in 10/13 points, Times by Cepha Imaging Pvt. Ltd
Printed in Singapore by Saik Wah Press Pte Ltd
10 9 8 7 6 5 4 3 2

Contents

Profile

Satyajit Das is an international specialist in the area of financial derivatives, risk management, and capital markets. He presents seminars on financial derivatives/risk management and capital markets in Europe, North America, Asia and Australia. He acts as a consultant to financial institutions and corporations on derivatives and financial products, risk management, and capital markets issues.

Between 1988 and 1994, Mr. Das was the Treasurer of the TNT Group, an Australian based international transport and logistics company with responsibility for the Global Treasury function, including liquidity management, corporate finance, funding/capital markets and financial risk management. Between 1977 and 1987, he worked in banking with the Commonwealth Bank of Australia, Citicorp Investment Bank and Merrill Lynch Capital Markets specialising in fund raising in domestic and international capital markets and risk management/derivative products.

In 1987, Mr. Das was a Visiting Fellow at the Centre for Studies in Money, Banking and Finance, Macquarie University.

Mr. Das is the author of *Swap Financing* (1989, IFR Publishing Limited/The Law Book Company Limited), *Swaps and Financial Derivatives: The Global Reference to Products, Pricing, Applications and Markets* (1994, IFR Publishing Limited/The Law Book Company Limited/McGraw-Hill), *Exotic Options* (1996, IFR Publishing/The Law Book Company), *Structured Notes and Derivative Embedded Securities* (1996, Euromoney Publications) and *Structured Products & Hybrid Securities – Second Edition* (2001, John Wiley & Sons). He is also the major contributor and editor of *The Global Swaps Market* (1991, IFR Publishing Limited), *Financial Derivatives & Risk Management: A Guide to the Mathematics* (1997, Law Book Company/McGraw-Hill/MacMillan Publishing), *Credit Derivatives* (1998, John Wiley & Sons) and *Credit Derivatives & Credit Linked Notes – Second Edition* (2001, John Wiley & Sons). He has published on financial derivatives, corporate finance, treasury and risk management issues in professional and applied finance journals (including Risk, Journal of International Securities Markets, Capital Market Strategies, Euromoney Corporate Finance, Futures & OTC World (FOW), Financial Products and Financial Derivatives & Risk Management).

Mr. Das holds Bachelors' degrees in Commerce (Accounting, Finance and Systems) and Law from the University of New South Wales and a Masters degree in Business Administration from the Australian Graduate School of Management.

Introduction

1 Introduction

The development of derivative instruments has emerged as perhaps the most significant aspect of capital markets in the last 20 years. Exchange-traded and over-the-counter derivatives have radically altered the practice of borrowing, investment and risk management. The changes affect the fundamental nature of financial activities and the manner in which financial transactions are undertaken.

The availability of derivative instruments provides benefits to market participants. These benefits include the ability to manage the price exposure and create exposure synthetically to assets. There are additional benefits in terms of enhancing the liquidity of the underlying asset markets and in reducing the volatility of asset prices. The availability of these types of instruments enhances the attractiveness of investment (both direct and portfolio) in asset markets.

Derivative markets exhibit the following characteristics:

- Derivatives have rapidly expanded to cover a variety of asset classes. Derivatives are available in debt/interest rates, currency, equities and commodities (particularly energy, metal and agricultural markets). Derivatives have also expanded into other markets including previously non-tradeable assets. This includes credit risk, inflation risk, insurance, weather risk, property, bandwidth/telephone minutes, macro-economic indexes and emissions quotas.
- The product range has developed. Non-generic and structured products increasingly complement standard derivative product structures. For example, exotic/non-standard options have emerged as a powerful instrument for risk structuring and transformation.
- The range of market participants is broad. Participants include financial institutions, corporations, investors (both institutional and retail), supra-national entities and governments. A number of dealers (primarily banks and securities dealers) are active in trading in derivative products providing liquidity. Derivatives are used for a wide range of funding, investment and risk management applications. Derivative elements are frequently embedded in structured

investment products for a wide range of investors. Derivatives are available in developed markets and increasingly in emerging markets.

2 Background and Objectives of Book

Structured Products Volume 1 (The Swaps & Financial Derivatives Library) – Third Edition Revised is the successor to *Swaps & Financial Derivatives*. This book was first published in 1989 (as *Swap Financing*). A second edition was published in 1994 (as *Swaps & Financial Derivatives – Second Edition* (in most of the world) and *Swaps & Derivative Financing – Second Edition* (in the USA)). The changes in the market since the publication of the second edition have necessitated this third edition.

Structured Products Volume 1 – Third Edition Revised is not an updated version of the previous edition. The book has been completely rewritten and reorganised. Extensive new material has been added to all sections to update existing areas of coverage. In addition, several new chapters covering areas of market development have been included. This has resulted in a significant expansion in the size of the text. *Structured Products Volume 1 – Third Edition Revised* is more than double the size of its predecessor. This has necessitated the book being structured as a four-volume work.

Structured Products Volume 1 – Third Edition Revised is designed to bring together all aspects of derivative instruments within a cohesive and integrated framework in a single work. The text covers all aspects of derivatives including:

- Design of derivative instruments.
- Pricing, valuation and trading/hedging of derivatives.
- Management of market, credit and other risk associated with derivatives trading.
- Documentation, accounting, taxation and regulatory aspects of derivatives.
- Applications of derivatives.
- Different types of derivative structures including synthetic asset structures using derivatives, exotic options, interest rate/currency, equity, commodity, credit and new derivative markets.
- Impact of electronic trading markets on derivative markets.
- Evolution and prospects of derivative markets.

Structured Products Volume 1 – Third Edition Revised is designed to be a comprehensive reference work for practitioners and students of derivative instruments and markets. It covers all aspects of the market. The focus is global, with coverage of exchange-traded markets, over-the-counter markets and all asset classes (including emerging asset classes).

The approach taken is practical rather than theoretical. Derivatives are examined from the different perspective of the investor, the issuer and the dealers/traders in these instruments. The emphasis is on *actual* transactions that are stripped down to analyse and illustrate the dynamics of individual structures and to understand the types of products available.

The book is intended for bankers/dealers, investors and issuers seeking either an understanding of the market or a reference work on the market. The book will also appeal to regulators, analysts, accountants, lawyers and consultants active in advising market participants involved in or contemplating involvement in these products. It will be of use to academics and students interested in derivatives.

The text is structured either to be read through from start to finish or, for the more experienced user of these products, to be used as a reference source where individual sections are read as required.

3 Structure of Book

The book is structured as follows:
- **Part 1** focuses on applications of derivatives. There are 3 chapters structured as follows:
  - **Chapter 1** sets out the generic applications of derivatives.
  - **Chapter 2** sets out the applications of exchange-traded derivatives (futures/ options) and over-the-counter derivatives (forwards, options and swaps).
  - **Chapter 3** sets out the use of swaps in funding transactions in new issue or funding arbitrage.

- **Part 2** outlines the structure of synthetic assets using derivatives. There is one chapter. **Chapter 4** sets out the structure of asset swaps, structured notes and repackaged assets created using special purpose vehicles.

- **Part 3** describes exotic options. There are 8 chapters structured as follows:
  - **Chapter 5** sets out an overview of exotic options.
  - **Chapter 6** sets out packaged products using combinations of forwards and options.
  - **Chapter 7** sets out path dependent options including average rate, lookback, ladder and swing structures.

- **Chapter 8** sets out time dependent options including preference/chooser, cliquet and forward start structures.
- **Chapter 9** sets out limit dependent options including barrier (knock-in/knock-out options) and defined exercise structures.
- **Chapter 10** sets out payoff modified structures including binary/digital and range/touch structures.
- **Chapter 11** sets out multifactor structures including best-of/worst-of, spread, basket and quanto structures.
- **Chapter 12** sets out the structure of volatility swaps and options.

- **Part 4** focuses on non-generic derivative structures used in interest rate and currency markets. There are 8 chapters structured as follows:
  - **Chapter 13** sets out non-generic swap structures including overnight index, amortising, delayed start, forward and cash flow modified swaps.
  - **Chapter 14** sets out the structure of basis (floating-to-floating) swaps including index, arrears reset and index differential swaps.
  - **Chapter 15** sets out the structure of swaptions (options on interest rate swaps).
  - **Chapter 16** sets out the structure of callable bonds.
  - **Chapter 17** sets out the structure of constant maturity (CMT) products.
  - **Chapter 18** sets out the structure of index amortising products.
  - **Chapter 19** sets out various interest rate structured products including reverse/inverse floating rate notes and range/accrual products.
  - **Chapter 20** sets out various currency linked structured products including dual currency bonds and currency option linked notes.

Each chapter includes selected references designed to allow readers to expand their knowledge of individual subjects as required. There is a detailed index to facilitate use of the work as a reference source.

4 Contributions

Structured Products Volume 1 – Third Edition Revised has a number of inclusions:
- There are Chapters on accounting and taxation aspects of derivatives contributed by PricewaterhouseCoopers. I would like to thank PricewaterhouseCoopers and the individual authors within the firm for contributing the Chapters. In particular, I would like to thank John Masters for arranging the participation of PricewaterhouseCoopers. I would also like to thank Jacqui Fawcett/Jane Docherty for coordinating the project.

- There is a Chapter on documentation of legal issues relating to derivatives contributed by Ben Bowden of Linklaters. I would like to thank Ben Bowden for his participation.
- Bloomberg agreed to allow a number of screen shots to be re-printed. I would like to thank Wendy de Cruz, Amanda Dobbie and Craig Davies for their assistance.
- Several authors and organisations agreed to make available material to be reproduced in the Work. The authors and organisations are acknowledged within the text itself.
- Several individuals read portions of the text and offered helpful comments. The individuals are acknowledged within the text itself.

5 Publisher

I would like to thank Law Book Company/IFR Publishing/McGraw-Hill for publishing the previous edition of this Book.

I would like to thank the Publishers of this Edition – John Wiley – for agreeing to publish the third edition of the Book. I would like to thank Nick Wallwork for agreeing to publish the work. I would like to thank Karen Noack who copy edited the book. I would also like to thank Hot Fusion for the cover design. I would particularly like to acknowledge the work of Selvamalar Manoharan who worked extremely hard to edit and co-ordinate the publication of the book.

6 Personal Acknowledgments

The first edition of *Swaps/Financial Derivatives* published in 1989 was the first book I wrote. Since that time, there have been 10 publishing projects including *Structured Products Volume 1 – Third Edition Revised.* Each of these books has only been possible because of the faith, support and understanding of three individuals – my parents (my father Sukumar Das and my mother Aparna Das) and my friend Jade Novakovic. I would like to thank my parents Sukumar and Aparna Das for their support and encouragement in my work. It is their sacrifices and efforts that made my life and work possible. I would like to thank my friend Jade Novakovic. Her belief, support, patience and understanding made this Book, like the others before it, possible. My debt to these three people is immeasurable. I can never repay my debt to my mother, father and Jade. This book is dedicated to these three people.

Satyajit Das

This Book is dedicated to

My friend Jade Novakovic

My mother Aparna Das

My father Sukumar Das

DERIVATIVE
APPLICATIONS

1

Applications of Derivative Products[1]

1 Overview

Derivative products are principally used to transfer risk or replicate positions in the underlying asset. Transactions combining positions in the asset and derivatives or cash and derivatives can be used to reduce risk or acquire asset exposure. In this Part of the Book, the major applications of derivative products (primarily the major building block products (forwards, swaps and options)) are discussed[2]. This Chapter sets out the general applications of derivatives and the principal drivers of derivative product applications. Chapter 2 sets out some examples of applications of exchange-traded and OTC derivative products. Chapter 3 outlines the concept of new issue arbitrage that is a special application of derivatives combined with debt issues to improve efficiency of funding.

The structure of this Chapter is as follows:
- Key applications of derivative products are outlined.
- The structure of risk transfer using derivative building blocks (forwards and options) is described. This includes discussion of generic applications/strategies using forwards and options.

---

[1] Derivatives applications/strategies for the use of forwards, futures, swaps, options etc., in this Chapter are described in general terms only. The Chapter does not purport to be complete or comprehensive. In particular, the description of general strategies is not intended to be a recommendation of a specific strategy/approach or particular solution to a specific risk problem. Intending users of derivatives should seek full advice from professional advisers in respect of any transactions planned.

[2] For discussion of the application of derivative products, see Smithson, Charles (1998) Managing Financial Risk – Third Edition; McGraw-Hill, New York.

- The use of derivative products in risk management is considered. This focuses on the types of financial risk. It also focuses on the linkage between risk management and value including the rationale for hedging.
- Key applications of derivatives by different types of entities (corporations, financial institutions and investors) are outlined.

The focus of this Chapter and Chapter 2 is on the *generic* framework for the application of derivative products. The focus is on the principal uses of key building block derivative products such as forwards/swaps and options. Specific applications of non-generic derivative structures or derivatives on different asset classes are set out in subsequent Chapters where the individual products are discussed. These applications represent more complex and specialised uses of derivatives within the general framework outlined in this Chapter.

2   Derivative Products – Key Applications[3]

The key factors that drive financial derivative applications include[4]:
- Ability to isolate and trade individual risks or return attributes of assets *independent of trading in the underlying asset itself.*
- Separation of the price movements from liquidity/cash investment, enabling the trading of risk without any cash investment.
- Ability to construct synthetic assets and liabilities from combinations of cash assets and derivatives.

The features allow derivatives to be used to isolate risks or attributes of assets. This allows:
- Separation of the management of/trading in the price risk of an asset from trading in the asset itself.
- Creation of desired combination of risks through synthetic asset and liability structures.

---

[3]   See Smithson, Charles W. "A LEGO® Approach to Financial Engineering: An Introduction to Forwards, Futures, Swaps and Options" (Winter 1987) Midland Corporate Finance Journal 16–28; Smith, Donald J "The Arithmetic of Financial Engineering" (Winter 1989) Journal of Applied Corporate Finance 49–58; Bernasconi, Jean-Luc "Derivatives – Another Look at the Basics" (1994) Swiss Bank Corporation Prospects – Special Edition 5–11.

[4]   See Das, Satyajit (2004) Derivative Products & Pricing; John Wiley & Sons (Asia), Singapore at Chapter 1.

The application of derivatives to manage risk with forward contracts can be readily illustrated as follows:

- The holder of an asset can minimise exposure to price fluctuations in the asset by selling the asset forward. During the term of the forward, changes in value of the asset position will be offset by changes in the value of the forward sale, reflecting the opposite direction of the two positions. This enables the holder to minimise risk without the need to sell the asset. This allows the minimisation of the asset price exposure with no change in the holder's liquidity position.
- An entity with a short position can hedge its price exposure by entering into a forward purchase. The changes in value of the short position will be offset by changes in the value of the forward purchase. This enables the entity to reduce risk without the necessity to commit capital to purchase the asset or finance the position until the required date in the future.

The use of options is similar. Options allow the separation of liquidity and price risk in a manner similar to that allowed by forwards. Options also allow the creation of asymmetric risk positions. This can be illustrated as follows:

- The holder of the asset can minimise price risk through a purchase of a put option. The put option will effectively reduce the holder's risk of loss from a decline in the price of the asset. The holder will maintain exposure to any price appreciation of the asset. This benefit will be achieved in exchange for the payment of the option premium. The premium will have the effect of reducing the return to the holder of the asset.
- The entity with the short position can hedge its price risk through the purchase of a call option. The call option will minimise the risk of the short position from an increase in the price of the asset. The entity will maintain exposure to any decrease in the price of the asset. The option premium paid will have the impact of reducing the return to the entity on its short position.

Options have a number of additional benefits. These include the ability to create structured risk reward profile (by altering the strike price of the option or using combinations of options), selling options to generate income/enhance earnings and trade volatility. Each of the applications is considered below.

The applications identified are relevant irrespective of whether the instrument is exchange-traded or OTC. Futures and options can be used to hedge in a manner similar to that described above. The applications of swaps and OTC options (currency options and cap/floors) are driven by the fact that the instruments are essentially portfolios of forward contracts or options.

Swaps have additional applications that derive from their cash flow characteristics. Interest rate and currency swaps are frequently used in conjunction with debt issues to synthesise assets or liabilities. These synthetic structures are designed to allow access to markets or create assets and liabilities with superior economics to those available directly[5].

3   Generic Risk Transfer

3.1   Overview

In this Section, the basic concept of risk transfer is outlined. Two examples (based on generic positions) outline the fundamental structure of hedging. Derivatives (forwards and options) are used to hedge inherent exposures. Options are also used to create structured risk profiles.

The underlying economic driver of generic risk transfer is the relationship between assets, forwards and options captured by put call parity[6]. This relationship forms the basis of all risk transfer possibilities[7].

3.2   Examples

Exhibit 1.1 sets out an example of hedging of a short asset position. **Exhibit 1.2** sets out an example of hedging a long asset position.

The analysis illustrates the following key aspects of the hedging/risk transfer process:

- Derivative transactions can be used to rearrange underlying risk exposures. They are generally used to align risk exposures to the entity's required risk profile. Different combinations of derivatives can be used to align the risk position to the required risk profile, creating different payoffs.
- Use of derivative transactions entails assumptions regarding expected changes in underlying prices. This can entail expectations about directional changes in asset prices (forwards) or volatility of asset prices (options).

---

[5]   See discussion on new issue arbitrage (Chapter 3) and asset swaps (Chapter 4).

[6]   See Das, Satyajit (2004) Derivative Products & Pricing; John Wiley & Sons (Asia), Singapore at Chapters 1 and 7.

[7]   See Smithson, Charles W. "A LEGO® Approach to Financial Engineering: An Introduction to Forwards, Futures, Swaps and Options" (Winter 1987) Midland Corporate Finance Journal 16–28.

3.3 Forwards – Applications

The basic applications of forwards revolve around the following transactions:
- **Long hedge** – this entails a forward purchase of the underlying asset to cover a short position.
- **Short hedge** – this entails a forward sale of the underlying asset to cover a long position.

Exhibit 1.1   Risk Transfer – Short Asset Case

1. Overview

Assume a purchaser of a commodity required as an input to its product. The purchaser has a short position in the commodity. The following analysis focuses on the potential alternative ways of managing this risk exposure.

2. Risk Exposure/Hedging Alternatives

The purchaser has a short position in the commodity. This reflects the fact that it is exposed to increases in the price of the commodity. As prices increase, the purchaser suffers losses as it has to pay higher prices.

The purchaser has the following hedging alternatives available:
- **Do nothing** – by taking no action, the purchaser would remain exposed to increases in the commodity price. The purchaser would also retain the ability to benefit from decreases in the commodity price as that would have the effect of reducing the purchase price of the commodity.
- **Forward purchase** – this would entail the purchaser entering into a forward purchase of the commodity. The effect of the forward purchase would be to fix the purchase price of the commodity at the contracted price. This would eliminate exposure to changes in the commodity price. The purchaser would minimise exposure to increases in the commodity price, but would also forgo the ability to benefit from decreases in the commodity price. The forward would not entail any cash commitment at the time of entry into the forward. This means that no cash would be required[8]. This would enable the purchaser to match its cash flows to its normal cash flow pattern where it would pay for the commodity at the required time.
- **Purchase call option** – this would entail the purchaser buying a call option on the commodity. The option would convey the right to purchase the commodity at the strike price of the option. This would have the effect of placing a maximum price for the purchase of the commodity. As the option does not have to be exercised, the purchaser would be able to benefit from commodity prices lower than the strike price. The purchaser would therefore minimise its risk to increases in the commodity price, but would retain its ability to benefit from lower commodity prices.

---

[8] For simplicity, no collateral or margin requirements have been assumed.

The purchaser would be required to pay a premium for the option. Other than the option premium, the purchaser would not incur any cash flow requirements until the maturity of the option. This would enable the purchaser to match cash flows to its normal cash flow pattern where it would pay for the commodity at the required time.

• **Sell put options** – this would entail the purchaser selling a put option on the commodity. The option would mean that the purchaser would have sold the right (to the buyer of the option) to sell the commodity to the purchaser at the strike price. The sold option would have the effect of placing a minimum price on the purchase of the commodity. This reflects the fact that the option would be exercised where the commodity price is below the strike price. The sold option would not provide protection for the purchaser when the commodity price increased. This is because the option would not be exercised. The purchaser would therefore remain exposed to increases in the price of the commodity. The purchaser would have forgone its ability to benefit from lower commodity prices. The purchaser would receive a premium for the sold option. This option premium would have the effect of reducing the purchaser's price of the commodity. Where the option is exercised (commodity price below the strike price), the effective price paid would be the strike price less the option premium received. Where the option is not exercised (commodity price above the strike price), the effective price would be the market price of the commodity at the maturity of the option less the option premium received. The option premium received would only insulate the purchaser from price increases up to the amount of the premium received. Other than the option premium, the purchaser would not incur any cash flows until the maturity of the option. This would enable the purchaser to match cash flows to its normal cash flow pattern, where it would pay for the commodity at the required time.

The hedging alternatives summarised exhibit the following features:
• The hedging structures are created using basic building block products (forwards and options). More complex hedging structures are structured using a similar approach. This reflects the fact that all derivative instruments are fundamentally forwards and options.
• The hedging structures are applicable irrespective of whether the instruments are exchange-traded or OTC. For example, the forward could be structured as a futures contract or a commodity swap. Similarly, the options could be structured as a cap (call option) or a floor (put option).
• The sold put option alternative is sometimes not considered a "true" hedge. This reflects the fact that it does not provide protection beyond the amount of the premium received when the commodity price increases. It is an alternative strategy to minimise the purchase price where the market price remains relatively stable. It is also necessary in this regard to differentiate between *naked* and *covered* option selling strategies. The option sold in this case is covered. This is because the commodity purchased, where the option is exercised against the purchaser, would have been purchased in any case. The option requires it to be purchased at the strike price (above the market price at the time of exercise). This should be contrasted with a naked option that is written with no natural underlying long or short position in the asset.

The hedging alternatives are summarised in the diagram below[9]:

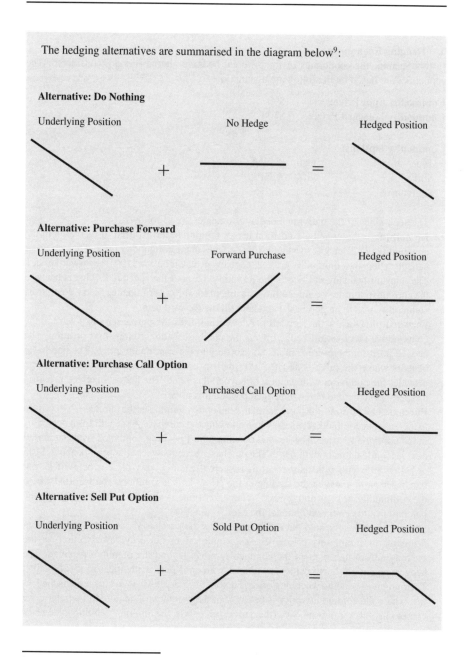

Alternative: Do Nothing

Underlying Position   No Hedge   Hedged Position

Alternative: Purchase Forward

Underlying Position   Forward Purchase   Hedged Position

Alternative: Purchase Call Option

Underlying Position   Purchased Call Option   Hedged Position

Alternative: Sell Put Option

Underlying Position   Sold Put Option   Hedged Position

---

[9]   The diagram depicts pay-offs for each strategy. For ease of exposition, only the position payoff is displayed. The horizontal axis (asset price) and vertical axis (gain/loss) is not displayed.

3. Hedging Economics

In this Section, the economics of the different hedging alternatives are considered. The economics are based on the following assumptions:

Commodity Spot Price:	$90
Commodity Forward Price:	$100

Commodity Options:

Type	Call	Put
Strike Price	$100	$100
Premium	$5	$5

The economics of the individual hedging strategies are as follows:

- **Do nothing** – the unhedged position leaves the purchaser exposed to increases in the commodity price but able to benefit from declines in the commodity price. The purchaser benefits where the commodity price at the relevant date is below $100 (the forward price). The relevant benchmark price is the forward price, not the spot price. This is because the current spot price would require adjustment for the cost of finance (carry cost) if the commodity was to be purchased and held till the forward date.
- **Forward purchase** – the forward purchase minimises the purchaser's exposure to the commodity. The forward hedge offsets the purchaser's underlying short position. The hedged position therefore exhibits no exposure to the commodity price. The purchaser benefits where the price is above $100 (the forward price). This is because the hedge provides the purchaser with gains at or beyond this price. The hedge, in effect, provides a superior outcome to being unhedged beyond this price.
- **Purchase call option** – the purchase of the call option minimises the purchaser's exposure to increases in commodity prices, while allowing the purchaser to benefit from decreases in the commodity price. The hedged position (short position combined with purchased call) is identical to a bought put[10]. The purchaser benefits where the price is above $105 or below $95. This reflects the fact that where the commodity price is below $95, the purchaser participates in the decline in the price. This also reflects the fact that where the commodity price is above $105, the market price is above the effective cost to the purchaser of the commodity under the exercised option.
- **Sell put option** – the sold put option minimises the purchaser's ability to benefit from decreases in commodity prices. The sold option does not provide protection for the purchaser from increases in the commodity price beyond the premium received. The hedged position (short position combined with sold put) is identical to a sold call[11]. The purchaser benefits where the price is below $105 or above $95. This reflects the fact that where the commodity price is below $95, the purchaser is required to purchase the commodity at a price of $95 (the strike price less the option premium received),

---

[10] This reflects put-call parity; see Das, Satyajit (2004) Derivative Products & Pricing; John Wiley & Sons (Asia), Singapore at Chapters 1 and 7.

[11] This reflects put-call parity; see Das, Satyajit (2004) Derivative Products & Pricing; John Wiley & Sons (Asia), Singapore at Chapters 1 and 7.

above the market price of the commodity. This also reflects the fact that where the price is above $105, the purchaser's actual cost of acquisition (market price adjusted for the premium received) exceeds the forward price of the commodity.

Several aspects of the economics of the different hedging strategies should be noted:
- Each individual hedge embodies inherent expectations of future market prices. This implies that the purchaser is required to formulate expectations of the future commodity market price in order to select between competing strategies. The no hedge and forward hedge strategies entail directional views on the commodity price at the relevant future date. The no hedge strategy would be most effective in the case where the commodity price was below the forward price. The forward hedge strategy would be most effective where the commodity price was above the forward price. The option strategies entail views on the volatility of commodity prices. In specific terms, the options embody views on actual volatility relative to the implied volatility used to price the options. For economic success, the strategies rely on whether actual volatility exceeds the implied volatility (bought option), or actual volatility is less than the implied volatility (sold option). The bought call option is most effective where the commodity price is volatile. The sold put option is most effective where the commodity price is relatively stable.
- The forward hedge strategy is deceptive in that it appears to imply that the purchaser has *no* exposure to commodity price fluctuations. This is misleading. The purchaser has no exposure to commodity prices. It is locked into the forward price. In the event that commodity prices fall, the purchaser will incur above market prices for the commodity. This may affect its competitive position. If the purchaser operates in a competitive market, then where its competitors are unhedged, the purchaser (because of its higher cost structure) may suffer a loss of market share or diminished profits/losses if an unhedged competitor cuts product prices.

The impact of each of the strategies is set out in the graphs below:

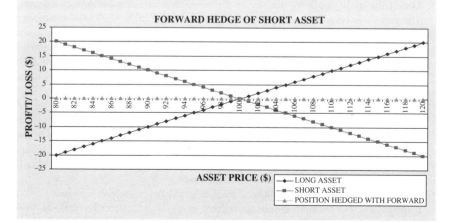

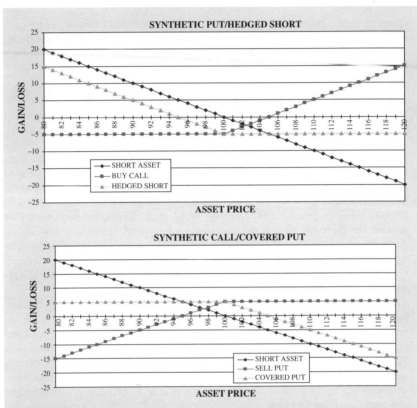

4. Other Hedging Alternatives

Hedging strategies that are variations or combinations of the above generic strategies are also feasible. These include:

- **Out-of-the-money options** – the options discussed above are struck at the forward rates. The purchaser could customise its hedging strategy by purchasing out-of-the-money options. This would entail buying a call option with a strike of say $110 at a lower premium (say $2). This would have the effect of protecting the purchaser from price increases above $112 and allowing it to participate in decreases in prices below $98. This would be analogous to purchasing *insurance* against a large unexpected increase in commodity prices.

- **Collars** – the bought call and sold put could be combined in a collar. This may have the advantage of eliminating the cost of the option, as the sold put could be used to finance the purchase of the call. The purchaser would be protected against an increase in the commodity price above $105 (the strike price of the purchased call option) but would only be able to participate in price declines to $95 (the strike price of the sold put option). The impact of the collar is set out in the graph below.

- **Option combinations** – the option strategies could be expanded to include option combinations. For example, the purchaser could have bought a call option (strike of $100 and premium of $5) and simultaneously sold a call option (strike of $110 and a premium of $2). This would have the effect of limiting the purchaser protection to an increase in the commodity price up to $110 (excluding the premium cost). If the commodity price increases beyond this price, then the purchaser would be exposed to higher prices. The effect of the call spread is a lower net cost ($3 versus $5) of the hedge.

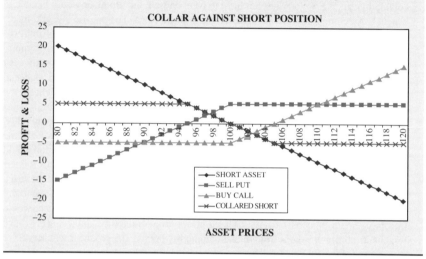

COLLAR AGAINST SHORT POSITION

ASSET PRICES

Exhibit 1.2   Risk Transfer – Long Asset Case

1. Overview

Assume a producer of a commodity seeks to manage its exposure to the price of the commodity. The producer has a long position in the commodity. The following analysis focuses on the alternative ways of managing this risk exposure.

2. Risk Exposure/Hedging Alternatives

The producer has a long position in the commodity. This reflects the fact that it is exposed to decreases in the price of the commodity. As the commodity price decreases, the producer suffers losses as it has to sell the commodity at lower prices.

The producer has the following hedging alternatives available:

- **Do nothing** – By taking no action, the producer would remain exposed to decreases in the commodity price. The producer would also retain the ability to benefit from increases in the commodity price that would have the effect of increasing the price of the commodity received when sold.
- **Forward sale** – this would entail the producer entering into a forward sale of the commodity. The effect of this forward sale would be to fix the sale price of the commodity at the contracted price. This would eliminate exposure to changes in the commodity price. The producer would minimise exposure to decreases in the commodity price, but would forgo the ability to benefit from increases in the commodity price. The forward would not entail any cash flow at the time of entry into the forward. This means that no cash

would be generated[12]. This would enable the producer to replicate its normal cash flow pattern where it would receive cash for the commodity at the time of the sale.

- **Purchase put option** – this would entail the producer buying a put option on the commodity. The option would convey the right to sell the commodity at the strike price of the option. This would have the effect of placing a minimum price on the sale of the commodity. As the option does not have to be exercised, the producer would be able to benefit from commodity prices higher than the strike price. The producer would therefore minimise its risk to decreases in the commodity price, but would retain its ability to benefit from higher commodity prices. The producer would be required to pay a premium for the option. Other than the option premium, the producer would not incur any cash flow requirements until the maturity of the option. This would enable the producer to match cash flows to its normal cash flow pattern where it would receive payment for the commodity at the time of the sale.

- **Sell call options** – this would entail the producer selling a call option on the commodity. The option would mean that the producer would have sold the right (to the buyer of the option) to buy the commodity from the producer at the strike price. The sold option would have the effect of placing a maximum price on the sale of the commodity. This reflects the fact that the option would be exercised where the commodity price is above the strike price. The sold option would not provide protection for the producer if the commodity price decreased. This is because the option would not be exercised. The producer would therefore remain exposed to decreases in the price of the commodity, and would also have forgone its ability to benefit from higher commodity prices. The producer would receive a premium for the sold option. This option premium would have the effect of increasing the producer's price of the commodity. Where the option is exercised (commodity price above the strike price), the effective price received would be the strike price plus the option premium received. Where the option is not exercised (commodity price below the strike price), the effective price would be the market price of the commodity at the maturity of the option plus the option premium received. The option premium received would only insulate the producer from price decreases up to the amount of the premium received. Other than the option premium, the producer would not have any cash flows until the maturity of the option. This would enable the producer to match cash flows to its normal cash flow pattern where it would receive payment for the commodity at the time of sale.

The hedging alternatives summarised exhibit the following features:
- The hedging structures are created using basic building block products (forwards and options). More complex hedging structures are structured using a similar approach. This reflects the fact that all derivative instruments are fundamentally forwards and options.
- The hedging structures are applicable, irrespective of whether the instruments are exchange-traded or OTC. For example, the forward could be structured as a futures contract or a commodity swap. Similarly, the options could be structured as a floor (put option) and a cap (call option).
- The sold call option alternative is sometimes not considered a "true" hedge. This reflects the fact that it does not provide protection beyond the amount of the premium received where the commodity price decreases. It is an alternative strategy to maximise the

---

[12] For simplicity, no collateral or margin requirements have been assumed.

purchase price where the market price remains relatively stable. It is also necessary in this regard to differentiate between *naked* and *covered* option selling strategies. The option sold in this case is covered. This is because the commodity to be delivered where the option is exercised against the producer would have been available for sale in any case. The option requires it to be sold at the strike price (below the market price at the time of exercise). This should be contrasted with a naked option that is written with no natural underlying long position in the asset.

The hedging alternatives are summarised in the diagram below[13]:

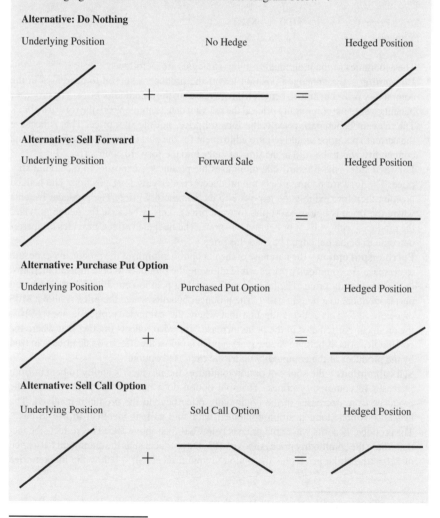

Alternative: Do Nothing

Underlying Position · · · No Hedge · · · Hedged Position

Alternative: Sell Forward

Underlying Position · · · Forward Sale · · · Hedged Position

Alternative: Purchase Put Option

Underlying Position · · · Purchased Put Option · · · Hedged Position

Alternative: Sell Call Option

Underlying Position · · · Sold Call Option · · · Hedged Position

---

[13] The diagram depicts pay-offs for each strategy. For ease of exposition, only the position payoff is displayed. The horizontal axis (asset price) and vertical axis (gain/loss) is not displayed.

3. Hedging Economics

In this Section, the economics of the different hedging alternatives are considered. The economics are based on the following assumptions:

Commodity Spot Price: $90
Commodity Forward Price: $100

Commodity Options:

Type	Call	Put
Strike Price	$100	$100
Premium	$5	$5

The economics of the individual hedging strategies are as follows:

- **Do nothing** – the unhedged position leaves the producer exposed to decreases in the commodity price but able to benefit from increases in the commodity price. The producer benefits where the commodity price at the relevant date is above $100 (the forward price). The relevant benchmark price is the forward price, not the spot price. This is because the current spot price would require adjustment for the cost of finance (carry cost) if the commodity was to be sold at the time of entry into the forward contract.

- **Forward sale** – the forward sale minimises the producer's exposure to the commodity price. The forward hedge offsets the producer's underlying long position. The hedged position therefore exhibits no exposure to the commodity price. The producer benefits where the price is below $100 (the forward price). This is because the hedge provides the producer with gains at or beyond this price. The hedge, in effect, provides a superior outcome to being unhedged beyond this price.

- **Purchase put option** – the purchase of the put option minimises the producer's exposure to decreases in commodity prices while allowing the producer to benefit from increases in the commodity price. The hedged position (long position combined with purchased put) is identical to a bought call[14]. The producer benefits where the price is above $105 or below $95. This reflects the fact that where the commodity price is above $105, the producer participates in the price increase. This also reflects the fact that where the commodity price is below $95, the market price is below the effective sale price achieved by the producer of the commodity under the exercised option.

- **Sell call options** – the sold call option minimises the producer's ability to benefit from increases in commodity prices. The sold option does not provide protection for the producer from decreases in the commodity price beyond the premium received. The hedged position (long position combined with sold call) is identical to a sold put[15]. The producer benefits where the price is below $105 or above $95. This reflects the fact that where the commodity price is above $105, the producer sells the commodity at a price of $105 (the strike price plus the option premium received) – below the market price

---

[14] This reflects put-call parity; see Das, Satyajit (2004) Derivative Products & Pricing; John Wiley & Sons (Asia), Singapore at Chapters 1 and 7.

[15] This reflects put-call parity; see Das, Satyajit (2004) Derivative Products & Pricing; John Wiley & Sons (Asia), Singapore at Chapters 1 and 7.

of the commodity. This also reflects the fact that where the commodity price is below $95, the producer sells the commodity at the market price plus the option premium received – below the forward price of the commodity.

Several aspects of the economics of the different hedging strategies should be noted:
- Each individual hedge embodies an inherent expectation of future market prices. This implies that the producer is required to formulate expectations on the future commodity market price in order to select between competing strategies. The no hedge and forward hedge strategies entail directional views on the commodity price at the relevant future date. The no hedge strategy would be most effective in the case where the commodity price was above the forward price. The forward hedge strategy would be most effective where the commodity price was below the forward price. The option strategies entail views on the volatility of commodity prices. In specific terms, the options embody views on actual volatility relative to the implied volatility used to price the options. For economic success, the strategies rely on whether actual volatility exceeds the implied volatility (bought option), or actual volatility is less than the implied volatility (sold option). The bought put option is most effective where the commodity price is volatile. The sold call option is most effective where the commodity price is relatively stable.
- The forward hedge strategy is deceptive in that it appears to imply that the producer has *no* exposure to commodity price fluctuations. This is misleading. The producer has no exposure to commodity prices. It is locked into the forward price. In the event that commodity prices increase, the producer will incur below market prices for the commodity. This may affect its competitive position. If the producer operates in a competitive market, then where its competitors are unhedged, the producer will show diminished profits/losses relative to an unhedged competitor. This may allow the competitor to cut prices to increase market share or use higher profits to increase capacity.

The impact of each of the strategies is set out in the graphs below:

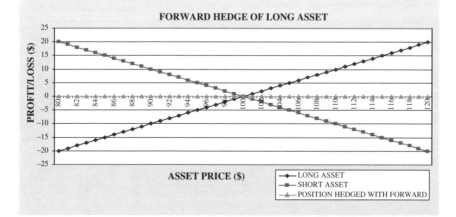

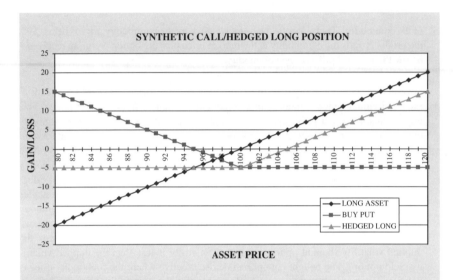

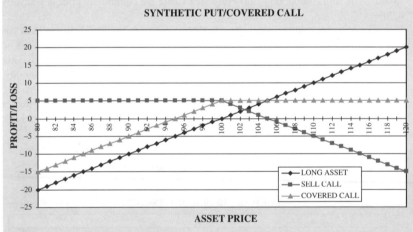

4. Other Hedging Alternatives

Hedging strategies that are variations or combinations of the above generic strategies are also feasible. These include:

• **Out-of-the-money options** – the options discussed above are struck at the forward rates. The producer could customise its hedging strategy by purchasing out-of-the-money options. This would entail buying a put option with a strike of say $90 at a lower premium (say $2). This would have the effect of protecting the producer from price decreases above $90 and allowing it to participate in increases in prices above $88. This would be analogous to purchasing *insurance* against a large unexpected movement in commodity prices.

- **Collars** – the bought call and sold put could be combined in a collar. This could have the advantage of eliminating the cost of the option, as the sold call may finance the purchase of the put. The producer would be protected against a decrease in the commodity price below $95 (the strike price of the purchased put option) but would only be able to participate in price increases to $105 (the strike price of the sold call option). The impact of the collar is set out in the graph below.
- **Option combinations** – the option strategies could be expanded to include option combinations. For example, the producer could have bought a put option (strike of $100 and premium of $5) and simultaneously sold a put option (strike of $90 and a premium of $2). This would have the effect of limiting the producer's protection to a decrease in the commodity price up to a price of $90 (excluding the premium cost). If the commodity price increases beyond this price, then the producer would be exposed to higher prices. The effect of the call spread is a lower net cost ($3 versus $5) of the hedge.

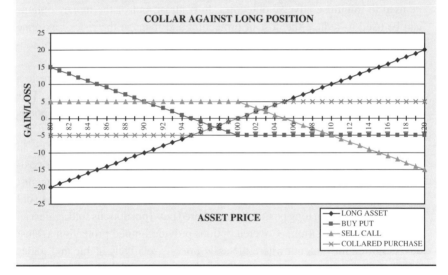

The principal uses of forwards include:
- **Risk transfer** – this covers using forwards to reduce exposure to price movements. For example, an entity with an underlying long (short) position can hedge its exposure by entering into a forward sale (purchase).
- **Replication** – this entails using forwards to synthesise positions in the underlying asset or cash. For example, by entering into a forward sale the holder of an asset minimises exposure to the price of the underlying asset. The combined position is equivalent to a position in cash (to the maturity of the forward). Similarly, an entity can synthetically create an exposure to the underlying asset by holding a cash investment and entering into a forward purchase.

The combined position will have the same economics as an outright purchase of the asset.

3.4   Options – Applications

3.4.1   General

The basic applications of options are based around the following objectives:

- **Asymmetric exposure** – this entails using bought options to protect against adverse price movements. For example, an entity with a long (short) position can hedge its price risk by buying a put (call) option to minimise its exposure to decreasing (increasing) prices. The level of protection may be customised by adjusting the strike price of the options. For example, at-the-money options can be used to minimise adverse outcomes. In contrast, out-of-the-money options can be used to reduce the cost of protection and manage the risk of extreme adverse price changes. **Exhibit 1.3** sets out the payoffs of in and out-of-the-money options.

- **Structured exposure** – this entails trading in option combinations to create a specific exposure to a specific range of asset prices or price movements. This will typically involve trading in combinations of put and call options or options with different strike prices and/or expiry dates.

- **Yield enhancement** – this entails selling options to earn the premium in exchange for assuming the risk of adverse price movements. Sold options positions are classified as *covered* or *naked*. Covered sold options are traded against underlying asset positions. Examples include covered calls (call options sold against an underlying long position) and covered puts (put options sold against an underlying short position). Covered options provide limited protection against adverse price movements where the asset price is relatively stable and trades within a very narrow range. Covered positions are generally used to improve the investment returns or subsidise the cost of the asset. Covered positions are not true hedges. Naked positions are options that are traded *without any underlying position*. They are used to seek premium income against the risk of an unexpected (by the trader) price movement. **Exhibit 1.4** sets out an example of covered call writing.

- **Volatility trading** – this entails using options to capitalise on changes in asset volatility. For example, purchased options can be used to position against increases in volatility. Similarly, sold options can be used to position for decreases in volatility. Volatility trading can be undertaken in two ways:
  1. *Delta hedged* – this entails trading in the options and offsetting the delta (asset price risk) of the options by a position in the asset. This ensures that the trader is not exposed to directional changes in asset price. The delta hedged option

position allows the trader to assume a position on actual volatility against the implied volatility used in the traded options[16].

2. *Not delta hedged* – this entails trading in the options with no offsetting trades in the asset. This means that the trader has a position in both volatility and the asset price. This is reflected in the exposure to both changes in the asset price and price volatility. The non delta hedged option position allows traders to trade the actual volatility of asset prices.

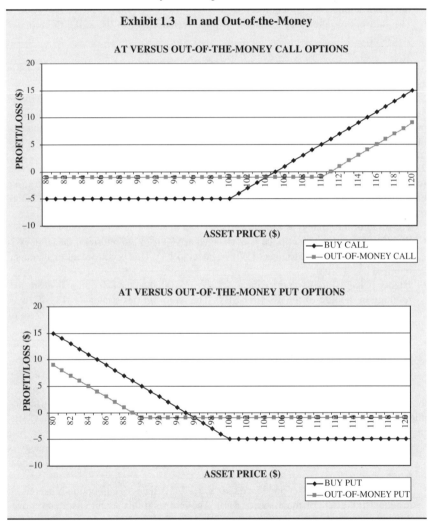

Exhibit 1.3   In and Out-of-the-Money

---

[16] See discussion in Das, Satyajit (2004) Derivative Products & Pricing; John Wiley & Sons (Asia), Singapore at Chapter 16.

Exhibit 1.4   Covered Call Writing

1. Strategy

Covered call writing is a common investment strategy used by asset holders. The asset holder sells a call option against the underlying asset position. This is also known as a buy-write strategy. The basic economics of the strategy are as follows:

- The premium received provides income in a stable price market.
- The premium received also provides protection against small falls in the price of the asset (up to the amount of premium received).
- The sold option allows appreciation in price increases up to the strike price of the sold call.

It is important to note that covered calls only offer minor protection against decreases in asset price. In this regard, it should not be regarded as a true hedge.

Covered call writing is commonly employed by asset holders to reduce the cost of purchasing or holding the asset and provide protection against minor movements in asset price. It is commonly used by asset managers on bonds and equity investments to enhance investment performance.

2. Example

Assume an asset is trading at $90. The asset holder sells call options on the asset at a strike of $100 for premium income of $5 for a period of 3 months. This has the impact of reducing the entry price into the asset to $85 (price ($90) minus premium ($5)).

The result of the strategy is as follows:

- **Stable price** – if the asset price is unchanged at $90 then the return on the strategy is 5.56% over 3 months (earnings ($5)/investment ($90)). This is equivalent to an annual return of 24.14% pa.
- **Higher price** – if the asset price increases above $100, then the call option is exercised, resulting in the sale of the asset for $100. The return on this strategy is 17.65% over 3 months (earnings ($15)/investment ($85)). This is equivalent to an annual return of 91.57% pa.
- **Lower price** – if the asset price falls, then the asset holder is protected until the asset price falls below $85 (the effective entry price into the original purchase of the asset).

The option could be struck out of the money. The asset holder may sell call options on the asset at a strike of $110 for premium income of $3 for a period of 3 months. This has the impact of reducing the entry price into the asset to $87 (price ($90) minus premium ($3)).

The result of the strategy is as follows:

- **Stable price** – if the asset price is unchanged at $90 then the return on the strategy is 3.33% over 3 months (earnings ($3)/investment ($90)). This is equivalent to an annual return of 14.01% pa.
- **Higher price** – if the asset price increases above $110, then the call option is exercised, resulting in the sale of the asset for $110. The return on this strategy is 26.44% over 3 months (earnings ($23)/investment ($87)). This is equivalent to an annual return of 155.59% pa.

- **Lower price** – if the asset price falls, then the asset holder is protected until the asset price falls below $87 (the effective entry price into the original purchase of the asset).

In both cases, if the share price continues to decrease below the option premium adjusted purchase price, then the asset holder is exposed to the risk of losses. The asset holder can hedge or sell the asset. An alternative is the technique of rolling the strike. This entails selling a new call option with a lower strike while simultaneously buying back the original call options. This would normally result in the receipt of a premium (the option sold is closer to the money than the out-of-the-money option re-purchased). This would move the purchase price down and therefore reduce the price below which the asset holder suffers losses.

In both cases, the asset holder forgoes any gains from price increase above the strike price of the sold call option.

The strategies outlined can be used for the following purposes:
- Options can be used for hedging either against a complete range of prices or for price movements within nominated price ranges.
- Options can be used to create trading positions in the underlying asset. This application of options is interesting. Forwards can be used to create the equivalent of the underlying asset. In contrast, options can be used to create structured exposure to the asset price. This is achieved by using combinations of options, adjusting strike prices and adjusting the expiry dates. This allows traders to design and assume exposure to *defined* price movements rather than *general* price movements.
- Options can also be used to trade volatility. This includes trading the actual volatility of asset prices and/or actual volatility versus implied volatility.

3.4.2   Option Strategies[17]

In this Section, typical option strategies are outlined. Option combinations are generally structured as combinations of put and call options, combinations of options with different strike prices and combinations of options with different expiry dates. In addition, option strategies can be leveraged by increasing the face value of one or other options traded in a combination.

---

[17]   See Becker, H. Phillip and Degler, William H. "19 Option Strategies and When to Use Them" (June 1984) Futures 46–50; McMillan, Lawrence G. (1986) Options as a Strategic Investment; New York Institute of Finance, New York at Chapters 3 to 24; Natenberg, Sheldon (1988) Option Volatility and Pricing Strategies; Probus Publishing, Chicago at Chapters 8, 10 and 11; Tompkins, Robert (1994) Options Explained[2]; MacMillan, Basingstoke at Chapters 6 and 7; "Customising Investment Return and Risk Using Derivatives" (April 1997) AsiaMoney 20–23.

Option strategies may be classified into the following types of transactions[18]:

- **Vertical spreads** – this entails a combination of options with the same expiry dates and different strike prices. There are a variety of vertical spreads that can be structured. These trades are all driven by expectations of asset price movements. **Exhibit 1.5** sets out a description of the major types of vertical spread strategies.

- **Time (Calendar) spreads** – this entails combinations of options with different expiry dates but the same strike prices. These strategies are designed to benefit from time decay (theta). The key value driver is the differential rate of time decay in the different options. **Exhibit 1.6** sets out a description of time (calendar) spread strategies.

- **Complex combinations** – this entails more complex strategies such as butterfly and condor option strategies. They are generally combinations of option spreads. They are designed to have low exposure to asset price movements and small exposure to volatility changes. **Exhibit 1.7** sets out a description of complex option combinations.

- **Volatility trades** – this entails combinations of put and call options. Volatility trades are designed to specifically benefit from increases or decreases in volatility. **Exhibit 1.8** sets out a description of volatility trades. **Exhibit 1.9** sets out the payoff of a straddle (a common type of volatility trade).

Exhibit 1.5 Option Strategies – Vertical Spreads[19]			
Strategy	**Components**	**Characteristics**	**Applications**
Bull Call Spread	Buy at-the-money call & sell out-of-the-money call (at higher strike)	• Lower premium cost • Known maximum gain (difference between strike prices less net premium) • Known maximum loss (net premium) • Delta positive (lower than outright call)	• Trading – to position for increase in asset price not exceeding the higher strike • Hedging – to place lower cost but limited hedge (up to higher strike price) on a short position

---

[18] There are literally a very large number of option combinations and the strategies set out here are merely the most common.

[19] Vertical spreads can be structured using gearing. For example, higher face value options may be sold than bought (ratio option spreads) to take advantage of expected volatility changes. These are known as ratio back spreads.

Strategy	Components	Characteristics	Applications
Bear Call Spread	Buy out-the-money call & sell at-the-money call (at lower strike)	• Net premium income • Known maximum loss (difference between strike prices less net premium) • Known maximum gain (net premium) • Delta negative (lower than outright call)	• Trading – to position for decrease in asset price with exposure to price increase not exceeding the higher strike
Bear Put Spread	Buy at-the-money put & sell out-of-the-money put (at lower strike)	• Lower premium cost • Known maximum gain (difference between strike prices less net premium) • Known maximum loss (net premium) • Delta negative (lower than outright put)	• Trading – to position for decrease in asset price not exceeding the lower strike • Hedging – to place lower cost but limited hedge (up to lower strike price) on a long position
Bull Put Spread	Buy out-the-money put & sell at-the-money put (at higher strike)	• Net premium income • Known maximum loss (difference between strike prices less net premium) • Known maximum gain (net premium) • Delta negative (lower than outright put)	• Trading – to position for increase in asset price with exposure to price decrease not exceeding the lower strike

Exhibit 1.6   Option Strategies – Time (Calendar) Spreads

Strategy	Components	Characteristics	Applications
Time Spread (Put or Call)	Sell call or put near expiry & buy call or put with later expiry	• Low premium cost • Maximum profit where markets stay stable and short dated position expires unexercised • Delta neutral, vega neutral, theta positive	• Trading – relative time decay of shorter and longer dated options.

Exhibit 1.7   Option Strategies – Complex Combinations

Strategy	Components[20]	Characteristics	Applications
Butterfly Spread	Buy (sell) 1 low strike option and 1 high strike option; sell (buy) 2 short options with a strike halfway between the low and high strikes; all options have same expiry.	• Low premium cost • Known maximum profit (spread between strikes less net premium) • Known loss (net premium cost) • Neutral or low delta; vega negative	• Trading – long butterfly benefits from stable market (profit is maximised where asset price is at the mid strike); short butterfly benefits from increased volatility with profit capped at the low and high strikes.
Condor Spread	Same as for Butterfly Spread except the 2 middle options have different strike each 1/3 away from the high and low strikes.	Similar to Butterfly Spread	Similar to Butterfly Spread

Exhibit 1.8   Option Strategies – Volatility Strategies

Strategy	Components	Characteristics	Applications

Straddle	Buy or sell 1 call and 1 put at the same strike with the same expiry	• For long straddle:
		  1. High premium cost
		  2. Maximum gain is unlimited
		  3. Maximum loss is limited to premium
		  4. Low/neutral delta, vega positive
			• Trading – long straddles are positioning for increases in volatility; short straddles are positioning for decreases in volatility

---

[20] Can be done with call or put options.

Strategy	Components	Characteristics	Applications
		• For short straddle: 1. High premium income 2. Maximum gain limited to premium 3. Maximum loss unlimited 4. Low/neutral delta, vega negative	
Strangle	Similar to straddle except both call and put options are out-of-the-money	Similar to Straddle	Similar to Straddle

Exhibit 1.9   Option Strategies – Option Straddle

Sold Straddle

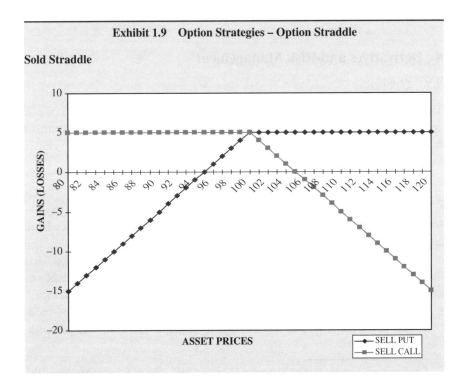

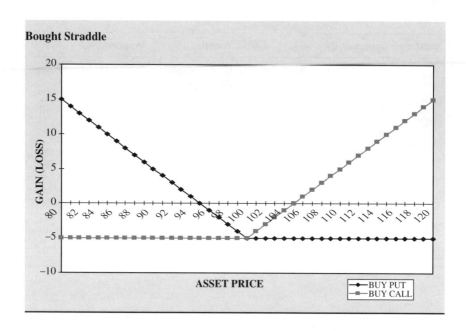

Bought Straddle

4   Derivatives and Risk Management

4.1   Overview

The use of derivatives in risk management is driven by the impact of financial risk on corporations, investors and financial institutions. In this Section, the nature of financial risk, the types of risk and the use of risk management to add value is examined.

4.2   Financial Risk

Interest in risk management is driven primarily by the presence of financial risk and its impact on participants in financial markets.

There is general agreement that the level of financial risk in markets has increased[21]. This increase in the *level* of financial risk is driven by a number of general and specific (affecting particular assets) factors. General factors include:

*   **Complexity of modern economies** – the increasing complexity of modern economic activity and relationships is a major factor in financial risk.

---

[21]   See Smithson, Charles (1998) Managing Financial Risk – Third Edition; McGraw-Hill, New York at Chapter 1.

For example, fluctuations in rates of economic growth and increasing price uncertainty (inflation/deflation) have all increased volatility of financial asset prices/rates.

• **Deregulation of industries and markets** – a broad range of countries and industries (telecommunications, banking, transport etc.) have been deregulated. In addition, government intervention (both direct and indirect) in establishing prices and rates in financial markets has decreased.

• **Globalisation/internationalisation of economies** – the growth in trade between nations and the creation of trading zones (the European Economic Union; NAFTA; Mercosur etc.) has led to a high degree of integration between economies. It has also created higher degrees of exposure to exchange rates and relative cost of capital (interest rates and exchange rates).

• **Cross border investment** – the pattern of investment (both direct and portfolio) has become internationalised. Capital flows are volatile and often short term in nature. This is driven from both the asset and liability side. Investors aggressively seek to capture maximum returns from foreign investors. Borrowers seek to access markets with a view to obtaining funding on the best available terms.

Specific factors include:

• **Exchange rates** – the breakdown of the Bretton Woods system of fixed exchange rates, abandonment of fixed or pegged exchange rates in various emerging countries, and the creation of a single European currency (the Euro), have all significantly altered the behaviour of exchange rates and contributed to price volatility.

• **Interest rates** – deregulation of domestic interest rates combined with "free" floating exchange rate systems has altered the dynamics of interest rate behaviour. This has also contributed to increased rate volatility. Long term structural changes in inflation (both actual and expected) have resulted in major changes in absolute levels of interest rates.

• **Commodity prices** – deregulation of commodity markets and the creation of coordinated commodity producer cartels (most notably the Organisation of Petroleum Exporting Countries ("OPEC")) have contributed to volatility in commodity prices. For example in energy markets, the formation of OPEC and the exercise of the oil cartel's powers (often in pursuit of non economic objectives) initially contributed to the volatility of energy prices. The deregulation of energy markets in the USA, Australia and Europe has added to the volatility of energy prices. Similar patterns are evident in other commodity markets.

All the identified factors (both general and specific) have contributed to increasing volatility in prices/rates of traded financial assets.

The impact of financial risk on corporations, investors and financial intermediaries is complex. The fundamental impact is as follows:

- **Corporations** – the primary effect of volatility of financial asset prices/rates on corporations is the impact on earnings (income or expenses), cash flows and balance sheets (values of assets and liabilities). For example, changes in exchange rates, interest rates, commodity prices and (less frequently) equity prices affect corporate earnings and cash flows. This is generally in the form of the impact upon sales revenues, expenses or financing charges. Changes in exchange rates also affect the value of balance sheet investments or liabilities denominated in foreign currency.
- **Investors** – the impact of asset price/rate volatility on investors is primarily on the current value of investments and the returns earned by investors. The volatility of asset prices/rates also represents an opportunity for investors to enhance returns and the value of investments through active trading and asset selection.
- **Financial intermediaries** – the volatility of asset prices/rates impacts upon financial intermediaries in several ways:
  1. *Demand for risk management products* – corporations and investors affected by financial risk increasingly require risk management instruments (such as derivatives) to manage exposure to this risk. Financial intermediaries are the primary dealers in these products. The contribution to the profitability of financial institutions of risk management products and related services is significant. The provision of risk management products exposes intermediaries to financial risk through the assumption of risk through trading in derivatives. This risk will generally be hedged by trading in financial assets. However, the financial intermediary will generally be exposed to the risk of any mismatch (basis risk).
  2. *Trading opportunities* – the volatility of asset prices/rates provides financial intermediaries with trading opportunities. Trading revenues are an increasingly important source of earnings to financial intermediaries. This trading may be related to supporting client demand for risk management products (referred to as flow trading) or standalone speculative trading (referred to as proprietary trading).

The impact of financial risk on all market participants has led to increased focus on risk management and the application of derivative products.

4.3 Types of Financial Risk

The types of financial risk are classified by asset class as follows:

- **Currency risk** – this refers to the exposure to changes in the exchange rate. Currency risk is usually classified as follows[22]:

  1. *Transaction exposure* – this is also known as cash or receivables/payables currency exposure. This refers to changes in value in the relevant base currency of cash amounts to be paid or received under commercial or financial contracts as a result of fluctuations in currency rates. This exposure is generally cash and realised. The exposure is driven by the need to actually sell or purchase foreign currency to generate or use local currency liquidity to buy or sell goods and services.

  2. *Translation exposure* – this is also known as accounting or balance sheet exposure. This refers to changes in value as expressed in the relevant base currency of balance sheet assets or liabilities (balance sheet translation) or revenue or expense items (earnings translation) as a result of fluctuations in currency rates. This exposure is generally non cash and unrealised. The exposure is driven by the need to convert foreign currency assets/liabilities or revenues/expenses into the base currency for reporting purposes.

  3. *Economic exposure* – this is also known as strategic or long term operating exposure. This refers to changes in the value of the enterprise resulting from long run changes in currency rates. This exposure is driven by the impact on the competitive position of the enterprise (in terms of cost structure or product costs) of currency rate changes.

- **Interest rate risk** – this refers to the exposure to changes in interest rates. The primary impact of interest rate changes is on interest rate sensitive assets or liabilities such as bonds or loans. The impact is seen in changes in interest income/expense or the value of debt instruments. Interest rate risk can be classified as follows:

  1. *Structural exposure* – this refers to the mismatch between assets and liabilities in terms of interest rate re-pricing or the re-pricing exposure on existing liabilities. The interest rate re-pricing structure of loans and deposits in a financial institution is a primary example of the interest rate structural exposure

---

[22] For example, see Shapiro, Alan C. (1986) Multinational Financial Management – Second Edition; Allyn and Bacon, Boston at Chapters 5 to 9; Pringle, John J. and Connolly, Robert A. "The Nature and Causes of Foreign Currency Exposure" (Fall 1993) Journal of Applied Corporate Finance 61–72.

created by the mismatch between assets and liabilities. The exposure on floating rate debt is a primary example of the re-pricing exposure on existing liabilities.

2. *Anticipatory exposure* – this refers to the interest rate exposure on future issuance of debt or the future price of debt to be purchased. Structural exposure refers to existing debt or investments. In contrast, anticipatory exposure refers to planned or known future issues of debt or investment in interest rate sensitive assets.

- **Equity price risk** – this refers to the exposure to changes in equity prices. This covers both changes in the general market (equity market index) or specific risk (individual stock prices). The primary impact is on holdings of equity securities. Interest rate risk can be classified as follows:
  1. *Structural exposure* – this refers to the change in value in existing positions (both long and short) in equity securities.
  2. *Anticipatory exposure* – this refers to the equity price exposure on future issuance of equity or the future price of equity to be purchased.
- **Commodity price risk** – this refers to the exposure to changes in commodity prices. The primary impact is on the sales price of commodity producers or on the input price of commodity users. Commodity price changes may also impact upon financial investments in commodities by asset managers.

4.4   Risk Management and Value

4.4.1   Rationale for Risk Transfer

The use of derivative instruments is predicated upon the financial risks evident in the normal business operations and the ability to transfer risks to a third party. The third party is prepared to assume the risk because it has an offsetting position and/or a superior ability to bear the risk. Alternatively, the third party is prepared to assume the risk in return for receipt of payment of a fee that compensates it economically for the risk assumed or the cost of synthetically hedging the risk. This is the position for financial institutions, investors and corporations.

Individual entities should only use derivatives to transfer risk where the transaction adds value to its business operations. The value created by hedging is different between financial institutions, investors and corporations. The differences are driven by a number of complex factors[23].

---

[23] The differences are similar to the factors that require VAR to be modified for corporations and investors; see Das, Satyajit (2004) Risk Management; John Wiley & Sons (Asia), Singapore at Chapter 2.

Financial institutions incur financial risk in two ways:
- Risk arising from entering into transactions with clients. This risk may be immediately minimised by entering into a matching transaction or an offsetting hedge.
- Risk assumed deliberately as part of the trading function to benefit from expected price/rate movements. This activity may be related to the risk arising from transactions entered into by clients where the exposure is not hedged. Alternatively, the risk may be assumed independently as part of proprietary trading operations.

This means that financial institutions use derivatives to hedge exposure incurred in trading with clients or in providing financial products with clients. Financial institutions also use derivatives to increase/decrease risk in their trading operations.

Investors are driven by the desire to maximise return relative to a benchmark. This benchmark may be a market index, model portfolio return or an absolute return/total return benchmark. The benchmark embodies the risk of the investments. This means that investor application of derivatives is conditioned upon increasing/decreasing risk relative to the benchmark.

Corporations incur financial risk from the underlying business activity. Shareholders provide capital to the entity to incur risks in the expectation of returns sufficient to compensate for the risk of the investment. This means that it is not immediately obvious that the *corporation* should hedge its exposures. This is because in hedging, the corporation changes the risk profile of the investment and the corresponding expected return received by the investor. This creates complexity in creating an appropriate policy framework to govern the application of derivatives.

An additional complication is that for financial institutions, both assets and liabilities are financial in nature. This means that it is relatively easy to establish a risk neutral or hedged position. In contrast, the position with investors and corporations is different. For investors, the assets are financial but the liabilities are complex payments (for example, driven by contingencies such as insurance or pension claims) that are not directly driven by financial asset prices/rates. For corporations, the liabilities are financial in nature but the assets are real. The value/income flows of corporate assets are not directly driven by financial asset prices/rates. This means that for investors and corporations, it is inherently more difficult to establish a risk neutral or hedged position. This has implications for the application of derivative instruments.

The nature of financial risk incurred by financial institutions, investors and corporations conditions the ability to generate value from hedging and drives derivative applications. The position is simplest for financial institutions. This is because there is no inherent requirement for financial institutions to incur and maintain exposure to financial risk. Financial institutions incur risk as a conscious decision with the objective of benefiting from favourable changes in asset prices/rates. This means that the value of risk management for financial institutions is driven simply by the ability of derivatives to alter the risk profile to the desired position.

The position for investors is driven by the inherent motivation of investors to maximise return within a given risk framework. The risk framework is prescribed by the return benchmark against which the investor's performance is to be measured. The investor will seek to increase or decrease risk relative to this benchmark. This means that the value of risk management for investors is similar to that for financial institutions. Risk management within investors is driven by the ability to use derivatives to alter the risk level of investments to the desired level.

The position for corporations is more complex. This reflect the fact that changes in financial market rates and prices affect the returns (earnings) generated by the assets of the corporation and the corporation's financial assets and liabilities in different ways. Maximisation of returns requires the management of the impact of fluctuations of financial prices and rates. This means that the relationship between risk management and value is more complex. It also varies significantly from that applicable to financial institutions and investors. The complex relationship between risk management and value within corporations is considered in the following Section.

4.4.2   Corporate Hedging – Risk Management and Value

The relationship between risk management and value for corporations is complex. The mere existence of exposure to financial risk and the availability of risk management instruments does not constitute sufficient reason to undertake risk management. If there is no value created through risk transfer, then corporate hedging or use of derivatives incurs costs and reduce returns to shareholders. The research suggests that if certain conditions exist, then risk management does have the potential to enhance the value of the firm[24].

---

[24] There is a large body of literature on the subject of risk management and value in non-financial institutions. The references listed here are a small selection of this literature. See Rawls, Waite S. and Smithson, Charles, W. "Strategic Risk Management" (Winter 1990) Continental Bank Journal of Applied Corporate Finance 6–18; Smithson, Charles "Something or Nothing" (December 1992) Risk 70–74; Froot, K., Scharfstein, D. and Stein, J. "Risk Management: Co-ordinating Corporate Investment and Financing Policy" (1993) Journal of Finance 48 1629–1658; Froot, K., Scharfstein, D. and Stein, J. "A Framework for Risk Management" (Fall 1994) Journal of Applied Corporate Finance 22–32; Crapp, Harvey "A Primer on Corporate Financial Risk Management" (December

The value of a firm can be given by the following:

Expected value of the firm $= \Sigma\,[(\text{expected future net cash flows})$
$\times\,(\text{discount factor calculated at the firm's cost of capital})]$

This means that any change in the value of the firm must be driven by changes in the future cash flows or the firm's cost of capital. In practice, risk management/derivatives can create value from its impact upon expected cash flows and the firm's cost of capital.

Risk management has the ability to increase future net cash flows by allowing investment in projects that may otherwise not have been feasible. This is because the risk of the cash flows may be reduced through hedging. Risk management also has the ability to reduce the volatility of the cash flows of the firm. This has the effect of lowering the cost of capital.

The primary drivers of risk management in corporations include:

- **Increasing investment capacity** – risk management may facilitate investment. Risk management achieves increased certainty of cash flows that can allow positive net present value/shareholder value enhancing investments to be made. Risk management prevents cash flow shortfalls from delaying investments or (in extreme cases) failing to invest in sound investment projects. In theory, *any* sound project should have access to external financing at a competitive price. In practice, capital market financing for projects is not always readily available at competitive prices, for example during market disruptions or recessions.
- **Access to financing** – risk management may allow investment in marginal projects by allowing risks to be reduced to allow finance to be raised. This is an extension of the idea of increasing investment capacity. This focuses on projects where hedging increases the certainty of project cash flows, enabling the project to be financed. This is common in the minerals/resources industry. Project finance is predicated upon the provision of funding against reasonably certain cash flows. Risk management is a mechanism to increase the certainty of cash flows to allow capital to be raised.

1994) The Australian Corporate Treasurer 17–19; Froot, K., Scharfstein, D. and Stein, J. "A Framework for Risk Management" (November–December 1994) Harvard Business Review 91–102; Shimko, David "Derivatives and the Bottom Line" (November 1995) Risk 29; Smithson, Charles "A Financial Risk Management Framework for Non Financial Institutions" (December 1995) Financial Derivatives and Risk Management Issue 4 8–16; Smithson, Charles "Theory Versus Practice" (September 1996) Risk 128–131; Smithson, Charles (1998) Managing Financial Risk – Third Edition; McGraw-Hill, New York at Chapter 20; Brown, Gregory and Toft, Klaus Bjere "Re-engineering Corporate Finance" (May 1998) Risk 44–47.

- **Reduction in cost of financing** – risk management can be used to reduce the cost of financing in several ways:
  1. *Capital market arbitrage* – risk management instruments such as swaps can be used in combination with issues of debt. This reduces funding costs by enabling borrowers to reduce the transaction costs of funding (bid-offer spreads, liquidity premium etc.) and to take advantage of comparative advantages in borrowing access/cost to lower funds costs in the required currency[25].
  2. *Monetisation of volatility* – borrowers may be able to reduce funding costs by monetising optionality inherent in their business or investments through the sale of embedded options. This includes the use of callable debt[26] or equity options/convertible debt[27].
- **Reduced distress costs** – risk management can decrease the cost of financial distress that may be faced by a firm. The risk of default is driven by the volatility of cash flows and the level of fixed commitments (debt service/financing claims). If cash flow falls below the level of fixed commitments, then to the extent that the firm is unable to finance the deficit, the risk of default increases. The cost of default includes direct costs (the actual costs of default such as legal costs) and indirect costs (the changes in incentives of various stakeholders and the loss of value from the sub-optimal management of the firm). In practice, the indirect costs of default risk are the most important. This includes the inability to make sound investments and the impact on customers (who are unable or unwilling to trade normally with the firm because of concerns regarding product quality, warranties or service agreements). This means in practice that firms with high default risk are unlikely to operate to maximise shareholder wealth. In this context, hedging can reduce default risk through increasing certainty of cash flows relative to committed cash flows. In this way, risk management can reduce default risk and potential distress costs. This can contribute to shareholder value though allowing investment, normal trading and access to financing.
- **Reduction in taxes** – risk management can decrease taxes in the following circumstances:
  1. *Convex tax profile* – if the firm's tax schedule is convex (that is, tax rates increase as income rises) then risk management can allow management of

---

[25] See discussion of comparative advantage in the context of using swaps in Das, Satyajit (2004) Derivative Products & Pricing; John Wiley & Sons (Asia), Singapore at Chapter 11. See also discussion on new issue arbitrage in Chapter 3.

[26] See Chapter 16.

[27] See Das, Satyajit (2004) Structured Products Volume 2; John Wiley & Sons (Asia), Singapore at Chapters 1, 2, 3 and 6.

earnings to minimise the tax payments. For example, under a minimum tax regime (such as the Alternative Minimum Tax ("AMT") rules in the US), firms should seek to ensure that the net income does not fall below the AMT threshold. Hedging, through its effect of stabilisation of the firm's cash flows, can increase control over the net income and allow effective tax planning. As taxes represent a net cash outflow, increased value is created as net cash flow available to shareholders is increased.

2. *High levels of tax deductions* – if the firm has a high level of tax deductions (such as investment tax allowances (tax credits or depreciation), interest costs or tax loss carry forwards) then the tax benefits have a cash flow value in the form of reduced tax payments. The ability to use the tax deductions is contingent upon the firm having sufficient net income to offset against these deductions. Reduced income through financial risk factors can reduce the value of the tax deductions. This can be through a delay in the use of the benefit or (in extreme cases) loss of the benefit (for example, where the tax credit must be used in the year of receipt or the tax loss carry forward is restricted to a specific period of time). Risk management can add value by ensuring the timely or accelerated use of these tax benefits. This is achieved by ensuring income stability. This would add value by increasing the present value of the benefit or the increase in net cash flows that will result.

• **Increased debt capacity** – risk management may increase debt capacity. Debt capacity of a firm will depend upon its ability to service the debt from its cash flows. Volatility of cash flows reduces the potential coverage of debt payments or the quality of the coverage. This has the effect of reducing the level of debt that can be maintained. Risk management, through the reduction of the volatility of income, can enhance debt coverage and increase debt capacity. This has several effects. It allows higher levels of investment to be sustained. It also allows higher level of debt to be sustained as part of the capital structure, thereby lowering the weighted average cost of capital.

The factors identified affect both expected cash flow and the firm's cost of capital. Factors such as increasing investment capacity, improving access to financing, reduction in tax costs and improved debt capacity can potentially enhance expected cash flows. Reduction in cost of financing, reduced distress costs and increased debt capacity can potentially decrease the firm's cost of capital. Both contribute to increased shareholder value.

The value from risk management is driven by market imperfections. For example, the impact of risk management in increasing investment capacity is driven by imperfection in capital markets where sound projects may fail to find financing at competitive market rates. Similarly, the presence of taxes, agency/contracting costs and information asymmetry all affect the opportunities for risk management.

Proponents of risk management argue that the presence of these factors allows risk management to be undertaken to enhance shareholder value. Opponents of risk management argue that risk management instruments (such as derivatives) are a zero sum game that destroys value[28]. There are two main arguments against risk management:

- **Portfolio hedging argument** – this is based on the fact that firms are artificial constructs used by investors to invest in specific projects. This means that the ultimate risk of the project is borne by the investor. This means that the investor can hedge at *a portfolio level*. This may take the form of diversification or specific hedges. This also means that to the extent that the firm hedges, it *prevents* the investor from obtaining its preferred risk position. For example, assume an investor purchases the shares in a Canadian gold producer. The investor is seeking exposure to the gold price and the US$/C$ exchange rate. To the extent that the gold producer specifically hedges the gold price and/or exchange rate risk, the investor's investment objectives are defeated. Under this approach, there is no role for *corporate risk management*. All risk management action is undertaken by the investor at the portfolio level.
- **Market efficiency** – this is based on the fact that the markets are efficient. Hedges must be executed at prevailing market rates. This means that unless the firm has superior forecasting abilities or forward rates/implied volatility are poor predictors of future spot rates, there is no value created by hedging. This is exacerbated by the transaction costs of hedging that would be incurred in entering into hedging transactions. This argument would militate against hedging of any kind.

In practice, the above arguments are flawed. Investors are not necessarily able to hedge at the portfolio level. This may be the result of a number of factors, including the transaction costs of hedging (particularly applicable to retail or smaller investors), the inability to fully diversify portfolios due to portfolio/market constraints and the inability to enter into hedges directly. This means that firms may

---

[28] For an interesting perspective on the hedging debate, see Ralfe, John "Betting Your Hedges" (July 1994) Risk 22–23; Ralfe, John "Value Added" (October 1994) Risk 46–47; Westby, David "Caveat Emptor" (June 1995) Risk 24–25; Copeland, Thomas and Joshi, Yash "Why Derivatives do not Reduce FX Risk" (May 1996) Corporate Finance 35–41; Ralfe, John "Reasons to be Hedging" (July 1996) Risk 20–21; Amrolia, Zar "Why FX Risk Must be Hedged" (August 1996) Corporate Finance 9–10.

enjoy comparative advantages in hedging. In addition, firms may be able to create specific value in hedging or financing that would be unavailable to investors. It includes factors such as the ability to use operating techniques or embedded correlations between financial risks. It may allow the monetisation of the embedded correlations and volatility positions through the design of specific hedges or funding structures.

It is also unlikely that the condition of market efficiency is satisfied. For example, forward rates are not generally accurate predictors of future spot rates[29]. In addition, information asymmetry and market inefficiency may confer trading advantages on firms with specific industry knowledge that may allow them to have superior hedging performance.

The debate about hedging can be simplified. The firm has to manage the financial risk incurred in its operations in some way. In practice, this entails either holding equity capital or entering into specific hedges. The choice between the two alternatives is driven by the relative costs. In effect, the issue of hedging and an inefficient capital structure is intrinsically linked[30]. This means that in reality, most firms will undertake *some level of hedging* to manage their portfolio of financial risks.

The theoretical evidence on corporate hedging favours the view that financial risk management can increase shareholder value. The evidence is not conclusive[31]. In practice, risk management instruments are used extensively[32]. Risk management is perceived to provide the opportunity to add value. Most firms have developed

---

[29] See Smithson, Charles "A Financial Risk Management Framework for Non Financial Institutions" (December 1995) Financial Derivatives and Risk Management Issue 4 8–16 at 10; Smithson, Charles (1998) Managing Financial Risk – Third Edition; McGraw-Hill, New York at Chapter 20 at 497–498.

[30] See discussion on using cash flaw VAR to establish economic hedges in Das, Satyajit (2004) Risk Management; John Wiley & Sons (Asia), Singapore at Chapter 2.

[31] There are a number of academic studies on the actual behaviour of corporate risk managers; for a summary see Smithson, Charles "Theory Versus Practice" (September 1996) Risk 128–131; Smithson, Charles (1998) Managing Financial Risk – Third Edition; McGraw-Hill, New York at Chapter 20; Raposo, Clara C. "Corporate Hedging: What Have We Learned So Far" (Spring 1999) Derivatives Quarterly 41–51; Smithson, Charles "Who Uses Risk Management?" (June 1999) Risk 47–49; Smithson, Charles "Does Risk Management Work?" (July 1999) Risk 44–45. For greater detail, see the original studies mentioned in the above articles.

[32] For a discussion of actual application of risk management instruments, see Dolde, Walter "The Trajectory of Corporate Financial Risk Management" (Fall 1993) Continental Bank Journal of Applied Corporate Finance 33–41; Stulz, Rene "Rethinking Risk Management" (Fall 1996) Journal of Applied Corporate Finance 8–24.

risk management frameworks that are designed to ensure that derivatives are used to enhance shareholder wealth[33].

5 Derivatives and Risk Management

5.1 Generic Applications

Derivatives allow the isolation and trading of risks separate from cash assets. The use of derivatives is predicated upon several types of generic applications[34]:

- **Replication** – this entails using derivatives in combination with cash borrowing/investment transactions to create economic equivalents of cash market assets. This may involve mere replication of the cash asset. It may also entail a relative value driven transaction where derivatives are used to compare the cost or return of the cash asset. This may then be used to arbitrage the value of the cash asset.
- **Risk separation and transfer** – this uses derivatives to separate specific identified risk and then hedge each risk (as required) independently to realign the risk profile of the entity.

Each of the generic applications is relevant to corporations, investors and financial institutions.

5.2 Derivative Products – Corporate Applications

Non-financial corporations use derivatives for the following primary purposes:

- **Fund raising** – this entails using derivatives in combination with actual borrowing to synthesise liabilities consistent with the requirements of the firm[35]. This involves the use of replication techniques. In general terms, it entails using forwards or swaps in combination with funding transactions (loans or capital

---

[33] See Shapiro, A.C. and Titman, S. "An Integrated Approach to Corporate Risk Management" in Stern, Joel and Chew, Donald (Editors) (1986) The Revolution in Corporate Finance; Basil Blackwell, Oxford at 215–229; Bauman, Joseph, Saratore, Steve and Liddle, William "A Practical Framework for Corporate Exposure Management" (Fall 1994) Journal of Applied Corporate Finance 66–72; Drennan, Anne S. "Keys to Successful Risk Management: Part 1" (Summer 1995) Derivative Quarterly 54–58; Drennan, Anne S. "Keys to Successful Risk Management: Part 2" (Winter 1995) Derivative Quarterly 46–51; Drennan, Anne S. "Keys to Successful Risk Management: Part 3" (Spring 1996) Derivative Quarterly 47–51.

[34] See Hancock, Peter "Derivative Applications: An Investor's Perspective" (May 1995) Financial Derivatives and Risk Management 1 55–64.

[35] See Yngwe, Peter "Derivative Applications: A Borrower's Perspective" (May 1995) Financial Derivatives and Risk Management 1 49–54.

market transactions) to generate funding in a specific currency, fixed or floating rate or maturity. It may also entail the sale of options to monetise volatility or the issue of hybrid securities/structured notes to raise funding[36]. It is driven by the ability to access markets otherwise unavailable, or the ability to lower the cost of funding relative to direct access. This practice is referred to as new issue arbitrage[37].

- **Risk transfer** – this entails the use of derivatives to transfer risk from business operations or financing transactions. It may also entail monetising inherent exposure to volatility of financial market prices and rates. This uses derivative products to hedge currency, interest rate, commodity and equity price risks, and is driven by the risk separation and transfer techniques[38]. The objective is to generally alter the risk profile and better align it with the desired risk profile of the entity.

5.3   *Derivative Products – Investment Applications*[39]

Investment managers use derivatives for the following primary purposes:

- **Replication** – this entails using derivatives in combination with cash borrowing/investments to create synthetic assets for investment purposes. This use of replication techniques is used for asset allocation, creating investment assets not directly available in the market[40] and to achieve superior returns. The principal value from the use of replication arises from lower transaction costs (including taxes), liquidity factors and market mis-pricing.

- **Relative value/arbitrage** – this entails using derivative instruments to unbundle and reconstruct cash instruments as combinations of borrowings/investments and derivative contracts. This provides a value benchmark against which the available cash instrument is compared. Differences in value arising from mis-pricing or capital market imperfections allow relative value/arbitrage trades to be constructed to seek to enhance returns on investment.

---

[36] For a discussion of hybrid securities/structured notes, see Chapter 4.
[37] See Chapter 3.
[38] Examples of risk transfer are discussed in Chapter 2. See also Das, Satyajit (2004) Structured Products Volume 2; John Wiley & Sons (Asia), Singapore at Chapters 6, 8, 9, 10, 14 and 17.
[39] See Hancock, Peter "Derivative Applications: An Investor's Perspective" (May 1995) Financial Derivatives and Risk Management 1 55–64.
[40] For a discussion of the use of hybrid securities/structured notes to create synthetic investment structures, see Chapter 4. For examples of specific types of synthetic investments, see Chapters 16, 17, 18, 19 and 20 and Das, Satyajit (2004) Structured Products Volume 2; John Wiley & Sons (Asia), Singapore at Chapters 2, 3, 4, 5, 7, 12, 14, 15, 16 and 17.

- **Risk separation and transfer** – this entails the disaggregation of risk and the hedging of a specific risk element through a derivative transaction. Investors will generally enter into transactions to either reduce risk or use derivatives to enhance exposure to specific market movements. The enhanced exposure to market movements may entail using leverage to increase the sensitivity of investment portfolios to specific expected market price/rate changes.

5.4   Derivative Products – Financial Institution Applications

The use of derivatives by financial institutions is more varied. This reflects the fact that the use of derivatives may be driven by the activities of the financial institution or to manage the risk of transactions entered into with clients (corporations, investors and other financial institutions).

Financial institutions will generally use derivatives for the following primary purposes in relation to their own activities:

- **Fund raising** – this entails using derivatives in combination with actual borrowing to synthesise liabilities consistent with the requirements of the entity. This involves using forwards or swaps in combination with funding transactions (loans or capital market transactions) to generate funding in a specific currency, fixed or floating rate, or maturity. It may also entail the sale of options to monetise volatility or the issue of hybrid securities/structured notes to raise funding. It is driven by the ability to access markets otherwise unavailable, or the ability to lower the cost of funding relative to direct access.
- **Risk transfer** – this entails the use of derivatives to transfer risk from banking operations. Derivative products are used to hedge currency and/or interest rates. The objective is generally to alter the asset liability risk profile and better align it with the desired risk profile of the entity.

Financial entities will use derivatives for the following primary purposes in relation to their trading activities:

- **Hedging** – this entails managing the risk of derivatives and other financial transactions entered into with clients. The traders will use combinations of cash borrowing/investments and derivatives to hedge exposure assumed in the course of trading with clients.
- **Trading** – this entails the use of derivatives in its own trading operations, and involves both low and high risk strategies. For example, derivative instruments may be used to unbundle and reconstruct cash to set up relative value/arbitrage trades to earn returns on a risk adjusted basis. It will also entail more aggressive use of derivatives to enhance exposure to specific market movements. This will

be driven by the inherent leverage of derivative contracts, lower transaction costs of trading and liquidity factors.

6 Summary

Derivative products are principally used to transfer risk or replicate positions in the underlying asset. Transactions combining positions in the asset and derivatives or cash and derivatives can be used to reduce risk or acquire asset exposure. Derivatives (forwards and options) are used to hedge inherent exposures. Options are also used to create structured risk profiles and to monetise views/positions on volatility.

The use of derivative instruments is predicated upon the financial risks evident in the normal business operations and the ability to transfer risks to a third party. The third party is prepared to assume the risk because it has an offsetting position, a superior ability to bear the risk, or is prepared to assume the risk in return for receipt of payment of a fee that compensates it economically for the risk assumed.

Individual entities will only use derivatives to transfer risk where the transaction adds value to its business operations. The value created by hedging is different between financial institutions, investors and corporations. Financial institutions use derivatives to manage risk incurred in transactions entered into with clients. Financial institutions also use derivatives to assume risk in their trading operations due to the efficiency of derivative instruments, lower trading costs and the ability to leverage positions. Investors use derivatives to replicate/synthesise investment assets, establish relative value/arbitrage trades to take advantage of market inefficiencies, hedge risk or enhance exposure to selected risks. Corporations use derivatives primarily to transfer risks and/or in the context of fund raising. Corporations use derivatives in fund raising to access markets or lower cost of funding (through taking advantage of market anomalies or selling optionality to monetise embedded optionality).

2

Application of Forwards/Futures, Swaps and Options[1]

1 Overview

Derivative products are principally used to transfer risk or replicate positions in the underlying asset. This Chapter sets out examples of applications of exchange-traded and over the counter ("OTC") derivative products, in particular, forwards/futures, swaps and options[2]. The primary focus in this Chapter is risk management/hedging. Chapter 3 outlines the concept of new issue arbitrage; that is, the use of derivatives combined with debt issues to improve cost and efficiency of funding.

The structure of this Chapter is as follows:
- A framework of applications is outlined, including the process of hedging.
- Applications of forwards and futures are outlined.
- Applications of swaps are examined.
- Applications of options are set out.

The focus of this Chapter and Chapter 1 is on the *generic* framework for the application of derivative products. The focus is on the principal uses of key building

---

[1] Derivative applications/strategies for the use of forwards, futures, swaps, options etc., in this Chapter are described in general terms only. The Chapter does not purport to be complete or comprehensive. In particular, the description of general strategies is not intended to be a recommendation of a specific strategy/approach or particular solution to a particular risk problem. Intending users of derivatives should seek full advice from professional advisers in respect of any transactions planned.

[2] For discussion of the application of derivatives, see Smithson, Charles (1998) Managing Financial Risk – Third Edition; McGraw-Hill, New York at Chapters 4, 5, 6, 7, 8, 9 and 10.

block derivative products such as forwards/swaps and options. Specific applications of non-generic derivative structures or derivatives on different asset classes are set out in subsequent Chapters where the individual products are discussed. These applications represent more complex and specialised uses of derivatives within the general framework outlined in this Chapter.

2 Hedging Framework

2.1 Hedging Process

Derivatives are frequently used to hedge financial price/rate risk. The hedging process will generally follow these discrete steps:

- **Identification of exposure** – this entails identifying the source of risk. This will cover examining the operations of the entity and isolating potential changes in value from unanticipated changes in financial market prices/rates. The objective is to identify the sources of value shifts, isolate the cause of the change in value, and measure the quantum of the change. This can be done using simple metrics (such as sensitivity analysis) or more complex approaches to risk measurement/quantification (such as VAR[3]).
- **Decision to adjust risk** – this covers the review of the exposure and the subsequent decision to enter into a transaction (either in the operating business or a financial transaction) designed to minimise/neutralise the identified risk. The basis for the decision to hedge is complex. It entails consideration of the value created from/preserved by hedging[4].
- **Hedging alternatives** – this entails identifying the available alternatives to restructure the risk exposures to realign these with the risk management objectives of the relevant entity. This will include consideration of:
  1. *Operating strategies* – this includes contractual arrangements and other rearrangements of aspects of the business such as changing invoicing currency, altering supplier arrangements etc.
  2. *Financial hedges* – this includes cash transactions (borrowing or investments) or derivatives.
- **Structure of hedge** – this is focused on structuring the hedge to ensure that it achieves the desired outcome and provides a close match to the underlying exposure being hedged. This involves the management of basis risk.

---

[3] See Das, Satyajit (2004) Risk Management; John Wiley & Sons (Asia), Singapore at Chapter 2.

[4] See Chapter 1.

- **Entry into/management of hedge** – this covers the entry into the hedging transaction and the subsequent management of the hedge. The focus is to ensure that the hedge performs as planned and maintains the offset to the underlying exposure. This will include adjustment to the hedge (as required) as a result of changes in the exposure or changes affecting the hedge. This will also cover the measurement of hedging performance.

2.2 Basis Risk in Hedging

2.2.1 Concept

The concept of hedging is based on assuming a position (the hedge) where the changes in value in the underlying position are offset by equal but opposite changes in value in the hedge. This assumes that the changes in value in the asset and the hedge instrument are equal and exactly identical for a given change in market prices/rates.

In practice, the strict definition of a hedge will frequently not be met exactly. There will be small differences between the changes in value of the underlying position and the hedging instrument. This difference is referred to as "basis risk". Basis risk will generally reduce the effectiveness of the hedge.

Basis risk can generally only be avoided where the instrument used to hedge is *identical* to the asset being hedged. In effect, the only true or exact hedge will be an equal but opposite position in the same asset or instrument. This is equivalent to closing out the underlying position. In practice, this is unrealistic. The reality is that most hedges will have some degree of basis risk. In effect, the hedger exchanges exposure to the outright price/rate risk of the underlying asset for basis risk. This means that the minimisation/control of basis risk is critical to successful hedging.

Basis risk results from a combination of the following factors:

- **Underlying asset** – this refers to the position where the asset being hedged is materially different from the asset underlying the derivative that is used to hedge. This is sometimes the case in interest rates (mismatches in the interest rate index or security), equities (mismatch between the security being hedged and the index used to hedge) and commodities (mismatch between the exact commodity being hedged and the commodity/commodity contract used to hedge). Where the price of the asset and the hedge do not move exactly in the same manner, there is a risk that there will be deviation in the performance of the hedge from the performance of the underlying asset.
- **Maturity mismatch** – this refers to differences between the holding period of the asset and the maturity of the hedge. Where the hedge is for a shorter maturity

than the underlying asset, the hedger will be exposed to price fluctuations for the period between the maturity of the hedge and the time of the transaction involving the underlying asset. Where the hedge is for a longer maturity than the underlying asset, the hedger must close out the hedge prior to maturity. This creates an exposure to the pricing of the hedge instrument, as the price of the underlying asset and the hedge may not converge at the date the hedge is terminated. This is a common problem where derivatives are used. Where the price deviation is significant, the performance of the hedge will be adversely affected.

Basis risk is present in hedges involving exchange-traded and OTC derivatives. The level of basis risk can be controlled more easily with OTC instruments. This reflects the fact the OTC instruments can be structured to closely replicate the underlying asset. In addition, the maturity of the hedge can be matched closely to the maturity of the underlying transaction. This means that the hedge can be structured to be more exact. This may entail the hedger incurring additional cost. The dealer will generally need to be compensated for any additional risk assumed as a result of the mismatch assumed in structuring a hedge specifically to suit the client.

The level of basis risk in exchange-traded instruments will generally be higher. This reflects the fact that the more standardised nature of the underlying instrument creates a greater degree of potential mismatch to the underlying asset being hedged.

Where exchange-traded instruments (futures and options) are used, additional basis risk results from the following factors:

- **Contract specification** – this refers to the fact that futures/options on futures contracts are specifically defined. This refers to the specific characteristics of the underlying asset, the contract face value and the contract maturities. In addition, limitations on settlement by physical delivery and trading price limits may create difficulties in using the contracts. This means that to the extent that there is any mismatch between the underlying asset and the exchange-traded contract, the performance of the hedge will be adversely affected.
- **Contract maturity** – this refers to the fact that exchange-traded futures contracts will have designated maturities. At maturity, the contract will need to be renewed or "rolled" (the existing contract will be closed out and a new position opened in a contract trading at a future date). This creates exposure to the cost of the roll and market liquidity. Where it is not possible to roll the contract at fair value, the performance of the hedge will be adversely affected.
- **Cash flow mismatch** – this refers to the requirement for initial and variation margins on exchange-traded products. The margins result in cash payments or

receipts that may not match the cash flows on the underlying asset. This will affect the efficiency of the hedge[5].

Any hedge with basis risk is often referred to as a "cross hedge". This is designed to indicate that the underlying asset is being hedged with a similar but different asset, or derivative on that asset.

2.2.2   *Basis in Futures Hedging*[6]

The term basis has a specific meaning in futures hedging. Basis risk is defined as:

$$\text{Basis risk} = \text{cash price of asset} - \text{futures price}$$

This reflects the logic that hedging using futures entails using the futures contract to offset a position in the underlying asset. The relationship between the two prices (futures and asset price) determines the cost and performance of the hedge.

The basis should approximate the carry cost (interest rate adjusted for income on the asset) on the futures contract[7]. The basis can be positive or negative. This reflects the quantum of the interest rate and the income on the asset. The basis will also change over time reflecting changes in the interest rate, asset income and the remaining time to maturity. The basis should reduce over time. At maturity of the futures contract, the basis should theoretically be zero as the asset price and the futures price converge[8].

In the futures market, the changing relationship between the asset price and the futures price is referred to as the basis risk of the hedge. In effect, the hedger substitutes the exposure to the price variation of the underlying asset with the exposure to changes in the basis. The basis must have smaller variability than the asset price for the hedge to work effectively. The re-statement of basis risk for the purposes of futures hedging highlights the need for the characteristics of the cash and futures contract to display a high degree of correlation for the hedge to be effective.

---

[5]   For example, the margins create interest rate risk that may need to be separately managed by "tailing" the hedge; see Das, Satyajit (2004) Derivative Products & Pricing; John Wiley & Sons (Asia), Singapore at Chapter 13.

[6]   See Schwartz, Edward W., Hill, Joanne M. and Schneeweis, Thomas (1986) Financial Futures; Irwin, Homewood, Illinois at Chapter 7 at 171–176.

[7]   See discussion in Das, Satyajit (2004) Derivative Products & Pricing; John Wiley & Sons (Asia), Singapore at Chapter 6.

[8]   See discussion in Das, Satyajit (2004) Derivative Products & Pricing; John Wiley & Sons (Asia), Singapore at Chapter 6.

2.3 Hedge Structuring

The objective of structuring of the hedge is to minimise the basis risk. It is focused on construction of a derivative position such that the $ price change in the derivative is equal but opposite in direction to the $ price change on the underlying asset. This requires the hedge to be structured so that the change in price of the asset and derivative are matched for a given change in the underlying market price/rate. This process is referred to as the hedge ratio or volatility matching. Hedge structuring requires the analysis of the hedging transaction to limit exposure to possible gains and losses due to changes in the basis.

There are several approaches to establishing hedge ratios/volatility matching, including[9]:

- **Face value hedging** – this entails setting the face value of the hedge to the principal value of the underlying position. This approach is deficient in that the changes in price may be different, reflecting the differences in price sensitivity for a given change in the relevant price/rate between the asset and the derivative.
- **Delta/Present Value of Basis Point ("PVBP") matching** – this approach entails matching the relative price movement of the asset and the derivative instrument. The objective is usually to match the $ price change in the underlying asset and the $ price change of the hedge. The $ price change is calculated as the delta of the position[10]. Alternatively, the $ price change is calculated as the PVBP of the position or the modified duration of the position (in case of fixed income securities)[11]. The hedge ratio is calculated as follows:

$$\text{Hedge ratio} = \$\text{ value price change of asset being hedged}/$$
$$\$\text{ value price change of hedge}$$

The delta/PVBP approach recognises the differing price sensitivity of the under-lying asset and the hedge. It assumes that the delta/PVBP of the asset and hedge is relatively stable. Where the delta/PVBP is unstable, the hedge ratio itself changes. This means that the hedge ratio must be continuously monitored and the hedge adjusted[12]. This problem occurs primarily with fixed income securities

---

[9] See Schwartz, Edward W., Hill, Joanne M. and Schneeweis, Thomas (1986) Financial Futures; Irwin, Homewood, Illinois at Chapter 7 at 171–176; Hull, John (2000) Options, Futures and Other Derivatives – Fourth Edition; Prentice-Hall Inc., Upper Saddle River, NJ at 35–40.

[10] See Das, Satyajit (2004) Derivative Products & Pricing; John Wiley & Sons (Asia), Singapore at Chapter 15.

[11] See Das, Satyajit (2004) Derivative Products & Pricing; John Wiley & Sons (Asia), Singapore at Chapter 5.

[12] This is similar to the problem of delta hedging; see Das, Satyajit (2004) Derivative Products & Pricing; John Wiley & Sons (Asia), Singapore at Chapter 16.

(due to convexity) and options. The approach also assumes that the changes in the underlying prices of the underlying asset and the derivatives are perfectly correlated. The delta /PVBP matching approach does not adjust for the different price or yield volatility of the two instruments.

- **Correlation based** – this approach extends the delta / PVBP matching approach to incorporate the estimated differences in price or yield volatility of the asset and the derivative. This is designed to overcome the deficiency identified in delta / PVBP matching. The objective is to match the $ price change in the underlying asset and the $ price change of the hedge adjusted for the fact that the asset and the hedge have different price/yield volatility. The hedge ratio is calculated as follows:

> Hedge ratio = ($ value price change of asset being hedged /$ value price change of hedge) × relative price/yield change of the cash asset to the hedge(β).

β is calculated using past historical price/yield changes in the asset and the hedge. This is generally calculated by regressing the historical price changes in price/yield changes in the asset against the price/yield changes in the hedge. The correlation based approach assumes stability of the historical price/yield relationship between the price/yield changes of the asset and the hedge.

In practice, the correlation based method is the most effective methodology for structuring the hedge. The establishment of the hedge ratio/volatility match must be undertaken with caution. This is because of the assumptions underlying the various approaches. Examples of the relevant techniques are set out below in the examples of applications of forwards/futures, swaps and options.

3   Applications of Forwards/ Futures

3.1   Currency Forwards[13]

Currency forwards may be used to offset exposure to changes in currency rates. **Exhibit 2.1** sets out an example of using currency forwards to hedge transaction exposures arising from export and import transactions. **Exhibit 2.2** sets out an example of using currency forwards to hedge a foreign currency borrowing. **Exhibit 2.3** sets out an example of using currency forwards to simulate foreign currency denominated borrowing and investments.

---

[13]   See Anthony, Steve (1989) Foreign Exchange in Practice; Law Book Company Limited, Sydney at Chapter 7 and 8.

Exhibit 2.1   Using Currency Forwards to Hedge Transaction Exposure

1. Hedging Export Receivables

Assume a Japanese exporter has sales denominated in US$. The exporter has expected revenues due in 6 months of US$10,000,000. The exporter will need to convert the US$ upon receipt into Yen. This means that the exporter is long US$/short Yen. This means that the exporter is exposed to any increase in the value of Yen. It receives a lower amount of Yen in exchange for the US$ cash flow where the Yen appreciates. Conversely, it benefits where the Yen depreciates. It receives a higher amount of Yen in exchange for the US$ cash flow where the Yen depreciates.

The exporter can sell forward the US$ export receivables to lock in the Yen value of the future cash flow. The hedging may be motivated by expectations that the Yen is likely to strengthen relative to the US$ or by the need to attain cash flow certainty by locking in the Yen value of the US$ receivables.

The market rates are as follows:

Rate	Value Date	Bid (buy Yen)	Offer (sell Yen)
Spot	15 November 2001	120.00	120.10
6 month Forward – Points	15 May 2002	−2.60	−2.50
6 month Forward – Rates	15 May 2002	117.40	117.60

The exporter can hedge by selling forward US$10,000,000 for value 15 May 2002 at a rate of US$1 = Yen 117.40. This means that the exporter receives a locked in amount of Yen 1,174,000,000 against delivery of US$10,000,000.

The cost of the hedge is the difference between the spot exchange rate (Yen 120.00) and the forward rate (Yen 117.40). This is equivalent to Yen 26,000,000 in amount. In percentage terms, the cost is equivalent to 4.42% pa (26,000,000/1,200,000,000 = 2.17% which is annualised as $(1 + 0.0217)^{(365/181)} - 1$).

Several aspects of the hedge should be noted:

- The hedge is executed on the face value of the exposure. This is to match the price changes as for a given change in the exchange rate both exposures will move by the equivalent amount.
- The hedge assumes that the amount and timing of the future cash flows are known with certainty.
- The hedge can generate both costs and benefits for the hedger. In the present case, the hedger incurs a loss, reflecting the interest rate differential between the US$ rate and Yen rate for 6 months.

2. Hedging Import Payables

Assume a Japanese importer has payments denominated in US$ for products to be purchased. The importer has expected payments due in 6 months of US$10,000,000. The importer will need to convert Yen into US$ to make the necessary payments. This means that the importer is short US$/long Yen. This means that the importer is exposed to any decrease in the value of Yen. It has to pay a higher amount of Yen to purchase the required US$ where the Yen depreciates. Conversely, it benefits where the Yen appreciates. It requires a lower amount of Yen to purchase the required US$ where the Yen appreciates.

The importer can sell forward Yen to lock in the Yen value of the future US$ payment. The hedging may be motivated by expectations that the Yen is likely to depreciate relative to the US$ or by the need to attain cash flow certainty by locking in the Yen value of the US$ payment.

The market rates are set out in the example of hedging export receivables:

Rate	Value Date	Bid (buy Yen)	Offer (sell Yen)
Spot	15 November 2001	120.00	120.10
6 month Forward – Points	15 May 2002	−2.60	−2.50
6 month Forward – Rates	15 May 2002	117.40	117.60

The importer can hedge by selling forward Yen for value 15 May 2002 at a rate of US$1 = Yen 117.60. This means that the importer receives US$10,000,000 against delivery of Yen 1,176,000,000.

The benefit of the hedge is the difference between the spot exchange rate (Yen 120.00) and the forward rate (Yen 117.60). This is equivalent to Yen 24,000,000 in amount. In percentage terms, the benefit is equivalent to 4.07% pa (24,000,000/1,201,000,000 = 2.00% which is annualised as $(1 + 0.02)^{(365/181)} - 1$).

The aspects of the hedge of the export receivable noted above are equally applicable to this hedge. In the present case, the hedger receives a benefit, reflecting the interest rate differential between the US$ rate and Yen rate for 6 months.

Exhibit 2.2   Using Currency Forwards to Hedge Debt

Assume a borrower undertakes an issue of Yen denominated debt. The terms of the transaction are as follows:

Amount (Yen)	25,000,000,000
Maturity	5 years
Issue Price	100.50%
Fees	2.00%
Coupon (pa annual)	5.00%

The all-in cost of the Yen issue is 5.35% pa (incorporating the issue premium and the fees).

The borrower's functional currency is US$. The transaction would entail the borrower being exposed to changes in the US$/Yen exchange rate in relation to future Yen interest and principal repayments on the debt. If the Yen appreciates, then the effective cost of funding for the borrower increases. This reflects the fact that the borrower will be required to use more US$ to purchase the required Yen to make the contracted interest and principal payments on the debt.

The borrower wishes to hedge the issue into US$ to avoid exposure to Yen. This may reflect the borrower's expectations on future currency rates or the desire to achieve a known cost of funding.

The hedge would entail the following currency transactions:
- Spot transaction where the Yen proceeds are sold in the spot US$/Yen market to generate US$.
- Forward transactions where Yen amounts covering each interest and principal payments are purchased against sales of US$ for value at the relevant payment dates.

The currency rates prevailing at the time of the issue are as follows:

Year	Bid (US$1= Yen)	Offer (US$1 = Yen)
Spot	120.00	120.10
	Forward Points	**Forward Points**
1	−4.80	−4.70
2	−9.35	−9.20
3	−13.50	−13.30
4	−16.10	−15.90
5	−17.65	−17.40

The fully hedged cash flows are as follows:

Year	Bond Cash Flows (Yen)	Bid (US$1= Yen)	Offer (US$1= Yen)	Conversion Rate (US$1=Yen)	Hedged Cash Flow (US$)
0	24,625,000,000	120.00	120.10	120.10	205,037,469
1	−1,250,000,000	−4.80	−4.70	115.20	−10,850,694
2	−1,250,000,000	−9.35	−9.20	110.65	−11,296,882
3	−1,250,000,000	−13.50	−13.30	106.50	−11,737,089
4	−1,250,000,000	−16.10	−15.90	103.90	−12,030,799
5	−26,250,000,000	−17.65	−17.40	102.35	−256,472,887

The all-in cost to the borrower in US$ is 8.85% pa (annual).

Several aspects of the hedge should be noted:
- The hedge is executed on the face value of the exposure equivalent to the interest and principal payment amounts. This is to match the price changes, as for a given change in the exchange rate both exposures will move by the equivalent amount.
- The net effect of the hedge is to eliminate any exposure to Yen on the underlying debt. The combined debt and the currency forwards have the effect of hedging the Yen debt into US$.
- The effect of the currency forwards in hedging the Yen debt into US$ is to alter the cost of the debt to an equivalent US$ interest cost.

Exhibit 2.3   Using Currency Forwards to Simulate Foreign Currency Loans/ Investments

Currency swaps (where a spot currency transaction is combined with a currency forward) can be used to simulate foreign currency loans and foreign currency investments[14]. The following two examples set out cases of simulating foreign currency loans and investments.

1. Simulated Foreign Currency Loan

Assume a US$ borrower wants to simulate a 6 month Yen loan in preference to directly accessing Yen borrowings. Assume the currency market rates are as follows:

Rate	Value Date	Bid (buy Yen)	Offer (sell Yen)
Spot	15 November 2001	120.00	120.10
6 month Forward – Points	15 May 2002	−2.60	−2.50
6 month Forward – Rates	15 May 2002	117.40	117.60

Assume the US$ interest rates for 6 months are 5.875/6.00% pa.

A simulated Yen 1,500,000,000 loan can be structured as follows:

- The borrower draws down a US$ loan of 12,500,000 for 6 months at a rate of 6.00% pa. The terms of the loan would commit the borrower to repaying the US$12,500,000 principal and the US$377,083 interest (US$12,500,000 × 6.00% × 181/360 = US$377,083) at the end of 6 months.
- The borrower enters into a spot transaction to sell US$ and purchase Yen at US$1 = Yen 120.00. The transaction would generate Yen 1,500,000,000 for the borrower.
- The borrower would simultaneously enter into a forward transaction to sell Yen and purchase US$ to cover the principal and interest repayment under the loan. This forward would be undertaken at US$1 = Yen 117.60. This would require the borrower to sell Yen 1,514,345,000 in return for receiving US$12,877,083.

The transaction results in the borrower receiving Yen 1,500,000,000 and repaying Yen 1,514,345,000 in 6 months. The effective cost is 1.91% pa annual (Yen 14,345,000/Yen 1,500,000,000 = 0.96% pa which is annualised as $(1 + 0.0096)^{(360/181)} - 1)$.

Several aspects of the hedge should be noted:

- The transaction results in the borrower being exposed to Yen as all the US$ cash flows of the borrowing are fully hedged into Yen.
- The currency swap involves uneven amounts (the spot and forward transactions are for different amounts). This reflects the need to cover the US$ interest and principal into Yen.
- The effective Yen cost of the transaction should equate to the approximate cost of Yen funding for the relevant maturity.

---

[14] Simulated loans/investments are sometimes driven by tax considerations; see Das, Satyajit (2004) Structured Products Volume 2; John Wiley & Sons (Asia), Singapore at Chapter 19.

2. Simulated Foreign Currency Investment

Assume a US$ investor wants to simulate a 6 month Yen investment in preference to directly accessing the Yen deposit market. Assume the currency market rates are as follows:

Rate	Value Date	Bid (buy Yen)	Offer (sell Yen)
Spot	15 November 2001	120.00	120.10
6 month Forward – Points	15 May 2002	−2.60	−2.50
6 month Forward – Rates	15 May 2002	117.40	117.60

Assume the US$ interest rates for 6 months are 5.875/6.00% pa.

A simulated Yen 1,500,000,000 deposit can be structured as follows:

- The investor makes a US$ deposit of 12,500,000 for 6 months at a rate of 5.875% pa. The terms of the deposit would mean that the investor would receive the US$12,500,000 principal and the US$377,083 interest (US$12,500,000 × 5.875% × 181/360 = US$369,227) at the end of 6 months.
- The transaction generates an investment equivalent of Yen 1,500,000,000 (US$12,500,000 converted at US$1 = Yen 120) for the investor.
- The investor would simultaneously enter into a forward transaction to sell US$ and purchase Yen. This is to cover the principal and interest under the US$ deposit into yen. This forward would be undertaken at US$1 = Yen 117.40. This would require the investor to sell US$12,869,227 and receive Yen 1,510,847,300.

The transaction results in the investor investing the equivalent of Yen 1,500,000,000 and receiving Yen 1,510,847,300 in 6 months. The effective return is 1.44% pa annual (Yen 10,847,300/Yen 1,500,000,000 = 0.72% pa which is annualised as $(1 + 0.0072)^{(360/181)} - 1)$. Several aspects of the hedge should be noted:

- The transaction results in the investor being exposed to Yen, as all the US$ cash flows of the borrowing are fully hedged into Yen.
- The currency swap involves uneven amounts (the spot and forward transactions are for different amounts). This reflects the need to cover the US$ interest and principal into Yen.
- The effective Yen cost of the transaction should equate to the approximate cost of Yen funding for the relevant maturity.

3.2 Interest Rate Forwards

Interest rate forwards (typically in the form of FRAs or bond forwards) are used to manage exposure to interest rate changes. Interest rate forwards are used to guarantee interest rates on future borrowing or investments. This can be for new borrowings or investments (anticipatory hedging) or adjusting the rate on an existing borrowing or investment.

Interest rate forwards are used as an instrument for managing assets and liabilities as follows.

- **Locking in interest rates on future borrowings/investments** – interest rate forwards are used to fix or guarantee a future rollover rate or repricing on either a loan or an investment. Generally, the underlying loan or investment will be on a floating interest rate basis. The interest rate forward is used to lock in future borrowing or investment rates on the relevant repricing dates of the loan. Interest rate forwards are used to fix the borrowing or investment return for a single period. Alternatively, a series of interest rate forwards can be used to lock in the rates on a series of repricing dates to lock in investment or borrowing rates for an extended period (this is equivalent to entry into an interest rate swap). Interest rate forwards can be used in a similar manner to guarantee the interest rate on a new issue of debt.

- **Creating exposures to floating interest rates** – interest rate forwards can also be used to create an exposure to floating rates for an investor or borrower with a fixed rate investment or borrowing. A borrower with fixed rate debt can create synthetic floating rate exposure for the period of the borrowing by buying interest rate forwards (selling FRAs). Due to anomalies in the forward markets, it may be possible to create cheaper borrowing or high-yielding investments through these strategies.

- **Locking in future reinvestment rates** – interest rate forwards can also be used to lock in future reinvestment rates on intermediate cash flows such as interest coupons on a term borrowing. In this context, the interest rate forwards function in a manner similar to zero coupon rates where a periodic coupon flow is swapped for a lump sum amount, payable at maturity. This type of strategy is applicable not only to investment managers seeking to eliminate reinvestment risk within their asset portfolios, but also to corporate liability managers creating sinking funds for the repayment of future liabilities.

- **Trading yield curves** – more complex and speculative strategies use interest rate forwards to trade a yield curve. Where interest rates are expected to be static at or about current levels, investors and borrowers can both potentially benefit from using interest rate forwards under certain circumstances. This type of strategy is predicated on the fact that the forward rates lie above or below the current physical market yield curve. For example, if the yield curve is normal or upward sloping, the forward rates lie above the cash market yield curve. Where the yield curve is inversely shaped or downward sloping, the forward rates lie below the cash market yield curve. In an environment where the yield curve is not expected to change significantly, borrowers and investors can benefit where they plan to undertake short-term borrowing or lending activities.

In the case where the forward rates lie above the cash market yield curve, it may be profitable for investors to lock-in forward investment rates. If the yield curve does not change significantly, then the forward rate achievable will be higher than the likely cash market rate at the time the investment must be undertaken. For borrowers, the reverse applies. Borrowers can benefit by locking in lower forward borrowing costs for short time frames than would be physically possible in the cash market – provided the inverse yield curve which prevails is not expected to shift significantly. The strategies are not riskless; they entail speculative trading based on expectations of future changes in interest rates.

Exhibit 2.4 sets out an example of using interest rate forwards to hedge asset liability mismatches within a financial institution. **Exhibit 2.5** sets out an example of using interest rate forwards to extend duration within a fixed income portfolio.

Exhibit 2.4   Using Forward Rate Agreements to Hedge Asset Liability Gaps

Assume a bank has an asset liability mismatch in its portfolio. The bank has assets (primarily loans) with longer term fixed maturities that are funded with short term deposits. This mismatch exposes the bank to interest rate risk. Increases in short term rates raise the cost of funding of the bank and reduce interest rate margins. Conversely, decreases in short term rates cut the cost of funding and increase the bank's interest rate margin.

The bank may wish to reduce its sensitivity to short term interest rate movements. This may be driven by a requirement to reduce volatility of earnings or protect its net interest margin. This may also be driven by the bank's desire to position itself for expected movements in interest rates. The bank can reduce its exposure to short term interest rates by buying a FRA (equivalent to shorting/selling forward interest rates).

Assume the bank wants to lock in its interest cost on forthcoming rollover of its short term deposits in 3 months time. These deposits are raised from both retail and wholesale depositors. The deposits take the form of 3 month certificates of deposit ("CDs") priced off US$ 3 month LIBOR. 3 × 6 FRAs (covering a 3 month period in 3 months time) are quoted at 5.75/5.80% pa.

The banks can buy a 3 × 6 FRA at 5.80% pa to lock in its borrowing cost on the refinancing of its short term deposits. The FRA would be cash settled in 3 months time, coinciding with the maturity of the underlying funding. If interest rates increase, then the bank's higher funding cost on the rollover of the CDs will be offset by the gain on the FRA. If interest rates decrease, then the bank's lower funding cost on the rollover of the CDs will be offset by the loss on the FRA. The FRA locks in the bank's interest rate cost out of the forward date. This will have the effect of locking in the bank's interest margin for the relevant period.

Several aspects of the FRA hedge should be noted:
* As with all hedges, the bank locks in the *implied forward rate*. This rate may be above the current spot 3 month interest rate if the yield curve is positive/upward sloping. This would represent a cost to the borrower. The forward rate may be below the current spot

rate if the yield curve is inverse/negatively sloped. This would represent a gain to the borrower. The actual benefit of the hedge would result from the extent to which the actual spot rate at the maturity of the FRA exceeds (gain to the borrower) or is below (cost to the borrower) the implied forward rate locked in through the FRA.

- The structure of the hedge will depend upon the nature of the bank liabilities sought to be hedged. In this case, a FRA based on US$ 3 month LIBOR provides an effective hedge, reflecting the fact that the bank CDs are 3 months in maturity and priced-off LIBOR. If this was not the case, then the borrower would need to structure the hedge to provide a match to the underlying liability. This would require adjustment for potentially two mismatches – the maturity of the CDs and the fact that the pricing of the bank's liabilities are not perfectly correlated to LIBOR. This would require determination of a hedge ratio based on PVBP/delta matching and incorporating the correlation of the bank's funding costs to the benchmark LIBOR rate.

Exhibit 2.5   Using Forward Rate Agreements to Extend Duration

Assume an investment manager seeks to extend the duration of a short term cash/money market investment portfolio. In the physical market, this would entail the investor buying longer dated assets. This may reduce the liquidity of the portfolio and also create greater price volatility in the value of the investment assets.

One possible way of extending the duration of the cash/money market investment portfolio is to enter into sold FRAs (equivalent to buying forward short rates) to capture value from the pattern of forward rates where the yield curve is upward sloping. Assume the following yield curve and implied forward rates (mid rates):

Maturity (years)	Interest Rates (% pa)	6 month Forward Rates (% pa)
0.50	5.50	5.80
1.00	5.65	5.80
1.50	5.70	7.10
2.00	6.05	6.40
2.50	6.12	6.30
3.00	6.15	6.79
3.50	6.24	7.12
4.00	6.35	

Assume 42×48 FRA (6 month LIBOR in 3.5 years) is quoted at 7.10/7.15% pa. The investor sells a 42×48 FRA at 7.10% pa. This allows the investor to lock in the premium of 1.60% pa (the implied 6 month LIBOR (7.10% pa) minus the current spot 6 month LIBOR (5.50% pa)). If 6 month LIBOR in 3.5 years is below 7.10% pa, then the FRA will result in a positive return to the investor, enhancing returns on the portfolio. If rates are above 7.10% pa, then the FRA results in a loss to the investor, as it locks in a return below market rates at the relevant time.

Several aspects of the transaction should be noted:
- The strategy is risky. It is based on expectations of future interest rates relative to the implied forward rates.
- The FRA is designed to extract value from the upward sloping yield curve. The expectation is that interest rates will not increase at the rate implied by the underlying yield curve.
- The transaction enables the separation of liquidity of the underlying investments and its duration. The underlying portfolio can continue to be invested in short dated (3 or 6 month) money market investments. The FRA enables the investor to extend duration without the need to change the composition of the underlying investments.

3.3 Interest Rate Futures

Interest rate futures contracts are used in a manner very similar to interest rate forwards. The major difference relates to the specification of interest rate futures, in particular bond futures contracts. The incorporation of the conversion factors and cheapest-to-deliver bond features in the determination of the hedge ratio is complex[15]. **Exhibit 2.6** sets out an example of using a bond futures contract to hedge the issuance of new debt.

Exhibit 2.6   Using Interest Rate Futures to Hedge Debt Issuance

Assume a borrower is scheduled to undertake a new issue of bonds in approximately 7 months. The details of the planned issue are as follows:

Current date:	10 January 2001
Issue date:	Mid August 2001
Amount:	US$250 million
Structure:	Amortising 30 year bonds with a modified duration of 6.85 years

The borrower is exposed to the following risks between now and the scheduled date of the issue:
- Exposure to movements in benchmark rates (Treasury or swap rates).
- Exposure to changes in the credit spread relative to the benchmark applicable to the borrower.

The borrower wishes to enter into a hedge to lock in the cost of issuance. This may be driven by the desire to guarantee the borrowing cost or reduce volatility of interest costs.

---

[15] See Das, Satyajit (2004) Derivative Products & Pricing; John Wiley & Sons (Asia), Singapore at Chapter 2.

The borrower decides to use the CBOT September 2001 Treasury Bond contract[16]. The details of the selected contract are as follows:

Contract Price: 66 28/32 (66.875%)

Cheapest to deliver ("CTD") bond: 12% pa coupon Treasury Bond with final maturity
                                     February 2019 trading at 112.02 (clean price) to
                                     yield 10.50% pa with a modified duration of
                                     7.53 years

The hedge must be structured to enable the borrower to minimise the variance of its hedged overall position. There are two ways of establishing the hedge:

1. Sell the following number of futures contracts:

   Number of contracts = (Par value of corporate bonds/par value of futures contract)
                        × coefficient of the bond price regression (β)
                        × conversion factor of CTD bond.

2. Sell the number of futures contracts determined with reference to the following hedge ratio:

   Hedge ratio = (modified duration of corporate bond/modified duration of CTD bond)
               × (price of corporate bond/price of CTD bond)
               × (change in corporate yield/change in CTD bond yield)
               × ((1+ yield of CTD bond)/(1+ yield of corporate bond)).

In practice, Method 1 is generally unavailable as there may be no historical price data for the issuer's debt or the specific *new* issue sought to be hedged. This means that Method 2 is normally used. This entails a number of discrete steps:

- The conversion factor of the CTD bond is calculated.
- The relationship between the issuer's yield and benchmark rates must be estimated.
- The hedge ratio is then established.

The conversion factor for a bond is calculated as follows:

- The value of the bond on the first day of the delivery month on the assumption that the interest rate for all maturities equals 6% pa compounded semi-annually[17].
- The bond maturity and coupon payments are rounded down to the nearest 3 months. If after rounding, the bond has an exact number of six monthly or semi-annual periods, then the first coupon is paid at the end of the first six month period. If after rounding the bond does not have an exact number of six month periods, which means there is a "stub" three month period (as a result of the rounding to the nearest three month period), then the first coupon is assumed to be paid after 3 months and accrued interest is subtracted.

Applying the above approach, the CTD can be restated as a 12% coupon bond with 18 years and 1 month to maturity. Applying the rounding rules (round down to nearest 3 months), the bond is assumed to have a life of 18 years or 36 semi-annual periods, and the

---

[16] For a description of the contract, see Das, Satyajit (2004) Derivative Products & Pricing; John Wiley & Sons (Asia), Singapore at Chapter 2.

[17] This was originally 8.00% pa but was changed to reflect lower market yields.

first coupon is assumed to be paid at the end of the first six month period. Using $100 as face value, the bond price is calculated using 36 payments of $6 coupon ($12/2), and a future value of $100 at the end of 36 semi-annual periods discounted at 3.00% per each semi-annual period (6.00% pa/2). This equates to a value of the bond of: $165.50. This gives a conversion factor as follows:

$$\text{Conversion factor} = \text{value of bond/face value} = 165.50/100 = 1.6550$$

The relationship between the issuer's yield and benchmark rates (the term (change in corporate yield/ change in CTD bond yield) in the hedge ratio calculation) is more difficult to estimate. In practice, it is estimated by regressing historical yields for a credit rating quality equivalent to that of the issuer against the underlying benchmark Treasury or swap rate.

In this case, the issuer is A rated and the results of the regression are as follows:

$$\text{A rated issuer's interest rate} = -0.0912 + 1.15 \times (\text{Treasury bond rate})$$

This allows the required inputs to the hedge ratio to be specified as follows:
- Modified duration of corporate bond = 6.85
- Modified duration of CTD bond = 7.53
- Price of corporate bond = 100.00 (the new bond is assumed to be priced at par)
- Price of CTD bond = 112.02
- Change in corporate yield/change in CTD bond yield = 1.15 (derived from the regression analysis)
- Yield of corporate bond = 12.00% pa (this is the spot yield for an A rated issuer)
- Yield of CTD bond = 10.50% pa

The hedge ratio is given by:

$$\text{Hedge ratio} = (6.85/7.53) \times (100.00/112.02) \times (1.15) \times ((1 + 0.1050)/(1 + 0.1200))$$

$$= 0.9214$$

In order to achieve a $ price equivalent position between the bond issue and the futures price, the hedge ratio is adjusted by the conversion factor as follows:

$$0.9214 \times 1.6550 = 1.5249$$

The number of Treasury bond futures contracts that the issuer will have to sell is now determined as follows:

$$\text{US\$250,000,000(Issue Amount)/US\$100,000(Contract Face Value)} \times 1.5249$$
$$= 3{,}812 \text{ contracts}$$

The effective rate locked in through the futures transaction can be estimated approximately, using the regression equation giving the relationship between the A rated yield and benchmark rates. This requires the assumption that the futures contract is equivalent to a forward on the CTD bond. In effect, this assumes that the issuer has sold forward the 12% pa coupon Treasury Bond with final maturity February 2019 trading at 110.678% of face value

(66.875% (bond future price) × 1.6550 (the conversion factor)). This equates to a yield from the future maturity date of 10.64% pa on the CTD bond. This allows the estimation of the issuer's cost after the hedge:

$$A \text{ rate} = -0.0912 + 1.15 \times 10.64\% = 12.14\% \text{ pa}$$

The difference between the current yield on A rated debt (12.00% pa) and the forward yield (12.14% pa) reflects the cost of carry of the positive yield curve. This represents the cost of hedging for the borrower.

The following aspects of the hedge should be noted:
- The structuring of the hedge is designed to match the volatility of the underlying debt issue to that of the bond futures contract.
- The hedge is a cross hedge as the issuer uses a derivative on a different underlying to effect the hedge.
- The cross hedge means that the hedge is not perfect. It leaves the issuer exposed to changes in the relationship between A rated issues and the benchmark rates (effectively, the credit spread). This may affect the efficiency of the hedge.
- The futures contract matures in September 2001. This is 1 month after the planned date of the issue. This means that the issuer is also exposed to changes in the futures basis in the period between establishing the hedge (January 2001) and the closeout of the hedge (August 2001). This may affect the effectiveness of the hedge.

4 Applications of Swaps

Swaps are used in risk management to convert fixed rate exposures to floating rate and vice versa. In the case of currency swaps, the swap is also used to convert assets and liabilities from one currency to another. This capacity makes swaps an important potential means of managing interest rate and currency exposures on existing assets and liabilities. In contrast, new issue arbitrage focuses on utilising swaps to create synthetic liabilities on the basis of cost advantages or issues of access[18].

The primary applications of swaps include:
- Using interest rate swaps to hedge floating rate debt to fixed rate (or vice versa) to manage interest rate risk.
- Using currency swaps to hedge foreign currency debt into a selected currency to manage currency risk.
- Using combinations of swaps and debt to create synthetic liabilities and assets.

---

[18] See Chapter 3.

The applications of swaps are similar to the uses of currency and interest rate forwards. This reflects the fact that swaps are portfolios of currency or interest rate forwards. The major relevant differences include:

- Interest rate and currency forward contracts entail the management of *single* cash flows as distinct from swaps that entail the exchange of a *series* of future cash flows.
- The pricing of *individual* interest rate and currency forward contracts varies. The interest rate or currency forward rate will generally be above or below the current spot rate. In contrast, under the terms of a swap, the contract is structured at par, with any interest rate differential being built into the different interest rates on the two sets of cash flows that are exchanged.

The differences between the two types of instruments dictate the application of the products. Swaps are generally used in conjunction with debt instruments or bond-like cash flow instruments. This reflects the ability of swaps to closely match the cash flows of the underlying instrument and alter its interest rate and/or currency denomination.

Interest rate and currency forward contracts are used in managing existing portfolios of assets and liabilities in the following cases:

- Interest rate and currency forward contracts are used to manage uneven cash flows. Where cash flows are of different amounts or are not at regular periodic intervals, interest rate and currency forward contracts are more flexible in changing the interest rate and currency basis of the cash flows. In contrast, where evenly spaced equal sets of cash flows are involved, it is usually more economical to use swaps to effect the interest rate or currency basis conversion.
- Interest rate and currency forward contracts allow each cash flow within a stream of cash flows to be managed individually. In contrast, interest rate and currency swaps convert all the relevant cash flows.
- Interest rate and currency forward contracts can be more flexible than swaps in adjusting or optimising a hedge. This is because it allows each cash flow to be treated independently, but also allows the cost of the hedge to be attuned to particular market environments.

Exhibit 2.7 and **Exhibit 2.8** set out two examples of using an interest rate swap to synthesise fixed rate debt. **Exhibit 2.9** sets out an example of using a currency swap to hedge debt in one currency into a second currency[19].

---

[19] Interest rate and currency swaps are also capable of being used to create synthetic assets (known as asset swaps); see Chapter 4.

**Exhibit 2.7   Using Interest Rate Swaps to Create Synthetic Fixed Rate Debt –
Example 1**

Assume a borrower with floating rate debt seeks to eliminate the exposure to fluctuations
in the cost of the debt. The borrower could enter into an interest rate swap matched to the
underlying floating rate debt to eliminate the exposure to the floating interest rates.

The transaction will be driven by:

* Requirement for certainty of interest costs and reduction of volatility of net earnings.
* Matching the interest rate profile of the borrower's assets.
* Reduction in the cost of the fixed rate debt relative to a direct issue of fixed rate debt[20].

The diagram sets out the structure of the transaction:

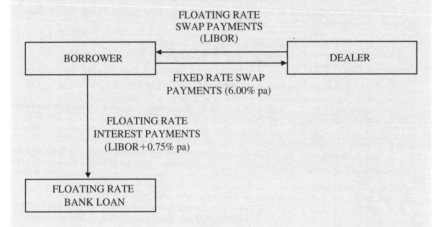

The effective net cost of the transaction is as follows:

Transaction	Payment
Bank Loan	−(6 month LIBOR + 0.75% pa)
Interest Rate Swap	
Fixed Rate Payments	−6.00% pa
Floating Rate Payments	+(6 month LIBOR)
Net Cost	−6.75% pa

The effect of the interest rate swap is to convert the borrower's floating rate debt (priced
off US$ 6 month LIBOR) into fixed rate debt. The net cost of the debt is 6.75% pa (calculated
as the swap rate (6.00% pa) and the bank debt margin (0.75% pa)).

---

[20] See Chapter 3 and Das, Satyajit (2004) Derivative Products & Pricing; John Wiley &
Sons (Asia), Singapore at Chapter 11.

**Exhibit 2.8   Using Interest Rate Swaps to Create Synthetic Fixed Rate Debt –
Example 2**

The transaction described in **Exhibit 2.7** is relatively simple. In practice, the degree of
match between the underlying debt issue and the interest rate swap varies. In this example,
a more complex scenario entailing hedging floating rate debt into fixed rate debt is set out.

Assume a borrower wishes to convert floating rate debt into fixed rate liabilities. Assume
the following facts:

- The underlying floating rate debt used by the borrower is US$ commercial paper ("CP")
  issued in the domestic market. The CP is issued at around the A1/P1 index[21] plus 5 bps[22].
- As the CP issuance is not underwritten, borrowers generally maintain committed standby
  revolving credit facilities to back-up the CP funding. The standby funding arrangements
  may be required by the Rating Agencies involved in rating the borrower's CP program.
  The standby credit line will also have a same day funding swingline facility allowing the
  refinancing of maturing CP. The borrower has a 5 year committed term standby credit
  facility priced as follows:
  1. *Arrangement Fee*: 0.25% pa (flat)
  2. *Commitment Fee*: 0.375% pa (payable semi-annually in advance)
  3. *Interest Cost*: LIBOR plus 0.75% pa (payable only on drawing under the Facility).
- The interest rates swap market (fixed rates versus US$ 6 month LIBOR) is trading at
  6.10/6.15% pa (semi-annual).

The structure of the hedge is set out below:

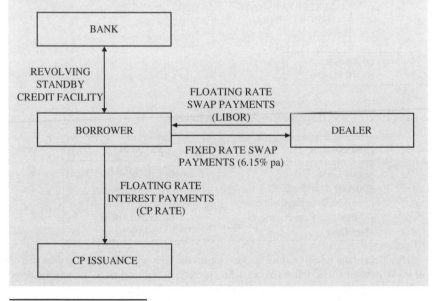

---

[21] The A1/P1 index is the reported commercial paper rates (discount basis) of AA rated com-
      panies. This index is compiled by the Federal Reserve and is known as the H-15 Series.

[22] This margin includes the dealer commissions and issuance costs, including amortised
      rating costs.

The effective cost to the borrower is summarised below:

Transaction	Payment
CP Issuance	−(A1/P1 + 0.05% pa)
Standby Credit Facility	−0.45% pa
Interest Rate Swap	
Fixed Rate Payments	−6.15% pa
Floating Rate Payments	+(6 month LIBOR = A1/P1 + 0.35% pa)
Adjustment	
Compounding of CP rate	−0.05% pa
Net Cost	6.35% pa

Notes:
1. The costing of the standby credit facility is calculated using the following methodology. The arrangement fee (25 bp) is amortised over 5 years at 6.15% pa (swap rate) to equate to 5.9 bps pa. The commitment fee (37.5 bps) is converted into an equivalent semi-annual arrears payment at 6.15% pa (swap rate) to equate to 38.7 bps pa.
2. The borrower pays out CP rates (calculated off A1/P1 rates) and receives 6 month LIBOR. This means that the borrower has an index mismatch (LIBOR versus CP rates)[23] and maturity mismatch (in general, the borrower issues short dated CP with maturities of around 30 days versus 6 month LIBOR). This is relevant to the determination of the effective total cost. In order to facilitate this comparison, the 6 month LIBOR is re-stated as a margin over the 1 month CP rate (35 bps). This margin is based on historical relationships between the two rates.
3. The compounding effect of 1 month CP rates relative to 6 month LIBOR must be recognised. This is done using the following methodology. The discount rate on the CP is converted into yield to maturity terms – assuming a discount rate of 5.00% pa, the equivalent yield to maturity is 5.09% pa. This rate is equivalent to a monthly rate of 0.42% pa (5.09%/12). The monthly rate is compounded for 6 months and re-stated as an annual rate to give a semi-annual rate of 5.14% pa ($[1 + .0042]^6 - 1] \times 2$). This gives the additional cost of the monthly compounding as 0.05% pa (5.14% pa (the semi-annual equivalent of the CP rate) − 5.09% pa (the monthly yield equivalent)). This is a cost to the borrower.

The effect of the interest rate swap is to convert the borrower's floating rate debt (priced off US$ CP) into fixed rate debt. The net cost of the debt is 6.35% pa.

Several aspects of the series of transactions should be noted:
• The interest rate swap hedge is not an exact match for the underlying CP debt. This reflects differences in index (LIBOR versus CP), interest rate mismatches (6 month LIBOR versus 1 month CP) and payment/cash flow mismatches (monthly CP versus semi-annual swap payments).

---

[23] The index and maturity mismatch can be minimised by using a basis swap (floating to floating interest rate swap); see Chapter 14.

- The cost of the hedged borrowing is not known with certainty. There are several unknown costs:
  1. CP/LIBOR spread.
  2. Standby credit costs.
  3. CP issuance rates (spread to A1/P1 composite).
  4. Absolute level of rates (this affects the compounding of the CP rate).

Exhibit 2.9   Using Currency Swaps to Create Synthetic Currency Debt

Assume the same position as in **Exhibit 2.2**. Assume a borrower undertakes an issue of 5 year Yen denominated debt. The terms of the transaction are as follows:

Amount (Yen)	25,000,000,000
Maturity	5 years
Issue Price	100.50%
Fees	2.00%
Coupon (pa annual)	5.00%

The all-in cost of the Yen issue is 5.35% pa (incorporating the issue premium and the fees).

The borrower's functional currency is US$. The transaction would entail the borrower being exposed to changes in the US$/Yen exchange rate in relation to future Yen interest and principal repayments on the debt. If the Yen appreciates, then the effective cost of funding for the borrower increases. This reflects the fact that the borrower will be required to use more US$ to purchase the required Yen to make the contracted interest and principal payments on the debt. This exposure is transactional (on the actual debt servicing cash flows) and translation (on the conversion of the Yen debt into US$ for the preparation of the financial statement).

The borrower wishes to hedge the issue into US$ to avoid exposure to Yen. This may reflect the borrower's expectations on future currency rates or the desire to achieve a known cost of funding. The hedge entails entry into a 5 year US$/Yen fixed rate to fixed rate currency swap.

Assume the currency swap rate is as follows[24]:

Pay:	US$ 8.40% pa (annual)
Receive:	Yen 5.02% pa (annual)

---

[24] The fixed to fixed swap rate reflects the pricing of US$ and Yen interest rate swaps adjusted for the pricing of the cross currency basis swap; see Das, Satyajit (2004) Derivative Products & Pricing; John Wiley & Sons (Asia), Singapore at Chapter 10.

The effective cost of the transaction is summarised below[25]:

Transaction	Payments (Yen)	Payments (US$)
Yen Bond Issue	−5.35% pa	
Currency Swap		
Yen Payments	+5.02% pa	
US$ Payments		−8.40% pa
Net Payments	**−0.33% pa**	**−8.40% pa**

The shortfall in Yen is converted into US$ using the Yen/US$ currency conversion factors/FX basis points[26]. The currency conversion factor is as follows: 100 bps in Yen is equivalent to 109.5 bps in US$. This means that the Yen 33 bps is equivalent to US$ 36.1 bps. This equates to an all-in cost in Yen of 8.761% pa.

5　Applications of Options

5.1　Overview

Options are asymmetric risk management instruments. This characteristic means that there are some significant differences as well as similarities in their use in hedging asset and liability portfolios. In particular, the risk profiles and payoffs to buyers and sellers of these instruments are different. The purchaser of the option benefits from the insurance features of such a transaction that limit the risk from adverse price/rate changes without the need to give up any potential benefits from a favourable movement in price/rates. In contrast, the seller of an option assumes a potentially unlimited liability in exchange for the premium or fee received. This difference in payoffs dictates the use of options in hedging.

There are two general classes of users of options:

- Purchasers of options use the instruments as an alternative to price fixing mechanisms such as interest rate/currency forwards or swaps. The objective is to establish a *maximum* cost or *minimum* rate of return while maintaining the possibility of lower costs or higher returns if favourable movements in price/rates occur.

- Sellers of options seek to gain (particularly in stable market environments) from the premium received from option writing activities. The option sold can

---

[25] Please note that this cost is an approximation. In practice, the swap would be structured to precisely match the cash flows of the bond issue; see Das, Satyajit (2004) Derivative Products & Pricing; John Wiley & Sons (Asia), Singapore at Chapter 10.

[26] See Das, Satyajit (2004) Derivative Products & Pricing; John Wiley & Sons (Asia), Singapore at Chapter 10.

be speculative or written against offsetting portfolio positions. The premium acts as a means of lowering borrowing costs or enhancing investment returns while providing a cushion or limited hedge against minor market movements.

The structuring issues in relation to hedging with options are very similar to the issues relevant to the use of forwards. The option hedge is generally structured so that the $ value change on the underlying position is matched by equal but opposite changes in the value of the option. The approach to matching the two positions using hedge ratios is identical to that described with forwards/futures.

The only complication with structuring of the hedge where it involves an option is the price behaviour of the option. The price sensitivity of the option is given by the option's delta. Under certain circumstances, the delta of the option may be sensitive to changes in the underlying asset price. This raises the issue as to whether the hedge involving the option should be delta matched *instantaneously* (that is, at all times) or only at maturity. In practice, delta matching at all times over the life of the hedge is expensive as it requires dynamic management of the hedge. This means that hedges involving options are usually delta/PVBP matched *at the maturity of the hedge*. This will generally ensure that the value changes in the hedge will approximately offset the changes in the value of the underlying position at maturity of the hedge. This will have the desired effect of protecting the hedger from price changes in the value of the underlying asset.

5.2   Currency Options[27]

Currency options can be used to provide protection against adverse price changes in currency values. **Exhibit 2.10** sets out an example of using currency options to hedge transaction exposures arising from exports or imports. Currency options can be used in a similar manner to hedge foreign currency denominated debt or investments (interest/dividend payments/receipts or principal amounts).

Exhibit 2.10   Using Currency Options to Hedge Transaction Exposures

1.   Hedging Export Receivables
Assume a US$ based exporter is expecting a Yen payment in 3 months time of Yen 100 million. The spot exchange rate is US$1 = Yen 120 and the 3 month forward rate is US$1 = Yen 116.50. The exporter purchases a put option on Yen (call on US$) for value in 3 months at a strike of Yen 116.50 for payment of a premium of Yen 1.165 (1%).

---

[27]   See Anthony, Steve (1989) Foreign Exchange in Practice; Law Book Company Limited, Sydney at Chapter 10.

In 3 months time, the exporter undertakes the following transactions:
- If the US$ is trading above Yen 116.50 (weaker yen), then the exporter exercises the option and purchases US$ at Yen 116.50. The effective level of the Yen achieved is 117.6650 (reflecting the option premium cost).
- If the US$ is trading below Yen 116.50 (stronger yen), then the exporter abandons the option and purchases US$ in the spot market at a more favourable rate than under the option. The effective breakeven for the exporter is Yen 115.3350 (the level of the strike price adjusted for the premium below which the exporter gains).

The result of the hedging strategy is summarised in the table below:

US$ Receipts to Exporter (per Yen 100 million)

	US$ Depreciates	US$ Appreciates
US$/Yen	115.00	125.00
Outright Forward	858,369	858,369
Put Option on Yen	860,844	849,870

2. Hedging Import Payable

Assume a US$ based importer is required to make a Yen payment in 3 months time of Yen 100 million. The spot exchange rate is US$1 = Yen 120 and the 3 month forward rate is US$1 = Yen 116.50. The importer purchases a call option on Yen (put on US$) for value in 3 months at a strike of Yen 116.50 for payment of a premium of Yen 1.165 (1%).

In 3 months time, the importer undertakes the following transactions:
- If the US$ is trading below Yen 116.50 (stronger yen), then the importer exercises the option and purchases Yen at Yen 116.50. The effective cost of the Yen is 115.3350 (reflecting the option premium cost).
- If the US$ is trading above Yen 116.50 (weaker yen), then the importer abandons the option and purchases yen in the spot market at a more favourable rate than under the option. The effective breakeven for the importer is Yen 117.6650 (the level of the strike price adjusted for the premium above which the importer gains).

The result of the hedging strategy is summarised in the table below:

US$ Cost to Importer (per Yen 100 million)

	US$ Depreciates	US$ Appreciates
US$/Yen	115.00	125.00
Outright Forward	858,369	858,369
Call Option on Yen	867,039	807,526

5.3 Interest Rate Options

Interest rate options can be used to provide protection against adverse changes in interest rates. **Exhibit 2.11** sets out an example of using interest rate caps to hedge floating rate debt. **Exhibit 2.12** sets out an example of using interest rate floors to create a synthetic floating rate liability. **Exhibit 2.13** sets out an example of using interest rate floors to manage floating rate debt.

Exhibit 2.11   Using Caps to Hedge Floating Rate Debt

This example compares the cost of four hedging alternatives on a 5 year 6 month LIBOR based loan. Current 6 month LIBOR is 6.00% pa.

The hedging alternatives available to the borrower are as follows:
* No hedge.
* Interest rate swap at fixed rate of 8.12% pa semi-annually against six month LIBOR.
* Interest rate cap with a strike at 8.12% pa (same as the swap rate and 2.12% pa higher than current 6 month LIBOR). The interest rate cap premium is 3.90% (equivalent to 0.96% pa).
* Collar agreement combining a cap at 8.12% pa (swap rate) and a floor at 6.00% pa (spot). The collar premium fee is 1.85% (equivalent to 0.46% pa).

The effective all-in costs of the hedging alternatives are summarised below. All-in cost calculations do not include the borrower's credit spread. The credit spread would be the same in all cases. All front end fees are converted to per annum equivalents using a discount rate of 8.12% pa (the swap rate).

Market Rate									
Average 6 month LIBOR (% pa)	3.00	4.00	5.00	6.00	7.00	8.00	9.00	10.00	11.00
Alternatives									
No Hedge (% pa)	3.00	4.00	5.00	6.00	7.00	8.00	9.00	10.00	11.00
Interest Rate Swap (% pa)	8.12	8.12	8.12	8.12	8.12	8.12	8.12	8.12	8.12
Cap									
Average LIBOR (% pa)	3.00	4.00	5.00	6.00	7.00	8.00	9.00	10.00	11.00
Cap Payment (% pa)	0.00	0.00	0.00	0.00	0.00	0.00	0.88	1.88	2.88
Amortised Premium (% pa)	0.96	0.96	0.96	0.96	0.96	0.96	0.96	0.96	0.96
Net Cost (% pa)	3.96	4.96	5.96	6.96	7.96	8.96	9.08	9.08	9.08
Collar									
Average LIBOR (% pa)	3.00	4.00	5.00	6.00	7.00	8.00	9.00	10.00	11.00
Collar Payment (% pa)	−3.00	−2.00	−1.00	0.00	0.00	0.00	0.88	1.88	2.88
Amortised Premium (% pa)	0.46	0.46	0.46	0.46	0.46	0.46	0.46	0.46	0.46
Net Cost (% pa)	6.46	6.46	6.46	6.46	7.46	8.46	8.58	8.58	8.58

The outcomes under the different hedging alternatives are summarised in the graph below:

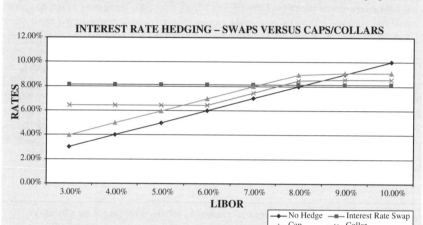

The results of the selected hedging alternatives at various rate levels indicate that there is no single preferred hedging strategy. The no hedge alternative appears to be the best strategy if rates fall. Fixed rates (via the interest rate swap) provide the best protection in the future if interest rates increase above the implied forward rates embedded in the swap. The cap provides protection against high interest rate levels but allows the borrower to participate in falls in interest rates. The collar provides protection against increases above the cap rate. The collar allows the borrower to achieve lower costs if rates are below the cap rate, but above the floor. While break-evens at any particular rate level are simple to ascertain, the true benefits of these alternative hedges can only be determined with reference to actual interest rates achieved over the life of the transaction.

A possible means of analysing the hedging alternatives is to take a probabilistic approach to future interest rate scenarios. Using actual historical interest rates/projected future interest rates it is theoretically possible to calculate the expected cost or benefit of any particular hedging strategy. The problem of hedging floating rate debt against the potential increase in interest expense as a result of increasing interest rates can be analysed in terms of establishing the economics of each hedging alternative, and then calculating expected values for the outcome with various instruments. Applying this approach, it is necessary to specify the actual economic cost of each alternative.

The economics of the various hedging alternatives can be summarised as follows:

- The economics of a swap into a fixed rate can be specified in terms of a borrower incurring a cost if the floating rate remains *below* the fixed rate (on average) for the term of the swap. Conversely, an economic gain to the borrower accrues where the floating rate averages a level above the fixed rate paid under the swap.
- The economics of the purchase of a cap relates to the cost of the cap, with an economic gain accruing to the borrower if the floating rate remains well above or remains well below the cap rate (on average) for the term of the transaction.

• The economics of the collar is similar to the economics of the cap combined with the sale by the borrower of the floor. The sale results in a premium being paid to the borrower, and this partially offsets the cost of the cap, with an economic loss arising if the floating rate index remains below the floor rate agreed under the collar agreement.

In each case, for the purpose of constructing a mathematically analytical model, the expected loss or gain over the life of each transaction can be calculated based on an assumed probability distribution of interest rates for the relevant index. This type of probabilistic analysis enables comparison of the relative cost effectiveness of different hedging strategies as a function of interest rate expectations using different probability estimates and levels of confidence. The framework allows outcomes to be simulated using techniques such as historical or Monte Carlo simulations.

Exhibit 2.12   Using Floors to Create a Synthetic Floating Rate Liability

A fixed rate borrower can create an exposure to a floating interest rate index by purchasing a floor at a level equal to the cost of its fixed rate debt. If interest rates fall, then the borrower benefits by an amount equivalent to the difference between the market level of the index relative to the floor level adjusted for the amortised purchase price of the floor. This type of strategy means that the borrower participates in any rate declines below the floor level on the relevant index, while having no exposure to rate increases. This is because if the floating rate index exceeds the floor level, the borrower's cost of funds equates to its fixed rate debt costs. This strategy is identical to purchasing a cap[28].

Assume a borrower has a five year fixed rate borrowing at 8.12% pa (generated via an interest rate swap). The borrower purchases a five year floor on 6 month LIBOR at a floor level of 6.00% pa (the current level of 6 month LIBOR) for a fee of 2.05% (equivalent to 0.51% pa utilising a discount rate of 8.12% pa (the swap rate)).

The impact of the strategy is set out below:

Market Rate									
Average 6 month LIBOR (% pa)	3.00	4.00	5.00	6.00	7.00	8.00	9.00	10.00	11.00
Alternatives									
No Hedge (% pa)	3.00	4.00	5.00	6.00	7.00	8.00	9.00	10.00	11.00
Interest Rate Swap (% pa)	8.12	8.12	8.12	8.12	8.12	8.12	8.12	8.12	8.12
Swap/Bought Floor									
Interest Rate Swap (% pa)	8.12	8.12	8.12	8.12	8.12	8.12	8.12	8.12	8.12
Floor Payments (% pa)	3.00	2.00	1.00	0.00	0.00	0.00	0.00	0.00	0.00
Floor Premium (% pa)	0.51	0.51	0.51	0.51	0.51	0.51	0.51	0.51	0.51
Net Cost (% pa)	5.63	6.63	7.63	8.63	8.63	8.63	8.63	8.63	8.63

---

[28] This entails an application of put-call parity.

The outcomes under the different hedging alternatives are summarised in the graph below:

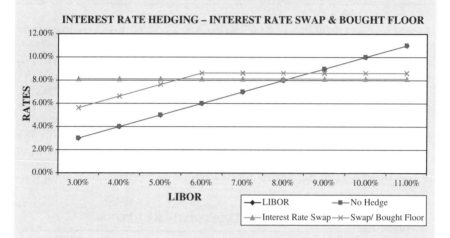

A conceptually similar strategy can be utilised by a fixed rate investor holding a portfolio of fixed rate assets such as bonds. The investor engineers an exposure to floating rates by purchasing a cap where the cap level is set at the level of interest receipts on the fixed rate portfolio. If interest rates on the relevant index increase, then the investor receives cash inflows equal to the excess of the index above the cap rate level (adjusted for the premium). This allows the investor to participate by way of increased interest earnings if rates increase, while maintaining a floor on portfolio interest earnings. The portfolio will earn a minimum of the fixed interest rate accruing on the portfolio, adjusted for the option premium paid.

Exhibit 2.13   Using Floors to Manage Floating Rate Liabilities

A floating rate borrower can seek to lower its cost of borrowing while simultaneously achieving limited protection from rate increases by selling floors against its borrowing. Under this strategy, if interest rates decline, then the borrower does not participate in the fall in interest rates beyond the floor level. This is because it must make payments to the purchaser of the floor that brings its cost of funding to the floor level adjusted by the premium received. If rates increase, then the borrower has limited protection equal to the amortised premium level, that partially offsets increased costs. However if rates increase sharply, then the borrower is exposed to increased interest cost under the strategy.

Assume a borrower has floating rate liabilities for 5 year pricing off 6 month LIBOR. The borrower sells a five year floor on LIBOR at a floor level of 6.00% pa (the current level of LIBOR) for a fee of 2.05% (equivalent to 0.51% pa utilising a discount rate of 8.12% pa (the swap rate)).

The impact of the strategy is set out below:

Market Rate									
Average 6 month LIBOR (% pa)	3.00	4.00	5.00	6.00	7.00	8.00	9.00	10.00	11.00
Alternatives									
No Hedge (% pa)	3.00	4.00	5.00	6.00	7.00	8.00	9.00	10.00	11.00
Interest Rate Swap (% pa)	8.12	8.12	8.12	8.12	8.12	8.12	8.12	8.12	8.12
Swap/Bought Floor									
Average 6 month LIBOR (% pa)	3.00	4.00	5.00	6.00	7.00	8.00	9.00	10.00	11.00
Floor Payments (% pa)	−3.00	−2.00	−1.00	0.00	0.00	0.00	0.00	0.00	0.00
Floor Premium (% pa)	0.51	0.51	0.51	0.51	0.51	0.51	0.51	0.51	0.51
Net Cost (% pa)	5.49	5.49	5.49	5.49	6.49	7.49	8.49	9.49	10.49

The outcomes under the different hedging alternatives are summarised in the graph below:

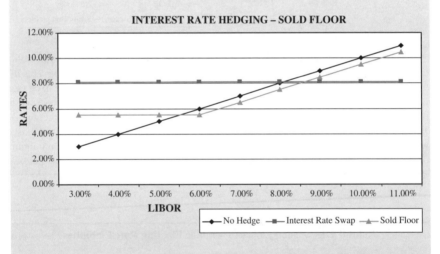

In an asset-based variation of the strategy, an investor holding a portfolio of floating rate assets may seek to enhance the yield on the portfolio by selling caps. Under this strategy, if interest rates increase above the cap level, then the investor's return is limited to the level of the cap adjusted for the premium received. If rates drop, then the investor earns the market interest rate, adjusted for the premium which allows it to earn a margin above the usual floating rate earnings that would accrue to the investor.

6   Summary

Derivative products are used principally to transfer risk or replicate positions in the underlying asset. This Chapter has set out examples of applications of exchange-traded and OTC derivative products; in particular, forwards/futures, swaps and options for risk management/hedging. The focus has been primarily on interest rate and currency risk. The principal issue identified is the need to precisely match the price movements in the underlying position and the instrument used to hedge. This is essential to ensuring the efficiency of the hedge. A number of techniques (delta/PVBP matching and correlation techniques) are used to achieve the required degree of matching.

The focus in this Chapter has been on the *economics* of hedging. In practice, the process of hedging is complicated by a number of other important factors. This relates to the accounting treatment and taxation position of the hedge[29]. Capital market participants seeking to manage risk will, of necessity, seek to ensure that the hedge simultaneously achieves economic efficiency as well as treatment as a hedge *for accounting purposes.* The efficiency of the hedge will need to be considered *on a post tax level.*

---

[29] See Das, Satyajit (2004) Risk Management; John Wiley & Sons (Asia), Singapore at Chapters 15 and 16.

3
New Issue Arbitrage

1 Overview

Derivatives (in particular, interest rate and currency swaps) can be utilised as an instrument for new issue arbitrage as well as an efficient method of hedging/risk transfer. New issue arbitrage is defined as combining the issuance of debt with a concurrent interest rate or currency swap to create a synthetic liability. The specific driver is that in the specific circumstances, new issue arbitrage can provide financing at a cost less than that available through conventional direct access to the relevant market.

The possibility of new issue arbitrage derives from the basic origin of swaps and in the fundamental economics of swap transactions. New issue arbitrage is based on the fact that the swap transaction allows the party seeking to raise funds to arbitrage differential access and relative cost across different markets[1]. In effect, where the borrower wishes to raise funds in a market where the terms available to that specific borrower are *relatively* less favourable, it may be less expensive to issue debt in a market where the terms are more favourable. The new debt is then converted using an interest rate or currency swap to create a liability corresponding to the borrower's favoured form of funding.

Analysis of the process of new issue arbitrage requires consideration of the following issues:
- Approach and economic criteria for new issue arbitrage.
- Concept of arbitrage funding that is the most developed form of new issue arbitrage.
- The impact of these techniques on the primary debt markets.

---

[1] See Das, Satyajit (2004) Derivative Products & Pricing; John Wiley & Sons (Asia), Singapore at Chapter 11.

This Chapter examines the theory and practice of new issue arbitrage. The structure of the Chapter is as follows:
- The basic concept and approach to new issue arbitrage is described.
- The benefits and risks of arbitrage funding are identified.
- The evolution of new arbitrage funding practices is discussed.
- Impact of new issue arbitrage on primary debt markets is detailed.

2   New Issue Arbitrage – Rationale

At the simplest level, new issue arbitrage transactions entail the issuance of new debt combined with a swap transaction. The basic types of arbitrage involve:
- Transactions in the same currency involving swapping fixed rate funding to floating rate funding and vice versa.
- Transactions across currencies involving swapping of debt in a particular currency to another currency. This will usually (at least initially) require the funding to be transformed into US$ floating rate funding priced off LIBOR.

A basic pattern permeates the types of new issue arbitrage undertaken. The economic theory of swaps suggests that highly rated borrowers would use their comparative advantage in fixed rate markets to swap their liabilities to a more cost effective floating rate basis in the same currency, or alternatively issue in a foreign currency then swap into their required currency. Similarly, the theory would predict that lower rated borrowers will raise floating rate funding and swap it into fixed in the same currency, or into floating or fixed in a foreign currency. The predictions are consistent with actual market practice.

The analysis of new issue arbitrage generally tends to focus on term borrowings. The process of arbitrage can exist in short-term markets. An example of this type of transaction would entail the issue of say 90 day short-term securities in one currency, with the simultaneous execution of a spot and forward currency contract to convert the liability into a different currency. This would be motivated by the fact that the all-up achieved cost is superior to direct access to the relevant currency.

The process of new issue arbitrage also tends to over emphasise the role of securities. For example, it is commonplace to talk about "swap driven primary issue markets" or "swap driven securities issues". This reflects the fact that the basic debt underlying swap transactions has, in recent times, involved the issue of securities. This reflects general trends in capital markets where the use of swaps has become commonplace. The whole concept of new issue arbitrage operates independently of the underlying source of the funding. It should be noted that access to direct funding through securities issues is, at least in part, the basis of the cost differences that allow the process of arbitrage to take place.

The process of new issue arbitrage is primarily driven by the potential availability of lower cost financing. In practice, the process of new issue arbitrage is considerably more complex. The factors motivating new issue arbitrage include:

- Minimisation of borrowing cost.
- Diversification of funding sources.
- Success of the borrowing transaction and ensuring continued market access.
- Specific factors inhibiting access to particular capital markets.
- Liability management flexibility.

The identified factors operate in a number of ways. Minimisation of cost operates as a first order factor that provides the primary incentive for new issue arbitrage. In contrast, the other identified factors are secondary to the basic cost minimisation objective. The additional factors usually serve to set up minimum arbitrage profit targets that must be satisfied before a new issue funding involving a swap can be undertaken.

The cost minimisation objective is self evident. This objective alone is not decisive. This is because it does not, of itself, provide guidance as to the desirability of a transaction per se. For example, the concept of cost minimisation only has significance within a defined asset liability management framework or funding profile. For each borrower where the relevant currency and interest rate exposure basis of the borrowing has been specified, the borrowing cost can be considered a factor. Key relevant factors include the nature of the underlying assets that are being funded, the desired maturity profile of debt, and liquidity considerations.

An additional issue in cost minimisation is the need to set a minimum improvement on the cost of funds before undertaking the swap driven new issue arbitrage transaction. This is because the cost minimisation argument *in extremis* would dictate that even a marginal improvement in cost would dictate undertaking a swap-driven transaction. Given that a particular funding transaction may have implications for future access to the market and hence future arbitrage possibilities, it is necessary to consider some of the other identified factors.

An additional consideration is that at a given point in time, a number of competing swap driven arbitrage opportunities may be available. The borrower may have the choice of a number of issues in various formats that can be swapped to provide cost effective funding. The likelihood of success of individual transactions in terms of market reception etc may vary significantly. Consequently, the risks of a transaction must be considered against the potential cost savings of individual transactions.

The difficulty in precisely quantifying some of the factors further complicates the process.

A major factor affecting the process of new issue arbitrage is the desire on the part of borrowers to diversify the sources of funding on a global basis. The need to diversify the sources of funding for a particular borrower through broadening the investor base of its debt is self evident. The problem is exacerbated in the case of a number of borrowers whose borrowing requirements, relative to the size of their domestic capital market, are large. This type of imbalance is one of the key factors underlying swap arbitrage profits[2]. The process of new issue arbitrage seeks to carefully balance the supply and demand for an issuer's debt both on a global and a market by market basis.

The issue of diversification of the investor base is a complex and controversial one. In theory, distinctions between markets, particularly given the increased trend towards global markets, should not be severe. The use of debt securities that are tradeable freely should, of itself, ensure distribution to the potential investors. This will generally be the case despite the presence of restrictions involving registration and listing etc that govern the sale/distribution of securities. Theoretically, this impedes the process of selling/distributing securities to investors in different markets. Investors are usually able to purchase securities from different markets as and when their investment requirements dictate. This would, in theory, lead to an automatic diversification of a borrower's investor base. This would occur as individual investors would diversify their portfolios in terms of borrower credit risk by buying the existing securities *irrespective of which market the securities were originally issued in.*

However, there is evidence to suggest that international investors only participate in certain sectors of the respective markets. This appears to be motivated primarily by reasons of legal restrictions, liquidity and convenience factors. In fact, there is evidence to suggest that a significant portion of the total international bond market is not readily accessible or liquid enough for active international participation[3]. The presence of restrictions on international fund flows means that borrowers can tap different classes of investors by issuing in different currencies, utilising different instruments and using different issuing formats. This is because the different formats will appeal to particular investor clientele. The factors dictate

---

[2]   See Das, Satyajit (2004) Derivative Products & Pricing; John Wiley & Sons (Asia), Singapore at Chapter 11.

[3]   See Marki, Frederick R V (1986) Size and Structure of World Bond Markets Special Report No 14 – Domestic and International Bond Markets (As of December 1985); Merrill Lynch Capital Markets, International Fixed Income Research Department, New York.

that borrowers need to identify potential investors for their securities. The borrowers specifically need to target these investor bases with the objective of balancing supply and demand to each segment with a view to maximising their arbitrage profits.

The availability of continued market access is also relevant. This dictates that any new issue must be perceived as successful by the market at large. This is designed to allow the borrower to return to access this particular investor base at a future point in time. This requirement, while largely vouchsafed by borrowers, is sometimes neglected, with issuers grossly mis-pricing issues (sometimes unintentionally due to changes in market conditions).

The need to ensure success of the transaction and to maintain continued market access relates to the desire of borrowers to maximise their arbitrage gains from a particular market segment over a medium to long time horizon.

There are restrictions that may impact upon individual institutions' capacity to enter into certain types of new issue arbitrage transactions. The major restriction of relevance is regulatory factors such as registration requirements, that must be satisfied as a precondition to the issue of debt securities. For example, a public issue of securities in the United States domestic market requires a Securities and Exchange Commission registration, equivalent or exemption. In contrast, the self-regulated Eurobond market does not require such registration processes. The documentary and listing requirements are considerably less onerous than in certain domestic markets. An additional factor may be the operation of a queuing system where issuers must formally register their intention to undertake a securities transaction in the particular market. In certain jurisdictions, taxation factors, like the imposition of withholding tax, may limit the capacity to enter into new issue arbitrage transactions.

An additional factor relevant to the new issue arbitrage decision is the difference in flexibility between a direct borrowing and a synthetic funding transaction (borrowing combined with a swap). For example, where a fixed rate debt issue is swapped into floating rate funding, in the same or a different currency, the rollover or repricing timing of the floating rate debt is fixed at the time at which the original swap transaction is undertaken. There are minor exceptions to this. The timing of the repricing dates can be varied either through a separate swap, special arrangements within the swap transaction itself, or by using other instruments (direct borrowings/investments or futures/forward interest rate transactions). This underlying inflexibility may reduce the benefits of a new issue arbitrage transaction. For example, the funding may need to be matched up against an existing portfolio of assets. The characteristics of the assets may not align totally with the synthetic liability created. The residual risk and/or the cost of managing the risk will influence the decision to undertake a new issue arbitrage transaction.

The use of a swap may enhance flexibility. Where floating rate funding is swapped into fixed rate funding, the opportunity to vary the underlying source of liquidity can be seen as adding flexibility for the borrower. Other issues relating to flexibility include the potential to terminate both types of transaction as well as the opportunities for early redemption that vary between a direct borrowing and a synthetic liability entailing the use of a swap.

The factors that underlie the process of new issue arbitrage are complex. This means that the decision to undertake a particular arbitrage transaction requires a balance between the competing considerations. In practice, the factors are summarised in a target cost level set relative to a particular funding benchmark. Common funding benchmarks in this regard include floating rate benchmarks (US$ LIBOR or the floating rate benchmark in the relevant currency rates) or fixed rate benchmarks (rates relative to government securities such as United States Treasury bonds or its equivalent in the particular currency).

In deference to the complexity of determining the economics of any new issue arbitrage transaction, swap targets are set at levels in cost terms below the level of funds available from alternative sources or direct access funding. The arbitrage margin is designed to capture (in quantitative terms) factors such as diversification, the utilisation of scarce market access, restrictions of access to particular markets and flexibility concerns. The benchmarks evolve over time, reflecting the changing conditions in the capital market. Benchmark rates are usually adjusted as a result of changing market opportunities for arbitrage funding.

The whole approach to new issue arbitrage can be best understood in the context of a special category of borrower (referred to as arbitrage funders) who represent the most developed case of new issue arbitrage practices. This aspect of new issue arbitrage is considered in the next Section.

3   Arbitrage Funding

3.1   Concept[4]

The concept of arbitrage funding is merely an extreme case of new issue arbitrage. Specifically, it refers to the practice by a borrower of a highly opportunistic borrowing strategy entailing access to almost any market at short notice[5]. Funding is undertaken on the basis that the issue proceeds are swapped into the borrower's

---

[4]   See Stillit, Daniel "Switching on to Swaps" (May 1987) Corporate Finance 68–75.
[5]   An alternative title of this group is "opportunistic funders".

desired form of funding (interest rate and currency) at a cost lower than a nominated benchmark. The basic concept is best exemplified by the title of an article published in Euromoney in 1985 – "*How SEK [6] Borrows at Fifty Below (LIBOR)*"[7].

The concept involves a highly rated borrower attuned and exposed to market innovations and price/rate movements. The borrower is prepared to take advantage of short-term windows to issue debt in particular forms, currencies and/or structures, with a view to generating cheaper funding elsewhere. The common operational benchmark in this regard is US$ floating rate LIBOR. Arbitrage funders usually nominate a margin *relative* to LIBOR as the relevant benchmark that must be equalled/surpassed if the transaction is to be considered. For example, given a benchmark of LIBOR minus 50 bps, SEK would be prepared to issue say NZ$ securities, provided the accompanying swap could generate US$ floating rate funding at a cost of LIBOR minus 50 bps or better. The fact that SEK did not require NZ$ funding would not constrain the issue.

The distinguishing feature of arbitrage funding is the willingness of the borrower to issue debt on a swapped basis almost totally unfettered by liquidity or asset liability management considerations. Arbitrage funders borrow on a purely opportunistic basis to optimise their costs of borrowing, irrespective of funding requirements. The funding generated is matched against specifically acquired investments (cash, deposits or short term securities) that are later exchanged for normal business assets (loans or other assets required within the relevant business). The maturity of the debt or the availability of offsetting assets are usually not major constraints on particular new fund raising structures/opportunities.

The requirements for effective use of arbitrage funding limit the types and numbers of entities that can engage in the practice. A number of key requirements to undertake arbitrage funding activities can be readily identified:

• **Credit quality** – an important criterion is that the borrower enjoys a high credit standing (usually an AA or AAA rating). This is driven by the fact that the issuer must be acceptable in terms of credit risk to the relevant group of investors. This limits the scope of arbitrage funding for entities other than major banks, sovereign or quasi-sovereign entities, supra-national organisations and a select group of corporations.

• **Funding benchmark** – an additional requirement is the ability for setting targets in terms of universally acceptable interest rate benchmarks. The setting of a benchmark (such as LIBOR plus/minus a margin) implicitly assumes that such

---

[6] SEK is the Swedish Export Credit agency.
[7] See Ollard, Will "How SEK Borrows at 50 Below" (May 1985) Euromoney 13–23.

a cost is relevant to the institution and that the nominated cost level is a realistic estimation of the cost advantage. The need to nominate this benchmark assumes in the case of financial institutions that the entity has assets priced off the same benchmark, or in the case of non-financial institutions that the benchmark represents an alternative source of funding for the borrower. The benchmark issue is relatively straight forward in the case of banks which have substantial portfolios of loans/assets priced off a number of indexes against which opportunistic borrowing can be matched. The opportunistic funding represents significant cost savings relative to alternatives to funding the assets. However, in the case of non-financial institutions, the argument is more complex. It assumes that the funding cost achieved is better than an alternative source of funding priced against the same benchmark. It may be difficult to establish the relative attractiveness of a number of benchmarks. The difficulty arises largely because non-financial institutions tend not to have financial assets. This creates complex asset liability management matching requirements. The benchmark issue also assumes that the borrower has a relatively diverse range of funding facilities or instruments available, allowing the borrower to establish alternative costs of borrowing *directly* in a number of markets. This tends to limit arbitrage funding practices to highly rated borrowers. The traditional benchmarks for arbitrage funding are floating rate indexes such as US$ LIBOR or the relevant floating rate benchmark in a particular currency. Alternatively, the benchmark may be represented as a spread relative to the relevant government bond rate in the currency. The important role of US$ LIBOR in arbitrage funding derives partially from the fact that it is a major market benchmark of interest rates. It is also driven by the fact that arbitrage funders have assets (or alternatively can readily acquire assets) priced relative to this index, creating the opportunity to match off opportunistic borrowings against these investments. An additional reason underlying the use of LIBOR in this particular role relates to the fact that US$ LIBOR functions very much as a central hub against which all currency swaps are transacted. Currency swaps tend to be quoted as a fixed rate against US$ LIBOR.

- **Scale** – the borrower must be of a portfolio size that allows it to readily absorb new opportunistic borrowings with limited dislocation. For example, an attractive funding opportunity may be less attractive if the particular pattern of repricing/rate setting on the floating rate funding generated creates significant mismatches against the borrower's asset portfolio. The resultant exposure on the portfolio may offset the cost advantage achieved. This means that borrowers with substantial portfolios are at a distinct advantage, as their portfolios are likely to be large enough to absorb particular fundraisings without creating this type of additional exposure. In addition, such borrowers are likely to be less sensitive as to the types of liability, maturity, rate reset details etc, as the marginal effect of a new borrowing on the overall portfolio is limited.

- **Access to temporary investments** – an additional requirement is the ability to issue attractively priced new debt and to match them off against specifically purchased investments. The transaction may lock in an arbitrage spread between the borrowing and the investment. This activity is undertaken on a short-term basis. The intention is to ultimately sell off the short-term investments and acquire the basic business assets requiring funding. This means that the borrower's balance sheet must be capable of absorbing significant size transactions without creating undue gearing or other balance sheet pressures.

- **Speed of response** – a critical element in using arbitrage funding is the capability to respond flexibly and quickly to market opportunities. This requires a management structure that is market sensitive and capable of reacting to often short lived opportunities in capital markets. A key requirement in this regard is a funding team with the necessary knowledge and experience to work with financial intermediaries to take advantage of opportunistic borrowing possibilities.

The opportunities available through new issue arbitrage have encouraged large/substantial borrowers with high credit ratings to operate an arbitrage funding strategy. This entails public issues linked to interest rate and currency swaps to generate (at least initially) floating rate US$ at attractive margins relative to LIBOR. In the case of borrowers seeking funding in currencies other than US$, subsequent swap transactions are used to convert the funding advantage relative to LIBOR into lower cost funding in the desired currency or interest rate basis.

Central to this fundraising approach are the following:

- An opportunistic approach to borrowing and willingness to raise funds at short notice, with excess liquidity being invested at a positive spread in anticipation of future funding requirements.
- Significant internal expertise, understanding of capital markets and the capacity to analyse and execute complex transactions within a relatively short time frame to take advantage of market opportunities.
- Receptivity to new issue structures and instruments that are innovative by nature and designed to take advantage of specific investment requirements of particular investors.
- Capacity to use swaps and other derivatives to manage the total debt portfolio.

In the case of arbitrage funders, a review of the list of issues undertaken (particularly, the types of structures) highlight the fact that the currencies and issues structures used are, often, totally at odds with the basic currency and interest rate basis of the requirement of each entity. The discrepancies can only be explained on the basis that the issues are primarily designed to generate lower cost funds in each entity's preferred currency and to allow these borrowers to diversify their fund raising activities.

The range of issuers that can be truly called arbitrage funders is relatively limited. The group is primarily limited to a number of supranationals and sovereign or quasi-sovereign issuers. A number of sovereign borrowers, multilateral development agencies, export credit agencies, banks/financial institutions and corporations operate their funding in this way. In some cases, the nature of the underlying portfolios and range of activities of the entity provides limitations to the extent to which they can operate as purely opportunistic borrowers.

A relatively specialised group of entities that use arbitrage funding techniques are the structured investment vehicles ("SIVs")[8]. These are primarily arbitrage vehicles designed to take advantage of pricing anomalies in capital markets. The SIVs issue debt opportunistically at attractive margins relative to LIBOR. The proceeds are then invested on a closely matched basis in high quality assets to lock in a profitable margin. The SIVs are highly rated and generally borrow opportunistically using arbitrage funding techniques.

3.2   Arbitrage Funding Case Study [9]

In this Section, the mechanics of an arbitrage funding transaction are outlined. **Exhibit 3.1** sets out an example of an arbitrage involving a yen bond issue with accompanying currency and interest rate swap.

4   Benefits/Risks of Arbitrage Funding

The benefits of arbitrage funding are self evident. The issuer will generally achieve a lower cost of funding, increased diversification of its funding and/or access to certain markets. The practice of arbitrage funding also has inherent risks.

---

[8]   See Chapter 4.

[9]   For example, see Massey, Les "One Borrower's Experience of a Eurobond Issue Case Study of a Straight Issue and Swap"; Paper presented at "Globalisation of Capital Markets" Conference organised by IIR Pty Ltd, 12 and 13 March 1987, Hilton International Hotel, Sydney; Shah, Ayesha and Bass, Michael "Case Study of a New Issue Swap" in Das, Satyajit (Editor) (1991) The Global Swaps Market; IFR Publishing, London at Chapter 24.

Exhibit 3.1   Arbitrage Funding Case Study

1. Background
Assume that the borrower/issuer is a AAA rated major international multilateral development agency. The issuer has substantial asset portfolios, primarily loans denominated in US$. The loan portfolio is floating rate and priced off US$ 3 or 6 month LIBOR. The bank is an opportunistic borrower willing to access a variety of markets to obtain cost effective funding to support its asset portfolio.

Major sources of funding for the bank (apart from shareholders' equity) include the following facilities:
- **Short term funding** – this is primarily directly sourced from the following markets:
  1. US$ deposits at around LIBOR.
  2. Euro-Commercial Paper ("ECP") facility, allowing for the issue of ECP or Euro CDs at rates around US$ LIBOR minus 5/6 bps.
  3. US CP program which generates very short-term 30 to 45 day funding at a small margin under US$ LIBOR. The margin varies according to the US CP/LIBOR funding spread.
- **Term funding** – this is primarily sourced from the following markets (for maturity of 5 years):
  1. Bank facilities at around LIBOR plus 25/30 bps.
  2. Public bond issues in a variety of currencies (primarily in Europe) swapped into US$. In recent years, the margins on the borrowings achieved have been in the range US$ LIBOR minus 10 bps to US$ LIBOR minus 15 bps.

2. Funding Opportunity
The specific opportunity that currently exists involves the issue of a Yen denominated bond with an accompanying swap into US$ LIBOR to produce funding for the bank at LIBOR minus 15 bps. The transaction has been proposed by a Japanese securities house. The dealer has approached the issuer with the full funding package (bond and swap).

In practice, the opportunity could have arisen in a number of different ways:
- A proposal from a securities firm or investments (as in this case).
- A specific funding requirement that has prompted the issuer to seek bids for funding.
- Movements in market rates/prices that may have created the funding opportunity (a demand for Yen debt/increases in Yen swap rates).

Frequent issuers constantly/regularly monitor the market for funding opportunities. There is a parallel effort by the investment banks/dealers aware of the funding requirements of different issuers. Frequent issuers who use arbitrage funding practices may seek indicative pricing from particular market segments on a regular basis for major markets, and on a more opportunistic basis in other markets. This means the borrowers are well attuned to market conditions, and are well placed to react to particular opportunities within a relatively short time frame.

In this case, the transaction satisfies the general funding and asset liability matching requirements of the issuer. There is also, in the view of the issuer, a reasonable assurance of a successful reception for the issue. The issuer decides to proceed with the transaction.

The basic structure of the proposed yen issue and the accompanying swap are detailed below:

Structure

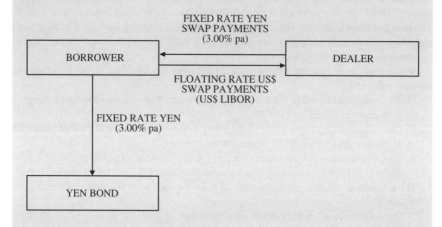

Cash Flows

Dates	Bond Issue (Yen million)	Swap (Yen million)	Swap (US$ million)	Net (US$ million)
27 August 2001	+19,700	−19,700	+157.6	+157.6
27 February 2002	−600	+600	−(US$ 6 month LIBOR − 15 bps)	−(US$ 6 month LIBOR − 15 bps)
27 August 2002	−600	+600	−(US$ 6 month LIBOR − 15 bps)	−(US$ 6 month LIBOR − 15 bps)
27 February 2003	−600	+600	−(US$ 6 month LIBOR − 15 bps)	−(US$ 6 month LIBOR − 15 bps)
27 August 2003	−600	+600	−(US$ 6 month LIBOR − 15 bps)	−(US$ 6 month LIBOR − 15 bps)
27 February 2004	−600	+600	−(US$ 6 month LIBOR − 15 bps)	−(US$ 6 month LIBOR − 15 bps)
27 August 2004	−600	+600	−(US$ 6 month LIBOR − 15 bps)	−(US$ 6 month LIBOR − 15 bps)
27 February 2005	−600	+600	−(US$ 6 month LIBOR − 15 bps)	−(US$ 6 month LIBOR − 15 bps)
27 August 2005	−600	+600	−(US$ 6 month LIBOR − 15 bps)	−(US$ 6 month LIBOR − 15 bps)
27 February 2006	−600	+600	−(US$ 6 month LIBOR − 15 bps)	−(US$ 6 month LIBOR − 15 bps)
27 February 2006	−19,700	+19,700	−157.6	−157.6

Notes:
1. The initial yen receipts are calculated based on an issue amount of Yen 20,000 million, issued at 100.50 with fees of 2.00%, giving net issue proceeds of Yen 19,700 million (calculated as Yen 20,000 million at 98.50% (issue price net of fees)).
2. The US$ amount on initial exchange (US$157.6 million) is calculated at an exchange rate of US$1.00 = Yen 125.00.
3. The US$ 6 month LIBOR flows are based on a US$ borrowing of US$157.60 million. For example, assuming LIBOR of 6.00% pa, the actual interest payment for the relevant six month period (184 days) is US$4,712,240 (calculated as US$157,600,000 × (6% − 0.15%) × 184/360).
4. The Yen payment (Yen 600 million) is based on yen coupon rate of 3.00% pa.

3. Executing the Transaction
The negotiation of the terms of the funding package is more complex than for a conventional funding. This is because the two elements (bond and swap) must be separately negotiated but must correspond to create a cohesive funding transaction.

The key elements in negotiating the actual bond issue include the following:

- **Selection of lead manager** – selection of the lead manager will depend upon the particular borrower's attitudes. The dealer that has brought the opportunity to the attention of the issuer will usually be awarded the mandate. Some borrowers may have established lead managers in particular markets that they will try to use for this particular transaction. "Deal shopping" (that is, awarding the transaction to a dealer other than the one that brought the transaction to the issuer) is not well regarded by dealers. It may lead to the issuer not being shown future attractive borrowing opportunities by the dealer.

- **Pricing and negotiating details of the bond issue** – the dealer that brought the funding opportunity to the issuer will provide indicative pricing. This will be progressively refined as the deal nears execution. The focus will be on the all-in borrowing cost as represented by the final margin relative to LIBOR achieved by the issuer. The issuer may seek a second opinion on pricing for the bond issue from another independent investment bank/dealer with whom it has a relationship in this particular market. This is usually done to mitigate the risk of a mis-priced transaction. The strategy is risky as each house may try to denigrate its competitors and will tend to talk its own "book". Important terms and conditions such as conditions of default, negative pledges, the issuing vehicle to be used and credit support (such as guarantees (if applicable)), must be agreed. The dealer will provide firm final pricing prior to agreement to undertake the issue. The need to provide firm pricing requires the transaction to be structured as a "bought deal" (that is, the lead manager submits a firm offer to the borrower with an underwriting syndicate to be formed only after the borrower has accepted this offer). The technique of the bought deal is designed to transfer the entire market risk from the borrower to the lead manager to ensure that the securities transaction underlying the swap is assured. The "bought deal" should be contrasted with a "best efforts" or classical "open priced" bond transaction. In the best efforts/open priced bond deal, the bond pricing is not pre-agreed and is subject to adjustment based on investor demand[10]. A best efforts/open priced bond issue to be swapped would expose the issuer to a market risk of price movements on the bond and/or swap. Most borrowers regard this risk as unacceptable. Typical offer and acceptance terms for the bond component of the transaction are set out below:

Bond Issue Terms

Issuer:	[Multilateral development agency]
Lead manager:	Japanese securities company
Co-lead managers:	(up to) 2 co-lead managers recommended by the lead manager
Principal amount:	Yen 20 billion
Maturity:	27 August 2006
Coupon:	6.00% pa (annual)
Issue price:	100.50
Gross commissions:	2.
Out-of-pocket expenses:	Reimbursable lead manager's expenses to be a maximum of US$60,000
Payment date:	27 August 2001
Form/denomination of notes:	To be specified
Optional redemption:	None, except in the event of the imposition of withholding taxes and then in whole, but not in part
Payments:	All payments of principal and interest will be made without deductions or withholding for, or on account of, any present or future taxes or duties of whatever nature
Governing law:	The law of England.
Conditions precedent:	Any required approvals to undertake the issue

- **Selection of Eurobond management group for the Eurobond issue** – it is usual to offer the provider of the swap to the bond issue (where it is not provided by the dealer leading the issue) the opportunity to join the lead management group for the securities transaction. Other lead managers may be selected by virtue of their market presence in the relevant sector and/or relationship with either the issuer or the book running lead manager. Underwriters and co-managers will be selected similarly with regard to relationships with the borrower and lead manager, as well as with reference to their placement power and market making capabilities in the particular market. Frequent borrowers to a particular market segment will have favoured co-management groups based on experience gained through the course of a number of transactions. Additions and deletions from

---

[10] For a description of primary market practices in bonds, see Fisher III, Frederick G. (1997) Eurosecurities and Their Related Derivatives; Euromoney Publications, London. See also Kerr, Ian M. (1984) A History of the Eurobond Market; Euromoney Publications, London; Bowe, Michael (1988) Eurobonds; Dow Jones Irwin, Homewood, Illinois; Gallant, Peter (1988) The Eurobond Market; Woodhead-Faulkner, New York.

this co-management group may be designed to create flexibility for particular transaction structures as well as to create incentives for improved performance[11].

The key points of negotiation on the swap component of the transaction will include a range of equally important but significantly different issues. These include:

- **Counterparty credit risk** – it will be necessary to assess the creditworthiness of the swap counterparty, as the issuer will be exposed to the credit risk of the swap counterparty for the term of the transaction.
- **Negotiating pricing, terms and conditions** – as in the case of the bond issue, the issuer will negotiate the terms and conditions as well as the pricing of the swap leading up to final commitment. A particular problem may be getting swaps on truly comparable terms because of the variety of swap structures that can be used in connection with a particular issue[12]. In addition, where there is a series of swaps, the necessity to match different elements of the securities transaction, the initial swap and any subsequent swap create an extra level of complexity. For example, in this example, the issuer could swap the Yen issue into US$ LIBOR and then subsequently swap into fixed rate US$ or another currency.
- **Swap conditional on completion of bond issue** – a key issue in negotiating the swap will be the necessity from the viewpoint of the borrower to ensure that the swap is conditional on the successful closing of the underlying securities transaction. This is designed to minimise any market exposure for the issuer. Swap counterparties usually attempt to resist this condition as it transfers the market risk from the issuer to the swap counterparty.
- **Structuring swap cash flows** – the swap that will be transacted is not a generic swap. The swap will be structured to match the cash flows of the bond transaction. This will include recoupment of issue fees/expenses[13].

Once the final negotiations are completed and swap prices are agreed upon, the parties will confirm the terms of the swap in a form similar to that set out below:

Yen / US$ LIBOR Currency Swap Terms

Yen Payer:	The dealer or counterparty acceptable to issuer (counterparty).
US$ Payer:	Issuer
Commencement Date:	27 August 2001
Maturity Date:	27 August 2006.
Yen Notional Principal:	Yen 20 billion.
US$ Notional Principal:	US$157.6 million

---

[11] The market trend is to small underwriting groups or sole or co-managed transactions.

[12] See discussion in Das, Satyajit (2004) Derivative Products & Pricing; John Wiley & Sons (Asia), Singapore at Chapter 10.

[13] For a discussion of structuring the swap to match a bond issue, see Das, Satyajit (2004) Derivative Products & Pricing; John Wiley & Sons (Asia), Singapore at Chapter 10.

Yen Payments:	The Yen payer will make annual payments on each 27 August Yen 600 million corresponding to Yen coupon payments payable by Issuer on its Yen issue.
US$ Payments:	The US$ Payer will make semi-annual payments on 27 August and 27 February in arrears at 6 month LIBOR less 0.15% pa calculated on the US$ Notional Principal
Initial Exchange:	At the Commencement Date, Yen Payer will pay the US$ Notional Principal and the US$ Payer will pay Yen 19.7 billion
Principal Re-exchange:	At the Maturity Date, US$ Payer will pay the US$ Notional Principal and the Yen Payer will pay Yen Notional Principal
Governing Law:	The law of England
Documentation:	ISDA
Condition Precedent:	Successful closure of Issuer's Yen 20 billion bond issue

Some of the key issues encountered with arbitrage funding transactions include:

- **Issue pricing** – a regular issuer in the relevant market will require that the issue be regarded as fairly priced and trade successfully. This is a particularly vexed issue. One approach to overcoming the difficulties should be noted. A number of borrowers now disaggregate the securities issue and the swap. The book running lead manager of the issue may not be allowed to bid for the swap. This disaggregation is intended to provide fair pricing for both elements of the transaction, as the lead manager is not allowed to cross-subsidise one element of the transaction with profits on the other. This is understandably not popular with dealers who suffer a loss of earnings as a result.

- **Legal issues** – specific problems in arbitrage funding relate to legal considerations, including differences in default conditions in the securities transaction and the swap, or jurisdictional differences between the securities transaction and the swap. Care should be taken to ensure that required linkages between the swap and the issue are inserted into the documentation. Tax effects of the transaction must also be carefully considered.

- **Returning to the market sector** – most frequent issuers will wish to preserve the opportunity to return to a particular sector to undertake a future issue. Consequently, issuers inevitably analyse and rate the performance of participants in a particular transaction. Both the issue and the swap performance are analysed with reference to independent benchmarks. The performance of the underwriters/managers on the securities transactions as well as the swap provider must be recognised, rewarded or punished as merited. One problem may be dealing with unsuccessful bidders as well as those parties not invited to form part of the management group for the issue, a particular problem for a well received transaction.

The major risk is rigid adherence to target spreads without flexibility. This may encourage mis-pricing of securities transactions. This may result in poor secondary market performance and poor distribution, ultimately damaging the borrower's reputation and capacity to access the market over the long term. In essence, a rigid arbitrage funding approach, with insufficient emphasis on the success of the underlying borrowing transaction, may reduce borrowing costs in the short-term. It may in fact, through reduced longer-term market access, cause the borrower's cost of funding to rise. This problem may be exacerbated where the borrower is slow in adjusting target spreads in rapidly moving market conditions.

An often bitter controversy surrounding the borrowing program of the Kingdom of Denmark highlights some of the risks in respect of arbitrage funding. The Kingdom of Denmark established a reputation as one of the premier borrowers in international markets. Denmark approached the Eurobond market 32 times in 1986 alone, raising the equivalent of Danish Krone 45 billion (around US$6.5 billion). Denmark established a reputation as an opportunistic arbitrage funder. The Kingdom used swap-driven securities issues as a means of lowering its all-in cost of borrowings. The debt strategy of Denmark is highlighted in an explanatory note that was released by the Ministry of Finance and is set out as **Exhibit 3.2**. The note provides an interesting insight into the behaviour of opportunistic issuers and arbitrage funding.

Exhibit 3.2   Kingdom of Denmark Foreign Debt Management Strategy

The Kingdom of Denmark (KoD) is one of the most important sovereign borrowers with, in 1986, its gross foreign borrowing reaching a record of US$6.5 billion.

The KoD, that is the Ministry of Finance, does not go abroad to finance the budget (which showed a surplus for 1986) but is a residual or buffer borrower.

The Danish authorities do not want to adapt domestic economic policies to whatever change there may be in private capital movements which are free, except for certain short-term financial transactions.

Private capital movements have, indeed, shown big shifts, for example, from 1985 to 1986 when foreign borrowing by Danish businesses and movements of securities, especially domestic Danish krone bonds, made a swing of about US$7 billion. Furthermore, the borrowing activity in recent years had been enlarged because of prepayments ranging from US$1.5 billion to more than US$3 billion. In 1984, the KoD in fact reduced the outstanding debt whereas in 1987 net borrowing will amount to US$3 billion, assuming that there will be no private capital net inflow.

By the end of 1986 the total foreign debt of the KoD was US$15 billion, corresponding to 18.00% of GDP. For the country as a whole net foreign debt amounted to US$33 billion or nearly 40.00% of GDP.

The KoD and the Euromarket

The Euromarket has developed remarkably during the last few years. Because it is flexible and characterised by non-bureaucratic requirements for documentation, it is here that the growing competition among banks has been most visible and here that changes in borrowing techniques and products have gone furthest. The KoD has, since 1983, raised between 80% and 85% of its new funds in the Euromarket and we see no reason for immediate change.

"Normal" Loans and "Profit" Loans

The KoD conceptually divides its borrowings into two parts, the so-called "profit loans" and the "normal loans". The profit loans are those that would be undertaken even in the absence of a financing need, because it would be possible to place the proceeds at a higher yield. Unfortunately only something like one quarter to one third of the borrowing needs have been covered in this way, and it has been necessary to supplement these with normal market transactions. The difference in the cost of funds between the two types of borrowing was around 40 bps in 1986.

It might be asked whether it would not have been better to relax the target for profit borrowing somewhat and thus increase the volume forthcoming, but it has been found that when the KoD through normal transactions had covered the substantive needs, it could set relatively high standards for further transactions and exploit its unusually quick decision process to take advantage of possibilities cropping up in the markets.

Use of Swaps to Cheapen and Balance the Debt

Until 1983 the KoD used relatively traditional instruments in fund raising. The tremendous development in the swap markets and the willingness, indeed eagerness, of banks to make firm offers for an issue have changed the situation dramatically. Therefore, a borrower can tap the markets where its relative advantage is greatest and reach the desired currency and interest structure through swaps, knowing in advance precisely what the result will be.

The KoD made its first swap-driven new issue in 1983. In the beginning most transactions were fixed rate US$ issues transformed into floating rate money. In later years there has been a rise, especially in swap transactions from yen but also A$, NZ$ and C$. Altogether one third of the amounts raised by the Kingdom in the period 1983–1986 have been through transactions with simultaneous swaps mostly into floating rate US$.

This has left the KoD with a big proportion of dollars in the debt. To avoid the risk which lies in having too much debt in one currency, the KoD in 1986 began to make secondary market swaps out of floating rate dollars into fixed rate European currencies, with a view to a combination of relatively low interest rates combined with the low risk of dramatic exchange rate increases. In 1986 through May 1987 the KoD has swapped more than US$2 billion.

Even stronger change has been caused by the decline in the dollar exchange rate so the KoD's dollar debt fell from 67.00% in 1983 to 46.00% at the end of 1986. Since then it has been further reduced to 40.00%. It is difficult to determine where to go from there, but tentatively it is felt that the share of US$ in present circumstances should be reduced still further, perhaps to around one third of the debt.

While most of our deutschmark and Swiss franc debt has been raised through swaps from US$, ECU debt is provided through direct issues in the Eurobond market. This is due to the fact that it is cheaper getting ECU directly than through swaps. The KoD has normally only raised ECU when the interest rate has been lower than the one which could be theoretically calculated on the basis of the market rates for debt in the component currencies.

Avoiding being Seduced by Options

Many offers look advantageous because the underlying issue has some particular feature in which there is, at least temporarily, a special investor interest, for instance options, especially warrants. Our view is, however, that proceeds from the sale of the warrants cannot be deducted when determining the cost of the loan unless the warrants are covered in some way. This is not to say that the KoD will in no circumstances issue warrants which are harmless, but to say that the question is whether the price for the warrants is high enough to cover the risk. The KoD has made seven transactions with attached warrants, of which five have been harmless.

Eurokrone Market Stabilisation
In 1985 the KoD began raising funds in the Euromarket for its own currency, the krone. It was not caused by a wish to include Danish krone in the portfolio, but rather to reduce the possibilities for arbitrage operations in which a foreign (or other Danish) entity would make Eurokrone issues and place the proceeds in domestic krone bonds at a higher yield. So whenever the interest differential between the Euromarket and the domestic market exceeds a certain level, the KoD is disposed to move with a view to reduce the spread.

Source: (16 May 1987) International Financing Review Issue 673 at 1596–1597.

The opportunistic borrowing strategies of Denmark made it the "darling" of investment bankers/dealers in the Eurobond market. Denmark's willingness to undertake innovative borrowing structures, provided certain cost targets could be met, provided dealers with the opportunity to introduce innovations in security structures and accompanying swaps into the Euromarkets through 1985 and 1986. However, by 1986 there were disturbing signs, suggesting some difficulties with this particular strategy.

Denmark, through 1986, brought to the market a series of aggressively priced transactions. The result was a series of securities which, by general consensus, performed particularly poorly both in syndication/primary market and in secondary market trading. The difficulties encountered appeared driven by a combination of factors including:

- Aggressive pricing (often irrationally so) from underwriting banks competing for international bond business and "league table" status.
- Denmark's use of competition among Eurobond underwriters to lower its borrowing costs.

Denmark used market conditions brilliantly, arguing that the banks making such aggressively priced offers to it must be the ultimate arbiter of how its securities could be sold and distributed in the international market. However, by the end of 1986, there were signs that the strategy had the potential to damage Denmark's reputation with the investor community and capital markets generally[14].

---

[14] See "The Kingdom of Denmark: Why Copenhagen's Debt Strategy is Going Badly Wrong" (28 February 1987) International Financing Review Issue 662 688–689.

The signs were manifested in two particular ways:

- Private indications from a number of major investment banks to the effect that they had no wish to lead manage or indeed participate in any Danish issue while this particular type of debt strategy prevailed.
- Recurrent appearance of a series of repackaged (usually asset swapped[15]) Danish securities issues at pricing levels that were clearly undermining Denmark's future price levels in certain market segments.

The two factors were clearly interrelated. The willingness of Denmark to issue in response to aggressively priced offers from investment banks/dealers led to a series of sometimes arguably ill-conceived transactions that proved profitable only to the lead manager or in a number of cases, to nobody other than Denmark. Problems of structure and pricing rapidly led to other underwriters and market makers becoming extremely reluctant and reticent to participate in Danish issues. This resulted in poor syndication and poor subsequent secondary market trading performance. The poor trading performance allowed financial institutions to repackage Danish securities at very attractive prices *to the investor*. By early 1987, these repackaged issues included the following transactions[16]:

- US$300 million fixed rate issue from Morgan Stanley International that represented a re-marketing of a US$300 million fixed-to-floating issue undertaken late in 1986.
- US$200 million synthetic FRN (dubbed TOPS) created by Bankers Trust International out of a US$1 billion 2 year fixed rate Eurobond launched late in 1986 by Shearson Lehman Brothers International.
- Repackaging by Morgan Guaranty Limited of a historic US$1 billion ten year FRN priced at 0.125% under LIBID (the lowest priced FRN in history until that time) into Deutschmarks and Sterling FRNs respectively totalling DEM 300 million and GBP100 million.

Parallel to the public re-packaged issues, a series of privately repackaged Danish issues were also placed amongst investors. In each case, the repackaging was made feasible by the poor original syndication of the host debt, as well as its poor secondary market trading. The secondary market trading suggested that the real price for Danish securities was much lower (higher spread to LIBOR) than that

---

[15] See discussion of asset swaps/repackaged assets in Chapter 4.

[16] See "The Kingdom of Denmark: Why Copenhagen's Debt Strategy Is Going Badly Wrong" (28 February 1987) International Financing Review Issue 662 688–689.

being obtained by Denmark's relentless use of competitive pressures to achieve the tightest terms each time it came to market. The poor secondary market performance was translated through the repackaging exercises into market clearing levels at which the issues, at least in their repackaged form, could be placed with genuine investors.

What was particularly disturbing was that the repackaged issues (both private and public) emerged at a much higher yield than what market sources estimated Denmark would have attained on any direct borrowing in the particular market segment. For example, on the repackaged Deutschmark and Sterling FRNs (known as Stars and Stripes) the coupons were set at 0.1875% pa and 0.20% pa over Deutschmark and Sterling LIBOR respectively. The levels at the time were significantly above the levels at which Denmark could have issued directly on a floating rate basis in Deutschmark or Sterling.

Essentially, the terms of the repackaged debt had dramatically impacted on Denmark's ability to tap those market segments in future. Investors had available to them a supply of richly priced Danish assets against which any future Danish transaction would be compared. The repackaged issues were essentially determining Denmark's future pricing in the relevant markets.

The re-packaged transactions also had implications for the relationship between Denmark and its investment bankers, underwriters and investors. Its use and reliance on unfettered competition between market participants had inevitably eroded any direct loyalty between borrower, intermediary and investor. This is evident in the fact that in the case of the repackaged issue, the transactions were undertaken with minimum consultation with Denmark. Consequently, Denmark had effectively lost control of the secondary market trading and the repackaging of its debt that ultimately would influence the terms on which Denmark could hope to access particular markets in the future.

Denmark issued a strongly worded reply to these allegations. **Exhibit 3.3** reproduces the reply by Denmark in full. Despite the refutation defending its behaviour, there was evidence that Denmark was aware of the problems. Denmark was looking at means of ensuring a more orderly market for its securities transactions.

The case of the Kingdom of Denmark's debt strategy and the controversy surrounding it highlights some of the risks of arbitrage funding. It is difficult to disentangle the problems of Denmark's debt strategy from the particular market environment that prevailed in the mid to late 1980s. During this period, intense competition between financial institutions, unprecedented growth in capital market activity and generally favourable market conditions may have, to a large extent, influenced events. With the market downturn in the late 1980s following the collapse of global equity markets, the change in market environment from

Exhibit 3.3 "Is the Kingdom of Denmark's Debt Strategy Going Badly Wrong?" – A Reply

If "Big firms" do not want to do business with the Kingdom, it would be more business-like to tell us so directly, rather than do it in a defaming way under the cover of IFR. We have never received a message like that from any bank. On the contrary several prime banks have strongly asked us to be invited to bid for the next deal. By the way, only in eight out of 32 issues made in 1986 competitive bidding was used.

Furthermore, your article touches upon the performance of our issues when they come to market. As everybody knows forecasting the reception of the market is very difficult. However, that key point in bond issuing cannot be avoided so it is no wonder that banks in the market put their very best resources to tackle those problems. From time to time the market is not as good as expected but I fail to see how we are to be blamed, especially when considering that our knowledge and feeling of the market cannot be as deep as is the case for the prime banks.

That brings us to the next issue. Is it true that Danish bonds perform poorly in the secondary market? We do not think so. If you consider the major fixed rate issues we did in 1986, we think they perform reasonably satisfactorily. As far as the US$1 billion Morgan Guaranty FRN is concerned, we must admit that it has never performed well. But we think, as you also mention in the article, that there have been some special reasons for that, especially the United Kingdom super-jumbo FRN a few days later and the general development in the FRN market.

Thirdly, the question of repackaging our issues, which the article take[s] as writing on the wall. It should be noted that a lot of repackaging takes place in the market. It is not only bonds of the Kingdom of Denmark that are involved in such operations. Even the FRN from the United Kingdom has been used in such an operation. We do not think that repackaging operations necessarily is a bad thing. The Euromarket has over the years been very successful. One of the reasons is that the players accept innovations and arbitrage and repackaging is precisely an effort to overcome imperfections of the market. Looking from the borrowers' point of view repackaging could have a positive effect since the neutralising of the repackaged bonds may make it easier for us to sell new issues.

The article mentioned that we are considering to ask the Danish Central Bank to act as "a purchaser of last resort". For information, I can say that our line of thinking is different. The purpose of such operations would be to improve the market efficiency and to make a profit by making purchases in some of the old illiquid outstanding issues.

To sum up it is our conclusion that our strategy has been fairly successful. Quite often in the past the IFR has quoted sources saying that our strategy would backfire and make it difficult for us to place new issues at reasonable prices. Consistently this view has been shown to be erroneous since subsequent issues have been on advantageous conditions. We believe that it will be no different in the future. Quite another matter is that the ultra-competitive phase of the markets may well pass so that profit margins for the banks will improve.

Source: (7 March 1987) International Financing Review Issue 663 at 781.

a borrower's market to a lender's market dictated changed attitudes that mitigated the more extreme aspects of arbitrage funding.

There is little doubt that the opportunistic basis of arbitrage borrowing continues to exist as a legitimate part of borrowers' strategies. In effect, despite the risks of arbitrage funding, its impact on primary debt markets and the way in which new borrowing activity is conducted has not changed significantly.

5 Evolution of New Issue Arbitrage Funding Practices

5.1 Key Evolutionary Factors

New issue arbitrage practices are not static. The opportunistic borrowing behaviour of key borrowers in global capital markets has evolved significantly in response to a variety of market and competitive factors.

The key elements of the initial development and growth of new issue arbitrage funding practices are the environment of growth and innovation that prevailed in the middle to late 1980s. The prevalence of the bought deal and the intense competition between new issue underwriters provided a strong basis for the development of these techniques. This was assisted by the strong growth in the swaps/derivatives market and the high levels of competition that existed among financial institutions seeking to build strong competitive positions in the market for swaps/derivative products. Significant changes in the global financial markets forced adjustment in the business emphasis of dealers and in debt/derivative markets. The changes, in turn, forced changes in arbitrage funding techniques. The changing competitive dynamics were not confined to financial institutions. Increased competition for lower cost funding from an increasingly larger group of borrowers has also greatly impacted upon arbitrage funding practices.

There are approximately five clearly identifiable phases in the evolution of new issue arbitrage practices[17]. Each of these is considered below.

5.2 New Issue Arbitrage – Pre-Swap Age

The predominant characteristics of this period were highly regulated markets and close relationships between borrowers and the lead manager/underwriter. Borrowing transactions were typically negotiated over extended periods of time.

---

[17] See Ljunggren, Bernt "New Issue Arbitrage – Designed Bond Swap Packages at SEK" in Das, Satyajit (Editor) (1991) The Global Swaps Market; IFR Publishing, London at Chapter 23.

Critical elements in determining pricing advantages depended upon the skills of the borrower, the appropriateness of the selection of the lead underwriter and timing of the issue. The ability to ensure liquidity of the borrowers' debt and engineering good distribution of securities was a major determinant of pricing and continued access to markets on a long-term basis.

5.3   New Issue Arbitrage – Early Swap Age

The emergence of swaps in the early 1980s (primarily, as purely counterparty transactions) began to alter the funding equation for high quality borrowers. The critical element in achieving lower cost funding in this period was the capacity and sophistication of borrowers in understanding swap transactions and the ability to negotiate bond/swap packages.

For market participants with no experience of this period, it is difficult to appreciate the radical changes that swap transactions, when linked to bond issues, necessitated. Borrowers needed to decide upon a whole variety of unfamiliar considerations. This included calculation/valuation of cash flows and counterparty credit risks. Transactions required negotiating highly individualised swap transactions where even trivial matters (such as day count and business day conventions) were not standardised and needed to be negotiated on a transaction by transaction basis. An added risk derived from the fact that the borrowing transaction and the accompanying swap would need to be negotiated and completed simultaneously.

Only a few borrowers at this point in time were able to develop the necessary expertise in swap technology to take advantage of the significant cost savings available from these transactions. The transactions undertaken were extremely conventional in nature, usually taking the form of straight bond issues in various currencies with accompanying interest rate or currency swaps to generate funding in the borrowers desired currency or interest rate basis.

5.4   New Issue Arbitrage – The Growth of Swaps

As the swap market grew and the understanding and knowledge of swap techniques proliferated, the practice of new issue arbitrage funding enjoyed rapid growth.

Standardisation within the swap market and a general pattern where dealers presented bond/swap funding packages to borrowers allowed greater numbers of borrowers to take advantage of opportunistic funding techniques.

From the borrowers' perspective, the principal requirements were reaction time and capacity to understand innovation. Swap market opportunities to generate low cost funding were still relatively plentiful. The borrower's reaction time became a crucial factor enabling a particular borrower to take advantage of a market opportunity. Particular borrowers were seen as being receptive to and capable of reacting within an appropriate time horizon, leading financial institutions to focus their efforts on these borrowers. Similarly, receptivity to innovation allowed borrowers to take advantage of arbitrage opportunities. A number of borrowers encouraged innovation and were willing to undertake innovative transactions, allowing them to benefit from a substantial reduction in borrowing costs.

The concept of a funding priced purely as a LIBOR margin emerged. The market conditions were such that it was still possible to bring issues to market with an accompanying swap where it was not essential to aggressively misprice the bond, allowing the borrower the opportunity to both achieve a successful bond issue as well as an acceptable cost of funds.

5.5 New Issue Arbitrage – Maturity of the Swap Market

By the late 1980s, the commoditisation of swaps and the intensity of competition among dealers and borrowers to take advantage of new issue arbitrage opportunities led to a significant deterioration in opportunistic funding practices.

As more and more borrowers understood the advantages of new issue arbitrage and sought to take advantage of funding opportunities, the arbitrage opportunities themselves became more limited. The funding cost achievable and the arbitrage gain also reduced. An additional factor was the increased sophistication on the part of investors, who learned through the development of the asset swap market to look through the packages of bonds and swaps to the floating rate equivalent return of any transaction.

The borrower's role became one of nominating a target funding and waiting for investment banks/dealers to structure a bond/swap package that met the targets. Dealers could now meet investment demand with a list of borrowers, of comparable high credit rating with estimated borrowing targets, all capable of entering into transactions at relatively short notice. As the list of borrowers with their targets increased, the cost savings themselves were eroded. Some degree of trading between credit risk and sub-LIBOR margin began to occur.

For the dealers, this phase of the evolution of the new issue arbitrage market had both positive and negative features. The positive feature was that the increasing indifference of borrowers to the type of bond issue and the swap (provided the borrower's target could be met) allowed the development of a variety of financial instruments, usually with derivative elements embedded. For example, structured notes emerged during this phase[18]. A small group of dealers developed expertise in structured products and concentrated in developing products where profit margins continued to be high.

A larger group of dealers without the technical expertise to engineer the more innovative bond/derivative packages were, in the face of increased competition, caught in a profit squeeze on both the underlying bond and the derivative. The result was often grotesque mis-pricing of the bond and/or the derivative. Dealers competed with almost primeval voracity in an effort to win mandates and execute transactions.

5.6   New Issue Arbitrage – The Late Maturity of the Swap Market

By the early 1990s, a combination of more limited arbitrage opportunities and the presence of a substantial number of borrowers actively seeking to take advantage of such opportunities greatly reduced the scope for new issue arbitrage. Arbitrage transactions were still completed. Fewer arbitrage transactions were completed, the savings in funding costs lower and the types of transaction used to generate funding advantage more varied. An increasing feature of this period was the withdrawal of a large number of dealers from various elements of the new issue arbitrage business (primarily, the debt underwriting side as well as the swap/derivative side)[19]. The developments ushered in a new competitive environment. The market environment was characterised by a greater degree of rationality than at any time since the early 1980s.

In the debt markets, a number of trends were evident:
* In the main bond markets, increased focus on underwriting, pricing and distribution practices led to changes in market practice. This included the introduction of the fixed price re-offer structure in preference to the bought deal. This had the impact of avoiding some of the mis-pricing practices on debt transactions in the past. The bought deal continued to be used selectively but the worst of the excesses of the late 1980s were avoided. The trend was also to very large issue sizes (benchmark issues). There was also increased focus on credit quality, issue liquidity, development of globally fungible distribution settlement and trading in particular issues.

---

[18]   See Chapter 4. See also Das, Satyajit (2001) Structured Products & Hybrid Securities – Second Edition; John Wiley & Sons, Singapore.

[19]   See Das, Satyajit (2004) Structured Products Volume 2; John Wiley & Sons (Asia), Singapore at Chapter 21.

- Bond markets in a variety of new, relatively minor currencies developed in conjunction with parallel swap markets in those currencies. Swap arbitrage opportunities in these markets continued to be available and became a feature of the activity of arbitrage funding. For example, markets in European currencies (Polish Zloty, Hungarian Forint, Czech Koruna), Asian currencies (Korean Won, NT$) and African currencies (South African Rand) emerged.
- The use of continuous issue formats for borrowers, usually in the form of medium term note ("MTN") programs, became increasingly popular. A significant component of issues under these programs was structured quasi-private placements of highly customised securities. These were structured notes, usually incorporating currency, interest rate, equity, commodity and credit derivatives specifically designed to individual investor specifications. The issues were typically combined with specifically engineered swap/derivative structures to generate attractively priced funding for borrowers. MTN programs emerged effectively as the preferred pre-packaged and pre-documented issuance format for structured private placements.

In essence, debt markets bifurcated into two parallel markets:
- A market for large scale issuance in traditional bond issuance format. This market was based on an increasingly negotiated pricing environment where underwriters would agree on the appropriate pricing of the bonds, with controls binding underwriters in terms of syndication and after market pricing.
- A market for issue of structured debt or debt in minor currencies using the MTN format.

Through the 1990s, major borrowers altered their funding practices to fit the new markets' exigencies as follows:
- New issue arbitrage borrowers continued to function as previously. The issuers seek to fund opportunistically and establish debt formats (such as MTN programs) to allow them to take advantage of market opportunity. The approach continues to emphasise rapid reaction time (to allow borrowers to take advantage of market windows) and expertise in analysing innovative debt formats.
- Funding arbitrage transactions are sometimes disaggregated into stages. For example, an issuer seeking to swap a Yen denominated issue in US$ may undertake the swap in stages. The issue may be swapped into floating rate Yen priced off Yen LIBOR initially. The proceeds may be invested in short dated Yen deposits/securities. The issuer may subsequently enter into a cross currency basis swap (receive floating yen/pay floating US$) to convert the funding into US$ as required. The separation of the swap into two components is designed

to allow optimisation of the pricing of each element to increase the benefit of the arbitrage.

- Increasing recognition that borrowers are required to accept, as part of the new issue arbitrage process, some risk elements of the transactions. The risk elements include:
  1. *Amount uncertainty* – where the borrower would not be certain of the amount of funding generated by the transaction, although its cost would be predetermined.
  2. *Maturity uncertainty* – where the borrower was certain of the amount of funding and its cost but not of its precise maturity, although the possible range of maturities would be known.
  3. *Interest basis uncertainty* – that is, whether the borrowing was on a fixed or floating rate basis.
  4. *Currency uncertainty* – where the borrower was subject to uncertainty about the currency in which the borrowing was denominated.

The presence of the risk elements dictated that new issue arbitrage borrowers were increasingly forced into risk reward trade-offs in undertaking transactions. Sophisticated borrowers were usually prepared to accept some of these risks. Most large borrowers were prepared to accept uncertainty in respect of amount and/or maturity that could be absorbed into their overall liability portfolios. A number of large borrowers, particularly sovereign entities, were prepared to accept uncertainty as to the fixed or floating nature of the underlying funding generated. A limited number of borrowers were willing to accept the currency uncertainty of certain types of transactions. In practice, amount and maturity uncertainty are the most common forms of risk assumed.

- A small group of borrowers were willing to extend their opportunistic funding practices in an effort to further reduce borrowing costs at the expense of an increased risk profile. The focus of this approach was to seek to capture the profit of dealers structuring/trading the complex debt/derivative packages. This latter type of approach was exemplified by SEK. In late 1989 SEK entered into arrangements with a specialist risk management consultancy firm (Westminster Equity) to initially analyse and subsequently to design and manage suitable risk positions using dynamic hedging and risk management techniques[20]. Utilising this approach, SEK was prepared to enter into transactions where the borrower issued debt instruments with embedded derivative elements as required

---

[20] See Chew, Lillian "Enticing, But Dangerous" (April 1990) Risk 31–33; Ireland, Louise "SEK's Safety Net Under Nikkei Wire" (May 1990) Corporate Finance 15–17.

by investors. The major difference was that SEK did not immediately immunise itself from the risk of the derivative structure by simultaneous execution of a swap/derivative that passed the risks of derivative elements on to a financial institution. SEK (in conjunction with Westminster Equity) assumed the risk of the position and sought to manage it dynamically. The major advantage to SEK was the capacity to generate the funding and significant margins under LIBOR (claimed to be in the range of 200–300 bps below LIBOR). The approach sought to dis-intermediate dealers from the structuring and risk management role in these transactions. The approach has had mixed success. The approach has not been adopted by a large number of borrowers, presumably because of the increased risks involved.

The current state of arbitrage funding continues to be characterised by the features identified.

6   Impact of New Issue Arbitrage on Primary Debt Markets[21]

Swap/derivative transactions increasingly unbundle the process of fund raising. New issue arbitrage separates the decision to raise funds in a particular market and the conversion of the funds raised into the desired currency and interest rate basis. This means that all the major global debt markets increasingly became arbitrage markets. This resulted in the development of the concept of "swap-driven primary issues". The exact extent to which new debt issuance is driven by swaps is not clear. It is evident that a significant portion of issuance is driven by the availability of the swap[22].

The emergence of swap-driven primary issues has a number of major implications:

- The pricing approach to the issuance of new debt changes radically. As an ever higher percentage of issues become swap-driven, the pricing in almost every segment of the bond market comes to be arbitrage driven. The relevant

---

[21] See Lipsky, John and Elhabaski, Sahar (30 January 1986) Swap-Driven Primary Issuance in the International Bond Market; Salomon Brothers Inc., New York; Benavides, Rosario and Lipsky, John "A Survey of Swap Driven Issuance in the International Bond Market" in Das, Satyajit (Editor) (1991) The Global Swaps Market; IFR Publishing, London at Chapter 17; Das, Satyajit (1994) Swaps and Financial Derivatives – Second Edition; LBC Information Services, Sydney/McGraw-Hill, Chicago at Chapter 19 at 631–640.

[22] For example, see Das, Satyajit (1994) Swaps and Financial Derivatives – Second Edition; LBC Information Services, Sydney/McGraw-Hill, Chicago at Chapter 19 at 631–640.

pricing is not the absolute interest cost of an issue per se. The relevant pricing is that achievable in US$ terms in floating rate terms as a margin relative to US$ LIBOR[23]. Floating rate US$ priced relative to LIBOR emerged as a useful medium against which cross currency swaps were transacted. The exact pricing in US$ terms does not matter, as the existence of deep liquid markets in US$ interest rate swaps means that floating rate could be converted to its fixed rate equivalent and vice versa.

- Swap driven primary issues results in a radical change in the currency distribution of international bond issues. The emergence of swap-driven primary issues of debt appears to have promoted or assisted in the development of international bond markets in a number of currencies, previously unknown outside their national markets.

The pattern of swap-driven issuance in individual currencies is volatile. There are significant changes in the relative share of swap-driven primary issuance in a specific currency from one period to the next. This reflects investor appetite for securities in a particular currency, dictated by anticipated movements in interest rate and currency values.

The impact on the primary debt markets extends well beyond these factors. It includes certain effects on the characteristics of bonds, which themselves started to evolve in response to their function as the host debt for often complex swap-driven fund raising exercises. The primary changes to the characteristics of the bonds include:

- Increased use of non-callable bullet maturities designed to help match counterparties in the swap transaction[24].
- Emergence of structured debt security structures (combinations of fixed or floating securities with embedded derivative elements) designed for investors with specific investment objectives[25].

The emergence of swap driven primary issues also had a profound impact on how the new issue business itself operated. Issuers increasingly saw the actual

---

[23] See Chapter 4 and Das, Satyajit (2004) Structured Products Volume 2; John Wiley & Sons (Asia), Singapore at Chapter 13.

[24] This is ironic in that swap driven issuance reduced the use of call options in bonds. However, a new class of *specifically engineered* callable bonds emerged. These specifically used swaptions to create the optionality. See discussion in Chapter 50.

[25] See Chapter 4. See also Das, Satyajit (2001) Structured Products & Hybrid Securities – Second Edition; John Wiley & Sons, Singapore.

securities/debt transaction and accompanying swap as a single integrated transaction. This meant that the financial institutions active in raising funds for clients had to increasingly acquire new skills and/or re-structure their operations. For intermediaries traditionally strong in the issuance of securities, it meant the acquisition of swap/derivative skills. For intermediaries with strong derivative skills, it provided an opportunity to increase their share of new issue business.

As the practice of arbitrage funding developed, the approach to originating securities transactions and the investment banking business was forced to evolve. Dealers were increasingly required to provide the total package with an all-up cost of funds stated as a margin relative to US$ LIBOR. In addition, as markets became increasingly volatile with short lived issuance opportunities and derivatives became standardised commodity products, the debt origination business moved rapidly into a trading room environment. The process of originating securities transactions had previously often stretched out over a period of months and, in some cases, years. This involved the client being courted by investment banks/dealers. This gave way to highly opportunistic securities transactions on a swapped basis driven by the existence of short lived opportunities.

The opportunities increasingly came to be offered to potential borrowers through the medium of small units working closely with the securities issuance/syndicate desk and swap desks to develop all-in funding packages. These units were referred to variously as "debt transactions group" (Merrill Lynch), "capital market services" (Salomon Brothers), "frequent issuers' desk" (Citicorp and Nomura Securities), "financing desk" (Lehman Brothers) etc. The groups would stay in touch with the borrower (particularly, frequent issuers), advising them of changing opportunities in the international capital markets. In particular, the desks would keep targeted opportunistic borrowers aware of the relatively rapid changes in funding arbitrages available via primary market transactions in various currencies.

As the practice of arbitrage funding evolved, a number of dealers focused almost exclusively on these borrowers, offering them various opportunities as and when they arose. This type of approach to the new issue business is evident from an advertisement in Euromoney in late 1987 placed by Bankers Trust Company. The advertisement was headed: "*If Your Bank Has Never Delivered Money at 200 Points Below LIBOR, Try The One That Has*". The advertisement also indicated that: "*over the last two years, Bankers Trust has lead managed 10 issues for SEK. We were book runners not only on their history-making US$200 million Eurobond issue at more than 200 basis points below LIBOR, but also on the US$200 million 40 year Eurobond issue – the longest term ever done*". Given the status of SEK as a premier arbitrage funder, the strategy of Bankers Trust of centralising its resources to originate capital markets transactions by focusing the attention of various specialists, in a small unit delivering bond swap packages to key large opportunistic borrowers, is self-evident.

The impact on the new issue business of swap-driven primary issues also has a more disturbing aspect. The emergence of primary issues that were swap-driven changed the profit equation on capital market business. There were two sources of earnings – the securities issue and the swap or related derivatives transaction. This meant that the financial institution involved had the opportunity to maximise its own earnings from the transaction by separating the pricing of the two elements to its own advantage. Increasingly through the 1980s, the underlying securities issue was often priced aggressively, sometimes beyond the tolerance of the market. This reflected aggressive pricing by the book running lead manager who, if it provided the swap, used the swap fees to compensate for the terms on the bond. The lead manager essentially relied on competition for market share by underwriters to limit the lead manager's underwriting commitment and therefore its risk of loss on the securities transaction.

The changing profit equation led to mis-priced issues that traded poorly and were not effectively distributed. The mis-priced issues allowed substantial opportunities for asset swap transactions and repackaging of issues into alternative formats, usually involving a swap, to be undertaken[26].

This practice is particularly true of a number of currency segments of the bond and swap market. Dealers take their earnings on the swap which are clearly attributable to them, while structuring a tightly priced securities issue with the objective of syndicating the risk to lower any potential risk on placement of the securities. **Exhibit 3.4** sets out an example of the cross-subsidisation of a new issue transaction.

The pattern of mispricing on the bond side, with the lead manager laying off bonds on the syndicate and making money on the swap, underwent substantial revision in the 1990s. This was particularly true in certain markets such as the Yen where subsidies on the swap as a means of "buying business" had historically been a common, though often heatedly denied, practice[27].

Issuers concerned with market reputation and the desire to maintain longer term access to debt markets increasingly dictated terms on the securities transactions to guard against mis-pricing. Dealers, given that the borrower still wishes to satisfy certain cost targets, increasingly built the subsidy (if any) into the swap/derivatives transaction. This shift in the profit equation had an interesting subsidiary effect. Lead managers can only subsidise to the extent of the proportion of the new issue

---

[26] This aspect is considered in detail in the context of asset swaps in Chapter 4.

[27] These were known colourfully as "hari kari" swaps.

they control. This results in book runners tending to control and distribute a very high percentage of issues. Allotments to other underwriters and selling group participants were confined to relatively small amounts[28]. This also manifests itself as the trend to sole managed issues or smaller underwriting groups.

Exhibit 3.4   Cross-Subsidisation of New Issue Transactions

Consider the interest swap transaction related to a new issue detailed in **Exhibit 10.38** (Das, Satyajit (2004) Derivative Products & Pricing; John Wiley & Sons (Asia) Singapore at Chapter 10).

Assume the issuer has a funding target of 50 bps under LIBOR. The transaction structure generates a cost of LIBOR minus 46 bps. This is below the target level.

The bank arranging the swap can seek to improve the borrower's cost of funds in the following way:

- Increase the rate paid under the swap.
- Lower the yield on the bond issue.

The structure and economics of the alternative strategies are set out below.

Adjusting the Swap Rate
The borrower's target could be met if the swap counterparty was willing to pay 8.53% pa annual (based on the structure utilised). Assuming the adjustments are constant, this equates to an equivalent swap rate of 9.03% pa annual or 8.84% semi-annual (adjusted by the 1 bps reinvested risk premium for the semi-annual-annual conversion). This rate is only 1 bps off the offer spread in the market and translates into a subsidy on a present value basis equivalent to approximately US$238,671 (calculated as a subsidy of 6 bps pa (US$30,000 on US$100 million each semi-annual payment date discounted at 8.78% pa semi-annual).

Adjusting the Bond Yield
The borrower's sub-LIBOR target could be met if the yield on the bond issue could be adjusted by approximately 4 bps. This could be achieved in a number of ways (adjusting coupon as well as issue price). The method outlined below is only one manner in which this adjustment is effected.

The bond is structured as follows:

Coupon	8.00% pa annual
Issue Price:	100
Fees & Expenses:	2.00%

This is equivalent to a yield (net of fees) of 8.51% pa annual.

---

[28] This was evident in a celebrated case where Credit Suisse First Boston pulled out of a syndicate for an issue led by County Natwest for the Kingdom of Belgium. The basis was that County, the book running lead manager, was holding back too much of the issue for itself. This was allegedly in order to offset the reputedly substantial subsidy on the swap it had provided to win the particular mandate.

The bond yield could be adjusted as follows:

Coupon   8.00% pa annual
Issue Price: 100.15
Fees & Expenses: 2.00%

This is equivalent to a yield (net of fees) of 8.47% pa annual (4 bps lower than the original bond yield).

The new adjusted swap rate is as follows:

Item	(% pa annual)
Swap rate	8.96
Amortisation of fee reimbursement	−0.48
Adjustment for delay	+0.04
Adjusted swap rate	8.52

Notes:
- The annualised equivalent of 8.78% pa semi-annual is 8.97% pa annual (a 19 bps gross up). However, the swap rate utilised is adjusted by 1 bp to reflect the added reinvestment risk to the counterparty.
- The swap rate is reduced by 0.48% pa to recover the 1.85% up front payment (1.875% for fees and 0.125% for expenses adjusted for the issue premium of 0.15%) amortised over five years. The discount rate used is the swap rate (8.97% pa annual) but could be higher or lower reflecting the cost of funding the payment to the dealer and the credit risk of the issuer.
- The swap rate is increased by a 0.04% adjustment to cover the delayed start of 4 weeks. This represents the positive carry or earning on the hedged or offsetting swap with immediate start. This is calculated as earnings of 2.00% (based on short-term rates of 6.00% pa semi-annual versus bond rates of 8.00% pa semi-annual) over four weeks (around 15 bps) amortised over five years at the swap rate (8.97% pa annual).

The net result of the swap is that the dealer would pay 8.52% pa annual. The dealer makes annual payments of 8.00% pa annual to match the bond coupon and receives a spread under LIBOR. The swap dealer receives LIBOR minus a margin every six months. The margin under LIBOR would be the floating rate equivalent of 52 bps. The 52 bps requires adjustment as the fixed rate and floating rate payments are not calculated on the same day count basis and paid on the same frequency. The 52 bps annual bond basis would be adjusted by 2 bps to an equivalent spread of 50 bps semi-annual LIBOR or money market basis[29].

The economic cost of this transaction to the financial institution will depend on whether the institution is providing the swap only or is underwriting the bond (and if so, the underwriting commitment).

---

[29] This is calculated as the swap rate (8.97% pa annual) minus the spread (52 bps annual) de-compounded into semi-annual equivalent to derive the semi-annual spread by deducting the semi-annual swap rate (8.78% pa semi-annual) which is then converted to a LIBOR/money market basis to provide the final spread.

Assume the following:

*   The swap counterparty underwrites, as book running lead manager, US$20 million of the issue.
*   The investor demands a return of 8.51% pa annual to purchase the bond. This implies a bond price in new issue trading of 98.00. This is below the trading price assuming deduction of full fees of 98.275 (issue price (100.15%) less fees (1.875%)).

The swap counterparty, in relation to its underwriting, incurs a loss of US$55,000 (0.275% (the market price less the price at which the underwriter acquires the bond) on US$20 million). This is presumably acceptable as it is covered by the earnings on the swap (approximately US$139,225 based on the spread from the mid of the bid-offer spread on the swap).

The other underwriters will, in this situation, make commensurately higher relative losses depending on their fee entitlement (which may be lower).

The change in the distribution of profits between the securities and the swap is not without its critics. The critics argue that it might be more desirable to take a loss on the mis-priced bonds than to book an off-market rate swap. This is because the latter is a term commitment that will stay on the books of the particular institution, and will require capital to be held against it over the full term.

The change in environment in international capital markets at the end of the 1980s and in the early 1990s eliminated the worst of the excesses identified. Reduced competition between financial institutions and investor unwillingness to purchase mis-priced securities have led to broadly more rational new issuance practices. The adoption of the fixed price re-offering system and the trend to consensus pricing represents manifestations of this general movement. The developments do not obviously ensure that all bonds are appropriately priced, or that no element of subsidisation is present in bond/swap combination transaction. In reality, subsidisation and mis-pricing of issues continues to be a factor, albeit a less important one than previously in capital markets.

7 Summary

Derivatives (in particular, interest rate and currency swaps) can be used as an instrument for new issue arbitrage. New issue arbitrage entails combining the issuance of debt with a concurrent interest rate or currency swap to create a synthetic liability. The specific driver is that in the specific circumstances, new issue arbitrage can provide financing at a cost less than that available through conventional direct access to the relevant market.

In a practice referred to as arbitrage funding, frequent/opportunistic borrowers exploit the potential advantages of new issue arbitrage. This practice also has risks. The advantages significantly outweigh the potential risks. A small number of highly rated entities undertake this form of opportunistic borrowing. They raise funds at attractive costs, taking advantage of market opportunities to issue. The proceeds are swapped initially into US$ LIBOR based funding. The proceeds may be invested in short term liquid investment pending deployment in the operations of the issuer. The defining characteristic of this arbitrage funding is the ability to borrow without the constraint of liquidity requirements and asset liability matching constraints.

The opportunistic borrowing practices have evolved since the mid 1980s. They have had a major effect on the primary debt markets and the operation of new issue/debt underwriting businesses. The primary debt markets have come to be swap or derivatives driven. While changes in the market environment have led to some changes, the basic impact of swaps/derivatives persists. This reflects the fact that swap-driven primary issuance is now an established and important part of the structure of the international capital market.

SYNTHETIC ASSETS

4

Synthetic Assets – Asset Swaps, Structured Notes, Repackaging and Structured Investment Vehicles

1 Overview

Applications of derivative instruments focus on using derivatives to transfer risk. The risk transferred typically derives from business cash flows or funding transactions. Derivatives can also be used to manage the financial risk of investments. An extension of this form of derivative application is the *creation of synthetic assets*. This entails the use of combinations of debt instruments and derivative contract(s) to create a synthetic investment asset. The defining feature of synthetic assets is that the transaction is driven by the investor's requirement for an investment not directly available, or the ability to create an investment with superior economics to a direct investment.

In this Chapter, the use of derivatives to create synthetic assets is discussed. The structure of the Chapter is as follows:
- The basic concept of synthetic assets and the various types of structures used are outlined.
- Asset swap transactions are examined.
- Structured notes are described.
- Synthetic assets created using special purpose repackaging vehicles are discussed.
- Structured investment vehicles are outlined.

The focus in this Chapter is on the basic concept of synthetic assets including types, structures, design/trading and the market for these instruments. Synthetic assets are available and used in each asset class. These structures are discussed in relation to derivatives on the individual asset class in the relevant Parts of the Book focused on these transactions[1].

2   Synthetic Assets – Concept & Types

The term synthetic asset is generic. It is used to indicate a transaction where an investment asset is created by combining a debt (fixed or floating interest rate) instrument with a derivative transaction. The objective is to synthetise an investment with specified characteristics nominated by the investor. This may include the following features of the asset:
* Currency.
* Interest rates (fixed or floating).
* Contingency on any cash flow.
* Linkage of interest or principal to price/rate fluctuations in a nominated asset.

The motivations driving the transaction will generally include:
* Ability to create an investment asset that is not available directly in the market.
* Capacity to generate higher returns than available on an equivalent investment with similar characteristics.
* Ability to assume specified exposure in exchange for commensurately adjusted returns on the investment.

There are a number of identifiable types of synthetic asset structures including:
* **Asset swaps** – this covers a group of transactions where derivatives (primarily interest rate and currency swaps) are used to alter the currency or interest rate profile of investment assets. The focus is on altering some of the features/attributes of the underlying asset available in the market.
* **Structured notes** – this entails the issue of debt instruments (fixed or floating interest rate notes) where a derivative transaction is engineered into the structure to create a synthetic investment asset. The differentiating feature of the structured notes compared to asset swaps is that there need not be a direct investment asset available in the market. The complete investment asset is manufactured/synthetised.

---

[1]   See Chapters 16, 17, 18, 19 and 20, and Das, Satyajit (2004) Structured Products Volume 2; John Wiley & Sons (Asia), Singapore at Chapters 2, 3, 4, 7, 12, 15, 16 and 17.

Synthetic assets often use special repackaging structures. This entails the use of special purpose repackaging vehicles or entities to act as the issuer of the security. There are several types of structures including:

- **Repackaging vehicles** – this entails the use of a special purpose repackaging vehicle to act as the issuer of the synthetic asset. The underlying asset structure is not altered. It is designed to enable the creation of synthetic investment assets predicated purely on the nominated investment parameters of the investor.
- **Structured investment vehicles** ("SIVs") – this covers a special class of repackaging vehicles that operate actively managed portfolios of synthetic assets. These are specifically funded through the issue of securities that rely on the cash flow of the synthetic investments to provide return of capital and returns. The distinguishing feature of SIVs is that the investor in the SIV does not obtain specific exposure to a nominated asset as in the case with repackaging vehicles.

Each of the types of synthetic asset structures is considered in detail below.

3   Asset Swaps[2]

3.1   Concept

Asset swaps involve extending the underlying concept of liability swaps to the creation of synthetic assets. "Asset swap" is a generic term for the repackaging of a security, usually a debt security. It entails altering the features of the underlying asset in terms of either interest rate (fixed or floating rate) or currency. For example, an asset swap may entail altering the interest rate of a debt security, paying fixed interest rates into floating interest rates, or from floating rate into fixed rate. It may also alter the cash flows of a debt instrument with interest and principal payments in one currency (yen) into interest and principal payments in another currency (US$).

The market for assets swaps (consistent with other synthetic assets) exists primarily for the following reasons:

- Existence of an arbitrage (similar to a liability arbitrage), enabling the creation of a higher yielding investment than an equivalent asset directly available in the market.

---

[2]   See Partridge-Hicks, Stephen, and Hartland-Swann, Piers (1988) Synthetic Securities; Euromoney Publications, London, England. See also Krishnan, Suresh E. "Asset Based Interest Rate Swaps" in Beideleman, Carl R. (1991) Interest Rate Swaps; Business One Irwin, Homewood, Illinois at Chapter 8; Efraty, Ravit (2 October 1995) An Introduction to Asset Swaps; Salomon Brothers, New York; Arbitrage Research and Trading "Two Become One" (June 2000) FOW 74–78.

- Lack of availability of a particular investment with the desired credit, interest rate or currency characteristics in conventional form that creates the opportunity to generate a synthetic investment using the asset swap.

Asset swaps are predicated on the fact that investors often require a set of cash flows that is unavailable directly in capital markets. In order to create the desired cash flows, the investor combines an existing cash market instrument and a swap to create the synthetic asset.

3.2 Asset Swap Structures

3.2.1 Mechanics

The basic mechanics of an asset swap are similar to that of a liability swap. The asset swap will usually entail a series of linked steps:
- The underlying physical security is purchased for cash.
- Cash flows (both interest and principal (in the case of a cross-currency asset swap)) are linked to either an interest rate or a currency swap to change the interest rate or currency denomination of the investment into the desired form.
- The overall package is held by the investor, or if assembled by a dealer, is sold to an ultimate investor as an asset in its synthetic form.

Exhibit 4.1 sets out the basic structure of an asset swap involving an interest rate swap. **Exhibit 4.2** sets out the basic structure of an asset swap involving a currency swap.

In practice, the structuring of an asset swap is more complex. Investors in synthetic assets will generally prefer an investment at par with the fixed or floating coupons equal to the purchase yield of the synthetic asset. Structural problems are created by factors such as accrued interest on the underlying security and/or any discount or premium on the purchase of the debt security (reflecting differences between the coupon of the security and the current market yield for the asset). This requires significant adjustments to the asset swap to convert the cash flows of the security to the desired pattern[3]. **Exhibit 4.3** sets out an example of structuring an asset swap, including the required adjustments.

Asset swap structures are related to the underlying market for these types of transactions. The market for asset swaps has evolved over the period since the

---

[3] The adjustments required in structuring an asset swap are similar to those required in relation to structuring non-generic swaps; see Das, Satyajit (2004) Derivative Products & Pricing; John Wiley & Sons (Asia), Singapore at Chapter 10.

early 1980s. It has a number of clearly identifiable dimensions:
- Type of asset swap transaction classified by category of investor.
- Type of underlying securities used in structuring the asset swap.
- Private versus public/securitised asset swaps. Private asset swap structures can be separated into investor made swaps and synthetic securities.

The basic asset swap structures used are largely dictated by the interaction of these various structural dimensions. Each of these aspects of asset swaps is examined in the following Sections.

Exhibit 4.1   Asset Swap Involving Interest Rate Swap

Assume the underlying transaction in this case is the purchase of a US$10 million fixed rate US$ bond with a maturity of three years and a coupon of 8.00% pa payable semi-annually. The fixed rate US$ bond is swapped into a floating interest rate asset (synthetic FRN) yielding LIBOR plus 75 bps through an interest rate swap.
The structure of the transaction is set out below:

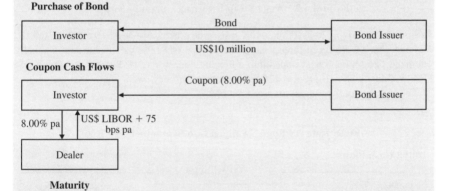

Fixed Rate US$ Bond Swapped to Synthetic FRN

The detailed cash flows (from the viewpoint of the investor) are set out below:

Year	Bond Cash Flows ($)	Swap Payments ($)	Swap Receipts ($)	Net Cash Flows ($)
Spot	−10,000,000			−10,000,000
0.5	+400,000	−400,000	+6 month LIBOR + 75 bps	+6 month LIBOR + 75 bps

Year	Bond Cash Flows ($)	Swap Payments ($)	Swap Receipts ($)	Net Cash Flows ($)
1.0	+400,000	−400,000	+6 month LIBOR + 75 bps	+6 month LIBOR + 75 bps
1.5	+400,000	−400,000	+6 month LIBOR + 75 bps	+6 month LIBOR + 75 bps
2.0	+400,000	−400,000	+6 month LIBOR + 75 bps	+6 month LIBOR + 75 bps
2.5	+400,000	−400,000	+6 month LIBOR + 75 bps	+6 month LIBOR + 75 bps
3.0	+400,000	−400,000	+6 month LIBOR + 75 bps	+6 month LIBOR + 75 bps
	+10,000,000			+10,000,000

The combination of the purchase of the bond and the entry into the interest rate swap enables the investor to create a synthetic FRN investment. The investor has no exposure to fixed rates under the structure. The investor's exposure under the asset swap includes:
- Exposure to the credit risk of the issuer of the bond.
- Exposure to the credit risk of the swap counterparty.
- Market risk on the floating interest rate.

Exhibit 4.2   Asset Swap Involving Currency Swap

Assume the underlying transaction in this case is the purchase of an A$10 million fixed rate A$ bond with a maturity of three years and a coupon of 8.00% pa payable semi-annually. The fixed rate A$ bond is swapped into a floating interest rate US$ assets (synthetic US$ FRN) yielding US$ LIBOR plus 125 bps through a currency swap.

The structure of the transaction is set out below:

Fixed Rate A$ Bond Swapped Into Synthetic US$ FRN

Initial Cash Flows

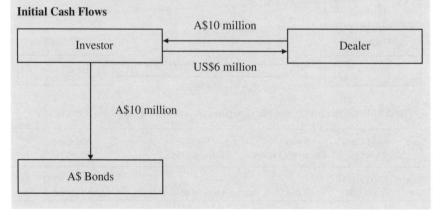

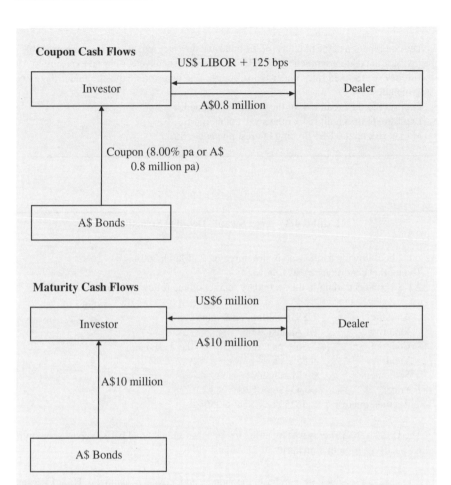

Coupon Cash Flows

Maturity Cash Flows

The detailed cash flows (from the viewpoint of the investor) are set out below:

Year	Bond Cash Flows (A$)	Swap Payments (A$)	Swap Receipts (US$)	Net Cash Flows (US$)
Spot	−10,000,000	+10,000,000	−6,000,000	−6,000,000
0.5	+400,000	−400,000	+6 month LIBOR + 125 bps	+6 month LIBOR + 125 bps
1.0	+400,000	−400,000	+6 month LIBOR + 125 bps	+6 month LIBOR + 125 bps
1.5	+400,000	−400,000	+6 month LIBOR + 125 bps	+6 month LIBOR + 125 bps
2.0	+400,000	−400,000	+6 month LIBOR + 125 bps	+6 month LIBOR + 125 bps
2.5	+400,000	−400,000	+6 month LIBOR + 125 bps	+6 month LIBOR + 125 bps
3.0	+400,000	−400,000	+6month LIBOR + 125 bps	+6 month LIBOR + 125 bps
	+10,000,000	−10,000,000	+6,000,000	+6,000,000

The combination of the purchase of the bond and the entry into the currency swap enables the investor to create a synthetic US$ FRN investment. The investor has no exposure to A$ in currency or A$ fixed rates under the structure. The investor's exposure under the asset swap includes:

- Exposure to the credit risk of the issuer of the bond.
- Exposure to the credit risk of the swap counterparty.
- Market risk on the US$ floating interest rate and US$.

Exhibit 4.3   Asset Swap – Detailed Structure

Assume the following asset swap is structured on 23 March 2001.

The market conditions are as follows:

- A US$ bond is trading in the secondary market on the following terms:

Amount:	US$10 million face value
Maturity:	21 August 2006
Coupon:	7.50% pa (Annual 30/360 day basis)
Yield:	9.85% pa
Settlement:	30 March 2001
Price:	90.43436 or US$9,043,436
Accrued interest:	4.56250 or US$456,250

- The US$ swap market is trading at 8.23/8.30% pa (annual bond basis) versus six month US$ LIBOR for a final maturity of 21 August 2006.

The investor decides to purchase the bonds and create a synthetic US$ FRN as follows:

- On 30 March 2001, the investor pays US$9,499,686 to purchase the bonds.
- To convert the investment into the desired synthetic US$ FRN at an investment value of US$10 million or the par value of the bond, the following swap is also transacted:
  1. Investor pays swap counterparty an additional US$500,314 on 30 March 2001 to bring its investment to US$10 million.
  2. Investor pays swap counterparty US$750,000 every 21 August commencing 21 August 2001 and ending 21 August 2006. Note that the first payment reflects the full annual coupon rather than the accrual from settlement.
  3. Investor receives from swap counterparty a margin over 3 month LIBOR based on a principal amount of US$10 million. The first payment is on 21 May 2001 (for a broken or stub period) and then quarterly thereafter on 21 August, 21 November, 21 February and 21 May with the final payment on 21 August 2006.

The margin relative to three month LIBOR is calculated as follows:

	(% pa)
Bond Coupon	+7.50
Swap Fixed Rate	−8.30
Adjustments	
1. Additional initial payment	+1.15
2. Full first coupon	+1.02
Margin	+1.37

Notes:
1. All rates on an annual basis.
2. Calculated as US$456,250 discounted back to 30 March 2001 from the coupon payment date of 21 August 2001 from and then amortised over each coupon date at swap rate (8.30% pa).
3. Amortisation of US$500,314 over each coupon date at swap rate (8.30% pa).

The margin of 1.37% pa is on an annual bond basis and must be converted to quarterly money market basis. The margin on a quarterly money market basis to the investor would be 1.27% pa (127 bps)[4].

The investor receives US$ 3 month LIBOR plus 127 bps quarterly on its initial investment of US$10 million.

The combination of the purchase of the bond and the entry into the interest rate swap enables the investor to create a synthetic FRN investment. The investor has no exposure to fixed rates under the structure. The investor's exposure under the asset swap includes:
• Exposure to the credit risk of the issuer of the bond.
• Exposure to the credit risk of the swap counterparty. The exposure under the swap is greater than for a normal interest rate swap. This is because the investor makes two additional payments (the initial payment and the full coupon payment) that are recovered over the term of the transaction.
• Market risk on the floating interest rate.

3.2.2 Variations

The basic asset swap structure entails swapping of a fixed rate asset into a floating rate of return or vice versa. Alternatively it entails the swapping of the currency denomination of the asset as well as the interest rate basis. A number of variations

---

[4] This is calculated as the swap rate (8.30% pa annual) plus the spread (137 bps annual) de-compounded into quarterly equivalent (9.34% pa) to derive the quarterly spread (bps) by deducting the quarterly swap rate (8.05% pa) which is then converted to a LIBOR/money market basis to provide the final spread of 127 bps (129 bps × 360/365).

of the basic asset swap structures are also feasible[5]. Typically the more complex types of asset swaps fall into the following categories:

- Variations resulting from differences in the underlying securities used as the basis of the asset swap.
- Adjustment swaps involving alteration of the basic cash flow of the security, usually using a structured swap.

An example of the first type of transaction may be a floating-to-floating asset swap where a basis swap transaction is used to convert a US$ LIBOR-based floating rate certificate of deposit into a floating rate asset yielding a return relative to US$ Commercial Paper rates[6]. Other variations may involve an asset swap with an amortising or sinking fund provision where the underlying instrument must be swapped using an amortising swap[7]. It may involve a callable bond that must be swapped using a swaption/option on swap[8].

The concept of an adjustment swap is more complex. Investors may prefer to change the cash flow characteristics of the underlying security for tax or accounting reasons. For example, an investor buying a fixed rate bond or FRN at a substantial discount may convert it into a par security by entering into an interest rate swap. Under the swap, the investor pays fixed or floating interest rates at a rate equal to the coupon on the security. This rate will usually be less than the market rate on the swap of that maturity. In return for paying less than a market return, the investor will make a one-time up-front cash payment to the swap counterparty, equal to the difference between the par value and the purchase price of the security. The difference compensates the swap counterparty for receiving a sub-market coupon, with the up-front payment being repaid to the investor over the life of the swap in the form of a premium on the swap payments it receives. In the opposite situation, an investor buying a bond at a premium may choose to pay an above market rate on the swap equivalent to the bond coupon, in return for an up-front payment from the swap counterparty equal to the premium on the bond. This payment is recovered by the swap counterparty by the fact that the investor pays an above market coupon under the swap.

---

[5] For a description of a range of these types of transactions, see Lecky Jr, Robert P (1987) Synthetic Asset Handbook; First Boston, Derivative Product Group, New York. Increasingly, asset swaps feature embedded credit derivative elements; see Das, Satyajit (2004) Structured Products Volume 2; John Wiley & Sons (Asia), Singapore at Chapter 11.

[6] See Chapter 14.

[7] See Chapter 13.

[8] See Chapter 15.

The adjustment swaps allow investors to smooth out and adjust the cash flows connected with specific investments. Swap coupons can be set equal to bond coupons, while margins above or below market coupons can be exchanged for up-front or in some cases, back end payments. This allows the investor to rearrange cash flows from an investment into a structure that the investor finds more suitable.

Examples of these types of adjustment swaps include:

- Par/par flat swap where an investor wishing to invest in a par asset at a stated return with no accrued interest needs to convert a security trading at a discount through the specific swap structure.
- A zero coupon issue swapped into a three or six month floating rate coupon.
- A discount floating rate coupon swapped to full floating coupon. Where a FRN is trading at a substantial discount to par and the investor wants current income, the investor would prefer to buy the bonds at par and receive the current market yield to maturity spread rather than the difference between the purchase price and face value of the notes at maturity. **Exhibit 4.4** illustrates an adjustment swap involving swapping of the discount on a FRN to a full floating coupon.
- A zero coupon bond swapped to a full fixed coupon. For example, where the zero coupon is priced attractively but the investor desires to shorten the duration and improve the cash flow of the investment.

Exhibit 4.4   Adjustment Asset Swap

An investor has the opportunity to buy the following FRN:

Amount:	US$5 million
Maturity:	30 June 2005
Interest rate:	6 month LIBOR payable semi-annually
Price:	98.80
Yield to maturity spread:	LIBOR + 34 bps pa
Current coupon:	6.3125%
Settlement date:	30 June 2001

The investor has a preference for current income. The investor would prefer to purchase the FRN at par and receive the current market yield to maturity spread as coupon income. The investor achieves this by entering into an asset swap whereby:

- Investor pays the counterparty six month LIBOR flat semi-annually as well as an up-front payment of 1.20% or US$60,000 on US$5 million.
- Investor receives six month LIBOR plus 34.44 bps semi-annually over the life of the transaction.

The spread over LIBOR earned by the investor equates to the 1.20% being amortised over the outstanding life of the security at an assumed rate of 7.00% pa semi-annually adjusted for the LIBOR day count basis.

3.3   Asset Swaps – Types

The types of asset swap transaction are dictated by the investor base for such synthetic assets. This in turn is driven by the objectives that drive investment in asset swaps. The main factors include:

- Increasing securitisation of capital markets that has led borrowers to increasingly issue securities to raise funding. This is driven by the fact that capital markets provide funding on more competitive terms than that available from financial intermediaries, primarily banks. This is particularly the case with borrowers of high credit quality (investment grade, particularly A or better). In the US and to a lesser extent in Europe, the trend to securitisation has extended to non-investment grade borrowers. This is driven by the rapid growth of high yield debt markets in the US and Europe. This development has created shortages of conventional loan assets issued, particularly by better credit quality borrowers. As a result, many banks face lower growth of the asset base, as these entities lose their historic corporate customer base to the securities markets.
- The (often substantial) improvement in return that is achievable through synthetic assets relative to the purchase of direct investments. Under certain market conditions, there are opportunities for a yield pick-up through asset swaps. This creates a ready-made market for the synthetic assets, primarily among banks.
- Use of asset swaps also helps banks to increase the level of diversification of their asset portfolios. This has the effect of reducing the credit risk of the portfolio[9].

Similar factors have attracted traditional investors (such as insurance companies, pension funds and investment managers) to the asset swap market.

The major types of asset swaps include:

- Assets denominated in any currency swapped into synthetic US$ LIBOR based FRNs for placement primarily to banks. This can be extended to asset swaps designed to create synthetic FRNs in currencies other than US$ to match demand for non-US$ floating rate assets from banks.
- Asset swaps that entail the creation of synthetic fixed rate bonds (in currencies such as US$, Euro and Yen) using either fixed or floating rate securities in a variety of currencies for sale to institutional investors.

A number of variations of special structured transactions are also feasible, including:

- Insurance company deposit transactions. **Exhibit 4.5** sets out an example of an insurance company deposit transaction.

---

[9]   See Das, Satyajit (2004) Structured Products Volume 2; John Wiley & Sons (Asia), Singapore at Chapters 13 and 14.

- Matched zaitech transactions. **Exhibit 4.6** sets out an example of a matched zaitech transaction.

Asset swaps involving the creation of synthetic US$ LIBOR based FRNs placed with banks constitute the most significant sector of the asset swap market[10]. The predominance of this structure primarily reflects the nature of the underlying investment demand. This demand is from commercial banks seeking floating rate assets (loan type assets) that can be match funded. The continued need for high quality and relatively high yield assets by a large group of commercial banks seeking asset growth drives this particular market segment. The major source of demand for this type of asset swap is medium to smaller banks. The banks are driven by the absence of direct access to the underlying credit assets, need for portfolio diversification and the inability to finance foreign currency assets. The yield pick-up often available from asset swaps, compared with the return available on equivalent direct investments, provides an additional incentive for these banks.

The attraction of synthetic US$ FRNs created using asset swaps also relates to the call features on normal FRNs. The call option on a FRN allows the borrower to redeem the issue prior to maturity. In the late 1980s/early1990s, the absence of high quality assets and competition among financial intermediaries led to decreasing levels of call protection on FRN issues. FRNs with protection against calls tend to trade at a premium to par, causing significant erosion in margin that are unattractive to investors. Asset swaps are particularly attractive for the investor as the underlying asset will have, in most cases, higher levels of call protection. A similar argument is relevant for banks. This is because most bank loans are callable/pre-payable at short notice. The asset swap, in contrast, provides significant call/pre-payment protection.

Exhibit 4.5   Structured Asset Swap – Japanese Insurance Company Transaction

Japanese insurance companies were the primary factor driving insurance company deposit transactions. These companies had a requirement to invest substantial volumes of funds in assets denominated in currencies other than Yen. This particular investment requirement could usually not be satisfied directly for the following reasons:
- The institution in question could not actually undertake foreign investments and was limited to domestic investments within Japan such as bank deposits.
- The institution was allowed to invest overseas but had already reached or was near the maximum limit imposed by the Ministry of Finance[11].

---

[10]   For an analysis of the dynamics of the market, see Hartland-Swann, Piers "Asset Swaps – Bringing Technology to Investors" in Das, Satyajit (Editor) (1991) Global Swaps Market; IFR Books, London at Chapter 16.
[11]   In the 1980s, this limitation was 10% of their overall investment portfolio.

- Direct investment in a foreign market was problematic because of unfamiliarity with the credit quality of issuers of the underlying securities, settlement difficulties and the impact of withholding tax on cross-border interest flows.

In these circumstances, a number of structures were developed to circumvent some of the difficulties. In a typical transaction, an insurance company would make a deposit in the desired currency (C$) with a Japanese bank. The Japanese bank in turn would buy a matching synthetic asset in C$ that provided the necessary cash flows to make interest payments and repay the original principal invested by the institution. The synthetic C$ asset would usually consist of floating rate US$ assets (either a US$ FRN or US$ CD's that were rolled over on maturity) combined with a C$ fixed/US$ LIBOR currency swap.

The structure of the transaction is set out below:

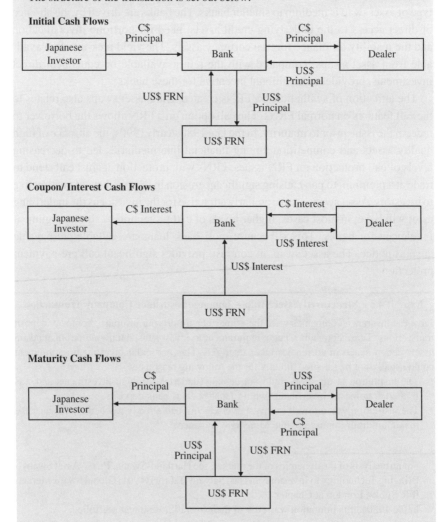

This particular structure satisfied all the investor's requirements. The deposit with the Japanese bank was usually within the allowed investment categories of the investor. The deposit with the Japanese bank did not usually constitute a foreign security for Ministry of Finance purposes, and therefore did not represent utilisation of any foreign asset allocation[12].

An additional benefit of this structure was that the Japanese bank (usually a major bank) was in a better position to assess the underlying credit risk of the security purchased and the swap counterparty. Settlement was relatively easy and the swap cash flows were not usually subject to withholding tax. This type of transaction involving deposits was undertaken in a wide variety of currencies including C$, A$ and NZ$.

Exhibit 4.6   Structured Asset Swap – Zaitech Transaction

The practice of zaitech transactions[13] occurred primarily in the period 1986 to 1990[14]. Japanese corporations undertook the practice of zaitech financing. The companies undertook financial arbitrage transactions to generate profits to subsidise basic business earnings in a period when the appreciating Yen led to a severe downturn in the profitability of their export businesses.

A popular practice during this time was for these companies to undertake borrowing transactions, where the funds raised were immediately reinvested at usually a higher return to provide a locked in annuity stream of earnings for the issuer. One form of this transaction was the issue of bonds with attached equity warrants. The equity option element led to the cost of financing being significantly reduced for the issuer. This allowed the issuer to generate substantial spread earnings by reinvesting the funds raised. In extreme cases, a number of borrowers were able to generate a negative cost of funds in yen. The funds raised were usually reinvested in yen assets. Some of these yen assets were in fact asset swaps, usually with the final synthetic asset being a fixed rate yen bond.

A typical transaction would be structured in the following form[15]. A Japanese corporation would undertake a US$100 million debt with equity warrants issued for 5 year maturity with a coupon of 1.00% pa. Assume that the following market rates are applicable:

US$ swap rate:	8.00% pa versus 6 month LIBOR
JPY/US$ swap rate:	4.77% pa versus 6 month LIBOR
US$/JPY spot rate:	140.00
US$/JPY five year forward:	104.72 (discount of 25.2%)

Under these conditions, the issuer's JPY cost was equal to approximately −2.03% pa (4.77% − (8 × 0.85) where 0.85 is the JPY/US$ currency conversion factor).

---

[12]   The rule deficiency was later rectified.
[13]   For a description of zaitech practices, see Das, Satyajit "Key Trends in Corporate Treasury Management" (April 1992) Corporate Finance 40–43 and (May 1992) Corporate Finance 33–39.
[14]   The term zaitech derives from the Japanese word *zaiteku* that means financial engineering.
[15]   This example is based on Stillit, Daniel and Ireland, Louise "Equity Warrants: Why Japanese Want that Negative Feeling" (July 1987) Corporate Finance 20–23.

The issuer can undertake the swap in one of two ways:
- A series of interest rate and currency swaps.
- A combination of LFTX contracts and a structured interest rate swap.

The structure involving the swaps would be set up as follows:

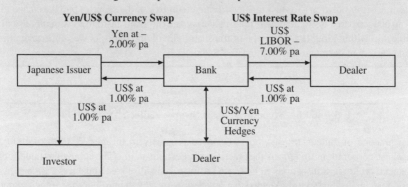

The structure involving the currency forwards would be set up as follows:

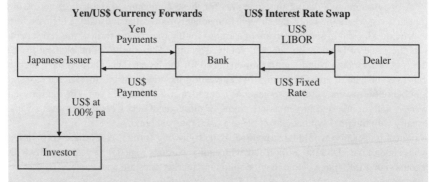

The issuer would then purchase a fixed rate JPY asset to lock in a spread. This would typically be an asset swap matched to the cash flows of the funding transaction.

3.4 Securities Used in Asset Swaps

The construction of the asset swap requires trading in the underlying debt security and entry into a swap transaction. The availability of the underlying debt securities is essential to the asset swap process. The existence of a discrepancy in the relationship between the yield on the assets and swap rates is also desirable. The discrepancies provide the basis of the arbitrage/higher returns available on asset swap transactions.

The discrepancies in market values arise from the differential pricing of assets in different segments of financial markets. This reflects different credit criteria or restrictions on asset choice. These create supply and demand imbalances that lead to asset pricing anomalies that provide opportunities for arbitrage[16].

Discrepancies in the relationship between asset returns and swap rates are more complex[17]. Opportunities for arbitrage emerge when asset yields move to a level that allows the securities to be asset swapped. The objective is based on the prevailing structure of swap rates to generate a coupon stream in excess of that on equivalent direct investment. The process is effectively one of transferring the particular security from one market segment to another to equalise supply and demand at a given price.

The types of securities used in asset swaps include:
- Bonds available in the secondary market.
- Structured debt issues such as equity linked securities (ex-warrant debt component of a bond with equity warrants issue or convertibles) and mortgage/asset backed securities. Other types of structured securities used in asset swaps have included perpetual FRNs and tax advantaged securities.
- New issues specifically designed to be asset swapped.

A major source of securities for asset swaps has been older (seasoned) bonds available in the secondary market. These bonds are often relatively illiquid and/or mis-priced. The bonds frequently provide attractive opportunities for asset swap transactions. The use of the bonds in asset swaps is driven by the trading pattern of non-government debt securities.

The behaviour of a liquid high credit quality bond issue tends to follow a specific trading pattern. During the term of the bond, the trading history of the security in spread (to a government or swap benchmark rate) generally approximates the following behaviour. The spread is credit related. This means that it should be greatest at issue date and decline over the life of the transaction to almost zero close to maturity when the credit risk is negligible. This assumes that the credit quality of the issuer remains unaltered. This also assumes that the issue is successfully priced and placed. It assumes that the bond is liquid, high/consistent credit quality of the issuer, and the presence of a substantial number of major market makers willing to make consistent two-way prices in the issue throughout its life. These conditions are only satisfied infrequently. The issues that generally satisfy the conditions are

---

[16] These discrepancies are similar to those that drive new issue arbitrage, see Chapter 3 and Das, Satyajit (2004) Derivative Products & Pricing; John Wiley & Sons (Asia), Singapore at Chapter 11.

[17] For a discussion of swap spreads, see Das, Satyajit (2004) Derivative Products & Pricing; John Wiley & Sons (Asia), Singapore at Chapter 11.

large 'bellwether" or benchmark issues undertaken by large frequent issuers of reasonable credit quality (generally investment grade).

Most bonds typically behave more erratically. Most bonds, even if launched at the same spread relative to the benchmark as a liquid benchmark issue, will tend to trade at wider spreads over time. This reflects the lack of liquidity in the issue. This is a function of a number of factors including the lower size of the issue, the (sometimes) lower credit quality of the issuer and the lack of market makers in the particular issue. It will also reflect a lack of trading interest among investors in these issues.

As the spread of the issues increases relative to more liquid and better traded issues, the higher yield on these bonds facilitates asset swap arbitrage. This arbitrage is facilitated by the fact that the investors in floating rate assets will traditionally be commercial banks or other financial intermediaries. These institutions match fund their assets, usually through the short-term money market at a cost relative to LIBOR or equivalent benchmark. These institutions are seeking good quality assets equivalent to traditional loans that are likely to be held to maturity. These investors will be less concerned about the factors that are driving the bond's poor performance in the secondary market (such as lack of liquidity).

Specific events also facilitate asset swap transactions. These include:

• Changes in credit quality may precipitate sudden changes in values of bonds. The relevant change may affect the market generally, a country (or group of countries), an industry or a specific issuer.

• General market shifts may cause a flight to quality during periods of market uncertainty and dislocation. The changes frequently lead to disinvestment from specific sectors of the market. Investor focus is on reducing exposure to riskier less liquid securities, and increasing exposure to high credit quality, liquid securities. It might also entail changes in investor preference for maturity with an increased demand for short dated securities.

• Mis-priced bonds may prove difficult to place resulting in poor trading performance[18]. Mis-pricing can occur for a variety of reasons. Mis-pricing may be the result of unanticipated changes in market conditions. It may also result from errors in the judgment of underwriters. A frequent source of mis-pricing is an issue being priced to accommodate the new issue swap arbitrage on the liability side for the issuer[19].

The special events all tend to lead to rapid changes in market values as trading activity is focused on rapidly adjusting portfolio positions. This frequently leads to the market generally over-shooting in a particular direction, or individual issues

---

[18] These issues are referred to as "dogs" or of "canine variety".

[19] See Chapter 3.

being mis-priced (as they trade indiscriminately with the market/sector at large). This creates opportunities for asset swap transactions.

Structured debt securities frequently provide opportunities for asset swap transactions. These include equity linked securities[20], mortgage/asset backed securities and a variety of structured issues.

A large source of securities for asset swap transactions historically was the ex-warrant debt component of a debt with equity warrants issue package. The major source was Japanese corporations. In many cases, a bank guarantee or letter of credit securing the debt component of the issue enhanced the Japanese issuer's credit. The practice is more general and not confined to Japanese issuers.

The primary attraction of the equity linked issues is the equity warrants. The warrants were stripped off and sold separately from the underlying debt component. The debt component itself usually has a below market coupon because of the economic value of the equity warrants. Consequently, the debt component trades at substantial discount to its face value shortly after issue once the warrants have been stripped off and sold. The ex-warrant bond usually trades at a higher yield relative to comparable securities. This primarily reflects its illiquidity and deep discount structure.

The use of ex-warrant bonds in asset swaps was a major feature of the markets in the late 1980s and early 1990s. More recently, asset swaps involving convertible bonds have emerged as a major part of the market for asset swaps[21].

An important source of securities for asset swapping is collateralised mortgage obligations ("CMO") (effectively mortgage backed securities ("MBS"))/asset backed securities ("ABS"). Mortgage-backed and asset-backed securities typically offer higher yields than comparable corporate or financial institution paper. The added return is partially in return for the investor in the securities accepting the risk of prepayment. If interest rates fall, then the underlying mortgages or assets tend to be prepaid, resulting in the mortgage backed security itself being called. This risk of prepayment does not preclude the use of CMO/ABS for asset swaps.

The market has evolved a number of approaches for dealing with the prepayment risk on the asset underlying the asset swap package. They include:
- **Amortising swap** – the basic approach uses an amortising swap structure[22]. In a typical asset swap structure involving CMO/ABS, the investor would

---

[20] See Das, Satyajit (2004) Structured Products Volume 2; John Wiley & Sons (Asia), Singapore at Chapters 2 and 3.

[21] For a discussion of asset swaps in the context of convertible arbitrage, see Das, Satyajit (2004) Structured Products Volume 2; John Wiley & Sons (Asia), Singapore at Chapter 2.

[22] Amortising swap structures are detailed in Chapter 13.

purchase the security and enter into an amortising swap. The investor receives the coupon on the security. The coupon is based on the actual remaining balance of the asset (for example, mortgage) pool. The investor pays a fixed rate and receives a floating rate plus a margin on an amortising interest rate swap. The amortising interest rate swap is structured so that the notional principal reduces. The rate of reduction is based on the *expected rate of amortisation* of the underlying asset. Under this structure, the investor is exposed to pre-payment risk. Any deviations in pre-payments from the assumed amortisation will result in a mismatch between the CMO/ABS host debt and the payments under the swap.

- **Option on swaps** – this combines the amortising swap with an option on swaps to minimise the underlying pre-payment risk. This approach uses putable swaps (a combination of a swap and a receiver swaption/option on swaps) to convert the CMO/ABS security to a floating rate asset[23]. As interest rates decrease, the putable swap terminates. This is designed to match the prepayment on the underlying securities. **Exhibit 4.7** sets out an example of this type of asset swap. The structure of the swap provides some protection against prepayment on the CMO/ABS. The protection is imperfect. This reflects the fact that as interest rates decline, the prepayment on the CMO/ABS may be faster/slower than the pre-agreed termination schedule on the putable swap.

- **Index amortising swap** – as swap technology has improved, specially structured CMO swap arrangements developed. This involved the use of index amortisation swaps ("IAS") to swap CMO/ABS debt[24]. Under the structure, the investor swaps the CMO issue into floating rate return with lower prepayment risk. The swap counterparty, in return for paying a lower floating rate return to the investor, absorbs some or all of the duration risk of the transaction. If interest rates fall, then the duration of the swap will correspondingly decline as mortgagors accelerate their principal repayment in order to refinance at lower interest rates. The structures generally amortise based on movements in a nominated interest rate (such as constant maturity Treasury ("CMT") rates) that is expected to be closely related to the rates that drive pre-payment on CMO/ABS debt. This is assumed to enable the investor to closely match the weighted average life sensitivity of the CMO/ABS to the interest rate swap. This approach, while more complex than the amortising swap and swaption/option on swaps, is expected to provide a more accurate amortisation match. The actual

---

[23] Swaptions/options on swaps are detailed in Chapter 15.
[24] Index amortisation swaps are detailed in Chapter 18.

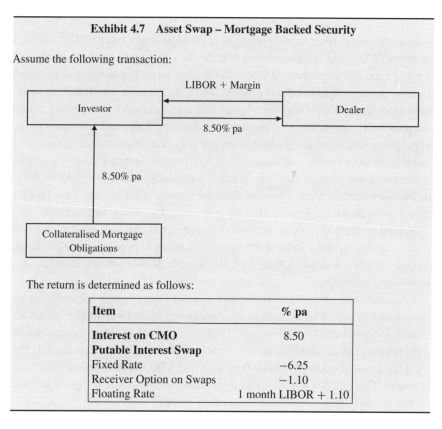

Exhibit 4.7   Asset Swap – Mortgage Backed Security

Assume the following transaction:

The return is determined as follows:

Item	% pa
Interest on CMO	8.50
Putable Interest Swap	
Fixed Rate	−6.25
Receiver Option on Swaps	−1.10
Floating Rate	1 month LIBOR + 1.10

performance of the IAS will depend on the degree to which the design of the swap will be able to replicate the pre-payment pattern of the CMO/ABS.

Asset-backed securities (particularly short-term credit card and auto receivables) used in asset swaps have produced different problems. Shorter term receivables demonstrate a more volatile and random repayment pattern. This necessitates that the swaps designed to convert income streams from these securities into floating rates for investors be structured on the basis of an assumed repayment schedule for the underlying debt. As actual repayments occur, the swap counterparty is forced to assume the residual position generated by variations from the *assumed* repayment schedule. In the event that interest rates decrease and prepayments are higher than anticipated in the repayment schedule, the swap counterparty may end up with an out-of-the-money swap, as the swap related to the asset backed issue is extinguished before its scheduled maturity. Swap market makers can use swaptions/options on swaps to neutralise the risk of prepayment at a cost.

Structured and hybrid securities also provide frequent opportunities for asset swap transactions. Most structured products are created as a result of demand from investors. Where the investor wishes to trade the structured note, it is usually not feasible to on-sell the structured note in the original form. This means that the notes must be "reverse engineered" to be placed with new investors. This is usually structured as an asset swap, where the original note is repackaged by combining it with a derivative(s) transaction(s) to eliminate the embedded derivative features of the note. The re-structured note (which is usually a fixed or floating interest rate note) is sold as an asset swap to traditional investors. A central feature of the repackaging of these complex security structures is that it is typically an attractive way to generate liquidity for the holder. The re-engineered security will generally have broader appeal to investors, facilitating disposal of the asset by the original investor.

A number of other forms of structured securities have created opportunities for asset swap transactions. **Exhibit 4.8** sets out an example of asset swaps involving perpetual FRNs. **Exhibit 4.9** sets out an example of asset swaps involving tax advantaged securities.

A separate category of securities used in asset swaps is new securities issues specifically designed to be sold in synthetic/asset swap format. The issues are usually for lower credit rated issuers. They are designed to allow them to access the fixed rate bonds market from which they would be otherwise precluded. The fixed rate bond is sold in synthetic form as a US$ LIBOR FRN, primarily to bank investors. This practice is used primarily in markets where there is limited demand for low credit quality issuers (non investment grade).

Exhibit 4.8   Asset Swap – Perpetual FRNs

In 1986, the market for subordinated perpetual FRNs (that had been used by banks to raise regulatory primary capital) collapsed[25]. Subordinated perpetual FRNs were used in asset swaps. The use of perpetual FRNs in asset swaps was facilitated by the fact that they were trading at one stage at 60–70% of face value.

The asset swap structures devised were typically as follows[26]:
* The investor purchased the perpetual FRN at say 70% of face value.

---

[25] For a description of the perpetual FRN market, see Parente, Gioia M. and Weintraub, Jay M. (March 1987) Eurodollar Perpetual Floating-Rate Note Markets; Salomon Brothers Inc, New York. For an overview of the collapse, see Evan, John "Perpetual FRNs – Eurobond Market's Great Debacle" (10 January 1987) International Financing Review Issue 655 103.

[26] See Cooper, Dr. Ian "Repackaging Perpetual FRNs" (Spring 1988) Journal of International Securities Market 55–60; Chew, Lillian "Zeroing in on Perpetuals"

- The investor simultaneously invested approximately 26.70% of face value of the notes in high credit quality short term securities yielding around LIBOR. This deposit was for a term of 3/6 months. The short term deposit was re-invested at maturity over the life of the transaction.
- The investor entered into a 15 year zero coupon interest rate swap[27] on a notional principal amount equivalent to the amount of the deposit (26.70% of the face value of the notes).
- Under the terms of the swap, the investor had the following cash flows:
  1. The investor paid either quarterly or semi-annual LIBOR to the swap dealer.
  2. At maturity, the investor received from the dealer a sum equivalent to the accumulated interest on the notional principal amount of the swap. Assuming an interest rate of 9.00% pa payable semi-annually, this equates to 73.30%.
- The net effect of the swap and deposit was to return to the investor 100% of the face value of the notes (26.70% from the maturing deposit together with 73.30% accumulated interest under the zero coupon swap).

The net effect of the transaction was to create a fixed maturity (15 year) conventional bank FRN at an attractive floating rate yield.

Assuming the perpetual FRN had a coupon of LIBOR plus 0.25% pa, the investor under the asset swap was able to create a 15 year floating rate asset at a cost of 96.70% of face value. This is equivalent to an effective asset yield of around LIBOR plus 0.65% pa that, on a relative value basis, was an attractive return for high credit quality bank obligations.

Transactions of this type were undertaken both in the form of private asset swaps as well as public securitised repackaging transactions of the type discussed below[28].

Exhibit 4.9   Asset Swap – Tax Advantaged Securities

Asset swaps occasionally rely on the inconsistent tax treatment of obligations. An example of this type of transaction uses Certificates del Tresor in ECU ("CTEs"). CTEs were securities denominated in ECU issued domestically by the Italian government.

CTE's were issued originally in 1982. The original issues of CTE's were free from withholding tax for foreign investors. In September 1986 the rules were altered and the

---

(October 1988) Risk 2–3. See also Perpetual Floating Rate Notes: Exchange Brilliance from Schroeders But at What Cost?" (25 July 1987) International Financing Review Issue 683 2462–2464; "FRN Repackaging: Another Stab at that Perpetual Problem" (31 October 1987) International Financing Review Issue 697 3474–3475.

[27] Zero coupon swap structures are detailed in Chapter 13.

[28] In an interesting variation, a new product (instantly repackaged perpetuals) was created as a form of primary capital for banks. The transaction involved a tax arbitrage whereby the redemption cost can be captured as a tax deduction. See Lancaster, Brian "Innovations Corner: Instantly Repackaged Perpetuals (IRPs)" (Winter 1988) Journal of International Securities Markets 281–284; "The Two-in-One Tax Trick" (December 1991) Euromoney 38–42.

Italian government imposed a 6.25% (subsequently increased to 12.5%) withholding tax on interest payments. The interest withholding tax was potentially recoverable under double taxation treaties between Italy and the country of residence of the relevant investor.

CTE's generally traded at a *pre tax* yield that is significantly above that of comparable ECU Eurobonds (CTE's trade on *a net of withholding tax* basis at yields below equivalent *tax free* ECU Eurobonds). This facilitated the use of CTE's to structure asset swaps generating floating rate returns to investors in a specified currency. This was achieved by combining a purchase of CTE's with an interest rate or currency swap.

The structure of the asset swap is as follows:

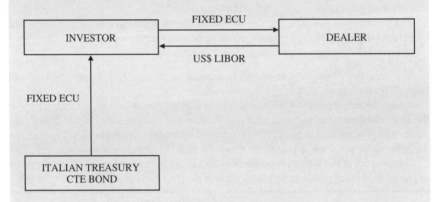

The detailed structure was as follows:
- The term of the swap exactly matches that of the underlying CTE.
- The investor makes fixed rate ECU payments equal to the gross coupon of the CTE. The investor will only receive 87.5% of the coupon and will need to recover the 12.5% withholding tax through an offsetting tax credit. The tax credit will be available after a delay, resulting in a funding cost to the investor that will need to be incorporated in the return calculation. This structure proved more efficient than seeking to recoup the tax from the Italian authorities.
- The investor will receive a floating rate return on its investment in its currency of choice.
- A principal exchange at commencement and at maturity will be required using the principal cash flows of the underlying CTE where the asset created is in a currency other than ECU.

This type of structure was attractive to investors for a number of reasons:
- The attractive returns available. CTE asset swaps offered yield pick-ups of around 30–40 bps pa relative to comparable FRN assets.
- CTE's were highly rated assets reflecting Italy's AAA credit rating. In addition, CTE's represented Italian sovereign risk that made them an attractive investment under the applicable BIS capital adequacy regulations.

As the asset swap market developed, a number of problems associated with using these particular assets became apparent. For example, the use of CTE's in asset swaps created some difficulties in regard to the following:

- Some asset holders experienced difficulties in recovering the withholding tax from the Italian (other than where there is an Italian tax liability) and Swedish authorities, resulting in a reduction in the yields on the transaction.
- Recovery of the interest withholding required the investor to have taxable profits over the life of the transaction. As circumstances changed, some investors found themselves unable to use the credit due to changes in their underlying tax position.

3.5 Private Versus Synthetic Security Structure

A critical element in creating an asset swap is the specific structuring of the swap for the investor. The asset swap can be structured as a private transaction, synthetic security or alternatively a public or securitised asset swap. In this Section, private asset swap structures and synthetic security structures are considered.

Where the asset swap is to be structured as a private transaction, there are two possible structures:

- A private or investor constructed asset swap.
- A synthetic security.

Exhibit 4.10 sets out the two structures.

Under the private asset swap structure, the investor purchases the underlying security and enters into the swap to convert the return into its preferred form. The implications of this particular structure include:

- The investor is responsible for multiple sets of cash flows, including the coupon on the bond and the flows under the swap.
- The credit risk on this transaction is complex. The investor has credit risk on both the issuer *and* the swap counterparty. The swap counterparty has credit risk on the investor. This will require both the investor and dealer to allocate credit lines against the other party to the swap.
- The recording of the total package in the books of record of the investor is complex. The security and the swap must be treated separately. This creates complexity in valuation of the package. For example, where the security is on an accrual basis and the swap on a mark-to-market basis, there is considerable potential for mismatches. Even where such mismatches in treatment are absent, the investor requires expertise in valuation of both transactions. In this regard, the structured interest rate or currency swap presents considerable challenges. The accounting and taxation treatment of the transaction is also complex.

Exhibit 4.10   Asset Swap – Private Structure Versus Synthetic Securities

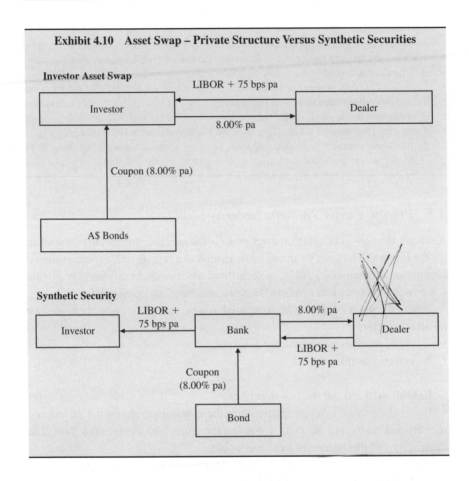

The treatment is complicated by the need to treat both transactions separately in contrast to the economic basis of the transaction.

- The liquidity of the asset swap will generally reflect the liquidity of the bond and the swap. The cost of liquidating the investment will essentially be the sum of the cost of the bid-offer spread for both the bond and the swap. Depending on the liquidity/issuer credit quality of the underlying security, the cost of selling the bonds may range from 0.15% to 0.30% of the price of the bond. Similarly, the cost of reversing the swap will typically be between 0.03% and 0.08% pa in major currencies. The exact cost of trading the bond or the swap will depend upon maturity. The combined cost of liquidating both the bond and swap for a 5 year transaction will be around 0.25% to 0.60% of the principal value of the transaction.

The factors limit the entities that are prepared to undertake asset swaps on a private basis. Banks and investors that possess the requisite expertise usually undertake private asset swaps. The key expertise includes the ability to structure the transaction and account for the structures, along with no significant requirement for any secondary market liquidity of the package.

The synthetic security structure was specifically designed to overcome some of the difficulties of the first structure. It was designed to provide investors with the benefit of a simpler structure, lower transaction costs and enhanced liquidity. The synthetic security structure was originally developed by Citicorp Investment Bank Limited ("Citicorp")[29]. Under the structure, Citicorp effectively interposes itself between the issuer and the investor with regard to the cash flows of the transaction. Citicorp strips and collects the fixed coupon from the bond and simultaneously enters the swap. Under the structure, Citicorp pays the investor a synthetic floating rate coupon.

The major structural advantages of the synthetic security include:

- Cash flows are considerably simplified by the combination of the bond and the swap, resulting in only a single set of cash flows for the investor.
- The credit risk factors are identical to a normal asset swap.
- The accounting and revaluation of the asset swap are simplified for the investor. The investor may be able to account for and revalue the synthetic FRN as a normal FRN. This may have certain administrative advantages as existing accounting procedures and systems can be used for the investment.
- The synthetic security is potentially more liquid than the private asset swap structure. This is because in theory, the permanent linkage of the bond to the swap creates a tradeable package that can be traded as a unit. This eliminates the requirement to liquidate the bond and swap separately. An additional factor is the absence of counterparty risk on the investor for the dealer. In theory, this allows the synthetic securities to be traded between investors in the secondary market, provided the investors entered into a master synthetic securities agreement. Synthetic securities generally traded on bid-offer spreads comparable with equivalent conventional FRNs. This cost was lower than that applicable on a private asset swap.

The importance of Citicorp's synthetic security structure has diminished over time. The value of the innovation lies less in the structural simplicity and enhancement of the original private asset swap than in the tentative attempt *to securitise*

---

[29] See Synthetic Securities; Citicorp Investment Bank, London.

the asset swap. In fact, the synthetic security structure has, to a large extent, been superseded by the emergence of public or securitised asset swaps and repackaging vehicles.

3.6   Securitised Asset Swaps

3.6.1   Structure

Until September 1985, asset swaps had been traditionally undertaken as private transactions, structured primarily as private transactions or synthetic securities. In September 1985, the concept of the public or securitised asset swap was introduced with two transactions. Hill Samuel led the first transaction. Merrill Lynch Capital Markets arranged the other transaction. An analysis of the Merrill Lynch transaction provides an insight into the mechanics of the securitised asset swap. **Exhibit 4.11** sets out the structure of the securitised asset swap.

The end result of the repackaging was the creation of a conventional fixed interest security for the investor. The securitised asset swap structure helped the investor avoid any need to either purchase the underlying securities or enter into the swap transaction. The structure met investor requirements in terms of:
- Credit quality.
- Interest rate and currency requirements.
- Capacity to have the security listed, rated, cleared and settled through existing clearing systems.
- Liquidity and ability to be traded.

The structure also subtly changes the risks of the asset swap structure. The dealer has no credit exposure to the investor. This is because the swap is secured over the collateral held by the special purpose vehicle. In contrast, the investor continues to be exposed to the credit risk of both the collateral and the derivative dealer.

The basic structure described continues to be the basis of the design of all repackaging vehicles.

3.6.2   Securitised Asset Swaps – Evolution

The two 1985 transactions undertaken involving the United Kingdom government US$2.5 billion 1992 FRN clearly demonstrated the advantages of securitising the underlying asset swap. The ability to list the investment, obtain credit rating of the synthetic security (if required) and improvement in liquidity/trading significantly increased the market for asset swaps.

Exhibit 4.11   MECS Securitised Asset Swap Structure

Towards the end of September 1985, the United Kingdom raised US$2.5 billion through the issuance of seven year FRNs due October 1992. The notes were originally priced at 99.70% of face value (net of fees) with a coupon of three month US$ LIBID. The notes were callable after 3 years at the option of the issuer and putable at the option of the investors (effectively making it a 3 year maturity transaction). Following the launch of the issue, the sales force of Merrill Lynch noted that there was considerable interest from its investors in *fixed rate* United Kingdom government US$ denominated debt. In particular, the sales force had reported a coupon of approximately 9.375% pa for a 3 year maturity as acceptable to these investors. However, no fixed rate United Kingdom government debt denominated in US$ was available. Consequently, the Merrill Lynch swap and Eurobond syndicate desk set about designing the largest securitised asset swap at that time.

The structure of the transaction was as follows:

* Merrill Lynch bought US$100 million of United Kingdom FRNs.
* The US$100 million of United Kingdom 1992 FRNs were then sold into a special purpose vehicle known as Marketable Eurodollar Collateralised Securities Limited ("MECS").
* Simultaneously, Merrill Lynch arranged an interest rate swap between MECS and Prudential Global Funding Corporation (rated AAA). Under the swap, MECS made payments of US$ LIBID every three months in return for Prudential making payments equivalent to 9.375% pa to MECS. This effectively converted the floating rate US$ cash flow that MECS earned from the United Kingdom FRNs into a fixed rate US$ flow. The swap between Prudential Global Funding and MECS was collateralised by the United Kingdom FRNs held by MECS.
* Merrill Lynch then arranged a Eurodollar bond issue in the name of MECS with a coupon of 9.375% pa and a final maturity of October 1988. The bonds issued by MECS were collateralised with the assets of the trust which was a holding of US$100 million of United Kingdom FRNs and also the contingent liability reflecting the interest rate swap with Prudential. Essentially the package constituted a high quality (AAA) credit risk.

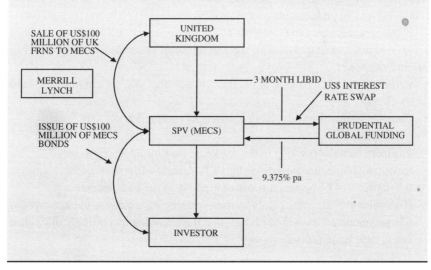

However, the market for public asset swap structures remained stagnant for almost one year. In September 1986, Morgan Guaranty Limited undertook a US$250 million repackaging of a subsequent US$4 billion United Kingdom FRN. Significantly, in September 1986, Banque Paribas Capital Markets undertook the first securitised synthetic asset transaction involving a currency swap. Utilising a vehicle known as Republic of Italy Euro Repackaged Asset Limited (dubbed "Ferraris"), the French investment bank used approximately ECU 200 million of Italy 1993 Treasury certificates as the basis of a synthetic asset US$ paying a coupon of LIMEAN.

The securitised asset swap market entered its growth phase in 1987. Bankers Trust undertook two transactions within one month of each other that created the basis for rapid growth in these transactions. Using a vehicle known as Trust Obligation Participating Securities ("TOPS"), Bankers Trust repackaged Kingdom of Denmark 7.00% 1988 bonds into US$200 million of 2 year FRNs paying a coupon of LIBOR plus 0.0625% pa. More significantly, in a second transaction Bankers Trust swapped a portfolio of Japanese bank guaranteed ex-warrant bonds into a US$100 million 5 year US$ FRN paying LIBOR plus 0.125% pa. The structure of the second transaction was significant in that for the first time it used ex-warrant bonds (mainly from Japanese issuers with usually bank guarantees) in a public securitised asset swap transaction.

The structure of the TOPS 2 transaction was extremely complex. The complexity derived from the fact that the package of ex-warrant bonds contained a variety of maturities. This required the FRNs to incorporate a complex sinking fund provision that reduced liquidity. However, the transaction aroused sufficient interest from Japanese regional banks seeking US$ floating rate assets to allow further transactions to be undertaken.

In the period January to December 1987, approximately US$4 billion of public securitised asset swap transactions were undertaken. The transactions fell into two distinct categories:
• Repackaging of Japanese ex-warrant bonds for sale to commercial bank investors.
• Complex transactions involving a variety of currencies.

The main factors operating in the market at the time appeared to be:
• Unsustainable decline in yields in the FRN market and the subsequent calamitous fall in prices of FRNs and the loss of liquidity in the FRN market.
• High volume of Japanese equity warrant issues being brought to market, creating a large amount of ex-warrant bonds that were proving increasingly difficult to sell in their basic format.

- Interest rate environment where expectations of increased interest rates (primarily in US$) was forcing investors to seek refuge in floating rate assets.

The combination of the factors served to create an environment particularly conducive to this type of securitised asset swap activity. The repackaging of Japanese ex-warrant bonds into US$ FRNs for placement with bank investors quickly became a highly standardised issue structure dominated by the Japanese securities houses and the subsidiaries of Japanese banks. The institutions were the primary players in the equity warrant markets. Initial problems involving differences in maturity of bonds requiring repackaging and cash flow timing were solved simply and elegantly. Issues were structured in groups of equity warrant issues with the same maturity and coupon dates to facilitate the repackaging process. The availability of a number of dealers willing to structure discount swaps to generate the required even coupon and maturity date cash flows assisted in this process.

The other category of securitised asset swaps was considerably more complex. In particular a large part of the activity appeared to be repackaging of originally unsuccessful issues into saleable form. The most notable example of this type of transaction was the repackaging of the hallmark Kingdom of Denmark 1996 US$ FRN that had carried a coupon of 0.125% pa *below* LIBID (the lowest coupon on a US$ FRN in history up until that time). The transaction had met with considerable criticism. It never found favour from end investors. The original lead manager (Morgan Guaranty) elegantly repackaged the issue to produce Deutschmark and Sterling synthetic FRNs. The original US$ FRN was combined with a Deutschmark/US$ floating-to-floating currency swap and a Sterling/US$ floating-to-floating currency swap respectively to create the synthetic FRNs. Taking advantage of a weakening US$, the general depression in the FRN market and a window in the currency swap market, Morgan Guaranty placed the two synthetic assets (named Stars and Stripes) with different investor groups. The Deutschmark FRN was mainly distributed into Europe. The sterling FRN was sold to banks as a commercial banking asset and to British building societies requiring floating rate assets.

Ironically, the repackaging of bonds to create a tradeable instrument came under severe criticism for several reasons:
- The argument that the repackaging in the public or securitised asset swap form created liquidity rapidly disintegrated. Investors tended to hold the security as a term asset, thereby limiting the development of a secondary market.
- Repackaging activity was seen by a number of observers as a means of improving individual investment banks' standing in the "league table" (comparisons in terms of volume of new issues brought to market). In particular, there was

an element of double counting as investment banks essentially got credit for the original bond issue as well as the repackaged security where the latter was publicly syndicated.

The yields on the public securitised asset swap transactions during this period merit comment. They provide some indication of the shifts in the pattern of pricing within the asset swap market as a whole (which is difficult to discern given that a high portion of activity is private). In the initial stages, the arbitrage spreads were particularly large and margins of LIBOR plus 0.30-0.40% pa were available on *AA/AAA rated sovereign risk* (well in excess of directly available rates for these types of issuers). As the demand for asset swapped investments developed and the asset swapped ex-warrant bond became the staple of the market, margins on securitised asset swaps stabilised in the range 0.125% to 0.25% over LIBOR (depending on the underlying credit quality of the banks guaranteeing the ex-warrant bonds). The spreads declined to a low of around 0.10% to 0.15% in late 1986/early 1987. The spreads widened, reflecting credit pressures within the global banking system, capital constraints and reduced asset growth targets.

Securitised asset swaps generally continue to trade at attractive spreads relative to FRNs of similar duration and credit quality. The differences in pricing reflect general credit conditions as well as supply/demand conditions in the synthetic asset market.

3.7 Impact of Asset Swaps on Debt Markets

The emergence of asset swaps as an important aspect of capital market activity has considerable implications for issuers, investors, and dealers[30].

---

[30] For a discussion of the market for asset swaps see Das, Satyajit (1989) Swap Financing; LBC Information Services, Sydney; IFR Publishing, London at 336–345; Das, Satyajit (1994) Swaps & Financial Derivatives; LBC Information Services, Sydney; McGraw-Hill, Chicago at 594–598. See also Crabbe, Matthew "If It Doesn't Sell – Swap It" (April 1986) Euromoney 1–13; "The Fast-Moving World of the Asset Swap" (12 July 1986) International Financial Review Issue 630 2043–2044; "Real Flavour of Synthetics" (July 1986) Corporate Finance 44–45;"Asset Swap – The New Global Synthesis" (8 November 1986) International Financing Review Issue 647 3314–3317; Stillit, Daniel "Unravelling the Asset Swap" (April 1987) Corporate Finance 24–27; "Repackaging: Flying in the Face of Misfortune" (April 1987) Corporate Finance 54–66; Shah, Ayesha "Asset Swaps: The Repackaging Game" (Summer 1988) Journal of International Securities Markets 83–88; Shirreff, David "Not So Sexy" (June 1990) Risk 26–42; Hartland-Swann, Piers "Asset Swaps – Bringing Technology to Investors" in Das, Satyajit (Editor) (1991) Global Swaps Market; IFR Books, London at Chapter 16; Hagger, Euan "Making the Most

Asset swaps allow investors to access investments that would otherwise be unavailable and generate higher returns than those available directly in the capital market. Investors are able to create customised investments to precisely match the cash flow requirements of the particular investor. An additional advantage for investors is that the presence of asset swaps allows a greater degree of portfolio diversification by allowing investors the opportunity to better manage the composition of credit risks in a portfolio, without necessarily being constrained by the types of securities actually on issue[31].

The benefits are available in exchange for assumption of some additional risks. The principal additional risks of asset swaps include the credit risk on the swap counterparty, the structural complexity (including valuation, accounting and taxation) and the potential limitations on liquidity.

For borrowers, the significance of asset swaps is more complex. Asset swaps have several implications including:

- Asset swaps highlight the existence of a particular investor clientele potentially available to purchase securities issued by the relevant borrower. However, the investor demand for issuer risk is in a form other than that currently available. Consequently, one possible response would be for the borrower to issue a security, similar in substance to the synthetic asset, directly to the investor base.
- Asset swaps using securities issued by a particular borrower highlight the potential arbitrage and mis-pricing of issues. By definition, a synthetic security should not be possible where the borrower has issued similar instruments in the relevant market. In this way, asset swaps point to potential mis-pricing of transactions. The availability of poorly trading bonds in the secondary or primary market that lends itself to repackaging is of obvious concern to issuers[32].
- Asset swaps also often allow borrowers to undertake transactions that would otherwise not be feasible. For example, a low rated corporation may not have

---

of Wide Spread Assets" (April 1993) Euromoney 79–83; Parsley, Mark "The End of Easy Profits" (April 1994) (November) Euromoney 35–39; van Duyn, Aline "Assets Enhanced by Swaps" (March 1995) Euromoney 48–53; van Duyn, Aline "Boosting Profits the Credit Way" (May 1995) Euromoney 10–12; Gordon-Walker, Rupert "Can the Growth Continue?" (April 1996) Euromoney 181–182; Reed, Nick "Swaps Yield Variety" (November 1996) AsiaRisk 19–22.

[31] To a substantial degree, the credit derivatives market also fulfils this function; see Das, Satyajit (2004) Structured Products Volume 2; John Wiley & Sons (Asia), Singapore at Chapters 11 to 14 (inclusive).

[32] The potential impact of asset swaps involving poorly performing outstanding issues on the issuer's capacity to access certain markets and/or the cost of such access is discussed in Chapter 3.

direct access to fixed rate bond markets. Where a high yielding fixed rate bond can be swapped into a synthetic FRN which would be attractive to certain investors, the borrower may be able to proceed with the direct fixed rate bond issue which otherwise would not be feasible. In these cases, the transaction undertaken is inefficient from an economic and pricing viewpoint, as the issuer pays a premium to gain this type of access to particular market segments.

Some issuers have sought to control the opportunity to repackage their outstanding debt by repurchasing the available bonds. This is an option that is available where the issuer has the cash or liquidity resources to fund the repurchase[33].

In an interesting variation on this theme, Swiss Bank Corporation in late 1991 undertook the following transaction. Swiss Bank offered to repurchase *on its own account* two outstanding Commonwealth of Australia issues (11% May 1995 US$83 million outstanding and 11.5% October 1995 US$147 million outstanding) at a spread of 65 bps over the relevant US treasury bond. This spread was at least 20/25 bps better than the bid spread relative to Treasuries for the securities in the traditional secondary market. In addition, Swiss Bank offered other banks a 50 bps commission for locating and submitting the bonds through a tender panel mechanism. It is understood that the repurchased bonds were then swapped to create a US$ floating rate asset yielding LIBOR flat. It is not clear whether the asset was held by Swiss Bank Corporation or re-placed with investors as an attractive 3 year sovereign floating rate investment. Swiss Bank subsequently launched a similar repurchase offer for an outstanding bond issued by the Australian Wheat Board. This issue was then swapped into a two year floating rate asset at around LIBOR plus 10 bps. This compares to euro-commercial paper issues by the same borrowers at yields of *LIBID flat/minus 2/3 bps*.

The fundamental consequence of asset swaps is that the market provides a boundary to the price fluctuations or yield differences of securities held in a particular portfolio. The fact that bonds can have their basic structure altered through swaps and therefore be placed with a different group of investors, tends to place a bound on its value. For example, a fixed rate bond will have its trading performance bounded by its relativity to swap market spreads. If the yield on the bond increases to a high level, then the bond can be repackaged as a floating rate asset at an attractive spread. The asset swap is placed with an investor that will accept the issuer's credit risk but would prefer the asset in a floating rate form. This influence on the trading performance of securities is of significance not only to investors but also to financial institutions.

---

[33] For example, see "Unlocking Bonds from the Balance Sheet" (January 1988) Risk 30–31.

The first category of financial institutions affected by asset swaps is investment banks/dealers active in new issue markets or in trading bonds in the secondary market. Essentially, the value bounding process of the underlying asset arbitrage means that relatively illiquid issues or offerings that have, for a variety of reasons, performed poorly and proved difficult to place can be repackaged for sale in a new form. The repackaged asset is distributed to investors who find the security attractive in its new form. This effectively creates a new option for investment banks to reduce the risk in new issue activity and in trading. In theory, it provides them with an additional mechanism for selling and distributing securities.

For financial institutions active in swap trading/market making, asset swaps provide a new dimension in their activities. At the most basic level, asset swap activity creates additional transaction volume that increases the underlying liquidity of the relevant swap market. It provides the other side to the liability swap arbitrage. It thereby creates an incentive for swap activity during periods when the liability swap arbitrage window is not operating. This additional liquidity improves the pricing performance and efficiency of the relevant swap market.

In essence, the asset and the liability swap are the opposite ends of the same transaction. This is because many new issues are undertaken on a fixed rate basis with an accompanying swap where the issuer receives the fixed rate to service the issue and pays floating rates. The pattern of payment under the liability swap in the new issue arbitrage is exactly the opposite side of the swap needed to generate synthetic assets. In an asset swap, the purchaser of the asset will generally pay a fixed rate in return for receiving a floating rate of return. Essentially, the presence of the asset swap therefore enables financial institutions active in swap trading/market making to operate more or less continuously in the expectations of liquidity generated from both ends of the arbitrage.

For swap counterparties, the evolution of the form of the asset swap is also significant. Of particular significance is the development of the public or securitised asset swap structure. The major advantage to swap counterparties is the changing credit risk implications of this particular structure. From the swap dealer's perspective, the public or securitised structure through a special purpose vehicle significantly reduces its exposure to the investor. This is because the issue vehicle is collateralised by the bonds being repackaged. The dealer has first call on that collateral. This allows swap counterparties to enter into asset swaps with investors that the dealer would not be able to deal with directly. In essence, under the public or securitised asset swap structure, the investor takes a risk on the dealer, but the dealer removes exposure to the investor. This absence of credit risk improves the pricing efficiency of the swap market.

4 Structured Notes[34]

4.1 Overview

The second group of synthetic assets is structured notes. Structured notes have emerged as an important instrument in financial markets. The combination of a fixed income security (typically a fixed or floating rate bond) and a derivative contract (a forward or option) to create a financial product has become a standard mechanism for enabling investors to broaden the range of investment opportunities to monetise their market expectations. This Section looks at the structure, rationale and design of structured notes.

There are major differences between asset swaps and structured notes. Asset swaps generally entail transformation of the interest rate or currency basis of an *existing* asset. The asset swap is designed to customise *an existing asset* to the requirements of an investor. In contrast, structured notes are driven purely by an investor's requirement for an investment with specific investment characteristics. The *entire* investment is constructed for the investor using debt securities and derivatives. Structured notes free the investor from the constraints of investments directly available in the market to a more significant extent than asset swaps.

4.2 Structured Notes – Concept

The concept of a structured note is a security that combines the features of a fixed income instrument with the characteristics of a derivative transaction (in effect, the return profile of a forward or option on a selected class of asset). The types of instruments are often referred to as structured notes or as derivative embedded securities.

Structured notes represent a special class of fixed income instruments. The principal demand for structured notes is the capacity of these instruments to

---

[34] See Das, Satyajit (2001) Structured Notes & Hybrid Securities – Second Edition; John Wiley & Sons, Singapore. See also Koh, Kenny (1986) Option or Forward Swap Related Financing Structures Unpublished research paper presented to course on Swap Financing, Centre for Studies in Money, Banking and Finance, Macquarie University; Cunningham, Michael M (1987) Selected Analysis of Recently Issued Index-Linked and Option Embedded Securities; unpublished research paper presented to course on Swap Financing, Centre for Studies in Money, Banking and Finance, Macquarie University; Crabbe, Leland E. and Argilagos, Joseph D. "Anatomy of the Structured Note Market" (Fall 1994) Journal of Applied Corporate Finance 85–98; Klotz, Rick and Pilarinu, Efi (22 December 1994) Understanding the Structured Note Process; Salomon Brothers US Derivative Research, Fixed Income Derivatives, New York; Peng, Scott and Dattatreya, Ravi (1994) The Structured Note Market; Probus Publications, Chicago.

generate highly customised exposures for investors consistent with their nominated investment objectives.

While structured notes have proliferated in recent times, there is a long history of fixed income securities with embedded derivative elements. The most common types of *traditional* derivative securities have included fixed income bonds with call options (callable bonds), allowing the issuer to retire the security before its scheduled maturity, or equity convertible securities which embodied call options on the equity of the issuer.

The distinguishing feature of modern structured notes is the different role played by the derivative element. In traditional configurations such as the callable bond or convertible note, the call option is used to make the security more attractive to investors as part of the overall investment package. In contrast, in modern structured notes the derivative element being incorporated is highly engineered and is specifically used to allow the creation and transfer of the risk embodied in the derivative component. For example, this may entail an investor creating the derivative element that is then securitised through the security structure. The issuer transfers the derivative element to a derivative dealer that in turn reallocates the risk element to ultimate users of that particular instrument. In this way, modern structured notes are utilised as a complex basis for transference of risk through an often long chain of transactions.

4.3 Creation of Structured Notes

A structured note is usually defined as a conventional fixed income debt security combined with a derivative transaction. The derivative element is generally incorporated into the normal fixed income security structure by linking either the redemption value and/or the value of coupons payable to movements in the price of a specified asset. Typically, linkages to financial market variables such as interest rates[35], currencies[36], equity (market indexes or individual stocks)[37] and commodities (both indexes and individual stocks)[38] are used. The derivative element usually incorporated is either a symmetric position such as a forward contract, or an asymmetric position such as an option. Increasingly, non standard hybrid and exotic

---

[35] See Chapters 16, 17, 18 and 19.

[36] See Chapter 20.

[37] See Das, Satyajit (2004) Structured Products Volume 2, John Wiley & Sons (Asia), Singapore at Chapters 2 to 4 (inclusive).

[38] See Das, Satyajit (2004) Structured Products Volume 2, John Wiley & Sons (Asia), Singapore at Chapter 7.

option structures[39] as well as newer asset classes (credit, insurance risk and inflation risk)[40] are also incorporated in structured note structures.

The combination of the base security and the derivative component is designed to produce the required sensitivity to the asset price movement sought. The derivative element is the mechanism by which the essential exposure to the market price component is created.

The essential elements of a structured note transaction include:

- **Identification of the investor requirements** – a number of distinct elements relating to the investor requirements will be identified. This will encompass identifying the exposure to be introduced into the investment portfolio within a traditional investment management framework. This will include identifying the specific economic outlook and the specific asset price expectations sought to be captured. Risk-reward parameters as well as asset-liability/portfolio considerations will be considered.

- **Structuring of the instrument** – when the underlying exposure sought to be created has been identified, then the issue of the most effective means through which the exposure can be captured is considered. Where the exposure sought is either customised or where, for regulatory, credit or other reasons the exposure cannot be created directly, the structured note represents an important alternative *mechanism* for creating the desired exposure. The structured note format will also, under certain circumstances, create the desired exposure in a format that is more efficient or incurs lower transaction costs. The process will, by its intrinsic nature, be iterative. The structured note may be either designed to investor specification or may be offered unsolicited to the investor. The latter forces the investor to examine its investment strategy in the process of evaluating *the specific security*.

- **Execution of the transaction** – this includes arranging the issuer and undertaking the hedging of all relevant exposures and risks. The structured note will be designed by a dealer based on the investor specifications or requirements. The principal components will be a fixed or floating rate security and the derivative elements that are engineered into the security structure.

- **Secondary market in the note** – the secondary market component entails the sale and purchase of the structured note prior to maturity. The liquidity of structured notes is generally lower than that of comparable conventional securities.

---

[39] See Chapters 5 to 11 (inclusive).

[40] See Das, Satyajit (2004) Structured Products Volume 2, John Wiley & Sons (Asia), Singapore at Chapters 12, 15 and 16.

The process of design of a structured note transaction requires further consideration.

A dealer generally designs the structured note based on the investor's specification or requirement. The principal components will be the following:

- A fixed or floating rate security.
- One or more derivative elements that are engineered into the security structure.

In general, the derivative elements will be relatively standard instruments available in the market. This will encompass either exchange-traded or more typically over-the-counter ("OTC") instruments on the relevant asset class.

The principal design elements will include:

- The nominated credit risk and issuer.
- The exposure embedded and in particular, the level of risk entailed.

Structured note issuers are usually of high credit quality. The vast majority of issuers are rated AA or better. The minimum credit rating will generally be A, although a limited number of issues by lower rated issuers have been undertaken. The use of high credit quality issuers is directly linked to the investor requirement for credit enhancement and the separation of credit risk from market risk. Structured notes are viewed as a mechanism for taking market risk[41].

As an alternative to arranging a highly rated issuer to undertake the issue of the structured note, the note may be created using a repackaging vehicle. The design of such structured notes is considered in greater detail below.

The creation of the desired market risk exposure requires the linkage or indexation of either the coupon or redemption value (in effect, the principal) to the nominated asset price or index. The critical issue in this context is the value placed at risk and the conditions under which the value is at risk of loss. In practice, the risk components are determined by the investor and will encompass:

- Coupon (in part or full) at risk.
- Principal (in part or full) at risk.
- The type of instrument (forward or option).
- (In the case of optionality) whether the option is purchased or written.
- The degree of leverage (if any) sought to be introduced.

In general, the dynamics of structuring will entail the following process. The investor seeking lower risk will seek to risk only coupon. In contrast, the higher

---

[41] For a discussion of issuer selection, see Das, Satyajit (2001) Structured Notes & Hybrid Securities – Second Edition; John Wiley & Sons, Singapore at Chapter 17.

risk investor may risk coupon and/or part or all of principal. The latter may also seek to enhance the risk through incorporating leverage.

Where a forward is embedded, the element linked (coupon or principal) will change in value in a linear and symmetric manner, both rising and falling in accordance with the movement in the asset price index. Where optionality is entailed, the structure reflects whether the option is purchased or written. Where purchased, the option premium payment must be funded, requiring a reduction in either the coupon or principal. Where written, the option premium will allow payment of a higher economic return most often in the form of a higher coupon. The payout under the option (if required) where the option expires in the money is made by reducing the coupon paid or the principal amount redeemed.

The issue of leverage relates to the *face value amount* of derivative contracts embedded in the structured note. The structured product concept does not limit the level of derivative components embedded. This allows the degree of derivative exposure (the mechanism by which the exposure to the required asset price movement is engineered) to be varied to both *increase or decrease* the sensitivity of the instrument's value to movements in the underlying asset price movements.

The investor requirement will shape the design and structure of the note[42].

The execution of the transaction entails the following steps:
*   The desired issuer is identified and approached to issue the security.
*   The security is issued.
*   Simultaneous to the agreement of the security terms between issuer, investor(s), and the dealer, the dealer executes all the required hedge transactions to insulate the issuer from any exposure to the embedded derivative element.
*   The transaction is settled.

The execution of the hedge is central to the completion of a transaction for two reasons. It is essential to the pricing of the transaction[43]. It is also essential to allow the issuer to participate in the transaction. Issuers are typically participating on the basis of a guaranteed and known funding cost. Therefore, insulation from any exposure to the market risk elements embodied in the note is central to the transaction. In order to eliminate this exposure, the issuer enters into a separate derivative contract with the investment bank or dealer.

---

[42] For a discussion of the universe of structured note investors and their objectives in participating in this market, see Das, Satyajit (2001) Structured Notes & Hybrid Securities – Second Edition; John Wiley & Sons, Singapore at Chapter 17.

[43] For discussion of pricing mechanics, see Das, Satyajit (2001) Structured Notes & Hybrid Securities – Second Edition; John Wiley & Sons, Singapore at Chapter 16.

4.4   Structured Note Transaction – Example

Exhibit 4.12 sets out an example of the collared FRN transactions which originally emerged to take advantage of the relatively steep slope of the US$ interest rate yield curve in 1992 and 1993[44]. The basic economics of the collared FRN are driven by the fact that it combines a standard FRN structure with a US$ LIBOR interest rate cap and floor. The investor, through the structure, effectively sold a cap and purchased a floor which equates to a sold interest rate collar on US$ LIBOR. **Exhibit 4.13** sets out the structure in terms of the individual components.

A number of key structural elements of this transaction should be noted:
* The issuer of the securities was typically a highly rated entity (usually AA rated or better).
* As a general rule, the issuer in the transactions did not position or absorb the risk of the derivative elements created through the FRN structure. The issuer, in fact, typically on-sold the derivative elements. It hedged its exposures to the derivative elements through the derivative market itself. Its primary motivation was the margin that it could make between the derivative element captured through the sale of the security, and the price for which the derivative element could be hedged, repackaged or on-sold in capital markets generally. The overall result for the issuer is that the issuer's overall cost of funds is attractive, based on

---

	Exhibit 4.12 Structured Note Transaction – Collared Floating Rate Notes ("FRN")
Issuer	JP Morgan
Amount	US$200 million of Subordinated FRNs
Maturity	10 years (due August 19 2002)
Spread	Three month LIBID flat
Fixed re-offer price	99.85
Minimum interest	5%
Maximum interest	10%
Amortisation	Bullet
Call option	None
Denominations	US$5,000, US$100,000
Commissions	0.50% (management & underwriting 0.25%; selling 0.25%)

Source: (1 August 1992) International Financing Review Issue 940 56.

---

[44]   A discussion of collared FRN structures is set out in Chapter 19.

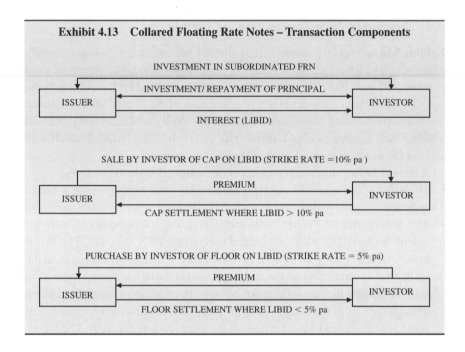

Exhibit 4.13   Collared Floating Rate Notes – Transaction Components

the margin earned between the purchase and on-sale of the derivative element acting as a subsidy on its overall borrowing cost.

• The maturity of the structured note in the case of collared FRNs was quite long – (up to) 10/12 years. This contrasts with the more common structured note structures that usually entail shorter maturities (typically one to three years), although longer transactions are not unknown.

• Key elements in the cash flow structuring of the security are central to the efficacy of the arrangement. In the case of the collared FRN, the transaction entails the investor purchasing a package consisting of:

1. Conventional FRN.
2. Selling a cap on US$ LIBOR at the maximum rate (10% per annum).
3. Purchasing a US$ LIBOR interest rate floor at the minimum interest rate level (5% per annum).

The structure entails the investor both purchasing and selling option elements.

The discussion regarding structural elements of the structured notes is related to the collared FRN example identified. In practice, almost all structured note transactions must, of necessity, embody similar structural features.

4.5 Rationale for Structured Notes

4.5.1 Overview

There are a number of possible explanations for the use of such structured notes, including:

- **Regulatory arbitrage** – where investors and less frequently issuers use derivative embedded structures to circumvent barriers to trading directly in the relevant derivatives.
- **Customisation** – using such structures to monetise positions/expectations in a particular manner.
- **Credit enhancement** – using such structures to provide credit enhancement to facilitate participation in the derivative market.
- **Denomination arbitrage** – allow derivative transactions to be undertaken in denominations that might otherwise not be feasible.

A number of other advantages that may be relevant in such structures include accounting or taxation factors, ease of administration and tradeability/liquidity of the instrument.

4.5.2 Regulatory Arbitrage

Structured notes are frequently used to circumvent regulations that would otherwise prevent an investor, or alternatively an issuer, from undertaking the underlying derivative transaction itself. For many investors, the use of structured notes is driven by the desire to overcome restrictive investment mandates. It is difficult to get direct evidence of the regulatory arbitrage element that motivates structured notes.

The capacity to use derivatives in this format is a necessary means by which issuers and investors, that would otherwise be prevented from managing their financial risks to the fullest extent possible, undertake required risk management actions. This is particularly true of investors constrained by constituent documents/investment powers created in an era before the availability of derivative instruments to implement appropriate investment strategies or manage risks. Such constituent documents/investment powers may be difficult and cumbersome to change. The use of structured notes is predicated on the fact that investors are allowed to purchase or sell securities as part of normal operations. Structured notes are a means of overcoming the transaction costs of effecting the necessary change in the constituent documents of the relevant entity.

Structured notes are also used by investors to satisfy a number of investment requirements. This includes the requirement for fully funded investment. This is primarily to enable the investor to deploy available capital/investment funds.

The creation of fully funded investments also overcomes the potential problem with derivatives of leverage. Many investors are restricted from borrowing or of leveraging investments in any other way. The use of fully funded investments intrinsically eliminates leverage, as any derivative position is fully backed by a cash investment. The maximum amount at risk is the face value that represents the amount that can be lost.

A significant factor in the design and sale of structured notes is the importance of transforming a derivative transaction into a security (for legal purposes) and a listed instrument (on a stock exchange). This is designed to overcome the investment constraints on investors who are only empowered to purchase *listed securities*. The prohibition limits the capacity of investors to use over-the-counter derivative products. This limitation can be overcome through the use of structured note transactions.

A related issue is the legal restriction (under gambling legislation) still in operation in a number of jurisdictions that prevents the entry into derivative transactions by institutional and retail investors. The use of structured note formats can be designed to overcome these difficulties.

4.5.3 Customisation

Customisation entails the creation of specifically designed risk exposures for the investors to allow monetisation of asset price expectations. Structured notes are customised to fit the unique requirements of particular investors. They are designed to facilitate the creation of risk-return trade offs that would not be readily available to investors directly. This enables investors to capture higher returns on their investments, provided their expectations about asset prices are realised[45].

Central to this process of customisation is the ability to access markets that would otherwise be difficult for investors to access directly. This difficulty of access may arise from two sources:
- The asset is synthetic, such as equity market or commodity indexes, and consequently not tradeable directly.
- Transaction costs of participation are high, such as commodity markets and foreign equity investments.

---

[45] For an interesting analysis or example of the process of creating/designing a structured note, see Dabansens, Frederic "Relative Risk" (April 1997) AsiaRisk 30–32; Dare, Laurence "How the Investor can Enhance Yield" (1996) Corporate Finance Risk Management & Derivatives Yearbook 34–36.

In addition, the use of structured notes may allow creation of particular risk return payoffs that are difficult or expensive (in the sense of transaction costs) to create in the market for physical assets.

This allows structured notes to be frequently used to monetise positions and/or expectations regarding capital market variables. The advantage of structured notes in this regard is that they allow capture of value in a particular way that is of interest to the investor or issuer. The major elements of this monetising aspect include:

- The transactions allow value to be captured by essentially allowing say an investor's expectation regarding particular values of financial assets to be embedded in the derivative. For example, a collared FRN or a reverse/inverse FRN structure[46] can be characterised as monetising an investor view that forward rates currently implied by an yield curve are significantly above the actual rates that will prevail in the future.
- Monetising positions or expectations within the structured note format may allow a degree of liquidity/tradeability that cannot be achieved in another manner. For example, in the case of a collared FRN, the investor can effectively trade a series of options indirectly, embodying views on forward interest rates in combination by purchasing and then selling the FRN itself. The FRN eliminates the need to enter into a complex series of transactions that may require the availability of credit facilities in the form of counterparty risk lines. The liquidity or tradeability potential (at least in theory) is an important incentive to use structured notes to monetise such positions and expectations.
- Using structured notes in this manner allows interesting combinations of positions to be created. An example of this concept is evident in the case of reverse FRNs, where the security combines a fixed bond with an interest rate swap in which the investor receives fixed and pays floating rates. Under this combined structure, the investor has several sources of value:
  1. Realised short-term money market rates relative to that embodied in the current yield curve.
  2. Movement in term rates will determine the value of the underlying bond and the embedded interest rate swap.

The particular combination of expectation/views may, in practice, allow value to be created from combinations of positions in a unique way. Importantly, creating such instruments in a package that is potentially both tradeable and liquid may enhance the value of the transaction.

---

[46] Inverse FRN structures are discussed in detail in Chapter 19.

4.5.4   Credit Enhancement

A key element of structured notes is that the mechanics facilitate a shift of all performance obligations onto the issuer (usually highly rated and considered to be relatively free of credit or default risk). Consider the example in **Exhibit 4.12**. This is most relevant in the case of the option created by the investor (the cap sold by the investor to the issuer). This would normally entail performance obligations on the investor to make cash payments where US$ LIBOR exceeded the cap level. However, the structure obviates this requirement by effectively requiring the *issuer* to effectively assume the credit risk of the option writer (from whom the issuer purchases the cap to on-sell). This also means that the ultimate buyer of the cap has the *issuer* as its counterparty for credit risk purposes.

The issuer assumes minimal risk on the derivative transaction because of the structure. From a mechanical perspective, in the case of the collared FRN this is achieved by two separate mechanisms:

- The sale of the cap by the investor to the issuer is fully cash collateralised by the face value of the FRN itself. The investor invests this amount with the issuer through the purchase of the FRN.
- There is also no performance obligation on the investor. The issuer only pays interest *up to* the maximum interest rate to the investor. Any payment that relates to the inherent value of the cap (reflecting the difference between US$ LIBOR and the maximum rate where LIBOR is above the maximum rate) is made to the ultimate purchaser of the cap.

In this manner, the performance obligations under the derivative element shifts to the issuer, allowing the issuer's credit risk to be substituted for that of the investor. In the reverse case, where the investor purchases an option, in the case of the collared FRN the floor purchased by the investor, the performance obligation is with the issuer from the outset.

The elements identified are all present in the transactions described in **Exhibit 4.12**. **Exhibit 4.14** illustrates the importance of the cash flow structuring to shift the performance obligation onto the issuer using a second transaction (a World Bank transaction that entails a securitisation of the collared FRN). In this transaction, the issue of FRNs is combined with a maximum interest rate (the Capped FRN). The FRN is issued in conjunction with the issue by the borrower of floor certificates that are detachable. The economic benefit of such an arrangement is that the floor certificates (effectively the minimum interest rate element of the transaction) are allowed to be traded freely by the investor and quite separately from the capped FRN itself. From a cash flow structuring viewpoint, the two option

Exhibit 4.14 Structured Note – Capped FRN with Floor Warrants	
Issuer	World Bank
Capped FRN	
Amount	US$200 million of FRNs
Maturity	10 years (due April 28 2003)
Coupon	Six month LIBOR plus 0.25% payable semi-annually on April 28 and October 28
Maximum interest	7.25% from the beginning of the fifth interest period
First interest determination date	April 26
Issue price	100%
Amortisation	Bullet
Call option	None
Denominations	DEM 10,000 and DEM 250,000 (global note)
Commissions	0.20% (management & underwriting combined 0.10%; selling 0.10%)
Floor Certificates	
Issuer	World Bank
Number 20,000 certificates	
Exercise	Each certificate entitles the holder to payment on April 28 and October 28 corresponding to the positive difference between 7% pa and six month LIBOR. Each certificate relates to DEM 10,000.
Issue price	DEM 695 per certificate
Expiration	April 28 2003
Selling concession	0.25%

Source: (13 March 1993) International Financing Review Issue 970 72.

elements – the cap *written by the investor* and the floor *purchased by the investor* – are treated differently. The floor element, where the performance obligation is on the issuer as the grantor of the option, can be freely securitised. In contrast, the cap element (where the performance obligation is on the investor as the grantor of the cap) cannot be structured as a tradeable security. This is because this would prevent the transfer of the performance obligation from the investor to the issuer.

The cash flow structuring entailed in a structured note typically allows the investor to transfer the credit exposure of the transaction to the issuer. This effectively allows the investor to use the credit quality of the issuer in derivative transactions. This is particularly important in the case of investors dealing in small face value amounts of derivatives, or investors whose structure such as a mutual or pooled fund may make it difficult for such entities to have access to the required credit arrangements to participate in derivative transactions more generally.

The case of mutual funds (or unit trust structures) is particularly important. This reflects the increasing amount of investment funds channelled through these investment vehicles. The use of mutual funds/unit trusts reflects the major benefits provided through the process of aggregation, including economies of scale/scope and diversification of smaller investor portfolios.

The counterparty credit risk of the mutual fund structure is problematic. As the arrangement entails no permanent capital or guarantee from a creditworthy party, the credit assessment must focus on the capacity of the fund itself to meet its contractual obligations. This is dependent on the liquidity of the fund and the continued retention of investment funds at a sufficient level to meet the relevant obligations. This risk is difficult to assess, particularly over long periods. This inherently limits the participation of mutual funds in derivative transactions. Structured notes play a central role in overcoming this limitation.

4.5.5   Retail Denomination

A related issue is what is termed the denomination arbitrage feature. The use of structured notes allows investors (in particular) to participate in the derivatives market in denominations that are significantly lower than that which might be achieved through direct participation. In the case of the capped FRN transactions, the low denominations of the FRNs allows investors to purchase and sell derivative elements for relatively modest amounts (say, $5,000 and above)[47]. Structured notes allow retail participation in the derivative market within a wholesale and institutional market structure.

The capacity of retail investors to use derivatives through structured notes also has a value arbitrage element. Through its structure, the structured note market entails *wholesale prices* for derivatives. This facilitates retail investor access to derivative products at prices that are significantly better than prices at which the products would be available to them without the availability of structured notes.

4.5.6   Other Considerations

Other factors that may enhance the demand for structured notes include accounting or taxation factors, ease of administration, ability to rate the structure and tradeability/liquidity of the instrument.

---

[47] In reality, the typical investment is significantly higher, being in the region of US$50,000/100,000 and higher.

The accounting and taxation benefits of embedding derivatives in a structured note format *should* not necessarily provide any significant advantages. In practice, there may be major advantages as the structured note may not be bifurcated into components and treated separately for accounting and tax purposes.

For accounting purposes, the structured note may be treated as a security and either held at book value (where it is a term or hold to maturity asset), or marked to market based on the market value *of the structured note*. The secondary market value of the structured note will be based on market prices or dealer quotes. The prices will encompass the market value of the derivative components but indirectly in the price of the security.

There may be accounting advantages in the treatment of option premiums. Premiums paid can be amortised over the life of the note (as embodied in the note cash flows), in contrast to being recognised immediately as is required under certain circumstances for particular categories of investors in specific jurisdictions. Premiums received can be recognised gradually (as also embodied in the note cash flows) rather than have to be recognised upon receipt or deferred until the option expires. The nature of the income may also be altered where the option premium is built into the interest or other cash flows of the security.

An advantage for mutual funds is the ability to avoid the complexity of option accounting, with the premium being captured by the note cash flows. This allows the avoidance of complex issues for the investors regarding maintaining equality amongst the fund investors at different points in time as well as distribution of earnings.

The taxation advantages are similar to those identified in the context of accounting. The major benefit is in the area of option premium treatment.

The ease of administration derives from the fact that the structured notes can be settled, processed and administered as essentially a fixed interest security, albeit with customised cash flows. This is an additional advantage over outright derivative transactions for investors that are not appropriately equipped in an operational and administrative sense to handle derivative trades.

The incorporation of the derivative into a note format enables the instrument to be rated. This may be an important factor for investors restricted to investments rated by major rating agencies[48].

---

[48] For a discussion of the process of rating a structured note, see Efrat, Issac, Gluck, Jeremy, and Powar, David (3 July 1997) "Moody's Refines its Approach to Rating Structured Notes"; Moody's Investors Service Global Credit Research, New York.

The liquidity and tradeability aspect of the structured note as an instrument may be relevant. The major advantage in this regard is the capacity to reduce exposure to the market risk and the Derivative component through the sale of the note. The sale also eliminates any counterparty credit risk. This contrasts with derivative transactions where eliminating the exposure would require the investor to either cancel the transaction with the existing counterparty, or enter into an offsetting transaction *with an alternative counterparty*. The second alternative requires the commitment of additional credit lines and continued usage of the credit capacity used in the original transaction.

4.6   Pricing and Valuation of Structured Notes

4.6.1   Overview

The structural elements and rationale for structured notes have direct implications on pricing of such transactions. The implications exist at two levels:
• Value capture issues.
• The apportionment of value between various parties involved in the transactions.

Given the nature of the transactions, the investor seeking to purchase or sell the derivative element incorporated in the security structure is likely to have relatively low price sensitivity. This is particularly if it has no alternative means of participating in the derivative market. In addition, it is probable that the investor will be prepared to pay a premium for the structure that allows the investor to monetise its particular position/expectation in a desirable manner. The investor will also be required to pay an additional premium for the credit enhancement elements of the transaction and the implicit denomination reduction process that allows more widespread participation.

Against this background, investors will typically pay a higher price for the structured note than the individual component values based on theoretical values under normal market trading conditions.

In this context value for the overall transaction will be driven by several elements:
• Investor's desired position and the value that the investor accords to the structure.
• Issuer's target cost of funds and the value it places on its credit enhancement role in the transaction.
• Return objectives of the intermediary arranging the overall package.

There is significant competition between investors, issuers and intermediaries. This creates a volatile market for such structures. The value exchange equation is dynamic and alters depending on changes in any of the variables identified[49].

4.6.2   Valuation Approach

The pricing and valuation of structured note transactions must, by definition, follow the inherent structure of the transaction. As a consequence, it must follow the components of the transaction. The components in a typical transaction will include the following elements:
*   A fixed or floating rate security.
*   The embedded derivative component(s) that will be a forward or option on an identified financial market variable or asset.

The pricing and value of the instrument will reflect the sum of the value of the components.

The approach can be applied uniformly across all transaction structures. It can also be applied irrespective of the valuation context (that is, new transaction, risk evaluation and secondary market pricing).

4.6.3   Pricing and Valuation of Components

The approach outlined uses existing valuation techniques *for the individual transaction components*. This means that the identified components are valued as follows:
*   The fixed income component (either a fixed rate bond or FRN) is priced using normal fixed income valuation techniques such as internal rate of return or yield to maturity.
*   The derivative components are valued using the appropriate valuation technique[50]:
    1. *Forward components* – carry cost based models.
    2. *Option components* – using the relevant option pricing model.

The pricing or valuation of the structured note is the sum of the values of the individual components, adjusted for some special factors.

---

[49] For discussion of pricing and value dynamics see Das, Satyajit (2001) Structured Notes & Hybrid Securities – Second Edition; John Wiley & Sons, Singapore at Chapter 16.
[50] See Das, Satyajit (2004) Derivative Products & Pricing, John Wiley & Sons (Asia), Singapore at Chapters 4 to 10 (inclusive).

A key aspect of the valuation approach is the ability to unbundle *any* structured note into its constituent elements. This is important for the following reasons:

- It allows the transaction to be engineered by combining the individual elements. The trader enters into a series of transactions to create the desired structure. The decomposition is essential to the hedging process.
- It places boundary values on the instrument. This dictates that if required, the transaction can be *reverse engineered* into the relevant elements. This allows the transaction to be repackaged and re-placed with counterparties prepared to purchase or trade in the constituent elements. Given the generic nature of many of the components, the liquidity of the components will typically be greater than that for the structured note. This allows an enhancement of the liquidity of the instrument (albeit at a price). The fact that the structured note must trade at a value *no lower* than that of its unbundled constituents also facilitates arbitrage (between the value of the structured note and the components) that assists in the liquidity of these types of instruments.
- It overcomes the difficulty of seeking to price and manage the risk elements of the structured note *as a security* by breaking the risks into discrete and separately hedgeable components.

4.6.4   Structured Note Valuation – Special Issues

The special issues in the pricing and valuation of structured notes relate (in general terms) to structural aspects of the instruments, including:

- Structured notes seek to isolate credit or default risk (the risk of failure to perform on the cash flow or payment obligations of the instrument) from market risk (the risk of fluctuations in the value of the instrument from changes in the value of the key market variables embedded in the instrument).
- A number of different value drivers (financial market variables) are typically combined within the structured note. For example, a commodity linked note will combine an exposure to interest rate (on the fixed income component) and an exposure to the price of the relevant commodity (through the embedded derivative element).

The factors impact upon the valuation of these instruments in a number of ways. The isolation of credit risk and market risk dictates the following value effects:

- The typical structured note is issued by high quality (AA or better rated) issuers. This means that the risk of value fluctuations from credit quality is lower than for comparable traditional securities.

- The fact that the structured note format uses the issuer's credit rating as a form of credit enhancement dictates that the cost of this enhancement charged by the issuer must be factored into the valuation (usually expressed as the issuer's funding target).

The second consideration is not present where the structured note is created using a special purpose repackaging vehicle.

The combination of value drivers requires the correlation relationships between the fixed income component of the structured note (the bond value) and the embedded derivative component (the market or derivative value) to be incorporated. It is unlikely that the two variables (the interest rates driving the bond value and the asset price driving the market or derivative value) are unrelated. For example, a change in commodity prices that impacts upon the value of the structured note may be accompanied by a change in interest rates (through the commodity price to inflation to interest rate linkages). This will either reinforce or partially offset the change in value of the structured note created by the shift in commodity prices alone. Interestingly, the market values of structured notes frequently do not appear to totally incorporate the embedded correlation relationships. A factor in this may be the relatively short tenor of structured note transactions where the market or derivative value element may dominate the value of the package.

4.6.5 Valuation Context

In examining the process and issues related to pricing and valuing structured notes, it is useful to separate the process into a number of distinct contexts. This is dictated by the fact that the key areas of focus are different in each of these contexts. While the analytical basis will remain substantially the same in each of the valuation contexts, the nature of the analysis has significant differences of emphasis. In part this reflects the fact that each context emphasises the different perspective of the issuer, investor and the dealer involved in engineering the transaction.

The three major contexts are as follows:
- Initial pricing.
- Risk evaluation.
- Secondary market pricing.

Each of these phases is considered in detail in the following Sections.

4.6.6   Structured Note Transactions – Initial Pricing

The initial pricing phase is focused on the structuring or construction of the security. The key participants are:

- **Investor** – the investor nominates the parameters of the transaction. This includes the issuer universe, the market risk to be assumed (the position sought to be taken in respect of the market variable sought to be traded) and the risk parameters (for example, interest or principal at risk/protected, minimum income requirement and time horizon at risk).
- **Issuer** – the issuer nominates the target funding cost that will determine the issuer's willingness to issue the security. This incorporates the cost of credit enhancement required by the issuer.
- **Financial institution/dealer** – the dealer must match investor and issuer requirements within the following constraints:
  1. The cost of the hedges that must be executed to engineer the structured note.
  2. The earnings required to compensate for the creation, hedging, ongoing risk management and capital commitment required by the transaction (if relevant).

The key elements of the process can be summarised as follows:
- The issuer's funding target.
- The component values based on appropriate market value (including bid-offer spreads and other transaction costs).

The first element is difficult to specify scientifically. The issuers are opportunistic new issue arbitrage funders that set benchmark funding costs[51]. This funding cost is based on the supply of financing opportunities on offer relevant to their financing requirements at a given point in time.

The process underlying this decision has been identified as follows[52]:
- Identify a base borrowing cost usually taken as a direct FRN issue for the relevant maturity (effectively a zero cost or base transaction).
- Identify the risks of the structured note or swapped transaction through a system of risk factors. This process will incorporate the volatility of the relevant asset price as well as correlation between the relevant parameters. This risk should capture the credit risk of the transaction that will be recorded against the

---

[51] See Chapter 3.
[52] See Yngwe, Peter "Derivative Applications: A Borrowers' Application" (1995) Financial Derivatives & Risk Management vol 1 no 1 pp 49–54.

issuer and reflected in the capital allocated by the counterparty to the derivative transaction.

- The target cost for the issuer should be the base borrowing adjusted for the risks/capital cost of the transaction.

The second element is purely market driven, reflecting the cost of the constituent elements using appropriate market pricing parameters.

The value of the security is driven by the two factors. The difference between the market value of the structure and the price *paid by the investor* represents:

- Cost to the investor in the structure (including the regulatory arbitrage, credit enhancement etc motivating entry into the transaction in the form of a structured note).
- Profit to the dealer in facilitating the transaction as well as compensation for any hedging and underwriting risk assumed in the transaction.

Exhibit 4.15 examines the pricing and initial valuation of a collared FRN transaction in the primary market.

Exhibit 4.15   Pricing and Valuation of Collared FRN Transaction – Primary Market

1. Transaction
Assume the example of a collared FRN[53] that is structured in response to investor demand. The potential issuer is an AA rated financial institution that is willing to undertake the transaction on the basis that the dealer hedges out its exposure to the embedded derivative elements and guarantees it an acceptable funding cost.

The components of the transaction are as follows:
1. US$100 million 10 year subordinated FRN priced off LIBOR issued by the issuer.
2. Cap on 6 month LIBOR with a strike price of 10% pa sold by the investor and purchased by the issuer.
3. Floor on 6 month LIBOR with a strike price of 5% pa purchased by the investor and sold by the issuer.

The structure of the transaction will take the form of a privately placed issue of the FRNs to be documented under an existing Medium Term Note ("MTN") program. The issue is expected to be placed with a small number (3–4) of investors who have indicated interest in the transaction. The issuer will be hedged on its cap/floor exposure through the entry into a hedge with the dealer. Under the hedge, the dealer will sell a floor to the issuer and purchase the embedded cap in the FRN to completely insulate the issuer from any market risk exposure under the cap or floor. This will be engineered so that where LIBOR rates are under 5% pa, the issuer will receive from the dealer the difference between 5% pa and the

---

[53] A transaction similar to that set out in **Exhibit 4.12**.

LIBOR rate for the relevant interest period on a principal equal to the face value of the transaction. Where LIBOR rates are over 10% pa, the issuer will pay to the issuer the difference between 5% pa and the LIBOR rate for the relevant interest period on a principal equal to the face value of the transaction.

2. Pricing and Valuation

The pricing and valuation of the transaction will reflect the value of the individual components. The only additional elements requiring identification (to enable pricing of the transaction) are the issuer's funding cost target and the dealer's fees in facilitating the issue.

Assume the prevailing market prices of the elements of the transaction are as follows:
- Subordinated FRN of the type identified is trading at around LIBOR plus 0.25% pa.
- Cap and floor prices are as follows[54]:
  Cap Price – 2.88% flat
  Floor Price – 1.64% flat.

Assume the investor is willing to buy this asset at a coupon of LIBOR plus 0.0625% pa. The issuer's target is LIBOR minus 6.25 bps on this financing. Given a discount rate applicable over 10 years of 7.10% pa (payable semi-annually), the 12.5 bps pa reduction in cost to the issuer is equivalent to 88 bps in present value terms. The amount due to be received by the issuer from the dealer for the sold cap and bought floor transaction is equivalent to 124 bps (this is the net of the cap premium (288 bps) received and the floor premium (164 bps) paid by the dealer). This amount is realised when the dealer sells the cap into and buys the floor from the derivatives market. This leaves a surplus of 36 bps for the dealer after it has paid 88 bps (or 12.5 bps pa) to the issuer to enable it to achieve its target cost of funds.

The surplus is available to either:
- Be paid as fees to investors.
- Retained as profit by the dealer.

Assume that in this case the dealer uses 10 bps of the surplus as management fees to be paid to the investor. The remaining 26 bps is available as remuneration to the dealer for facilitating this transaction.

4.6.7 *Structured Note Transactions – Risk Evaluation*

Overview

The risk evaluation context is relevant to the investor seeking to evaluate the investment characteristics of an individual transaction. The pricing and valuation focus

---

[54] The cap and floor prices are derived using Black's Option Pricing Model utilising the implied forward 6 month LIBOR rates calculated off the prevailing yield curve (which is steeply upward sloping with a spread between 6 month LIBOR (3.50% pa) and 10 year swap rates (7.10% pa) of approx. 360 bps) and based on volatility levels of 14% pa (for the floor) and 13% pa (for the cap). The different volatility reflect the bid and offer volatility levels, which reflect the fact that the trader – in hedging the issuer's exposure – is purchasing the cap and selling the floor.

in this context seeks to identify the risk return characteristics of the structured note from the viewpoint of an investor in terms of:
• Market risk.
• Cash flow risk.
• Liquidity risk.

This risk evaluation can encompass the evaluation of a transaction on a number of bases:
• Standalone versus portfolio basis.
• Hold to maturity versus active trading basis.

The risk evaluation process has a number of different components covering alternative methods of evaluation of the various risks identified.

A central element in this process is to ensure evaluation of all the risk elements of the transaction within a framework that allows the risks to be incorporated into the investors' overall portfolio management process.

Risk Evaluation Techniques
The major risk evaluation techniques used in this context are similar to those generally used in investment management of fixed income portfolios. They include:
• **Duration concepts** – as a measure of the interest rate risk of the instrument.
• **Market price sensitivity concepts** – using the concept of the sensitivity of the instrument to the major pricing parameters.
• **Scenario or simulation approaches** – based on either fixed (deterministic) combinations of market price events or probabilistic (stochastic) combinations of events to observe the value changes in the price of the instrument.

Duration Based Approaches
The concept of duration (in particular modified duration) is commonly used to measure the interest rate sensitivity of a security or portfolio of cash flows[55].

The use of duration as a measure of risk in structured notes requires significant adaptation of the concept reflecting the nature of the underlying security. For example, some analysts[56] suggest expansion of the concept to cover multiple valuation and risk analysis techniques predicated upon key rate duration based around the following:
• Duration with respect to the interest rate applicable to the interest rate(s) used to value the fixed or floating rate host bond.

---

[55] See Das, Satyajit (2004) Derivative Products & Pricing; John Wiley & Sons (Asia), Singapore at Chapter 5.
[56] See Peng, Scott and Dattatreya, Ravi (1994) *The Structured Note Market*; Probus Publications, Chicago at 23–40.

- Duration with respect to the market rates relevant to the embedded derivative element. This rate may be identical to the rate applicable to that identified above, or may be a different rate to that used to value the bond component.

In cases where the structured notes contain embedded optionality, the duration analysis is supplemented with measures of the sensitivity of the structured note to the option component, with reference to traditional measures of option risk, such as delta, gamma or vega[57].

In practice, this approach entails the following steps:
- Identifying the rates determining the value of the structure, separating the rate affecting the bond component and that determining the embedded element.
- Measure sensitivity to *each rate* by measuring the key rate duration of the structured note by perturbing the yield curve by, say 1 bps, at the selected key points in the yield curve.
- [Optional] For structures with embedded option elements, calculate the price sensitivity of the option to changes in the rate determining the embedded component and volatility in that rate.

The approach outlined has a significant advantage in that it provides a measure of risk consistent with other components of fixed income portfolios. However, the approach has a number of disadvantages including:
- It provides a reasonable measure of risk for structured notes with embedded exposure to *interest rates*. It does not provide a corresponding basis for the measure of risk in structured note transactions where the embedded component is related to a different asset class; for example, currency, commodity, equity, credit etc.
- It must be complemented by a measure of option risk where the embedded risk element has an option component.
- It does not provide a measure of the inter-relationship of risk, namely the correlation risks relating to the interaction of the bond component with the market risk component.

Market Price Sensitivity Approaches
An alternative approach to risk evaluation focuses on measuring the market price sensitivity of the structured note within a general risk framework. Within this

---

[57] See Das, Satyajit (2004) Derivative Products & Pricing; John Wiley & Sons (Asia), Singapore at Chapter 15.

framework, the risk of the transaction is measured in term of the traditional measure of market risk (the Greek alphabet of risk) as follows:

- **Absolute price (or rate) risk (delta Δ)** – this measures the exposure of the price of the note to a given change in the price of the underlying asset or instrument. The concept is identical to the concept of PVBP (present value of a basis point) or DVO1 (dollar value of 1 basis point). In the case of a structured note, there would generally be at least two deltas. The first delta will be with reference to the interest rate applicable to the bond component. The second or additional deltas will be with reference to the asset element underlying the embedded derivative element. Where the debt elements are valued using zero coupon interest rates which are perturbed at each point in the yield curve, the fixed interest elements (whether bond or embedded element) will have *multiple* deltas corresponding to each zero coupon rate[58].

- **Convexity risk (gamma γ)** – this measures the exposure to a change of delta as a result of the change in the interest rate and the market price or rate element. There would also be cross gammas reflecting the change in convexity as a result of changes in the underlying price elements and the correlation between the two components.

- **Volatility risk (vega κ)** – this measures the exposure to a change of the volatility of the price of the underlying asset price embedded in the structured note in price terms for usually a 1% change in volatility.

- **Time decay risk (theta τ)** – this represents the exposure in price terms of the structured note to a change of the maturity of the contract. The key elements will be the interest rate accrual on the fixed income components, as well as the impact of time decay on the embedded instrument.

- **Discount or riskless interest rate (rho ρ)** – this measures the exposure to a change in the rate used to discount future cash flows; usually the risk free interest rate element used to value any embedded option element.

- **Correlation or basis risk** – this measures the exposure to changes in the correlation values between the interest rate of the bond component and the asset price element embedded.

The advantages of the market price sensitivity approach include:
- Uniformity and consistency of risk capture irrespective of the asset class of instrument embedded in the structured note.
- Total capture of risk of the instrument, including correlation elements.

---

[58] See Das, Satyajit (2004) Derivative Products & Pricing; John Wiley & Sons (Asia), Singapore at Chapters 13 and 14.

The disadvantage relates to the potential inability to compare this risk measure to traditional risk measurement approaches used in the management of fixed income security portfolios (such as duration).

Scenario/Simulation Approaches

An alternative set of risk evaluation tools focuses on simulation type approaches. These fall into two classes:

*   **Deterministic** – usually entailing the use of designated fixed sets of financial market rates to calculate the impact on the price of the structured note to measure its price sensitivity or risk profile.
*   **Stochastic** – usually entailing the use of probability based techniques such as Monte Carlo Simulations to model the price of the structured note. This entails using potential distributions of the price elements (the bond interest rate, the embedded asset price element and other relevant price drivers such as volatility). The distributions are based on spot prices, a volatility based distribution centred on the implied forward price of the variable, and the correlation between the elements. The distribution of price outcomes is used to determine the risk of the instrument. A common method is to identify the underlying movements that generate unacceptable price outcomes in the value of the security at any time during its life.

Risk Evaluation – In Practice

In practice, the approaches used will vary, depending upon the type of risk measured. In this regard, it is usually important to identify the different risk elements:

*   **Market risk** – reflecting potential changes in the price of the note in the event of changes in the key market variables that determine the value of the note.
*   **Cash flow risk** – this is similar to market risk but focuses on the change in cash flow to the investor as a result of changes in market variables. In effect, this does not incorporate the *unrealised* and *future* changes in cash flow. It concentrates on changes in the level of coupon payment during the life of the instrument and the principal repayment at maturity.
*   **Liquidity risk** – reflecting the risk of loss (primarily from transaction costs) from the need to sell the note prior to maturity.

The risk measures identified are all available to measure the *market* risk of transactions. The cash flow risk is best able to be identified using simulation approaches. The liquidity risk is more difficult to measure. In practice, it might be identified in qualitative terms only, or by looking at the value loss by using the adjusted bid-offer spreads for all value elements reflecting unfavourable market conditions to quantity the potential loss.

Active Versus Passive Investment Management – Risk Evaluation Elements

Risk evaluation is inherently related to the type of investment management approach adopted in relation to the portfolio of structured notes or the portfolio in which the note is incorporated.

Passive portfolio management is defined as the management of a portfolio consistent with the objective of generating returns to match the relevant performance benchmark. This is achieved through the replication of the investment asset selection in the index. The replication may be complete or partial. It may also be either direct or indirect (usually synthetic, entailing the application of derivative technology). Active portfolio management is defined as the management and trading of investment assets with the objective of generating returns relative to a benchmark or maximising the total return of the portfolio (possibly within some risk-return framework). The distinction is as much one of approach as in the activity levels in trading the underlying assets.

Structured notes can be used in both types of portfolios. For example, a structured note with an embedded forward or call option on an equity index can be incorporated in a passive portfolio to replicate tracking of the equity index performance. A structured note that incorporates yield curve positions combined with leverage can be incorporated into an active investment management portfolio to seek to create exposure to changes in the yield curve, or to capture value from the implied forward shape of yield curves in order to increase investment returns.

The implications for risk measurement relate to the fact that in the case of the passive portfolio manager, the focus of risk measurement is substantially the degree of *tracking error* representing the deviation from the portfolio manager's replication objectives. In the case of the active portfolio manager, the focus of risk measurement is the general market risk of the instrument and potential movements in value of the structured note as a result of movements in the underlying rates/asset prices.

The implications flow to a large extent from the likelihood that the structured note designed for the passive investment manger will be held until maturity. This focuses on tracking risk (a subset of market risk) and cash flow risk. The active manager is more likely (at least in theory) to trade the note prior to maturity, presumably to reflect changes in market rates that either allow capture and crystallisation of the expected movement in rates/price or elimination of the risk. This means that the active manager emphasises market and liquidity risk in the risk evaluation process.

4.6.8 *Structured Note Transactions – Secondary Market Pricing*

The final approach to pricing focuses on the pricing of transactions in the secondary market. In this context, the secondary market is taken to mean the sale and purchase of structured notes *after* initial placement and *before* final maturity. The valuation in the secondary market will typically be provided by the dealer asked to provide a bid price to purchase the structured note. The dealer will generally be the same entity that originally designed and placed the note with the investor.

The pricing and valuation approach in this context is predicated on establishing the value of a structured note at the time of the secondary market transaction. There are a number of mechanisms for determining value in this context, including:

- **Pricing the structured note as a security** – this entails the straight purchase and subsequent on-sale of the security to an end investor. The pricing in this case reflects the price the ultimate investor is willing to pay for the instrument.
- **Pricing on an issuer buy-back basis** – this enables the original investor to *re-purchase* the structured note.
- **Pricing on asset swap basis** – this involves unbundling the note into its constituent elements and stripping the note value to re-place the instrument in the form of a fixed or floating bond with traditional fixed interest investors.

In theory, the valuation on all three bases should be similar. In practice, the value will typically vary. This reflects the impact of a number of factors, including segmentation of markets, the valuation parameters used to value individual elements of the transaction by different parties, the lot size factor and the note maturity. These factors will typically be reflected in the supply and demand of the specific security and the market clearing price.

Pricing the structured note as a security entails the dealer making a price to the investor based on the *anticipated* price at which the dealer can on-sell the note to *another investor*. The key element of the approach is that as the note is sold as a security, no additional transactions (to strip out the derivative elements or re-package the asset) are required. The pricing logic will dictate that the dealer will bid the investor a price reflecting the purchasing investor's valuation, or a price adjusted (reduced) by the dealer's profit margin.

In practice, structured notes are priced only as a security under limited circumstances. For example, there was an active market for collared FRNs in the early phase of the introduction of the product. This was characterised by liquidity and tight bid-offer spreads for the instruments during this period.

Pricing on an issuer buyback basis is predicated on two bases:
* Repurchase designed to generate significant arbitrage profits through pricing the structured note on an asset swap basis.
* Repurchase on a no or low gain basis designed primarily to provide liquidity to the investor and ensure an orderly after market in the securities.

In each case, the repurchase requires the use of asset swap pricing to reverse engineer the embedded derivative components. The major difference in practice is that in the first case, the issuer seeks to earn the above market return on its securities *in an approach which reflects the return that an external investor would require to purchase the re-packaged note.*

The issuer buyback pricing should reflect the reversal of the credit enhancement built in to the transaction. The re-purchase of the note and the cancellation or buy-out of the embedded derivative element should eliminate the use of capital and credit resources required by the original transaction structure. This should be reflected in the pricing. The additional factor that will impact on pricing is the opportunity cost in terms of the forgone funding cost saving over the remaining life of the transaction by the issuer.

The repurchase pricing on an asset swap basis is predicated on the reverse engineering of the transaction to create a synthetic asset (generally, a fixed rate or more typically floating rate note). This repackaged asset is placed with investors seeking a traditional investment. The pricing in this case requires incorporation of:
* The cost of the derivative components *at the time of repackaging.*
* The return required by the investor on the repackaged asset.

The return required by the investor will generally be higher than for an equivalent conventional asset of the type. This reflects the following considerations:
* Complexity of the structure (reflecting the elimination of the embedded derivative components).
* Capital and credit requirements of entering into the derivative transactions to eliminate the derivative generated market risk.
* Compensation for the relative illiquidity of the asset.

Other factors in practice that may impact upon the pricing of structured notes in the secondary market include:
* **Credit risk of issuer** – changes in credit quality may positively or negatively affect the pricing of the structured note.
* **Parcel size** – secondary market prices are affected adversely by the size of parcel offered. Sizes smaller than US$10 million will attract a penalty while parcel sizes

in excess of around US$50–100 million (depending on market conditions) may be reflected in pricing pressure.

- **Maturity** – secondary market prices for long dated structured notes are generally lower. The price adjustment for maturity like the adjustment for parcel size reflects the universe and preferences of purchasers of the asset (either in the original or repackaged format) and the transaction costs associated with the repackaging transactions.
- **Market conditions** – in particular, supply and demand conditions for particular types of investments or structures can place temporary pressure on prices.

The relationship of the level of secondary market prices derived from the different valuation bases is interesting. **Exhibit 4.16** sets out the typical pricing relationship in practice.

The importance of the different valuation techniques in the secondary market is also relevant. In practice, inevitably asset swap/repackaging pricing is the most important. This reflects the depth and liquidity (in terms of number and range of investors) of the segment. This basis of pricing tends to place the floor price level for structured notes in the secondary market.

Exhibit 4.17 sets out the pricing and valuation of a collared FRN transaction in the secondary market.

4.6.9   Pricing and Valuation of Structured Notes – Summary

The pricing and valuation of structured notes follows the separation of the structures into the relevant component elements and the pricing of the individual building blocks transactions. The valuation of the components follows traditional pricing techniques.

Exhibit 4.16 Structured Notes Pricing Hierarchy	
Structured Note Price	**Pricing Basis**
High	New Issue (Primary Market)
⇓	⇓
⇓	Security Basis (Secondary Market)
⇓	⇓
⇓	⇓
⇓	Issuer Buyback (Secondary Market)
⇓	⇓
Low	Asset Swap/Repackaging (Secondary Market)

Exhibit 4.17   Pricing and Valuation of Collared FRN Transaction –
Secondary Market

1. Assumptions
This example focuses on the pricing and valuation of the capped FRN transaction detailed
in **Exhibit 4.15** in the secondary market.

Assume the subordinated capped FRN was originally issued with a final maturity of
10 years and a coupon of LIBOR plus 0.0625% pa. The remaining maturity of this note
is currently 8 years. The investor now seeks to sell the capped FRN and seeks bids from
the trader at the investment bank. The trader's bid to purchase the note is based on the
premise that the note will be repackaged and placed as a straight FRN with traditional FRN
investors.

2. Pricing & Valuation
The relevant pricing levels for the components are as follows:
- A subordinated FRN of the type identified is trading at around LIBOR plus 0.20% pa.
- Cap and floor prices reflecting movements in the yield curve and in volatility levels are
  as follows:

Cap Price – 2.75% flat.

Floor Price – 0.82% flat.

The difference between the cap and floor price (193 bps) reflects a cash outflow to the
trader, who must purchase the cap to hedge out the purchasing investor's exposure under
the sold cap embedded in the note, and sell the floor to be re-purchased from the investor.

Assume also that the investor who is prepared to purchase the collared FRN repackaged
into a conventional FRN requires a return of LIBOR plus 35 bps (a premium of some 15 bps
above that applicable to a comparable conventional FRN).

Using the parameters outlined above, the pricing is determined as follows:
- The adjustment to the margin above LIBOR required to increase the coupon to the
  required 35 bps from the coupon of 6.25 bps equates to 28.75 bps pa or 178 bps in
  present value terms, based on a discount rate of 6.40% pa payable semi-annually.
- The cost of hedging the cap and floor elements is 193 bps.
- The total cost of repackaging the note into a conventional FRN yielding LIBOR plus
  35 bps is 371 bps.
- The trader's breakeven price would therefore be 96.29% of face value. Assuming a bid
  offer spread of 10 bps (in price terms), the trader would bid the investor a price of 96.19%
  of face value.

Other required adjustments would include accrued interest and broken period calculation
where the note is to be traded in between interest payment dates.

Prices for the cap and floor will be derived using the relevant bid-offer prices, reflecting
the actual transactions required to be executed to re-package the risk of the transaction.

The complexity of the pricing and valuation of these types of instruments is related to capturing accurately and precisely all the risk elements and the correlation relationship between the bond or fixed interest element and the embedded market risk element. Additional complexity is generated by the necessity of evaluating the risk of the structure from the perspective of the investing institution. In this regard, a major consideration is the requirement to match the risk of the structured note *with more general risk concepts used to measure the risk of fixed interest portfolios generally*. The final complexity is created by the availability of a variety of mechanisms for pricing such transactions in the secondary market.

5   Repackaging Vehicles

5.1   Overview

Synthetic assets often use special repackaging structures. Special purpose repackaging vehicles are used to act as the issuer of the synthetic asset. The underlying asset structure is not altered. It is designed to enable the creation of synthetic investment assets predicated purely on the nominated investment parameters of the investor. Structured Investment Vehicles ("SIVs") are a special class of repackaging vehicles. In this Section, the evolution, structure and types of repackaging vehicles are outlined. SIVs are discussed in the following Section.

5.2   Evolution

The form of structured notes described to date uses a highly rated issuer to undertake the issue of structured notes. Increasingly, structured notes are created through special purpose repackaging vehicles. The concept of repackaging vehicles evolved out of the asset swap market; specifically out of the concept of securitised asset swaps. Securitised asset swaps were the effective precursors of the repackaging vehicle.

Repackaged structured notes are a special class of structured notes. They involve using a special purpose issuance vehicle or asset repackaging structure to repackage the risk of securities to create structured notes. The repackaging vehicle purchases securities in the secondary market and then re-profiles the cash flows of the underlying securities by entering into derivative transactions with a dealer. The repackaged cash flows are then bundled up as a security and placed with investors. Structurally, repackaged notes are fundamentally based on asset swap technology.

The motivations underlying repackaged notes and repackaging vehicles are similar to that underlying the market for structured notes generally. These include:
• Investor demand for investments and risk that is not directly available in the market.

- Relative value considerations under which the exposure can be created at a more attractive value through structured notes.
- Regulatory and market considerations that favour indirect assumption of the exposure relative to direct investment or entry into a derivative transaction.

The demand for repackaged structured notes *over traditional structured notes* is predicated upon the following additional factors:
- Absence of requirement to compensate the issuer for issuing the structured note.
- Relative value considerations where the repackaging structure provides the opportunity to purchase undervalued securities in the secondary market to collateralise the structure reducing the cost.
- Greater flexibility to structure investments consistent with investor requirements, without the restriction of needing to satisfy the requirements of the note issuer[59].
- Enhanced freedom to select the credit and issuer profile of the underlying securities that allows customisation of issuer risk and diversifies the universe of issuers of structured notes.

The factors (in particular the first two factors) have greatly contributed to the development of repackaged notes. Repackaged structured notes complement and compete with standard structured notes. The market also operates parallel to the asset swap market.

5.3   Structured Note Repackaging Vehicles

The use of the structure described gradually gained in popularity as a means for repackaging secondary markets assets. An important step in the evolution of the repackaging markets was the development of a secondary market in structured notes[60].

The impetus to secondary market trading in structured notes derived from the market distress period of 1994/1995. Prior to that, secondary market interest had been spasmodic. The activity that had occurred had been related to investors exiting structured investments with the dealer purchasing the note, engineering the reversal

---

[59]   This is relevant despite the fact that the issuer is perfectly insulated from the impact of the embedded derivative and is fully hedged back into LIBOR based funding at an attractive cost. This may be related to some elements of reputation risk.

[60]   See Das, Satyajit (2001) Structured Notes & Hybrid Securities – Second Edition; John Wiley & Sons, Singapore at Chapter 17.

of the derivative component(s), and distributing the security as a higher yielding fixed or floating note security to conventional investors in asset swap products. The latter continues to be the basic mechanism for providing any required secondary market liquidity and establishing benchmark secondary market bid prices for these notes.

In late 1994 and early 1995, the volume of structured notes that began to appear for sale increased dramatically as investors exited their investments[61]. The market conditions resulted in dealers rapidly re-positioning their secondary market trading in these instruments to allow them to be repackaged. The major buyers of the structured notes were asset swap buyers prepared to purchase structured notes that had been asset swapped to reverse engineer the market risk component. The asset swap was used to typically create a FRN priced off LIBOR targeted to banks, or a fixed rate bond priced off US Treasuries targeted to the fixed income investor.

The development of the secondary market in structured notes saw the introduction of a number of structured note repackaging vehicles. These vehicles were modelled on the securitised asset swap vehicles identified. Such vehicles include Merrill Lynch's STEERS (Structured Enhanced Return Trusts), Salomon Brothers' TIERS (Trust Investment Enhanced Return Securities)[62] as well as similar vehicles operated by other investment banks[63].

The central concept of the trust based structures was their ability to create trust receipts/securities that represented either repackaged structured notes or structured

---

[61] The most notable transaction during this period was the sale of the very large portfolio of structured notes held by Orange County; see Irving, Richard "County in Crisis" (March 1995) Risk 27–32. See also "Earthquake in Southern California" (3 December 1994) International Financing Review Issue 1059 102; "Salomon to Clock Orange County's Work" (10 December 1994) International Financing Review Issue 1060 82; "Orange County Begins Sale of Portfolio" (17 December 1994) International Financing Review Issue 1061 86; "Banks Suck Up Orange Juice" (24 December 1994) International Financing Review Issue 1062 60.

[62] For example, see Klotz, Rick, Dominguez, Nestor, Roy, Sumit, Schwartz, Mike, and Shaffran, Alan (30 March 1995) Trust Investment Enhanced Return Securities (TIERS[SM]); Salomon Brothers US Derivatives Research.

[63] For examples of other vehicles, see "Laser Shows at Paribas" (21 January 1995) International Financing Review Issue 1065 100; "Laser on Laser" (25 January 1995) IFR Swaps Issue 10 12; "BT TOPS out" (10 February 1996) International Financing Review Issue 1119 54; Rutter, James "Repackaging of All Kinds of Credits" (July 1997) Euromoney 29; Nicholls, Mark "TICs Tap into Swap Spreads" (March 1999) Risk 15; de Teran, Natasha "Warburg Begins Multi-Issue Asset Repackaging Program" (27 June–3 July 2000) Financial Products 9.

notes specifically created through repackaging which are sold to investors[64]. The trust receipts/securities were rated by one or more of the major rating agencies. The trust receipt/security is tradeable to facilitate liquidity. In essence, it is the conversion of asset swaps into public and tradeable securities.

The process of utilising a trust vehicle/special purpose company ("SPC") is set out in **Exhibit 4.18**. The diagram illustrates the creation of a trust receipt by re-profiling the risk of a structured note. The transaction entails the following steps:

- Purchase of a security in generally secondary markets (the collateral).
- The lodgement of the security in the trust vehicle/SPC.
- The entry by the trust/SPC into a series of derivative transactions with a counterparty to engineer the required cash flow/risk profile. This can entail either reverse engineering a structured note to remove the derivative element to allow the security to be placed as a fixed income bond. Alternatively, a conventional fixed or floating rate security can be combined with the relevant derivative components to create a structured note.
- The trust/SPC then issues trust certificates/notes representing the restructured cash flows of the security (combining the security and the derivative transactions) to the investor in return for payment of the face value.

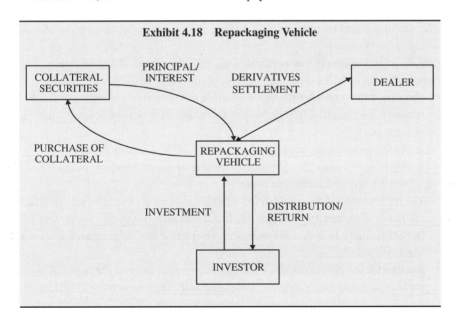

Exhibit 4.18   Repackaging Vehicle

---

[64] In non US jurisdictions, as discussed below, a special purpose vehicle is used. The vehicle issues bonds instead of trust receipts.

- The trust/SPC collects all cash flows (principal/interest from the collateral securities and derivative settlements from the dealer). The net cash flows are passed through to the investor over the life of the transaction.

The credit rating of this trust/SPC arrangement is the rating of the collateral plus the derivative transaction(s). The typical counterparty to the derivative transaction is a dealer with a high credit rating (minimum A with a significant number of dealers being AA or better). The issuer selects the credit quality of the underlying security. The resulting transaction can, at the option of the investor, be issued as a rated or unrated security.

The original purpose of the repackaging vehicles was to re-engineer large volumes of structured notes that investors wanted to sell. The notes were converted into conventional fixed income (primarily floating or fixed rate) bonds for re-placement with investors. The capacity of these structures to *create* structured notes, as distinct from reverse engineer them into conventional securities, was recognised. This led to the emergence of the modern structure of repackaging vehicles. These vehicles currently operate both in the primary and secondary markets.

5.4   Primary Market Repackaging Vehicles

The use of the special purpose repackaging vehicles in both the creation of *new* structured notes (the primary market) and in repackaging existing structured notes (the secondary market) was predicated on the advantages of the structure. The major advantages of the repackaging vehicle structures include:

- **Relative value considerations** – the structures can provide significantly higher returns to the investors. The sources of the enhanced return derive from a number of sources:
  1. Ability to purchase undervalued securities in the secondary market.
  2. Avoiding payment to the issuer of the required funding margin on a customised structured note issue.

  The higher costs of the repackaging vehicle structure do not significantly affect the return. The majority of costs are fixed, and on a per transaction basis may be substantially less than the enhanced return that can be generated from the identified sources.
- **Restructuring risk exposure** – a major advantage relates to the re-profiling of the investor's exposure under the structured note. The restructuring of risk under a traditional structured note requires the entry into an offsetting series of derivatives transactions to adjust the cash flow and risks. The required transactions may be difficult, for regulatory or credit reasons, for the investor to undertake. The alternative is to sell the structured note and if appropriate, purchase a *new*

structured note with the new risk profile. The second alternative is expensive in practice. Under the repackaging vehicle structure, the restructuring is achieved by selling back the trust certificate to the vehicle. The vehicle executes a series of derivative trades designed to eliminate the original exposure and create the desired profile. The trust re-issues a certificate with adjusted cash flows. The cost or benefit of the re-profiling is captured by either payment at the time of the restructuring, or over the life of the transaction. The flexibility and cost economies of this flexibility are considerable.

- **Credit selection** – the repackaging vehicle enables the use of *any available security*. This allows significant expansion in credit selection processes that are no longer constrained by the issuer universe prepared to undertake the issue of the required structured note.
- **Liquidity** – secondary market liquidity should be comparable to that for traditional structured notes. In practice, secondary market liquidity is enhanced by the repackaging vehicle structure as the receipts or notes are tradeable. The underlying process of gaining liquidity is at worst unaltered, and at best, improved.

In overall terms, the structure significantly enhances the potential of repackaging of structured notes. The repackaging structure effectively allows securitised and tradeable asset packages. The repackaging vehicles currently operate in competition to the primary issuer market in these types of transactions.

5.5   Generic Structure

The basic design of the repackaging vehicles is largely standardised. It follows the structure set out above in **Exhibit 4.18**[65].

The basic repackaging vehicle used is either a trust structure (favoured in the US) or a single purpose special company. The vehicles are associated with, but not owned by, dealer or investment banks[66]. The critical issues in structuring the vehicle include:

- The dealer does not own the vehicle. This is to avoid the need to consolidate the assets of the vehicle and maintain regulatory capital against the exposures incurred by the vehicle.
- The vehicle should be bankruptcy remote to the sponsoring entity. This means that the default or bankruptcy of the sponsor does not result in the default or bankruptcy of the special vehicle.

---

[65] See Fuller, Geoff and Sethupathy, Joan "Repackagings in 1998: Old Tunes, New Songs..." (March 1999) Futures & OTC World 72.

[66] The vehicle is often referred to as an "orphan subsidiary".

The steps in creating a structured note using a repackaging vehicle take the following (fairly standard) steps:

- The investor requirements are determined in terms of credit risk, risk profile and exposure required.
- The dealer purchases the required collateral in the secondary market.
- The dealer sells the collateral for value into the repackaging vehicle. The repackaging vehicle generates the liquidity needed to purchase the collateral from the issue of the structured note to the investor.
- The repackaging vehicle enters into derivative transactions with the dealer to:
  1. Convert a conventional security into a structured note with a defined risk profile by embedding the required exposure into the transaction through the derivative transaction.
  2. Convert a structured security into a conventional fixed or floating rate bond by hedging out the derivative elements through the derivative transaction.

  The derivative transaction is secured over the assets (the collateral securities) of the repackaging vehicle.
- The repackaging vehicle issues notes (in the case of a company) or trust receipts (in the case of a trust) to the investor in return for value. The proceeds of the structured note are used to purchase the collateral securities and if necessary, finance any payment required under the derivative contract. The securities are typically issued under a continuous issuance program such as a MTN program.
- The repackaging vehicle collects the cash flows from the underlying collateral as well as the settlements under the derivative contracts. The net cash flow is paid to the investor over the term of the transaction and at maturity. The structured note is cleared and settled through normal accepted mechanics.
- The investor in the structured notes is generally secured with:
  1. A charge over the collateral. This is usually a second ranking security interest. The dealer/derivatives counterparty will have a first charge securing payments required under the derivative contract.
  2. A charge (first charge) over the derivative contract.
- In the event of default under either the collateral securities or the derivative contract, the investor in the notes is fully exposed to the risk of loss. The investor receives any payment received by the repackaging vehicle based on the realisation of the collateral securities adjusted for the benefit/cost of closing out the derivative contracts. The investor's loss is limited to the face value of the note.
- The structured notes issued by the vehicle can (if required) be rated by a rating agency. The rating is dependent upon both the collateral and the credit risk of the derivative counterparty.

In effect, the repackaging vehicle acts as a conduit to allow the investor to access the underlying security and overlay the specific risk exposure required through the derivative contract. The repackaging vehicle funds itself through the issue of the structured notes. The risk and return profile of the structured note is attributable to the underlying collateral and the derivative contract.

There are a number of repackaging vehicles active in the market. These include the vehicles mentioned above, as well as other vehicles such as those associated with major investment banks. Examples include: JP Morgan (CRAVE – Custom Repackaged Asset Vehicle Trust), Barclays (ALTS – Asset Linked Trust Securities), Deutsche Bank (CROWNs, EARLs, etc.), ING (SNAP – Structured Note Asset Packages), UBS (SPARC – Special Purpose Asset Repackaging Company) etc.

5.6 Types of Vehicle

The types of vehicles used are:

- **Single purpose standalone issuers** – where a separate entity is established *for each issue* of structured notes.
- **Multiple issuance structures** – where a broad flexible structure is in place that allows the same entity to undertake different issues of structured notes.

The selection between the types of vehicles is dictated by the desire to maximise administrative flexibility and speed of execution, and minimise the costs of establishing the repackaging vehicles.

Multiple issuance structures have grown in popularity. Their popularity derives from:

- Lower cost of such structures reflecting the capacity to amortise the set up and ongoing costs over a larger volume of issues.
- Speed of execution; as the structure is *permanently in place*, transactions can be completed in a relatively short time scale.
- Benefits of administration of fewer vehicles.
- Opportunity for individual investment banks to brand their repackaged products. The brand awareness has significant benefits in terms of achieving the status of an established issuer, facilitating ready acceptance by investors.

Two types of multiple issuance vehicles are commonly used:

- Program Issuers.
- Multiple Issuer or "Umbrella" Programs.

Program issuers are designed as single legal entities that issue multiple series of structured notes. Each note is specifically secured over the specific assets and derivatives used to create the note. This is achieved by a combination of specific charges and limited recourse agreements that limit the recourse of the investor (as creditor) to specified assets and derivative transactions. Each series of notes is isolated from other assets and the contract held by or entered into by the issuer through the non-recourse mechanism – often referred to as a "firewall". **Exhibit 4.19** sets out the structure.

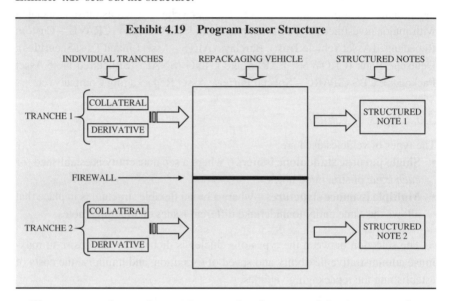

Exhibit 4.19   Program Issuer Structure

The program issuer format is attractive because of its low cost, lower administrative requirements and speed and flexibility in use.

The critical issue is in relation to the effective segregation of assets. This is important both from a legal and ratings perspective, as well as from the point of view of investors. In the event that assets underlying one issue were in default and the required separation had not been achieved, then the investors could potentially seek recourse to *all assets and contracts of the vehicle*. This phenomenon (referred to as "tainting") would have far reaching effects. The issuer itself could be in default, compromising *all issues*, not just the one in default. This may lead to litigation *against the issuer* and could prevent the operation of the vehicle.

This means that the program issuance format is not used in all jurisdictions. It is only used in jurisdictions where an appropriate level of legal comfort on the firewalls can be established. In practice, two other provisions are generally also used to manage this risk:

• Program issuance structures are not used where the underlying assets being securitised vary significantly in terms of credit quality from one issue of structured notes to another.

• The structure incorporates substitution rights, enabling assets to be removed from the structure in order to protect the rating of the vehicle[67].

The alternative is the multiple issuers or umbrella structure, where a separate vehicle is used for each issue, but a master documentary framework governing the individual issuers is established. **Exhibit 4.20** sets out the structure.

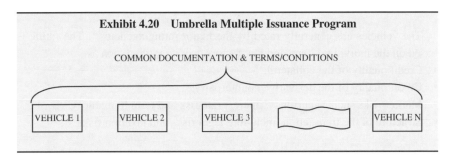

Exhibit 4.20   Umbrella Multiple Issuance Program

This type of structure has the following characteristics:
• The problems of tainting are avoided.
• Individual companies must still be established and administered over the transaction term.
• The process is facilitated by the common master documentation, with speed being increased by advance creation of a number of issuance vehicles.
• Cost is higher and the threshold size of the transaction and/or its profitability must be larger to support the higher cost.

The multiple issuer structure is generally favoured where the underlying assets are of higher risk, or the underlying assets are of significantly *different* credit risk.

The vehicles are generally based in favourable tax and regulatory environments such as Holland, Netherlands Antilles, Channel Islands (such as Jersey) Cayman Islands or British Virgin Islands. The major factors driving selection between the jurisdictions include:
• Tax regimes,
• Legal framework; particularly in terms of contract law, segregation, and bankruptcy remoteness.
• A benign regulatory framework.

---

[67] Following the emerging market collapse in 1997/8, this provision was used to remove Korean assets from some vehicles. This reflected the sharp deterioration in Korea's credit rating during this period.

- Political stability.
- Cost factors.
- Availability of services such as legal firms, accounting firms, and management companies.
- Physical location in terms of distance from major financial centres.
- Time zones that allow trading overlap with normal trading hours in key trading jurisdictions.

The vehicles are generally rated by the major rating agencies[68]. The rating is based on the individual issue and key factors driving ratings such as:
- Credit quality of the collateral.
- Credit quality of the derivative counterparty.
- Market risks such as currency, interest rate risk and term to maturity.
- Structure of the transaction, including legal risks and taxation risks.

5.7 Repackaged Structured Notes

The concept of repackaged structured notes is based firmly on asset swap/asset repackaging principles. The rationale is to deliberately create market risk exposure to selected risks and price movement using a derivative contract.

In general, there are two types of repackaged structured note transactions:
- **Introduction of market risk** (primary market trades) – these are generally *new* structured notes created in response to investor specifications. The dealer purchases high quality assets in the secondary market and then enters into the required derivative transactions to create the risk profile sought by the investor. The synthetic structured note is then placed with the investor.
- **Reduction in market risk** (secondary market trades) – these are generally structured notes that are purchased in the secondary market from existing investors and then repackaged using derivatives to reduce or eliminate the embedded market risk exposure. The repackaged security (a high quality fixed or floating rate bond) is then placed with a new investor (typically a bank or institutional investor). The major objective is to provide secondary market liquidity for the original holder. The new investor can usually achieve a higher return on a relative value basis for the underlying credit (even after adjusting for the structural complexity).

---

[68] See Das, Satyajit (2001) Structured Notes & Hybrid Securities – Second Edition; John Wiley & Sons, Singapore at Chapter 17.

The two structures are now an essential component of the market for structured notes. Primary market repackaging transactions now compete with traditional issuer based structured notes. The essential rationale for the structures remains identical to that of structured notes in general. The benefits of regulatory arbitrage, risk customisation, credit enhancement and denomination arbitrage remain available to investors, irrespective of the structure used.

6 Structured Investment Vehicles

6.1 Concept

SIVs cover a special class of repackaging vehicles. SIVs operate actively managed portfolios of synthetic assets that are specifically funded through the issue of securities that rely on the cash flow of the synthetic investments to provide return of capital and returns. They are also referred to as Limited Purpose Investment Companies ("LPICs") or Limited Purpose Finance Companies ("LPFCs").

The basic concept of a SIV entails a limited purpose investment company that manages a portfolio of assets and liabilities. The assets are generally of high credit quality. The SIV does not take any market risk. The SIV funds the portfolio by the issue of debt. The SIV debt is rated on the basis of the high credit quality investments and its market risk neutral structure. The SIV debt is highly rated (AAA/Aaa) based on the high credit quality of its diversified investment portfolio and its capital structure.

The objectives of SIVs include:
- Generation of high risk adjusted returns by investing in a high quality well diversified portfolio of investment grade securities.
- Funding the asset portfolio using capital and highly rated (AAA/Aaa (long term) or A1+/P1 (short term)) debt.
- Minimisation of exposure to credit, market and liquidity risk.

The distinguishing features of SIVs include:
- SIVs are arbitrage vehicles designed to operate in a manner analogous to financial institutions without the restrictions/regulations that affect banks.
- SIVs entail the specific debt investments being funded within the vehicle. Investors obtain off-balance sheet funding using the credit quality of the SIV. The funding does not use the investor's debt capacity or funding lines.
- Investors in the SIV do not obtain exposure to specific nominated investments designed to investor requirements as is the case with other synthetic assets

(including issues from repackaging vehicles). Investors in the SIV obtain net returns from a large diversified portfolio of debt assets.

• SIVs do not provide market risk exposure for the investor.

6.2 Structure

In this Section, the detailed structure of a SIV is outlined[69]. The key elements of the structure include:

• **Vehicle structure** – SIVs are generally limited purpose investment companies. The vehicles are generally incorporated in a tax neutral jurisdiction. The majority of SIVs are incorporated in the Cayman Islands. The use of the Cayman Islands is driven by a number of factors including[70]:

  1. Tax exempt status for the SIV is achievable. There is a structure whereby a 20 year exemption from tax (renewed every 10 years) is available.
  2. The jurisdiction is politically stable and uses English law.
  3. The jurisdiction has good legal, financial etc infrastructure.

  The early SIVs were designed with finite lives (around 10 to 15 years). The more recent structures have no fixed maturity. In some cases, the limited term SIVs were restructured to extend the initial maturity[71]. The capital structure and business purpose of the SIV cannot be changed. The activities of the SIV are managed by a third party under contract. The manager is generally an investment bank/dealer or specialist fund manager.

• **Capital structure** – the SIV has substantial paid up capital. The amount varies between vehicles and the structure. SIVs typically have capital of around US$1.0 to 1.5 billion. The capital is subscribed by the sponsor entity and institutional investors. In most cases, the individual investors are limited to a maximum percentage of the SIV's capital (around 15%). This is designed to avoid the need for individual investors to consolidate the SIV. Investors are generally anonymous. The capital of the SIV is supplemented by external debt (typically a mixture of short term funding (commercial paper ("CP")) and term funding (MTNs). The amount of leverage that the SIV can assume varies, depending

---

[69] For example, see Marrinan, Edward B. and Derrick, Simon (13 August 1997) "Beta Finance Corporation" JP Morgan, London.

[70] The considerations are very similar to those that drive selection of jurisdiction choice for a repackaging vehicle.

[71] For example, the shareholders in Beta Finance Corporation, which in accordance with its Articles of Association would have been voluntarily wound up in 1999 (it was created in 1989), extended its life in 1994. In contrast, Alpha Finance Corporation (a sister vehicle) was wound up in 1998.

upon the structure. The leverage permitted is driven by the credit quality and maturity of the investment portfolio. Typical leverage levels are around 10 times (that is, 10% equity/90 % debt within the capital structure). The leverage structure is designed to create incentives for the manager to generate higher returns without significantly increasing risk.

- **Investment assets** – the SIV investment portfolio is generally of very high credit quality. The investments are subject to strict investment guidelines that are monitored by the rating agencies, manager and trustee (if appointed under the structure). The investments must be investment grade. In general, the SIVs only invest in AA or better assets. A significant portion (around 75% or more) of the investment portfolio is generally of AA or better rated. There are specific limitations (as % of the investment portfolio) on holdings of individual assets of different credit rating. There are also concentration limits for individual issuers. This is to ensure that the portfolio is well diversified and a diverse range of securities is held. Typical restrictions are that the largest individual investment exposure within the portfolio cannot exceed a limit around 25% to 33% of capital or around 1% to 15% of the investment portfolio. The limits are based around credit quality. Greater concentration is permitted for higher rated issuers. Most SIVs hold well diversified portfolios with exposure to financial institutions, sovereigns, corporations and structured finance issuers (for example, securitisation vehicles). Each category of issuer is usually further sub-divided into sub-groups to ensure a high level of diversification. The SIV can hold a limited amount of non investment grade assets. This is generally limited to BB/Ba rated assets and the total of such investments cannot exceed 10% of the investment portfolio. This limit does not permit the outright purchase of non-investment grade assets. This allowance is designed to permit the SIV to continue to hold investments where an investment grade asset has been downgraded.
- **Risk Management** – the SIV is subject to tight risk management guidelines that are monitored closely. The SIV is required to be market-risk neutral at all times. The SIV is only permitted to assume credit and liquidity risk within prescribed guidelines. The risk management guidelines generally used are as follows:
    1. *Market risk* – the SIV is generally required to minimise exposure to market risk. Interest rate risk is minimised by matching assets and liabilities and/or the use of derivatives. Currency risk is minimised by matching funding in the relevant currency and/or the use of derivatives. Most SIVs use interest rate and currency forwards, swaps and options to convert all assets and liabilities into appropriate floating rate instruments that are closely matched. The SIV's book will generally be structured to have a liquidity mismatch, with the average maturity of its liabilities being less than the average maturity

of its assets. However, the SIV portfolio will be matched as to interest rate re-pricing. For example, a 5 year FRN with semi-annual interest may be match funded by a 1 year floating rate MTN, where the floating rate on the liability will reset on the same dates as the asset. The risk limits for interest rate and currency mismatches applied to SIVs are very conservative. For examples, risk limits may be set around the following levels: 0.05 bps change in portfolio value for a 1 bps change in interest rates (parallel or yield curve shape) and 0.5 bps change in portfolio value for a 1% change in currency rates.

2. *Credit risk* – the SIV will generally incur credit risk in relation to its investments and derivative counterparties. In relation to investments, the SIV's assets must be formally rated investment grade by major rating agencies at the time of purchase. The investment portfolio must meet ratings and maturity limits. There are additional limits on diversification, country and industry exposure. The limits are generally more restrictive at lower credit ratings. This has the effect of capping exposure to an obligor if its credit quality declines. In relation to derivative counterparties, the SIV is subject to several layers of risk control. Counterparties are restricted to entities with a minimum credit rating of A or better. The SIV is also allowed to enter into transactions that are cleared through established clearing houses and exchanges. In practice, SIVs only deal with high quality counterparties and all derivatives are marked to market daily. There is generally a capital charge for changes in value by rating category. All transactions are documented under the standard ISDA documentation. There is use of netting agreements with all counterparties. There is also increased use of collateral and other types of credit enhancement to manage the risk of non performance by a derivatives counterparty.

3. *Liquidity risk* – SIVs have significant liquidity risk. This is in the form of re-financing risk driven by the mismatch in maturity between the assets and liabilities. The quantum of liquidity risk is controlled by conservative limit structures designed to limit the possibility of losses from liquidity risk. The SIV is required to limit the amount of liabilities that can become due over any 1 week, 2 week and 1 month period. In addition, the SIV is required to have access to liquidity. This is from asset holdings of short dated, high quality securities (usually government or A1+/P1 rated bank certificates of deposit) that can readily liquidated if required. In addition, the SIV will generally be required to have committed liquidity facilities provided by high quality (A1+/P1 rated) banks. The liquidity facilities will generally require a same day funding facility to cover maturing CP (known as a "swingline").

In practice, SIVs manage the liquidity risk of the operations conservatively. On the asset side, holdings of short term, liquid, highly rated assets, diversification of the asset portfolio and access to the repo markets is used to provide potential liquidity. On the liability side, conservative net cumulative outflow limits, committed liquidity facilities and liability management (extending the maturity structure of debt issued and diversification of the funding) is used to avoid re-financing risk. In general, SIVs will hold liquidity reserves of around 10% of the total investment portfolio.

4. *Operational* – the SIV is exposed to various forms of operational risk. It is controlled by a variety of measures. The major form of control is the establishment of appropriate procedures and strict reporting/monitoring requirements. This is reinforced in some SIVs by the use of external independent trustees. All securities are required to be held by established reputable trustees (such as Euroclear and CEDEL). Where the SIV is associated with a dealer, additional procedural controls are required. These are in the form of organisational controls. The SIV manager must be functionally separate from other functions (trading etc) of the dealer. This is to ensure complete independence and avoid potential conflicts of interest.

- **Liability management** – the SIV's funding is generally sourced from capital markets directly. The high credit rating/quality (SIVs are generally rated AAA/Aaa) facilitates direct access to investors. Debt is generally issued under continuous issuance formats such as global CP and MTN programs. The programs are generally structured to allow access to all potential markets (in practice, the US and international markets are the most important). This requires compliance with the requisite regulatory requirements (such as SEC registration). The focus of liability management is on achieving low cost of funds and diversification of the liabilities. SIVs maintain sophisticated and flexible treasury operations with a very high level of expertise. The SIVs are extremely responsive to investor demands for investments. SIV issuance focuses on a mixture of issuance combining conventional fixed and floating rate funding and structured issues. SIVs are able to issue MTNs or CP in any currency, interest rate basis or structure. The issue is swapped/hedged with derivatives to obtain funding of the required type. The ability to issue flexibly allows the SIVs to significantly reduce their cost of funding. SIVs also maintain good investor relations and undertake extensive global investor marketing to facilitate access to funding.
- **Control process** – SIV operations are subject to rigorous disclosure and control processes. These are focused on: daily monitoring of the operations, daily mark-to-market of all positions, weekly reporting to rating agencies/ trustee (if applicable), quarterly verification by external auditors and

semi-annual/annual audits by external auditor. An independent risk control unit undertakes all control processes. This unit reports directly to the Board of the Manager and the external auditors.

- **Termination structure** – a key feature of the SIV structure is defined tolerance for loss. This is set at a prescribed amount (say 3% to 5% of the total investment portfolio). The limit is set at a level that represents a loss that the SIV could sustain, and still maintain its financial viability. If the loss limit is exceeded, then the structure goes into defeasance. This means that the liquidity support facilities would be drawn down. Holders of SIV debt may have the option to redeem their securities prior to maturity *at market value*. All assets and liabilities would be pooled into annual maturity buckets. The credit support for each defeasance pool would be sized on a per pool basis, weighted by the amount of liabilities in the pools. This is designed to enable each pool to withstand a significant level of obligor defaults. The defeasance process will be administered by a Trustee with the objective of ensuring that the SIV debt holders are repaid in full on a timely basis. If a SIV goes into defeasance, then dividends/returns to equity holders are suspended.
- **SIV Rating** – the SIV achieves it high ratings (generally AAA/Aaa) on the basis of its fundamental structure. Key factors include: the high credit quality of its asset portfolio, diversification of its assets, maturity restrictions on its assets, limits on credit quality of assets, restriction on credit quality of derivative counterparties, level of committed capital, liquidity support, market risk neutral position, termination structure (if incorporated) and rigorous operational controls.

The SIV return is the net spread between the income stream from the high quality investment portfolio and its low funding cost (based on its high credit quality). The return to the SIV equity investors is the net spread adjusted for administration and funding costs.

Exhibit 4.21 sets out the basic structure of a typical SIV.

6.3   Market[72]

SIVs originally emerged around 1987[73]. The concept evolved from the asset swap market. The following conditions were the major drivers of SIV structures:
- Availability of attractive returns on high credit quality assets through asset swaps.

---

[72]   See Sandiford, Jane "Building a Structured Credit Solution" (April 2001) FOW 38–47.

[73]   The concept is generally attributed to a small group of individuals from Citicorp led by Stephen Partridge–Hicks) who were involved in the asset swap market. The group

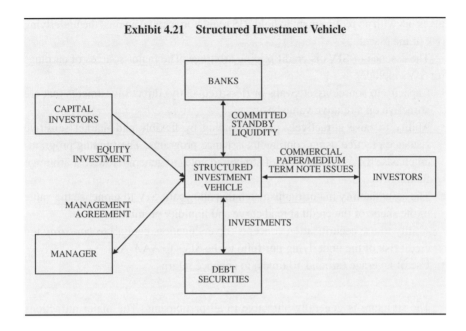

Exhibit 4.21   Structured Investment Vehicle

- Ability for highly rated issuers to generate attractive funding through new issue arbitrage; in particular, through structured notes.
- The requirement for banks/financial institutions regulated under BIS credit capital guidelines to hold credit capital against high quality assets in excess of the economic risk on the assets. This made it difficult for banks to hold such investments. This was despite the fact that the assets were attractively priced relative to risk.

The presence of these factors led to the creation of SIVs. The major activity of SIVs is the purchase of asset swapped investments funded by low cost funding generated by active new issue arbitrage. The attractive investment returns (derived from the asset swap arbitrage) funded by low cost funding (derived from the liability arbitrage) generated attractive risk adjusted returns. The returns were attractive to

---

created Alpha Finance Corporation ("Alpha"), Beta Finance Corporation ("Beta") and Centauri Finance Corporation ("Centauri"). This Group of entities came to constitute the Credit Structures Group within Citicorp (that subsequently evolved into the Citibank Alternative Investment Strategies Group). The original creators of the Citicorp SIV structures subsequently formed an entity (Gordian Knot) that established and manages Sigma Finance Corporation (a vehicle associated with Deutsche Bank).

investors with no requirement to hold BIS regulatory capital against the underlying risk of the assets.

The essence of SIVs is credit pricing arbitrage. The major sources of earnings for SIVs include:

- Capacity to source asset swaps or (less frequently) direct investments that are attractive on a relative value basis.
- Ability to raise attractively priced funding by flexible and market sensitive issuance practice using continuous issuance programs. The funding programs emphasise the aggressive use of structured notes to generate low cost arbitrage funding[74].
- The asset liability maturity mismatch that allows the SIV to monetise the value of the shape of the credit spread curve and liquidity premiums.
- Ability to use securitisation concepts (diversification, capital) to *bootstrap* the credit risk of the underlying portfolio to the SIVs to AAA/Aaa.
- Use of leverage (around 10 times) to enhance returns.

The structure is generally attractive to all participants. The major attractions include:

- Investors in the SIV equity gain the capacity to invest in a portfolio of high credit quality securities with minimal market risk. Investors also gain access to credit investment and arbitrage expertise that they may not possess internally. A major attraction of the structures is the ability for investors to leverage their investments. The SIV structure provides the investor with access to a leveraged portfolio of attractively funded credit assets. The investor gains access to off balance sheet funding that does not rely on the investor's credit rating or debt capacity. In this way, the SIV represents a mechanism for exploiting investor's unused investment capacity for high quality securities to generate attractive risk adjusted returns.
- Investors in debt issued by the SIV gain access to an attractive source of investments. The high rating of the SIV provides the investor with the opportunity to diversify its AAA/Aaa issuer base. The responsiveness of the SIVs to structured issuance is also attractive to investors seeking structured investment products.
- The SIV structure is attractive to dealers both as a purchaser of asset swap investments and issuer of structured product. The potential transaction flows that SIVs generate have led a number of dealers to establish these structures. However, the

---

[74] For a description of the issuing practices of SIVs, see "Best User of EMTNs" Beta Finance Corporation" (June 1996) Euromoney 80–82.

manager of the SIV must maintain independence and avoid conflicts of interest. This means that the dealer must compete with other market participants for a share of the SIV's transactions.

The major vehicles active in the market include Citicorp vehicles (Beta, Centauri, Five Finance), JP Morgan (Argo), Deutsche Bank (Sigma), Bank of Montreal (Links) and European Sovereign Investment ("ESI")[75]. The structures are all similar. However, there are some differences, reflecting the type of activity undertaken. In recent years, interest in SIVs has grown in parallel with increased interest in credit risk. The structures continue to evolve, with interest in structuring SIVs for investment in loan assets and non investment grade assets.

7 Summary

Synthetic assets entail the use of combinations of debt instruments and derivative contract(s) to create an investment asset. The objective is to synthetise an investment with specified characteristics nominated by the investor. This may include adjusting the currency, interest rate (fixed or floating), contingency on any cash flow and/or linking the interest or principal to price/rate fluctuations in a nominated assets. The defining feature of synthetic assets is that the transaction is driven by the investor's requirement for an investment not directly available, or the ability to create an investment with superior economics to a direct investment.

There are a number of identifiable types of synthetic asset structures, including asset swaps and structured notes. Asset swaps entail the use of derivatives (principally, interest rate and currency swaps) to alter the currency or interest rate profile of investment assets. Structured notes entail the issue of debt instruments (fixed or floating interest rate notes) where a derivative transaction has been engineered into the structure to create a synthetic investment asset. The differentiating feature of the structured notes compared to asset swaps is that there need not be a direct investment asset available in the market. The complete investment asset is manufactured/synthetised.

---

[75] For examples of other vehicles, see "The Big ESI" (24 November 1993) IFR Swaps Issue 45 1–2; "Dressing Mutton as Lamb" (26 November 1994) International Financing Review Issue 1058 16; "Arbitrage Angles" (17 December 1994) International Financing Review Issue 1061 39; "Sigma Extends the Alphabet" (4 February 1995) International Financing Review Issue 1067 34–36; Lee, Peter "Citicorp's New Constellation" (November 1996) Euromoney 14–16; Hargreaves, Tim "New Vehicles for Credit Arbs" (September 1999) Risk 6.

Synthetic assets often use special repackaging structures. This entails the use of special purpose repackaging vehicles or entities to act as the issuer of the security. Synthetic assets also include activities involving SIVs – a special class of repackaging vehicles that operate actively managed portfolios of synthetic assets, that are specifically funded through the issue of securities that rely on the cash flow of the synthetic investments to provide return of capital and returns.

Synthetic assets are an increasingly important part of the capital market. The major use of synthetic asset technology is to create structured investment products for investors. Structured notes also play a major role in frequent issuers' liability portfolios. These types of issues are used to access low cost funding from investors seeking customised investment structures.

EXOTIC OPTIONS

5
Exotic Options

1 Overview

Exotic options have emerged as an important instrument for risk management. The increased interest in exotic option structures reflects the growth of derivatives generally. It also reflects the increased demand for highly customised risk management / hedging structures.

The importance of exotic options derives from a number of factors:

- Exotic options expand the available range of risk management/risk transfer opportunities.
- Exotic options create unique valuation, pricing and hedging problems that provide additional insights into the pricing and hedging of options generally.
- Exotic options provide insight into risk dimensions such as correlation/ covariance and uncertain cash flow hedging.

This part of the Book examines exotic options and related products. The objective of this Chapter is to provide an overview to exotic options. Chapters 6 to 11 discuss specific types of exotic options.

The structure of this Chapter is as follows:

- The evolution of risk management products and the key factors underlying this evolutionary process are outlined.
- The hierarchy of risk management instruments and types of exotic options are examined.
- General issues relating to the valuation, pricing and hedging of exotic options are analysed.
- The market for exotic options is described.

2 Evolution of Risk Management Products

The emergence of exotic options is driven by the overall evolution of risk management itself. The key factors underlying this evolutionary process include:
- Uncertainty/volatility in asset markets.
- Increased focus on financial risk management.
- Demand for highly customised risk reward profiles.
- Developments in option pricing and hedging technology.
- The politics of risk management.

A key driver of the evolution of risk management products is the problems confronted by borrowers and investors as a result of uncertainty and volatility[1]. Financial market volatility has increased since the early 1970s. This has necessitated instruments that facilitate hedging and position taking amongst investors and borrowers. Volatility in foreign exchange markets increased dramatically. Similar increases in interest rate volatility occurred in the late 1970s, early 1980s and the 1990s. Equity prices and commodity prices have also shown significant volatility over recent times. The available evidence does not support an increase in volatility over the period from the early 1970s. However, the pattern of volatility has shifted.

While overall volatility levels may be comparable to previous periods of history, short term periods of *high volatility* have been evident. This means that periods of low or normal volatility are punctuated by short periods of much higher volatility. For example, temporary short term volatility increases have been evident in currency markets (breakdown in the European Rate Mechanism in the early 1990s; emerging market currencies in the late 1990s/early 2000s); interest rates (US rates in 1994 and 2000/2001; credit/swap spreads in 1997/1998 and 2001); equity markets (various episodes since the late 1980s) and commodities (various episodes in the energy market; gold market in the late 1980s).

The temporary surges in volatility have increased demand for financial derivatives to manage risk. The interspersion of periods of low and high volatility complicates hedging. Generally borrowers and investors will seek to hedge against high volatility in asset prices/rates. Hedging is not required during periods of low volatility. This is because the cost of hedging may exceed the benefit of the hedge, reducing shareholder value/investor returns. However, it is unlikely that borrowers/investors can accurately anticipate periods of high volatility. Periods of high volatility also affect the cost of hedging. High volatility can translate into high

---

[1] See Chapter 1.

hedging costs. This also makes it difficult to hedge. The *pattern* of volatility has driven demand for more structured hedging products that seek to minimise the identified problems.

The increase in/change in the pattern of volatility is compounded by uncertainty. Uncertainty relates to the fact that cash flows/underlying positions held by investors and borrowers are also uncertain variables. Uncertainty relates to the impact of financial market variables (such as commodity price/equity/interest rate fluctuations) on hedging requirements in currencies. It also relates to fundamental changes in the underlying real assets, and business or operating/financial strategy of the industrial or investing entity. The changes alter hedging requirements. This uncertainty relates to the size, timing and contingent nature of the underlying cash flows that are to be hedged. This creates problems in risk management. This uncertainty has also prompted innovation in risk management instruments.

Development of innovative risk management products is driven by increased focus on risk management by both corporations and investors. The uncertainty and volatility factors identified have led to increased focus on risk management. The increasingly global and cross border nature of business, with attendant financial risk, has increased focus on risk management techniques. The increased focus on risk management has created demand for highly customised risk reward profiles. Corporations, investors and financial institutions increasingly seek to separate financial risks in a specific and precise manner. This necessitates the availability of instruments to facilitate hedging and position taking consistent with the desired level and type of exposure. The demand for highly customised risk reward profiles is allied to an increasing trend towards active management of financial risk. It is also driven by investor demand for yield enhancement in return for assumption of specific types of risk.

The supply of innovative risk management products has been facilitated by developments in option pricing and hedging technology. The evolution of financial technology, allied to dramatic advances in computer and hardware software, now allows the routine application of sophisticated mathematical techniques for pricing and management of derivative products. This has been central to the evolutionary process allowing the design of new risk management structures. The development process is mutually accommodating. Client demand has prompted innovation. Trading opportunities/portfolio risk positions have also prompted creation of products designed to separate and unbundle price risks, and redistribute the risks to those best able to assume and manage them.

An often underestimated factor in the development of exotic options is *the politics of risk management*. The politics of risk management revolve around corporate/investment processes involving the adoption by entities of appropriate policies and procedures relating to the measurement, management and evaluation of financial risk and activities in managing risk.

Organisations frequently fail to adopt risk management practices commensurate with their business. In addition, there is evidence of the use of speculative strategies as means of generating earnings unrelated to their basic business. This has resulted in a number of cases of significant losses. These losses can be traced to the inappropriateness of risk management policy or control procedures[2]. The increased focus on risk management in a number of cases is not allied to a willingness to use all possible available risk management products. This is driven by a variety of factors. One factor is the difficulty of hedging in conditions of volatility and uncertainty. This creates significant problems by way of hedging gains/losses and opportunity costs in terms of missed profit potential. A further factor is the reluctance to pay (sometimes substantial) hedging costs in periods of high volatility to purchase insurance against financial risk. Lack of information/expertise has also limited the adoption of sound hedging practice. For example, use of sold options to generate earnings against underlying positions is frequently excluded from the range of permitted hedging actions. The political nature of the risk management decision has encouraged the development of innovative risk management products that seek to address these factors.

In summary, the volatility/uncertainty of global markets, the risk management requirement of corporations (to protect income streams/balance sheets) and investor requirement for risk/yield enhancement has created an environment conducive to the development of specialised risk management products.

3 Risk Management Instruments – Hierarchy

The evolution of risk management products has created successive generations of instruments. **Exhibit 5.1** sets out a hierarchy of risk management products. It is important to note that the products are generic in nature. The various types of risk management products are applicable, irrespective of underlying asset types (for example, interest rate/debt securities, currencies, commodities, equities etc).

First generation risk management products consist of the basic building block derivative instruments: forwards and option contracts. The building block instruments can be traded in different markets (exchange-traded markets (futures) or OTC markets (swaps)). The basic instruments facilitate traditional risk

---

[2] See Das, Satyajit "Controlled Experiments" (24 August 1994) IFR Swaps no 83 10–15; Das, Satyajit "Guidelines for Utilisation of Derivative Instruments in Risk Management" (2nd Quarter 1995) ASX Perspectives 25–32.

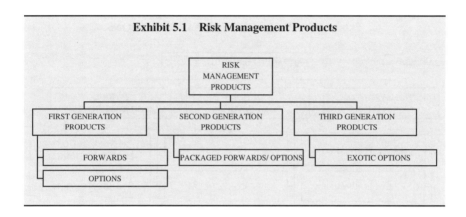

Exhibit 5.1   Risk Management Products

transfer applications. The basic instruments, in conjunction with a spot or physical market in the relevant asset, complete the principal opportunities to separate, unbundle and redistribute price risks in financial instruments.

The second generation of risk management products consists of packaged forwards/options. There are three specific classes of instruments:

• Option/forward combinations.
• Option combinations.
• Hybrid structures.

The products are constructed using combinations of first generation risk management products. The various combinations of options and forwards are primarily designed to achieve a number of objectives:

• Customise risk profiles to overcome the difficulty of traditional forward contracts that eliminate the opportunity for the user to benefit from any favourable movements in underlying asset prices/rates.
• Combinations of bought and sold options to effectively reduce the premium required to be paid in connection with an option.
• Particular combinations of options to create a higher degree of leverage.
• Hybrid structures designed to assist in managing the problem of uncertainty or contingent hedging.

Exhibit 5.2 sets out a hierarchy of packaged forwards/options. Chapter 40 examines packaged forwards/options in detail.

Third generation risk management products are "true" exotic options. Each instrument seeks to vary one or more elements of the fundamental structure of an option contract.

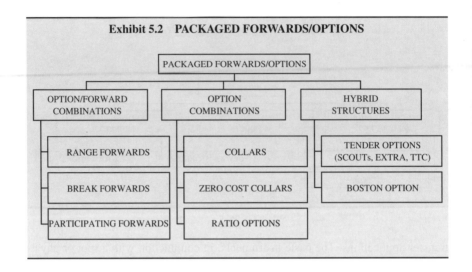

Exhibit 5.2 PACKAGED FORWARDS/OPTIONS

4 Exotic Options[3]

4.1 Definition

Exotic options can be defined as:

Any option whose characteristics, including strike price calculations/determinations, payoff characteristics, premium payment terms or activation/expiration mechanisms

---

[3] See (1992) From Black-Scholes to Black Holes – New Frontiers in Options; Risk Publications, London; Tompkins, Robert (1994) Options Explained[2]; Jarrow, Robert (Editor) (1995) Over the Rainbow – Developments in Exotic Options and Complex Swaps; Risk Publications, London; Das, Satyajit (1996) Exotic Options; LBC Information Services, Sydney; Macmillan Press Limited, England; Nelken, Israel (Editor) (1996) The Handbook of Exotic Options; Irwin Professional Publishing, Chicago; Ravindran, K. (1998) Customised Derivatives; McGraw-Hill, New York; Bhansali, Vineer (1998) Pricing and Managing Exotic and Hybrid Options; McGraw-Hill, New York; Nelken, Israel (2000) Pricing, Hedging and Trading Exotic Options; McGraw-Hill, New York. See also K. Duker "Derivative Products" (November 1989) The Treasurer 6–13; Gerard Ducros "New Strategies for a Corporate Treasurer" (November 1989) The Treasurer 23–24; Yvon Sinnah "Exotic Currency Options: An Introduction" (Autumn 1991) The Journal of International Securities Markets 203–208; Citibank (undated) Exotic Options: New Flexible Instruments for Foreign Exchange Rate Hedging; Stambaugh, Fred "The First Choice for FX Hedging" (1994/95) Corporate Finance Foreign Exchange Yearbook 11–18; Rowe, David "In Defence of Exotics" (September 2000) Risk 105; Smith, Craig "All that Glitters" (March 2002) FOW 71–74.

vary from standard call and put options, or where the underlying asset involves combined or multiple underlying assets.

Exotic options are primarily focused on varying one or more elements of the fundamental structure of an option contract. This can be illustrated by the following examples:

- In the case of an average rate option, the dimension that is altered is the payoff determination. The option payoff is calculated through a comparison of the strike price of the option and the average price of the underlying commodity as sampled over the relevant period. This is in contrast to the traditional option contract where the payoff is determined by a comparison of the strike price and the *final* price of the underlying asset.

- In the case of a barrier option, the existence of the option is itself contingent upon a specified event occurring. Typically, a barrier option (such as a knock-in) will only be activated if the underlying asset price reaches some specified level, or in the case of a knock out, will continue to remain active unless the asset price achieves the nominated level.

4.2 Exotic Options – Hierarchy

Exhibit 5.3 sets out a classification of exotic options. The classification follows the approach generally followed by practitioners[4]. The classification used is arbitrary. This is because a specific type of option may exhibit a combination of different characteristics. For example, a structure may be both path and limit dependent. The classification is only useful as a means of identification of the predominant themes underlying exotic optionality.

The major types of exotic options are as follows:

- **Path Dependent Options** – path dependent options are characterised by payoffs that are a function of the particular path that asset prices follow over the life of the relevant option. The path of the underlying asset price can determine not only the payoff, but also the structure of the option. Path dependent structures include:
  1. *Average rate (or Asian) options* – where the payoff upon settlement is determined by comparing the strike price with the average of the spot asset price over a specific period during the life of the option.

---

[4] See Chase Securities Inc. "Mundane Problems, Exotic Solutions" (August 1992) Euromoney 42–48; Ong, Michael "Exotic Options: The Market and Their Taxonomy" in Nelken, Israel (Editor) (1996) The Handbook of Exotic Options; Irwin Professional Publishing, Chicago at Chapter 1; Smithson, Charles "Path Dependency" (April 1997) Risk 65–67.

2. *Average strike rate option* – where the strike rate itself is not fixed, and the payoff is determined through a comparison of the underlying price of the asset at expiration with the strike price computed as the average of the underlying asset price over a specified period.
3. *Lookback options* – where the purchaser has the right at expiration to set the strike price of the option at the most favourable price for the asset that has

---

Exhibit 5.3   Exotic Options – Hierarchy

Exotic options can be classified into five categories:

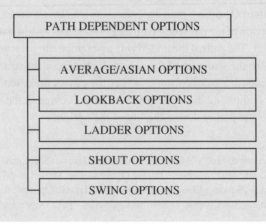

Each category can then be further classified into different types of options. Path dependent options consist of the following major types of options:

Time dependent options consist of the following major types of options:

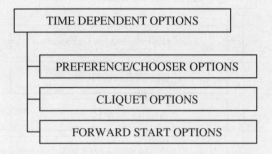

Limit dependent options consist of the following major types of options:

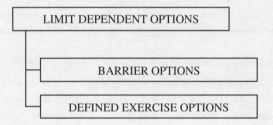

Payoff modified options consist of the following major types of options:

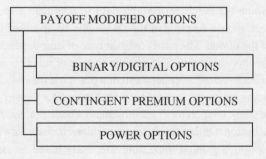

Multi-factor options consist of the following major types of options:

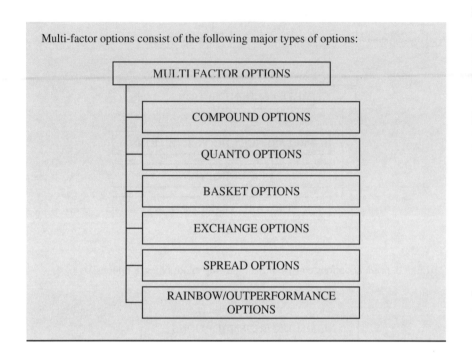

occurred during a specified time. In the case of a lookback call (put), the buyer
can choose to purchase (sell) the underlying asset at the lowest (highest) price
that has occurred over a specified period, typically the life of the option.

4. *Ladder options* – where the strike price of the option is periodically reset
based on the underlying evolution of the asset price. A ladder option is not
dissimilar to a lookback option. In the most extreme cases, if the number of
resets is set to infinity, the ladder option approximates the economics of a
lookback option.

- **Time Dependent Options** – time dependent options can be characterised as
options in which the purchaser has the right to nominate a specific characteristic of the option as a function of time – usually on specified dates before the
expiration of the option. The most common type of time dependent option is the
preference or chooser option. The specific feature of this option is that it is not
specifically characterised as either a call or a put at the time of entry. At a predetermined date, usually after commencement but no later than expiration (known
as the choice date), the purchaser can nominate whether or not the transaction is
a call or a put option. Other time dependent options include forward start options
(where the option is granted some time after entry based on asset prices at the
grant date) and cliquet options (where the option has a lock-in feature similar to

a ladder option except that it is based on the asset price on a pre-specified future date or dates). All time dependent options are also path dependent.

- **Limit Dependent Options** – limit dependent options are a special class of options incorporating a mechanism where the option contract is activated or deactivated as a function of the level of the underlying asset price. These types of options are usually known as barrier options. In a typical structure, a barrier option may appear or disappear, depending on the contractual arrangements agreed based on the performance in price terms of the underlying asset. Barrier options are, in a sense, both limit and path dependent. A variety of types of barrier options exist. Defined exercise options are a special type of barrier option where the option is triggered in or out, based on the price evolution of an asset *other than the underlying asset of the option.*
- **Payoff Modified Options** – payoff modified options entail adjustment to the normal payoffs that are associated with conventional options. The major types include:
  1. *Digital (binary) options* – where the payout under the option contract is a fixed pre-determined amount payable if the strike price is reached, irrespective of the asset price performance (that is, how far the option is in the money).
  2. *Contingent premium options* – this option links the option premium to be paid to the writer to the asset price performance. In the classical structure of a contingent premium option, no premium is payable at the commencement of the transaction. The premium becomes due and payable at expiration *only* if the option expires in the money. Technically, the contingent premium structure is a combination of a conventional option and a digital option.
  3. *Power (exponential) options* – where the option payout is enhanced upon exercise. A standard option return is a clear linear function of the difference between the underlying asset price and the option strike at exercise or at maturity. In the case of a power option, the option payoff is a defined function of the difference between the underlying asset price and the option strike raised to a power eg higher than 1.
- **Multi-Factor Options** – multi-factor options typically involve a pattern of payoffs based on the relationship between multiple assets. This is in contrast to conventional options, where a single asset drives the option performance. A variety of structures exist, including:
  1. *Compound options* (options on options) – where the holder has the right but not the obligation to buy or sell another predetermined option at a pre agreed price.
  2. *Basket options* – where the payout under the contract is related to the cumulative performance of a basket of underlying assets.

3. *Exchange options* – where the purchaser has the right to exchange one asset for another.

4. *Quanto options* – where the option contract is denominated in a currency other than that of the underlying asset to which exposure is sought or being hedged. The quanto contract will typically allow the quantity or notional principal of the transaction to be adjusted, reflecting the fact that the face amount of the currency cover required fluctuates to cover changes in the foreign currency value of the underlying asset.

5. *Spread options* – where the option payout is based on the difference between two nominated assets.

6. *Rainbow options* – where the option payout is based on the relationship between multiple assets as opposed to a price of a single asset. Typical structures include best-of or worst-of options (often known as out performance options).

Other types of exotic options are also available. These often represent changes in the basic structure outlined.

4.3   Exotic Options – Rationale

The exotic option structures identified are predicated on the achievement of one or more of the following objectives:

- **Reduction in option premium** – effectively to lower the cost of purchasing the option.
- **Alteration in risk profile** – this can take one of a number of forms, including:
  1. *Increased probability of gain* – creating the ability to restructure the strike, type or other aspect of the option to ensure that the prospect of positive economic value at exercise or maturity is increased for the purchaser.
  2. *Quantification of loss* – ensuring that *the option writer's* potential payout, if the option expires in the money at maturity, is known at the time the option is traded, or ensuring the premium on the option is *only payable* by the buyer under defined conditions.
  3. *Optimal exercise timing* – ensuring that the option pays out the maximum value or close to this value, irrespective of whether the option is exercised at the optimal time.
- **Asset liability matching** – the option payoff profile matches the underlying asset or liability required to be hedged or managed through the option transaction.

The capacity of exotic options to reduce option premiums and also alter risk profiles makes them particularly suitable for use in structured notes. In practice, the major types used in designing structured notes include average rate options, ladder options, barrier options, basket options and digital options[5].

5   Exotic Options – Valuation/Pricing and Hedging Issues

5.1   Overview[6]

The demand for customised risk management structures such as exotic options places increased demands on the capacity of dealers to price and hedge/trade complex products. The problems of valuation, pricing and hedging are important at several levels, including:

- The ability to value/price is fundamental to the creation, provision and trading of exotic options.
- Efficient valuation and hedging techniques are essential to enable dealers to manage the risk of such transactions and portfolios.

The special characteristics of exotic options and the special risk management hedging problems posed provide insight into pricing/management of derivative portfolios.

In this Section, the key issues in valuation/pricing and hedging exotic options are considered. Issues examined include the valuation/pricing approach used, model issues in pricing exotic options and trading/hedging issues. The discussion in this Chapter is generic. It focuses on common issues affecting exotic options *generally*. Specific valuation and hedging issues affecting individual types of exotic options are examined in the Chapters dealing with the relevant type of exotic options.

5.2   Exotic Options – Valuation/Pricing Approach[7]

Since the original publication of the Black-Scholes-Merton approach to option pricing, there has been rapid and significant development of option pricing

---

[5]   See Chapters 19 and 20, and Das, Satyajit (2004) Structured Products Volume 2; John Wiley & Sons (Asia), Singapore at Chapter 4. See also Das, Satyajit (2001) Structured Notes & Hybrid Securities – Second Edition; John Wiley & Sons, Singapore at Chapter 13.

[6]   For a discussion of the general issues in valuation and hedging exotic options, see de Jager, Garry "Pricing Models for Complex/Exotic Options" in Das, Satyajit (Editor) (1997) Risk Management & Financial Derivatives: A Guide to the Mathematics; LBC Information Services, Sydney; McGraw-Hill, Chicago; MacMillan Publishing, England at Chapter 9.

[7]   There is significant literature on valuation/pricing exotic options; see Wilmott, Paul, Dewynne, Jeff and Howison, Sam (1994) Option Pricing: Mathematical Models and Computations; Oxford Financial Press, Oxford; Brys, Eric Bellalah, Mondher, Mai, Huu Minh and De Varenne, Francois (1998) Options, Futures and Exotic

theory[8]. A major part of the development in option pricing is focused on the valuation of exotic options.

Valuation of exotic options is based on the generalised approach to valuation of contingent contracts. This entails the generation of the expected value of the option that is then discounted back to the valuation date. The valuation of exotic options poses significant problems. This complexity reflects the following factors:

- Exotic option payoffs may depend on asset prices over the life of the option, rather than the values *only* at maturity[9].

- Exotic option pay-offs may be more sensitive than conventional options to the shape of the distribution (skews) or to large unexpected price changes (jumps). rather than the overall realised actual volatility.

- Exotic option pay-offs may be driven by the relationship between multiple assets (correlation).

Derivatives: Theory, Application and Practice; John Wiley & Sons, Chichester; Wilmott, Paul (1998) Derivatives: The Theory and Practice of Financial Engineering; John Wiley & Sons, Chichester; Hull, John (2000) Options, Futures and Other Derivatives – Fourth Edition; Prentice-Hall Inc., Upper Saddle River, NJ; Nelken, Israel (2000) Pricing, Hedging & Trading Exotic Options; McGraw-Hill, New York. See also (1992) From Black-Scholes to Black Holes – New Frontiers in Options; Risk Publications, London; Jarrow, Robert (Editor) (1995) Over the Rainbow – Developments in Exotic Options and Complex Swaps; Risk Publications, London; Nelken, Israel (Editor) (1996) The Handbook of Exotic Options; Irwin Professional Publishing, Chicago; Ravindran, K. (1998) Customised Derivatives; McGraw-Hill, New York; Bhansali, Vineer (1998) Pricing and Managing Exotic and Hybrid Options; McGraw-Hill, New York. For a bibliography of the literature of exotic option pricing models, see Lyden, Scott "Reference Check: A Bibliography of Exotic Options Models: (Fall 1996) Journal of Derivatives 79–91; see also Smith Jr., Clifford W. "Option Pricing: A Review" (1976) Journal of Financial Economics Vol 3 15–24; Smithson, Charles "Wonderful Life" (October 1991) Risk 37–44; Smithson, Charles "Extended Family (1)" (October 1995) Risk 19–21; Smithson, Charles "Extended Family (2)" (November 1995) Risk 52–53; Smithson, Charles "Extended Family" (December 1997) Risk 158–163; Whaley, Robert "Building on Black-Scholes" (December 1997) Risk 149–156; Smithson, Charles "Extended Family" (September 1998) Risk 1Black Scholes Merton Supplement 14–18.

[8] See Das, Satyajit (2004) Derivative Products & Pricing, John Wiley & Sons (Asia), Singapore at Chapter 4 for the epistemology of option pricing. See Das, Satyajit (2004) Derivative Products & Pricing, John Wiley & Sons (Asia), Singapore at Chapter 7 for a description of the Black-Scholes-Merton approach to option pricing.

[9] This is evident in the case of an American (or Bermudan) option that is a simple example of a path dependent option; see Das, Satyajit (2004) Derivative Products & Pricing, John Wiley & Sons (Asia), Singapore at Chapter 7.

The identified factors create a number of difficulties including:

* The specific path followed by the asset price must be known to generate an option value.
* Constant volatility cannot be assumed. as the value of the exotic option will be sensitive to the volatility skew and the relationship between spot price changes and volatility.
* The term structure of interest rates is needed as the discounting back of the payoffs cannot be undertaken using a fixed interest rate to the final maturity of the option.

In this Section, the principal approaches to overcoming the issues created by path dependency are discussed. The issue of volatility estimation for exotic options is discussed in the next Section. The requirement for variable discount factors is dealt with by using interest rate term structure models[10].

Approaches to valuation/pricing of exotic options generally focus on a two tier approach:

* Adapt Black-Scholes-Merton approach where feasible to price/value the contract.
* Where either Black-Scholes-Merton itself or a variant cannot be applied, a variety of numerical and/or simulation approaches are used.

Where Black-Scholes-Merton approaches are appropriate, exotic options are priced either by adjusting the Black-Scholes-Merton formula itself, or breaking the options into components that can be priced within the original framework. Some examples of this approach include:

* Preference options, where the purchaser chooses whether the option is a call or a put, can be priced by separating the payoff profile and equating it to a portfolio of puts and calls at different strikes and different maturities that are then priced using Black-Scholes-Merton.
* Compound options can be priced using Black-Scholes-Merton adjusted by changing the characteristics of the asset to equate to that of the underlying option.

In the case of a number of products, Black-Scholes-Merton approaches are not appropriate. This is particularly the case where the options are path dependent, as typically closed form solutions are unavailable. In these cases, pricing is undertaken

---

[10] See Das, Satyajit (2004) Derivative Products & Pricing, John Wiley & Sons (Asia), Singapore at Chapter 8.

using one of the following approaches[11]:

- **Binomial/tree approaches** – this uses a discrete time version of the Black-Scholes-Merton model[12]. The approach requires specification of a particular process for the underlying asset price, modelling the asset price movement over time, and then using an iterative (numerical) approach to solve the value of the option by working backward from maturity. The approach models the underlying asset price evolution as a binomial or (more recently) trinomial/multinomial tree that is then solved using mathematical programming techniques. Standard binomial/multinomial trees are adjusted to accommodate interest rate term structure models to allow pay-offs to be discounted at different discount rates at different points of the tree.
- **Analytic solution** – this entails solving for the option value by solving the partial differential equation that the exotic option contract satisfies. The solution uses advanced mathematics including:
  1. *Finite difference schemes* – this converts the partial differential equation into a finite difference scheme that is solved.
  2. *Integrals or numerical methods* – this uses integration techniques to solve for the option value using a variety of mathematical or numerical techniques.
- **Simulation techniques** – this uses Monte Carlo simulation techniques to generate random asset price/rate paths to simulate the behaviour of the asset over time. It is similar to the application of binomial/multinomial processes to simulate the underlying asset price/rate movements. Price paths of the underlying asset/rate are created, with each simulation allowing expected option values to be extracted. Where a large number of simulations are used, the distribution of possible option values can be generated. This allows derivation of the fair value of the exotic option contract. The difficulty with simulation techniques includes the need to simulate or solve using iteration for the relevant value or hedging information. Depending on the type of option, a large number of sample paths or increases in simulation trials are required to derive a robust valuation. This creates problems of processing speed and accuracy.
- **Approximation techniques** – this involves estimation of the value of an exotic option by using a connection with a similar problem that has a known answer. For example, one approach to pricing average rate options uses an approximation

---

[11] See de Jager, Garry "Pricing Models for Complex/Exotic Options" in Das, Satyajit (Editor) (1997) Risk Management & Financial Derivatives: A Guide to the Mathematics; LBC Information Services, Sydney; McGraw-Hill, Chicago; MacMillan Publishing, England at Chapter 9; Smithson, Charles "Path Dependency" (April 1997) Risk 65–67.

[12] See Das, Satyajit (2004) Derivative Products & Pricing, John Wiley & Sons (Asia), Singapore at Chapter 7.

technique. The first two moments of the probability distribution of the arithmetic average are calculated. It is assumed that the distribution of the arithmetic average is log normal with those first two moments. This allows an analytic solution to be used[13].

5.3 Pricing/Valuation of Exotic Options – Model Issues

The difficulties in valuing and pricing exotic options focus on the assumptions used in option pricing generally[14]. For example, traditional assumptions used in option pricing (log normal distribution of price changes, proportionality of volatility to the underlying asset price, and the use of interest rates to determine the drift of the asset price) create important modelling errors that distort exotic option values significantly. The errors also reduce hedging efficiency. In addition, discontinuous asset price/rate changes (jumps) have a larger impact upon the valuation of certain exotic options than on corresponding conventional options.

The major problems include the impact of the smile/skew and term structure of volatility and relationship between volatility and spot price changes on exotic option prices[15]. The problems have significant impact on the hedging/trading of exotic options. This aspect is considered in the next Section. Many of the problems identified are in fact *not unique* to exotic options. The problems are probably more significant in relation to pricing/valuing exotic options.

Traditional Black-Scholes-Merton option price approaches assume that the asset price/rate follows a random walk over time. Returns on the asset are assumed to be normally distributed with a constant volatility. In practice, volatility is both dependent upon the strike price of the option and the remaining time to maturity. This means that the market distribution is non log normal and "fat tailed". The observed second order effect of asset price paths has a major effect on the valuation of exotic options. This is because a path dependent option will be sensitive to both the distribution of the asset prices *and* the evolution of this distribution from one period to the succeeding period. This means that different processes may be

---

[13] See Turnbull, S. and Wakeman, L. "A Quick Algorithm for Pricing European Average Options" (September 1991) Journal of Financial Quantitative Analysis 377–389.

[14] See Hewett, Thomas and Igolnikov, Roman "Option Valuation: Key Issues in Option Pricing" (2000) Balance Sheet Vol 8 No 4 11–16.

[15] See Hyams, Gideon and Weinberger, Jonothan "Exotic Options" (September 1999) Risk Special Supplement – Euro Derivatives 18–19; JP Morgan "Pricing Exotics Under the Smile" (November 1999) Risk 72–75; Savery, Howard "Quantifying Volatility Convexity" (February 2000) Derivatives Strategy 54–55; Blacher, Guillame "Stochastic Volatility" (14–20 March 2000) Financial Products 8–9; Fabery, Fabrice and Cornu, Sebastian "From Theoretical Value to Dealing Price" (September 2000) Risk Special Supplement – Euro Derivatives 14–15.

consistent with the observed volatility, but produce different values for a path dependent option.

In practice, the pricing of exotic options must be undertaken consistent with the observed volatility smile[16]. This involves the use of a number of different classes of models, including:

- **Stochastic volatility models** – this defines a stochastic process for instantaneous volatility with a number of free parameters that are chosen to best fit market implied volatility.
- **State dependent volatility models** – this uses local instantaneous volatility that is defined as a function of asset value and time[17].
- **Discrete jump process models** – this uses jump processes to model the asset price movements over time and uses this to drive the option value[18].

In practice a number of hybrid models are used[19]. The models use elements of the various approaches outlined so as to generate realistic exotic option prices.

An additional problem with exotic options relates to the sensitivity of the value to changes in the spot price. This occurs at two levels. Discontinuous large price changes in a time series of asset prices/rates potentially have significant effects on the expected value of the option. For example, a large jump may trigger in or out a barrier option. Similarly, a large change in asset prices may have a large price impact on a digital option with a large fixed payout. In effect, the *pattern* of price changes is potentially significant.

A further problem is the relationship between spot price changes and the sensitivity of the option premium to volatility. For example, in the case of a normal option, its vega is greatest when the option is at-the-money. In the case of some exotic options, the behaviour of the option's vega displays sensitivity to spot prices as well as changes in implied volatility[20]. This type of cross convexity means that the value of the option is sensitive to correlation between the underlying asset price/rate and volatility. For example, this may dictate large changes in hedges to maintain vega neutrality where the spot moves a large amount.

---

[16] See discussion of stochastic or local volatility based option pricing models in Das, Satyajit (2004) Derivative Products & Pricing; John Wiley & Sons (Asia), Singapore at Chapter 9.

[17] See Dupire, Bruno "Model Art" (September 1993) Risk 118–124; Dupire, Bruno "Pricing with a Smile" (January 1994) Risk 18–20; Derman, Emanuel and Kani, Iraj "Riding on a Smile" (February 1994) Risk 32–39; Rubinstein, Mark "Implied Binomial Trees" (July 1994) Journal of Finance 771–818.

[18] See JP Morgan "Optional Events and Jumps" (September 1999) Risk 111–114.

[19] See JP Morgan "Pricing Exotics Under the Smile" (November 1999) Risk 72–75.

[20] These sensitivity measures are referred to as second order Greeks. They are also referred to as cross gammas (reflecting the fact that the pricing model is being differentiated with respect to a risk measure rather than the value of the option).

This creates significant difficulties in hedging exotic options. The impact on pricing/valuation derives from the fact that the option value must cover the cost of hedging. The difficulty of hedging dictates that options cannot be priced simply at a simple premium to the implied volatility of a conventional option. The order of difficulty of hedging and re-hedging must be incorporated into the valuation process. In practice, this presents difficulties that can only be dealt with using simulation technology[21].

The primary objective of the approaches outlined is to ensure that the model captures (as closely as possible) the actual market price changes. The manner is which dealers in the market assign value to the risk of asset price and volatility changes must be captured by the model. This is designed to ensure that the exotic options can be hedged/traded accurately. In addition it attempts to ensure that exotic option values are consistent with the market valuation of conventional options.

A final problem is that some exotic options introduce correlation into option pricing. This is explicit in the case of many multi-factor option structures. This requires estimation of correlation[22]. The required correlation is the *actual correlation to be experienced* over the life of the option. As with volatility estimation, the estimation of correlation is difficult. This creates significant difficulties in accurately pricing/valuing exotic options.

5.4 Trading/Hedging Exotic Options

Exotic options represent significant challenges in trading and risk management. This relates to two specific aspects of exotic options. The behaviour of the option sensitivities (the Greeks) for exotic options can be dramatically different to that for conventional options[23]. In addition, the actual hedging/risk management of exotic options is complex because of the sensitivity of the options simultaneously to changes in spot prices, volatility and the spot price-volatility cross convexity.

The behaviour of the Greeks for exotic options is complex[24]. The differences can be readily illustrated with a few examples including:

- In the case of an average rate option, the fact that the payoff is based on a moving average has a stabilising effect on the behaviour of the option premium.

---

[21] See Murphy, David "Setting the Scene" (June 1997) Risk 43–47.

[22] See Das, Satyajit (2004) Derivative Products & Pricing; John Wiley & Sons (Asia), Singapore at Chapter 9.

[23] See Das, Satyajit (2004) Derivative Products & Pricing; John Wiley & Sons (Asia), Singapore at Chapter 15.

[24] See de Jager, Garry "Pricing Models for Complex/Exotic Options" in Das, Satyajit (Editor) (1997) Risk Management & Financial Derivatives: A Guide to the Mathematics;

The price of the average rate option is generally more stable than a comparable conventional option. This reduces the gamma and vega of the option. The sensitivity of the option is also time dependent. As the remaining time to maturity diminishes, the fact that the average becomes more fixed has the effect of reducing the gamma and vega of the average rate option.

- In a number of exotic options, delta and gamma are discontinuous. This reflects the underlying structure of payoffs for the particular option. For example in barrier options, the Greeks behave in a manner similar to that for a conventional option where the asset price is trading well away from barrier levels. The discontinuous payoff of barrier options creates extreme behaviour at or near the barrier levels. This is reflected in rapid changes in delta and high gammas. It may also be reflected in high sensitivity to spot-volatility relationships. Digital options also exhibit similar extreme behaviour in the Greeks at or around the strike levels; in particular, where a large payout is triggered.

- In a number of exotic options, the vega behaviour is complex. For example, in a range binary (where the investor receives a high rate of interest as long as a nominated asset price stays within a range), a higher volatility is associated with a lower expected payout to the buyer. This reflects the fact that increased volatility would increase the chance of the option expiring with no value, as the asset price would be more likely to move outside the nominated range. Similarly, spread options can often exhibit negative vega. This is a result of the fact that a decrease in volatility of one of the two assets in the spread option can increase the likelihood of the spread increasing, resulting in a higher value of the option.

Traditional hedging and risk management of options is based on establishing the sensitivities of the option premium (using partial derivatives of the option valuation model) to model the behaviour of individual options or portfolios. The principal focus is matching the option/portfolio delta, gamma and vega. The dealer seeks to offset the risks to a substantial degree by trading in the underlying asset (delta hedge) and/or options (gamma and vega)[25]. This level of risk management is not adequate for portfolios of exotic options[26].

LBC Information Services, Sydney; McGraw-Hill, Chicago; MacMillan Publishing, England at Chapter 9.

[25] See Das, Satyajit (2004), Derivative Products & Pricing; John Wiley & Sons (Asia), Singapore at Chapter 16.

[26] See Hyams, Gideon and Weinberger, Jonothan "Exotic Options" (September 1999) Risk Special Supplement – Euro Derivatives 18–19; Blacher, Guillame "Stochastic Volatility" (14–20 March 2000) Financial Products 8–9; Thombre, Prasanna and Sim, Eric "Monitoring Discontinuous Risk" (4 September 2000) Derivatives Week 6–7.

Hedging/risk management of exotic options requires additional derivatives that allow quantification of the higher order risks of this type of instrument. It also requires more sophisticated risk management/trading to manage the risks present. Exotic options generally demonstrate significant cross convexity. The major types of cross convexity are between spot price changes/vega changes and vega changes/implied volatility changes (volatility gamma).

The impact of the higher order risks is complex. For example, where an exotic option's vega is sensitive to changes in spot, the dealer will need to recognise this relationship in hedging. Exotic options also create problems of volatility gamma (known as "vol gamma"). Exotic option portfolios that have positive (negative) vol gamma will become longer (shorter) vega as implied volatility increases. In both cases, the additional vega risk will need to be hedged. The additional hedging risk may be significant.

For example, assume the dealer is short a call on an asset with a strike of $110 and with a knock out set at $125 (known as reverse knockout options). Where the underlying asset is trading at levels well below the knock out level (say at $100), the position exhibits positive vol gamma. This means that implied volatility increases (decreases) make the dealer longer (shorter) vega. The positive vol gamma benefits the dealer. Where the underlying asset is trading at prices closer to the knock out level (say $120), the position exhibits *negative* vol gamma. This means that implied volatility increases now increase the dealer's risk by reducing the vega of the position (making the dealer short vega). The negative vol gamma forces the dealer to re-hedge when implied volatility increases. This means that the dealer must buy volatility as implied volatility increases, or sell volatility as implied volatility decreases. The adjustment of the hedge is potentially very expensive.

An additional aspect of risk management relates to the discontinuous payoff functions of exotic options. Assume a digital option that has a large payout if a pre-agreed asset price level is hit at anytime over the life of the option (a one touch digital option). Where the asset price is below the pre-agreed strike, the option has low gamma. If the asset price approaches the strike price, then the option gamma increases rapidly. This reflects the fact that if the asset price breaches the strike, the large payout is triggered. The option gamma becomes extremely sensitive to changes in the spot price and changes in implied volatility. The size of the hedge can become very large, depending upon the size of the fixed payout relative to the notional value of the option.

The risk management requirements of exotic options have systemic implications. As volatility exhibits increased sensitivity to spot changes or implied volatility changes, option volatility itself becomes extremely unpredictable. The need to manage the large gamma risk also increases the volatility of the underlying asset market.

The potential negative feedback loops within markets create significant difficulties in hedging. The position is further complicated by concentration of barrier levels or strike levels on digital options. This means that dealers frequently seek to anticipate changes in the spot market or implied volatility. The dealers seek to hedge aggressively to avoid being caught with excessive risk. This introduces auto-correlation of volatility and discontinuous asset price changes that further complicate hedging.

Efficient hedging and risk management of exotic options requires that the identified factors be incorporated into the pricing/valuation and determination of the sensitivity of the option. This includes incorporating the volatility smile/local volatility surface in exotic option valuation/trading. This also requires using an appropriate hedging strategy with a strong emphasis on managing the volatility risk. The problems of risk management have driven traders to examine static hedging approaches[27].

Static hedging focuses on trading in conventional options to replicate the payout of exotic options. The problems of hedging barrier options led dealers to replicate these instruments with conventional European options using symmetry arguments[28]. The attraction of this approach is that in theory, such a hedge would immunise the dealer from any move of the implied volatility surface. However, the presence of a volatility skew or drift in the asset price may adversely affect the strategy.

Alternative hedging approaches include vega bucket/super bucket hedging[29]. This uses a pricing model that incorporates a term structure of implied volatility (vega bucket hedging) or a complete volatility surface including sensitivity to both strike and term (super bucket hedging). In theory, these approaches immunise the trader from small moves in implied volatility, skew and/or term structure. The hedge must be dynamic with frequent adjustment. It is reliant on obtaining required implied volatility data and efficient pricing/hedging methods.

---

[27] See Derman, Emanuel, Ergener, Demiz and Kani, Iraj "Static Options Replication" in Konishi, Atsuo and Dattatreya, Ravi E. (1997) Frontiers in Derivatives; Irwin Professional Publishing, Chicago at Chapter 10; Blacher, Guillaume "Vega Hedging" (7–13 March 2000) Financial Products 8–9; Blacher, Guillaume "Hedging Exotic Options with Europeans" (August 2000) Derivatives Strategy 45–47.

[28] Specific design of these hedges is discussed in Chapter 9.

[29] See Blacher, Guillaume "Vega Hedging" (7–13 March 2000) Financial Products 8–9; Blacher, Guillaume "Hedging Exotic Options with Europeans" (August 2000) Derivatives Strategy 45–47.

6 Market for Exotic Options

6.1 Overview

The emergence of exotic options has been a significant factor in derivative markets. The development of exotic option products is significant in a number of respects, including:

- Increased flexibility for risk transfer and hedging.
- Highly structured expression of expectations of movements in asset prices.
- Insights into the nature of *optionality* and the management of risks associated with options generally.
- Facilitation of trading in new risk dimensions such as the correlation between key financial variables, allowing in part a better and more complete understanding of risk.

The features of exotic option products have generated considerable discussion about and research into these products. The market for exotic options has demonstrated rapid growth. It is now established as a significant component of the options market[30]. This is particularly the case in certain asset classes such as currencies.

The dominant characteristics of the market for exotic options include:

- Complexity of the risk profiles of these instruments.
- Difficulty in pricing, hedging/replicating and trading in these instruments (reflecting the complex structures and risk profiles).
- Low secondary market trading volumes and relative lack of liquidity in the market for exotic options other than a few structures (principally barrier and digital options).

In this Section, the structure of the market for exotic option instruments is examined. The analysis examines the underlying dynamics of the market. The principal user groups and applications of the products are considered. The market for individual products is then analysed. Differences in the market for these instruments by asset class and/or geography are considered[31].

---

[30] This has led to an increasing debate on what constitutes a "true" exotic, see Webb, Andrew "What's Exotic?" (July 1999) Derivatives Strategy 17–21.

[31] For discussion of the market for exotic options, see Martyn Turner and Richard Attrill "Exotic Currency Options" (May 1993) Corporate Finance Derivatives Supplement 21–23; Simon Brady and Helen Murphy "Exotic Cures for Currency Headaches" (October 1993) Corporate Finance 18–21; Simon Brady "Handle Exotics with Care" (March 1994) Corporate Finance 38–39; Reed, Nick "Tales of Exotica" (June 1995)

6.2 Exotic Options – Users and Applications

The key user groups for exotic options include:
* Investors/asset managers.
* Non-financial institutions.
* Derivatives dealers.
* Non dealer financial institutions.

The key applications are focused upon:
* Yield enhancement.
* Trading/positioning.
* Structured protection.
* Option premium reduction strategies[32].

Major users of exotic option products are investors. It is useful in this context to differentiate between institutional investors/professional asset managers and retail investors.

Institutional investors and professional asset managers have used these types of products to primarily enhance portfolio returns or monetise expectations on asset price movements. The major impetus for the use of exotics by this group includes:
* Low absolute returns in fixed income instruments in the early 1990s.
* Shift to asset allocation strategies and the practice of benchmarking portfolios that forced asset managers to monetise expectations in order to outperform index performance benchmarks.
* Increased involvement outside traditional investment markets, including investment in emerging markets.
* Use of leverage to enhance investment returns.

The low nominal returns from fixed income markets forced asset managers to seek to enhance returns through the use of derivative instruments. A major focus was the capture of return from value differentials in asset prices or positioning

---

Risk 27–29; Falloon, William "Hedges for Export" (July 1995) Risk 20–26; Ogden, Joan "Free Falling Derivative Prices" (July 1996) Global Finance 23–28; Ogden, Joan "Complex Derivatives for a Placid Environment" (February 1997) Global Finance 36–37; Nusbaum, David "March of the Exotics" (June 1997) Risk 24–28; Parsley, Mark "Exotics Enter the Mainstream" (March 1997) Euromoney 127–130; Webb, Andrew "What's Exotic?" (July 1999) Derivatives Strategy 17–21.

[32] For an interesting discussion of option premium reduction strategies, see Smith, Craig "All that Glitters" (March 2002) FOW 71–74.

against implied market prices. This was characterised by a significant migration from outright positioning for asset price movements (simple directional trading) to trading second and third order variables on asset prices. This style of investment strategy is referred to as *relative value trading*.

For example, fixed income portfolio managers increasingly trade implied forward rates in the yield curve, spreads between securities at different maturities in the yield curve/different currency markets, volatility or correlations between different financial market variables. This shift in trading techniques encourages the use of exotic structures that are often an efficient and focused means of expressing the asset manager's expectations on the evolution of the asset price. An example of this phenomenon is the practise of using barrier options as part of covered call writing programs and the use of preference options to trade extremes of volatility.

The shift to asset allocation strategies created the impetus for exotic option structures in a different manner. Exotic options based on return indexes (global bond indexes, equity market indexes, commodity price indexes) allowed the price performance characteristics of each asset class to be captured in its purest form. A more complex benefit related to the use of multi-factor option structures such as quantos to capture returns (say the return on an equity market or differential between two bond markets) without the need to incur the currency risk that would normally be associated with the investment strategies. The use of exotic structures to amend the currency risk profile, albeit at a cost, was a significant impetus to the development of these structures.

The pressure to outperform indexes forced the monetisation of specific and complex expectations regarding asset price movements. This was undertaken through increasingly more intricate and precisely defined structures. This also created demand for specific exotic option structures. Multi-factor structures (exchange or out performance (rainbow) options) and path dependent structures (lookback, ladders and average rate options) were specific responses to investor demands. The focus was on relatively passive instrument structures that, to a greater or lesser degree, allowed optimisation of the return from identified asset classes in which the investor had invested. For example, the use of an out performance option structure (between various European bond markets) combined with a cash investment in European bond markets increased the asset manager's prospects for outperforming the benchmark index used to measure the portfolio's returns.

A specific factor that also encouraged the use of exotic options is the increased shift of investment funds from established developed markets to emerging markets. This shift created pressures on asset managers who were, on the whole, less familiar with these markets and generally more hesitant about the liquidity of these assets. This forced the increased management of their exposure through derivatives generally, and exotic structures in particular.

A significant development in investment markets during this period was the emergence of hedge funds or total return investors[33]. This universe of investors was characterised by the objective of maximisation of *absolute return* (not performance relative to a benchmark), use of leverage, use of short positions and investment in non-traditional investment markets. The inherent ability of exotic options to create desired levels of leverage and/or monetise event risk was attractive to these investors. This led to significant demand for exotic options (for example, barrier and digitals) from hedge funds.

The retail investment demand for exotics is different. It derives from the passive nature of some of these products. A key element is that exotic option structures are not true options in the sense that exercise is voluntary. Exotic options generally have mandatory exercise rules based on the economic performance of the instrument. This is of great benefit in structuring products for retail investors that, for a cost, allows the investor to benefit from optimal exercise of the option without the need for intervention by the investor. Path dependent structures (average rate options, lookbacks, ladders) and time dependent structures (chooser and cliquets) proved attractive for this group of investors. An additional motivation relates to the opportunities for premium reduction that increases the attractiveness of options for retail investors. Average rate and barrier option structures are typical examples of this type of innovation. Retail investors also proved an important source of exotic optionality. Some retail investors were willing to sell exotic optionality to monetise expectation of asset prices, asset price paths and correlation. This entailed the use of limit dependent structures (barriers), modified payoff options (digital options) and multi-factor options (spread and out performance options).

---

[33] See (1998) Hedge Funds Demystified – Their Potential Role in Institutional Portfolios; Financial Risk Management Ltd, London; Schneeweis, Thomas and Spurgin, Richard "Traditional and Alternative Investments: Market Structure, Product Structure and Security Design" (Fall 1999) Journal of Alternatives Investments 9–29. See also Ogden, Joan "Now Banks are Offering Their Own Derivatives Funds" (March 1994) Global Finance; Bennett, Rosemary and Shireff, David "Let's Bash the Hedge Funds" (April 1994) Euromoney 26–37; Cook, Stephanie "In Pursuit of Absolute Return" (August 1994) Euromoney 45–48; Celarier, Michelle "Clipped" (December 1995) Euromoney 42–46; Steinberger, Mike "Overgrown and Full of Deadwood" (August 1998) Euromoney 29–32;"You Should be in an Institution . . ." (October 1998) FOW – Hedge Fund Risk & Reward 18–21; Webb, Andrew "Hedge Fund Fever" (October 1998) Derivatives Strategy 33–36; Atlas, Riva "Founders Keepers" (September 1999) Institutional Investor 134–141.

Exotic structures for both institutional and retail investors have sometimes, for regulatory as well as convenience reasons, been designed as securities; typically structured notes.

Use of exotic options structures by non-financial (industrial) corporations revolves around different applications[34]. The major applications include:

- Using exotic embedded structures to generate cost effective funding.
- Creating complex hedge structures to match underlying exposures.

A key motivation is the ability to lower the premium cost of options – traditionally an obstacle to using options as part of corporate hedging programs.

The use of exotic option embedded securities to generate attractively priced financing operates at a number of levels. Highly credit rated borrowers issue structured notes with embedded exotic options, usually under continuous issue formats such as Medium Term Note ("MTN") programs. The notes are then hedged with a derivative dealer (usually the originator of the note), to provide the issuer with cost effective funding without exposure to the underlying derivative elements. This type of use of exotic option structures is not substantively different to arbitrage funding techniques generally. In particular, its fundamental purpose is to provide exotic options packaged as securities for investors[35].

A parallel development focused on corporations using exotic option structures on the underlying equity securities as a means for providing structured equity exposure for investors and attractively priced financing for the company. An example of this type of transaction is a series of issues by Roche, the Swiss pharmaceutical company, through Swiss Bank Corporation. This entailed the issue of equity linked debt and featured a number of exotic option structures, including barrier options, *on Roche equity securities*[36]. The Italian company Benetton has also undertaken similar structures[37].

---

[34] See Shimko, David "Safe Executions" (September 1995) Risk 107; Rowe, David "In Defence of Exotics" (September 2000) Risk 105.

[35] See Chapter 3.

[36] See Das, Satyajit (2004) Structured Products Volume 2; John Wiley & Sons (Asia), Singapore at Chapter 3. See also "Dashing Debut Offering from Roche" (May 1991) Corporate Finance 6–8; Chew, Lillian "SBC's Roche Prescription " (May 1991) Risk 4; "Roche's Euro is a Knock Out" (April 1993) Corporate Finance 6–8; Cooper, Graham "Knock Out Drug is the Issue" (May 1993) Risk 6–7; "A Yen 100 bn Sleight of Hand" (November 1994) Corporate Finance 5–6; Reed, Nick "Samurais Cut it for Roche" (November 1994) Risk 7.

[37] See Bennett, Rosemary "Benetton Clothes Naked Exposure" (July 1993) Euromoney 12–14; "Benetton Styles a New Lira Bond" (August 1993) Corporate Finance 8.

The second class of corporate applications focuses on the management of financial risk. In particular, the availability of exotic option structures has facilitated the evolution of increasingly precise dissection and management of corporate risk profiles. In general, the major thrust of applications of structured risk management have concentrated upon one or more of the following:

- **Lower cost hedges** – this entails the use of exotic options designed to lower option premiums (barrier options, basket option structures, digital options or contingent premium options) to create more cost effective hedges. The lower cost entails the assumption by the hedger of different risks, including correlation risks, and implicitly forces the user to develop more detailed views on the likely future path of asset prices.
- **Application of products to precisely offset underlying cash flow exposures** – this includes use of average rate options to match a series of cash flows. This would also include the use of preference options by multinationals where the currency pairing of the exposure is known, but the direction of that exposure is subject to uncertainty.
- **Correlation based hedges** – this type of hedge recognises the inter-related nature of some corporate risks. Examples of these strategies include:
  1. Use of quanto structures to hedge the currency component of commodity prices.
  2. Use of spread options by a refiner to hedge the margin between feedstock prices and product prices.
  3. Use of defined exercise options to hedge correlated exposures between interest rates/commodity price and currency rates.

Financial institution use of exotics varies between dealers and non-dealers. Non dealer financial institution use is analogous to that of the asset managers identified above. Specific applications include:

- **Trading/hedging yield curve risks** – using products such as spread options to hedge or monetise asset liability gaps and positions generated from traditional financial intermediation activities.
- **Creating synthetic mortgage assets** – US banks have been aggressive users of exotic option products to synthesise assets with mortgage type characteristics, particularly pre-payment profiles. The creation of synthetic assets has been predicated on the relative yield, credit/market risk profile and comparative liquidity of the synthetic against more traditional mortgage assets such as mortgage backed securities.
- **Creating higher yielding assets** – during certain periods, the lack of traditional banking assets combined with an aversion to credit risk led financial institutions

to assume increased market risk in order to generate higher yielding assets. An example of using exotic structures to create higher yielding assets is the use of range/accrual floating rate notes. This structure entailed the sale by the purchaser of the security of digital options on a nominated asset. The premium captured from the sale of the options allowed the financial institution to create high yielding assets, albeit at the cost of increased market risk.

Dealer financial institution participation was predicated on generating returns from trading/distributing exotic options. A major attraction was the non-commodity nature of the products that allowed the capture of higher earnings relative to traditional derivatives. This feature is most marked at the early stages of the product life cycle for each product. Pricing, hedging and trading of these instruments was complex. This meant that early entrants gained experience in and built a larger portfolio of transactions that, in some cases, allowed efficiencies in risk management and pricing. This combination often assisted in entrenching an individual dealer's market position. It also facilitated development of new products and built on the institution's experience in the market.

An underestimated motivation for dealer involvement in these products was the opportunity to trade second and third order variables that were seen as both more complex and providing above average returns. An additional factor eliciting dealer involvement was the often profound insight into derivative risk generally which trading in these instruments afforded. A further factor was the additional flexibility in risk management of existing derivative portfolios that these instruments afforded traders.

Over time, exotic options have become increasingly commoditised. Knowledge of structure, pricing and hedging/risk management has become more widespread. This has been most marked in the case of common exotic options (barriers and digital options). In these products, margins have diminished but have been compensated by higher trading volumes and increased liquidity. The complexity of hedging/risk management continues to be a barrier to the complete commoditisation of many exotic options.

6.3 Exotic Options – Markets

6.3.1 Asset Classes

The market for individual exotic option products reflects the complexities of the users and common applications identified. Some general trends in relation to individual product groupings are evident.

The application of exotic option concepts varies significantly between asset classes[38]. **Exhibit 5.4** sets out the availability of exotic options in the different asset classes.

The predominant asset class in which exotic option products are available is foreign exchange. A large number of the products were originally engineered with reference to currency exposure problems. This reflects the 24 hour trading in and globalisation of currency markets. The penetration of derivative product concepts to other types of assets is different between asset classes.

Interest rate exotic option structures include:
- **Barrier options** – usually to provide customised protection based on expectations regarding the evolution of interest rates.
- **Swing options** – to provide lower cost structured protection against interest rate risk.
- **Digital options** – to provide structured protection or to generate leverage/yield enhancement.
- **Spread products** – structured to either capture value from money market rate differentials, spreads between bond rates in different currency markets or yield curve option structures.

Equity products have included:
- **Path and time dependent structures** – in particular, the structures featuring inherently passive optimisation structures, or lower cost optionality incorporated in investment products targeted (in particular) at retail investors. This includes average rate, ladder and cliquet options.
- **Barrier options** – this is focused on structured/contingent forms of risk protection and creating lower cost optionality.
- **Basket structures** – designed to primarily create effective basis for hedges of portfolios of equities.
- **Exchange/out-performance options** – primarily based on indexes or individual stock pairs within the same industry sector designed to capture relative performance characteristics.
- **Currency protected/quanto structures** – to isolate the equity value and embed the currency hedge through the quanto structure.

Commodity products include average rate options, barrier options, currency protected quanto structures and baskets. Average rate options are particularly popular as they provide a cash flow match to trading cash flows in the underlying commodities.

---

[38] See Smithson, Charles "Path Dependency" (April 1997) Risk 65–67.

Exhibit 5.4 Exotic Options – Markets	
Type of Options	**Markets**
Conventional	
European/ American	Available/used in all asset classes including interest rate, currency, equity and commodity markets.
Bermudan	Available/used extensively in interest rate markets (callable/ puttable bonds/swaptions). Occasionally used in equity markets (usually combined with another exotic form).
Path dependent	
Average rate	Available/used extensively in currency and commodities markets. Available but used less frequently in interest rates and equity markets.
Lookback	Limited use in any asset class.
Ladder	Available/used extensively in equity markets. Limited use in other asset classes.
Shout	Limited use in any asset class.
Swing	Available/used occasionally in commodity and interest rate markets. Limited use in other asset classes.
Time dependent	
Chooser	Limited use in any asset class.
Forward start	Limited use in equity markets (employee stock option plans). Limited use in other asset classes.
Cliquet	Available/used extensively in equity markets. Limited use in other asset classes.
Limit dependent	
Barriers	Available/used in all asset classes including interest rate, currency, equity and commodity markets.
Defined exercise	Available/used occasionally in combinations of commodity, interest rate and currency market transactions.
Payoff Modified	
Digitals	Available/used in all asset classes including interest rate, currency, equity and commodity markets.
Contingent premium	Available/used occasionally in any asset class.
Power	Limited use in any asset class.
Multi-factor	
Compound	Limited use in any asset class.
Quantos	Available/used in equity markets and interest rates. Limited use in other asset classes.
Basket	Available/used in all asset classes including interest rate, currency, equity and commodity markets.
Rainbow (best of/ worst of)	Available/used occasionally in equity markets. Limited use in other asset classes.
Spread	Available/used extensively in interest rates. Limited use in other asset classes.
Exchange	Limited use in any asset class.

The bulk of exotic options are traded in the OTC market. There are a number of instances of exchange-traded markets involving exotic options. The primary instance is commodity exchanges that have listed average rate options on certain commodities for trading[39].

6.3.2 Types of Exotic Options

Path Dependent Structures

The most popular path dependent structure is probably the average rate option structure that is generally used in two contexts:

- Corporations with regular streams of cash flows (exports, imports or royalties) seeking protection from currency risk have found these structures afford cost effective protection. Similarly, average price structures on commodities have found acceptance amongst organisations with underlying commodity price exposures.
- Retail investors concerned about the exercise risk of standard option structures (in the case of a European option, the return on the transaction is a function of the final asset price) have found average rate structures attractive. Average rate option based retail products are attractive to these investors as it simultaneously lowers the cost of the option and provides a return linked to the series of prices (decreasing exposure to the price on a specific date).

The demand for other path dependent products (lookbacks, ladders and shout options) reflect demand for structures that inherently optimise option value by (generally) passive exercise rules embedded within the option. This demand is motivated by the type of investor (retail investment products) or asset liability matching requirements (regular streams of cash flows similar to the position that motivates the use of average rate options).

The advantage of optimal exercise characteristics is only available at a cost to the purchaser. Lookback option structures are ideal for the purchaser who wishes to ensure a very high probability of a positive payoff for the option. The structure is generally extremely expensive. Structures such as ladders and shouts have developed as they use the concept of path dependency, and extend it to provide many of the benefits of such structures, but with a lower cost than the lookback structure.

---

[39] See Nicholls, Mark "In Praise of the Average" (May 1996) Risk 53–55; Banks, Jim "No Exchange of Asians" (October 1997) Futures & Options World 31.

Increasingly, these types of path dependent structures are incorporated in retail targeted securities, or through pooled fund structures that are based around an embedded exotic option of this type.

Path dependent structures such as swing options have generally been used to lower the cost of insurance against adverse price movements and/or provide structured protection from volatility in interest rates or commodity prices.

Time Dependent Structures

The key benefit of time dependent structures such as preference or chooser options is the capacity of the instruments to be used to trade or hedge against extreme volatility. This is evident in the extensive use of these instruments to capture returns during periods of high asset price/rate volatility. For example, during the Gulf War in 1991, a number of structures encompassing preference options were successfully used to monetise high oil price volatility.

The demand for preference options and other time dependent structures have traditionally been from traders and investors seeking to capture the returns from volatility in the most efficient manner. One particular application has entailed embedding preference options in notes or warrants in order to enable retail investors to express their views on asset price movements.

Corporate use of time dependent structures is modest. There is interest in the use of preference option structures to hedge against currency risk where the specific currency pairing is known, but the direction of the exposure is unknown. This type of exposure is prevalent in multinational or international businesses where global sourcing and distribution of products is common. In addition, cross border investments where the currency risk is sought to be hedged, pose difficulties where the performance of the operation may determine the polarity of the exposure. Preference option structures may allow these types of exposure to be effectively managed.

Forward start options are used almost exclusively in employee share option schemes. Cliquet options are used primarily for structured investment products for retail investors.

Limit Dependent Structures

Limit dependent structures such as barrier options are among the most the popular exotic option structures. The key reasons for the popularity of barrier options include the lower premiums achievable and the limit dependency. Limit dependency facilitates both positioning for particular asset price changes and the use of barrier options in the creation of very specific hedge structures. The applications contribute to the attractiveness of barrier structures. This can be illustrated with simple examples.

Assume the case of a US$ based exporter with revenues denominated in Euros. Exposed to the weakening of the Euro, the exporter can sell forward its Euro revenues or alternatively purchase a put option on Euro/call on US$. The exporter can incorporate a barrier option into the hedging strategy in a number of ways. For example, if the exporter is unhappy with the present spot level of Euro against US$ and anticipates a strengthening in the Euro, it can buy a knock-in Euro put that is triggered if the Euro appreciates to the barrier level. This strategy has various benefits, including lower premium cost and the fact that if triggered, it is at a more attractive price level. An added advantage is that execution of the option is automatic if the barrier level is reached. This reduces the exporter's execution risk. This strategy leaves the exporter at risk if the Euro depreciates without reaching the nominated barrier level. An alternative strategy may be to purchase a knock-out Euro put based on the view that if the Euro appreciates to a certain level, then the exporter is willing to forgo further immunisation from a weaker Euro. If the Euro put is knocked out, then the exporter would need to enter into a new transaction to hedge. This knock-out level may be set with reference to a budget or other target rate for the exporter. This type of hedge is predicated on the lower cost of the knock-out put that effectively reduces the hedging cost of the exporter.

Similar transactions involving investors are feasible. Take the example of an investor seeking to generate income against an underlying asset position by selling calls. Assume the original asset was purchased at $100 and the call is struck at $105. If the asset price falls, then the call position falls in value. Assume the investor sells a knock-out call with the same strike but an out-strike of $95. If the asset price falls to that level, then the knock-out call is extinguished. This enables the investor to sell additional calls to generate additional premium against the asset. The major difference between the two approaches is that the lower premium received for the barrier option is offset by the elimination of the requirement to transact to buy back the call sold initially before initiating the sale of the further call. The elimination of trading or execution risk is an important element of this approach.

The sale of barrier products to generate premium income by both investors and corporations is another common application. The primary motivation for the sale of a barrier as against a standard option is that the lower premium captured is offset by the reduction in risk for the writer. This is because the exposure under the sold option is extinguished where the barrier is reached and the option extinguished.

Barrier structures are frequently packaged with either forwards or other options to create highly specific risk transfer instruments for both corporations and investors.

Pay-off Modified Structures

The demand for payoff modified structures is based on different dynamics, depending upon the application. Investors frequently use digital options because of the known and fixed loss. Investors also frequently sell digital options, with the premium received being used to increase the yield on fixed income assets. Digital options are used to hedge where the hedger is willing to effectively *cap* the level of protection (to the agreed payout). This is used to align the hedge with the trader's view of future market prices.

Contingent premium option demand derives from corporations and asset managers seeking to hedge against large changes in asset values, particularly currency values. The absence of a premium, except where the option expires in-the-money, makes this instrument a favoured *disaster* hedging vehicle. For example, corporations seeking to hedge translation exposures use this type of structure to achieve their objectives.

Multi-Factor Structures

Multi-factor structures encompass a broad range of risk transfer instruments that are motivated by a range of potential applications. In general terms, multi-factor products can be separated into two specific categories:

- **Correlation based instruments** – basket, spread, compound, exchange or rainbow/out performance options.
- **Currency protected instruments** – primarily, quanto options.

The market for correlation based products is generally driven by a combination of the following factors:

- **Lower cost of the instrument** – this uses the imperfect correlation between the underlying assets (for example, in a basket) to reduce the cost of the option. A major driver of the market is the use of basket options on currency portfolios to hedge currency exposures from normal operations at a lower cost than hedging individual currency positions separately.
- **Nature of the underlying exposure** – this is focused on hedging or monetising existing positions. Types of positions traded in this way include yield curve risk positions inherent in balance sheet management in financial institutions, and multi-currency/multi-stock exposures in the portfolios of corporations and/or investors. This activity takes the form of demand for spread options, basket options or compound options to create contingent hedges.
- **Intrinsic correlation risk** – this is focused on hedging/monetising correlation exposure incurred by corporations and investors. The positions frequently entail

the relationship between asset values and currency prices. The opportunity for dealers to trade correlation relationships directly is also a key factor in the market for multi-factor products.

The demand for currency protected structures is driven by investors and corporations seeking to separate asset returns from currency movements. Corporations use quanto structures to simultaneously hedge commodity/currency or interest rate/currency exposures. For currency protected investments, investor demand is focused in equity and interest rates.

6.4   Exotic Option – Markets

There are differences in the market for exotic options in different geographic jurisdictions. The pattern of use varies significantly.

In North America, investors (in particular, hedge funds) dominate the use of exotic options. Exotic options are used to aggressively monetise asset price expectations. The applications are driven by a traditional focus on total returns and experience in trading complex securities such as mortgage backed securities. Corporate use of exotic products is less well developed, except for the more common exotic structures such as average rate products.

European markets are significantly more varied in their use of exotics. Investor use is more complex. Retail investment demand for certain structures (particularly path dependent options) is a major component of the market. Institutional investor demand is also a component of the market. Corporate use is confined to a relatively modest sized group of sophisticated derivative market users.

European institutional investor demand for exotic option products has been driven by different factors. In the period leading up to the implementation of the Euro, exotic option based products in European currencies were used by investors to implement convergence and/or de-convergence strategies. This focused on trading/monetising price/rate expectations and relative value between the relevant European markets. Institutional investor use of exotic options has increased following the implementation of the Euro. This simply reflects the reduced trading opportunities in European currencies. This forced investors to seek new trading strategies to generate returns. Many of the strategies focused on using exotic options to trade expected asset price movements.

The Japanese market is a significant component of the overall exotic options market. Japanese demand is focused on hedging and trading. Hedging applications include the use of average rate options as currency and commodity price hedges. Trading applications for investors, trading companies and corporations are a large part of the market for these products in Japan. For example, the Japanese market is characterised by significant interest in selling barrier and digital options for premium capture.

Exotic options have also penetrated emerging markets in Eastern Europe, Latin America and Asia. A major component of the demand has been from financial institutions seeking to create higher yielding assets. The institutions have frequently achieved such returns by assuming increased market risk rather than credit risk. The increased market risk profile is achieved through the sale of exotic options such as digital options, spread structures and barrier option based products. The Asian crisis of 1997/98, the Russian crisis of 1998 and multiple crises in Latin America have impeded the rate of development of exotic options in emerging markets.

7 Summary

The rapid development of new generation risk management products reflects a market response to factors such as uncertainty/volatility, increased demand for highly customised risk reward profile and the corresponding improvements in option pricing/hedging technologies. The products (like traditional derivatives) permit the separation, unbundling and redistribution of price risk in financial markets. The increased capacity to delineate risks more precisely should theoretically improve the capacity of markets to redistribute and reallocate risks based on the economic value of that market risk. This should facilitate more efficient allocation of economic resources.

The emergence of exotic options has added an extra dimension to derivative markets. A number of barriers to the further development of the markets exist, including:

- Limited understanding and knowledge about the products; in particular, about the valuation, hedging and trading of exotic options.
- The market for most of the products is characterised by low levels of liquidity, except in a few products (barrier and digital options).
- Limited standardisation of terminology, terms for quoting and trading conventions and pricing models/methodology.
- Developing applications of the products in the management of financial risks encountered by corporations and investors.

The attractiveness of exotic options for dealers derives in part from the inefficiency in the market structure. Low liquidity, lack of standardisation, difficulties of pricing/trading, and the evolving range of applications are precisely the factors that allow dealers to add value and capture higher returns from exotic options relative to more standardised products.

The market for exotic option products has an importance in derivative markets out of proportion to its absolute size. This reflects the interesting products and the insights available in terms of the valuation, trading and risk management of traditional derivatives. It also reflects the additional levels of exposure that the structures inherently isolate and facilitate trading in. This process of risk dissection, and its contribution in the identification and analysis of correlation risk, significantly enhances the understanding of risk and its management.

6
Packaged Forwards and Options

1 Overview

Packaged forwards and options are a specific class of risk management products. The products are constructed as combinations of options and forwards. In this Chapter, packaged forwards and options are discussed.

The structure of the Chapter is as follows:
- The overall structure of packaged forwards/options is outlined.
- A number of common types of packaged forward/options are described.

2 Packaged Forwards/Options – Structures

Packaged forwards/options are generally regarded as second generation risk management products. The various combinations of options and forwards are primarily designed to achieve a number of objectives, including:
- Customised risk profiles can be used to overcome the difficulty of traditional forward contracts that eliminate the opportunity for the user to benefit from any favourable movements in underlying asset price/rate.
- Combinations of bought and sold options are used to effectively reduce the premium paid to purchase an option. Hedgers are frequently reluctant to pay option premiums. This is particularly the case during periods of high or extreme volatility. The cost of options increases precisely at the time that they potentially have the greatest benefit for hedgers. This has created demand for packaged forwards/options where the premium is embedded within the structure, or where sold options are used to lower the cost of the hedge.
- Packaged forwards and options are used to enter into sold option positions. Most packaged forwards/options entail sales of options. Many financial market participants are unable to enter into sold option positions because of trading restrictions. The ability to sell optionality within packaged forwards/options is attractive.

- Particular combinations of options can be used to create a higher degree of leverage to asset price/rate movements. This can be extended to generate yield enhancement through receipt of net premium on the embedded options.
- Packaged forwards/options include a number of special hybrid structures that are designed to assist in managing the problem of uncertainty or contingent hedging.

The creation of packaged forwards/options uses basic financial engineering concepts. The underlying constituent elements are conventional forward and option contracts. Packaged forwards/options primarily use multiple options (in the form of collars and/or option spreads) and the relationship between forwards and options (put-call parity[1]). This means that the structures pose no special valuation problems. Traditional approaches to the valuation of forward contracts and option contracts are adequate.

Exhibit 6.1 sets out the major types of packaged forwards/options[2]. The packaged option structures are generic in nature and are applicable to any asset class[3].

Packaged forwards/options increasingly use embedded exotic options (primarily barrier and digital options)[4] to create more complex customised hedging structures[5].

3 Option Forward Combinations

3.1 Range Forwards[6]

A range forward entails an agreement to buy or sell an asset of a specified future date at a price *that lies within a particular range of prices*. The actual price at

---

[1] See Das, Satyajit (2004) Derivative Products & Pricing; John Wiley & Sons (Asia), Singapore at Chapter 7.

[2] See Showers, Janet L. and Lindenberg, Eric B. (September 1987) Strategies for Using Foreign Exchange Products to Hedge a Foreign Equity Investment; Salomon Brothers Inc. Financial Strategy Group, New York; Guido Furer "Currency Hedging with Low Cost Options" (April/May 1992) Swiss Bank Corporation Prospects No. 2/1992 1–4.

[3] See Warren, Geoffrey "Quick Brown Fox Breaks Forward Over Lazy Scout" (May 1987) Euromoney 245–264; Batchelor, Gwen and Perera, Ranil "Keeping Options Open for Hedging Exchange Risk" (July 1987) Corporate Finance 70–71; Cohen, Edi "Banker's Alchemy" (June 1987) The Banker 75–81.

[4] See Chapters 9 and 10.

[5] See "Outperforming the Forward Rate" (April 1997) AsiaMoney 10–13; Klein, Matthias "Currency Derivatives" (November 1998) Germany – Supplement to Risk 6–7; Winton, Leigh "Making Volatility Your Ally" (April 1999) Asia Risk 35–37.

[6] See Gadkari, Vilas and Khadjavi, Laya (November 1985) Range Forward Contracts – A New Tool for Currency Exposure Management; Salomon Brothers, New York.

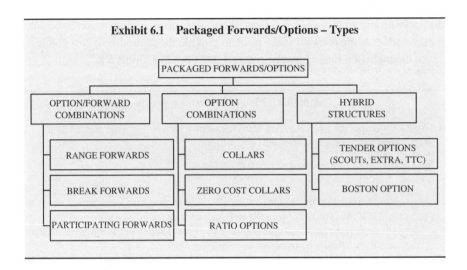

Exhibit 6.1   Packaged Forwards/Options – Types

which the purchase or sale is completed depends on the actual price of the asset at maturity of the contract. This is in contrast to a conventional forward contract that is an agreement to buy or sell the asset at a specified future date *at the agreed price*.

From a functional viewpoint, the range forward is effectively a combination of bought and sold puts and calls (effectively a collar arrangement). The strike prices of the relevant options are set at a level designed to create a zero cost collar. The pricing of the range forwards is driven by the values of the separate component options. The pricing of the range forward is generally sensitive to the volatility skew in the market as the options have the same maturity but are at different strike prices.

The major features of the range forward include:

- Absence of an up-front cost as a result of the embedded zero cost premium structure.
- Protection against adverse changes in the asset price through the embedded purchased option.
- Capacity of the user to benefit from favourable movements in asset price, but only within the specific range.

The major advantage of the range forward is its flexibility. The hedger will typically nominate the range within which it is willing to allow the asset price to fluctuate. The hedger will frequently nominate the upper (for a short position) or lower (for a long position) price level of the range. The dealer will then determine the opposite end of the range. In effect, the dealer solves for the option to be sold for the hedger at the relevant strike price to provide the desired zero cost collar.

An example of a range forward contract is set out in **Exhibit 6.2**.

Exhibit 6.2   Range Forward Contracts

Assume a US corporation needs to buy Euro for value 6 months from the present date.
The current market rates (Euro/US$) are as follows:

Spot rate	Euro 1 = US$0.8
6 month forward rate	Euro 1 = US$0.84

Assume the corporation enters into a range forward to purchase Euro with a range of US$0.81 and US$0.88. The range forward will operate as follows:
- If the spot exchange rate at contract expiration is Euro 1 = US$0.81 or lower (stronger US$), then the corporation buys Euro at US$0.81.
- If the spot exchange rate is between US$0.81 and US$0.88, then the corporation buys Euro at the prevailing spot rate for Euro.
- If the spot exchange rate at contract expiration is Euro 1 = US$0.88 (weaker US$), then the corporation buys Euro at US$0.88.

When executing the range forward contract, the corporation selects one of the levels in the range and the final expiration date of the contract. The dealer determines the other end of the range. The corporation would generally select the adverse side of the range level. In this example, the corporation would specify US$0.88 as the highest price (in US$ terms) at which it would be prepared to buy Euro. The dealer would then specify the other end of the range (in this case US$0.81).

In effect, the corporation is purchasing a 6 month US$ put/Euro call with a strike price of US$0.88. To finance this option, the corporation is selling a 6 month US$ call/Euro put with a strike price of US$0.81. The premium on the sold US$ call exactly equals the premium paid to purchase the US$ put option. Where the corporation nominated the worst case exchange rate (Euro 1 = US$0.88) that it was prepared to accept, the dealer would have worked out the strike on the US$ call that the corporation sells by working back from the premium required to purchase the US$ put.

The payoffs (in US$) from the range forward (based on Euro 1 million of underlying exposure) are specified below:

Spot (Euro 1=)	Unhedged (US$)	Forward (US$)	Range Forward (US$)
0.9500	950,000	840,000	880,000
0.9400	940,000	840,000	880,000
0.9300	930,000	840,000	880,000
0.9200	920,000	840,000	880,000
0.9100	910,000	840,000	880,000
0.9000	900,000	840,000	880,000

Spot (Euro 1=)	Unhedged (US$)	Forward (US$)	Range Forward (US$)
0.8900	890,000	840,000	880,000
0.8800	880,000	840,000	880,000
0.8700	870,000	840,000	870,000
0.8600	860,000	840,000	860,000
0.8500	850,000	840,000	850,000
0.8400	840,000	840,000	840,000
0.8300	830,000	840,000	830,000
0.8200	820,000	840,000	820,000
0.8100	810,000	840,000	810,000
0.8000	800,000	840,000	810,000
0.7900	790,000	840,000	810,000
0.7800	780,000	840,000	810,000
0.7700	770,000	840,000	810,000
0.7600	760,000	840,000	810,000
0.7500	750,000	840,000	810,000
0.7400	740,000	840,000	810,000

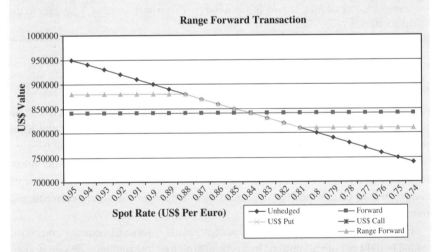

Range Forward Transaction

Under the range forward structure, the corporation is protected against any strengthening in the Euro beyond US$0.88 (purchased US$ put). This protection is financed by forgoing any weakening in the Euro below US$0.81 (sold US$ call).

The range forward contract can be traded prior to maturity. The range forward contract to buy Euro may be reversed by executing another range forward contract with an identical range to sell the currency. To reverse the range forward contract, the corporation would need to execute a contract to sell Euro/buy US$ where the range is also chosen to be between US$0.81–US$0.88. Although the initial range forward contract does not incur any premium, a reversal may result in a net gain or cost. The gain or cost will depend upon the changes in the value of the embedded currency options.

The corporation may wish to reverse the position prior to maturity. In order to achieve this objective, the holder would need to execute another range forward contract. In this reversal, the corporation would sell Euro with a range of US$0.81–US$0.88. The following examples quantify the gains or losses that the corporation would incur given assumed currency movements:

- Assume that the spot rate moves to US$0.7650 (10% depreciation in the value of the Euro) and that the forward rate for the remaining maturity of the original range forward is US$0.76. The spot and the outright forward are below the lower end of the range forward contract. To reverse the contract, the range forward contract holder would have to repurchase the sold US$ call/Euro put (that is now in-the-money) and sell the US$ put/Euro call (that is now out-of-the-money). This would result in a net cost to the corporation.

- Assume that the spot rate moves to US$0.9350 (10% appreciation in the value of the Euro) and that the forward rate for the remaining maturity of the original range forward is US$0.93. The spot and the outright forward are above the higher end of the range forward contract. To reverse the contract, the range forward contract holder would have to repurchase the sold US$ call/Euro put (that is now out-of-the-money) and sell the US$ put/Euro call (that is now in-the-money). This would result in a net gain to the corporation.

3.2 Break Forwards[7]

A break forward contract entails an agreement to purchase or sell an asset at an agreed price, with the ability to close out the contract if the price of the asset moves in the purchaser or seller's favour. An alternative name for break forward contracts is a forward with optional exit ("FOX"). The key driver of the break forward structure is related to the ability to terminate the forward where a favourable change in asset price would result in an adverse hedging result under a conventional forward contract.

Functionally, the break forward concept entails a forward contract combined with a bought put or call option. In a typical structure, the purchase or sale is at an off market forward rate. The adjustment to the forward rate allows the present value of the difference to be used to pay for the option to cancel the forward agreement

---

[7]   See "Foreign Exchange Hedging: Anticipating Forex Fluctuating with Midlands "Break Forwards" and "Scouts" (1986) (June 28) International Issue 628 1939–1940; Edwardes, Warren and Levy, Edmond "Break-Forwards: A Synthetic Option Hedging Instrument" (Summer 1987) Midland Corporate Finance Journal 59–67.

at a pre-determined strike price. The break forward structure is usually constructed on a zero premium cost basis.

The economics of a break forward contract is determined by the combination of forward price and the option premium. The forward price is adjusted to cover the price of purchasing the requisite option. The dynamics of valuation entail a trade off between the forward rate and the close out rate to maintain the zero cost structure.

The principal features of the break forward contract include:

- No upfront cost, as the premium paid to purchase the option is effectively built into the adjustment to the forward rate.
- Provision of protection against adverse changes in asset prices.
- Opportunity to benefit from favourable asset price movements (above or below the agreed break rate), thereby overcoming the difficulties of traditional forward contracts.

The advantage of break forward contracts derives from the fact that they enable the hedger to obtain an option like asymmetric risk exposure without the necessity of paying a premium.

An example of a break forward contract is set out in **Exhibit 6.3**.

Exhibit 6.3 Break Forward Contract

Consider the same example set out in **Exhibit 6.2**. A US corporation needs to buy Euro for value 6 months from the present date.

Assume the corporation enters into a break forward contract for 6 months to buy Euro/sell US$. The forward purchase of the Euro is equivalent to a purchase of a Euro call/US$ put and a sale of a Euro Put/US$ call at the forward rate. The adverse outcome under the forward is the result of the payoff under the sold Euro put/US$ call. This occurs where the Euro weakens against the US$ relative to the forward rate. In order to structure the break forward, the corporation must purchase a Euro put/US$ call to cancel the effect of the sold Euro put/US$ call. The cost of the purchased option is built into the forward contract by structuring the transaction at an off-market rate. The present value benefit of the off market rate (effectively the mark to market value of the forward) is equivalent to the option premium paid.

Assume the corporation enters into a break forward contract for 6 months to buy Euro/sell US$. The corporation is willing to lower the level of the forward rate by 2.50% to pay for the right to break. The pricing of the break forward rate is calculated below.

The current market rates (Euro/US$) are as follows:

Spot rate	Euro 1 = US$0.85
6 month forward rate	Euro 1 = US$0.84
Break loading	2.50% × US$0.84 = US$0.0210
Adjusted forward rate	Euro 1 = US$0.8610

The dealer then calculates the break rate at US$0.83.

In effect, the corporation has the following option positions:

- The forward purchase of Euro at US$0.8610 is equivalent to a purchase of a Euro call/US$ put and a sale of a Euro Put/US$ call at a strike price of US$0.8610.
- Long a Euro Put/US$ call at a strike price equal to the break rate of US$0.8300.

The break forward operates as follows:

- If the Euro strengthens/US$ weakens above the US$0.83 (the break rate), then the corporation purchases Euro at the agreed fixed rate of US$0.8610. This means the corporation pays US$861,000 per Euro 1,000,000.
- If the exchange rate is equal to the break rate (Euro 1 = US$0.83), then the break facility is activated. The corporation buys Euro 1,000,000 at the fixed rate of US$0.8610 (US$861,000). The corporation immediately sells back the Euro 1,000,000 at the break rate of US$0.83 (receives US$830,000). This locks in a loss of US$31,000. The corporation then purchases the required Euro 1,000,000 at the spot rate – in this case equal to the break rate (US$830,000). This means the total cost to the corporation for the Euro 1,000,000 is US$861,000 (effective exchange rate of Euro 1 = US$0.8610).
- If the Euro weakens/US$ strengthens below the break rate (Euro 1 = US$0.83) then the break facility is also activated. The corporation buys Euro 1,000,000 at the fixed rate of US$0.8610 (US$861,000). The corporation immediately sells back the Euro 1,000,000 at the break rate US$0.83 (receives US$830,000). This locks in a loss of US$31,000. The corporation then purchases the required Euro 1,000,000 at the spot rate. This means the total cost to the corporation for the Euro 1,000,000 is the spot rate plus the locked in loss (the difference between the off-market forward rate and the break rate (the strike of the purchased Euro Put/US$ call)).

The payoffs (in US$) from the break forward (based on Euro 1 million of underlying exposure) are specified below:

Spot (Euro 1=)	Unhedged (US$)	Forward (US$)	Break Forward (US$)
0.9500	950,000	840,000	861,000
0.9400	940,000	840,000	861,000
0.9300	930,000	840,000	861,000
0.9200	920,000	840,000	861,000
0.9100	910,000	840,000	861,000
0.9000	900,000	840,000	861,000
0.8900	890,000	840,000	861,000
0.8800	880,000	840,000	861,000
0.8700	870,000	840,000	861,000
0.8600	860,000	840,000	861,000
0.8500	850,000	840,000	861,000
0.8400	840,000	840,000	861,000
0.8300	830,000	840,000	861,000
0.8200	820,000	840,000	851,000

Spot (Euro 1=)	Unhedged (US$)	Forward (US$)	Break Forward (US$)
0.8100	810,000	840,000	841,000
0.8000	800,000	840,000	831,000
0.7900	790,000	840,000	821,000
0.7800	780,000	840,000	811,000
0.7700	770,000	840,000	801,000
0.7600	760,000	840,000	791,000
0.7500	750,000	840,000	781,000
0.7400	740,000	840,000	771,000

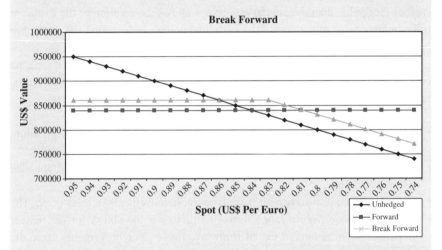

Under the break forward structure, the corporation is protected against any strengthening in the Euro beyond US$0.8610 (off market forward purchase). This is at a level below the forward rate (US$0.84). The corporation maintains the ability to participate in any appreciation in the US$ above a level of Euro 1 = US$0.83. This is achieved by terminating the forward (selling the Euros at US$0.83) and purchasing Euro in the spot market at a better exchange rate.

3.3 Participating Forwards

A participating forward entails an agreement to buy or sell an asset at an agreed price. The contract specifies a worst case price at which the hedger can buy or sell the asset. The contract also specifies an agreed participation rate. The hedger receives a portion of any favourable movement in the asset price. The portion is equivalent to the agreed participation rate. The participating forward allows the hedger to obtain protection from an unfavourable price movement. Unlike a normal forward contract, the hedger retains the capacity to benefit from favourable movements in price up to the agreed participation rate (zero to 100%).

From a functional viewpoint, the participating forward is effectively a combination of bought and sold puts and calls (effectively a collar arrangement). The strike prices of the relevant options are set at a level designed to create a zero cost collar. The major distinguishing feature of the participating structure is that *the face value of the two options is different.* The option purchased is for the full face value of the amount of the hedge. The option sold to finance the option purchase is for a percentage of the face value of the bought option. Premium neutrality is achieved by adjusting the strike price of the option. The fact that the sold option is for a smaller face value than the purchased options allows the creation of the exposure to favourable price movements. The participation rate is driven by the difference between the face value of the option purchased and the option sold.

The pricing of the participating forwards is driven by the values of the separate component options. The pricing is generally sensitive to the volatility skew in the market, as the options have the same maturity but are at different strike prices.

The major features of the participating forward include:

- Absence of an upfront cost as a result of the embedded zero cost premium structure.
- Protection against adverse changes in the asset price through the embedded purchased option.
- Capacity of the user to benefit from favourable movements in asset price. The major difference from a range forward structure is the ability for the hedger to benefit to an *unlimited* extent from favourable price movements up to the participation rate.

The major advantage of the participating forward is its flexibility. The hedger will typically nominate the price level at which it requires protection. The hedger will frequently nominate the upper (for a short position) or lower (for a long position) price level of the range. The hedger will nominate either the degree of participation in any favourable price movement required, or the level above or below which participation is required. The dealer will then determine either the price at which participation commences, or the level of participation. In effect, the dealer solves for the face value of the option to be sold, or the strike price of the options to be sold. The basic constraint is the requirement to provide the desired zero cost collar (that is, cover the cost of the option to be purchased).

An example of a participating forward contract in currencies is set out in **Exhibit 6.4**. An example of a participating forward in interest rates (participating swap/cap) is set out in **Exhibit 6.5**.

Exhibit 6.4   Participating Forward Contract

Consider the same example set out in **Exhibit 6.2**. A US corporation needs to buy Euro for value 6 months from the present date.

Assume the corporation enters into a participating forward contract for 6 months to buy Euro/sell US$. Under the terms of the contract, the corporation is protected from a weaker US$ below Euro 1 = US$0.88. However, the corporation will participate in any appreciation in the US$ above Euro 1 = US$0.84. The agreed participation ratio is 50%.

The participating forward will operate as follows:

- If the spot exchange rate at contract expiration is Euro 1 = US$0.88 (weaker US$), the corporation buys Euro at US$0.88.
- If the spot exchange rate at contract expiration is Euro 1 = US$0.84 or lower (stronger US$), then the corporation buys Euro at US$0.84 for 50% of the total amount of the face value, and buys Euro at the prevailing spot rate for Euro for the remaining 50%. In practice, this is expressed as an effective rate formula ([(Participating ratio (50%) × Spot Rate) + ((1− Participating ratio (50%) × Agreed Price (Euro 1 = US$0.84))] × Notional Value).

When executing the participating forward contract, the corporation selects one of the levels in the range and the final expiration date of the contract. The corporation also selects either the price level above which participation is sought, or the participating ratio. The dealer then determines either the participation ratio or the price above which participation will operate. The corporation would generally select the adverse side of the range level. In this example, the corporation would specify US$0.88 as the highest price (in US$ terms) at which it would be prepared to buy Euro. The corporation would specify either the price level above which participation is sought (Euro 1 = US$0.84) or the participating ratio (50%). The dealer then determines either the participation ratio (50%) or the price above which participation will operate (Euro 1 = US$0.84).

In effect, the corporation is purchasing a 6 month US$ put/Euro call with a strike price of US$0.88. This option is on a notional principal equal to the value of the position to be hedged. To finance this option, the corporation is selling a 6 month US$ call/Euro put with a strike price of US$0.84. The sold option is on 50% (100% less the participation ratio) of the face value of the US$ put/Euro call purchased. The premium on the sold US$ call exactly equals the premium paid to purchase the US$ put option. Assume that the corporation nominated the worst case exchange rate (Euro 1 = US$0.88) that it was prepared to accept. The dealer would have worked out the strike on the US$ call ((Euro 1 = US$0.84) or the amount of call that would need to be sold (50%) to ensure the premium required to finance the purchase of the US$ put.

The payoffs (in US$) from the participating forward (based on Euro 1 million of underlying exposure) are specified below:

Spot (Euro 1=)	Unhedged (US$)	Forward (US$)	Participating Forward (US$)
0.9500	950,000	840,000	880,000
0.9400	940,000	840,000	880,000
0.9300	930,000	840,000	880,000

Spot (Euro 1=)	Unhedged (US$)	Forward (US$)	Participating Forward (US$)
0.9200	920,000	840,000	880,000
0.9100	910,000	840,000	880,000
0.9000	900,000	840,000	880,000
0.8900	890,000	840,000	880,000
0.8800	880,000	840,000	880,000
0.8700	870,000	840,000	870,000
0.8600	860,000	840,000	860,000
0.8500	850,000	840,000	850,000
0.8400	840,000	840,000	840,000
0.8300	830,000	840,000	835,000
0.8200	820,000	840,000	830,000
0.8100	810,000	840,000	825,000
0.8000	800,000	840,000	820,000
0.7900	790,000	840,000	815,000
0.7800	780,000	840,000	810,000
0.7700	770,000	840,000	805,000
0.7600	760,000	840,000	800,000
0.7500	750,000	840,000	795,000
0.7400	740,000	840,000	790,000

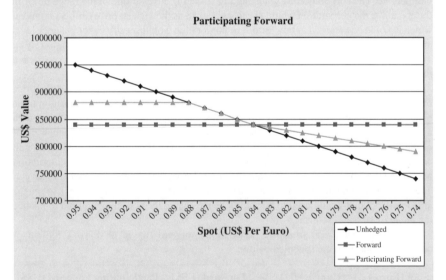

Under the participating forward structure, the corporation is protected against any strengthening in the Euro beyond US$0.88 (purchased US$ put). This protection is financed by forgoing any weakening in the Euro below US$0.84 (sold US$ call) on 50% of the face value of the position sought to be hedged.

Exhibit 6.5   Participating Swap/Cap Transaction

Assume US$ 6 month LIBOR rates are at 6% pa. A corporation seeks protection from higher short-term interest rates on its short term floating rate debt. The corporation would like to benefit, at least in part, from any potential decline in rates.

To achieve its objectives, the corporation enters into a participating swap or participating cap transaction.

The participating cap is structured as follows:
* The corporation elects the maximum interest rate level it is prepared to pay.
* The dealer works out the effective participation ratio below this rate.

There is a trade off between the maximum rate and the participation ratio. The higher the maximum interest rate level the corporation accepts, the higher the level of participation (in % terms) in a fall in interest rates below this level.

Assume the structure of the market allows the dealer to offer the following rates for a participating swap/cap transaction:

Maximum Interest Rate (% pa)	7.00	7.25	7.50	8.00
Participation Rate (%)	0	41	55	64

Under the structures available, if the corporation chose a maximum interest rate level of 7.50%, then the corresponding participation rate in a fall in interest rates would be 55%.

The participating swap/cap would operate as follows:
* If 6 month LIBOR rates are above 7.50% pa in any interest rate period, then the corporation's cost of funding is capped at 7.50% pa.
* If 6 month LIBOR rates are below 7.50% pa in any interest rate period, then the corporation participates (by 55% of the notional face value of the transaction) on any declines in the interest rate. The effective rate to the corporation when LIBOR is under the maximum interest rate level is determined by the following formula:

Interest Rate = Maximum Rate − Participation Rate × (Maximum Rate − LIBOR)

For example, if LIBOR is at 5% pa then the interest rate payable under the transaction is 6.125% pa (7.50% − 0.55 (7.50% − 5%)).

Under the participating swap, if LIBOR increases above 7.50%, then the corporation's interest cost would be capped at that level. If LIBOR falls, then the corporation participates on 55% of any decline. Under the structure, the corporation has purchased protection at no up-front premium, and benefits if interest rates decline.

The structure of the participating swap/cap can be readily reverse engineered. A conventional interest rate swap is equivalent to a portfolio of forwards on interest rates[8].

---

[8]   See Das, Satyajit (2004) Derivative Products & Pricing; John Wiley & Sons (Asia), Singapore at Chapter 10.

This means that paying fixed rate/receiving floating rate in an interest rate swap is equivalent to buying a cap/selling a floor[9]. The strike price of the cap and the floor contract is equal to the swap rate. The maturity date of the cap and floor are identical to the maturity of the swap. The cap and floor are on the underlying interest rate (for example, 6 month LIBOR against which the interest rate swap is settled).

The participating cap is a cap with a strike price at the maximum interest rate level (in this case 7.50% pa). The premium for the cap is funded by the sale of a floor at a strike equivalent to the maximum interest rate level. The sold floor is on a lower face value than the purchased cap. The face value of the floor sold is equal to (1 – participation ratio). In this case, this is equivalent to 45% of the notional face value of the transaction. The economics are driven by the differential in value between the cap and the floor. The cap is out-of-the-money (as it has a strike above the swap rate for the maturity). In contrast, the floor is in-the-money (as it has a strike above the swap rate). This means a lower amount of floors can be sold to finance the cap, allowing the participation in lower rates.

In this case, the lowest maximum interest rate that gives zero participation is equivalent to the swap rate for paying fixed/receiving floating under an interest rate swap. A 100% participation ratio would be equivalent to being fully unhedged.

The payoff (in % pa) from the participating swap/cap is specified below:

US$ LIBOR (% pa)	Unhedged/Floating Rate Borrowing (% pa)	Interest Rate Swap (% pa)	Participating Swap/ Cap (% pa)
10.00	10.00	7.00	7.500
9.50	9.50	7.00	7.500
9.00	9.00	7.00	7.500
8.50	8.50	7.00	7.500
8.00	8.00	7.00	7.500
7.50	7.50	7.00	7.500
7.00	7.00	7.00	7.225
6.50	6.50	7.00	6.950
6.00	6.00	7.00	6.675
5.50	5.50	7.00	6.400
5.00	5.00	7.00	6.125
4.50	4.50	7.00	5.850
4.00	4.00	7.00	5.575
3.50	3.50	7.00	5.300
3.00	3.00	7.00	5.025

[9]   Based on put call parity, see Das, Satyajit (2004) Derivative Products & Pricing; John Wiley & Sons (Asia), Singapore at Chapter 7.

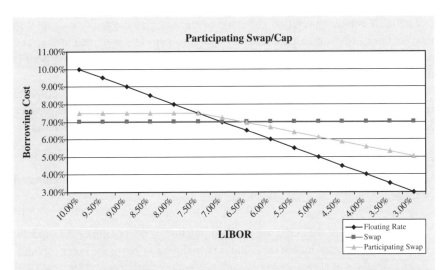

Under the participating swap/cap structure, the corporation is protected against any increases in interest rates above 7.50% pa. However, this protection is financed by forgoing any benefits from lower interest rates on 45% of the face value of the position to be hedged.

4 Option Combinations

4.1 Overview

Option combinations are a major component of the market for packaged options. In reality, the packaged forwards are constructed from option combinations. For example, a range forward and break forwards are merely option collars. Similarly, a participating forward is equivalent to a ratio option transaction. This means that there is considerable overlap between packaged forwards and option combinations.

4.2 Collars[10]

A collar contract (also referred to as an option cylinder or mini-max contract) is an agreement to buy or sell an asset at a specified future date at a price within a particular range of prices. The collar functionally combines bought and sold puts

---

[10] See James Capel Bankers "Hedging Strategies: How to Reduce the Cost of Using Foreign Currency Options" (4 April 1987) International Financing Review Issue 667 1164; Curnutt, Dean "Introduction to Collar Analytics" (8 January 2001) Derivatives Week 7–8.

and calls. It entails a premium reduction or financing strategy. For example, in interest rates, a borrower purchases an option (a cap) at a specified strike, and sells an option (floor) at a much lower strike interest rate. The sale of the floor is designed to recoup some or all of the premium paid to purchase the cap.

A zero cost collar uses adjustments to the strike prices of the relevant options to equate the premiums on the bought and sold contracts. This is designed to create a zero net option premium position to eliminate any cost to the option purchaser.

The key features of a collar include:

- Reduction in the net premium paid.
- Capacity to benefit from favourable movements in price within the nominated range.

The economics of the collar are purely a function of the pricing of the separate components. The behaviour of the collar is very similar to that of the range forward.

4.3 Ratio Options

Ratio options involve the simultaneous purchase and sale of options, but on different face value or notional amounts. In contrast, in a collar transaction both purchased and sold contracts are on identical notional face value amounts.

Ratio option positions are typically used to achieve the following objectives:

- Achieve premium neutrality through varying the amount of the options bought and sold. This requires the strike prices of the two options to be adjusted (relative to a collar structure).
- Create capacity to benefit from either an appreciation or depreciation in the relevant asset price.

The participating forward structure is a typical application of ratio option structures.

Ratio options can also be structured as the simultaneous purchase of a specific quantity of options and sale of a larger quantity of out-of-the-money options. In this strategy, the purchase of the in-the-money options is funded by the sale of larger amounts of out-of-the-money options. Alternatively, the purchase of an in-the-money option can be financed by the sale of a higher amount of out-of-the money options. The ratio option strategies are usually entered into to create structured exposure to particular movements in the underlying asset price[11]. A typical example

---

[11] See discussion of option spreads in Chapter 1.

of this type of transaction is a leveraged risk reversal undertaken by investors. In a typical trade, an investor would buy a US$ put/Euro call and sell double the volume US$ call/Euro put at a higher strike price. The structure is designed to provide a net premium to the investor. The strategy provides the investor with protection against a fall in the value of the US$ in exchange for limiting the opportunity to benefit from a favourable movement in the US$. The amount of the two options is different. The strategy is used to generate yield enhancement on investments.

5 Hybrid Structures

5.1 Overview

There are a number of hybrid packaged option structures. These are focused on:
- Contingency hedging structures.
- Transactions designed to defer payment of or disguise the option premium payable.

5.2 Contingency Hedging Structures

The contingency hedging structures attempt to deal specifically with the situation confronting tenderers in a contract bidding situation. The problem is that an individual entity may incur a financial exposure where it is bidding for a contract. The major difficulty with hedging such exposures is that the risk is only relevant *where the bid is successful*. This situation creates a complex hedging problem.

Two structures were developed to deal with this problem. They were known as Shared Currency Option Under Tender ("SCOUT") and Export Tender Risk Avoidance ("EXTRA")[12].

The SCOUT is an arrangement where the *contract awarder* buys the option required to hedge the underlying exposure. The premium is then allocated among the tenderers on a pro rata basis. This structure recognises the fact that each tenderer had an identical exposure, but only one (the successful bidder) would require the option. By switching the onus of hedging onto the contract awarder, the SCOUT structure increases the efficiency of the hedging arrangement. The EXTRA structure involves the dealer refunding 50% of the option fee if the bid was unsuccessful.

---

[12] See 'Foreign Exchange Hedging: Anticipating Forex Fluctuations with Midland's "Break-Forwards" and "Scouts"' (28 June 1986) International Financing Review 1939–1940; Katsouris, Christina "ECGD Squares the Circle" (November 1991) Risk 10–12.

In practice, contingency hedging structures are not commonly used. Compound options are also available to create contingency hedges[13].

5.3 Premium Deferred Structures

Premium deferred structures are predicated upon deferring the payment of the premium or disguising the premium payable. The basic structure used is that the option premium is not paid up-front, but paid at maturity or built into the spot or forward price of the asset. An example of this type of packaged option is a deferred premium option (also known as a 6 month forward)[14].

Structurally, the deferred premium option involves a loan to fund the premium and matched buy – sell contracts and options (with differential forward rates/strike prices)[15]. Functionally, the structure entails combinations of forwards and options (based on put call parity):
- To simulate a put call option, the counterparty bought a forward and bought a put option.
- To synthesise a put option position, the counterparty sold a forward and bought a call option.

Key features of this structure include:
- Deferred premium cost.
- An exposure identical to the purchase of the underlying option.

The economics of the structure entailed the basic option premium, adjusted for the funding cost through to expiration. An example of the deferred premium option is set out in **Exhibit 6.6**.

6 Applications of Packaged Forwards/Options

The demand for packaged forwards/options is driven by the demand for specifically structured hedging profiles, and reduction/elimination of the premium cost

---

[13] See Chapter 11.
[14] See Cicchetti, Claude "The Beauty of the Boston Option" (February 1985) Euromoney 45; Attfield, Chris "Can't Pay? Don't Pay – Deferred Premium Options" (3 April 2000) Derivatives Week 8–9.
[15] Structurally, it is similar to the break forward contract.

associated with the purchase of an option. The various structures described consist of a continuum of potential hedging strategies. **Exhibit 6.7** sets out a comparison of the different hedging structures using the examples outlined in this Chapter.

Exhibit 6.6 Deferred Premium Option

Assume a corporation needs to purchase Pound Sterling (GBP)/sell US$ forward 6 months to cover a payment. Assume that the market rate to buy GBP/sell US$ purchase 6 month forward is GBP 1 = US$1.45. Under the deferred premium option, the forward rate is adjusted by the option premium (say 2.00%) to establish a new forward rate of GBP 1 = US$1.4790.

Under the terms of the deferred premium option, the corporation would buy GBP at the US$1.4790 rate and have the option to sell sterling back to the bank at the rate of US$1.45 (the market forward rate).

The deferred premium option would operate as follows:
- If GBP were to strengthen to US$1.50 then the corporation would deliver under the forward at US$1.4790. The corporation would gain by US$0.0210 for every GBP1 of underlying value.
- If GBP were to weaken to US$1.40, then the corporation would exercise the option to sell GBP back to the bank at US$1.45. The corporation would then be free to buy GBP at the spot rate. If the GBP weakened to US$1.40, then the corporation would gain by US$0.05 for every GBP 1. The net gain is US$0.0210 per GBP 1. This represents the gain from the option exercise rate of US$0.05 (US$1.45 − US$1.40) adjusted by the option premium (the difference between the option exercise rate and the forward purchase rate of US$0.0290 (US$1.4790 − US$1.4500).

The deferred premium option is a packaged synthetic option. Using put call parity, it is possible to demonstrate that:

Option	Equivalent Synthetic Position
Call	Forward Purchase + Purchased Put
Put	Sold Forward + Purchased Call

This relationship is used to construct the deferred premium option. The corporation wants to purchase a GBP call/US$ put to hedge its GBP payment in 6 months. It could purchase this option but this would require immediate payment of the premium. In this case, the corporation buys GBP forward and simultaneously purchases a GBP put/US$ call. The call is struck at the forward rate. The premium is not paid immediately. The premium, together with the cost of funding the premium, is built into the off-market forward rate.

Exhibit 6.7   Packaged Forwards/Options – Case Study

1. Assumptions

Consider the position of a US corporation that needs to buy Euro for value 6 months from the present date.

The current market rates (Euro/US$) are as follows:

Spot rate   Euro 1 = US$0.85
6 month forward rate   Euro 1 = US$0.84

Typically, the corporation would hedge using a forward (purchase Euro/sell US$) or a purchased option (US$ put/Euro call). The two strategies suffer from a number of difficulties, including:

- The forward prevents the corporation from benefiting from an appreciation in the US$.
- The option requires the corporation to incur the premium cost.

The corporation considers the following alternative hedging strategies to overcome some of the identified problems with the basic hedging strategies:

1. Range forward and reverse range forward contract.
2. Break forward contract.
3. Participating forward.

2. Range Forward

Assume the corporation enters into a range forward to purchase Euro with a range of US$0.81 and US$0.88. The range forward will operate as follows:

- If the spot exchange rate at contract expiration is Euro 1 = US$0.81 or lower (stronger US$), then the corporation buys Euro at US$0.81.
- If the spot exchange rate is between US$0.81 and US$0.88, then the corporation buys Euro at the prevailing spot rate for Euro.
- If the spot exchange rate at contract expiration is Euro 1 = US$0.88 (weaker US$) then the corporation buys Euro at US$0.88.

Under the range forward structure, the corporation is protected against any strengthening in the Euro beyond US$0.88 (purchased US$ put). However, this protection is financed by forgoing any weakening in the Euro below US$0.81 (sold US$ call).

3. Reverse Range Forward

The range forward allows the corporation to benefit within the nominated range. As the corporation purchases an out-of-the-money put and sells an out-of-the money call, the corporation only benefits relative to the forward where the US$ strengthens above the forward rate. The use of a reverse forward can be used to change the price exposure.

In a reverse range forward, the corporation buys an in-the-money put (strike price equal to Euro 1 = US$0.81) and finances the premium by selling an in-the-money call (strike price equal to Euro 1 = US$0.87). The effect of the reverse range forward is very similar to that of the range forward. The corporation has a worst case exchange rate of Euro 1 = US$0.87 and a best case exchange rate of Euro 1 = US$0.81. Within the range, the corporation benefits (relative to the forward) where the US$ is weaker.

4. Break Forward

Assume the corporation enters into a break forward contract for 6 months to buy Euro/sell US$. The corporation is willing to lower the level of the forward rate by 2.50% to pay for the right to break. The adjusted forward rate is Euro 1 = US$0.8610. The dealer then calculates the break rate at US$0.83.

The break forward operates as follows:
- If the Euro strengthens/US$ weakens above the US$0.83 (the break rate), then the corporation purchases Euros at the agreed fixed rate of US$0.8610. This means the corporation pays US$861,000 per Euro 1,000,000.
- If the exchange rate is equal to the break rate (Euro 1 = US$0.83), then the break facility is activated. The corporation buys Euro 1,000,000 at the fixed rate of US$0.8610 (US$861,000). The corporation immediately sells back the Euro 1,000,000 at the break rate of US$0.83 (receives US$830,000). This locks in a loss of US$31,000. The corporation then purchases the required Euro 1,000,000 at the spot rate, in this case equal to the break rate (US$830,000). This means the total cost to the corporation for the Euro 1,000,000 is US$861,000 (effective exchange rate of Euro 1 = US$0.8610).
- If the Euro weakens/US$ strengthens below the break rate (Euro 1 = US$0.83), then the break facility is also activated. The corporation buys Euro 1,000,000 at the fixed rate of US$0.8610 (US$861,000). The corporation immediately sells back the Euro 1,000,000 at the break rate US$0.83 (receives US$830,000). This locks in a loss of US$31,000. The corporation then purchases the required Euro 1,000,000 at the spot rate. This means the total cost to the corporation for the Euro 1,000,000 is the spot rate plus the locked in loss (the difference between the off-market forward rate and the break rate (the strike of the purchased Euro Put/US$ call)).

Under the break forward structure, the corporation is protection against any strengthening in the Euro beyond US$0.8610 (off market forward purchase). Notice that this is below the forward rate (US$0.84). However, the corporation maintains the ability to participate in any appreciation in the US$ above a level of Euro 1 = US$0.83. This is achieved by terminating the forward (selling the Euros at US$0.83) and purchasing Euro in the spot market at a better exchange rate.

5. Participating Forward

Assume the corporation enters into a participating forward contract for 6 months to buy Euro/sell US$. Under the terms of the contract, the corporation is protected from a weaker US$ below Euro 1 = US$0.88. However, the corporation will participate in any appreciation in the US$ above Euro 1 = US$0.84. The agreed participation ratio is 50%.

The participating forward will operate as follows:
- If the spot exchange rate at contract expiration is Euro 1 = US$0.88 (weaker US$), the corporation buys Euro at US$0.88.
- If the spot exchange rate at contract expiration is Euro 1 = US$0.84 or lower (stronger US$), then the corporation buys Euro at US$0.84 for 50% of the total amount of the face value and buys Euro at the prevailing spot rate for Euro for the remaining 50%.

Under the participating forward structure, the corporation is protected against any strengthening in the Euro beyond US$0.88 (purchased US$ put). However, this protection is financed by forgoing any weakening in the Euro below US$0.84 (sold US$ call) on 50% of the face value of the position sought to be hedged.

6. Comparison of Strategies

The alternative strategies have a number of common elements:

- No up-front premium payment.
- Ability for the corporation to benefit from favourable changes in exchange rate to varying degrees.

The different strategies described provided different outcomes under different future exchange rate scenarios. The Graphs below compare the different hedging strategies in terms of US$ cost per Euro 1 million and US$ gain (loss) relative to the forward rate:

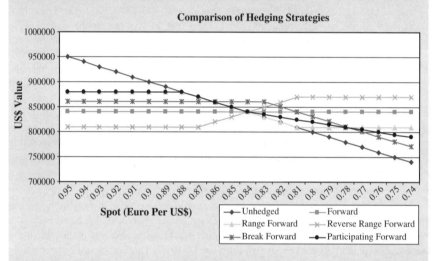

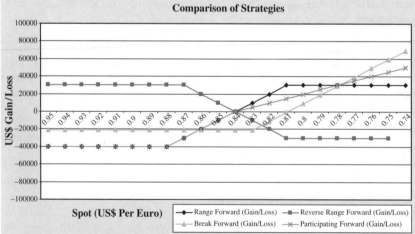

The choice between the identified hedging strategies requires the corporation to form views on the likely future evolution of the exchange rate.

7 Summary

Packaged forwards/options represent a significant evolution in risk management products. Packaged options are a combination of traditional risk management building blocks (forwards and option contracts). Packaged forwards/options represent the initial attempt by dealers to tailor risk management instruments to client requirements. It also represents an attempt to overcome weaknesses of traditional risk management instruments (inability to benefit from favourable price movements or the premium cost of options). While the objectives of the packaged forward/option structures can now arguably be achieved more efficiently through more exotic option structures, these products continue to be a significant part of the market for risk management products.

7
Path Dependent Options

1 Overview

Path dependent options are an important type of exotic options. In conventional options, the value of the option is based on the price of the underlying asset at expiry of the option. This is the case, particularly with European options. The value of path dependent options depends upon the asset price path over the life of the options. In this Chapter, the major types of path dependent forms of exotic options are discussed.

The structure of the Chapter is as follows:

- The key dynamics of path dependent options are outlined.
- Each of the major types of path dependent exotic options is described. Path dependent options covered include average rate options, average strike options, ladder options, shout options and swing options.

2 Path Dependent Options[1]

Path dependent options are characterised by payoffs that are a function of the particular path that asset prices follow over the life of the relevant option. The path of the underlying asset price is used to determine the payoff or the structure of the option. American and Bermudan options are examples of simple path dependent options[2]. **Exhibit 7.1** sets out the major types of path dependent options.

---

[1] For a discussion of path dependent options, see Gastineau, Gary "Path-Dependent Options" (Winter 1993) 78–86; Smithson, Charles "Path Dependency" (April 1997) Risk 65–67; Ong, Michael "Exotic Options: The Market and their Taxonomy" in Nelken, Israel (Editor) (1996) The Handbook of Exotic Options; Irwin Professional Publishing, Chicago at Chapter 1; Smithson, Charles (1998) Managing Financial Risk – Third Edition; McGraw-Hill, New York at Chapter 13.

[2] See Das, Satyajit (2004) Derivative Products & Pricing; John Wiley & Sons (Asia), Singapore at Chapters 7 and 8.

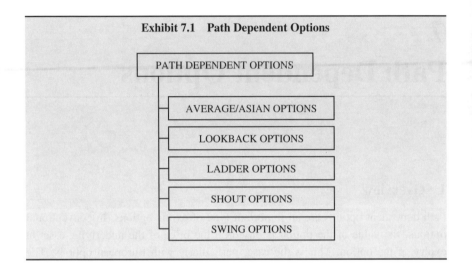

Exhibit 7.1   Path Dependent Options

The major types of path dependent exotic options include:

- **Average rate (or Asian) options** – options where the payoff at settlement is determined by comparing the strike price with the average of the spot asset price over a specific period during the life of the option.
- **Average strike rate options** – options where the strike rate itself is not fixed, and the payoff is determined through a comparison of the underlying asset price at expiration with the strike price computed as the average of the underlying asset price over a specified period.
- **Lookback options** – options where the purchaser has the right at expiration to set the strike price of the option at the most favourable price for the asset that has occurred during a specified time. In the case of a lookback call (put), the buyer can choose to purchase (sell) the underlying asset at the lowest (highest) price that has occurred over a specified period (typically the life of the option).
- **Ladder options** – options where the strike price of the option is periodically reset, based on the underlying evolution of the asset price. A ladder option is not dissimilar to a lookback option. In the most extreme cases, if the amount of resets is set to infinity, the ladder option approximates a lookback option.
- **Shout options** – options where the purchaser has the right to fix the intrinsic value of the option at the difference between the strike price and the asset price at a given time by advising the seller ("shouting"). The value of the shout is the greater of the value of the option at the time of the shout, and the intrinsic value at maturity. The shout combines some of the features of lookback, ladder and cliquet options.

• **Swing options** – options where the purchaser buys a package of several European options where the total number of options that can be exercised is set at a number lower than the number of the total options purchased. In effect, the purchaser has an option on exercising some, but not all, of the purchased options.

There are a number of variations on the structures outlined. These represent structural changes to the basic elements of the primary path dependent options.

Exotic option structures are generally driven by the following objectives:
• Reduction in option premium.
• Alteration in risk profile, including increased probability of gain, quantification of loss, or optimal exercise timing.
• Asset liability matching.

Path dependent options are primarily driven by the capacity of the structures to reduce option premium, increase the probability of gain and match underlying assets or liabilities. The exact factor driving individual path dependent structures varies between types of options.

Path dependency in option structures is a source of value to option users. Demand for path dependent structures is driven by a number of factors, including:
• The nature of the underlying asset or liability allows a path dependent hedge.
• The fact that the value of the option will rarely be at its maximum level at the maturity of the option.

Average rate, average strike and swing options are examples of path dependent structures driven by the nature of underlying assets or liabilities. These types of options are used to hedge regular series of cash flows where the price risk or performance is driven by the average of prices/rates over a period. The existing path dependency within the underlying assets or liabilities can be used to reduce the cost of the option. This derives from the fact that the volatility of an average is lower than the volatility of an asset price. It also derives from the fact that the payoff based on an average is inherently more stable than the payoff based on an asset price.

Lookback, ladder and shout options are examples of path dependent structures designed to increase the probability of gain on the option. The structures inherently attempt to optimise option value by generally passive exercise rules being embedded within the option features. This demand can be motivated by the type of investor (retail investment products), investment style or asset liability matching requirements.

The optimal exercise characteristics can typically only be achieved at a cost to the purchaser. The lookback option structure is the ultimate example of this structure. It is ideal for the purchaser who wishes to ensure a very high probability of a positive payoff for the option. The lookback option is generally extremely expensive. A number of path dependent structures seek to use the concept of path dependency to increase the probability of a positive payout, but at a lower cost than for a lookback option. Structures such as ladder and shout options are examples of this structure.

3 Average Rate Options

3.1 Average Rate Options – Concept[3]

The average rate option is a path dependent option. Average rate options are also referred to as Asian options.

The average rate option is similar to a conventional option. The major difference with conventional options is the applicable payoff at maturity or exercise. Under a conventional option, the payoff is determined as the difference between the strike price/rate of the option and the spot price/rate at maturity or exercise date. Under an average rate option, the payoff is determined as the difference between the strike price/rate of the option and the average spot rate over a specified period (usually the life of the option).

The major features of average rate options include:
- Ability to hedge a series of regular or irregular cash flows with option payoffs being based on the *average* price/rate rather than a single final price/rate observation. There is an effective reduction in premium costs relative to using a series of options to hedge this type of exposure.
- Lower premium cost relative to comparable conventional options.

Average rate options are used in all asset classes. They are used extensively in foreign exchange and commodity markets where the averaging structure facilitates hedging of series of regular cash flows.

---

[3] See Ong, Michael "Exotic Options: The Market and their Taxonomy" in Nelken, Israel (Editor) (1996) The Handbook of Exotic Options; Irwin Professional Publishing, Chicago at Chapter 1 at 19–21; Smithson, Charles (1998) Managing Financial Risk – Third Edition; McGraw-Hill, New York at Chapter 13 at 267–269; Ravindran, K. (1998) Customised Derivatives; McGraw-Hill, New York at Chapter 3 at 80–94; Nelken, Israel (2000) Pricing, Hedging and Trading Exotic Options; McGraw-Hill, New York at Chapter 15.

3.2 Average Rate Options – Structure

The payoff of an average rate option is linked to the average spot price of the underlying asset/rate. The key structural features of the average rate option include:

- **Option Payoff** – the average rate option is typically cash settled against the average of the specified series of asset price fixings (rather than the spot rate at maturity). The payoff can be defined as follows:

Type of Option	Payoff of Call Options	Payoff of Put Options
Conventional	Maximum $[0; S_m - K]$	Maximum $[0; K - S_m]$
Average rate option	Maximum $[0; S_{avge} - K]$	Maximum $[0; K - S_{avge}]$

Where:

K = strike price

S_m = spot price at maturity

S_{avge} = average spot price

- **Averaging mechanism** – the average rate can be determined utilising a variety of means:
  1. Geometric average – defined as: $[S_1 \times S_2 \cdots \times S_n]^{(1/n)}$
  2. Arithmetic Average – defined as: $\Sigma (S_1 + S_2 + \cdots + S_n)/n$

     Where

     S_n = spot price at time n

     n = number of price observations

  The most common structure used is arithmetic averaging.

- **Averaging Timing** – the average can be calculated over the option term using different sampling processes. The frequency and interval between the underlying price observations can be adjusted to suit the particular user. The major choice is between an average based on continuous and discrete (infrequent) price samples. In practice, a variety of structures are utilised. Average rate options, where the average is calculated using daily price/rate observations, are common. Infrequent sampling (weekly or monthly) is generally used primarily to capture the price behaviour of underlying positions that are hedged using average rate options.

- **Partial versus Full Average** – in a normal average rate option, the average is calculated over the full term of the option. The average can be calculated over a subset of the option's term to expiry (referred to as a partial average rate option).

- **American versus European Style** – average rate options are generally European. However, unlike a conventional European style option, average rate options is sometimes settled at discrete times over the life of the option. For example, the purchaser of a 1 year average rate option can choose to settle the option monthly against the average price/rate of the underlying previous month.

The design of average options assumes the availability of suitable market prices/rates that are used to calculate the average. In practice, the price/rate source will be an accepted market benchmark. The key criteria in this regard include transparency, ease of price discovery and accuracy of the price. The criteria are relatively easy to satisfy in certain asset classes (currency, interest rates and equity indexes) and markets (developed markets and exchange-traded products).

3.3   Average Rate Options – Economics & Applications[4]

The economics of average rate options are driven by the following factors:
- The payoff of the average rate option is driven purely by the behaviour of the average price of the underlying asset/rate. The individual prices only affect the economic payoff to the extent that the individual price affects the average. **Exhibit 7.2** sets out the payoff structure of an average rate option. The average rate call option will only have value to the extent that the average is above the strike price. Similarly, the average rate put will only have value to the extent that the average is below the strike price. This means that individual price movements above or below the strike will not in themselves have any impact upon the payoff of the average.
- The volatility of the average of prices is lower than the volatility of the individual asset prices. This reflects the fact that as an increasing proportion of asset prices is known, a greater component of the average price is known. This means that individual prices have proportionately lower impact upon the average price. **Exhibit 7.3** sets out the behaviour of the average price relative to the asset price.

---

[4]   See Coward, Martin and Thomas, Lee "When Average Can be Good" (July 1988) Risk 42–43; Cunctator "Optional Hindsight" (October 1988) Risk 48; Cole, Joseph B. (December 1989) Cash Flow Management Using Asian Options; Drexel Burnham Lambert, Chicago; Kryzak, Krystyna "Asian Elegance" (December 1989/January 1990) Risk 30–49; Curran, Michael "Beyond Average Intelligence" (November 1992) Risk 60; Sullivan, Sara "Average Rate Options Offer the Benefit of Hindsight" (February 1993) Corporate Finance 15–16; Jones, David "The Flexible ARO" (1994) Corporate Finance Risk Management & Derivatives Yearbook 39–42; Cook, Julian "On Averages" (October 1996) Futures & Options World 64–67.

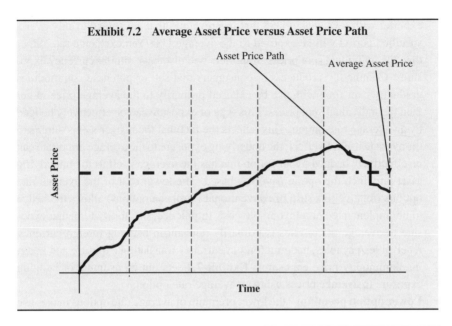

Exhibit 7.2   Average Asset Price versus Asset Price Path

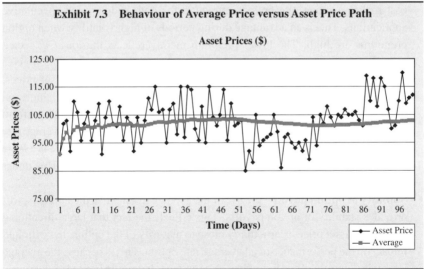

Exhibit 7.3   Behaviour of Average Price versus Asset Price Path

The identified factors also drive applications of average rate options. The primary applications are based around the following factors:

- **Hedging exposure to average prices/rates** – hedgers are frequently exposed to the average price rather than to individual asset prices. For example, a Yen based exporter with revenues in US$ that has revenues that are spread evenly over a specified period will be exposed to the average US$/Yen exchange rate rather than the individual spot prices. Importers will also have similar currency exposures. Commodity producers or consumers that sell or purchase commodities gradually over time will also be exposed primarily to the average price rather than the individual spot prices. This type of exposure can be effectively hedged by an average rate option. This reflects the fact that the hedger's exposure is to the average itself. In effect, the underlying exposure to the average price/rate can be effectively hedged by an option that has the average itself as the underlying asset on which the option payoff is based. The lower cost of the average rate options (relative to a strip of conventional European options) allows the hedge to be implemented at a favourable cost. In practice, the ability to hedge exposure to average prices/rates is primarily relevant in hedging foreign currency receivables/payables, hedging foreign currency translation exposure and hedging commodity price exposures. **Exhibit 7.4** sets out an example of hedging exposure to average prices using an average rate option.

- **Lower option premium** – the lower premium of average rate options makes use of these structures cheaper than comparable conventional options. The lower cost makes average rate options attractive for both hedging and speculative applications. This is an advantage during periods of high volatility when option premiums are high. The lower premium merely reflects the *lower* expected payoff of the average rate option. In effect, the purchaser of the option gives up the opportunity to benefit from large directional changes in asset prices. This is because the averaging reduces the impact of large prices changes on the option payoff. This means that the average rate options may under perform conventional options in certain market conditions. In particular, the average rate option will have a lower payoff than a conventional option where there is a large favourable movement in asset prices close to expiry of the option. This under performance may offset the lower premium cost.

- **Stability of option payoff** – the use of the average to establish the option payoff provides stability of option payoffs. This reflects the fact that large directional changes in asset prices, particularly close to maturity of the option, have limited impact on the performance of an average rate option. This is because the average is largely determined and individual price changes have only limited impact upon the average. This contrasts with conventional options where the performance of the options is significantly affected by large price changes close to maturity. The large price changes may increase or decrease the value of the option as it moves the option into or out-of-the-money. The stability of option payoff is attractive to option purchasers who want to avoid exposure to large price changes close to option expiry. The stability of option payoff combined with the lower option cost makes average rate options attractive for use in retail investment products[5].

Exhibit 7.4   Average Rate Options – Hedging Regular Cash Flows

Assume a Japanese exporter whose revenue is denominated in US$. The exporter is confronted with the risk of a weaker US$/appreciating Yen. Such a market environment would reduce the exporter's Yen revenue. The exporter has Yen based cost of production. This means that a weaker US$ would adversely impact revenues and the exporter's profitability. The problem is further compounded by the need to set the US$ price of the company's product for the forthcoming year. Furthermore, the price is to be held constant over the whole of the year.

In seeking to hedge the US$/Yen currency exposure (at a transactional exposure level), the exporter focuses on the following considerations:
- Total cash flows are expected to be around US$100 million over the whole year.
- Exact timing is uncertain but based on past history, the revenues will be steady throughout the year and average around US$1.92 million per week.
- The Yen has strengthened against the US$ over the near past and the exporter is uncertain about the future exchange rate.

Against this background, the exporter favours using options rather than locking in the current forward rates for selling US$/purchasing Yen. The exporter considers two separate option strategies:
- Purchasing a series of 52 options (US$ put/Yen call) on a face value of US$1.92 million maturing at weekly intervals (the serial option strategy).
- Purchasing a US$100 million face value average rate option covering the year (the average rate option strategy).

The exporter plans to sell its US$ revenue weekly upon receipt in the spot market, and cash settle its options to achieve the economic hedge it seeks.

The US$/Yen rate at the time of entry into either strategy is US$1 = Yen 104.50. Both the conventional options (under the serial option strategy) and the average rate option have a strike price equal to the spot rate.

The cost of the options is as follows:
- Serial options: 3.60% of face value (equivalent to Yen 376.2 million)
- Average rate option: 3.00% of face value (equivalent to Yen 313.5 million).

The performance of the alternative hedges over the year is now considered:
- The exporter received US$100 million in revenue from sales and this was exchanged into Yen in the spot market at the prevailing spot rate (which averaged Yen 91.51) generating Yen cash flow of Yen 9,151 million.

---

[5]   See Das, Satyajit (2004) Structured Products Volume 2; John Wiley & Sons (Asia), Singapore at Chapter 4.

- If the exporter had hedged using the serial options, then most of the options would have been exercised. The gain on the options would have been Yen 799.6 million that, adjusted for the cost of the options (Yen 376.2 million), would have been Yen 423.4 million. The Yen revenue and effective exchange rate achieved would have been Yen 9,574 million and Yen 95.75.
- The actual average daily exchange rate over the year was Yen 91.51(this uses the average rate calculation mechanism under the average rate option). The gain on the average rate option is Yen 1,299 million that, adjusted for the cost of the options (Yen 313.5 million), would have been Yen 985.5 million. The Yen revenue and effective exchange rate achieved would have been Yen 10,136.5 million and Yen 101.37

The effective exchange rate achieved under the average rate option is significantly higher. The difference between the two strategies relates to a number of factors:
- The premium on the average rate option (computed using the same volatility) was lower by approximately Yen 62.7 million.
- The option payout was different, reflecting the *path* of the Yen over the year. The Yen moved sharply in one direction and most of the serial options finished in the money. If more of the serial options had finished out of the money, then the average rate option strategy would have been more significantly superior to the serial option strategy.

In this case, the average rate option settlement is payable at maturity. This defers the settlement cash flows under the average rate option. If this is a concern, then it would be feasible to construct a 1 year average rate option that settled on a monthly basis. This would be constructed as a series of deferred average rate options.

3.4   Average Rate Options – Product Variations

3.4.1   Overview

A number of variations to the basic average rate options exist, including:
- Deferred average rate options.
- Double average rate options.
- Cumulative average rate options.
- Average strike rate options.

3.4.2   Deferred Average Rate Options[6]

The deferred start average rate option structure provides for averaging to commence not at the commencement of the option transaction, but at a nominated point in

---

[6]   See Kryzak, Krystyna "Asian Elegance" (December 1989/January 1990) Risk 30–49 at 31.

time in the future. The typical use of the deferred start average rate option is to hedge seasonal cash flows. This is a special case of hedging a series of regular cash flows where the cash flows are not even, but subject to seasonal fluctuation. In this case, the traditional average rate option structure on a fixed principal is not appropriate. Accordingly, the transaction structure designed to hedge these particular cash flows entails a series of deferred start average rate options to hedge the seasonal fluctuations in the cash flows. **Exhibit 7.5** sets out an example of using deferred average rate options to hedge seasonal cash flows.

Exhibit 7.5   Deferred Average Rate Options – Hedging Seasonal Cash Flows

Assume the Japanese exporter (in **Exhibit 7.4**) has seasonal case flows. The US$ revenues are not spread evenly throughout the year but fluctuate from month to month. The pattern of cash flows is set out in the Graph below:

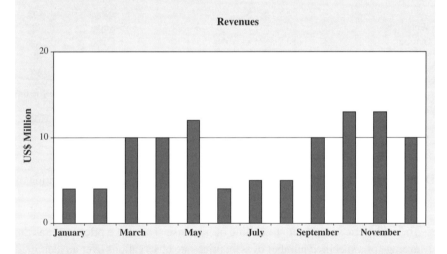

The use of a normal average rate option would not exactly hedge the underlying currency exposure. This reflects the fact that the seasonal pattern will mean that the actual average achieved from the sale of US$ receipts at spot rates will differ (potentially very significantly) from the average determined for the average rate option. The difference will be caused by the different amounts of the actual transactions. The actual currency transactions will reflect the seasonal pattern of revenues. In contrast, the average rate option will reflect evenly spread cash flows throughout the year.

A more accurate hedge is achieved by using a series (12) of deferred average rate options. The deferred average rate options required will have the following features:
• The options are all purchased at the commencement of the year.
• The options have different maturities ranging from 1 to 12 months.

- The average will be calculated over a specified period (an identified month).
- Each option will have a different face value, reflecting the actual cash flow in the specific period.

The specific options required are summarised below:

Month	Revenues (US$ Million)	Maturity	Averaging Period	
			Start	**End**
January	4	31-Jan	2-Jan	30-Jan
February	4	28-Feb	1-Feb	27-Feb
March	10	30-Mar	1-Mar	29-Mar
April	10	30-Apr	2-Apr	27-Apr
May	12	31-May	1-May	30-May
June	4	29-Jun	1-Jun	28-Jun
July	5	31-Jul	2-Jul	30-Jul
August	5	31-Aug	1-Aug	30-Aug
September	10	28-Sep	3-Sep	27-Sep
October	13	31-Oct	1-Oct	30-Oct
November	13	30-Nov	1-Nov	29-Nov
December	10	28-Dec	3-Dec	27-Dec

The series of deferred average rate options will provide a more accurate hedge for the exporter's seasonal cash flows.

3.4.3 Double Average Rate Options[7]

Double average rate options (often referred to as "DAROs") are a combination of average rate and average strike options.

The principal features of the double average rate options are as follows:

- The strike price is not set at the time of purchase. The strike price is set as the average of a specified number of asset price/rate observations over an identified period.
- The option payoff is based on the difference between the strike price (set as described above) and the average asset price calculated as the average of asset price *over a different period*.

The primary application of the double average rate option is in currency hedging (specifically hedging currency translation exposure). For example, a multinational

---

[7]   See Falloon, William "Forex Managers Go for DAROs Option" (October 1999) Risk 32–33.

corporation would need to translate foreign currency earnings at the end of each quarter for financial reporting purposes. In practice, analysts will compare the current quarter earnings against the comparable quarter in the previous year. Changes in the translation rate used will affect the earnings in comparative terms.

Minimisation of currency translation gains (losses) is difficult in practice. A conventional average rate option is not effective as a hedge. In contrast, the double average rate option is well suited to hedging this type of exposure. For example, in January of the current year, the multinational could hedge the earning currency translation exposure for the final quarter of next year using a double average rate option. The strike would be set at the average rate for the final quarter *in the current year*. Th option payoff would be based on comparison of the strike rate to the average exchange rate for the final quarter *the next year*. This would have the effect of hedging the currency translation between the current year and the following year.

A key driver of double average rate options is the lower cost of this structure compared to a conventional average rate option. The value of the double average rate option is driven by the difference implied by current forward rates between the average that determines the strike and the average that determines the payoff. The shape of the forward price curve drives the value.

An unusual feature of double average rate options is that the option initially has no gamma. This is because the option strike is not fixed. The risk for the dealer is the exposure to changes in volatility. The dealer has a position similar to a calendar option spread where it has sold the front end and purchased the back end of the volatility term structure curve.

3.4.4 Average Rate Options – Miscellaneous Structures

A number of other average rate options have also emerged, including cumulative average rate options. A typical structure is a cumulative average interest rate cap[8]. This structure provides a payoff to the purchaser only if the purchaser's interest cost over the specified period exceeds the strike price. This means the payoff is related to the average of the interest rates at the relevant interest rate fixing dates on the borrower's underlying debt. The fact that specific interest rates exceed the strike price is irrelevant to the option payoff. It is only the cumulative interest rate that

---

[8]   This is also known as the Q-Cap (a proprietary name used by Chase Manhattan); see Chase Securities Inc. "Mundane Problems, Exotic Solutions" (August 1992) Euromoney 42–48 at 46.

drives the option payoff. The structure allows the purchaser to hedge its interest cost over the term of the option[9].

3.4.5 Average Strike Options[10]

The average strike rate option is a variation on the average rate option concept. It entails a moving (floating) strike rate. The payoff of the average strike option at maturity is the difference between the spot price at maturity and the strike price set at the average of the asset prices over the relevant period.

The relationship between average strike rate options and average rate options is easily understood by considering the payoffs under the structures:

Type of Option	Payoff of Call Options	Payoff of Put Options
Conventional	Maximum $[0; S_m - K]$	Maximum $[0; K - S_m]$
Average rate option	Maximum $[0; S_{avge} - K]$	Maximum $[0; K - S_{avge}]$
Average strike option	Maximum $[0; S_m - S_{avge}]$	Maximum $[0; S_{avge} - S_m]$

Where:

K = strike price
S_m = spot price at maturity
S_{avge} = average spot price

In the case of the average strike rate option, the option *strike rate* is uncertain and determined at maturity or exercise. Average strike rate options are similar to lookback options.

Average strike rates are not frequently used. Potential applications include the use of an average strike rate option to hedge currency exposures where a company has known periodic receipts in a local currency followed by a single aggregate disbursement in a foreign currency. An average strike rate call on the foreign currency would preserve the relative foreign exchange rate between receipts and disbursements, without forgoing the opportunity to gain on the disbursement.

---

[9] See Smithson, Charles (1998) Managing Financial Risk – Third Edition; McGraw-Hill, New York at Chapter 13 at 270; Smithson, Charles "What's New in the Options Markets?" (May 2000) Risk 54–55.

[10] See Ong, Michael "Exotic Options: The Market and their Taxonomy" in Nelken, Israel (Editor) (1996) The Handbook of Exotic Options; Irwin Professional Publishing, Chicago at Chapter 1 at 19–21; Smithson, Charles (1998) Managing Financial Risk – Third Edition; McGraw-Hill, New York at Chapter 13 at 269–270.

3.5 Average Rate Options – Pricing/Valuation & Hedging

3.5.1 Average Rate Options – Premium Behaviour

The price/value of average rate options is driven by a number of factors, including:

- Average rate options are path dependent. The payoff depends upon the history of asset prices/rates over the relevant period that is used to calculate the average.
- The relevant volatility is the volatility of the average asset price. The volatility of the average of the asset price will generally be lower than the volatility of the asset price itself.

Average rate option premiums will generally be lower than comparable conventional options. The exact difference will depend upon the maturity, strike price relative to the forward price, length of the averaging process and the sampling frequency used to determine the average.

Exhibit 7.6 sets out an analysis of the premium behaviour of an average rate option relative to a comparable conventional option.

Exhibit 7.6   Option Premium – Average Rate Options versus Comparable Conventional Options

1. Assumptions
Assume the following parameters:

Asset Price ($)	100.00
Strike Price ($)	See below
Maturity	See below
Volatility (% pa)	See below
Interest rates (% pa)	6.00
Asset income (% pa)	3.50
Exercise	European

Additional assumptions in relation to average rate options include:

Type of average	Arithmetic average
Averaging	Continuous averaging over the full term of the option commencing upon the trade date

Conventional options are valued using a binomial tree with 500 steps. Average rate options are valued using an analytic approximation model.

2. Option Premiums – Average Rate Options versus Conventional Options

Comparative option premiums ($) for average rate options and comparable conventional options are set out below:

Maturity: 6 month

Assuming volatility = 20% pa

		Conventional Options		Average Rate Option	
		Call	Put	Call	Put
Strike	110	2.50	10.98	0.59	9.68
Strike	100	6.14	4.92	3.49	2.88
Strike	90	12.41	1.48	10.61	0.30

Assuming volatility = 25% pa

		Conventional Options		Average Rate Option	
		Call	Put	Call	Put
Strike	110	3.75	12.24	1.11	10.20
Strike	100	7.51	6.29	4.29	3.68
Strike	90	13.40	2.47	10.97	0.66

Maturity: 12 month

Assuming volatility = 20% pa

		Conventional Options		Average Rate Option	
		Call	Put	Call	Put
Strike	110	4.94	11.97	1.61	9.84
Strike	100	8.85	6.47	5.00	3.82
Strike	90	14.60	2.80	11.45	0.84

Assuming volatility = 25% pa

		Conventional Options		Average Rate Option	
		Call	Put	Call	Put
Strike	110	6.83	13.87	2.55	10.78
Strike	100	10.73	8.34	6.10	4.91
Strike	90	16.11	4.31	12.14	1.53

3.5.2   Average Rate Options – Valuation Approaches[11]

The pricing/valuation of average rate options must incorporate the following factors in practice:
- Path dependency of the average asset price, the type of average (arithmetic or geometric), and the nature of the distribution of the average price.
- The averaging process is not continuous in practice. The average price in practice must be calculated on a discrete basis (daily etc).
- The averaging process may not be over the *full* term of the option.

Where the average rate option is based on a geometric average, analytic solutions for pricing of the average rate options are available. This reflects the fact that the product of a series of lognormal random variables is lognormal. Where the underlying asset price/rate is assumed to be log normal and the average is calculated continuously, the expectation and variance of the underlying asset price/rate can be calculated directly. This allows closed form solutions for pricing geometric average rate options to be derived by discounting the expected value of the payoffs at expiration by the discount rate.

Where the average rate option is based on an arithmetic average, analytic closed form solutions for pricing are not available. This reflects the fact that the arithmetic average of a log normally distributed asset price is not lognormal. This means that the distribution of the arithmetic average is not known.

The approach to pricing/valuation of average rate option structures is categorised as follows:
- The use of adjusted volatility within a Black-Scholes framework.
- Analytic closed form solutions available for geometric averaging processes using the concept of a pseudo spot or forward parameter[12].

---

[11] See Briys, Eric Bellalah, Mondher, Mai, Huu Minh and De Varenne, Francois (1998) Options, Futures and Exotic Derivatives: Theory, Application and Practice; John Wiley & Sons, Chichester at Chapter 20; Wilmott, Paul (1998) Derivatives: The Theory and Practice of Financial Engineering; John Wiley & Sons, Chichester at Chapter 16; Hull, John (2000) Options, Futures and Other Derivatives – Fourth Edition; Prentice-Hall Inc., Upper Saddle River, NJ at Chapter 18 at 467–469; Nelken, Israel (2000) Pricing, Hedging & Trading Exotic Options; McGraw-Hill, New York at Chapter 15.

[12] For analytical models for pricing of average rate options, see Heenk, B.A., Kemna, A.G.Z. and Vorst, A.C.F. "Asian Options on Oil Spreads" (1990) Review of Futures Markets 511–528; Conze, Antoine and Vishwanathan, R. "European Path-Dependent Options: The Case of Geometric Averages" (June 1991) Finance 7–22; Boyle, Phelim P. "New Life Forms on the Options Landscape" (September 1993) Journal of Financial

- Approximation models used to value arithmetic average rate options[13].
- Numerical/simulation approaches such as binomial trees or Monte Carlo simulations.

The approaches outlined have deficiencies. The major problems relate to the use of discrete rather than continuous sampling to calculate the average. In practice, the average price will inevitably need to be calculated on a discrete basis (daily etc prices). Continuous averaging simplifies the pricing of average rate options. In practice, it is common to simplify the pricing of average rate options by assuming that prices are observed continuously. Where the averaging period varies from the term of the option or sampling is infrequent, continuous averaging cannot be assumed. In this case, numerical or simulation approaches may need to be used.

3.5.3 Average Rate Options – Adjusted Volatility Pricing Approach

An approximation technique available to estimate the price of an average rate option is to adjust the volatility of the asset used to price an average rate option. This technique relies on the fact that the average rate option has a lower premium cost than conventional options because the averaging process reduces volatility.

Under this approach, the volatility used for an Average Rate Option is adjusted as follows:

$$\text{Normal Volatility} \times 1/\sqrt{3}$$

This is effectively around 58% of normal volatility.

Engineering 217–252; Bouaziz, Laurent, Briys, Eric and Crouhy, Michel "The Pricing of Forward-Starting Asian Options" (October 1994) Journal of Banking and Finance 823–839; Longstaff, Francis A. "Hedging Interest Rate Risks with Options on Average Interest Rates" (March 1995) Journal of Fixed Income 37–45; Helyette, Geman and Eydeland, Alexander "Domino Effect" (April 1995) Risk 65–67.

[13] For numerical models for pricing average rate options, see Ruttiens, Alain "Classical Replica" (February 1990) Risk 33–35; Carverhill, Andrew and Clewlow, Les "Flexible Convolution" (April 1990) Risk 25–29; Levy, Edmond "Asian Arithmetic" (May 1990) Risk 5 7–8; Levy, Edmond and Turnbull, Stuart "Average Intelligence" (February 1992) Risk 53–59; Curran, Michael "Beyond Average Intelligence" (November 1992) Risk 60; Ritchken, Peter and Sankarasubramanium, L "Averaging and Deferred Payment Yield Agreements" (February 1993) Journal of Futures Markets 23–41; Hull, John C. and White, Alan "Efficient Procedures for Valuing European and American Path-Dependent Options" (Fall 1993) Journal of Derivatives 21–31; Turnbull, Stuart and Wakeman, Lee Macdonald "A Quick Algorithm for Pricing European Asian Options" (September 1991) Journal of Financial and Quantitative Analysis 377–389; Zhang, Peter G. "Flexible Arithmetic Asian Options" (Spring 1995) Journal of Derivatives 53–65.

The rationale for the approximation approach is based on an argument proposed by William Margabe in the context of exchange options[14]. The argument proposes that the volatility that is relevant is the volatility of the price ratio of the asset being exchanged. In the case of an average rate option, the average is being exchanged for a fixed strike price. It can be shown mathematically that the volatility of the average is related to the price volatility divided by $\sqrt{3}$. Based on the further fact of the specific and positive correlation between the final price at maturity and the average price over the relevant sampling period, the *initial* volatility applicable to the average rate option is also equal to the *initial* price volatility divided by $\sqrt{3}$.

This approximation provides a crude estimate of the value of an average rate option. The major advantage is the ease of computation. The approach also has a number of defects, including:

- The implicit assumptions and inaccuracies create errors.
- Averages are correlated and the addition of a series of log normal distribution is not log normal.

3.5.4 Average Rate Options – Closed Form Pricing Models

Mathematical approaches to option valuation are available for the valuation of geometric average rate options. If the asset price/rate is assumed to be distributed log normally and the average is geometric, then the average is also log normal. This allows the expectation and variance of the average price/rate to be calculated explicitly. This allows derivation of a closed form solution for pricing geometric average rate options based on discounting the expected value of payoffs at expiration. The earliest model proposed was that by Kemna and Vorst[15].

The model is only applicable to continuous, geometric averaging processes. In practice, most average rate options use an arithmetic average.

3.5.5 Average Rate Options – Approximation Approaches to Pricing

The valuation of arithmetic average options is complicated by the fact that the distribution of the average of a log normally distributed asset is not known. The most common approach used is to approximate the probability distribution for the arithmetic average. The price of the arithmetic average rate option is then calculated from this distribution.

---

[14] See Margrabe, William "The Value of an Option to Exchange One Asset for Another" (March 1978) Journal of Finance Volume 33 177–186.

[15] See Kemna A.G.Z. and Vorst A.C.F. "A Pricing Method for Options Based on Average Asset Values" (1987) Journal of Banking and Finance Vol. 14 113–129.

The basic approach requires the first two moments of the probability distribution of the arithmetic average to be calculated. It is assumed that the distribution of the arithmetic average is log normal with those first two moments. This approach requires the mean and variance of the true distribution to be calculated using a recursive relationship. The true distribution is then approximated using an Edgeworth series transformation to a log normal density function with mean and variance equal to the moments calculated of the true distribution. This allows an analytic solution to be used.

In practice, the model usually used is that proposed by Levy and Turnbull[16]. **Exhibit 7.7** sets out the Levy–Turnbull approach. The Levy–Turnbull approximation approach is relatively robust when tested against Monte Carlo simulations and is faster[17].

Exhibit 7.7   Average Rate Options – Levy/Turnbull Approximation Model[18]

Assuming the asset price is log normal and the average is calculated through continuous sampling, an average rate option is similar to an option on a futures contract. This allows the price of the average rate option to be calculated as:

$$\text{Call option premium} = e^{-rt}[\ F.N(d_1) - K.N(d_2)]$$
$$\text{Put option premium} = e^{-rt}[\ K.N(-d_2) - F.N(-d_1)]$$

Where

$$d_1 = [\ln (F/K) + (\sigma^2/2)\ T]/\sigma\sqrt{T}$$
$$d_2 = [\ln (F/K) - (\sigma^2/2)\ T]/\sigma\sqrt{T} = d_1 - \sigma\sqrt{T}$$
$$F = M_1$$
$$\sigma^2 = 1/t\ \ln(M_2/M_1)$$

M_1 (the first moment) and M_2 (the second moment) are calculated as follows:

$$M_1 = [(e^{(r-y)t} - 1)/((r - y)t)]S$$

---

[16]   See Turnbull, S. and Wakeman, L. "A Quick Algorithm for Pricing European Average Options" (September 1991) Journal of Financial Quantitative Analysis 377–389.

[17]   See Levy, Edmund and Turnbull, Stuart "Average Intelligence" in (1992) From Black Scholes to Black Holes; Risk Magazine, London at Chapter 23.

[18]   The version described is that from Hull, John (2000) Options, Futures and Other Derivatives – Fourth Edition; Prentice-Hall Inc., Upper Saddle River, NJ at Chapter 18 at 467–469.

$$M_2 = \{[(2e^{[2(r-y)+\sigma^2]t}S^2]/[(r - y - \sigma^2)(2r - 2y + \sigma^2)t^2]\}$$
$$+ \{[2S^2/((r - y)t^2)][(1/(2(r - y) + \sigma^2)) - (e^{(r-y)t})/(r - y + \sigma^2)]\}$$

Where

S = spot price of the asset
K = strike price of the option
σ = volatility
t = time to option expiry
r = discount rate
y = income on asset

3.5.6 Average Rate Options – Numerical/Simulation Approaches

Where the average rate option uses infrequent, discrete averaging and/or where the averaging period does not cover the term of the option, it is often necessary to use numerical/simulation approaches. This requires simulating the paths of the asset price based on an assumed stochastic process, distributional assumptions and assumed volatility. The average rate option price is derived from the generated distribution of the average price[19].

3.5.7 Average Rate Options – Hedging/Risk Management

Average rate option transactions are typically hedged using dynamic replication techniques. The use of dynamic replication techniques will typically require the use of not only the spot asset, but also forward contracts corresponding to the averaging dates. This reflects the higher interest rate risk in the structures.

The behaviour of the hedge is different to that of a conventional option. The average rate option will typically be characterised by reduced volatility as time to maturity reduces. An increasing portion of the average price, upon which the settlement value would be based, is known. This reduces the gamma of the option (reflecting the fact that its delta becomes more stable as time to maturity reduces). This makes the average rate options relatively easier to hedge. This is particularly the case on a portfolio basis.

---

[19] This includes identifying a partial differential equation that must be satisfied by the option and solving it numerically; see Vecer, Jan "Unified Asian Pricing" (June 2002) Risk 113–116.

4 Lookback Options

4.1 Lookback Options – Concept[20]

Lookback options are a path dependent option. Lookback options are also referred to as reset, "no regrets" or "hindsight" options. Lookback options entail an option where the strike price of the option is set at maturity of the option. The strike price is set at the minimum asset price (for a call) or maximum asset price (for a put) over a pre-determined prior period (the lookback period).

Lookback options allow the purchaser to look back over the life of the option and set the strike price at the most favourable asset price that has prevailed during the relevant time horizon. The purchaser can, by using a lookback call (put) option, purchase (sell) the underlying asset at the lowest (highest) price that has occurred over the life of the option. The strike is then used to determine the option payoff at expiration normally. **Exhibit 7.8** sets out the structure of a lookback option.

4.2 Lookback Options – Structural Features

The payoffs for a lookback option are summarised below:

Type of Option	Payoff of Call Options	Payoff of Put Options
Conventional	Maximum $[0; S_m - K]$	Maximum $[0; K - S_m]$
Lookback option	Maximum $[0; S_m - S_{min}]$	Maximum $[0; S_{max} - S_m]$

Where:

K = strike price
S_m = spot price at maturity
S_{min} = lowest spot price attained over lookback period
S_{max} = highest spot price attained over lookback period

There are a number of structures for lookback options, including:
- **Full lookback options** – where the purchaser can select the strike price based on asset prices over the entire period from commencement of the transaction to expiry of the option.

---

[20] See Ong, Michael "Exotic Options: The Market and their Taxonomy" in Nelken, Israel (Editor) (1996) The Handbook of Exotic Options; Irwin Professional Publishing, Chicago at Chapter 1 at 16–17; Smithson, Charles (1998) Managing Financial Risk – Third Edition; McGraw-Hill, New York at Chapter 13 at 274; Ravindran, K. (1998) Customised Derivatives; McGraw-Hill, New York at Chapter 3 at 149–160; Nelken, Israel (2000) Pricing, Hedging & Trading Exotic Options; McGraw-Hill, New York at Chapter 16.

Exhibit 7.8   Lookback Options – Structure

The graph below sets out the path of prices for an asset. The call and put strike for a lookback option (based on this asset price path) are set out on the graph.

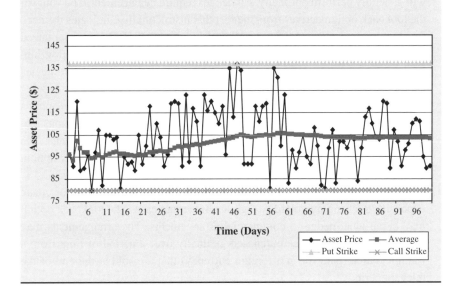

- **Partial lookback options** – where the purchaser selects a subset of the period from commencement to expiry as the lookback period for determining the option strike price based on asset prices achieved.

The issue of sampling frequency identified in relation to average rate options is also relevant to lookback options.

4.3   Lookback Options – Economics and Applications

Lookback options represent a variation on traditional option structures, allowing the purchaser to nominate the strike price at maturity *rather than commencement*. The change in the timing of determination of the strike price creates highly structured risk transfer possibilities.

The value of the lookback option will be greater than or equal to that of a comparable conventional option. This greater expected value will result in a higher premium cost of a lookback option.

The logic underlying lookback options points to the subtle interaction between risk management objectives of option purchasers and the characteristics of options. The major attractions for the purchaser of a lookback option include:

- Lookback options provide hedgers with the capacity to implement a hedge that will generally perform optimally. All hedges require management. The value of the lookback option derives from the fact that it structurally eliminates the need for this ongoing management. In effect, the purchaser is always guaranteed optimal performance, thereby eliminating the risk of errors in entering into hedges. The errors include the specific timing of entry into option strategies and/or selection of the strike price.
- Lookback options entail less trading than strategies where ordinary options are used. The purchaser effectively eliminates the need to replace options that have moved deep out-of-the-money as a result of asset price movements. The lookback option structure automatically replaces the out-of-the-money option, creating new at-the-money options on a continuous basis.
- Lookback options create the capacity to trade particular price paths or create exposures to changing volatility regimes. In certain cases, the lookback option may be an ideal hedge to commercial arrangements. The arrangements may entail selling commodities purchased gradually over a period of time from a foreign source (paid for in a foreign currency) that are sold at the end of the relevant period.

The benefits of the lookback option are obtained at the cost of the higher premium cost. The lookback option is ideal for a purchaser who wishes to be absolutely certain of the best asset price and is prepared to pay for this right. For the purchaser, the payoff on a lookback option will be greatest where the actual realised volatility of the underlying asset price is higher than the implied volatility used to price the option. The purchaser will also benefit if there is be a discontinuous jump in the underlying asset price.

In practice, the high cost of lookback options has discouraged use of the product. Lookback options are most often used in currency, equity and commodity markets. The principal types of applications include:

- **Hedging** – hedging activities are driven by the ability to guarantee purchase or sale at the best price. This may be attractive in periods of high volatility or uncertainty.
- **Speculation** – lookback options may be attractive for speculation during periods of high volatility or uncertainty. The volatility would allow the speculator to take advantage of a favourable shift in the asset price by the automatic adjustment to the lookback strike. This increases the likelihood of a gain on the option.

- **Separation of investment and currency decisions** – investors are often faced with complex investment choices where the investment involves currency risk. Movements in currency values affect the return on the asset. In practice it may be difficult to optimise both asset and currency decisions simultaneously. Lookback options provide a mechanism for decoupling the asset investment and currency timing decision. **Exhibit 7.9** sets out an example of this type of application.

Exhibit 7.9   Lookback Options – Application

Assume a US investor wishes to purchase Japanese stocks. This is based on an expectation that Japanese stocks will appreciate over the investment horizon of 1 year. The investor is uncertain about the direction of the US$/Yen exchange rate. A weaker Yen/stronger US$ will adversely affect the investment returns. The loss on the currency may reduce or exceed the expected gain on the Japanese stocks.

Assume the investor wishes to purchase US$10 million of stocks. At the current spot rate (US$1 = Yen 120), the investor will have a Yen currency exposure equivalent to Yen 1,200 million. Assume that the Japanese stocks appreciate by 10% over the 1 year period. The value of the Japanese stock investment will be Yen 1,320 million. If the US$ strengthens/Yen weakens to an exchange rate higher than US$1 = Yen 132.00, then the investor will suffer a loss in US$ terms. If the US$/Yen exchange rate is in the range of Yen 120 to 132, then the investor will show a positive return but less than the 10% increase in the underlying stocks.

The US investor could hedge the currency exposure using a forward (sell yen/buy US$) or a purchased option (Yen put/US$ call). As the investor does not know the future Yen value of the investment, there are difficulties in structuring a hedge[21].

An alternative is to purchase a Yen put/US$ call lookback option. The expiry of the option is set at 1 year (the investment horizon). Under the lookback option, if the Yen is lower than the US$/Yen exchange rate in 1 year (investment maturity) at any point over the 1 year period, then the investor will receive a payoff based on the difference between the final exchange rate and the lowest Yen rate.

The economic effect of the currency lookback option is that the US$ investor enters the Yen investment at the most favourable exchange rate over the 1 year period. This has the effect of minimising the potential loss due to currency movements. In effect, it separates the asset investment decision from the currency timing decision. Although the currency lookback option will be significantly more expensive than a conventional option, the expected investment returns (after adjustment for the premium cost) may be sufficiently attractive for the strategy to be considered.

---

[21] This problem is known as the quanto problem. It can be hedged using a quanto (quantity adjusting option); see Chapter 11.

4.4   Lookback Options – Pricing/Valuation and Hedging

4.4.1   Lookback Options – Valuation Approach

The value of the lookback option will be greater than or equal to that of a comparable conventional option. This greater expected value will result in a higher premium cost of a lookback option. In practice, lookback options are significantly more expensive than comparable conventional options (up to 2/3 times greater than the premium on a conventional option). The premium of a lookback option (both in absolute terms and relative to a conventional option) increases with increased volatility, the term of the option and the length of the lookback period.

The valuation approach for lookback options relies on a rollover replication strategy[22]. Under this approach, the seller of a lookback option initially replicates the sold option position by buying a comparable conventional option with the same expiration date and strike price as the lookback option sold. The hedge is adjusted dynamically by selling the bought option and purchasing a new option with a lower (higher) strike price each time the asset price achieves a new low (high) price in the case of a call (put) option. The new options have an expiry date corresponding to that of the original option. The process is repeated each time a new low or high is achieved.

Under the rollover replication strategy, the cost of simulating the lookback option is the price of the initial option and the expected cost of successive rollovers in new options. The rollover results in cost because the seller must purchase a more expensive option (closer to at-the-money strike) and sell a cheaper option (out-of-the-money strike). The timing of the rollovers is not known in advance. This is similar to the classical delta neutral option replication strategy where the exact timing of the hedge adjustments is also unknown at the outset.

4.4.2   Lookback Options – Valuation Models[23]

There are primarily two approaches to valuation of lookback options:
• Closed form mathematical models.
• Numerical/simulation approaches.

---

[22] See Garman, Mark "Recollection in Tranquillity" (March 1989) Risk 16–18.
[23] See Briys, Eric Bellalah, Mondher, Mai, Huu Minh and De Varenne, Francois (1998) Options, Futures and Exotic Derivatives: Theory, Application and Practice; John Wiley & Sons, Chichester at Chapter 19; Wilmott, Paul (1998) Derivatives: The Theory and Practice of Financial Engineering; John Wiley & Sons, Chichester at Chapter 17; Hull, John (2000) Options, Futures and Other Derivatives – Fourth Edition; Prentice-Hall Inc.,

A closed form model for pricing a lookback option can be derived based on the rollover replication strategy. The value of the lookback option is separated into two components:

- Premium for the ordinary option.
- Value of a strike bonus option.

The pricing of the ordinary option is undertaken normally. The strike bonus option derives its value from the capacity to lower the strike price. The value of the lookback option is equal to the sum of the value of the ordinary option struck at the achieved minimum, plus the value of the strike bonus option[24].

Several researchers have proposed a mathematical solution to the valuation of lookback options[25]. **Exhibit 7.10** sets out the closed form solution to pricing lookback options. **Exhibit 7.11** sets out an example of valuation of a lookback option.

The closed form solution has a number of weaknesses, including[26]:

- The model assumes continuous sampling. In practice, sampling will generally be discrete. This means that the lookback option will generally be worth less than the value obtained using the continuous sampling model. The closed form solution also does not hold for partial lookbacks.
- Lookback options are sensitive to the term structure and volatility of interest rates. In a conventional European option, the relevant interest rate is the rate to option maturity. In the case of lookback options, the value of the option will be sensitive to the term structure and volatility of interest rates. The model does not incorporate this effect.
- Lookback options are also sensitive to the term structure and smile/skew of volatility. This is because discontinuous price jumps will significantly affect the value of a lookback option.

Upper Saddle River, NJ at Chapter 18 at 465–466; Nelken, Israel (2000) Pricing, Hedging & Trading Exotic Options; McGraw-Hill, New York at Chapter 16.

[24] The solution for a strike bonus option was presented in Garman, Mark "Recollection in Tranquillity" (March 1989) Risk 16–18. there is a singularity ("black hole") in the formula. For a way around this, see Briys, Eric Bellalah, Mondher, Mai, Huu Minh and De Varenne, Francois (1998) Options, Futures and Exotic Derivatives: Theory, Application and Practice; John Wiley & Sons, Chichester at Chapter 19 at 405–407.

[25] See Garman, Mark "Recollection in Tranquillity" (March 1989) Risk 16–18. See also Goldman, M. Barry, Sosin, Howard B., and Gatto, Mary Ann "Path Dependent Options: Buy at the Low, Sell at the High" (December 1979) Journal of Finance 1111–1128; Heynen, Ronald and Kat, Harry "Selective Memory" (November 1994) Risk 73–76; Cheng, Wai-Yan and Zhang, Shuguang "The Analytics of Reset Options" (Fall 2000) Journal of Derivatives 59–71.

[26] See Garman, Mark "Recollection in Tranquillity" (March 1989) Risk 16–18.

- The closed form model only holds for European lookback options. This is because the lookback option is valued as a combination of a conventional option and a strike bonus option. If the conventional option is exercised early, then the purchaser must also give up the strike bonus option which must be cancelled. This means that the value of the American lookback does not satisfy the additive property of a European lookback option that is used to derive the closed form solution.

Many of the weaknesses identified can be addresses using numerical/simulation approaches. Numerical or simulation approaches use a binomial tree or a Monte Carlo to generate asset price paths. The strike is then reset based on the asset price path. The expected value of the option is then calculated. It is then discounted back to provide the value of the lookback option[27]. Numerical/simulation models can incorporate discrete sampling, interest rate terms structures and volatility skews/term structures.

Exhibit 7.10 Lookback Options – Pricing Model[28]

Assume

S = spot price of the asset
S_{min} = minimum stock price achieved to date (as at trade date $S_{min} = S$)
S_{max} = maximum stock price achieved to date (as at trade date $S_{max} = S$)
K = strike price of the option
σ = volatility
t = time to option expiry
r = discount rate
y = income on asset

The value of a European lookback call is:

$$Se^{-yt}N(a_1) - Se^{-yt}[(\sigma^2/2(r-y))N(-a_1)] - S_{min}e^{-rt}[N(a_2)$$
$$- ((\sigma^2/2(r-y))e^{Y1}N(-a_3))]$$

---

[27] For numerical models for pricing lookback options, see Hull, John C. and White, Alan "Efficient Procedures for Valuing European and American Path-Dependent Options" (Fall 1993) Journal of Derivatives 21–31; Kat, Harry M. "Pricing Lookback Options Using Binomial Trees: An Evaluation" (December 1995) Journal of Financial Engineering 375–397.

[28] The version described is that from Hull, John (2000) Options, Futures and Other Derivatives – Fourth Edition; Prentice-Hall Inc., Upper Saddle River, NJ at Chapter 18 at 465–466.

Where

$$a_1 = [\ln(S/S_{min}) + (r - y + \sigma^2/2)t]/\sigma\sqrt{t}$$
$$a_2 = a_1 - \sigma\sqrt{t}$$
$$a_3 = [\ln(S/S_{min}) + (-r + y + \sigma^2/2)t]/\sigma\sqrt{t}$$
$$Y1 = -[2(r - y - \sigma^2/2)\ln(S/S_{min})]/\sigma^2$$

The value of a European lookback put is:

$$S_{max}e^{-rt}[N(b_1) - ((\sigma^2/2(r - y))e^{Y2}N(-b_3))] + Se^{-yt}[(\sigma^2/2(r - y))N(-b_2)]$$
$$- Se^{-yt}N(b_2)$$

Where

$$b_1 = [\ln(S_{max}/S) + (-r + y + \sigma^2/2)t]/\sigma\sqrt{t}$$
$$b_2 = b_1 - \sigma\sqrt{t}$$
$$b_3 = [\ln(S_{max}/S) + (r - y + \sigma^2/2)t]/\sigma\sqrt{t}$$
$$Y2 = [2(r - y - \sigma^2/2)\ln(S_{max}/S)]/\sigma^2$$

Exhibit 7.11   Option Premium – Lookback Options versus Comparable Conventional Options

1. Assumptions

Assume the following parameters:

Asset Price ($)	100.00
Strike Price ($) (for conventional options)	100.00
Current Strike ($) (for lookback options) set at asset price	100.00
Maturity	See below
Volatility (% pa)	See below
Interest Rates (% pa)	6.00
Asset Income (% pa)	3.50
Exercise	European

Additional assumptions in relation to lookback options include:

Sampling	Discrete daily sampling over the full term of the option commencing upon the trade date

Conventional options are valued using a binomial tree with 500 steps. Lookback options are valued using a closed form model.

2. Option Premiums – Lookback Options versus Conventional Options
Comparative option premiums ($) for lookback options and comparable conventional options are set out below:

Maturity: 6 month

		Conventional Options		Lookback Option	
		Call	Put	Call	Put
Volatility	20% pa	6.14	4.92	11.16	10.92
Volatility	25% pa	7.51	6.29	13.65	13.96
Volatility	30% pa	8.88	7.66	16.08	17.06

Maturity: 12 month

		Conventional Options		Lookback Option	
		Call	Put	Call	Put
Volatility	20% pa	8.85	6.47	15.52	15.04
Volatility	25% pa	10.73	8.34	18.81	19.40
Volatility	30% pa	12.61	10.22	21.99	23.89

4.4.3   Lookback Options –Hedging/Risk Management

A lookback option position can be replicated by a static hedge (by a series of rollover transactions) or a dynamic hedge (using the underlying asset based on the hedge ratios). Under the static approach, the premium received for the sale of the strike bonus option (effectively the difference between the premium of the lookback and a conventional option) is used to finance the rollovers required to hedge the lookback position. The dynamic replication of lookback options is more complex.

The hedging risks of lookback options are more complex than for conventional options. The complexity includes:

• The delta of a lookback option is typically smaller in value than for conventional options. As new minimum (maximum) asset price levels are established, the delta may become fixed and not subject to change (that is, it becomes asymmetrical).

• The gamma of lookback options (the rate of change of hedge ratio) is typically higher than for ordinary options. In addition, gamma can become one sided (where the delta becomes fixed). It is also very high as the asset price approaches either new minimum or maximum levels.

- The theta (or time decay) of lookback options is higher than for corresponding conventional options. In certain circumstances, the theta of a lookback option behaves unconventionally. For example, it may become positive where the theta of the European option component becomes so positive that it outweighs the otherwise negative influence of the strike bonus option.

The difficulties increase the complexity of managing the risk of lookback option portfolios. Historical studies conducted suggest that using historical data on major currencies lookback options can be replicated through the hedging techniques identified. The empirical analysis indicates that lookback option payoffs for both purchasers and writers vary significantly from initial estimations[29].

5 Ladder Options

5.1 Concept [30]

Ladder options entail a special type of path dependent option where the *strike price* is periodically reset (automatically) and the intrinsic value guaranteed when the price of the asset underlying the option trades at or above pre-specified asset price levels. For example, in the case of a ladder call on an asset with an initial strike price of $100 and ladder re-set level set at $5 intervals, if the price rises above $105, then the strike price is automatically reset to $105 and the $5 price appreciation is locked in.

The major attraction of the ladder option structures is the automatic ability to lock in gains from movements in asset prices. This increases the probability of optimal exercise of the option. This is achieved at a cost that is favourable relative to other comparable option products such as look back options. A ladder option operates in some respects as a *discrete* lookback option.

---

[29] See Garman, Mark "Recollection in Tranquillity" (March 1989) Risk 16–18.

[30] See Ong, Michael "Exotic Options: The Market and their Taxonomy" in Nelken, Israel (Editor) (1996) The Handbook of Exotic Options; Irwin Professional Publishing, Chicago at Chapter 1 at 17; Smithson, Charles (1998) Managing Financial Risk – Third Edition; McGraw-Hill, New York at Chapter 13 at 274–275; Ravindran, K. (1998) Customised Derivatives; McGraw-Hill, New York at Chapter 3 at 149–160; Nelken, Israel (2000) Pricing, Hedging & Trading Exotic Options; McGraw-Hill, New York at Chapter 14.

5.2   Structural Features

The payoffs for a ladder option are summarised below:

Type of Option	Payoff of Call Options	Payoff of Put Options
Conventional	Maximum $[0; S_m - K]$	Maximum $[0; K - S_m]$
Ladder option	Maximum $[0; S_m - K;$ $L_i - K]$	Maximum $[0; K - S_m;$ $K - L_i]$

Where:

  K = strike price

  S_m = spot price at maturity

  L_i = highest (lowest) ladder level reached during the term of the call
     (put) option

The key structural features of ladder options include:

- **Ladders** – the number of ladder levels (referred to as "rungs" or "steps") is agreed between the purchaser and seller of the ladder option. As the number of ladder rungs increases, the ladder option starts to approach the economic characteristics of a lookback option.
- **Ladder levels** – the asset price/rate levels of each ladder level are agreed between the purchaser and seller of the ladder option.
- **Price sampling** – the sampling process (daily etc) must be agreed between the purchaser and seller of the ladder option.
- **Ladder operation** – the period during the life of the option that the ladder option operates must be agreed between the purchaser and seller of the ladder option.

5.3   Economics & Applications

The value of a ladder option will be greater than or equal to the value of a comparable conventional option. The payoff of a ladder option at expiry is the higher of:

- Zero.
- Payoff of a conventional European option.
- Difference between strike price and highest ladder level achieved.

Exhibit 7.12 sets out the general pattern of payoffs under a ladder option. **Exhibit 7.13** sets out the payoff of a ladder option under different asset price paths.

Exhibit 7.12   Ladder Options – Payoff Behaviour

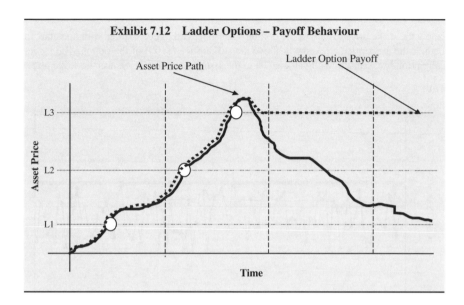

Exhibit 7.13   Ladder Options – Payoff Behaviour (Detailed)

Assume a ladder call option with a strike price of $100 and 2 ladder levels set at $110 and $120. Assume that there are 5 possible asset price paths. The payoff under each of the asset price paths is set out below:

Path 1 and Path 2

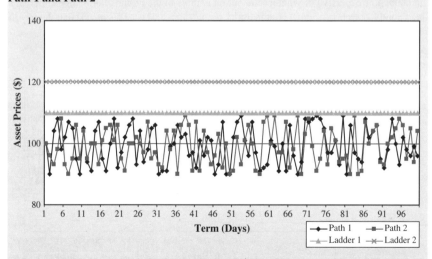

Paths 1 and 2 do not reach the first ladder level ($110). This means that the ladder option payoff is the same as that for a conventional option. In Path 1, the asset price at expiry is below the strike price ($100) of the option. The ladder call option expires with no value. In Path 2, the asset price at expiry is above the strike price ($100) of the option. The ladder call option is exercised, with value equal to the asset price at maturity, less the strike price.

Path 3

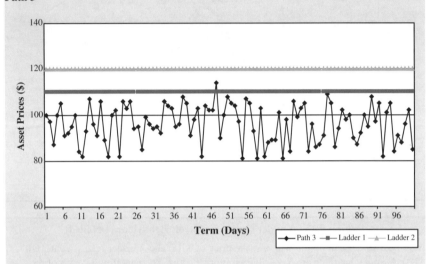

Path 3 reaches the first ladder level ($110). This means that the ladder option payoff is a minimum of the ladder level ($110) and the strike price ($100) or $10. This value is guaranteed, irrespective of whether the option expires in the money. Path 3 does not reach the second ladder level ($110) or at maturity remain above $110. This means that the payoff of the ladder call option is $10.

Path 4 and Path 5

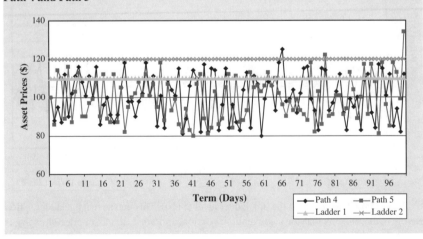

Paths 4 and 5 reach the first ladder level ($110) and the second level ($120). This means that the ladder option payoff is a minimum of the ladder level ($120) and the strike price ($100) or $20. This value is guaranteed, irrespective of whether the option expires in the money. Path 4 at maturity is below the second ladder level ($120). This means that the payoff of the ladder call option is $20. In Path 5, the asset price at expiry is above the second ladder price ($120). This means that the ladder call option has a value equal to that for a conventional call option. This equals the asset price at maturity less the strike price.

The major attraction of ladder options is the ability to lock in gains from favourable movements in asset prices, increasing the probability of gain from the option. A ladder option allows this to be achieved at a lower cost than comparable structures such as lookback options.

Ladder options are used primarily in equities. The structure is used less frequently in currency and commodity transactions. Ladder options are generally used in the following applications:

- **Structured hedges** – this involves using ladder options to hedge exposures where the impact of favourable directional movements in the underlying asset price/rate are locked in. This is the case, irrespective of the final asset price/rate. In effect, the ladder option is used to maximise the value of the option. The optimisation of exercise timing is entirely passive and dependent upon the preset ladders (number and price/rate levels). The key factor is the desire to improve the performance of the option. **Exhibit 7.14** sets out an example of using a ladder option for structured hedging.
- **Structured investment products** – this is focused primarily on retail investors attracted by the passive optimisation feature of ladder options. There is demand from investors for structures that inherently optimise option value by (generally) passive exercise rules embedded within the option. This demand can be motivated by the type of investor (retail investment products) or asset liability matching requirements (regular streams of cash flows that often motivate the use of average rate options). The key factor is the fact that the value of option will rarely be at its optimal level at the maturity of the option. This makes it unlikely that investors (particularly retail investors) will be able to optimise the value of the option through sale or early exercise[31].

---

[31] See Das, Satyajit (2004) Structured Products Volume 2; John Wiley & Sons (Asia), Singapore at Chapter 4.

Exhibit 7.14   Ladder Options – Application

Assume a US manufacturer imports electronic components priced in Yen. The importer seeks to protect itself against a stronger Yen/weaker US$. The importer wishes to obtain protection against a weaker US$ through the purchase of a US$ put/Yen call option.

Assume the spot exchange rate is US$1 = Yen 120. The importer expects the Yen to strengthen to Yen 115 and potentially to Yen 110.

In order to hedge its Yen exposure, the importer purchases a European style 6 month Yen call/US$ put ladder option with a strike of US$1 = Yen 120 and two ladder levels of Yen 115 and Yen 110. The ladder option payoff will be the maximum of:

• Zero.
• Difference between the spot rate at option maturity and the highest ladder levels reached over 6 months.
• Difference between US$/Yen exchange rate and option strike at maturity option expiry.

The payoffs under this option at maturity are as follows:

1. If the US$/Yen exchange rate never trades at Yen 115 and at maturity is below the strike (Yen 120), then the option payoff is zero. The importer obtains a benefit as it can now enter the spot market and purchase Yen at a lower US$ cost. The importer's effective exchange rate is the actual spot rate at which it purchases Yen, adjusted for the cost of the option.
2. If the US$/Yen exchange rate never trades at Yen 115 and at maturity is above the strike (Yen 120), then the option payoff is the difference between the US$/Yen exchange rate and option strike at maturity option expiry. For example, assume the US$/Yen exchange rate at option maturity is Yen 118. The ladder option payoff is Yen 2. The importer exercises the option and purchases Yen at an exchange rate of US$1 = Yen 120 to lock in the gain on the option. The importer's US$ cost is at the level guaranteed by the option strike level (Yen 120), less the premium cost.
3. If the US$/Yen exchange rate trades at Yen 115 at any time over the life of the option, but not above Yen 110, and at maturity is below Yen 115, then the option payoff is a guaranteed Yen 5. The importer's effective exchange rate is the actual spot rate at which it purchases Yen, adjusted for the Yen 5 payoff of the ladder option and the cost of the option.
4. If the US$/Yen exchange rate trades at Yen 120 at any time over the life of the option and at maturity is below Yen 120, then the option payoff is a guaranteed Yen 10. The importer's effective exchange rate is the actual spot rate at which it purchases Yen, adjusted for the Yen 10 payoff of the ladder option and the cost of the option.
5. If the US$/Yen exchange rate trades at Yen 120 at any time over the life of the option and at maturity is above Yen 120, then the option payoff is the difference between the US$/Yen exchange rate and option strike at maturity option expiry. For example, assume the US$/Yen exchange rate at option maturity is Yen 100. The ladder option payoff is Yen 20. The importer exercises the option and purchases Yen at an exchange rate of US$1 = Yen 120 to lock in the gain on the option. The importer's US$ cost is at the level guaranteed by the option strike level (Yen 120), less the premium cost.

The ladder option hedges the importer's currency exposure. In cases 1, 2 and 5, the ladder option behaves exactly like the purchase of a conventional Yen call/US$ put option. The only difference is that the cost of the ladder will typically be higher than for a conventional option. This will reduce the effective exchange rate achieved (increase US$ cost of the imports). In cases 4 and 5, the payoff of the ladder option exceeds the loss suffered by the importer as a result of movements in the spot rate. This is because the payoff on the ladder is based on the highest level achieved by the Yen (relative to the pre-set ladder levels) during the life of the option. The Yen moved in one direction (stronger Yen/weaker US$) but then reversed its direction. This allows the importer to achieve a lower US$ cost of its Yen imports than under a conventional option.

5.4   Variations

There are a number of variations on the ladder option structure. The major variation is cliquet options[32] (also known as ratchet or reset options). Cliquet options entail a structure where the strike price is reset *on pre-determined dates*. The intrinsic value of the option is also locked in on the pre-determined date. Cliquet options are treated as time dependent options[33].

5.5   Pricing/Valuation & Hedging[34]

The value of a ladder option will be greater than or equal to the value of a comparable conventional option. Ladder options are path dependent. This means that closed form solutions to valuation of these structures are not available. Pricing of ladder options is based on decomposing the ladder options into components.

Ladder options are constructed using combinations of conventional options and barrier options[35]. The value of the ladder is the sum of the prices of the component options. The hedging of ladder options follows this replication logic. The individual components are hedged by trading in the underlying asset or more typically the component options.

Exhibit 7.15 sets out a replication methodology for the creation of the ladder option.

---

[32] The term cliquet is based on the French *vilbrequin a cliquet* for ratchet brace.
[33] See Chapter 8. There is debate as to whether cliquet options are path or time dependent options.
[34] See Street, Andrew "Stuck up a Ladder?" (May 1992) Risk 43–44; Nelken, Israel (2000) Pricing, Hedging & Trading Exotic Options; McGraw-Hill, New York at Chapter 14.
[35] See Chapter 9.

Exhibit 7.15   Ladder Options – Replication/Pricing

1.   Ladder Option

Consider a ladder call option on a stock index. The index is trading at a level of 500.00. The ladder call option has a strike price of the spot level of the index (500.00) and has 1 ladder level of 5% (index levels of 525). The option is for 6 months.

The purchaser is guaranteed a payout of the ladder levels (i.e., 5%) in the event where the index *trades* above those levels, even if the index level *at maturity* is below the relevant ladder level or option strike price. If the index is above the upper ladder level, then the purchaser benefits to the full extent that the index exceeds the strike price.

2.   Ladder Option – Replication

The construction of the ladder option requires the following decomposition involving a series of standard and barrier options on the index:

1. Purchase a European 6 month call option with a strike of 500.
2. Sell a 6 month European put option with a strike of 500.
3. Purchase a knock out put with a strike level of 500 and an outstrike level of 525.
4. Purchase a European 6 month put option with a strike of 525.
5. Sell a 6 month knock out put option with a strike of 525 with an out strike level of 525.

The operation of this set of options can be analysed as follows:

- If the index value of 525 (the ladder level) is not reached over the life of the option, then Options 2, 3, 4 and 5 either expire unexercised or cancel themselves out, leaving only Option 1. This means that the transaction has the normal payoff of a European option.
- If the index value of 525 (the ladder level) is reached, then Options 3 and 5 is knocked out. Options 1 and 2 combine to create a synthetic long position. The combination of the synthetic long position and the purchased put at the index level of 525 (Option 4) locks in a minimum value of 25 (525–500) where the asset price at maturity is below 525. It also enables the holder to participate in any rise above 525 through the synthetic long position that is then sold at maturity.

In essence, the structure combines a call option with a series of put spreads/knock-out put spreads.

The process can be repeated to create additional steps in the ladder if required. Additional ladder levels are created by adding additional put spreads/knock-out put spreads at the relevant ladder levels.

3.   Ladder Option – Pricing

The ladder option value is the total premiums paid and received in creating the structure. Hedging of the ladder option is based on trading the option components.

The value of the ladder option is calculated below. The following assumptions are used to derive the individual option values:

Asset Price	500.00
Strike Price	500.00 or 525
Outstrike Levels (for barrier options)	500 or 525
Maturity	6 months

Volatility (% pa)	20[36]
Interest Rates (% pa)	6.00
Asset Income (% pa)	1.50
Exercise	European

The individual option premiums (index points) are as follows:

Option	Option Premium (Index Points)
Purchase a European 6 month call option with a strike of 500	−33.52
Sell a 6 month European put option with a strike of 500	+22.48
Purchase a knock out put with a strike level of 500 and an outstrike level of 525	−13.97
Purchase a European 6 month put option with a strike of 525	−35.44
Sell a 6 month knock out put option with a strike of 525 with an out strike level of 525	+19.87

The net cost of the options is 40.58 index points. The premium cost of the ladder call option is 8.12% (40.58/500). This can be compared to the cost of a conventional call option (strike of 500) of 6.70% and the cost of a comparable lookback option of 11.74%.

6 Shout Options[37]

Shout options are a variation on ladder options. Shout options allow the purchaser to select (actively) the minimum payout of the option while retaining the right to gain from further favourable movements in the underlying asset's price. Shout options combine features of lookback, ladder and cliquet options.

Under the term of a shout, at any one time during the term of the option the purchaser can lock in the then current intrinsic value of the option. The payoff of the shout option is the greater of the intrinsic value guaranteed at the time of the shout or at expiry of the option. The term "shout" refers to the fact that the option purchaser must contact the seller ("shout") to lock in the intrinsic value at any time prior to expiry of the option. The purchaser in effect shouts to lock in a price high (low) for a shout call (put) option.

---

[36] No adjustment is made for the effect of the volatility skew/smile.

[37] See Thomas, Bryan "Something to Shout About" (May 1994) Risk 56–58; Smithson, Charles (1998) Managing Financial Risk – Third Edition; McGraw-Hill, New York at Chapter 13 at 275–277; Nelken, Israel (2000) Pricing, Hedging & Trading Exotic Options; McGraw-Hill, New York at Chapter 9.

The key characteristic of the shout option is the ability of the purchaser to *actively select* the asset price level at which to lock in the guaranteed intrinsic value of the option. This is in contrast to the ladder option where the ladder levels are pre-agreed.

The payoffs for a ladder option are summarised below:

Type of Option	Payoff of Call Options	Payoff of Put Options
Conventional	Maximum $[0; S_m - K]$	Maximum $[0; K - S_m]$
Ladder option	Maximum $[0; S_m - K; L_i - K]$	Maximum $[0; K - S_m; K - L_i]$
Shout option	Maximum $[0; S_m - K; S^* - K]$	Maximum $[0; K - S_m; K - S^*]$

Where:

K = strike price
S_m = spot price at maturity
L_i = highest (lowest) ladder level reached during the term of the call
      (put) option
S^* = the asset price nominated (shouted) by the purchaser

Shout options can be structured with single or multiple opportunities to lock in intrinsic value prior to maturity. The period over which the shout can be exercised can also be limited.

The shout option will only be "shouted" to specify the minimum payout levels where the option has intrinsic value. The rational shout strategy for the purchaser would be to seek to exercise the right to shout at any time during the life of the option, if the value of the option by shouting is greater than the value of the option without shouting. This allows the purchaser to presumably act on expectations of future asset price movements. The structure is ideal for a trader who believes that they have the ability to call turns in market direction.

Shout options are used infrequently. The major asset class in which shout options are used is currency. The demand for shout options is driven by the lower option premium relative to competing structures (primarily lookback options). Shout options are also potentially attractive to investment/asset managers and liability managers who believe themselves capable of accurately predicting future market asset price movements.

Shout options will have greater value than a comparable conventional option. This reflects the ability to lock in a guaranteed intrinsic value. The higher expected value translates into a higher premium cost. A shout option should be more expensive than a ladder option as the lock in level can be chosen at the option of the purchaser. The value of the shout option is also related to the number of shouts permitted.

The value of a shout option at the shout date is equivalent to the intrinsic value at the time of the shout, and the price on an at-the-money European option on that date. Shout options can be priced using a binomial approach. The expected values of the option, including the value at the date of the shout, are discounted back to calculate the price of the shout option[38].

Exhibit 7.16 sets out an example of a shout option.

Exhibit 7.16   Shout Options – Example

1. Shout Option

Consider a shout call option on a stock index. The index is trading at a level of 500.00. The shout call option has a strike price of the spot level of the index (500.00). The purchaser has 1 shout at any time till expiry of the option. The option is for 6 months.

2. Shout Option Payoff

The shout option has the characteristics of a normal call option on the index until the shout. At the date of the shout, the purchaser is guaranteed a payout of the intrinsic value on the day of the shout in the event that the index is below the relevant shout level or option strike price at maturity. For example, if the purchaser shouts when the index is trading at 550, a minimum payoff of 50 index points is locked in. If the index at maturity is below 550, then the purchaser receives 50 index points. If the index is above the shout level (550), then the purchaser benefits to the full extent that the index exceeds the strike price.

3. Shout Option – Pricing

The value of the shout option is calculated based on the following assumptions:

Asset Price	500.00
Strike Price	500.00
Maturity	6 months
Volatility (% pa)	20[39]
Interest Rates (% pa)	6.00
Asset Income (% pa)	1.50
Exercise	European
Shout	1 shout at any time in the time to expiry

The premium cost of the shout option is 8.42% (42.10/500). This can be compared to the cost of a conventional call option (strike of 500) of 6.70%, the cost of a ladder call option (single ladder level of 525) of 8.12%, and the cost of a comparable lookback option of 11.74%.

---

[38] See Thomas, Bryan "Something to Shout About" (May 1994) Risk 56–58; Nelken, Israel (2000) Pricing, Hedging & Trading Exotic Options; McGraw-Hill, New York at Chapter 9.

[39] No adjustment is made for the effect of the volatility ske/smile.

7 Swing Options

Swing options are options where the purchaser buys a package of several European options. The total number of options that can be exercised is set at a number lower than the number of the total options purchased. In effect, the purchaser has an option on exercising some but not all of the purchased options.

The key factor underlying swing options is the ability to lower the cost of options. The lower cost is achieved at the cost of limiting the protection offered by the options. This assumes that only *some* but *not all* the purchased protection will be required.

Swing options have proved popular in interest rates and commodity markets (in particular, the electricity market). Typical applications and swing option structures include:

- **Interest rate swing options** (also known as the auto or flexible cap)[40] – in a typical structure, a borrower purchases an interest rate cap to manage the risk on its floating rate borrowing. The cap is for 5 years on 3 month LIBOR at a strike of 6.50% pa. The normal cap would provide the borrower with a payoff in *any* period that 3 month LIBOR is above 6.50% pa. This means that the borrower is buying protection on 19 quarterly interest rate set dates (excluding the first period for which the interest rate fixing is known). The swing option provides the borrower with protection on, say 10 quarterly periods. This means that the borrower can exercise the cap-lets on *only 10 interest rate set dates*. The borrower can exercise on any 10 of the 19 possible interest rate set dates. This means that the borrower is only protected from interest rates above the cap level on around half the interest rate periods. The borrower's interest rate cost will only be affected if the actual spot 3 month LIBOR rate is above the strike price on more than 10 interest rate periods. If interest rates increase significantly and stay at high levels, then the interest rate swing option will *delay* but not completely protect against the impact of higher interest rates. There are two possible exercise structures – automatic (where all the cap-lets that expire in-the-money are automatically exercised up to the maximum permitted number) or voluntary exercise (where the purchaser has the right to choose to exercise on any interest rate date where the interest rate fixing is above the strike rate up to the maximum permitted number).
- **Commodity swing options** – in a typical structure, a commodity producer or consumer will agree to sell or buy a commodity at a fixed price over say a

---

[40] See Bjerregaard, Morten and Sidenius, Jakob "Flexible Caps" (20 April 1998) Derivatives Week 7.

180 day period, but be limited to say 30 deliveries. This means that the producer (consumer) obtains protection against lower (higher) commodity prices for part of the period. To the extent that prices are generally above (below) the strike price, the swing option provides equivalent protection to a conventional option. If prices fall (increase) sharply and remain at the new levels for periods in excess of the specified number of deliveries, then the producer and consumer are unprotected beyond the number of exercises permitted.

The value of swing options is generally calculated using a modified binomial tree or Monte Carlo simulation. The asset price paths are generated and the expected payoff discounted to provide the current price of the option. The valuation of interest rate swing options requires the use of interest rate term structure models[41].

Exhibit 7.17 sets out an example of a swing option.

Exhibit 7.17   Swing Options – Example

1.   Swing Option
Consider a swing put option on electricity. A producer purchases a swing option that gives the producer the right to buy electricity at a strike price of $200/megawatt hour. The option has a term of 6 months. The producer is permitted to deliver up to 30 megawatt hours over the term of the option. The producer can deliver, at most, 1 megawatt hours in a single day.

2.   Swing Option Payoff
The swing option has the characteristics of a normal put option on the electricity. If electricity prices are above $200/megawatt hour then the option will not be exercised. The producer will sell electricity normally in the spot market at prices higher than $200/megawatt hour. If the electricity prices are below $200/megawatt hour, then the producer will exercise the swing put option. The option can only be exercised for up to 30 megawatt hours and no more than 1 megawatt hours in any one day. This means that the producer will be protected from lower electricity prices only if the prices infrequently falls below the strike price. The producer also has protection on a limited amount of electricity.

3.   Swing Option – Pricing
The value of the shout option is calculated based on the following assumptions:

Asset Price ($)	200
Strike Price ($)	200
Maturity	6 months
Volatility (% pa)	30

---

[41] See Das, Satyajit (2004) Derivative Products & Pricing; John Wiley & Sons (Asia), Singapore at Chapter 8.

Interest Rates (% pa)	6.00
Asset Income (% pa)	0.00
Exercise	European
Swing	Up to 30 megawatt hours with up to 1 megawatt hours in a single day

The premium cost of the swing put option is $418.93. This can be compared to the cost of a conventional American put option (on 30 megawatt hours for the full 6 months) of $434.37.

8   Other Path Dependent Options

A number of other path dependent options have also emerged:

- **Mirage options**[42] – these are European style options where the payoff is the compounded value of returns on a specified asset over a part of the term of the option. In the mirage structure, the highest or lowest returns over part of the term of the option are excluded. For example, in a typical example involving a commodity, a consumer purchases a mirage call option on the cumulative increase in commodity prices over 1 year. The mirage feature entails the highest compounded return over any 3 month period during the 1 year term of the option being excluded. The payoff to the purchaser is based on the compounded return over the other 9 months. The structure is designed to lower the cost of the option by reducing the expected payoff of the option.

- **Passport options**[43] – these are options on actively traded accounts. The purchaser pays a premium. The purchaser retains any gain from trading but is immunised against any loss. The payoff is driven by the changes in the value of the asset held in the trading account and also the trading strategy employed by the trader. The payoff is path dependent. The payoff is also dependent upon the strategy of the trader. The purchaser of the option will rationally seek to maximise the gain on the contract[44]. This means that the value of the passport option will correspond to the trading strategy that is most likely to maximise the value of the option. Valuation of the option is complex as it needs to incorporate

---

[42] See Smithson, Charles "What's New in the Options Markets?" (May 2000) Risk 54–55.

[43] See Hyer, Tom, Lipton-Lifschitz, Alexander and Pugachevsky, Dmitry "Passport to Success" (September 1997) Risk 127–131; Lipton, Alexander "Similarities and Self Similarities" (September 1999) Risk 101–105.

[44] This will be the case unless the seller places constraints on the trading strategy employed.

the trading strategy used. The valuation of the model must establish the value maximising trading strategy in relation to the asset, as it will drive the value of the passport option.

9 Summary

Conventional European options have payoffs that are dependent upon the asset price at maturity. Path dependent options are characterised by payoffs that are a function of the particular path that asset prices follow over the life of the relevant option. The path of the underlying asset price is used to determine the payoff or the structure of the option. A variety of path dependent option structures are available. Common path dependent options include average rate options, lookback options, ladder options and swing options. Variations on individual structures are also available.

Path dependent options are driven primarily by the ability to reduce option premium, increase the probability of gain and match underlying assets or liabilities. Path dependency in option structures is a source of value to option users. The value of path dependent options frequently derives from the nature of underlying assets or liabilities that are consistent with a path dependent hedge. Path dependent options are also frequently used to implement passive or active exercise rules to maximise the value of the option. This reflects recognition of the fact that the value of the option will rarely be at its maximum level at the maturity of the option.

8
Time Dependent Options

1 Overview

Time dependent options are options where the purchaser has the right to nominate a specific characteristic of the option as a function of time. In this Chapter, the major types of time dependent forms of exotic options are discussed.

The structure of the Chapter is as follows:

- The key dynamics of time dependent options are outlined.
- Each of the major types of path dependent exotic options is described. This includes preference (chooser) options, cliquet options and forward start options.

2 Time Dependent Options[1]

Time dependent options are options where the purchaser has the right to nominate/alter specific characteristics of the option at a certain time before the expiration of the option. The specific characteristics of the option that can be set/altered are the call or put feature (preference or chooser option), strike price/guaranteed intrinsic value (cliquet option) or the strike price (forward start option). The specified dates on which certain characteristics of the option can be altered/set are pre-set. All time dependent options are also path dependent.

Exhibit 8.1 sets out the major types of time dependent options. The most common types of time dependent options include:

- **Preference (chooser) options** – the specific feature of this option is that it is not specifically characterised as either a call or a put at the time of entry. At a predetermined date, usually after commencement but no later than expiration

---

[1] For a discussion of time dependent options, see Ong, Michael "Exotic Options: The Market and their Taxonomy" in Nelken, Israel (Editor) (1996) The Handbook of Exotic Options; Irwin Professional Publishing, Chicago at Chapter 1; Smithson, Charles (1998) Managing Financial Risk – Third Edition; McGraw-Hill, New York at Chapter 13.

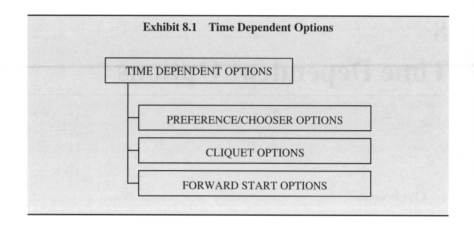

Exhibit 8.1   Time Dependent Options

(known as the choice date), the purchaser can nominate whether or not the transaction is a call or a put option.

- **Cliquet options** – where the option has a lock in feature similar to a ladder option, except that is based on the asset price on a pre-specified future date or dates.
- **Forward start options** – where the option is granted some time after entry, based on asset prices at the grant date.

There are a number of variations on the structures outlined. The variations represent structural changes to the basic elements of the primary time dependent options.

Exotic option structures are generally driven by the following objectives:

- Reduction in option premium.
- Alteration in risk profile, including increased probability of gain, quantification of loss, or optimal exercise timing.
- Asset liability matching.

Path dependent options are driven primarily by the capacity of the structures to reduce option premium, increase the probability of gain and match underlying assets or liabilities. The exact factor driving individual path dependent structures varies between types of options.

Preference options are used primarily to create exposure to asset price/rate volatility where the direction of the price change is not anticipated. Preference options are also used to hedge exposures where the *direction of the exposure* is not known with certainty. Cliquet options are primarily used to improve the payoff on the option by locking in the intrinsic value of the option on pre-specified days over the term of the option. Forward start options are used to hedge future exposures at the market rate on a given future date. Forward start options are used primarily in equities in connection with employee share option schemes.

3 Preference Options

3.1 Preference Options – Concept[2]

Preference options are time dependent options. Preference options entail a structure where the type of option (put or call option) is not set at the time of purchase. At the time of purchase, the purchaser and the seller agree the underlying asset, strike price, expiry date and the option premium. The purchaser selects the type of option on or by a predetermined date (the choice or put/call determination date) prior to expiration of the preference option. At the choice date, the purchaser of the preference option elects whether the option is going to be a call or a put option. Preference options are also known as chooser options.

The use of preference options first gained in popularity during the 1991 Gulf conflict. During this period, some oil producers and purchasers used preference options to hedge against the extreme volatility in oil prices. Preference options were also used by investors to monetise expectations on oil prices and speculate on future oil prices.

3.2 Preference Options – Structure

The key structural feature of preference options is the choice date. There are in fact two relevant dates – the choice date and the expiry of the option. The purchaser of the preference option selects whether the option is to be a put or call option on the choice date. In a typical structure, the purchaser can select the put or call feature at any time until the choice date. The expiry date of the option operates normally. Once selected, the put or call option is settled normally at the expiry date. All other features of a preference option are identical to the characteristics of a comparable conventional option.

---

[2] See Ong, Michael "Exotic Options: The Market and their Taxonomy" in Nelken, Israel (Editor) (1996) The Handbook of Exotic Options; Irwin Professional Publishing, Chicago at Chapter 1 at 27–28; Smithson, Charles (1998) Managing Financial Risk – Third Edition; McGraw-Hill, New York at Chapter 13 at 283–284; Ravindran, K. (1998) Customised Derivatives; McGraw-Hill, New York at Chapter 3 at 119–129.

There are two types of preference options:
- **Standard Chooser Options** – where the call and put options have identical strikes and expiry dates.
- **Complex Chooser Options** – where the call and put options have different strike prices and expiry dates.

3.3 Preference Options – Economics & Applications

The payoff of a preference option at maturity is identical to that of a conventional put or call option with similar terms. This reflects the fact that at the choice date, the purchaser selects whether the preference option is a call or put option.

The payoff of a preference option *at the choice date* is the maximum of the values of a call or put option with the same strike and remaining time to expiry. Both the call and put are valued at the asset price *at the choice date*. This means that the purchaser will economically select the call or put feature based on the value of the respective options at choice. In practice, this will mean the option in-the-money will be selected.

Analytically, a preference option has a similar payoff profile to that of a purchased European straddle (entailing the simultaneous purchase of put and call options with the same strike price and expiry date). The unique feature of the preference option is that the purchaser *must choose* the put or call option (effectively cancelling the other option) by or at the choice date. The preference option will have a lower premium than a comparable straddle. This is because the purchaser must choose the call or put option prior to expiry date.

Preference options are not common. Standard preference options are more commonly used than complex preference options.

The structure is used infrequently; primarily in currency, commodity and equity markets. The primary applications of preference options are focused on the following situations:
- **Trading in conditions of extreme volatility in asset prices** – this involves taking positions in asset prices during periods of high price volatility or uncertainty. It involves trading around events (for example, elections or major profit/economic announcements) that have the potential to significantly affect asset prices/rates. In both cases, the actual outcome of the event is highly uncertain. It is probable that the event will affect the asset price and cause *a large change* in prices. The preference option allows the trader to take positions under these conditions at a lower cost than the comparable option straddle. **Exhibit 8.2** sets out an example of using preference options to trade in this way.

- **Hedging where the direction of the exposure is unknown**[3] – this relates to situations when the direction of the underlying price exposure is unknown. For example, a company invests in a venture in a foreign location. The investor seeks to hedge the currency exposure. In order to hedge its currency exposure, the economic outcome of the venture (whether it will be profitable or incur losses) must be projected. A normal hedge (using a forward or option) is difficult when there is uncertainty about the direction of the exposure. It may inadvertently *increase* the investor's currency exposure *through the position in the hedge*. The company can potentially use a currency preference option to hedge against changes in value in the investment. **Exhibit 8.3** sets out an example of using preference options to hedge exposure where the direction of the exposure is potentially unknown.

Exhibit 8.2   Preference Options – Trading Price Volatility

Assume a company has scheduled a special analyst briefing regarding a new product. The analyst briefing is to be held in 2 weeks. It is anticipated that the company will reveal new information at the analyst briefing regarding progress on a research and development project vital to the future of the company. The release of this information will provide considerable impetus to the equity price of the company. It is not clear whether the information will be positive or negative.

Assume a trader wants to take a position in the stock. This is based on the expectation that the news will cause the stock to move outside its current trading range. The trader expects the news to be positive. However, the outcome is clearly uncertain. The trader wants to use options to take the position to limit potential losses. The trader's time horizon is 6 months.

Assume the following facts:

Stock price:	$100.00
Dividend:	1.00% pa
Interest rate:	6.00% pa (for 6 months)
Volatility:	25% pa

Three potential strategies are considered:

1. **Purchase a European call option** (strike of $100 and 6 months to expiry) – this is designed to take advantage of the anticipated increase in the stock price. The premium cost of this option is 8.18%.
2. **Purchase a straddle entailing the purchase of a call and put option** (strike of $100 and 6 months to expiry) – this is designed to take advantage of the increase *or decrease* in the stock price. The premium cost of the straddle is 13.93% (8.18% for the call and 5.75% for the put option).

---

[3]   See Kaufman, Jim "Will it be a Put or a Call? You Choose" in (1994) Corporate Finance Risk Management and Derivatives Yearbook 35–38.

3. **Purchase a preference option** (strike of $100, 6 months to expiry and a choice date of 1 month from purchase date) – this is designed to take advantage of any increase or decrease in the stock price. The strategy is time dependent. The purchaser must select the call or put feature of the option no later than 1 month after the purchase of the option. This is after the announcement. It is designed to allow the information to be impounded in the stock price. The premium cost of the preference option is 9.98%.

Assume the company announces that the research and development project has been discontinued. It also announces that it is taking a large charge to earnings as a result of writing off the research and development expenditure. The stock falls sharply (by say 25%). The outcome under the three strategies is as follows:

1. **Purchase a European call option** – the call option loses value and the trader suffers a loss of the premium (8.18% pa).
2. **Purchase a straddle** – the call option component of the straddle loses value. The put option component of the straddle is now in-the-money. The gain to the trader is approximately 10.07% (the fall in the stock price (25%) adjusted for the cost of the straddle (13.93%)).
3. **Purchase a preference option** – the purchaser selects the put option under the preference option as it is in-the-money. The gain to the trader is approximately 15.02% (the fall in the stock price (25%) adjusted for the cost of the preference option (9.98%)).

The preference option offers similar exposure to the straddle for the trader at a lower cost. The preference option requires the choice to be exercised by 1 month from the date of purchase. The trader can only take advantage of directional movements up to that time. If the directional move takes place after that time, then the trader has greater capacity to benefit from the straddle than the preference option.

Exhibit 8.3   Preference Options – Hedging Uncertain Exposures[4]

Assume a corporation has currency exposure generated by its manufacturing operations in Singapore. The exposure is to the US$/S$ exchange rate.

The firm's Singapore operations consist of two operations. There is a local market sales function. The other is a manufacturing operation. The budget for the forthcoming year indicates that the operations will result in a loss of S$15 million. The loss is the result of the net exposure of the two operations.

Based on the forecasts, the corporation anticipates a short S$/long US$ position. It is exposed to S$ strength/US$ weakness. In order to hedge this exposure, the corporation purchases S$/sells US$ for 1 year to cover the loss.

Assume the following exchange rates:

Spot rate: US$1 = S$1.40
Forward rate (1 year)   US$1 = S$1.50

---

[4]   This example is similar to but not identical to that mentioned in Kaufman, Jim "Will it be a Put or a Call? You Choose" in (1994) Corporate Finance Risk Management and Derivatives Yearbook 35–38.

The corporation's budget is based on the forward rate of US$1 = S$1.50. Based on the market rates, the corporation locks in the US$ value of the loss at US$10 million (S$15 million/US$1 = S$1.500) by buying forward S$/selling US$.

The actual performance of the Singapore operations differs from the forecast. The revised forecast (3 months into the budget period) projects a profit of S$15 million. The S$30 million swing in projected earnings is driven by the better than expected performance of the local market sales function.

The impact of this change is that the corporation is now long S$/short US$. The forward hedge exacerbates this position. The forward position makes the corporation further long S$/short US$. The total position is long S$30 million ($15 million profit from operations and the $15 million currency hedge). During this period the S$ has weakened against the US$, compounding the problem. The current forward rate to the end of the year is US$1 = S$1.65.

The net loss for the corporation is as follows:

Item	Operating Earnings	Forward Hedge
Amount	S$15,000,000	S$15,000,000
Budgeted/contracted exchange rate	US$1 = S$1.50	US$1 = S$1.50
Budgeted/contracted US$ Value	US$10,000,000	US$10,000,000
Current exchange rate	US$1 = S$1.65	US$1 = S$1.65
Current US$ value	US$9,090,909	US$9,090,909
Gain/loss	−US$909,091	−US$909,091

The total loss is US$1,818,182 (around 18% of the exposure).

The use of a conventional option would not have effectively hedged the corporation's currency exposure as the direction of the exposure is not known. The corporation would have purchased a US$ put/S$ call to hedge the forecast short S$/long US$ position. When the position changed into a long S$/short US$ position, the option would have lost value as it was out-of-the money. The premium on this option would have been lost. The long S$/short US$ position would have been unhedged exposing the corporation to the risk of loss from a weaker S$. The use of option would not have been an effective hedge. It would have *capped the losses on the hedge to the option premium paid.*

A preference option strategy may have offered a more effective hedge. This would entail the corporation purchasing a preference option on the US$/S$. The preference option would have face value of S$15 million, a strike of S$1.50, an expiry of 12 months (the risk horizon) and a choice date of 3 months. The selection of the choice date is dictated by the corporation's belief that the revised forecasts available by that time will provide a better projection of the likely financial performance of the unit.

Under this strategy, at the choice date the corporation will select the put or call feature, depending upon the projected exposure. If the forecast continues to show losses, then the US$ put/S$ call is selected. If the forecast now shows a profit, then the US$ call/S$ put is selected.

The performance of the preference option based hedge is complex. The major factors driving this complexity include:

• **Exchange rate movements** – movements in exchange rate will affect the performance of the hedge. If the forecast shows losses, then the US$ put/S$ call should be selected.

If the S$ has appreciated during this period, then this will be the case. If the S$ has depreciated, then the S$ put/US$ call will be in-the-money. The rational exercise strategy entails selecting the S$ put/US$ call that is immediately closed out in the market. The corporation would then be free to hedge in the market (using either forwards or options) at an improved exchange rate (lower amount of US$ required to finance losses). A similar situation would exist where the forecast was for profits 3 months into the budget year. This highlights the ability to use preference options to optimise the performance of the hedge.

- **Exposure amount** – the preference option is effective in hedging changes in the direction of the exposure. Changes in the *face value or amount to be hedged* are not covered by the use of preference options. In this example, the amount of the exposure (S$15 million) remains the same, although the position changes from a short to a long position. In practice, this may not be the case, as the amount of the exposure may also change. The preference option does not protect against this change.

Preference options offer potential benefits in the implementation of hedging strategies when the forecast exposure is uncertain due to factors beyond the control of the corporation.

3.4   Preference Options – Pricing/Valuation and Hedging

The approach to the valuation of preference options depends on whether the instrument is a standard or complex chooser. The valuation approaches commonly used are as follows:

- **Standard preference options**[5] – put-call parity relationships are used to derive a closed form valuation model. **Exhibit 8.4** sets out the approach used to derive the value of a standard preference option. **Exhibit 8.5** sets out an example of the value of a standard preference option under different assumptions.
- **Complex preference option**[6] – unlike a standard preference option, there are no closed form solutions for a complex preference option where the strike prices

[5]   See Rubinstein, Mark "Options for the Undecided" (April 1991) Risk 43; Nelken, Izzy "Square Deals" (April 1993) Risk 56–59. See also See Briys, Eric Bellalah, Mondher, Mai, Huu Minh and De Varenne, Francois (1998) Options, Futures and Exotic Derivatives: Theory, Application and Practice; John Wiley & Sons, Chichester at Chapter 14; Wilmott, Paul (1998) Derivatives: The Theory and Practice of Financial Engineering; John Wiley & Sons, Chichester at 183–185; Hull, John (2000) Options, Futures and Other Derivatives – Fourth Edition; Prentice-Hall Inc., Upper Saddle River, NJ at Chapter 18 at 461–462.

[6]   See Rubinstein, Mark "Options for the Undecided" (April 1991) Risk 43; Nelken, Izzy "Square Deals" (April 1993) Risk 56–59. See also See Briys, Eric Bellalah, Mondher, Mai, Huu Minh and De Varenne, Francois (1998) Options, Futures and Exotic Derivatives: Theory, Application and Practice; John Wiley & Sons, Chichester at Chapter 14;

and/or time to expiry of the call or put option are not identical. Numerical solutions can be used to value complex preference options. The approaches rely on numerically solving the critical value of the spot asset price at the choice date, so that the value of the underlying call and put options is the same. This allows an analytical solution for the complex preference option to be determined[7].

Exhibit 8.4   Preference Options – Pricing Approach[8]

A standard preference option is priced using the assumption that the option payoff will be the maximum of the value of a put or call option. This assumes that the spot price on the choice date is known and both options have the same strike and expiry date.

This is driven by the fact that the purchaser will always choose the more valuable option on the choice date. If the call is more valuable than the put, then the preference option purchaser will select the call. If the put is more valuable than the call, then the call is exercised and a synthetic put created by shorting the underlying asset forward at the strike price to the expiry date.

This means that if both the call and put options are European and have identical strike prices and time to expiry, the preference option at the choice time will have a value equal to:

$$\text{Maximum } (C; P)$$

Where

C = value of a call option with strike price (K), time to expiry (t) at asset price (S_{t*})
P = value of a put option with strike price (K), time to expiry (t) at asset price (S_{t*})
S_{t*} = asset price at time t^*
t^* = choice date

Assume:

r = interest rate to expiry date
y = income on asset

Hull, John (2000) Options, Futures and Other Derivatives – Fourth Edition; Prentice-Hall Inc., Upper Saddle River, NJ at Chapter 18 at 461–462.

[7] Mark Rubinstein has presented a solution to the valuation of complex preference options that is similar to the valuation of compound options; see Rubinstein, Mark "Options for the Undecided" (April 1991) Risk 43. An alternative approach to the pricing of complex preference and compound options using numerical quadrature has been proposed by Izzy Nelken; see Nelken, Izzy "Square Deals" (April 1993) Risk 56–59.

[8] The version described is that from Hull, John (2000) Options, Futures and Other Derivatives – Fourth Edition; Prentice-Hall Inc., Upper Saddle River, NJ at Chapter 18 at 461–462.

Using put call parity, the value of the preference option can be re-stated as:

$$\text{Maximum } (C; P) = \text{Maximum } (C, C + Ke^{-r(t-t^*)} - S_{t^*}e^{-y(t-t^*)})$$

$$= C + e^{-y(t-t^*)}\text{Maximum } (0, Ke^{-(r-y)(t-t^*)} - S_{t^*})$$

This demonstrates that the preference option can be replicated as follows:
- Buying a call option with strike price K and time to expiration t.
- Buying $e^{-y(t-t^*)}$ put options with strike price $Ke^{-(r-y)(t-t^*)}$ and time to expiration t^*.

The value of the preference option can now be calculated as the value of the two options (using Black-Scholes-Merton or binomial models).

Exhibit 8.5   Preference Options – Valuation Example

The value of the preference option is calculated based on the following assumptions:

Asset Price	100.00
Strike Price	100.00
Maturity	6 months
Volatility (% pa)	20
Interest Rates (% pa)	6.00
Asset Income (% pa)	1.50
Exercise	European
Choice Date	3 months

The premium cost of the preference option is 9.62%. This can be compared to the cost of the equivalent straddle of 11.21% (6.82% for the call and 4.39% for the put option).

The sensitivity of the preference option premiums is set out below. All parameters are the same as above, unless specified otherwise.

Volatility	Strike Price	Choice Date (1 month)	Choice Date (3 month)	Choice Date (5 month)	Premium for Straddle
20%	90	13.43%	13.82%	14.38%	14.67%
20%	100	8.09%	9.62%	10.74%	11.21%
20%	110	10.46%	11.57%	12.56%	13.00%
30%	90	15.62%	16.83%	18.05%	18.60%
30%	100	11.89%	14.24%	15.94%	16.65%
30%	110	13.86%	15.95%	17.60%	18.30%

The hedging and risk management of preference options depends on the underlying product. In the case of standard preference options, it is possible to replicate the relevant option by trading in a portfolio of calls and puts. The trader will trade in one of the options. At the choice date, the trader will either maintain the position or use put call parity to convert the option held to the one selected. For example, assume that the trader initially purchased a call, but due to asset price changes the purchaser selects a put. The trader would need to create a synthetic put by selling the asset forward to the expiry date of the option.

Complex preference options are replicated in a similar manner. Complex preference shares are more difficult to hedge. This usually occurs by trading in portfolios of underlying options to replicate the underlying straddle.

Both standard and complex preference options can be hedged by dynamic replication techniques to hedge the risk of the options underlying the preference options.

4   Cliquet Options[9]

Cliquet options[10] (also known as ratchet or reset options) are a variation on ladder options[11]. Cliquet options entail the ability to lock in the intrinsic value of the option based on market asset prices *on a pre-determined date*. The purchaser is guaranteed a minimum payoff of the intrinsic value calculated on the prescribed date, irrespective of asset price changes over the remaining time to expiry of the option.

The payoffs for a cliquet option are summarised below:

Type of Option	Payoff of Call Options	Payoff of Put Options
Conventional	Maximum $[0; S_m - K]$	Maximum $[0; K - S_m]$
Ladder option	Maximum $[0; S_m - K; L_i - K]$	Maximum $[0; K - S_m; K - L_i]$
Cliquet option	Maximum $[0; S_m - K; S_i - K]$	Maximum $[0; K - S_m; K - S_i]$

Where:

K = strike price
S_m = spot price at maturity

---

[9]   See Ong, Michael "Exotic Options: The Market and their Taxonomy" in Nelken, Israel (Editor) (1996) The Handbook of Exotic Options; Irwin Professional Publishing, Chicago at Chapter 1 at 17; Smithson, Charles (1998) Managing Financial Risk – Third Edition; McGraw-Hill, New York at Chapter 13 at 274–275; Nelken, Israel (2000) Pricing, Hedging and Trading Exotic Options; McGraw-Hill, New York at Chapter 7.
[10]   The term cliquet is based on the French *vilbrequin a cliquet* for ratchet brace.
[11]   See Chapter 7.

L_i = highest (lowest) ladder level reached during the term of the call
(put) option

S_i = the spot price at the agreed time at which the intrinsic value of the option
is determined.

The key structural features of cliquet options include:
- **Dates** – the number of dates on which the lock in feature operates is agreed between the purchaser and seller of the cliquet option.
- **Price sampling** – the sampling process (daily etc) must be agreed between the purchaser and seller of the cliquet option.

The value of a cliquet option will be greater than or equal to the value a comparable conventional option. The payoff of a cliquet option at expiry is the higher of:
- Zero.
- Payoff of a conventional European option.
- Difference between the strike price and the asset price on the relevant date(s).

Exhibit 8.6 sets out the general pattern of payoffs under a cliquet option.

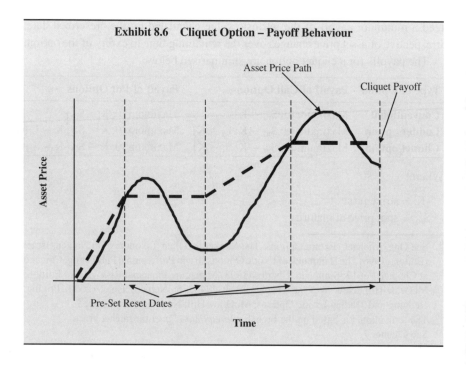

Exhibit 8.6   Cliquet Option – Payoff Behaviour

The benefits of cliquet options are similar to the benefits of ladder options. There is a difference between cliquet and ladder options. The ladder option's performance is *asset price based* while the cliquet option's performance is based *on the asset price on specific dates*. The cliquet option is both path and time dependent.

The major attraction of cliquet options is the ability to lock in gains from favourable movements in asset prices, increasing the probability of gain from the option. A cliquet option allows this to be achieved at a lower cost than comparable structures such as lookback options.

Cliquet options are used primarily in equities. The structure is used less frequently in currency and commodity transactions. Cliquet options are generally used in the following applications:

• **Structured hedges** – this involves using cliquet options to hedge exposures where the impact of favourable directional movements in the underlying asset price/rate is locked in. This is the case irrespective of the final asset price/rate. In effect, the cliquet option is used to maximise the value of the option. The optimisation of exercise timing is entirely passive and dependent upon the preset lock in dates. The key factor is the desire to improve the performance of the option.

• **Structured investment products** – this is focused primarily on retail investors attracted by the passive optimisation feature of cliquet options. There is demand from investors for structures that inherently optimise option value by (generally) passive exercise rules embedded within the option. This demand can be motivated by the type of investor (retail investment products) or asset liability matching requirements (regular streams of cash flows that often motivate the use of average rate options). The key factor is the fact that the value of option will rarely be at its optimal level at the maturity of the option. This makes it unlikely that investors (particularly retail investors) will be able to optimise the value of the option through sale or early exercise[12]. The cliquet option maximises the return on the option be locking in the intrinsic value on the prescribed dates.

The value of a cliquet option is calculated using numerical or simulation approaches. In practice, this entails the use of binomial trees or Monte Carlo simulations to generate asset price paths. The value of the cliquet is calculated by establishing the expected payoff that is then discounted back to the valuation date[13].

Exhibit 8.7 sets out an example of a cliquet option.

---

[12] See Das, Satyajit (2004) Structured Products Volume 2; John Wiley & Sons (Asia), Singapore at Chapter 4.

[13] See Nelken, Israel (2000) Pricing, Hedging and Trading Exotic Options; McGraw-Hill, New York at Chapter 7. For a discussion of the pricing in the market, see Patel, Navroz "The Evolving Art of Pricing Cliquets" (July 2002) Risk 22–24.

Exhibit 8.7   Cliquet Options – Example

1. Cliquet Option
Consider a cliquet call option on a stock index. The index is trading at a level of 500.00.
The cliquet call option has a strike price of the spot level of the index (500.00). The option
is for 6 months. There is a single lock-in date 3 months from commencement.

2. Cliquet Option Payoff
The cliquet option has the characteristics of a normal call option on the index until the lock
in date. At the lock in date, the intrinsic value of the option is calculated. The purchaser
is guaranteed a payout of the intrinsic value on the relevant day in the event that the index
is below the locked in value or option strike price at maturity. For example, if the index is
trading at 550 on the lock in date, a minimum payoff of 50 index points is locked in. If the
index at maturity is below 550, then the purchaser receives 50 index points. If the index is
above the lock in level (550), then the purchaser benefits to the full extent that the index
exceeds the strike price.

3. Cliquet Option – Pricing
The value of the cliquet option is calculated based on the following assumptions:

Asset Price	500.00
Strike Price	500.00
Maturity	6 months
Volatility (% pa)	20[14]
Interest Rates (% pa)	6.00
Asset Income (% pa)	1.50
Exercise	European
Lock in Date	Single lock in date in 3 months

The premium cost of the cliquet option is 7.92% (39.61/500). This can be compared
to the cost of a conventional call option (strike of 500) of 6.70%, the cost of a ladder call
option (single ladder step at 525) of 8.12% and the cost of a comparable lookback option of
11.74%.

---

5   Forward Start Options[15]

Forward start options entail an option where the purchaser buys the right to receive
an option on a future date (the grant date). The option received has a strike price
set at the asset price on the grant date.

---

[14] No adjustment is made for the effect of the volatility skwe/smile.
[15] See Ong, Michael "Exotic Options: The Market and their Taxonomy" in Nelken, Israel
     (Editor) (1996) The Handbook of Exotic Options; Irwin Professional Publishing, Chicago

Forward start options are used primarily in the following applications:

- **Interest rate forward start options** (known as periodic caps or floors) – this structure entails non conventional interest rate caps and floors. In a conventional cap or floor, the strike price of the cap-lets or floor-lets is agreed at the time of entry into the transaction. In a periodic cap or floor, the strike of each cap-let and floor-let is set at the start of each period, usually as a margin relative to the spot interest rate. **Exhibit 8.8** sets out an example of this type of application of forward start options.
- **Employee equity option schemes** – this entails employee incentive schemes where the employees are awarded options that will commence with at-the-money spot strikes at future dates.

The major attraction of forward start options is the lower cost of the structure. The lower structure reflects the lower expected payout under a forward start option. The fact that the option is not received until the grant date and the strike is set *at the spot price on the grant date* means that the purchaser is unprotected up to this price/rate level. This lowers the value of the protection offered by a forward start option.

Forward start options can be valued using a number of approaches[16]:

- **Closed form solution** – a number of analytic solutions have been derived[17]. These approaches rely on using the expected value of the option at the grant date. **Exhibit 8.9** sets out the approach used in practice. **Exhibit 8.10** sets out an example of pricing forward start options.

---

at Chapter 1 at 28; Smithson, Charles (1998) Managing Financial Risk – Third Edition; McGraw-Hill, New York at Chapter 13 at 283–284; Ravindran, K. (1998) Customised Derivatives; McGraw-Hill, New York at Chapter 3 at 149–160.

[16] See Briys, Eric Bellalah, Mondher, Mai, Huu Minh and De Varenne, Francois (1998) Options, Futures and Exotic Derivatives: Theory, Application and Practice; John Wiley & Sons, Chichester at Chapter 14; Wilmott, Paul (1998) Derivatives: The Theory and Practice of Financial Engineering; John Wiley & Sons, Chichester at 234–237; Hull, John (2000) Options, Futures and Other Derivatives – Fourth Edition; Prentice-Hall Inc., Upper Saddle River, NJ at Chapter 18 at 460; Nelken, Israel (2001) Pricing, Hedging & Trading Exotic Options; McGraw-Hill, New York at Chapter 6.

[17] See Longstaff, Francis A. "Pricing Options with Extendible Maturities: Analysis and Applications" (July 1990) Journal of Finance 935–957; Rubinstein, Mark "Pay Now, Choose Later" (February 1991) Risk 13; Bouaziz, Laurent, Briys, Eric and Crouhy, Michel "The Pricing of Forward Starting Asian Options" (October 1994) Journal of Banking and Finance 823–839.

- **Numerical approach** – this entails the use of binomial trees or Monte Carlo simulations to generate asset price paths. The value of the forward start option is calculated by establishing the expected payoff that is then discounted back to the valuation date.

Exhibit 8.8   Periodic Cap Transaction[18]

Assume a borrower wishes to hedge its floating rate US$ borrowing pricing of 6 month LIBOR for 3 years. The borrower wishes to hedge with a 3 year cap on US$ 6 month LIBOR to limit its exposure to increased interest rates.

The current US$ yield curve is steeply upward sloping. This means that a conventional cap is expensive. This reflects the higher forward rates implied by the current yield curve. The borrower expects that *actual* spot US$ 6 month LIBOR will remain relatively constant. The borrower's expectation is that the *implied* forward rates are overestimating the rate of increase in US$ 6 month LIBOR.

The borrower can take advantage of its expectation and lower the cost of the cap by entering into a periodic cap. The periodic cap is a series of forward starting options on US$ 6 month LIBOR. The borrower purchases a 3 year US$ 6 month LIBOR cap at a strike set at the US$ 6 month LIBOR, set at the previous interest rate set date plus 50 bps.

The operation of the periodic cap is as follows:

- At the time of purchase of the cap, US$ 6 month LIBOR is at 4.50% pa.
- The strike rate for the first cap-let in 6 months time (6×12) is set at commencement LIBOR (4.50% pa) plus 50 bps. The strike rate is 5.00% pa. If US$ 6 month LIBOR sets at a rate above 5.00% pa, then the borrower will receive a payoff under the periodic cap. Assume that the actual US$ 6 month LIBOR sets at 4.80% pa. The cap-let expires out-of-the-money.
- The strike rate for the second cap-let in 12 months time (12×18) is set at LIBOR at 6 months (4.80% pa) plus 50 bps. The strike rate is 5.30% pa. If US$ 6 month LIBOR sets at a rate above 5.30% pa then the borrower will receive a payoff under the periodic cap. Assume that the actual US$ 6 month LIBOR sets at 5.50% pa. The cap-let expires in-the-money.
- The strike rate for the third cap-let in 18 months time (18×24) is set at LIBOR at 12 months (5.50% pa) plus 50 bps. The strike rate is 6.00% pa. If US$ 6 month LIBOR sets at a rate above 6.00% pa, then the borrower will receive a payoff under the periodic cap. Assume that the actual US$ 6 month LIBOR sets at 5.50% pa. The cap-let expires out-of-the-money.
- The process is repeated in an identical manner for each of the remaining interest rate periods over the remainder of the term of the cap.

The purchaser of a periodic cap incurs a lower premium cost for the forward start option relative to a package of conventional options. The purchaser benefits where the actual US$

---

[18] For examples of this type of application see Ravindran, K. (1998) Customised Derivatives; McGraw-Hill, New York at Chapter 3 at 149–160.

6 month LIBOR rates remain below the level implied by the US$ yield curve at the time of purchase. If US$ rates increase sharply and rapidly, then the purchaser is exposed to increased interest rate costs. In particular, the periodic cap will under perform a conventional cap. This reflects the fact that the protection offered by the periodic cap is based on *the higher prevailing market rates.*

Exhibit 8.9   Forward Start Options – Pricing Approach[19]

Forward start options are priced using expected value of the option received on the grant date.
Assume:

S = spot asset price on trade date
t = time to expiry
r = interest rate
y = asset income
S_{t*} = spot asset price at time t^*
t^* = grant date
C = value at trade date of an in-the-money option that has a term equal to $(t - t^*)$

The value of an at-the-money forward start option on the grant date is:

$$C[S_{t*}/S]$$

This is based on the fact that the premium of an European at-the-money call option is proportional to the asset price.
The value of the forward start option at trade date is:

$$e^{-rt^*}E\{C[S_{t*}/S]\}$$

Where
E = expectations in a risk neutral world.
C and S are known. $E[S_{t*}]$ is equal to $Se^{(r-y)t^*}$. This means that the value of the forward start option is given by:

$$Ce^{-yt^*}$$

Where the asset pays no income, the value of the forward start option is equal to the value of a comparable conventional at-the-money option.
An identical approach is used where, under the terms of the underlying forward start option, the strike price is set proportional to the asset price at the grant date. A similar approach is used with forward start put options.

---

[19] The version described is that from Hull, John (2000) Options, Futures and Other Derivatives – Fourth Edition; Prentice-Hall Inc., Upper Saddle River, NJ at Chapter 18 at 460.

Exhibit 8.10   Forward Start Options – Valuation Example

The value of the forward start option is calculated based on the following assumptions:

Asset Price	100.00
Maturity	1 year
Volatility (% pa)	20
Interest Rates (% pa)	6.00
Asset Income (% pa)	1.50
Grant Date	6 months

The premium cost of the forward start call option is 6.05%. The equivalent forward start put option is 4.39% pa. This can be compared to the costs of the comparable conventional options (strike price equal to $100 and expiry 6 months) that are 6.85% (call option) and 4.40% (put option).

---

6 Summary

Time dependent options are options where the purchaser has the right to nominate/alter specific characteristics of the option at certain times before the expiration of the option. The specific characteristics of the option that can be set/altered are the call or put feature (preference option), strike price/guaranteed intrinsic value (cliquet option) or the strike price (forward start option). The specified dates on which certain characteristics of the option can be altered/set are pre-set. All time dependent options are also path dependent.

Path dependent options are driven primarily by the capacity to reduce option premium, increase the probability of gain and match underlying assets or liabilities. Preference options are used primarily to create exposure to asset price/rate volatility where the direction of the price change is not anticipated. Preference options are also used to hedge exposures where the *direction of the exposure* is not known with certainty. Cliquet options are primarily used to improve the payoff on the option by locking in the intrinsic value of the option on pre-specified days over the term of the option. Forward start options are used to hedge future exposures at the market rate on a given future date. Forward start options are used primarily in equities in connection with employee share option schemes.

9
Limit Dependent Options

1 Overview

Limit dependent options are dependent upon the underlying asset price reaching a specified level over a nominated period (generally the maturity of the option). Limit dependent options are path dependent options. They are not only driven by the path taken by the asset price, but specifically the asset price reaching a nominated *price level*[1]. Limit dependent options are therefore both limit and path dependent. This feature gives rise to a number of unique features, which means that limit dependent options are a separate class of exotic option in their own right. Limit dependent options are examined in this Chapter.

The structure of the Chapter is as follows:
- General features of limit dependent options are outlined.
- Barrier (knock in/knock out) options are described.
- Valuation and hedging issues of barrier options are discussed.
- Structural variations of barrier options, including packaged forward structures incorporating barrier options, are examined.
- Defined exercise options (a special case of limit dependent options) are outlined.

2 Limit Dependent Options[2]

Limit dependent options are a special class of options incorporating a mechanism where the option contract is activated or deactivated as a function of the level of

---

[1] Limit dependent options are sometimes referred to as "extremum dependent" options; see Ong, Michael "Exotic Options: The Market and their Taxonomy" in Nelken, Israel (Editor) (1996) The Handbook of Exotic Options; Irwin Professional Publishing, Chicago at Chapter 1 at 14; Smithson, Charles (1998) Managing Financial Risk – Third Edition; McGraw-Hill, New York at Chapter 13 at 270.

[2] For a discussion of limit dependent options, see Ong, Michael "Exotic Options: The Market and their Taxonomy" in Nelken, Israel (Editor) (1996) The Handbook of Exotic

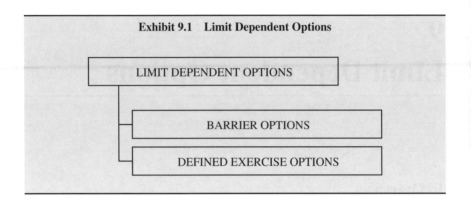

Exhibit 9.1   Limit Dependent Options

the underlying asset price. **Exhibit 9.1** sets out the major types of limit dependent options. The most common types of time dependent options include:

- **Barrier options** – barrier (knock in/knock out) options are the most common type of limit dependent option. In a typical structure, a barrier option may appear or disappear (depending on the agreed contractual arrangements) based on the performance in price terms of the underlying asset.
- **Variations on barrier options** – a variety of barrier options exist. Major variations include combinations of barrier options with forwards, or structural extensions to the barrier option itself. Structural extensions to barrier options include products where the option is knocked in or out gradually as a function of price movements and/or time.
- **Defined exercise options** – defined exercise options are a special type of barrier option where the option is triggered in or out based on the price evolution of an asset *other than the underlying asset of the option.*

Exotic option structures are driven generally by the following objectives:
- Reduction in option premium.
- Alteration in risk profile, including increased probability of gain, quantification of loss or optimal exercise timing.
- Asset liability matching.

Limit dependent options are driven primarily by the capacity of the structures to reduce option premiums and provide structured hedges that provide more accurate

---

Options; Irwin Professional Publishing, Chicago at Chapter 1; Smithson, Charles (1998) Managing Financial Risk – Third Edition; McGraw-Hill, New York at Chapter 13.

matching of underlying assets or liabilities. The exact factor driving individual path
dependent structures varies between types of options.

3 Barrier Options

3.1 Barrier Options – Concept[3]

Barrier options are the most important type of limit dependent options. Barrier
options are similar to conventional European options. If at any point in the option's
lifetime a specific price level is reached, then the option is either activated (knocks
in) or expires (knocks out). The price that triggers the option in or out is the price
of the asset upon which the option is based.

   Barrier options are among the most common types of exotic options. The structure is used frequently in most asset classes, primarily in currency, interest rate
and equity markets. Based on some estimates, barrier options and variations on
barrier options may make up in excess of 60–70% of the exotic option market in
currencies.

   In this Section, the structure, economics and applications of barrier options are
considered.

3.2 Barrier Options – Structure

3.2.1 General

Barrier options are identical to conventional options in most aspects. Similar to
conventional options, barrier options pay the difference between the asset price at
maturity and the strike price at expiry. Barrier options are characterised by both
a strike price and a specific *barrier asset price level*. The strike price is used to
calculate the actual option pay-off at maturity. The pay-off is contingent on *whether
the asset price attains the barrier level* over the term of the option.

   The barrier level specified can be one of the following types:
- **Outstrike (out barrier/knock out)** – in this case the option (which is initially
  active) is extinguished upon achievement of the relevant price level. This means
  that the option will only payoff where the option is in-the-money at maturity

---

[3]   See Ong, Michael "Exotic Options: The Market and their Taxonomy" in Nelken, Israel
      (Editor) (1996) The Handbook of Exotic Options; Irwin Professional Publishing, Chicago
      at Chapter 1 at 14–16; Smithson, Charles (1998) Managing Financial Risk – Third
      Edition; McGraw-Hill, New York at Chapter 13 at 270–273; Ravindran, K. (1998)
      Customised Derivatives; McGraw-Hill, New York at Chapter 3 at 195–202.

*and the asset price has not reached the outstrike price during the term of the
option.*

- **Instrike (in barrier/knock in)** – in this case the option (which is initially not
active) is activated upon the relevant asset price level being reached. This means
that the option will only payoff where the option is in-the-money at maturity
and the asset price has reached the instrike price during the term of the option.

Under market practice, barrier options are classified in a number of ways :

- The location of the barrier and the direction in which the asset price crossing
will affect the option payout. **Exhibit 9.2** sets out a classification based on this
approach.
- The location of the barrier and the in or out-of-the money status of the option if
it is triggered. **Exhibit 9.3** sets out a classification based on this approach.

The classification approaches are similar.
Key variations on the basic structure of the barrier structure include:

- **Partial barriers** – this is where the barrier feature operates for a period that is
shorter than the full term to expiry of the option. This allows the option purchaser
to benefit from the barrier feature, but limits exposure to the contingency of the
barrier to a shorter period than the full life of the option.
- **Discontinuous barriers** – under this structure, the relevant asset price level
that activates or extinguishes the option only operates on specific dates and/or
at specific times.

Exhibit 9.2 Barrier Options – Classification – Approach 1[4]			
Barrier Option – Type	**Barrier Location (Relative to Spot Asset Price)**	**Option Payout If Barrier Reached**	**Option Payout If Barrier Not Reached**
Down-and-out call	Below	0	Standard call
Down-and-in call	Below	Standard call	0
Up-and-out call	Above	0	Standard call
Up-and-in call	Above	Standard call	0
Down-and-out put	Below	0	Standard put
Down-and-in put	Below	Standard put	0
Up-and-out put	Above	0	Standard put
Up-and-in put	Above	Standard put	0

---

[4]   The table is based on Derman, Emanuel and Kani, Iraj "The Ins and Outs of Barrier
Options: Part 1" (Winter 1996) Derivatives Quarterly 55–67 at 56.

Exhibit 9.3 Barrier Options – Classification – Approach 2[5]		
Barrier Option – Type	**Barrier Location**	**Barrier Option Payout**
Regular knock out/ knock in options	Barrier is out-of-the-money: • Below strike for call. • Above strike for put.	For knock out if barrier is not reached or for knock in if barrier is reached, payout is identical to standard call or put. Otherwise, the option has 0 value.
Reverse knock out/ knock in options	Barrier is in-the-money: • Above strike for call. • Below strike for put.	For a knock out if barrier is reached, the option has 0 value (it loses intrinsic value rapidly). For a knock in if barrier is reached, payout is identical to standard call or put (it gains intrinsic value rapidly).

• **European/American options** – barrier options are feasible with either European and American exercise structures. In practice, European barrier options are most frequently used.

3.2.2   Barrier Options – Establishing Price Events

A critical aspect of barrier options is the ability to establish that the agreed barrier level has been reached. Dealers have historically used similar but different criteria for establishing whether a barrier event has occurred[6]. The key problems in establishing the occurrence/non-occurrence of a barrier event include[7]:

• **Barrier period** – this focuses on the trading period during which asset prices can be sampled to establish whether a barrier event has occurred. Some dealers restrict barrier events to "normal" trading hours, or periods when markets are perceived to be reasonably liquid (generally around 6:00 am Sydney time to 5:00 pm New York time). Prices reached outside this period are ignored in establishing whether a barrier event has occurred. Other dealers will use prices *at any time* (theoretically, even prices over a weekend) to determine whether a barrier event has occurred.

---

[5]   The table is based on Combalot, Lauren "Getting to Know Barrier Options" (September 1995) AsiaMoney 33–39.

[6]   See Hsu, Hans "Surprised Parties" (April 1997) Risk 27–29.

[7]   See Hsu, Hans "Surprised Parties" (April 1997) Risk 27–29.

- **Quoted versus transacted rates** – this focuses on whether the barrier event is based on a price quoted but not transacted, or an actually transacted market price. The difference is based on a variety of factors. Proponents of quoted prices base their position on the fact that pricing models are predicated on a distribution of prices (not transactions) and quotation must be used during illiquid periods. Proponents of transacted prices seek to avoid the risk of arbitrary or artificial quoted prices being used to manipulate markets.
- **Transaction size** – this focuses on the size of the transaction that will be considered as a barrier event. Some dealers specify a minimum transaction size required to qualify as a barrier event.
- **Internal versus customer transactions** – this focuses on whether the transactions qualifying as a barrier event can include internal transactions (intra-group or with a related party), or must be transactions with an arms length external counterparty. This reflects concern that internal transactions may not be consistent with actual market prices and may also be more susceptible to manipulation.
- **Off market transactions** – this focuses on whether transactions occurring at "off market" rates will qualify as barrier events. This includes transactions involving manifest errors or collusion.

Additional issues include[8]:
- **Calculation party** – a specific party is usually responsible for determining whether a barrier event has occurred. Dealers will generally act in this capacity. In inter-bank trades, the market maker will generally act in this capacity. In transactions with customers, the dealer will generally perform this function. The dealer will generally have a potential conflict of interest in performing this role as a party to the transaction.
- **Evidentiary requirements** – irrespective of the criteria used, evidence is required to establish a barrier event. Major issues relate to problems of unobservable transactions. Some dealers restrict asset prices used in determining barrier events to transactions or prices that dealers can reasonably observe, or those that can be established from acceptable information sources (such as transactions through inter dealer brokers or reported/verifiable transactions).

Specific problems also exist in relation to cross rates. This problem is exaggerated in the case of illiquid currency cross rates. In practice, the cross rate barrier

---

[8]   See Hsu, Hans "Surprised Parties" (April 1997) Risk 27–29.

event can be based on actual transactions or theoretical cross rate calculations based on quotation in one or both relevant currencies[9].

The problems identified mean that there is potential scope for confusion or disagreement on whether a barrier event has actually occurred.

The problems identified have forced dealers, under the auspices of regulators (primarily, the New York Federal Reserve Bank), to develop standards for barrier events. Recent industry efforts have been directed at creating greater standardisation, certainty and transparency in the process. The proposals have focused primarily on specifying minimum size (suggested US$3 million), use of transacted prices and exclusion of internal or off market transactions[10].

3.3   Barrier Options – Economics and Applications

3.3.1   Barrier Options – Economics

The performance of a barrier option at maturity is similar to that of a conventional put or call option with similar terms where the option exists. Where the barrier option is not extinguished as a result of a barrier event not occurring (knock out barrier option), or is activated as a result of a barrier event occurring (knock in barrier option), the pay-off of a barrier option is identical to that of a conventional option. The existence of the barrier feature means that the barrier option has different economics to that of conventional options.

The economics of barrier options is driven by the following factors:

- **Premium economics** – barrier options usually have lower premiums than comparable conventional options. This lower premium amount reflects the possibility that the option will be extinguished or not activated. The premium difference is dependent upon a number of factors, including the relationship between the forward asset price level, the barrier level and the maturity of the option.
- **Impact of volatility** – the premium for conventional options will generally increase with higher levels of volatility. The impact of volatility increases on barrier options is more complex. Higher volatility decreases the relative premium for a knock out barrier option. This reflects the fact that increased volatility makes it more probable that the option will be extinguished, reducing the potential cost to the writer. In contrast, for a knock in barrier option, higher volatility increases the chance of activation of the option. This will increase the cost of the

---

[9]   See Hsu, Hans "Surprised Parties" (April 1997) Risk 27–29.
[10]   See Dunbar, Nicholas "Breakthrough for Barrier Hedging" (February 2000) Risk 7.

knock in barrier option. The impact of lower volatility is similar but opposite in direction. Lower volatility increases the relative cost of knock out barrier options and decreases the cost of knock in barrier options.

- **Contingency feature** – the barrier feature central to knock in and knock out barrier options allows the structuring of links between specific asset price events and the nature of the option. This contingency feature allows specific risks to be eliminated or assumed. This is generally not available with traditional options. This creates the ability to create highly structured forms of protection/exposures in line with asset price expectations. This is usually feasible with lower transaction costs and/or lower execution risk than traditional trading or option structures.

The economic characteristics of barrier options are related.

Exhibit 9.4 sets out examples of the premium dynamics of barrier options.

Exhibit 9.4   Barrier Options – Premium Behaviour

1. Assumptions

In this Exhibit, the premium behaviour of knock out and knock in barrier options is set out. The examples assume the following parameters:

Asset Price ($)	1,000.00
Strike Price ($)	1,000.00
Expiry	6 months
Volatility (% pa)	20
Interest Rates (% pa)	6.00
Asset Income (% pa)	1.50
Exercise	European

Prices are set out for both calls and put options with different barrier structures (knock in, knock out etc) and different barrier levels.

2. Knock Out Barrier Options

2.1 Down and Out Call Barrier Option

Assume a down and out call barrier option with the characteristics set out above, and with the barrier level set at $950 (95% of current spot price). The structure operates as follows:

- The option behaves like a normal call option unless the asset price trades at $950 at any time before expiry.
- The option is extinguished if the asset price trades at $950 at any time before expiry.

The premiums (premium expressed as % of asset value) for the down and out call barrier option and a conventional call option are set out below:

Down and Out Call Barrier Option	Conventional Call Option
4.51	6.72

The change in premium (premium expressed as % of asset value) for changes in the barrier level is set out below:

Barrier Level	Down and Out Call Barrier Option	Conventional Call Option
999	0.12	6.72
975	2.68	6.72
950	4.51	6.72
900	6.24	6.72
800	6.70	6.72
700	6.71	6.72

The change in premium (premium expressed as % of asset value) for different volatility levels is set out below:

Volatility (% pa)	Down and Out Call Barrier Option			Conventional Call Option
	Barrier = 950	Barrier = 900	Barrier = 800	
15	4.25	5.24	5.35	5.35
20	4.51	6.24	6.70	6.72
30	4.74	7.52	9.30	9.42
40	4.84	8.24	11.46	12.20

2.2 Up and Out Put Barrier Option

Assume an up and out put barrier option with the characteristics set out above, and with the barrier level set at $1,050 (105% of current spot price). The structure operates as follows:
- The option behaves like a normal put option unless the asset price trades at $1,050 at any time before expiry.
- The option is extinguished if the asset price trades at $1,050 at any time before expiry.

The premiums (premium expressed as % of asset value) for the up and out put barrier option and a conventional put option are set out below:

Up and Out Put Barrier Option	Conventional Put Option
2.79	4.50

The change in premium (premium expressed as % of asset value) for changes in the barrier level is set out below:

Barrier Level	Up and Out Put Barrier Option	Conventional Put Option
1,001	0.08	4.50
1,025	1.64	4.50
1,050	2.79	4.50
1,100	4.00	4.50
1,200	4.48	4.50
1,300	4.50	4.50

The change in premium (premium expressed as % of asset value) for different volatility levels is set out below:

Volatility (% pa)	Up and Out Put Barrier Option			Conventional Put Option
	Barrier = 1,050	Barrier = 1,100	Barrier = 1,200	
15	2.33	3.01	3.14	3.14
20	2.79	4.00	4.48	4.50
30	3.35	5.35	6.90	7.23
40	3.66	6.17	8.77	9.97

3. Knock-in Barrier Options

3.1 Up and In Call Barrier Option

Assume an up and in call barrier option with the characteristics set out above, and with the barrier level set at $1,050 (105% of current spot price). The structure operates as follows:

* The option behaves like a normal call option if the asset price trades at $1,050 at any time before expiry.
* The option does not come into existence if the asset price does not trade at $1,050 at any time before expiry.

The premiums (premium expressed as % of asset value) for the up and in barrier call option and a conventional call option are set out below:

Up and In Call Barrier Option	Conventional Call Option
6.68	6.72

The change in premium (premium expressed as % of asset value) for changes in the barrier level is set out below:

Barrier Level	Up and In Call Barrier Option	Conventional Call Option
1,001	6.71	6.72
1,025	6.71	6.72

Barrier Level	Up and In Call Barrier Option	Conventional Call Option
1,050	6.68	6.72
1,100	6.41	6.72
1,200	4.53	6.72
1,300	2.23	6.72

The change in premium (premium expressed as % of asset value) for different volatility levels is set out below:

Volatility (% pa)	Up and In Call Barrier Option			Conventional Call Option
	Barrier = 1,050	Barrier = 1,100	Barrier = 1,200	
15	5.29	4.75	2.25	5.35
20	6.68	6.41	4.53	6.72
30	9.42	9.34	8.44	9.42
40	12.17	12.13	11.68	12.20

3.2 Down and In Put Barrier Option

Assume a down and in put barrier option with the characteristics set out above, and with the barrier level set at $950 (95% of current spot price). The structure operates as follows:
* The option behaves like a normal put option if the asset price trades at $950 at any time before expiry.
* The option does not come into existence if the asset price does not trade at $950 at any time before expiry.

The premiums (premium expressed as % of asset value) for the down and in put barrier option and a conventional put option are set out below:

Down and In Put Barrier Option	Conventional Put Option
4.47	4.50

The change in premium (premium expressed as % of asset value) for changes in the barrier level is set out below:

Barrier Level	Down and In Put Barrier Option	Conventional Put Option
999	4.50	4.50
975	4.50	4.50
950	4.47	4.50
900	4.12	4.50
800	1.88	4.50
700	0.27	4.50

The change in premium (premium expressed as % of asset value) for different volatility levels is set out below:

Volatility	Down and In Put Barrier Option			Conventional Put
(%pa)	Barrier = 950	Barrier = 900	Barrier = 800	Option
15	3.08	2.49	0.48	3.14
20	4.47	4.12	1.88	4.50
30	7.22	7.09	5.59	7.23
40	9.96	9.91	9.04	9.97

4. Premium Behaviour

Barrier options usually have lower premiums than comparable conventional options. This lower premium amount reflects the possibility that the option will be extinguished or not activated. The premium difference is dependent upon a number of factors that vary depending upon the features of the barrier option. Some of the key behavioural aspects are summarised below:

- For knock out options, the option premium behaves as follows:
  1. The differential between the premium for a conventional option and a knock out option will generally decrease (in absolute terms) as the barrier level is moved further away from the current forward asset price. Higher barrier levels for an up and out put, or lower barrier levels for a down and out call, will increase the premium. As the barrier level is moved further away from the current forward price, the premium for the knock out barrier will approach the premium for a conventional option with similar characteristics. This reflects the fact that for a given volatility level, the chance of the option being knocked out decreases.
  2. Increases in volatility levels will generally reduce the cost of a knock out barrier option relative to that of a conventional option. This reflects the fact that higher volatility levels increase the chance of the option being knocked out prior to expiry.
- For knock in options, the option premium behaves as follows:
  1. The differential between the premium for a knock in barrier option and a conventional option will generally increase (in absolute terms) as the barrier level is moved further away from the current forward price. Higher barrier levels for an up and in call, or lower barrier levels for a down and in put, will decrease the premium. This reflects the fact that for a given volatility, the chance of the option being knocked in decreases.
  2. The relationship between the strike price and the barrier level is an important factor in determining the premium of a knock in option. This reflects the fact that the option may be in-the-money *at the time of the barrier event*. This dictates that the barrier option value will incorporate the intrinsic value of the option at the time of the option being knocked in.
  3. Increases in volatility levels will generally increase the cost of a knock in barrier option relative to that of a conventional option. This reflects the fact that higher volatility levels increase the chance of the option being knocked in prior to expiry.

3.3.2 Barrier Options – Applications[11]

Applications of barrier options are driven primarily by the underlying economics of the structure. The lower premium cost, the relationship to volatility and the contingency feature are all central to the use of barrier options.

The major applications of barrier options are focused on the following areas:

- **Structured hedging** – this application is focused on using the contingency feature of barrier options to structure hedges that closely match the risk exposure of the party. The barrier option is used to create a hedge that is matched to the actual risk incurred. This enables the hedger to lower the cost of hedging by avoiding the requirement to pay for protection under conditions that do not require hedging, or are considered unlikely[12]. Examples of structured hedging are set out in **Exhibits 9.5, 9.6, 9.7** and **9.8**.
- **Re-structuring existing hedging arrangements** – this application is focused on using barrier options to restructure existing hedges (particularly out-of-the-money hedging arrangements) to re-align risk exposures[13]. This type of application is also potentially applicable where the asset price has moved

---

[11] See Barrett, Gilles "Ins and Outs of Barrier Options" (1994) Corporate Finance Risk Management and Derivatives Yearbook 26–36; Combalot, Lauren "Getting to Know Barrier Options" (September 1995) AsiaMoney 33–39; Cook, Julian "Trigger Happy" (August 1996) Futures & Options World 55–56; Cook, Julian "Double Barriers" (September 1996) Futures & Options World 58–61; Derman, Emanuel and Kani, Iraj "The Ins and Outs of Barrier Options: Part 1" (Winter 1996) Derivatives Quarterly 55–67; Derman, Emanuel and Kani, Iraj "The Ins and Outs of Barrier Options: Part 2" (Spring 1997) Derivatives Quarterly 73–80.

[12] See Stone, Daniel "Knock-Out Options: When and How to Use Them" (June 1993) Corporate Finance 11–13; Turner, Marilyn "Break-Even Analysis of Knock Out Options" (September 1993) Corporate Finance 43–45; Jaatinen, Satu "Constructive Barriers" (December 1996) Risk Management Focus – Futures & Options World III–VI.

[13] The most extreme example of using barrier options to re-structure existing exposures was in the Dharmala case. In this transaction, an Indonesian company (PT Dharmala Sakti Sejaharta ("DSS")) entered into 2 swaps with Bankers Trust ("BT") in February 1994. The first was a US$50 million swap under which DSS paid 5% and BT paid 5% times n/183 where n was the number of days that LIBOR fixed below 4.125% pa. The second swap entailed DSS paying 6 month LIBOR and receiving from BT 6 month LIBOR plus 1.25% pa. Under the structure, if US$ LIBOR rose above 4.125% pa then DSS would receive no payment from BT and would have a net loss of 3.75% pa on the transaction. At the time the swaps were entered, US$ 6 month LIBOR was 3.625% pa. Shortly after the swaps were entered into, US$ interest rates increased as the Federal Reserve tightened monetary policy. DSS re-structured the swap with a barrier swap. The new swap was designed to replace the original swap. Under the new swap DSS would receive 6 month LIBOR plus 1.25% pa and pay 6 month LIBOR less 2.25% pa

unfavourably before the position could be hedged. An example of using barrier options to re-structure hedging arrangements is set out in **Exhibit 9.9**.

- **Volatility trading** – as noted above, the impact of volatility on barrier options is different to the impact on conventional options, in particular for knock out barrier options. This allows both traders and hedgers to use barrier options to take structured positions on volatility and future asset price movements. In part, this is driven by the fact there is generally a premium difference between barrier options and conventional options. This is despite the fact that the pay-offs will be identical under certain conditions. Examples of using barrier options to assume volatility positions are set out in **Exhibits 9.10** and **9.11**.

- **Premium capture/positioning strategies** – this type of application is based on similar principles to those that drive structured hedging. In structured hedging, the cost of hedging is reduced by eliminating protection against certain contingencies. In premium capture/positioning strategies, barrier options are used to capture premium or value by selling a barrier that will payoff under asset price outcomes that are considered improbable. Examples of using barrier options to generate premium are set out in **Exhibit 9.12**.

Exhibit 9.5   Applications of Barrier Options – Structured Hedging Example 1

Assume an investor is long an asset at $1,000. The investor is concerned about declines in the value of the asset. The market is volatile and the investor believes that the prices may rally significantly. The investor decides to use a put option to hedge the position against the risk of price declines. The investor is concerned that in these circumstances, the value of the put will be lost if the asset price increases. In this situation, the investor could use a knock out barrier option to provide structured protection of the position.

---

plus a spread. If the spread is zero, then DSS would receive a net 3.50% pa. This was presumably designed to ameliorate the position under the original swap. The spread was zero if 6 month LIBOR was below an agreed amount (5.25% on one tranche of US$25 million and 5.3125% on a second tranche of US$25 million). Where 6 month LIBOR was above these levels, DSS paid the spread which was calculated as: (LIBOR/4.50% pa) –1. Following interest rate increases in March and April 1994, the spread was around US$19 million for the swap, implying a negative mark-to-market on the swap of US$34/35 million. This increased to around US$45 million by May 1994. See "Bankers Trust Takes Dharmala to Court" (12 July 1995) Financial Products Issue 22 1, 14, 15; "Dramatis Personae" (26 July 1995) Financial Products Issue 23 20; "Innocence and Experience" (26 July 1995) Financial Products Issue 23 14–19; "Judgement Reserved" (9 August 1995) Financial Products Issue 24 5–6; Ball, Matthew "Dharmala Hits the Barrier in Swaps Trial" (February 1996) Corporate Finance 38–40; "BT-Dharmala Settle Dispute" (6 March 1996) Financial Products Issue 37 1,3.

The investor could purchase the following options:

- **Conventional put option** – the cost of a conventional put (strike of $950; maturity of 6 months) for 2.58%.
- **Knock-out put barrier option** – the cost of a knock out put barrier option (strike of $950; maturity of 6 months; outstrike of $1,050) for 1.76%.

The conventional put option would protect the investor from declines in asset prices below $950. The knock out put barrier option would provide identical protection, provided that the asset price does not trade at or above $1,050. If the asset trades above $1,050, then the knock out put barrier option would be extinguished. The inclusion of the barrier feature reduces the cost of the hedge by 0.82% (32 %).

There are several aspects relating to the use of barrier options, including:

- The barrier feature reduces the cost of the hedge by eliminating the option if the asset price moves in favour of the position. In these circumstances, the protection afforded by the put option is not required.
- The barrier feature creates a path dependency in the risk profile of the position. If the asset price trades above the barrier level ($1,050), then the option is extinguished, leaving the position unprotected. If the barrier event occurs early in the life of the option, then the investor may be exposed to a sudden and unexpected fall in the asset price. In practice, this risk must be managed. This requires the investor to cover or re-hedge the position *at the more favourable asset price*. This can be done in a number of ways. A common way (for example, in the currency market) is to leave a standing spot limit order at the barrier level to hedge the position (when the barrier level is breached).

Exhibit 9.6   Applications of Barrier Options – Structured Hedging Example 2

Assume an investor is short an asset. The asset price is currently $1,000. The investor has already suffered a loss in that it was seeking to purchase the asset at $900. The investor is concerned about further rises in the asset price that would increase its loss. The investor decides to use a call option to hedge the potential price risk of the position. The investor is concerned that in these circumstances, the value of the call will be lost if the asset price decreases. In this situation, the investor could use knock out and knock in barrier options to provide structured protection for the position.

The investor could select from the following options:

- **Conventional call option** – the cost of a conventional call (strike of $900; maturity of 6 months) for 13.22%. This strategy provides the investor with protection against increases in the asset price above $900. The option is expensive, reflecting the significant intrinsic value of the structure. The option premium will be lost if the asset price decreases below $900, although the investor will be able to purchase the asset at the lower price.
- **Knock-in call barrier option** – the cost of a knock in call barrier option (strike of $900; maturity of 6 months; instrike of $1,100) for 11.13%. The strategy provides no protection if the asset price does not increase above $1,100. The investor will be protected against increases in the asset price beyond $1,100 *from the target price level of $900*. This means that the investor's maximum loss is capped at $200. The structure lowers the cost of protection by 2.09% (16%).

- **Knock-out (down and out) call barrier option** – the cost of a down and out call barrier option (strike of $900; maturity of 6 months; outstrike of $950) for 7.45%. The strategy provides protection *from the target price level of $900* if the asset price does not decrease below $950. Under this structure, the investor's maximum loss is $50. If the asset price falls to $950, knocking out the call option. The investor would be able to purchase the asset at the lower price but would lock in the loss above its target price level of $900. The investor is also exposed to losses where the asset price falls to $950 (knocking out the option) and then increases. The amount of this loss would depend on the actual asset price level. The structure lowers the cost of protection by 5.77% (44%).

- **Knock-out call (up and out) barrier option** – the cost of an up and out call barrier option (strike of $900; maturity of 6 months; outstrike of $1,200) for 6.57%. The strategy provides protection *from the target price level of $900* if the asset price does not increase above $1,200. Under this structure, the investor's maximum level of protection is capped at $300 (to the asset price level of $1,200). If the asset price increases above $1,200, then the investor is unprotected, as the call option is extinguished. The investor would be able to purchase the asset at the higher price but would lock in the loss of at least $300. The structure lowers the cost of protection by 6.65% (50%).

The hedging structure is driven by the investor's asset price expectations and risk reward profile. The incorporation of barrier features creates a path dependency in the risk profile of the position. If the barrier event occurs, then the investor may be exposed to a sudden and unexpected increase or decrease in the asset price. In practice, this risk must be managed. This requires the investor to cover or re-hedge the position at the time of the barrier event.

Exhibit 9.7   Applications of Barrier Options – Structured Hedging Example 3

Assume a corporation is long US$ against Yen for a value date in 6 months. The US$/Yen spot rate is at Yen 100. The corporation has a down side price limit of Yen 95. The investor may choose to hedge by purchasing a knock out US$ put/Yen call barrier option with a strike price of Yen 95 with outstrike level of Yen 105. If the US$/Yen spot rate reaches Yen 105 before expiry, then the option ceases to exist. If the option is knocked out, then the corporation can sell the US$ at the improved rate. If the option is not knocked out, then the option functions like a conventional US$ put/Yen call option. The option is either exercised or expires out-of-the-money.

The premium for a conventional 6 month European US$ put/Yen call with strike Yen 95.00 is 2.25%. The cost of a knock out US$ put/Yen call barrier option with a strike price of Yen 95 with an outstrike level of Yen 105 is 1.75%. This represents a saving of 0.50% (22%).

The knock out option offers a structured hedge of the underlying currency position. The hedging structure provides protection beyond a worst case level (Yen 95). It also allows the investor to take advantage of a favourable rate movement and close out its long US$ position at an exchange rate of Yen 105. The purchase of the knock out option would generally be combined with an order to sell US$/buy Yen at Yen 105 (the barrier level) to cover the position where the barrier option is extinguished.

The major advantage of the strategy is the ability to purchase protection at a lower premium cost.

Exhibit 9.8   Applications of Barrier Options – Structured Hedge Example 4

This type of application is focused on structuring a hedge where the asset price has moved unfavourably before the position could be hedged[15]. It entails buying a knock out option that is already in the money with a barrier level close to the strike. This is designed to reduce the cost of the option where the underlying conventional option will generally be expensive because it is deep in-the-money.

Assume an investor is long an asset at $1,000. The price of the asset has declined to $950 (a fall of 5%). The investor is concerned about further declines in the asset price and is seeking to hedge. The fall in the asset price means that it either locks in a loss or incurs higher hedging costs (through buying an option that is in-the-money).

The investor could purchase the following options:

- **Conventional put option** – the cost of a conventional put (strike of $1,000; maturity of 6 months) for 7.24%. This strategy provides the investor with protection against decreases in the asset price below $1,000. The option is expensive, reflecting the significant intrinsic value of the structure. The option premium will be lost if the asset price increases above $1,000, although the investor will be able to hedge the asset at the higher price.

- **Knock-out (up and out) put barrier option** – the cost of a knock out put barrier option (strike of $1,000; maturity of 6 months; outstrike of $1,000) for 4.19%. The investor obtains protection against decreases in the asset price below $1,000 *(the entry level into the position)*. The barrier put option is extinguished if the asset price increases above $1,000. If the asset price increases from current levels, the investor would be able to re-hedge at a better rate. The structure lowers the cost of protection by 3.05% (42%).

Exhibit 9.9   Applications of Barrier Options – Restructuring Existing Hedge[16]

Assume a corporation enters a three year interest rate collar on 6 month US$ LIBOR to hedge its borrowing costs. The collar is structured as follows: bought cap with strike of 6.50% pa and sold floor with strike of 5.00% pa. At the time of entry into the transaction, the three year swap rate against 6 month US$ LIBOR is 5.95% pa and 6 month US$ LIBOR is 5.50% pa.

US$ short term interest rates fall unexpectedly. By the end of the first year (2 years remaining under the collar), US$ 6 month LIBOR declines by 1.00% pa to 4.50% pa. The floor component of the collar is now in-the-money, increasing the borrowing cost of the corporation. The corporation could reduce the impact of the floor by buying back the floor component of the collar. The cost of re-purchasing the floor is 4.00% pa flat.

---

[15] See Combalot, Lauren "Getting to Know Barrier Options" (September 1995) AsiaMoney 33–39 at 38.

[16] This type of transaction was used quite frequently in the French market in the early 1990s to unwind a position taken by a borrower in interest rate collars where the floor moved into-the-money causing losses; see Barrett, Gilles "Ins and Outs of Barrier Options" (1994) Corporate Finance Risk Management and Derivatives Yearbook 26–36.

The corporation can reduce the cost of re-purchasing the floor by incorporating barrier features in the transaction. Assume that the corporation expects that 6 month US$ LIBOR interest rates will decline gradually over the remaining life of the collar to around 3.75% pa at a rate of approximately 0.25% every 6 months. The corporation may monetise this view by offsetting the existing floor with the purchase of a 2 year knock out (down and out) floor on US$ 6 month LIBOR.

The knock out (down and out) floor would be structured as follows:
- Strike rate of 5.00% pa (equivalent to the strike on the existing floor).
- Barrier levels set at 6 month US$ LIBOR levels of 4.25% pa, 4.00% pa, 3.75% pa and 3.75% pa for each of the successive semi-annual interest rate set dates under the floor.

The knock out (down and out) floor would operate as follows:
- If the barrier levels are not reached, then the original floor is eliminated, allowing the corporation to lower its funding costs.
- If any of the barrier levels are reached, then the knock out (down and out) floor is extinguished. The corporation's funding cost reverts to the 5.00% pa level of the original floor (which is no longer offset by the purchased knock out (down and out) floor).
- The corporation continues to have the protection of the 6.50% pa cap against an increase in interest rates.

The cost of the knock out (down and out) floor is 1.10% (a reduction of 2.90% (72%) relative to a conventional floor). The amortised cost of the knock out floor is around 0.60% pa. This means that where US$ 6 month LIBOR averages below 4.40% pa for the remaining 2 years of the collar, the corporation achieves a cost saving relative to leaving the original floor in place. This saving is only achieved where US$ 6 month LIBOR does not fall below the specified barrier level at the relevant dates.

The lower cost of the knock out (down and out) floor allows the corporation to restructure its out-of-the-money hedge consistent with its rate expectations. The restructuring is achieved at a lower cost than that feasible with a conventional floor. The corporation assumes the risk that the barrier levels will be reached and its funding costs will revert to the original levels adjusted for the cost of the knock out floor.

Exhibit 9.10   Applications of Barrier Options – Volatility Trading: Example 1

Assume equity market volatility has increased sharply. Current implied volatility for 6 month put options has risen to 40% pa (well above historic levels of around 20% pa). The increase reflects recent sharp movements in stock prices and general market uncertainty.

An investor wants to purchase put options to provide contingent protection against any decline in equity values. The increase in volatility has sharply increased the premium for put options. The investor believes that the increase in *implied* volatility for equity index options is unwarranted. The investor believes that the *actual* realised volatility will be below current *implied* volatility levels. In these circumstances, the investor can use barrier options to significantly lower its cost of hedging. This entails using the specific impact of volatility on the value of barrier options in the hedging strategy.

Assume the equity index is trading at 1,000 and the investor seeks protection for 6 months. The investor could purchase the following options:

- **Conventional put option** – the cost of a conventional put (strike of 950 (95% of current market level; maturity of 6 months) for 7.60%. This strategy provides the investor with protection against decreases in the equity index below 950. The option is expensive, reflecting the high implied volatility levels. The option premium will be lost if the equity index remains above 950.
- **Knock-out (up and out) put barrier option** – the cost of a knock out put barrier option (strike of 950; maturity of 6 months; outstrike of 1,100 (110% of current market level)) for 4.92%. The investor obtains protection against decreases in the equity index below 950. The barrier put option is extinguished if the equity index increases above 1,100. If the equity index increases from current levels, the investor would be able to re-hedge at a better rate. The structure lowers the cost of protection by 2.68% (35%).

The performance of the two options is identical *as long as the barrier level of 1,100 is not breached*. If the investor's expectation is that the actual volatility of the equity market will be lower than the current implied volatility levels, then the investor is able to significantly lower its hedging cost by using the barrier option. The reduction in hedging cost is driven by the fact that at higher volatility levels, the relative cost of a knock out barrier is significantly lower than that for a conventional option with comparable features. The central feature of this strategy is the use of the barrier feature to monetise volatility expectations.

Exhibit 9.11   Applications of Barrier Options – Volatility Trading: Example 2

Assume equity market volatility has decreased sharply. Current implied volatility for 6 month put options has fallen to 12% pa (well above historic levels of around 20% pa). The decrease reflects recent stability in stock prices and the fact that the equity market has traded in a tight range over recent times.

An investor is short the equity index within its portfolio. The investor wants to purchase call options to provide some contingent exposure against an increase in equity values. The investor believes that the low levels of *implied* volatility for equity index options are unwarranted. The investor believes that the *actual* realised volatility will be above current *implied* volatility levels. In these circumstances, the investor can use barrier options to significantly lower its cost of hedging. This entails using the specific impact of volatility on the value of barrier options in the hedging strategy.

Assume the equity index is trading at 1,000 and the investor seeks protection for 6 months. The investor could purchase the following options:

- **Conventional call option** – the cost of a conventional call option (strike of 1,000 (current market level); maturity of 6 months) for 4.54%. This strategy provides the investor with *immediate* protection against increases in the equity index above 1,000. The option premium will be lost if the equity index remains below 1,000.
- **Knock-in (up and in) call barrier option** – the cost of a knock in call barrier option (strike of 1,000; maturity of 6 months; instrike of 1,100 (110% of current market level)) is 3.59%. The investor obtains protection against increases in the equity index above 1,000

if the option is activated. The barrier call option is activated only if the equity index increases above 1,100. The structure lowers the cost of the call option by 0.95% (21%).

- **Knock-in (down and in) call barrier option** – the cost of a knock in call barrier option (strike of 1,000; maturity of 6 months; instrike of 950 (95% of current market level)) is 0.56%. The investor obtains protection against increases in the equity index above 1,000 if the option is activated. The barrier call option is activated only if the equity index decreases below 950. The structure lowers the cost of the call option by 3.98% (88%).

The performance of the different option strategies is as follows:

- The knock in (up and in) call barrier option is identical to the conventional call *provided the barrier level of 1,100 is breached* (ie the asset price increases by at least 10%).
- The knock in (down and in) call barrier option is identical to the conventional call *provided the barrier level of 950 is breached* (ie the asset price decreases by at least 5%).

If the investor's expectation is that the actual volatility of the equity market will be higher than the current implied volatility levels, then the investor is able to significantly lower its hedging cost by using the barrier option. The reduction in hedging cost is driven by the fact that at lower volatility levels, the relative cost of a knock in barrier is significantly lower than that for a conventional option with comparable features. The central feature of this strategy is the use of the barrier feature to monetise volatility expectations. The specific strategy adopted will depend upon the specific expectations (actual volatility levels and directional asset price movements) of the investor.

Exhibit 9.12   Applications of Barrier Options – Premium Capture/Positioning: Examples

Assume an asset is trading at $1,000. A trader may monetise its expectation on future asset prices to generate premium income in a number of ways:

- **Sell a conventional call option** – a conventional call option (strike price $1,000; maturity of 6 months) would generate premium income for the trader of 6.70%. The trader would gain from the premium as long as the asset price did not increase above $1,000. The trader would incur losses where the asset price increases above $1, 067 (an increase of 6.70%). The call option has a high delta (59%), indicating a high probability of exercise.
- **Sell a knock in (down and in) call barrier option** – a knock in (down and in) call barrier option (strike price $1,000; maturity of 6 months; instrike of $950 (95% of current asset price)) would generate premium income for the trader of 2.20% (a reduction of 4.50% (67%)). The risk of the sold barrier option is different to that of the conventional call option. The option is not initially in operation. Unless the asset price trades at $950, then the option is never activated. This means that the trader has no exposure to increases in the asset price unless the option is knocked in. The trader also has no exposure under the knock in (down and in) call barrier option where the option is triggered (asset price trades at $950) but the asset price at maturity is below the strike price ($1,000).

- **Sell a knock in (up and in) call barrier option** – a knock in (up and in) call barrier option (strike price $1,000; maturity of 6 months; instrike of $1,200 (120% of current asset price)) would generate premium income for the trader of 4.53% (a reduction of 2.17% (32%)). The risk of the sold barrier option is different to that of the conventional call option. The option is not initially in operation. Unless the asset price trades at $1,200, then the option is never activated. This means that the trader has no exposure under the option to increases in the asset price above the strike price where the asset price remains below $1,200. The premium reflects the fact that if the barrier event occurs, then the call option will have significant intrinsic value.
- **Sell a knock out (down and out) call barrier option** – a knock out (down and out) call barrier option (strike price $1,000; maturity of 6 months; outstrike of $950 (95% of current asset price)) would generate premium income for the trader of 4.50% (a reduction of 2.20% (33%)). The risk of the sold barrier option is different to that of the conventional call option. The option is initially in operation. Unless the asset price trades at $950, the pay-off of the option is identical to that of the conventional option. This means that the trader has exposure under the option to increases in the asset price above $1,000 (the strike price). The trader has no exposure under the knock out (down and out) call barrier option where the option is triggered out (asset price trades at $950). This would be the case even if after the barrier event, the asset price at maturity is above the strike price ($1,000).
- **Sell a knock out (up and out) call barrier option** – a knock out (up and out) call barrier option (strike price $1,000; maturity of 6 months; outstrike of $1,200 (120% of current asset price)) would generate premium income for the trader of 2.18% (a reduction of 4.52% (68%)). The risk of the sold barrier option is different to that of the conventional call option. The option is initially in operation. Unless the asset price trades at $1,200, the pay-off of the option is identical to that of the conventional option. This means that the trader has exposure under the option to increases in the asset price above $1,000 (the strike price). The trader has no exposure under the knock out (up and out) call barrier option where the option is triggered out (asset price trades at $1,200). This would be the case even if after the barrier event the asset price at maturity is above the strike price ($1,000).

In each of the cases incorporating barrier options, the trader can monetise its expectations of future asset price expectations. The barrier options are used to capture premium or value by selling a barrier option that will only pay-off under asset price outcomes that are considered improbable. This allows customised risk profiles to be constructed and monetised.

The premium capture/positioning strategies are also influenced by expectations of volatility – specifically the current market *implied* volatility and the trader's expectations regarding *actual realised* volatility likely to be experienced over the term of the option. This reflects the fact that higher implied volatility increases the relative value of knock in options and decreases the value of knock out options.

The premium capture/positioning strategies can be extended to assume very high levels of risk. This is done by selling barrier options that would be deeply in-the-money if triggered in or not triggered out. Examples of this type of strategy (in the situation identified) include:
- **Sell a knock in (up and in) call barrier option** – a knock in (up and in) call barrier option (strike price $500; maturity of 6 months; instrike of $1,200 (120% of current asset price)) would generate premium income for the trader of 15.21%. The option is

not initially in operation. Unless the asset price trades at \$1,200, then the option is never activated. This means that the trader has no exposure under the option where the asset price remains below \$1,200. If the asset trades at or above \$1,200, then the trader is short a significantly in-the-money option resulting in a large loss.

- **Sell a knock out (up and out) call barrier option** – a knock out (up and out) call barrier option (strike price \$500; maturity of 6 months; outstrike of \$1,200 (120% of current asset price)) would generate premium income for the trader of 35.52%. The option is initially in operation. Unless the asset price trades at \$1,200, pay-off of the option is identical to that of the conventional option. The trader has no exposure under the knock out (up and out) call barrier option where the option is triggered out (asset price trades at \$1,200). If the asset does not trade at or above \$1,200, then the trader is short a significantly in-the-money option, resulting in a large loss.

The high premium reflects the fact that the call option underlying the barrier will have significant intrinsic value if it is operational. A comparable conventional call option would generate premium income of 50.73%, but the option would have a very high probability of exercise (because of the low strike price). The strategies represent an aggressive application of the concept of capturing premium by selling optionality that will only require pay-offs under asset price conditions that are considered unlikely.

4   Barrier Options – Pricing / Valuation & Hedging

4.1   Overview[17]

Barrier options demonstrate pay-offs that are identical to that of comparable conventional options *at least where the option is in existence*. The presence of the barrier feature means that there is a possibility that a knock out barrier option will be extinguished or that a knock in option will not be activated. This factor drives the differential in value between conventional and barrier options.

The similarity in pay-off between barrier and conventional options establishes the following direct value relationship:

Premium of conventional option = premium of a knock out option

+ premium of a knock in option

Exhibit 9.13 sets out an example of this arbitrage relationship.

---

[17]   See Briys, Eric Bellalah, Mondher, Mai, Huu Minh and De Varenne, Francois (1998) Options, Futures and Exotic Derivatives: Theory, Application and Practice; John Wiley & Sons, Chichester at Chapter 18; Wilmott, Paul (1998) Derivatives: The Theory and Practice of Financial Engineering; John Wiley & Sons, Chichester at Chapter 14; Hull, John (2000) Options, Futures and Other Derivatives – Fourth Edition; Prentice-Hall Inc., Upper Saddle River, NJ at Chapter 18 at 462–464, 477–481; Nelken, Israel (2001) Pricing, Hedging & Trading Exotic Options; McGraw-Hill, New York at Chapter 11.

Exhibit 9.13   Premium Relationship – Conventional and Barrier Options

Assume the following parameters:

Asset Price ($)	1,000.00
Strike Price ($)	1,000.00
Maturity	6 months
Volatility (% pa)	20
Interest Rates (% pa)	6.00
Asset Income (% pa)	1.50
Exercise	European

The premium for a conventional call option is 6.70% pa.

The conventional call option can be replicated by a portfolio of the following barrier options:

- **Knock-out (down and out) call barrier option** – the option is structured with an outstrike barrier level of $950.00. This means that the knock out (down and out) call barrier option behaves identically to a conventional call unless the asset price reaches $950. If the asset price reaches $950, then the option is extinguished. The premium for this option is 4.50%.

- **Knock-in (down and in) call barrier option** – the option is structured with an instrike barrier level of $950.00. This means that the knock in (down and out) call barrier option behaves identically to a conventional call only if the asset price reaches $950 and the option is triggered in. If the asset price does not reach $950, then the option is never activated. The premium for this option is 2.20%.

The combination of barrier options has the same pay-off profile as the conventional call options. The combined premium is also identical to that of the conventional call option.

The adjustment to the value of a conventional option to reflect the possibility of extinguishment (knock out barrier option) or non activation (knock in barrier option) requires adjustment to the normal pricing models. A variety of approaches (analytic and numerical) have emerged. These approaches are examined in the following Sections. The basic valuation approaches are used for both standard and non-standard barrier options. For non-standard barrier options, numerical approaches are generally required.

4.2   Analytic Models

Analytic solutions for the value of barrier options are feasible. The analytic solutions generally assume a Black-Scholes-Merton valuation framework, including the standard assumptions regarding asset price movements and the distribution of asset price changes[18]. The analytical solutions typically use conditional probability distributions. The basic distribution is the log normal distribution of the asset price changes. The conditional distribution is focused on the probability of the asset price reaching the barrier price level at some time. This allows a closed solution to be derived.

A number of analytic formulations for pricing barrier options have been proposed[19]. **Exhibit 9.14** sets out the general analytic pricing formulation for barrier options.

Exhibit 9.14   Barrier Options – Analytic Pricing Models[20]

1. Terminology
Assume:

S = asset price
K = strike price
H = barrier level
t = time to expiry
r = interest rate
q = income on the asset
σ = volatility

2. Barrier Call Options
If $H \leq K$ then the value of a knock in (down and in) call barrier options is given by:

$$Se^{-qt}(H/S)^{2\lambda}N(y) - Ke^{-rt}(H/S)^{2\lambda-2}N(y - \sigma\sqrt{t})$$

Where

$$\lambda = (r - q + \sigma^2/2)/\sigma^2$$
$$y = [\ln(H^2/(S.K))/\sigma\sqrt{t}] + \lambda\sigma\sqrt{t}$$

---

[18] For a discussion of the assumptions underlying traditional option pricing, see Das, Satyajit (2004) Derivative Products & Pricing; John Wiley & Sons (Asia), Singapore at Chapter 7.

[19] See Hudson, Mike "The Value in Going Out" (March 1991) Risk 29–33; Benson, Robert and Daniel, Nicholas "Up Over and Out" (June 1991) Risk 17–19; Rubinstein, Mark and Reiner, Eric "Breaking Down the Barriers" (September 1991) Risk 28–35; Heynen, Ronald and Kat, Harry "Crossing Barriers" (June 1994) Risk 46–51; Rich, Don R. "The Mathematical Foundations of Barriers Options" (1994) Advances in Futures and Options Research, 7 267–311; Zhang, Peter G. "A Unified Formula for Outside Barrier Options" (December 1995) Journal of Financial Engineering 335–349.

[20] The analytical solutions set out are those suggested by Hull, John (2000) Options, Futures and Other Derivatives – Fourth Edition; Prentice-Hall Inc., Upper Saddle River, NJ at Chapter 18 at 462–464.

Using the arbitrage relationship between knock in and knock out barrier options, the value of a knock out (down and out) call barrier options is given by:

Premium of knock out (down and out) barrier call option = premium of call option − premium of knock in (down and in) barrier call option

If $H \geq K$ then the value of a knock out (down and out) call barrier options is given by:

$$SN(x_1)e^{-qt} - Ke^{-rt}N(x_1 - \sigma\sqrt{t}) - Se^{-qt}(H/S)^{2\lambda}N(y_1)$$
$$+ Ke^{-rt}(H/S)^{2\lambda-2}N(y_1 - \sigma\sqrt{t})$$

Where

$$x_1 = [(\ln(S/H))/\sigma\sqrt{t}] + \lambda\sigma\sqrt{t}$$
$$y_1 = [(\ln(H/S))/\sigma\sqrt{t}] + \lambda\sigma\sqrt{t}$$

The value of a knock in (down and in) call barrier options is given by:

Premium of knock in (down and in) barrier call option = premium of call option − premium of knock out (down and out) barrier call option

If $H < K$, then the value of a knock out (up and out) call option is 0 and the value of the knock in (up and in) call option is equal to the value of a conventional call option.

If $H \geq K$, then the value of a knock in (up and in) call barrier options is given by:

$$SN(x_1)e^{-qt} - Ke^{-rt}N(x_1 - \sigma\sqrt{t}) - Se^{-qt}(H/S)^{2\lambda}[N(-y) - N(-y_1)]$$
$$+ Ke^{-rt}(H/S)^{2\lambda-2}[N(-y + \sigma\sqrt{t}) - N(-y_1 + \sigma\sqrt{t})]$$

The value of a knock out (up and out) call barrier options is given by:

Premium of knock out (up and out) barrier call option = premium of call option − premium of knock in (up and in) barrier call option

3. Put Options

If $H \geq K$, then the value of a knock in (up and in) put option is given by:

$$-Se^{-qt}(H/S)^{2\lambda}N(-y) - Ke^{-rt}(H/S)^{2\lambda-2}N(-y + \sigma\sqrt{t})$$

The value of a knock out (up and out) put barrier options is given by:

Premium of knock out (up and out) barrier put option = premium of put option − premium of knock in (up and in) barrier put option

If $H \leq K$, then the value of a knock out (up and out) put option is given by:

$$-SN(-x_1)e^{-qt} + Ke^{-rt}N(-x_1 + \sigma\sqrt{t}) + Se^{-qt}(H/S)^{2\lambda}[N(-y_1)]$$
$$- Ke^{-rt}(H/S)^{2\lambda-2}[N(-y + \sigma\sqrt{t})]$$

The value of a knock in (up and in) put barrier options is given by:

Premium of knock in (up and in) barrier put option = premium of put option −
premium of knock out (up and out) barrier put option

If $H \geq K$, then the value of a knock out (down and out) put option is 0 and the value of the knock in (down and in) put option is equal to the value of a conventional put option. If $H \leq K$, then the value of a knock in (down and in) put option is given by:

$$-SN(-x_1)e^{-qt} + Ke^{-rt}N(-x_1 + \sigma\sqrt{t}) + Se^{-qt}(H/S)^{2\lambda}[N(y) - N(y_1)]$$
$$- Ke^{-rt}(H/S)^{2\lambda-2}[N(y - \sigma\sqrt{t}) - N(y_1 - \sigma\sqrt{t})]$$

The value of a knock out (down and out) put barrier options is given by:

Premium of knock out (down and out) barrier put option = premium of put option −
premium of knock in (down and in) barrier put option

4.3 Numerical Models

The analytic solutions assume that the barrier is continuously monitored. This is consistent with the continuous time framework within which the analytic solutions are derived. This creates difficulty where the barrier is only monitored at discrete times. In this case, an analytic solution is not available and numerical approaches must be used. This is a common approach used with other path dependent exotic options.

For non-standard barrier options, analytic solutions are frequently not available. For these options, numerical solutions are generally required.

The primary numerical approaches used in relation to the valuation of barrier options are[21]:

- **Monte Carlo simulations** – this entails the generation of random asset price paths, calculating the barrier option pay-off and discounting the pay-off. The value of the barrier option is determined by running multiple samples and

[21] See Hull, John (2000) Options, Futures and Other Derivatives – Fourth Edition; Prentice-Hall Inc., Upper Saddle River, NJ at Chapter 18 at 471–481. See also Derman, Emanuel, Ergener, Deniz and Kani, Iraj "Forever Hedged" (September 1994) Risk 139–145; Kat, Harry and Verdonk, Leen "Tree Surgery" (February 1995) Risk 53–56; Ritchen, Peter "On Pricing Barrier Options" (Winter 1995) Journal of Derivatives 19–28; Cheuk, Terry H.F. and Vorst, Ton C.F. "Complex Barrier Options" (Fall 1996) Derivatives Quarterly 8–21.

calculating the mean value from the distribution. Monte Carlo simulations, while relatively straightforward, are computationally slow and expensive. This reflects the fact that a high number of sample paths must be run to obtain satisfactory levels of accuracy.

- **Binomial/trinomial models** – this entails adapting the basic binomial or trinomial approach to barrier options[22]. The approach is similar to normal binomial pricing approaches. The only difference is that the contractual feature of the barrier option must be incorporated in the asset price tree. This is done by setting the option value equal to zero (where the option is knocked out or where the option has not been knocked in). **Exhibit 9.15** sets out this approach diagrammatically using a trinomial tree.

Exhibit 9.15   Barrier Options – Valuation Using Binomial Tree

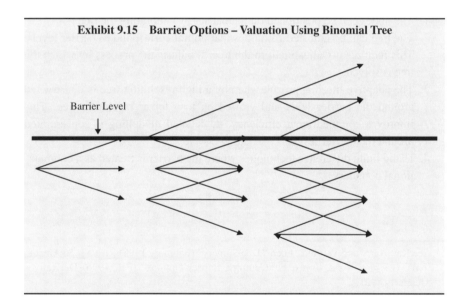

In practice, binomial/trinomial models are commonly used to value barrier options (particularly where the barrier is not continuously monitored). There are several related issues regarding the use of binomial/trinomial models for pricing barrier options, including:

- The solution may be slow and a large number of tree steps may be required to obtain accurate results. The need to use a large number of

---

[22] For a discussion of binomial option pricing models, see Das, Satyajit (2004) Derivative Products & Pricing; John Wiley & Sons (Asia), Singapore at Chapter 7.

steps is related in part to the problem of positioning tree nodes on the barrier[23]. Trinomial trees are generally used because they are generally more accurate and converge to a solution more easily than comparable binomial trees[24].

- There may be difficulties in fitting the barrier to the nodes of the tree[25]. The difficulty derives from the fact that the binomial/trinomial tree has a rigid relationship between node placement and time step. This relationship creates complex problems if nodes have to be placed arbitrarily to coincide with barrier levels. A simple way to overcome this problem is to increase the time steps to decrease the chance of barriers not coinciding with nodes in the tree. This is expensive and computationally slow. A number of approaches have been suggested to overcome this problem, including[26]:

1. The nodes can be positioned on the barrier by calibrating the tree.
2. The tree can be adjusted for nodes that do not correspond to barrier levels. This requires no adjustment to the tree. It adjusts the process by which the tree is solved.
3. The adaptive mesh approach whereby a high resolution tree is constructed around the barrier level and grafted on to a lower resolution tree. This improves computational efficiency, as detailed modelling is concentrated around the barrier levels.
4. Using finite difference techniques where the barrier is treated as a computational boundary[27].

---

[23] See Kat, Harry and Verdonk, Leen "Tree Surgery" (February 1995) Risk 53–56; Cheuk, Terry H.F. and Vorst, Ton C.F. "Complex Barrier Options" (Fall 1996) Derivatives Quarterly 8–21.

[24] See Cheuk, Terry H.F. and Vorst, Ton C.F. "Complex Barrier Options" (Fall 1996) Derivatives Quarterly 8–21.

[25] See Boyle, Phelim P. and Lau, Sok Hoon "Bumping Up Against the Barrier with the Binomial Method" (Summer 1994) Journal of Derivatives 6–14; Derman, Emanuel, Ergener, Deniz and Kani, Iraj "Forever Hedged" (September 1994) Risk 139–145; Kat, Harry and Verdonk, Leen "Tree Surgery" (February 1995) Risk 53–56; Ritchen, Peter "On Pricing Barrier Options" (Winter 1995) Journal of Derivatives 19–28; Cheuk, Terry H.F. and Vorst, Ton C.F. "Complex Barrier Options" (Fall 1996) Derivatives Quarterly 8–21; Gentle, David "Mind the Curves" (16 October 1996) Financial Products Issue 52 16–18.

[26] See Hull, John (2000) Options, Futures and Other Derivatives – Fourth Edition; Prentice-Hall Inc., Upper Saddle River, NJ at Chapter 18 at 478–481.

[27] See Randall, Curt "Pricing Barrier Options with PDEs" (1 March 1999) Derivatives Week 6–7; Tavella, Domingo "Barrier Monitoring" (August 2001) Risk 36.

4.4   Barrier Options – Behaviour of "Greeks"[28]

The sensitivity of the barrier option to changes in key parameters (spot price, volatility, time etc) is complex. The behaviour is often significantly different to that for conventional options[29]. This makes the management of the risk of barrier option positions potentially complex. The difference reflects the fact that barrier option values are dependent upon a small sample of future asset price paths and the discontinuous nature of the knock in/out feature.

The major differences relate to the behaviour of the following "Greek" letters:

*   **Delta** – the delta of barrier options is significantly different to that of a comparable conventional option. Deltas of normal options are between 0 and 1 (call option) and 0 and −1 (put option). A barrier option can have delta value less than zero (negative) or greater than 1. A reverse knock out option (for example, a deep in-the-money up and out call) will have a negative value. This reflects the fact that the delta is positive when it is operative because the option has intrinsic value. As it approaches the barrier, the potential loss of a large value forces delta to change sign as the underlying hedge position has to be reversed.
*   **Gamma** – the fact that the delta of the option may change rapidly under certain situations (for example, when the asset price approaches the barrier) means that the gamma of barrier options can be high. The fact that delta is effectively discontinuous means that gamma can become infinite.
*   **Vega** – conventional option value are positively related to increases in volatility. The value of some barrier options (knock outs) will, in certain circumstances, be inversely related to increases in volatility. This reflects the fact that higher volatility increases the possibility of the barrier option being extinguished.
*   **Impact of time to maturity** – the value of conventional options increases with maturity[30]. Barrier options exhibit similar behaviour. For knock out options, increases in maturity will increase the premium by smaller amounts and for significant increases in maturity, decrease the premium. This reflects the fact that the longer the maturity of the option, the greater the chance that the option will be knocked out.

---

[28]   See Combalot, Lauren "Getting to Know Barrier Options" (September 1995) AsiaMoney 33–39; Julian Cook "Trigger Happy" (August 1996) Futures & Options World 55–56; Derman, Emanuel and Kani, Iraj "The Ins and Outs of Barrier Options: Part 1" (Winter 1996) Derivatives Quarterly 55–67.

[29]   For a discussion of option value sensitivities, see Das, Satyajit (2004) Derivative Products & Pricing; John Wiley & Sons (Asia), Singapore at Chapter 15.

[30]   This is true of call options but put options may decrease in value with significant increases in term to expiry; see discussion in Das, Satyajit (2004) Derivative Products & Pricing; John Wiley & Sons (Asia), Singapore at Chapter 7.

Exhibit 9.16 sets out an analysis of the behaviour of the "Greeks" for some typical barrier options.

Traditional risk measures of options are generally not adequate to fully capture the risk/sensitivity of barrier (and other) exotic options. As a result, traders now use a number of additional measures to measure the risk of barrier options. These include[31]:

- **Vomma** – this is the change in vega for a change in implied volatility.
- **Vanna** – this is the change in vega for change in spot rate.

The additional measures are designed to attempt to overcome weaknesses in vega (particularly important for exotic options). They are also attempts to capture the changes in volatility for a change in spot prices and also the impact of the volatility smile/skew. **Exhibit 9.17** sets out an example of the use of these measures.

Exhibit 9.16   Barrier Options – Behaviour of "Greeks"[32]

All analysis is based on 6 month European options with the strike price set at the spot asset price. For the barrier options, the barrier level is set at 90% (down) and 110% (up) of the current spot asset price.

1. Call Options

1.1 Conventional Call Option
- Delta ranges between 0 and 1, increasing as the asset price increases relative to the strike price, increasing the intrinsic value of the option.
- Gamma is always positive and is at the highest level where the asset price is trading around the strike price and the remaining time to maturity is short.
- Vega is positive, reflecting the fact that the option value increases with increases in volatility.

1.2 Down and Out Call Option
- Delta behaviour is a function of where the asset price is relative to the barrier level. Below the barrier level, the option is extinguished and delta is zero. Above the barrier level, delta is positive. It increases rapidly when the asset price increases. Where the asset price is high and above the barrier level, the impact of the barrier is not significant and the delta of the barrier approximates that of the conventional call. In this case,

---

[31] See Webb, Andrew "The Sensitivity of Vega" (November 1999) Derivatives Strategy 17–24.

[32] The analysis is based on Combalot, Lauren "Getting to Know Barrier Options" (September 1995) AsiaMoney 33–39; Derman, Emanuel and Kani, Iraj "The Ins and Outs of Barrier Options: Part 1" (Winter 1996) Derivatives Quarterly 55–67.

the option is not significantly in-the-money. If the call is structured to have significant intrinsic value, then if the asset price falls towards the barrier level, the delta may become negative (the long asset position must be adjusted to a short asset position), reflecting the fact that the barrier option will lose value rapidly. Where the asset price is above the barrier level, the delta on this type of barrier option may be larger than that of the corresponding standard call.

- Where the asset price is high and well above the barrier level, the gamma of the barrier option approximates that of the conventional call. Gamma will increase rapidly where the asset price trades around the barrier level. This reflects the fact that the risk of the option being knocked out is high. Gamma may become infinite at the barrier level. For a long dated option, gamma may go negative. This reflects the fact that the barrier feature is analogous to being short options (short volatility) at the barrier level.
- Vega will be positive but generally lower than for a conventional option. For long dated options, vega may be negative, reflecting the fact that an increase in volatility would make a knock out more likely, decreasing overall option value. This may also be the case where the asset price is trading around the barrier level, as an increase in volatility would make a knock out more likely.

1.3 Down and In Call Option

- Delta behaviour is a function of where the asset price is relative to the barrier level. Above the barrier level, the option is not activated and delta is low. As the asset price increases, if it has not reached the barrier level first, delta declines, as the possibility of the option being triggered in declines. If the barrier level is reached, then the delta of the barrier option approximates that of the conventional call. Delta reaches a peak at the barrier level. If the underlying call is structured to have significant intrinsic value, then if the asset price falls towards the barrier level, the delta may become very large, reflecting the fact that the barrier will gain value rapidly. Delta is discontinuous around the barrier. Below the barrier, the delta is positive. Just above the barrier, delta is negative, reflecting the fact that the position is analogous to being short the asset as an increase in asset price will reduce the chance of the barrier being triggered.
- Gamma is positive throughout. Gamma may be infinite at the barrier level because of the discontinuous nature of delta.
- Vega will be positive. Increases in volatility would make a knock in more likely. Vega is particularly significant where the asset price is trading around the barrier level because an increase in volatility makes a knock in more probable.

1.4 Up and Out Call Option

- Delta below the barrier level is similar to that of a conventional call. As the asset price approaches the barrier, delta decreases and becomes negative. This reflects the fact that the risk of knock out increases with the resulting loss of intrinsic value. Where the option is deep in-the-money, the delta can become very large.
- Gamma is positive near the strike price but negative near the barrier. This reflects the rapid change in delta from positive to negative. Gamma may be infinite at the barrier.
- Vega behaviour will be similar to that for the down and out call option.

1.5 Up and In Call Option

- Delta behaviour of the option is dominated by the fact that the option will be in-the-money if the barrier level is reached. Delta is low where the asset price is below the barrier level. As the asset price approaches the barrier level, delta increases rapidly. The delta reflects the potential for sudden acquisition of significant value. At this point, the delta is substantially above that for a conventional call. Above the barrier level, the barrier option delta behaviour is similar to that for an in-the-money conventional call.
- Gamma is positive throughout. Gamma increases rapidly as the asset price approaches the barrier level. Gamma may be infinite at the barrier level because of the discontinuous nature of delta. Gamma is relatively low for other asset prices. At low prices the option is unlikely to be activated, and at high prices above the barrier the position is that of a deep in-the-money call option.
- Vega behaviour will be similar to that for the down and in call option.

2. Put Options

2.1 Conventional Put Option

- Delta ranges between 0 and −1, increasing as the asset price decreases relative to the strike price, increasing the intrinsic value of the option.
- Gamma behaviour is identical to that for the conventional call.
- Vega is positive, reflecting the fact that the option value rises with increases in volatility.

2.2 Down and Out Put Option

- Delta above the barrier level is similar to that of a conventional put. As the asset price approaches the barrier, delta increases and becomes positive. This reflects the fact that the risk of knock out increases with the resulting loss of intrinsic value. Where the option is deep in-the-money, the delta can become very large.
- Gamma is positive near the strike price but negative near the barrier. This reflects the rapid change in delta from negative to positive. Gamma may be infinite at the barrier.
- Vega will be positive but generally lower than for a conventional option. For long dated options, vega may be negative, reflecting the fact that an increase in volatility would make a knock out more likely, decreasing overall option value. This may also be the case where the asset price is trading around the barrier level, as an increase in volatility would make a knock out more likely.

2.3 Down and In Put Option

- Delta behaviour of the option is dominated by the fact that the option will be in-the-money if the barrier level is reached. Delta is low where the asset price is above the barrier level. As the asset price approaches the barrier level, delta increases rapidly. The delta reflects the potential for sudden acquisition of significant value. At this point, the delta is substantially above that for a conventional put. Below the barrier level, the barrier option delta behaviour is similar to that for an in-the-money conventional put.
- Gamma is positive throughout. Gamma increases rapidly as the asset price approaches the barrier level. Gamma may be infinite at the barrier level because of the discontinuous nature of delta. Gamma is relatively low for other asset prices. At high prices, the option

is unlikely to be activated and at low prices below the barrier, the position is that of a deep in-the-money put option.
- Vega will be positive. Increases in volatility would make a knock in more likely. Vega is particularly significant where the asset price is trading around the barrier level because an increase in volatility makes a knock in more probable.

2.4 Up and Out Put Option
- Delta behaviour is a function of where the asset price is relative to the barrier level. Above the barrier level, the option is extinguished and delta is zero. At the barrier level, the put would have minimal value as it is out-of-the money. Below the barrier level, the delta of the barrier is very similar in behaviour to a conventional put. It is only if the option was deep in-the-money (high strike) that the behaviour would be significantly different. This would reflect the sudden large loss of value at the barrier level. This is similar to the situation with an up and out call option.
- Gamma is similar to that for a conventional put. Gamma may be infinite at the barrier level.
- Vega behaviour will be similar to that for a down and out put option.

2.5 Up and In Put Option
- Above the barrier level, the option is activated and would behave in a manner similar to a conventional put. The put would have minimal value as it is out-of-the money. Below the barrier level, the delta of the barrier is zero. As the asset price approaches the barrier level, the delta increases. Delta peaks at the barrier level. It is also discontinuous at the barrier level as the delta moves from positive to negative (the need to switch from shorting to purchasing the asset).
- Gamma is positive. It peaks at a very high level at the barrier level. Gamma may be infinite at the barrier level.
- Vega behaviour will be similar to that for a down and in put option.

Exhibit 9.17   Barrier Options – Additional Risk Measures

Assume the spot asset price is $100. The trader is short a reverse knock out (up and out) call barrier option with a strike of $80 and a barrier level of $110. The trader is long the asset to hedge the short barrier option position. The hedge reflects the fact that the call has significant intrinsic value as it is in-the-money.

The behaviour of the barrier option and the hedge is driven by the position of the asset price relative to the barrier. If the asset price falls, then the barrier option behaves in a manner similar to a conventional call option. The barrier option value falls. The trader reduces the hedge position in the underlying asset to match the reduction in delta.

If the asset price increases, then the position is more complex:
- If the asset price reaches $110, then the barrier option is extinguished and the delta goes to zero.

- If the asset price increases but remains below $110, then the delta increases in line with the increasing value of the barrier option.

Assume the asset price is $109. The barrier option has significant intrinsic value ($29). However, the risk of a barrier event is high. The value of the barrier option will generally be low, reflecting the risk of knock out.

The hedging and risk of the position is complex. The option delta is low, reflecting the risk of the barrier being triggered. If the asset price does not reach $110, then the delta will be high. The position is extremely difficult to manage because of the high gamma.

The sensitivity of the position to both changes in volatility and spot rate is high. Additional risk measures are therefore useful in measuring the risk of the position. These would include:

- The position is very sensitive to changes in volatility (high vomma) as it affects chances of the barrier option knocking out.
- The position is sensitive to spot rate changes (high vanna) as it also affects the chances of the barrier option knocking out.

4.5 Hedging

There are several approaches to hedging barrier option portfolios:

- **Dynamic replication**[33] – this entails trading in the asset to offset the delta of the barrier option as the asset price evolves over time. Barrier options are difficult to hedge dynamically[34]. This reflects the behaviour of the option's delta. The discontinuous behaviour of delta and the high (sometimes infinite) gamma at the barrier makes hedging problematic. The sensitivity to volatility changes is also a complicating factor. The difficulty in estimating hedging costs and re-balancing/tracking error of the hedge make it difficult to price and manage barrier option positions. The difficulties are exacerbated in discontinuous markets where the asset price displays jump behaviour. These factors make it difficult to replicate barrier options efficiently within acceptable risk tolerances[35].
- **Static replication** – the difficulties with dynamic hedging of barrier options have encouraged the development of alternative approaches such as static replication[36]. This involves replicating the profile of the barrier option by trading

---

[33] See Das, Satyajit (2004) Derivative Products & Pricing; John Wiley & Sons (Asia), Singapore at Chapter 16.

[34] See Taleb, Nassim (1997) Dynamic Hedging; John Wiley & Sons, New York at Chapters 19 and 20.

[35] For an interesting case of some of the practical difficulties in hedging, see Reed, Nick "Aussies Get their Betting Slips" (January 1997) Risk 10.

[36] See Bowie, Jonathan and Carr, Peter "Static Simplicity" (August 1994) Risk 44–49; Derman, Emanuel, Ergener, Deniz and Kani, Iraj "Static Options Replication" in Konishi, Atsuo and Dattatreya, Ravi E. (1997) Frontiers in Derivatives; Irwin Publishing, Chicago

in a portfolio of conventional options. The key principle of static hedging is to match the behaviour of the barrier option and the replicating portfolio at specified boundaries. This allows the barrier option to be replicated, as the two portfolios will have equal values and pay-offs at all interior points of the boundaries. The advantages of the static replication approach are:

1. Re-balancing error is lowered as the portfolio does not have to be continuously adjusted.
2. As the hedge is based on a replicating portfolio of options, the gamma risk is reduced.
3. Increased certainty of hedging transaction costs.
4. Unlike dynamic hedging, there is minimal exposure to volatility estimation as static replication only requires the implied volatility of the conventional options used to hedge. In contrast, dynamic hedges are susceptible to tracking error where the volatility estimate used to hedge is incorrect.

4.6 Barrier Options – Volatility Estimates

A key issue in the valuation of barrier option is the volatility to be used. Standard barrier option pricing models use a single volatility. The problem arises because of the existence of the barrier level and the strike price. If a volatility smile/skew is used, then the volatility will be different between the strike and the barrier as they will be at different points on the smile.

In practice, a number of approaches to accommodate different volatility at the barrier and the strike have developed[37]:

• **Local volatility surfaces** – this entails fitting a tree to the implied volatility smile/skew and term structure and solving for the barrier value within this framework[38]. This approach is useful, but suffers from computational complexity, problems of obtaining the required implied volatility, and slow computational speeds.

• **Two volatility models** – this approach extends the standard model by adding a separate volatility for the trigger. In simple terms, this approach adjusts the theoretical barrier option values. For a reverse knock out, increasing the volatility

---

at Chapter 10; Carr, Peter and Chou, Andrew "Breaking Barriers" (September 1997) Risk 139–144; Hull, John (2000) Options, Futures and Other Derivatives – Fourth Edition; Prentice-Hall Inc., Upper Saddle River, NJ at Chapter 18 at 487–489.

[37] See Cook, Julian "Breaking Breakers" (December 1996) Futures & Options World 22–23; Wilmott, Paul (1998) Derivatives: The Theory and Practice of Financial Engineering; John Wiley & Sons, Chichester at Chapter 14 at 198–200.

[38] See description of local volatility surfaces in Das, Satyajit (2004) Derivative Products & Pricing; John Wiley & Sons (Asia), Singapore at Chapter 9.

around the barrier level will reduce the barrier option premium, reflecting the higher probability of the option being extinguished. Lowering the volatility around the barrier level will increase the barrier option premium. The approach is relatively simple and captures the impact of the volatility smile/skew.

5 Barrier Options – Structural Variations

5.1 Overview[39]

Barrier options are extensively used in hedging and trading. This reflects the capacity to use the contingency feature to develop structured hedges and also to take positions in asset markets. A number of structural variations on barrier options have evolved. The major structural variations on the basic barrier option concepts include:

- **Adjustment to the terms of barrier options** – the focus is on amending the key terms of a barrier option to alter the economic impact of the structure. This includes structures such as rebate structures, gradual barriers that reduce the discontinuity of the pay-off, double barriers and capped options. This also includes combinations of binary/digital and barrier option features.
- **Packaged barrier options** – the focus is on embedding barrier options within forward structures, or combinations of conventional and barrier options to create specific hedging structures.
- **Defined exercise options** – the focus is on altering the barrier mechanism. In standard barrier options, the payoff under the option and the barrier feature are based on the *same* asset. In a defined exercise option, the barrier feature is based on price movements in a *different* asset to that underlying the payoff of the option.

5.2 Barrier Options – Structural Variations

Variations to barrier options generally alter some of the structural features (premium; operation of the barrier etc). The objective is to alter the economic impact of the structure.

The major structural variations include:

- **Premium rebate structure** – this entails a knock out barrier option where a cash payment is received if the option is extinguished. A common structure is that the initial premium paid is refunded if the option knocks out. The cash

---

[39] See Cook, Julian "Double Barriers" (September 1996) Futures & Options World 58–61; Derman, Emanuel and Kani, Iraj "The Ins and Outs of Barrier Options: Part 2" (Spring 1997) Derivatives Quarterly 73–80.

payment can be structured to be either at the time of the barrier event (at hit) or at the original option maturity (at maturity). The structure is designed to make it attractive for the purchaser. The purchaser does not suffer a loss of premium where the option ceases to exist. Valuation of the structure entails incorporating the payment to the purchaser where the barrier is reached. **Exhibit 9.18** sets out an example of a premium rebate structure barrier option.

- **Capped/floored options** – this entails a structure where the option pay-off is subject to a maximum or minimum amount driven by the asset price attaining a nominated barrier level[40]. The structure operates as follows:
  1. *Capped call* – the option has a strike price and a cap barrier above the strike price. The option pay-off is:
     - If the asset price does not reach the barrier level, then the pay-off is the same as for a standard call.
     - If the asset price reaches the barrier level, then the option is extinguished and the option payout is the difference between the strike and the barrier.
  2. *Floored put* – the option has a strike price and a floor barrier below the strike price. The option pay-off is:
     - If the asset price does not reach the barrier level, then the pay-off is the same as for a standard put.
     - If the asset price reaches the barrier level, then the option is extinguished and the option payout is the difference between the strike and the barrier.

  The cash payment can be structured to be either at the time of the barrier event (at hit) or at the original option maturity (at maturity). The structure is similar to the rebate structure.

- **Continuous barrier structures** – this entails options with continuous strike prices and barriers producing proportional payouts and proportional knock ins and outs respectively. The primary objective is to reduce the risk of the barrier event on the option payout. Several structures are utilised[41]:
  1. *Step barriers* – under this structure the option is knocked in or out gradually, amortising the principal for each unit of time the underlying asset is above or below the barrier.

---

[40] See Derman, Emanuel and Kani, Iraj "The Ins and Outs of Barrier Options: Part 2" (Spring 1997) Derivatives Quarterly 73–80; Smithson, Charles (1998) Managing Financial Risk – Third Edition; McGraw-Hill, New York at Chapter 13 at 273. For a discussion on pricing, see Boyle, Phelim P. and Turnbull, Stuart M. "Pricing and Hedging Capped Options" (1989) Journal of Future Markets 41–54.

[41] See Hart, Ian and Ross, Michael "Striking Continuity" (June 1994) Risk 51–56; Linetsky, Vadim "Steps to the Barrier" (April 1998) Risk 62–65; Qu, Dong "Managing Barrier Risks Using Exponential Soft Barriers" (15 January 2001) Derivatives Week 6–7.

2. *Soft strike barriers* – under this structure the option is knocked in or out gradually for each price unit that the underlying asset is above or below the barrier.

Exhibit 9.18   Barrier Options – Rebate Structure

Assume a barrier option (in this case an up and out call option) with premium rebate on an equity index. The structure is designed to allow the purchaser to create an exposure to the equity index whilst reducing the premium required to create that exposure. This is consistent with the motivation for standard barrier option structures. The additional feature in this case is the rebate feature that allows the investor to recover the initial premium cost paid.

The terms of the option are as follows:

Current Index Level	524.00
Option Strike Price	524.00
Barrier (Outstrike) Level	650.00
Option Expiry	1 year
Premium	22.5 Index Points (4.30%)

The option return at maturity is as follows:
- If Index ≥ Barrier (650.00) at any time before maturity then the option is de-activated and ceases to exist. The purchaser receives a rebate equal to the option premium.
- If Index < Barrier (650.00) at all times before expiry then the purchaser's pay-off is:

Maximum of [0; Index at maturity – Strike Price (524.00)]

The option provides the purchaser with an exposure to the asset as follows:
- If the index trades above 524.00 and below 650.00 during the life of the option, then the purchaser receives a return equal to the appreciation in the index adjusted for the premium. For example, if the index at maturity is at 570.00, then the purchaser receives a benefit of 46.00 which, after premium, gives a net return of 23.50 which is equivalent to an annualised return of 104% pa on the premium amount on a market move of approx. 8.78%.
- If the index trades above 650.00, then the option is knocked out. But as the rebate operates, the purchaser recovers the premium paid.
- If the index trades below 650.00, then the purchaser loses the premium paid.

The rebate structure, combined with the barrier option, isolates the purchaser's risk of loss to the premium amount only where the market falls. A rise in the market of around 4.30% is needed to recover the premium amount paid. The reduction in option premium achieved by incorporation of the barrier eliminates the option if the market rises past 650.00 (a rise of some 24% over a 1 year period). This is not at the expense of a loss of premium that is recovered through the rebate mechanism.

The structure is attractive where the purchaser is seeking to monetise a view of a rise in the index but not beyond 650.00. The structure allows the purchaser to lower the cost of the option while eliminating any loss of premium if the option is knocked out.

3. *Parisian barriers*[42] – under this structure the option is knocked in or out only if the underlying asset is above or below the barrier and stays there for longer than a specified period.

- **Double barriers**[43] – this entails barrier options that have *two* barriers. In the case of a double barrier knock out, the option is extinguished at either a maximum or minimum level. The structure is driven by the purchaser's desire to reduce the cost of the option and/or place the barriers further away from the current market price. **Exhibit 9.19** sets out an example of a double barrier option.
- **Binary/digital and barrier combinations** – this entails barrier options that pay out a fixed amount if the asset price does not trade above or below a specific asset price. In effect, the options have no strike as the payout is fixed. Structures involving double barriers are common. A typical structure would be a binary/digital knock in up and in call option. The structure would pay out the agreed amount if the asset price increases to the barrier price level. A typical double barrier structure would be a binary/digital double no touch option. The structure would payout out a fixed amount if the asset price remained within the upper and lower barrier level in the period until option expiry. These structures combine features of digital/binary options and barrier options. The structures are considered as special cases of digital/binary options[44].

5.3 Packaged Barrier Options

The focus of packaged barrier options is on embedding barrier options within forward structures, or combinations of conventional and barrier options to create specific hedging structures. The key drivers of packaged barrier options are as follows:

- **Improving the hedge rate** – a key objective of the structures is to improve the hedging cost relative to the available current market prices. A key element is the desire by hedgers to outperform the current market forward price/rate.

---

[42] See Chesney, M., Cornwall, J., Jeanblance-Picque, M., Kentwell and Yor, M. "Parisian Pricing" (January 1997) Risk 77–79; Vorst, Ton "Parisian Option Valuation" (22 February 1999) Derivatives Week 6–7.

[43] See Julian Cook "Double Barriers" (September 1996) Futures & Options World 58–61; Smithson, Charles (1998) Managing Financial Risk – Third Edition; McGraw-Hill, New York at Chapter 13 at 273.

[44] See Chapter 10.

Exhibit 9.19   Barrier Options – Double Barrier Structure

Assume the following currency double barrier on the US$/Yen exchange rate. The market parameters are as follows:

Structure	Double barrier knock in US$ call/Yen put option
Spot rate (US$1:Yen)	120.00
Strike rate (US$1:Yen)	119.00
Upper barrier (US$1:Yen)	125.00
Lower barrier (US$1:Yen)	115.00
Maturity	3 months

The basic structure operates as follows:
- The barrier option is not activated unless the US$/Yen spot rate trades at the upper or lower barrier level.
- The barrier option is activated if the US$/Yen spot rate trades at the upper or lower barrier level. In this case, the option functions like a conventional US$ call/Yen put option.

The double barrier structure requires that the upper barrier is above the strike and the lower barrier is below the strike. The option strike does not have to be within the range specified by the barriers. In the case of double barrier knock out structure, the strike would not be placed above the upper barrier for a call option or below the lower barrier for a put option. This reflects the fact that the option would always be knocked out before it reached the strike and would be incapable of acquiring value.

The primary motivation for this structure is cost reduction within specific risk parameters. The purchaser has the objective of reducing the premium of buying a US$ call/Yen put option. For a standard knock out option, the barrier has to be placed close to the current spot rate to achieve the targeted premium reduction. The use of the double barrier structure allows the barrier to be placed at a level that is further away from the spot, reducing the risk of a barrier event. The structure may also allow the purchaser to take advantage of the implied volatility smile/skew to lower the cost of the option.

- **Creating structured risk profiles** – the packaged barrier options are used to create precise risk profiles. The structured profiles allow the hedger or trader to develop risk profiles consistent with expectations of directional asset price movements, volatility and asset price evolution over time.

There are a large number of possible structures that can be developed consistent with individual requirements. The basic structures are follows:
- Combinations of conventional options and barrier options.
- Combinations of forwards and barrier options.

- Combinations of standard packaged options (such as range forwards)[45] and barrier options.

The structures are similar. Forward can be replicated by a combination of purchased and sold conventional call and put options (using put-call parity[46]). Similarly, packaged options are a zero cost combination of conventional call and put options. This means that the structures are equivalent.

The typical dynamics of the structures are as follows:

- **Preservation of potential upside** – this structure entails accepting a hedged cost that is *worse* than the forward price/rate. The structure allows the possibility of improving the hedge (for example, the forward or sold option component of a packaged product is extinguished) if a specific market event occurs (generally the market price/rate moves in a favourable direction and reaches the barrier level).

- **Reduced hedge cost** – this structure entails generating a hedged cost that is *better* than the forward price/rate. The structure allows the possibility of losing the protection of the hedge (for example, the forward or bought option component of a packaged product is extinguished) if a specific market event occurs (generally, the market price/rate moves in an unfavourable direction and reaches the barrier level).

In practice, the use of packaged barrier options (rather than entering into a series of separate forward or option transactions) is driven by the zero cost nature of the structures, the inability of the parties to trade the separate components, and the administrative convenience of the packaged structure[47].

In the remainder of this Section, a number of examples of packaged barrier structures are set out[48]. **Exhibit 9.20** sets out an example of roll up options (a combination of conventional and barrier options). **Exhibit 9.21** sets out examples of a number of structures combining forward contracts with barrier options. **Exhibit 9.22** sets out examples of a number of structures combining range forward contracts with barrier options. **Exhibit 9.23** sets out a number of structures involving currency contracts. **Exhibit 9.24** sets out a number of structures involving interest rate contracts.

---

[45] See Chapter 6.
[46] See Das, Satyajit (2004) Derivative Products & Pricing; John Wiley & Sons (Asia), Singapore at Chapter 7.
[47] These factors are similar to the key drivers of packaged options generally; see Chapter 6.
[48] The examples are not comprehensive but seek to provide an indication of the types of structures in use.

Exhibit 9.20   Packaged Barrier Options – Roll-Up Options[49]

This entails a standard option with an additional feature. If the asset price reaches a pre-specified level (the roll up or roll down strike), then the option changes to a knock out barrier option with a reset strike price. For example, assume a roll up put with a roll up strike above the initial strike price. If the asset price reaches the roll up strike, then the standard put is replaced by a knock out (up and out) put at a more favourable strike price. The roll up strike and the terms of the knock out barrier option are pre-agreed. The structure is a combination of a conventional put option and a barrier option. The purchaser is undertaking 3 separate option transactions:

1. Purchase a standard put.
2. Sell a knock in put (underlying terms same as the standard put) that is triggered at the barrier level (the roll up strike).
3. Purchase a knock in put (underlying terms of the knock out put triggered at the barrier) that will be triggered at the barrier level.

The structure is used to give the hedger the ability to participate in any favourable movement in the asset price with low risk. The cost of the structure is the net premium cost of the components. Generally, the roll up option is structured to have a cost that is close to the cost of the corresponding standard option.

Exhibit 9.21   Packaged Barrier Options –Forward/Barrier Option Combinations[50]

The central element in structuring forward barrier options is the fact that under put call parity:

• A bought forward is equivalent to a bought call/sold put.
• A sold forward is equivalent to a sold call/bought put.

The sold option component of the forward prevents the holder of the contract from benefiting from favourable movements in the asset price. Similarly, the bought option component has value that can be monetised.

Forward/barrier option combinations can be used to improve the forward price/rate achieved or improve the ability to participate in favourable movements in asset prices.

---

[49] See Gastineau, Gary L. "An Introduction to Special Purpose Derivatives: Roll-up Puts, Roll Down Calls and Contingent Premium Options" (Summer 1994) The Journal of Derivatives 40–43; Smithson, Charles (1998) Managing Financial Risk – Third Edition; McGraw-Hill, New York at Chapter 13 at 272–273.

[50] See Combalot, Lauren "Getting to Know Barrier Options" (September 1995) AsiaMoney 33–39; Deutsche Morgan Grenfell "Outperforming the Forward Rate" (April 1997) AsiaMoney 10–13.

The basic strategies are:

- **Conditional forward purchase** – for a forward purchase, the structure entails purchasing a call and simultaneously selling a put that knocks in at a specified barrier level. The trade is done for zero cost. This is achieved by adjusting the strike prices of the call and knock-in put. The pay-offs of this structure are as follows:
  1. If the barrier is not reached, then the purchased call will provide protection above the strike price. The holder of the option will be able to benefit from decreases in the asset price.
  2. If the barrier is reached, then the put is triggered in. The combination of the bought call and the sold put is equivalent to a bought forward. The holder is locked in at the relevant forward rate.

  The economics of the structure are driven by the fact that the sold knock-in put will result in the receipt of a premium that is lower than the premium equivalent conventional put. This means that in order to achieve a zero cost structure, the strike price of the option will be at a level that is worse than the forward rate. This means that if the barrier is reached, the hedger is locked into a forward rate that is less attractive than the prevailing forward rate at the time of entry into the contract. In return for this additional cost, where the barrier is not reached the contract allows participation in favourable movements in the asset price. An equivalent structure for a forward sale can be devised.

- **Knock out forward** – for a forward purchase, the structure entails the simultaneous purchase of a knock out call and the sale of a knock out put barrier option. The options have the same maturity, strike rate and barrier levels. The trade is done for zero cost. This is achieved by adjusting the strike prices of the knock out call and knock in put. The pay-offs of this structure are as follows:
  1. If the barrier is reached, then both options are extinguished, leaving the underlying position exposed to price movements.
  2. If the barrier is not reached, then both options remain in place. The combination of the bought call and the sold put is equivalent to a bought forward. The holder is locked in at the relevant forward rate.

  The economics of the structure are driven by the location of the barrier. If the barrier is set at a level that represents a favourable movement in the price/rate (in this case, a decline in the price), then there will be a net cost in establishing the option position. This means that in order to achieve a zero cost structure, the strike price of the option will be at a level that is worse than the forward rate. This means that if the barrier is not reached, the hedger is locked into a forward rate that is less attractive than the prevailing forward rate at the time of entry into the contract. In return for this additional cost, where the barrier is reached the contract allows participation in favourable movements in the asset price. When the forward is extinguished, the hedger has the opportunity of purchasing the underlying asset at a price that is below the rate embedded in the options. The barrier can be set at a level that represents an unfavourable movement in the price/rate (in this case an increase in the price) then there will be a net premium receipt in establishing the option position. This means that in order to achieve a zero cost structure, the strike price of the option will be at a level that is better than the forward rate. This means that if the barrier is not reached, the hedger achieves a forward rate that is attractive relative to the prevailing forward rate at the time of entry into the contract. In return for this benefit, where the barrier is reached the contract is extinguished and the hedger is exposed to the unfavourable movement in the asset price. This means that conservative or aggressive structures can be devised as required. Equivalent structures for a forward sale can be devised.

Different combinations of forwards and options can be used to achieve equivalent structures.

Exhibit 9.22   Packaged Barrier Options – Range Forward/Barrier Option Combinations[51]

Range forward/barrier option combinations are predicated on adjusting the basic components of range forwards using embedded barrier options.

The range forward consists of a bought and a sold option[52]. The options have the same face values and maturity. The strike prices of the two options are adjusted to realise a zero premium cost structure. The sold component of the option combination prevents the hedger from fully benefiting from any favourable movement in prices. Barrier options are used to adjust the cost and risk profile of the basic structure as follows:

• **Range forward with purchased barrier option** – this entails a combination of:
  1. Selling a normal call or put to cap the profit of the position.
  2. Buying a knock out put or call to protect the value of the position.

The knock out option will be less expensive than an equivalent conventional option. This means that the hedger is able to adjust the strike of the sold option to a more favourable level and maintain the zero premium cost structure. The barrier can be set at a level considered unlikely to be attained by the hedger. The conservative approach entails setting the barrier at a level that represents a favourable movement in the asset price. This is designed to ensure that the structure allows the hedger to re-cover the position without additional risk of loss if the barrier is reached.

• **Range forward with sold barrier option** – this entails a combination of:
  1. Buying a normal call or put to protect the value of the position.
  2. Selling a knock out put or call to finance the purchased option by capping the profit of the position.

The knock out option sold generates a lower premium than the equivalent normal option. This means an adjustment of the strike of the sold option (lower profit) or bought option (lower level of protection). The benefit of the structure is that unfavourable movement in the asset price has a beneficial effect on the hedge. This is because the sold option is extinguished.

---

[51] See Combalot, Lauren "Getting to Know Barrier Options" (September 1995) AsiaMoney 33–39.

[52] See Chapter 6.

- **Range forward with sold reverse barrier option** – this entails a combination of:
  1. Buying a normal call or put to protect the value of the position.
  2. Selling a reverse knock out put or call to finance the purchased option by capping the profit of the position.

The performance of this structure is similar to that of a normal range forward. If the asset price moves in a favourable direction, then the performance of the range forward is enhanced. This is because as the asset price moves favourably, the sold option limits the gain to the extent of the difference between the strike price and the barrier level. If the barrier is reached, then the sold option is extinguished. This means that the full gains from the favourable asset price move are received. The structure also benefits from the fact that the reverse knock out will attract a larger premium than a conventional option. Where the barrier is not reached, the sold reverse knock out option's large payout will reduce the benefit of the structure. The knock out option sold generates a lower premium than the equivalent normal option. This means an adjustment of the strike of the sold option (lower profit) or bought option (lower level of protection). The benefit of the structure is that unfavourable movement in the asset price has a beneficial effect on the hedge. This is because the sold option is extinguished.

Exhibit 9.23   Packaged Barrier Options – Currency Structures[53]

1. Knock Out Forwards

Assume a company needs to purchase US$/sell Euros to cover a payment in 6 months. The foreign exchange market is volatile. The company expects the Euro to appreciate, although periods of short-term weakness are considered possible. The company can use a knock out forward to hedge its exposure in line with its expectations.

Assume the following market parameters:

Spot rate	Euro 1 = US$0.9500
6 month forward rate	Euro 1 = US$0.9520

The knock out forward is structured as follows:
- Purchase a standard Euro put/US$ call with a strike of US$0.9370
- Sell knock out (down and out) Euro call/US$ call with a strike of US$93.70 and barrier of US$93.40.
- All options are for the same face value.
- The premium for the two options is offsetting, providing a zero premium cost hedge.

The hedge structure operates as follows:
- If the Euro does not reach US$0.9340, then the two options are operative. The combination of the bought Euro put and sold Euro call is equivalent to a short Euro/long US$ forward position at US$0.9370. This means that the company is hedged at US$0.9370.

---

[53] For an excellent overview of a number of currency strategies, see (1999) Structured Risk Management Products; National Australia Bank, Melbourne.

- If the Euro reaches US$0.9340 then the sold put is extinguished. This leaves the bought standard Euro put/US$ call. This means that the company participates in any strength in the Euro above US$0.9370 but is protected against any decline below that level.

The economics of the structure are as follows:
- The company has a worst case cost in US$ terms of US$0.9370. This is Euro 0.0150 worse than the forward rate at the time of the hedge.
- If the barrier level is reached then the company has the full benefit of the standard Euro put at US$0.9370. The company is protected fully against any weakness in the Euro (below US$0.9370) but has the opportunity to participate in any appreciation in the Euro (above US$0.9370).
- The hedge does not incur any immediate premium cost for the company.

The knock out put provides a worst case Euro cost of the US$ while allowing participation in any appreciation of the Euro, provided the Euro trades at US$0.9340. The expectation of short term Euro volatility and setting the worst case Euro cost at a level below the forward rate achievable allows the company to create a zero premium cost structure that has potential for significant gains from improvements in value of the Euro.

2. Convertible Currency Options (Trigger Forwards)
Assume a company need to purchase Euro/sell US$ to cover US$ cash flow receipts.
Assume the following market parameters:
Spot rate   Euro 1 = US$0.9500
6 month forward rate   Euro 1 = US$0.9520

The company uses a convertible Euro call/US$ put option (strike at Euro 0.9470 and a barrier level at Euro 93.00) to hedge this exposure.
The convertible option operates as follows:
- If the Euro does not trade at US$0.9300, then the structure operates as a normal Euro call/US$ put structure. The company sells US$ in the market where the Euro is weak (below the US$0.9470 strike) and exercises the Euro call/US$ put to lock in the Euro value of the receipts where the Euro is strong (above the US$0.9470 strike).
- If the Euro trades at US$0.9300, then the structure converts into a bought Euro/sold US$ forward at a rate of US$0.9470 (the strike price of the initial option).

The convertible option is constructed as follows:
- Purchase standard Euro call/US$ put with a strike of US$0.9470.
- Sell knock in (down and in) Euro put/US$ call option with a strike rate of US$0.9470 and a barrier of US$0.9300.
- All options are for the same face value and maturity.
- The premium for the two options is offsetting, providing a zero premium cost hedge.

Where the barrier level is reached, the knock in option is triggered, creating the synthetic forward position.
The convertible option allows the company to hedge its position at a rate better than the forward rate and maintain exposure to depreciation of the Euro to a level of US$0.9300.

3. Knock Out Range Forwards

Assume a company needs to purchase US$/sell Euros to cover a payment in 6 months. Knock out range forwards use sold barrier options to achieve a rate superior to the available forward rate, while assuming the risk of the barrier event.

Assume the following market parameters:

Spot rate	Euro 1 = US$0.9500
6 month forward rate	Euro 1 = US$0.9520

The knock out range forward is structured as follows:
- Sell knock out (down and out) Euro call/US$ put option with a strike rate of US$0.9670 and a barrier of US$0.9300.
- Purchase standard Euro put/US$ call with a strike of US$0.9520 (the forward rate).
- Sell standard Euro put/US$ call option with a strike of US$0.9300.
- All options are for the same face value.
- The premium for the three options is offsetting, providing a zero premium cost hedge.

The knock out range forward would operate as follows:
- If the Euro does not trade at US$0.9300 then:
  1. If the Euro is above US$0.9670, then the knock out (down and out) Euro call/US$ put option is exercised against the company. This means that the company purchases US$ at Euro 0.9670 (Euro 0.0150 above the original forward rate).
  2. If the Euro is between US$0.9520 and US$0.9670, all options expire out-of-the-money. This means that the company purchases US$ at the spot rate that is above the original forward rate.
  3. If the Euro is between US$0.9520 and US$0.9300, then the purchased standard Euro put is exercised. This means that the company purchases US$ at US$0.9520 (the forward rate).
- If the Euro trades at US$0.9300, the knock out option is extinguished, then:
  1. If the Euro is above US$0.9520, the two remaining options expire out-of-the-money. This means that the company purchases US$ at the spot rate that is above the original forward rate.
  2. If the Euro is between US$0.9520 and US$0.9300, then the purchased standard Euro put is exercised. This means that the company purchases US$ at US$0.9520 (the forward rate).
  3. If the Euro is below US$0.9300, then the company has a net gain of US$0.0220 (the difference between the strike (US$0.9520) of the bought put and the strike (US$0.9300) of the sold put). This means that the company purchases US$ at a rate of US$0.0220 above the spot but below the forward rate.

The effect of the knock out range forward is to achieve any effective Euro cost that is, under certain circumstances, at least equal to or superior to the forward rate. This improvement is obtained by taking a number of risks:
- If the barrier level is not reached, then if the Euro rallies, the company caps its participation at US$0.9670. This means that in the case of a significant increase in the value of the Euro, the hedge under performs the spot rate (i.e., the unhedged position).

- If the barrier level is reached, then the company is unprotected where the spot is below US$0.9300, except for the US$0.0220 put spread gain. This means that below US$0.9080, the company suffers an economic loss.

The company would enter into this transaction where it does not expect the spot rate to trade above US$0.9670 or below US$0.9080.

**Exhibit 9.24   Packaged Barrier Options – Interest
Rate Structures**

1.   Knock Out (Up and Out) Barrier Interest Rate Swap
Assume the US$ yield curve is steep – current 3 month US$ LIBOR is 4.00% pa and the 5 year US$ swap rate against 6 month LIBOR is 6.25% pa payable quarterly. This means a borrower swapping floating rate funding into fixed rate incurs a high cost. Effectively, the borrower pays the difference between current US$ LIBOR and the swap rate immediately. A possible mechanism for reducing the swap cost is to enter into a knock out (up and out) barrier interest rate swap.
   The structure of the knock out (up and out) barrier interest rate swap is as follows:
- Swap fixed rate: 5.25% pa payable quarterly if the barrier level is not reached.
- Barrier level: 7.00% pa on 3 month US$ LIBOR.

The operation of the swap is as follows:
- If the 3 month US$ LIBOR does not trade above 7.00% pa, then the swap will operate, locking in a cost of 5.25% pa.
- If 3 month US$ LIBOR trades above 7.00% pa, then the swap is extinguished and the borrower has no protection against higher interest rates. The borrower's cost on funds will be equal to the then current 3 month US$ LIBOR rate.

The economics of the knock out (up and out) barrier interest rate swap is based on its lower fixed rate (a reduction of 1.00% pa) relative to a conventional swap. The lower cost is achieved by eliminating the protection of the swap if US$ 3 month LIBOR trades above 7.00% pa (presumably a rate that is considered unlikely to be reached).
   Under the basic structure, the swap is knocked out *in its entirety* for the complete remaining maturity. A variation would entail a periodic knock out structure. Under the periodic knock out (up and out) barrier interest rate swap, the barrier is monitored at each interest rate period. If the barrier level is reached, then the swap is extinguished *only for that 3 month interest rate period*. The swap is reinstated in future interest rate dates where 3 month US$ LIBOR trades below 7.00% pa. The periodic knock out (up and out) barrier interest rate swap fixed rate is 5.75% (a reduction in cost of 0.50% pa). The higher cost reflects the lower risk to the borrower.

The construction of the knock out (up and out) barrier interest rate swap is as follows:

- The underlying swap is a series of sold interest rate forwards (of FRAs) on US$ 3 month LIBOR.
- The forwards can be restated as a series of bought puts on price/calls on interest rates and sold call options on price/put options on interest rates.
- In the knock out (up and out) barrier interest rate swap, the conventional call and put options are replaced by barrier (knock out (up and out)) structures. The barriers are not continuous and only operate on the interest rate setting dates.
- In the cases of the standard knock out (up and out) barrier interest rate swap, the barriers operate on all interest rate setting dates prior to the expiry of the option. In the periodic knock out (up and out) barrier interest rate swap structure, the barrier only operates on the interest rate setting date that coincides with the expiry date of the relevant option.

2. Knock Out (Down and Out) Interest Rate Swaps[54]

Assume US$ 3 month LIBOR is 3.25% pa. US$ short term interest rates are expected to fall further. The expectation is that 3 month US$ LIBOR rates will fall by 0.25% pa. The current US$ yield curve has the 3 month LIBOR forward curve at 3.00% pa in 6 months and increasing rapidly thereafter. Implied forward 3 month LIBOR rates are at current spot levels in 1 year. The implied forwards indicate that short term rates are expected to increase within the next 18–24 months.

A borrower seeks to gain from the expected decrease in short term rates, and also seeks protection against the potential future rise in rates. Traditional hedging strategies used would be as follows:

- 3 year interest rate swap at fixed rate at 4.50% pa. This strategy will benefit the borrower if the 3 month US$ LIBOR fixes at levels higher than the current implied forward 3 month LIBOR curve. The borrower would be locked in to a high cost of funds where 3 month LIBOR decreases. The cost of carry of the interest rate swap would be high because of the upward slope of the yield curve.
- 3 year interest rate collar with a sold 3.00% pa strike floor and a purchased 5.00% pa cap. The cost of this collar would be around 150 bps (or 54 bps pa). This strategy would allow the counterparty's debt rate to fluctuate between an effective minimum and maximum cost (inclusive of the amortised premium) of 3.54% pa and 5.54% pa. Within this range, the borrower's cost would be LIBOR plus 54 bp pa.

One structure that may achieve additional flexibility for the borrower is a knock out (down and out) swap (also referred to as the floored swap). This structure offers the borrower protection at a fixed rate but allows the borrower to benefit from a decrease in rates down to a nominated level.

---

[54] See Barrett, Gilles "Ins and Outs of Barrier Options" (1994) Corporate Finance Risk Management and Derivatives Yearbook 26–36.

On each fixing date, the LIBOR fixing is compared to the limit (see Table below):

3 Month US$ LIBOR Rate (% pa)	Payments Under Knock Out (Down and Out) Swap	Net Cost to Borrower (% pa)
> 4.80	Pay 4.80% pa/receives 3 month US$ LIBOR	4.80% pa
2.95 < or < 4.80	No Payments	3 month LIBOR
< 2.95	Pay 4.80% pa/receives 3 month US$ LIBOR	4.80% pa

The borrower's pay-off profile is as follows:
- If US$ 3 month LIBOR interest rates increase above 4.80% pa, the borrower has a fixed cost of funding under the swap of 4.80% pa.
- If US$ 3 month interest rates are below 4.80% pa and the barrier level of 2.95% pa is not breached, the borrower has a borrowing cost equivalent to US$ 3 month LIBOR.
- If US$ 3 month interest rates fix below the barrier level of 2.95% pa, then the borrower has a fixed cost of funding under the swap of 4.80% pa.

The knock out (down and out) swap provides the borrower with zero premium cost protection with no cost of carry if the barrier level (2.95% pa) is not reached. The barrier level is set at a level below which US$ 3 month LIBOR is not expected to fall. The structure simultaneously provides protection in the event of a rise in interest rates. If the borrower expects a small decrease in short term rates over the near term followed by an increase in rates then the knock out (down and out) swap provides an effective hedge.

The knock out (down and out) swap is constructed as follows:
- A normal fixed against US$ 3 month LIBOR interest rate swap.
- Purchase of a knock out (down and out) interest rate floor that is triggered out if US$ 3 month LIBOR trades below the barrier level. The barrier floor neutralises the effect of the sold floor embedded in the interest rate swap, unless the barrier is triggered.
- The cost of the knock out interest rate floor is incorporated in the higher swap rate and the adjustment of the strike price of the floor itself.

5.4   Defined Exercise Options

In standard barrier options, the option payoff and the barrier feature are based on the *same* asset. This means that in standard barrier options, price movements of a single asset determine whether the option is knocked out or in *and* the value of the option. In a defined exercise option (also referred to as outside barrier options), the barrier feature is based on price movements in a *different* asset to that underlying the option. This means that the value of the option is determined by the price of one asset. Price movements of a second asset determine whether the option is knocked in or knocked out[55].

---

[55]   See Heynen, Ronald and Kat, Harry "Crossing Barriers" (June 1994) Risk 46–51; Klotz, Rick and Efraty, Ravit (8 December 1994) "Analyzing Defined Exercise Options";

An example of a defined exercise option is an interest rate cap on 6 month US$ LIBOR with a strike rate of 6.50% pa which only pays off if gold prices are below US$250/ounce. The pay-off of this defined exercise option is given as:

$$\text{Maximum } [0; 6 \text{ month US\$ LIBOR} - 6.50\% \text{ pa}] \text{ if Gold} < \text{US\$250/ounce}$$
$$0 \text{ if Gold} \geq \text{US\$250/ounce}$$

The structure means that the payoff under the interest rate cap will knock in or out depending upon gold price movements.

Defined exercise option structures include links between interest rates and currency or commodity prices, currency and commodity prices, and equity value and interest rates.

The major application of defined exercise options is the design of integrated hedges where contingent price movements drive risk. The structured hedge effectively monetises the embedded price relationship to lower the cost of the hedge.

Defined exercise options, despite the similarity to limit dependent options, are multi-factor options. This reflects the fact that the correlation between the two underlying asset prices is a key driver of the value of defined exercise options. These structures are examined in the context of multi-factor options[56].

6 Summary

Limit dependent options are dependent upon the underlying asset price reaching a specified level over a nominated period (generally the maturity of the option). Limit dependent options are both limit and path dependent. Limit dependent options, particularly barrier options, are among the most important types of exotic options. The structures, either in standard format or in packages, are extensively utilised in capital markets for the purpose of hedging and trading. Limit dependent options are driven primarily by the capacity of these structures to reduce option premium and provide structured hedges that provide more accurate matching of underlying assets or liabilities.

Salomon Brothers US Derivatives Research Fixed Income Derivatives, New York; Ong, Michael "Exotic Options: The Market and their Taxonomy" in Nelken, Israel (Editor) (1996) The Handbook of Exotic Options; Irwin Professional Publishing, Chicago at Chapter 1 at 15.

[56] See Chapter 11.

10
Payoff Modified Options

1 Overview

Traditional options have linear continuous functions above or below the strike price. Payoff modified options alter the payoff of the options. The adjustments include the incorporation of a fixed payoff or enhancing the payoff. In this Chapter, payoff modified exotic option structures are examined.

The structure of the Chapter is as follows:

- An overview of payoff modified options is set out.
- Binary/digital options, the major types of payoff modified option, are described.
- The pricing/valuation and hedging of payoff modified structures are outlined.
- Contingent payment options, a specific application of binary/digital options, are examined.
- Power options, a special type of payoff modified option where the return is amplified, are outlined.

2 Payoff Modified Options[1]

Payoff modified options entail adjustment to the normal payoffs that are associated with conventional options. **Exhibit 10.1** sets out the major types of payoff modified options.

The major types include:

- **Digital (binary) options** (referred to as "digital" options) – where the payout under the option contract is a fixed pre-determined amount payable if the strike

---

[1] For a discussion of payoff modified options, see Ong, Michael "Exotic Options: The Market and their Taxonomy" in Nelken, Israel (Editor) (1996) The Handbook of Exotic Options; Irwin Professional Publishing, Chicago at Chapter 1; Smithson, Charles (1998) Managing Financial Risk – Third Edition; McGraw-Hill, New York at Chapter 13.

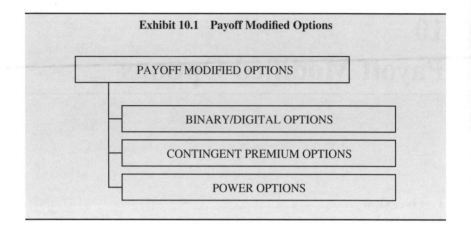

Exhibit 10.1   Payoff Modified Options

price is reached, irrespective of the asset price performance (that is, how far the option is in the money).

- **Contingent premium options** – this option entails linking the option premium to be paid to the writer to the asset price performance. In a contingent premium option, no premium is payable at the commencement of the transaction. The premium becomes due and payable at expiration only if the option expires in the money. The contingent premium structure is a combination of a conventional option and a digital option.
- **Power (exponential) options** – where the option payout is enhanced upon exercise. A standard option return is a simple linear function of the difference between the underlying asset price and the option strike at exercise or at maturity. In the case of a power option, the option payoff is a defined function of the difference between the underlying asset price and the option strike raised to a power; for example, higher than 1.

There are a number of variations on the structures outlined, in particular, to the standard digital option. The variations represent structural changes to the basic elements of the primary payoff modified option structure.

Exotic option structures are generally driven by the following objectives:

- Reduction in option premium.
- Alteration in risk profile, including increased probability of gain, quantification of loss or optimal exercise timing.
- Asset liability matching.

Payoff modified options are driven primarily by the capacity of the structures to reduce/increase option premium, reduce the risk of loss on a sold option position and improve matching of underlying assets or liabilities. The exact factor driving individual payoff modified structures varies between types of option.

3 Digital Options

3.1 Concept[2]

Digital options are options where the payout is discontinuous. Normal options have smooth payout profiles (that is, the further the option is in-the-money, the higher the option payout to the purchaser). In contrast, digital options have a fixed payout. The payout is an agreed amount, or nothing. In a standard digital option, if the strike price is reached, then the payout is a fixed predetermined amount. This is the case irrespective of how far the asset price at maturity is above (call options) or below (put options) the strike price (that is, the extent that the option is in-the-money).

The term digital refers to the "digitised" payout. These options are also referred to as binary as the fixed option is either switched on or off (a *binary* payout). These options are also often termed cash-or-nothing options, all-or-nothing options or "bet" options.

Digital options are relatively common. The structure is frequently used in currency and interest rate markets. They are also used less frequently in equity and commodity markets. Digital options are the second most commonly used exotic option structure after barrier options.

3.2 Digital Options – Structure

The payoff of a digital option can be given as the following:

Digital call option: if $Sm > K$ then X; if $Sm \leq K$ then 0

Digital put option: if $Sm < K$ then X; if $Sm \geq K$ then 0

Where

Sm = asset price at maturity

---

[2] See Ong, Michael "Exotic Options: The Market and their Taxonomy" in Nelken, Israel (Editor) (1996) The Handbook of Exotic Options; Irwin Professional Publishing, Chicago at Chapter 1 at 22–26; Smithson, Charles (1998) Managing Financial Risk – Third Edition; McGraw-Hill, New York at Chapter 13 at 285–286; Ravindran, K. (1998) Customised Derivatives; McGraw-Hill, New York at Chapter 3 at 105–119; Nelken, Israel (2000) Pricing, Hedging & Trading Exotic Options; McGraw-Hill, New York at Chapter 3.

K = strike price
X = fixed payout

Exhibit 10.2 sets out the payoff of a standard digital option. The structure indicates the truncated payoff (representing the digitised payout amount) and the limited loss profile represented by the premium paid. The digital payoff is similar to that of a vertical option spread. The major difference is that the payout between the two strikes is fixed, unlike a normal spread where it tracks the increase or decrease in the asset price.

There are two basic types of digital options:

* **Cash or nothing** – the payoff for a cash or nothing option is a predetermined amount if the option is in-the-money.
* **Asset or nothing** – this structure is very similar to the cash or nothing digital, except that the payoff for an asset or nothing option is the underlying asset itself if the option is in-the-money.

The standard digital is not path dependent. The payout is driven by the asset price at maturity relative to the strike price.

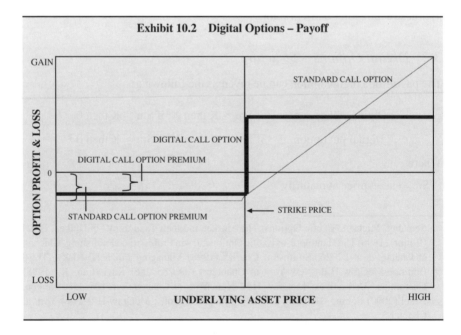

Exhibit 10.2   Digital Options – Payoff

3.3 Digital Options – Economics and Applications[3]

3.3.1 Digital Options – Economics

The economics of digital options are driven by the following factors:

- **Fixed and known payout** – digital structures are attractive to option sellers as the digital structure guarantees a known maximum loss in the event that the option is exercised. This overcomes a fundamental problem with standard options where the potential loss is unlimited. For the purchaser of a digital option, the fact that the option payoff is a known constant amount may be advantageous. The amount can be adjusted to provide the exact quantity of protection required. The fixed payout also overcomes the problem for a purchaser of an option that expires at or slightly in-the-money. In this case, the option payout will generally not cover the option premium cost. In the case of a digital option, the digitised payout can be set at a level that ensures recovery of the premium.
- **Premium cost** – the digital payout can be used to adjust the cost of the option relative to a conventional option. This allows the simultaneous optimisation of the level of protection purchased or the risk assumed by the digital option seller against the premium.
- **Impact of volatility** – digital options are affected by changes in volatility in a manner different to the impact on conventional options. The cost of digital options becomes cheaper relative to the cost of conventional options with increases in volatility.

Exhibit 10.3 sets out an analysis of the premium dynamics of digital options.

3.3.2 Digital Options – Applications

Applications of digital options are driven primarily by the underlying economics of the structure. The fixed payout, relative premium cost and the relationship to volatility are all central to the use of digital options.

The major applications of digital options are in the following areas:

- **Structured hedging** – this application is focused on using the fixed payout feature of digital options to structure hedges that closely match the risk exposure

---

[3] See Liu, Ralph Yiehmin "The Alchemy of Asian Exotics" (November 1995) AsiaRisk 50–52; Barret, Gilles "The Binary Option Mechanism" in (1995) Corporate Finance Risk Management & Derivatives Yearbook 24–29; Cook, Julian "Digital Lines" (July 1996) Futures & Options World 55–57; Davies, David "Switched on to Digitals" (July 2001) FOW 31–32.

Exhibit 10.3   Digital Options – Premium Behaviour

1. Assumptions

In this Exhibit, the premium behaviour of cash payout digital options is set out. The examples assume the following parameters:

Asset Price ($)	1,000.00
Strike Price ($)	1,000.00
Expiry	6 months
Volatility (% pa)	20
Interest Rates (% pa)	6.00
Asset Income (% pa)	1.50
Exercise	European
Digital Payout ($)	100.00

Premium behaviour of digital call and put options are examined and compared to the behaviour of conventional call and put options. The sensitivity to the size of digital payout, volatility changes and maturity is examined.

2. Digital Options – Premium Behaviour

The following Table sets out the premium (% of asset price) of digital call and put options and the premium for conventional call and put options:

Type	Call	Put
Conventional	6.67	4.48
Digital	5.19	4.51

The digital call is cheaper than the conventional call, while the digital put and conventional put are very similar. The relationship is driven by the fact that the conventional call and put option provides unlimited profit opportunities. In contrast, the digital option payout is fixed. This means that where the digital payout is smaller than the expected payout of the conventional option, the digital option will be cheaper. The relativity of the digital payout and the expected payout is driven by the forward price and forward asset price distribution (which is affected by the volatility level).

3. Digital Options – Premium Sensitivity

3.1 Sensitivity to Digital Payout

The following Table sets out the premium (% of asset price) of digital call and put options for different payout levels and the premium for conventional call and put options:

Type	Call	Put
Conventional	6.67	4.48
Digital		
Payout = $25	1.30	1.13
Payout = $50	2.60	2.26

Type	Call	Put
Payout = $100	5.19	4.51
Payout = $150	7.79	6.77
Payout = $200	10.39	9.03
Payout = $300	15.58	13.54
Payout = $400	20.78	18.05

The premium of the digital options increases with the size of the digital payout. This is driven by the fact that where the digital payout is small, it is lower than the expected payout of the conventional option. This makes the digital option cheaper. As the size of the digital payout increases, the fixed payout is larger than the expected payout of the conventional option. This increases the premium of the digital option.

3.2 Sensitivity to Volatility
The following Table sets out the premium (% of asset price) of digital call and put options (fixed payout $100) and the premium for conventional call and put options for different volatility levels:

Volatility (% pa)	10	20	30	40	50
Conventional Call	3.99	6.67	9.39	12.13	14.84
Digital Call	5.93	5.19	4.85	4.61	4.42
Conventional Put	1.80	4.48	7.20	9.94	12.65
Digital Put	3.78	4.51	4.85	5.09	5.29

The premium of the digital options displays a lower sensitivity to volatility than the corresponding conventional option. This reflects the fact that the fixed payout means that the expected asset price does not have a significant impact upon the value of the option. In addition, as the payout is fixed, the value is not affected by the higher volatility that increases the chance of more extreme price outcomes and option values that increases the value of the conventional options.

Where volatility increases, the digital option premium relative to the premium for conventional options decreases. This decrease is most marked at higher levels of volatility. This reflects the fact that higher volatility implies higher expected values that affect the value of the conventional options, as extreme price outcomes increase in likelihood. This means that the expected value of the conventional option become larger than the fixed payout of the digital.

3.3 Sensitivity to Maturity
The following Table sets out the premium (% of asset price) of digital call and put options (fixed payout $100) and the premium for conventional call and put options for different maturities:

Maturity	3 months	6 months	1 year	2 years	3 years
Conventional Call	4.50	6.67	10.04	15.14	19.27

Maturity	3 months	6 months	1 year	2 years	3 years
Digital Call	5.17	5.15	5.18	5.06	4.89
Conventional Put	3.40	4.48	5.70	6.78	7.20
Digital Put	4.68	4.51	4.24	3.81	3.46

The premium of the digital options displays lower sensitivity to changes in maturity than the corresponding conventional option. This change in value of the conventional options represent gains in intrinsic value (for the conventional call) and the gain in time value (for both conventional calls and puts) as a result of the combined impact of volatility and time. The digital options with a fixed payout are less affected by increases in maturity. This has the effect of significantly decreasing the relative cost of the digital options.

of the party. The digital option is used to create a hedge that is matched to the actual level of protection required. This enables the hedger to lower the cost of hedging by avoiding the requirement to pay for protection under conditions that do not require hedging or are considered unlikely. Examples of structured hedging are set out in **Exhibits 10.4** and **10.5**.

- **Premium capture/positioning strategies** – this type of application is based on similar principles to those that drive structured hedging. In structured hedging, the cost of hedging is reduced by eliminating protection against certain contingencies. In premium capture/positioning strategies, digital options are used to capture premium or value by selling a digital option that only pays off under asset price outcomes that are considered improbable. Examples of using digital options to generate premium are set out in **Exhibit 10.6**.

Digital options are frequently packaged with fixed interest securities or other conventional derivatives. Digital option embedded structured notes include Range Note structures (also known as Corridor or Accrual notes). These structures are discussed in the context of interest rate, currency and equity linked notes[4]. **Exhibit 10.7** sets out an example of a derivative (an interest rate swap) with an embedded digital option.

Digital options can also be regarded as building blocks for other exotic option structures. The major example is contingent premium options that combine a conventional option with simultaneous sale of the digital option[5].

---

[4]   See Chapters 19 and 20 and Das, Satyajit (2004) Structured Products Volume 2; John Wiley & Sons (Asia), Singapore at Chapter 4.

[5]   See later in this Chapter.

Exhibit 10.4   Digital Option Application – Hedging

Assume an investor has a position in an asset. The current price is $1,000. The investor is concerned about a decrease in asset prices. The investor expects a market correction of around 10% (to $900) over a 6 month time horizon. The volatility of asset prices drives the investor to consider the use of options to hedge.

The investor considers the following options:

• Purchase a 6 month conventional put with strike of $975 (97.5% of current market). The premium is 3.44%.

• Purchase a 6 month digital put with a strike of $975 and a fixed payout of $75. The premium is 2.87% (a saving of 0.57% or 17% to the cost of the conventional option).

The options are priced at a volatility level of 20% using comparable parameters.

The operation of the two options is as follows:

• Both options will protect the position against any decline in the asset price below the strike price of $975.

• The conventional option will recover the premium paid when the asset price reaches $940.60. The conventional put will provide protection against any decline irrespective of size.

• The digital option will payout $46.30 (the digital payout less the premium paid) if the option is exercised. The digital put will only provide protection (excluding the effect of the premium) against a decline in the asset price to $900 (a decline of 10%). The digital put will not provide any protection below this level except to the extent of the $46.30 net payout.

The digital option allows the investor to lower the cost of hedging where it is willing to monetise its expectation of a limited price decline. The lower cost of the digital option reflects the fact that the investor is willing to forgo protection below $900. By solving for the fixed payout for a digital put premium equivalent to the cost of a conventional put (3.44%), it is possible to establish the level to which the conventional put is providing protection. A digital put with a cost of 3.44% would give a payout of around $90. This indicates that the conventional put is implying a larger price decline to around $885 (11.5%). This is below the investor's expectation.

The difference in premium is even more marked for higher volatility levels and where the risk horizon is longer:

	Conventional Put	Digital Put
Volatility 30%	6.06%	3.29%
Maturity 1 year	4.70%	2.83%

Digital options can be used in this way to align hedge structures to market price expectations. The primary objective is to align the hedge to the actual risk to be eliminated at the lowest cost.

Exhibit 10.5   Digital Option Application – Interest Rate Hedging[6]

Assume an investor seeks to hedge a portfolio of money market instruments against declines in US$ 3 month LIBOR rates.

The investor purchases a 1 year digital interest rate floor with a strike price at 3.01% pa and a fixed payout of 75 bps. Under the digital floor, the investor receives the payout of 75 bps where US$ 3 month LIBOR rates fall to 3.00% pa or lower levels. The premium cost of the digital floor is 32 bps. A 1 year conventional interest floor with a strike price of 3.01% pa would cost 15 bps.

The relevant performance of the digital floor and a conventional floor (calculated as the option payout (bps) at the relevant LIBOR level adjusted for the option premium (bps)) is set out below:

3 month LIBOR (%)	Digital Floor Payout (bps)	Conventional Floor Payout
3.10	−32	−15
3.00	43	−14
2.85	43	1
2.60	43	26
2.50	43	36
2.43	43	43
2.20	43	66

The digital floor achieves an enhanced performance relative to the conventional floor in all cases except where US$ 3 month LIBOR rates fall below 2.43% pa or remain above 3% pa.

The purchase of the digital floors would be the preferred hedge where the investor expects US$ 3 month LIBOR to decline modestly over the term of the hedge. The digital option structure ensures that the investor does not pay for protection that is not likely to be required. The digital floor means the investor can avoid incurring the premium for deep-in-the-money protection that is not required. This, allied to the fact that the structure increases the payout when the option is closer to the strike price, improves the hedge performance in the specified interest rate scenario.

Exhibit 10.6   Digital Option Application – Premium Capture/Positioning

Assume the investor holds an asset in its investment portfolio. The current price of the asset is $1,000. The investor considers that the asset price is likely to fall but not significantly. The investor wishes to monetise its expectation by selling covered call options against the asset position.

---

[6]   See Konotey-Ahulu, David "Options as an Alternative" (1994) Corporate Finance Risk Management & Derivatives Yearbook 20–25.

The investor considers the following options:
- Sell a 6 month conventional call with strike of $1,025 (102.5% of current market). The premium is 5.46%.
- Sell a 6 month digital call with a strike of $1,025 and a fixed payout of $75. The premium is 3.39% (a reduction of 2.07% or 38% to the premium of the conventional option).

The options are priced at a volatility level of 20% using comparable parameters. The operation of the two options is as follows:
- Both options will not be exercised if the asset price is below the strike price of $1,025. The conventional option premium will provide protection against price declines on the position to $945. The digital call premium will provide protection against price declines to $966.
- If the asset price is above $1,025, then both options will be exercised. All price increases above $1,025 will be lost where the conventional call is used. Where the digital option is used, the fixed payout caps the loss at $75. The investor maintains exposure to the asset above that level.

The digital option allows the investor to manage the risk of unlimited losses that may be unacceptable. The structure also refines the risk profile. The structure is effectively a 2.21 to 1 "bet". The investor receives $1 of premium in return for assuming $2.21 (fixed payout ($75)/digital premium ($33.90)) of potential loss if the option is exercised. The bet is contingent on the asset price not increasing above $1,025.

The structure is best used for short maturities and where volatility is low:

	Conventional Call	Digital Call
Volatility 10%	2.68%	3.44%
Maturity 3 months	3.33%	3.15%

The structure can be aggressively used to generate premium income. For example, assume that the investor expects asset prices to be relatively stable over the next 6 months and monetises this view by selling a digital call on the same terms as above except *with a fixed payout of $250 (25% of asset value)*. The premium generated is 11.29% (double the premium of the normal call). The higher premium is driven by the larger fixed payout. In effect, the investor agrees to make a very large payout in the event of an unexpected price move occurring (namely, the asset price reaching the strike price).

An alternative approach might entail selling a digital call option with a fixed payout of $250 but a strike of $1,126. This option generates the same premium as the conventional call (5.46%). As the option is less likely to be exercised, the risk of the option is reduced.

Digital options can be used in this way to generate premium by monetising market price expectations. The primary objective is to manage the risk of loss in case of exercise. A further objective may be to generate significant premium income by taking exposure to events considered unlikely to occur. A related objective may be to monetise expectations for adequate reward during periods of low volatility.

Exhibit 10.7   Packaged Digital Options – Range LIBOR/Accrual Swap[7]

The range LIBOR/Accrual swap is structured as follows:
- Dealer receives US$ 6 month LIBOR.
- Dealer pays US$ 6 month LIBOR plus a margin if US$ 6 month LIBOR sets between two predetermined levels – a lower range boundary value and an upper range boundary value of US$ 6 month LIBOR. Dealer does not make any payments if US$ 6 month LIBOR sets outside the range – below the lower range or above upper range value.

For example, a typical transaction would be structured as follows:

Maturity: 1 year
Dealer receives: US$ 6 month LIBOR
Dealer pays: US$ 6 month LIBOR + 150 bp on any fixing date on which 6 month LIBOR sets within the following bands:

Fixing Dates	Lower Boundary (% pa)	Upper Boundary (% pa)
6 months	3.50	4.50
12 months	3.25	4.50
18 months	3.00	4.50

If LIBOR sets outside the relevant band no coupon is payable.

The structure is designed for an investor that has an expectation that US$ 6 month LIBOR will set between the lower and upper boundaries on the relevant fixing dates. The investor monetises this expectation to boost investment returns. The structure is aggressive in that the investor stands to lose all income (for the relevant interest rate period) if the expectations on rates (trading within the range) are not realised.

The structure is constructed using a combination of digitals and conventional caps as follows:
- In respect of each interest rate band, the investor:
  1. Sells a digital floor option with a strike price set at the lower boundary.
  2. Sells a digital cap option with a strike price set at the upper boundary.
- The digital payout of both the cap and the floor are set equal to the expected interest accrual over the relevant interest rate period which is locked in using interest rates forwards (FRAs or Swap).

---

[7] See Konotey-Ahulu, David "Options as an Alternative" (1994) Corporate Finance Risk Management & Derivatives Yearbook 20–25; Barret, Gilles "The Binary Option Mechanism" in (1995) Corporate Finance Risk Management & Derivatives Yearbook 24–29. This structure has been widely used. An alternative term is Swap with Embedded Leverage ("SPEL").

Variations on this structure include:
- **Frequent fixings** – the enhanced return is paid based on daily or weekly fixings of US$ 6 month LIBOR. The investor receives the enhanced return only where US$ 3 month LIBOR stays within the range at each relevant date. The investor also does not suffer a total loss of income if the rate sets outside the range for any one fixing. The interest accrual is lost only for that fixing (ie for 1 day or 1 week).
- **Reset-able structures** – the upper and lower boundaries are reset at each quarterly fixing. The investor will be allowed to set either the upper or lower boundary and the other boundary will be set at a pre-specified level relative to the selected boundary level.

4 Digital Options – Pricing/Valuation & Hedging

4.1 Overview[8]

The valuation of digital options presents specific problems. The key features of digital options that drive valuation include:

- The payoff of the digital option is switched completely one way or the other depending on whether the asset price is above (call option) or below (put option) the strike price.
- The payoff, provided the option is in-the-money, is fixed.

In practice, the valuation of digital options is relatively uncomplicated. Both analytic and numerical approaches are available. Hedging and trading of digital options is more difficult. The instruments present significant complexities in trading and risk management.

The values of digital options are inherently related to the value of equivalent conventional European options as follows[9]:

> European call option
> = purchase of asset or nothing call and a short position in a
>   cash or nothing call (fixed payout equal to the strike price)

---

[8] See Briys, Eric Bellalah, Mondher, Mai, Huu Minh and De Varenne, Francois (1998) Options, Futures and Exotic Derivatives: Theory, Application and Practice; John Wiley & Sons, Chichester at Chapter 18; Hull, John (2000) Options, Futures and Other Derivatives – Fourth Edition; Prentice-Hall Inc., Upper Saddle River, NJ at Chapter 18 at 464–465; Nelken, Israel (2000) Pricing, Hedging & Trading Exotic Options; McGraw-Hill, New York at Chapter 3.

[9] See Hull, John (2000) Options, Futures and Other Derivatives – Fourth Edition; Prentice-Hall Inc., Upper Saddle River, NJ at Chapter 18 at 465.

European put option

= a long position in a cash or nothing put (fixed payout
equal to the strike price) and a short position in asset or
nothing put.

4.2   Analytic Models

Analytic models for the valuation of digital options are based on the fact that the option only pays out a fixed amount if the option finishes in-the-money. A closed form solution based on the Black-Scholes-Merton option pricing model can be derived[10]. This means that the value of a cash or nothing digital option is the present value of the fixed payout conditioned upon the probability that the option expires in-the-money (this is given by N(d2) in the cash of a call option in the Black-Scholes formula). Using a similar logic, the value of an asset or nothing digital option is given as the present value of the underlying conditioned upon the probability that the option expires in-the-money. **Exhibit 10.8** sets out the general analytic pricing formulation for digital options.

Exhibit 10.8   Digital Options – Analytic Pricing Models[11]

Terminology
S = spot asset price
X = fixed payout
r = interest rate
y = income on the asset
t = time to expiry

N(d2) is the same as for the standard Black-Scholes option pricing model[12].

---

[10] See Rubenstein, Mark and Reiner, Eric "Unscrambling the Binary Code" (October 1991) Risk 75–83; Turnbull, Stuart M. "Interest Rate Digital Options and Range Notes" (Fall 1995) Journal of Financial Engineering 92–101; Hull, John (2000) Options, Futures and Other Derivatives – Fourth Edition; Prentice-Hall Inc., Upper Saddle River, NJ at Chapter 18 at 464–465; Nelken, Israel (2000) Pricing, Hedging & Trading Exotic Options; McGraw-Hill, New York at Chapter 3.

[11] The version set out here is that suggested in Hull, John (2000) Options, Futures and Other Derivatives – Fourth Edition; Prentice-Hall Inc., Upper Saddle River, NJ at Chapter 18 at 464–465.

[12] See Das, Satyajit (2004) Derivative Products & Pricing; John Wiley & Sons (Asia), Singapore at Chapter 7.

Cash or Nothing Digital Options
- Call options: $Xe^{-rt} N(d2)$
- Put options: $Xe^{-rt} N(-d2)$

Asset or Nothing Digital Options
- Call options: $Se^{-yt} N(d2)$
- Put options: $Se^{-yt} N(-d2)$

4.3 Numerical Models

Numerical approaches to the valuation of digital options are also feasible. The most typical approach is a binomial model. The approach is similar to normal binomial pricing approaches. The only difference is the contractual feature of the digital option must be incorporated in the asset price tree. This is done by setting the option value equal to the fixed payout where the option is in-the-money. The binomial tree is then solved normally.

Numerical approaches are primarily required for more complex types of digital structures. Path dependent digital structures (range digitals or barrier digital combinations) are generally not capable of being valued using analytical solutions. This is especially the case where the range or barrier level is not continuously monitored. In practice, this means that numerical approaches (binomial models or Monte Carlo simulations) are used to value these structures.

4.4 Digital Options – Hedging/Trading and Risk Management

The hedging/trading and risk management of digital options presents significant difficulties. Digital options can be dynamically hedged. The discontinuous nature of the digital option payoff creates hedging difficulties. Like barrier options, digital options are difficult to hedge because around the strike level, small moves in the underlying asset price can have large effects on the value of the option.

The behaviour of the "Greeks" of digital options is as follows[13]:
- **Delta** – the delta of a digital option is large around the strike. This reflects the fact that if the option expires in-the-money, then the option will have significant value. The delta of a digital option can take on positive as well as negative values. The behaviour is driven by exactly the same dynamics that

---

[13] See Cook, Julian "Digital Lines" (July 1996) Futures & Options World 55–57; Davies, David "Switched on to Digitals" (July 2001) FOW 31–32.

drives delta changes in a reverse knock out barrier option – that is, the potential loss of a large fixed payout if the option expires out-of-the-money. The absolute value of delta can be large. This reflects the fact that a marginally in-the-money digital option will have a much larger payout than a comparable conventional option. The delta of a digital option is also prone to change rapidly, especially where the asset price is trading around the strike and the time to expiry is short.

- **Gamma** – digital options also have large gammas under certain circumstances. This reflects the fact that the value and delta of a digital option can exhibit rapid changes where the underlying price is trading around the strike price and the option is close to expiry. The problem of delta and gamma is exacerbated where the fixed payout is large.

- **Vega** – digital options, like barrier options, are sensitive to changes in volatility around the strike price. This reflects the fact that a change in volatility where the asset is trading around the strike price affects the chances of the option being exercised.

The risk behaviour of digital options makes these instruments difficult to hedge[14]. This is particularly the case for digital options where the asset is trading around the strike and the remaining time to maturity is short. The size of the fixed payout, if large, also affects the risk management. In practice, it is difficult to hedge/trade digital options on a dynamic basis[15].

The difficulties of dynamically hedging digital options have forced traders to use static hedging techniques[16]. The factors driving this move are identical to those that affect the hedging/trading of barrier options[17].

Static hedging may take the form of using a conventional option spread to hedge the digital position. The basic premise is that the spread accurately replicates the digital payoff in most price ranges. The problem with this approach comes when the price is in the range between the strike prices of the two options. The fixed payout

[14] See Taleb, Nassim (1997) Dynamic Hedging; John Wiley & Sons, New York at Chapter 18.
[15] For a discussion of problems encountered by traders in managing the risk of digital options; see Priest, Andrew "Banks Hit by Exotic Losses" (January 1997) Risk 7.
[16] See Bowie, Jonathan and Carr, Peter "Static Simplicity" (August 1994) Risk 44–49; Derman, Emanuel, Ergener, Deniz and Kani, Iraj "Static Options Replication" in Konishi, Atsuo and Dattatreya, Ravi E. (1997) Frontiers in Derivatives; Irwin Publishing, Chicago at Chapter 10; Carr, Peter and Chou, Andrew "Breaking Barriers" (September 1997) Risk 139–144.
[17] See Chapter 9.

of the digital will generally be larger than the payout of the spread. This means that the face value of the spread may need to be adjusted to ensure that the digital option payout is covered. In practice, this means that the trader will enter into an option spread with a small difference between the strike of the sold and bought option. The amount of the hedge will be adjusted to equate to the digital option payout. An added complication is that the behaviour of the digital option and the conventional option spread will be different during the term of the hedge. Alternatively, more sophisticated static replication approaches using portfolios of options to replicate the boundary conditions of the digital option may be utilised[18].

5 Digital Options – Structural Variations

There are a number of variations to the standard digital options described. The major structural variations include:

• **Adjusted payout** – the principal feature of this type of structure is an adjustment to the payout mechanism. Typical examples include:

1. *Gap options*[19] – in a standard option, the strike price determines both the exercise of the option and the payout (the difference between the strike price and the asset price at maturity). In a gap option there are two strike prices – a normal strike price that determines whether the option is exercised and a separate strike price (known as the gap or pay strike) that determines the payout. The payout under a gap option is determined by the difference in price between the asset price at maturity and the gap or pay strike. The payout under a gap option is as follows:

   For a call gap option: Sm – P if Sm > K or 0 if Sm < K

   For a put gap option: P – Sm if Sm < K or 0 if Sm > K

   Where
   Sm = asset price at maturity
   K = strike price
   P = strike on which the payout is based (referred to as the "paystrike")

   The term gap is used to describe the difference between the strike price and the paystrike. A positive gap (paystrike above the strike) will reduce the cost

---

[18] See Chriss, Neil and Ong, Michael "Digitals Defused" (December 1995) 56–69.
[19] See Rubenstein, Mark and Reiner, Eric "Unscrambling the Binary Code" (October 1991) Risk 75–83 at 78; Zhang, Peter G. "Correlation Digital Options" (March 1995) Journal of Financial Engineering 75–96.

of a call option. A positive gap will increase the value of a put option. Gap options are constructed from digital options (cash or nothing and asset or nothing options) as follows:

Gap call option = long asset or nothing call and short a cash or nothing call

Gap put option = long a cash or nothing put and short an asset or nothing put

The gap option is used to hedge positions from a price level that is different from the strike price.

2. *Supershares*[20] – this is a structure where the holder, on expiration date, is entitled to a pre-specified proportion of the assets underlying a portfolio of securities provided the asset price is between two strike prices (a lower and upper strike level). The structure is equivalent to a spread of asset or nothing call options where the holder has purchased an asset or nothing call (strike set at the lower strike) and sold an asset or nothing call (strike set at the upper strike).

• **Path dependent digital options**[21] – in a standard digital option, the option payoff is only dependent upon the asset price at maturity relative to the strike price. In the case of path dependent digital options, the option depends upon whether the option is in-the-money *at any time prior to expiry of the option*. These structures are often referred to as "one touch" or "no touch" options. The structure requires the option to be out-of-the-money at the time of purchase. In the case of a one touch digital call (put) option, the option will pay out a fixed amount if the asset price trades above (below) the strike at any time prior to expiry. In the case of a no touch digital call (put) option, the option will pay out a fixed amount if the asset price does not trade above (below) the strike at any time prior to expiry. The digital payout can be paid at the normal expiry (for example, one touch at expiration) or at the time the option goes in-the-money (for example, one touch at hit). Cash or nothing payouts and asset or nothing payouts are both feasible. The structure is analogous to American style exercise digital options. Path dependent digital options are used for similar applications to standard digital options. Closed form analytic solutions for the

---

[20] See Hakansson, Nils "The Purchasing Power Fund: A New Kind of Financial Intermediary" (November/December 1976) Financial Analyst Journal 49–59.

[21] See Nelken, Israel (2000) Pricing, Hedging & Trading Exotic Options; McGraw-Hill, New York at Chapter 13.

value of these options can be derived[22]. The solutions are generally derived using similar approaches to that used to value barrier options. Numerical and Monte Carlo valuation approaches are also available. These approaches are required where the asset price is monitored discretely.

- **Barrier-digital option combinations** – these structures involve digital options that have a barrier feature. The primary application is structured risk assumption to generate premium income. Investors use the structures to enhance investment returns. The structures are used either in standalone formats or more frequently in the form of structured notes[23]. There are a variety of structures[24] that are used, including:

  1. *Knock in or knock out digital options* – these structures involve a combination of a barrier option and a digital option. For example, assume a knock in (down and in) digital option. In this structure, the option would only pay out the fixed amount where the option expires in-the-money and the asset price trades below the barrier price level prior to expiry of the option. The options must be structured so that the asset price is above or below the barrier level at commencement. There are a number of combinations available based on:
     - Payout – the digital amount can be a fixed cash amount or the asset.
     - Barrier structure – the barrier can be set to create up and out, up and in, down and out and down and in structures.
     - Rebate – where a cash amount (for example, the initial premium payment) is rebated to the purchaser if the option is knocked out.

     These options can be valued using either an analytic[25] or numerical solution. Numerical valuation techniques are used where the barrier is monitored discretely.

  2. *Range digital option* – these structures combine double barrier options and digital options. The option has an upper and lower barrier level. The options have no strike prices as the payout is fixed. There are two basic structures:
     - Range barrier no touch option – the structure pays out a fixed payout if the asset price trades within an agreed range. The asset price is assumed

---

[22] See Rubenstein, Mark and Reiner, Eric "Unscrambling the Binary Code" (October 1991) Risk 75–83.

[23] See Chapters 19 and 20 and Das, Satyajit (2004) Structured Products Volume 2; John Wiley & Sons (Asia), Singapore at Chapter 4.

[24] For example, see Briys, Eric Bellalah, Mondher, Mai, Huu Minh and De Varenne, Francois (1998) Options, Futures and Exotic Derivatives: Theory, Application and Practice; John Wiley & Sons, Chichester at Chapter 18 at 361–364.

[25] See Rubenstein, Mark and Reiner, Eric "Unscrambling the Binary Code" (October 1991) Risk 75–83.

to be within the range at commencement. The purchaser pays a premium. The purchaser receives the fixed payment if the asset price does not trade outside the range at any time prior to the expiry of the option.

- Range barrier one touch option – the structure pays out a fixed payout if the asset price trades outside an agreed range. The asset price is assumed to be within the range at commencement. The purchaser pays a premium. The purchaser receives the fixed payment if the asset price trades outside the range at any time prior to the expiry of the option. The fixed payment is received either at the time the range is reached (at hit), or at the expiry of the option (at expiration).

Range digitals can be valued using either analytic or numerical solutions. The valuation approach used is similar to that used with double barrier options. Analytical solutions are predicated upon valuing the option using Black-Scholes approaches within the barrier levels. This is combined with various boundary conditions at the barriers and at expiration. The equation can then be solved numerically. Where analytic solutions are not available (for example, when the barriers are monitored discretely), numerical methods are used. This approach is computationally slow as the number of steps used increases.

6 Contingent Premium Options[26]

6.1 Concept

Contingent premium options are a special application of digital options. A contingent premium option is an option where the option premium is not payable at the commencement. The premium is only payable at expiration and is conditional on the option expiring in-the-money.

Under this structure, the option payoff is as follows:

- If the option expires out-of-the-money, then the option is not exercised and no premium is payable.
- If the option expires in-the-money, then the option is exercised and the premium is payable.

---

[26] See Gastineau, Gary L. "An Introduction to Special Purpose Derivatives: Roll-up Puts, Roll Down Calls and Contingent Premium Options" (Summer 1994) The Journal of Derivatives 40–43; Ong, Michael "Exotic Options: The Market and their Taxonomy" in Nelken, Israel (Editor) (1996) The Handbook of Exotic Options; Irwin Professional Publishing, Chicago at Chapter 1 at 22–23; Smithson, Charles (1998) Managing Financial Risk – Third Edition; McGraw-Hill, New York at Chapter 13 at 286; Nelken, Israel (2000) Pricing, Hedging & Trading Exotic Options; McGraw-Hill, New York at Chapter 4.

Exercise is automatic. If the option expires in-the-money, then the option is automatically exercised and the premium must be paid.

This structure is also referred to as cash on delivery options, money back options and refundable premium options.

Contingent premium options are used in a variety of asset classes, including currencies and interest rates (typically in the form of contingent caps, floors, swaps and swaptions).

6.2 Economics and Applications

The economics of contingent premium options are driven by the following factors:

* The purchaser of a contingent premium option does not pay for the option in the case where it expires out-of-the-money. This has significant appeal for users reluctant to pay the premium for an option.
* The contingent or conditional nature of the premium payment dictates that it is more expensive than a conventional option with similar characteristics. This reflects the fact that the premium is only payable if the option expires in the money and the writer is not guaranteed receipt of this premium.

Exhibit 10.9 sets out the payoff diagram for a contingent premium option and a comparable conventional option. The payoff diagram set out is for a contingent call option. The pattern of payoff for a put is similar.

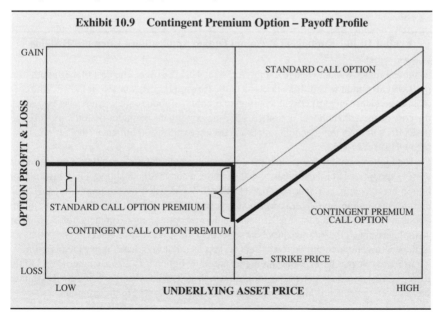

Exhibit 10.9   Contingent Premium Option – Payoff Profile

The payoff diagram indicates that the contingent premium option has no cost if the option expires out-of-the-money. If the option expires in-the-money, then the contingent premium option is automatically exercised and the premium paid. If the option expires just in-the-money, then the larger premium on a contingent premium option dictates that the option may not be sufficiently in-the-money to recover the premium. This is effectively the worst case for the purchaser. The effect of the higher premium is that the option must expire out-of-the-money or sufficiently deep in-the-money to recoup the contingent premium to provide the purchaser with any benefit. Any gain on the contingent premium option is also lower than for a conventional option because of the impact of the larger premium. In contrast, the worst case for the writer is that the option expires just out-of-the-money.

Contingent premium options are designed to provide protection against large unanticipated price movements (both up and down). This reflects the fact that the structure isolates a range (defined by the strike and the contingent premium option premium) within which the purchaser suffers a loss. Where the asset price is outside this range, the purchaser benefits. This benefit is in the form of either non payment of the premium as the option is not exercised (favourable movement in the asset price), or gain from the option (after the premium) to protect the underlying position (large unfavourable movement in the asset price).

Exhibit 10.10 sets out an example of a contingent premium option on currencies. **Exhibit 10.11** sets out an example of a contingent premium option on interest rates.

Exhibit 10.10   Contingent Premium Option Application – Currency Hedging

Assume a trader wants to hedge a long Yen/short US$ position. The cost of a 3 month Yen put/US$ call option with a strike price set at the forward (US$1:Yen 115) is 2.50%. The cost of an equivalent Yen put/US$ call contingent premium option is 5.25% (just over two times the cost of the conventional option). Under the contingent premium option structure, the trader does not pay the premium unless the option expires in-the-money (the Yen weakens below US$1:Yen 115).

The higher premium means that the contingent premium option requires a much higher closing spot price in order to breakeven than under a conventional option. The conventional option breakeven is at a spot rate Yen 117.88 (strike adjusted for the premium paid). The contingent premium option breakeven is at a spot rate of Yen 121.04. The contingent premium option will also show a gain smaller than the normal option (approximately Yen 3.16). The advantage is that if the Yen at expiry is stronger than the strike (above Yen 115), the purchaser of the contingent premium option suffers no loss as it does not have to pay the premium.

In effect, the purchaser of the contingent premium option is isolating a range (Yen 115.00 to Yen 121.04) within which the position shows a loss. Outside that range, the position either breaks even or profits. Within the range, the loss itself is limited to the premium.

Exhibit 10.11   Contingent Premium Option Application – Interest Rate Hedging

Assume US$ LIBOR rates are relatively low. A borrower wishes to hedge its borrowing cost to protect itself against potential increases in interest rates. Assume US$ 3 month LIBOR is currently 3.75% pa and the 3 year US$ swap rate is 4.75% pa.

The borrower considers the following hedging alternatives:
- Purchase a 3 year interest rate cap with a strike of 5.50% pa. The premium cost is 65 bps.
- Purchase a zero cost collar (cap at 5.50% pa and floor at 3.75% pa).
- Purchase a contingent premium cap with a strike of 5.00% pa. The premium cost is 90 bps for any interest rate period. The premium for the contingent premium cap is only payable if the cap expires in the money at each of the relevant rate set dates[27].

The impact of the different hedging alternatives is summarised below:
- The cap protects the borrower against increases in 3 month US$ LIBOR rates above 5.50% pa but allows the borrower to benefit from lower interest rates. The effective maximum cost of borrowing is 5.735% pa (the strike of the cap adjusted for the amortised premium). The premium increases the cost of funding by 23.5 bps pa.
- The collar protects the borrower from increases in interest rates (above 5.50% pa). The borrower cannot benefit from any decrease in interest rates below 3.75% pa. The borrower's cost of funds fluctuates in line with market 3 month US$ LIBOR rates between 3.75% pa and 5.50% pa.
- The contingent premium cap does not incur any premium cost unless 3 month US$ LIBOR rates increase above 5.00% pa. This means where rates are below this level the borrower's cost of funds is the market 3 month US$ LIBOR rates. If 3 month US$ LIBOR rates are set above 5.00% pa, then the borrower's cost of the fund will be 5.90% pa *for that 3 month period.*

The major features of the contingent premium cap include:
- The borrower benefits from lower interest costs (below 5.00% pa) without any premium cost.
- If the cap level is hit, then the option premium is paid and the cap triggered, guaranteeing the borrower a maximum cost of funds of 5.90% (above the cost under a conventional cap).

The major benefit of the contingent premium cap is where the borrower expects rates to be below 5.00% pa, but would like to have protection against an unexpected sharp rise in interest rates (above 5.90% pa).

---

[27] Contingent premium caps and floors have an added complexity. This reflects the fact that the cap or floor consists of a series of cap-lets or floor-lets. The contingent cap or floor structure is effectively a series of contingent premium options on the individual cap-lets or floor-lets. This means that the premium for the *individual* contingent premium options is only received for the specific cap-lets or floor-lets that expire in-the-money.

6.3   *Valuation and Hedging*[28]

The valuation of a contingent premium option is based on decomposing it into the constituent elements. A contingent premium option is effectively made up of the following options:
- Purchase of a conventional option.
- Sale of a digital option with an identical strike price to that of the conventional option and a fixed payout equal to the premium of the conventional option.

Exhibit 10.12 sets out the construction of a contingent premium call option from a conventional call option and digital call option. A similar approach is used for contingent premium put option.

Using this approach, the contingent premium option is priced as a combination of the constituent elements.

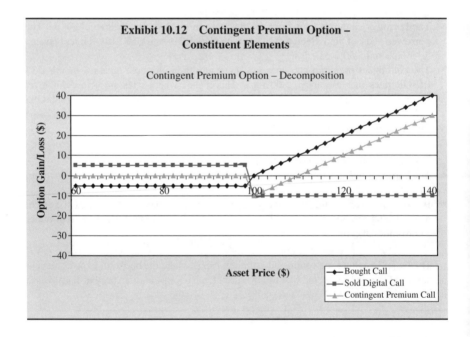

**Exhibit 10.12   Contingent Premium Option –
Constituent Elements**

Contingent Premium Option – Decomposition

---

[28]   See Turnbull, Stuart "The Price is Right" (April 1992) Risk 56–57; Kat, Harry M. "Contingent Premium Options" (Summer 1994) Journal of Derivatives 44–54; Nelken, Israel (2000) Pricing, Hedging & Trading Exotic Options; McGraw-Hill, New York at Chapter 4.

7 Power Options

7.1 Concept[29]

The concept of modified option payoffs can be extended to alter the payoff to *increase* the return to the option purchaser. The major example is a special type of option structures that is referred to as power or exponential options. These options are also often referred to as polynomial or squared options. The nomenclature reflects the design of the instrument where the option return is expressed as a power of the underlying asset or intrinsic value; for example, $LIBOR^2$. These types of options are referred to as power options.

The central feature of a power option relates to the option payoff at maturity. The return on a standard option is a linear function of the difference between the underlying asset price at exercise or maturity. The return function on a power option is a function of the difference (intrinsic value) raised to a power higher than 1. For example, assume a power option with a strike price of $100 whose return is squared. The option payout would provide a payoff (if the option expires in-the-money) that is equal to the asset price less the exercise price squared. For an asset price at expiry of $105, the power option payoff would equal $25 (calculated as $(\$105 - \$100)^2$). This compares to the payoff of an equivalent standard option of $5[30].

The design of a power option is not dissimilar to the payoff modification inherent in digital option structures. The linear and continuous payoff of a standard option is replaced by an agreed payoff amount. Unlike a digital option, in the case of a power structure the payoff of the option is amplified by the introduction of the exponent rather than restricted to the agreed amount.

7.2 Economics

The payoff for a power option is as follows:

$$\text{Power Call Option} - \text{Maximum } [0, (S_m - K)^n]$$

$$\text{Power Put Option} - \text{Maximum } [0, (K - S_m)^n]$$

---

[29] See Ong, Michael "Exotic Options: The Market and their Taxonomy" in Nelken, Israel (Editor) (1996) The Handbook of Exotic Options; Irwin Professional Publishing, Chicago at Chapter 1 at 37–38.

[30] There is a variation in the structure where the payoff is based on squaring the *underlying* asset price. Under this structure, the payoff for a call is either 0 where the option is out-of-the-money or asset price at maturity^2 – strike where the option is in-the-money. The return amplification in this case is higher than for the standard power call. In this example, the payoff would be $9,900 ($10,000 - $100).

Where:

K = Strike Price
S_m = Asset Price (at maturity or exercise)
n = Power exponent of option

Exhibit 10.13 sets out the payoff profile of a power option in graphical form. The modification of the payoff profile has a number of implications, including:
- For the purchaser, the power feature has the effect of increasing the sensitivity of the option's payoff for relatively small movements in the underlying

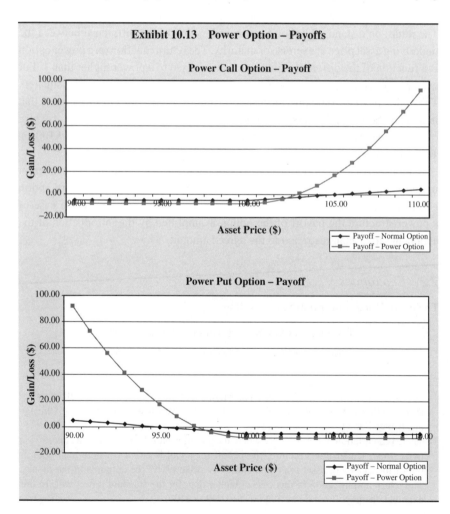

Exhibit 10.13   Power Option – Payoffs

asset price. This enhances the return, allowing the option purchaser to recover its premium payment for a small favourable movement in the underlying asset price. The structure also increases the degree of protection for a particular specified directional movement in the underlying asset price.

- For the seller, the power feature increases the risk, as the potential payout is increased proportional to the exponent used for a given movement in the underlying asset price. In effect, the writer increases the level of price insurance or protection offered to the option purchaser.
- The alteration in the payoff is reflected in a higher option premium than for a comparable standard option. The higher premium reflects the higher payoff/ expected value of the structure.

The power structure is applicable across all asset classes. It is typically structured as a cash settled option with European exercise.

7.3 Structures

The power option structure is used in a variety of formats:
- **Option format** – this is a standalone option format where the normal terms and features of an option transaction are preserved, with the addition of an adjustment to the exponent to amplify the return.
- **Warrant structures** – this incorporates power option features in a warrant. **Exhibit 10.14** sets out an example of 3 power warrant issues undertaken in Germany in 1995. The 3 warrant issues cover debt, equity and currency asset classes. The transactions are, in substance, power option spreads, with the warrant purchasers both purchasing and selling the relevant options. The sold power option effectively caps the purchaser's returns. The transactions were motivated, at least in part, by the investors' expectations of a small move in the underlying asset price. For example, in the currency tranche, the maximum payoff is set at DEM 25. In the case of a normal warrant, this would require an appreciation in the US$ to DEM 1.70 (an increase of 17.24%). In contrast, the power warrant provides a similar return to the option purchaser for an increase in the US$ to DEM 1.50 (an increase of 3.45%). The amplification of the return provided by the power feature allowed investors to maximise the expected return in the context of their expectations of modest price movements.
- **Embedded in swaps or other derivatives** – in this structure, power options are embedded in swaps or other derivatives. This entails using the premium on the power option to adjust the return profile and/or the cost level of the transaction. **Exhibit 10.15** sets out an example of this type of structure involving an interest rate swap.

Exhibit 10.14   Power Options – Warrant Structures[31]

The following issues were undertaken by Trinkhaus & Burkhardt (the German merchant banking arm of HSBC Markets) in May 1995. All warrants were listed on the Berlin, Dusseldorf, Frankfurt, Hamburg and Stuttgart stock exchanges. All warrants were denominated in Deutschemarks (DEM).

The issues of warrants were divided into three tranches.

1.   10 Year Bund Tranche
The Bund tranche was structured as follows:
- Three tranches with strike prices ranging from 101%, 102% and 103% of par.
- European style exercise on 4 March 1996.
- Payouts were as follows:

Strike   Payout (based on underlying notional value of DEM100)
101%   (Change in bond price above strike)^2 capped at DEM 9 per warrant
102%   (Change in bond price above strike)^2 capped at DEM 16 per warrant
103%   (Change in bond price above strike)^2 capped at DEM 16 per warrant

2.   DAX Warrants
The Dax tranche was structured as follows:
- Strike price 2,000.
- European style exercise on 23 May 1996.
- Payouts were (Change in DAX above strike)^2 capped at DEM 25 per warrant based on an underlying warrant value of DEM100 (implying a capped DAX level of 2,500).

3.   US$/DEM Warrants
The DEM currency tranche was structured as follows:
- Two tranches with strike prices of US$/DEM at DEM 1.45 and DEM 1.55.
- European style exercise on 17 June 1996.
- Payouts were 100 × (positive difference between spot above strike)^2 capped at DEM 25 per warrant based on an underlying warrant value of US$100.

Exhibit 10.15   Power Options – Embedded in Interest Rate Swap

The structure is as follows:

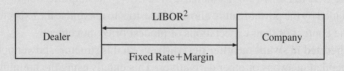

---

[31]   See Reed, Nick "The Power and the Glory" (August 1995) Risk 8; International Financing Review (19 August 1995) 1095 at 88.

In the transaction set out, the dealer pays fixed rate to the client company fixed rate (equivalent to a fixed rate plus an additional margin) in return for receiving floating rate at a rate equivalent to 3 or 6 month LIBOR[2]. The transaction can be unbundled into two separate components:

- Normal US$ fixed-floating interest rate swap.
- Power option component – in this case, a power option on LIBOR.

The power option is a series of options on US$ LIBOR sold by the company to the dealer. As LIBOR increases, the Company's swap payments increase, reflecting the payout under the power options. The return for the Company is the premium captured through the sale of the power options. The premium increases the fixed rate received under the swap[32].

7.4 Applications

The leveraged payoff structure of a power option has a number of applications, including:

- Creating exposure to a large payoff for small movement in the underlying asset price.
- Providing a volatility hedge.
- Hedging non-linear price risk.

Each of the applications is considered in detail below. The last of the applications is potentially the most important, reflecting the non-linear nature of financial risk faced by risk managers in both non-financial and financial enterprises.

The leveraged option payoff inherent in the power option design allows the purchaser to capture a larger return for a given movement in the underlying asset. The benefit may be offset by the higher premium for the power option. To the extent that the curvature of the option payoff exceeds the increased payoff, the purchaser benefits. The structure is particularly well suited to trading or seeking to monetise

---

[32] The most notorious/famous example of a power swap is that between Gibson Greeting Cards and Bankers Trust. Commencing in 1992, Gibson Greeting Cards ("Gibson") entered into what would become a series of complex swap transaction (including a LIBOR[2] contract) with Bankers Trust ("BT"). The transactions ultimately resulted in a loss to Gibson of around US$27.5 million. See Dyer, Geoff "Half-a-billion Gibson Plays it Dumb" (October 1994) Euromoney 26–30; Irving, Richard "Bankers Bites Back" (October 1994) Risk 8–9; Overdahl, James and Schachter, Barry "Derivatives Regulation and Financial Management: Lessons from Gibson Greetings" (Spring 1995) Financial Management 68–78; Kramer, Andrea "SEC Settlement with Gibson Greetings Sends a Strong Message to End-Users of Derivatives" (Spring 1996) Derivatives Quarterly 7–9.

market expectations under conditions where the anticipated move in the asset price is small.

The volatility characteristics of power options also facilitate their use as a hedge against changes in volatility[33]. For example, assume the case of a commodity hedge. The transaction involves an option straddle entailing the simultaneous purchase of both put and call options. The strike price is at-the-money. Instead of using standard options, the strategy uses power call and put options (where the payoff is the square of the expiry asset price and the strike price). The position in this case can be delta hedged to neutralise exposure to directional movements in the underlying asset, leaving only an exposure to volatility, gamma (reflecting the need to adjust the hedge)[34] and time decay (theta).

The impact of using this strategy on the payoff profile is as follows:

* The straddle payout will take on a "U" rather than the characteristic "V" shape, reflecting the power payoff feature of the options.
* The payoff of the straddle involving power options will preserve volatility exposure to a much greater degree than the equivalent standard option straddle. This is because under conventional options, movements in the underlying asset price in one or other direction (the option moves into-the-money) have the effect of reducing the volatility sensitivity of the position.

The behaviour is consistent with the structural difference between the two instruments. The value of a standard option is affected by:

* Changes in the applicable volatility as the asset price moves away from the strike price (the impact of the volatility smile).
* Reduced sensitivity of the option premium to volatility as the underlying asset price moves away from the strike price (the option moves into or out-of-the-money).

In contrast, a power option is essentially a series of options with differing strike prices where the *number* of options increases as the option moves further into-the-money. This means that irrespective of the movement in the asset price, a greater sensitivity to volatility is present.

The capacity to create and sustain an exposure to volatility can be attractive to both traders seeking exposure to volatility (often without exposure to the underlying asset price) or risk managers with a desire to hedge exposure to volatility.

---

[33] See Reed, Nick "Square Deal" (December 1994) 6.

[34] The fact that the power option payout is squared means that the option will have relatively constant gamma; see Reed, Nick "Square Deal" (December 1994) 6.

The potentially greatest appeal of power options relates to the application of these instruments to the hedging of non-linear risk price risk[35]. In financial risk management terms, traditional approaches to hedging rely significantly on the linear nature of the risk profile.

For example, a commodity producer will typically hedge by selling forward its commodity production at an agreed price. The strategy assumes that for a given movement in the price of the commodity, there will be a linear change in the value of its production (change in price times volume). If the commodity producer has hedged through a forward sale, then there will be an offsetting change in the value of its hedge. In reality, the hedge approach described fails to incorporate the fact that the revenue amount sought to be hedged is a function of price, volume and the relationship between price and volume (the elasticity of demand). If for a given change in asset price the volume sold changes, then the amount being hedged itself changes in a non-linear function that traditional hedging instruments cannot capture[36]. Power options, because of their non-linear payoff functions, have the potential to be applied to the management of such exposures[37].

The type of demand function discussed can generate the non-linearity of price risk. Non-linearity can also be generated by deliberate policy frameworks that assume curved risk behaviour. For example, an asset manager operating an insured type of portfolio will often be required to buy more puts to hedge the portfolio value as the asset price declines. A power option can be used to replicate the deliberate action that would be required to hedge portfolio values through the payoff modification inherent in the design.

7.5   Valuation And Hedging[38]

The valuation and hedging of power option products is undertaken by decomposing the structure into its constituent components. This process of decomposition can be undertaken in a number of ways.

---

[35] See Hart, Ian and Ross, Michael "Striking Continuity" (June 1994) Risk 51–56; Reed, Nick "Square Deal" (December 1994) 6; Shimko, David "Non Linear Risk Management" (December 1995) Financial Derivatives & Risk Management 36–38.

[36] For a discussion of non linearity of risk profiles in hedging, see Das, Satyajit (2004) Risk Management; John Wiley & Sons (Asia), Singapore at Chapter 2.

[37] For a discussion of an application of power options in financial institution asset liability management, see Jarrow, Robert and Van Deventer, Donald "Disease or Cure" (February 1996) Risk 54–57.

[38] See Hart, Ian and Ross, Michael "Striking Continuity" (June 1994) Risk 51–56; Jarrow, Robert and Van Deventer, Donald "Disease or Cure" (February 1996) Risk 54–57.

A power option is equivalent to a series of options with different strike prices where the *number* of options increases the further into-the-money the option moves. This allows power options to be hedged and priced with a hedge constituted from a series of options with a mix of different strike prices and maturities and a mix of purchased and sold positions. The hedge portfolio is constructed taking into account the sensitivity of the options to movements in the underlying asset price.

The second method of decomposition would entail re-stating a power option (say a call) as a standard call option combined with barrier options. In this case, the barriers would be structured as a series of knock-in options with a strike equal to the strike of the standard call, and instrike barrier levels corresponding to asset prices, reflecting the appreciation of the asset. The power option would then be priced and hedged as the combination of the different options[39].

8 Summary

Payoff modified options alter the payoff of the options. The adjustments include the incorporation of a fixed payoff (digital options) or enhancing the payoff (power options). Payoff modified options are driven primarily by the capacity to reduce/increase option premium, reduce the risk of loss on a sold option position, and improve matching of underlying assets or liabilities.

Payoff-modified options (particularly digital options) are commonly used in financial markets in a wide variety of asset classes. They are used in a standalone form to hedge or assume risk. They are also commonly used or in combination with other derivatives or securities to create highly customised risk-reward profiles.

---

[39] This approach can be generalised so that power option structures are an example of a more general class of exotic option – the continuous strike or parameter option ("CSO"). The CSO structures produce the proportional payout associated with power options. A closed form solution for the CSO can be derived. This can be used to price and hedge power options. Within the CSO framework, power options can be hedged either statically with a portfolio of standard options or replicated dynamically using the underlying asset and cash within a traditional delta hedging framework. See Hart, Ian and Ross, Michael "Striking Continuity" (June 1994) Risk 51–56.

11
Multifactor Options

1 Overview

Multifactor options are exotic options where the option payoff is based on the relationship of more than one asset. This directly introduces the impact of correlation between the asset prices into the behaviour of the option. In this Chapter, multifactor exotic option structures are examined.

The structure of the Chapter is as follows:
- The general concept of multifactor options is outlined.
- Individual types of multifactor options (including relative performance structures (rainbow, outperformance, maximum/minimum options), exchange options, spread options, compound options, basket options and quanto options) are described.

2 Multifactor Options[1]

Multifactor options are characterised by payoffs that are driven by the performance of two or more asset prices. This is different from conventional options, where the option payoff is driven by the performance of a single asset price. Multifactor options have two sources of price risk dictated by the multiple underlying assets on which the option contract is structured. Multifactor options allow traders to achieve the following objectives:
- Capture the volatility of each of the underlying asset prices.

---

[1] For a discussion of multifactor options, see Ong, Michael "Exotic Options: The Market and their Taxonomy" in Nelken, Israel (Editor) (1996) The Handbook of Exotic Options; Irwin Professional Publishing, Chicago at Chapter 1 at 28–37; Smithson, Charles (1998) Managing Financial Risk – Third Edition; McGraw-Hill, New York at Chapter 13 at 278–283. See also Gastineau, Gary "An Introduction to Special Purpose Derivatives: Options with a Payout Depending on more than one Variable" (Fall 1993) 98–104; Smithson, Charles "Multifactor Options" (May 1997) Risk 43–45.

- Trade/manage the correlation between the price movements of the respective assets.

Exhibit 11.1 sets out the major types of multifactor options. Multifactor options can be categorised as follows:

- **Relative performance structures** – the option payouts under these structures are driven by the *relative* price performance of two or more underlying assets. For example, the payoff of a spread option is based on the difference between two asset prices at option expiry. Examples of relative performance structures include:

1. *Rainbow options*: these are options where the option payout is based on the relationship between multiple assets, as opposed to a price of a single asset. Typical structures include best-of or worst-of options, out performance option or maximum/minimum options.
2. *Exchange options*: these are options where the purchaser has the right to exchange one asset for another.
3. *Spread options*: these are options where the option payout is based on the difference between two nominated assets relative to a specified strike price.

- **Complex underlying asset structures** – these structures are based on underlying assets that are non-standard. The non standard underlying asset includes options where the underlying is an option (compound option) and a basket of

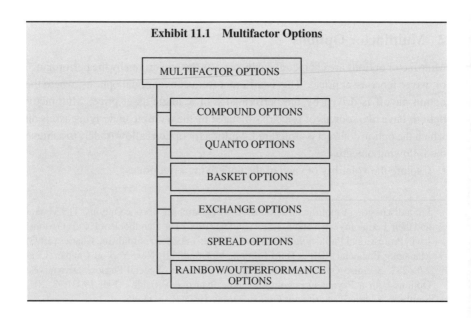

Exhibit 11.1   Multifactor Options

MULTIFACTOR OPTIONS

- COMPOUND OPTIONS
- QUANTO OPTIONS
- BASKET OPTIONS
- EXCHANGE OPTIONS
- SPREAD OPTIONS
- RAINBOW/OUTPERFORMANCE OPTIONS

underlying assets (basket option). It also includes structures where the option payout is modified by the relationship between the asset into which the option is capable of exercise and the price of another asset. Examples of this structure include linkages to currencies (quanto options) and any other asset (defined exercise options). Examples of multifactor options with complex underlying asset structures include:

1. *Compound options* (options on options): these are options where the holder has the right but not the obligation to buy or sell another predetermined option at a pre agreed price.
2. *Basket options*: these are options where the payout under the contract is related to the cumulative performance of a basket of underlying assets.
3. *Quanto options*: these are options where the option payout is converted at a pre-agreed exchange rate to a currency different to that of the underlying asset. The quanto contract will typically allow the quantity or notional principal of the transaction to be adjusted, reflecting the fact that the face amount of the currency cover required fluctuates to cover changes in the foreign currency value of the underlying asset.
4. *Defined exercise options*: these are options where two different assets are used to determine the option payoff. One asset is used to determine if the option is exercised. A second asset is used to determine the option payout[2].

Exotic option structures are generally driven by the following objectives:
• Reduction in option premium.
• Alteration in risk profile, including increased probability of gain, quantification of loss or optimal exercise timing.
• Asset liability matching.

Multifactor options are driven primarily by the capacity of these structures to hedge or trade specific types of *relative* asset price movements. Multifactor options are also used to hedge complex exposures where there are inherent correlation relationships that can be monetised to reduce the cost of the hedge and provide a better match to the underlying position.

Multifactor options are based on the price performance of multiple assets. This means that the value of the option is driven by two asset prices and the volatility of two assets[3]. The payoff of these structures is dependent upon the correlation

---

[2] Defined exercise options have certain similarities to barrier options; see Chapter 9.
[3] For a general discussion of valuation of multifactor options see Briys, Eric Bellalah, Mondher, Mai, Huu Minh and De Varenne, Francois (1998) Options, Futures and

between the asset prices. Pricing/valuation and hedging of the structures requires the correlation between the asset price movements. This requires estimation of correlation[4]. The required correlation is the *actual correlation to be experienced* over the life of the option. As in the case with volatility estimation, the estimation of correlation is difficult[5].

The requirement to estimate correlation creates significant difficulties in accurately pricing/valuing exotic options[6]. Traders must estimate correlation from primarily historical information. This estimate will be adjusted for the trader's expectations regarding asset price behaviour over the term of the option. Traders will generally be unable to hedge the correlation risk assumed. If *actual* correlation is different from *assumed (implied)* correlation used to price and hedge the option, then the difference will manifest itself as the cost of the dynamic or static hedge used by the trader. The trader would like to hedge this correlation risk in the market. The absence of a liquid market in correlation products or correlation hedging instruments limits the capacity of the traders to manage the risk[7].

Exotic Derivatives: Theory, Application and Practice; John Wiley & Sons, Chichester at Chapters 15, 17 and 20; Hull, John (2000) Options, Futures and Other Derivatives – Fourth Edition; Prentice-Hall Inc., Upper Saddle River, NJ at Chapter 18; Nelken, Israel (2000) Pricing, Hedging & Trading Exotic Options; McGraw-Hill, New York at Chapters 10, 17, 18, 19, 20 and 21. See also Boyle, Phelim P. "A Lattice Framework for Option Pricing with Two State Variables" (March 1988) Journal of Financial and Quantitative Analysis 1–12; Boyle, Phelim P., Evnine, Jeremy and Gibbs, Stephen "Numerical Evaluation of Multivariate Contingent Claims" (1989) Review of Financial Studies 241–250; Cheyette, Oren "Pricing Options on Multiple Assets" (1990) Advances in Futures and Options Research 69–81; Okunev, John and Tippet, Mark "A Multi-Factor Option Pricing Model" (1993) Advances in Futures and Options Research 67–80.

[4]   See Das, Satyajit (2004) Derivative Products & Pricing; John Wiley & Sons (Asia), Singapore at Chapter 9.

[5]   For a discussion of issues in estimation of correlation, see Levy, Edmund "Capitalising on Correlation" (May 1991) Risk 30–33; Eisenberg, Larry "Somebody Else's Money" (August 1993) Risk 44–49; Alexander, Carol "History Debunked" (December 1994) Risk 59–63; Sullivan, Greg "Correlation Counts" (August 1995) Risk 36–37.

[6]   See Cookson, Martin "Dangerous Liasons" (March 1993) Risk 30–36; Parsley, Mark "The Last Piece of the Jigsaw" (November 1993) Euromoney 29–32; Lousi, J.C. "Worrying about Correlation" (March 1997) Derivatives Strategy 53–55; Paul-Choudhury, Sumit "Taking Care of Correlation" (February 1998) Risk S9–S11. See also Mahtani, Arun "Correlation Concerns Rise as SG Rolls Out Himalaya" (16 October 1999) International Financing Review Issue 1305 92.

[7]   There are attempts to start trading in correlation risk; see Dunbar, Nicholas "Correlation Swaps Take Off" (May 1999) Risk 6; Crossman, Alexander "Searching for Solutions to Correlation Risk" (18 September 1999) International Financing Review Issue 1301 88.

Certain types of multifactor options (in particular, basket options and quanto options) are commonly used by traders and hedgers. Other multifactor structures are less frequently used.

3   Rainbow Options

3.1   Concept

Rainbow option is a generic term that is used to describe a number of similar option structures[8]. The key feature of the structures is that the option payoff is dependent upon the *relative* price performance of two or more assets. There are a number of different structures, including:

- Best-of/worst-of options.
- Out-performance options.
- Maximum/minimum options.

It is common to refer to the "colours" of a rainbow. This refers to the *number* of underlying assets. For example, a 4 colour rainbow best-of option refers to an option that pays off the highest increase in the value of 4 underlying assets over the term of the option.

3.2   Best-of/Worst-of Options[9]

Best-of/worst-of options (also known as alternative options) entail a structure where the purchaser receives the highest (best-of) or lowest (worst-of) price change

---

[8]   See Gastineau, Gary "An Introduction to Special Purpose Derivatives: Options with a Payout Depending on More Than One Variable" (Fall 1993) 98–104; Ong, Michael "Exotic Options: The Market and their Taxonomy" in Nelken, Israel (Editor) (1996) The Handbook of Exotic Options; Irwin Professional Publishing, Chicago at Chapter 1 at 29–31; Smithson, Charles "Multifactor Options" (May 1997) Risk 43–45; Smithson, Charles (1998) Managing Financial Risk – Third Edition; McGraw-Hill, New York at Chapter 13 at 279–280; Nelken, Israel (2000) Pricing, Hedging & Trading Exotic Options; McGraw-Hill, New York at Chapter 17.

[9]   See Gastineau, Gary "An Introduction to Special Purpose Derivatives: Options with a Payout Depending on More Than One Variable" (Fall 1993) 98–104; Ong, Michael "Exotic Options: The Market and their Taxonomy" in Nelken, Israel (Editor) (1996) The Handbook of Exotic Options; Irwin Professional Publishing, Chicago at Chapter 1 at 29–31; Smithson, Charles "Multifactor Options" (May 1997) Risk 43–45; Smithson, Charles (1998) Managing Financial Risk – Third Edition; McGraw-Hill, New York at

(in percentage terms) of two or more assets. The payoff is equal to the positive or negative percentage change from the strike on the best or worst performing asset multiplied by the face value of the option.

The payoff of these types of options can be described as follows:

> **Best-of option**: Maximum $(\Delta S_1, \Delta S_2, \Delta S_3, \ldots \Delta S_n)$
>
> **Worst-of option**: Minimum $(\Delta S_1, \Delta S_2, \Delta S_3, \ldots \Delta S_n)$
>
> Where ΔS_n = the percentage change in price in asset n relative to the strike price.

The strike of the option is normally set at the spot rate of each asset. As the return is based on the percentage return, the price of each asset is scaled so that a common strike price can be used. If the underlying assets are two stocks, then the best-of/worst-of option could be based on their return relative to the spot price at the time of entry into the option.

Assume a best-of option structured on two stocks (X and Y stocks) where the purchaser receives the higher of the percentage increase in the price of the two assets. Assume that at expiry, X stock has increased by 6% and Y stock has increased by 2.50%. The best-of option will pay the higher percentage gain of 6%.

Structurally, the best-of option is similar to buying separate call options on the underlying assets. The difference relates to the payoff at expiry. Under a best-of structure, the purchaser receives the higher of the percentage increases in the prices of the stock or 0 if the stocks have decreased. In contrast, the two call options will payoff the two separate intrinsic values. The best-of option will only payoff the highest increase in price (or 0 if there is no increase). There is no payoff on the other option even if the option was in-the-money. Worst-of options can also be analysed similarly.

The economics of the best-of/worst-of options are based on the lower premium cost of the structure relative to the purchase of two separate options. The lower cost reflects the fact that the payoff will generally be lower than the payout of the two separate options. The lower premium is directly related to the assumed correlation of the two asset price changes. The higher the correlation in asset price changes, the greater will be the premium saving relative to the purchase of two separate options. This reflects the fact that where the correlation is high, the performance of the best-of or worst-of will be similar to that of the conventional option on one of the assets.

Chapter 13 at 279–280; Nelken, Israel (2000) Pricing, Hedging & Trading Exotic Options; McGraw-Hill, New York at Chapter 17.

The economics of best-of/worst-of options allows the purchaser to monetise expectations on future relative asset price movements. This may reflect a trading decision or the nature of the underlying exposure being hedged. This structure is used where the purchaser expects that both assets will move in a similar direction but not at the same rate.

In practice, the major users of best-of/worst-of options are asset managers. This drives the types of structures used. Common structures include best-of/worst-of options on baskets of equity stocks or equity indexes. Other common structures include best-of/worst-of options on the performance of different asset classes (for example, equity versus fixed income/bonds).

Best-of/worst-of options are also used in currency markets to provide exposure to the better or worst performing currency. This can be used by corporations to hedge specific correlation exposures or competitive risks[10]. **Exhibit 11.2** sets out an example of a dual currency option involving currencies.

Maximum/minimum options are a variation on the best-of/worst-of structure. The maximum/minimum option will pay off based on the maximum or minimum of two or more assets. The maximum/minimum options are similar to best-of/worst-of options when the strikes of each asset are set to zero[11].

Exhibit 11.2   Best-of/Worst-of Options – Dual Currency Option Example

Assume the case of a UK (pound sterling (GBP) based) manufacturer of capital equipment whose principal competitors are based in the USA (US$ based) or Japanese (Yen based).

The UK manufacturer's competitive position is affected by currency movements as follows:
• An appreciation in the GBP relative to the US$ reduces the competitiveness of the UK Company, reflecting the increased US$ cost of its products.
• An appreciation of the GBP relative to the Yen also reduces its competitiveness as it improves the competitive position of its Japanese competitors (through reduced US$ cost of the Japanese manufacturer's product in US$ terms).

The UK Company's exposure is a multifactor exposure reflecting the following:
• It is exposed to both the GBP/US$ and US$/Yen (effectively the GBP/Yen cross rate).
• The economic exposure is only to the currency that *depreciates by the highest amount* against GBP, reflecting the fact that this will determine its competitive position.

The strategic currency exposure is complex and one increasingly faced by international businesses competing for sales against competitors based in a number of currencies.

---

[10] See Benson, Robert and Levy, Ed "Bouncing Your Rivals" (November 1989) Risk 13–14.
[11] See Smithson, Charles "Multifactor Options" (May 1997) Risk 43–45 at 43–44.

The UK Company's hedging alternatives to seek to manage this complex exposure are as follows:

1. Purchase a GBP call/US$ put option (to provide protection against the strengthening of GBP against US$) *and* a GBP call/Yen put (to provide protection against the appreciation of GBP against Yen).
2. Purchase a multifactor best-of option that allows the UK Company to buy GBP and sell *either US$ or Yen, whichever is cheaper.*

The major difference between the two alternatives identified is the cost and the degree to which the options match the underlying exposure.

Assume that the UK Company seeks to hedge at the start of 2001 using the multifactor structure. Assume the rates and option premium are as follows:

* Currency rates for spot transactions:

    GBP 1:   US$1.50
    US$1:   Yen 120.00
    GBP 1:   Yen 180.00

* The premium on the two separate options struck at the forward rates of GBP 1:US$1.49 and GBP 1: Yen 176 with an expiry in 1 year are as follows:

    GBP Call/ US$ Put – 4.08% of GBP amount
    GBP Call/ Yen Put – 1.50% of GBP amount

* A multifactor best-of currency option (final payout is a function of the appreciation of GBP relative to either US$ or Yen, whichever is greater) is 4.61% of GBP amount.

Assuming total sales total US$100 million pa (equivalent to GBP 67.1 million at the forward rate), the cost of the multifactor option is GBP 3.09 million (GBP 0.65 million lower than the cost of the separate options of GBP 3.74 million).

The performance of the hedge can be considered where at hedge maturity at the expiry of 1 year, the currency rates are as follows GBP 1: US$1.40 and GBP 1: Yen 200.

The weakening of the GBP against the US$ and its strengthening against the Yen has the following implications for the hedges implemented:

* If the UK Company had taken out the individual options then it would exercise its GBP call/Yen put at Yen 176 and the GBP call/US$ put would expire out-of-the-money.
* If the UK Company had taken out the multifactor option, then the economic consequences would be identical with the GBP call being exercised against the Yen.

The benefit from the option would be equal to the appreciation of the GBP against the Yen (Yen 24.00) on the GBP face value which totals Yen 1,610.7 million (GBP 8.05 million at prevailing spot rates). The net gain would be lower, reflecting the cost of the option. The cost of the multifactor option would be significantly lower than the cost of the two separate options.

The gain from the option offsets potential losses resulting from the loss of competitiveness of the UK manufacturer. These losses would be reflected in lower revenues as sales are lost to Japanese competitors.

3.3 Outperformance Options

Outperformance options are structures that provide the purchaser with a payoff based on the difference in performance of two nominated assets. The payoff of an outperformance option is the percentage return on one asset minus the percentage return on the second asset multiplied by the face value of the option.

The payoff of these types of options can be described as follows:

$$\text{Maximum}(\Delta S_1 - \Delta S_2; 0)$$

Where

ΔS_1 = the percentage change in price of asset 1 relative to the strike price.

ΔS_2 = the percentage change in price of asset 2 relative to the strike price.

The strike of the option is normally set at the spot rate of each asset. If the underlying assets are two stocks, then the outperformance option could be based on their return relative to the spot price at the time of entry into the option.

Assume an outperformance option structured on two stocks (X and Y stocks) where the purchaser receives the higher of the percentage increase in the price of the two assets. Assume that at expiry, X stock has increased by 6% and Y stock has increased by 2.50%. The outperformance option will payoff 3.50%. In contrast, the best-of option will payoff 6%. If at expiry X stock has increased by 6% and Y stock has decreased by 2.50%, then the outperformance option will payoff 8.50% (versus 6.00% pa for a best-of option).

Structurally, the outperformance option is similar to buying separate options on the underlying assets – in the above example, a call on X stock and a put on Y stock. The difference relates to the payoff at expiry. Under an outperformance structure, the purchaser receives a payoff only if the percentage increase in the price of X stock exceeds the percentage change in Y. In contrast, the two options will pay off the two separate intrinsic values.

The economics of the outperformance options is based on the lower premium cost of the structure relative to the purchase of two separate options. The lower cost reflects the fact that the payoff is the difference between price changes of the two assets. The lower premium is directly related to the assumed correlation of the two asset price changes. The higher the correlation in asset price changes, the greater the premium saving relative to the purchase of two separate options. This reflects the fact that where the correlation is high, the expected difference will be lower.

The economics of outperformance options allows the purchaser to monetise expectations on future relative asset price movements. This may reflect a trading decision or the nature of the underlying exposure being hedged. This structure is used where the purchaser expects that the asset prices will move in a different direction.

The outperformance structure is similar to the best-of/worst-of structure discussed above. Both structures use embedded correlations to lower the cost of the option. The performance of both structures is enhanced where actual correlations are lower than the assumed correlations used to price the option. There are also differences between the two structures. The outperformance option entails monetisation of the view that one asset will have a positive return and the other a negative return. In contrast, the best-of/worst-of structure seeks to capture value from the higher performance of one asset where both assets are potentially expected to increase. The purchaser of the outperformance structure must also identify the better performing asset within the structure. In contrast, the purchaser of the best-of/worst-of structure is not required to identify the better performing asset.

In practice, the major users of outperformance options are asset managers. This drives the types of structures used. Common structures include outperformance options on baskets of equity stocks or equity indexes. Other common structures include outperformance options on currencies or the performance of different asset classes (equity versus fixed income/bonds etc). For example, a fund manager short the S & P 500 against the DAX (relative to model or index weight) can protect the portfolio from losses by purchasing an outperformance option on the difference between the S & P 500 and the DAX. Alternatively, a similar structure could be used to monetise expectations of relative performance where the fund manager expected the S & P 500 to outperform the DAX.

The use of outperformance structures is especially attractive where the asset manager's performance is measured against a benchmark (relative rather than absolute returns). In this situation, outperformance options can be an effective way of monetising expectations on individual assets. Where the outperformance option is purchased, the loss (the premium paid) is also known and capped[12].

Outperformance options have been increasingly embedded in fixed income securities as follows:

- Equity linked notes, where the payoff is linked to relative price performance in different ways. This structure entails investors either purchasing correlation or selling correlation (in return for premium income used to enhance yields)[13].

---

[12] For example, see comments attributed to Ontario Teachers Pension Fund in Falloon, William "Teaching Aids" (February 1998) Risk 68–70 at 69–70. See also Wood, Duncan "Pension Managers in UK Funding Crisis" (November 1998) Risk 6.

[13] See Das, Satyajit (2004) Structured Products Volume 2; John Wiley & Sons (Asia), Singapore at Chapter 4.

- Exchangeable bonds (convertible and exchangeable into shares other than that of the issuer) with embedded outperformance bonds have also been used[14]. In one transaction, Swiss Reinsurance ("Swiss Re") issued a 5 year US$450 million bond that could be exercised into the shares of either Swiss Re itself, Credit Suisse or Novartis[15]. The investor effectively purchased a best-of rainbow option on the 3 underlying stocks. The additional value received for the option allowed Swiss Re to achieve better terms than that available for a conventional transaction.

3.4 Valuation

As with other types of exotic options, several alternative ways of valuing rainbow options are available[16]. In practice, the principal approaches include:
- Analytic solutions.
- Numerical methods (primarily binomial models or Monte Carlo simulations).

The problems in pricing rainbow options include:
- Difficulty of assuming log normality of the underlying asset price distribution. This is because the sum or difference of two log normally distributed assets may not be log normal.
- Need to incorporate the correlation between the asset price changes.

In practice, two approaches exist for rainbow options:
- Closed form analytic solutions are available. These assume either of the following approaches:
  1. The earliest approach[17] assumes that both asset prices are log normal and derives a partial differential equation that must be satisfied by a European best-of/worst-of option on two assets. A closed form analytic solution to the equation that satisfies the boundary conditions is then derived.

---

[14] See Das, Satyajit (2004) Structured Products Volume 2; John Wiley & Sons (Asia), Singapore at Chapter 3.

[15] See Mahtani, Arun "Swiss Re Narrows Convertible/Derivatives Gap" (15 May 1999) International Financing Review Issue 1283 93.

[16] See Briys, Eric Bellalah, Mondher, Mai, Huu Minh and De Varenne, Francois (1998) Options, Futures and Exotic Derivatives: Theory, Application and Practice; John Wiley & Sons, Chichester at Chapter 15; Hull, John (2000) Options, Futures and Other Derivatives – Fourth Edition; Prentice-Hall Inc., Upper Saddle River, NJ at Chapter 18 at 482–485; Nelken, Israel (2000) Pricing, Hedging & Trading Exotic Options; McGraw-Hill, New York at Chapter 17.

[17] See Stulz, Rene "Options on the Minimum or Maximum of Two Risky Assets' (July 1982) Journal of Financial Economics 161–185; Johnson, Herb "Options on the Maximum or Minimum of Several Assets" (September 1987) 277–283.

2. An alternative approach[18] assumes that the asset prices are jointly log normal. Using this approach, the expected option payoffs at maturity can be determined using a cumulative bi-variate normal distribution function. The expected values are discounted back to valuation date to derive the fair value of the option. This approach also allows a closed form analytic solution to be generated[19].

Exhibit 11.3 sets out the formula for a rainbow option. **Exhibit 11.4** sets out an example of valuing a rainbow option.

- Numerical solutions can be used to derive the value of the options[20]. These are specifically used where closed form solutions are not available. Where numerical techniques are used, a number of alternative approaches are available[21]. For example, where a binomial tree approach is used, a tree that represents the movements in two correlated variables must be constructed. This involves the following steps:

1. Construct a two dimension tree for each variable. The trees are then combined into a single three dimensional tree where there are 4 branches emanating from each tree node.

2. Correlations between the variables are incorporated in a number of alternative ways:
   - Use the correlations to define two new uncorrelated variables that are then modelled using separate binomial trees, with probabilities being chosen so that the tree gives the correct values for the first two moments of the distribution of the new uncorrelated variables. As the new variables are uncorrelated, they can be combined into a single three dimensional tree that can be solved in a similar manner as a normal two dimensional tree.
   - A three dimensional tree can be constructed for 2 correlated asset prices using a non rectangular arrangement of the nodes[22].

---

[18] See Rubinstein, Mark "Somewhere Over the Rainbow" (November 1991) Risk 63–66.

[19] This approach (identified in Rubinstein, Mark "Somewhere Over the Rainbow" (November 1991) Risk 63–66) has applications beyond rainbow options and can be utilised to value basket and spread options.

[20] See Boyle, Phelim P. and Tse, Y.K. "An Algorithm for Computing Values of Options on the Maximum or Minimum of Several Assets" (June 1990) Journal of Financial and Quantitative Analysis 215–227; Rubinstein, Mark "Return to Oz" (November 1994) Risk 67–71.

[21] See Hull, John (2000) Options, Futures and Other Derivatives – Fourth Edition; Prentice-Hall Inc., Upper Saddle River, NJ at Chapter 18 at 482–485.

[22] See Rubinstein, Mark "Return to Oz" (November 1994) Risk 67–71.

- Construction of the three dimensional tree assuming no correlation, but then adjusting the probabilities at each node to reflect the correlation.

A number of aspects of the valuation and hedging of rainbow options should be noted:

- The option creates exposure to two asset prices, volatility of two assets and the correlation between the two assets.
- The option will have two deltas. Hedging the option requires trading in two assets.

Exhibit 11.3   Rainbow Options – Pricing Model[23]

Assume:

S_1 = price of asset 1
S_2 = price of asset 2
σ_1 = volatility of asset 1
σ_1 = volatility of asset 2
ρ = correlation of asset price changes between asset 1 and asset 2
K = strike price of option (purchaser pays K and receives the greater of S_1 and S_2)
r = interest rate for maturity t
t = time expiry of the option
The value of a best-of option is given by:

$$S_1 N2[d1, \gamma 1, v1] + S_2 N2[d2, \gamma 2, v2] - Ke^{-r.t}(1 - N2[-d1 + \sigma_1\sqrt{t}, -d2 + \sigma_2\sqrt{t}, \rho])$$

The value of a worst-of option is given by:

$$S_1 N2[d1, -\gamma 1, -v1] + S_2 N2[d2, -\gamma 2, -v2] - Ke^{-r.t}(1 - N2[d1 - \sigma_1\sqrt{t}, d2 - \sigma_2\sqrt{t}, \rho]$$

Where

$d1 = [\ln(S_1/K) + (r + \sigma_1^2/2)t]/\sigma_1\sqrt{t}$
$d2 = [\ln(S_2/K) + (r + \sigma_2^2/2)t]/\sigma_2\sqrt{t}$
$\sigma^2 = \sigma_1^2 + \sigma_2^2 - 2\rho\sigma_1\sigma_2$
$v1 = (\sigma_1 - \rho\sigma_2)/\sigma$
$v2 = (\sigma_2 - \rho\sigma_1)/\sigma$
$\gamma 1 = [\ln(S_1/S_2) + (\sigma^2/2)t]/\sigma_1\sqrt{t}$
$\gamma 2 = -\gamma 1 + \sigma\sqrt{t}$
N2[y1, y2, ρ] = cumulative bi-variate normal distribution function with correlation
coefficient ρ

---

[23] The version set out here is that from Gastineau, Gary "An Introduction to Special Purpose Derivatives: Options with a Payout Depending on More Than One Variable" (Fall 1993) 98–104 at 101–102. See Stulz, Rene "Options on the Minimum or Maximum of Two Risky Assets' (July 1982) Journal of Financial Economics 161–185; Rubinstein, Mark "Somewhere Over the Rainbow" (November 1991) Risk 63–66.

Exhibit 11.4   Rainbow Options – Valuation Example

Assume a European 1 year best-of call option with face value $100,000 where the purchaser has the right to either buy government bonds or an equity index. The strike of the option is as follows:
- Government bonds: 100% of face value.
- Equity index: 1,000.

The example assumes the following parameters:

Asset Price – Government Bond ($)	98.00
Asset Price – Equity Index (index points)	950.00
Strike Price	See below
Maturity	1 year
Volatility – Government Bond (% pa)	15
Volatility – Equity Index (% pa)	22
Asset Income – Government Bond (% pa)	6.00
Asset Income – Equity Index (% pa)	2.00
Interest Rates (% pa)	5.00
Exercise	European
Correlation	0.4

The option strike price must be calculated. The asset prices are denominated in different units. This means that it is necessary to work in one of the units ($ or index points). Assume that in this example, the valuation is undertaken in index points. The option (as structured) allows the purchaser to buy the following:
- 100 units of the equity index at 1,000 (total $100,000).
- 1,000 units of the government bond at 100 (total $100,000).

To convert the bond price to index units, the following adjustments must be made:
- Multiply the strike price and current asset price of the bond by 10 (1,000/100).
- Multiply the option premium by 1000, reflecting the fact that there are 100 equity index units in the option.

The adjustment means that the strike price ($1,000) is the same for both assets.

The best-of call option premium is 100.72. This is the price on one unit. This means that the premium is 10,072 (100.72 times 100 units).

The following Table sets out the premium of digital call and put options for different correlation levels:

Correlation	−1.0	−0.5	0	+0.5	+1.0
Premium (per unit)	123.67	118.64	110	97.91	76.85

- The option will have multiple gammas. There will be gammas with respect to each asset and cross gammas (the change in the delta of asset 1 for a change in the price of asset 2 and vice versa). In practice, this cross gamma can only be hedged by trading in a portfolio of the underlying assets and conventional options of the assets.
- The option premium and consequently the option delta and gamma will be sensitive to changes in correlation. This will result in the need to adjust the hedge as correlation changes. This will trigger hedge losses.
- The exposure to volatility changes will be complex. This is because the payoff is dependent upon the relative performance of the assets. If the volatility of one asset decreases relative to the volatility of the other asset, then the difference between the two prices may increase, impacting upon the value of the option. The relationship between volatility and correlation changes will also affect the outcome.

4 Exchange Options

An exchange option specifically refers to an option structure where the purchaser has the right to exchange one asset for another[24].

The payoff from an exchange option is set out below:

$$\text{Maximum } [O; S_2* - S_1*]$$

Where

$S_1* = $ Final price of underlying asset 1

$S_2* = $ Final price of underlying asset 2

The exchange option payoff is based on the difference between the two assets at expiry of the option. An exchange option is equivalent to a call option on the second asset with a strike price equal to the forward price of the first asset. An exchange option is also equivalent to a put option on the first asset with a strike price equal to the forward price of the second asset. The exchange option is similar to a two colour rainbow option. The value of a rainbow worst-of option on the two assets is equivalent to the present value of the second asset and an exchange option that allows the purchaser to exchange the first asset for the second asset[25].

---

[24] See Ong, Michael "Exotic Options: The Market and their Taxonomy" in Nelken, Israel (Editor) (1996) The Handbook of exotic Options; Irwin Professional Publishing, Chicago at Chapter 1 at 31.

[25] See Rubinstein, Mark "One for Another" (July–August 1991) 30–32; Hull, John (2000) Options, Futures and Other Derivatives – Fourth Edition; Prentice-Hall Inc., Upper Saddle River, NJ at Chapter 18 at 469–470.

Exchange options are relevant in several contexts. For example, many types of options in financial markets are exchange options. This includes currency options (the right to exchange a currency for a second currency), takeovers financed by stock (the right to exchange one stock for another) and futures delivery options (the right to deliver one bond for another) [26]. **Exhibit 11.5** sets out an example of an exchange option involving two indices.

A modified Black-Scholes model can be used to value an exchange option[27]. **Exhibit 11.6** sets out the valuation model. **Exhibit 11.7** sets out an example of the valuation of an exchange option.

Exhibit 11.5   Exchange Options – Example

The following example sets out a structured note with an embedded exchange option. The Double Index Bull ("DIB") Note was designed for investors that believed that two specified indices will increase in value over a given term. The note typically pays no coupon. It has a redemption value linked to the lowest value of the two indices at maturity. The redemption value is:

Gearing × Minimum [(Index1, Index2)]

Where Index1 and Index2 are the $ values of the two indices on the maturity date of the note, and gearing is the degree of leverage of the note. Generally, the two indices are standardised to have identical forward values.

This structure is similar to a best-of note where the redemption value is linked to the highest value of the two indices and defined as:

Gearing × Maximum (Index1, Index2)

---

[26] See Chapter 2. See also Gay, Gerald D. and Manaster, Steven "The Quality Option Implicit I Futures Contracts" (September 1984) Journal of Financial Economics 353–370; Boyle, Phelim P. "The Quality Option and Timing Option in Futures Contracts" (March 1989) Journal of Finance 101–113; Ritchken, Peter and Sankarasubramanian, L. "Pricing The Quality Option in Treasury Bond Futures" (July 1992) Mathematical Finance 197–214; Ritchken, Peter and Sankarasubramanian, L. "A Multifactor Model of the Quality Option in Treasury Futures" (Fall 1995) Journal of Financial Research 261–279.

[27] See Margrabe, William "The Value of an Option to Exchange One Asset for Another" (March 1978) Journal of Finance 177–186; Rubinstein, Mark "One for Another" (July–August 1991) 30–32. See also Hull, John (2000) Options, Futures and Other Derivatives – Fourth Edition; Prentice-Hall Inc., Upper Saddle River, NJ at Chapter 18 at 469–470.

The important difference between the two notes lies in the embedded option. In the case of the DIB note, the redemption payoff can be decomposed as follows:

Gearing × Minimum (Index1, Index2) = Gearing × [Index1 − Maximum (Index1 − Index2), 0)]

The payoff of a best-of note can be decomposed as follows:

Gearing × Minimum (Index1, Index2) = Gearing × [Index1 + Maximum (Index2) − Index1, 0)]

The DIB note embeds an exchange option sold by the investor. The option premium is used to increase the gearing of the note. In contrast, the best-of note embeds the purchase of an exchange option. In this case, the option premium decreases the gearing of the note. As a result, in most cases the DIB note will pay in excess of 100% of the upside of the minimum of the two indices, whereas the best-of note will pay less than 100% of the maximum of the two indices.

For example, consider an investor who expects increases in the price of oil and gold. Assume a 3 year structured note with US$20 million face value. The note pays no coupon and has a redemption value of 107% of the minimum value of 44,444 ounces of gold and 1,975,268 barrels of oil. The payoff of the note (stated in US$ million redemption values) for gold and oil prices is provided in the Table below.

Price of gold ($/oz)

Oil Price ($/barrel)	375	400	425	450	475	500	525	550	575	600
16	17.83	18.41	18.41	18.41	18.41	18.41	18.41	18.41	18.41	18.41
17	17.83	19.02	19.56	19.56	19.56	19.56	19.56	19.56	19.56	19.56
18	17.83	19.02	20.21	20.71	20.71	20.71	20.71	20.71	20.71	20.71
19	17.83	19.02	20.21	21.40	21.86	21.86	21.86	21.86	21.86	21.86
20	17.83	19.02	20.21	21.40	22.59	23.01	23.01	23.01	23.01	23.01
21	17.83	19.02	20.21	21.40	22.59	23.78	24.16	24.16	24.16	24.16
22	17.83	19.02	20.21	21.40	22.59	23.78	24.97	24.97	25.31	25.31
23	17.83	19.02	20.21	21.40	22.59	23.78	24.97	26.16	26.46	26.46

The investor receives full principal repayment if the price of oil per barrel is greater than US$17.38 and the price of gold per ounce is greater than US$420.57. For an investor anticipating increases in both indices, the structure offers a higher expected return than an equal weighted portfolio in the two indices. Specifically, this transaction will provide a return of 17.70% if both indices rally 10%.

Source: Broer, Sydney, Durland, Michael, Engel, Mark and Vohra, Anil "Double Index Bull Note" (27 April 1994) IFR Swaps Weekly Issue 66 10.

Exhibit 11.6   Exchange Options – Pricing Model[28]

Assume:

U = price of asset 1 at commencement
V = price of asset 2 at commencement
σ_u = volatility of asset 1
σ_v = volatility of asset 2
ρ = correlation of asset price changes between asset 1 and asset 2
q_u = income on asset 1
q_v = income on asset 2
t = time expiry of the option

The value of an exchange option where the purchaser can deliver asset 1 worth U_t at time t and receive asset 2 worth V_t is given by:

$$Ve^{-q_v t}N(d1) - Ue^{-q_u t}N(d2)$$

Where

$d1 = [\ln(V/U) + (q_u - q_v + \sigma^2/2)t]/\sigma\sqrt{t}$
$d2 = d1 - \sigma\sqrt{t}$
$\sigma = \sqrt{(\sigma_u^2 + \sigma_v^2 - 2\rho\sigma_v\sigma_u)}$

Exhibit 11.7   Exchange Options – Valuation Example

Assume two bonds that are eligible for delivery into the Treasury bond futures contract. The value of the delivery option can be estimated as an exchange option.

The example assumes the following parameters:

Asset Price – Treasury Bond 1	98.50
Asset Price – Treasury Bond 2	104.125
Maturity	1 month
Volatility – Treasury Bond 1 (% pa)	18
Volatility – Treasury Bond 2 (% pa)	14
Coupon – Treasury Bond 1 (% pa)	5.00
Coupon – Treasury Bond 2 (% pa)	6.00
Interest Rates (% pa)	4.50
Correlation	0.78

The exchange option premium is 5.58.

---

[28] The version set out here is from Hull, John (2000) Options, Futures and Other Derivatives – Fourth Edition; Prentice-Hall Inc., Upper Saddle River, NJ at Chapter 18 at 469–470. For a version of this model which shows the solution where the second asset is denominated in a foreign currency, see Brotherton-Ratcliffe, R. and Iben, Ben "Yield Curve Applications of Swap Products" in Schwartz, R. and Smith, C (ed) (1993)

5 Spread Options

5.1 Concept[29]

Spread options refer to an option structure where the underlying asset is the differential between the prices of two underlying assets. In a typical structure, the underlying assets are two indices such as interest rates or equity indexes. The spread option payout is determined by the difference if positive (negative) for a call (put) between the identified indexes. Spread options, like other multifactor options, have two sources of price risk dictated by the multiple underlying assets on which the option contract is structured.

The payoff for a spread option can be stated as[30]:

$$\text{Maximum } [0; (a.S_1 + b.S_2 + c)]$$

Where

a, b, and c are constants

S_1 is equivalent to price or yield on the first asset

S_2 is equivalent to price or yield on the second asset

Where the spread option was on the yield differential between two interest rate instruments, b would be equal to -1. Where c is equal to zero, the spread option is identical to an exchange option.

Spread option settlements can be structured on the following basis:

• **Cash settlement** – this entails cash payment equal to the in-the-money value of the option (the most common structure).

• **Physical settlement** – this entails a purchase and sale of the two securities underlying the option. Physical settlement of spread options can be complex, reflecting the fact that physical transactions are necessary in multiple securities

---

Advanced Strategies in Financial Risk Management; New York Institute of Finance: New York at Chapter 15.

[29] See McDermott, Scott "A Survey of Spread Options for Fixed Income Investors" in Klein, Robert A. and Lederman, Jess (Editors) (1993) The Handbook of Derivatives & Synthetics; Probus Publishing: Chicago, Illinois at Chapter 4; Ong, Michael "Exotic Options: The Market and their Taxonomy" in Nelken, Israel (Editor) (1996) The Handbook of Exotic Options; Irwin Professional Publishing, Chicago at Chapter 1 at 31; Smithson, Charles "Multifactor Options" (May 1997) Risk 43–45; Smithson, Charles (1998) Managing Financial Risk – Third Edition; McGraw-Hill, New York at Chapter 13 at 279–280; Ravindran, K. (1998) Customised Derivatives; McGraw-Hill, New York at Chapter 3 at 68–80; Nelken, Israel (2000) Pricing, Hedging & Trading Exotic Options; McGraw-Hill, New York at Chapter 19.

[30] See Ravindran, K. "Low Fat Spreads" (October 1993) Risk 66–67.

and a number of securities can underlie each rate. Investors sometimes require physical settlement[31].

5.2 Applications

Conceptually, spread options can be used to capture price differentials between commodities that are related in one of the following ways:
- **Demand substitution** – for example, between alternative investments such as bonds or equity indexes either in the same currencies or between currencies.
- **Transformation potential** – asset related by one asset being a price input into the other, such as "crack" spreads that refer to the price differentials between refined and unrefined energy products (for example, crude oil into gasoline).

The key application of spread option structures is the capacity to trade *relative* risk. For example, a spread option on the spread between Euro and US$ interest rates enables an asset manager to create and trade a specific exposure to the differential/relativity between the interest rate in the two markets without exposure to absolute underlying rate movements in either market. This allows capture and monetisation of views on the differential in a manner sought by asset or liability managers. In essence, the market for spread options facilitates trading in second order relationships between certain assets in financial markets, effectively trading in correlation relationships between the relevant assets. A key advantage is that it is difficult to replicate the economic profile of spread options by trading in the standard form put and call options on the underlying asset.

Interest rate spread options are one of the most important types of spread option products. They typically fall into the following categories:
- **Single currency structures** – covering the differential between interest rates in the same currency including:
  1. *Yield curve options* – these structures allow trading in the shape of the yield curve as embodied in rates at two nominated points in the yield curve.
  2. *Intra-market spread options* – these structures allow trading in the relative rates between two instruments. This structure includes options on:
     - Spreads between instruments where relative value is driven by credit factors; for example, spreads between government bonds and bonds issued by non-governmental issuers.

---

[31] This requirement has led to the development of proprietary products designed to facilitate physical settlement. An example of this structure would be Goldman Sach's DUOP[SM] (Dual Option Exercise) structure which allows a spread option to be settled by a simultaneous sale and purchase of underlying Treasury securities at a strike price spread.

- Spreads between cash instruments and derivatives on the underlying asset; for example, interest rate swap spreads.
- Spreads between instruments where relative value is driven by cash flow or contingency factors; for example, spreads between conventional government bonds and mortgage/asset backed securities (the latter is subject to pre-payment risk).

- **Cross Currency Structures** – covering the differential in rates between two different currency markets such as:
  1. *Cross currency bond spread options* – these structures allow trading in yield differentials in medium to long term interest rates in two separate currencies.
  2. *Cross currency money market rate spread options* – these structures allow trading in yield differentials in short term or money market interest rates in two separate currencies.

Each of these structures allows the monetisation and capture of value from expectations regarding interest rates at different points in the yield curve or across markets. Alternatively, the structures facilitate the hedging of exposures to changes in yield curve shape or spreads between markets. The terminology[32], structure and potential applications of these structures are discussed in the examples set out below.

Exhibit 11.8 sets out an example of a yield curve spread option. **Exhibit 11.9** sets out an example of a cross market bond yield spread option.

An application of cross market interest rate spread options is index differential swap transactions that are structured to capture the positive or negative differential between money market indexes in two currencies[33]. Other structures include options on the spread between US Treasury securities and mortgage securities and options on swap spreads.

A significant volume of interest rate spread options is related to the US interest rate market. This reflects the maturity of the US market, established interest rate relationships between various securities traded in the market, liquidity and sophistication of participants. An additional area of significant activity is cross market spread options between the major reserve currencies (US$, Euro and yen). During the late 1990s, a significant component of spread option volume was trading in interest rate spreads between European currencies in the lead up to the introduction of the Euro. Anticipation of convergence in interest rates in member countries led to spread options being used to monetise expectations.

---

[32] The terminology for spreads is not fully standardised.
[33] See Chapter 14.

Exhibit 11.8   Spread Options – Yield Curve Option[34]

This example focuses on a yield curve option on the 2 year to 10 year yield spread on US Treasury securities[35].

The general terminology in regard to such options is as follows:

- **Call options** – this is equivalent to a long position in the shorter maturity security and a short position in the longer maturity security. The position allows the purchaser to gain from a steepening of the shape of the yield curve where short rates rise less or fall more than longer rates. This is referred to as "buying" the yield curve. The face value amounts are volatility matched (using modified duration, present value of a basis point ("PVBP") or dollar value of 1 basis point ("DVOI") methods) to equate the relative price sensitivity of the different securities to yield movements.
- **Put options** – this is equivalent to a short position in the shorter maturity security and a long position in the longer maturity security. The position allows the purchaser to gain from a flattening of the shape of the yield curve where short rates rise more or fall less than longer rates. This is referred to as "selling" the yield curve. The face value amounts are volatility matched.

The key terms of the transaction include:
- **Strike spread level** – this is usually quoted as a yield spread in bps between two underlying securities[36]. This is set at the time of entry into the transaction.
- **Type of exercise** – European and American option structures.
- **Expiry date**.

Assume an investor purchases a put option on the yield spread between the 2 year US Treasury bonds and the 10 year US Treasury bond. The terms of the option are as follows:

Notional amount:	US$10 million
Strike spread level:	100 bps
Type of exercise right:	European
Expiration date:	3 months

The put option will expire:
- In-the-money – where the yield spread between the identified securities is less than 100 bps.

---

[34] See McDermott, Scott "A Survey of Spread Options for Fixed Income Investors" in Klein, Robert A. and Lederman, Jess (Editors) (1993) The Handbook of Derivatives & Synthetics; Probus Publishing: Chicago, Illinois at Chapter 4.

[35] These options are traded under a variety of proprietary trade names eg Goldman Sachs' SYCURVE (Slope of the Yield Curve) Options.

[36] The strike spread level can be set as the yield spread between the current on-the-run Treasury securities at expiry of the option. This would increase the complexity of any settlement calculation. This type of structure would approximate a constant maturity structure; see Chapter 17.

- Out-of-the-money – where the yield spread between the identified securities is greater than 100 bps.

The payoff on the option is typically structured to equate to a dollar value per basis point of the spread. A typical structure entails $10,000 per basis point per $1 million of notional principal of the option. The standardised dollar value amount is based on adjusting the face value of securities underlying the option.

The option premium is also typically quoted in basis points. Assume that the option premium in this case is 15 bps or $150,000.

For example, if the yield curve spread between the nominated securities at expiration was less than 100 bps (60 bps) then the return to the investor would be 40 bps (strike spread (100 bps) minus expiration spread (60 bps)). This equates to a $ gain (net of the premium) to the buyer of $250,000 (intrinsic value $400,000 (40 bps × $10,000) less premium paid $150,000 (15 × $10,000)). If the option expires out-of-the-money, then the option buyer would have lost the premium paid.

The yield curve option is essentially an option on the forward yield spread between the two securities. This is based on the implied forward prices out of the expiry date of the option at the time of entry into the transaction based on the shape of the yield curve. The intrinsic value of the spread option at commencement (whether it is out-of or in-the-money) is a function of yield curve slope.

In a positively sloped yield curve environment, a call (put) option on the yield curve spread (where the strike yield spread is set *at the current or spot yield spread*) will tend to be substantially in-the-money (out-of-the-money) and its premium will reflect the high (low) intrinsic value. The relative value is dictated by the relative pace at which forwards increase (or decrease) in a positive (or negative) yield curve environment for the two securities. The rate of increase in the implied forward rates for the shorter maturity security will typically be faster than that for a longer maturity security. This creates the implied narrowing or widening of the forward yield curve spread[37].

The yield curve option of this type is used to trade expectations regarding the yield curve shape. Assume that in a positive yield curve environment, the investor anticipates a continuation of the positive shape structure. The investor can capture the value of the narrower yield curve spread, implied by the forwards embedded in the yield curve, by selling yield curve shape put spread options or purchasing equivalent call options. Conversely, investors anticipating a faster flattening of the yield curve than implied by the forward rates (and corresponding forward yield spread) can sell call options or purchase put options on the spread.

Asset managers use yield curve options to seek to increase returns or minimise losses on bond portfolios. Similar strategies may be utilised by liability managers (including those in financial institutions) faced with the problem of funding mismatches between assets and liabilities.

---

[37] See discussion regarding CMT transactions in Chapter 17.

Exhibit 11.9   Spread Options – Cross Currency Spread Option[38]

This example focuses on a yield spread option between the US$ and the German government bond markets.

The terminology and structure of a cross currency yield spread option is similar to that described in **Exhibit 11.8**. The yield spread is specified in relation to two identified bonds. Each bond is quoted in a manner consistent with the underlying market convention. A call option implies the right to buy the spread and will increase in value when the yield spread increases. A put option implies the right to sell the spread and will increase in value when the yield spread decreases. The only additional element in such structures is the necessity to nominate the currency in which the option is denominated. Typically, the yield spread option is denominated in one or another of the underlying bond currencies. It can also be denominated in a third currency, usually the currency in which the asset or liability manager's performance is measured.

Assume an investor purchases a put option on the spread between the current 10 year US$ government bond and the current 10 year German Bund. The current spread between the bonds is 78 bps (US government yields are above the German Bund rates). The terms of the option are as follows:

Notional amount:	US$10 million
Strike spread level:	65 bps
Type of exercise right:	European
Expiration date:	3 months

The option is denominated in US$. The quoting convention is standardised to equate each basis point to represent 1% of the notional principal of the option. For example, if this option was quoted at a premium of 10 bps, the net cost to the investor to purchase US$10 million notional principal of the put would be determined as follows:

Premium times cost per US$1 notional $10 \, \text{bps} \times 0.01 \, \text{per bp} = 0.10 \times \text{US\$1 million}$
principal (bps) equals US$ cost per US$1 $= \text{US\$100,000}$
notional principal times notional principal
amount equals net option cost

The put option will expire:
- In-the-money – where the yield spread between the identified securities is less than 65 bps.
- Out-of-the-money – where the yield spread between the identified securities is greater than 65 bps.

The put option will provide a positive payoff to the investor where the yield spread between the two markets narrows (US$ 10 year rate falls more (rises less) than 10 year German rates). Where the option expires in the money (the yield spread at maturity is 40 bps), the investor makes a gross gain on the option position of 25 bps (US$250,000). This equates to a net gain after adjustment for the premium cost of 5 bps (US$50,000).

---

[38] See McDermott, Scott "A Survey of Spread Options for Fixed Income Investors" in Klein, Robert A. and Lederman, Jess (Editors) (1993) The Handbook of Derivatives & Synthetics; Probus Publishing: Chicago, Illinois at Chapter 4.

Cross market yield spread options allow asset as well as liability managers to effectively trade relative performance of fixed interest/bond markets. This structure facilitates asset allocation decisions (without cash investments in the foreign market) or trading spreads between markets.

For example, assume that a multi currency bond portfolio investor anticipates that the US$ bond market will outperform the German market. The investor can take advantage of this expectation by increasing exposure to US$ bonds and decreasing the exposure to German bunds. The asset manager intends to return the portfolio to its neutral allocation if the spread decreases to 65 bps. The asset manager could sell the US$ Treasury/German bund put at a strike spread of 65 bps. If the spread decreases below this level, then the portfolio is effectively adjusted from its overweight position to a neutral configuration. The investor earns the premium from the sale of the option. Where the spread widens, the option premium provides a limited hedge (up to the value of the premium received) to the deterioration in bond portfolio value.

5.3   Valuation

5.3.1   Approach

The key factors that drive the value of spread options are the forward yield spread and the volatility of the spread. Other required parameters include the strike yield spread, the time to expiry and the interest to expiry.

The spread option structure is effectively an option on the forward yield spread between the nominated securities. The forward yield spread is economically the differential between the forward rates of the two securities at the option expiry date. The forward rates are usually estimated using the current spot yield for the security and the financing rate (repo or money market (LIBOR) rate) to the option expiry[39]. The forward rate estimated using this technique is not exactly equal to the security's forward yield at the theoretical forward price. This is because the security has a non-zero convexity. For short dated options, the difference is not material[40].

The value of spread options is based on the relationship between forward rates on shorter versus longer maturity securities in different yield curve environments. The differential between the implied forward rates is largely dictated by the fact that the difference between spot and forward rates for shorter term securities is greater than the difference between the spot and forward rates for longer term securities. This creates substantial changes in the implied forward yield spread relative to the spot yield spread, leading to value creation opportunities. The price of the option prior to expiration is also sensitive to both the spot rates for the relevant securities and the financing rate to expiration (that in combination, determines the forward spread).

---

[39]   See Das, Satyajit (2004) Derivative Products & Pricing; John Wiley & Sons (Asia), Singapore at Chapter 6.

[40]   For discussion on the convexity adjustment, see Das, Satyajit (2004) Derivative Products & Pricing; John Wiley & Sons (Asia), Singapore at Chapter 6.

5.3.2   *Volatility Estimation*

The volatility of the forward spread is complex. It reflects the volatility of the underlying securities and the correlation between yield movements between the two securities. There are a number of ways to model the volatility of the forward spread, including:

- Historical volatility of the spread between the *actual* two securities.
- Historical volatility of the spread between two securities *having constant maturities* equivalent to the actual underlying securities (say, 2 year constant maturity bond against 10 year constant maturity security[41]).
- Estimated yield spread volatility based on the average yield of each security, the historical yield volatility of each security and the historical correlation between the two.
- Estimated expected future yield spread based on the actual yields on the securities at transaction date, the implied volatility of options on each security, and an estimate of the future correlation coefficient.

In practice, the forward credit spreads appear to be relatively more volatile than the underlying securities. This higher spread volatility reflects the following:

- Lower absolute level of spread (a 1 bps change in credit spread results in a larger *percentage change* than an equivalent change in the absolute yield level on the security).
- Imperfect correlation between the security and risk free rate.

Exhibit 11.10 sets out an example of the calculation of the volatility of the credit spread as well as the yield volatility of the underlying security.

Exhibit 11.10 Historical Spread Volatility – Calculation		
Assume the following rates and spreads:		
Period	**Risk Free Interest Rate (% pa)**	**Spread (% pa)**
0	6.030	0.450
1	6.010	0.460
2	5.990	0.430
3	5.990	0.430
4	6.000	0.410
5	6.040	0.440
6	6.010	0.450
7	6.020	0.430
8	6.050	0.430
9	6.040	0.410

---

[41] For a discussion of the concept of constant maturity securities, see Chapter 17.

Period	Risk Free Interest Rate (% pa)	Spread (% pa)
10	5.980	0.420
11	5.950	0.440
12	5.960	0.430
13	5.960	0.410
14	5.930	0.450
15	5.950	0.420
16	5.980	0.440
17	5.970	0.410
18	6.010	0.410
19	6.040	0.420
20	6.020	0.400

The rates and spreads are depicted in the graphs below:

RATES (% pa)

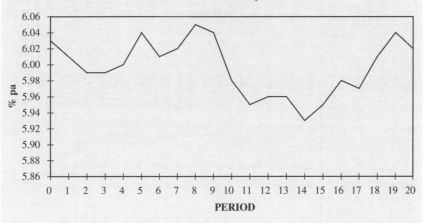

SPREADS (bps)

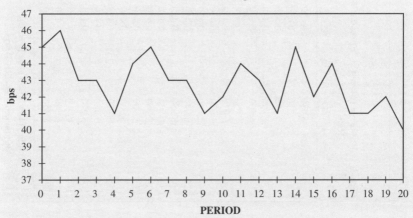

The rate and spread volatility is calculated in the Table below:

Period	Risk Free Interest Rate (% pa)	Spread (% pa)	Interest Rate (% pa)	Yield Volatility Calculations		Spread Volatility Calculations	
				Spread Relative $(S_t/(S_{t-1}))$	Daily Return $U_i = \ln(S_t/(S_{t-1}))$	Yield Relative $(S_t/(S_{t-1}))$	Daily Return $U_i = \ln(S_t/(S_{t-1}))$
0	6.030	0.450	6.480				
1	6.010	0.460	6.470	1.02222	0.02198	0.99846	(0.00154)
2	5.990	0.430	6.420	0.93478	(0.06744)	0.99227	(0.00776)
3	5.990	0.430	6.420	1.00000	0.00000	1.00000	0.00000
4	6.000	0.410	6.410	0.95349	(0.04763)	0.99844	(0.00156)
5	6.040	0.440	6.480	1.07317	0.07062	1.01092	0.01086
6	6.010	0.450	6.460	1.02273	0.02247	0.99691	(0.00309)
7	6.020	0.430	6.450	0.95556	(0.04546)	0.99845	(0.00155)
8	6.050	0.430	6.480	1.00000	0.00000	1.00465	0.00464
9	6.040	0.410	6.450	0.95349	(0.04763)	0.99537	(0.00464)
10	5.980	0.420	6.400	1.02439	0.02410	0.99225	(0.00778)
11	5.950	0.440	6.390	1.04762	0.04652	0.99844	(0.00156)
12	5.960	0.430	6.390	0.97727	(0.02299)	1.00000	0.00000
13	5.960	0.410	6.370	0.95349	(0.04763)	0.99687	(0.00313)
14	5.930	0.450	6.380	1.09756	0.09309	1.00157	0.00157
15	5.950	0.420	6.370	0.93333	(0.06899)	0.99843	(0.00157)
16	5.980	0.440	6.420	1.04762	0.04652	1.00785	0.00782
17	5.970	0.410	6.380	0.93182	(0.07062)	0.99377	(0.00625)
18	6.010	0.410	6.420	1.00000	0.00000	1.00627	0.00625
19	6.040	0.420	6.460	1.02439	0.02410	1.00623	0.00621
20	6.020	0.400	6.420	0.95238	(0.04879)	0.99381	(0.00621)
Standard Deviation (Per Period)					4.894%		0.527%
Annualised Volatility (Days)			250		77.386%		8.334%

The relative volatility is as follows:

Rate volatility: 8.33% pa
Spread volatility: 77.39% pa

5.3.3   Valuation Models

Spread options can be priced using a variety of models. Spread options can be equated to and valued as exchange options in certain circumstances[42]. Two separate approaches exist to the valuation of spread options. These include:

- **Modelling the spread as an underlying asset** – this approach will generally allow analytical solutions based on the Black-Scholes-Merton[43] model to be derived[44]. The advantage of this approach is its relative simplicity. The approach creates significant problems. It assumes that the spread will never become negative. This may be a reasonably tractable assumption where the spread is likely to be positive (yield on a risky security is compared to the yield on a risk free security). This is clearly inconsistent where the spread is between two assets where negative spreads are feasible. This problem is introduced by the implicit assumption of the log normal distribution of the spread as an asset price. In addition, the log normal assumption suggests that spread fluctuation size would increase for large spreads and decrease for small ones (the proportionality impact), which is not supported by evidence. One possible means of coping with the difficulties posed by the assumption of log normality (particularly in respect of the spread price being negative) is to assume a normal as opposed to log normal distribution where volatility is calculated on the *absolute price change* annualised standard deviation.

---

[42] For an adoption of the Margrabe approach, see Bhansali, Vineer (1998) Pricing and Managing Exotic and Hybrid Options; McGraw-Hill, New York at 69–79.

[43] See Das, Satyajit (2004) Derivative Products & Pricing; John Wiley & Sons (Asia), Singapore at Chapter 7. The version used is Black's commodity forward/futures pricing model; see Black, Fischer "The Pricing of Commodity Contracts" (March 1976) Journal of Financial Economics 3 167–179.

[44] See Garman, Mark "Spread the Load" (December 1992) Risk 68–84; McDermott, Scott "A Survey of Spread Options for Fixed Income Investors" in Klein, Robert A. and Lederman, Jess (Editors) (1993) The Handbook of Derivatives & Synthetics; Probus Publishing: Chicago, Illinois at Chapter 4 at 102–111. See also Heenk, B.A., Kemna, A.G.Z. and Vorst, A.C.F. "Asian Options on Oil Spreads" (1990) Review of Oil Spreads" 511–528; Bhansali, Vineer (1998) Pricing and Managing Exotic and Hybrid Options; McGraw-Hill, New York at 29–33.

- **Utilising multi (two) factor options models** – this approach is generally implemented using a numerical approach[45]. It is assumed that each security has a log normal distribution. A binomial distribution or Monte Carlo simulation is used to find the expected value of the option at expiry. This is then discounted back to the valuation date to derive the present value of the option. This approach incorporates the separate volatility of the underlying assets and the correlation between the two assets to derive the spread option value. This approach is preferable in that it does not suffer the same restrictions as the first approach.

Exhibit 11.11 sets out an example of an analytical option pricing model for spread options. **Exhibit 11.12** sets out an example of pricing a spread option.

Exhibit 11.11   Spread Options – Analytical Pricing Model[46]

The pricing of a call option is:

$$C_t = e^{-rt}[(S_t - K)N(h) + \sigma\sqrt{t}N'(h)]$$

where

$$h = (1/\sigma\sqrt{t})(S_t - K)$$

where

K = strike yield spread
S_t = forward yield spread at time t
σ = volatility (standard deviation of yield spread)
r = risk free rate
t = time to option maturity
$N(h)$ = standard normal distribution

The equivalent pricing for a put option is:

$$P_t = e^{-rt}[(K - S_t)(1 - N(h)) + \sigma\sqrt{t}N'(h)]$$

where

$$h = (1/\sigma\sqrt{t})(S_t - K)$$

---

[45] See Garman, Mark "Spread the Load" (December 1992) Risk 68–84; Ravindran, K. "Low Fat Spreads" (October 1993) Risk 66–67; Ravindran, K. "Exotic Options" in Dattatreya, Ravi E. and Hotta, Kensuke (1994) Advanced Interest Rate and Currency Swaps: State-of-the Art Products, Strategies & Risk Management Applications; Probus Publishing: Chicago, Illinois; Pearson, Neil D. "An Efficient Approach for Pricing Spread Options" (Fall 1995) Journal of Derivatives 76–91; Ravindran, K. (1998) Customised Derivatives: A Step-by-Step Guide to Using Exotic Options, Swaps and Other Customised Derivatives; McGraw-Hill, New York at 274–278, 331–332.

[46] The version set out here is from McDermott, Scott "A Survey of Spread Options for Fixed Income Investors" in Klein, Robert A. and Lederman, Jess (editors) (1993)

Exhibit 11.12   Spread Options – Valuation Example

Assume an option on the spread between two bonds. The example assumes the following parameters:

Bond 1 Current Yield (% pa)	6.70
Bond 2 Current Yield (% pa)	6.30
Current Spread (% pa)	0.40
Strike Spread (% pa)	0.40
Maturity	3 months
Volatility – Bond 1 (% pa)	14.00
Volatility – Bond 2 (% pa)	18.00
Interest Rates (% pa)	5.50
Correlation	0.80

The spread option premium is 0.14%[47].

5.3.4   Hedging/Trading Spread Options

Spread options are usually created dynamically through trading in the underlying assets. For example, yield curve options can be equated to positions in the underlying bonds designed to have an equivalent dollar equivalent (PVBP or DVO1) and/or duration position. Consistent with normal delta hedging approaches, the amount of the hedge portfolio held is adjusted continuously to synthetically replicate the returns on the option. The approach to hedging cross market spread options is similar.

Spread options cannot usually be efficiently replicated by trading in options on the underlying assets. The portfolio of options is generally more expensive, reflecting the separate payoff that allows each option to be separately exercised to maximise the value of individual options. This reflects the fact that the yield curve option is insensitive to absolute rate levels while the option portfolio is generally sensitive to the overall absolute level of rates[48].

It should be noted that the one factor approach creates significant hedging difficulties. This reflects the fact that this type of model indicates a single delta

---

The Handbook of Derivatives & Synthetics; Probus Publishing: Chicago, Illinois at Chapter 4 at 109–110.

[47] The option is priced using a binomial model.

[48] This is often expressed as the fact that the $ duration of the option portfolio is not zero, while the $ duration of the yield spread option is zero.

governing synthetic replication or hedging of the spread option. The two factor approach creates more complex valuation parameters including two deltas, multiple gammas and at least two vegas. It requires, for computation purposes, the volatility of both assets involved in the spread and the correlation coefficient between them.

A particularly significant factor of spread options when priced using the multifactor approach is the phenomenon of negative vega. This reflects the fact that lower volatility levels can result, under certain circumstances, in higher option premiums. This is because if the volatility of one asset diminishes (at least with other variables held constant), the diminished volatility in one asset price performance can in fact *increase* the value of the spread option as it increases the possibility of the spread increasing or decreasing.

6   Compound Options

6.1   Concept[49]

A compound option (also known as an option on an option) is an option that gives the purchaser the right but not the obligation to buy or sell another agreed *option* at a pre agreed price on or by the expiry of the compound option. Compound options are an example of multifactor option structures where the underlying asset is varied.

6.2   Structural Features and Economics

The compound option is often referred to as the "overlying" or "mother" option. The option underlying the compound option is termed the "underlying" or "daughter" option.

There are four possible variations:
- A call on a call option (the right to buy a call option).
- A put on a call option (the right to sell a call option).
- A call on a put option (the right to buy a put option).
- A put on a put option (the right to sell a put option).

---

[49]   See Ong, Michael "Exotic Options: The Market and their Taxonomy" in Nelken, Israel (Editor) (1996) The Handbook of Exotic Options; Irwin Professional Publishing, Chicago at Chapter 1 at 35–37; Ravindran, K. (1998) Customised Derivatives; McGraw-Hill, New York at Chapter 3 at 129–141; Nelken, Israel (2000) Pricing, Hedging & Trading Exotic Options; McGraw-Hill, New York at Chapter 10.

The key elements of the compound option that are agreed at the commencement of the transaction include:

- Strike price and expiry of the underlying option (the daughter option).
- Strike price and expiry of the compound option.
- Underlying asset price, volatility and interest rate.

The major attraction of compound option structures is the premium economics. The premium for the compound option is generally low. The total premium for the option (the sum of the compound option and the premium payable for the daughter option) will generally be higher than the premium of a conventional option on comparable terms. The lower *initial* premium cost facilitates hedging certain types of exposures and/or trading strategies.

An additional advantage of compound options is the ability to trade volatility. The premium on the daughter option is agreed at the time of entry into the compound option. This means that the volatility of the option is fixed. This allows compound options to be used to take positions on changes in asset volatility with relatively low outlays (the compound option premium).

The major applications of compound options include[50]:

- Contingency hedging situations such as contract tenders where the party hedging is uncertain as to the requirement of the hedge. The low initial cost of the compound options allows cost effective hedging structures to be devised[51].
- Trading/positioning on underlying asset price movements or changes in volatility. This is driven by the low initial cost of the compound option that allows the purchaser to gear itself into a more expensive option at a later stage if required.

Exhibit 11.13 sets out an example of using compound options to hedge a contingent exposure. **Exhibit 11.14** sets out an example of using an option on a cap to manage interest rate exposures.

Compound options are not common. They are used mainly in currency and interest rate markets. Compound option structures are sometimes used in equity markets.

---

[50] See Krsyzak, Krystyna "Insurance Against the Unknown" (October 1989) Risk 17–23; Duker, K. "Derivative Products" (November 1989) The Treasurer 6–13; Bailey, Trevor "Exploiting Compound Options" (July 1993) Corporate Finance 9–10.

[51] Alternative structures for hedging contingency risk of this type have often been suggested. This can take the form of packaged option structures; see Chapter 40. Other structures include the FX Tender Hedge Product suggested by one bank; see Patel, Navroz "Try a Little Tender Hedge" (July 2001) Risk 32–34.

Exhibit 11.13   Compound Option Application – Contingent Hedging

Assume a European company is bidding on an export contract to the US. The contract will be awarded in six months. If the European company is awarded the contract, then it will generate US$60 million in revenue from the sale in 9 months from the contract date. If the company does not hedge the long US$/short Euro exposure, then it is exposed to losses from a depreciation of the US$ against the Euro. This is because lower US$ would reduce the Euro value of the US$ revenue.

The company has a contingent currency exposure. The company could purchase a 6 month compound call option on a 9 month US$ put/Euro call option (the daughter option) to hedge the contingent exposure. The option would give the company the right in 6 months to buy a US$ put/Euro call option with 9 month maturity and a set strike price for an agreed premium.

The payoffs from the compound option are as follows:
*   If the company is awarded the contract, then the outcomes would be:
    1. If the US$ put/Euro call has increased in value (the US$ has depreciated against the Euro), then the company would exercise the compound option and buy the US$ put/Euro call. The underlying option would be purchased at a lower premium than its market value.
    2. If the US$ put/Euro call has decreased in value (the US$ has appreciated against the Euro), then the company would let the compound option expire. It would then buy a new US$ put/Euro call in the market or hedge by selling forward US$/purchasing Euro. If it expected the US$ to continue to appreciate, then it would have the option of leaving the exposure unhedged.
*   If the company is not awarded the contract, then the outcomes are as follows:
    1. If the US$ put/Euro call increases in value (the US$ has depreciated against the Euro), then the compound option will have value. The company can sell the compound option or exercise into and sell the underlying option to capture the value from the position.
    2. If the US$ put/Euro call decreases in value (the US$ has appreciated against the Euro), then the compound option will have no value. The loss to the company will be limited to the premium paid at the beginning of the compound option contract.

The economics of the transaction are as follows:
*   Assume that the 6 month forward exchange rate is US$1: Euro 0.95.
*   The cost of a standard US$ put/Euro call with a strike at US$1: Euro 0.95 and 15 month expiry is 4.68% of the Euro amount.
*   This can be compared to the following costs of 6 month compound call options. All compound options are structured with a daughter US$ put/Euro call option with strike of US$1: Euro 0.95, and expiry of 9 months from expiry of compound option (15 months from spot).
    1. Under the first structure, the company purchases a compound option for a premium of 2.63% for the right to buy the US$ put/Euro call option in 6 months. If the company decides in 6 months time to buy the daughter option, then the company would pay an

additional premium of 2.63% for the 12 month US$ put/Euro call option. The total cost of the daughter option, if exercised, would be 5.26%.

2. Under the second structure, the company purchases a compound option for a premium of 1.70% for the right to buy the US$ put/Euro call option in 6 months. If the company decides in 6 months time to buy the daughter option, then the company would pay an additional premium of 4.55% for the 12 month US$ put/Euro call option. The total cost of the daughter option, if exercised, would be 6.25%.

The choice between the two compound option structures is driven by the likelihood of the contract being awarded to the European company. If the company has a strong expectation that it will be awarded the contract, then it may select the structure with the higher initial premium and lower overall cost.

Under both compound option structures, the cost to the company is higher than for the standard US$ put/Euro call. The compound option has lower cost where the contract is not awarded and the option is not required. This creates additional flexibility for the company in structuring its risk management.

Exhibit 11.14   Compound Option Application – Low Cost Hedging

Assume a liability manager wishes to hedge a portfolio of US$ floating rate debt priced off 3 month LIBOR. The liability manager seeks to hedge using options. This reflects an expectation of a positive yield curve and lower short term interest rates. The liability manager requires a level of protection to unexpected increases in US$ interest rates over its 3 year hedging time horizon.

The liability manager considers two strategies:

- Purchase of a standard cap on 3 month LIBOR for 3 years at a strike of 6.50% pa. The cost of this cap is 2.1% of the face value of the underlying debt being hedged (equivalent to 79 bps pa when amortised).
- Purchase of a compound cap or option on cap (also referred to as a "caption") where the liability manager purchases the *right to buy a cap* on 3 month LIBOR with a strike of 6.50% pa at an agreed total premium of 1.75% (for all 11 caps if exercised). The premium for this compound cap is 0.74% (equivalent to 28 bps pa when amortised).

The second strategy involving the compound cap offers the hedger a substantial cost saving on the initial premium. The contingent protection provided would be triggered only if the cap level is breached at any 3 month LIBOR fixing date, where the hedger would pay the relevant agreed premium *for that particular period*. This means the hedge is effected for a lower cost, except where interest rates rise sharply and all (or substantially all) of the caps are triggered, reflecting a sharp and immediate increase in US$ interest rates. In that case, the higher combined premium (2.49%) versus the standard cap premium (2.1%) will increase the cost of the hedge.

6.3 Valuation and Hedging

The valuation of compound options is relatively straightforward. This reflects the fact that the structure is identical to a standard option, except that the underlying asset itself is an option.

A compound option is essentially a purchase of the underlying option where the premium is paid in multiple instalments. In a compound option there are two instalments – a compulsory first payment (the compound option premium) and the second optional payment for the underlying (daughter) option. This means that the value of the compound option is influenced by the factors that drive the value of a normal option and a number of additional factors. The additional factors include[52]:

- **Instalment structure** – this includes the size of the initial compulsory and the subsequent optional payment. It also includes the number of instalments. In a standard compound option there are only two instalments. In other variations of a compound option, there may be additional instalments.
- **Payment timing** – this refers to the time period between the instalment payments.

Within this general framework, European compound options can be valued analytically[53]. This uses integrals of bi-variate normal distributions[54].

---

[52] See Ravindran, K. (1998) Customised Derivatives; McGraw-Hill, New York at Chapter 3 at 133–141.

[53] The original analytical solution was suggested by Robert Geske. Geske's closed form formula is based on an interesting insight. The original Black Scholes formula for stock options was developed in the context of seeking to value the *equity* of a traditional firm. This reflects the fact that the equity or ordinary share capital of a firm can be viewed as a call option. This reflects the fact that an ordinary share provides a return or payoff to the holder that is a function of the net value of the firm (defined as the value of the firm minus the face value of outstanding debt). If the net value of the firm is negative, then the shareholder would abandon the option (the premium cost foregone would be the actual equity subscribed). In contrast, if the value of the firm is in excess of the value of its debt, then the holder of share capital captures all returns resulting from the increase in the value of the firm. Geske extended this original Black Scholes approach to encompass the position. He argued that an option on an ordinary share (standard equity option) must, by inference, be a compound option. The compound option is an option on the ordinary share capital that is itself an option on the value of the firm adjusted for the face value of outstanding debt. See Geske, Robert "The Valuation of Compound Options" (March 1979) Journal of Financial Economics 63–81.

[54] See Geske, Robert "The Valuation of Compound Options" (March 1979) Journal of Financial Economics 63–81; Rubinstein, Mark "Double Trouble" (December 1991–January 1992) Risk 73. See also Hull, John (2000) Options, Futures and

Numerical solutions using binomial or Monte Carlo techniques are also available[55]. The numerical solutions are generally used for more complex compound option structures where analytic solutions are not available.

Exhibit 11.15 sets out the analytical solution for the valuation of a compound option. Exhibit 11.16 sets out an example of the valuation of a compound option.

Compound option structures are, in practice, created and hedged synthetically. The optionality of the underlying asset of a compound option creates a number of unique hedging dimensions. This includes:

- The gamma of compound options is relatively high.
- Compound options tend to magnify volatility risk. This is because unlike traditional underlying assets, the underlying option's value is impacted by changes in volatility.
- The theta of the option behaves differently to the theta behaviour of a conventional option. This is because it must take into account the passage of time that affects the remaining time to expiration of the compound option and the remaining time to expiration of the underlying option. This means that it is insufficient to move the maturity of the underlying option alone, but the maturity of both the mother and daughter option must be adjusted in conjunction.

Exhibit 11.15   Compound Options – Pricing Formula[56]

Assume:

S = price of asset

$S*$ = the asset price at time t_1 for which the option price at time t_1 equals K_1

y = income on the asset

σ = volatility of asset

r = interest rate

t_1 = the first exercise date (the compound option exercise date)

t_2 = the second exercise date (the underlying option exercise date)

K_1 = the first strike price (the compound option strike price or the price of the underlying option)

K_2 = the second strike price (the underlying option strike price)

Other Derivatives – Fourth Edition; Prentice-Hall Inc., Upper Saddle River, NJ at Chapter 18 at 460–461.

[55] See Schroeder, Mark "A Reduction Formula Applicable to Compound Options" (July 1989) Management Science 823–827; Selby, Michael and Hedges, Stewart "On the Evaluation of Compound Options" (March 1987) Management Science 347–355; Nelken, Izzy "Square Deals (April 1993) 56–59.

[56] The version set out here is from Hull, John (2000) Options, Futures and Other Derivatives – Fourth Edition; Prentice-Hall Inc., Upper Saddle River, NJ at Chapter 18 at 460–461.

The value of a compound European call option on a call option is given by:

$$Se^{-yt_2}M(a_1, b_1; \sqrt{(t_1/t_2)}) - K_2e^{-rt_2}M(a_2, b_2; \sqrt{(t_1/t_2)}) - e^{-rt_1}K_1N(a_2)$$

Where

M is the cumulative bi-variate normal distribution function[57].

$a_1 = [\ln(S/S*) + (r - y + \sigma^2/2)t_1]/\sigma\sqrt{t_1}$

$a_2 = a_1 - \sigma\sqrt{t_1}$

$b_1 = [\ln(S/K_2) + (r - y + \sigma^2/2)t_2]/\sigma\sqrt{t_2}$

$b_1 = b_1 - \sigma\sqrt{t_2}$

The value of a compound European put option on a call option is given by:

$$K_2e^{-rt_2}M(-a_2, b_2; -\sqrt{(t_1/t_2)}) - Se^{-yt_2}M(-a_1, b_1; -\sqrt{(t_1/t_2)}) + e^{-rt_1}K_1N(-a_2)$$

The value of a compound European call option on a put option is given by:

$$K_2e^{-rt_2}M(-a_2, -b_2; \sqrt{(t_1/t_2)}) - Se^{-yt_2}M(-a_1, -b_1; \sqrt{(t_1/t_2)}) - e^{-rt_1}K_1N(-a_2)$$

The value of a compound European put option on a put option is given by:

$$Se^{-yt_2}M(a_1, -b_1; -\sqrt{(t_1/t_2)}) - K_2e^{-rt_2}M(a_2, -b_2; -\sqrt{(t_1/t_2)}) + e^{-rt_1}K_1N(a_2)$$

Exhibit 11.16   Compound Options – Pricing Example

Assume a compound call option to purchase a call option. The example assumes the following parameters:

Underlying Asset Price ($)	100
Asset Income (% pa)	0.00
Volatility (% pa)	20.00
Interest Rates (% pa)	5.00
Strike Price (compound option) ($)	4.00
Strike Price (underlying option) ($)	125
Expiry Date (compound option)	6 months
Expiry Date (underlying option)	12 months (from commencement)

The compound call option premium is $1.97 (1.97% of current asset price). The premium for a comparable 18 month conventional option is $4.41 (4.41% of current asset price).

---

[57] For the procedure for calculating M see Hull, John (2000) Options, Futures and Other Derivatives – Fourth Edition; Prentice-Hall Inc., Upper Saddle River, NJ at Appendix 11C at 272.

The total cost of the option if the compound option is exercised is $5.97 (5.97% of current asset price). This is $1.56 or 35% more expensive than the conventional call option. If the compound option is abandoned after 6 months, then the cost of abandonment is $1.97; that is, $2.44 lower than the cost of the conventional option.

The Table below sets up the cost of a compound option and the comparable conventional options for different compound option strike prices to illustrate the effect of altering the instalments of the option premium.

Strike Price (compound option) ($)	3.00	3.50	4.00	4.50	5.00
Premium (compound option) ($)	2.37	2.16	1.97	1.79	1.64
Total Option Premium ($) (if compound option exercised)	5.37	5.66	5.97	6.29	6.64
Premium (conventional option) ($)	4.41	4.41	4.41	4.41	4.41
Difference ($)	0.96	1.25	1.56	1.88	2.23
Difference (%)	22	28	35	43	50

6.4   Variations on Compound Options

A variation on the compound option structure is the instalment option (often referred to as the deferred premium, pay-as-you-go or rental option)[58]. This structure entails an option whose premiums are paid in instalments at regular intervals. This structure is similar to the compound option. It entails purchasing the option by paying the instalment in a series of premiums more than the two generally used in a standard compound option. The instalment option gives the purchaser the advantage of being able to make a decision to abandon the option and cut the premium cost at each instalment payment date. **Exhibit 11.17** sets out an example of an instalment cap agreement.

Exhibit 11.17   Instalment Options – Example

Assume a borrower has floating rate debt priced off 3 month LIBOR. The borrower is concerned about potential increases in interest rate cost if US$ interest rates increase. The borrower seeks protection from higher interest rates. The borrower is not certain about the duration of its debt. It is planning a major equity issue that would be used to repay the outstanding debt. This contingency creates complexity in designing the hedge.

---

[58]   See Karsenty, Franck and Sikorav, Jacques "Instalment Plan" (October 1993) Risk 36–40; Chance, Don "The Pricing and Hedging of Limited Exercise Caps and Spreads" (Winter 1994) Journal of Financial Research 561–584; Thompson, Andrew C. "Valuation of Path Dependent Contingent Claims with Multiple Exercise Decisions Over Time: The Case of Take-or-Pay" (June 1995) Journal of Financial and Quantitative Analysis 271–293.

The following structures are available:
- **Standard cap** – the company can purchase a 3 year standard cap on US$ 3 month LIBOR with a strike of 6.00% pa for a premium of 180 bps.
- **Instalment cap** – the company can purchase a 3 year instalment cap. Under the structure, the purchaser pays the premium over time in multiple instalments. The purchaser can terminate the cap by ceasing to make further premium instalment payments. If the company continues to make the instalment payments, then the cap operates normally. In this case, the instalment cap costs the company 25 bps per 3 month period.

The economics of the structure are as follows:
- The cost of the instalment cap is dependent upon the term of the option and the number of instalment payments made. The premium cost of the instalment cap will be higher than the conventional cap where all instalments are paid to keep the cap in operation over the total term (300 bps for the instalment cap versus 180 bps for the standard cap).
- The instalment cap allows the company to terminate the cap when required by simply ceasing to make any future payments. This will be valuable where the company no longer needs the hedge. This will allow the company to lower the cost of hedging where it is uncertain about the requirement for the hedge (as in this case because of the uncertainty of the duration of the funding requirement). It provides considerable flexibility for a hedger that requires the ability to adapt the hedge to changing circumstances. In this case if the funding is terminated after 1 year, vitiating the need for the hedge, the company would have achieved a cost saving of 80 bps (the cost of the standard cap (180 bps) against the cost of 4 instalments (100 bps)).
- The instalment cap can be terminated for any reason. It may provide value maximisation opportunities where, due to market rate movements, it is possible to hedge at more attractive rates.
- A disadvantage of the instalment structure is that if an instalment is not paid, the cap is terminated and cannot be entered into again on the original terms.

7   Basket Options

7.1   Concept[59]

A basket option is an option where the payout is related to the cumulative performance of a specified basket of underlying assets. Typical examples include options

---

[59] See Ong, Michael "Exotic Options: The Market and their Taxonomy" in Nelken, Israel (Editor) (1996) The Handbook of Exotic Options; Irwin Professional Publishing, Chicago at Chapter 1 at 29; Smithson, Charles "Multifactor Options" (May 1997) Risk 43–45; Smithson, Charles (1998) Managing Financial Risk – Third Edition; McGraw-Hill, New York at Chapter 13 at 282; Ravindran, K. (1998) Customised Derivatives; McGraw-Hill, New York at Chapter 3 at 94–104; Nelken, Israel (2000) Pricing, Hedging & Trading Exotic Options; McGraw-Hill, New York at Chapter 21.

on baskets of currencies and equity stocks. In a basket option, the multifactor element is the multiple underlying assets incorporated in the option structure. Basket options are a frequently used form of correlation based product.

7.2 Structural Features and Economics

The payoff in a conventional option is based on the value at expiry or exercise of an individual asset. In contrast, the payoff of a basket option is based on the aggregate value of a specified basket of assets.

The payoff of a basket option is as follows:

$$\text{Call option} = \text{Maximum} \left[\sum_{i=1}^{n} w_i S_i - K; 0 \right]$$

$$\text{Put option} = \text{Maximum} \left[\sum_{i=1}^{n} K - w_i S_i; 0 \right]$$

Where

S_i = the price of asset i in the basket
w_i = weighting (in percentage terms) of asset i within the basket
K = the strike price

The design of a basket option follows a specific process. For example, an index is created that represents the base value of the predetermined portfolio of assets. The strike price of the basket option is defined in terms of the aggregate value of the basket of assets. The strike price is set frequently as a percentage (110% or 90%) of the value of index at commencement. **Exhibit 11.18** sets out an example of the construction and performance of a basket option.

The economics of the basket option is driven by the fact that it is similar to purchasing an option on the individual assets within the basket. However, there are major difference as the basket option payout is driven by the aggregate performance of the basket, *not the individual performance of the basket elements.*

The structure of the basket option means that the premium of a basket option should generally be lower than the option premium on the individual components. The lower premium is driven by the correlation between the assets in the basket. If the assets within the basket are less than perfectly correlated (correlation less than 1), then the basket option will be lower in cost than the total cost of purchasing options on the individual elements of the basket.

The basic concept underlying basket options is based on portfolio theory. In particular, diversification and imperfect covariance within the basket is used to

---

Exhibit 11.18   Basket Options – Example

Assume a call option is structured on a basket of 6 equity stocks (Stocks A, B, C, D, E and F). The initial index value is established as follows:

Assets	Quantity	Price ($)	Value ($)
Stock A	1	110.00	110.00
Stock B	1	75.00	75.00
Stock C	1	40.00	40.00
Stock D	1	125.00	125.00
Stock E	1	92.00	92.00
Stock F	1	56.00	56.00
Basket			498.00

Based on an initial value of the basket of $498.00, assume the basket call option strike is set at 100% of initial value or $498.00.

Assume that at expiry, the value of the asset is as follows:

1. Out-of-the-money Case

Assets	Quantity	Price ($)	Value ($)
Stock A	1	95.00	95.00
Stock B	1	91.00	91.00
Stock C	1	45.00	45.00
Stock D	1	110.00	110.00
Stock E	1	76.00	76.00
Stock F	1	55.00	55.00
Basket			472.00

In this case, the value of the basket option is 0 as the aggregate value of the basket is below the strike price.

Note that if individual call options on the basket components had been purchased, then the options on Stocks B and C would have expired in-the-money. This is irrelevant where the option is on the basket itself.

2. In-the-money Case

Assets	Quantity	Price ($)	Value ($)
Stock A	1	115.00	115.00
Stock B	1	92.00	92.00
Stock C	1	38.00	38.00
Stock D	1	110.00	110.00
Stock E	1	104.00	104.00
Stock F	1	64.00	64.00
Basket			523.00

In this case, the value of the basket option is $25.00, as the aggregate value of the basket is above the strike price.

Note that if individual call options on the basket components had been purchased, then the options on Stocks A, B, E and F would have expired in-the-money. The value of these options at expiry would be $42, exceeding the value of the basket option.

---

lower the cost of the option. The basic concept is that the volatility of the basket is lower than the volatility of the individual assets, reflecting the impact of imperfect correlations. The concept is similar to the logic of creating an index (such as an equity or stock index) to diversify risk and reduce volatility. Basket design is driven by the desire to reduce correlation between the basket components.

In some basket options, assets denominated in different currencies are used within the basket. There are two types of baskets in this case:

- **Currency unhedged** – under this structure, each asset is converted into the base currency of the basket option. The exchange rate used is the spot rate at the date of entry into the option (to establish the initial value of the basket) and the spot rate at the expiry date (to establish the final value of the basket). Under this structure, the purchaser is exposed to both asset price and currency risk.

- **Currency hedged** – under this structure, the basket option is combined with quanto features[60] (referred to as quanto basket options). This has the effect of eliminating the currency risk on the assets denominated in foreign currency for the option purchaser. Under this structure, a pre-agreed exchange rate (generally the spot rate at the time of entry into the transaction) is used to convert the asset price at expiry to calculate the final value of the basket.

Basket options are generally European options.

7.3 Applications[61]

The major applications of basket options are driven by the lower premium. An additional feature is the ability to monetise existing correlations within asset and liability portfolios.

---

[60] See discussion later in this Chapter.
[61] For examples of applications of basket options see Grannis, Scott "An Idea Whose Time Has Come" (September 1989) 72–74; Falloon, William "Funds in the Sun" (August 1993) Risk 21–25; Stambaugh, Fred "Put All Your Exposures in One Basket" (October 1993) Corporate Finance 22–23; Dillon, Gary and Darley, Brett "There's Value in a Basket" (February 1994) The Australian Corporate Treasurer 6–8.

Corporate treasurers or investment/asset managers use basket options to hedge currency and equity price risks. Typical applications include:

- **Hedging currency risk** – this is focused on structuring baskets of currencies to which the hedger has exposure. A call or put option on the basket is then used to hedge the exposure. Alternatively, the basket is designed to enable the liability or asset manager to position against future currency movements. The structure is used to hedge the underlying exposure at lower cost than purchasing options on each basket component. The structure also allows the trading position to be constructed at lower cost than the equivalent separate option. In cases where the underlying exposure is to a specified group of assets, the basket option allows the cost of hedging/trading to be reduced by monetising the implicit correlations in the basket.

- **Creating equity baskets** – this entails the creation of baskets to replicate the synthetic return profiles on specified stock groupings. The primary driver is the frequent focus of asset managers on *sectors* or *groups of stocks*. The basket option allows a lower cost hedge to existing positions to be developed. The basket option allows the construction of customised exposure to selected stocks included in the basket. The lower cost is achieved by the monetisation of the embedded equity correlations within the baskets.

Basket options are also used in structured notes. For example, basket options are used extensively in equity linked notes, including structures targeted at retail investors[62].

Basket options are generally inflexible. The structure assumes that the basket components will remain at the pre-fixed weighting within the basket till expiry. This implicitly assumes that the underlying position being hedged or the assets to which exposure is sought remains fixed. In practice, this may not be case. Any required re-structure is generally expensive and difficult. This reflects the lack of liquidity in basket options (that is a characteristic of correlation products generally). This means that the position will generally need to be traded with the original counterparty. The cost that will be incurred will reflect the bid-offer spread on volatility of the basket assets and the correlation between basket components. The trading cost

---

[62] See Das, Satyajit (2004) Structured Products Volume 2; John Wiley & Sons (Asia), Singapore at Chapter 4. See also Newman, David "Hedging Total Portfolio Value" (1995) Corporate Finance Risk Management & Derivatives Yearbook 19–23; Bensman, Miriam "Hedging Multiple Currency Exposures the Easy Way" (April 1997) Derivatives Strategy 28–29; Falloon, William "Basket Cases" (March 1998) Risk 44–48; Margrabe, William "Equity Basket Swaps and Options: Part 1" (11 December 2000) Derivatives Week 7–8.

may be significant. These trading costs mean that basket options are frequently used for passive positions and hedges rather than positions that are likely to be actively traded.

7.4   Valuation and Hedging[63]

Basket option values are driven by factors similar to the factors that affect the valuation of other options. There are a number of additional factors that specifically affect the value of a basket option, including:
- Number of assets and the specific weighting of the individual components.
- Volatility of *each asset* is required.
- Correlation between the components of the basket.

The overall premium of basket options is influenced by the level of covariance between the basket components. Depending on the nature of the covariance, volatility is generally lower for the basket than for the individual components. In the event that the correlations between basket components are negative, then moves in the value of one component will tend to be neutralised by opposite movements of another. Consequently, unless all the components are highly correlated, the option will be cheaper than a series of individual currency options.

There are several approaches to the valuation of Basket Options:
- Numerical approaches such as binomial and Monte Carlo simulations can be used. One approach involves the creation of a bi-variate binomial lattice to price basket options[64]. Monte Carlo simulations are where a large number of asset paths are simulated to provide a distribution of the value of the basket. The expected payout is discounted back to provide the value of the options. The numerical techniques are powerful where a large number of steps/paths are utilised. The large number of steps required creates problems of the speed of pricing. An additional problem relates to the fact that the bi-variate binomial

---

[63] See Briys, Eric Bellalah, Mondher, Mai, Huu Minh and De Varenne, Francois (1998) Options, Futures and Exotic Derivatives: Theory, Application and Practice; John Wiley & Sons, Chichester at Chapter 15; Hull, John (2000) Options, Futures and Other Derivatives – Fourth Edition; Prentice-Hall Inc., Upper Saddle River, NJ at Chapter 18 at 471; Nelken, Israel (2000) Pricing, Hedging & Trading Exotic Options; McGraw-Hill, New York at Chapter 21. See also Margrabe, William "Equity Basket Swaps and Options: Part 1" (11 December 2000) Derivatives Week 7–8.

[64] See Rubenstein, Mark "Somewhere Over the Rainbow" (November 1991) Risk 63–66.

techniques, when extended to baskets of more than two assets, involve longer and longer calculation times.

- Approximation techniques, where the value of the option is estimated by the use of assumptions regarding the distribution of the basket value. One approach is moment matching. Under this approach, the first two moments of the basket at maturity are calculated and are used to generate the distribution of the basket value under the assumption that the value of the basket is log normally distributed. This allows the value of the option to be obtained by integration[65]. The approximation methods are useful in overcoming the computational difficulties of numerical approaches.

Exhibit 11.19 sets out an example of pricing a basket option.

Basket options are generally hedged using option replication technology. Hedging requires trading in all the basket components. Pricing models generate multiple deltas, cross gammas and multiple vegas. Changes in correlation also create shifts in deltas that require re-hedging.

In the case of large baskets, a variation used is the use of a modified hedging basket (the tracking basket), representing a sub-set of the components of the actual asset basket created. The tracking basket is selected using statistical methods to closely track the performance of the *actual basket*. This is designed to allow replication of the basket efficiently by reducing trading costs.

The major risks in replicating a basket option include:

- **Correlation risks** – changes in correlation can have significant impact on the value of the option. The absence of a liquid and tradeable market in correlation risk means that the risk must be assumed and held by the trader through to expiry. Incorrect estimates of correlation will result in a replication cost that is significantly above the originally estimated value of the option.
- **Re-balancing costs** – where basket options are synthetically replicated, it is necessary to trade in a series of underlying assets rather than one single asset. This substantially increases the hedging and re-balancing costs.
- **Tracking error** – where a tracking basket is used to hedge a diverse currency or equity portfolio, this introduces tracking error to the performance of the hedge. This reflects the cumulative difference between the value of the hedge and the value of the portfolio over time. This is analogous to a basis risk on the hedge.

---

[65] See Gentle, David "Basket Weaving" (June 1993) Risk 51–52; Huynh, Chi Ban "Back to Baskets" (May 1994) Risk 59–61.

Exhibit 11.19   Basket Options – Pricing Example

Assume a call option on a basket of two stocks (Stocks A and B).
The assumed parameters of the two stocks for valuation are as follows:

Assets	Quantity	Price ($)	Value ($)	Asset Volatility (% pa)	Asset Income (% pa)
Stock A	1	10.00	10.00	20.00	2.50
Stock B	1	11.50	11.50	25.00	1.00
Basket			21.50		

Other parameters are as follows:

Interest Rates (% pa)	5.00
Strike Price ($)	21.50
Expiry	1 year
Correlation (Stock A to Stock B)	0.30

The value of a basket call option with a strike of 21.50 (the current value of the basket) is $2.00 (9.28%).

This compares to the price of two separate at-the-money spot options of $2.24 (10.42%). The basket option represents a saving in premium cost of $0.24 (10.71%).

The sensitivity to correlation changes is set out in the Table below:

Correlation	−0.60	−0.30	0.00	.30	.60
Premium ($)	1.39	1.62	1.82	2.00	2.15
Premium (%)	6.47	7.56	8.47	9.28	10.02

The premium of the basket option decreases with lower correlation and increases with higher correlation.

---

8   Quanto Options

8.1   Concept[66]

A quanto option refers to a special class of option where the underlying amount of the asset being hedged is driven by movements in a separate financial

---

[66] See Gastineau, Gary "An Introduction to Special Purpose Derivatives: Options with a Payout Depending on More Than One Variable" (Fall 1993) 98–104; Ong, Michael "Exotic Options: The Market and their Taxonomy" in Nelken, Israel (Editor) (1996) The Handbook of Exotic Options; Irwin Professional Publishing, Chicago at Chapter 1 at 31–35; Smithson, Charles "Multifactor Options" (May 1997) Risk 43–45; Smithson,

market variable. A quanto option is effectively a derivative product denominated in a currency other than that of an underlying asset to which exposure is to be hedged. The term *quanto* usually refers to the quantity adjustment feature of the option. This type of product is sometimes referred to as a currency protected product.

The concept of a quanto option can be illustrated with an example. Assume a US investor (base currency US$) seeks to invest in the Japanese stock market (the Nikkei index). The investor would be exposed to two separate risks – the equity price risk and the currency risk (long Yen/short US$). Any depreciation in the value of the Yen has the potential to reduce any gain on the equity position.

Hedging this currency exposure is difficult. This reflects the fact that the amount to be hedged (the equity position) is uncertain. This is because the amount to be hedged is driven by changes in the value of the Nikkei index. As the index increases, the amount of exposure increases. In contrast, as the index decreases, the amount of exposure also decreases. This means that any currency hedge based on a fixed amount (say the initial investment) will potentially be mismatched to the underlying exposure. If the Nikkei index increases, then the investor will be under hedged (long Yen/short US$). If the Nikkei index decreases, then the investor will be over hedged (short Yen/long US$). This will be the case irrespective of whether the hedge is implemented with forwards or options. This is because the face value of the hedge must be nominated in each case.

Hedging this type of exposure requires a hedge that adjusts the face value of the hedge consistent with the evolution of the underlying asset price (in the above case, the Nikkei index). There are several ways that this linkage can be created. One possible way of linking the returns on the Nikkei index and the currency risk is a quanto option. In this case, a quanto option entails a call option on the Nikkei stock index denominated in US$. Under this structure, the payoff is based on the value of the Nikkei stock index call option converted to US$ at an agreed exchange rate (say the spot exchange rate prevailing at the start of the option contract). The structure allows the investor to create an exposure to the underlying asset free from exchange rate risk.

The critical element is that the amount of currency exposure of this transaction is variable. The amount to be hedged depends on the value of the Nikkei index. The option writer must convert the returns from the index from its original currency (Yen) into US$ at expiry. The quantity to be hedged matches the receipts from the

---

Charles (1998) Managing Financial Risk – Third Edition; McGraw-Hill, New York at Chapter 13 at 280–281; Ravindran, K. (1998) Customised Derivatives; McGraw-Hill, New York at Chapter 3 at 172–193; Nelken, Israel (2000) Pricing, Hedging & Trading Exotic Options; McGraw-Hill, New York at Chapter 21.

index call option. It also reflects the correlation between changes in value in the stock index (the Nikkei) and fluctuations in the value of the Yen/US$ exchange rate. Quantos represent a special case of multifactor options. Quantos provide protection against exposure to the asset price fluctuations where the asset is denominated in a currency other than that of the hedger. It overcomes the difficulty of hedging uncertain future cash flows by creating an explicit linkage between the asset price fluctuations and the amount of the currency hedge.

8.2 Structure and Economics

The principal focus of quanto options is the linkage of asset price movements and currency exposure. There are a number of possible alternatives for linking the foreign asset and currency exposures. **Exhibit 11.20** sets out the different structures linking the foreign asset and the currency risk.

Variations on standard structures are also feasible. This includes the joint quanto option. This structure combines an option on the asset and a currency option. For example, the investor has exposure to any price appreciation in the asset and can convert any gain into the domestic currency at the better of a guaranteed exchange rate and the exchange rate at maturity[67].

Exhibit 11.20   Alternative Structures for Linking Asset and Currency[68]

1.   Potential Structures

There are a number of possible linkages between the asset price and the currency exposure:
- Foreign currency asset call struck in foreign currency.
- Foreign asset call struck in domestic currency.
- Fixed exchange rate foreign asset call.
- Asset linked foreign call.

The structures are illustrated below with an example. The example used is as follows:
- Assume a US investor (base currency US$) seeks to invest in the Japanese stock market (the Nikkei index denominated in Yen). The investor would be exposed to two separate

---

[67] See Smithson, Charles (1998) Managing Financial Risk – Third Edition; McGraw-Hill, New York at Chapter 13 at 281.

[68] See Reiner, Eric "Quanto Mechanics" (March 1992) Risk 59–63; Ong, Michael "Exotic Options: The Market and their Taxonomy" in Nelken, Israel (Editor) (1996) The Handbook of Exotic Options; Irwin Professional Publishing, Chicago at Chapter 1 at 31–35; Smithson, Charles (1998) Managing Financial Risk – Third Edition; McGraw-Hill, New York at Chapter 13 at 280–281; Briys, Eric Bellalah, Mondher, Mai, Huu Minh and De Varenne, Francois (1998) Options, Futures and Exotic Derivatives: Theory, Application and Practice; John Wiley & Sons, Chichester at Chapter 17 at 342–345.

risks – the equity price risk and the currency risk (long Yen/short US$). Any depreciation in the value of the Yen has the potential to reduce any gain on the equity position.
- Assumed rates are as follows:

Nikkei index level: 12,000
Spot exchange rate: US$1 = Yen 125
Investment amount: US$1,000,000 (Yen 125 million)

2. Foreign Currency Asset Call Struck in Foreign Currency

The position is similar to that under a conventional call option. Under this structure, the investor seeks to capture the appreciation in the Nikkei index above the agreed strike price (spot level of the Nikkei index 12,000) but is not concerned about the Yen/US$ currency risk.

The payoff of this instrument is as follows:

$$FX_m \times [\text{Maximum} (S_m - K_{fx}; 0)]$$

Where

K_{fx} = strike price denominated in the foreign currency.
S_m = spot price of asset at option expiry.
FX_m = exchange rate at option expiry.

In the example above, the payoffs on the call option are as follows:
- If the Nikkei index is below 12,000 then the option has no value.
- If the Nikkei index is above 12,000 then the option has value. For example, if the index is at 13,200 (an increase of 10%) then the option will have a payoff of Yen 12,500,000.
- The US$ value of the payoff will depend upon the exchange rate at expiry. The payoffs are summarised below:

Exchange Rate (US$1: Yen)	US$ Return (US$)	US$ Return (%)
110.00	113,636	11.36
125.00	100,000	10.00
140.00	89,286	8.93

3. Foreign Asset Call Struck in Domestic Currency

The position is similar to that under a conventional call option except that the foreign currency is translated into domestic currency terms. Under this structure, the investor seeks to capture the appreciation in the Nikkei index above the agreed strike price (spot level of the Nikkei index 12,000) but in US$ currency terms.

The payoff of this instrument is as follows:

$$\text{Maximum} [(FX_m \times S_m) - K_{domestic}; 0)]$$

Where

$K_{domestic}$ = strike price denominated in the domestic currency.
S_m = spot price of asset at option expiry.
FX_m = exchange rate at option expiry.

In the example above, assume the strike price is set at the spot value of the index (12,000) converted at the spot exchange rate (US$1: Yen 125.00) equivalent to 96.00. The payoffs on the call option are as follows:

*   If the US$ Nikkei index (defined as the value of the Nikkei index converted at the exchange rate at maturity) is below 96, then the option has no value.
*   If the US$ Nikkei index is above 96.00, then the option has value.

The structure means that the US$ value of the option is dependent on *both* the equity index value and the exchange rate at expiry. If the Nikkei is below the commencement value (the Yen strike), then the option will have no value unless the Yen has appreciated by an amount sufficient to offset the decline in asset value. If the Nikkei is above the commencement value (the Yen strike), then the option will have value unless the Yen has depreciated by an amount sufficient to offset the increase in asset value.

The payoffs are summarised below:

Nikkei below 12,000 at 10,800 (decrease of 10%)

Exchange Rate (US$1: Yen)	US$ Return (US$)	US$ Return (%)
110.00	22,727	2.27
125.00	0	0.00
140.00	0	0.00

Nikkei above 12,000 at 13,200 (increase of 10%)

Exchange Rate (US$1: Yen)	US$ Return (US$)	US$ Return (%)
110.00	250,000	25.00
125.00	100,000	10.00
140.00	0	0

4. Fixed Exchange Rate Foreign Asset Call

The position is similar to that under a conventional call option except the payoff on the option is converted at a fixed pre-agreed exchange rate. Under this structure, the investor seeks to capture the appreciation in the Nikkei index above the agreed strike price (spot level of the Nikkei index 12,000). The investor hedges the Yen/US$ currency risk by agreeing the exchange rate at which the payoff on the option will be converted into domestic currency. This is often referred to as the true quanto option.

The payoff of this instrument is as follows:

$$FX_{fixed} \times [Maximum(S_m - K_{fx}; 0)]$$

Where

K_{fx} = strike price denominated in the foreign currency.

S_m = spot price of asset at option expiry.

FX_{fixed} = fixed exchange rate.

In the example above, assume the fixed exchange rate is US\$1 = Yen 125. The payoffs on the call option are as follows:
- If the Nikkei index is below 12,000, then the option has no value.
- If the Nikkei index is above 12,000, then the option has value. For example, if the index is at 13,200 (an increase of 10%), then the option will have a payoff of Yen 12,500,000.
- The US\$ value of the payoff will be calculated at US\$1 = Yen 125.00 *irrespective of the spot exchange rate at expiry.*

5. Asset Linked Foreign Call

This structure links a currency option with an asset forward. Under this structure, the investor seeks exposure to the asset price. This exposure is on a linear basis; that is, the investor is exposed to increases as well as declines in the asset price. The investor purchases a currency option to hedge the currency exposure. The face value of the currency option adjusts to the amount of the asset exposure, based on the asset price at expiry.

The payoff of this instrument is as follows:

$$S_m \times [\text{Maximum} (FX_m - FX_{strike}; 0)]$$

Where

S_m = spot price of asset at option expiry.

FX_m = exchange rate at expiry.

FX_{strike} = strike exchange rate.

In the example above, assume the strike exchange rate is US\$1 = Yen 125. The payoffs on the asset linked option are driven by the movements in the exchange rate. If the Yen is weaker than US\$1 = Yen 125.00, the currency option is exercised. If the Yen is stronger than US\$1 = Yen 125.00, the currency option is not exercised. The payoffs (final investment value in US\$) are set out below:

Exchange Rate (US\$1: Yen)	110.00	125.00	140.00
Nikkei Index			
10,800	1,022,728	900,000	900,000
12,000	1,136,364	1,000,000	1,000,000
13,200	1,250,000	1,100,000	1,100,000

8.3 Applications[69]

The economics of quanto products is driven by the capacity to use the correlation between the currency and the underlying asset return to create a more

---

[69] See "Portfolio Management: Hedging Uncertain Foreign Cash Flows with Quantity Adjusting Options and Forwards" (2 May 1987) International Financing Review Issue 671 1501; Chew, Lillian "ELF and Efficiency" (October 1991) Risk 4; Chew, Lillian

exact hedge of the underlying risk profile. This hedge structure has several benefits:
• Creation of an exposure to the underlying asset price while minimising the currency risk.
• Avoidance of the deficiency of traditional hedging instruments in dealing with an uncertain notional amount to be hedged.
• Increasing or decreasing the cost of the option, depending upon the interest differential between the currencies and the correlation between the asset and exchange rate.

Major examples of quanto products include:
• Currency hedged equity options or equity market indexes.
• Currency hedged fixed income products.
• Currency hedged differentials or spreads between equity and/or fixed income markets. An important application of quanto options is indexed differential swaps. This entails hedging the currency risk on interest differentials between money market rates in two currencies[70].

Major applications of quanto options include:
• Investors using quantos to take advantage of the interest rate differential between two currencies to create favourable pricing for the underlying asset call. For example, a call on the US$ equity market denominated in a high coupon currency is less expensive than a call denominated in US$. This reflects the wide interest differential between the two currencies that will be reflected in the forward currency rate through the swap points. Using the forward points and discounting them to the present can generate savings that can be used to reduce the price of the call on the US equity market.
• Traders selling quantos to monetise the value of the interest rate differential. For example, assume an Australian client who wants to hedge its US$ equity portfolio. In order to reduce the premium payable, the investor wishes to sell a call to finance the put on the currency. If the investor were to undertake this transaction in US$, the transaction may be unattractive, as it may have to sell the call at a relatively low strike price to generate enough premium to finance the put. This reflects the fact that US$ interest rates are lower than A$ rates. However, a sale of a quanto option in A$ using the interest rate differential to advantage

---

"Quanto Leap" (April 1993) Risk 21–28; Davies, David "Quanto Leap" (September 2001) FOW 33–35.
[70] See Chapter 14.

may lower the cost of hedging the portfolio. The sale of the quantos creates a complex risk profile and can potentially reduce the value of the underlying equity portfolio.

Exhibit 11.21 sets out an example of the application of quanto options.

Exhibit 11.21   Quanto Options – Application

A US Investor invests in 100,000 shares in a UK firm (Company X) at GBP 30 per share. The current exchange rate is GBP 1: US$1.45. The total investment is GBP 3,000,000 or US$4,350,000. Company X does not pay dividends. The investor expects the share price to increase to GBP 40 over the next year.

The investor is seeking a US$ return. In order to hedge the currency risk, the investor sells forward GBP 4,000,000 (the number of shares (100,000) at the expected price (GBP 40)) for value 1 year forward. The forward rate is GBP 1: US$1.43. This means that the terminal US$ value locked in through the forward is US$5,720,000.

The structure of the hedge is problematic. This is because the value of the underlying stock is not known with certainty. If the shares increase to only GBP 32, then the investor will be over hedged. This means that the investor will need to buy GBP 800,000 in the spot market to fulfil the obligation to deliver GBP 4,000,000 into the sold GBP/bought US$ forward contract. If the pound has appreciated to GBP 1: US$1.50 then the GBP 800,000 purchase will result in a loss to the investor of US$56,000. This will reduce the US$ return to the investor, despite the fact that the stock has appreciated in GBP terms.

In contrast, the investor could use a quanto product. Under this structure, the investor would have been required to deliver GBP 32 only per share or GBP 3,200,000 in return for US$ at a guaranteed exchange rate.

A problem of the quanto hedge is the lack of flexibility. The investor cannot change the underlying position (shares) as the quanto hedge is linked to it. This type of hedge is better suited to portfolios where the composition remains stable over time. It is less suitable for actively traded portfolios as the underlying position may change significantly over time.

8.4   Valuation and Hedging[71]

Traditional Black-Scholes approaches to option valuation and hedging can be used to develop analytic solution to the pricing of quanto options[72].

---

[71] See Briys, Eric Bellalah, Mondher, Mai, Huu Minh and De Varenne, Francois (1998) Options, Futures and Exotic Derivatives: Theory, Application and Practice; John Wiley & Sons, Chichester at Chapter 17; Hull, John (1998) Options, Futures and Other Derivatives – Third Edition; Prentice-Hall Inc., Upper Saddle River, NJ at Chapter 13 at 298–301; Nelken, Israel (2000) Pricing, Hedging & Trading Exotic Options; McGraw-Hill, New York at Chapter 20.

[72] See Rubinstein, Mark "Two into One" (May 1991) Risk 49; Reiner, Eric "Quanto Mechanics" (March 1992) Risk 59–63; Wei, Jason Z. "Pricing of Nikkei Put Warrants"

The difference between the valuation technique for quantos and conventional options is the impact of the interest rate differential between the two currencies and the correlation between the underlying asset price and the relative exchange rate. **Exhibit 11.22** sets out an analytic solution to the valuation of quanto options. The solution is for a fixed exchange rate foreign asset call[73]. **Exhibit 11.23** sets out an example of the valuation of a quanto option.

The behaviour of quanto option value is complex. The example indicates that where correlation is zero, the cost of a quanto is almost identical to that of a conventional option. There is a marginal difference in the price because of the interest differential between the currencies. Where the option has a short remaining time to expiry, this difference is low, as the impact of discounted forward points is lower. For quanto options with longer times to expiry, the quanto should theoretically cost more or less because of the compounding impact of the interest differential and forward points.

Where the correlation between the stock price and the relative exchange rate is positive, then the call quanto costs less and the put quanto cost is greater than a conventional option. This is reversed in the case of negative correlation. This reflects the fact that the quanto feature will only improve the payoff to the purchaser on the underlying option where the exchange rate is weaker than the guaranteed exchange rate. Positive correlation means that an increase in the value of the underlying asset is accompanied by a change in the exchange rate whereby the foreign currency strengthens. This means the effective gain to the investor is reduced. This is

---

(November 1992) Journal of Multinational Financial Management 45–75; Dravid, Ajay, Richardson, Matthew and Sun, Tongsheng "Pricing Foreign Index Contingent Claims: An Application to Nikkei Index Warrants" (Fall 1993) Journal of Derivatives 33–51; Gruca, Edward and Ritchken, Peter "Exchange Traded Foreign Warrants" (1993) Advances in Futures and Options Research 53–66; Jamshidian, Farshid "Corralling Quantos" (March 1994) Risk 71–75; Jamshidian, Farshid "Hedging Quantos, Differential Swaps and Ratios" (September 1994) Applied Mathematical Finance 1–20. See also Rumsey, John "Pricing Cross-Currency Options" (February 1991) Journal of Futures Markets 89–93; Brooks, Robert "Multivariate Contingent Claims Analysis with Cross-Currency Options as an Illustration" (September 1992) Journal of Financial Engineering 196–218; Yu, G. George "Financial Instruments to Lock In Payoffs" (Spring 1994) 77–85. For an application of quanto concepts in the context of index differential swaps and their valuation, see Jamshidian, Farshid "Price Differentials" (July 1993) Risk 48–51 and Jamshidian, Farshid "Corralling Quantos" (March 1994) Risk 71–75.

[73] For analytic solutions to other types of quanto products, see Reiner, Eric "Quanto Mechanics" (March 1992) Risk 59–63; Briys, Eric Bellalah, Mondher, Mai, Huu Minh and De Varenne, Francois (1998) Options, Futures and Exotic Derivatives: Theory, Application and Practice; John Wiley & Sons, Chichester at Chapter 17.

because the purchaser is giving up any appreciation from positive movements in the exchange rate.

Quanto options are generally dynamically hedged. The hedge of a quanto option uses a portfolio of instruments including:

- Underlying asset.
- Currency forwards or spot positions in foreign and domestic currency.

The structure of the hedge is dictated by the fact that it is not possible to trade directly in a security that will have a value equal to the underlying asset in the

---

Exhibit 11.22   Quanto Options – Pricing Formula[74]

Assume:

   S = price of asset in foreign currency
   K = strike price in foreign currency
   FX = fixed exchange rate at which option proceeds will be converted into
           domestic currency
   y = income on the underlying asset
   σ_s = volatility of asset
   σ_{fx} = volatility of exchange rate
   r_f = interest rate in foreign currency
   r = interest rate in domestic currency
   t = time to expiry
   ρ = correlation between the asset price and exchange rate

The premium for a European call is:

$$FX(Se^{-(r-r_f+y+\rho\sigma_s\sigma_{fx})t}N(d) - Ke^{-rt}N[d - \sigma_s\sqrt{t}])$$

The premium for a European put is:

$$FX(Ke^{-rt}N[-d + \sigma_s\sqrt{t}] - Se^{-(r-r_f+y+\rho\sigma_s\sigma_{fx})t}N(-d))$$

Where

$$D = [\ln(S/K) + (r_f - y + \sigma_s^2/2 - \rho\sigma_s\sigma_{fx})t]/\sigma_s\sqrt{t}$$

---

[74] See Dravid, Ajay, Richardson, Matthew and Sun, Tongsheng "Pricing Foreign Index Contingent Claims: An Application to Nikkei Index Warrants" (Fall 1993) Journal of Derivatives 33–51. The version set out here is from Gastineau, Gary "An Introduction to Special Purpose Derivatives: Options with a Payout Depending on More Than One Variable" (Fall 1993) 98–104 at 103.

Exhibit 11.23   Quanto Options – Pricing Example

Assume a call on the Nikkei stock index denominated in Yen where the return is translated into US$ at a guaranteed US$/Yen exchange rate. The parameters assumed are as follows:

Spot price of asset in foreign currency (index points)	12,000.00
Strike price in foreign currency (index points)	12,000.00
Fixed exchange rate (Yen = US$)	0.0080 (1/125.00)
Income on the underlying asset (% pa)	0.50
Volatility of asset (% pa)	25.00
Volatility of exchange rate (% pa)	12.00
Interest rate in foreign currency (% pa)	1.00
Interest rate in domestic currency (% pa)	5.00
Correlation	0.40
Time to expiry	6 months

The value of the quanto option is 6.85% pa. The premium for a comparable conventional yen denominated call on the Nikkei index is around 7.11% pa.

The sensitivity to correlation changes is set out in the Table below:

Correlation	−1.00	−0.80	−0.40	0.00	0.40	0.80	1.00
Premium (%)	8.02	7.84	7.50	7.17	6.85	6.54	6.39

The premium of the quanto option decreases with higher correlation and increases with lower correlation.

---

relevant currency. The hedge structure outlined overcomes this. The hedge portfolio must be continuously managed as the asset price and/or the exchange rate changes. As with other correlation products, pricing models generate multiple deltas, cross gammas and multiple vegas. Changes in correlation also create shifts in deltas that require re-hedging.

It is necessary to make a number of assumptions in structuring the hedge:

- The structure of the hedge assumes the level of the underlying asset, converted into the relevant currency at the relevant exchange rate, provides the basis of the hedge. It implicitly assumes that these two random variables are jointly log normally distributed. It also assumes that their product is also log normally distributed.

- It is also assumed that the correlation estimate used to calculate the premium for the option and the hedge ratio remains constant.

In practice, the assumptions may not hold in entirety.

9 Defined Exercise Options

Defined exercise options are similar to barrier options. In a defined exercise option (also referred to as outside barrier options or gap correlation products), two assets are used to determine the option payoff. The value (size of payoff) of the option is determined by the price of one asset. Price movements of a second asset determine whether the option is exercised and will pay out to the purchaser[75].

An example of a defined exercise option is an interest rate cap on 6 month US$ LIBOR with a strike rate of 6.50% pa that only pays off if gold prices are below US$250/ounce. The payoff of this defined exercise option is given as:

Maximum [0; 6 month US$ LIBOR − 6.50% pa] if Gold < US$250/ounce

0 if Gold > US$250/ounce

The structure means that the payoff under the interest rate cap will knock in or out depending upon gold price movements.

Defined exercise option structures include links between interest rates and currency or commodity prices, currency and commodity prices and equity value and interest rates. The major application of defined exercise options is the design of integrated hedges where contingent price movements drive risk[76]. The structured hedge effectively monetises the embedded price relationship to lower the cost of the hedge.

Exhibit 11.24 sets out an example of a defined exercise option that can be used in a commodity hedge. **Exhibit 11.25** sets out an example of an interest rate swap linked to oil prices.

The correlation between the two underlying asset prices is a key driver of the value of defined exercise options. A modified Black-Scholes model or numerical methods are used to price defined exercise options[77].

---

[75] See Heynen, Ronald and Kat, Harry "Crossing Barriers" (June 1994) Risk 46–51; Klotz, Rick and Efraty, Ravit (8 December 1994) "Analyzing Defined Exercise Options"; Salomon Brothers US Derivatives Research Fixed Income Derivatives, New York; Ong, Michael "Exotic Options: The Market and their Taxonomy" in Nelken, Israel (Editor) (1996) The Handbook of Exotic Options; Irwin Professional Publishing, Chicago at Chapter 1 at 15.

[76] See Sabloff, Michael and Turner, Christopher "Integrated Risk Management" in Smith, Kathleen Tener and Kennison, Pam (Editors) (1996) Commodity Derivatives and Finance; Euromoney Books, London at Chapter 7; Quarmby, David "Cross-Market Risk Management and Commodity-Linked Finance" in (1997) Managing Metals Price Risk; Risk Publications, London at Chapter 4.

[77] See Boyle, Phelim P. and Kirzner, E.F. "Pricing Complex Options: Echo Bay Ltd. Gold Purchase Warrants" (December 1985) Canadian Journal of Administrative Sciences

---

Exhibit 11.24   Defined Exercise Options – Application Example 1

Assume an Australian gold producer. Gold production is exported with sales being denominated in US$. Production costs are in A$.

The producer has two price risks:

* US$ Gold price – the producer is exposed to lower US$ gold prices.
* Exchange rate (A$/US$) – the producer is exposed to any depreciation in the US$ against the A$.

Traditionally, the producer would hedge the two exposures separately. The traditional form of hedge may result in the producer being over hedged. This has cost implications for the producer as the hedges incur significant costs.

The position of the producer can be analysed using the following assumptions:

* Gold price – US$300/ounce (for 1 year forward delivery).
* A$/US$ exchange rate – A$1: US$0.50 (for 1 year forward delivery).
* Assumed production – 100,000 ounces.

At current forward prices, the producer can lock in US$ revenues from gold sales of US$30 million (A$60 million)

The Table sets out the producer's position under different gold price and exchange rate scenarios:

	Stronger A$ Case (A$1 : US$0.55)	Weaker A$ Case (A$1 : US$0.45)
Lower Gold Price (**Gold Price : US$270/ounce**)	Revenue is US$27 million (A$49.1 million)	Revenue is US$27 million (A$60 million)
Higher Gold Price (**Gold Price : US$330/ounce**)	Revenue is US$33 million (A$60 million)	Revenue is US$33 million (A$73.3 million)

The analysis indicates that the gold price and exchange rate *jointly* affect the producer's revenue. The analysis indicates that the worst case for the producer is where a combination of lower gold prices and stronger A$ is experienced. In all other cases, the combination of gold price movements and exchange rates (at least) maintains the (A$) revenue position without the need for a hedge.

In these circumstances, the separate hedging of the gold price (purchase of gold put options) and exchange rate (purchase of US$ put/A$ call options) would significantly over hedge the producer and also result in substantially higher hedging costs. A lower cost and effective hedge would be to purchase a defined exercise put option on gold with a strike rate of $300/ounce which only pays off if the A$ is stronger than A$1: US$0.50. The payoff of this defined exercise option is given as:

Maximum [0; US$300 – Gold price at maturity] if A$ > US$0.50

0 if A$ ≤ US$0.50

294–306; Carr, Peter "A Note on the Pricing of Commodity Linked Bonds" (September 1987) 1071–1076.

The hedge cost would depend upon the correlation between the gold price and the A$/US$ exchange rate. The higher the correlation, the lower the cost of the gold/A$/US$ defined exercise option. This is because the higher the correlation, the more likely the movements in the gold price and the exchange rate will offset each other, thereby reducing the option payoff.

In practice, the hedge cost would be significantly below the cost of the two separate (gold and exchange rate) options. The lower cost is generated by the producer monetising the embedded correlation in its business operations.

Exhibit 11.25   Defined Exercise Options – Application Example 2

A number of oil consumers (including airlines) have undertaken oil linked interest rate swaps[78]. The typical structure is as follows:
- The oil consumer enters into a US$ interest rate swap where it pays the fixed rate and receives US$ 3 or 6 month LIBOR. The fixed rate on the swap is below prevailing market levels. For example, if market rates are say 6.50% pa, then the fixed rate is say 5.50% pa (a saving of 1.00% pa).
- The fixed rate on the swap is linked to the oil price. For example, the structure may entail the oil consumer paying 5.50% pa only if the benchmark West Texas Intermediate oil price is equal to/above US$20.00/barrel. If the oil price falls below US$20.00/barrel, then the oil consumer pays a higher fixed rate (say 7.50% pa). The higher fixed rate is generally significantly higher than the prevailing swap rate at the time of entry into the transaction.

The structure provides the oil consumer with a lower fixed interest cost where oil prices are higher. This is presumably where the consumer requires protection to maintain its net revenue. If oil prices decline and the interest cost increases, then the higher interest cost is offset in part or full by the effect of lower oil prices. The oil consumer lowers the cost of its interest rate hedge by monetising its inherent correlation position between interest rates and oil prices.

In economic terms, the oil consumer in these structures sells a defined exercise option. The option is a digital interest rate option, where the option is triggered by the oil price.

---

10   Summary

Multifactor options are exotic options where the option payoff is based on the relationship of more than one asset. This introduces the impact of correlation between

---

[78]   See Castell, Helen "Taiwan Airline Eyes Maiden Exotic Swaps Flight" (26 June 2000) Derivatives Week 1, 10.

the asset prices into the behaviour of the option. Multifactor options, as a group, allow traders to capture the volatility of each of the underlying asset prices and trade/manage the correlation between the price movements of the respective assets.

There are a number of types of multifactor options, including relative performance structures (where the option payouts under the structures are driven by the relative price performance of two or more underlying assets such as rainbow options, exchange options and spread options) and complex underlying asset structures (where the option structure is based on underlying assets that are non standard such as compound options, basket options, quanto options and defined exercise options).

Multifactor options are driven primarily by the capacity of these structures to hedge or trade specific types of *relative* asset price movements. Multifactor options are also used to hedge complex exposure where there are inherent correlation relationships that can be monetised to reduce the cost of the hedge and provide a better match to the underlying position.

12
Volatility Products

1 Overview

Volatility of asset prices/rates is central to financial markets. It forms the basis of trading of assets and rates. In derivative products, volatility is central to option pricing. The importance of volatility has led to the development of a number of products that are designed primarily to allow volatility itself to be traded *separately* as an asset. The products are designed to hedge the risk of volatility itself changing, or to acquire exposure to volatility changes. In this Chapter, products designed to allow trading in volatility are discussed.

The structure of the Chapter is as follows:
- The process of volatility trading is described.
- Volatility futures are examined.
- Volatility or variance swaps are discussed.
- Some product extensions (volatility options and structured notes with embedded exposure to volatility) are outlined.

2 Volatility Trading[1]

Volatility trading is driven by a number of factors, including:
- **Volatility risk** – a variety of traders have explicit volatility risk. This includes option traders that, in the process of market making, acquire long or short positions in implied volatility in their option positions. This also includes asset managers who have implicit volatility positions, either from trading in options or in terms of portfolio tracking error against a benchmark index.

---

[1] See Heron, Dan "Volatility Traders Widen Their Nets" (May 1997) Risk 13; Hunter, Robert "Prepackaged Volatility Plays" (April 1998) Derivatives Strategy 7–8; Pelham, Mark "Vol of Vol" (September 1998) Futures & OTC World 66.

- **Acquiring exposure to volatility risk** – traders or investors may seek exposure to volatility with the object of benefiting from anticipated movements in market volatility. This may take the form of changes in implied volatility or from the differences between actual realised volatility and implied volatility. This focuses on volatility as a trading asset *in its own right*.
- **Volatility as an asset class** – this focuses on volatility as a separate asset class. This would mean that volatility would display return, changes in level and liquidity. It would also display correlations to other asset classes (cash, fixed interest, property, equity, commodity etc). Where volatility displays these characteristics, investment in volatility within a portfolio may be used to generate significant returns or manage the risk of existing portfolios. Research suggests that addition of volatility as a separate asset class in this way can significantly add value to portfolios[2].

Traditionally, transfer of or acquisition of exposure to volatility risk has only been feasible through trading options. This is because volatility is an essential input in pricing options. Changes in implied volatility affect the value of the options[3].

Trading in options requires assumption of complex risks. Trading in options will generally expose the trader to directional changes in asset prices and implied volatility changes. In addition, the presence of the volatility smile/skew and term structure will expose the trader to other risks such as the relativity of the asset price to the option strike and time decay. This means trading options provides, at best, an imperfect exposure to market volatility.

Traders generally use particular option strategies to create specific exposure to volatility[4]. This entails trading in options and then hedging away the directional exposure to asset prices. In practice, this will entail the trader entering into a straddle (long or short both a put and a call option)[5] and then entering into offsetting asset positions to reduce the net delta of the position to zero. The straddle is used to ensure there is no directional bias. The delta hedge is

---

2   See Gross, Leon and Mezrich, Joe (January 1998) Introducing Volatility Swaps; Salomon Smith Barney - Equity Derivative Sales, Derivative Products, New York at 34–35.
3   See Das, Satyajit (2004) Derivative Products & Pricing; John Wiley & Sons (Asia), Singapore at Chapters 7 and 9.
4   See Gross, Leon and Mezrich, Joe (January 1998) Introducing Volatility Swaps; Salomon Smith Barney - Equity Derivative Sales, Derivative Products, New York at 9–15; Blacher, Guillaume "Volatility Power" (October 2000) FOW 55–59; Qu, Dong "Hedging Volatility Dynamics In Equity Derivatives" (9 October 2000) Derivatives Week 6–7.
5   See Chapter 1.

used to hedge away any exposure to asset price changes. The position will need to be managed dynamically over time as asset prices change or time to expiry changes[6].

The transaction will provide the trader with exposure to implied volatility (the mark-to-market value of the position) and the realised volatility (the actual cost of the delta hedge over the time to expiry of the options). Traders will buy the straddle to go long volatility to benefit from expected increases in implied volatility or higher actual realised volatility levels relative to implied volatility used to price the options. Traders will sell the straddle to short volatility to benefit from decreases in implied volatility or lower actual volatility levels relative to implied volatility to price options.

The transactions described to create exposure to *pure* volatility are not efficient. Costs of establishing and managing the position include:

- **Transaction costs** – trading to replicate the pure exposure to volatility will result in significant transaction costs, including the bid-offer costs of buying and selling the options and trading in the asset. It may also include items such as commissions, taxes and clearing costs.
- **Institutional restrictions on trading** – the strategy assumes the ability to trade in the asset without limitation. This may not be the case in practice. Restrictions would include market liquidity and ability to fund positions. In practice, the capital required to support this trading might be significant, limiting the capacity to trade in this way. A special problem relates to the ability to short assets. This may be restricted, further limiting the capacity to trade[7].
- **Path dependency** – the effectiveness of the delta hedge strategy is both volatility *and* path dependent. This means that the result of the trading strategy is not purely a function of realised versus implied volatility. The need to dynamically re-balance the hedge dictates that the position is exposed to gamma or convexity risk. This means that depending on the path followed by the asset over time, even at identical realised overall volatility levels, may result in different profit

---

[6] For a discussion of delta hedging, see Das, Satyajit (2004) Derivative Products & Pricing; John Wiley & Sons (Asia), Singapore at Chapter 16.

[7] For example, the "up-tick" rule applicable in certain equity market may restrict the ability to short assets such as individual equity stocks in the US market. This would particularly be the case in a long or short position that requires a short asset hedge. Positions requiring shorting may only be done on the zero plus tick basis. This would make it difficult to stay delta neutral, particularly where selling is required when the market is falling. This is because it may be impossible to short where a zero plus tick is required. See Gross, Leon and Mezrich, Joe (January 1998) Introducing Volatility Swaps; Salomon Smith Barney - Equity Derivative Sales, Derivative Products, New York at 13.

and loss positions on the trades. This means that the desired *pure* exposure to volatility may not be achieved[8].

- **Infrastructure requirements** – the ability to manage the trading positions required assumes the availability of and investment in appropriate risk management and trading infrastructure. This would generally be available to traders. Other market participants wishing to hedge or trade volatility may not have similar infrastructure available, limiting the ability to trade in this manner.

These factors mean that in practice, creating pure exposure to volatility is difficult through trading in options.

3 Volatility Futures

Futures and options contracts on volatility offer an obvious instrument for the management of volatility. The idea has been frequently proposed[9].

Volatility futures and options, where available, would assist in the following economic functions, including:

- **Trading and hedging volatility risk acquired in option trading or portfolio management** – the contract would allow volatility risk to be shifted in an efficient and cost effective framework.
- **Trading the volatility forward curve** – the term structure of volatility would be visible and tradeable.
- **Capture of mean reversion tendencies** – volatility displays mean reversion characteristics[10]. Volatility futures would allow trading to position against mean reverting changes in volatility.

The range of applications would include trading/hedging volatility of the underlying of the contract as well as trading/hedging volatility on related assets.

---

[8] For a detailed discussion of this issue, see Das, Satyajit (2004) Derivative Products & Pricing; John Wiley & Sons (Asia), Singapore at Chapter 16.

[9] See Brenner, M. and Galai, D. "New Financial Instruments For Hedging Changes In Volatility" (July/August 1989) Financial Analysts Journal 61–65; Whaley, Robert E. "Derivatives on Market Volatility: Hedging Tools Long Overdue" (Fall 1993) Journal of Derivatives 71–84; Fleming, J., Ostdiek, B. and Whaley R. "Predicting Stock Market Volatility: A New Measure" (1995) The Journal of Futures Markets Volume 15 Number 3 265–302; Rolfes, Bernd and Henn, Eric "A Vega Notion" (December 1999) Risk – Equity Risk Special Report 26–28.

[10] See Salter, Suzanne "Utility of Volatility Futures" (24 March 1997) Derivatives Week 9; Werner, Elmar and Roth, Randolf "The Volax Future" (February 1998) Risk S16–S17.

This would entail the design and execution of cross hedges based on the correlation of volatility between different assets/rates[11].

The central issue in designing futures or options is standardisation of the underlying commodity – volatility. One possible approach is the creation of a volatility index that represents an average implied volatility. Examples of such indexes include the VIX index (constructed by the Chicago Board Options Exchange in 1993) and the VDAX on DAX options (constructed by Deutsche Borse in 1997). Both indexes use at-the-money options with an average time to expiry of 30 days (for the VIX) and 45 days (for the VDAX). Implied volatility for the construction of the index uses either available options or is obtained by interpolation of implied volatility of options with nearby strikes and expiries[12].

The major advantages of volatility indexes include the concept of a standardised volatility measure and the correlation between the index and underlying option portfolios. These characteristics should facilitate liquid trading and hedging. There is no universally agreed methodology for construction of a volatility index. This has meant that futures and option contracts on such indexes have not developed.

Exhibit 12.1 summarises the two major volatility futures contracts that have emerged. The design of both contracts has been criticised. The OMLX contracts avoid the problem of defining a volatility index. The mixture of historical and expected volatility is problematic. In particular, the changing combination of past and expected volatility as the contract approaches expiry creates complexity. The Volax contract is simpler. The choice of the underlying has been criticised as limiting. Both the OMLX and Volax contract design do not encompass the problems of the volatility smile/skew.

In practice, the existing futures contracts on volatility have had limited success. The contracts failed to reach trading volumes and liquidity levels that were economically viable. This failure can be attributed to a mixture of the following factors[13]:

• The contract design was considered flawed by traders and hedgers.
• Difficulties in establishing arbitrage positions to replicate the contract. For example, in the Volax contract, the contract design required the trader to buy

---

[11] See discussion in Chapter 2.
[12] For a discussion of the issues in construction of volatility indexes, see Whaley, Robert E. "Derivatives on Market Volatility: Hedging Tools Long Overdue" (Fall 1993) Journal of Derivatives 71–84; Fleming, J., Ostdiek, B. and Whaley R. "Predicting Stock Market Volatility: A New Measure" (1995) The Journal of Futures Markets Volume 15 Number 3 265–302; Rolfes, Bernd and Henn, Eric "A Vega Notion" (December 1999) Risk – Equity Risk Special Report 26–28.
[13] Tompkins, Robert "What Volax Lacks" (May 1998) Futures & OTC World 13–15.

or sell an at-the-money DAX straddle. If the contract traded was the 3 month Volax contract, then the trader would need to trade a 3 month straddle and take an opposite position in a 6 month straddle. This hedge is not efficient as the Volax future had a constant exposure to implied volatility (vega). In contrast, the exposure to vega of the straddles is subject to changes. This reflects the fact that the vega will depend on the relativity of the strike price to asset prices, remaining time to expiry and the absolute level of volatility. This would mean that the hedge would need to be dynamically managed to replicate the Volax future. This impedes efficiency of market pricing[14].

- The failure of the contracts to achieve liquidity levels that encouraged participation.
- The parallel over the counter ("OTC") volatility swap market that was available drained trading interest from the volatility futures market.

Exhibit 12.1 Volatility Futures Contracts	
Contract	**Structure**

OMLX Contracts[15]	• Underlying is the price volatility of equity markets.
	• Volatility futures on the following markets:
	  1. FTSE 100 based on a contract multiplier of GBP 250.
	  2. DAX based on a contract multiplier of DEM 500.
	  3. OMX based on a contract multiplier of SKr 2,500.
	• Measure of volatility is the Expiration Settlement Rate ("ESR") determined as the annual deviation of the natural logarithms of the relative change in closing prices of the stock index during the 3 month contract period (the rate setting period ("RSP")). The volatility level consists of the actual historical volatility in the index over the period to date over the term of the contract and the expected volatility over the remaining term of the contract.
	• Minimum price movements are 0.01%.
	• Cash settlement.

---

[14] A possible solution to this problem is allowing deliverability of DAX index options into the Volax contract using a system of contract conversion factors; see Tompkins, Robert "What Volax Lacks" (May 1998) Futures & OTC World 13–15.

[15] See "On The VOLX Wagon" (23 November 1996) International Financing Review Issue 1160 122; Salter, Suzanne "Utility of Volatility Futures" (24 March 1997) Derivatives Week 9.

Contract	Structure
Volax Contract[16]	• Underlying is the implied volatility of a DAX option with 3 months to expiry and an at-the-money strike. • Underlying value is the % 3 month forward volatility based on a contract multiplier of DEM 100. • Minimum price movement is 0.01%. • Cash settlement.

4 Volatility Swaps

4.1 Concept/Structure

The volatility swap is designed to allow traders to achieve a long or short position in market volatility. The basic structure of the contract entails the trader receiving (paying) a fixed volatility in return for paying (receiving) the *actual realised volatility* on the underlying asset over the term of the swap. The structure allows the trader to buy or sell volatility by receiving or paying the difference between the fixed volatility and the actual experienced volatility.

Exhibit 12.2 sets out the terms and structure of a volatility swap[17]. The key features of the volatility swap are as follows:

• The contract is structured as an OTC derivative contract.
• The contract underlying is the volatility of an agreed asset. In practice, this is primarily the volatility of equity indexes. The underlying can be based on the volatility of a futures contract rather than cash. In practice, this is frequently the case. The fact that trading in futures has lower transaction costs and higher liquidity means that volatility swaps based on futures rather than cash prices may be more cost effective.
• The counterparties agree the fixed volatility level (in the example equal to 20% pa) and the multiplier (effectively the $ value of 1 bps pa in volatility that in this case is $1,000).

---

[16] See Werner, Elmar and Roth, Randolf "The Volax Future" (February 1998) Risk S16–S17.
[17] See Gross, Leon and Mezrich, Joe (January 1998) Introducing Volatility Swaps; Salomon Smith Barney - Equity Derivative Sales, Derivative Products, New York at 20–26; Curnutt, Dean "The Art of the Variance Swap" (February 2000) Derivative Strategy 52–53.

- The contract pay-off is based on the actual realised volatility (on an annual basis) over the term of the contract, calculated as the standard deviation of the continuously compounded asset returns against the fixed volatility level. In this case, if actual historical volatility is 25% pa, then the contract payout is $500,000 (500 × $1,000/0.01% pa in volatility).
- The volatility buyer receives the contract payout where actual historical volatility increases above the fixed volatility level. The volatility buyer pays the contract payout where the actual historical volatility decreases below the fixed volatility level. In this case, the investor receives payment from the dealer where volatility increases above 20% pa (for example, if realised volatility is 25% pa the investor receives $500,000). The investor pays the dealer where volatility decreases below 20% pa.

A variation on the basic volatility structure is the variance swap. **Exhibit 12.3** sets out the terms and structure of a variance swap[18]. The key features of the variance swap are as follows:
- The basic elements of the contract are identical to the volatility swap structure.
- The key difference is that the contract payout is based on the variance (square of the volatility). For example, in the case described below, if actual historical volatility is 25% pa, then the contract payout is $225,000 (225 ($25^2 - 20^2 =$ $625 - 400$) × $1,000/0.01% pa in volatility).

The variance swap differs from the volatility swap in economic impact. In a variance swap, each volatility point is not worth the same $ amount. For example, the variance points from 20% pa to 21% pa are valued at 41 variance points. In contrast, the variance points from 30% pa to 31% pa are valued at 61 variance points. In a volatility swap, a volatility change of 1% pa would have identical value, irrespective of the absolute level of volatility. This means that the variance swap payout is curved (it is convex rather than linear). **Exhibit 12.4** sets out the comparative pay-offs of a volatility swap and a variance swap. The volatility swap has, in effect, a constant vega position. In contrast, the variance swap has a constant gamma position. In practice, variance swaps are easier to hedge. This dictates that the variance swaps are generally cheaper to transact than volatility swaps[19].

---

[18] See Gross, Leon and Mezrich, Joe (January 1998) Introducing Volatility Swaps; Salomon Smith Barney - Equity Derivative Sales, Derivative Products, New York at 21–22.

[19] See Gross, Leon and Mezrich, Joe (January 1998) Introducing Volatility Swaps; Salomon Smith Barney - Equity Derivative Sales, Derivative Products, New York at 20–26; Curnutt, Dean "The Art of the Variance Swap" (February 2000) Derivative Strategy 52–53.

Exhibit 12.2   Volatility Swap – Terms & Conditions

Underlying Asset	Equity Index (S & P 500) Realised Volatility
Maturity	1 month to 1 year
Volatility Buyer	Investor
Volatility Seller	Dealer
Fixed Volatility Level	20% pa
Contract Payout	Multiplier × [Realised Volatility – Fixed Volatility Level]
Multiplier	$1,000 per 0.01% pa volatility movement
Realised Volatility	Calculated as[20]:

$$\sqrt{(1/n \sum_{i=1}^{N} [\ln(S_i/S_{i-1})^2 \times \sqrt{\text{number of days in the year}}])}$$

Where

S_i = the price of the asset on i trading day

Number of days in the year = either 250 or the exact number of trading days in the year

Payments	• Volatility Buyer receives the Contract Payout from the Volatility Seller where the Contract payout is positive.
	• Volatility Buyer pays the Contract Payout to the Volatility Seller where the Contract Payout is negative.

4.2   Applications

Applications of volatility swaps include[21]:

- **Acquiring exposure to volatility** – volatility swaps allow traders/investors to easily acquire exposure to volatility changes. This allows monetisation of expectations of future volatility. For example, after sharp price shocks, implied volatility often increases. This was experienced during the Gulf war, the Asian monetary crisis, the Long Term Capital Management crisis and the technology stock collapse. Volatility swaps allow traders/investors to short volatility in the expectation that over time, market volatility will mean revert to more "normal" levels. Similarly, traders/investors can purchase volatility where volatility is low and expected to increase.

---

[20] This is standard deviation of the continuously compounded annual return on the asset; see Das, Satyajit (2004) Derivative Products & Pricing; John Wiley & Sons (Asia), Singapore at Chapter 9.

[21] See Gross, Leon and Mezrich, Joe (January 1998) Introducing Volatility Swaps; Salomon Smith Barney - Equity Derivative Sales, Derivative Products, New York; Demeterfi, Kresmir, Derman, Emanuel, Kamal, Michael and Zou, Joseph "A Guide to Variance Swaps" (June 1999) Risk 54–59; Curnutt, Dean "The Art of the Variance Swap" (February 2000) Derivative Strategy 52–53.

Exhibit 12.3   Variance Swap – Terms & Conditions

Underlying Asset	Equity Index (S & P 500) Realised Volatility
Maturity	1 month to 1 year
Volatility Buyer	Investor
Volatility Seller	Dealer
Fixed Volatility Level	20% pa
Contract Payout	Multiplier × [Realised Volatility^2 – Fixed Volatility Level^2]
Multiplier	$1,000 per 0.01% pa volatility movement
Realised Volatility	Calculated as:

$$N\sqrt{(1/n \sum_{i=1}^{N}[\ln(S_i/S_{i-1})^2 \times \sqrt{\text{number of days in the year}}])}$$

Where
S_i = the price of the asset on i trading day
Number of days in the year = either 250 or the exact number of trading days in the year

Payments
- Volatility Buyer receives the Contract Payout from the Volatility Seller where the Contract payout is positive.
- Volatility Buyer pays the Contract Payout to the Volatility Seller where the Contract Payout is negative.

Exhibit 12.4   Volatility versus Variance Swap Payoff

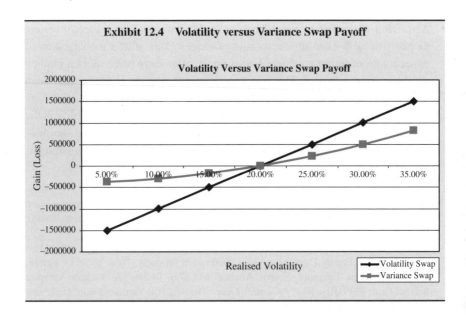

Volatility Versus Variance Swap Payoff

- **Hedging risk to volatility changes** – volatility swaps also allow traders with existing volatility positions to hedge exposure to unexpected changes in volatility. Option traders with net volatility positions in their trading portfolios can use volatility swaps to hedge the risk. Investors can hedge volatility that may affect the tracking error relative to benchmarks of their investments. Other potential hedgers include corporate issuers of convertible securities, where changes in volatility impact upon the value received from the sale of equity options embedded in the convertible at some planned future date.

- **Arbitrage** – volatility swaps can allow potential arbitrage between different segments of the volatility market. This may take the form of selling or buying options at implied volatility levels that are different from the values available in the volatility swap market. The bought or sold option would be hedged as to the implicit volatility exposure to obtain the arbitrage profit. This could also take more complex structures such as convertible arbitrage[22], where the low embedded volatility stripped from convertible securities can be monetised through an offsetting volatility swap. More complex forms of trading/arbitrage, including term structure and skew/smile trading may also be feasible where liquidity in volatility swaps permits. For example, forward volatility swaps are feasible and could be used to trade volatility term structure.

- **Price discovery** – in theory, volatility swaps should allow discovery of observable volatility estimates from the market. This would provide useful information of expected volatility to traders. There is debate about the significance/information content of the volatility information embedded in a volatility swap. There is an arbitrage relationship between the implied volatility of traded options and the volatility swap volatility. This is because traders use a portfolio of traded options to hedge a position in a volatility swap. This means that the volatility swap captures the market's expectations of the realised volatility of the asset between the relevant date and the expiry of the contract. The volatility swap is useful for analysis of market option volatility and the skew/term structure of volatility. This is because the at-the-money option benchmark volatility represents the expected volatility *only if the asset price remains at the current price level*. In this context, the volatility swap volatility represents a more meaningful benchmark of expected volatility. This means option traders will find the embedded volatility of a volatility swap a useful benchmark to compare to the

---

[22] See Das, Satyajit (2004) Structured Products Volume 2; John Wiley & Sons (Asia), Singapore at Chapter 2.

trader's own estimate of the forecast implied volatility over any particular time horizon[23].

In practice, volatility swaps are predominantly used to hedge equity volatility, in particular equity index volatility[24]. Volatility swaps have also been completed in currencies. The major driver of activity in volatility swap trading appears to be taking volatility risk. In this context, volatility swaps are seen as an alternative to option trading strategies.

Increased investor interest in volatility trading is evident. The major focus of asset managers using volatility swaps is the management of benchmark tracking error. Few investment managers currently treat volatility as a separate asset class. Interest from asset managers has prompted product innovation including:

- **Volatility options** – these are options on volatility or volatility swaps[25]. The structure is analogous to an out-of-the-money put. The instrument gains value rapidly where volatility increases sharply. These instruments can be used to provide protection against sharp movements in market price such as that experienced in a major market correction.
- **Capped volatility swaps** – this entails investors buying or selling volatility swaps where the pay-off is restricted. The structure is designed to limit the loss to the difference between the cap or floor volatility level[26].
- **Volatility swaps combined with equity futures trades** – volatility swaps entail an implicit directional view on market price movements. This is because in practice, where the equity market falls, implied and actual volatility generally increases. This negative correlation means that the volatility swap has an implicit exposure to equity market changes. A seller of volatility swaps has an implicit expectation that the equity market will increase in value. A buyer of volatility has an implicit expectation that the equity market will decrease in value.

---

[23] See Avellaneda, Marcus "Variance Swap Volatility and Option Strategies" (30 October 2000) Derivatives Week 7–8. See also Taleb, Nassim (1997) Dynamic Hedging; John Wiley & Sons, New York.

[24] See Paul-Choudhury, Sumit "Volatility Swaps In Vogue" (September 1996) Risk 7; Mehta, Nina "Equity Vol Swaps Grow Up" (July 1999) Derivatives Strategy 11–12.

[25] See Gross, Leon and Mezrich, Joe (January 1998) Introducing Volatility Swaps; Salomon Smith Barney - Equity Derivative Sales, Derivative Products, New York at 31–32; Mahtani, Arun "Banks Seek Comfort In Volatility Options" (6 February 1999) International Financing Review Issue 1269 86; Rolfes, Bernd and Henn, Eric "A Vega Notion" (December 1999) Risk – Equity Risk Special Report 26–28.

[26] See Gross, Leon and Mezrich, Joe (January 1998) Introducing Volatility Swaps; Salomon Smith Barney - Equity Derivative Sales, Derivative Products, New York at 31–32.

This exposure can be hedged by trading in equity futures to reduce the implicit asset exposure (delta) [27].

• **Volatility bonds** – structured bond issues to provide investors (including retail investors) the ability to trade volatility have also been designed. An example of this structure was an issue undertaken in 2000 by Banca Monte dei Paschi di Siena. The issue was for Euro 20 million and 15 year maturity. The bond coupon is proportional to the difference in 20 year swap rates between the start and end of each year. The structure is also leveraged (by 12 times). The structure entails the investor buying a series of cash settled 1 year into 20 year swaption straddles. The swaptions are reset at-the-money each year. The structure provided the investors with direct exposure to Euro interest rate volatility[28].

4.3 Pricing/Valuation and Hedging

The pricing/valuation and hedging of volatility swaps is driven by the cost of replicating the contract payout. In practice, the trader hedges the position in the volatility swap by purchasing/selling a portfolio of options that is then delta hedged. The net return on the hedge portfolio (either positive or negative) is equivalent to the payout on the volatility swap[29].

The price/value behaviour of volatility swaps over its term is as follows[30]:

• The volatility swap has no value at commencement of the transaction.

---

[27] See Gross, Leon and Mezrich, Joe (January 1998) Introducing Volatility Swaps; Salomon Smith Barney - Equity Derivative Sales, Derivative Products, New York at 31–32.

[28] See Dunbar, Nicholas "Vol Bonds A Hit with Investors" (August 2000) Risk 6.

[29] See Carr, Peter and Madan, Dilip "Introducing The Covariance Swap" (February 1999) Risk 47–51; Demeterfi, Kresmir, Derman, Emanuel, Kamal, Michael and Zou, Joseph "A Guide to Variance Swaps" (June 1999) Risk 54–59; Brockhaus, Oliver and Long, Douglas "Volatility Swaps Made Simple" (January 2000) Risk 92–95; Overhoaus, Marcus, Brockhaus, Oliver, Farkas, Michael, Ferraris, Andrew and Long, Douglas "Pricing Issues For Volatility Contracts: Part I" (1–7 February 2000) Financial Products 8–9; Overhoaus, Marcus, Brockhaus, Oliver, Farkas, Michael, Ferraris, Andrew and Long, Douglas "Pricing Issues For Volatility Contracts: Part II" (8–14 February 2000) Financial Products 8–9; Overhoaus, Marcus, Brockhaus, Oliver, Farkas, Michael, Ferraris, Andrew and Long, Douglas "Pricing Issues For Volatility Contracts: Part III" (15–21 February 2000) Financial Products 8–9; Blacher, Guillaume "Volatility Power" (October 2000) FOW 55–59. See also Brockhaus, O., Farkas, A., Gallus, C., Long, D., Martin R. and Overhaus M. (1999) Modelling and Hedging Equity Derivatives; Risk Books, London.

[30] See Gross, Leon and Mezrich, Joe (January 1998) Introducing Volatility Swaps; Salomon Smith Barney - Equity Derivative Sales, Derivative Products, New York at 22–24.

- At maturity the value of the volatility swap is the difference between the realised volatility and the fixed volatility.
- At any point prior to expiry, the value of the volatility swap is based on a combination of realised volatility to date and expected volatility over the remaining term to maturity. The expected volatility is determined by the implied volatility of the underlying options.

The hedging/replication logic dictates that the pricing of the volatility swap reflects the following:

- **Cost of the hedge portfolio** – the volatility swap is hedged by an offsetting position in a weighted combination of options with different strikes. The hedge is designed to ensure that the volatility exposure (vega) is constant across different strikes[31]. The cost of this portfolio is equivalent to the implied volatility paid or received from trading in the options. This means that future realised volatility is a function of current implied volatility. This reflects the fact that the value of the volatility swap is affected by both the realised and implied volatility.
- **Convexity cost** – this relates to the need to maintain delta neutrality of the portfolio. It will reflect the convexity (gamma) exposure. The portfolio re-balancing will be affected by the volatility surface (smile/skew and term structure)[32]. This hedging cost will be driven by the interaction of time to expiry, volatility and the relationship between the option strikes and asset price levels. The hedging/re-balancing cost is uncertain. It must be estimated at commencement of the swap. There are significant differences between the convexity cost of a volatility swap and a variance swap.

The presence of convexity cost means that the volatility swap will be more expensive than the current implied volatility levels for the asset.

Modelling of volatility products has focused on variance swaps. The risks of hedging a variance swap include[33]:

- **Availability of options with relevant strike prices** – hedging assumes the availability of a complete set of options with a theoretically infinite set of

---

[31] A common weighting scheme is to weight the number of options based on the inverse of the strike squared for a variance swap.

[32] See Das, Satyajit (2004) Derivative Products & Pricing; John Wiley & Sons (Asia), Singapore at Chapter 9.

[33] See Demeterfi, Kresmir, Derman, Emanuel, Kamal, Michael and Zou, Joseph "A Guide to Variance Swaps" (June 1999) Risk 54–59; Chriss, Neil and Morokoff, William "Market Risk of Variance Swaps" (October 1999) Risk 55–59.

strike prices. In practice, there will only be a limited range of options with specified strikes available as hedges. In addition, liquidity factors and transaction costs may further limit available hedging instruments. If the asset price remains within the strike range of the hedging portfolio of options, then the hedge will function with reasonable efficiency. If the asset price moves outside the range of the strikes, then the sensitivity to volatility changes is reduced. This will have the effect of introducing hedging error as the replicating portfolio becomes less sensitive to volatility changes.

* **Non continuous price changes** – asset price jumps will also affect hedge efficiency. A large price jump may take the asset price outside the strike range, reducing sensitivity to volatility changes. In addition, the price jump will introduce hedging error, causing the hedge portfolio value changes to diverge from the value changes of the variance swap. For example, assume the trader is short variance in a swap and holds an offsetting hedge portfolio of options. If the price falls sharply in a discontinuous fashion, moving the asset price outside the strike range, then the trader would enjoy a convexity gain. The vega and gamma of the hedge would be reduced and would not match the position in the variance swap. If the price jumped up sharply, then the hedge portfolio would suffer both an immediate loss from the convexity effect of the price change and also lose hedging efficiency[34].

The pricing/hedging of variance swaps follows the replication structure described. The pricing/hedging of a volatility swap is inherently more complex. This is because the volatility swap has a constant vega and a variable gamma. This implies that the hedging cost of a volatility swap and the corresponding price is higher than for a comparable variance swap. The higher convexity cost of the volatility swap is also highly model dependent. This reflects the sensitivity to the structure and modelling of the volatility surface[35].

---

[34] See Demeterfi, Kresmir, Derman, Emanuel, Kamal, Michael and Zou, Joseph "A Guide to Variance Swaps" (June 1999) Risk 54–59 at 59.

[35] See Brockhaus, Oliver and Long, Douglas "Volatility Swaps Made Simple" (January 2000) Risk 92–95; Overhoaus, Marcus, Brockhaus, Oliver, Farkas, Michael, Ferraris, Andrew and Long, Douglas "Pricing Issues For Volatility Contracts: Part I" (1–7 February 2000) Financial Products 8–9; Overhoaus, Marcus, Brockhaus, Oliver, Farkas, Michael, Ferraris, Andrew and Long, Douglas "Pricing Issues For Volatility Contracts: Part II" (8–14 February 2000) Financial Products 8–9; Overhoaus, Marcus, Brockhaus, Oliver, Farkas, Michael, Ferraris, Andrew and Long, Douglas "Pricing Issues For Volatility Contracts: Part III" (15–21 February 2000) Financial Products 8–9.

The risks of hedging a volatility swap are greater. This reflects the fact that there is no simple replication strategy for the volatility swap. The primary difference between the two structures relates to the fact that the variance swap makes no assumption about future volatility. In contrast, volatility swaps are dependent upon changes in volatility and actual realised volatility. This makes the structure difficult to price and hedge[36].

5 Summary

Volatility of asset prices/rates is crucial to financial markets. It forms the basis of trading of assets and rates and is central to option pricing. Products that are primarily designed to allow volatility to be traded *separately* as a traded asset itself have emerged. The products include exchange-traded futures on volatility and OTC volatility and variance swaps. The OTC products have enjoyed limited success. However, difficulties in hedging volatility swaps have impeded the rapid development of the market. The concept of volatility hedging has also led to attempts to create tradeable correlation hedges. The market remains in an early stage of development[37].

---

[36] See Demeterfi, Kresmir, Derman, Emanuel, Kamal, Michael and Zou, Joseph "A Guide to Variance Swaps" (June 1999) Risk 54–59 at 59.

[37] There are attempts to start trading in correlation risk; see Dunbar, Nicholas "Correlation Swaps Take Off" (May 1999) Risk 6; Crossman, Alexander "Searching for Solutions to Correlation Risk" (18 September 1999) International Financing Review Issue 1301 88.

INTEREST RATE & FX STRUCTURES

13
Non-Generic Swaps

1 Overview

Conventional forwards, options and swaps constitute the most significant portion of transactions completed in financial markets. A wide variety of non-standard or non-generic transactions are also transacted. The non-generic structures are designed to allow participants to achieve hedging or trading objectives that cannot be satisfied by conventional products. In this Chapter and following Chapters, non-generic swap structures are considered. This Chapter focuses on variations on conventional interest rate and currency swaps. Chapter 14 focuses on basis (floating to floating) interest rate swaps. Chapter 15 focuses on options on swaps/swaptions.

The structure of this Chapter is as follows:

- The rationale for non-generic swap structures is outlined.
- Different types of non-generic swaps are then described. Structures covered include overnight index swaps, amortising swaps, timing variations (deferred start swaps, forward swaps and spreadlocks), cash flow variations (non-par/discount or premium swaps and zero coupon swaps), swaps with embedded optionality and different swap execution structures.

2 Non-Generic Swaps – Rationale

Conventional derivative structures (forwards, options and swaps) form the basis of *all* non-generic transactions[1]. Non-generic swaps and/or hybrid structures represent structural variations on the conventional swap/derivative structure. Non-generic structures are used for both liability and asset applications[2].

---

[1] See Das, Satyajit (2004) Derivative Products & Pricing; John Wiley & Sons (Asia), Singapore at Chapters 1, 2 and 3.

[2] For a discussion of the market for non-generic swap structures, see Keller, Paul "The Rocket Men Are Still" (September 1989) Euromoney 148–158; Krzyzak, Krystyna "Don't Take Swaps at Face Value" (November 1988) Risk 28–31; Brady, Simon "How To Tailor Your Assets" (April 1990) Euromoney 83–89; Brady, Simon "Derivatives

Non-generic swaps are primarily driven by the following factors:

- **Cash flow matching** – this is focused on facilitating the ability of asset and liability managers to match the cash flows of underlying investments and liabilities. The structures focus on the pattern and timing of cash flows that are being hedged. A special case of cash flow matching is structures required to match the cash flows of capital market issues (bonds and other securities). This reflects the fact that the availability of derivatives leads to an increased opportunity for the separation of cash flow profiles for investors and borrowers. Capital market issues are structured to provide investors with specified cash flows that match investment requirements. The borrower then enters into a derivative transaction that is designed to strip out the elements *engineered* for investors to provide the borrower with its preferred cash flow profile for the liability. A number of the non-generic structures are driven by this phenomenon.

- **Flexibility** – this covers structures focused on incorporating additional flexibility within the basic swap structure to cater for various asset liability management strategies. This may be designed to enable asset and liability managers to structure hedging and trading decisions that more accurately match expectations of future changes in asset prices/rates and underlying transactions.

Non-generic swap structures are classified as follows:

- **Non-generic swaps** – this involves variations on the basic parameters of interest rate and currency swaps. The structures include variations in floating rate index (overnight index swaps), variations in principal (amortising swaps), timing variations (deferred start swaps, forward swaps and spreadlocks), cash flow variations (non-par/discount or premium swaps and zero coupon swaps), swaps with embedded optionality and different swap execution structures. Non-generic swaps are discussed in this Chapter.

- **Basis (floating to floating basis swaps)** – this involves swap transactions where both streams of cash flows are variable and re-set periodically. Basis swaps entail swaps where the cash flows are priced off different short term/money market indexes in the same currency or in different currencies. The structures include floating to floating swaps in the same currency, arrears reset swaps

Sprout Bells and Whistles" (August 1992) Euromoney 29–39; Irving, Richard "Biting the Bullet" (November 1994) Risk 20–26; Sweeney, Stuart "Using Swaps To Enhance Yield" in (1994) Corporate Finance Risk Management & Derivatives Yearbook 12–15; Reed, Nick "Bear Necessities" (July 1994) Risk 16–20; Fraser, K. Michael "Refitting Exotics For A Bear Market" (July 1994) Global Finance 68–71; Brady, Simon "New Ways with Derivatives" (June 1996) Corporate Finance 23–31; Fink, Peter "Elegant Solutions In Complex Deals" in (1998) Corporate Finance Risk Management & Derivatives Yearbook 9–12.

and index differential swaps. Basis swaps are discussed in Chapter 14. Yield curve or constant maturity swaps (collectively referred to as constant maturity or CMT products) are a special type of basis swap. Constant maturity products are discussed in Chapter 17.

• **Options on swaps/swaptions** – this involves a variety of transactions where an option is combined with a swap. The structure entails an option on the fixed rate component of an interest rate swap. Swaptions are considered in Chapter 15. Swaptions are frequently used in conjunction with callable bonds (the callable bond being equivalent to a non callable bond and an embedded swaption). Callable bonds are discussed in Chapter 16.

There are a number of other variations on conventional structures. The structures are mainly focused on the creation of synthetic assets where the interest rate or currency derivatives are embedded in a fixed or floating rate security. There are a variety of structures in common use. The structures include index amortising products ("IAR") (detailed in Chapter 18), interest rate linked notes (detailed in Chapter 19) and currency linked notes (detailed in Chapter 20).

Non-generic swaps are priced/valued by decomposing the transaction into simpler derivatives. This will generally entail decomposition of the transactions into simpler forwards and options that can be priced using standard valuation approaches. The decomposition provides a theoretical valuation of the structures. In practice, the market values of the structures are predominantly based on the ability of dealers to hedge the structure using conventional derivatives. The dealer will closely replicate the non-generic structure using combinations of existing conventional derivatives. The price quoted for the non-generic structure will reflect the cost of the hedges. The approach used reflects the desire by dealers to use existing and liquid markets to transfer the market risk of the non-generic structure. The process of pricing the structures *off the hedge* may lead to some differences from theoretical prices. The difference reflects the presence of transaction costs and market frictions.

3   Overnight Index Swaps

3.1   Concept/Structure[3]

The basic concept of an overnight index swap ("OIS") is related to a variation on the floating rate index or benchmark used in an interest rate swap. In a conventional swap, the floating rate index is typically the 1, 3 month or 6 month short term/money

---

[3] See de Coudenhove, Bernard, Porter, William and Newman, David "Using the Overnight Indexed Swap" in (1996) Corporate Finance Risk Management & Derivatives Yearbook at 29–33.

market rate. The rate typically used is the inter-bank rate[4]. In a OIS transaction, the floating rate is based on an overnight rate that is reset daily. This will typically be the inter-bank overnight or call interest rate. In some cases, the tom/next rate for foreign currency transactions may also be used. Other elements of the OIS are similar to those used in a conventional interest rate swap[5].

OIS transactions are used to manage the interest risk on overnight rates. **Exhibit 13.1** sets out the typical terms of an OIS transaction. All terms are similar to those used in a standard interest rate swap. The major differences include:

*   **Term** – OIS transactions are for relatively short maturities (up to 6 or 12 months).
*   **Floating interest rate calculation** – the floating rate side must be reset daily. The floating rate must be compounded over the period[6].

OIS transactions originated in Europe. The transaction commenced in the early 1990s and active markets existed in a number of European currencies including Deutschemarks, French Francs[7], Italian Lira, Spanish Pesetas and a number of other currencies[8]. Following the creation of the Euro, a substantial market in Euro denominated OIS transactions has also emerged[9]. Other OIS markets include US$ overnight rate[10] and Federal Funds swaps in the US$, sterling[11] and yen[12].

---

[4]   See Das, Satyajit (2004) Derivative Products & Pricing; John Wiley & Sons (Asia), Singapore at Chapter 3.

[5]   The OIS structure should be distinguished from interest rate swaps in certain emerging markets that use overnight cash rates as the floating rate benchmark. This is because in these markets, the overnight rate is used for the floating rate because of the absence of reliable price discovery of short term interest rates. See discussion in Das, Satyajit (2004) Derivative Products & Pricing; John Wiley & Sons (Asia), Singapore at Chapter 3.

[6]   It can also be averaged if required.

[7]   The French Franc market was among the most active reflecting the use of the T4M and TAM indexes; see Das, Satyajit (1994) Swaps and Financial Derivatives – Second Edition; McGraw-Hill, Chicago/LBC Information Services, Sydney at Chapter 26.

[8]   See "Overnight Swaps Market Debuts In Frankfurt" (10 July 1996) Financial Products Issue 46 3; Sorries, Bernd "Forward with FIONA" (November 1996) Risk 36–37; Elliot, Margaret "Europe Wakes Up To Overnight Swaps" (July–August 1997) Derivatives Strategy 40.

[9]   See Priest, Andrew "BIS Opens New Swaps Market" (April 1996) Risk 9; Hargreaves, Tim "Eonia Traders Stalk ECB" (December 1999) Risk 9.

[10]   See "Morgan Launches US Dollar OIS Market (10 July 1996) Financial Products Issue 46 3.

[11]   See Nicholls, Mark "UK Election Spurs Sterling OIS Market" (March 1997) Risk 6; "Sterling Swaps Market To Debut In April" (5 March 1997) Financial Products Issue 61 12; "Early OIS Launch Breaks with Convention" (3 April 1997) Financial Products Issue 63 7.

[12]   See Locke, Jane "Japan's OIS Launch Boosts Loan Market" (June 1997) Risk 8.

OIS markets have also developed in a number of other emerging currencies such as HK\$[13], S\$[14] and Czech Koruna[15].

Exhibit 13.1	**Overnight Index Swaps – Terms and Structure**

Term	Specification
Value Date	Consistent with market convention but generally 2 business days. Forward start transactions are also feasible.
Maturity	Between 1 week and 12 months.
Fixed Rate	Agreed at the time of entry into the transaction.
Floating Rate	Consistent with market convention but generally the benchmark overnight or call money market interest rate such as the Eonia (Euro overnight interest rate), Sonia (Sterling overnight interest rate) etc.
Payment/Settlement	Final payment/ settlement is usually at maturity of the transaction based on the difference between the floating and fixed rate on a net payment basis.
Floating Rate Calculation	The floating rate used to calculate the settlement is based on converting the daily overnight rates into a single interest rate on a compounded basis using the following formula: $$R_{\text{floating rate}} = [\prod_{i=1}^{N_b} (1 + OR_i \times n_i/\text{basis}) - 1] \times \text{basis}/N$$ Where $R_{\text{floating rate}}$ = floating rate for OIS i = ith day of the transaction N_b = number of business days over the term of the OIS OR_i = overnight rate for the ith day of the transaction n_i = the number of days for which the overnight rate OR_i is applicable basis = day count basis consistent with market convention (either 360 or 365 days) N = the number of days in the OIS The floating rate payment is given by: $$\text{Notional Principal} \times R_{\text{floatingrate}} \times N/\text{basis}$$
Documentation	ISDA

---

[13] "Hong Kong Opens Up to the Overnight Swap" (November 2000) Asia Risk 8.

[14] See Bergin, Tom "First Singapore Overnight Index Swap Dealt" (18–24 April 2000) Financial Products 2.

[15] See Bergin, Tom "Prague Agrees Index For Overnight Swaps" (25 April–1 May 2000) Financial Products 1, 12.

In the major markets, the OIS market is characterised by the following features:
- **Established market conventions** – mechanics of the overnight rate calculation are established and accepted by market participants.
- **Low transaction costs** – OIS transactions generally trade at tight bid-offer spreads (around 1–5 bps) that are attractive relative to cash deposits.
- **Liquidity** – in some currencies the liquidity of OIS transactions is high, allowing liquid trading and hedging.

The low transaction costs and market liquidity reflect the low levels of counterparty credit exposure on OIS contracts. The low credit exposure reflects the structure of the contract. This includes the derivative nature of the contract (net settlement).

3.2 Pricing/Valuation[16]

The approach to pricing and valuation is similar to interest rate swaps generally. The OIS market trades relative to money market deposits and futures for the same maturity.

Pricing/valuation involves derivation of zero rates for the relevant currency and solving for the swap fixed rate on the OIS. In the liquid OIS markets, the zero curve for OIS can be constructed from available benchmark OIS rates. The benchmark OIS rates are typically for 1, 2, 3, 6, 9 and 12 months. Non-benchmark rates are derived by interpolation techniques.

In practice, OIS transactions trade at a small premium against the theoretical values. Traditionally, OIS transactions have traded at a discount (up to 5–10 bps pa) to the deposit and futures curves. This difference is also volatile. The difference reflects the difficulties of hedging OIS transactions.

3.3 Applications[17]

The primary applications of OIS transactions reflect the ability to use the contract to manage exposure to short term interest rates. The major users include financial

---

[16] See de Coudenhove, Bernard, Porter, William and Newman, David "Using the Overnight Indexed Swap" in (1996) Corporate Finance Risk Management & Derivatives Yearbook at 29–33.

[17] See de Coudenhove, Bernard, Porter, William and Newman, David "Using the Overnight Indexed Swap" in (1996) Corporate Finance Risk Management & Derivatives Yearbook at 29–33.

institutions and corporations. Major applications include:

- **Hedging overnight interest rate exposures** – this application focuses on the management of the risk of changes in overnight interest rates. Typical transactions include:
  1. *Managing bank funding positions* – most banks are active in the overnight cash market to manage their balance sheets. Conventional interest rate products (based on 1, 3 or 6 month rates) are inadequate to hedge the exposures as they expose the bank to some level of yield curve risk. OIS contracts (where the bank pays fixed rate and receives the overnight rate or vice versa) are well suited to management of this type of exposure.
  2. *Managing repo exposures* – most trading operations use repo transactions to finance trading positions in cash instruments or derivatives. Repo rates are generally for very short durations and are correlated to overnight/call rates. OIS contracts (where the bank pays fixed rate and receives the overnight rate) can be used to manage the risk to changes in the repo rates.
  3. *Managing non bank treasury cash positions* – non bank treasuries generally borrow term funds (priced off 1, 3 or 6 month rates) using bank provided credit lines or commercial paper issues. Centralised corporate treasuries have to invest surplus cash overnight. In some cases, the centralised treasury also charges individual business units at rates related to overnight rates. This creates an intrinsic mismatch between the interest income and expenses of the centralised corporate treasury. The mismatch can be hedged using OIS contracts (where the corporate treasury receives the fixed rate and pays the overnight rate).
- **Creating synthetic deposits** – this application focuses on creating synthetic deposits by investing in overnight deposits and entering into an OIS where the investor receives the fixed rate and pays the overnight rate. The strategy is used can be used to create value in different ways. The strategy may provide incremental returns on cash investments where the yield curve is inverted. The strategy may also provide additional returns where the OIS market is trading at a yield above the comparable cash yield for the relevant maturity. Additional value is created from the restructuring of the credit risk. The investor's credit risk on the underlying deposit is on an overnight basis rather than on a term basis. This means that the credit risk is lower than for a comparable term deposit. The additional credit exposure on the OIS (as noted above) is relatively low. The structure may provide the investor with comparable returns to a normal deposit but with lower credit risk and the additional flexibility to manage the deposit credit risk (by placing the deposit with another counterparty if required).

- **Trading overnight rates** – the OIS allows traders to monetise expectations of overnight interest rate movements. As monetary policy most directly affects the overnight rates, OIS allows trading of expected changes in policy settings.

4 Amortising Swaps

4.1 Concept/Structure

Conventional swap transactions are based on a notional principal that is fixed and non-amortising prior to maturity. Amortising swaps entail transactions based on amortising (decreasing or increasing) notional principal amounts.

Amortising swap structures are required in hedging non-bullet assets and liabilities, including:

- **Mortgage or other amortising loans** – these types of loans entail equal repayments in a fixed annuity stream. This means that each repayment is made up of amortising principal (increasing over time) and interest (decreasing over time).
- **Project loans** – these entail structured loans linked to projects such as infrastructure loans, resources/mining project finance transactions, property transactions and other specific cash flow related finance transactions[18]. In these transactions, loan repayments (both principal and interest) are matched to the cash flows generated by the underlying project. This means that the principal of the loan is periodically amortised as cash flows allow over the term of the loan. This contrasts with simpler corporate loans where there is no amortisation of principal over the term of the loan, with repayment of the total principal in a single payment at maturity. A common application is construction funding where the construction funding facility has a specific principal amortisation schedule. This includes a drawdown period where the loan balance increases as the project is undertaken, and funding utilised and then reduced as the project begins operation. The amortising swap includes both an increasing and decreasing principal basis, giving rise to a "roller coaster" amortising swap.
- **Leases and other asset backed transactions** – these focus on asset leases, hire purchase, title retention security[19] and other instalment finance/asset based loans[20]. The principal characteristic of the structures is the pattern of repayments.

---

[18] See Nevitt, Peter K. (1983) Project Financing - Fourth Edition; Euromoney Publications, London; Clifford Chance (1991) Project Finance; IFR Publishing Ltd, London.

[19] These are sometimes referred to as "Romalpa Clause" transactions.

[20] See Nevitt, Peter K. and Fabozzi, Frank J.(1985) Equipment Leasing – Second Edition; Dow Jones – Irwin, Homewood Illinois; Clark, Tom (Editor) (1990) Leasing Finance – Second Edition; Euromoney Books, London.

Repayments (of principal and interest) take the form of a series of equal instalments followed by a larger principal repayment at maturity of the transaction. This structure means that individual repayments consist of amortising principal (increasing over time) and interest (decreasing over time).

Amortising structures are used for interest rate and currency swaps. The discussion in this Section is focused on interest rate swaps. The basic concepts are equally applicable to amortising currency swaps. Some amortising currency swap structures are outlined in the next Section.

4.2 Pricing/Valuation

An amortising swap is replicated by a *series* of conventional bullet notional principal swaps. **Exhibit 13.2** sets out the process of replication of an amortising swap.

The amortising swap is priced using current market swap rates. The approach is to derive a blended rate for the combination of swaps that replicate the cash flow profile of the amortising structure. Using the blended rate approach, the amortising swap is treated as a number of separate swaps where the quoted swap rate reflects a weighted average of the individual swap rates. **Exhibit 13.3** sets out an example of calculating the blended rate pricing of an interest rate swap. The blended rate is used primarily because it accurately reflects the way the dealer will hedge an amortising swap using the underlying swap.

The pricing of an amortising swap reflects the theoretical price adjusted for a number of factors:

*   **Hedging considerations** – this focuses on the need to transact a series of swaps to replicate the amortisation profile. The individual amortisation profile may not be even or entail market dealing sizes of swaps. This will result in difficulties in hedging the amortising swap exactly. The swap price will generally be adjusted for the additional risk and/or hedging cost.
*   **Cash flow risk** – this focuses on the fact that the amortising swap rate is a blended rate. This means that the individual swaps transacted to hedge the amortisation patterns will have coupons higher or lower than the blended rate. This will entail funding or re-investment of cash flows over the term of the transaction. In effect, the amortising swap will entail the dealer either funding or borrowing from the counterparty. The dealer should charge a funding spread (to compensate for default risk) on amounts advanced to the counterparty.
*   **Credit risk** – the amortising swap will have credit risk that differs from that of an equivalent conventional swap. There are several factors that affect the

---

Exhibit 13.2   Amortising Interest Rate Swaps – Replication Structure

Assume a swap with initial notional principal of $100 million with a final maturity of 5 years where the principal is reduced by $25 million after 3 years, $25 million after 4 years and $50 million at maturity. The amortising swap is replicated by simultaneously transacting 3 swaps as follows:
* 3 year US$25 million swap.
* 4 year US$25 million swap.
* 5 year US$50 million swap.

The combination of the three transactions replicates the cash flow profile of the amortising transaction as follows:

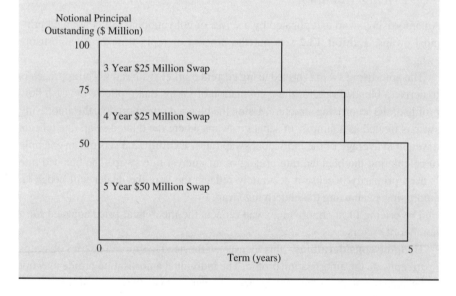

credit risk. The amortisation pattern will reduce the credit risk relative to a conventional swap of equivalent maturity. The cash flow risk (the transaction will result in the dealer lending or borrowing cash from the counterparty) will result in a loan or deposit like exposure that will need to be incorporated in the measurement of the credit risk.

The maturity characteristic of an amortising notional principal swap is often reduced to a single measure. This measure is either the duration or the average

Exhibit 13.3   Amortising Interest Rate Swaps – Pricing

Assume the swap outlined in **Exhibit 13.2**. The pricing of the swap is set out below:

Days to Cash Flow	Tenor (years)	Notional Principal ($)	Principal Amortisation ($)	Swap Rate (% pa)	Tenor × Amount	Tenor × Amount × Rate
		100,000,000				
184	0.50	100,000,000		5.40		
365	1.00	100,000,000		5.55		
549	1.50	100,000,000		5.73		
730	2.00	100,000,000		5.90		
914	2.50	100,000,000		6.05		
1095	3.00	75,000,000	25,000,000	6.58	75,000,000	4,935,000
1279	3.50	75,000,000		6.85		
1461	4.00	50,000,000	25,000,000	7.05	100,068,493	7,054,829
1645	4.51	50,000,000		7.25		
1826	5.00	0	50,000,000	7.50	250,136,986	18,760,274
				Total	425,205,479	30,750,103

Notes:
1. The tenor × amount is calculated as the product of the principal amortisation amount of the swap by the tenor (years).
2. The tenor rate amount is calculated as the product of the tenor amount and the swap rate for the relevant maturity.
   The amortising swap rate is 7.23% pa (calculated as the tenor amount rate (30,750,103)/tenor amount (425,205,479)).

life of the amortising swap. **Exhibit 13.4** sets out an example of an average life calculation for an amortising swap.

4.3   Applications

Amortising swap transactions are used to hedge non-bullet asset and liability structures. Typical applications include:
- **Hedging amortising loans** – this includes the conversion of the interest rate or currency basis of an amortising loan. Common examples would be the types of underlying transactions identified such as mortgage loans, project loans and lease/asset backed financing.

Exhibit 13.4   Amortising Interest Rate Swaps – Average Life

Assume a 10 year $100 million amortising swap where the principal reduces by 20 equal payments of $5 million every 6 months. The average life of the swap is calculated as follows:

Days to Cash Flow	Tenor (years)	Notional Principal($)	Principal Amortisation ($)	Tenor × Amortisation
182	0.50	100,000,000	5,000,000	0
365	1.00	95,000,000	5,000,000	5,000,000
547	1.50	90,000,000	5,000,000	5,000,000
730	2.00	85,000,000	5,000,000	10,000,000
912	2.50	80,000,000	5,000,000	10,000,000
1095	3.00	75,000,000	5,000,000	15,000,000
1278	3.50	70,000,000	5,000,000	20,000,000
1461	4.00	65,000,000	5,000,000	20,000,000
1643	4.50	60,000,000	5,000,000	25,000,000
1826	5.00	55,000,000	5,000,000	25,000,000
2008	5.50	50,000,000	5,000,000	30,000,000
2191	6.00	45,000,000	5,000,000	30,000,000
2373	6.50	40,000,000	5,000,000	35,000,000
2556	7.00	35,000,000	5,000,000	35,000,000
2739	7.50	30,000,000	5,000,000	40,000,000
2922	8.01	25,000,000	5,000,000	40,000,000
3104	8.50	20,000,000	5,000,000	45,000,000
3287	9.01	15,000,000	5,000,000	45,000,000
3469	9.50	10,000,000	5,000,000	50,000,000
3652	10.01	5,000,000	5,000,000	50,000,000
		Total	100,000,000	535,000,000

Notes:
The tenor × amortisation is calculated as the principal amortisation times the tenor.

The average life of the amortising swap rate is 5.35 years (calculated as the tenor amortisation (535,000,000)/face value amount (100,000,000).

- **Asset swaps** – where amortising swap structures are used to convert amortising (via sinking fund or early redemption provisions) fixed interest securities into floating rate securities. This may include amortising swaps structured to match the expected prepayment schedule of mortgage backed securities or receivable backed securities to reduce reinvestment risk[21].

---

[21]   Swaptions are frequently used to hedge the embedded optionality in these types of assets; see Chapters 15 and 18.

- **Yield curve arbitrage** – in the early 1990s amortising swap structures were used in the US$ capital market to take advantage of the prevailing historically steep yield curve. The structure entailed issues of 5 year debt incorporating an amortising repayment schedule where half of the issue was paid down after 3 years and the remaining 50% after 4 and 5 years. The average life of the debt was approximately 3 years. The issue was then swapped using an amortising swap structure into floating rate US$ funding. The rate achieved was better than that available for conventional 3 year bullet maturity issues. The advantage derived from a market anomaly. While the debt issue had an average life of approximately 3 years, the amortising structure entails a concentration of cash flows in the final two years of the life of the bond. The debt markets priced the bond slightly more attractively than an orthodox 3 year bullet issue. In contrast, the swap was priced as a series of bullet notional principal swaps based on yields further along the yield curve. In the market environment existing, the amortising bond was priced against the 3 year US Treasury note yielding approximately 5.60% pa. The swap was priced closer to the 5 year US Treasury note that was yielding 6.75% . The structure of the swap spread curve between 3 and 5 years was relatively flat. This meant that the steepness of the government bond curve allowed this transaction.

4.4 Amortising Currency Swaps

Amortising currency swap structures are similar to the amortising interest rate swaps described. In a typical amortising currency swap, the notional principal in one currency either decreases or increases in accordance with a specified schedule. The amortisation pattern in the second currency follows the amortisation pattern in the original currency. The amortising currency swap can be replicated by trading in a series of currency swaps with different notional principal at different maturities. Amortising currency swaps are used to hedge amortising currency assets and liabilities.

A special case of amortising currency swaps is the foreign exchange annuity or amortising currency annuity swaps[22]. This structure is used to exchange a set of constant even cash flows in one currency for an equivalent annuity cash flow in a second currency. **Exhibit 13.5** sets out the structure and pricing of a currency annuity swap. The structure can be replicated quite simply by a series of currency forward contracts. The advantage of the annuity swap structure is that it avoids the

---

[22] See Haghani, Victor J (4 April 1986) Foreign Exchange Annuity Swaps; Salomon Brothers Inc., New York.

impact of premiums and discounts on forward currency rates that would create an increasing or decreasing series of cash flows in one currency[23].

The foreign exchange annuity swap transaction is typically used by corporations with regular future inflows or outflows in a foreign currency arising from exports, investments or known commitments to fund projects. A major advantage of this type of structure is that the expected foreign currency cash flows can be translated into its equivalent in the base currency of the organisation, providing certainty for planning purposes. Currency annuity swaps are frequently used for tax based applications of derivatives[24].

Exhibit 13.5   Currency Annuity Swaps

Assume Company A wants to hedge an annuity stream of US$1 million pa over 5 years into an equivalent Yen annuity. This can be done in several ways:
- Treating the US$ annuity as an amortising loan and executing an amortising principal US$/Yen currency or equivalent US$/Yen LTFX contracts.
- Entering into a series of currency forwards where it sells US$/buys Yen.
- Transacting a currency annuity swap.

Assume A wants to use a currency annuity swap to establish a single conversion rate for the future US$ cash flows.
The US$ interest rates, Yen interest rates and US$/Yen currency rates are as follows:

Year	US$ Zero Coupon Rates (% pa)	Yen Zero Coupon Rates (% pa)	US$/Yen Currency Rates (US$1:Yen)	Premium/ Discount(Yen)
0/Spot			120.00	
1	4.50	1.00	115.98	(4.02)
2	4.60	1.50	112.99	(7.01)
3	4.75	1.75	109.98	(10.02)
4	5.00	2.00	106.86	(13.14)
5	5.50	2.50	103.88	(16.12)

The annuity swap rate is calculated as follows:
- Calculate the present value of the US$ annuity using the US$ zero coupon interest rates for each maturity.
- Calculate the present value of an equivalent Yen annuity using the Yen zero coupon interest rates for each maturity.
- Use the spot US$/Yen rate to convert the present value of the US$ annuity into Yen equivalent.

---

[23] Conceptually, the annuity swap structure is similar to the par forward foreign exchange contract arrangement described in Das, Satyajit (2004) Derivative Products & Pricing; John Wiley & Sons (Asia), Singapore at Chapter 3.

[24] See Das, Satyajit (2004) Structured Products Volume 2; John Wiley & Sons (Asia), Singapore at Chapter 19.

- Divide the Yen value of the US$ annuity by the present value of the Yen annuity to generate the annuity swap rate.

Year	US$ Amount	Present Value of US$ Cash Flow	Yen Amount	Present Value of Yen Cash Flow
1	1.00	0.9569	1.00	0.9901
2	1.00	0.9140	1.00	0.9707
3	1.00	0.8700	1.00	0.9493
4	1.00	0.8227	1.00	0.9238
5	1.00	0.7651	1.00	0.8839

Annuity Period (years)	Present Value of US$ Annuity (US$)	Present Value of US$ Annuity (Yen)	Present Value of Yen Annuity (Yen)	Annuity Swap Rate (US$1:Yen)
1	0.9569	114.83	0.9901	115.98
2	1.8709	224.51	1.9608	114.50
3	2.7410	328.91	2.9100	113.03
4	3.5637	427.64	3.8339	111.54
5	4.3288	519.46	4.7177	110.11

In this example, the 5 year annuity swap rate is US$1 = Yen 110.11. Company A would enter into the annuity swap to exchange US$1 million pa for Yen 110.11 million pa.

The following features of the currency annuity swap should be noted:

- The annuity swap rate is within the range of outright currency rates.
- The currency annuity swap rate effectively provides the Company in the early part of the transaction with higher cash flows and a more favourable exchange rate to translate the US$ (assuming the US$ cash flows are inflows) into Yen. The early higher cash flows are "borrowed" from later cash flows to create the annuity swap rate (which is higher than the outright currency forward rates). Where the interest rate differential is reversed, then the pattern of cash flow surplus is also reversed.
- Changes in the maturity of the annuity will have varying effects, depending on the pattern of interest differentials. If the maturity is increased, then when swapping into a premium (discount) currency, the level of the annuity is increased (decreased), reflecting the fact that additional cash flows can be borrowed (forgone) from (to) later payments. Shortening the maturity of an annuity swap has the reverse impact.

5 Swaps – Timing Variations

5.1 Concept

Conventional swaps entail transactions that commence either two days or 1 day from the date of entry into the transaction, depending upon the market convention.

Timing variations focus on altering the time of commencement of the underlying swap.

Timing variations entail agreement on the fixed rate payable under the swap at the time of entry into the transaction. The actual commencement of the transaction itself is deferred. The rate fixed can be the swap rate itself or the swap spread, depending upon the type of transaction. Timing variations on conventional swaps include:

• **Deferred start or forward swaps** – this entails a delayed commencement date for the underlying transactions. The swap rate is fixed at the time of entry. The fixed and floating rates do not begin to accrue until the actual commencement date (which is deferred in time beyond the normal commencement date).

• **Spreadlocks** – this entails a delayed commencement date for the underlying swap where the swap spread *but not the swap rate* is fixed at the time of entry into the transaction.

Timing variations are also available for currency swaps. For example, deferred start/forward currency swaps are feasible.

5.2   Deferred Start Swaps

Deferred start swaps (also known as a delayed start or forward commencement swap) entail a swap where the swap rate is fixed but the transaction does not commence at the normal start date. The swap is effective and commences on a future date. The future date is usually between 1 week and 3/6 months forward. **Exhibit 13.6** sets out the structure of a deferred start swap transaction.

A forward swap is conceptually similar to a deferred start swap. The difference between a deferred start and a forward swap is the length of the delay. The commencement date in a forward swap is usually deferred for a significantly longer time.

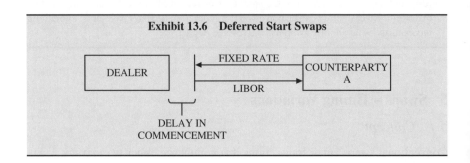

Exhibit 13.6   Deferred Start Swaps

In a forward swap, the commencement date is deferred by up to 10 years (and in some cases for a longer period).

Deferred start swaps are used primarily for the following applications:

- **Cash flow matching** – this is focused on matching funding or investment requirements. For example, a borrower/investor may wish to precisely match either a drawdown or rollover date on an underlying transaction. This entails entering into a deferred start swap, where the fixed swap rate is agreed at the time of entry into the transaction and the swap commences on an agreed date in the future.
- **Trading forward rates** – this focuses on agreeing a fixed rate on the deferred start swap where the accrual on the transaction does not commence until the delayed commencement date. This allows the trader to benefit from rate movements (in the forward swap rate or in the relationship between the spot start swap rate and the agreed deferred swap rate) without incurring the cost of the transaction.

The delayed start swap equates economically to a *forward* on the interest rate swap that can be derived from the swap yield curve itself. There are several ways to price this transaction. They include calculating the theoretical forward on swap rate or adjusting the cash flows resulting from the delayed start. **Exhibit 10.27** and **Exhibit 10.28** (Das, Satyajit (2004) Derivative Products & Pricing; John Wiley & Sons (Asia), Singapore at Chapter 10) sets out an example of pricing of a deferred start swap.

5.3 Forward Swaps

5.3.1 Concept

A forward swap is an interest rate swap that commences at a specified time in the future. A typical example is a US$ interest rate swap commencing in 2 years from the time of entry, with a final maturity 3 years from commencement (5 years from the time the transaction is entered into) (a 2 × 5 forward swap[25]). The forward rate is agreed at the time of entry into the transaction. The agreed forward rate commences accruing only at the forward commencement date. **Exhibit 13.7** sets out the structure of a forward swap transaction.

The forward start swap is similar to the deferred start swap. The difference is the extent of the delay in commencement. In the case of the forward swap, the delay may be lengthy. For example, forward swap transactions such as 10 × 30 (20 year swap with deferred commencement date in 10 years from entry) or

---

[25] The terminology is similar to that used in FRA's; see Das, Satyajit (2004) Derivative Products & Pricing; John Wiley & Sons (Asia), Singapore at Chapter 3.

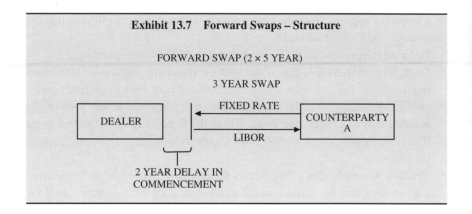

Exhibit 13.7   Forward Swaps – Structure

FORWARD SWAP (2 × 5 YEAR)

3 YEAR SWAP

FIXED RATE

DEALER ← COUNTERPARTY A

LIBOR →

2 YEAR DELAY IN COMMENCEMENT

10 × 40 (30 year swap with deferred commencement date in 10 years from entry) are feasible.

There are two types of forward swaps:

- **Forward swaps** – where the party entering into the transaction is a fixed rate payer.
- **Reverse forward swaps** – where the party entering into the transaction is a fixed rate receiver.

Forward currency swaps are similar in structure to forward interest rate swaps. In a forward currency swap, no payments occur until the forward start date. All terms of the forward currency swap (including forward start dates, principal amounts, implicit exchange rates, interest rates, payment amounts and payment dates) are agreed at the time of entry. At the forward commencement date, the initial exchange is undertaken and interest payments start to accrue. Forward currency swaps can be structured as fixed rate to floating rate, fixed rate to fixed rate, or floating rate to floating rate as required. The typical forward currency swap involves a currency swap between a fixed rate in the non US$ currency and floating rate US$ LIBOR commencing at an agreed time in the future.

Forward currency swaps can be decomposed into a series of currency forward contracts and a forward interest rate swap. For example, assume that a borrower wants to enter into a forward currency swap where it receives A$ fixed rate against payment of US$ LIBOR. The transaction commences in 2 years with a final maturity 3 years from commencement (a 2 × 5 year transaction). The cross-currency forward swap is constructed in several steps. The borrower creates a 3 year deferred synthetic US$ liability commencing in 2 years by entering into a series of currency forward contracts (buy A$/sell US$). The currency forwards convert A$ cash flows into a synthetic US$ liability. The liability would have a known fixed cost. This is because the US$ outflows are known at the outset through the currency forward contracts. The borrower would hedge the fixed rate US$ liability into floating rate. This is done through entry into a 3 year US$ forward interest rate swap commencing in 2 years time to convert the fixed rate US$ liability into floating rate US$ priced off LIBOR.

5.3.2   Pricing/Valuation of Forward Swaps

A forward start swap equates economically to a *forward* on the interest rate swap that can be derived from the swap yield curve itself. There are several ways to price this transaction. They include:

- **Calculating the theoretical forward swap rate** – this entails using the swap rates or zero rates to the delayed commencement date and the final maturity to derive the implied forward swap rate.
- **Replicating the forward swap as two offsetting swaps** – this entails trading in two offsetting swaps with identical notional principal but different maturity. The dealer pays (or receives) in one maturity (the commencement date of the forward swap) and undertakes the opposite transaction (receives or pays) to a second maturity (the final maturity of the forward swap). The cash flows of the two offsetting swaps will substantially offset during the initial period to the commencement date of the forward swap. At the commencement date, the first swap (to the commencement date) terminates. The second swap remains in place. The maturity of the swap exactly matches the maturity of the forward swap that has commenced. The forward swap rate is calculated by allocating the net cash flow deficit or surplus in the period to the commencement of the swap over the term of the forward swap. The cost of the forward swap is dependent on the shape of the yield curve that determines the cash flow surplus or deficit between the two swaps in the period to commencement.

Exhibit 13.8 sets out the offsetting swap approach. **Exhibit 13.9** sets out an example of calculating the forward swap rate using the offsetting swap approach.

The two approaches described are theoretically comparable. In practice, the two models may yield slightly different forward swap rates. Dealers generally prefer to use the offsetting swap method as it corresponds to the hedge used to manage the market risk of a forward swap. The differences between the two pricing models are driven by factors including different transaction costs and balance sheet impact issues.

The pricing of a forward swap reflects the theoretical price adjusted for a number of factors, including:
- **Hedging considerations** – this focuses on the need to transact two swaps with a total face value equal to *twice* the notional principal of the forward swap. This increases the dealer's use of credit lines and capital.
- **Cash flow risk** – this focuses on the fact that the forward swap hedge entails funding or re-investment of cash flows over the term of the transaction. In effect, the forward swap will entail the dealer either funding or borrowing from the counterparty. The dealer should charge a funding spread (to compensate for default risk) on amounts advanced to the counterparty.
- **Credit risk** – the forward swap will have credit risk that differs from that of an equivalent conventional swap. The cash flow risk (the transaction will result in the dealer lending or borrowing cash from the counterparty) will result in a loan or deposit like exposure that will need to be incorporated in the measurement of the credit risk.

Exhibit 13.8   Forward Swaps – Hedging Structure

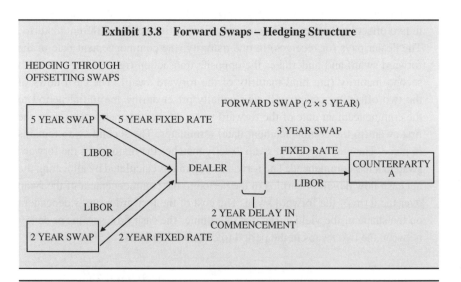

Exhibit 13.9   Forward Swaps – Pricing

Assume a company wants to enter into a 2×5 forward swap with a dealer where it pays fixed rates and receives LIBOR (a 3 year forward swap commencing in 2 years from the time of entry). The dealer will decompose the transaction into two separate swaps and hedge the transaction as follows:
- Enter a 5 year swap where the dealer pays the fixed rate and receives LIBOR.
- Enter a 2 year swap where the dealer receives the fixed rate and receives LIBOR.

Assuming that the swap rates are as follows:

Maturity (years)	2	5
Bid Swap Rate (% pa semi annual)	6.25	6.50
Offer Swap Rate (% pa semi annual)	6.27	6.53

The cash flows under the hedge (based on notional principal of $100) for the dealer would be as follows:

Year	2 Year Swap (Fixed Payments at 6.25% pa)	2 Year Swap (Floating Payments)	5 Year Swap (Fixed Payments at 6.53% pa)	5 Year Swap (Floating Payments)	Net Flows (Fixed)	Net Flows (Floating)
0.0						
0.5	3.125	−LIBOR	−3.265	LIBOR	−0.140	0
1.0	3.125	−LIBOR	−3.265	LIBOR	−0.140	0
1.5	3.125	−LIBOR	−3.265	LIBOR	−0.140	0
2.0	3.125	−LIBOR	−3.265	LIBOR	−0.140	0
2.5			−3.265	LIBOR	−3.265	LIBOR
3.0			−3.265	LIBOR	−3.265	LIBOR
3.5			−3.265	LIBOR	−3.265	LIBOR
4.0			−3.265	LIBOR	−3.265	LIBOR
4.5			−3.265	LIBOR	−3.265	LIBOR
5.0			−3.265	LIBOR	−3.265	LIBOR

The hedges result in a cash flow shortfall to the dealer at the first 4 settlement dates (2 years) of the transaction equal to 0.14% of notional principal (equivalent to the yield curve loss of 28 bps pa (6.53% versus 6.25% pa)). This cash flow loss must be funded and recovered together with funding cost over the term of the forward swap.

Assuming a funding cost of 6.53% pa (semi-annual compounding), the value of the losses (including funding cost) is approximately 59 bps *at the end of year 2 of the transaction* (the commencement of the forward swap). The annuity stream over 3 years (assuming the same funding cost of 6.53% pa (semi-annual compounding)) to recover this cost is equal to 21.9 bps pa. This equates to a forward swap price of:

Spot Swap 5 Year Rate (% pa)	6.530
Forward Start Adjustment (% pa)	0.219
2 × 5 Forward Swap Rate (% pa)	6.749

If the company wants to enter into a 2 × 5 forward swap with a dealer where it receives fixed and pays LIBOR, then the dealer will decompose the transaction into two separate swaps and hedge the transaction as follows:

- Enter a 5 year swap where the dealer receives the fixed rate and receives LIBOR.
- Enter a 2 year swap where the dealer pays the fixed rate and receives LIBOR.

Assuming the same swap rates, the cash flows under the hedge (based on notional principal of $100) for the dealer would be as follows:

Year	2 Year Swap (Fixed Payments at 6.27% pa)	2 Year Swap (Floating Payments)	5 Year Swap (Fixed Payments Payments at 6.50% pa)	5 Year Swap (Floating Payments)	Net Flows (Fixed)	Net Flows (Floating)
0.0						
0.5	−3.135	LIBOR	3.25	−LIBOR	0.115	0
1.0	−3.135	LIBOR	3.25	−LIBOR	0.115	0
1.5	−3.135	LIBOR	3.25	−LIBOR	0.115	0
2.0	−3.135	LIBOR	3.25	−LIBOR	0.115	0
2.5			3.25	−LIBOR	3.25	−LIBOR
3.0			3.25	−LIBOR	3.25	−LIBOR
3.5			3.25	−LIBOR	3.25	−LIBOR
4.0			3.25	−LIBOR	3.25	−LIBOR
4.5			3.25	−LIBOR	3.25	−LIBOR
5.0			3.25	−LIBOR	3.25	−LIBOR

The hedges result in a cash flow surplus to the dealer at the first 4 settlement dates (2 years) of the transaction equal to 0.115% of notional principal (equivalent to the yield curve gain of 23 bps pa (6.50% versus 6.27% pa)). This cash flow loss must be invested and paid together with interest over the term of the forward swap.

Assuming an investment rate of 6.50% pa (semi-annual compounding), the value of the surplus (including interest) is approximately 48 bps *at the end of year 2 of the transaction* (the commencement of the forward swap). The annuity stream over 3 years (assuming the same investment rate of 6.50% pa (semi-annual compounding)) to recover this cost is equal to 18 bps pa. This equates to a forward swap price of:

Spot Swap 5 Year Rate (% pa)	6.50
Forward Start Adjustment (% pa)	0.18
2 × 5 Forward Swap Rate (% pa)	6.68

5.3.3 Forward Interest Rate Swaps – Applications

Forward interest rate swaps are used for a number of applications:

- **Forward rate setting transactions** – this entails using forward swaps to set fixed rates commencing at a specified time in the future. This application is used in projects with a known schedule of funding drawdowns in the future, or to lock in a known fixed cost of funds for future funding. The rationale is to provide certainty of funding costs or the expectation that interest rates will increase between now and when the funding is required. Forward swaps can also be used to extend existing swaps or fixed rate liabilities to suit a changing asset or liability profile.

- **Forward rate trading transactions** – this entails using forward swaps to trade yield curves[26]. **Exhibit 13.10** sets out an example of using forward swaps to trade changes in yield curve shape to create value in a liability portfolio.
- **Structured capital market transactions** – this focuses on using forward swaps in connection with the re-financing of high coupon bonds under specific interest rate conditions[27]. **Exhibit 13.11** sets out an example of this type of application.

Exhibit 13.10   Application of Forward Interest Rate Swaps – Trading Forward Rates[28]

Assume company A has 7 year fixed rate debt. The rate on this debt is 7.75% pa. The fixed rate debt has been created by converting a 7 year US$ LIBOR based floating rate loan into fixed rate funding through a 7 year US$ interest rate swap under which A pays fixed rate and receives LIBOR[29].

Shortly after this transaction is implemented, the yield curve steepens significantly between 5 and 7 years. The yield spread between 5 and 7 years increases from approximately 15 bps pa (at the time of the swap) to 45 bps pa. This results in the rate for a 5 × 7 forward swap (two year swap commencing in approximately five years) reaching 9.25% pa.

Under these circumstances, the company can convert the rate advantage of approximately 150 bps pa over years 6 and 7 of the original financing by shortening the term of the original fixed rate borrowing from 7 years to 5 years. This is done by A entering into a 5 × 7 forward swap where it receives fixed rate (at 9.25% pa) and pays LIBOR.

---

[26] Forward swaps were used to trade interest rate differentials between swap rates in currencies in the run up to the introduction of the Euro; see Payne, Beatrix "On Course For Convergence" (November 1998) Risk 47–49.

[27] See Brown, Keith and Smith, Donald J. "Forward Swaps, Swap Options and the Management of Callable Debt" (Winter 1990) Journal of Applied Corporate Finance 59–71. See also "No More Call Waiting" (1 May 1996) Financial Products Issue 41 1, 20.

[28] See "TNT: Reverse Forward Swap Shaped to the Yield Curve" (January 1987) Corporate Finance Supplement 23.

[29] The loan margin is ignored as it does not materially affect the transaction economics.

The overall position is as follows:

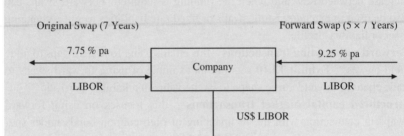

The company can take the economic benefit of the locked in gain of 150 bps pa on the forward swap in a number of ways:

- A can leave the two swaps in place and maintain the underlying borrowing. The borrowing rate is effectively LIBOR minus 150 bps pa in years 6 and 7.
- A can terminate the last 2 years of the original 7 year swap (effectively shortening the maturity to 5 years). This generates a present value benefit of 1.82% of transaction principal amount (using a discount rate of 8.00% pa). This benefit could be realised as an up-front cash benefit or as a reduction in the five year fixed rate payable under the swap of 46 bps pa.

If the company chooses the first alternative, then it could potentially benefit from reversing the forward swap if the yield curve falls in absolute rate terms or it flattens in shape.

Irrespective of the alternatives selected, the company would be left with a floating rate borrowing for 2 years in 5 years time. It would have the choice of either terminating the underlying funding (if a call option on the loan was available) or maintaining the borrowing.

Exhibit 13.11   Applications of Forward Interest Rate Swaps – Re-financing High Coupon Bonds

The opportunity developed in an environment where there was a sharp decline in US$ interest rates. This resulted in a corresponding increase in the value of call options on existing fixed rate bonds. The transactions involved bonds where the call option on the existing debt could not be exercised until some time in the future. This delay in the exercise of the call meant that the value of the call was uncertain. This was because an increase in interest rates between early 1986 (the timing of the original transactions) and the time the call was capable of being exercised would erode or eliminate the value of the option.

In this environment, two particular types of transactions evolved:

- Transactions that entailed ordinary callable fixed rate bonds.
- Transactions involving callable fixed rate bonds that had been swapped to generate LIBOR based floating rate funds.

In the first case, the issuers entered into a forward swap coinciding with the call option on the outstanding callable bonds. The borrower's intention was to call the bond and simultaneously re-finance with new floating rate funds which, through the forward swap, would generate fixed rate funds at the lower locked-in interest rates.

The second type of transaction was more complex[30]. The borrower had unrealised value from two sources - the value of the call and the value in the original interest rate swap where the fixed rate received was above current market rates. In this environment, the borrower could call the original bond, leaving it with a swap where it was receiving an above fixed market rate.

The value of the swap was realised by entering into a forward swap. Under the forward swap, the borrower made payments matching the fixed rate receipts from the original swap in return for receiving LIBOR payments that were passed onto the original swap counterparty. The forward swap simply reversed the original swap between the call and final maturity of the original fixed rate issue. This reversal left the borrower with a profit representing the difference in swap rates. The value of the swaps was realised as follows:

- A periodic flow, being the difference between the two swap rates.
- An up-front payment representing the present value of the future cash flows.

In one case, the difference was taken as a subsidy on a new issue and related swap. The transaction dramatically reduced the cost of funds to the borrower. In that case, the borrower effectively pre-funded the call by issuing debt swapped into floating rate funds with maturity coinciding with that on the original issue. The value of the forward reversal of the original swap was applied to the new issue. This pre-funding of the call resulted in the borrower having additional cash for the period until the call on the original issue that was consistent with its financing requirements.

Forward swap structures compete with swaptions and deferred call debt warrant issues as a means of realising the current value in a call option. This is particularly the case where the call cannot be exercised until some time in the future. Under the deferred call debt warrant structure, a borrower with a callable high coupon bond monetises the call option by issuing debt warrants. The warrants are exercisable on the call date into the borrower's debt on terms coinciding with the original callable issue. If interest rates fall, then the warrants are exercised. The borrower simultaneously calls the original issue being left with funding on largely identical terms, but with a lower effective cost as a result of the premium received from the issue of warrants. If interest rates increase, then the warrants will expire unexercised. The borrower is left with the original debt. The borrower can use the premium received to lower its all-in borrowing cost.

The forward swap structure and the debt warrant were effectively different techniques designed to achieve similar economic objectives. The choice between the techniques is based on market conditions and the competing economics of the debt warrant and forward swap transactions. Key market factors include the shape of the swap yield curve (which affects the pricing dynamics of the forward swaps) and value characteristics of the

---

[30] A number of these type of transactions, including a much publicised one for SEK, were concluded in early 1986; see "SEK Digs Up the Treasure Chest" (2 July 1988) International Financing Review Issue 731 2134–2136.

debt warrant (the warrant exercise period (the period until call), the life of the back bonds underlying the warrants, and the exercise period for the warrant). The attitude of the borrower is also critical. In particular, the issuer's attitude to doubling up debt until call date is important in determining the choice between the two techniques.

5.3.4   *Forward Currency Swaps – Applications*[31]

Forward currency swaps are structurally similar to forward interest rate swaps. Forward currency swaps are used for the following applications:

* Setting future fixed rate funding costs in the relevant currency.
* Management of currency exposures within an asset or liability portfolio.
* Re-financing or refunding callable foreign currency debt transactions.

Exhibit 13.12 sets out an example of using forward currency swaps to hedge future financing costs. **Exhibit 13.13** sets out an example of using forward currency swaps to refund high coupon callable debt.

Exhibit 13.12   Applications of Forward Currency Swaps – Hedging Future Financing Costs

Assume company A has a funding commitment of Euro 100 million in 2 years to fund the acquisition of a European asset (for example, a contractual obligation to acquire a business from its existing proprietors). A wishes to lock in the funding rate on the financing as well as the US$ equivalent of the Euro purchase price. In order to achieve its objectives, A enters into a forward currency swap.

The company enters into a 2 × 7 forward currency swap (5 year currency US$/Euro swap commencing in 2 years time). Under the swap, the company agrees to:
* Pay fixed rate Euro at 6.50% pa.
* Receive floating rate at US$ 6 month LIBOR.
* The exchange rate applicable will be the 2 year US$/Euro forward rate of Euro 1: US$0.9250. This implies initial and final principal amounts to be exchanged of US$92.5 million and Euro 100.0 million.

The transaction would be as follows:
* **Initial Exchange** (2 years from entry) – the company raises US$92.5 million in funding (a bank loan or US$ FRN issue) at say, LIBOR plus a margin[32]. The company pays

---

[31] See Showers, Janet L (October 1986) Forward Currency Swaps – A Product for Managing Interest Rate and Currency Exposure; Salomon Brothers, New York.

[32] The loan margin is ignored as it does not materially affect the transaction economics. The effective rate achieved by A is equivalent to 6.50% pa plus the margin over LIBOR (which must be translated from US$ into a Euro equivalent).

the US$ borrowing proceeds to the dealer and in return receives Euro 100 million that is used to make the committed Euro payment.

- **Interest Payments** (Years 3–7 inclusive) – the company pays approximately Euro 3.25 million semi-annually (6.50% pa on the Euro 100 million principal) to the dealer in return for receiving US$ 6 month LIBOR on US$92.5 million semi-annually. The US$ LIBOR receipts cover the US$ LIBOR payments on the company's floating rate US$ borrowing. The company's Euro outflows are offset by Euro earnings/surplus cash flow from the Euro denominated asset acquired.
- **Final Exchange/Re-Exchange of Principal** (Year 7) – the company pays Euro 100 million to the dealer and receives US$92.5 million from the dealer at maturity of the swap. The company uses the US$ receipts to repay the US$ floating rate borrowing. The Euro 100 million can be funded by liquidation of the asset or by re-financing in Euro (either directly or indirectly via a borrowing converted to Euro via another currency swap).

The structure of the transaction is set out diagrammatically below:

Initial Exchange (at Year 2)

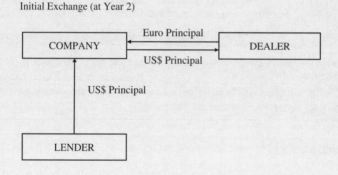

Interest Payments/ Final Exchange (at Years 3–7)

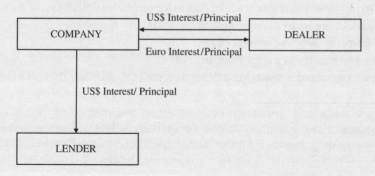

The transaction cash flows are summarised below:

Forward US$/Euro Currency Swap

	Year	US$ Borrowing – Principal (US$ m)	US$ Borrowing – Interest (US$ m)	US$ Principal (US$ m)	US$ Interest (US$ m)	Euro Principal (Euro m)	Euro Interest (Euro m)	Net Cash Flows (Euro m)
Entry into	0.0							
forward	0.5							
swap	1.0							
	1.5							
Forward	2.0	92.500		(92.500)		100.000		100.000
swap	2.5		– LIBOR		LIBOR		(3.250)	(3.250)
commences	3.0		– LIBOR		LIBOR		(3.250)	(3.250)
	3.5		– LIBOR		LIBOR		(3.250)	(3.250)
	4.0		– LIBOR		LIBOR		(3.250)	(3.250)
	4.5		– LIBOR		LIBOR		(3.250)	(3.250)
	5.0		– LIBOR		LIBOR		(3.250)	(3.250)
	5.5		– LIBOR		LIBOR		(3.250)	(3.250)
	6.0		– LIBOR		LIBOR		(3.250)	(3.250)
	6.5		– LIBOR		LIBOR		(3.250)	(3.250)
Forward	7.0	(92.500)	– LIBOR	92.500	LIBOR	(100.000)	(3.250)	(103.250)
swap								
terminates								

The forward currency swap transaction allows the company to guarantee itself financing in Euro at 6.50% pa in 2 years time. The company also locks in a US$/Euro rate of Euro 1: US$0.9250. The company will benefit (lose) if Euro five year interest rates rise (fall) or the US$ depreciates (appreciates) against the Euro.

5.4   Spreadlocks[33]

Spreadlocks (also known as deferred rate setting swaps) allow traders and hedgers to separate interest rate risk from swap spread risk. Under the structure, the party entering into the swap spreadlock fixes the swap spread, and separately fixes the underlying government rate at a later date to lock in the total fixed rate of the swap. Spreadlocks are undertaken to lock in the swap pay spread (pay spreadlock) or receive spread (receiver spreadlock).

The key features of a spreadlock include:

- The swap spread is fixed over a defined period (generally less than six months).

---

[33] See Shanahan, Terence "Horses For Courses" (March 1990) Risk 62–64; Chandrasekhar, Krishnan "Using Spreadlocks" in Das, Satyajit (Editor) (1991) Global Swaps Markets; IFR Publishing, London at Chapter 20. See also Ireland, Louise "Spread-Locks: Safe Combinations" (July 1989) Corporate Finance 11–13; "Flat's Where It's At" (14 July 1993) IFR Swaps Issue 27 1, 2.

Exhibit 13.13 Applications of Forward Currency Swaps – Re-financing High Coupon Bonds

At June 2002, a company has an outstanding Yen 20,000 million issue with a coupon of 6.50% pa maturing in June 2008. The Yen issue was swapped into floating rate US$125.0 million funding at a rate of US$ 6 month LIBOR minus 0.20% pa at the time the issue was undertaken. The issue is callable at June 2004 at 102% of par value. Yen interest rates have fallen since the time the issue was undertaken. There is value in the call option. The company can realise the value by entering into a Yen/US$ forward currency swap.

The company can capture the call value by entering into a 2 × 6 Yen/US$ forward currency swap (a 4 year currency swap commencing in 2 years time (June 2004)). The terms of the swap are as follows:

- The company agrees to pay fixed rate Yen at a rate of 5.50% pa annually.
- The company agrees to receive US$ 6 month LIBOR flat semi-annually.
- The company agrees with the dealer that the exchange rate applicable will be the 2 year US$/Yen forward rate of US$1:Yen 138.00. This implies an initial and final exchange amount of US$144.928 million and Yen 20 billion.

The forward currency swap transaction has the effect of locking in a positive spread between the original Yen/US$ currency swap and the forward currency swap in the period between June 2004 (the date of commencement of the forward swap) and June 2008 (the maturity date of the original swap).

The transaction will operate as follows:

- **Initial Cash Flows (June 2004)** – The company calls the bond issue and redeems the bond for Yen 20.4 billion (102% of par value). The company simultaneously enters into a 4 year new US$ borrowing whereby it borrows US$144.928 million. Assume the company completes this re-financing at a rate of US$ LIBOR flat. The US$ proceeds of the new borrowing are delivered to the swap counterparty who in return provides Yen 20.0 billion to the company, which then uses it to fund the call on the Yen bond. There is a shortfall of Yen 400 million (US$2.899 million at US$1:Yen 138.00) that is funded by the company out of general resources.

- **Periodic Interest Flows (December 2004 to June 2008)** – on 20 June (commencing June 2005 and ending June 2008), the company receives Yen 1,300 million (under the original swap) and pays Yen 1,100 million (under the forward swap), resulting in a cash surplus of Yen 200 million at each payment date. On 20 June and 20 December (commencing December 2004 and ending June 2008) The company has the following US$ cash flows:
  1. The company pays US$ 6 month LIBOR on US$144.928 million (on its 4 year borrowing).
  2. The company receives US$ 6 month LIBOR on US$144.928 million (under the forward currency swap).
  3. The company pays US$ 6 month LIBOR minus 20 bps on US$125.00 million (under the original swap).

The net result is the company pays US$ 6 month LIBOR minus 20 bps on US$125.0 million.

- **Final Cash Flows (June 2008)** – The company repays the US$144.928 million borrowing of 4 years undertaken in June 2004. Under the two swaps, the following principal exchanges are completed:
  1. The company receives Yen 20.0 billion (under the original swap) and pays Yen 20.0 billion (under the forward swap).
  2. The company receives US$144.928 million (under the forward swap) and uses this to repay its US$144.928 million borrowing. The company pays US$125.0 million (under the original swap).

The net result is the company has a net cash outflow of US$125.0 million, representing its original borrowing. This amount is funded by liquidating the asset acquired (for example, repayment of a loan funded through this transaction in the case of a financial institution) or by re-financing the US$ borrowing.

The structure of the transaction is set out diagrammatically below:

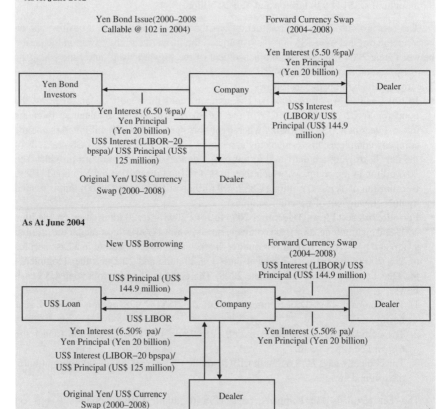

The transaction cash flows are summarised in the following Table:

Year		Yen Bond		Original Yen/US$ Swap		US$ Borrowing	Forward Yen/US$ Swap		Net Cash Flows	
	Principal (Yen m)	Call Premium (Yen m)	Interest (Yen m)	US$ Payment (US$ m)	Yen Payment (Yen m)	US$ Payment (US$ m)	US$ Payment (US$ m)	Yen Payments (Yen m)	Yen m	US$ m
0.00										
0.50										
1.00			−1,300.00	−2.688	1,300.00	144.980	−144.980			−2.688
1.50				−2.688		−3.261	3.261			−2.688
2.00	−20,000.00	−400.00	−1,300.00	−2.688	1,300.00	−3.261	3.261	20,000.00	−400.00	−2.688
2.50				−2.688		−3.261	3.261			−2.688
3.00				−2.688	1,300.00	−3.261	3.261	−1,100.00	200.00	−2.688
3.50				−2.688		−3.261	3.261			−2.688
4.00				−2.688	1,300.00	−3.261	3.261	−1,100.00	200.00	−2.688
4.50				−2.688		−3.261	3.261			−2.688
5.00				−2.688	1,300.00	−3.261	3.261	−1,100.00	200.00	−2.688
5.50				−2.688		−3.261	3.261			−2.688
6.00				−127.688	21,300.00	−148.241	148.241	−21,100.00	200.00	−127.688

Entry into forward swap — 0.00

Forward swap commences — 2.00 / 3.00

Forward swap terminates — 6.00

Notes:
The cash flows assume a US$ LIBOR rate of 4.50% pa for the purposes of the calculation.

The net result of the transaction is that the company continues to have a borrowing of US$125 million at an interest cost of US$ 6 month LIBOR minus 20 bps. In addition, it has a series of Yen flows where it has a Yen 400 million outflow (the call premium) at June 2004 and a series of Yen 200 million inflows on June 2005 to June 2008 (the difference between the Yen swap rates). The present value of the Yen cash flows to June 2002 (at a Yen interest rate of 5.50% pa for years 2004 to 2008 and a rate of 5.35% pa for the years 2002 to 2004) is equivalent to Yen 271.2 million. This is equivalent to US$2.01 million (assuming a spot rate of US$1:Yen 135). This is equivalent to an annuity of US$0.19 million over 12 semi-annual periods using a US$ interest rate of 4.50% pa. Based on the borrowing amount of US$125 million, this is equivalent to 31 bps pa. The locked in interest gain on the Yen swaps can be used to lower the borrowing cost of the company from LIBOR minus 20 bps to LIBOR minus 51 bps.

In the period prior to the call (that is, to June 2004), the company enjoys an additional trading opportunity where, if Yen interest rates rise, then it may be able to close the forward currency swap and maintain the bond issue and the related swap. The gain or the swap closeout lowers the company's borrowing cost.

- The purchaser of the spreadlock agrees to enter into a swap (pay or receive the fixed rate) at the agreed spread over a reference rate for an agreed maturity
- The purchaser of the spreadlock must enter into the swap. It only has the option of determining the timing of setting the underlying government benchmark fixed rate.

Exhibit 13.14 sets out an example of a spreadlock.

Spreadlocks are hedged by trading in the underlying swap and simultaneously hedging the Treasury component of the swap. **Exhibit 13.15** sets out the hedging structure. The cost or benefit of the spreadlock is driven by the cost of the hedge. **Exhibit 13.16** sets out an example of hedging and pricing of a spreadlock.

The applications of spreadlocks include:

- **Hedging exposure to swap spread** – spreadlocks are used to hedge exposures to changes in swap spreads. This involves several types of transaction including:
  1. *Hedging credit spreads* – swap spreads are a surrogate for credit spreads[34]. This allows spreadlocks to be used to hedge movements in generalised credit risk.
  2. *Efficient hedging* – entry into a normal swap fixes the total swap rate (spread and underlying government rate). The spreadlock only fixes the swap spread

---

[34] See Das, Satyajit (2004) Derivative Products & Pricing; John Wiley & Sons (Asia), Singapore at Chapter 11.

over the relevant reference rate. This allows traders to separate the swap spread risk from the risk of changes in the underlying government rate. This allows the hedge to be optimised by timing the two markets (swap spreads and government rates) separately. For example, a payer spreadlock allows the borrower to take advantage of any expected decrease in the underlying government interest rates without exposure to movements in the swap spread.

- **Trading swap spreads** – spreadlocks are used to trade the volatility of swap spreads. This can involve directional trading of movements in swap spreads. In addition, spreadlocks can be used for more structured forms of trading where it is used to trade anomalies between the repo market and swap spreads[35]. **Exhibit 13.17** sets out examples of this type of trading.

There are variations on the spreadlock structures. The most significant variation is the deferred rate setting structure. This type of transaction has been used by the World Bank[36].

In 1991, the World Bank commenced a program of global bond issues primarily in US$. Such transactions entailed issuance of large volumes of US$ debt securities (usually at least US$1,000 million). These global issues exposed the World Bank to the risk of setting the underlying Treasury rate. This related to the fact that a transaction was completed and priced on a single date.

In order to reduce this pricing risk, the World Bank developed a structure analogous to spreadlocks to defer the Treasury price setting on its global bond issues over a more extended time frame. Under this arrangement, the World Bank would undertake its global bond issue and price the transaction at an agreed margin over the relevant US Treasury bond of equivalent maturity. Simultaneously, or in the period prior to the launch of the issue, the World Bank would purchase US Treasury bonds of equivalent maturity for an amount (up to) the full issue volume. The net result of the transactions was to leave the World Bank with an agreed spread over the US Treasury bond but with the underlying absolute Treasury rate undetermined. The World Bank would liquidate its Treasury hedge position to gradually establish the effective borrowing cost over a period of time. The gains and losses on the sale of the Treasury hedge would either increase or decrease the cost of borrowing. This would effectively adjust the Treasury rate set on the day the global bond issue

[35] See Fidelholtz, Peter "Playing the 10 Year" (September 1997) Derivatives Strategy 38.
[36] See "DRS Adds Flexibility" (14 December 1991) International Financing Review Issue 908 77.

was priced. This type of structure is similar to a spreadlock in economic terms. The structure allowed the World Bank to spread the Treasury pricing risk over an acceptable period.

In 1993, Kreditanstalt Fuer Weideraufbrau ("KfW") undertook a variation on the deferred rate setting structure[37]. KfW issued US$500 million of 5 year bonds. KfW entered into a series of swaps designed to obtain US$200 million of the issue as 10 year funds. The swaps (undertaken with Deutsche Bank) were as follows:

- KfW swapped US$200 million of the issue for 5 years. KfW paid US$ LIBOR and received fixed rates covering the fixed interest cost of the bond.
- KfW entered into a swap where it paid fixed US$ rates for 10 years against receipt of US$ LIBOR on US$200 million.
- KfW entered into a deferred rate setting for US$200 million of the proceeds at 18 bps over US Treasury rates. This effectively allowed KfW to lock in a fixed rate liability before the expiration of the rate setting period.
- US$100 million of the issue was left in fixed rate US$.

The first two swaps allowed KfW to lock in 10 year fixed rates (at below current 10 year swap rates). KfW had to re-finance US$200 million of the 5 year bonds at maturity. KfW's cost of finance is fixed as long as it re-finances at US$ LIBOR flat. Any improvement in its funding cost under LIBOR will improve its cost of funds. The transaction achieved KfW's objective of 10 year financing. This was during a period when market conditions would have made a 10 year issue expensive for the German State guaranteed agency.

Spreadlocks are used primarily in the US$ market. This reflects the fact that swaps are traded (at least historically) as a spread to Treasury rates[38].

Exhibit 13.14 Spreadlocks – Structure

Assume that US$ 5 year swaps are trading at the 5 year Treasury bond rate + 51/54 bps. A company considers that the swap spread is attractive and wishes to lock in the pay or offer

---

[37] See "Deutsche Bank Implements Novel Swap Structure For KfW" (13 January 1993) IFR Swaps Issue 1 11.

[38] In the late 1990s, the US government ran substantial budget surpluses, allowing reduction in the volume of government debt. This led to concern about the liquidity of the Treasury market and the ability to price swaps off Treasury notes/bonds. For example, see Youngdahl, John, Stone, Brad and Boesky, Hayley "Implications of a Disappearing Debt Market" (March 2001) Journal of Fixed Income 75–86; Smithson, Charles "Swaps Become the Benchmark" (April 2001) Risk 78–79.

spread (54 bps) for a period of 3 months. The company enters into a payer spreadlock agreement with a dealer on the following terms:

Commencement Date	15 November 2002
Expiry Date	15 February 2003
Maturity date of underlying swap	5 years (final maturity 15 November 2007)
Counterparty pays	US Treasury Rate plus the Payer Spread (on a semi-annual basis based on actual/365 day basis)
Counterparty receives	6 month LIBOR (on a semi-annual basis based on actual/360 day basis)
Payer Spread	54 bps pa
US Treasury Rate	5 year on-the-run US Treasury rate on the Fixing Date
Fixing Date	Any business day of the Counterparty's choice between the Commencement Date and the Expiry Date

The following aspects of the spreadlock terms should be noted:

- The final maturity of the underlying swap is 5 years *from commencement date of the spreadlock*. It is feasible to structure a transaction where the final maturity is 5 years from the date of exercise of the spreadlock or the expiry date of the spreadlock. The cost of the transaction is adjusted where the maturity is changed.
- The structure allows exercise *at any time in the period to expiry of the spreadlock*. A structure where the spreadlock is only capable of exercise at the expiry date of the spreadlock is also feasible.

Under the spreadlock, the company has locked in the payer swap spread of 54 bps pa. The US Treasury rate is not fixed. The company has the right to set the US Treasury rate at any time within 3 months. At any time during the 3 month period, the company can enter into a 5 year US$ interest rate swap where it pays the then prevailing 5 year US Treasury rate plus 54 bps and receives 6 month US$ LIBOR.

Exhibit 13.15   Spreadlocks – Hedging Structures

Pay Spreadlock Hedge

Receive Spreadlock Hedge

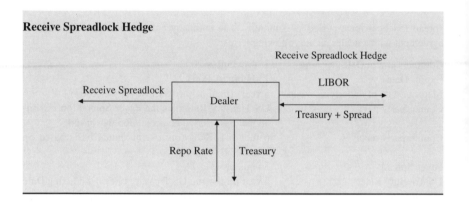

Exhibit 13.16   Spreadlocks – Pricing

Assume the transaction described in **Exhibit 13.14.** The fee payable to or receivable from the dealer is determined by the cost of the hedge. The structure of the hedge is as follows:
- The dealer enters into a 5 year swap under which it pays T + 54 bps. Assuming a current 5 year US Treasury rate of 6.00% pa, the swap rate is 6.54% pa.
- The dealer hedges the 5 year US treasury component of the swap by purchasing a 5 year Treasury (generally the on-the-run or equivalent Treasury note or bond). The dealer funds the purchase at the repo rate or other short-term rate. The Treasury hedge is designed to compensate for the fact that the swap (under which the dealer receives fixed rate) has not commenced and the absolute rate has not been set.
- The dealer sells the 5 year Treasury held as a hedge when the company exercises its right under the spreadlock to fix the Treasury rate and enters into the swap.

The effective cost of hedging the spreadlock is the cost of the swap and the Treasury hedge.
Assume the following rates[39]:

5 year US Treasury rate: 6.00% pa (semi-annual compounding).
6 month LIBOR: 5.00% pa (semi-annual compounding).
Repo rate: 4.50% pa.

The net position of the dealer under the hedge (based on a notional principal of $1,000,000) is that it has the following cash flows:
- Under the 5 year swap, the dealer will have the following cash flows over the term of the spreadlock:

Fixed rate ($)   −16,484
Floating rate ($)   12,778
Net ($)   −3,707

---

[39]   Please note that bid-offer spreads have been ignored for convenience.

- Under the bond purchase and repo to fund the bond position, the dealer will have the following cash flows over the term of the spreadlock:

Bond coupon ($)   15,123
Repo cost ($)   −10,082
Net ($)   5,041

- The net cash flow of the hedge is a gain of $1,334 or 13.3 bps.

The dealer gains from the hedge and will be prepared to pay a fee to the counterparty to enter into the spreadlock. The fee is equivalent to 13.3 bps upfront or around 3.2 bps pa. If paid over the life, then the dealer may offer the counterparty the opportunity to pay an adjusted spread (around 50 bps pa reflecting the benefit of the hedge).

Several aspects of the hedging and pricing of the spreadlock require comment:

- The spreadlock is set as a spread over the *current* on-the-run US Treasury bond for the relevant maturity at the time the spreadlock is arranged. Where the spreadlock is of significant duration, there is a likelihood that the spreadlock will be affected by a change of benchmark. This will usually result from the issuance of new Treasury bonds and the changing maturity of the old benchmark. This necessitates that for longer term spreadlocks, there is provision for a change in Treasury benchmark during the life of the spreadlock. This requires adjustment for the difference in yield between the old and new benchmark bond. Typically, as the new Treasury benchmark yields less than the old benchmark, the purchaser of a payer (receiver) spreadlock will incur a slight cost (benefit).

- The dealer has several uncertainties:
  1. The dealer does not know the duration of the hedge (the counterparty can fix at any time) so the exact cost or benefit of the hedge is difficult to calculate at the time of entry.
  2. The dealer incurs risk on the financing cost of the long Treasury position or the cost of maintaining the Treasury short position. This is because the dealer can exercise its spreadlock at any time within the contract period. This generally means the Treasury position is "rolled" on a short term basis.
  3. The dealer's cash position is affected by the various accruals under the swap entered into to hedge the position, as well as the treasury position. This is particularly significant where the spreadlock is of a significant duration.

The pricing of the spreadlock will incorporate the hedging risk. For a payer spreadlock, during the period the spreadlock is in place prior to exercise, the dealer's net cash flows are: LIBOR − Repo rate − Swap Spread. Assuming LIBOR is equal to the Repo rate, in the worst case the cash flow deficiency will be equal to the swap spread for the relevant period. For a receiver spreadlock, the dealer's net cash flows are: − LIBOR + Repo rate + Swap Spread. Assuming that the repo rate is low (as can be the case when the bond goes "on special" and is difficult to borrow), the maximum net cash flow is the swap spread minus LIBOR. The actual pricing for a spreadlock would incorporate these factors and the dealer's view on these rate relationships.

Exhibit 13.17   Application of Spreadlocks – Trading Swap Spreads Against Repo Rates

Assume the 10 year US Treasury bond is trading "on special" in the repo market. This means that the bond is difficult or expensive to borrow. The scarcity may be driven by a variety of factors, including an excess of borrowing demand (from dealers and mortgage/corporate bond traders to hedge fixed income security inventories) over available supply of the bonds. The fact that the bonds are "on special" means that the notes can be financed at a substantial discount to the prevailing federal funds rate.

Spreadlocks can be used to trade this market situation. The trade is structured as follows:
- The dealer buys the 10 year note and then repos the note to finance the purchases.
- The dealer pays fixed in a 10 year US$ swap against receipt of US$ 3 or 6 month LIBOR.

The strategy allows the dealer to take advantage of the fact that the swap is funded at LIBOR while the 10 year bonds are financed at the low repo rate. The position has low interest rate risk as the swap and the bond position are offsetting.

The level of this discrepancy can be significant. During certain periods in the late 1990s[40], the 10 year swap rate was 6.51% pa against the 10 year bond rate of 6.10% pa. At this time, LIBOR was 5.75% pa while overnight repo rates were 3.00% pa. This meant that the dealer lost 41 bps pa (the pay swap spread) but received 275 bps pa (the difference between LIBOR and the low repo rate). The dealer was earning 234 bps pa.

The risk of the transaction is that the repo rates change. For example, if repo rates went back to the federal funds rate at the time of 5.50% pa, then the position would lose 16 bps (the spread of 41 bps would not be offset by the 25 bps difference between LIBOR and the repo rates).

The transaction risk may be reduced by entering into a term repo and using a forward start interest rate swap. For example, assume the 3 month repo rate is around 4.00% pa. The impact of locking in the repo rate means that the dealer has locked in a forward swap spread (in this case of around 35 bps versus the 41 bps spot payer swap spread). If the swap spread stays at the current level (41 bps), then the dealer earns around $4,100 per $ million. If the swap spread increases, then the profit on the position increases. If the swap spread decreases below 35 bps, then the position will show a loss.

In practice, the strategy described is used where swap spreads are at a low level based on historical trading patterns to reduce the risk of the transaction.

---

6   Swaps – Cash Flow Variations

6.1   Concept

Cash flow variations in swap transactions entail adjustments to the normal coupon cash flow associated with standard transactions.

---

[40] The market scenario described is that set out in Fidelholtz, Peter "Playing the 10 Year" (September 1997) Derivatives Strategy 38.

The cash flow structure under a conventional swap meets the following conditions:

- Swap fixed rate coupon is set at the swap rate at the time of entry into the transaction.
- Coupon is paid at pre-specified intervals throughout the term.
- The net present value of the transaction is equal to zero other than any profit margin on the transaction.
- There are no other payments associated with the transaction.

In the case of a currency swap, the initial exchange and final exchange is undertaken at the spot rate for value at the commencement date of the transaction.

In a swap involving some form of cash flow variation, the swap coupon is set at a level that is different from the swap rate. This creates an initial positive or negative net present value of the transaction. In addition, the coupon may not be paid at pre-specified regular intervals through the life of the transaction, but either deferred or accelerated.

The major types of cash flow variations on swaps include:

- **Premium or discount swaps** (also known as off-market swaps) – these transactions entail a swap coupon that is higher or lower than the swap rate. This creates an initial negative or positive cash flow. For example, the structure may entail an up-front payment by the dealer where the swap is structured so that the counterparty pays a higher coupon payment than the swap rate.
- **Structured coupon swaps** – this entails changes in the payment pattern. Under this structure, the swap coupon is not paid normally. The swap payment may be deferred (a deferred or zero coupon swap) or accelerated (a reverse zero coupon swap).

6.2 Pricing/Valuation of Structured Cash Flow Swaps

The pricing of a structured cash flow swap follows the normal convention of swap valuation. Under this approach, the initial value of the transaction must be zero. This is achieved in the following way:

- **Premium/discount swaps** – the structure entails a swap coupon that is set above or below the swap rate. This means that the dealer is either making a loan (swap coupon above the swap rate) or taking a deposit (swap coupon below the swap rate). In both cases the value of the swap incorporating the up-front payment or receipt should still equal zero. **Exhibit 10.28** and **Exhibit 10.29** (Das, Satyajit (2004) Derivative Products & Pricing; John Wiley & Sons (Asia), Singapore at Chapter 10) set out an example of pricing a swap where the dealer makes an up-front payment in return for receiving higher than market coupons. A number of other factors must be priced in to the valuation process. This includes the fact that the transaction entails a loan or deposit, the differences in credit risk of the transaction, and the different re-investment risk of the transaction.

- **Structured coupon swaps** – the structure entails changing the timing of the payment of the swap coupon. This means that the dealer is re-investing or borrowing cash equivalent to the normal swap coupon. The value of the swap needs to reflect the re-investment or funding of the cash flows. The cash flows are generally assumed to be funded or re-invested at the assumed forward rates implicit in the zero coupon yield curve at the time the transaction is entered into. This means that the value of the swap based on the accrued coupon (including re-investment returns) must equal zero in present values at the time of entry into the transaction. In practice, this means that the swap rate will effectively equate to the zero coupon rate for the relevant maturity. The zero coupon pricing must be adjusted for additional factors such as the embedded loan/deposit transaction, the credit risk of the transaction and the different re-investment risk.

In practice, structured cash flow swaps are priced using zero coupon rates. The rate derived must be adjusted for a number of additional factors, including:

- **Embedded loan/deposit transaction** – the structured cash flow swap will entail an embedded loan by or deposit with the dealer. Where zero coupon methodology is used, this assumes that the dealer is financing the counterparty or paying interest to the counterparty at a rate equivalent to the swap rates (or LIBOR flat). The rate charged or paid may be inappropriate. This will reflect the credit risk on the loan or the credit quality of the dealer and its funding costs. This means that the transaction must be bifurcated into the conventional swap and a separate loan or deposit transaction. The relevant zero rates must be adjusted for the credit margin on the loan or deposit and valued appropriately. **Exhibit 10.30** (Das, Satyajit (2004) Derivative Products & Pricing; John Wiley & Sons (Asia), Singapore at Chapter 10) sets out an example of pricing the swap where the dealer makes an up-front payment in return for receiving higher than market coupons incorporating the credit spread on the loan component.

- **Credit risk issues** – the swap pricing must also reflect the different credit risk profile created by the adjustment for the cash flows. In a premium/discount structure, the change in credit risk is directly related to the embedded loan or deposit transaction. The embedded loan increases the counterparty credit risk for the dealer. In contrast, the embedded deposit decreases the counterparty credit risk for the dealer. The altered credit risk of the transaction is reflected in the pricing of the embedded loan or deposit within the transaction. In a structured coupon swap, the change in credit risk derives from the delay or acceleration in receipt of cash flows. This can be illustrated with a zero coupon swap. Under a normal swap, the swap coupon is received quarterly or semi-annually.

In contrast, in a zero coupon swap, the swap coupon is accrued and reinvested and paid at maturity. This means that the dealer is exposed to the counterparty for the full amount of *all the swap coupons plus accrued interest on the unpaid coupon* until maturity. This exposure is exacerbated by the fact that the dealer is also paying regular floating rate coupons to the counterparty. In practice, the second risk is mitigated by the practice of the floating rate payments being accrued, compounded and only paid to the swap counterparty at maturity. This provision is designed to reduce the credit risk on the transaction for the dealer. The different credit risk profile of the cash flow structured swap should be reflected in the pricing.

*   **Re-investment risk issues** – the cash flow structured swaps effectively require the dealer to either assume reinvestment risks or alternatively to fund payments to the counterparty that are then recovered over the life of the swap. The pricing reflects the assumptions as to reinvestment rates and funding costs. The problem for the dealer is that the cash flow variations increase the reinvestment risk of the portfolio and must be hedged. This hedging will be undertaken at a portfolio level. The additional costs should be incorporated into the transaction pricing and recovered from the counterparty.

The complex structure of structured cash flow swaps creates special issues when pricing a reversal/cancellation. **Exhibit 13.18** sets out an example of pricing a zero coupon swap reversal that highlights the technical issues.

Exhibit 13.18   Pricing Zero Coupon Swap Reversals

Assume a counterparty entered into a zero coupon swap where it paid US$ 6 month LIBOR semi-annually in return for receiving a zero coupon pound sterling (GBP) amount at maturity. The basic terms of the swap are as follows:

Term	10 years
US$ Notional Principal	US$79,908,905
US$ Notional Principal	GBP 53,272,604 (based on an initial exchange rate of GBP1.00:US$1.50)
GBP fixed rate (payable at maturity)	6.50% pa annual compounding
US$ floating rate (payable semi-annually)	6 month LIBOR (the most recent rate set was 4.25% pa)

The swap cash flows are as follows:
*   At commencement date, the counterparty receives US$79,908,905 from the dealer and pays GBP 53,271,604 to the dealer.
*   Every 6 months up to and including the termination date, the counterparty pays US$ 6 month LIBOR on US$ principal amount to the dealer.

- At termination date, the counterparty pays US$79,908,905 to the dealer and receives GBP 100,000,000 calculated as follows:
  1. GBP principal amount of GBP 53,272,604
  2. Fixed payment of GBP 47,726,396 (being compounded interest on the GBP amount at an interest rate of 6.50% pa).

The swap has a special feature in respect of the floating rate US$ LIBOR payments. Interest on the principal amount is to be compounded at the relevant US$ 6 month LIBOR rate and paid to the swap dealer at maturity. This provision is designed to reduce the credit risk on the transaction for the counterparty.

Assume that the counterparty wishes to unwind this swap where there is just over 8 years remaining time to original maturity. The prevailing market rates at the date are:

- Exchange rate is equal to GBP1:US$1.5500.
- US$ LIBOR rate (to the next coupon date) is 4.5625% pa.
- GBP zero coupon swap rate (to original swap maturity) is 5.80% pa

The valuation of the swap is undertaken in discrete steps. The first step is to value the currency swap conventionally.

The Table below sets out the transaction cash flows that are then discounted back to the valuation date. Please note that both fixed and floating rate components are decomposed into security equivalents and the principal amount is included in the calculation.

The GBP fixed rate position is as follows:

Time to Cash Flows (Days)	Principal (Original) (GBP)	Fixed Rate (Original) (GBP)	Total Cash Flows (Original) (GBP)	Zero Rates (% pa)	Discounted Net Cash Flows (GBP)
2922 Total	(53,272,604)	(46,727,396)	(100,000,000)	5.80	(63,676,692) (63,676,692)

The US$ LIBOR position is as follows:

Time to Cash Flows (Days)	Principal (Initial) (US$)	LIBOR (Initial) (US$)	Total Cash Flows (Initial) (US$)	Zero Rates (% pa)	Discount Net Cash Flows (GBP)
135 Total	79,908,905	1,735,799	81,644,704	4.00	80,468,891 80,468,891

The value of the swap at the valuation date can be established by taking the present values in each currency (translated into the other currency at the spot rate at the valuation date) and taking the net of the two:

Currency	GBP	US$
Current Value	(63,676,692)	80,468,891

Currency	GBP	US$
Foreign Currency Value	(98,698,872)	51,915,414
Total Value	(11,761,278)	(18,229,980)

The analysis indicates that the dealer would pay and the counterparty would receive a cash payment of US$18,229,980 to cancel the swap at the assumed rates[41].

The value of the swap derived must be adjusted for the accumulated floating rate US$ LIBOR payments that have been accrued but not paid. The counterparty would have to pay to the swap dealer the accumulated floating rate interest (that has been compounded but not paid) calculated as follows:

Days to Cash Flows	US$ LIBOR Rate (% pa)	US$ Principal (US$)	US$ Interest (US$)	Cumulative Balance (US$)
0	6.125	79,908,905		79,908,905
181	5.750		2,460,806	82,369,711
365	5.375		2,348,434	84,718,145
546	4.875		2,159,483	86,877,628
730			1,991,064	88,868,691

The total accumulated interest is US$8,959,786 (the cumulative balance (US$88,868,691) minus the US$ Principal (US$79,908,905). This amount of US$8,959,786 would need to be paid to the swap dealer on termination.

The total settlement sum upon cancellation of the zero coupon swap would be a payment of US$9,270,194 by the dealer to the counterparty (calculated as the value of the swap of US$18,229,980 adjusted for the accumulated floating rate interest of US$8,959,786).

The focus hitherto has been on interest rate swaps. The methodology of pricing structured cash flow currency swaps is identical. This reflects the fact that premium/discount or structured coupon structures affect the coupons in each currency. The currency basis of the transaction is not, strictly speaking, affected by the manipulation of the coupon flow. A zero coupon fixed to fixed currency swap is structurally identical to a currency forward contract.

[41] The "gain" on the reversal of the zero swap is somewhat illusory as it must be offset against the accrual of the zero coupon foregone as a result of the cancellation of the swap. The swap coupon accrual to date must be deducted from the theoretical mark-to-market value to derive a true economic gain on the transaction. In this case, the accrual to date would be approximately US$12,629,390 (calculated as the compound interest (at the original swap rate of 6.50% pa) on the GBP notional principal (GBP 53,272,604) for 2.26 years (the time elapsed since the start of the swap) being GBP 8,147,994 converted into US$ at the exchange rate of GBP1:US$1.55).

6.3 Applications

Overview

The demand for cash flow variations within the swap structure are driven by a number of different factors including:

- **Cash flow management** – this focuses on:
  1. Creating funding or investment structures by setting the swap coupon at a rate above or below the swap rate.
  2. Deferring gains/losses on existing transactions.
  3. Matching cash flows of underlying investments or liabilities.
  4. Management of transaction credit risk.
- **Taxation factors** – this focuses on the deferral or acceleration of payments to adjust the tax liabilities of the counterparty.
- **Capital market transactions** – this is driven by capital market issues where the coupon structure is not standard. This includes zero coupon bonds, graduated coupon bonds or premium/discount bond structures. The bonds are generally created to meet demand from investors seeking protection from reinvestment risks or seeking to take advantage of the tax treatment on discounts or premiums. Issuers of the bonds generally seek protection from the coupon structure. This requires the development of structured cash flow swaps designed to insulate the issuer from the cash flow structure of the issue.

Cash Flow Management

Cash flow variations on swaps can be used for cash flow management. The focus is generally on the following:

- **Creating funding or investment** – this focuses on premium/discount swap structures. The swap can be used to generate funding by paying a swap coupon at a rate above the swap rate. Alternatively, swaps can be used to synthesise a deposit by paying a swap coupon at a rate below the swap rate. This entails the combination of a loan or deposit and an off-market swap. The loan or deposit is repaid in the form of an annuity stream that is built into the swap rate. The annuity stream has the impact of increasing or decreasing the swap rate. The loan or deposit should be priced using the zero coupon rates adjusted for the relevant funding or deposit credit spread.
- **Deferring recognition of gains/losses** – this application entails using off-market swaps to defer cash flows and/or profits/losses on existing transactions. These types of transactions are usually undertaken to defer payment or alternatively disguise/defer recognition of gains and losses. An example of this type of application is a reputed transaction undertaken by a European sovereign country that used a currency swap in 1997 to defer payments to reduce the country's

fiscal deficit. This was designed to allow the country to conform to the Maastricht treaty's budget deficit targets required in order to qualify for entry to the Euro[42]. Adjusting the recognition of gains/losses entails the combination of off-market derivatives and a loan or deposit transaction. Deferring recognition of profits on existing transactions entails entry into transactions where the gain is built into the derivative that is entered into at rates/prices superior to those available in the market. Deferring recognition of losses entails entry into transactions where the derivative counterparty enters into a loan to finance the loss. The loan is then recovered by repayment (including funding costs) through a derivative contract that is at a rate/price above current market levels. The use of derivatives to defer losses is controversial[43]. **Exhibit 10.39** (Das, Satyajit (2004) Derivative Products & Pricing; John Wiley & Sons (Asia), Singapore at Chapter 10) sets out an example of using swaps to defer currency gains on a borrowing. **Exhibit 13.19** sets out an example of a foreign exchange historic rate roll-over contract where derivatives are used to defer recognition of existing currency losses on a forward.

• **Matching cash flows of underlying investments or liabilities** – this focuses on using structured coupon swaps to defer cash flows to match underlying cash flows. This can entail deferring interest payments to match the income flows on a project or investment. **Exhibit 13.20** sets out an example of using structured cash flows to match cash flows on underlying transactions. Structured coupon swaps (such as zero coupon swaps) can also be used to manage currency risk. **Exhibit 13.21** sets out an example of this type of application in cross border leasing transactions.

• **Management of transaction credit risk** – this is focused on the creation of off-market transactions or structuring of derivatives with non-standard cash flows to minimise credit exposure to a counterparty in such transactions. For example, assume a low credit quality company wishes to hedge its interest exposure by entering into an interest rate swap where it pays fixed and receives floating. In order to reduce its credit exposure, the dealer could enter into the swap at a rate *significantly above the current market rate*. The above market rate would be compensated for by payment of a lump sum amount *at the maturity of the swap*. This structure has the effect of reducing the dealer's risk, as the off-market structure would decrease the chance that the transaction has negative

---

[42] See "Italian Fiddle?" (10 November 2001) The Economist 99; Evans, Jules "How Italy Shrank Its Deficit" (December 2001) Euromoney 22; Thind, Sarfraz "Italy's Use of Derivatives For EMU Access Under Scrutiny" (January 2002) Risk 17.

[43] See "Squabble Over HRRs" (April 2000) Asia Risk 6. In Japan, the use of "tobashi" transactions by banks to defer unrealised losses has attracted controversy; see Irvine, Steven "Cruel and Unusual Punishment" (September 1999) Euromoney 48–51.

mark-to-market value (that is, the dealer is exposed to the risk of default by the counterparty). The above market coupon effectively creates a reserve fund (as payments are received) that could be used to offset any replacement cost of the transaction in the event of default of the counterparty[44].

Exhibit 13.19   Applications of Structured Cash Flow Swaps – Historical Rate Rollovers

Assume an Australian exporter has purchased A$/sold US$ for a face value amount of US$10,000,000 at a rate of A$1:US$0.7560. Under the contract, the exporter would receive A$13,227,513 in exchange for delivery of US$10,000,000. The position was taken some time ago and is currently due to settle spot. The current spot rate is A$1:US$0.5920/30. The forward points for 90 days are 47/42.

The position is clearly out-of-the-money as A$/US$ has depreciated relative to the forward rate. The exporter does not wish to realise the loss on the out-of-the-money position. The exporter requests that the bank roll over the position at historic rates to avoid realisation of the currency loss. The bank is prepared to undertake a historic rate rollover of the currency position.

The bank prices the historic rate rollover using the following methodology:
* The current position loss (A$3,664,379) is calculated as follows:

Position	Exchange Rate (A$1:US$)	A$ Cash Flow	US$ Cash Flow
Original Position	0.7560	13,227,513	−10,000,000
Spot Position	0.5920	−16,891,892	+10,000,000
Net Gain/Loss		−3,664,379	

* The loss must be funded. It is effectively a loan from the bank to the exporter. Assume that the exporter cost of funds is equivalent to 7.00% pa (interest rate for 90 days of 6.00% pa plus a risk margin of 1.00% pa). The interest cost over 90 days is equivalent to A$64,126 (calculated as A$3,664,379 × 7% × 90/360).
* The contract would normally be transacted as 0.5878 (spot (0.5920) adjusted for the forward points (0.0042)).
* The adjusted forward rate of A$1:US$0.7528 (calculated as A$13,284,084/ US$10,000,000) is derived as follows:

Position	A$ Cash Flow	US$ Cash Flow
Contract at current market rates (A$1: US$0.5878)	17,012,589	−10,000,000
Adjust for loss	−3,664,379	
Adjust for interest on loss	−64,126	
Net	13,284,084	−10,000,000

---

[44] For a detailed discussion of this approach to credit enhancement, see Das, Satyajit (2004) Risk Management; John Wiley & Sons (Asia), Singapore at Chapter 6.

The contract is re-negotiated at a forward rate for 90 days of A$1:US$0.7528. The bank, in agreeing to the historic rate rollover, must be prepared to take the credit risk on the exporter for the 90 day forward and the loan exposure equivalent to the loss embedded within the structure.

Exhibit 13.20   Applications of Structured Cash Flow Swaps – Cash Flow Matching

In early 1987, an Australian company Westfield Capital Corporation ("Westfield") arranged a funding package to finance its investments in a number of companies (including Coles Myer). The dividend yield on the investments was well below the interest coupons on the debt financing. Westfield used a zero coupon interest rate swap to generate fixed rate funding on which no payment was due until 5 years in the future. The zero coupon swap deferred the cash outflow. This overcame the problem of the negative spread between dividend income and interest expense in the short run. It was consistent with Westfield's objective of achieving capital growth on its share investments.

Exhibit 13.21   Applications of Structured Cash Flow Swaps – Currency Matching

During the 1980s, Japanese cross-border tax based leasing structures developed[45]. Under these arrangements, Japanese equity investors in leveraged lease transactions purchased capital equipment (mainly mobile transportation equipment such as aircraft) and leased them to corporations who were non-residents of Japan. The transaction used depreciation/capital allowances on the equipment and interest deductions (from the debt component of the leveraged lease) to defer taxation liabilities of the Japanese investor. This generated a lower effective implicit cost of finance to the non Japanese lessee. The transactions were typically pure funding transactions. The lease entailed no exposure for the Japanese lessor to the residual value of the asset. The lessee generally acquired the asset at the end of the transaction or indemnified the lessor against risk of loss on the disposal of the equipment at the end of the lease term.

The lease stream payable by the lessee under such transactions was typically denominated in a currency relevant to the lessee (typically US$), matching the debt component of the leveraged lease. The lease structure required some Yen rentals to be paid, usually towards the maturity of the lease term. Often the Yen payments were effectively structured as the final residual value payment to the lessor.

The Yen payment typically created a currency exposure for the lessee. Initially, the lessees hedged this exposure by placing a deposit (denominated in Yen) at the commencement of

---

[45] For a discussion of cross border leasing, see (1989) Cross Border Aircraft Leasing; Clifford Chance, London; Hall, Simon A. D. (Editor) (1993) Aircraft Financing – Second Edition; Euromoney Books, London.

the transaction with Japanese financial institutions. The institution would then assume the Yen obligations under the lease (effectively eliminating the cash and currency exposure of the lessee). This arrangement represented a defeasance of the Yen liability by the lessee.

The deposit taking institution, in order to hedge the interest rate exposure under this arrangement, hedged using the following transactions:

- Entering into a Yen interest rate swap where it made periodic payments of Yen LIBOR (usually matching income generated by depositing the Yen on a short term basis) in exchange for a receipt of a lump sum at maturity matching the payment to be made under the lease.
- Non Japanese institutions used the Yen deposit to generate low cost US$ funding by entering into a Yen zero coupon/US$ floating LIBOR currency swap. Under the swap, it received the Yen zero amount (required to service its commitment under the lease) and paid floating rate US$ LIBOR (usually at a margin under LIBOR).

As the lessees grew in sophistication, a number of them bypassed the deposit process and entered into the Yen zero coupon/US$ LIBOR swap directly. This allowed the lessees to insulate themselves from any currency exposure, as the zero JPY amount received under the currency swap at maturity effectively matched the cash outflow under the lease payments.

Tax Driven Applications

Tax driven applications of structured cash flow swaps are based on the different treatment of derivative payments and traditional securities/transactions in a number of jurisdictions. For example, derivative payments/receipts may be treated on a cash basis rather than the accrual basis for traditional securities. Where taxation on derivative payments is on a cash basis, deductions (assessable income) on payments (receipts) arise when the payment is incurred. This allows the use of swap transactions to accelerate or defer cash flows to manage tax liabilities[46].

Capital Market Transaction Driven Applications

Structured coupon swaps are frequently required in relation to capital market issues where the coupon structure is not standard. This includes different structures such as zero coupon bonds, graduated coupon bonds or premium/discount bond structures. The bonds are generally created to meet demand from investors seeking protection from reinvestment risks or seeking to take advantage of the tax treatment on discounts or premiums[47]. Issuers of the bonds generally seek

---

[46] For a detailed discussion of these types of applications of structured cash flow swaps, see Das, Satyajit (2004) Structured Products Volume 2; John Wiley & Sons (Asia), Singapore at Chapter 19.

[47] See Das, Satyajit "Zero Coupon Securities" (1987 No. 1) Bulletin of Money, Banking and Finance 1–51.

protection from the coupon structure. This requires the development of structured cash flow swaps designed to insulate the issuer from the cash flow structure of the issue.

Issues of zero coupon bonds in the capital market have taken place at various periods. In the 1980s, yields on zero coupon Eurodollar bonds were significantly lower than normal coupon conventional bonds. This reflected strong demand by foreign investors wanting to lock in relatively high US$ interest rates (avoiding the reinvestment rate risk implicit in a normal coupon paid bond) or take advantage of favourable tax treatment of the discount. For example, in August 1984 a high credit quality borrower could issue a 10 year Eurodollar bond at an all-in cost of 30 bps pa over the comparable United States Treasury bond. The issue could be swapped into floating rate at a cost of 25 bps under LIBOR. The same issuer could issue a 10 year Eurodollar zero coupon bond at an all-in cost of at least 60 bps pa *below* the comparable United States Treasury. Similar opportunities to issue zero coupon bonds have occurred at various times in other currencies including Pound Sterling, Deutschemarks, Lira, Spanish Pesetas, Yen, A$, NZ$ and South African Rand.

Issuers of zero coupon bonds are attracted by the significant interest cost saving on the zero coupon bond. The issuer generally does not want exposure to the zero coupon structure. The issuer will generally enter into a swap to re-profile the cash flow of the issue. This will generally be in the form of structured cash flow swaps to convert the zero coupon fixed rate into floating rate either in the same currency or into US$ LIBOR based funding.

The design of the structured cash flow swaps against zero coupon capital market issues will usually take the following forms:

- **Interest rate swaps** – this is where the issue is being swapped into floating rate in the same currency. This will entail a normal zero coupon swap where the fixed rate coupons are accrued and compounded over the maturity of the swap. The fixed rate amount (the swap coupons and accrued interest) is paid at maturity to match the coupon on the zero coupon bond. The notional principal of the swap is based on the present value or proceeds of the bond issue. Structured swaps against the zero coupon bond issue are also undertaken. **Exhibit 13.22** sets out examples of two structured forms of zero coupon interest rate swaps. All transactions are designed to enable an issuer to issue zero coupon bonds and to enter into swaps such that the borrower's net cash flow is that of a conventional floating rate funding transaction.
- **Currency swaps** – this type of transaction entails entry into a cross currency swap where the fixed rate (in a non US$ currency) is paid on a zero coupon basis against regular fixed or floating rate payments in US$. The transaction would be

used to hedge a zero coupon bond in a foreign currency into US$. The currency swap can be transacted as either a fixed zero coupon in the foreign currency/fixed or floating rate US$ swap or a currency forward contract. **Exhibit 13.23** sets out an example of a zero coupon currency swap transacted against an A$ zero coupon bond. **Exhibit 13.24** sets out the structuring of a zero coupon currency swap against a new issue.

Other types of non-standard coupon capital market issues requiring a structured coupon swap to convert/hedge the bond cash flows include:

• **Deferred coupon bonds** – these are architecturally similar to zero coupon bonds. Deferred coupon bonds entail the issue of a security with a maturity of 7 years and a coupon of 8.00% pa. The issue structure requires a payment of the coupon for the first four years and at the end of that period, as a rolled up lump sum of 32.00% of the principal value of the bond with level 8.00% pa coupon payments thereafter. The structure was designed to circumvent regulations against the purchase of zero coupon securities by investors. The deferred coupon bonds had similar cash flow characteristics to zero coupon bonds for the first part of its maturity. Swap structures similar to those utilised with zero coupon bonds are used to swap these types of issues.

• **Deferred coupon FRNs** – these structures emerged in early 1986. Typical issues had a maturity of approximately five years. The coupon structure required that the issuer made no coupon payment for the first 2 years but paid a relatively high margin of say 4.50% pa over 6 month LIBOR for years 3 to 5. The security issues were tailor-made for investors presumably seeking to defer income into future periods. The issuers of deferred coupon FRNs entered into swaps to obtain LIBOR based funding. The swap structure entailed the dealer covering the cash flows under the security issue in return for receiving a substantial margin under LIBOR throughout the 5 years. Under the structure, the dealer has a positive cash flow initially followed by a negative cash flow. In effect, the dealer uses the cash flow surplus to finance the larger cash flows in the later part of the transaction. The swap transaction takes the form of a deposit that is returned with interest in the later years. A variation on the deferred coupon FRN structure is the high initial spread FRN. This reverses the cash flow pattern with large payments in the early years and no/very low payments in the distant years. These transactions were swapped, providing the opposite problem for the dealer. The dealer was required to fund large payments in the early years that were recovered in the latter half of the transaction.

Exhibit 13.22   Structured Zero Coupon Interest Rate Swaps Against Bond Issues

Structure 1

The transaction outlined entails the borrower issuing a zero coupon 10 year bond. The bond has net proceeds of US$50 million and face value of US$135.7 million. The bond yield is 10.50% pa annual.

The zero coupon issue is then swapped in two stages:

- **Transaction A** – the issuer enters into a conventional interest rate swap with a dealer A. The swap is based on a notional principal amount of US$50 million for 10 years. The issuer pays floating rate interest at a margin under LIBOR and receives fixed rate interest payments at a rate of 10.60% pa annual.
- **Transaction B** – the issuer reinvests the fixed interest rate payments received under the interest rate swap. This is to guarantee a maturity value equal to the face value of the bonds to repay the bond holders at maturity. The issuer entered into a commitment to deposit each fixed rate interest receipt under the swap with a bank. The bank, in turn, enters into an interest rate swap (with a dealer B) to fix the yield on the floating rate deposit. The size of the deposit increases and the corresponding notional principal under the swap increases over the term of the transaction. The swap with dealer B enables the bank to guarantee the issuer a fixed rate on its deposits which continue to roll forward until the final maturity of the bond.

The structure is set out below:

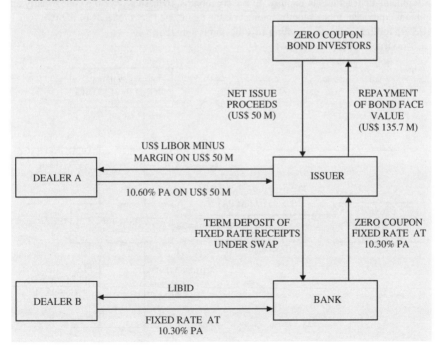

Structure 2

This structure entails two separate issues:

- **Issue A** – this is an issue of zero coupon 10 year bonds. The bond net proceeds are US$29.4 million (after fees). The face value is US$95 million. The yield on the bond is 12.44% pa on an annual basis.
- **Issue B** – this is an annuity loan (usually arranged as a private placement). The loan is repaid at the end of each year until maturity by equal level repayments composed of interest and annual redemption of principal. This would entail a 10 year loan for US$65.6 million repayable by annual instalments of US$11.54 million which equates to an interest rate of 11.85% pa annual.

The two issues provide the issuer with total net proceeds of US$95 million (net proceeds US$29.4 million from the zero coupon bond issue and net proceeds of US$65.6 million from the annuity loan). The issuer has an annual commitment for 9 payments of US$11.54 million (corresponding to the interest and principal repayments under the annuity loan). The issuer must make a final repayment of US$106.54 million after 10 years (the repayment of the US$95 million face value of the zero coupon issue and the final US$11.54 million instalment of the annuity loan). The overall package implies a net interest cost to the issuer of 12.81% pa annual.

The issuer undertakes a conventional interest rate swap transaction with a dealer. On each annual interest date, the dealer pays the issuer US$11.54 million, corresponding to the instalments under the loan annuity. Every six months, the issuer pays the counterparty an amount equivalent to six months interest on the aggregated net proceeds of the two issues (US$95 million) at a rate equalling LIBOR minus a margin.

The structure is set out below:

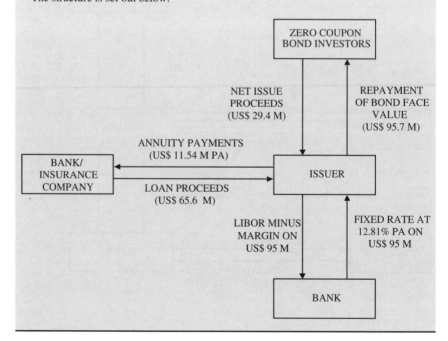

Exhibit 13.23   Zero Coupon Currency Swaps

The transaction depicted is an A$200 million zero coupon A$ Eurobond issue and associated currency swap and currency forward transaction undertaken by Eastman Kodak Company in early 1987. The transaction entailed 2 separate swap transactions to convert the issuer's A$ zero coupon exposure into fixed rate US$. Part of the issue proceeds were hedged into A$ using LTFX contracts.

INITIAL EXCHANGE

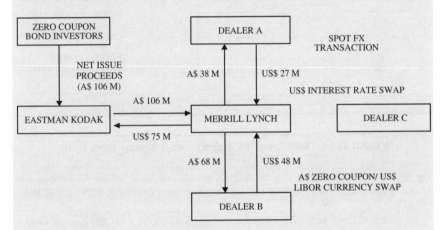

SPOT EXCHANGE RATE IS A$ 1.00: US$ 0.7075

PERIODIC PAYMENTS

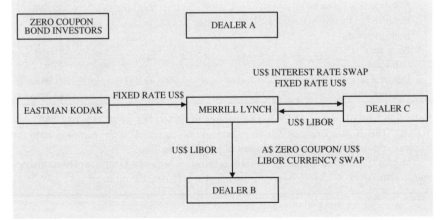

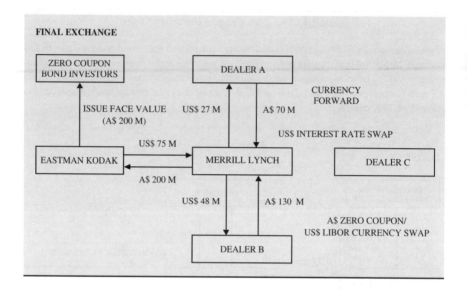

Exhibit 13.24   Zero Coupon Currency Swaps Against Bond Issues

The objective in this example is to derive the available yield on a zero coupon new issue denominated in NZ$ that will provide the issuer with funding at US$ LIBOR minus 25 bps pa.

Assume that the 5 year zero swap rate for fixed NZ$/US$ LIBOR currency swap is 16.50% pa annual and the current spot exchange rate is NZ$1/US$0.58.

A NZ$ 5 year zero coupon issue with face value of NZ$100 million yielding 16.50% pa annual would have proceeds of NZ$46.598 million (US$27.027 million).

All-in pricing of the new NZ$ issue is calculated as follows:

	US$ million	NZ$ million
Net proceeds (at swap rate)	27.027	46.598
Reserve fund to generate sub LIBOR funding	0.270	0.465
Issue expenses	0.125	0.216
Issue fees		0.659
Sub-total		47.938
Dealer's profit	0.500	0.862
Net proceeds		48.800

Note: Sub-LIBOR margin of 25 bps pa equates to US$67,568 pa (0.25% of US$27.027 million). This is discounted at 8.00% pa annual (the current US$ 5 year swap rate) for 5 years to produce a present value amount of US$0.270 million.

The gross proceeds required for the issue is therefore NZ$48.800 million. This translates into an issue yield of 15.43% pa annual for a 5 year NZ$100 million issue.

7 Structured Swaps

7.1 Concept

Structured swaps are essentially non-standard "packaged" swap products. The structures primarily entail combinations of swaps and other derivative instruments (typically forward and option positions). The linkages may be within the same asset class (an interest rate swap with engineered exposure to interest rates) or across asset classes (an interest rate swap with embedded currency or commodity exposure).

Structured swaps are driven by the efforts of dealers to "bundle" or "package" derivative products for clients. This is referred to as *financial engineering* or *risk management/hedging solutions*. In reality, structured swaps are motivated by a number of factors:

• Repackage (from a cosmetic perspective) existing products to increase margins and/or enable the existing products to be marketed in a different manner[48].

• Disguise the cost of the structure or product from the counterparty by reducing structural and pricing transparency[49].

• Enable investors and borrowers to circumvent restrictions on the ability to transact in derivatives or enter into specific types of transactions[50].

• Generate (somewhat infrequently) genuine innovative solutions to asset liability management requirements of the investors and borrowers and thereby create value.

The analysis of structured swaps and hybrid instruments is complicated by several factors:

• The structures are customised to individual user specifications.

• The nomenclature of the structures is highly individualised. Individual dealers use their own trademark names for specific structures.

• The structures are frequently undertaken confidentially for competitive reasons.

---

[48] This is similar to the motivations driving packaged forward and options (see Chapter 6) and packaged exotic options (see Chapters 9 and 10).

[49] This is similar to the motivations driving packaged forward and options (see Chapter 6) and packaged exotic options (see Chapters 9 and 10).

[50] This is similar to the motivations driving structured notes; see Chapter 4.

7.2 Structured Swaps – Examples

In the following Sections, some examples of structured swaps are examined. It should be noted that the structures examined are by no means comprehensive. The structures outlined are merely indicative of the structuring possibilities available to satisfy individual risk management requirements[51].

Examples of structured swaps include the following types of transactions:

- **Disguised (hidden) optionality** – this entails transactions where the counterparty enters into a swap that is, in effect, a disguised option. **Exhibit 13.25** sets out an example of a flexible swap that is, in effect, a disguised sold floor position. **Exhibit 13.26** sets out an example of a variable swap that is, in effect, also a disguised sold floor position.

- **Swaps combined with forwards/ordinary or exotic options** – this entails traditional swaps or similar derivative transactions where the pay-off is adjusted by embedding additional forwards or options within the structure. Packaged options (both conventional and exotic options) are examples of this type of structure[52]. Other examples of this type of structure include swap/swaption combinations[53]. **Exhibit 6.5** sets out an example of a participating swap or cap that entails the combination of a swap with a purchased floor. **Exhibit 13.27** sets out an example of a window swap that combines a swap with a conventional floor spread. **Exhibit 13.28** sets out an example of a super floater swap that combines a ratio option spread with a conventional interest rate swap. **Exhibit 13.29** sets out an example of a two tier cap that combines a traditional cap with a barrier cap spread.

- **Cross market structures** – this involves structures where an interest rate swap may be combined with embedded currency or commodity exposure. It may also entail currency structures with embedded interest rate exposures. **Exhibit 13.30** sets out an example of a currency linked interest rate swap. **Exhibit 13.31** sets out an example of a currency swap with embedded yield curve optionality. **Exhibit 13.32** sets out an example of a currency option with a floating interest rate structure.

---

[51] See Chapters 6, 9 and 10. See also McKeith, Colin and L'Estrange, Jim "Variations on Conventional Swap Structures - Swap Option Combination" in Das, Satyajit (Editor) (1991) Global Swaps Markets; IFR Publishing, London at Chapter 20; (1999) Structured Risk Management Products; National Australia Bank, Melbourne.

[52] See Chapters 6, 9 and 10.

[53] See Chapter 15.

Exhibit 13.25   Structured Swaps – Flexible Swaps[54]

1. Concept

The flexible swap structure evolved in response to borrowers seeking to take advantage of expectations of a gradual decline in interest rates in the relevant currency. The borrowers were reluctant to enter into interest rate swaps at the prevailing level as they believed interest rates would decline over the relevant time horizon. The borrowers were often not allowed to sell interest rate options.

The flexible swap structure operated as follows:
- The dealer paid the client a floating rate (3 or 6 month LIBOR).
- The borrower paid the higher of a floating rate (3 or 6 month LIBOR) minus a margin or a fixed rate. The dealer had the alternative payment receipt rights at each coupon date over the life of the transaction.

From the viewpoint of the borrower, if interest rates behaved in accordance with its expectations and decreased gradually, the borrower's cost of funds was reduced until such time as rates fell below the fixed rate under the flexible swap. The fixed rate that the borrower would be required to pay was significantly lower than the swap rate for the equivalent maturity prevailing at the time the transaction was entered into. In the event that interest rates increased, the borrower paid a margin under the floating rate index. The borrower had minimal protection against higher short term interest rates.

Analytically, the flexible swap structure was identical to the sale of a floor at the implicit fixed rate by the borrower to the dealer. The amortised premium for the sold floor was incorporated into the margin under the floating rate index.

2. Example

Assume that company A has floating rate debt priced off 6 month LIBOR. Swap rates for three years (the hedging time horizon) are 6.00% pa payable semi-annually. Currently 6 month LIBOR is 5.00% pa. A expects that 6 month LIBOR rates will decline gradually over the next 3 years to around 4.50% pa.

The company wishes to hedge but is concerned about locking in current swap rates. The company is also concerned about the current difference between 6 month LIBOR and the swap rate. This is because entering into the swap will lock in a negative carry of around 1.00% pa (6.0% minus 5.00% pa). The company enters into a 3 year flexible swap to hedge its interest rate exposure.

The flexible swap is structured as follows:
- The company receives LIBOR from the dealer every semi-annual settlement date.
- At each semi-annual settlement date, the company pays the higher of fixed rate of 4.50% pa or floating rate of 6 month LIBOR less 25 bps pa.

Under the flexible swap, the company has an interest cost of:
- 4.50% pa if LIBOR is equal to/falls below 4.50% pa.
- LIBOR minus 25 bps if rates are above 4.50% pa.

---

[54] See Curry, David "Bend the Rate with a Flexible Swap" (June 1991) Corporate Finance 48.

The company's interest cost under this structure is summarised in the Table below. The company's borrowing costs are set out on three bases: unhedged floating rate (LIBOR); fixed rate (3 year swap rate); and the flexible swap.

6 Month LIBOR (% pa)	Unhedged Borrowing Cost (% pa)	Interest Rate Swap (% pa)	Flexible Swap (% pa)
3.00	3.00	6.00	4.50
3.50	3.50	6.00	4.50
4.00	4.00	6.00	4.50
4.50	4.50	6.00	4.50
5.00	5.00	6.00	4.75
5.50	5.50	6.00	5.25
6.00	6.00	6.00	5.75
6.50	6.50	6.00	6.25
7.00	7.00	6.00	6.75
7.50	7.50	6.00	7.25
8.00	8.00	6.00	7.75

The pay-off is set out in the form of a graph below:

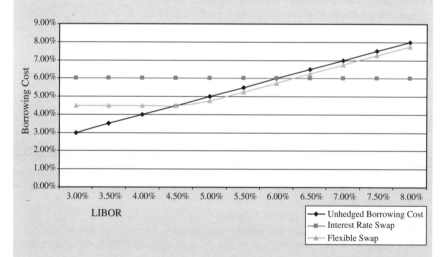

The company benefits most where LIBOR rates are above 4.50% pa and below 6.25% pa. The flexible swap transaction is equivalent to the sale of a floor by A to the dealer with a strike price of 4.75% (the flexible swap rate minus the flexible swap margin (25 bps pa)). The premium received is equivalent (on an amortised basis) of 25 bps pa.

Exhibit 13.26   Structured Swaps – Variable Swaps

1. Concept

The variable swap is similar to the flexible swap. The variable swap entails a sold floor position embedded in a swap. The structure involves the following cash flows:

- The dealer pays the client 3 or 6 month LIBOR.
- The borrower pays the higher of 3 or 6 month LIBOR minus a margin or 2 times LIBOR minus a fixed rate. The dealer has the alternative payment receipt rights at each coupon date over the life of the transaction.

Analytically, the variable swap structure is identical to the sale of a floor at the implicit fixed rate by the borrower to the dealer. The amortised premium for the sold floor is incorporated into the margin under the floating rate index.

2. Example

Assume a company enters into the following variable rate swap:

- The company receives LIBOR from the dealer every semi-annual settlement date.
- At each semi-annual settlement date, the company pays the higher of 6 month LIBOR less 20 bps pa or 2 times 6 month LIBOR minus 6.00% pa.

Under the variable swap, the company has an interest cost of:

- 6.00% pa if LIBOR is equal to/falls below 6.20% pa.
- LIBOR minus 20 bps if rates are above 6.20% pa.

The company's interest cost under this structure is summarised in the Table below. The company's borrowing costs are set out on three bases: unhedged floating rate (LIBOR); fixed rate (3 year swap rate of 6.50 % pa); and the flexible swap.

6 Month LIBOR (% pa)	Unhedged Borrowing Cost (% pa)	Interest Rate Swap (% pa)	Flexible Swap (% pa)
3.00	3.00	6.50	6.00
3.50	3.50	6.50	6.00
4.00	4.00	6.50	6.00
4.50	4.50	6.50	6.00
5.00	5.00	6.50	6.00
5.50	5.50	6.50	6.00
6.00	6.00	6.50	6.00
6.50	6.50	6.50	6.30
7.00	7.00	6.50	6.80
7.50	7.50	6.50	7.30
8.00	8.00	6.50	7.80

The pay-off is set out in the form of a graph below:

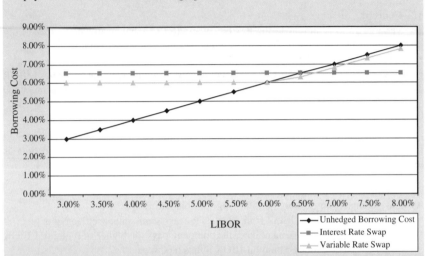

The flexible swap transaction is equivalent to the sale of a floor by A to the dealer with a strike price of 6.20%. The premium received is equivalent (on an amortised basis) of 20 bps pa.

Exhibit 13.27   Structured Swaps – Window Swaps[55]

1. Concept

The window swap structure is designed to provide borrowers with fixed rates under an interest rate swap, with protection against lower short term interest rates up to a prescribed level. The structure allows the borrower to fix rates while maintaining the ability to benefit from lower rates in an agreed "window". The structure is designed to lower the cost of fixing rates in a positive yield curve environment and to monetise expectations of steady/lower short term rates within the "window" range.

The window swap is similar to a participation swap or cap structure. The structure combines a normal interest rate swap (where the borrower is paying fixed) with a floor

---

[55] See (1999) Structured Risk Management Products; National Australia Bank, Melbourne at 10–11.

spread (bought floor at a strike equal to the swap rate and a sold floor at the lower end of the range). The floor spread is paid for through a higher swap rate.

2. Example

Assume a company has floating rate debt priced off 6 month LIBOR. Current swap rates for 3 years (the hedging time horizon) are 6.00% pa payable semi-annually. Currently 6 month LIBOR is 5.50% pa. The company expects that 6 month LIBOR rates will decline gradually over the next 3 years to around 5.00% pa.

The company wishes to hedge but is concerned about locking in current swap rates. The company is also concerned about the current difference between 6 month LIBOR and the swap rate. This is because entering into the swap will lock in a negative carry of around 0.50% pa (6.0% minus 5.50% pa). The company enters into a 3 year window swap to hedge its interest rate exposure.

The flexible swap is structured as follows:
- The company receives LIBOR from the dealer every semi-annual settlement date.
- At each semi-annual settlement date, the company pays the following rates:
  1. If LIBOR fixes above 6.50% pa, then the company pays 6.50% pa.
  2. If LIBOR fixes below 6.50% pa and above 5.00% pa, then the company pays LIBOR.
  3. If LIBOR fixes below 5.00% pa, then the company pays 6.50% pa.

Under the flexible swap, the company has an interest cost of:
- 6.50% pa, if LIBOR is above 6.50% pa or below 5.00% pa.
- LIBOR, if LIBOR is above 5.00% pa and below 6.50% pa.

The company's interest cost under this structure is summarised in the Table below. The company's borrowing costs are set out on three bases: unhedged floating rate (LIBOR); fixed rate (3 year swap rate); and the flexible swap.

6 Month LIBOR (% pa)	Interest Rate Swap (% pa)	Window Swap (% pa)
3.00	6.00	6.50
3.50	6.00	6.50
4.00	6.00	6.50
4.50	6.00	6.50
5.00	6.00	6.50
5.50	6.00	5.50
6.00	6.00	6.00
6.50	6.00	6.50
7.00	6.00	6.50
7.50	6.00	6.50
8.00	6.00	6.50

The pay-off is set out in the form of a graph below:

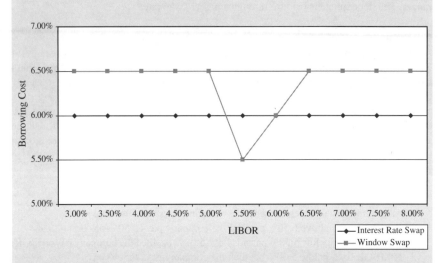

The company benefits most where LIBOR rates are above 5.00% pa and below 6.00% pa (relative to the conventional swap strategy). The structure allows the borrower to remain protected against increases in interest rates, but allows participation in lower short term rates within the window range.

The window swap transaction is equivalent to the entry into a swap where the company pays fixed rate of 6.50% pa and receives LIBOR. The swap is combined with the purchase of a floor with a strike of 6.50% pa. The bought floor allows the company to participate in falls in interest rates below 6.50% pa. The company simultaneously sells a series of barrier options on each of the floor-lets. The barrier option are knock-in floors with a strike of 6.50% pa and a instrike of 5.00% pa. If LIBOR trades at our below 5.00% pa, then the company enters into a sold floor that offsets the bought floor. The sold option reduces the net cost of the bought floor. The net premium cost for the floor spread is paid by way of the higher swap rate. The floors are on a face value amount equivalent to the notional principal of the swap.

Exhibit 13.28   Structured Swaps – Super Floater Swaps

1. Concept

The super floater swap structure is used by borrowers seeking protection against higher interest rates. The structure operates as follows:

- The borrower pays the fixed rate under the swap and receives floating rates (LIBOR).
- The borrower also selects an upper and lower strike rate. The floating payments on the reset dates under the swap are scaled (by a preselected multiplier) relative to the level of the floating rate.

The operation of the structure is as follows:
- If floating interest rates increase above the upper strike level and the multiplier factor is 2, then for each basis point that floating rates increase above the selected strike, the borrower would receive a 2 basis point increase in the floating rate received.
- If floating interest rates fall below the lower strike rate and the multiplier factor is 1.5, then the floating rate received by the borrower will decrease by 1.5 bps for every 1 bps that short term rates are below the lower strike.

In effect, the borrower's cost increases as rates fall below the lower strike band, but decreases as rates increase above the upper strike level. The structure is designed to provide interest rate protection with significant reductions in borrowing costs where there are increases in short-term rates. The structure is attractive for borrowers anticipating sharp rises in short term floating rates.

Analytically, the super floater structure combines a conventional interest rate swap (the borrower pays fixed rate and receives floating rates) and the purchase of a cap at the upper strike level and the sale of a floor at the lower strike level. Notional principal values of the cap and floor are determined by the selected multiplier. The cap and floor (adjusted for the multiplier) are structured on a zero premium cost basis.

A number of variations on the basic structure are feasible. A super floater structure can be structured with the swap rate payable being set at a level below the current swap rate. The lower swap cost is generated by structuring the options to generate net premium (the sold floors result in a higher premium than the purchased cap). The net premium income can be created by manipulating the face value of the options (the multiplier) and/or the strike of the cap and floor.

This structure developed in an environment where borrowers expected floating interest rates to increase sharply. The structure is flexible and can be tailored to suit individual borrowers' requirements. A major advantage is that the super floater can be reversed at any time. For example, if short term interest rates increase sharply, then the floor component of the super floater structure could be repurchased at minimal cost. This would eliminate the cost incurred if interest rates were to fall over the life of the transaction.

2. Example

Assume a company is a floating rate borrower with liabilities priced off LIBOR. The company anticipates that short-term interest rates will rise.

The company enters into a super floater swap to hedge its borrowing costs on the following terms:
- Maturity: 2 years
- Swap payments payable semi-annually:
  1. The company pays fixed rate of 6.00% pa payable semi-annually.
  2. The company receives 6 month LIBOR subject to the super floater conditions.
- Super Floater Terms:
  1. Upper Strike: 8.50% pa
  2. Upper Multiplier: 2
  3. Lower Strike: 4.00% pa
  4. Lower Multiplier: 1.5

Under the super floater swap, the company's cash flows are as follows:
- The company pays the fixed rate of 6.00% pa.
- The company receives LIBOR under the swap as calculated below:
  1. If LIBOR is between 4.00% pa and 8.50% pa, then the company receives LIBOR rate.
  2. If LIBOR is higher than 8.50% pa (say 9.50% pa), then the company receives the following adjusted floating rate: $8.50 + [2 \times (9.50 - 8.50)] = 10.50\%$ pa.
  3. If LIBOR is less than 4.00% pa (say 3.00% pa), then the company receives the following adjusted floating rate: $4.00 - [1.5 \times (4.00 - 3.00)] = 2.50\%$ pa.

Under the super floater swap, the company's borrowing cost is as follows:
- If LIBOR is between 4.00% and 8.50% (the upper and lower strike level), then the company's cost is 6.00% pa (the swap rate).
- If LIBOR increases above the upper strike level of 8.50%, then the higher floating rate receipts reduce the cost of the swap fixed rate.
- If LIBOR decreases below 4.00%, then the reduced floating rate receipts increase the cost of the swap fixed rate.

The company's interest cost under this structure is summarised in the Table below. The company's borrowing costs are set out on two bases: unhedged floating rate (LIBOR) and the super floater swap.

Floating Rate (% pa)	Unhedged Borrowing Cost (% pa)	Super Floater Swap-Fixed Rate Payment (% pa)	Super Floater Swap-Floating Rate Receipts (% pa)	Super Floater Swap-Effective Cost (% pa)
2.00	2.00	6.00	1.00	7.00
2.50	2.50	6.00	1.75	6.75
3.00	3.00	6.00	2.50	6.50
3.50	3.50	6.00	3.25	6.25
4.00	4.00	6.00	4.00	6.00
4.50	4.50	6.00	4.50	6.00
5.00	5.00	6.00	5.00	6.00
5.50	5.50	6.00	5.50	6.00
6.00	6.00	6.00	6.00	6.00
6.50	6.50	6.00	6.50	6.00
7.00	7.00	6.00	7.00	6.00
7.50	7.50	6.00	7.50	6.00
8.00	8.00	6.00	8.00	6.00
8.50	8.50	6.00	8.50	6.00
9.00	9.00	6.00	9.50	5.50
9.50	9.50	6.00	10.50	5.00
10.00	10.00	6.00	11.50	4.50
10.50	10.50	6.00	12.50	4.00

The pay-off is set out in the form of a graph below:

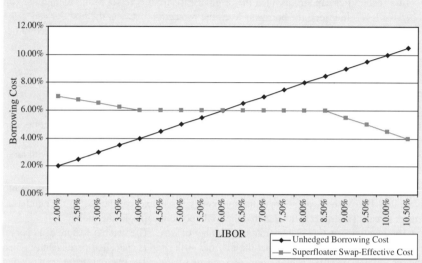

The company benefits most where LIBOR rates are above 6.00% pa (relative to the conventional swap strategy).

The super floater swap transaction is equivalent to the entry into a swap where the company pays the fixed rate of 6.00% pa and receives LIBOR. The swap is combined with the purchase of a cap with a strike of 8.50% pa and the sale of a floor with a strike of 4.00% pa. There is no net premium cost for the cap and floor. The zero cost of the option is created by adjusting the face value of the options. The purchased cap is on a face value amount equivalent to two times (the upper strike multiplier) the notional principal of the swap. The floor is on a face value amount equivalent to 1.5 times (the lower strike multiplier) the notional principal of the swap.

Exhibit 13.29   Structured Swaps – Two Tier Cap[56]

1. Concept

The two tier cap reduces the premium cost of an interest rate cap by monetising expectations of short term rates remaining at current levels or increasing above current levels, but not above a pre-specified level.

The structure operates as follows:

- The borrower purchases a cap at a specified strike rate (the first tier cap strike). The cap operates conventionally.

---

[56] See (1999) Structured Risk Management Products; National Australia Bank, Melbourne at 6–7.

- If short term rates rise above the first tier cap strike and reach an agreed higher strike rate (the second tier cap strike), then the original cap strike is re-set to the second tier cap strike level. In effect, the borrower loses the protection between the first tier cap strike and the second tier strike rate. The cap then operates conventionally at the second tier cap strike level.
- The two tier structure results in the cap premium being significantly lower than for a conventional cap with a strike set at the first tier cap strike level.

The structure can be decomposed into:
1. Purchase of a conventional cap with a strike equal to the first tier cap strike.
2. Sale of a knock in cap (on identical terms) with an instrike equal to the second tier cap strike.
3. Purchase of knock in cap with strike price equal to the second tier cap strike with an in strike equal to the second tier cap strike[57].

The total premium cost is the sum of the 3 option premiums. The reduction of the premium is achieved because the premium of the sold knock in cap exceeds the cost of the purchased knock in cap. This reflects the fact that the sold knock in cap is in-the-money.

The two tier structure can operate in a number of ways. The two tier feature can operate on a one-off basis. This means that the first tier strike cap is cancelled permanently when the second tier cap strike is hit *on any interest rate set date*. The two tier feature can operate on *each interest rate set date*. This means that the first tier strike cap is only cancelled for the specific interest period.

2. Example

Assume a company wishes to hedge its LIBOR based borrowing. The company can purchase a 3 year conventional cap on 3 month LIBOR with a strike rate of 6.00% pa for 1.22% (equivalent to 45 bps pa). The company purchases a two tier cap on 3 month LIBOR with a first tier strike of 6.00% pa and a second tier strike of 7.50% pa for 0.75% (equivalent to 28 bps pa).

The two tier cap structure operates as follows on each interest rate set date:
- If LIBOR is below 6.00%, then the cap does not operate and the company's borrowing cost is current LIBOR.
- If LIBOR is above 6.00% but below 7.50%, then the cap pays the difference between LIBOR and 6.00% and the company's borrowing cost is capped at 6.00% pa.
- If LIBOR is above 7.50% pa, then the cap with a strike at 6.00% is cancelled. The cap strike is reset at 7.50% pa. The cap pays the difference between LIBOR and 7.50% and the company's borrowing cost is capped at 7.50% pa.

The two tier cap has a significantly lower premium cost. The structure provides identical protection to a conventional cap as long as rates do not increase above 7.50% pa.

The premium saving of 47 bps is equivalent to the extra interest cost of around 3 quarterly periods at the second tier cap level. In effect, unless LIBOR sets at the second tier cap level for at least 3 of the 12 quarterly periods, the two tier cap will provide the company with cost savings.

---

[57] For a discussion of barrier options, see Chapter 9.

Exhibit 13.30   Structured Swaps – Currency Indexed Swaps

1. Concept

The currency indexed swap (also known as the dual coupon swap) combines an interest rate swap with a strip of currency options. The fixed rate on the swap is reduced in consideration for payments being made either in the base currency or a nominated alternative currency at a predetermined exchange rate. The structure uses the premium received on the sold currency options embedded in the coupons to lower the fixed rate payable under the swap.

2. Example

Assume a company has A$100 million of floating rate debt. The company wants to swap the debt into fixed rate for 3 years to fix the borrowing. The current three year A$ swap rate is 7.50% pa payable quarterly.

In order to lower the swap fixed rate, the company enters into a currency indexed swap on the following terms:

- The company receives floating rate (A$ bank bill rates).
- The company pays a fixed rate 6.50% pa payable quarterly (below the current market swap rate).
- The company's fixed rate payments are indexed to a currency exchange rate of A$1:US$0.6000 (currency index level).

The fixed rate payment under the currency indexed swap at each quarterly payment date is calculated as follows:

- If A$ appreciates above the currency index level (exchange rate above A$1:US$0.60 then the company pays 6.50% pa on A$100 million as under a conventional swap. The payment is A$1,625,000 (calculated as A$100 million × 6.50%× 0.25).
- If the A$ depreciates below the currency index level (exchange rate below A$1:US$0.60) then the company must pay either:
  1. US$ equivalent of A$1,625,000 at A$1.00:US$0.60, that is,US$975,000; or
  2. A$ equivalent of US$975,000 at the exchange rate current on the payment date. For example if A$1:US$0.55) then the company must pay A$1,772,727.

The borrowing cost of the company (in A$ terms) is either 6.50% pa or higher if the A$ declines in value below the currency index level. The Table below sets out the interest cost of the company at varying A$/US$ exchange rate levels. The company gains when the exchange rate at each payment date averages above A$1:US$0.5200.

Exchange Rate (A$1:US$)	Fixed Rate Payment (A$)	Fixed Rate Payment (US$)	Effective Borrowing Cost (% pa)
0.6500	1,625,000	975,000	6.50
0.6400	1,625,000	975,000	6.50
0.6300	1,625,000	975,000	6.50
0.6200	1,625,000	975,000	6.50
0.6100	1,625,000	975,000	6.50
0.6000	1,625,000	975,000	6.50
0.5900	1,652,542	975,000	6.61

Exchange Rate (A$1:US$)	Fixed Rate Payment (A$)	Fixed Rate Payment (US$)	Effective Borrowing Cost (% pa)
0.5800	1,681,034	975,000	6.72
0.5700	1,710,526	975,000	6.84
0.5600	1,741,071	975,000	6.96
0.5500	1,772,727	975,000	7.09
0.5400	1,805,556	975,000	7.22
0.5300	1,839,623	975,000	7.36
0.5200	1,875,000	975,000	7.50
0.5100	1,911,765	975,000	7.65
0.5000	1,950,000	975,000	7.80

The pay-off is set out in the form of a graph below:

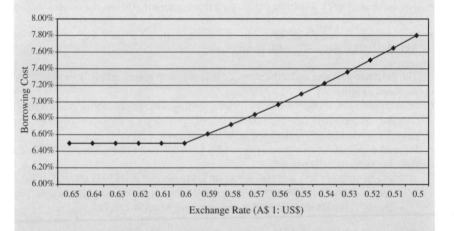

The currency indexed swap entails the company writing a series of 12 A$ put/US$ call options with a strike price set at A$1:US$0.60. The options have expiry dates coinciding with the interest payment dates under the swap. Each currency option is on A$ face value of A$1,625,000. The premium received for selling the currency options is used to reduce the swap rate by 1.00% pa.

If the company is an exporter with underlying US$ receivables, then it is a natural buyer of A$. This means that where the exchange rate is below the currency index level, the company can service the swap payments from its US$ receivables. The company must be prepared to purchase A$ at US$0.60 and suffer any opportunity loss where the A$ declines below this level. In effect, the company trades off the exchange rate loss against the lower swap fixed rate. Where the exchange rate is above the currency index level, the embedded options are not exercised. In this case, the company sells its US$ receivables at the prevailing exchange rate.

Exhibit 13.31   Structured Swaps – Currency Swap with Yield Curve Option

This structure combines a conventional cross currency swap with a yield curve differential option[58]. Under the structure, a conventional cross currency swap is combined with an option which pays an agreed amount of US$ for each basis point by which the difference between the Sterling ("GBP") 5 year swap rate exceeds US$ 5 year swap rates. The combination of the yield curve option with the cross currency swap allows the company entering into this transaction to improve the cost of the swap. This reduction in cost is achieved by the cash flow generated by entering the swap (where the company is paying GBP/receiving US$, reflecting the rate differential in favour of the GBP at the relevant time).

This type of structure can be used by a company with substantial net assets/equity in GBP that is therefore exposed to changes in the US$/GBP exchange rate. The company can use a conventional cross currency swap (where it pays GBP) to hedge this balance sheet exposure. In effect, the combination of the swap and the option enables the currency hedging cost to be lowered where high GBP interest rates would make the hedging cost high.

Exhibit 13.32   Structured Currency Options – Option with Floating Interest Rate Structure

1. Concept

Long dated currency forwards or option transactions are based on fixed *interest rates* in both currencies. For example, dealer quotes for a currency option are based on the existing and fixed interest differential between the fixed rates in the relevant currencies. Similarly, corporations entering into forward FX contracts for long tenors are based on fixed rates in both currencies. The party hedging may prefer to transact on the basis of a floating interest rate for one or both of the currencies.

The trader may seek to use floating rates for the following reasons:

• Expectations on interest rates.
• Floating rates provide a better hedge of the underlying exposure.

A structured currency option can modify the option structure and base the price on a floating interest rate.

Additional value on the currency option (increase the value of sold options or decrease the value of bought options) is created by the trader entering into an interest rate swap. The swap is in the currency that has a strike price that is in-the-money from the dealer's point of view. For example, the client will receive fixed US$ for 3 years at 4.00% pa when the market rate is 4.70% pa against an expectation that the floating rate over the period of the swap will average below 4.00% pa. The benefit from the in-the-money swap is converted to an equivalent adjustment of the option premium. The structure yields maximum value where actual rates differ significantly from rates currently implied in the existing yield curve.

---

[58] See discussion in Chapter 11.

2. Example

Assume an Australian exporter is hedging forward its US$ export receivables. In hedging forward, the exporter receives A$ fixed rate and pays US$ fixed rate. If the exporter expects A$ rates to be above the current fixed level or US$ floating rates to be below their current fixed level, then the company should re-structure the hedge to have floating interest rates in one or both of the currencies. Where yield curves are steeply positive (upward sloping) or interest rates are expected to decrease, the hedger will benefit where the rate on the pay side of the transaction is floating. Where interest rates are expected to increase, the hedger will benefit where the receiver side of the transaction is on a floating rate basis.

Assume the exporter wants to hedge a receivable of US$10 million with a 3 year A$ call/US$ put option. The structure of a standard option is as follows:

- Spot currency rate is A$1:US$0.6640.
- Option strike is set at A$1:US$0.6500 (exporter sells US$10,000,000 and purchases A$15,384,615)
- Option premium for a standard option is 4.30% of strike (US$430,000).

The currency option is restructured to create exposure to floating US$ interest rates as follows:

- The exporter enters into a zero coupon US$ swap where it receives fixed rate and pays LIBOR. The swap is on a notional amount of US$8.70 million (on a present value basis) at a fixed rate of 4.75% pa payable annually.
- The mark-to-market value of the swap at the current market swap fixed rate is US$184,000 (in present value). This reflects the fact that the exporter has entered into the swap at off market rates.

The present value of the swap is used to reduce the structured currency option (with floating interest rates) premium to 2.46%.

Under the structured currency option, the exporter pays the floating rate (3 month LIBOR) and receives the fixed rate under the swap. There is a net settlement based on the US$ LIBOR rate compared to the swap rate. If US$ 3 month LIBOR over the 3 year period does not exceed the swap rate, then the exporter will retain the full benefit of the lower premium.

8   Swaps – Execution Structures

Swap transactions are generally executed as follows:

- **End user transactions** – the transactions are generally entered into between the counterparty and the dealer. End users approach dealers or vice versa with the objective of executing the transaction. Both parties act as principals to the transaction.

- **Inter-bank transactions** – the transactions are entered into between the dealers directly or via an inter-dealer broker[59].

In recent years, electronic execution structures (primarily for inter-bank transactions) have been promoted[60].

A number of innovative arrangements were developed in the 1980s to facilitate entry into swap transactions. The structures primarily reflected the size and complexity of the particular transaction requirements. The structures were motivated at that time by the difficulty of executing particular transactions. The arrangements were generally used in the development phase of the swap market. The arrangements are in part, cosmetic in nature, and generate no clearly quantifiable economic value. The growth in liquidity and availability of swaps and derivative transactions has rendered the structures largely obsolete. The innovations are mainly of historic interest, although from time to time the concepts have been used for specific transactions. For example, in the managed liquidation of derivative positions relating to Long Term Capital Management ("LTCM"), a tender process was used.

The swap execution structures used include:

- **Swap tender panels** – this structure entails the use of a tendering process to arrange the required swaps. The concept was introduced in 1984 when Morgan Grenfell arranged a US$50 million Euro-note facility for the Export Finance and Insurance Corporation of Australia ("EFIC"). The facility included a tender panel that allowed members to bid for the right to swap the floating rate debt raised by the notes into fixed rate funding. Subsequently, the United Kingdom Export Credit Guarantee Department and Grand Metropolitan, faced with very large swap programs, used the same concept. The Grand Metropolitan transaction illustrates the basic concept[61]. The company was faced with the need to put

---

[59]   See Shireff, David "What's In A Name?" (August-September 1988) Risk 58–61; Shireff, David "The Wins of Change" (February 1992) Risk 19–25; Shireff, David "Uncommon Market" (March 1993) Risk 49–57; Isaacs, Jonothan "Fingers on The Pulse" (April 1994) Risk 46–54; Irving, Richard "Patriot Games" (April 1995) Risk 25–29; Irving, Richard "Going for Broke" (April 1996) Risk 25–28; Cooke, Stephanie "Will Brokers Go Broke?" (May 1996) Euromoney 90–93; Boughey, Simon and Elliot, Margaret "Fear and Loathing in the Interdealer Swap Market" (February 1997) Derivatives Strategy 20–23; Nusbaum, David "Strategies for Survival" (April 1997) Risk 30–32; Louis, J.C. "Squeezing the Brokers" (May 1998) Derivatives Strategy 15–17; Hunter, Robert "Clash of the Titans" (May 1998) Derivatives Strategy 24–27; Sandiford, Jane "Broker Breaks" (June 1998) Futures & OTC World 47–49.

[60]   See discussion in Das, Satyajit (2004) Structured Products Volume 2; John Wiley & Sons (Asia), Singapore at Chapter 20.

[61]   See "Tender Panel Fits into Grand Met Scheme" (June 1987) Corporate Finance 21–24.

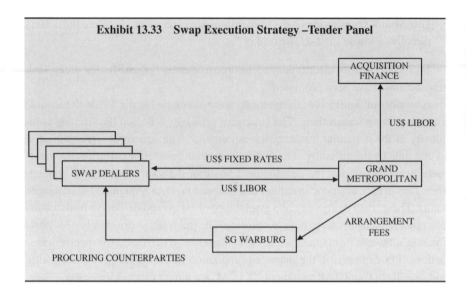

Exhibit 13.33   Swap Execution Strategy –Tender Panel

in place a program of US$ interest rate swaps totalling US$750 million. In order to avoid the administrative complexity of dealing with separate counterparties given timing constraints, Grand Metropolitan appointed SG Warburg (a United Kingdom investment bank) to arrange the program. **Exhibit 13.33** sets out the structure of the Grand Metropolitan swap tender panel.

• **Revolving swap facility** – this is a variation on the swap tender panel concept. SG Warburg developed the revolving swap facility. In this case, the transaction was arranged for Booker, the international food distribution and health products company. The company had an ongoing need to convert US$ assets into GBP. **Exhibit 13.34** sets out the structure of the revolving currency swap facility. In late 1987, the Mass Transit Railway Corporation of Hong Kong arranged a similar revolving currency swap facility to convert liabilities from a variety of other currencies into Hong Kong dollars[62].

• **Swap arranger** – this entails using a third party to arrange the relevant transaction. This is similar to using inter-dealer brokers in the inter-bank market. In late 1989, SG Warburg arranged swap programs totalling approximately GBP

---

[62] See Stillit, Daniel "The Booker Prize to Warburg For Some Fairly Novel Work" (June 1987) Corporate Finance 20–21; "The Revolving Currency Swap" (June 1987) The Banker 18.

Exhibit 13.34   Swap Execution Strategy – Revolving Swap Facility

The company wants to convert its US$ asset return into Pound Sterling (GBP) through the revolving swap facility.
Under the structure the company:
- Pays US$ LIBOR and receives GBP LIBOR minus a spread.
- Pays the US$ notional principal amount and receives the GBP notional principal amount at maturity.
- Determines the date when the swap is entered into.
- Determines maturity date.

The counterparty arranges the maturity of its US$ funding to match possible termination dates chosen by the company. The counterparty achieves attractively priced funding in GBP.

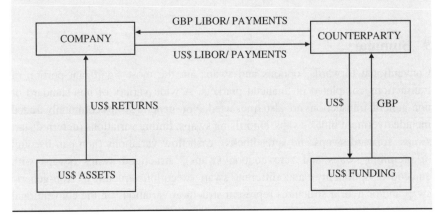

2,500 million for two leveraged transactions in the UK (Magnet and Isosceles)[63]. In each case, to avoid the risk of adverse market movements in GBP swap rates, SG Warburg acted as an arranger of the required swaps for and on behalf of the borrowers. In this case, rather than using a swap tender panel structure, SG Warburg directly sourced swap counterparties by arranging receivers of GBP fixed rates in the new issue market either through public bond issues or private placements. The arranger took advantage of buoyant market conditions in GBP. In this way, by creating a natural demand for the receipt of fixed rate GBP in the new issue market, SG Warburg was able to reduce the potential impact on GBP swap rates as a result of the transactions. In late 1991/early 1992,

---

[63]   See "Isosceles Illustrates Some Swaps Synergy at Warburg" (5 August 1989) International Financing Review Issue 787 29.

a further variation on the execution of large swap programs emerged with the use of a specialist swap broker (Intercapital) by the African Development Bank ("ADB") to arrange approximately US$1,200 million of interest rate and currency swaps[64]. The ADB was interested in executing the program of currency swaps to correct an asset/liability mismatch in its liability portfolio and to re-balance its currency mix. Swaps required to be undertaken included 2 fixed rate Yen/fixed rate US$ swaps for a total of US$475 million, US$600 million of swaps to fixed rate French Francs, cancellation of 2 swaps totalling DEM 200 million and assignment of one SFR 150 million swap. Transactions ranged in maturity from three to nine years. Intercapital arranged transactions for and on behalf of the ADB with a number of major international banks in return for receipt of a brokerage fee.

9 Summary

Conventional forwards, options and swaps are the most significant portion of transactions completed in financial markets. A wide variety of non-standard or non-generic transactions are also transacted. Non-generic swaps commonly traded include overnight index swaps, amortising swaps, timing variations (deferred start swaps, forward swaps and spreadlocks), cash flow variations (non par/discount or premium swaps and zero coupon swaps), structured swaps (swaps with embedded optionality) and different swap execution structures. Non-generic swap and/or hybrid structures represent structural variations on the conventional swap/derivative structure. The non-generic structures are driven by the need for cash flow matching and additional flexibility of asset and liability managers. These structures are designed to allow participants to achieve hedging or trading objectives that are not met by conventional products.

---

[64] See "AfDB Move Sparks Dollar Swap Drama" (23 November 1991) International Financing Review Issue 905 41; "London's African Program" (18 January 1992) International Financing Review Issue 912 39.

14
Basis Swaps

1 Overview

Basis swaps represent a special type of non-generic swap structure. Basis swaps are floating-to-floating interest rate swaps. In this Chapter, basis swap transactions are examined.

The structure of the Chapter is as follows:
- The types of basis swaps are outlined.
- Specific basis swap structures (basis swaps, arrears reset swaps and index differential swaps) are described.

2 Basis Swaps – Types

Basis swaps are floating-to-floating interest rate swaps. The major distinguishing characteristic of basis swaps is that both streams of cash flows exchanged are variable. The two streams are priced off different indexes in the same currency. In certain cases, the cash flows are based off indexes in different currencies but are paid in one currency, eliminating currency risk.

There are four types of basis swap transactions:
- Basis swaps (also known as floating-to-floating interest rate swaps).
- Arrears reset swaps.
- Index differential swaps.
- Yield curve or constant maturity swaps.

Basis swaps, arrears reset swaps and index differential swaps are examined in this Chapter. Yield curve or constant maturity swaps are part of the universe of constant maturity treasury or swap products. These are considered separately in Chapter 17.

3 Basis Swaps

3.1 Concept

Basis swaps (or floating-to-floating interest rate swaps) entail the conversion of one floating rate index into another in the same currency. Basis swaps operate in the same way as normal interest rate swaps. The principal features of basis swaps include:

- All cash flows (receipts and payments) are reset based on the notional principal amount at each payment date. The payments are based off different short term floating interest rates.
- The payments are paid and received on a net basis.
- The notional principal is never exchanged.

The market for basis swaps consists of several components:

- **Basis swaps between different money market/short term indexes** – this entails floating-to-floating interest rate swaps between *different* money market indexes in the same currency. For example, in US$ there are a number of short term interest rate indexes (Treasury bill ("T-Bills"); Federal Funds ("Fed Funds"); Cost of Funds Index ("COFI"); Certificate of Deposit ("CD"); Bankers Acceptance ("BA"); Bank Prime Rate ("Prime"); Commercial Paper ("CP"); LIBOR). This creates opportunities to exchange/convert funding priced off one index into funding priced off an alternative index. This type of activity is common in the US$ market. It is less common in other markets because of the absence of a multiplicity of money market indexes. Prior to the introduction of the Euro, there was a basis swap in French Francs and (to a more limited extent) in Italian Lira[1]. The introduction of the Euro has eliminated these markets.
- **Basis swaps based on the same index but different interest rate periods** – this entails floating-to-floating swaps between the *same* money market index but based on a different interest rate period. For example, a basis swap between 1 month US$ LIBOR and 6 month US$ LIBOR. This type of structure is used to create exposure to different parts of the yield curve. Basis swaps based on different interest rate periods are available in most currency markets.

Basis swaps originally developed in US$ primarily between Prime and LIBOR. The transactions were driven by foreign banks that were participants in loan

---

[1] See Das, Satyajit (1994) Swaps and Financial Derivatives – Second Edition; LBC Information Services, Sydney/McGraw-Hill, Chicago at Chapter 26.

syndicates where the borrower was able to draw down Prime based funding. The foreign banks were forced to fund loan assets priced off Prime in the LIBOR market that was their traditional US$ funding source. In order to eliminate the asset liability mismatch, the foreign banks entered into a Prime/LIBOR basis swap. Under the swap, the foreign banks paid a specified margin under Prime and in return received LIBOR. This allowed the foreign banks to match their assets and their liabilities and lock in the margin on the Prime based loans.

3.2   Structure

The structure of the basis swap is similar to that of a conventional interest rate swap. **Exhibit 14.1** sets out a confirmation of a LIBOR/CP basis swap.

The key structural issues are as follows:

- **Rate source** – an acceptable price source for the relevant money market index is required. For US$ indexes, a common source is the Federal Reserve Bank of New York H.15 publication ("H.15") that uses a prescribed method to determine the relevant rate for T-Bills, Fed Funds, COFI, CD, BA, Prime and CP. Alternative price sources include a system of sampling reference banks[2].

- **Rate calculation** – the rate obtained must be used in the calculation in accordance with a prescribed approach. This is illustrated with a CP based basis swap. In CP/LIBOR basis swaps, it is common practice to use the 1 month US$ CP rate. The rate used is the CP rate published by the Federal Reserve Bank in its weekly H.15 bulletin. The published rate is a discount rate. The discount rate is converted into a money market yield equivalent as follows:

    $(360 \times d)/(360 - (30 \times d/100)$ where d = the discount rate in % rounded to 2 decimal places

    The CP rate (stated as a money market yield equivalent) is paid on the basis of an actual/360 year[3]. The CP rate is set at the commencement of the basis swap. The CP rate is re-set at an agreed frequency (monthly in the case of 1 month CP).

- **Rate compounding** – the floating rate may need to be compounded. This will be required where the payment frequency and the interest rate period of the rate are mismatched. In the CP/LIBOR swap, the transaction is between 6 month LIBOR and 1 month CP. If the LIBOR payments are semi-annual and the 1 month CP payments are monthly, then there is no need for compounding.

---

[2]   There have been some accusations that dealers have distorted some of these indexes such as CP; see "No Basis to Trade" (29 November 1999) IFR Financial Products Issue 31 13.

[3]   The CP rate can be paid on bond equivalent basis if required. For conversion formulas, see Das, Satyajit (2004) Derivative Products & Pricing; John Wiley & Sons (Asia), Singapore at Chapter 5.

Exhibit 14.1   CP/LIBOR Basis Swaps – Structure

To [Party A]

The purpose of this letter agreement is to confirm the terms and conditions of the Swap Transaction entered into between us on the Trade date specified below (the "Swap Transaction"). This letter agreement constitutes a confirmation as referred to in the Interest Rate and Currency Exchange Agreement specified below.

The definitions and provisions contained in the 1991 ISDA Definitions (as published by the International Swap Dealers Association, Inc.) are incorporated into this Confirmation. In the event of any consistency between those definitions and provisions and this Confirmation, this Confirmation will govern.

This confirmation supplements, forms part of, and is subject to, the Interest Rate and Currency Exchange Agreement dated [   ], as amended and supplemented from time to time (the "Agreement") between you and us. All provisions contained in the Agreement govern this confirmation except as expressly modified below.

General

Notional Amount	US$100 million
Trade Date	15 May 2001
Effective Date	17 May 2001
Termination Date	17 May 2004 subject to the [Following/Modified/Preceding Business] day Convention

CP Amounts

CP Payer	Party A
CP Payment Dates	Every 17 November and 17 May commencing 17 November 2001 and terminating on 17 May 2004 subject to the [Following/Modified/Preceding Business] day Convention
CP	US$ CP-H-15 of the Designated Maturity reset monthly plus the Spread payable semi-annually in accordance with the Floating Rate Day Count Fraction
Designated CP Maturity	1 Month
CP Spread	0.05% pa
CP Day Count Fraction	Money market basis calculated on an actual/360 day year compounded at the rate set at the commencement of the month

LIBOR Amounts

LIBOR Payer	Party B
LIBOR Payment Dates	Every 17 November and 17 May commencing 17 November 2001 and terminating on 17 May 2004 subject to the [Following/Modified/Preceding Business] day Convention
LIBOR	US$ LIBOR of the Designated Maturity reset semi-annually plus the Spread payable semi-annually in accordance with the Floating Rate Day Count Fraction
Designated LIBOR Maturity	6 Months
LIBOR Spread	Nil

LIBOR Day Count Fraction	Semi-annual money market basis calculated on an actual/360 day year
Other Terms	
Netting of Payments	Applicable
Documentation	Standard ISDA
Calculation Agent	Party B
Governing Law	London
Account Details	
Payments to Party A	
Account for Payment	
Payments to Party B	
Account for Payments	
Offices	
Party A	
Party B	
Broker/Arranger	
(if applicable)	

Please confirm that the forgoing correctly sets forth the terms of our agreement by executing the copy of this Confirmation enclosed for that purpose and returning it to us or sending us a letter or telex substantially similar to this letter which letter or telex sets forth the material terms of the Swap Transaction to which this confirmation relates and indicates agreement to those terms.

Party B

In practice, the payment frequency will be mismatched on at least one side of the basis swap. If the basis swap settlements on the CP/LIBOR swaps are semi-annual, then the CP payments will need to be compounded[4]. This will entail the CP payments being compounded each month. The CP rates are compounded at the applicable monthly CP rate, with settlement taking place semi-annually.

The structural issues identified are generally more relevant to basis swaps between different money market/short term indexes. The structure of basis swaps based on different interest rate periods is less problematic in terms of rate source and rate calculation. This reflects the fact that these types of basis swaps are generally undertaken on the common short term interest rate index (for example US$ LIBOR) for different interest rate maturities. The rate compounding issue is relevant to both structures.

---

[4]   The process is identical to that used in overnight index swaps; see Chapter 13.

The major market for basis swaps is US$. This reflects the multiplicity of money market/short term indexes available in US$. It also reflects the fact that different market participants have assets and liabilities indexed off the different indexes. This creates a natural demand for transactions designed to match assets and liabilities or trade between the relative valuations of the indexes. **Exhibit 14.2** sets out the major US$ money market rates.

Active basis swap markets exist between LIBOR, T-Bills, Fed Funds, CP and Prime. **Exhibit 14.3** sets out market quotations for the main types of basis swaps between US$ money market indexes. The various basis swap markets vary significantly as to liquidity and depth. For example, the LIBOR/CP and the LIBOR/T-Bills are relatively liquid. This reflects the popularity of CP as a form of short-term funding for high quality borrowers. These borrowers use CP as the underlying liquidity for US$ interest rate swaps. The large funding requirements of the US government sponsored entities ("GSE") (including Government National Mortgage Association ("GinnieMae"), Federal National Mortgage Association ("FNMA"), Federal Home Loan Mortgage Corporation ("FHLMC"), Student Loan Mortgage Association ("SallieMae") that use T-Bills as a benchmark for funding provides the LIBOR/T-Bill basis market with liquidity.

Exhibit 14.4 sets out market quotations for basis swaps in US$ between different interest rate periods.

Exhibit 14.2   Major US$ Floating Rate Indexes[5]

Index	Comments	Price Source[6]
T-Bills	Rates for US government obligations for designated maturities.	Auction average rate (H.15 bulletin) or secondary market rate based on sampling of reference dealers.
Fed Funds[7]	Rates for lending/borrowing federal funds (held by law by US banks with Federal Reserve system) for designated maturities (Overnight or term (1 week to 6 month)).	Market rate (H.15 bulletin) or last transaction rate for Fed Funds based on sampling of reference dealers.

---

[5]   See Mahtani, Arun "Basis Swap Hedges Pay Dividends" (9 October 1999) International Financing Review Issue 1304 96.

[6]   The price sources are defined in detail in the ISDA Swap definitions (see Das, Satyajit (2004) Risk Management; John Wiley & Sons (Asia), Singapore at Chapter 16).

[7]   See Hiemstra, Martin "Fed Funds Feeding Frenzy" (September 1999) FOW 23.

Index	Comments	Price Source
COFI	Cost of funds of retail mortgage banks as measured by the monthly weighted average cost of funds paid by member institutions of the 11th Federal Home Loan Bank District of San Francisco ("FHLBSF").	Dow Jones Telerate (7175) or COFI rate announced by FHLBSF.
CD	Rates for bank funds for designated maturities in the wholesale money markets as measured by rates on negotiable US$ CDs of major US money market banks.	Market rate (H.15 bulletin) or secondary market rate based on sampling of reference dealers.
BA	Rates for top rated US$ bankers acceptances for designated maturities in the US money market.	Market rate (H.15 bulletin) or secondary market rate based on sampling of reference dealers.
Prime	Base/benchmark lending rates charged by banks for credit.	Market rate (H.15 bulletin), Reuters (NYMF) or market rate based on sampling of reference banks.
CP	Rates for commercial paper issued by high grade (AA rated) non-financial corporations for designated maturities	Market rate (H.15 bulletin), Reuters (ISDD) or market rate based on sampling of reference banks.
LIBOR	Rates for US$ deposits placed with leading international banks in London for designated maturities.	Market rate (based on Reuters (LIBO or ISDA) or Telerate (3750) or market rate based on sampling of reference banks.

Exhibit 14.3   US$ Basis Swap (Money Market Index) Quotations

Commercial Paper/3 Month LIBOR Swaps

Maturity (years)	Pay	Receive
1	8.8	12.8
2	8.0	12.0
3	7.5	11.5
5	6.5	10.5
7	6.3	10.3
10	5.8	9.8

Treasury Bills/3 Month LIBOR Swaps

Maturity (years)	Pay	Receive
1	29.0	39.0
2	37.0	47.0
3	46.0	56.0
5	60.0	70.0
7	60.0	70.0
10	59.0	69.0

Prime Rate/3 Month LIBOR Swaps

Maturity (years)	Pay	Receive
1	−284.0	−280.0
2	−282.0	−278.0
3	−280.5	−275.5
5	−278.5	−274.5
7	−278.0	−274.0
10	−277.5	−273.5

Fed Funds/3 Month LIBOR Swaps

Maturity (years)	Pay	Receive
1	17.0	21.0
2	17.8	21.8
3	18.5	22.5
5	20.3	24.3
7	21.0	25.0
10	21.5	25.5

Notes:
All spreads are on the money market index. The 3 month LIBOR is paid flat.

Exhibit 14.4   US$ Basis Swap (Interest Periods) Quotations

1 Month/3 Month LIBOR Swaps

Maturity (years)	Pay	Receive
1	2.0	6.0
2	1.0	5.0
3	0.5	4.5
5	0.3	4.3
7	0.0	4.0
10	−0.3	3.8

1 Month/6 Month LIBOR Swaps

Maturity (years)	Pay	Receive
1	0.8	4.8
2	0.5	4.5
3	0.8	4.8
5	1.0	5.0
7	0.5	4.5
10	0.5	4.5

3 Month/6 Month LIBOR Swaps

Maturity (years)	Pay	Receive
1	−1.3	2.8
2	−1.5	2.5
3	−1.5	2.5
5	−1.5	2.5
7	−1.5	2.5
10	−1.8	2.3

Notes:
All spreads are on the money market index. The 3 month LIBOR is paid flat.

3.3 Applications

Basis swaps are used for the following reasons:

- **Asset liability matching** – this entails the use of basis swaps to alter the pricing basis of assets and liabilities to reduce risk. This can take several forms:

  1. *Matching the pricing basis of asset and liabilities* – for example, a bank with Prime based loans funded by LIBOR deposits can use a basis swap where it pays Prime/receives LIBOR to match its asset-liability position. **Exhibit 14.5** sets out an example of this type of application. COFI, CD, BA and Prime swaps are used by banks/financial institutions to improve the asset-liability mismatch (driven by the nature of their activities) within portfolios. Basis swaps between different interest rate periods (6 month LIBOR/1 month LIBOR) are used (extensively by banks/financial institutions) to reduce interest rate mismatches within portfolios.

  2. *Matching floating rate payments under a swap* – for example, a corporation with CP based funding entering into a conventional swap to fix rates would create a basis risk between its LIBOR based receipts (under the swap) and its CP based payments (on its funding). This mismatch could be managed by

Exhibit 14.5   US\$/Prime Basis Swaps – Structure

The transaction described below is driven by the following factors:

* A foreign (non US) bank has a portfolio of Prime based loans. The foreign bank funds the loan assets priced off Prime in the LIBOR market. In order to eliminate the asset liability mismatch, the foreign bank enters into a Prime/LIBOR basis swap. Under the swap, the foreign bank pays a specified margin under Prime and in return receives LIBOR. This allows the foreign bank to match its assets and liabilities and lock in the margin on the Prime based loans.

* Counterparty B (a US entity) has liabilities priced off Prime. The Counterparty can generate US\$ fixed rate funding by entering into a US\$ fixed rate/Prime interest rate swap. This allows the counterparty to match its liability flows exactly, avoiding any basis risk.

The overall transaction structure is as follows:

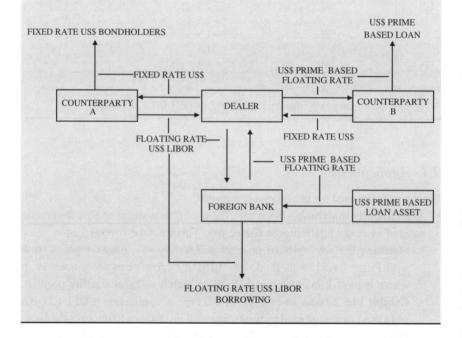

the corporation directly through entry into a basis swap (pay LIBOR/receive CP) or indirectly through entry into an interest rate swap (pay fixed/receive CP[8]). CP and Prime swaps are used by corporations to reduce the liability

---

[8]   In effect, the dealer undertakes the basis swap and embeds it in Fixed/CP interest rate swap.

mismatch within debt portfolios. **Exhibit 14.5** sets out a US$ fixed rate/Prime swap that is an example of this type of application.

- **Diversification of floating rate indexes** – this entails using basis swaps to diversify away from a single floating rate index[9]. The key driver of this type of activity is reduction of risk. The primary risk is the different underlying credit basis of the various indexes. The differences include credit risk (government, (different types of) bank or corporation), regulatory risk (regulatory framework and domestic or international) and type of obligation (deposits, trade obligations or securities). The differences dictate that the spread between rates changes over time, creating risks for borrowers and investors. This type of activity can take several forms:

1. *General diversification* – this is focused on structural diversification of indexes within the asset or liability portfolio. For example, a corporation with large CP borrowing can decrease its sensitivity to fluctuations in CP rates by employing basis swaps to convert the debt into T-bills or US$ LIBOR pricing basis. A benefit of this approach is that the diversification is feasible without the necessity of directly entering the relevant markets for funding. For example, some non-US companies can use LIBOR/CP swaps to convert LIBOR funding to a CP base without needing to qualify themselves (for example, obtaining credit ratings etc) to issue in the CP market. Conversely, United States companies with available CP lines use the swaps to generate LIBOR based funding for their European operations.

2. *Event risk management* – this is focused on using basis swaps to diversify away from indexes deemed susceptible to the risk of adverse movements. For example in late 1999, in anticipation of potential increases in LIBOR rates relative to other short term benchmark rates, some borrowers diversified away from LIBOR using basis swaps. In late September when 3 month LIBOR rates crossed into 2000, LIBOR rates increased sharply by more than 50 bps pa, driven by concern about excess demand for short term liquidity over the 1999/2000 (Y2K) transition. The borrowers captured value from the increased payments from the basis swaps. This insulated these borrowers from increases in interest costs[10].

---

[9] See Buchmiller, Jack "Diversifying Interest Rate Indices With Basis Swaps" (August 1992) Corporate Finance 41–43.

[10] See Mahtani, Arun "Basis Swap Hedges Pay Dividends" (9 October 1999) International Financing Review 96.

- **Trading basis relationships** – this is focused on assuming the risk of basis changes between short term interest rate indexes. The objective is to trade movements in the spreads between the rates. Value is generated by the monetisation of expectations of spread changes. Trading basis relationships is inherently speculative as adverse changes in the spread will result in losses. The risk of trading basis swaps relates to the relative performance of the different interest rate indexes rather than exposure to outright interest rate movements. This reflects the fact that short term rates will generally tend to be positively correlated. Basis swaps may also include some yield curve risk. This reflects the fact that the two short term rates may be for different maturities. For example, in a 6 month LIBOR/1 month CP swap, the trader assumes the exposure to the 1 month against 6 month rate. This type of activity takes several forms:
  1. *Trading basis swaps* – this entails receiving one index and paying another with a view to capturing value from changes in the spread. This activity may be driven by concern about the credit quality of the banking system. A deterioration of bank credit quality may have an adverse impact on LIBOR rates relative to T-Bill rates. Where the LIBOR-T-Bill spread is expected to increase, traders would receive LIBOR pay T-Bills. The position would register positive changes in value where the spread widens. The value could be realised by holding the position or terminating/reversing the basis swap.
  2. *Trading the floating rate under a swap* – this activity is undertaken by borrowers seeking to hedge floating rate debt into fixed rate funding. This deliberately assumes basis risk by creating an implicit basis swap position by mismatching the floating rate indexes. **Exhibit 14.6** sets out an example of trading the floating rate under a swap. Similar types of transactions can be created by traders within swap portfolios in order to trade basis relationships.

Exhibit 14.6   Trading Basis Swaps – CP/LIBOR Trading

1. Concept

This transaction is undertaken by borrowers seeking to hedge floating rate debt into fixed rate funding. This entails deliberately assuming basis risk by creating an implicit basis swap position by mismatching the floating rate indexes.

The transaction is predicated on the fact that when transforming a floating rate liability into a fixed rate basis, the all-in fixed rate cost is driven by two components:

1. Fixed rate payment under the swap.
2. Spread (if any) between the floating rate received under the swap and the floating rate funding cost payment.

If the second item is positive (cost of the borrower's underlying floating rate funding is lower than the floating rate payment received from the counterparty), then the *all-in* fixed rate cost to the borrower is reduced.

Typical transactions entail the borrower receiving LIBOR against payment of fixed rate under the interest rate swap. The borrower's underlying borrowing is in the CP market, priced off the CP rate. The borrower's funding cost is related to CP rates. If LIBOR rates are above CP rates on average over the term of the swap, then the all-in effective borrowing cost of the borrower is reduced.

2. Example

Assume company A raises short term floating rate funding in the CP market. A seeks to fix the rate on its borrowing. In order to match the underlying debt cash flows, the company would enter into a swap where it pays fixed and receives CP rates.

The company may elect to use interest rate swaps linked to LIBOR (rather than the CP rate). This allows the borrower to lower its fixed cost where CP rates are below LIBOR rates. If the historical pattern of rates (LIBOR higher than CP) is replicated over the term of the swap, then the company will achieve a more attractive cost of funding relative to a conventional swap. This structure is set out below:

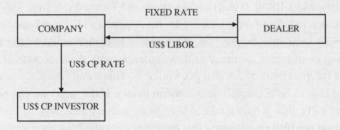

The effective cost to the borrower is set out below:

CP funding costs	−CP rates
Swap cash flows	
Swap payment (US Treasury + 60 bps) (% pa)	−6.60
Swap receipts	LIBOR
LIBOR-CP spread (%pa)	0.10
All-in funding cost (% pa)	−6.50

Notes:
1. Based on cost of funds equal to H.15 CP composite index for A1/P1 CP issuer but not including issuance costs or the cost of back-up credit lines.
2. Assumed spread between LIBOR and CP rates.

The transaction entails the borrower running the risk that CP rates will rise relative to LIBOR (the spread will become negative). The borrower is also exposed to the risk of yield curve shape. For example, an inverse yield curve (1 month CP rates are above 6 month LIBOR) will increase the company's effective cost.

The yield curve risk can be managed through a "reset" swap. The reset swap moderates the yield curve risk by sampling the 6 month LIBOR at more frequent (usually monthly) intervals.

For example, a typical 5 year interest rate swap against 6 month LIBOR entails 10 LIBOR rate setting and payment dates. A reset swap will have ten payment dates, but the rate that is paid every 6 months will be the compounded monthly rate settings (a total of 60) of 6 month LIBOR[11].

3.4 Pricing/Valuation

Basis swaps can be priced in a number of ways:

- **Theoretical pricing** – this uses conventional swap pricing techniques to price the basis swap. The approach would require the forward rates for the money market index and the LIBOR rates to be derived. The basis swap cash flows would be projected. The basis swap margin would be calculated as the margin required to equate the net present value of the payments and receipts to zero at commencement. The approach is difficult to implement in practice. Yield curves and forward rates for various money market rates are not readily available. Treasury and LIBOR (swap) yield curves and forward rates are available or can be derived. Fed funds, COFI, CD, BA, Prime and CP yield curves are not as readily available. In practice, the problem is compounded by the fact that hedging instruments for many of these indexes (with the exception of the Fed Funds futures contract) are also not available. This means the basis swaps may not be able to be accurately priced theoretically. If the structure can be priced theoretically, then it may not be able to be effectively hedged.

- **Residual portfolio positions** – this entails pricing the basis swaps off residual positions or mismatches resulting from other swap transactions. For example, a dealer can enter into two swaps where it pays fixed against 6 month LIBOR but receives fixed against 1 month CP. The dealer has a CP/LIBOR mismatch. This allows the dealer to enter into a CP/LIBOR basis swap where it receives CP against payment of LIBOR. **Exhibit 14.7** sets out an example of the construction of a LIBOR/CP basis swap. The value/price of the basis swap under this approach is the combination of prices of the individual swaps required to structure the hedge.

In practice, the pricing of basis swaps is based on residual position mismatches. This reflects the fact that it allows the dealer to effectively hedge its underlying position closely. The dealer will also be cognisant of the historical relationship

---

[11] This structure is similar to the structure of a mismatch FRN; see Ugeux, George (1985) Floating Rate Notes – Second Edition; Euromoney Publications, London at 148–149.

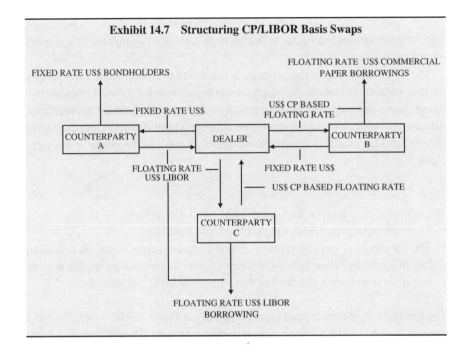

Exhibit 14.7   Structuring CP/LIBOR Basis Swaps

between the floating rate indexes and expectations of possible future movements in the spreads. This will be particularly important where the required swaps are not immediately available. This requires the dealer to "warehouse" the position and assume the trading risk until it can be matched out.

Dealers run active books in basis swaps. The risk of basis swaps is generally hedged using available swap or futures contracts. Dealers use the T-Bill futures contract or the US Fed funds futures contract[12] to hedge risk positions. Basis swaps against other indexes are much more difficult to hedge. This reflects, in part, the absence of futures contracts and/or other hedging instruments.

4   Arrears Reset Swaps

4.1   Concept

Arrears reset swaps (also known as delayed or deferred LIBOR set swaps) are a form of basis swap. The structure was introduced in September 1987. It has been popular at various times coinciding with steeply positive sloping yield curves.

Arrears reset structures are used in derivative formats (basis swaps) or structured note formats (arrears reset notes). Transactions have been completed in a number of currencies.

The major attraction of the structure is the ability to extract value from steeply positive yield curves where the progressively higher implied forward rates overestimate *the path or rate of increase* in actual short term money market interest rates. Arrears reset structures (like a number of other structures incorporating derivative instruments) are available to take advantage of changes in the *shape* of the yield curve.

4.2 Structure

The structure of an arrears reset interest rate swap is as follows:
* The counterparty receives or pays a fixed rate normally.
* The counterparty pays or receives floating rate payments based on a floating rate index set *two days before the payment date*. In a normal swap, the floating rate is set *three or six months and two days prior to the payment date*.

The fixed rate in an arrears reset swap is typically different (higher where the yield curve is upward sloping) than that in an interest rate swap. The different fixed rate reflects the actual floating rate (LIBOR) rates payable in an arrears reset swap. Given an interest rate swap represents a portfolio of forward interest rates, in an arrears reset swap the fact that the forwards payable entail a *different set of* forwards will result in a different fixed rate. In an arrears reset swap, the only rate payable that is different from that in a conventional swap is the last LIBOR set. This is *not* paid in a normal swap where the current spot LIBOR is paid. In a positive yield curve environment, the *implied* LIBOR for the last period is higher than the spot LIBOR, dictating that a receiver of floating rates will require a higher rate to be paid on the fixed rate side.

Arrears reset swap structures can be designed as fixed rate against floating rate (calculated in arrears) transactions or unbundled into a floating-to-floating swap structure. Under this floating-to-floating structure (referred to as an arrears reset basis swap), one floating rate leg is set in arrears, while the other is calculated normally.

Exhibit 14.8 sets out the equivalence of a fixed against floating rate in arrears transaction and the second type of floating-to-floating structure. Fixed Rate A will be higher than Fixed Rate B, with the difference being built into the floating rate-to-floating rate swap. For example, the swap dealer may receive 6 month LIBOR in arrears less a margin while paying 6 month LIBOR flat, or receive 6 month LIBOR in arrears flat while paying 6 month LIBOR plus a margin.

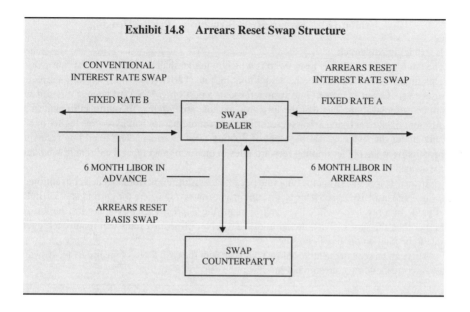

Exhibit 14.8   Arrears Reset Swap Structure

4.3   Pricing/Valuation

The pricing of an arrears reset structure revolves around extracting the value embedded in a steeply positive shaped (upwardly sloping) yield curve. The value derives from forward interest rates that are above prevailing spot rates. **Exhibit 14.9** sets out the detailed mechanics of pricing and valuing an arrears reset swap.

In arrears reset structures, especially with a long term to maturity, it is necessary to incorporate a convexity adjustment[13]. **Exhibit 14.10** sets out a possible methodology for making the convexity adjustment[14].

---

[13] The importance of the convexity adjustment is highlighted by an incident in mid 1995. At that time, several derivative dealers (JP Morgan and Goldman Sachs were reported to be among the dealers) arbitraged the valuation of other dealers on arrears reset swaps (1 year LIBOR in arrears in swaps of between 5 and 10 years in maturity). The dealers noticed that the swaps were valued *without the convexity adjustment*. The difference, that was supposed to be worth around 8–10 bps, arose from the long maturities of the transactions that accentuated the value of the convexity effect. See "Swap Model Arbitrage" (29 July 1995) International Financing Review Issue 1092 at 101; Rombach, Ed "Zen and the Art of Trading the Convexity Bias" (December 1995) Financial Derivatives and Risk Management 17–22 at 20, 21.

[14] For other approaches see Coleman, Thomas S. "Convexity Adjustment for Constant Maturity Swaps and LIBOR-in-Arrears Swaps" (Winter 1995) Derivatives Quarterly 19–27; Li, Anlong "LIBOR-In-Arrears" (Spring 1996) The Journal of Derivatives 44–48.

Exhibit 14.9   Arrears Reset Structures – Pricing/Hedging

1. Pricing Approach

The fixed rate in an arrears reset swap is typically higher than that in an interest rate swap. This higher fixed rate reflects the actual floating rate (LIBOR) rates payable in an arrears reset swap. Given an interest rate swap represents a portfolio of forward interest rates, in an arrears reset swap the fact that the forwards payable are *different* forwards will result in a different fixed rate. Using arrears reset structures, counterparties would receive higher fixed rates under the swap against payment of floating rates in arrears. The fixed rate receiver benefits from the higher implied forward rates in the form of a higher fixed rate flow under the swaps.

In an arrears reset swap, the only rate payable that is different from that in a conventional swap is the last LIBOR set. This is *not* paid in a normal swap where the current spot LIBOR is paid. In a positive yield curve environment, the *implied* LIBOR for the last period is higher than the spot LIBOR, dictating that a receiver of floating rates will require a higher rate to be paid on the fixed rate side.

This can be seen in the table below which sets out the cash flows of an arrears reset swap and a corresponding conventional interest rate swap.

Year	Arrears Reset Swap Cash Flows		Conventional Swap Cash Flows		Net Cash Flow
	Fixed	Floating	Fixed	Floating	
0.5	F	L(t1)	F	L(t0)	L(t0)−L(t1)
1.0	F	L(t2)	F	L(t1)	L(t1)−L(t2)
1.5	F	L(t3)	F	L(t2)	L(t2)−L(t3)
2.0	F	L(t4)	F	L(t3)	L(t3)−L(t4)

Notes:

F = Fixed rate payable under the swap

L(t) = US$ 6 month LIBOR

The net cash flows of an arrears reset structure is:

LIBOR (t4) − LIBOR (t0) (the 24 × 30 LIBOR minus 0 × 6/spot LIBOR).

If US$ 6 month LIBOR (as at time t4) is greater (less) than spot US$ 6 month LIBOR, then a floating rate receiver under an arrears reset structure gains (loses). The approximate size of the gain or cost is:

[LIBOR (t4) − LIBOR (t0)] × Notional Amount × (number of days/360)

2. Example

Assume the yield curve set out below exists. The rates set out are the current yield curve rates as well as implied 6 month LIBOR forwards derived from the yield curve.

Years	Days (to Maturity)	Current Rates (% pa)	Forward Rates (% pa)
0.00	0		
0.50	182	3.00	3.498
1.00	366	3.25	3.765

Years	Days (to Maturity)	Current Rates (% pa)	Forward Rates (% pa)
1.50	547	3.42	3.738
2.00	731	3.50	5.787
2.50	912	3.95	

The rate structure is set out below in the graph.

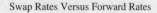

Swap Rates Versus Forward Rates

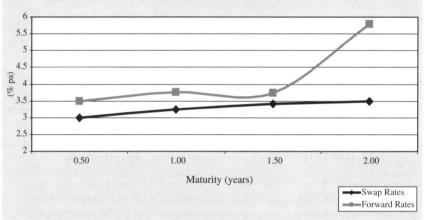

Based on the above rates, the benefit of the arrears reset structure can be estimated as follows: (5.787% pa − 3.00 % pa) × 182/360 = 1.409%

This gain can be amortised over the two year swap (at the swap rate) and built into the fixed rate side of the swap whereby the fixed rate payer increases the rate paid.

The approximation of the arrears reset structure benefit is only accurate where the yield curve is flat and all zero coupon rates are the same. In practice, the exact adjustment is based on using the theoretical forward rates to generate the actual arrears reset structure cash flows (relative to cash flows under a conventional swap) which are then discounted using the zero rates. The table below sets out this analysis for the above swap.

Days (Per Period)	Days (Cumulative)	6 month LIBOR (% pa)	Normal Swap – LIBOR Cash Flows	Arrears Reset Swap – LIBOR Cash Flows	Net Cash Flows	Discount Rate (% pa)	Discounted Cash Flows
		3.000					
182	182	3.498	1.517	1.768	0.252	3.000	0.248
184	366	3.765	1.788	1.924	0.136	3.250	0.132
181	547	3.738	1.893	1.879	−0.013	3.420	−0.013
184	731	5.787	1.911	2.958	1.047	3.500	0.978
		Total	7.108	8.530	1.422		1.345

The benefit derived from the arrears reset structure (on a net present value basis) is 1.345% or 70 bps pa (amortised over 2 years).

3. Hedging

A dealer will hedge the exposure under an arrears reset structure transaction as follows:

*   The change in the PV of the cash flows of the arrears reset structure for a 1 bps movement in interest rates is measured.
*   To offset the arrears reset structure swap risk, the counterparty maintains a hedge (using a portfolio of physical securities and/or derivatives (FRAs/futures)) to offset the NPV change in the arrears reset structure transaction.
*   This hedge portfolio is adjusted periodically to align it with changes in the net value of the arrears reset structure.

Alternatively, the swap counterparty can structure hedges using either FRAs, short term interest rate futures (if available) or deferred start swaps to seek to structure offsetting cash flows to immunise the arrears reset structure.

Exhibit 14.10   Arrears Reset Swaps – Convexity Adjustment[15]

Where interest rate derivatives incorporate an *unnatural* time lag, a convexity adjustment is required. A *natural* time lag is defined as where the pay-off on a derivative depends on the N period rate, the rate is observed at one point in time and is paid at a subsequent time exactly N periods later. Where the time lag is *natural*, the structure can be valued using the assumption that the expected future interest rate is equivalent to the forward rate. Where the time lag is *unnatural*, that is, a transaction such as an arrears reset swap, the expected future interest rate should be calculated as the forward rate adjusted for convexity.

One form of convexity adjustment is that proposed by Brotherton-Ratcliffe and Iben[16]. They show that the convexity adjustment that must be made to the forward rate (F) is:

$$-0.5F^2\sigma^2T[P''(F)/P'(F)]$$

---

[15]   For a discussion of the convexity adjustment see Hull, John (2000) Futures, Options and Other Derivatives – Fourth Edition; Prentice Hall, Upper Saddle River, NJ at 547–55. See also Brotherton-Ratcliffe, R. and Iben, B. "Yield Curve Applications of Swap Products" in Schwartz, R. and Smith, C (Editors) (1993) Advanced Strategies In Financial Risk Management; New York Institute of Finance at Chapter 15; Coleman, Thomas S. "Convexity Adjustment for Constant Maturity Swaps and LIBOR-in-Arrears Swaps" (Winter 1995) Derivatives Quarterly 19–27.

[16]   See Brotherton-Ratcliffe, R. and Iben, B. "Yield Curve Applications of Swap Products" in Schwartz, R. and Smith, C (Editors) (1993) Advanced Strategies In Financial Risk Management; New York Institute of Finance, New York at Chapter 15.

Where

F = forward rate
σ = volatility
T = time to maturity of the forward
$P'(F)$ = first derivative of the price of bond (P) with respect
to yield (Y)
$P''(F)$ = second derivative of the price of bond (P) with respect to yield (Y)

This means that the adjusted forward rate should be:

$$F - 0.5F^2\sigma^2 T[P''(F)/P'(F)]$$

The application of this adjustment can be illustrated with an example. Assume the following:

F = 6% pa
Y = 6% pa
σ = 15% pa

Assume that the instrument provides a payoff in 3 years time linked to the 1 year rate. The value of the instrument is given by:

$$P(Y) = 1/(1 + Y)$$

The first and second derivatives are given by:

$$P'(F) = -1/(1 + Y)^2 = -1/(1 + 0.06)^2 = -0.89$$
$$P''(F) = 2/(1 + Y)^3 = 2/(1 + 0.06)^3 = 1.68$$

The convexity adjustment is given by:

$$-0.5 \times .06^2 \times .15^2 \times 3 \times (1.6792/ - 0.89) = 0.0002 \text{ or } 2 \text{ bps}$$

This means that a forward rate of 6.02% pa (rather than 6.00% pa) should be used in the valuation.

4.4 Applications[17]

The economics of arrears reset swaps derive from the steepness of the yield curve. Where the forward rates are expected to be *over estimating* the rate of increase in

---

[17] See Falloon, William "Curves and the Fuller Figure" (May 1992) Risk 19–25; Monroe, Ann "Hedging the Steep Yield Curve – and Profiting Besides" (September 1992) Global Finance 18–19; Harpe, Michael and Simpson, Justin "The Interest Cost Lessons of 1993" in (1994) Corporate Finance Risk Management & Derivatives Handbook 7–11.

interest rates, the value can be extracted to enable borrowers to reduce the cost of debt and investors to enhance returns on the debt investments.

The major applications of arrears reset swaps include:

- **Reduction of borrowing cost** – this entails using the arrears reset value to reduce the debt cost. This is done in several ways:
    1. *Arrears reset swap against fixed rate debt* – the borrower enters into a swap where it receives fixed rate/pays floating rate (LIBOR in arrears). The higher swap rate received reduces the floating rate payments (to a more attractive margin relative to LIBOR). The absolute interest cost of the borrower depends upon the path of LIBOR rates.
    2. *Arrears reset swap against floating rate debt* – the borrower enters into an arrears reset swap where it receives LIBOR in advance plus a margin and pays LIBOR in arrears. The margin received lowers the cost of the borrower. The reduction is only to the extent that the LIBOR rate set at the end on any interest rate period does not exceed the LIBOR rate set at the start of the interest rate period by the arrears reset margin. The absolute interest cost of the borrower depends upon the path of LIBOR rates.
- **Enhancement of investment return** – this entails the investor seeking to receive the arrears reset value. This is done in several ways:
    1. *Fixed rate investment* – the investor receives the fixed rate/pays LIBOR in arrears against an underlying floating rate investment. This has the effect of enhancing the return on the fixed rate portfolio by the arrears reset margin. The absolute interest return to the investor depends upon the path of LIBOR rates. This is because the underlying floating rate investment returns (LIBOR in advance) are mismatched against the floating rate payments (LIBOR in arrears) under the swap. If LIBOR increases at a rate greater than that implied by the forward rates, then the investor's return will be adversely affected.
    2. *Floating rate investment* – the investor receives LIBOR in advance plus a margin/pays LIBOR in arrears against an underlying floating rate investment. This enhances the return by the arrears reset margin. The absolute interest return to the investor depends upon the path of LIBOR rates. This is because the underlying floating rate investment returns (LIBOR in advance) are mismatched against the floating rate payments (LIBOR in arrears) under the swap. If LIBOR increases at a rate greater than that implied by the forward rates, then the investor's return will be reduced.
- **Trading yield curve shape** – this entails using arrears reset swaps to trade changes in the shape of the yield curve shape. The value of an arrears reset swap derives from two sources:
    1. The actual term swap rate (unadjusted for the arrears reset benefit).

2. The arrears reset benefit that depends on the shape of the yield curve and specifically the difference between the final implied forward rate (as embodied in the forward yield curve) and current LIBOR.

Consequently, counterparties depending on the pattern of interest rate movements can derive value from one or both sources. For example, assume a transaction where a trader receives fixed rates and pays 6 month LIBOR in arrears. The transaction was entered into when the yield curve was strongly positively shaped. A flattening in the yield curve, combined with a decrease in term fixed interest rates, provides trading opportunities. There is value implied by the move in the term fixed rate. The flattening in the yield curve will result in the arrears reset benefit also being diminished. The arrears reset benefit may go to zero where the yield curve is perfectly flat, to a cost where the yield curve inverts. The trader with the arrears reset position in a flattening yield curve environment can reverse the 6 month LIBOR in arrears leg of the transaction and substitute it for a normal 6 month LIBOR in advance floating rate. This could be done at a reduced or no cost (potentially a benefit) if the yield curve shape changes in its favour. The arrears reset structure can be structured to take advantage of a variety of yield curve movements that are dependent purely on the changing term structure of interest rates and changes in the implied forward yield curve. For example, if the yield curve is flat and forward rates are underestimating the rate of increase in LIBOR, then a trader can enter into a arrears reset structure where it receives LIBOR in arrears/pays LIBOR in advance plus a margin. This margin will be small because of the flat yield curve. The position will grow in value if the yield curve steepens and becomes positively sloped.

In all cases, the use of arrears reset swaps entails exposure to yield curve changes. The higher implied forward rate is only an unbiased estimate of the actual future spot interest rate. The actual spot rate at the relevant future date may differ from that implied by the forward rate curve. The arrears reset structure allows traders to generate value based on expectations as to whether forward rates underestimate or overestimate actual future spot interest rates.

If the arrears reset swap entails paying LIBOR set in arrears, then the exposure is (to LIBOR) increasing at a rate exceeding that implied by the yield curve. For example, if the benefit of an arrears reset swap is 70 bps pa in a 2 year transaction (see **Exhibit 14.9**), then if rates increase by more than approximately 140 bps, the gain received will be lost by way of higher interest costs. The transaction also creates exposure to a steepening in the yield curve. This is because a steeper yield curve will increase the arrears reset benefit. This means that the mark-to-market value of the structure will show a loss. The loss will be realised if the position is closed out before maturity. If the position is held till maturity, then the loss will not be realised. If held to maturity, then the gain or loss is dependent purely on the path of LIBOR rates.

4.5   Arrears Reset Notes

Arrears reset products can be packaged as structured notes for investors. The arrears reset note structures usually combine a conventional LIBOR based FRN with an arrears reset swap. Two examples of the structures are set out in **Exhibit 14.11** and **Exhibit 14.12**.

The first structure pays LIBOR in arrears *minus* a margin. The investor will receive incremental returns under this structure where interest rates *rise* by an amount *greater* than the margin over the interest rate period. In the second structure, the investor will earn incremental returns where the interest rates *increase by less than* the margin over the relevant interest rate period. In each case, the comparable benchmark is a standard LIBOR based FRN with LIBOR set in advance. Under both structures, the investor is trading the implied forward rates in the yield curve.

Exhibit 14.11   Arrears Reset Note Structure (1)

Terms

Amount	US$100 million
Term	3 years
Coupon	3 or 6 month LIBOR in arrears minus [margin]
	LIBOR in arrears is calculated and reset two business days prior to payment

Structural Decomposition

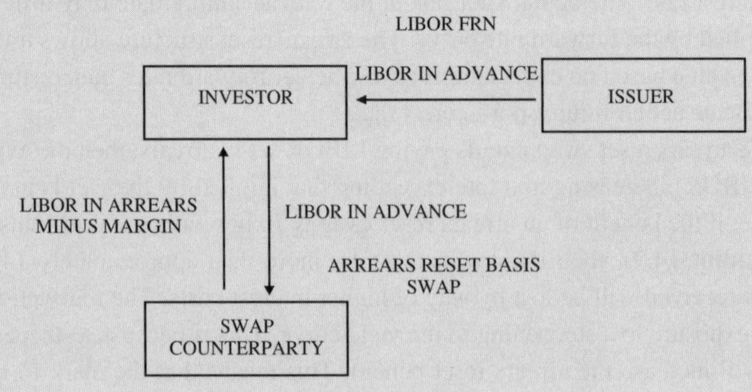

LIBOR FRN

INVESTOR ←— LIBOR IN ADVANCE —— ISSUER

LIBOR IN ARREARS MINUS MARGIN

LIBOR IN ADVANCE

ARREARS RESET BASIS SWAP

SWAP COUNTERPARTY

Exhibit 14.12   Arrears Reset Note Structure (2)

Terms

Amount	US$100 million
Term	3 years
First Format	
Coupon	3 or 6 month LIBOR plus [Spread]
Spread	(3 or 6 month LIBOR in advance minus 3 or 6 month LIBOR in arrears) plus [margin]
	LIBOR in arrears is calculated and reset two business days prior to payment
Alternative Format	
Coupon	[(2 times 3 or 6 month LIBOR in advance) minus 3 or 6 month LIBOR in arrears] plus [margin]
	LIBOR in arrears is calculated and reset two business days prior to payment

Structural Decomposition

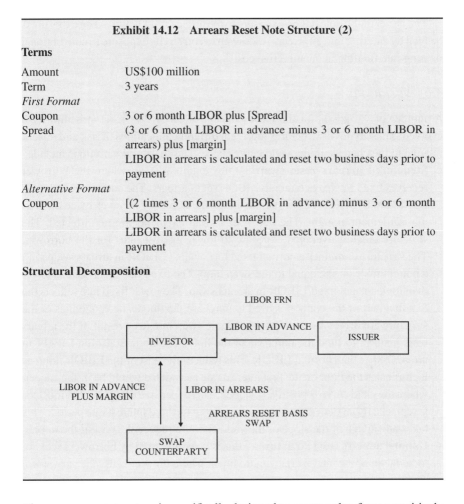

The arrears reset structure is specifically designed to create value from a positively sloped yield curve where implied forward rates lie successively higher above the current yield curve.

The use of arrears reset structures to trade forward expectations of the short term interest rates is similar to other forms of structured products such as inverse FRN structures. The major distinguishing feature is that the inverse FRN is designed to allow investors to buy the complete series (or strip) of interest rate forwards. In contrast, the arrears reset products allow the capture of value from *a single forward rate*[18].

---

[18]   See Chapter 19.

The issuer of the note has no exposure to the arrears reset feature. The exposure is hedged by entering into an arrears reset swap to convert its exposure to conventional floating rate funding at an attractive cost[19].

4.6 Variations

A number of variations on the basic concept of an arrears reset structure have evolved. These types of structures represent different allocations of risk and reward relative to the changes in the yield curve shape. The structural variations include:

- **Structured arrears reset swap**[20] – this entails a swap where the borrower receives fixed rate/pays 6 month LIBOR set in arrears. The additional feature is that where LIBOR is below the fixed rate, the borrower receives twice the normal settlement amount. The borrower's swap payments are not affected. The structure creates leveraged exposure to lower interest rates for the borrower. The structure combines a normal fixed rate against LIBOR in arrears swap with a bought floor (strike equal to the swap rate). The fixed rate receivable is lower than for a normal fixed/LIBOR in arrears swap. The lower fixed rate reflects the fact that part of the coupon is used to purchase the floor. The economics of the structure are driven by the higher available swap rate (as a result of the arrears reset feature) to fund the purchase of the floor. The floor is also on LIBOR in arrears rather than normal LIBOR. This reduces the cost of the LIBOR floor, as it eliminates the floor on the first interest rate period that would be in-the-money where the yield curve is positively sloped. This expensive component of the floor is replaced by an out-of-the-money floor-let in the final interest rate period. This takes advantage of the slope of the yield curve to reduce the cost of the floor.
- **Capped arrears reset structures** – this is generally used by borrowers seeking to hedge in a low interest rate environment where the yield curve is very steep. The shape of the yield curve means that fixing rates using a swap is unattractive because of the possibility of rates falling further and the negative carry under a normal swap. Under the capped arrears reset structure, the borrower receives US\$ 6 month LIBOR in advance and pays US\$ 6 month LIBOR in arrears. The borrower's payments are subject to a cap at level of say 3.50% pa (where 6 month US\$ LIBOR is trading at 1.25% pa). The structure entails the borrower using the implicit benefit of the arrears reset structure to fund the purchase of the cap to protect it against unexpected sharp increases in interest rates.

---

[19] For other variations, see Pilarinu, Efi and Klotz, Rick (7 July 1994) "Yield Enhancement Strategies for LIBOR Floaters In A Steep Yield Curve" Salomon Brothers US Derivatives Research Fixed Income Derivatives; New York.

[20] This structure is similar to the structured swap products described in Chapter 13.

- **Forward start arrears reset swap** – where the yield curve is steeply positively sloped in the short end but is then flatter, value can be extracted from the flat yield curve. The shape of the yield curve implies a relatively low value of the arrears reset swap. Value can be extracted from receiving the benefit by paying LIBOR in advance plus a (small) margin against payment of LIBOR in arrears *commencing out of the forward date*. The most attractive use for a forward start arrears reset swap is to reverse an existing position taken when the entire yield curve was steep. The flattening at the medium to long end of the yield curve can be monetised by reversing the forward component of an exiting arrears reset swap with this structure.
- **Arrears reset swap with optionality** – arrears reset swap with option or asymmetric elements are feasible. There are several examples of this type of transaction:
    1. *Choice of LIBOR swap* (also known as velocity cap or optional reset swap)[21] – under the basic structure, the dealer pays fixed rate and has the right to receive 3 or 6 month LIBOR set at the beginning of the period or at the end of the period, whichever is higher. The fixed rate paid is higher than that payable under a normal arrears reset structure. The additional yield pick up is based on the embedded options on forward rates sold by the receiver of the fixed rate under the structure. The value of the option reflects the shape of the yield curve (identical to the format of the arrears reset structure) and the volatility of forward rates implied by the yield curve. A typical structure is that the borrower pays a subsidised fixed rate and receives LIBOR. The LIBOR payments vary as a function of the change in LIBOR over a given interest period. The LIBOR payments vary according to the formula: LIBOR – Maximum [(LIBOR change (defined as LIBOR at the start of the interest rate period minus LIBOR at the end of the interest rate period) – (specified amount (say, 0.50%); 0]. The structure provides lower borrowing costs for the payer of fixed rates unless LIBOR rises by more than the specified percentage over any interest rate period. A typical structure involves the investor receiving an enhanced fixed rate coupon in return for paying the greater of 3 or 6 month LIBOR set at the start or end of each interest rate period.
    2. *Maximum reset swap* – this is an extension of the choice of LIBOR concept. A typical example of this structure is a 1 year transaction where the investor receives 3 month LIBOR plus a margin (say, 50 bps) and pays the maximum of 3 month LIBOR over the next 12 months. The 3 month LIBOR receipts are normally paid quarterly. The 3 month LIBOR payments are reset monthly

---

[21] See "Arrears Pay Up" (13 April 1994) IFR Swap Issue 64 4–5.

and paid in a single payment at maturity. The transaction is attractive to an investor who believes that LIBOR will remain at current levels over the term of the swap. The margin over LIBOR provides the investor with a level of protection against interest rate increases.

5   Index Differential Swaps

5.1   Concept

Index differential swaps (also known as differential ("diff") swaps, quanto/quanto basis swaps or cross currency interest rate swaps) are basis swaps with embedded quanto option features[22]. The structure entails payment or receipt of the difference between money market interest rates in two currencies. The structure entails no currency risk as all payments are made in a single currency.

Index differential swaps are designed to allow borrowers and investors to capture existing and expected differentials in money market rates between alternative currencies without incurring any foreign exchange exposure. This allows borrowers to reduce funding costs. It also allows investors to generate higher yields. The benefits are created by monetisation of the expected interest rate differential between the currencies and using the correlation between interest rates and exchange rates to hedge the currency risk.

5.2   Structure

The index differential swap structure entails payment or receipt of the difference between money market interest rates in two currencies. There is no currency risk as all payments are made in a single currency. Under a normal index differential swap, the cash flows are as follows:

- The counterparty receives payments in a specific currency on a notional principal amount for a specified term at the prevailing floating money market rate in that currency.
- The counterparty makes payments on the same notional principal amount based on the prevailing floating money market rate in a different currency. The notional principal is in the same currency. The transaction is for the same term.

The major features of the index differential swap include:

- All payments and receipts (based on the same notional principal amount) are floating rate. The rates are reset at specified intervals (usually quarterly or semi-annually). The payments and receipts are based on short term money market rates *in different currencies.*

---

[22]   See discussion of quanto options in Chapter 11.

- All payments under the transaction are made in the counterparty's nominated currency. This eliminates any currency exposure.
- There is no exchange of principal amounts.
- All payments are made in the nominated base currency on a net settlement basis.

Exhibit 14.13 sets out an example of an index differential swap. The transaction set out is a liability index differential swap.

A borrower enters into a Euro/US$ differential swap to benefit from the fact that US$ money market rates (LIBOR) are currently below equivalent Euro money market rates (Euro-IBOR). The borrower enters into a differential swap for 3 years. The borrower makes payments in Euro calculated as 6 month US$ LIBOR plus a margin on a notional principal amount of Euro 100 million (equivalent to US$90.0 million based on an exchange rate of Euro 1:US$0.90). The borrower will receive payments in Euro calculated as 6 month Euro-IBOR on the notional principal of Euro100 million.

Under the differential swap, the borrower will pay interest at a rate equivalent to the 6 month US$ LIBOR plus a margin (assumed to be 194 bps) in Euro. The margin represents the differential between interest rates of the relevant maturity (three years) in US$ and Euro markets and the currency hedging costs.

Exhibit 14.14 sets out the cash flows under the differential swap transaction from the perspective of the borrower. At the end of each interest period (semi-annually), the borrower makes payments on Euro 100.0 million at 6 month US$

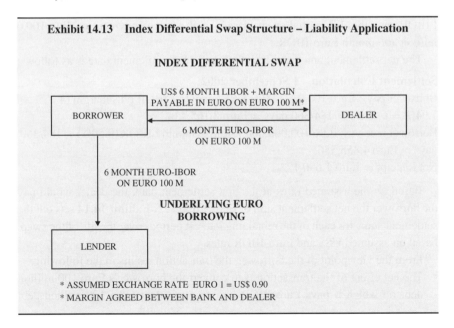

Exhibit 14.13   Index Differential Swap Structure – Liability Application

INDEX DIFFERENTIAL SWAP

US$ 6 MONTH LIBOR + MARGIN
PAYABLE IN EURO ON EURO 100 M*

BORROWER → DEALER

6 MONTH EURO-IBOR
ON EURO 100 M

6 MONTH EURO-IBOR
ON EURO 100 M

**UNDERLYING EURO
BORROWING**

LENDER

* ASSUMED EXCHANGE RATE EURO 1 = US$ 0.90
* MARGIN AGREED BETWEEN BANK AND DEALER

Exhibit 14.14   Index Differential Swaps – Cash Flows

Assume the transaction described in **Exhibit 14.13**. Assume the US$ LIBOR and Euro-IBOR floating rates are as follows:

Year	0.5	1.0	1.5	2.0	2.5	3.0
6 Month Euro-IBOR (% pa)	9.50	9.35	9.62	9.00	8.63	8.25
6 Month US$ LIBOR (% pa)	4.25	4.38	4.13	4.75	5.13	5.50
Margin (% pa)	1.94	1.94	1.94	1.94	1.94	1.94
US$ LIBOR + Margin (% pa)	6.19	6.32	6.07	6.69	7.07	7.44

The cash flows based on the above floating rates are as follows:

Date	Days (in interest rate period)	Borrower Payments (Euro)	Borrower Receipts (Euro)	Borrowers Net Cash Flow (Euro)
01-Mar-02				
01-Sep-02	184	3,165,434	4,855,556	1,690,122
01-Mar-03	181	3,176,671	4,700,972	1,524,302
01-Sep-03	184	3,101,545	4,916,889	1,815,344
01-Mar-04	181	3,365,212	4,525,000	1,159,788
01-Sep-04	184	3,612,656	4,408,333	795,677
01-Mar-05	181	3,742,296	4,147,917	405,621

LIBOR plus the differential swap margin, and receives payment on Euro100.0 million at 6 month Euro-IBOR.

The net settlement amount calculation at the first settlement date is as follows:

Settlement Calculation – 1 September 2002:

Borrower pays: Euro 100,000,000 × US$ 6 month LIBOR plus margin (4.25% + 1.94% = 6.19%) × 184/360 days = Euro 3,165,434.

Borrower receives: Euro 100,000,000 × Euro 6 month LIBOR (9.50%) × 184/360 days = Euro 4,855,556

Net Receipt = Euro 1,690,122.

Based on the assumed rates at the first settlement date, the dealer would pay the borrower the net settlement sum of Euro 1,690,122. **Exhibit 14.14** sets out the settlement sums for each of the remaining interest periods over the life of the swap, based on assumed US$ and Euro-IBOR rates.

From the viewpoint of the borrower, the transaction results in the following:

• The net effect of the transaction is to convert the borrower's Euro 100 million debt on which it pays Euro-IBOR into an equivalent Euro 100 million debt pricing off US$ LIBOR. This means that it benefits where US$ six month LIBOR rates are below Euro six month LIBOR rates by more than the margin.

- Under the terms of this differential swap, the borrower will receive a net settlement amount that equates to the net differential between Euro and US$ rates adjusted for the margin. If US$ LIBOR rates are below Euro-IBOR by an amount that exceeds the margin on the index differential swap, then the borrower reduces the cost of its borrowing. This reduction in interest cost is achieved by the net settlement amounts under the swap that reduces the borrower's interest payments under its underlying Euro borrowing. If 6 month US$ LIBOR plus the margin is above the 6 month Euro-IBOR rate on any particular rate setting date, then the borrower pays the dealer the difference in Euro. This has the effect of increasing the borrower's interest cost.
- This reduction is achieved without incurring any exposure to US$/Euro exchange rates. This is because all payments are in Euro.

Exhibit 14.15 sets out the structure of an index differential swap entered into by an investor. The transaction is used by the investor to convert an underlying US$ asset yielding a return linked to 6 month US$ LIBOR into a US$ asset yielding a return linked to 6 month Euro-IBOR.

Under this transaction structure, the base currency would be restructured to be US$90 million (equating to Euro 100 million at the assumed exchange rate).

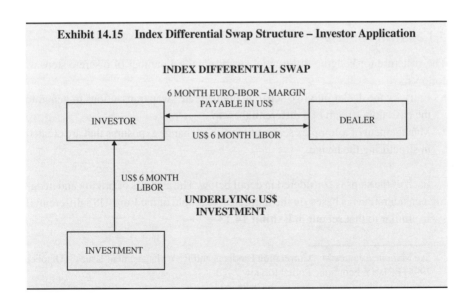

Exhibit 14.15   Index Differential Swap Structure – Investor Application

INDEX DIFFERENTIAL SWAP

6 MONTH EURO-IBOR – MARGIN
PAYABLE IN US$

INVESTOR

DEALER

US$ 6 MONTH LIBOR

US$ 6 MONTH
LIBOR

UNDERLYING US$
INVESTMENT

INVESTMENT

The investor would pay 6 month LIBOR on US\$90 million and receive 6 month Euro-IBOR *less* a specified margin on US\$90 million in US\$. Under the transaction, all payments would be in US\$ to insulate the investor from any foreign exchange risk. Such a transaction would allow the investor to benefit from the positive differential between Euro and US\$ floating rates, while maintaining its underlying US\$ investment position.

5.3 Pricing

5.3.1 Overview

The pricing of an index differential swap transaction is derived from the transactions entered into by the dealer to hedge the risk of the trade. In this Section, the pricing of and hedging structure for an index differential structure is set out.

The index differential swap can be decomposed into a series of forwards on money market interest rates in the two respective currencies, and a foreign exchange exposure management problem[23]. The trading in the forwards is designed to capture the *current implied interest rate differential* from the current yield curves. This is done using interest rate forwards (futures (if available)), FRAs or interest rate swaps in the respective currencies. The foreign exchange exposure problem relates to translating the implied differential into a single currency. The exposure is uncertain in quantum and direction and must be hedged using a quanto option[24].

5.3.2 Hedge Structure

The structure for hedging differential swaps entails a number of discrete steps as follows:

- Entry by the dealer into two separate interest rate swap transactions to generate the cash flow stream of a differential swap.
- Management of a complex series of foreign exchange exposures that are created in structuring the hedge.

Each of the steps is considered in detail below. The analysis of pricing and hedging considerations is based on the numerical example of the Euro/US\$ differential swap similar to that set out in **Exhibit 14.13**.

---

[23]   See Mahoney, James M. "Correlation Products and Risk Management Issues" (October 1995) FRBNY Economic Policy Review 7–20.

[24]   See discussion of quanto options in Chapter 11.

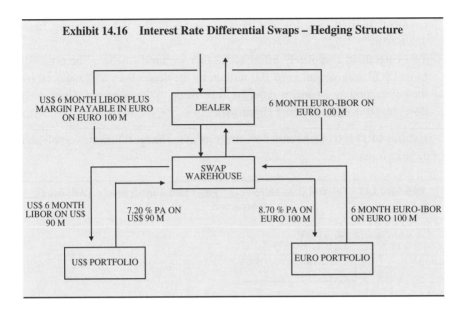

Exhibit 14.16   Interest Rate Differential Swaps – Hedging Structure

In order to hedge the underlying position, the dealer would enter into the following two 3 year interest rate swaps to replicate the cash flows of the differential swap:
- 3 year Euro 100 million interest rate swap under which the dealer:
  1. Pays 8.70% pa on Euro 160.0 million (payable semi-annually on an actual/365 basis).
  2. Receives 6 month Euro-IBOR on Euro 100 million.
- 3 year US$90.0 million interest rate swap in which the dealer:
  1. Pays US$ 6 month LIBOR on US$90 million.
  2. Receives 7.20% pa on US$90 million (payable semi-annually on an actual/365 basis).

The fixed rate on the US$ and Euro swaps are the market interest rate swap rates at the time of entry into the transaction. The currency values between the US$ and Euro interest rate swaps is established using the spot US$/Euro exchange rate at the time the transaction is entered (Euro 1 = US$ 0.90).

Exhibit 14.16 sets out the overall hedging structure.

The structure of the hedge is simplified in two steps as follows:
- The US$ interest rate swap is restructured to an off-market rate basis. The fixed rate under the US$ swap is restructured to match the fixed coupon of 8.70% pa payable under the corresponding Euro interest rate swap. This necessitates the dealer paying the present value equivalent of approximately 1.50% pa at the commencement of the swap to compensate for the off market coupon. The upfront

payment required to restructure the swap is US$3,585,510 (equivalent Euro 3,226,959)[25].

- Two cash flows completely offset each other within the hedge. The 6 month Euro-IBOR received on Euro 100 million by the dealer is exactly matched by the corresponding payments required to be made to the borrower. These cash flows that cancel or offset are eliminated.

Exhibit 14.17 sets out the cash flow structure of the hedge following completion of these two steps.

Exhibit 14.17   Interest Rate Differential Swap Hedging Structure – Adjusted Structure

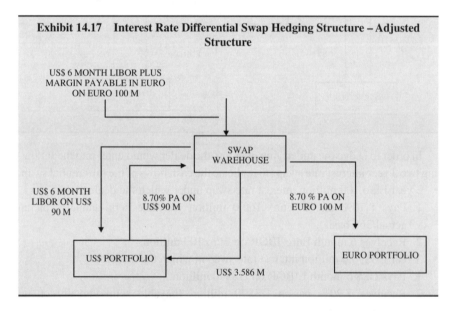

5.3.3   Currency Risk Management

Nature of Exposure

Under the differential swap, the dealer has a complex foreign exchange exposure to movements in the US$/Euro interest rates. This reflects the fact that the dealer has a series of US$ and Euro cash flows to manage.

The unique aspect of this currency risk management position is that:

- The dealer's US$ and Euro net cash flows at each settlement date are determined by an exogenous factor – US$ 6 month LIBOR. This rate is not known until the rate is set at the commencement of the relevant interest period.

---

[25] See discussion of off-market swaps in Chapter 13.

- The nature of the exposure to the US$/Euro rate *changes,* depending upon the nominal level of 6 month US$ LIBOR.

Exhibit 14.18 analyses the net cash flow exposures experienced by the dealer (within its hedge portfolio) at the first settlement date. Please note that while this discussion focuses on the first settlement date only, a similar problem exists in respect of each of the remaining five interest periods and settlement dates.

If US$ 6 month LIBOR is less than 8.70% pa (the fixed rate payable under the Euro swap), then the dealer will have a net receipt of US$ that will be needed to fund a net Euro outflow. Conversely, if US$ 6 month LIBOR exceeds 8.70% pa, then the dealer has a net Euro inflow that will be required to fund a net US$ outflow.

If US$ six month LIBOR (for the first settlement) is set at 4.25% pa, then the dealer has a net US$ inflow of US$1,992,178 and a net Euro outflow of Euro 2,213,531. If the US$/Euro exchange rate remains at Euro 1:US$0.90 (the rate of the commencement of the transaction) then the dealer's net cash flow position is zero (that is, the Euro equivalent of the net US$ inflow exactly matches the dealer's Euro shortfall). The dealer has a currency gain if the Euro depreciates against the US$ and has a currency loss if the Euro appreciates against the US$. The dealer's exposure to an appreciating Euro is *reversed* where US$ 6 month LIBOR is greater than 8.70% pa. Where US$ 6 month LIBOR is greater than 8.70% pa, the dealer has a net US$ outflow (US$882,822) that must be funded from a net Euro cash surplus (Euro 980,913). As a consequence, the dealer's exposure is to a depreciating Euro relative to the US$.

In analysing the complex foreign exchange exposures generated by the hedge structure, the exposure in regard to the *margin* over US$ six month LIBOR payable by the counterparty in Euro is ignored. In practice, part of the margin will represent an annuity designed to recover the up-front US$ payment made as part of restructuring the cash flows of the US$ interest rate swap to equate the fixed rate payable under the Euro interest rate swap. In practice, this exposure can be eliminated quite simply by the following strategies:

- The swap structure could have been realigned by reducing the Euro coupon to equate to the US$ interest rate swap coupon of 7.20% pa.
- Alternatively, the Euro equivalent of the US$ payment to the US$ swap portfolio could have been borrowed from the Euro swap portfolio, with the borrowing being repaid by the margin payable by the counterparty (in Euro).

This exposure is ignored in the remainder of this analysis.

The structure of the hedge requires the dealer to make a number of payments in one currency (either Euro or US$) while receiving the equivalent cash flow in the

Exhibit 14.18   Foreign Exchange Risk Analysis

1. Hedge Cash Flow at Settlement Date

The Tables below set out the total cash flows of the hedge portfolio at different US$ LIBOR rates. The calculations are as follows:

- Euro receipts are calculated as the payments received from the borrower (US$ 6 month LIBOR on Euro 100 million).
- Euro payments are calculated as the payments made under the Euro swap (8.70% pa on Euro 100 million).
- US$ receipts are calculated as the payments received under the US$ swap (8.70% pa on US$90 million).
- US$ payments are calculated as the payments made under the US$ swap (US$ 6 month LIBOR on US$90 million).

Case 1: US$ 6 Month LIBOR < 8.70% pa (say 4.25% pa)

US$ 6 month LIBOR (% pa)	Receipts (Euro)	Payments (Euro)	Payments (US$)	Receipts (US$)	Net Euro Flow (Euro)	Net US$ Flow (US$)	Exchange Rate (Euro 1:US$)	Net Cash Flow (US$)
4.25%	2,172,222	−4,385,753	−1,955,000	3,947,178	−2,213,531	1,992,178	0.9000	0
4.25%	2,172,222	−4,385,753	−1,955,000	3,947,178	−2,213,531	1,992,178	0.8000	221,353
4.25%	2,172,222	−4,385,753	−1,955,000	3,947,178	−2,213,531	1,992,178	0.8500	110,677
4.25%	2,172,222	−4,385,753	−1,955,000	3,947,178	−2,213,531	1,992,178	0.9500	−110,677
4.25%	2,172,222	−4,385,753	−1,955,000	3,947,178	−2,213,531	1,992,178	1.0000	−221,353

Case 2: US$ 6 Month LIBOR > 8.70% pa (say 10.50% pa)

US$ 6 month LIBOR (% pa)	Receipts (Euro)	Payments (Euro)	Receipts (US$)	Payments (US$)	Net Euro Flow (Euro)	Net US$ Flow (US$)	Exchange Rate (Euro 1:US$)	Net Cash Flow (US$)
10.50%	5,366,667	-4,385,753	3,947,178	-4,830,000	980,913	-882,822	0.9000	0
10.50%	5,366,667	-4,385,753	3,947,178	-4,830,000	980,913	-882,822	0.8000	-98,091
10.50%	5,366,667	-4,385,753	3,947,178	-4,830,000	980,913	-882,822	0.8500	-49,046
10.50%	5,366,667	-4,385,753	3,947,178	-4,830,000	980,913	-882,822	0.9500	49,046
10.50%	5,366,667	-4,385,753	3,947,178	-4,830,000	980,913	-882,822	1.0000	98,091

2. Currency Position Analysis

The Table below shows the change in the Euro and US$ positions as US$ 6 month LIBOR changes at each settlement date:

US$ LIBOR Rate (% pa)	4.250	5.250	6.250	7.250	8.250	8.700	9.700	10.500
US$ Cash Flows (US$)	1,992,178	1,532,178	1,072,178	612,178	152,178	-54,822	-514,822	-882,822
Euro Cash Flows (Euro)	-2,213,531	-1,702,420	-1,191,309	-680,198	-169,087	60,913	572,024	980,913
Breakeven Exchange Rate (Euro 1:US$)	0.9000	0.9000	0.9000	0.9000	0.9000	0.9000	0.9000	0.9000

other currency. The dealer must manage this complex foreign exchange exposure. The difficulty in managing this exposure is the inherent linkage between the nature of the underlying currency exposure to the US$ 6 month LIBOR rate for any interest period during the life of the differential swap. This exposure can be managed in one of a number of ways:

- The exposure can be left unhedged.
- The exposure can be managed on an opportunistic basis as a trading position in line with currency value expectations.
- The exposure can be hedged statically, assuming certain known cash flow ranges.
- The exposure can be managed dynamically, incorporating the correlation between the two variables (US$ LIBOR and US$/Euro in this example).

In practice, this exposure is hedged in either a static or a dynamic framework. Quanto option based pricing approaches are used by dealers active in trading index differential swaps.

Foreign Exchange Exposure Management – Static Model
Under the static replication model, the risk is treated as one where the cash flows are known. The currency exposure is then hedged through foreign exchange options.

To structure the currency option hedge, it is necessary to make assumptions regarding the anticipated maximum and minimum future level of the 6 month US$ LIBOR rate over the life of the differential swap transaction. This is because the exact quantum of the cash flows to be hedged is generated by the actual level of US$ six month LIBOR at any LIBOR set date.

For the purpose of illustration, assume that it is anticipated that US$ 6 month LIBOR will never be set below 4.25% pa or above 10.50% pa over the 3 year term of the differential swap. Using this assumption, to fully hedge against losses, the dealer would need to purchase the following options:

- **Purchase of Euro call/US$ put option** – the dealer would purchase a series of six Euro call options (with maturities corresponding with the payment date under the differential swap structure) at a strike price equal to the spot rate of Euro 1:US$0.90. The dealer would purchase the Euro call on Euro 2,213,531/US$1,992,178. The face value amount of the option is related to the long US$/short Euro position on any settlement date where US$ LIBOR sets at 4.25% pa (the assumed lowest LIBOR rate).
- **Purchase of Euro Put/US$ call** – the dealer would purchase a series of six Euro put options (with maturities corresponding with the payment date under the differential swap structure) at a strike price equal to the spot rate of Euro 1:US$0.90.

The dealer would purchase the Euro put on Euro 980,913/US$882,822. The face value amount of the option is related to the short US$/long Euro position on any settlement date where US$ LIBOR sets at 10.50% pa (the assumed highest LIBOR rate).

The structure of the static currency hedge is inefficient. In general, the hedger will be over hedged as it is hedging against both a rise and a fall in the currency and in reality only one option will be required. The effectiveness of the hedge also depends on the forecasting accuracy of the minimum and maximum US$ 6 month LIBOR rates over the life of the differential swap. If the dealer accurately estimates the minimum and maximum levels of US$ 6 month LIBOR over the swap, then where the US$ LIBOR rate is within the range, the dealer will be over hedged. It is possible that the hedger may be under hedged. Where the maximum or minimum is exceeded by a large amount, the face value of the hedge might be insufficient.

In the example, if US$ 6 month LIBOR is between the minimum level assumed (4.25% pa) and the break-even rate (8.70% pa), then where the Euro strengthens against the US$, the dealer will gain. This is because the Euro call/US$ put option purchased by the dealer will generate a higher gain than the actual cash flow loss incurred by the dealer under the hedge. The dealer will also gain from over hedging where US$ 6 month LIBOR is between 8.70% pa and the assumed maximum of 10.50% pa and the US$ strengthens. In order to avoid over hedging, the amount of the options purchased can be based on the US$ 6 month LIBOR *average* over the life of the transaction.

In summary, the static hedge model, while it allows modelling of the risk, does not provide an efficient hedge.

Foreign Exchange Exposure Management – Dynamic Model
The problem in structuring the hedge which lowers hedge efficiency is the inherent assumption that movements in US$ 6 month LIBOR rate are *not* correlated to movements in the US$/Euro exchange rate. In practice, there will be some correlation between movements in US$ 6 month LIBOR rate and the US$/Euro rate that will influence the *actual* currency exposure under the differential swap.

Correlation based hedging techniques (incorporating quanto options) can be designed to improve the efficiency of the currency hedge necessitated by the differential swap. Improving the efficiency of the currency risk management process necessarily minimises the cost of implementing and maintaining the hedge. For example, if it is assumed that increases in US$ LIBOR are likely to coincide with a stronger US$, then the hedge structure could be adjusted to lower the effective level of protection against a depreciation of the US$ against the Euro. This could entail the dealer purchasing a lower face value amount of options (in the extreme case, this exposure could be left unhedged).

The correlation concepts underlying the derivation of the option value are common to quanto (or quantity adjusting) options. The central feature of these instruments is the uncertainty underlying the value or amount of cash flow required to be hedged[26].

This type of transaction is equivalent to a purchase of a relevant option on the index and the simultaneous entry into a derivative transaction to hedge the return into its base currency, usually at rates prevailing at the commencement of the transaction. Given the uncertainty in the value of the index and therefore the maturity value of the option, the currency hedge must be structured to cater for the uncertainty of the value to be hedged. In effect, the hedge needs to recognise the correlation between the change in value of the index and the movements in the currency relativities. The problem in the case of the index differential swaps is that the underlying currency exposure is linked to the interest rate relativities as between the currencies.

Mathematical pricing models for valuing quanto options or derivatives of this type have been developed[27]. The approach to pricing quanto options is to use the correlation between the relevant variables as a parameter in the pricing of the option. For example, in the context of currency hedged structures, the relevant correlation is that between the returns on the relevant currency values and the return on the foreign market index in the currency of the index. In the case of index differential swaps, the relevant correlation is that between the relevant currency and the interest rate in the relevant currency (effectively the Euro and US$ LIBOR in the example). A problem underlying this approach to pricing is the need to assume stability of the relationship between the variables.

Using the quanto option methodology to price the currency risk management component of such transactions requires the separation of the risks of differential

---

[26] See Chapter 11.
[27] See Chapter 11. See also Reiner, Eric "Quanto Mechanics" (March 1992) Risk Vol. 5 No. 3 59–63; Rubinstein, Mark "Two Into One" (May 1991) Risk Vol. 4 No. 5 49; Jamshidian, Farshid "Price Differentials" (July 1993) Risk Vol. 6 No. 7 48–51 and "Corralling Quantos" (March 1994) Risk Vol. 7 No. 3 71–75; Wei, Jason "Valuing Differential Swaps" (Spring 1994) Journal of Derivatives 64–76; Mahoney, James M. "Correlation Products and Risk Management Issues" (October 1995) FRBNY Economic Policy Review 7–20. See also references in Chapter 13.

swaps into specific components (which are consistent with the approach discussed above)[28]:
- Exchange rate risk based on current yield curves in the relevant currencies and exchange rates.
- A contingent exposure based on future yield curves.

This approach seeks to manage and hedge the exchange rate and interest rate risks of differential swaps separately, the rationale being that this facilitates more efficient management of these risks.

Under this approach, the amounts to be received and paid under the differential swaps are determined using the forward rates in the relevant currencies implied by the respective yield curves. For instance, in the example used previously, the six month Euro-IBOR and the six month US$ LIBOR implied at the relevant points in time (for example, six, 12, 18, etc months in the future) from the existing yield curve would be determined. The determination of the forward rates would allow the differential to be paid or received under the differential swap to be established. The interest rate exposure is hedged using forwards in the respective currencies (this is done in the above example using the US$ and Euro interest rate swaps).

Once the net payments are established, the net amounts of a particular currency to be paid or received can be present valued to a current sum, with the resultant payable or receivable amount being hedged by:
- Purchase of the required quanto options.
- An offsetting spot position in the currency that is then dynamically adjusted as the yield curve in both currencies changes and the currency rates alter.

This procedure allows the interest rate exposure and the currency exposure of the transaction to be hedged.

An alternative is not to specifically hedge the interest rate exposure, but to hedge dynamically where the contingent exchange rate risk (which is driven by changes in interest rate risks) is immunised, if required, through option transactions. This approach only allows a perfectly immunised position to be created instantaneously at a given point in time. Maintenance of the hedge requires future transaction costs to be incurred that will be driven by the volatility of interest rates, foreign exchange rates and most importantly, the correlation between these variables.

---

[28] See, for example, Letter to the Editor by Putley, Jeremy (Lehman Brothers, New York) (1993) (March) Risk Vol 6, No 3, p 12; Mahoney, James M. "Correlation Products and Risk Management Issues" (October 1995) FRBNY Economic Policy Review 7–20.

The major difficulty with this approach is that the risk of interest rate movements and currencies are related and there are limited opportunities for hedging this correlation with liquid instruments.

In practice, the hedging and pricing of differential swap transactions is complex. This has led to multiple approaches to the management of the underlying risks of such transactions. There is also concern regarding the difficulties of hedging such exposures, particularly in periods of increased volatility in markets. For dealers in index differential swaps and other quanto products, a portfolio approach to risk management is generally used. Under this approach, the risk of differential swap transactions is aggregated into portfolios of other interest rate and currency transactions and the net position hedged.

Margin on Interest Rate Differential Swap Transaction
The actual margin payable under the differential swap requires the amortisation over the life of the transaction of the following items:
- The upfront payment required to be made by the dealer to re-write one of the interest rate swap coupons.
- The cost of purchasing or creating the options designed to hedge the foreign exchange exposure.

In the above example, the total cost that must be amortised over the life of the transaction is as follows[29]:
- Upfront payment in respect of US$ interest rate swap: US$3,585,510.
- Option premiums: US$946,745.

This total cost of US$4,532,254 (Euro 5,035,838) is amortised over the six payments (three years of semi-annual payments) and equates to approximately 194 bps pa payable semi-annually over US$ LIBOR payable in Euro.

Based on these calculations, the pricing of the differential swap requires the counterparty to pay US$ 6 month LIBOR plus 194 bps pa on a notional principal amount of Euro 100 million in return for receiving 6 month Euro-IBOR on Euro 1000 million. Accordingly, the counterparty would benefit from the transaction as long as US$ 6 month LIBOR was at least 194 bps pa below 6 month Euro-IBOR over the term of this transaction.

In general, pricing of a differential swap will closely approximate the net difference in swap rates in the relevant currencies for the maturities relevant to the

---

[29] For reasons of simplicity, the option cost of the static hedge has been used.

desired term of the differential swap, plus the dealer's cost of hedging the currency risk in the transaction. In effect, the borrower is extracting value from the current and expected interest differentials between the two currencies.

The cost of hedging will depend upon a variety of factors, including the assumptions regarding the future path of the relevant floating rate index and the exact structure of the currency hedge. The cost of hedging the currency risk will generally depend on the shape of the yield curve of the two relevant currencies. The wider the interest differential between the two currencies over the life of the transaction, the higher the hedging costs (or benefits). The importance of this factor relates to the fact that the strike price of the relevant options will be set at the prevailing spot rate at the commencement of the transaction. The prevailing forward rate (determined by interest differentials) will dictate whether the options are in or out-of-the-money and therefore their relative cost.

For example, in the above example, because of the positive interest rate differential in favour of the Euro, forward rates will be lower than the prevailing spot rate of Euro 1:US$0.90. This means that Euro call/US$ puts with the strike rise of US$0.90 required will be out-of-the-money, reducing the cost of the option. Conversely, the Euro put/US$ calls required to hedge will be in-the-money, increasing the cost.

The pricing of differential swaps is most favourable where the net difference in swap rates between the two respective currencies for the relevant maturities is low, and the shape of the yield curve for the two currencies means that the cost of hedging the currency risks is minimal.

5.4 Applications

Applications of index differential swaps focus on the ability to take advantage of existing/expected differences in short-term interest rates between currencies without incurring any currency exposure. Borrowers and investors use differential swaps to manage underlying liability and asset portfolios. Index differential swaps are also used by traders to engineer yield curve positions. This application focuses on assumption of an exposure to future short term interest rate differentials against long-term interest differentials in the relevant currencies.

The use of index differential swaps is predicated on the trader assuming an interest rate risk position across currencies. The transaction creates exposure to interest rate differentials. If interest rate differentials change or are different from expectations, the index differential swap will increase the cost of borrowing or reduce the return to investors. An issue in trading differential swaps is the relatively higher bid-offer spread that may increase the cost of such trading in these instruments.

Applications of index differential swaps include:

- **Reduction of borrowing costs** – this focuses on using the short term interest rate benchmark to reduce borrowing costs. This type of activity can take several forms:

  1. *Paying interest rates priced off the low coupon currency* – this entails a borrower with floating rate debt in a high coupon currency entering into a differential swap where it receives the money market rate in the high coupon currency and pays the money market rate in the low coupon currency[30]. The net payment from the index differential swap reduces the effective debt cost of the borrower. **Exhibit 14.13** sets out an example of this type of application.

  2. *Cross rate loans*[31] – this entails a conventional floating rate bank loan where the loan interest is based on money market rates in a low coupon currency. The structure entails a normal loan with an embedded index differential swap. **Exhibit 14.19** sets out an example of the cross rate loan structure.

  3. *Managing the floating rate under a swap* – this uses an index differential swap to manage the fixed rate cost under an interest rate swap. For example, assume a borrower enters into an interest rate swap in US$ to hedge underlying borrowings. If the yield curve is steeply and positively sloped, then the borrower incurs substantial cost. This cost is the differential between short-term US$ LIBOR and term fixed swap rates. The yield curve cost under the US$ interest swap transactions can be managed using differential swaps. The borrower enters into a US$ interest rate swap where it pays a fixed rate and receives US$ LIBOR. Simultaneously, the borrower enters into an index differential swap for the US$ notional principal amount, where the borrower agrees to pay Yen LIBOR plus a margin and receive US$ six month LIBOR. All payments are in US$. The result of this strategy is to generate positive margins where Yen LIBOR plus the differential swap margin is below US$ LIBOR. This lowers the effective fixed rate cost to the borrower. **Exhibit 14.20** sets out an example of the use of index differential swaps to manage the cost under an interest rate swap.

- **Enhancement of return** – index differential structures are used by investors to increase returns on money market interest related investment assets.

  1. *Receiving interest rates priced off the high coupon currency* – this entails investors with money market investments entering into a differential swap where they receive the money market rate in a high coupon currency. **Exhibit 14.15** sets out an example of this type of application.

---

[30] See Walker, Andrew and Warner, Eric "A Strategy for High Deutschemark Interest Rates" (June 1992) Corporate Finance 43–44.

[31] See Cookson, Richard "Cross Wise Companies" (September 1991) Risk 4.

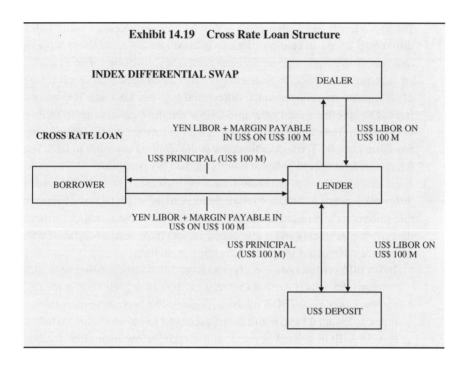

Exhibit 14.19   Cross Rate Loan Structure

INDEX DIFFERENTIAL SWAP

DEALER

CROSS RATE LOAN

YEN LIBOR + MARGIN PAYABLE
IN US$ ON US$ 100 M

US$ LIBOR ON
US$ 100 M

US$ PRINICIPAL (US$ 100 M)

BORROWER

LENDER

YEN LIBOR + MARGIN PAYABLE IN
US$ ON US$ 100 M

US$ PRINICIPAL
(US$ 100 M)

US$ LIBOR ON
US$ 100 M

US$ DEPOSIT

**Exhibit 14.20   Index Differential Swap Structure Against Existing Interest Rate
Swap**

INTEREST RATE SWAP

US$ FIXED RATE

DEALER

BORROWER

6 MONTH US$ LIBOR

6 MONTH YEN LIBOR +
MARGIN PAYABLE IN US$

US$ 6 MONTH
LIBOR PAYABLE
IN US$

INDEX DIFFERENTIAL SWAP

DEALER

2. *Trading interest rate differentials* – this focuses on investors using index differential swaps to take positions in interest rate differentials *in between any two currencies, without incurring currency exposures.* For example, an investor with a US$ investment portfolio could seek to take advantage of anticipated movements in the differential between US$ and Yen interest rates. The investor would enter into a US$/Yen differential swap to receive US$ and pay Yen money market rates. All payments are in US$, eliminating any currency risk. The transaction creates the required exposure to US$/Yen interest differentials to enhance returns on the US$ portfolio.

3. *Index differential notes* – investors frequently use notes with embedded index differential swaps to enhance return by monetising expectations of interest rate differentials between currencies. A number of security issues (primarily private placements and a few public issues) have been undertaken with embedded differential swap characteristics, including:

   • **Index differential note** – in a typical issue, the borrower issues securities (say in US$ which carry an interest coupon in a high short-term rate currency (say Euro-IBOR minus a spread)). The borrower enters into an index differential swap with a dealer to convert its payments stream linked to US$ LIBOR related payment at a margin below its normal funding costs. **Exhibit 14.21** sets out an example of this type of structure.

   • **Differential swap inverse FRN** – this entails differential swap transactions embedded in Inverse FRN issues[32]. **Exhibit 14.22** sets out an example of this structure. The investor receives an interest rate on its investment of 18.00% pa minus US$ LIBOR plus a margin. All payments are in A$. The investor receives enhanced where US$ LIBOR rates stay low. The issuer of the A$ Reverse FRN would convert its borrowing into a conventional floating rate borrowing relative to US$ LIBOR by entering into two swaps. The issuer enters into a differential swap under which it pays US$ LIBOR plus a margin and receives A$ Bank Bill Rates (all payments in A$). The issuer enters into a conventional A$ interest rate swap on *double the total amount of the face value of the Reverse FRN,* whereby it receives a fixed A$ rate (say, $2 \times 9.50\%$ pa $= 19.00\%$ pa) and pays A$ Bank Bill rates (2 times A$ Bank Bill Rates). The result of these swaps would be to leave the issuer with a borrowing (equivalent to the face value of the FRN) at a margin under A$ Bank Bill Rates (in this example, 1.00% pa).

---

[32] For a discussion of inverse FRN issues; see Chapter 19.

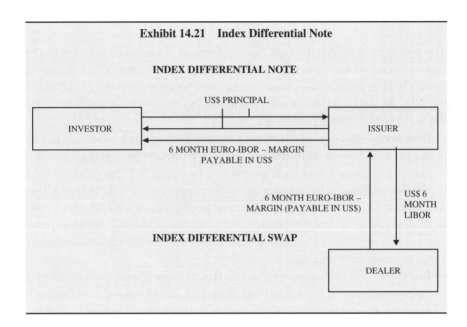

Exhibit 14.21   Index Differential Note

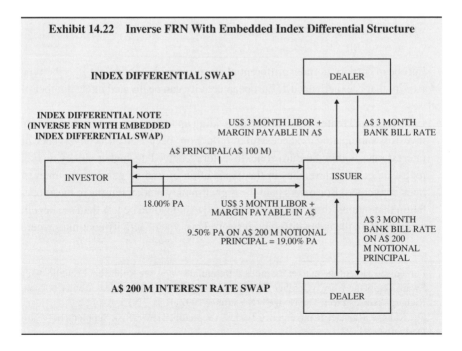

Exhibit 14.22   Inverse FRN With Embedded Index Differential Structure

5.5 Market[33]

The first index differential swaps were undertaken in late 1990/early 1991. The major impetus to the market has been the prevailing structure of global interest rates. The difference in short term interest rates between a number of currencies has been the major drivers of activity. Index differential swaps are used by the following capital market participants:

- **Borrowers** – this is mainly borrowers in currencies in which short-term money market rates have been relatively high. The borrowers have entered into differential swaps to reduce their interest cost by taking positions on the interest differential between the relevant currencies. In the early 1990s, European borrowers switched debt denominated in European currencies in US$ where rates were lower. In the late 1990s/early 2000s, borrowers in many currencies have tried to lower costs by switching borrowing into Yen and US$ where money market rates have been low.

- **Investors** – this enhances returns on relatively low yielding money market investment assets in low interest rate currencies. This has entailed transactions in currencies where money market rates have dropped to relatively low levels, such as US$ short-term investments in 1991–1993 and in 2001/2001, in Yen in the period since 1995, and in Euros and other European currencies in 1999. This has also involved trading interest rate differentials *between any two currencies* without incurring currency exposures.

European activity in index differential swaps provides an insight into the type of activity that is experienced[34]. European activity can be divided into a number of phases:

- **Convergence strategy** – in the period leading up to the introduction of the Euro, investors anticipating its successful introduction speculated on a convergence of interest rates within the Euro zone. Investors received the higher money market return on certain currencies in the expectation of trading gains as the interest rates converged. Borrowers paid the higher money market returns in the expectation that interest differentials would narrow and would be less than the benefit received from the index differential swap. This type of activity continues where

---

[33] For a discussion of the market for index differential swaps, see Robinson, Danielle "Diff Swaps Tempt the Wary" (October 1991) Euromoney 10–11.; Shireff, David and Cookson, Richard "Noises From The Hedge" (November 1992) Risk 21–25.

[34] See Kahane, Raphael "Convergence Trades" (September 1999) Risk Supplement – Euro Derivatives 21–22.

either event driven convergence/de-convergence (entry into the Euro) or economic cycle driven convergence/de-convergence (growth cycles) affect money market interest rate differentials.

- **Positive forward strategy** – these transactions were also undertaken in the period leading up to the introduction of the Euro. The transactions focused on identifying interest rate differential post-Euro conversion. The fact that the positive forward differential is free of interest rate risk where the currency risk is eliminated allows investors and borrowers to take advantage of interest rate differentials.

- **Positive carry strategy** – this is focused on currency pairs where there is a positive current spread but negative forward spreads. This allows investors to create positive carry trades. Borrowers can create lower cost debt where they are willing to switch borrowing indexes between currencies.

A major aspect of activity includes:

- **Economic convergence** – this focuses on the alignment of economic cycles (and monetary policies) in major economies. Index differential swaps have emerged as an efficient way of trading expected convergence or de-convergence of economic cycles.

- **Regulatory factors** – investment restrictions constrain the investment activities of many insurance companies and pension funds. The investors have found it attractive to use index differential swaps to trade interest differentials and monetise expected interest differentials without direct investment in foreign markets and without currency risk.

6 Summary

Basis swaps are floating-to-floating interest rate swaps. The major distinguishing characteristic of basis swaps is that both streams of cash flows exchanged are variable. The two streams are priced off different indexes in the same currency. In certain cases, the cash flows are based off indexes in different currencies but are paid in one currency, eliminating currency risk. There are several types of basis swaps (also known as floating-to-floating interest rate swaps) including arrears reset swaps, index differential swaps and yield curve or constant maturity swaps. Basis swaps generally create value by allowing improved asset-liability matching or trading. Trading opportunities focus on trading yield curve slope (arrears reset swaps and yield curve swaps) or interest rate differentials across currencies (index differential swaps).

15
Options on Swaps/Swaptions

1 Overview

Options on swaps (generally known as swaptions) are a specific type of non-generic swap. Swaptions entail an option on the fixed rate component of a swap transaction. Swaptions combine the features of interest rate options with swap transactions. A variety of structures (callable, putable, collapsible, extendible etc swaps) are available. Each structure effectively represents an option to either enter into or provide the swap at a known price over a specified period. Swaptions are discussed in this Chapter.

The structure of the Chapter is as follows:
* Basic features (structure, mechanics, terminology, characteristics and types) of swaptions are outlined.
* Pricing of swaptions is discussed, including hedging issues.
* Applications of swaptions are analysed.

Swaptions are integrally linked to the market for callable bonds. A callable bond is, in fact, a non-callable bond combined with a receiver swaption. Callable bonds and the relationship with swaptions is discussed in Chapter 16.

2 Swaptions

2.1 Concept[1]

Swaptions entail an option on the fixed rate component of a swap transaction. A swaption is an option on an underlying interest rate swap transaction. The structure and terminology of swaptions, in practice, is complex.

2.2 Structure and Terminology

A swaption provides the purchaser or holder of the option with the right but not the obligation to enter into a swap where it pays fixed rates against receipt of a floating rate index at a future date. The reverse type of transaction, where the holder of the option on the swap will, if the option is exercised, receive the fixed rate, is also feasible.

A swaption usually entails an option on the fixed rate component of a swap. It is designed to give the holder the benefit of the strike rate (that is, the *fixed* rate specified in the agreement) if the market rates are worse, with the flexibility to deal at the market rates if they are better.

The terminology associated with swaptions (much of it consistent with general option terminology) is as follows:

- **Receiver swaptions** – where the purchaser or holder has the right to receive fixed rates under the swap.
- **Payer swaptions** – where the purchaser or the holder has the right to pay fixed rates under the swap.
- **European style** – a swaption that can be exercised only on the expiry date.
- **American style** – a swaption that can be exercised on any business day within the swap option exercise period.
- **Bermudan style** – a swaption that can be exercised on more than one date, where the exercise dates are specified at the time of entry into the transaction[2].

---

[1] See Stavis, Robert M and Haghani, Victor J (1987) Putable Swaps Tools for Managing Callable Assets; Salomon Brothers Inc., New York.; Johnson, Cal (July 1989) Options on Interest Rate Swaps: New Tools for Asset and Liability Management; Salomon Brothers, New York; Tracy, J R, and Goldstein, Gregg "Swap Options: A Descriptive Approach" (August/September 1991) Swiss Bank Corporation Economic and Financial Prospects 1–4; Dare, Lawrence "Swaption Mechanics Explained" in (1994) Corporate Finance Risk Management & Derivatives Yearbook 16–19.

[2] See Sillet, Richard and Davies, David "The Benefits of Occasional Exercise" (August 2001) FOW 33–35.

- **Exercise or strike price** – the specified fixed rate at which the buyer has the right to enter into the swap.
- **Expiry date** – the last date on which the swaption can be exercised and the effective date (if exercised) the fixed and floating components of the swap begin to accrue.
- **Premium** – the consideration paid by the buyer for the swap option.

Exhibit 15.1 sets out the structure of a receiver and payer swaption. **Exhibit 15.2** sets out a typical confirmation of a swaption.

Swaptions generally operate as follows:

- At commencement of the transaction, the purchaser pays the premium to the seller of the swaption.

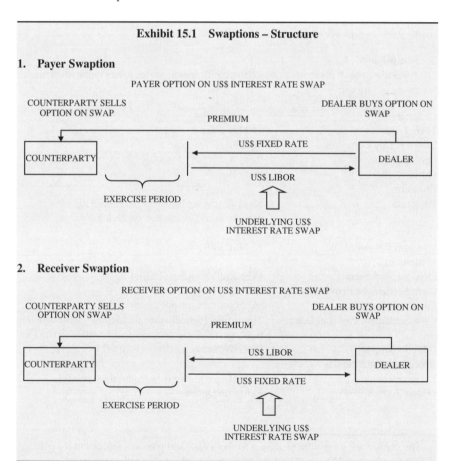

Exhibit 15.1   Swaptions – Structure

1. Payer Swaption

PAYER OPTION ON US$ INTEREST RATE SWAP

COUNTERPARTY SELLS
OPTION ON SWAP

DEALER BUYS OPTION ON
SWAP

PREMIUM

COUNTERPARTY

US$ FIXED RATE

US$ LIBOR

DEALER

EXERCISE PERIOD

UNDERLYING US$
INTEREST RATE SWAP

2. Receiver Swaption

RECEIVER OPTION ON US$ INTEREST RATE SWAP

COUNTERPARTY SELLS
OPTION ON SWAP

DEALER BUYS OPTION ON
SWAP

PREMIUM

COUNTERPARTY

US$ LIBOR

US$ FIXED RATE

DEALER

EXERCISE PERIOD

UNDERLYING US$
INTEREST RATE SWAP

Exhibit 15.2   Swaption – Confirmation[3]

To [Party A]

1. Introduction

The purpose of this letter agreement is to confirm the terms and conditions of the Swap Transaction entered into between us on the Trade date specified below (the "Swap Transaction"). This letter agreement constitutes a confirmation as referred to in the Interest Rate and Currency Exchange Agreement specified below.

The definitions and provisions contained in the 1991 ISDA Definitions (as published by the International Swap Dealers Association, Inc.) are incorporated into this Confirmation. In the event of any consistency between those definitions and provisions and this Confirmation, this Confirmation will govern.

This confirmation supplements, forms part of, and is subject to, the Interest Rate and Currency Exchange Agreement dated [ ], as amended and supplemented from time to time (the "Agreement") between you and us. All provisions contained in the Agreement govern this confirmation except as expressly modified below.

2. Swaption

The particular swap transaction to which this confirmation relates is an Option, the terms of which are as follows:

General

Trade Date	15 May 2001
Business Day Convention	Modified Following
Option Buyer	Party A
Option Seller	Party B
Premium	
Premium	$500,000 (being 0.50% of $100 million) amount payable in one instalment on each Premium Payment Date
Premium Payment Date	17 May 2001
Settlement	
Physical Settlement	[Applicable/Not Applicable]
Cash Settlement Provisions	
Cash Settlement	[Applicable/Not Applicable]
Cash Settlement Payment Date	The second Business day next following the date the rights or rights granted pursuant hereto are exercised
Cash Settlement	[Specify means for determination]
Procedure for Exercise	
Exercise Terms	[Identify terms Buyer is required to specify]
Option Style	European Option

---

[3]   The confirmation includes provision for both cash and physical settlement. In practice, one or other would be used and the confirmation adjusted to reflect the terms.

Exercise Period	15 May 2002 300 p.m. London Time
Written Confirmation	Applicable
Broker/Arranger (if applicable)	

3. Underlying Swap

The particular terms of the underlying swap transaction to which the Option relates are as follows:

General

Notional Amount	US$100 million
Trade Date	15 May 2001
Effective Date	17 May 2002
Termination Date	17 May 2005 subject to the Modified Following Business Day Convention
Fixed Amounts	
Fixed Rate Payer	Party A
Fixed Rate Payment Dates	Every 17 November and 17 May commencing 17 November 2002 and terminating on 17 May 2005 subject to the Following Modified Business Day Convention
Fixed Rate	6.25% pa payable semi-annually in accordance with the Fixed Rate Day Count Fraction
Fixed Rate Day Count Fraction	Semi-annual bond equivalent basis calculate on an actual/365 day year
Floating Amounts	
Floating Rate Payer	Party B
Floating Rate Payment Dates	Every 17 November and 17 May commencing 17 November 2002 and terminating on 17 May 2005 subject to the Following Modified Business Day Convention
Floating Rate	US$ LIBOR of the Designated Maturity reset semi-annually plus the Spread payable semi-annually in accordance with the Floating Rate Day Count Fraction
Designated Maturity	6 Months
Spread	Nil
Floating Rate Day Count Fraction	Semi-annual money market basis calculated on an actual/360 day year
Other Terms	
Netting of Payments	Applicable
Documentation	Standard ISDA
Calculation Agent	Party B
Governing Law	London
Account Details	
Payments To Party A	
Account For Payment	
Payments To Party B	
Account For Payments	

Offices
Party A
Party B

Please confirm that the forgoing correctly sets forth the terms of our agreement by executing the copy of this Confirmation enclosed for that purpose and returning it to us or sending us a letter or telex substantially similar to this letter which letter or telex sets forth the material terms of the Swap Transaction to which this confirmation relates and indicates agreement to those terms.

Party B

- The purchaser of the receiver swaption will exercise the swaption and enter into the swap where interest rates decrease. The purchaser of the receiver swaption will not exercise the swaption if interest rates increase, as it can receive at higher rates than the strike price on the swaption.
- The purchaser of the payer swaption will exercise the swaption and enter into the swap where interest rates increase. The purchaser of the payer swaption will not exercise the swaption if interest rates decrease, as it can pay at lower rates than the strike price on the swaption.
- Exercise will be at expiry of the swaption if the swaption is European. If the swaption is American, then the swaption can be exercised at any time. If the swaption is Bermudan, then the swaption can be exercised on the specified dates.
- Settlement will generally be on either a physical or cash settlement basis. This will operate as follows:
  1. *Physical Settlement* – where physical settlement is used upon exercise of the swaption, the purchaser enters into the underlying swap with the seller. The underlying swap may be for a fixed maturity. In most European and American swaptions, upon exercise the purchaser enters into a swap for a pre-agreed maturity. For example, in a 1×4 payer European payer swaption with a strike of 6.00% pa against LIBOR, the purchaser has the option to enter into a 3 year swap in 1 year. If swap rates in 1 year are above 6.00% pa, then the purchaser will exercise the swaption and enter into the swap. If the swaption was American, then the purchaser could exercise the swaption at any time within 1 year. Upon exercise, the purchaser would enter into a 3 year swap from the date of exercise. In the case of Bermudan options, the purchaser may have the right to enter into a swap *with a fixed final maturity*. This is in contrast to the structure where the swap has a fixed maturity. For example, if the 1×4 swaption described above was Bermudan, with exercises possible on quarterly intervals, then upon exercise the purchaser could enter into a swap with

a final maturity of 4 years (from the date of entry into the swaption). In effect, the purchaser has an option on a 3 year 9 month swap with 3 months expiry, an option on a 3 year 6 month swap with 6 months expiry etc. This is related to the use of Bermudan swaptions with callable debt issues.

2. *Cash settlement* – where cash settlement is used, the purchaser will receive from the seller a payment reflecting the intrinsic value of the swap (calculated normally) based on the actual market rate for the swap on the exercise date where the swaption is in-the-money.

2.3 Characteristics of Swaptions

Swaptions offer protection against interest rate uncertainty in a manner analogous to conventional debt options. The user of swaptions is able to limit risk in switching from fixed to floating interest rates or vice versa, without limiting potential benefits associated with unforeseen *favourable* interest rate movements. In return for this opportunity, the purchaser of a swaption pays a fee - the swaption premium.

Swaptions provide borrowers and investors with flexibility and certainty in managing their assets or liabilities[4]. This can be seen from the fact that before the emergence of these instruments, the only management tool for asymmetric risk management available to customers were exchange-traded options (usually on government bond rates) or to a lesser extent, over-the-counter markets in options on government bond rates.

There are a number of specific characteristics of swaptions that make the instruments particularly useful for asset or liability managers in managing interest rate exposures. These include:

- **Maturity** – swaptions are available with periods to expiration of (up to) 10 years[5]. This is significantly longer than the maturity of options available on futures exchanges and other over-the-counter options.
- **Options on term interest rates** – in contrast to caps and floors which are long dated options on short-term rates, swaptions represent options on intermediate and long-term rates, adding an extra dimension to interest rate risk management for asset and liability managers[6].
- **Spread component** – options and swaps provide an option on the all-in fixed cost of funds for borrowers (or return for investors) as they incorporate a credit

---

[4] For discussion of the emergence of the swaption market, see Krzyak, Krystna "Swaptions Deciphered" (February 1988) Risk 9–17.
[5] Longer swaptions up to 20–30 years may be available in US$, Yen, Euro and Sterling.
[6] See Rombach, Ed "The Cost of Insurance" (May 1991) Risk 12–14.

spread component (the swap spread). This allows borrowers or investors who traditionally use swaps to manage their portfolios to avoid exposure to changing spreads between swap rates and underlying government bond rates.

- **Flexibility** – options and swaps, like other over-the-counter products, are flexible. The user is able to specify exercise dates, amounts, specific strike rates and other structural aspects without the constraint of standardised exchange options and administrative procedures such as deposits and margins.
- **Markets** – swaptions are increasingly available in a wide range of currencies, facilitating their use. The market for swaptions is also increasingly liquid, particularly in major currencies, and that further facilitates their utilisation.

2.4 Types of Swaptions

There are various swap structures referred to variously as callable, putable, collapsible, extendible etc swaps[7]. The structures are ultimately versions of swaptions. The structures are equivalent to combinations of swaps and swaption transactions. The structuring, pricing, trading and hedging of the instruments is based on the capacity to decompose them into either the receiver or payer swaptions.

The structural features of the common types of packaged swaptions available are as follows[8]:

- **Callable swap** – under this structure, the fixed rate payer is allowed to enter into a swap (under the terms of which it pays a fixed rate and receives a floating rate) up to a maximum amount at a known cost up until the end of the expiry of the option. A callable swap is identical to a payer swaption. The reverse structure is also possible, allowing the purchaser of the option to, upon exercise, require the counterparty to pay fixed rate under the swap.

---

[7] It should be noted that the terminology associated with swaptions is far from standardised. There are significant differences in usage between jurisdictions. For example, as discussed in greater detail below, in the United States a putable swap would imply an option whereby the holder, a payer of fixed rates under a swap, would have the right to terminate a swap. In contrast, a callable swap would imply the right of the holder to enter into a swap as a payer of fixed rates. In some other jurisdictions, terminology is exactly opposite, with a callable swap giving the right to terminate the swap arrangement.

[8] The various structures described above are, by no means, a comprehensive listing of variations available. In addition, definitions of the various structures are not universal and variations in usage persist between jurisdictions and markets and even sectors within markets.

- **Putable swap** – under this structure, a fixed rate payer under a swap has the option to terminate the swap at some agreed future date without penalty. Analytically, a putable swap is identical to entry into an interest rate swap under which the holder pays fixed rate and receives floating rate combined with the purchase of a receiver swaption where the purchaser has the right to receive fixed rate and pay floating rate. The expiry date of the receiver swaption coincides with the date on which the fixed rate payer wishes to have the choice of terminating the interest rate swap. Upon exercise of the receiver swaption, the fixed rate and floating rate flows under the original interest rate swap and the swap entered into as a result of exercise of the receiver swaption match and offset each other, thereby effectively terminating the original transaction.
- **Extendible swap** – under the terms of an extendible swap, the fixed rate payer or receiver has the option to continue the swap (upon existing terms) for a fixed period beyond the term of the original swap. Analytically, an extendible swap can be unbundled as follows:
  1. A payer extendible swap is equivalent to a conventional interest rate swap under which the party pays fixed rates and receives floating rates combined with the purchase of a payer swaption where the expiry date of the option coincides with the maturity of the interest rate swap.
  2. A receiver extendible swap is identical to the payer extendible swap except that holder receives fixed rates under the original interest rate swap and purchases a receiver swaption.
- **Cancellable/collapsible swap** – under this structure, a fixed rate payer provides the counterparty with the right to terminate the transaction. Effectively, the fixed rate payer in an interest rate swap sells a payer swaption (where the counterparty at its option pays fixed rates and receives floating rates) on an underlying swap. The swap underlying the swaption commences at a specified time during the life of the original interest rate swap, and matures at the maturity of the original interest rate swap.
- **Contingent swap** – this structure is identical to a receiver or payer swaption. This type of structure is used both with interest rate swaps and currency swaps and linked to contingent assets and liabilities such as call options on debt instruments in the form of warrants or options.

The callable, putable, extendible etc structures incorporate bought or sold swaption positions. The premium can be paid up front. More typically, the premium is built into the swap rate (reflecting the amortisation of the option premium at a nominated funding cost).

3 Pricing Swaptions

3.1 Premium Characteristics

Swaptions are combinations of the swap (portfolios of forward rates) and options. The pricing of swaptions is based on traditional option pricing theory. For pricing purposes, a swaption is the purchase or sale of an option on interest rates (the fixed rate of the swap). The primary determinants of the price or premiums payable on swaptions include:

- **Strike fixed rate** – the level of fixed rates on the underlying swap is one of the key determinants of the value of the swaption. Where the fixed coupon (fixed rate minus any spread relative to the variable index) on the swap is higher, the value of a receiver swaption increases, and conversely the value of a payer swaption decreases.

- **Forward swap rate** – the swaption is an option on the forward swap rate (the swap rate out of the exercise date). Where the implied forward swap rate is higher, the value of the receiver swaption decreases and the value of the payer swaption increases.

- **Maturity of the underlying swap** – an increase in the maturity of the underlying swap will increase the value of the swaption. This reflects the increased price sensitivity of the swap with a longer maturity.

- **Exercise payments (if any)** – this reflects any payment that may need to be made if the swap is exercised. This is used where the swaption relates to a callable or putable bond issue where the call/put is at a premium[9]. Where the exercise payment that must be paid to exercise the option is large, the value of a receiver or payer swaption decreases. The payment can be equated to an increasingly out-of-the-money option that affects the value of the swaption.

- **Time outstanding until exercise** – the remaining time to expiry will affect the value of swaptions. The impact of outstanding time until exercise in the case of some swaptions can be complex. This is particularly the case where the swaption is Bermudan or the underlying maturity of the swap is fixed. If the time to expiration of a swaption is extended holding the final maturity of the swap constant, a variety of factors affect value. The increased time to expiration of the option increases the premium. However, the underlying swap is aging over the life of the option. This may in fact lower the value of the swaption. In the limiting case, where the expiration date of the option equals the maturity date of the swap, the option will, in theory, have no value at maturity.

---

[9] See discussion in Chapter 16.

- **Volatility of the forward swap rate** – as with all options, increases in volatility will increase the value of the swaption.

3.2 Pricing Swaptions – Approach[10]

The basic swaption pricing methodology uses option pricing techniques[11]. The price of a European swaption can be derived using the Black option on forward pricing model.

The pricing of swaptions is undertaken in a number of discrete steps;

- **Calculation of the forward swap rates** – this requires calculation of forward swap rates implicit in the swap yield curve. This is because the underlying asset of the swaption is effectively a forward swap[12].
- **Calculation of swaption price** – this requires the specification of the various inputs (necessary to determine option prices) and incorporating these into the selected option pricing model and calculating the price.

Exhibit 15.3 sets out an example of pricing a European swaption.

3.3 Swaption Pricing – Model Choice Issues

The swaption premium calculations above are derived using a modified Black-Scholes option pricing model (Black's forward pricing model). The modified Black-Scholes formula relaxes some of the assumptions applicable to the original Black-Scholes formula. The following restrictive assumptions remain:

- Prices are for European options *only*. The option is not exercised before expiration date.
- Underlying asset prices are log-normally distributed.
- Interest rates are fixed over the life of the option.
- Volatility is known and constant over the life of the option.

The problem of early exercise can be solved relatively easily. In practice, the binomial model is generally used to value American style exercise swaptions. This uses a discrete time binomial process to create a tree of price outcomes to derive

---

[10] See Tompkins, Robert "Behind the Mirror" (February 1989) Risk 17–23; Smith, David R. "A Simple Method for Pricing Interest Rate Swaptions" (May-June 1991) Financial Analyst's Journal 72–76.

[11] See Das, Satyajit (2004) Derivative Products & Pricing; John Wiley & Sons (Asia), Singapore at Chapters 7 and 8.

[12] See Chapter 13 and Das, Satyajit (2004) Derivative Products & Pricing; John Wiley & Sons (Asia), Singapore at Chapter 6.

Exhibit 15.3   Swaption Pricing – Example

Assume the following swaption:

- **Structure** – A 1 × 4 payer swaption where the buyer has the right to enter into a swap to pay fixed rate at 6.25% pa for 3 years. The option is European exercise and can only be exercised at the end of 1 year.
- **Swap rates** – the 1 year swap rate is 5.875% pa and the 4 year swap rate is 6.10% pa.
- **Volatility** – the volatility of the 3 year swap rate 1 year forward is assumed to be 5% (in price terms).

To calculate the price of the option, the parameters are reconfigured as input for the option pricing model and the price determined.

Face value	100
Dates	
Transaction date	1 October 2001
Exercise date	1 October 2002
Final maturity date	1 October 2005
Swap rates	
To Exercise Date (% pa)	5.88
To Maturity (% pa)	6.10
Implied Forward Rate (% pa)	6.18
Swaption details	
Strike Rate (% pa)	6.25
Discount Rate (% pa)	5.63
Volatility (% pa)	5.00
Type of option	European

The swaption premium is calculated as the price of a call option for a receiver swaption and a put option for a payer swaption. This reflects the fact that all calculation are undertaken in this case in price terms. It is also feasible to derive the swaption premium in yield terms[13].

The swaption premiums calculated are as follows:

Premium	Payer	Receiver
Premium (%)	1.79	1.98
Premium ($/ Million)	17,933	19,847

---

[13] See discussion in Das, Satyajit (2004) Derivative Products & Pricing; John Wiley & Sons (Asia), Singapore at Chapter 8.

The Tables summarises the swaption premiums (% flat) for a range of strike prices (volatility held constant) and volatility (strike price held constant):

Strike Rate (% pa)	Payer Swaption Premium (%)	Receiver Swaption Premium (%)
7.25	0.85	3.59
6.75	1.26	2.72
6.25	1.79	1.98
5.75	2.47	1.38
5.25	3.28	0.91

Volatility (% pa)	Payer Swaption Premium (%)	Receiver Swaption Premium (%)
7.00	2.55	2.74
6.00	2.17	2.36
5.00	1.79	1.98
4.00	1.42	1.61
3.00	1.04	1.23

the value of the option. Within the tree, early exercise possibilities are identified and the tree modified to enable the American option to be priced.

In the case of a swaption, the other breakdowns in the model assumptions include:

- Underlying asset price may not be log normally distributed.
- Interest rates are not fixed over the life of the option.
- Volatility estimates are especially problematic. This is because the swaption may be deep in or out-of-the money, depending on the positioning of the strike. This is especially problematic as the shape of yield curve will dictate the position of the forward swap rate. The impact of the volatility smile on valuation may be significant. A single volatility may also be inappropriate where the swaption is Bermudan.

The issues identified are similar to problems with the valuation of debt options generally[14].

This means alternative approaches must be used to price swaptions. The general approach uses interest rate term structure models[15]. These models seek to address

---

[14]　See Das, Satyajit (2004) Derivative Products & Pricing; John Wiley & Sons (Asia), Singapore at Chapter 8.

[15]　See Das, Satyajit (2004) Derivative Products & Pricing; John Wiley & Sons (Asia), Singapore at Chapter 8. See also Sillet, Richard and Davies, David "The Benefits of Occasional Exercise" (August 2001) FOW 33–35.

the problems identified. The approach used is to create a tree of interest rates that allow valuation of the underlying swap at any point in the future. The interest rate tree is derived from assumed volatility and distribution properties of interest rates. The interest rate tree is also calibrated to market interest rates and implied volatility (based on available cap/floor and swaption volatility).

The advantages of the term structure approach include:
- Ability to incorporate the volatility smile in pricing swaptions[16].
- Ability to value Bermudan exercise feature.
- Ability to value and hedge all interest rate instruments within a consistent framework.

The problems with using term structure models include:
- Computation requirements to provide an accurate valuation are significant.
- There are practical difficulties in calibrating the pricing approach. In practice, it is desirable to calibrate a term structure model for valuing swaptions to a set of European swaptions that underlie the swaption (such as Bermudans) being traded. The full range of instruments may not be available. This makes calibration difficult. It also creates risks that there are internal arbitrage opportunities within the model.
- Assumptions underlying the interest rate term structure models[17].

Increasingly, swaptions with exotic features (such as swaptions with barrier features) are also traded. These structures are valued in a manner similar to exotic options[18].

3.4   Volatility Estimation[19]

Volatility estimation for swaptions is usually undertaken using the following methods:
- Implied volatility (determined from market premiums for swaptions).
- Historical volatility.

---

[16]   See "Swaptions With a Smile" (August 1999) Risk 107–111.
[17]   For a discussion of the problem of interest rate term structure modelling in the context of swaption pricing, see discussion of the Sterling Swaption market later in this chapter. See also Das, Satyajit (2004) Derivative Products & Pricing; John Wiley & Sons (Asia), Singapore at Chapters 7 and 8.
[18]   See Chapters 5, 9 and 10. See Cheuk, Terry and Vorst, Ton "Breaking Down Barriers" (April 1996) Risk 64–67.
[19]   See Das, Satyajit (2004) Derivative Products & Pricing; John Wiley & Sons (Asia), Singapore at Chapter 9.

In the case of historical volatility, it is theoretically necessary to get the volatility of the appropriate forward swap prices. In practice, the volatility of spot swap rates for the relevant maturity may be used.

A variety of alternative approaches are used in practice, including:

- The volatility of government securities for the relevant maturity with an added element for swap spread volatility.
- The volatility of interest rate futures contracts (particularly where the underlying swap is of a relatively short maturity - less than two/three years - reflecting the use of interest rate futures to hedge the position).

3.5   Trading/Hedging Swaptions in Practice

Swaptions are hedged in a manner similar to that used to hedge options generally[20]. The trader matches the delta of the swaption with a position in the forward swap. In the case of portfolios or complex options, the trader may create a series of maturity "vectors" (buckets or points) and aggregate positions within the maturity vectors. The exposure at each point is then hedged. This is designed to increase the efficiency of hedging and reduce transaction costs. The hedge is re-balanced (the gamma) as the yield curve changes. Volatility risk is hedged by trading in swaptions or other interest rate options.

The hedging of swaptions is difficult in practice for a number of reasons[21]:

- Relatively high transaction costs make hedging difficult. The underlying instruments vary in liquidity and trading cost. In the case of longer dated and more complex products, the lack of liquidity and higher transaction costs reduce the ability to hedge effectively. Certain structures such as Bermudan swaptions may have high gamma that necessitates frequent re-hedging that exacerbates the problem.
- The trader has exposure to the complete yield curve (both absolute rates and yield curve shape). This makes hedging complex. The trader is required to hedge as many maturity points as possible and as closely as feasible to reduce risk. The availability of a complete set of market instruments is necessary to allow efficient hedging of the position. In practice, this condition may be difficult to meet in many markets.
- Volatility risk can be hedged by trading in swaptions and other interest rate options. High transaction costs, lack of liquidity and/or absence of a complete

---

[20]   See Das, Satyajit (2004) Derivative Products & Pricing; John Wiley & Sons (Asia), Singapore at Chapter 16.

[21]   For a discussion of the problems of pricing/hedging swaptions, see Polyn, Gallagher "Volatility Dealers' Conundrum" (August 2002) Risk 18–20.

set of instruments may restrict the ability of the trader to manage exposure to swaption volatility risk.

In practice, the pricing/hedging of swaptions exhibits the following patterns:
- In markets with high liquidity, the market swaption premiums trade close to the theoretical swaption values.
- In swaption markets characterised by depth, high trading volumes and the availability of good two way transaction flows, market swaption premiums trade close to the theoretical swaption values. This reflects the ability of traders to assume and hedge exposures.
- Availability of hedging instruments, hedging cost and efficiency of the hedge dictate the pricing efficiency of swaption markets.

Swaption markets vary significantly between currencies. A number of general trends are apparent. Shorter swaptions (that is, those with periods to expiry of less than one/two years) tend to be priced close to their theoretical values. This reflects the following factors:
- Arbitrage opportunities to force prices to theoretical levels.
- Liquidity of the market that facilitates position clearing.
- Availability of a variety of hedging instruments including:
  1. Options on traded interest rate futures contracts.
  2. Capacity to generate forward/forward positions in interest rate swap portfolios.
  3. Availability of option and forward markets in government securities in the relevant currencies.

Swaptions with longer maturities (that is, with periods to expiry in excess of say 3 to 10 years) are more problematic. This reflects the difficulty of hedging the swaption positions. Consequently, these types of swaptions tend to be driven by capital market arbitrage and in particular, the stripping of options from capital market instruments such as callable bonds[22].

The problems of swaption trading/pricing can be illustrated with an example. **Exhibit 15.4** sets out the problems encountered by dealers in the Sterling swaption market.

---

[22]   See discussion in Chapter 16. See also Louis, J.C. "Inside Tullet & Tokyo" (August 1998) Derivatives Strategy 52–53; Mahtani, Arun "Callable Benchmarks to Squeeze Swaption Dealers" (1 May 1999) International Financing Review Issue 1281 96.

Exhibit 15.4   Sterling Swaptions – Hedging Case Study[23]

1. Overview
In 1999, the UK pound sterling ("GBP") swaption market experienced problems. This resulted in losses being sustained by dealers. A significant component of the problems that emerged related to the difficulties in hedging long dated GBP swaptions. In this Exhibit, the nature of the problem and the issues raised are discussed.

2. Guaranteed Annuity Option ("GAO") Contracts
The problem that emerged related to the structure of the UK pension industry. Under UK law, retirees with a pension plan were required to cash in their investment and purchase an annuity upon reaching retirement. UK life insurance companies offered GAO contracts to retiring investors. The structure of the GAO contract was an annuity contract with a floor on the annuity rate received by the pension holders. The contracts were marketed for a lengthy period from the 1970s. The guaranteed rates were high, reflecting the high sterling interest rates prevailing in the 1980s and early 1990s[24].

The life insurance companies are required by the UK FSA and the Government Actuarial Department to fully reserve for all liabilities to policyholders. The liabilities under GAO contracts must be fully reserved. Liabilities must be determined on the basis of actuarial principles and prudent assumptions. The life insurers are allowed to invest in a narrow range of assets.

Historically, the life insurers invested in long dated UK government GBP bonds ("gilts") to fund the GAO contracts.

In the late 1990s, the life insurers began to experience problems with GAO contracts. This problem arose from a combination of the following factors:

- The annuity contract required the payment of the pension until death. Since the 1960s, UK pensioners' life expectancy improved from around 15 years post retirement to 20–30 years. This increased the size of the annuity liability. It also required the life insurers to purchase longer dated gilts to hedge the annuity payments.
- UK interest rates declined sharply in line with the decline in global interest rates. This reduced the investment earnings from the gilts held to hedge/fund the annuity payments.
- The supply of UK gilts decreased as the Government retired debt due to a reduced public sector borrowing requirement.

In effect, the life insurers had sold long dated interest rate options. The life insurers were short receiver swaptions on interest rates (represented by the commitment to pay the minimum guaranteed rates on the GAO rates). As rates fell, the options were in-the-money and the life insurers suffered losses on the GAO contracts. The embedded options were not directly hedged.

---

[23] For a discussion of the problems, see Dunbar, Nicholas "Sterling Swaptions: Volatility by the Pound" (September 1999) Risk 23–28; Dunbar, Nicholas "Sterling Swaptions: Under New Scrutiny" (December 1999) Risk 33–35; Hunter, Kim "Swaptions Scandal" (December 1998) Futures & OTC World 18; Donohue, Jennifer and Sheppard, Susannah "Transferring GAO Risk for UK Life Companies" (February 2000) Risk 49–51.

[24] Some of the policies offered a guaranteed return of around 10% pa.

A complicating factor was the fact that the life insurers were subject to an accrual accounting regime (rather than a mark-to-market regime for dealers). This delayed the recognition of the potential losses from the mismatch in the GAO contracts.

3. Hedging Interest Rate Risk on GAO Contracts

As the problem came to be recognised, the life insurers were forced to hedge the exposure to ensure compliance with solvency requirements.

The life insurers were constrained in their choice of hedging instrument by a number of factors:

- Availability of hedging instruments (direct and derivative) of the required maturity of 10 to 30 years in sufficient size.
- Limited range of eligible investment assets.
- Structure of the solvency margin requirements for life insurance companies.

In practice, the life insurers relied on the following hedging strategies:

1. **OTC derivatives** – this entailed entry into a forward swap or the purchase of a receiver swaption with a dealer. The favoured maturity was 10 × 30 (a 20 year swap commencing in 10 years). The structure allowed the investor to benefit from decreases in GBP rates, offsetting losses on the GAO contract.
2. **Structured notes** – this entailed investment in structured bonds (usually off medium term note/continuously offered debt programs). The structured bond was usually a fixed rate bond with an embedded forward swap or purchased receiver swaption[25]. The structured note was issued by a highly rated (AAA) entity (usually a AAA rated sovereign, supranational or corporation). The structure was used to avoid restrictions on using derivative contracts and the counterparty credit risk of the OTC derivative[26].
3. **Reinsurance** – this entails the life insurer entering into a reinsurance treaty with reinsurance companies to cover the risk of the GAO contracts. This structure takes the form of an excess of loss contract. The loss insured is the annuity payments (defined as potential future losses).

In practice, the principal hedging strategies used were OTC derivatives and structured notes. The hedge structures used entailed the entry into GBP forward swaps (receiving fixed) and purchased receiver swaptions.

4. Relative Value Trading Opportunities

A parallel development that was to impact upon the position was a trading opportunity that emerged in GBP interest rates. In late 1997/early 1998, traders in relative value funds (such as Long Term Capital Management ("LTCM")) and dealer proprietary trading operations identified a pricing anomaly. The forward swap spread in GBP 10 and 15 year forwards was

---

[25] Typical examples were issues by the European Investment Bank and European Bank for Reconstruction and Development. The issues were for GBP 530 million and 40 year maturity. The notes were structured with embedded receiver swaptions. See "Anatomy of a Deal: Scottish Widows and Morgan Stanley" (December 1999) Risk 34.

[26] See discussion of the rationale for structured notes in Chapter 4.

around 80 bps versus 20 bps in Deutschemarks ("DEM") (soon to be incorporated into the Euro).

The trading opportunity was attractive for a number of reasons:

- The expected convergence of GBP and DEM/Euro rates, driven by the anticipated ultimate entry by the UK into the Euro.
- A shortage of GBP assets that could be met by synthesising a GBP asset from long dated Euro denominated bonds. This required a change in regulations governing the UK life insurers.

The expectation was that the spreads would align as a result of these factors. Based on this view, traders went long sterling forward swap spreads and short DEM/Euro swap spreads. The positions were entered into in the expectations that the spread would narrow, allowing the trade to be unwound profitably.

In addition, some relative value traders/proprietary desks also identified an anomaly in interest rate volatility patterns. GBP swaption values were low in relative terms to cap volatility. Traders seeking the gain from a re-alignment in the volatility relationship purchased swaption volatility against sales of cap volatility. The positions were delta hedged to avoid exposure to outright interest rate movements.

The impact of the trading strategies was complex:

- Establishment of the positions exacerbated demand for receiving forward GBP swap rates and short 30 year gilts.
- It created an illusion of liquidity as the traders' willingness to take on this position began to allow the spread/rates to trade at the theoretical/expected level.

5. Hedging Sterling Swaptions

The combination of hedging demand from life insurers and trading demand from relative value investors/proprietary traders increased volumes in GBP forward swaps/swaptions. Dealers active in GBP swap/swaptions quickly acquired very large positions during this period.

Hedging of the positions presented difficult issues. Dealers generally used multi-factor interest rate term structure models to price and derive the hedges for these positions. The market constraints forced the dealers to structure imperfect hedges, albeit matched as to deltas/PVBPs.

The hedging instruments used included:

- **Gilts/gilt futures** – this involved trading in gilts or gilt futures to hedge the position. This entailed using the gilt yield as a proxy for the risk of the forward swap/swaption. The problem with the hedge was that it created significant basis risk. This included exposure to the swap spread. It also included risk to changes in the cash-future basis. It also exposed the dealer to yield curve risk. An additional problem was the shortage of GBP gilt stock.
- **GBP forward swaps** – this used forward GBP swaps or spot start GBP swaps to replicate the forward swaps. The problem with this hedge was the lack of liquidity of the GBP swap market beyond 10-15 years. Where shorter dated swaps had to be used, the hedge had significant yield curve risk. In addition, the higher hedging costs were problematic where the hedge had to be frequently re-balanced.

- **Euro swaps/bonds** – this used Euro denominated bonds, swaps and/or swaptions to hedge the equivalent GBP position. This hedging strategy was predicated on the increased supply of hedges in Euro and the higher liquidity of Euro denominated instruments. The fact that the hedges were cheaper was an additional factor in using Euro based hedges. The Euro based hedge is reliant on the assumed correlation between GBP and Euro rates, spreads and volatility.

6. Postscript

The problem with the hedges of the underlying forward swaps/swaptions emerged in late 1998. In August 1998, LTCM collapsed[27]. Instead of converging as expected, GBP-Euro spreads widened (to 200 bps). In addition, GBP swaption volatility increased to 17% pa from 11% pa.

The combination of the two changes was very significant for dealers. The positions previously entered into were marking to market at losses (the dealers were long the GBP-Euro spread and short GBP swaption volatility).

The unwinding of large positions as relative value funds/proprietary traders incurred losses and hit stop loss levels exacerbated the problem. Liquidity declined, making the position even more difficult to hedge.

The problems led to large losses being sustained by a number of dealers active in GBP swaptions.

4   Applications

4.1   Overview

Applications of swaptions are driven by the same factors that drive the use of options generally. This includes the use of swaptions for contingency hedging, creating asymmetric risk profiles, to monetise existing option positions and generate premium income. There are several aspects of the application of swaptions that are interesting, such as:

- **Swaptions versus caps**[28] – swaption and caps/floors are both OTC interest rate options. There is a tendency to consider swaptions and caps/floors as hedging alternatives. There are significant differences between the instruments:
  1. A swaption is generally on term (medium to long maturity) interest rates. In contrast, caps/floors are on short term money market rates. This means that the exposure hedged is to different interest rates at different points of the yield curve.

---

[27]   See discussion in Das, Satyajit (2004) Risk Management; John Wiley & Sons (Asia), Singapore at Chapter 8.

[28]   See Rombach, Ed "The Cost of Insurance" (May 1991) Risk 12–14.

2. A swaption is a *one-time* option that can be exercised into a swap to either receive or pay the fixed rate for the full term of the underlying interest rate swaps. In contrast, a cap or floor is a *series* of options on a short term interest rate (3 or 6 month LIBOR).

3. A swaption provides protection against the adverse movement in interest rates for the period of the swaption. At the end of this period, the swaption must be exercised or abandoned. If the swaption is exercised into the underlying swap, then the purchaser is locked into paying or receiving the fixed rate. If the swaption is not exercised, then the purchaser has no further protection from changes in interest rates. In contrast, a purchaser of a cap or floor receives the difference between market rate and the strike level over the full life of the contract.

4. Swaptions are priced as a one period option allowing exercise into an underlying swap. In contrast, a cap or floor is a series of options on the relevant interest rate index.

• **Structured swaptions** – swaptions are frequently packaged with conventional swaps to create structured hedging instruments[29]. This is designed to disguise the purchased or sold optionality. The packaging is used to reduce the hedging cost/enhance returns or provide additional flexibility. The benefits of lower cost or enhanced return are created through the sale of a swaption. This entails the assumption of risk to certain interest rate movements. The structures providing additional flexibility usually require the purchase of a swaption. This cost is built into the swap rate and increases hedging costs or reduces returns.

• **Relationship between swaptions and callable bonds** – swaptions are linked to the market for callable bonds. A callable bond is actually a non-callable bond combined with a receiver swaption. This means that swaptions are stripped from callable bonds or used to construct synthetic callable bonds.

In this Section, conventional applications of swaptions and structured swaptions are discussed. Callable bonds and the relationship with swaptions is discussed in Chapter 50.

4.2 Swaption Applications

Conventional applications of swaptions are driven by the need for contingency hedging, creation of asymmetric risk profiles, monetisation of existing option

---

[29] See Chapters 6 and 13.

positions and generation of premium income[30]. Typical applications include:

- **Contingency hedging** – this uses swaptions for hedging uncertain financing or investment requirements. Swaptions allow borrowers and investors to hedge contingent interest rate exposures at a known cost. **Exhibit 15.5** sets out an example of a contingency hedging with swaptions.

- **Anticipatory hedging** – borrowers and investors can use swaptions to hedge future borrowing costs and investment returns. A borrower can purchase a payer swaption to guarantee a maximum funding cost on existing floating rate debt. An investor can purchase a receiver swaption to guarantee a minimum investment return. The purchase of swaptions creates asymmetric protection against movements in term interest rates. The borrower and investor will only exercise the swaption where interest rates move adversely. For example, the borrower would not exercise the payer swaption unless interest rates had increased. If interest rates had decreased, then the borrower would abandon the swaption and would fund at lower market rates. A similar situation would be applicable to the investor. **Exhibit 15.6** sets out examples of anticipatory hedges by borrowers and investors using swaptions.

- **Generation of premium income** – sale of swaptions generates premium income that can be used to reduce borrowing costs or enhance returns. The swaptions can be sold on the following basis:
  1. *Covered* – this entails selling the swaption against an underlying position. If the swaption is exercised, it offsets the existing position within the portfolio. Covered writing of swaptions takes the form of targeted buying or selling of interest rates. For example, a borrower may consider selling an out-of-the-money receiver swaption. The fixed rate on the underlying swap is below the prevailing forward swap rate out of the swaption maturity. The borrower receives premium income for the sale of the option. In the event that interest rates do not fall, the premium income received assists in reducing the borrower's funding cost. In the event that interest rates fall, the payer

---

[30] See "How to Manage Exposures with Swaptions" (January 1986) Corporate Finance 51–52; Ireland. Louise "Call of the Swaptions Market" (July 1988) Corporate Finance 38; McGoldrick, Beth "Swaptions Have Charms for the Investors Too" (April 1989) Euromoney 49; Sheridan, Elayne "Swaptions Take Off." (June 1990) Global Finance 89–92; Sorab, Adam and Hodgson, Mike "Extendable Swaps: Two Way Solutions" (May 1991) Corporate Finance 52; Buchmiller, Jack "Using Swaptions in a Low-Rate Environment" (October 1992) Corporate Finance 40-42; Firth, Andrew "The Proof is in the Versatility" in (1996) Corporate Finance Risk Management & Derivatives Yearbook 37–40; Brown, Keith and Smith, Donald "The Good Banker/Bad Banker Exercise" (October 2000) Derivatives Strategy 43–45.

swaption is exercised. The borrower will have fixed the rate on its floating rate debt. The rationale of this transaction is that the borrower is prepared to swap its floating rate borrowing into a fixed rate at the strike rate of the swaption. Investors use the sale of payer swaptions to convert floating rates to fixed rates. In each case, the effective rate achieved would be the fixed rate under the swap, adjusted for the option premium element arising from the sale of the option on the swap. **Exhibit 15.6** sets out examples of using swaptions to generate premium income by borrowers and investors[31].

2. *Naked* – this is where the swaption sold is not related to an underlying position. It is designed purely as a means of capturing value from an anticipated movement in interest rates. Naked writing of swaptions to generate premium income is more risky than covered writing of swaptions. This reflects the fact that covered sales of swaptions will result in opportunity costs.

- **Monetisation of existing optionality** – this relates to existing option positions within debt or asset portfolios. The swaption is used to manage the embedded risk. This can entail several types of activity:

  1. *Existing debt* – this entails hedging or monetisation of the embedded debt optionality within a funding transaction. The typical case of this structure is the monetisation of embedded call options in callable issues[32]. **Exhibit 15.7** sets out an example of hedging an embedded interest rate option within an export credit loan using a swaption.

  2. *Gap/Prepayment risk* – banks/financial institutions have significant embedded optionality within their portfolios. This may be in the form of balance sheet interest rate exposures (often known as "gap positions"). Typical bank balance sheets are structured with long duration assets funded with short duration liabilities. This results in exposure to increases in rates. Asset liability managers can use purchased payer swaptions to manage the gap exposure. Banks/financial institutions generally have embedded optionality in the form of pre-payment risk. This is where the bank's asset portfolio contains a significant proportion of assets (mortgages or receivables) where the asset duration typically shortens in a low interest rate environment. This is the result of pre-payments as borrowers re-finance the loans. This is similar to call risk

---

[31] The risk of using sold swaptions to generate premium income as a source of cash flow was highlighted dramatically in the transactions involving the UK councils. The Councils collectively wrote a large volume of swaptions merely to generate income by speculating on future interest rate movements. See Das, Satyajit (2004) Risk Management; John Wiley & Sons (Asia), Singapore at Chapter 10.

[32] See Chapter 16.

on a callable bond. Swaptions can be used to hedge the pre-payment risk. This would entail purchasing receiver swaptions to hedge the pre-payment risk[33].

Exhibit 15.5   Applications of Swaptions – Contingency Hedging

Assume a company is tendering to construct a plant estimated to cost US$10 million. The company will fund the construction (if successful) with a floating rate funding facility priced off 6 month US$ LIBOR. The project requires a fixed cost of funding as the tender is on a fixed cost basis. The cost of funding is required on 15 January 2001. The contract will be awarded on 15 April 2001. The company needs to fix the cost of 5 year funds based on current information for a project that will not begin for at least three months, and will not necessarily be awarded to the company.

On 15 December 2000, the company decides to buy a European style payer swaption at a premium of 1.00% of the principal. The company, on exercise, will enter into a 5 year swap where it will pay a fixed rate of 6.00% pa and will receive 6 month LIBOR semi-annually for 5 years. The swaption exercise date is 15 April 2001 (coinciding with the date of award of the contract).

On 15 April 2001, the contract is awarded to the company. The pay-off under the swaption to the company in this case is as follows:
- If 5 year swap rates are above 6.00% pa (say 6.50% pa), then the company exercises the swaption. The result is that the company has fixed rate funding at 6.00% pa. Adjusting for the premium, the cost of funding is 6.23% pa. This is lower than the current market rate.
- If 5 year swap rates are below 6.00% pa (say 5.50% pa), then the company does not exercise the swaption. The company funds the project in the market at current rates. The result is that the company has fixed rate funding at 5.50% pa. Adjusting for the premium, the cost of funding is 5.73% pa. This is lower than the strike rate on the swaption.

In both cases, the company ensures that the cost of funding for the project will not be greater than the presumably acceptable level of 6.23% pa. This is done at a known cost through the purchase of the swaption.

If on 15 April 2001 the company was not awarded the contract, then the company's position would be as follows:
- If 5 year swap rates were above 6.00% pa, then the company would exercise the swaption to capture the intrinsic value (presumably through cash settlement of the position).
- If 5 year swap rates were below 6.00% pa, then the company would not exercise the swaption as it has no value.

In each case, the company has a known cost of buying the interest rate protection (1.00% or $100,000) that can be incorporated into the bid expenses.

---

[33] US mortgage providers use swaption or callable bonds to hedge this pre-payment risk.

Exhibit 15.6 Applications of Swaptions – Anticipatory Hedging

1. Swaption Hedge – Borrower

Assume a borrower with floating rate debt priced off LIBOR. Assume LIBOR rates have increased in the past year. The company is considering hedging to manage its borrowing cost. The company is reluctant to swap into fixed rate as it believes interest rates will not increase significantly (at least above implied forward rates embedded in the swap).

The company has the following hedging options:

- **Do nothing** – this would leave the company exposed to further increases in interest rates.
- **Buy a cap** – this would provide a maximum cost of the cap rate, allowing the company to enjoy the benefit of lower LIBOR rates at each interest rate set date. The 5 year cap with a strike of 6.50% pa on 6 month LIBOR will cost a premium of 3.25% (equivalent to 77 bps pa). This means it will have a maximum borrowing cost of 7.27% pa (cap strike adjusted for the amortised premium). If the cap is not exercised at any interest rate settlement date, then the company will have a borrowing cost of LIBOR plus 77 bps pa.
- **Buy a swaption** – this would provide protection from increases in interest rates to the swaption expiry date. The company 1 × 5 payer swaption (a 1 year European option into a 4 year swap) with a strike rate of 6.50% pa will cost 1.75% (equivalent to 50 bps pa if amortised over the 4 year swap term). Under the swaption, the company must exercise the swaption in 1 years time. It has a single option into 4 year swap rates. If swap rates in 1 year are higher than 6.50% pa, then the company will exercise the swap and fix its borrowing cost for 4 years. The effective fixed rate will be 7.00% pa (the swap rate under the swaption adjusted for the amortised premium). If LIBOR declines below the swap rate at any time over the 4 years, then it will not benefit. If swap rates in 1 year are lower, then the company will not exercise the swaption. It will continue to have LIBOR based borrowing. It will not have any protection against higher interest rates. Its effective cost will be LIBOR plus 41 bps pa (LIBOR adjusted for the borrowing cost of the swaption premium amortised over 5 years).

An alternative strategy would be for the company to sell a swaption. The company could sell a 1 × 5 receiver swaption with a strike rate of 6.00% pa. It receives a premium of 1.25%. The swaption will act as a partial hedge as follows:

- If 4 year swap rates decrease below 6.00% pa, then the dealer will exercise the swaption. The company will fix its borrowing cost at 6.00% pa. The company's effective cost will be 5.64% pa (the swaption strike adjusted for the premium received amortised over the 4 year swap term).
- If 4 year swap rates increase above 6.00% pa, then the dealer will not exercise the swaption. The company will continue to borrow floating rate of LIBOR minus 29 bps (the premium amortised over 5 years).

The sold swaption is not a complete hedge. If 4 year swap rates increase above 6.36% pa over 1 year, then the company is exposed to higher interest costs. If 4 year swap rates decrease below 6.00% pa, then the company will be locked into a fixed rate of 6.00% pa (a rate that will be above market at the time of exercise). The company may find that rate (adjusted for the premium) attractive relative to fixing at current market rates.

2. Swaption Hedge – Investor

Assume an investor with floating rate investments priced off LIBOR. Assume LIBOR rates have decreased in the past year. The investor is considering hedging to manage its investment returns. The investor is reluctant to swap into fixed rate as it believes interest rates will not decrease significantly (at least below implied forward rates embedded in the swap).

The investor has the following hedging options:

- **Do nothing** – this would leave the investor exposed to further decreases in interest rates.
- **Buy a floor** – this would provide a minimum return equivalent to the floor rate allowing the investor to enjoy the benefit of higher LIBOR rates at each interest rate set date. A 5 year floor with a strike of 5.00% pa on 6 month LIBOR will cost a premium of 2.50% (equivalent to 59 bps pa). This means it will have a minimum investment return of 4.41% pa (floor strike adjusted for the amortised premium). If the floor is not exercised at any interest rate settlement date, then the investor will have an investment return of LIBOR minus 59 bps pa.
- **Buy a swaption** – this would provide protection from decreases in interest rates to the swaption expiry date. A 1 × 5 receiver swaption (a 1 year European option into a 4 year swap) with a strike rate of 5.00% pa will cost 1.00% (equivalent to 28 bps pa if amortised over the 4 year swap term). Under the swaption, the investor must exercise the swaption in 1 year. It has a single option into 4 year swap rates. If swap rates in 1 year are lower than 5.00% pa, then the investor will exercise the swap and fix its investment returns for 4 years. The effective fixed rate will be 4.72% pa (the swap rate under the swaption adjusted for the amortised premium). If LIBOR increases above the swap rate at any time over the 4 years, then it will not benefit. If swap rates in 1 year are higher, then the investor will not exercise the swaption. It will continue to have LIBOR based investment. It will not have any protection against lower interest rates. Its effective return will be LIBOR minus 23 bps pa (LIBOR adjusted for the borrowing cost of the swaption premium amortised over 5 years).

An alternative strategy would be for the investor to sell a swaption. The investor could sell a 1 × 4 payer swaption with a strike rate of 6.00% pa. It receives a premium of 1.00%. The swaption will act as a partial hedge as follows:

- If 4 year swap rates increase above 6.00% pa, then the dealer will exercise the swaption. The investor will fix its investment return at 6.00% pa. The investor's effective return will be 6.28% pa (the swaption strike adjusted for the premium received amortised over the 4 year swap term).
- If 4 year swap rates decrease below 6.00% pa, then the dealer will not exercise the swaption. The investor will continue to invest at a floating rate of LIBOR plus 23 bps (the premium amortised over 5 years).

The sold swaption is not a complete hedge. If 4 year swap rates decrease below 6.00% pa over 1 year, then the investor is exposed to lower returns. If 4 year swap rates increase above 6.00% pa, then the investor will be locked into a fixed rate of 6.28% pa (a rate that will be below market at the time of exercise). The investor may find that rate (adjusted for the premium) attractive relative to fixing its returns at current market rates.

Exhibit 15.7   Applications of Swaptions – Monetisation of Embedded Options

1.   Concept
This hedging transaction is used with export credit funding or other subsidised financing available in relation to the acquisition of large capital goods (such as aircraft, ships, power generation equipment etc). Export financing agencies often guarantee a known cost of funding for the beneficiary of the subsidised financing - effectively, granting an interest rate option. There are lags and leads in the adjustment of export financing rates relative to movements in market rates. This means that the subsidy element may effectively increase or decrease (in extreme cases it may be eliminated) as a result of interest rate movements between the time of commitment and the time funding is drawn down. This exposure can be hedged using swaptions.

2.   Example
Assume a company enters into a contract to acquire heavy machinery. Delivery is scheduled in 12 months. The contractual arrangements incorporate a subsidised export credit finance package. Under the export credit, the company has the *option* in 12 months time to enter into an export credit loan for a period of 5 years at a fixed rate of 6.00% pa. The interest rate on the loan is approximately 2.00% pa below normal market rates (the equivalent forward rate in 12 months time).

The company has the following alternatives available to maximise the value of the subsidised financing:
1. **Do nothing** – the company may suffer an opportunity loss if as a result of a fall in interest rates, the subsidy implicit in the financing is eroded.
2. **Sell its interest rate option implicit in the export credit loan** – the company would be exposed to increases in interest rates that may adversely affect the economics of the project.
3. **Enter into a forward start swap** – this would lock in the subsidy at current levels.
4. **Purchase a receiver option on a swap** – This alternative is considered below.

Under the fourth alternative, the company purchases a 1 × 6 receiver swaption to receive fixed rate at 8.00% pa. The pay-offs under this strategy are as follows:
- If 5 year market rates rise, then the option is not exercised. The company uses the export credit financing. The value of the export subsidy has increased.
- If 5 year market rates fall, then the swaption is exercised to lock in the subsidy level.

The above analysis assumes that the company wishes to finance on a floating rate US$ LIBOR basis. Even if the company wishes to finance on a fixed rate basis, the changes in value of the swaption preserve the subsidy value of the export financing.

Assume a premium of the 1 × 6 8.00% pa payer swaption of 1.25%, payable by the company. The company will benefit where interest rates increase by approximately 0.31% pa (that is, 5 year rates increase to 8.31% pa). If rates fall, then the option on the swap locks in a subsidy value of 1.69% pa (being the 2.00% pa subsidy adjusted for the premium).

4.3 *Structured Swaptions*

Swaptions are frequently packaged with conventional swaps to create structured hedging instruments. This is designed to disguise the purchased or sold optionality. The packaging is used to reduce the hedging cost/enhance returns or provide additional flexibility. The premium cost of the swaption is incorporated into the swap rate.

There are a wide variety of structures feasible. Major examples of structured swaptions include:

* **Cancellable swaps**[34] – the basic structure entails entry into a swap that can be cancelled by one party at its option. The structure involves a normal swap in combination with a bought or sold swaption. The swaption incorporated depends on the dynamics of the structure. This includes factors such as the user (borrower or investor) and the objective of the transaction. **Exhibit 15.8** sets out an analysis of cancellable structures, including variations on the structure. The structures discussed are for a borrower. Similar structures could be designed for investors.

* **Extendible swaps**[35] – the basic structure includes entry into a swap that can be extended by one party at its option. The dynamics of the structure are similar to that of cancellable swaps. **Exhibit 15.9** sets out an analysis of extendible structures. The structures discussed are for a borrower. Similar structures could be designed for investors.

* **Exchangeable zero coupon swaps**[36] – this structure is driven by high swaption volatility and a relatively flat yield curve. The structure entails the optional exchange of a zero coupon swap for a normal par coupon swap, **Exhibit 15.10** sets out the structure of an exchangeable zero coupon swap[37].

Exhibit 15.8   Structured Swaptions – Cancellable Swaps

1. Cancellable Swaps – Structure
Under the basic structure, the cancellable swap structure entails entry into a swap that can be cancelled by one party at its option. The structure involves a normal swap in combination with a bought or sold swaption.

---

[34] See Firth, Andrew "The Proof is in the Versatility" in (1996) Corporate Finance Risk Management & Derivatives Yearbook 37–40.
[35] See Sorab, Adam and Hodgson, Mike "Extendable Swaps: Two Way Solutions" (May 1991) Corporate Finance 52.
[36] See Reed, Nick "Salomon's Swap on Stability" (September 1998) Risk 8.
[37] A variation on this structure is the callable zero coupon bond; see Chapter 16.

2. Cancellable Swaps – Example

Under the basic structure, the borrower would enter into a swap for 5 years where it pays fixed rates and receives LIBOR. The borrower or dealer would have the right to terminate the swap at the end of 2 years. There are two structures based on the party that has the option to cancel the swap.

The alternatives are as follows:

- **Borrower (fixed rate payer) has cancellation rights** – the structure can be decomposed as follows:
  1. A fixed rate swap (pay fixed). Assume current swap rates for 5 years are 6.00% pa.
  2. The purchase by the borrower of a 2 × 5 receiver swaption with a strike fixed rate equal to the swap rate.
  3. The borrower pays the premium to purchase of the swaption (the cancellation right). The premium would effectively increase the fixed rate payable under the swap. The premium can be captured in a number of ways:
     - The premium can be amortised into the swap rate. For example, a 5 year swap cancellable at the borrower's option after 2 years may be priced at 6.50% pa (50 bps above the current 5 year swap rate). This structure requires the strike rate of the swaption to be set at 6.50% pa[38]. This is the most common approach.
     - The premium can be paid separately as fee or annuity stream over the term of the swap. For example, a payment of 2.00% upfront or an annuity payment of 47 bps pa over the life of the transaction.

Under this structure, the borrower has fixed rate debt for a period of 2 or 5 years. The borrower has the right to cancel the swap after 2 years.

If 3 year swap rates decrease below 6.50% pa in 2 years, then the borrower will cancel the swap (effectively exercising the swaption that offsets the existing swap). In this case, the borrower is able to take advantage of lower rates. If 3 year swap rates increase above 6.50% pa in 2 years, then the borrower will not cancel the swap. In this case, the borrower is locked into fixed rates as rates are increasing. The borrower has an uncertain duration fixed rate borrowing. The borrowing is at a higher rate than the market non-cancellable swap rate at the time of entry into the transaction. The higher cost is the result of the premium paid for the purchase of the swaption.

- **Dealer (fixed rate receiver) has cancellation rights** – the structure can be decomposed as follows:
  1. A fixed rate swap (pay fixed). Assume current swap rates for 5 years are 5.50% pa.
  2. The sale by the borrower of a 2 × 5 receiver swaption with a strike fixed rate equal to the swap rate.
  3. The borrower receives the premium received from the sale of swaption (the cancellation right). The premium would effectively lower the fixed rate payable under the swap. The premium can be captured in a number of ways:
     - The premium can be amortised into the swap rate. For example, a 5 year swap cancellable at the dealer's option after 2 years may be priced at 5.20% pa (80 bps

---

[38] In practice, this requires an iterative process to solve for the premium and strike rate simultaneously.

below the current 5 year swap rate). This structure requires the strike rate of the swaption to be set at 5.20% pa[39]. This is the most common approach.
- The premium can be paid separately as fee or annuity stream over the term of the swap. For example, a payment of 3.50% upfront or an annuity payment of 82 bps pa over the life of the transaction.

Under this structure the borrower has fixed rate debt for a period of 2 or 5 years. The dealer has the right to cancel the swap after 2 years. If 3 year swap rates increase above 5.20% pa in 2 years, then the dealer will cancel the swap (effectively exercising the swaption that offsets the existing swap). In this case, the borrower is fully exposed to higher rates. If 3 year swap rates decrease below 5.20% pa in 2 years, then the dealer will not cancel the swap. In this case, the borrower is locked into fixed rates as rates are declining. The borrower has an uncertain duration fixed rate borrowing. The borrowing is at a lower rate than the market non-cancellable swap rate at the time of entry into the transaction. The lower cost is the result of the premium generated by the sale of the swaption.

3. Cancellable Swaps – Applications

In practice, the most common structure is the cancellable swap where the borrower sells the dealer the cancellation option. The cancellable swap structure is used by borrowers for the following reasons:
- To reduce interest expense in near term periods in return for taking interest rate risk in future periods.
- Generate up-front premiums (where the premium for the option on the swap is not amortised over the life of the transaction).
- Meet interest cost targets where the target rate cannot be met directly as current interest rates are above target levels.

4. Cancellable Swaps – Variations[40]

The basic structure has a number of variations which are driven by a number of factors:
- Risk preferences of the borrower.
- Yield curve, volatility environment and the value available from the sold swaption or cost of the purchased swaption.

Common variations on the basic cancellable swap structure include:
- **Bermudan cancellable swaps** – the structure described above has a single cancellation date (exercise date). The Bermudan structure allows either party to cancel at specified multiple dates. For example, the structure described could be adjusted to create a cancellable swap that can be terminated at the option of the dealer after 2 years and every

---

[39] In practice, this requires an iterative process to solve for the premium and strike rate simultaneously.

[40] For a discussion of cancellable swap variations, see Firth, Andrew "The Proof Is in the Versatility" in (1996) Corporate Finance Risk Management & Derivatives Yearbook 37–40.

6 months thereafter. This would have the effect of reducing the fixed rate to the borrower to 4.80% pa (120 bps below the swap rate). The lower rate reflects the additional optionality sold by the borrower.

- **Revisable swaps** – this structure allows the borrower to revise the fixed rate under the swap down if interest rates decline. For example, the fixed rate on the swap may be adjusted to 6.20% pa (an increase of 20 bps above the market swap rate). If rates decline below 6.20% pa in 2 years time, then the swap rate resets to a lower level of 5.60% pa (40 bps below the market swap rate). If rates are above 6.20% pa in 2 years time then the swap remains unaltered. The structure entails the following combination:
  1. A normal swap.
  2. Purchase by the borrower of a 2 × 5 receiver swaption at a rate of 6.20% pa.
  3. Sale by the borrower of a 2 × 5 knock in barrier swaption at a rate of 5.60% pa with an in strike of 6.19% pa.
  The higher swap rate is the result of the amortised net cost of the two options.
- **Range cancellable swaps** – this structure entails the borrower achieving lower fixed rate on the swap as long as 3 year swap rates trade in a specified range. For example, the fixed rate on the swap may be set at 6.20% pa (20 bps above the market swap rate). If 3 year swap rates set between 5.40% pa and 6.20% pa in 2 years time, then the swap rate resets to a lower level of 5.40% pa (60 bps below the market swap rate). If 3 year swap rates set outside the range, then the swap rate remains at 6.20% pa. The structure entails the following combination:
  1. A normal swap.
  2. Sale by the borrower of a 2 year range binary option (a double no touch between 5.40% pa and 6.20% pa). The premium received from the sale of the option is used to reduce the swap rate to the borrower. The fixed range binary payout is equal to the net present value payment required to increase the 3 year swap rate from 5.40% pa to 6.20% pa.

Exhibit 15.9   Structured Swaptions - Extendible Swaps

1. Extendible Swaps – Structure
Under the basic structure, the extendible swap structure involves entry into a swap that can be extended in maturity by one party at its option. The structure entails a normal swap in combination with a bought or sold swaption.

2. Extendible Swaps – Example
Under the basic structure, the borrower would enter into a swap for 2 years where it pays fixed rates and receives LIBOR. The borrower or dealer would have the right to extend the swap at the end of 2 years for a further 3 years. There are two structures based on the party that has the option to extend the swap.

The alternatives are as follows:
- **Borrower (fixed rate payer) has extension rights** – the structure can be decomposed as follows:
  1. A fixed rate swap (pay fixed). Assume current swap rates for 2 years are 5.50% pa.

2. The purchase by the borrower of a 2×5 payer swaption with a strike fixed rate equal to the swap rate.
3. The borrower pays the premium to purchase the swaption (the extension right). The premium would effectively increase the fixed rate payable under the swap. The premium can be captured in a number of ways:
   - The premium can be amortised into the swap rate. For example, a 2 year swap extendible at the borrower's option after 2 years into 3 years may be priced at 6.10% pa (60 bps above the current 2 year swap rate). This structure requires the strike rate of the swaption to be set at 6.10% pa[41].
   - The premium can be paid separately as a fee or annuity stream over the term of the swap. For example, a payment of 1.05% upfront or an annuity payment of 60 bps pa over the life of the initial swap.

Under this structure, the borrower has fixed rate debt for a period of 2 or 5 years. The borrower has the right to extend the swap after 2 years.

If 3 year swap rates decrease below 6.10% pa in 2 years, then the borrower will not extend the swap (effectively not exercising the swaption). In this case, the borrower is able to take advantage of lower rates. If 3 year swap rates increase above 6.10% pa in 2 years, then the borrower will extend the swap by exercising the swaption. In this case, the borrower is locked into fixed rates as rates are increasing. The borrower has an uncertain duration fixed rate borrowing. The borrowing is at a higher rate than the market non-extendible swap rate at the time of entry into the transaction. The higher cost is the result of the premium paid for the purchase of the swaption.

- **Dealer (fixed rate receiver) has extension rights** – the structure can be decomposed as follows:
   1. A fixed rate swap (pay fixed). Assume current swap rates for 2 years are 5.50% pa.
   2. The sale by the borrower of a 2×5 receiver swaption with a strike fixed rate equal to the swap rate.
   3. The borrower receives the premium received from the sale of swaption (the extension right). The premium would effectively lower the fixed rate payable under the swap. The premium can be captured in a number of ways:
      - The premium can be amortised into the swap rate. For example, a 2 year swap extendible at the dealer's option after 2 years for a further 2 years may be priced at 5.00% pa (50 bps below the current 2 year swap rate). This structure requires the strike rate of the swaption to be set at 5.00% pa[42].

---

[41] In practice, this requires an iterative process to solve for the premium and strike rate simultaneously. This is problematic as the borrower only pays the full amortised premium if the swap is extended. This means that the premium is amortised over the initial swap maturity.

[42] In practice, this requires an iterative process to solve for the premium and strike rate simultaneously. This is problematic as the borrower only receives the full amortised premium if the swap is extended. This means that the premium is amortised over the initial swap maturity.

- The premium can be paid separately as a fee or annuity stream over the term of the swap. For example, a payment of 0.88% upfront or an annuity payment of 50 bps pa over the life of the initial swap.

Under this structure, the borrower has fixed rate debt for a period of 2 or 5 years. The dealer has the right to extend the swap after 2 years.

If 3 year swap rates increase above 5.00% pa in 2 years, then the dealer will not extend the swap (effectively not exercising the swaption). In this case, the borrower is fully exposed to higher rates. If 3 year swap rates decrease below 5.00% pa in 2 years, then the dealer will extend the swap by exercising the swaption. In this case, the borrower is locked into fixed rates as rates are declining. The borrower has an uncertain duration fixed rate borrowing. The borrowing is at a lower rate than the market non-extendible swap rate at the time of entry into the transaction. The lower cost is the result from the premium generated by the sale of the swaption.

3. Extendible Swaps – Applications

In practice, the most common structure is the extendible swap where the borrower sells the dealer the extension option. The extendible swap structure is used for the same reasons as the cancellable swap. The two structures are very similar because of the equivalence provided through put call parity. The extendible swap structure can be varied in exactly the same way as the cancellable swap.

Exhibit 15.10   Structured Swaptions – Exchangeable Zero Coupon Swaps

The basic structure is as follows:

Notional Principal Amount ($)	10 million
Trade Date	1 July 2001
Maturity	1 July 2011
Initial Swap	Unless the dealer exercises the conversion option: • Counterparty pays fixed rate at 6.00% pa payable semi annually on a zero coupon basis at maturity (compounded at the fixed rate). • Dealer pays 6 month LIBOR re-set at each interest payment date and paid in a zero coupon basis at maturity (compounded at the current LIBOR rate for each period)
Conversion Option	The dealer can, on any reset date, convert the initial swap into a normal current coupon swap on the following terms: • Counterparty pays fixed rate of 6.00% pa payable semi-annually on each re-set date following the exercise of the conversion option. • Dealer pays 6 month LIBOR re-set at each interest payment date and paid on each re-set date following the exercise of the conversion option.

| Re-set dates | Every 6 months from the commencement date till maturity |

The structure operates as follows:

- The counterparty enters into a zero coupon swap with the dealer[43]. Counterparty pays the fixed rate in a zero coupon amount at maturity. Dealer pays LIBOR re-set semi-annually. The LIBOR payments are accrued, compounded at the current LIBOR rate and paid at maturity. This is to reduce the counterparty credit risk of the structure.
- The dealer has a one time option to convert the zero coupon swap into a normal par swap. This conversion option exists at each semi-annual LIBOR set date. If the conversion option is exercised, then the zero coupon swap is replaced by a normal par coupon swap as follows:
  1. Counterparty pays the fixed rate on each semi-annual payment date.
  2. Dealer pays LIBOR on each semi-annual payment date.
  3. On the conversion date, the counterparty pays the accrued zero coupon payment up to that date and the dealer pays the accrued LIBOR to that date. This is done as net cash flow settlement.

The structure involves the counterparty selling a string of receiver swaptions to the dealer. This is because the zero coupon swap entails the counterparty agreeing to re-invest the coupons under the swap at the zero coupon swap fixed rate. If rates decrease, then the re-investment rate is attractive to the dealer. If rates increase, then the re-investment rates are no longer attractive. In this case, the dealer would prefer to receive current cash flow that can be re-invested at (higher) current market rates. The position is equivalent to that under a bought receiver swaption. The swaption is a Bermudan structure with exercise every 6 months. The swaption is also on an increasing amount, reflecting the accrual of the coupon that is re-invested through the swap.

The sale of the swaptions reduces the effective fixed rate under the exchangeable zero coupon swap. The fixed rate is generally lower than the normal par coupon fixed rate and the zero coupon swap rate. The structure will benefit the payer of fixed rate where interest rates are stable or decline by a small amount.

5 Summary

Swaptions are a specific type of non-generic swap which combine the features of interest rate options with swap transactions. A variety of structures (callable, putable, collapsible, extendible etc swaps) are available. Each structure effectively represents an option to either enter into or provide the swap at a known price over a specified period. Swaptions are traded either on a standalone basis or in structured packages in combination with conventional swaps. The principal applications

---

[43]   See discussion of zero coupon swaps in Chapter 13.

include contingency hedging, creation of asymmetric risk exposures, generation of premium income and monetisation of embedded debt optionality. The last aspect is most relevant in the context of callable bonds. Pricing of swaptions is similar to the pricing of debt options generally. The long dated nature of some swaption structures creates special hedging risks.

16
Callable Bonds

1 Overview

A callable security is a fixed rate bond where the issuer has the right but not the obligation to repay the face value of the security at a pre agreed value prior to the final original maturity of the security.

Callable bonds are an example of structured notes. They are amongst the most common and traditional types of structured note transactions. A large universe of publicly traded as well as privately placed transactions including fixed rate bonds and equity linked securities (convertibles and preference shares/preferred stocks) incorporate call provisions. The concept has evolved over time and been extended to a variety of transactions where debt option features are embedded in securities. The variations include debt warrants, step-up/multi-step callable bonds and putable bonds.

This Chapter examines callable bonds. The Chapter is structured as follows:
- The structure of callable bonds is described.
- Valuation of callable securities is discussed.
- Applications of callable bonds for both issuers and investors are examined.
- Use of options on swaps to monetise callable bonds is outlined.
- Variations on callable structures, particularly detachable debt warrants, step-up/ multi-step callable bonds and putable bonds and the market for callable securities are described.

2 Callable Bonds – Structure

2.1 Concept

A callable security is a fixed rate bond where the issuer has the right but not the obligation to repay the face value of the security at a pre agreed value prior to the final original maturity of the security.

Exhibit 16.1 Callable Bonds – Structure	
Amount	US$100 million
Issue Date	15 September 2002
Maturity	15 September 2012 (10 years)
Coupon	8.00% pa (payable annually)
Call Provision	Callable, subject to 30 days notice, as follows:

Call Date	**Call Price**
5 years (15 September 2007)	103% of Face Value
6 years (15 September 2008)	102% of Face Value
7 years (15 September 2009)	101% of Face Value
8 years (15 September 2010)	100% of Face Value
9 years (15 September 2011)	100% of Face Value

Exhibit 16.1 sets out the terms and structure of a typical callable bond. The example is of a bond with an original final maturity of 10 years that is callable on each annual coupon date after 5 years; that is, the bond is *call protected* for a period of 5 years (referred to as the non-call period). The call is exercisable at a premium to the face value of the bonds. The initial call premium is 3% of face value, declining at the rate of 1% per annum. Callable bonds, where the call provision does not require payment of a premium (par call) upon repayment, are also commonly used.

The call provision, in this case, provides for the issuer to repay the bond in full at face value at its sole choice on the relevant dates. If interest rates decrease, then the issuer will call the bond and pre-pay the debt where interest rates decrease (the price of the bond increases). This reflects the fact that the issuer can re-finance at lower interest rates. If interest rates increase, then the issuer will not call the bond.

2.2   *Characteristics*

Callable bonds are a combination of a fixed interest security with an option on the price of the security. The structure of a callable bond is as follows:

Callable Bond = Straight (or Non-Callable) Bond plus Option

In practice, the embedded option is equivalent to a receiver swaption[1] sold by the investor to the issuer.

---

[1]   For discussion of swaptions, see Chapter 15.

The option element can be characterised in the following ways[2]:
- Call option on the price of the bond sold by the investor to the issuer. The option is on a bond with maturity identical to that of the final maturity of the bond, a strike price equal to the call price, and an expiry date equal to the call date. The call option allows the issuer to repay the bond before its original scheduled maturity as of the call dates at the prescribed call prices.
- Put option on the price of the bond sold by the investor to the issuer. The option is on a bond with a maturity equal to the period *from the call date to the final maturity of the bond*, a strike price equal to the call price, and an expiry date equal to the call date. The issuer issues a bond with a maturity equivalent to the first call date (5 years in the above example). The issuer has the option (sold by the investor) to issue additional debt with a maturity equivalent to the period between the call date and the final maturity of the original bond.

The different characterisation does not affect the fundamental economics of the option feature. In both cases, the option possesses economic value. This value derives from the fact that if interest rates decrease, then the issuer can refinance itself for the period between the call date and the original maturity of the bond at a lower effective cost than the coupon on the original bond adjusted for the call premium (if any).

Several features of the debt option embedded in the security should be noted:
- The underlying asset (the debt security) has a variable life (that will, at the very least, differ from that of the term of the original bond). This dictates that the value of the debt option will be a factor of the shape of the yield curve.
- The call option in the above example (a typical structure) has multiple exercise dates. It is a Bermudan option that is exercisable on specific dates prior to the final maturity of the option.
- The premium for the option sold by the investor is incorporated in the bond by way of a higher coupon (relative to a comparable non callable transaction).

In summary, the callable bond may be characterised as a classical option "buy-write" transaction where the investor purchases a fixed maturity bond and sells an option on *that bond* to the issuer. The unique element of the transaction is the incorporation of the optionality into the terms of the bond itself.

<hr>

[2] This is an application of put-call parity in relation to the underlying bond.

2.3   Price Behaviour

The structure of the callable bond dictates its economic characteristics. The characteristics can be analysed in terms of traditional measures such as bond price behaviour, duration and convexity. Each of the features is considered in turn.

The price behaviour of a callable bond relative to an identical non callable bond is dominated by the potential for early repayment of the callable bond where interest rates fall (the price of the bond rises). The possible shortening in the life of the callable bond means that as interest rates fall, the callable bond will begin to trade at a price lower than that of the comparable non callable bond, reflecting the possibility of early repayment. Economically, the accretion in value of the bond, resulting from the impact of discounting the bond cash flows at a lower interest rate, is offset by the increasing value of the option sold.

This characteristic dominates the trading price behaviour of callable bonds. Where the interest rate structure is at a level well above that of the bond coupon (the option has low value), the bond trades below par. In this circumstance, the callable bond should in fact outperform a comparable non callable issue, reflecting the higher coupon on the callable bond. A fall in interest rates will generally cause an appreciation both in the value of the callable and corresponding non-callable bond. The increase in bond value for the two bonds will be similar. In the case where the market interest rates are below the coupons on the bonds, the price behaviour of the two securities will diverge. The callable bond will underperform the non callable bond. The increasing value of the call dominates the price changes of the callable as the likelihood of a call increases. **Exhibit 16.2** and **Exhibit 16.3** set out the price characteristics of a callable and a non callable bond.

Fixed income investors traditionally use the concept of duration to measure the life of the series of fixed cash flows embodied in a bond. Duration, in this context, serves as a means of measuring the interest rate sensitivity of a security. The concept of duration is capable of being applied to callable bonds to provide a measure of the price behaviour of such securities[3].

The application of duration approaches to callable securities is problematic because typically the measure can only be calculated where the bond cash flows are known with certainty. In the case of a callable bond, the uncertain maturity that is interest rate related creates a number of difficulties. The central problem is that the

---

[3]   For a discussion on duration, see Das, Satyajit (2004) Derivative Products & Pricing; John Wiley & Sons (Asia), Singapore at Chapter 5. For a discussion on duration of a callable bond, see Latainer, Gary D., and Jacob, David P. (October 1985) Modern Techniques for Analysing Value and Performance of Callable Bonds; Morgan Stanley Fixed Income Analytical Research, New York at 7–10.

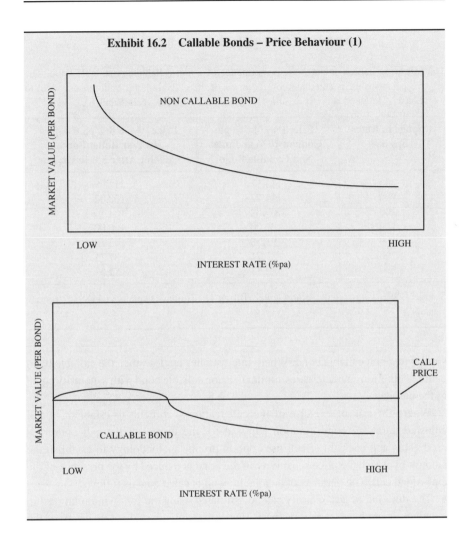

Exhibit 16.2   Callable Bonds – Price Behaviour (1)

embedded call option decreases the sensitivity of the price of a callable bond relative to that of a non callable bond as interest rates decrease (particularly below the callable bond coupon). The estimation of the sensitivity of the callable bond price to the embedded option is central to determination of its duration characteristics.

The duration characteristics of a callable bond are most difficult to estimate where there is uncertainty as to the risk of exercise of the call option (effectively when the option is trading at-the-money). This reflects the fact that where the interest rates are very high (low) relative to the bond coupon, the low (high) probability of early repayment dictates that the callable bond exhibits duration characteristics

---

Exhibit 16.3   Callable Bonds – Price Behaviour (2)

The following Table compares the performance of a non callable and callable bond. The relative performance is calculated on the basis of the callable bond trading on a yield to worst basis. The yield curve is assumed to remain flat between years 5 and 10.

Change in Rates (bps pa)	Price (%) of 8% pa Coupon 10 Year Bullet Non Callable Bond	Price (%) of 8% pa Coupon 10 Year Bullet Bond Callable After 5 Years at Par
−300	123.17	112.99
−200	114.72	108.42
−100	107.02	104.10
0	100.00	100.00
+100	93.58	93.58
+200	87.71	87.71
+300	82.33	82.33

Source: CSFB as quoted in Stillit, Daniel "Biting The Bullet" (September 1988) Corporate Finance 61–65 at 62.

---

similar to a non callable bond. Where interest rates are low, then the callable bond exhibits duration characteristics similar to a non callable bond with a maturity equal to the call date.

Where the risk of exercise of the call feature is difficult to establish, a call adjusted duration (bond duration adjusted for the impact of the call option) is used. This approach, in effect, uses option pricing methodology to establish the amount by which the price sensitivity of the bond is reduced by the presence of the embedded call. The duration of a callable bond is calculated as follows[4]:

• The duration of any security can be estimated using the following relationship which is predicated upon the basis that it measures the price sensitivity of the security with respect to interest rates:

$$D = -\Delta P/P \times (1 + y/2)/\Delta y$$

Where

   D = Duration

---

[4]   See Latainer, Gary D., and Jacob, David P. (October 1985) Modern Techniques for Analysing Value and Performance of Callable Bonds; Morgan Stanley Fixed Income Analytical Research, New York at 8.

ΔP = Change in price of the bond for a small change in interest rates

P = Current price of bond

y = Current bond equivalent interest rate.

- In the case of a callable bond, this formula is used with the following input adjustments:

  y = Bond equivalent yield on underlying *non callable* bond

  P = Price of callable bond using an option pricing model.

- The duration of a callable bond using this approach will typically need to be solved numerically, reflecting the absence of a closed form solution to the problem of pricing debt options.

Exhibit 16.4 sets out an example of calculating the adjusted duration of a callable bond.

The duration behaviour of a callable bond using the concept of call adjusted duration can be summarised as follows:

- The duration of a callable bond is most affected by the call feature where the call option has a high value, as it reduces the price appreciation of a callable bond relative to a comparable non callable bond.

- For bonds generally, duration falls (increases) as interest rates increase (decrease). In the case of callable bonds, the sold call option has the effect of *decreasing* duration as rates fall. This reflects the likelihood of early repayment (effectively the reduction in the number of cash flows that will only extend to the call date).

- Where the call value is high, it is more likely that a callable bond's duration falls (increases) as rates decrease (increase). For a given change in rates, the duration change for a callable bond will, in general terms, be lower than that for an equivalent non callable bond.

- The duration of a callable bond is sensitive to the passage of time. As the call protection period diminishes, the uncertainty regarding the remaining cash flows of the bond increases. The value of the call feature increases and impacts on duration to a greater degree.

An alternative measure of the price behaviour of a fixed interest security is convexity. This measures the change in price sensitivity of a bond for a given change in yields. Bonds generally have positive convexity characteristics, reflecting the fact that a fall in yields will result in an increasing level of price appreciation. Callable bonds under defined circumstances are characterised by negative convexity. This reflects the callable bond's duration behaviour. This characteristic is most marked in long remaining term to maturity securities with little remaining call protection.

Exhibit 16.4 Callable Bonds – Duration Behaviour

Consider the call adjusted duration of the following security:

Maturity	27 years
Coupon	12% pa
Call Provision	After 2 years at 109.60

Where the yield on the underlying bond is 11% pa and assuming an annualised yield volatility of 12%, the call adjusted duration is approximately 6.6 years. If the yield falls to 9% pa, then the callable bond's duration falls to 4.4 years. This contrasts with a duration of a non callable bond with the above characteristics of around 9 years and a duration of a bond with a maturity equal to the call date of around 1.8 years.

Source: Latainer, Gary D., and Jacob, David P. (October 1985) Modern Techniques for Analysing Value and Performance of Callable Bonds; Morgan Stanley Fixed Income Analytical Research, New York at 7,8.

These bonds are characterised by high negative convexity, reflecting the uncertainty associated with the bond's cash flows.

3 Callable Bonds – Valuation

The valuation of callable securities is predicated on the decomposition of the security into its components:

Price of a callable bond = price of comparable non-callable bond plus price of the call option

Using this approach, the callable bond value is calculated as the combination of a purchase of a non callable bond and a sold position in a call option where the purchaser has granted this option to the issuer. In practice, the price of the call option is based on the value of the embedded receiver swaption. The premium receipt for the sale of the option is embedded in the higher yield of the callable bond.

This relationship can be used to derive the value placed on the embedded call. For example, given the price of comparable callable and non callable bonds, the difference in value should equate in an arbitrage free world to the price of the call option.

An important point to note regarding the valuation of the debt option component of a callable bond is that it is essentially an option on the *forward* price of the underlying bond *at the call date*. Consequently, the value of the bond is driven by the changes in forward interest rates.

The fair value of the call option component can be valued using conventional option pricing techniques[5]. The factors impacting on the value of the option are consistent with those affecting other options. The specific characteristics of the embedded debt option mean that a number of other factors are relevant to the valuation including:

- The payout on the asset (effectively the bond coupon) must be adjusted for in one of two possible ways:
  1. The coupon is treated as a continuous return on the asset and used to adjust the carry cost or risk free discount rate.
  2. The present value of the coupon is deducted from the value of the bond that is then treated purely as a zero coupon bond.
- The structure of the underlying bond and the optionality embedded on that security dictates that the option value is a function of:
  1. Term structure of interest rates consistent with the declining remaining life of the bond dictates the accretion in the value of the bond that determines in turn the value of the debt option.
  2. Term structure of volatility that is related to the declining maturity profile of the underlying asset as with a shorter bond, the effective volatility will decline towards zero.

The identified issues are present in the pricing of debt options generally[6].

In practice, a common means of determining the value of the embedded call option is to establish the range of values that the bond underlying the option can assume at maturity. Once the distribution is determined, the expected value of the option at expiration or on call dates (where the option is Bermudan) can be established and discounted back to the time of valuation.

The key issues in this valuation approach are[7]:

- Treatment of uncertain interest rates inclusive of term structure changes in determining the potential distribution of bond values.

---

[5]   See discussion in Das, Satyajit (2004) Derivative Products & Pricing; John Wiley & Sons (Asia), Singapore at Chapters 7 and 8.

[6]   See discussion in Das, Satyajit (2004) Derivative Products & Pricing; John Wiley & Sons (Asia), Singapore at Chapter 8. See also Kish, Richard J and Livingston, Miles, "Estimating the Value of Call Options on Corporate Bonds" (Fall 1993) Journal of Applied Corporate Finance 91–94.

[7]   See Bookstaber, Richard, Hanley, William C., and Noris, Peter D. (December 1994) Are Options on Debt Issues Undervalued?; Morgan Stanley Fixed Income Analytical Research, New York at 4–16, 32.

- Incorporation of particular distributional assumptions in the pricing approach. Classical option pricing models assume a distribution of the changes in the underlying asset prices at maturity that is log normal. Given that bond prices are determined by complex movements in interest rates, the bond prices that would arise from the distribution of interest rates is unlikely to be log normal even if changes in the interest rates were log normal in distribution.
- Pricing consistency within the model must be maintained. The distribution of future bond prices based on an assumed interest rate process must ensure that the overall interest rate structure is consistent; for example, the distribution should not generate *negative* forward interest rates. Similarly the model must be constrained to ensure that logical valuation relationships are maintained. For example, working within a yield curve of returns, the failure of put-call parity is possible, leading to a fundamental inconsistency within the pricing logic.

An additional factor that influences the value of callable bonds is the possibility of early exercise of the call option. In the case of some bonds, exercise is only feasible on the specified call date. Where exercise is feasible at any time before the expiration of the call option (the Bermudan structure incorporates this feature in part as the call is exercisable on specific dates before maturity), the risk of early exercise is relevant to the value of the option.

The key determinants of early exercise are:

- The tendency of the bond price volatility to decline as the life of the underlying bond declines (reflecting the tendency of the bond price towards par at maturity).
- The ability to lower the interest rate on the borrowing from the rate equivalent to the bond coupon upon exercise. Assume a bond with a coupon of 10% pa that is currently callable at any time but has a further 5 years to final maturity. Where interest rates fall to 8% pa, early exercise would generate value equal to the 2% pa difference between the bond coupon and the current interest rate. This establishes the value of early exercise as the present value of the interest expense savings. For a callable bond, a sharp decrease in interest rates will generally favour early exercise as the intrinsic value of the option begins to dominate the remaining time value of the option.

4 Callable Bonds – Applications

4.1 Overview

The utilisation of callable bonds by issuers and investors is based on the performance characteristics and value dynamics of the instrument. The applications of callable bonds include:

- Inclusion of callable securities in liability and asset portfolios primarily as a means of managing interest rate risk in the portfolios.
- Monetisation of the value of the embedded call option through the use of swaptions.

In this Section, the first class of application that can be regarded as the traditional use of callable bonds is examined. In the following Section, the second class of application is analysed.

4.2   Issuer Applications[8]

The incorporation of call provisions in a fixed interest bond provides the issuer with the option to retire the debt and re-finance the borrowing at lower interest rates. The refunding would have the impact of reducing the interest cost of the issuer.

There are a number of separate issues regarding the inclusion of a call option in a bond, including:

- The rationale for the issuer, including a call option within the bond issue.
- The optimal refunding strategy for callable bonds.

Financial economists have questioned the advantage of incorporating a call feature. They argue that given a fair value of the call, any *expected* gains to the issuer from refinancing the bond at a lower interest rate represents a corresponding loss to the investor. The higher return demanded by the investor in a callable bond relative to equivalent non callable securities should offset any expected gain from the potential exercise of the call. In effect, if the call option is fairly valued, then the incorporation of the call feature will offer advantages to the issuer that will be *exactly offset* by the premium charged.

An additional element to this argument is that the yield curve, including the implied forward interest rates, already embodies market expectations about future interest rates that should reduce the advantage conferred by incorporation of the call feature.

Against this background, the incorporation of a call provision can only be justi-fied economically on the basis of the superior knowledge or forecasting of ability of the issuer in respect of future interest rates. This argument is unsustainable on

---

[8]   See Kraus, Alan "An Analysis of Call Provisions and the Corporate Refunding Decision" (Spring 1983) Midland Journal of Corporate Finance vol 1 no 1 46–60.

the following basis:

- There is no compelling basis for accepting that issuers can systematically outperform investors in predicting the path of future interest rates.
- Even if the issuer did possess such superior knowledge, then over time investors would interpret the incorporation of call features as signalling issuer expectations that rates were likely to fall below current expected and implied levels. The investors would increase the premium for the call option to levels that would negate any economic benefit of the call provision.

Consequently, it is difficult to attribute the incorporation of call features in bond issues *solely* to the interest rate expectations of the issuer.

Financial economists have identified at least three different possible reasons for issuers to issue callable bonds[9]:

- Use of call options to enable issuers to prepay debt to eliminate any restriction on the activities of the firm.
- Possible tax advantages.
- Reduction of interest rate sensitivity of a bond's value to changes in interest rates to manage the equity value of the firm.

The call provision allows the issuer to retire debt where the terms and conditions (particularly the covenants associated with the issue) are restrictive to the company. Bondholders generally impose covenants on issuers, imposing restrictions on the operating flexibility of the issuer.

The restrictions include maintenance provisions (requiring compliance with financial ratios such as leverage restrictions, fixed charge coverage, minimum capital levels etc) and negative provisions (preventing the issuer from undertaking certain investments, sale of business, corporate restructures etc). The inclusion of covenants is to protect bondholders that typically, in the absence of ownership rights or representation, are unable to control the activities of the issuer. The nature of the restrictions is related to the credit standing of the issuer. Issuers with lower credit standing are required to place more onerous restrictions on activities. The provision of covenants facilitates both issuer access to capital as well as effecting a reduction in the issuer's cost of debt funds.

Under certain circumstances, the restrictions may be of a magnitude that the cost to the issuer in terms of forgone business opportunities is greater than the savings on debt cost that are achieved through the provision of the covenants. The callable

---

[9]   See Kraus, Alan "An Analysis of Call Provisions and the Corporate Refunding Decision" (Spring 1983) Midland Journal of Corporate Finance vol 1 no 1 46–60.

structure in these situations would provide an upper limit on the retirement cost of the bonds. It does not place the issuer in a position of having to seek to re-purchase its bonds which is, of necessity, purely voluntary for the investor as an alternative means of repaying the debt.

The flexibility to use the call to undertake otherwise restricted activities provides a rationale for the incorporation of call features in funding transactions. In essence, the payment of the call premium allows the issuer to preserve operating flexibility.

The call provision may also benefit issuers where there is a tax rate asymmetry; that is, where the marginal tax rate of the issuer is *higher* than that of the investor. This reflects the fact that the higher interest cost is deductible to the issuer at a higher rate than it is taxable in the hands of the investor, thereby enhancing the present value of the debt tax shield for the company.

The call feature may also act as a mechanism to protect issuers from exposure to interest rate risk. The call provision decreases the interest rate sensitivity of a bond to movements in interest rates. Changes in bond prices equate to a risk for the investor. There is an implicit relationship between changes in interest rates, economic activity and the operating cash flows of a company. Changes in bond prices translate into changes in the market value leverage of the firm and the relative risk of the equity securities of a company. The incorporation of a call feature under these circumstances through a reduction in the sensitivity of bond prices benefits equity investors by lowering the risk to the capital providers. This may, in turn, lower the company's required return on equity capital.

As evident from the above discussion, the case for inclusion of call provisions in a bond issue is complex.

Where a bond is callable, the issuer must determine the optimal refinancing strategy that maximises the value of the embedded option. The key issue is the problem of early exercise that eliminates the remaining time value of the option.

The optimal refunding strategy has been the subject of considerable debate[10]. The basic strategy for calling a bond can be summarised as follows[11]:

* If there are no new issue costs associated with the refinancing issue, then the bond should be called if it trades above its call price.

---

[10] See Kraus, Alan "An Analysis of Call Provisions and the Corporate Refunding Decision" (Spring 1983) Midland Journal of Corporate Finance vol 1 no 1 46–60; Finnerty, John D. (1984) An Illustrated Guide To Bond Refunding Analysis; The Financial Analysts Research Foundation, Charlotteville, Virginia; Finnerty, John D., Kalotay, Andrew J. & Farrell Jnr., Francis X. (1988) The Financial Manager's Guide To Evaluating Bond Refunding Opportunities; Ballinger Publishing Company, Cambridge, Massachusetts.

[11] See Kraus, Alan "An Analysis of Call Provisions and the Corporate Refunding Decision" (Spring 1983) Midland Journal of Corporate Finance vol 1 no 1 46–60.

- If new issue expenses are present and significant, then the call should be exercised where interest rates decline sufficiently such that the bond has traded above the call price and then returned to the call price.

The optimal call strategy is dictated by the fact that the benefit to shareholders from calling the bond is a function of the repurchase of the coupon and principal at less than its market value and the difference is greater than the refinancing costs. This is reflected in the actual trading behaviour of callable bonds that trade close to the call price when the market anticipates that the security will be repaid. Callable bonds often trade at a level above the call price even where the interest rates have fallen below the bond coupon, reflecting investor consideration of issue expenses that will defer refunding.

The determination of the optimal refunding policy requires the issuer to estimate the critical interest rate at which exercise of the call is optimal. Alternatively, the issuer can rely solely on market pricing of the callable bonds or, for any given level of interest rates, compare the cash flow savings in present value terms against the cost of refunding. The latter strategy is not an optimal approach, although in practice it is easier to implement.

4.3 Investor Applications

Investor applications of callable bonds focus upon the following applications:
- Yield enhancement.
- Asset liability matching.

The use of callable bonds to achieve yield enhancement is based on the capture of premium from the sale of the call option. The intrinsic strategy is that of covered call writing. The underlying security in this instance is the fixed interest bond in which the option is embedded, with the issuer purchasing the bond from the investor through the call. Under the strategy, the investor trades off the potential appreciation of the bond above the call price against the premium received which is inherent in the higher yield to maturity of the callable instrument.

The strategy of using callable bonds for portfolio return enhancement can be undertaken at varying levels of analytical sophistication, including:
- **Naive strategies** – investing in callable securities and using the yield to call as the relevant return metric to generate higher nominal returns either relative to a benchmark or in absolute terms.
- **Structured risk return strategies** – entailing the use of covered call writing to generate premium income within specified risk reward criteria.

- **Value based strategies** – designed to value callable securities in terms of the underlying components and seek to sell expensive securities and purchase cheaper securities (based on the component values), arbitraging between the universe of comparable callable and non callable securities.

The asset liability matching application of callable bonds is more complex[12]. Traditionally, asset liability managers seek to match the relevant portfolios in terms of a nominated measure of interest rate risk. This measure is typically duration. The practice referred to as portfolio immunisation is commonly used by a wide variety of portfolio managers[13]. This includes:

- Asset liability managers in financial institutions responsible for the management of the overall interest rate risk of the institution's balance sheet.
- Insurance company asset managers seeking to match the interest rate characteristics of investment products that have cash flow characteristics that are defined and dependent on interest rates.
- Asset managers (seeking to manage fixed income portfolios within defined interest rate risk frameworks).

The process of asset liability matching efficiently requires matching of *not only duration but also convexity*. The major role of callable bonds in the context of such an immunised portfolio structure is in assisting in achieving this convexity match[14].

The duration and negative convexity feature of callable bonds is characterised by an underperformance in bond price performance in a falling rate environment. This can act as a hedge against the rest of the fixed interest portfolio. This entails selecting portfolio assets where the duration is matched. In addition, it entails ensuring that duration changes with interest rate movements in a manner consistent with the

---

[12] For a discussion of asset liability based applications of callable bonds, see Latainer, Gary D., and Jacob, David P. (October 1985) Modern Techniques for Analysing Value and Performance of Callable Bonds; Morgan Stanley Fixed Income Analytical Research, New York at 20–23; Bookstaber, Richard, Hanley, William C., and Noris, Peter D. (December 1984) Are Options on Debt Issues Undervalued?; Morgan Stanley Fixed Income Analytical Research, New York at 17–24.

[13] See Fabozzi, Frank J. (Editor) (1992) Investing: The Collected Works of Martin L. Lieibowitz; Probus Publishing, Chicago, Illinois at 611–989; Fabozzi, Frank J. and Christensen, Peter F. "Bond Immunisation: An Asset/Liability Optimisation Strategy" in Fabozzi, Frank J. (Editor) (2001) The Handbook of Fixed Income Securities – Sixth Edition"; McGraw-Hill, New York at Chapter 44.

[14] This characteristic is comparable to the price performance and characteristics of mortgage backed securities and index amortising structures.

corresponding changes in liability duration. This second order portfolio matching should result in greater efficiency in portfolio management.

The utility of callable bonds in portfolio composition to achieve nominated asset liability management targets is further enhanced where the inclusion of callable bonds, based on value analysis, allows the desired portfolio to be created on a more cost effective basis. This allows portfolio managers to increase returns on existing securities holdings by selling or purchasing callable versus non callable based on the component analysis techniques previously identified. The increased investment universe will tend, on the whole, to increase the capability to add value to the portfolio over time, even where the callable bonds are not significantly cheaper than equivalent non callable bonds.

5   Callable Bonds – Monetisation of Options

5.1   Overview

Traditional applications of callable securities have been increasingly supplanted by the issue of callable bonds where the issuer monetises the embedded call option. This entails issue of callable bonds with the objective of using the value captured from the on sale of the embedded option to lower borrowing cost.

This application is used to correct the supply demand imbalance of callable bonds. In practice, investor demand for callable structures exceeds potential direct issuers of callable bonds (prepared to pay the cost of the option). This is overcome by arranging issues of callable bonds where the issuer is insulated from the impact of the call option. This is achieved using the swaption market[15].

In this Section, this particular type of application is considered. The potential use of swaptions in combination with callable bonds is first examined. The role of these transactions in capital market arbitrage is then considered. The final section looks at using value differences between the various participants concerning the value of the embedded options which can be used by investors to synthetically create callable securities.

5.2   Using Swaptions with Callable Bonds

5.2.1   Overview

Swaptions are primarily used with callable bond structures in the following situations:

---

[15]   For a discussion of swaptions, see Chapter 15.

- To monetise the implicit call options on the underlying debt security (liability applications) [16].
- In conjunction with asset swaps where the underlying fixed rate security has an uncertain life as a result of call options embedded in the original issue terms (asset applications).

5.2.2   Liability Applications

The first type of transaction represents attempts to securitise the value of options embedded in debt securities. **Exhibit 16.5** sets out an example of a transaction involving a putable swap[17].

The basic structure entails a borrower issuing a 7 year callable bond that is non-callable for 5 years. After the expiry of the call protection period, the borrower can redeem the issue at par. The borrower uses the fixed rate bond to create a synthetic floating rate borrowing. The borrower enters into a simultaneous swap where it receives fixed rates and pays floating rates (LIBOR). The interest rate swap has an additional feature where the dealer has the right to terminate the swap at a future date (coinciding with the call date of the underlying bond). For example, in the situation described, the 7 year issue is swapped with the dealer. The dealer pays fixed rates for 7 years and receives LIBOR, but with the added right to cancel the swap after 5 or 6 years.

The economics of the transaction is predicated on the dealer paying a premium for the embedded option on the swap. The borrower achieves a lower floating rate cost of funding. If interest rates fell, then the dealer exercises the option and cancels the swap. Simultaneously, the borrower terminates the bond by exercising the call option. If interest rates increase, then the dealer does not terminate the swap. The swap runs its full term.

Under the structure, the borrower has no exposure to the call option on the bond. The call option is transferred to the dealer. The borrower achieves a lower cost of funding through the transaction.

The internal economics of the transactions relies on the borrower's bond call option. The bond call offsets the swaption sold to the dealer. Investors will demand

---

[16] For example see Buchmiller, Jack, "Stripping Options from Callable Debt" (February 1993) Corporate Finance 11–13.

[17] A putable swap is a combination of an interest rate swap (where the counterparty pays fixed rate and receives floating rate) and the purchase of a receiver option on an interest rate swap (where the counterparty has the right to receive fixed rates (equal to the fixed rate on the original swap) and pay floating rate). Exercise of the receiver swaption has the effect of cancelling the original swap. See Chapter 15.

a higher yield on callable bonds because of the interest rate risk assumed. The increased yield is offset by the swaption premium received from the dealer for the cancellation rights. The option premium charged by investors in the callable bond (the higher yield on the callable bond) for the call option is generally below what the dealer is willing to pay for the swaption. Consequently, there is an opportunity to monetise the call option on the bond via the swaption, to effectively allow the borrower to achieve a lower all-in cost of funding.

The swaption is initially transferred to the dealer. The dealer will generally hedge the position or transfer it to a natural buyer of the swaption. Natural takers of the swaption are borrowers seeking to hedge interest rate risk but also seeking some capacity to benefit from a favourable rate movement. Traders may also purchase the swaption to trade the direction or volatility of interest rates[18].

Exhibit 16.5   Using Swaptions to Monetise Callable Bonds

Assume the following transaction:

Terms of callable bond

Issue date	15 November 2001
Maturity	15 November 2008 (7 years)
Coupon	10.00% pa
Call provisions	At par on 15 November 2006 (5 year) and 15 November 2007 (6 year)
Issue price	100

Terms of putable swap

Maturity	15 November 2008 (7 years)
Fixed rate	10.00% pa
Floating rate	LIBOR minus 25 bps
Put provisions	On 15 November 2006 (5 year) and 15 November 2007 (6 years) with no penalty
Swaption fee	1.25% pa flat

---

[18] Some counterparties enter into putable swaps to buy the underlying call option on interest rates implicit in the putable swap. For example, in November 1987, Salomon Brothers, in a difficult market, brought approximately US$1.85 billion of fixed rate debt involving putable swaps to market. While the rationale for the transactions was not made public, observers speculated that the transactions were driven by an internal need by Salomon Brothers to purchase call options on United State Treasury bonds. Under one theory, the US Investment Bank was using the options to hedge positions in its proprietary option book where it had previously sold Treasury bond options or interest rate options positions. Under an alternative theory, Salomon Brothers was using the putable swaps to hedge prepayment of mortgage backed securities either in its own portfolio or a portfolio that it had sold to a client.

The combined transaction results in the following cash flows for years 1 to 5 (years 6 and 7 if the bond is not called) of the transaction:

YEARS 1 TO 5 (YEARS 6 AND 7 IF BOND NOT CALLED)

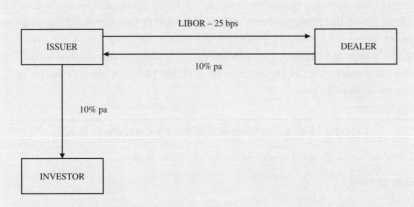

The all-in cost of funds to the borrower, after the proceeds of the up-front premium are incorporated, is LIBOR minus 51bps (assuming a discount rate of 10.25% pa).

If the swap is cancelled under the put feature of the swap, then the borrower calls the underlying bond, which means it achieves lower cost funding but for a shorter period:

6 years: LIBOR minus 54 bps
5 years: LIBOR minus 58 bps[19].

5.2.3 Asset Swaps Involving Callable Bonds

Swaptions are also used in asset swap transactions where the underlying asset is a callable bond. The putable swap allows investors to enter into transactions where a callable fixed rate bond is swapped into floating rate. If the bond is called, then the investor can terminate the original swap by cancelling the swap to the provider of the putable swap option. This allows the investor to terminate the swap at the time the underlying fixed rate bond is called[20].

---

[19] In order to ensure that the full amount of the premium is received, the typical structure of the swap would be for the issuer to pay LIBOR minus 58 bps for the first 5 years and LIBOR minus 25 bps for the last 2 years. In effect, the premium for the option on the swap is amortised in full over the non call period of the bond and swap.

[20] See Stavis, Robert M and Haghani, Victor J (1987) Putable Swaps Tools for Managing Callable Assets; Salomon Brothers Inc., New York.

Asset swaps, where synthetic floating rate assets at attractive spreads relative to LIBOR are created, are an important component of the growth of the swap market[21]. There is a limited universe of non-callable fixed rate bonds. As a result, many of the bonds used in asset based swaps have embedded call options. When interest rates decrease below the coupon, the bond is called. The investor is left with an out-of-the-money interest rate swap position (the swap fixed rate is above market rates). This swap is expensive to reverse, creating losses for investors. Putable swaps are structured as a means of mitigating the potential loss resulting from early redemption of the asset swap. **Exhibit 16.6** sets out an example of an asset based putable swap.

Exhibit 16.6   Using Swaptions to Asset Swap Callable Bonds

Assume the following bond is available in the secondary market:

Terms of bond
Issue Date	1 July 2001
Maturity	1 July 2011 (10 years)
Coupon	7.00% pa annual
Call provisions	Callable at the option of the issuer commencing 1 July 2006 (5 years) and annually thereafter on each coupon date.
	Initially callable at a price of 101 decreasing by 0.50 each year and thereby callable at par at 1 July 2008 and each coupon date thereafter.
Bond price	Issued at par

An investor purchases the bond and enters into the following swap to convert the fixed rate returns from the bond into floating rate payments priced off LIBOR. The terms of the swap are as follows:

Terms of swap
Final Maturity	1 July 2011
Fixed coupon	Investor pays 7.00% pa annually (matching the bond coupon).
Floating coupon	Investor receives 6 month LIBOR + 48 bps pa
Swap Termination	Investor has the right to terminate the swap commencing 1 July 2005 and each anniversary of the swap. At each termination date, the investor pays the following fee to the swap counterparty:

Date	Fee (%)
1 July 2006	1.00
1 July 2007	0.50
1 July 2008 to 1 July 2010	0.00

---

[21] See Chapter 4.

The swap combines a conventional interest rate swap (investor pays fixed rate and receives LIBOR) with a receiver swaption purchased by the investor to receive fixed rates (at 7.00% pa) and pay floating (at LIBOR plus 48 bps). The swaption is a Bermudan style exercise. The investor can exercise the option on any annual coupon date commencing 1 July 2006 (triggering a 5 year interest rate swap) and 1 July 2010 (triggering a 1 year interest rate swap). There are no initial cash flows under this swap. The only initial cash flow is the investment by the investor in the underlying bonds.

The investor's cash flow on each interest payment date will be as follows:

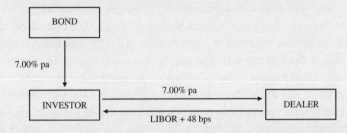

If the bond is called, then the investor is paid 101% of the face value of the bond by the issuer (assuming call on 1 July 2006). The investor passes 1% to the dealer for the right to trigger the swaption and cancel the original 10 year interest rate swap. This effectively gives the investor back 100% of its initial investment.

The pricing of the overall transaction will incorporate the following elements:
- Interest rate swap rate.
- Pricing of the swaption purchased by the investor.
- Call premium received in the event of exercise of the swaption. In effect, this can be treated as an adjustment to the effective strike rate on the swaption.

If the bond was not purchased in the primary market and was trading at a premium or discount, then the initial cash payment of receipt may also be incorporated in the swap pricing[22].

---

[22] For a discussion of the structuring of off-par interest rate swaps associated with asset swaps, see Chapter 4.

In addition, this type of structure can be used to swap assets that have uncertain lives. This can be particularly important in structuring asset swaps against mortgage and other asset backed securities.

5.2.4   Capital Market Valuation of Debt Options

Central to the use of swaptions for monetising the embedded options in callable bonds is the relative value of options in the fixed interest and derivative/swap markets. The securitisation of embedded options in callable debt relies on the relatively low priced options implicit within the bond. The embedded option is then sold through the swaption at a higher price in a different market segment (the interest rate derivative market). The apparent anomalous pricing of such options and the sources of relative value of such transactions merits comment.

Existence of this discrepancy in pricing suggests that implied volatility in the fixed interest market for callable debt is lower than that in the swap market itself. Research on fixed interest markets indicates that the implied volatility of fixed interest markets, particularly corporate securities, may be lower than historical realised volatility for a number of reasons, including[23]:

- Investors focus on security yields rather than on the total return, thereby systematically undervaluing the call option implicit in a callable bond.
- Investors often evaluate securities on the basis of their yield to worst or cash flow yield. This implicitly assumes that interest rate volatility is zero.
- Investors have a different information set regarding the probability of corporate bond calls than that incorporated in the market model. The market model estimates an option's value by assuming that any call will be exercised with perfect economic efficiency. The additional information about an individual issuer's behaviour may reduce the value of the option. This difference is reflected in the lower implied volatility.

An alternative explanation focuses on the pattern of implied forward credit spreads. Research on yield curve relationships between the swap and corporate market primarily undertaken in the US$ swap market tends to indicate that swap spreads track A or AA corporate spreads, although the relationship is not exact[24]. The difference in implied volatility can be explained in certain circumstances by the shape of the yield curve and the implied forward swap and corporate bond

---

[23] See William M Boyce, Webster Hughes, Peter S A Niculescu and Michael Waldman, (January 1988) The Implied Volatility of Fixed-Income Market; Salomon Bros Inc Research Department, New York

[24] See Das, Satyajit (2004) Derivative Products & Pricing; John Wiley & Sons (Asia), Singapore at Chapter 11. See Das, Satyajit (1994) Swaps and Financial Derivatives; LBC Information Services, Sydney; McGraw-Hill, Chicago at Chapter 23.

rates (the forward credit spread to the swap rate). For example, if the 3 year swap rate 7 years forward is lower than the corresponding forward corporate rate, then the swaption will be worth more than the embedded call, even if their implied volatility is equal. This reflects the embedded intrinsic value in the swaption.

Anecdotal evidence of swaption trading indicates that activity coincides with differences in the shape of the swap yield curve relative to the corporate bond yield curve. For example, this occurs in periods where the swap curve is inverted and the corporate bond curve is not inverted. This implies that when forward rates are lower in the swap market (generally when the swap curve is inverted relative to the corporate curve), receiver swaptions will be worth more than call options in the corporate market. Conversely, when forward rates are higher in the swap market, payer swaptions will be worth more than put options in the corporate market. This discrepancy between the shape of the swap and corporate bond yield curves facilitates the type of capital market arbitrage described.

An additional factor relates to an embedded quality spread differential within the corporate market. The swap market typically operates on the following pattern:

- Low quality issuers issue floating rate debt and swap into fixed rate debt using an interest rate swap.
- High quality issuers issue fixed rate debt that is then swapped through an interest rate swap into floating rate debt.

This pattern implies that for the investor, the swap market is an attractive source of high quality fixed rate assets through the purchase of highly rated floating rate assets that can be swapped into fixed rate. Conversely, it is an attractive source of low quality floating rate assets created primarily through asset swaps entailing purchase of lower quality fixed rate bonds that are then swapped into floating rate basis. Given that synthetic callable and putable securities can be created through the combination of actual physical non-callable or non-putable securities combined with swaptions, the synthetic component (that is, the part which relies on the underlying swap) that can be created will be as follows:

- Where the synthetic component is floating rate, the asset is more likely to be attractive when the underlying corporate security is low quality.
- When the synthetic part is fixed rate, the asset is likely to be attractive when the underlying corporate security is high quality. The embedded quality spread differential again implies under pricing of volatility in the corporate bond market, particularly for issuers of high quality[25].

---

[25]   See Johnson, Cal (July 1989) Options on Interest Rate Swaps: New Tools for Asset and Liability Management; Salomon Brothers, New York at 5–6.

Additional factors that may dictate differences in relative value include yield curve differences between the swap and corporate market. It may be that the relative value of synthetic securities created using swaptions embeds a quality spread differential *within the corporate market.*

For example, in the example of monetising the embedded call option described in **Exhibit 16.5**, the issuer through the transaction assumes an implicit maturity uncertainty. The funding in that case was for between 5 and 7 years, depending on the future path on interest rates. Implicit in that funding uncertainty is a credit *spread* position for the issuer. The current transaction is undertaken at a certain rate against LIBOR. The forward spread implied for the issuer, based on the implied forwards in the bond rate curve and the swap curve, indicates a widening in the spread. In monetising the call, in the event the call is exercised, the issuer will benefit from the on sale of the call only to the extent that its funding spread does not increase beyond that implied in the current yield curve structure.

5.2.5 Synthetic Callable Bonds

The development of substantial liquid markets in swaptions allows investors and borrowers to synthetically create callable/putable structures consistent with interest rate expectations and portfolio requirements. In particular, disparities in pricing between the fixed interest and swap markets allows the creation of synthetic callable and putable structures at values superior to that obtainable directly from the fixed interest market.

Asset managers can create synthetic callable or putable bonds by using a number of alternative combinations of physical securities and swaptions. For example, an asset manager can create a synthetic callable bond as follows:

*   Purchase a long-term straight bond and sell a receiver option on a swap.
*   Purchase a floating rate note, enter into a swap under which it receives fixed/pays floating and sells an option to cancel the swap.
*   Purchase a short term bond and sell a payer option on a swap.

Exhibit 16.7 details creating a synthetic callable bond using each of these methods.

The synthetic structures can be created using a variety of combinations that are economically equivalent. The availability of the alternative structures allows the creation of the most efficient structure to take advantage of relative value considerations at any point in time.

Liability managers can also create synthetic debt structures at attractive value levels to manage liability portfolios. For example, borrowers can create the

following synthetic structures:
- **Synthetic non callable debt** – this involves the issue of callable debt that is then converted into synthetic non callable funding by neutralising the embedded call by entering into a receiver swaption[26].

Exhibit 16.7   Synthetic Callable Bonds

Assume an investor wishes to create a synthetic callable bond to match its portfolio requirements.
Assume the following market conditions exist:
- 5 year AA corporate bonds with a one time par call at 3 years are trading at 7.60%pa.
- 5 year AA corporate non-callable bonds are trading at 7.50% pa.
- A 3 × 5 receiver swaption at 7.50% pa is priced at a 180 bps premium.

The investor can create a synthetic callable bond as follows:

Alternative 1
The investor enters into the following transactions:
- Purchase 5 year non-callable bond.
- Sell a receiver swaption where the dealer can require investor to pay 7.50% pa and receive US$ LIBOR for years 4 and 5 (if interest rates decrease).

The diagram below sets out the position:

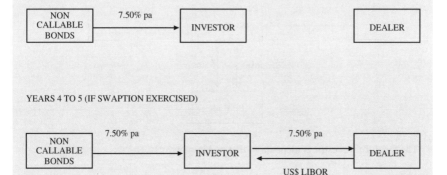

---

[26] This is essentially the logic of the monetisation of the call option discussed above (see **Exhibit 16.4**).

If interest rates rise, then the swaption is not exercised. The investor continues to receive the fixed coupon of 7.50% pa. If interest rates fall, then the swaption is exercised. The investor receives money market rates (LIBOR) on its investment. The return characteristics are identical to those under an actual callable bond.

The effective return to the investor incorporating the premium received is:

Over 3 years   8.19% pa.
Over 5 years   7.94% pa.

Alternative 2

The investor enters into the following transactions:
*   Purchases a 5 year floating rate asset yielding US$ LIBOR.
*   Enters into two swap transactions:
    1. 5 year swap under which it receives 7.50% pa.
    2. Sells a receiver option on a swap as in Alternative 1.
    The two swaps can be combined in a cancellable swap where the dealer can cancel the swap under which it pays fixed (if interest rates fall) after three years.

The diagram below sets out the position:

YEARS 1 TO 3 (YEARS 4 TO 5 IF SWAPTION UNEXERCISED)

YEARS 4 TO 5 (IF SWAPTION EXERCISED)

The result for investor is identical to that in Alternative 1.

Alternative 3

The investor enters into the following transactions:
*   Purchases a 3 year non-callable AA corporate bond which yields 7.50% pa (for convenience, a flat yield curve is assumed).
*   Sells a 3 × 5 payer swaption at 7.50% pa to the dealer.

The diagram below sets out the position:

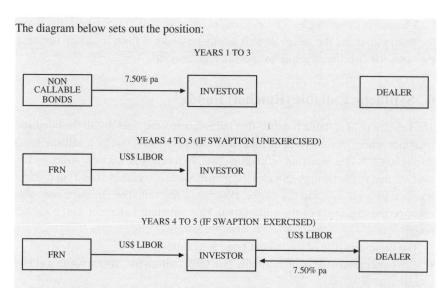

The return to the investor under various interest rate scenarios is identical to those in Alternatives 1 and 2.

For convenience, the above examples assume flat yield curves and the returns from the different strategies are identical. In practice, considerable scope exists to extract additional value from the alternatives based on:

- Slope of the swap and/or corporate bond yield curves.
- Structure of forward rates implicit in the two yield curves.
- Different implied volatility and anomalies in the pricing of swaptions.
- Capacity to enhance return by earning above US$ LIBOR return on floating rate investments.

Source: This example draws on Johnson, Cal (July 1989) Options on Interest Rate Swaps: New Tools for Asset and Liability Management; Salomon Brothers, New York.

- **Synthetic putable bonds** – this entails the issue of a conventional bond combined with the sale of a receiver swaption exercisable when the debt matures, effectively extending the maturity of the debt[27].
- **Synthetic portfolio shortening** – this involves selling payer swaptions where the issuer has the right to pay fixed converting callable debt to fixed rate debt effectively maturing at the call date. Through this transaction, the issuer has purchased a call (embedded in the callable debt) and sold a put (the option on the swap is a put on the market) that equates to a forward repurchase of the debt.

---

[27] See discussion of synthetic putable debt structures later in this Chapter.

A feature of the strategies is the capacity to tailor the strike price level (effectively the fixed rate under the swap) as well as other aspects of the transaction to match the synthetic liability structure to specific requirements.

6   Synthetic Callable (Ratchet) Bonds[28]

The key driver of callable bonds is that the issuer has the right to call the bond and refinance where interest rates decline. The traditional structure of a callable bond results in the issuer incurring refunding costs. In recent years, a new structure has evolved that synthetically replicates the performance of a callable bond but reduces transaction costs associated with the exercise of the call. The structure may also enhance the execution of the call option. This structure is known as the ratchet bond[29].

The basic structure of the ratchet bond is as follows:

- The issuer issues the bond normally (US$500 million for 10 years with a single call after 5 years).
- The coupon of the bond is fixed for the term of the bond (6.75% pa determined as the 10 year Treasury plus 100 bps).
- At the call date (5 years after issue), the coupon on the bond may be adjusted in accordance with a pre-agreed formula. This adjustment is based on an agreed credit spread over a benchmark Treasury bond[30] (in this case, 100 bps over the 5 year Treasury bond at the call date). If the new rate (Treasury bond plus spread) is greater than the coupon (6.75% pa), then the coupon on the bond remains unchanged. If the new rate is lower than 6.75% pa, then the coupon is reset to the new rate.

The structure results in the coupon declining if interest rates fall, but remaining constant if interest rates increase. The structure replicates the effective performance of a callable bond without requiring retirement of the original bond. From the perspective of the investor, the ratchet bond behaves like the callable bond. The structure assumes that the investor reinvests the maturing proceeds in a new bond for the remainder of the term of the original investment. The premium for the embedded call option is used to enhance the coupon of the bond as with conventional callable structures.

---

[28] For a discussion of Ratchet Bonds see Kalotay, Andrew and Abreo, Andrew "Ratchet Bonds" (Spring 1999) Journal of Applied Finance 40–47.

[29] The Tennessee Valley Authority introduced the structure in an issue known as PARRS.

[30] The Treasury rate used is usually a Constant Maturity Treasury ("CMT") rate; see Chapter 17.

7 Callable Bonds – Structural Variations

The concept of embedding a debt option within the format of a traditional fixed interest security has gradually been extended to encompass a broad variety of formats. There are three major variations: the putable bond, detachable debt warrants and multi-step callable structures. The structural variations considered have similar characteristics to callable bonds generally. The major driver of the structures is the desire to either overcome one or other deficiency of the traditional format of instruments or generate added value under specific market conditions by adjusting the structural features. Each of the major structural variations is discussed in the following Sections.

8 Putable Bonds

8.1 Concept[31]

A putable bond entails a fixed income security where *the investor* has the right to terminate the investment by selling back the security to the issuer. The bond can be put to the investor at a pre-agreed price (typically par or in some cases at a premium) on one or more predetermined dates prior to maturity of the security.

Exhibit 16.8 sets out an example of a putable bond. The transaction entails the borrower issuing a 10 year bond. The investor has the right to terminate the transaction and put the bonds to the issuer prior to maturity at the end of 5 years at face value. In return for receiving the right to put the bonds to the issuer, the investor accepts a lower return on the investment. The issuer receives the benefit of the lower borrowing cost. This reflects the option premium received from the sale of the put on the bond. The issuer assumes the interest rate and liquidity (maturity contraction) risk of the structure.

It is useful to differentiate the key features of a putable bond with that of a callable bond. The differences are as follows:

• The callable bond combines a bond with a call option sold by the investor to the issuer. In contrast, the putable structure consists of a bond combined with a put option sold by the issuer to the investor[32].

---

[31] See Fishbein, Mark "New Ways to Apply an Old Idea" (September 1988) Corporate Finance 43–46.

[32] Using put-call parity, the putable bond can be stated as a bond with a maturity equal to the put date combined with a call option on debt with coupon equal to that on the original bond and with a maturity equal to the original final maturity of the bond. The issuer sells the call option to the investor.

- The coupon on the putable bond is lower than that of a comparable non callable bond, reflecting the benefit of the option premium sold by the issuer to the investor. In contrast, the coupon on the callable bond is higher than a comparable non-callable bond, reflecting the purchase of the option by the issuer from the investor.
- The maturity extension risk is different. In the case of a callable bond, a fall in interest rates (under rational exercise conditions) will lead to the exercise of the call, resulting in maturity contraction. In the case of a putable bond, a fall in interest rates will lead to no exercise of the embedded option, resulting in maturity extension. Higher interest rates will result in the put bond being terminated and the maturity contracting.

Exhibit 16.8   Putable Bonds – Structure

Amount	US$100 million
Coupon	7.00% pa (payable annually)
Issue Date	15 September 2002
Maturity	15 September 2012 (10 years)
Put Date	15 September 2007 (5 years)
Put Provision	Investor has the right, subject to 30 days notice, to put the bond to the issuer at par (100% of face value) at the Put Date

---

8.2   Economics, Price Characteristics & Valuation

In economic terms, the investor is purchasing a combination of a bond and a call option on interest rates or a put on the price of the bond. The option acquired by the investor has an expiry date coinciding with the put date or dates and has a strike price equivalent to the pre-agreed put value of the bond. The option premium is built into the coupon of the security[33].

As with a callable bond, the structure can be decomposed in a variety of ways. For example, using swaptions, a putable bond can be restated from the perspective of the investor as follows:

- Putable bond = non-putable bond (final maturity equal to maturity of putable bond) plus purchased payer swaption (strike equal to bond coupon, swap maturity equal to difference between put date and final maturity date and exercise date equal to put date).

---

[33] For a discussion of the value of the put option in a putable bond, see Chatfield, Robert E. and Moyer, R. Charles "Putting-Away Bond Risk: An Empirical Examination of the Value of the Put Option on Bonds" (Summer 1986) Financial Management 26–33.

- Putable bond = non-putable bond (final maturity equal to put date) plus purchased receiver swaption (strike equal to bond coupon, swap maturity equal to difference between put date and final maturity date and exercise date equal to put date).

The valuation of the embedded option can be undertaken using the analytical basis used with callable bonds.

The embedded option features impact upon the price characteristics and behaviour of the putable bond. The major price characteristics of the putable bond include:

- The positive protection afforded by the put option against increases in interest rates dominates the price behaviour. The likelihood of maturity contraction, reflecting the exercise of the put option where interest rates increase, reduces the price risk of the security without given the asymmetric nature of the instrument pay-off reducing the sensitivity to price appreciation from decreasing interest rates.

- The putable bond has favourable duration characteristics with the security life and number of cash flows increasing (decreasing) with decreases (increases) in interest rates.

- The putable bond has high positive convexity where interest rates fall, reflecting the extension of the life of the security. Conversely, putable securities have negative convexity where interest rates increase. This is because the price does not fall for a rise in interest rates, reflecting the dominant influence of the embedded put option which dictates a shortening life of the security and a payout of the agreed put price where rates increase.

The valuation of putable bonds is complicated in practice by the fact that pricing is a function of two factors:

- Valuation of the fixed interest cash flows and the embedded debt option.
- Implicit credit or default risk option.

The valuation approach described above focuses on the first factor. The implicit credit or default risk option manifests itself in a number of ways. For example, to the extent that changes in credit risk of the issuer affect the spread relative to the benchmark risk free security, value changes of the bond will be reflected in the altered valuation of the fixed interest cash flows and the embedded debt option.

A second and potentially more complex impact of changes in the default or credit risk occurs where the risk of default increases to the level where the risk of issuer default and the potential loss upon default dominates any value change on the first factor. For example, interest rates may have fallen, dictating abandonment of the put in order to capture the price gains on the investment. Deterioration in the credit quality of the issuer (manifested in higher credit spreads) dictates exercise of the put in order to safeguard return of principal. Economically, under these circumstances, the present value of the capital received upon exercise of the put is greater than the amount that would be received under the bond if maturity is extended. The future receipt (in case of default) is effectively the recovery rate. The current receipt of capital (the difference between the face value and the recovery value) is greater than the present value gains on the bond as a result of the fall in interest rates.

The incorporation of put options in longer term securities as a mechanism for mitigating the credit risk of the transaction necessarily requires increased consideration of this second factor in valuation. The difficulty in estimating the parameters required to value the default option is problematic[34].

It should be noted that the implicit credit option applies equally to callable and putable bond transactions. Research undertaken by Moody's Investors Service indicates that the value of the implicit credit spread option is significantly less than that of the interest rate option. This is particularly the case where the issuer's credit rating is high. The credit option becomes increasingly relevant as the issuer's credit rating declines[35].

8.3 Applications

Putable bonds developed in response to a number of factors including:
- The demand for fixed interest instruments that have defensive characteristics but significant positive convexity to allow capture of maximum price benefit in a favourable interest rate environment.
- The need for credit enhancement in longer maturity debt and/or equity linked transactions.

As in the case of callable bonds, the ability under certain circumstances to arbitrage relative valuation of options between the fixed income investors and the swaptions market is also an important factor.

---

[34] The emerging market in credit derivatives shows considerable promise in allowing improved pricing of this aspect of value; see Das, Satyajit (2004) Structured Products Volume 2; John Wiley & Sons (Asia), Singapore at Chapters 11 to 14.

[35] See Pimbley, Joseph M. and Curry, Daniel A. (July 1995) Market Risk of the Step-Up Callable Structured Note; Moody's Investors Service, New York.

Investors use putable bonds to obtain protection from increases in interest rates. If rates increase, then investors protect the capital value of the investment by terminating the bond at the put date and reinvesting in higher yielding securities. In particular, the high positive convexity of this structure can be used to hedge the negative convexity arising from the prepayment risk in portfolios of mortgage securities. As interest rates decline, prepayment and refinancing of mortgages creates a general shortening in the term of mortgage securities. Holding putable bonds that lengthen in maturity as interest rates decline allows investors to use these securities to hedge portfolios of mortgage securities.

The second application relates to the ability of the put option to provide credit enhancement. It is typically used in both conventional debt and equity linked transactions.

The issuer undertakes an issue of debt with a final maturity of 10 years. The issue is putable to the issuer after say 5 years, or every year commencing at year 5. The embedded put provides interest rate protection for the investor. In addition, the put allows termination of the transaction prior to maturity where the issuer's credit quality deteriorates. The put is usually unconditional. Consequently, there is no precondition to its exercise. This facilitates exercise, irrespective of reason for exercise (including changes in credit quality).

There are several aspects of this type of transaction which merit comment. Such features are used particularly in long dated transaction (20 to 30 years in initial maturity) for lower investment grade (usually A/BBB) borrowers. The put in these cases is at year 7 to year 12.

The incorporation of the put feature in equity linked transactions (usually convertibles) is designed to achieve a wider range of different objectives including[36]:

• Credit enhancement similar to that used in bond issues.
• Protection for the investor against failure of the equity price to show anticipated appreciation. The put on an equity convertible is designed to convert the convertible into a debt instrument returning an interest rate comparable to the return on an equivalent non equity linked security. In practice, the return on exercise of the put may be equivalent to at least the return on a risk free security of the relevant maturity (for example, the Treasury yield for the maturity to put at the time of issue). This requires, in the case of a convertible, the put to be exercisable at a premium to par value of the bond. This reflects the fact that the coupon on the convertible is lower than that of equivalent debt for the same maturity at the time of issue.

---

[36] See Das, Satyajit (2004) Structured Products Volume 2; John Wiley & Sons (Asia), Singapore at Chapter 3.

Issuers of putable securities must assume the liquidity and interest rate risks resulting from the potential shorter life of the security (if interest rates rise). The issuers of putable bonds fall into the following categories:

- Direct issuers who do not hedge out the embedded option. The issuer prefers to generate cheaper funding and accept the maturity and liquidity risk. The risk is often assumed by issuers that find it difficult to access debt funding for the relevant term achieved without using the put structure.

- Arbitrage issuers who hedge out the embedded optionality through an offsetting derivative transaction. The issuers use the putable bond to generate lower cost floating rate funding by swapping the issue proceeds into a floating rate basis. This entails the use of extendible swaps. The issuer enters into a swap where it receives fixed rate and pays LIBOR to the put date on the bond. Simultaneously, the issuer purchases a receiver swaption to receive fixed rates (at the same rate) commencing on the put date to the final maturity of the putable bond. In the event that interest rates fell, then the put option will not be exercised. The issuer exercises its option under the extendible swap (the receiver swaption) to continue funding on a floating rate basis. The lower coupon on the putable bond allows the issuer to cover the cost of the purchase of the extendible swap or the receiver option on the swap. Typically the issuer all-in cost of funding is below direct term funding costs. The pricing advantage is driven by disparities in valuation of the embedded option between the debt and derivatives markets.

In the absence of putable bonds, an investor can create synthetic putable bonds. For example, an investor can create a synthetic putable bond using the following methods:

- Purchasing a long term conventional bond and purchasing a payer option on a swap where it pays fixed and receives floating.
- Purchase a short term bond and purchase a receiver option on a swap where it receives fixed and pays floating.

The reverse process is also feasible to arbitrage bond values. **Exhibit 16.9** sets out an example of creating a synthetic conventional bond from a putable bond.

Exhibit 16.9   Using Swaptions to Monetise Putable Bonds[37]

Assume an investor purchases a 10 year AA corporate bond that is putable to the issuer at year 5. The putable bond yields 7.00% pa (versus the comparable yield on conventional

---

[37] The example draws on Johnson, Cal (July 1989) Options on Interest Rate Swaps: New Tools for Asset and Liability Management; Salomon Brothers, New York.

ten year non putable 10 year AA corporate bond of 7.50% pa). In order to synthetically create a non-putable security, the investor simultaneously sells a payer swaption at 7.50% pa. The diagram below sets out the position:

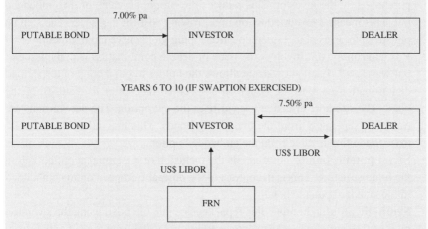

If interest rates fall, then the investor does not put the bonds at year 5. The swaption is unexercised and the investor receives the coupon of 7.00% pa for the full 10 years. If interest rates rise, then the investor puts the bond to the issuer at par. The proceeds are re-invested at a floating rate asset yielding US$ LIBOR. The swaption is exercised, converting the floating rate investment into a fixed rate investment yielding 7.50% pa.

The effective return to the investor (incorporating an option premium of 4.00% flat) is:
*   If option is unexercised: 7.59% pa.
*   If option is exercised: 7.79% pa.

8.4   Putable Bonds – Structural Variations

8.4.1   Overview

There are a number of variations to the standard putable bond structure. The various structures are designed to achieve the following objectives:
*   Accommodate issuer or investor requirements.
*   Extract value from the applicable yield curve shape and interest rate volatility environment.

The common variations on putable bonds include:
*   **Step up puts** – this entails a putable bond where the coupon of the bond steps up at the put date. The structure is similar to a step up callable bond. The coupon

increase after the put has the effect of increasing the yield to the investor. This means that yields have to increase significantly before the put is likely to be exercised. This reduces the risk of the bond being put to the issuer. The economic effect of the higher coupon is to increase the strike price of the receiver swaption purchased by the investor. This reduces the economic value of the embedded put. This means a lower reduction in borrowing cost for the issuer. The step up put structure is used in a steep upward sloping yield curve environment.

* **Put warrants** – this involves the issue of debt in combination with the issue of put warrants[38]. Each put warrant allows the holder to put a bond of a specified denomination back to the issuer on a specified date prior to maturity of the bond. The structure effectively securitises the put option. The put warrants are tradeable separately from the underlying bonds. This may allow the issuer to extract additional value from the embedded option.
* **Serial putable bonds** – this entails the inclusion of a Bermudan option within the bond structure. This is in contrast to the normal European option embedded in the standard putable bond.
* **Synthetic putable bonds** – this repackages a putable bond using the swaption market. The structure seeks to extract additional value from the put option from selling the receiver swaption in the derivative market.

Serial and synthetic putable bonds are described in the following Sections.

8.4.2 Serial Putable Bonds

One development in putable bond structures is the serial put bond. The structure first emerged around 1996/97 in the US domestic debt market[39].

The basic structure is a long dated bond (40 years) that is putable at year 1 or 2 *and every year thereafter*. Issuers of serial putable bonds are motivated by the high value paid by investors for the embedded Bermudan debt options. This enabled the issuers to achieve funding rates often below US Treasury yields for comparable maturities.

The original issues were undertaken in an environment of low nominal and decreasing interest rates. In this environment, there was strong demand from debt

---

[38] For example, Bank of Nova Scotia issued US$150 million of 5 year notes with 120,000 put warrants where each warrant allowed the holder to put a bond (US$1,000) back to the issuer after 3 years at a price of 98.375% of face value; see (17 May 1986) International Financing Review Issue 622 1462.

[39] See Salmon, Felix "Market Openings and Reopenings" (February 1998) Corporate Finance 32–37.

portfolio managers for putable bonds to hedge the prepayment risk of large mortgage portfolios. If interest rates fall, then the appreciation in the value of the embedded option within the putable bond offsets the decline in value of the mortgage investments. For the investors, the putable structures represent a lower cost mechanism for purchasing volatility. This is predicated on the pricing of the debt options embedded in these issues being lower than in the derivatives market.

For the issuers, the low nominal cost of funds was the major driver of issuance. The issuer accepted the prepayment risk. The issuers assumed this risk on the basis that the putable issues did not constitute a significant part of their overall liability portfolios and did not create unacceptable exposures to liquidity or re-financing risk.

In addition, the structure of the serial put bonds is such that even if interest rates rose, then the likelihood of an immediate put was low. This reflects the fact that the investor may not put the bond back to the issuer even if rates rise, because the options may further increase in value at a later date. In effect, the future put options retain significant embedded value. The combined value of the series of puts in a typical structure require interest rates to increase by around 100–150 bps in the first few years of the term of the bond before it becomes economically desirable to exercise the put. This exercise behaviour dictates that the issuer obtains attractive rates for 1 or 2 year funding. The borrower is likely to retain this funding in an environment where interest rates were rising, but not significantly.

8.4.3 Synthetic Putable Bonds

The synthetic putable bond structure developed in response to issuers seeking to issue putable bonds, but concerned about the value for the embedded debt options being paid by investors relative to the value of the options in the derivatives market (specifically the swaption market). The structure that evolved entailed the issue of a putable bond that was repackaged by the underwriter in a way that sought to extract a higher value for the embedded options[40]. This market evolved in the US debt markets over 1997 and 1998[41]. **Exhibit 16.10** sets out the basic structure of the synthetic putable bond.

---

[40] The structure appears to have been originated by UBS as the Pass through Asset Trust Securities ("PATS"); variants have since emerged including Morgan Stanley's Reset Put Securities ("REPs"); Merrill Lynch's Mandatory Par Put Re-marketed Securities ("MOPPRS"); CS First Boston's Term Enhanced Re-Marketable Securities ("TERMS").

[41] See Salmon, Felix "Market Openings and Reopenings" (February 1998) Corporate Finance 32–37; Rutter, James "Cross Capital Market Boundaries" (July 1998) Euromoney 140–142.

Exhibit 16.10   Synthetic Putable Bonds

The structure entails the issuer undertaking an issue of a putable bond (10 year issue with a 5 year put). The bond issue is placed with a special purpose trust vehicle arranged by the underwriter.

The trust undertakes two separate transactions:

- The trust issues a 5 year bond.
- The trust simultaneously arranges to sell the put option on the bond to the underwriter.

The 5 year bond is issued at par. The premium received for the put from the underwriter is 2.00%. The total cash flow paid to the issuer is 102% of face value of the issue.

The put option is either on sold or hedged in the swaption market. This swaption transaction (effectively the sale of the embedded option into the derivatives market) generates the premium that is paid through to the issuer.

The transaction operates as follows:

- For the first 5 years, the issuer makes payments to the trust which are directly passed through to the bond investors.
- At the end of 5 years, the operation of the transaction is contingent on interest rates. The constant to the operation is the need to repay the maturing principal to the investor *in the 5 year bond.*
    1. If interest rates increase, then the underwriter exercises its right to put the bond back to the issuer through the trust. The cash received is used to fund the redemption of the 5 year issue.
    2. If interest rates decrease, then the underwriter does not exercise its put. Instead the underwriter undertakes a new issue of *5 year* securities by the trust (effectively a sale of the original 10 year security which has 5 years remaining maturity). The bonds that are sold are an issue of high coupon bonds (reflecting the original coupon of the bonds that is now above current market levels). The sale of the bonds generates an amount in excess of par of the bonds. An amount equal to 100% of face value is used to redeem the original 5 year securities issued by the trust. The remaining value is dealt with as set out below.
- The embedded option that is stripped from the bond and purchased from the trust by the underwriter and on sold or hedged settles as follows:
    1. If rates rise, then the option expires out of the money and no settlement is required.
    2. If rates fall, then the option is exercised and the value of the option (in cash terms) is generated from the amount above par gained from the sale of the second 5 year bond by the trust. The sale of a high coupon bond generates a payment above par of which only par is required to retire the first 5 year issue.
- For the remaining 5 year life of the transaction, the issuer pays interest coupons and finally the principal redemption as per normal to the trust. That is then used to service the second 5 year issue normally.

The structure is set out in the diagram below:

Initial Position

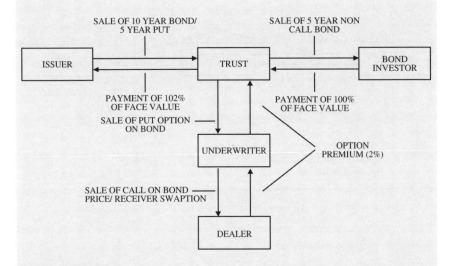

Coupon Payments (Initial 5 Years)

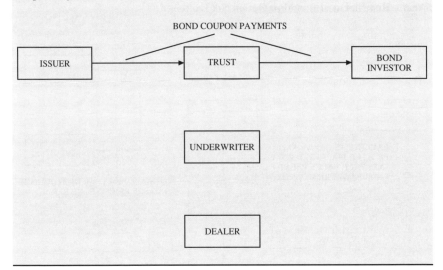

5 Year – Repayment of Bond/Put Option Exercised

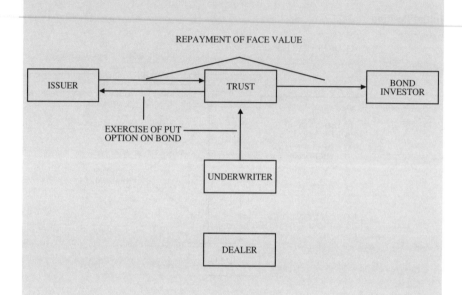

5 Year – Repayment of Bond/Put Option Not Exercised

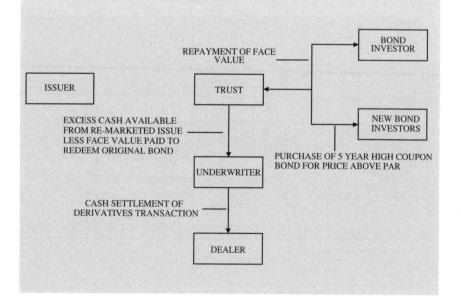

Coupon/Principal Repayment (Second 5 Years)

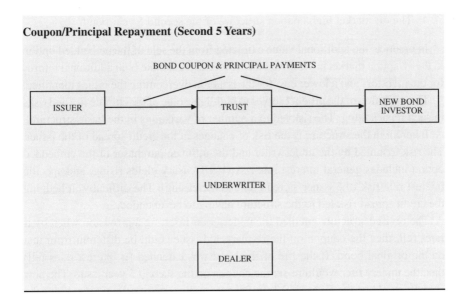

The dynamics of the structure are as follows:

- From the viewpoint of the issuer, the transaction operates in a liquidity/cash flow sense as a traditional directly issued putable bond. The only difference is that after 5 years if interest rates fall, then the underwriter will undertake an issue of 5 year securities *of the issuer* indirectly through the trust without the direct participation of the issuer.

- From the viewpoint of the investor in the bonds (effectively 2 separate 5 year bond issues), the transaction represents the traditional purchase of a bond. Investors have generally received higher yields on the straight bonds issued as a direct result of the repackaging of a synthetic putable security[42]. This has reflected a combination of factors:

  1. The fact that the issuer is a trust entity not the direct issuer.

  2. The securities issued because of the utilisation of a trust issuing entity are not SEC registered but are issued as a Rule 144a offering that usually requires a premium.

  3. A premium for illiquidity of the trust offering. The synthetic issue is considered unlikely to have the same liquidity as conventional securities of the same issuer.

---

[42] For example, an issue for GMAC was undertaken at a 5 bps premium to standard GMAC bond and subsequently widened to 12 bps in secondary market trading; see Salmon, Felix "Market Openings and Reopenings" (February 1998) Corporate Finance 32–37 at 36.

4. The off market high coupon structure of the second 5 year bond.

In practice, the additional value extracted from the sale of the embedded option in the swaption market has allowed the structure to generate both additional returns for the investors and a lower cost for the issuer in overcoming the issues identified.

The evolution of the product serves to highlight some of the complexity and risks in such repackaging. The risk led to a number of variations in the basic structure.

Inherent in the structure is the risk of changes in the credit spread of the issuer. The risk assumed by the underwriter and the ultimate purchaser of the embedded option includes general interest rate risk (US Treasury yields rising) and specific interest rate risk (the issuer's credit spread increasing). The difficulty in hedging the credit spread risk led to the structure having to be amended.

The revised structure entailed the underwriter inserting a provision whereby if rates fell, then the coupon on the re-marketed issue could be different from that on the original bond. If the life of the bond was extended (if interest rates fell) then the underwriter would re-set the coupon on the second 5 year issue. The new coupon would be the 5 year US Treasury rate at the time of original issue plus the issuer's credit spread *at the time of re-marketing* (that is, in 5 years). This structure is designed to shift the credit spread risk to the issuer.

This creates additional problems, including:
• The exact cost of the issue to the issuer is uncertain. It is contingent on the future credit spread at the time of the re-marketing.
• The credit spread applied might be high at the time the put decision is made. Given that the underwriter must re-market the bonds to generate liquidity to retire the original debt issue, there is little flexibility in undertaking the issue even if market conditions are difficult. The issuer also has little or no control over that process as the second issue is outside its control (at least technically).

In further developments, the product evolved to accommodate the following variations:
• The trust structure was discarded with the original longer dated bond being placed with the investor in combination with a *mandatory call* held by the underwriter. The bond is purchased back from the original investor at par at the put date and then either put back to the issuer (if rates have risen) or re-marketed (if rates have fallen).
• To increase flexibility, some issues have introduced a re-marketing window that allows some timing discretion as to the date of re-marketing the securities. This is designed to attempt to reduce the risk of the credit spread being reset in adverse market conditions.

In the late 1990s, the substantial cost savings available to issuers outweighed the market risks[43]. The savings derive primarily from the extraction of the higher value available for the options from the swaptions market as compared to the debt markets[44].

The synthetic putable bond market saw reduced activity after 1998. This reflected the shape of the yield curve and the level of interest rate volatility. This reduced the value that could be extracted for embedded receiver swaptions. The market re-emerged in early 2000. This reflected the flat/inverted yield curve and the increase in implied volatility of receiver swaptions. The higher value available for the receiver swaptions allowed synthetic putable bonds to be issued. The structure evolved during this time. The typical format (known as the reset put security[45]) now involved a call and a put option embedded within the bond. **Exhibit 16.11** describes the structure of the reset put security[46].

Exhibit 16.11   Reset Put Bonds[47]

The basic structure is as follows[48]:
* The issuer issues a 15 year bond.
* The bond has an embedded put/call at 5 years. The put and call option is held by the investor (or in a synthetic structure by the investment bank[49]).

---

[43] The importance of this structure can be seen from the fact that in 1998 (in the period to June) 95% of putable issuance totalling US$11.5 billion was synthetic (as distinct from direct cash). This is an increase from 1997 when only some 28% of putable issuance totalling US$13.6 billion was in synthetic form. [Statistics from Credit Suisse First Boston, as quoted in Rutter, James "Cross Capital Market Boundaries" (July 1998) Euromoney 140–142 at 142].

[44] An additional driver for the structures was the derivatives accounting directives of the US Federal Accounting Standards Board ("FASB"). The regulations require all derivative transactions to be marked to market. This discourages issuers from entering into OTC derivative transactions (for example. swaptions). However, the derivative in embedded form avoids the mark-to-market requirement under the current structure of the accounting framework. See discussion in Das, Satyajit (2004) Risk Management; John Wiley & Sons (Asia), Singapore at Chapter 17.

[45] The name is the name used by Morgan Stanley – Reset Put Securities ("REPS").

[46] See Boughey, Simon "Curve Inversion Renews Appetite for REPS" (March 2000) Credit 20–21.

[47] See Boughey, Simon "Curve Inversion Renews Appetite for REPS" (March 2000) Credit 20–21.

[48] For an example of the structure, see BMW's Money Market Targeted Reset Securities ("MoTRS") issued through Goldman Sachs; see Ferry, John "BMW's Crashing MoTRS" (October 2001) Risk 14.

[49] See discussion in **Exhibit 16.10** of the synthetic structure involving the investment bank.

The structure operates as follows:
- If interest rates increase, then the investors are obliged to put the bonds back to the issuer. The put is mandatory (if interest rates are higher).
- If interest rates are lower, then the call option is exercised and the issuer issues new bonds to the final maturity (10 years). The issued bonds are on the same terms as the original bond issue. The new bonds are then re-marketed by the underwriter. The high coupon on the bond means that the bonds are re-marketed at a premium. The premium is used to cash settle the receiver swaption sold by the underwriter to hedge the position in the call option under the reset put bonds.

The typical structures include 6 year final maturity/1 year put, 7 year final maturity/2 year put, 8 year final maturity/3 year put, 11 year final maturity/3 year put, 12 year final maturity/2 year put, 13 year final maturity/3 year put and 15 year final maturity/5 year put.

The reset put structure extracts value from the embedded receiver swaption. The value is derived from the shape of the yield curve (flat/inverted) and the high implied volatility in the swaption market. The shape of the yield curve means that the implied forward swap rates are below the current spot start swap rates. This means that the receiver option was in-the-money. This, combined with the high implied volatility, increases the value of the receiver swaption. The swaption value is also increased by the length of the term of the swap underlying the swaption.

The value received for the swaption decreases the funding cost for the borrower. The risk for the borrower is that rates fall sharply and it is effectively locked into a high cost borrowing. A secondary risk is that if the call is exercised, then the new bond issues are marketed at a potentially unfavourable credit spread. The borrowers are generally willing to accept the risks in return for the lower borrowing cost.

The structure is based on either swap rates or (more commonly) Constant Maturity Treasury ("CMT") rates[50]. This means that the embedded option is based on CMT rates. In the US$ market, the CMT rate is used because the bond is priced/re-marketed against a Treasury benchmark. This allows the underwriter to hedge its embedded call option position by selling CMT floors.

The structure also potentially involves the underwriter assuming the risk of changes in the issuer's credit spread. As with the synthetic putable bond structure, this risk is generally transferred to the issuer.

9   Debt Warrants

9.1   Concept

A variation on the embedded debt option theme relates to introducing detachability of the embedded option. In the case of both callable and putable bonds, the option

---

[50]   For a discussion of CMT products, see Chapter 17.

embedded is non detachable. Trading in the option requires the option purchaser to purchase or sell the underlying bond. The concept of facilitating the "stripping" out and separate trading of the debt option underlies the concept of debt warrants.

Debt warrants are effectively call options on the debt of the issuer sold by the issuer to the warrant purchaser. The warrants are created in exchange for the receipt of an explicit or implicit premium (that is, the premium may be built into a lower than market cost on a related issue of debt).

From the borrower's viewpoint, the sale of warrants produces cash that reduces the cost of the borrower's total funding program. Exercise of the warrants requires the issuer to undertake issues of additional debt on pre-agreed terms, creating additional debt funding for the issuer. The inclusion of the debt options allows the debt to be issued at an effective return to the investor that exceeds the current market yields for comparable debt at the time of issue.

The difference between the callable and putable bond structures considered above and debt warrant transactions should be noted. Debt warrants are sold by the *issuer*. In this regard, the debt warrant transaction replicates putable bonds rather than callable bonds. Conceptually, debt warrant transactions can be used to replicate putable bonds by combining a bond issue and the debt warrants. The bonds issued have a maturity coinciding with the proposed put date. Debt warrants are exercisable on the maturity date of the bond into a bond with terms identical to the original bond, with a final maturity equal to the planned final maturity of the transaction. The relationship between debt warrants and callable bonds derives from the fact that the call option purchased from the investor in a callable bond transaction can be securitised *by the issuer* and on-sold through the issue of debt warrants.

9.2   Pricing and Valuation

The pricing of debt warrants is analogous to pricing of normal interest rate options. However, the following aspects of valuation of these instruments should be noted:

- As the option is not embedded within a bond, the cost of the warrant is the explicit option premium. The lower absolute commitment of funds allows greater leverage (in the case of a buyer with low risk on a committed dollar amount basis). This feature may make the structure attractive to certain investors.
- The detachability of the warrants could influence valuation. The detachability allows liquidity and trading that may attract a separate group of option oriented investors.
- Warrants can be structured as American style exercise instruments due to the avoidance of a mechanical restriction derived from embedding the option in the bond. The possibility of early exercise may enhance debt value, although

the tendency of the bonds to move towards par as maturity approaches will affect the period of maximum option value, making early exercise less likely.

9.3 Debt Warrant Structures

9.3.1 Overview

The types of debt warrant transactions can be categorised as follows:
• Standalone issues of debt warrants.
• Fixed rate bonds with attached warrants.

The first type of transactions can be further sub-divided into two separate types of transactions. The first entails debt warrants issued on *existing* securities. This involves the creation, distribution and trading of options on bonds/debt securities by investors or dealers. The transactions are packaged as either warrant issues, over-the-counter options or exchange-traded option transactions.

The second class entails issues of debt warrants by *issuers* that are exercisable into new debt to be created and issued by the issuer. This necessarily entails the receipt of cash from the new issue of debt. Fixed rate bonds with attached warrants generally entail the second type of warrant identified. The focus in this Section is on this type of structure[51].

In most transactions involving the issuance of debt options and warrants, the underlying funding is swapped, with the option element being stripped off and sold and the interest rate or currency basis of the funding altered. The specific swap structure used can vary significantly depending on the overall structure of the debt warrant package.

9.3.2 Standalone Debt Warrant Issues

Standalone debt warrant issues entail the issue of call options on debt by the issuer. The holders of the warrants acquire the right to purchase fixed rate bonds of the issuer on predetermined terms. Upon exercise, the issuer receives cash, representing the sale proceeds of the fixed rate bond. The issuer also receives the premium from the sale of the warrant that lowers the funding cost of the borrower.

The initial debt warrant transactions emerged in an environment of falling interest rates. There was demand from investors for instruments that allowed leveraged and low risk increase in exposure to the anticipated decline in interest rates. The

---

[51] For a discussion of the evolution of this market, see Eilon, Amir "Debt Warrant Instruments" in (1987) Warrants and Options; IFR Publishing Limited, London 9–46.

demand for debt warrants was not matched by issuer interest. This reflected the fact that issuers were unwilling to issue warrants that obligated them to issue debt at above market rates as rates fell. This demand-supply imbalance was resolved by the use of issuers who were insulated from the risk of falling interest rates through the swaption market.

The earliest examples of the structures emerged under specific conditions. A number of floating rate borrowers seeking to hedge interest rate risk entered into transactions requiring them to enter into additional amounts of swaps where the borrowers paid fixed rates during a specified period of sometimes up to five years. In effect, the borrowers had sold receiver swaptions.

One of the first such swaps allowed the counterparty to call additional amounts of the swap when fixed rates fell in the future. The swaps were used to allow issuers to undertake warrant issues or bond issues with attached warrants for additional bonds. If the warrants were exercised, then the additional amounts of the swap could be called (the receiver swaption triggered) to convert the fixed rate funds into floating rate debt. The swaption seller received a premium for selling the option in return for absorbing the risk that rates might fall and the warrants would be exercised. The swaption guarantees the borrower's funding cost on the additional funds raised through the warrant exercise.

The market for standalone debt warrants evolved to encompass two specific categories of transactions. The first entailed the issue (usually by a high quality issuer) of standalone warrants where the warrant issuer hedged its own exposure through the entry into a contingent swap (effectively, the purchase of a receiver option on a swap). The issuer captured the value difference between the warrant premium and the cost of the swaption. The second structure entailed the issue of debt warrants by dealers. The dealers hedged the exposure by either re-purchasing the option, replicating the option dynamically and/or re-packaging existing options. The structure involving the issue of debt warrants by dealers is similar to the covered warrants issued in the equity market.

The first structure entailed a receiver swaption to hedge the contingent liability. The contingent liability was in the form of a call option on debt instruments (the warrants exercisable into fixed rate bonds). The warrants were issued either in conjunction with a host bond or on stand-alone ("naked") basis. The call option embedded in the debt instrument also took the form of an option to extend the maturity of an existing issue.

There were two types of transactions:
- **Contingent interest rate swaps** – this entails purely an interest rate option.
- **Contingent currency swaps** – this entails a combined interest rate and currency option.

The swaption structure designed to hedge a naked debt warrant issue illustrates the mechanics of these transaction.

Exhibit 16.12 sets out an example of a naked warrant issue and accompanying contingent swap. In this example, a contingent swap (effectively, a receiver swaption) is linked to debt warrants exercisable at interest rates below current market levels. When the warrants are issued, the two parties enter into a contingent swap agreement and the fixed rate payer receives an up-front fee from the issuer of the warrants. If and when the warrants are exercised, then the swap becomes effective. The swap is identical to a traditional interest rate or currency swap. If interest rate levels rise or remain constant, then the warrants will expire unexercised. The contingent swap provider will keep the premium. If interest rates fall, then the warrants are exercised. The parties enter into the swap as the contingent swap is triggered to hedge the bonds issued under the warrants. In the initial transactions, the ultimate seller of the receiver swaption was generally a borrower with large funding requirements seeking attractively priced fixed rate funding to match fund assets. For the seller of the receiver swaption, the structure generates significant savings compared to a standard swap. This saving is generated from two sources:

- The fixed rate on a contingent swap is generally substantially below the current market level.
- Fixed rate payer received an up-front premium. If the warrants expire unexercised, then the premium will be retained as income. If the warrants are exercised, then the premium will lower the all-in cost of the swap.

The issuer of the warrants is insulated from the fixed rate level on the swap. If the warrants are exercised, then the issuer immediately translates its fixed rate funding into floating rate funding at a predetermined margin under LIBOR.

Where the underlying debt warrants are exercisable into foreign currency bonds and say the US$ amount required to buy the relevant bonds is fixed at the outset, the warrants entail both a specific interest rate and currency option that is usually covered by the contingent currency swap. **Exhibit 16.13** sets out an example of a transaction involving a contingent currency swap.

One application entailing the use of debt warrants originally evolved in early 1986 when a marked decline in US$ interest rates resulted in a corresponding increase in the value of call options on existing fixed rate bonds. In all cases, the call option on existing debt could not be exercised until some time in the future. This delay in the exercise of the call meant that its value was uncertain, as an increase in interest rates between the present and the time the call was capable of being exercised would erode or eliminate the value of the option. In this environment, two particular types of transactions evolved. The first involved using forward swaps to realise the value of in-the-money call. The second involved using debt warrants to monetise the value of the in-the-money call options[52].

Exhibit 16.12   Naked Warrants Issue and Contingent Swap Structure

Assume a company issues warrants exercisable into A$ bonds on the following terms:

Back bonds (bonds into which the warrants are exercised)

Amount	A$50 million
Term	5 years
Coupon	14.00% pa payable annually

Warrants

Number of warrants	50,000 (based on assumed exchange rate) each exercisable into A$1,000 bonds on above terms
Assumed exchange rate	A$1.00 = US$0.70
Warrant price	See discussion below.
Expiry date	The warrants will expire, unless exercised approximately one year after issue (that is, February 2002). The warrant can be exercised at any point in time before expiry

The dealer provides a contingent currency swap (sells a receiver swaption) on the following terms:

Amount	A$50 million
Term	5 years
Dealer pays	14.00% pa payable annually
Dealer receives	6 month LIBOR
Up-front fee	See discussion below.
Commencement date	The swap can be triggered at any time within one year after issue (that is, by February 2002) at the option of the company.

The rationale for the transaction is as follows:

- The issuer is indifferent as to the outcome. If the warrants are exercised, then it triggers the contingent swap to achieve a margin under LIBOR.
- The purchaser of warrants gets a highly leveraged A$ interest rate play (possibly a currency play if exchange rate is fixed).
- Contingent swap provider benefits from:
  1. Receiving the theoretical value of the option (appropriate for a dealer which will seek to offset or hedge its exposure).
  2. Receives attractively priced funding if the contingent swap is called upon (appropriate for a liability manager with funding targets that are currently unachievable in the market).

---

[52]   See Chapter 13.

Where the counterparty for the contingent swap is a liability manager, the analysis of its position is as follows:
- The counterparty can obtain funding at say 14.70% pa payable semi-annually (15.24% pa payable annually) for 6 years (the A$ bond rate).
- The counterparty can obtain funding for one year (the swaption period) at 17.00% pa (payable semi-annually).
- If the counterparty can obtain funding at less than 14.24% pa payable semi-annually (14.75% pa payable annually) in 1 year from now, then it can achieve a cost saving.

The pricing dynamics of the transaction are as follows. Assume:
- The issuer requires LIBOR minus 25 bps.
- The dealer requires 13.75% pa payable annually (13.31% pa payable semi-annually) if the warrants and contingent swap are triggered to undertake the transaction.

Given the assumptions, it is possible to structure the transaction as follows:
- The dealer requires 25 bps under 14.00% pa (25 bps on A$50 million = A$125,000 pa discounted back at 15.24% pa (payable annually) (the bond rate)) equates to A$416,649 (US$291,654 at the assumed exchange rate). The swap may not be exercised for up to a maximum of one year, that is the dealer gets investment earning at 15.24% pa (payable annually) for this period, therefore allowing the up-front payment to be reduced (present valued at 15.24% pa) to A$361,549 (US$253,084). Therefore, depending on assumption of timing of warrant and swap exercises, the dealer needs between US$253,084 to US$291,654 to achieve 13.75% pa (payable annually).
- The issuer requires 25 bps under LIBOR (25 bps on US$35 million (A$50 million at A$1.00/US$0.70) = US$87,500 discounted back at 10.00% pa (payable annually) equates to US$ 331,694). Depending on assumption of timing of warrant and swap exercises, the issuer would need between US$301,540 and US$331,694 to achieve 25 bps spread under LIBOR.
- Given the size of the up-front payments to the issuer and the dealers, the warrants would have to be sold for at least:

$$[(US\$253,084 + US\$301,540)/50,000] = US\$11.09$$
$$[(US\$291,654 + US\$331,694)/50,000] = US\$12.47$$

Any price over and above that amount would be profit for the investment bank structuring and executing the transaction.

The dealer may require a considerably higher payment to enter into the contingent swap if it analyses the transaction in terms of option theory to price the implicit swaption being created.

Assume that the warrants are sold for US$24.00 per warrant (net of fees, commissions and expenses). This will result in a net inflow of US$1,200,000 (50,000 warrants at US$24.00 each). The warrant proceeds received are used as follows:
- The issuer is paid US$331,694 for acting as the issuer of the warrants.
- The provider of the swap is paid US$291,654 for entering into the contingent swap.
- The surplus of US$576,652 is retained by the investment bank.

The position for all participants in this transaction, under different interest rate scenarios, is as follows:

Scenario (Bond Rates % pa)	Warrant Purchaser	Warrant Issuer	Contingent Swap (Swaption) Provider
Above 14	Not Exercised	Payment Retained	Retain premium
Below 14	Exercised	Financing at LIBOR minus 25 bps pa	Fixed rate funding at around 13.75% pa (assumes US$ funding at LIBOR flat)

For the contingent swap provider, the opportunity loss (funding at 13.75% pa where market rates are lower) may not be relevant. For example, it may have an ongoing need for substantial fixed rate funding or is running an asset liability gap (a bank with high yielding fixed rate loans on its books that may be seeking a fixed rate liability to hedge its mismatch). In the case of a dealer, the position is hedged. The premium for the contingent swap is the theoretical option premium plus the dealer's profit.

As a variation, on exercise of the warrant the A$/US$ exchange rate can be fixed at or near the spot rate on the date of launch or settlement. This has the following effects:

* The purchaser of the warrants has a currency option as well as an interest rate option. If the A$ appreciates, irrespective of interest rate movements, then the warrants may have value.

* The issuer is indifferent because it knows the maximum cost of US$ funding it is obtaining if the exchange rate is not fixed:

  1. If the A$ appreciates, then it gets less US$ and achieves a higher margin under LIBOR.
  2. If the A$ depreciates, then it gets more US$ and achieves a lower margin under LIBOR.

The contingent swap provider is, in this case, granting a foreign exchange option on the A$/US$ rate. It has an exposure to an appreciation in the A$ where it would suffer a loss, as it would receive less A$, or conversely it would have to borrow more US$ to support the currency swap if it was to be triggered.

Exhibit 16.13   Warrant Issues and Contingent Currency Swaps[53]

In late 1985, a currency option swap was created by Credit Commercial de France ("CCF").

CCF structured such a swap by issuing a US$ floating rate note for the first counterparty with attached warrants into a European Currency Units ("ECU") issue. A contingent swap was then written with a second counterparty that wished to borrow ECU. If the warrants

---

[53]   See Bisquerra, Michel and Nijdam, Christophe "Currency Option Swap" in Antl, Boris (Editor) (1986) Swap Finance: Volume 2; Euromoney Publications, London at Part IX Chapter 11 243–246.

are exercised, then the contingent swap is invoked and the second counterparty pays the fixed rate coupons on the ECU bonds. The first counterparty then pays US$ LIBOR to cover the second counterparty's inter-bank funding cost.

The investors purchased the warrants for a premium that reflected the potential currency and interest rate option value. Since the ECU bond warrant premium is shared by both counterparties, the first party effectively raises dollars at a sub-LIBOR rate while the second counterparty raises fixed rate ECU at a borrowing cost well below current market levels, assuming that the warrants are exercised.

Contingent currency swaps involving Deutschmarks were also pioneered by CCF with an issue of 250,000 warrants to buy a 6.375% Deutschmark bond attached to a US$250 million floating rate note issue. If the warrants are exercised then a swap is automatically triggered where a counterparty agrees, in return for an option premium, to assume the fixed deutschmark liability on CCF's behalf and receive US$ coupon payments. CCF thus hedged its currency exposure into US$ should the warrants be exercised. Similar deals were undertaken by Swedbank and PKBanken.

9.3.3   Debt Warrants and Host Bond Packages

The second structural class of transactions involving debt warrants entails the issue of bonds (referred to as the host bond or debt) simultaneously with the issue of debt warrants into bonds issued by the issuer. The terms of the bonds to be issued under the terms of the warrants were similar or identical to that of the host bonds (referred to as the back bonds). The majority of the structures were arbitrage driven, seeking to capture value discrepancies between the market for debt warrants and the swaptions market.

The transactions entailed using one of the following arrangements:

• Where the total package has an uncertain level of proceeds over its life and/or an uncertain maturity.

• Debt warrant packages where the amount of debt remains relatively constant and the cost to the issuer does *not* change when and if the warrants are exercised.

For example, periods characterised by expectations of falling rates resulted in the offering of fixed rate bonds with attached warrants that allowed the holder of the warrant the right to purchase additional fixed rate bonds of the issuer at a predetermined coupon. The warrants had lives of anywhere between 1 and 7 years. The warrants allowed the cost of the initial fixed rate debt to be reduced by the proceeds of the warrant issue. This resulted in a saving in yield of between 50 and 100 bps pa relative to a conventional issue. The issuer was simultaneously exposed to issuing further debt at a coupon cost equal to that of the fixed rate bonds into which the warrants could be exercised. The cost of the back bonds was generally 25 to 50 bps pa lower than the host coupon bond. Given that there are no issuance costs or fees on issuance of the warrant bonds, the cost of the warrant bond could be 70 to 100 bps pa below the issuer's current fixed rate cost.

The overall yield savings (anywhere up to 100 bps compared to a conventional fixed rate offering) was achieved at the expense of not being able to determine in advance how many warrants will be exercised. The issuer therefore had a known cost of debt, but an uncertain amount of debt over the life of the transaction.

For fixed rate issuers with absolute interest rate targets, the uncertainty regarding the amount of debt was not problematic. However, certain issuers were only attracted to a warrant issue on the basis of the underlying issue being swapped into floating rate US$. If the borrower could insulate against the cost of the prospective issuance of additional fixed rate debt as a result of the warrants being exercised by being able to swap it into floating rate, then both parties could be accommodated simultaneously. The borrower no longer has an exposure to fixed interest rates, only to the uncertain amount of debt that might be outstanding at any time.

The perfectly matched interest rate swap allowed the issuer to swap the host issue immediately into floating rate US$. The swap provided for the swap notional principal to be increased at any time to accommodate further amounts of fixed debt created by the exercise of warrants (in effect, the purchase of a receiver swaption by the issuer). This structure allowed the issuer to substantially shift the exposure of warrant exercise to the swap counterparty.

The cost of the swaption could outweigh most or even all of the advantages gained by issuing warrants. Consequently, the structure of warrant swaps increasingly began to trade off the quantum of the spread below LIBOR and warrant exercise risk. Typical warrant swap structures designed to provide cost savings and limit risk would feature a 7 year host bond issue callable at par at any time after 4 years, with attached warrants into a 3 year bond. This structure was predicated on the assumption that warrants are not usually exercised until near to their expiry date, and at their expiry date the host issue can be called. This capacity to call the host bond allows the issuer to have a degree of control over the amount of outstanding debt, enabling it to keep the total volume of paper on issue constant. The issue is combined with a standard 7 year swap to convert the fixed rate into floating, with the value of the warrants being used to subsidise the cost of the swap. This structure is known as the harmless debt warrant structure.

Pioneered by the Kingdom of Denmark, debt and warrant issue packages were created to ensure that the amount of the debt outstanding remained relatively constant and the cost of the issue did not change significantly if the warrants were exercised. The host bond was made callable at any time should warrants be exercised. This ensured that the amount of debt outstanding remains constant, enabling a standard interest rate swap to be executed. This alternative entailed a higher cost on the host issue in terms of both coupon (approximately 0.125% pa) and call premium (approximately 1.00%). However, depending on the value of the attached warrants, the floating rate cost obtainable with this structure was considerably better than a standard fixed rate issue without warrants. Under this structure, a conventional interest rate or (if applicable) currency swap could be used as the security issue's cash flows resemble a straight bond issue.

This structure essentially gave borrowers access to cheap funds, designed in most cases to be swapped into floating rate at extremely competitive levels with extremely limited exposure to the implicit call option. **Exhibit 16.14** sets out the concept using the example of an issue for Westpac Banking Corporation.

Exhibit 16.14   "Harmless" Debt Warrant Issues and Swaps

The Westpac issue was on the following terms:
*   US$100 million 10 year (maturing 1996) 10.00% pa coupon issued at 100 with 2.00% fees. The issue was callable after five years at 101.50% of face value declining by 0.50% pa to par.
*   200,000 warrants at US$50 each. Each two warrants are exercisable after 5 years into one 11.25% non-callable bond due 1996 at par (that is, US$100 per bond). During the first 5 years, the warrants pay 10.00% interest and if not exercised, they are each redeemable at US$50 in 1996.

The Table below shows the cash flow (US$ million) to Westpac whether or not the warrants are exercised. It is assumed that the host bonds will be called if the warrants are exercised in years six to ten; the warrants will automatically be redeemed at maturity if they are not exercised.

Year	Not Exercised	Year Warrants Are Exercised (assumed warrants exercised at year end)					
		5	6	7	8	9	10
0	108.875	108.875	108.875	108.875	108.875	108.875	108.875
1	−11.000	−11.000	−11.000	−11.000	−11.000	−11.000	−11.000
2	−11.000	−11.000	−11.000	−11.000	−11.000	−11.000	−11.000
3	−11.000	−11.000	−11.000	−11.000	−11.000	−11.000	−11.000
4	−11.000	−11.000	−11.000	−11.000	−11.000	−11.000	−11.000
5	−11.000	−12.500	−11.000	−11.000	−11.000	−11.000	−11.000
6	−10.000	−11.250	−11.000	−10.000	−10.000	−10.000	−10.000
7	−10.000	−11.250	−11.250	−10.500	−10.000	−10.000	−10.000
8	−10.000	−11.250	−11.250	−11.250	−10.000	−10.000	−10.000
9	−10.000	−11.250	−11.250	−11.250	−11.250	−10.000	−10.000
10	−120.00	−111.250	−111.250	−111.250	−111.250	−111.250	−111.250

All in cost to Westpac as margin (bps pa) relative to US Treasuries:

Year	Not Exercised	5	6	7	8	9	10
	43	43	27	13	0	−8	−8

Note: Assumes host bonds are called from the end of year five. In the no-exercise case, warrants are redeemed at US$50.

From the Table, it is apparent that the issue is structured such that the issuer is guaranteed a maximum rate that can only decrease if the warrants are exercised. Through this structure, Westpac paid a maximum of 9.82% pa (9.59% pa semi annual or US Treasury bond plus 43 bps), a saving of approximately 20–25 bps pa on its normal cost of funds.

The issue was swapped into floating rate US$ LIBOR using a conventional US$ interest swap that would have been structured to accommodate the unusual cash flow pattern.

10 Step Up/Multi-Step Callable Bonds

10.1 Concept

Putable bond structures and debt warrant structures have a long history. In contrast, the concept of step up and multi-step callable bonds derives from recent history. The structures evolved in a period of low nominal interest rates and a very steep positive yield curve in the early 1990s.

Driving this innovation was the fact that in a callable bond, the value of the option component is related to the relativity of the bond coupon and the forward rate implied by the current yield curve. In the early 1990s, the high implied US$ forward rates meant that the option embedded in a callable bond was substantially out-of-the money, contributing to the low premium value for the option. This made the additional yield available on a callable bond less attractive. The compensation for the sale of the call option was particularly small in relation to the perceived risk of exercise of the call.

Investor behaviour reflected an expectation that the rate structure would stay relatively static and that forward rates were *overestimating* the rise in actual interest rates. Against this background, several types of callable structures emerged in order to increase the value of the embedded option and enhance the attractiveness of the bond. The structures included:

• Step up callable notes.
• Multi-step callable notes.

Exhibit 16.15   Step Up Callable Notes

Issuer	AAA/Aaa Rated Issuer	
Amount	US$100 million	
Maturity	10 years	
Issue Price	100	
Coupon	**Year**	**Coupon (% pa semi-annually)**
	1 to 5	6.75 (64 bps above 5 Year Treasury)
	5 to 10	8.25 (156 bps above 10 Year Treasury)
Call Options	Callable at the option of issuer at year 5	

The step up callable structure (also referred to as a single step callable) entails a callable bond with a two tier coupon. The initial (lower) coupon applies until the call date (usually only a single call date is used). The coupon increases if the bond is not called. The increase in the coupon gives rise to the term "step up". The typical structure of a step up call involves a yield to call that is significantly higher than that on a comparable non call bond with a maturity equivalent to the call date. The stepped up coupon was usually set at or higher than the implied forward interest rate[54].

Exhibit 16.15 sets out an example of the terms of a typical step up callable note. In this case, the step up callable returns around 64 bps above the 5 year Treasury at the time of issue and around 36 bps above the 5 year financing cost for the issuer. The step up coupon is 8.25% pa, which is 156 bps over the current 10 year Treasury. The multi-step callable structure is similar in concept to the step up callable structure. The major differences are as follows:

- The multi-step callable bond entails the issuer having the right to call the bond on a sequence of successive dates. The call dates usually coincide with the coupon payment dates until maturity (effectively, a Bermudan option).
- The initial coupon to the first call date is set at a level which is higher than the comparable non callable return to the call date. The coupon then increases *at each call date*. The step ups in the coupon on the multi-step callable note generally follow the shape of the implied forward yield curve.

A multi-step callable note typically has a higher nominal spread than the traditional callable issue of the same maturity or an equivalent step up callable note.

---

[54] See Chen, Shiuan and Macirowski, Tom (May 1994) Step-Up Callable Agency Notes; Goldman Sachs Fixed Income Research, New York.

Exhibit 16.16 Multi-Step Callable Notes – Example 1

Issuer	AAA/Aaa Rated Issuer	
Amount	US$100 million	
Maturity	7 Years	
Issue Price	100	
Coupon	**Year**	**Coupon (% pa semi-annually)**
	1	4.75(67 bps above 1 Year Treasury)
	2	5.00 (31 bps above 2 Year Treasury)
	3	5.50 (22 bps above 3 Year Treasury)
	4	6.00 (21 bps above 4 Year Treasury)
	5	6.50 (34 bps above 5 Year Treasury)
	6	6.75 (42 bps above 6 Year Treasury)
	7	7.00 (41 bps above 7 Year Treasury)
Call Options	Callable at the option of the issuer on each semi-annual coupon date commencing on the second coupon date (after 1 year)	

Exhibit 16.17 Multi-Step Callable Notes – Example 2

Issuer	AAA/Aaa Rated Issuer	
Amount	US$100 million	
Maturity Date	10 years	
Issue Price	100	
Coupon	**Year**	**Coupon (% pa semi-annually)**
	1	5.50
	2	5.75
	3–10	Previous Coupon Plus 0.30% pa
Call Options	Callable at the option of the issuer on each semi-annual coupon date commencing on the second coupon date (after 1 year)	

Exhibit 16.16 sets out an example of the terms of a typical multi-step callable note. The transaction described is 5 year non call 1 year. The coupon for the first year is set at an attractive spread over the 1 year Treasury rate and if the note is not called, the coupon rises. **Exhibit 16.17** sets out a longer dated multi-step callable note.

10.2 Economics, Price Characteristics and Valuation

The economics of the step up callable and multi-step callable structures derive from the objective of extracting additional value from the embedded debt options.

The additional value is created from the following sources:
- The adjustment in the coupon at the call dates has the effect of placing the call option at-the-money or closer to the money.
- In the case of the multi-step callable note structure, the option is structured as a Bermudan exercise option, allowing for exercise at various dates up until final maturity that serves to further enhance the value of the option.

The value impact is evident from the examples set out above. In practice, a major determinant of value is the valuation of the embedded option as calculated by the swaptions market that is used by the issuer to strip out the debt option and sell it to lower its borrowing cost.

Development of an appropriate measure of the price characteristics of this type of security focuses on multiple metrics, including:
- Duration and Price Convexity.
- Option Adjusted Spread ("OAS").
- Extension Risk.

The measurement of duration and price convexity of step up callable and multi-step callable notes is problematic. This is because of the uncertainty of the cash flows that are interest rate contingent. Assuming non exercise of the call allows estimation of the duration characteristics of such securities.

For example, the duration characteristics of the step-up callable note may be illustrated with a simple example. The analysis compares the effective duration of two securities – a 10 year non call note, a 10 year note callable after 5 years. The duration of the non call note declines with increasing rates, reflecting the positive price convexity. The duration of the callable bond approaches that of the non callable bonds for large movements in rates from present levels. The callable bond exhibits negative convexity characteristics for rate movements with duration increasing with yield, reflecting the increasing likelihood of non exercise of the calls. The step up callable demonstrates a lower duration, reflecting the higher probability that it will be called prior to maturity. Multi-step up callable will generally have duration that is even shorter than for step up callable structures.

An alternative means of estimating the duration characteristics is to measure the option adjusted duration. The option adjusted duration of the multi-step up callable will tend to be lower than that of a non call bond and a normal callable structure. This reflects the high probability that the note will be repaid prior to maturity. It is consistent with the fact that the bond has a maturity closer to the earlier call dates than the final maturity.

The concept of option adjusted spread ("OAS") calculates the effective spread of a callable bond to the underlying Treasury rate, by adjusting the nominal spread by subtracting the cost of the option[55]. The option cost is calculated in an arbitrage free framework by generating future scenarios of interest rates. In theory, in an efficient market the OAS of the callable note should equal the return on an equivalent non-callable security.

In practice, the concept of extension risk is perhaps the most important mechanism for analysing these types of instruments. This reflects, in part, the behaviour of issuers. Issuers normally set the front coupon at a higher level relative to their cost of borrowing for the shorter maturity. The step up rate is set with reference to implied forward rates. In contrast, investors view this type of callable bonds as *short term investments (to the call date) with extension risk*. This derives from the fact that unless interest rates rise at the rate implied by the forward curve, the higher step-up coupon on the call date dictates that the bond will be pre-paid. This will leave the investor with a short term investment at an enhanced yield. Consequently, the central value characteristic is the trade-off between the spread of the initial coupon to comparable investments and the risk of maturity extension.

The central factor determining extension risk is the likelihood of exercise of the call option. The factors that will generally dictate call include:
- Absolute level of interest rate.
- Yield curve shape.
- Volatility of interest rates.

The impact of changes in the absolute level of interest rates on call exercise relates primarily to the amount that rates will have to rise for the issuer not to exercise the call. The breakeven condition is the market rate from call date to maturity, relative to the yield to maturity of the bond if not called. The call will be exercised if the market rate is below the callable bond's yield to maturity.

The extension risk of the multi-step up callable note in practice is expressed as the amount interest rates will have to increase to economically dictate extension of note maturity. For example, in the issue described in **Exhibit 16.16**, the yield to maturity after 1 year for the remaining 9 year term is 5.00% pa. If the market rate for 9 years for the issuer is below this level, then the issuer would pre-pay the issue and re-finance. If the yield curve stays static between the time

---

[55] See Audley, David, Chin, Richard and Ramamurthy, Shrikant "OAS and Effective Duration" in Fabozzi, Frank J. (Editor) (2001) The Handbook of Fixed Income Securities – Sixth Edition"; McGraw-Hill, New York at Chapter 37.

of entry into the transaction and the call date in 1 year, and assuming parallel yield curve shifts, then the rate structure will have to rise for the bond not to be called.

Exhibit 16.18 sets out the expected final maturity of the bond assuming certain changes in interest rates.

Exhibit 16.18   Multi-Step Callable Notes – Extension Risk

The extension risk profile for a multi-step callable (on the terms set out in **Exhibit 16.16**) for parallel and instantaneous yield curve shifts is summarised below:

Yield Curve Shift (bps)	Yield (% pa)	Average Life (Years)
−150	4.75	1
−100	4.75	1
−50	4.75	1
0	4.75	1
+50	4.75	1
+100	5.00	2
+150	5.50	3

The analysis highlights that the call exercise is a function of how accurately the forward rates implied by the yield curve capture the actual increase of rates. The bonds are likely to be called where the forward rates are higher than the actual rates.

The change in the shape of the yield curve will impact upon extension risk. This will be through its effect on the implied forward rate and on the value of the embedded call. For example, in an upward sloping yield curve, the forward rates will lie above the yield curve. In addition, the rising yield curve will dictate that the forward rates will anticipate a flattening of the yield curve (generated by the fact that the short term implied forward rates (1 year) will be above the forward rates applicable for longer maturities). If the implied 1 year forwards are realised, then the call would not be exercised. A flattening of the yield curve would increase the value of the embedded options, thereby requiring a higher nominal yield to create the same bond, and making it more likely that the bond would not be called. For example, in **Exhibit 16.15** in a curve flattening scenario, the spread between short and long rates would have to decrease substantially before exercise of the call becomes uneconomical. In a curve steepening scenario, the spread would have to increase equally significantly for the call not to be exercised. In general terms, in the conditions identified, a flattening (steepening) in the yield curve increases (decreases) the expected final maturity of a multi-step callable.

The impact of changes in volatility is manifested through the direct impact on option values. An increase (decrease) in volatility levels will create a corresponding increase (decrease) in the value of the embedded debt option. Increases in volatility will therefore make it more expensive to purchase the option, with the result that the call will not be exercised. This is only relevant to the multi-exercise structure of the Bermudan call.

In practice, under conditions of stable interest rates, the multi-step callable structures have exhibited short duration with well defined average lives and limited extension risk. The volatility of future values of callable and step-up callable structures has been found to be significantly less than that of a corresponding non-callable note[56].

10.3 Applications

The application of step up/multi-step callable bonds is substantially investor driven. The major issuer interest has been arbitrage driven.

The bulk of issuance has been by high credit quality issuers. In the US, it has been concentrated among federal government agencies. The issuers have undertaken issues that are simultaneously swapped into attractively priced floating rate funding. The value basis of such transactions has been the higher premium paid by the derivatives market for the Bermudan style, step-up strike payer swaption relative to the additional return demanded by investors to take on the extension risk of these callable bonds.

There has been a limited volume of unswapped issuance, particularly by US mortgage financing institutions. These issuers use the embedded call as a mechanism for hedging the pre-payment risk on mortgage loans.

Investor demand for the structures reflects the underlying investment and price characteristics of the structure. Steep positive slope of the yield curve in many currencies and the relatively low nominal rates of interest return create an environment where investors have aggressively sought enhanced returns. The expectation that interest rates would not increase *at the rate* implied by the forward curve is monetised by the step up callable format. The additional coupon is used to enhance fixed income portfolio yields.

---

[56] See Pimbley, Joseph M. and Curry, Daniel A. (July 1995) Market Risk of the Step-Up Callable Structured Note; Moody's Investors Service, New York.

Step up callable notes compete with a variety of other types of investments that provide similar return enhancement possibilities. These include:
* Mortgage Backed Securities ("MBS")[57].
* Index Amortisation Rate ("IAR") Transactions[58].

In general, the single and multi-step up callable notes compare favourably with the competing investment alternatives, particularly MBS transactions. The major consideration in this regard appears to have been the relative stability of the average lives, lower extension risk and more predictable prepayment behaviour of the structures. These characteristics have proven particularly suitable for investors seeking a final repayment of principal and easily quantified prepayment risk.

A significant part of the demand for step-up structures is from retail investors, particularly in the US domestic market. This demand is both directly for the securities and indirectly through retail financial institutions. In the latter case, the retail financial institutions purchase the notes as investments, while simultaneously issuing retail deposit facilities including CDs or deposit accounts that replicate the return profile of the step up callable instrument.

10.4   Variations and Extensions

The development of the market for step up callable structure is reflected in the richer variety of structures that have become available. The major variations and product extensions include:
* Extending the credit range of issuers.
* Greater variety of maturity structures.
* Defined call structures.
* Zero coupon callable bonds.
* Expansion of concept into other currencies.

The initial market for the structures was focused almost exclusively on the US Agency market which was the largest single issuer group for these securities.

---

[57] See Fabozzi, Frank J. (Editor) (1992) The Handbook of Mortgage Backed Securities – Second Edition; Probus Publishing Company, Chicago, Illinois. See also Henderson, John and Scott, Jonothan P. (1988) Securitisation; Woodhead-Faulkner, New York; Rosenthal, James A. and Ocampo, Juan M. (1988) Securitisation of Credit; John Wiley, New York; Zweig, Philip (Editor) (1989) The Asset Securitisation Handbook; Dow Jones-Irwin, Homewood, Illinois; Shaw, Zoe (Editor) (1991) International Securitisation; MacMillans, London.

[58] See Chapter 18.

As the market has developed, high quality corporate issuers entered the market as issuers of multi-step callable notes.

The range of maturities has also broadened, with investors being able to choose from very short notes with 6 months final maturity (with almost no call protection - 3/6 months) to 20 year final maturities (with 1 to 5 years call protection). The major trend in this regard was a consistent shortening of maturities during the period 1994/1995. Two examples of such short dated structures – a three year non-call 6 month and a 1 year monthly callable note are set out in **Exhibit 16.19** and **Exhibit 16.20**.

The index or defined callable structure (referred to as defined callable notes) represents an interesting extension of the callable concept. In a defined callable note, the fixed interest instrument is combined with a call option on a nominated index (typically 3 or 6 month LIBOR). If LIBOR is below the strike level then the issuer must call the note. If LIBOR is above the strike level, then the call cannot be exercised and the note maturity is extended. Both single step and multi-step call

---

Exhibit 16.19   Short Term Multi-Step Callable Notes - 3 Year/6 Month Non Call

Issuer	AAA/Aaa Rated Issuer	
Amount	US$100 million	
Maturity	3 Years	
Issue Price	100	
Coupon	**Months**	**Coupon (% pa semi-annually)**
	0–6	5.50 (57 bps above 6 month Treasury)
	7–12	5.75 (44 bps above 12 month Treasury)
	13–18	6.00 (38 bps above 18 month Treasury)
	19–24	6.25 (39 bps above 24 month Treasury)
	25–36	6.50 (44 bps above 36 month Treasury)
Call Options	Callable at the option of the issuer on each semi-annual coupon date commencing on the first coupon date (after 6 months)	

The extension risk of the multi-step up callable note expressed as the amount interest rates will have to increase to economically dictate extension of note maturity is summarised below:

Maturity (Months)	Maximum Rate Rise Up to Call Date (bps)
6	27
12	89

Exhibit 16.20   Short Term Multi-Step Callable Notes - 1 Year/Monthly Call

Issuer   AAA/Aaa Rated Issuer
Amount   US$100 million
Maturity   1 year
Issue Price   100
Coupon   6.10% pa payable monthly
Call Options   Callable on each monthly date in whole only.

The yield advantage of the 1 year monthly call note over the 1 year Treasury was typically around 90 to 100 bps pa, reflecting investor requirements. The extension risk of the multi-step up callable note expressed as the amount interest rates will have to increase to economically dictate extension of note maturity was usually around 5–10 bps per month or around 25 bps per quarter, usually reflecting investor expectations about the course of US monetary policy.

Exhibit 16.21   Defined Callable Notes

Issuer   AAA/Aaa Rated Issuer
Amount   US$100 million
Maturity   3 year
Issue Price   100
Coupon   6.00% pa
Call Options   Callable at the option of the issuer after 1 year except if Index is above Index Strike Level
Index   6 Month LIBOR
Index Strike Level   6.625% pa (200 bps over spot 6 Month LIBOR)

---

structures are feasible within the defined callable framework. **Exhibit 16.21** sets out an example of a defined callable note.

In typical cases, the note structure allowed the investor around 200 bps of protection against rising interest rates, as the market rates must rise by at least this amount before these notes extend. If the forward rates overestimate the rate of increase of the nominated index, then the notes are unlikely to extend and provide investors with a high yielding investment to the call date. The structures offered investors a return pick-up in the region of between 70 to 90 bps pa over the equivalent yield for a similar security.

The major advantage of defined call instruments is the fact that the call decision is based solely on the level of the agreed market index. The call is also mandatory, providing the call condition is satisfied. This is in contrast to the call decision in the case of a traditional callable bond that will be dependent on changes in the *issuer's* funding cost (which will incorporate changes in the issuer's credit spread) and/or changes in the shape of the yield curve. Consequently, the use of the defined call structure is designed to create certainty in the exercise of the call.

A more recent innovation has been the callable zero coupon bond. The typical structure entails the investor purchasing a zero coupon bond with a long maturity (usually 30 years). The bond is callable annually, usually after a call protection period of around 5 years. The structure developed originally in Germany. The major investors were insurance companies seeking higher yielding securities. During the 1990s as interest rates fell, these investors found it increasingly difficult to generate the returns often guaranteed to insurance policy holders. This problem was exacerbated as high yielding bonds (with coupons of 8% and 9%) matured. The callable zero coupon bond proved valuable in this environment.

The rationale behind the structure was the steep German yield curve and the characteristics of the zero coupon bond itself. The structure effectively uses a Bermudan swaption to enhance the return to the investor. The reinvestment of interest creates considerable leverage through the call structure. This is because the embedded option is also on the reinvested interest component. This means that the option premium is larger relative to the amount invested in the bonds.

An additional motivation underlying the structure was the ability to use the callable zero coupon bonds to match asset return to liabilities. The callable zero coupon bonds provided the investor with a higher than market return. If the bonds were called, where rates did not rise significantly, then the investor would receive a high short term return and would face reinvestment risk. If the bonds were not called, if rates increased rapidly, then the investor is guaranteed the above market return over the life of the bonds. It is only where rates fall sharply, exposing the investor to lower returns on the funds to be reinvested, that the investors are in a disadvantageous position.

The concept of step up callable bonds has been extended into a number of other currencies – most notably, Japanese yen, Deutschemark ("DEM"), other European currencies and Canadian Dollars ("C$"). Examples of DEM and C$ Multi-step Callable structures are set out in **Exhibit 16.22** and **Exhibit 16.23**. The motivation for these transactions in other currencies is similar to that in US$. The steep upward sloping nature of the yield curve and the desire of investors to monetise expectations regarding the future path of actual rates create an environment where the additional return available is attractive relative to the extension risk assumed. An additional factor for foreign currency fixed income investors is the currency risk element. A major attraction has been the potential for appreciation as result of further strengthening in the currency.

Exhibit 16.22   DEM Multi-Step Callable Notes

Issuer	AAA/Aaa Rated Issuer
Amount	DEM 100 million
Maturity Date	10 years
Issue Price	100
Coupon	**Year** **Coupon (% pa payable annually)**
	1–3 6.50
	4–10 7.75
Call Options	Callable at the option of the issuer on each annual coupon date commencing from the 3rd coupon date

The yield advantage of the note is as follows:

Maturity (Year)	Step Up Yield (% pa)	Spread to German Swap Rate (bp)
3	6.50	52
5	6.95	51
7	7.14	34
10	7.28	32

The extension risk of the multi-step up callable note expressed as the amount interest rates will have to increase (assuming a parallel shift in DEM interest rates) to economically dictate extension of note maturity is summarised below:

Maturity (Years)	Maximum Rate Rise to Call Date (bps)
3	+25/35
5	+75/85

11   Callable Bonds – Market

The market for callable bonds is complex. The dynamics of the market are driven by the following factors:

- The market sectors can be separated as follows:
  1. In currency terms, US$ versus other currencies.
  2. In market terms, US domestic versus international markets, in particular the European markets.
- The market prior to and after the introduction and use of swaptions to monetise and trade the embedded debt options in callable bonds.

Exhibit 16.23 C$ Multi-Step Callable Notes	

Issuer	AA Rated Issuer	
Amount	C$100 million	
Maturity Date	5 Years	
Issue Price	100	
Coupon	**Year**	**Coupon (% pa payable annually)**
	1	7.00
	2	7.75
	3	8.00
	4	8.25
	5	8.50
Call Options	Callable at the option of the issuer on each annual coupon date commencing from the 3rd coupon date	

The yield advantage of this type of note required by investors was between 65 and 85 bps over the equivalent yield for a non callable security.

The extension risk of the multi-step up callable note, expressed as the amount interest rates increase in a typical transaction, was around 50 to 75 bps in the first year. The amount increased with a gradual step-up to anywhere between 200 and 300 bps at the final call date, depending on the shape of the yield curve at the time of issue.

Callable bonds are traditionally a more significant part of the US domestic capital market than international markets. The bulk of callable bond issuance has been in US$. While there has been activity in other currencies, the activity is both more sporadic/opportunistic and lower in absolute volume terms.

The difference between the market sectors appears based on a variety of factors:

- The fixed income investor in the US is predominantly institutional. In contrast, the corresponding investor base in European and Japanese markets has a stronger retail element.

- US investors tend, on the whole, to be among the most quantitative in their approach to fixed income portfolio management. In addition, US fixed interest investors are often benchmarked against indexes and are required to run interest rate immunised portfolios. In contrast, other markets/retail investors are less quantitative in investment approach. This group are total rate of return investors.

The difference in investor base and investment approach manifests itself in relation to investment in callable securities in a number of ways. Institutional investors such as those in the US view callable notes in a relative value framework and use these instruments for the following purposes:

- Arbitrage between securities on a "rich/cheap" basis, incorporating the option features of callable bonds to look for investment value.

- Adjust the return, duration and price convexity profile of a portfolio against identified liability funding constraints.
- Sell optionality and trade volatility of interest rates as a means for generating yield enhancement, effectively assuming extension risk in return for premium income generation.
- Implement strategies to extract value from the yield curve.

In contrast, other investors (including retail investors and other European investors) seek to maximise fixed interest returns through a combination of leverage to anticipated interest rate movements through trading in options and investment timing.

The former approach favours both traditional and more recent callable bond approaches as a means for incorporating debt options within fixed income portfolios. The latter approach does not favour the use of callable securities, but favours the use of debt options in the form of debt warrants. These instruments combine low dollar value commitment (particularly where the option is structured out-of-the-money), low and known risk (the premium) for the buyer, and the high leverage of returns to a favourable movement in the underlying bond. These instruments are particularly suitable for the type of investment approach identified.

This dichotomy in market structure results in a large thriving market for US$ callable notes in the US domestic markets. In contrast, other markets generally favour debt warrants. The advent of debt warrants as a means for securitisation of the embedded debt option in bonds was substantively a European market phenomenon that is consistent with this hypothesis.

In recent times, the demand for debt options packaged as warrants continues to thrive, with concentrated periods of activity in particular currencies reflecting changing investor expectations on rate movements. Increasingly, this demand is not met by genuine debt issuers, issuing debt warrants exercisable into new debt of the issuer. This demand is mostly met by the issue of debt warrants (either on a standalone basis or embedded in a structured note issued by either a dealer or arbitrage issuer). The underlying interest rate option exposure is hedged in the derivatives markets.

The above analysis is not designed to suggest that there is *no* activity in callable bonds in currencies other than US$ or in markets other than the US market. It is intended to convey the broad pattern of activity. Issuance of callable securities, when it occurs in these other currencies and markets, is in response to specific demand that is usually driven by particular market conditions. Such conditions have, in recent times, included investor demand for yield enhancement in a positive yield curve environment that has allowed investors to generate value through the sale of options embedded in callable bonds. The opportunities exist from time to time in a variety of currencies.

The other major dynamic of the market for callable securities has been the gradual development of the market for swaptions in the relevant currencies. The availability of swaptions has fundamentally altered the nature of the market in two separate ways:

• The capacity to allow issuers to undertake callable issue without exposure to the embedded option.
• The ability to value, securitise and trade the underlying debt option through the swaption market.

Traditionally, the market for callable securities suffered from problems of supply demand imbalance. Expectations on interest rates created either excess demand for or excess supply of callable securities. The fact that swaptions can be used to repackage the embedded debt option and re-sell it into a different market has allowed more consistent use of these structures. It allows the introduction of opportunistic arbitrage borrowers that use the callable issue as a means of capturing the value difference between the fixed income and swaption markets in terms of lower borrowing cost. These issuers basically trade off maturity uncertainty or liquidity risk on their underlying funding in return for an improvement in their cost of borrowing.

The second benefit relates to the ability to accurately value the embedded debt option. The availability of a market for swaptions facilitates the decomposition of the callable bond into a fixed interest security and a receiver or payer swaption, and accurately valuing the transaction. It also facilitates (as noted above) the capacity to re-create callable bonds and their variations by a process of reverse engineering using non-callable bonds and options on swaps. This naturally creates a deeper and more liquid market for callable securities[59].

Callable notes/swaptions are also available in a number of other currencies other than US$. The level of activity in other currencies varies significantly. Activity and liquidity is driven by the inter-relationship between callable bonds and swaptions.

The pattern of activity in swaptions in the German market illustrates the pattern of activity. The German swaption was historically driven by the German Federal Government and its appetite for fund raising. In the early 1990s, in an attempt to

---

[59] See Bookstaber, Richard, Hanley, William C., and Noris, Peter D. (December 1994) Are Options on Debt Issues Undervalued?; Morgan Stanley Fixed Income Analytical Research, New York; Latainer, Gary D., and Jacob, David P. (October 1985) Modern Techniques For Analysing Value and Performance of Callable Bonds; Morgan Stanley Fixed Income Analytical Research, New York.

keep coupons below 9% pa, German issuers offered investors in Schuldscheindar-lehen (often referred to as Schuldscheine) the ability to put the bonds back after 1, 2 and 3 years. Investors purchasing the Schuldscheine typically stripped out the put option and sold it to the swaption market. The government's role, as essential suppliers of long term options on government securities through this put option, effectively facilitated the development of the DEM swaptions market.

In summary, the market for callable bonds is, to a large degree, a market which focuses on US$ and the US market. However, the basic technology is readily available and adaptable to other currency markets and is increasingly being applied to those markets.

12 Summary

Callable bonds represent one of the most traditional forms of option embedded securities. In essence, such securities combine a traditional fixed income security with a call option written by the investor in favour of the issuer. The callable bond has particular price performance, duration and convexity characteristics that make such securities useful to both investors and issuers in terms of traditional asset and liability portfolio management. In recent times, the call feature has been effectively monetised or securitised through the use of swaption transactions which seek to capture the value differences between the pricing of these debt options between the fixed income and derivative markets. In response to market conditions, the structure has developed a rich and complex variety of extensions. The approaches focus on improving the value captured through the embedded option and/or adjustment of the investment characteristics to particular interest rate environments.

17
Constant Maturity Products

1 Overview

The concept of derivatives based around Constant Maturity Treasury ("CMT") rates and Constant Maturity Swap ("CMS") rates is relatively new in capital markets.

CMT/CMS structures are similar in concept to basis swaps. The central objective of these instruments is to hedge and trade positions on:

- Medium to long term interest rates in any currency.
- The spread between interest rates at different points in the yield curve (effectively the slope or shape of the yield curve).

The structure and applications of CMT/CMS based instruments are outlined in this chapter. The structure of the Chapter is as follows:

- The concept of CMT/CMS rates is outlined.
- CMT/CMS swaps and options are described.
- The pricing, valuation and hedging of CMT structures is outlined.
- Applications of CMT/CMS swaps and notes are analysed.

2 CMT/CMS Rates[1]

The concept of CMT/CMS rates focuses on an interest rate on securities with specified maturities. Observable rates in the market have a number of deficiencies, including:

- The observed rate for bonds is rarely the exact relevant maturity. For example, the current 10 year Treasury bond rate may be slightly longer or shorter than 10 years depending upon the actual maturity of the bond.
- Actual bonds or securities are subject to time decay. For example, the current 10 year bond will be a 9 year bond in 1 year.

CMT/CMS rates are designed to overcome both deficiencies.

---

[1] See Smithson, Charles "ABC of CMT" (September 1995) Risk 30–31.

Exhibit 17.1 sets out the manner in which the CMT rates (as published by the Federal Reserve) are determined.

Exhibit 17.1   CMT Rates

CMT Rates
CMT rates are equivalent par yield for a US Government Treasury security with an exact maturity of 1, 2, 3, 5, 7, 10, 20 or 30 years.

Methodology
The Federal Reserve of New York polls five primary dealers (selected from more than 30 primary dealers) for closing bids for "on the run" issues. This poll is conducted daily when the market is open at 3.30 PM.
   The bids are used to construct a complete Treasury yield curve. Cubic spline methodology is used to interpolate between data points. The CMT rate for each maturity is then interpolated from this yield curve.

Dissemination of CMT Rates
The Treasury posts the calculated rates in a number of ways:
• The CMT rates are available from the Commerce Department's economic bulletin board after 4.30 PM on the relevant day. A number of commercial data services disseminate the rates from the Commerce Department.
• The CMT rates are also published by the Federal Reserve Bank in its weekly H-15 Statistical Release.

Constant maturity yields on treasury securities are interpolated by the US Treasury from the daily yield curve. The curve relates the yield on a security to its time to maturity based on the closing market bid yields on actively traded treasury securities in the over-the-counter market. The market yields are calculated from composites of quotations reported by leading US Government Securities dealers to the Federal Reserve Bank of New York. The constant maturity yield values are read from the yield curve at fixed maturities: currently 1, 2, 3, 5, 7, 10 and 30 years. According to the Federal Reserve, this method would provide a yield for the exact 10 year maturity, even if no outstanding security has exactly 10 years remaining to maturity.

The concept of CMT rates is used predominantly in the US. In other markets, the concept of CMS rates has evolved. The rate used is the market interest rate swap rate for the relevant maturity, assuming a generic structure for the underlying swap transaction.

The use of CMS rates reflects the following factors:
• The central role played by swap rates in a number of markets where these rates are used as the major market interest rate indicator.

- The level of liquidity of swap rates relative to other fixed income benchmark rates (such as government bonds).
- The inherent constant maturity feature of swap rates. The maturity for a generic swap is inherently constant maturity as it is for the relevant maturity from start date, irrespective of the start date selected. This contrasts with bonds/debt securities that, by their nature, have fixed maturities, and the remaining life to maturity diminishes over time.

Both methodologies provide an exact rate for a relevant maturity that is not subject to time decay.

The use of CMT/CMS rates facilitates hedging and trading pure interest rates for a selected maturity without the impact of reducing term to maturity associated with physical securities. A further advantage of using CMT/CMS rates is that in the case of options on term rates, the fixed and constant maturity feature allows avoidance of some of the difficulties in pricing options on physical debt securities/bonds. This includes features such as a declining maturity and a declining volatility, reflecting the pull of the bond's price to par[2].

3 CMT/CMS Instruments[3]

3.1 Overview

The major CMT[4] instruments are forwards and options on CMT rates or spreads. The two major formats are:

- **Yield Curve Swaps** (also known as CMT swaps) – this entails a portfolio of forwards allowing the counterparties to take positions on the forward spread between two nominated CMT rates.

---

[2] See Das, Satyajit (2004) Derivative Products & Pricing; John Wiley & Sons (Asia), Singapore at Chapter 8.

[3] For a discussion of yield curve products, see Bennett, Rosemary "Creative Solutions for Interest Rate Uncertainty" (August 1993) Euromoney 50–52; Cornog, Peggy "Hidden Powers of the Yield Curve" (1994) Corporate Finance, Risk Management & Derivatives Yearbook 57–60; Klotz, Rick, Shah, Nilesh V., and Efraty, Ravit A. (26 May 1994) Structured Note Strategies: Alternatives to LIBOR Based Floating Rate Notes; Salomon Brothers Fixed Income Derivatives Research, New York; Britt, Patrick E. "CMT Plays" (14 December 1994) IFR Swaps Weekly 9; Patyne, Hans and McCarroll, Veronique "Beating the Positive Yield Curve" (1995) Corporate Finance, Risk Management & Derivatives Yearbook 30–32; Dago, Virginie and Lauwick, Vincent "Taking Advantage of the Steep Yield Curve" (1996) Corporate Finance, Risk Management & Derivatives Yearbook 18–22.

[4] For convenience, in the rest of this Chapter the term CMT is used to indicate CMT or CMS based structures.

- **Options on Yield Curve Spreads** – this entails call and put options on the forward spread between two nominated CMT rates.

3.2   Yield Curve/CMT Swaps

A yield curve swap is a floating-for-floating interest rate swap (similar conceptually to a basis swap). **Exhibit 17.2** sets out the structure of a yield curve swap diagrammatically. **Exhibit 17.3** sets out an example of the mechanics of the yield curve swap.

Under the structure, the swap counterparty:

- Pays (receives) one interest rate as set by one part of the yield curve (US$ 3 or 6 month LIBOR).
- Receives (pays) another interest rate at another point of the yield curve (10 or 30 year US$ Treasury yield or swap rate plus/minus a margin).
- Both rates are reset either quarterly or semi-annually.
- All calculations are based on an agreed notional principal. The principal is not exchanged.
- All payments are made on a net basis. All payments are in the same currency.
- The term of the yield curve swap ranges from 1 to 10 years.

The transaction is similar to the basis swap except that one of the interest indexes is a long term rate, although it is reset frequently.

Yield curve swaps have the following characteristics:

- The structure is generally insensitive to the absolute level of interest rates.
- Yield curve swaps are very sensitive to the shape of the yield curve.

Yield curve swaps create an exposure to the slope of the yield curve. Under a typical arrangement, the counterparty receives the 10 or 30 year rates and pays US$ LIBOR. If the yield curve steepens (flattens or inverts), then the net receipt under the yield curve swap will increase (decrease).

Yield curve swaps are feasible between any two selected points on the yield curve. Typical yield points used include 3 months, 6 months, 1 year, 2 year, 3 year, 5 year, 7 year, 10 year, 15 year, 20 year and 30 years. Any combination of 2 of these rates may be combined in a yield curve swap.

3.3   CMT Options

There are two types of options used in the CMT market:

- **CMT options** – these are options on CMT rates. These are traded as conventional call and put options on the synthetic rates. Alternatively, caps and floors on CMT rates are also traded.

Exhibit 17.2   Yield Curve Swaps

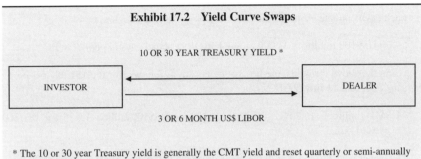

* The 10 or 30 year Treasury yield is generally the CMT yield and reset quarterly or semi-annually usually at the same time the 3 or 6 month LIBOR rates are reset

Exhibit 17.3   Yield Curve Swaps – Payment Calculations

An investor enters into a 5 year yield curve swap to pay 6 month LIBOR and receive the 10 year treasury minus 35 bps pa.

Trade details are as follows:

Trade Date	10 January 2001
1st Rate Setting Date	11 January 2001 (next business day)
Effective Date	13 January 2001 (2 business days later)
2nd Rate Setting Date	11 July 2001 (6 months after 1st rate setting)
First Payment Date	13 July 2001 (6 months after effective date)

The 10 year rate used will be the Constant Maturity Treasury ("CMT") rate for the relevant term as calculated by the US Treasury and the Federal Reserve Bank of New York by a process of interpolation from the existing yield curve (refer **Exhibit 17.1**). Both LIBOR and the US Treasury rate are set as of the rate setting date. The Treasury rate will not be known until the following Tuesday after the release of the Fed H.15 report, with calculation of the first payment being made after the release of the report.

The structure of the yield curve swap will be as follows:

Treasury Maturity	10 years
Payments per Year	2
Term	5 years
Swap Maturity Date	13 January 2006
Notional Principal	$100 million
Current 6 Month LIBOR	5.25% pa (calculated on an actual/360 day basis)
Current 10 year Treasury	6.20% pa (calculated on a semi-annual bond equivalent basis)
Yield Curve Swap Spread	−35 bps

Each payment date, the investor receives the following payment from the dealer:

US$100 million × (10 year CMT rate − spread) × actual days in period/365

Each payment date, A makes the following payment to the dealer:

US$100 million × US$ 6 month LIBOR × actual days in period/360[5].

Using the above formulas, the first payments are as follows (for the 181 day period 13 January 2001 and 13 July 2001):

US$100 million × (6.20% − 0.35%) × 181/365 − US$100 million × 5.25% × 181/360 = $261,376.

The dealer pays this amount to the investor on the first payment date (13 July 2001).

- **Yield curve options** – these are a category of spread options that are a special type of multi factor options[6]. The general terminology in regard to such options is as follows[7]:
  1. Call options are used to buy the yield curve. This is equivalent to a long position in the shorter maturity security and a short position in the longer maturity security (the amounts are volatility matched using duration, PVBP or DVO1 methods to equate the relative price sensitivities of the different securities to yield movements). This position will allow the purchaser to gain from a steepening of the shape of the yield curve where short rates rise less or fall more than longer rates.
  2. Put options are used to sell the yield curve. This is equivalent to a short position in the shorter maturity security and a long position in the longer maturity security (the amounts are volatility matched). This position will allow the purchaser to gain from a flattening of the shape of the yield curve where short rates rise more or fall less than longer rates.

4 CMT/Yield Curve Swaps – Pricing and Hedging

4.1 Pricing CMT/Yield Curve Swaps

The pricing of CMT based products is based on decomposition of each instrument into a CMT forward and/or a CMT option. The pricing of yield curve swaps derives

---

[5] The swap could also be structured as the investor receiving 10 year CMT and paying 6 month *plus 35 bps*. Economically, the two structures are similar.
[6] See Chapter 11.
[7] The terminology for these options, in common with other exotic structures, is far from standardised. See discussion in Chapter 11.

from the implicit forward rates embodied in the yield curve. Yield curve options are priced using a traditional option framework[8].

Pricing yield curve swaps requires determination of the spread that, at transaction commencement, will equate the *expected* transaction cash flows to the initial value of the swap. All cash flows, with the exception of the first settlement based on the current interest rates, are variable and unknown. Implied forward rates can be derived from the current yield curve. The forward rates are used to price the yield curve swap.

The pricing of a yield curve swap entails the following steps:

- Calculation of the forward LIBOR and CMT rates for the relevant maturity from the *current* yield curve.
- Implied forward spreads (reflecting the fact that the dealer is paying rates priced off one point in the yield curve and receiving rates priced off another point of the maturity spectrum) are then calculated.
- The implied spread is then discounted to the present using applicable discount rates. This allows the margin to be determined. The margin is the amount paid or received that, on a present value basis, equates the net present value of the swap to zero.
- The approach is then adjusted for the relative price sensitivity of the two rates which, given the term difference, are likely to be present. Yield curve swap cash flows are projected using the implied forward rates incorporating convexity based adjustments.

Exhibit 17.4 sets out the methodology for pricing a 3 year yield curve swap between 10 year swap rates and 3 month LIBOR.

The dynamics of value of a yield curve swap is purely a function of the shape of the two forward curves (the 3 or 6 month LIBOR forwards and the 10 or 30 year forward rates) and the *implied* forward spread. In an upward sloping or positive yield curve, the short term forwards typically increase at a faster rate than the longer term forwards. This reflects the mathematics of forward rates. The lower rate for the shorter maturity must be compensated for by the higher implied forward rate to equate the rate for the longer maturity to prevent yield curve arbitrage. The fact that the higher rate can be earned over a longer period in the case of a term security, rather than over a short period, dictates the relative rate of increase. This pattern of increase will inherently *imply* a contraction in the yield spread between the two rates, suggesting a *flattening* of the yield curve. In the case of a negatively sloped

---

[8]   See Chapter 11.

yield curve, the opposite will be the case. The shape of the yield curve is projected to steepen, with short forward rates declining at a faster rate than term forward rates.

In **Exhibit 17.4** the price derived is that the dealer pays 10 year swap rates minus 77 bps pa and receives 3 month LIBOR. This means that where the actual yield curve spread (10 year swap rate less 3 month LIBOR) exceeds 77 bps, the counterparty will benefit. The current spread between the 3 month and 10 year rates is 160 bps. This means that in the initial period, the counterparty will receive a positive cash flow equivalent to 83 bps pa. If the yield curve slope does not change (3 month LIBOR rate does not increase relative to 10 year swap rates as implied by the yield curve), then the counterparty will receive value from the yield curve swap.

The value of a yield curve swap is affected by:
• The *implied* interest rate differential at the relevant forward dates.
• The convexity position inherent in the structure[9].

The valuation/pricing methodology outlined in **Exhibit 17.4** only deals with the implied interest rate differential. A separate adjustment must be made for the convexity effect[10].

The convexity impact relates to the fact that the CMT payment is calculated in a linear fashion using the relevant index, while the underlying instrument itself is convex. This difference is exacerbated by the fact that the yield curve swap itself may be hedged using the underlying convex instrument. A different way of conceptualising the problem is to identify that the CMT pay-off does not relate to a single zero coupon rate but a series of payments related to the relevant rate on pre-agreed payment dates. Where the derivative (in this case the forward) is structured so that its pay-offs correspond to the payment pattern on the underlying instrument (bond or swap), then it is appropriate to set the expected rate used to calculate the implied spread to the derived forward rate. Where the pay-off does

---

[9]   The convexity adjustment in relation to CMT or yield curve swaps is similar to that impacting upon arrears reset structures, see Chapter 14.

[10] For a discussion of the convexity adjustment, see Hull, John (2000) Futures, Options and Other Derivatives – Fourth Edition; Prentice Hall, Upper Saddle River, NJ at 547–55. See also Brotherton-Ratcliffe, R. and Iben, B. "Yield Curve Applications of Swap Products" in Schwartz, R. and Smith, C (Editors) (1993) Advanced Strategies in Financial Risk Management; New York Institute of Finance at Chapter 15; Coleman, Thomas S. "Convexity Adjustment for Constant Maturity Swaps and LIBOR-in-Arrears Swaps" (Winter 1995) Derivatives Quarterly 19–27.

not follow the same payment pattern as in the case of CMT based products, then a convexity adjustment to the forward rate is required. This difference must be dealt with in the pricing. The linearity of the payment on the CMT side of the swap and the convexity of the underlying instrument lead to a benefit for the receiver of CMT rates under the swap. The exact same factor affects the valuation of CMS based yield curve transactions. This must be reflected in the pricing. There are a number of ways of making this convexity adjustment[11]. **Exhibit 17.5** sets out one form of this convexity adjustment that is used with CMT swaps.

The convexity effect increases the value of the receiving CMT payments under the CMT based yield curve swap. This means that the swap has a higher value relative to the valuation generated by simply pricing off the forward curve. This means that the CMT payments will generally be reduced below that implied by the forward rates (before adjusting for convexity). This allows the expected values of the transaction to be equated at the time of entry into the transaction.

Key problems in pricing yield curve transactions include:

- **Derivation of the underlying forward rates** – this requires the availability of an appropriate yield curve. This may be problematic where the maturity of the yield curve swap transaction and/or underlying long term index is long. For example, a 10 year yield curve swap of 30 year CMT rates against 6 month LIBOR requires availability of a yield curve out to 40 years. This is to allow derivation of the complete set of forwards required to price the transaction. In practice, the relevant curve may not be available. This requires the curve to be interpolated or extrapolated[12]. This introduces the risk of error in pricing the yield curve swap because of the risk of mis-specification of the underlying forwards.

- **Estimate of interest rate volatility** – a secondary problem relates to the inherent exposure to interest rate volatility because of the convexity adjustment. The required volatility is usually derived from the swaption market. Errors in the volatility estimate may distort the pricing of the yield curve swap by affecting the convexity adjustment.

---

[11] See Hull, John (2000) Futures, Options and Other Derivatives – Fourth Edition; Prentice Hall, Upper Saddle River, NJ at 547–55. See also Brotherton-Ratcliffe, R. and Iben, B. "Yield Curve Applications of Swap Products" in Schwartz, R. and Smith, C (Editors) (1993) Advanced Strategies in Financial Risk Management; New York Institute of Finance at Chapter 15; Coleman, Thomas S. "Convexity Adjustment for Constant Maturity Swaps and LIBOR-in-Arrears Swaps" (Winter 1995) Derivatives Quarterly 19–27.

[12] See Das, Satyajit (2004) Derivative Products & Pricing; John Wiley & Sons (Asia), Singapore at Chapter 5.

Exhibit 17.4   Yield Curve Swap Pricing

1. Calculation of Forward Rates

The initial step entails calculating the 3 month and 10 year forwards implied by the yield curve[13]. The current yield curve and the implied forwards are set out in the Table below:

Years	Interest Rates (% pa)	3 Month LIBOR Forward Rates (% pa)	10 Year CMS Forward Rates (% pa)	Forward Differential (% pa)
0.00		3.25	4.85	1.60
0.25	3.25	3.55	4.90	1.35
0.50	3.40	3.78	4.95	1.17
0.75	3.53	4.03	4.99	0.96
1.00	3.65	3.96	5.03	1.06
1.25	3.71	4.09	5.06	0.98
1.51	3.78	4.22	5.10	0.88
1.76	3.84	4.35	5.13	0.79
2.00	3.90	4.69	5.16	0.48
2.25	3.99	4.86	5.18	0.32
2.51	4.08	5.05	5.20	0.16
2.76	4.16	5.23	5.22	−0.02
3.00	4.25	4.41	5.23	0.81
3.25	4.26	4.44	5.26	0.82
3.51	4.27	4.46	5.29	0.83
3.76	4.29	4.49	5.32	0.83
4.00	4.30	4.51	5.35	0.84
4.25	4.31	4.54	5.38	0.85
4.51	4.32	4.56	5.41	0.85
4.76	4.34	4.59	5.45	0.85
5.01	4.35	4.74	5.48	0.74
5.26	4.37	4.78	5.49	0.71
5.51	4.39	4.82	5.50	0.68
5.76	4.41	4.86	5.51	0.65
6.01	4.43	4.89	5.52	0.63
6.26	4.44	4.93	5.53	0.60
6.51	4.46	4.97	5.54	0.57
6.76	4.48	5.02	5.55	0.53
7.01	4.50	5.34	5.56	0.21
7.26	4.53	5.40	5.55	0.15
7.51	4.56	5.47	5.55	0.08
7.76	4.59	5.54	5.55	0.01
8.01	4.62	5.58	5.54	−0.03
8.26	4.65	5.63	5.54	−0.10

---

[13] The interest rates utilised for the purpose of valuation will need to be made consistent in terms of compounding and day count basis. This is particularly important for yield

Years	Interest Rates (% pa)	3 Month LIBOR Forward Rates (% pa)	10 Year CMT Forward Rates (% pa)	Forward Differential (% pa)
8.51	4.67	5.70	5.53	−0.18
8.76	4.70	5.76	5.52	−0.24
9.01	4.73	5.81	5.51	−0.30
9.26	4.76	5.87	5.50	−0.37
9.51	4.79	5.94	5.48	−0.46
9.76	4.82	6.02	5.47	−0.56
10.01	4.85	5.36	5.45	0.09

The implied swap rate, forward 3 month LIBOR rates, forward 10 year swap rates and implied yield curve slope are set out in the diagrams below:

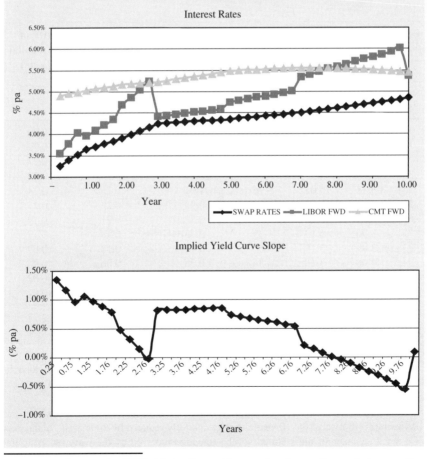

curve products as the CMT side is often paid quarterly whereas the market convention is to quote the rate on a semi-annual basis.

2. Calculation of Yield Curve Spread

The determination of the spread on the yield curve swap is undertaken using the following steps:

*   The forward rate at each pricing date of the yield curve swap is identified to calculate the implied forward spread.
*   The implied forward spread is then adjusted in two ways:
    1. The annualised spread is reduced to match the interest rate period under the swaps (quarterly).
    2. The quarterly forward spread is then discounted back to the commencement of the transaction using zero coupon swap rates for each maturity.
*   The discounted spread is then amortised over the term of the yield curve swap to calculate the margin on the transaction.

The Table below sets out the cash flows of the yield curve swap using the implied forward rates:

Days	Discount Rates (% pa)	10 Year Swap Forward Rates (% pa)	LIBOR – Forward Rates (% pa)	10 Year Swap – LIBOR Differential (% pa)	10 Year Swap – LIBOR Differential (% pa over number of days)	NPV of Differential (% pa)
92	3.25	4.85	3.25	1.55	0.39	0.39
184	3.40	4.90	3.55	1.30	0.33	0.32
275	3.53	4.95	3.78	1.12	0.28	0.27
366	3.65	4.99	4.03	0.91	0.23	0.22
458	3.71	5.03	3.96	1.01	0.25	0.24
550	3.78	5.06	4.09	0.92	0.23	0.22
641	3.84	5.10	4.22	0.82	0.21	0.19
731	3.90	5.13	4.35	0.73	0.18	0.17
823	3.99	5.16	4.69	0.41	0.10	0.09
915	4.08	5.18	4.86	0.25	0.06	0.06
1006	4.16	5.20	5.05	0.09	0.02	0.02
1096	4.25	5.22	5.23	−0.09	−0.02	−0.02
			Total		2.26	2.17

Notes: The LIBOR rates are calculated on actual/360 day basis. 10 year rates are calculated on an actual/365 day basis.

The discounted implied spread is then translated into an annualised margin equivalent to 0.77% pa. This is the amount that, paid quarterly, will equate the present value of the yield curve swap to zero at the time of entry into the transaction.

In this case, given the upward sloping nature of the yield curve, the receiver of the 10 year rate will receive the 10 year rate reset quarterly reduced by the margin. In the case of a negative shape of the yield curve, the spread is received by the party receiving the CMT rate.

Exhibit 17.5   Yield Curve Swap Pricing – Convexity Adjustment

Brotherton-Ratcliffe and Iben[14] show that the convexity adjustment that must be made to the forward rate (F) is:

$$-0.5F^2\sigma^2 T[P''(F)/P'(F)]$$

Where

    F = forward CMT rate
    σ = volatility
    T = time to maturity of the forward
    P(F) = the price at time t of a security that provides coupons equal to the forward CMT rate over the life of the bond as a function of yield (Y)
    $P'(F)$ = first derivative of the price of bond (P) with respect to yield (Y)
    $P''(F)$ = second derivative of the price of bond (P) with respect to yield (Y)

This means that the adjusted forward rate should be:

$$F - 0.5F^2\sigma^2 T[P''(F)/P'(F)]$$

This means that to obtain the expected forward rate, the convexity adjustment should be added to the forward bond yield.

The application of this adjustment can be illustrated with an example. Assume the following:

F = 6% pa
Y = 6% pa
σ = 15% pa

Assume that the instrument provides a payoff in 3 years time linked to the 3 year rate. The value of the instrument is given by:

$$P(Y) = F/(1 + Y) + F/(1 + Y)^2 + (1 + F)/(1 + Y)^3$$

The first and second derivatives are given by:

$$P'(F) = -F/(1 + Y)^2 - 2F/(1 + Y)^3 - 3(1 + F)/(1 + Y)^4 = -2.6730$$

$$P''(F) = 2/(1 + Y)^3 + 6F/(1 + Y)^4 + 12(1 + F)/(1 + Y)^5 = 11.4695$$

The convexity adjustment is given by:

$$-0.5 \times .06^2 \times .15^2 \times 3 \times (11.4695/ - 2.6730) = 0.0005 \text{ or 5 bps}$$

This means that a forward rate of 6.05% pa (rather than 6.00% pa) should be used in the valuation.

---

[14]   See Brotherton-Ratcliffe, R. and Iben, B. "Yield Curve Applications of Swap Products" in Schwartz, R. and Smith, C (Editors) (1993) Advanced Strategies in Financial Risk Management; New York Institute of Finance at Chapter 15.

4.2   Hedging CMT/Yield Curve Swaps

The hedging approach follows the approach to pricing/valuation. The CMT forward structures are hedged by trading in instruments to replicate the forward rates used in the structure.

In the example in **Exhibit 17.4**, assuming the dealer pays the CMT rate and receives 3 month LIBOR, the dealer would need to trade as follows:

- Buy forward/receive fixed 10 year swap rates out of 3 months, 6 months etc at quarterly intervals.
- Sell forward 3 month LIBOR (sell futures or buy FRAs) out of 3 months, 6 months etc at quarterly intervals.

The hedging of the short term interest rate leg is relatively uncomplicated. These positions can be hedged by trading in LIBOR forwards (in the form of FRAs or futures contracts (for example US$ Eurodollar contracts)).

Hedging the CMT forwards is more difficult. The position is different between a yield curve swap linked to CMT and a yield curve swap linked to CMS rates.

If the yield curve swap is linked to swap rates, then the CMS forwards are hedged with forward starting swaps[15]. Trading in the forward swaps is relatively straightforward. Potential benefits of this hedge include liquidity of the swap market and the off balance sheet nature of the hedges. The major constraint is the availability of swaps to the relevant maturity.

Replication of CMT forward rates is more difficult. This will be the case particularly where the maturity of the CMT forwards is significant. The following possible approaches are available:

- **Trading in the physical bonds** – this entails buying and selling the relevant bonds and then funding the positions to the relevant forward dates to replicate the forward. This is difficult in practice. The relevant bonds must be available and liquid. Trading in the underlying physical bonds is balance sheet and capital intensive. This is combined with difficulties in funding the bonds for the requisite maturities through the repo market. This creates interest rate risk for the dealer.
- **Use of bond futures contracts (where available)** – the use of bond futures is attractive as it minimises the balance sheet and capital use problems. However, the range of contracts available may be limited. Trading liquidity is concentrated in the contracts at the near term. This requires the position to be hedged in the more liquid shorter maturity contracts. The hedge must then be rolled.

---

[15]   See discussion of forward starting swaps in Chapter 13.

This exposes the dealer to significant basis risk in hedging. It also creates exposure to changes in the shape of the yield curve. This risk may be significant where the maturity of the forward sought to be hedged is long.

- **Use of forward interest rate swaps** – the use of forward interest rate swaps is efficient. The dealer is required to assume the risk of changes between the swap and underlying bond rate (the swap spread). This basis risk can be significant.

In practice, CMT yield curve swaps are hedged using interest rate swaps. This is driven by considerations of liquidity of the swap market, transaction costs, lower yield curve risk and efficient hedging structure (off balance sheet). The problem with this hedge is the dealer is exposed to the swap spread risk. The dealer must price for the spread risk in pricing the transaction. Alternatively, the dealer may use spreadlocks to manage the risk[16].

Hedging of CMT trades is both complex and capital intensive. The capital intensive nature of the hedge is driven by the large face value amounts that will need to be traded to hedge the position. The volume of hedges requires using significant counterparty/trading lines and credit capital in hedging the transaction.

CMT options are usually created dynamically through trading in the underlying assets. Consistent with normal delta hedging approaches, the amount of the model portfolio held is adjusted continuously to synthetically replicate the returns on the put option. Spread options cannot usually be efficiently replicated by trading in options on the underlying bonds. The portfolio of options is generally more expensive, reflecting the separate pay-off that allows each option to be separately exercised to maximise the value of individual options. This reflects the fact that the yield curve option is insensitive to absolute rate levels, while the option portfolio is generally sensitive to the overall absolute level of rates.

5   CMT Products – Variations

5.1   Overview

A number of extensions/variations to the basic CMT product concept are available. The product variations focus on extensions to CMT swaps and CMT notes. CMT notes are generally used to repackage CMT swaps and options for investors.

---

[16] See discussion of spreadlocks in Chapter 13.

5.2 CMT Swaps – Variations

The major product variations in CMT swaps are:

- **Forward starting yield curve swaps** – this entails a conventional yield curve swap with a deferred commencement date. For example, a 1 × 4 yield curve swap would entail a 3 year yield curve swap commencing in 1 year. The first rate set for both rates is in 1 year from trade date, and the first payment is in 1 year and 3 months (assuming quarterly payments). The forward starting yield curve swap is utilised where the yield curve is very steep at the short end but is then flatter. Under the forward starting yield curve swap, the receiver of CMT rates will benefit from a lower margin under CMT rates. This is because there is less value from the flatter part of the yield curve. If the yield curve shape does not change, then the transaction results in the receiver achieving a significant yield pick-up when the yield curve swap commences.

- **Quanto yield curve swaps** – this entails a yield curve swap where the CMT and short term rates are in different currencies. The payments are hedged with a quanto option to eliminate currency risk[17]. The objective is to take advantage of interest rate differentials across currencies without assuming currency risk. The quanto yield curve swap is used to trade yield curve differences between currencies and/or diversify interest rate index exposure. **Exhibit 17.6** sets out an example of a quanto yield curve swap.

Exhibit 17.6   Quanto Yield Curve Swaps

Assume UK pound sterling ("GBP") 5 year swap rates are trading at a significant premium to 5 year Euro swap rates. GBP 5 year rates are also above Euro-IBOR rates. An investor expects the yield curve differences to continue due to macro-economic factors (divergence in economic growth). A possible way to monetise this expectation is to enter into a quanto yield curve swap on the following terms:

Term	3 years
Investor Receives	GBP 5 year swap rate minus 0.75% pa reset and paid quarterly
Investor Pays	3 Euro-IBOR reset and paid quarterly
Currency of Payments	Euro
Payments	Quarterly

The quanto yield curve swap can be effectively de-composed into a yield curve swap and a quanto option hedging the GBP 5 year swap rate into Euro.

---

[17] See Chapter 11.

The advantages of the strategy include:
- **Yield enhancement** – the transaction provides immediate positive carry as 5 year GBP swap rates exceed 3 month Euro-IBOR by more than 75 bps. The investor achieves yield enhancement as long as GBP 5 year swap rates continue to exceed 3 month Euro-IBOR by at least 75 bps. The investor improves its position where the spread widens. In this case, the spread is better than would be achieved in an equivalent conventional Euro yield curve swap.
- **No currency exposure** – all payments are in Euro, ensuring that the investor has no GBP currency exposure.

The risk of the strategy is a contraction in the spread between GBP 5 year swap rates and 3 month Euro-IBOR rates.

5.3   CMT Notes

5.3.1   Overview

The CMT note structures typically are securities (usually floating rate securities such as a LIBOR based FRNs) combined with a yield curve swap or yield curve option based on CMT rates. The structures are usually attractive to counterparties seeking to hedge or trade yield curve risks.

The major types of structures used include:
- CMT based FRNs.
- CMT based Yield Curve Notes.
- CMT Option Notes.

Each of the structures is discussed below. Variations on the structures are also frequent, but the basic structural features identified are largely consistent. Consistent with the general structural features of the instruments, the notes can be designed to incorporate additional leverage by increasing the notional principal of the derivative component embedded in the security.

5.3.2   CMT FRNs

CMT based floaters originally emerged in the US market in an environment of tightening monetary policy and an extremely steep yield curve. The steepness of the yield curve made a LIBOR based FRN unattractive, while lengthening the term of the investment in an environment of expected increasing interest rates exposed portfolios to a risk of capital loss. In this environment, a FRN priced off CMT rates emerged as an attractive alternative format of floating rate investment.

Exhibit 17.7 CMT FRNs	
Issuer	AAA Rated Issuer
Amount	US$100 to 400 million
Maturity	5 year
Index	2 Year Constant Maturity Treasury (CMT2)
Coupon	CMT - 34 bps reset quarterly

Exhibit 17.7 sets out the terms of a typical 5 year FRN whose coupon is priced off 2 year CMT rates ("CMT2"). Functionally, the CMT2 FRN can be decomposed into an investment by the investor in a AAA rated 5 year FRN yielding 3 month LIBOR minus 10 bps and the simultaneous entry by the investor into a 5 year yield curve swap where the investor pays 3 month LIBOR and receives CMT2 - 24 bps. **Exhibit 17.8** sets out the structure in a diagrammatic format.

The CMT based FRN offers a higher return to the investor relative to a LIBOR based FRN investor. The return advantage was around 75–80 bps at the time of entry into this transaction (based on a yield on a comparable LIBOR based FRN of LIBOR minus 10 bps). The investor is assuming the risk that the spread between 3 month LIBOR and CMT2 will not decrease, or even if the curve flattens, that the spread will not narrow to an extent which will reduce the return performance

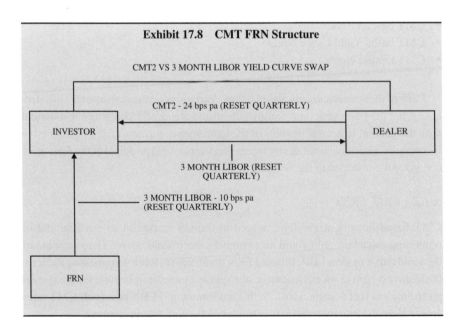

Exhibit 17.8   CMT FRN Structure

CMT2 VS 3 MONTH LIBOR YIELD CURVE SWAP

of the CMT2 FRN below that of the LIBOR FRN. The spread must decrease to a level below 34 bps before the CMT2 FRN under performs the LIBOR FRN.

At the time the transaction was undertaken, the spread between CMT2 and LIBOR was 94 bps. The 2 year forward rates implied a spread of 3 bps (a decrease of 91 bps). The investor is monetising its expectation that the implied narrowing of the yield curve spread (flattening) overestimates the actual narrowing that will occur. As long as the decrease in the spread does not occur at the rate or to the level implied by the current yield curve, the CMT2 FRN will outperform the LIBOR FRN.

5.3.3 CMT Yield Curve Notes

CMT yield curve notes are another category of structures entailing derivative return characteristics based on CMT rates to also emerge in the low nominal interest rate and steep yield curve environment of the early 1990s. An example of the structure is the Step Up Recovery FRNs ("SURFs") or deleveraged FRN (referred to hereinafter as a deleveraged FRN).

The deleveraged FRN entails a floating rate bond where the interest return is linked to the return on the CMT rate. In contrast to the type of CMT FRN described above (that pays CMT minus a margin), a CMT deleveraged FRN pays a coupon calculated as:

Leverage Factor × CMT plus/minus a margin.

The Leverage Factor is set between 0 and 100%.

The structure can be decomposed in a number of ways:
- A fixed rate bond with an embedded yield curve swap, where the notional principal of the yield curve swap is equal to the notional principal of the note multiplied the leverage factor.
- A fixed rate bond and a position in a CMT FRN. The amount of the investment in the bond is equal in percentage terms to 1 minus leverage factor. The position in the CMT FRN is equal to the leverage factor.

The major return characteristic of the structure is that the coupon does not increase or decrease as rapidly as the CMT index. The coupon participates only partially (in proportion to the leverage factor) in the movement of the relevant index.

It is possible to analyse the comparative return of three instruments: a fixed rate note, a CMT FRN returning a coupon of CMT minus a spread, and a deleveraged FRN (Leverage Factor of 50%). The analysis indicates that for low absolute CMT rates, the deleveraged FRN provides returns superior to that of the CMT FRN. For higher absolute values of CMT rates, the CMT FRN outperforms the deleveraged FRN.

The return characteristics can be adjusted by lowering the leverage factor. This has the effect of increasing the initial coupon rate on the transaction. This increase is achieved at the risk of reduction in potential returns where there are increases in CMT rates. The increase in initial coupon achievable is a function of the steepness of the yield curve. The steeper the curve, the greater the increase for a given change in leverage factor.

The investor will typically select the maturity of the CMT rate consistent with views on the shape of the yield curve and its evolution over the investment horizon. The deleveraged FRN will outperform a LIBOR based FRN at commencement as its initial coupon will be higher. Outperformance over the investment horizon will depend upon the performance of the selected CMT rate. If the differential between the selected CMT rate and short term rates flattens less than the decrease implied by the forward rates derived from the current yield curve, then the superior performance is likely to be sustained.

In order to lower the risk of the coupon becoming low on the deleveraged FRNs, the structures incorporate a floor component that ensures the coupon cannot go below an agreed level. This protection is achieved by embedding a floor on CMT rates within the note.

Exhibit 17.9 sets out an analysis of the deleveraged FRN structure together with the accompanying hedge arrangements incorporating a yield curve swap.

A variation on the structure is the CMT based *superfloater* that entails a leverage factor greater than 100%. The higher leverage factor has the following effect: the initial coupon is lowered (although it may still be above LIBOR) but the structure provides greater upside participation for a rise in the CMT rate.

Exhibit 17.9   Deleveraged FRNs

1.   Overview
In early 1993, a series of structured FRNs (introduced as SURFs or deleveraged FRNs) were issued in the Eurobond market. The first issues were undertaken for the World Bank and Eurofima by Lehman Brothers. The issues in the Eurobond market followed approximately US$1 billion of issues in the US domestic market.

2.   Structure
The basic structure is a floating rate bond where the interest rate is calculated in accordance with a formula linked to the theoretical ten year US Treasury bond rate.
The terms of the World Bank transaction are summarised below[18]:

Issuer	World Bank
Amount	US$100 million

---
[18]   See (1993) (February) International Financing Review Issue 967 at 59.

Maturity	5 years (due 17 March 1998)
Coupon	(Constant Maturity Treasury × 0.5) plus 1.45% where CMT is a theoretical 10 year treasury yield
Minimum coupon	4.60% pa
Maximum coupon	25.00% pa
Issue/fixed re-offer price	100.00
Amortisation	Bullet
Call option	None
Put option	None
Listing	Luxembourg
Denominations	US$1,000, US$10,000, US$100,000
Commission	0.40% (management and underwriting 0.15%; selling 0.25%).
Payment	17 March 1993
Swap	Into floating rate deutschmarks
Lead managers	Lehman Brothers Intl (books).
Co-lead managers	CSFB, Kidder Peabody Intl, Merrill Lynch Intl, Salomon Brothers Intl, SBC.

3. Issue Economics
The return to investors is dependent on the CMT yield. The Table below sets out the absolute return on the deleveraged FRN (inclusive of the minimum coupon level) on the transaction:

10 Year CMT Yield (% pa)	Deleveraged CMT Yield (% pa)
4.000	4.600
4.500	4.600
5.000	4.600
5.500	4.600
6.000	4.600
6.500	4.700
7.000	4.950
7.500	5.200
8.000	5.450
8.500	5.700
9.000	5.950
9.500	6.200
10.000	6.450
10.500	6.700
11.000	6.950
11.500	7.200
12.000	7.450
12.500	7.700

10 Year CMT Yield (% pa)	Deleveraged CMT Yield (% pa)
13.000	7.950
13.500	8.200
14.000	8.450
14.500	8.700
15.000	8.950
15.500	9.200
16.000	9.450
16.500	9.700
17.000	9.950

The Table below sets out the yield curve risk in the transaction by comparing the return on the deleveraged FRN with LIBOR, and deriving the breakeven CMT rate needed to equate the two returns.

LIBOR (% pa)	Breakeven (10 Year CMT) (% pa)	Deleveraged FRN Yield (% pa)	Breakeven CMT – LIBOR Spread (bps pa)
2.000	1.100	2.000	−90.0
2.500	2.100	2.500	−40.0
3.000	3.100	3.000	10.0
3.250	3.600	3.250	35.0
3.500	4.100	3.500	60.0
4.000	5.100	4.000	110.0
4.500	6.100	4.500	160.0
5.000	7.100	5.000	210.0
5.500	8.100	5.500	260.0
6.000	9.100	6.000	310.0
6.500	10.100	6.500	360.0
7.000	11.100	7.000	410.0
7.500	12.100	7.500	460.0
8.000	13.100	8.000	510.0
8.500	14.100	8.500	560.0
9.000	15.100	9.000	610.0
9.500	16.100	9.500	660.0
10.000	17.100	10.000	710.0
10.500	18.100	10.500	760.0
11.000	19.100	11.000	810.0
11.500	20.100	11.500	860.0
12.000	21.100	12.000	910.0
12.500	22.100	12.500	960.0
13.000	23.100	13.000	1010.0

For a LIBOR based investor, the return on the deleveraged FRN is attractive. For example, on the World Bank transaction, the CMT on the day of launch was just below 6.30% pa, meaning that the bonds would pay their minimum interest rate of 4.60% pa. This compared to 3 month US$ LIBOR of around 3.25% pa. The return to the investor over the life of the transaction will continue to be attractive where the shape of the US$ yield curve remains positive. Based on a price formula of [(CMT × 0.5) + 1.45% pa], the investor's return on a deleveraged FRN continues to be superior to LIBOR where the CMT − LIBOR rate differential is not less than that which prevailed approximately at the time of the issue (ignoring the minimum coupon level). The degree of yield curve steepness needed for the deleveraged FRN to outperform a LIBOR-based FRN increases as the LIBOR level rises.

The minimum or floor rate means that where the CMT rate is less than 6.30% pa, then the investor receives the minimum rate. This means that for CMT levels lower than or equal to 6.30% pa, LIBOR has to be below 4.60% pa (a yield spread of 170 bps) for the deleveraged FRN to outperform a LIBOR based FRN.

In essence, the deleveraged FRN will outperform LIBOR based FRNs where the yield curve remains positive and relatively steep. The major risk to the investor is a flattening or inversion of the US$ yield curve.

4. Hedging Structure

The issuer of the deleveraged FRN will typically seek to insulate itself from the full impact of the coupon structure. The issuer will seek to swap the issue into US$ LIBOR-based funding.

The hedge structure entails two separate transactions:
- A 5 year yield curve swap on 50% (equivalent to the leverage factor) of the total amount of the deleveraged FRN issue, where the issuer receives CMT minus a margin and pays US$ LIBOR.
- A conventional 5 year US$ interest rate swap where the issuer receives fixed rates and pays US$ LIBOR.

Algebraically, the position is as follows:

$$\text{Net Borrowing Cost} = \text{Deleveraged FRN Coupon} - \text{Yield Curve Swap Payment} - \text{Swap Payments.}$$

This translates into:

$$-[\text{CMT} \times 0.5 + M(S)] + 0.5\,[\text{CMT} - M(\text{YCS}) - \text{LIBOR}] + 0.5\,[\text{SR} - \text{LIBOR}]$$

Where:

$M(S) = $ Deleveraged FRN Margin
$M(\text{YCS}) = $ Yield Curve Swap Margin
$\quad\text{SR} = $ Swap Rate

The equation simplifies to:

$$-\text{LIBOR} - M(S) + 0.5(\text{SR} - M(\text{YCS}))$$

Assuming a transaction of US$100 million where:

$M(S) = +145$ bps
$M(\text{YCS}) = -155$ bps
$\quad\text{SR} = 650$ bps (or 6.50% pa)

The net borrowing cost is:

$$LIBOR - [145 + 0.5(650 - 155)] = LIBOR - 102.5 \text{ bps}$$

This is equivalent to a borrowing cost of LIBOR -102.5 bps.

This cost does not include the cost of the floor at 4.60% pa, which is designed to insulate the issuer from the risk of the minimum rate in the deleveraged FRN. The floor is on the 10 year CMT rate rather than on 6 month LIBOR, reflecting the interest formula of the deleveraged FRN structure. Given the steeply positive shape of the US$ yield curve, the bulk of the value in the floor is in the initial periods. The higher forward rates implicit in the yield curve dictate that the floors, as structured, are initially in-the-money. The longer dated floors are substantially out-of-the-money and are consequently relatively inexpensive. In the above case, the issuer has available (assuming a sub-LIBOR target of 50 bps pa) 52.5 bps pa (or 2.19% pa flat in present value) to cover the floor premium.

The 25% cap is more intriguing. CMT rates would have to rise above 47.10% pa for the deleveraged FRN coupon to reach the cap level. The 25% pa cap which the issuer can sell is not of significant value and therefore does not assist in reducing the cost of the floor premium. One theory is that the Euromarket transactions were priced in accordance with US domestic transactions where such a cap was necessitated to avoid the cost of the deleveraged FRN rising above legal upper limits on borrowing cost (for example, Fannie Mae has an official 24% pa cap on its borrowing cost).

The hedge arrangements underlying the deleveraged FRN issue highlight the price dynamics. The deleveraged FRN pricing depends on the interaction of the following variables:

• Price for yield curve swaps.
• Price for interest rate swaps.
• Cost of the CMT floors.

The variables reflect the prevailing yield curve shapes in the relevant markets.

Variations on the above structure have been undertaken. Seven year transactions with a higher minimum rate (5.00% pa) emerged, reflecting market opportunities as the US$ yield curve shifted.

5.3.4 CMT Option Notes

CMT option notes typically take the form of notes combined with the sale by the investor of a call or put option on the relevant CMT rates to monetise expectations on yield curve movements. The transactions are structured either as a conventional option trade, embedded in a yield curve swap or as a structured note. **Exhibit 17.10** sets out an example of how CMT option notes may be used.

Exhibit 17.10 CMT Options

1. Background

Assume an investor expects that the yield spread between the 2 year CMT rate ("CMT2") and 10 year CMT rate ("CMT10") will steepen. The investor's expectations are based on historical rate movements. These are characterised by steepening in this portion of the yield curve during periods of falling interest rates, while in a rising rate environment, this portion of the yield curve has flattened.

2. Transaction Structures

In order to capture value from the expected rate movements, the investor can buy interest rate floors on CMT2 and sell interest rate floors on CMT10. The interest rate floors represent calls on the price of the relevant securities of the particular maturity. The implementation of this strategy is shown in three transaction formats as follows:

Option trades

Investor Buys	Floor on CMT2 with Strike Price at 5.20% pa (Spot CMT2 = 5.50% pa)
Investor Sells	Floor on CMT10 with Strike Price at 5.65% pa (Spot CMT10 = 5.80% pa)
Option Expiration	2 Years
Floor Reset Frequency	Quarterly
Net Premium Paid	0.00%

Yield Curve Swap with Embedded CMT Floor Options

Investor Pays	3 Month LIBOR (payable and reset quarterly on actual/360 day count basis)
Investor Receives	CMT2 - 10 bps + Max [5.20% − CMT2; 0] − Max [5.65% − CMT10;0]
Payment/ Reset	Payable and reset quarterly
Maturity	2 Years

Structured Note with Embedded CMT Floor Options

Issuer	AAA Rated Issuer
Issue Price	100
Maturity	2 Years
Coupon	CMT2 - 20 bps + Max [5.20% − CMT2; 0] − Max [5.65% − CMT10;0]
Payment/Reset	Payable and reset quarterly
Minimum Coupon	0.00%

3. Economics

The essential value dynamics of the transactions are identical. The option transaction is used to examine the returns from this strategy.

The option transaction will be profitable for the investor in circumstances *except where* the CMT10 rallies below 5.65% pa and the spread between CMT10 and CMT2 is less than 45 bps (the difference between the strike rates of the two options). The investor has thus isolated a limited set of transactions where the transactions can result in a loss. The transaction would be predicated on the basis that the scenario where the investor would sustain a loss has occurred infrequently (based on historical data).

The transaction results in neither gain nor loss to the investor where the rates are unchanged or where both options are out of the money (CMT2 is higher than 5.20% pa and CMT10 is greater than 5.65% pa). The return to the investor where both options are in-the-money will vary with the slope of the yield curve. Where the yield curve steepens and rates increase, the CMT2 may be in-the-money but the CMT2 floor will be out-of-the-money.

The same transaction can be embedded in either a yield curve swap or combined with a security in the form of a structured note. In each case, the options are incorporated into the other instrument. In the case of the yield curve swap, the pricing reflects the combined values of the yield curve swap (receive CMT2 - 10 bps against payment of 3 Month LIBOR). In the case of the structured note, the pricing reflects the structure that combines a FRN yielding 3 Month LIBOR - 10 bps and the CMT Floor embedded yield curve swap.

6   CMT Products – Applications[19]

Yield curve swaps allow the counterparty receiving the term rate to price off the long rather than the short end of the yield curve. The major application of this type of arrangement includes:

- **Asset liability matching** – this has focused on converting liabilities to price off CMT rates to reduce interest rate risk within portfolios. This activity is mainly in relation to US mortgages. The activity is predicated in part on the view that US mortgage rates and mortgage pre-payment behaviour are closely related to changes in CMT rates[20]. This type of activity takes the following forms:
    1. *Mortgage hedging* – this focuses on investors with portfolios of mortgage assets/mortgage backed securities ("MBS")[21] converting the funding to a CMT basis. This entails entry into a swap where the entity pays

---

[19]   See Cataldo, James "Welcome to the CMT Jungle" (November 1996) Derivatives Strategy 20–26; Saunderson, Emily "Vive Le Tec" (November 1997) Risk 38–40; Viry, Alexis "Constant Maturity Swaps" (September 1999) Risk – Euro Derivatives Supplement 20; Yedinsky, Sarah and Gottel, Thorsten "Structured Products" (November 2000) Risk – Germany Supplement 6–8.

[20]   For example, see Cataldo, James "Welcome to the CMT Jungle" (November 1996) Derivatives Strategy 20–26.

[21]   See Fabozzi, Frank J. (Editor) (1992) The Handbook of Mortgage Backed Securities – Second Edition; Probus Publishing Company, Chicago, Illinois. See also Henderson,

CMT rates/receives LIBOR (or other relevant floating rate index) to convert its debt to CMT basis to match the interest rate behaviour of the assets.

2. *Mortgage servicer hedging* – this entails hedging by mortgage servicers that receive fee income from the administration of pools of mortgages. When mortgages are prepaid, the fee income falls. The value of the servicing rights depends significantly on the expected life of the mortgage pool. This means that value of the servicing rights is sensitive to prepayment forecasts[22]. Mortgage servicers use typically out-of-the-money CMT floors to hedge exposure to falling CMT rates. A number of variations on the basic theme are also used. These include CMT floor spreads (known as floor-idors) where the investor buys a CMT floor at a strike of 5.00% pa and sells an identical floor at 4.00% pa to reduce the premium cost. Path dependent exotic CMT products are also used. One structure is the auto floor, where the 5 year CMT floor is structured so that of the 19 floor-lets, only 10 can be exercised[23]. The structure is designed to lower the cost of the options. Another structure is the memory floor. This structure is designed to overcome a hedging problem of the basic CMT floor. If rates fall and mortgages are repaid, then the loss of servicing fees is permanent. If rates increase subsequently, then the loss is not recovered. Where rates decrease and subsequently increase, then the CMT floor is ineffective in hedging the actual exposure. The memory floor seeks to overcome this by a structure that replaces the annuity cash flows lost with an off-setting cash flow or payment. The memory floor pay-off is based on assumed duration and other features of the specified mortgage pool being hedged[24].

- **Hedging risk on investment products** – this entails using CMT products to hedge investment returns on different types of portfolios. This includes:

  1. *Synthetic mortgage assets* – CMT linked returns are seen as a substitute for direct MBS investments[25]. This entails investors converting the return on

---

John and Scott, Jonothan P. (1988) Securitisation; Woodhead-Faulkner, New York; Rosenthal, James A. and Ocampo, Juan M. (1988) Securitisation of Credit; John Wiley, New York; Zweig, Philip (Editor) (1989) The Asset Securitisation Handbook; Dow Jones-Irwin, Homewood Illinois; Shaw, Zoe (Editor) (1991) International Securitisation; MacMillans, London.

[22] Mortgage servicers must mark to market the servicing rights under FASB rules since 1994.

[23] This is identical to an auto-cap or swing option; see Chapter 7.

[24] See Cataldo, James "Welcome to the CMT Jungle" (November 1996) Derivatives Strategy 20–26.

[25] This is similar to the rationale for index amortising products; see Chapter 18.

a floating rate asset by receiving CMT rate and paying out US$ LIBOR, which is matched by the income from the underlying floating rate asset. An advantage is the ability to customise investment with precise investment and risk characteristics difficult to obtain from the mortgage or MBS market. There is also CMT activity linked to adjusting the interest rate or option characteristics of traditional MBS investments. This may include changing MBS tranche floors/caps or changing the interest rate basis to LIBOR.

2. *Structured investment products* – insurance companies are active users of CMT products to hedge exposures associated with insurance policies and structured investment products. Life insurance companies use CMT structures to create long term assets to match the underlying long term liabilities of the activity. Insurance companies provide a variety of structured investment products such as single premium deferred annuities and Guaranteed Investment Contracts ("GICs"). Many of the products have exposures to CMT rates. The exposures are hedged by insurance companies using yield curve swaps. The insurer receives CMT rates and pays LIBOR (or equivalent) payments. The CMT receipts offset the liability floating off the long-term rate. CMT products are also used to design insurance products for specific client demand.

- **Asset or liability index diversification** – this focuses on altering the index that determines the funding cost of the borrower. This entails diversification of floating rate indexes to CMT indexes. This is motivated usually by a combination of expected borrowing cost and also stability of interest costs.
- **Trading yield curves** – this entails trading the shape of the yield curve. Investors are increasingly seeking instruments that allow trading of irregularities/monetising expectations between different parts of the yield curve in a currency and the relationship between yield curves in different currencies. This type of trading takes several forms:
    1. *Outright yield curve trading* – for example, an investor expecting the yield curve to steepen would receive the 10 year or 30 year rate and pay short-term rates or vice versa. Similar strategies can be developed for borrowers.
    2. *Yield enhancement strategy* – this type of activity relies on the positive carry of a steep yield curve and the continuation of a steep yield curve. Under these conditions, traders benefit from receiving CMT rates and paying LIBOR.
    3. *Cross market yield curve trading* – this entails capturing the yield curve differentials across currencies. The use of quanto yield curve swaps allows this activity to be undertaken with no currency risk.
    4. *Lower cost borrowing strategy* – this focuses on borrowers using the positive carry and shape of the yield curve to capture positive cash flows that are used

to lower borrowing costs. This type of activity is not common. **Exhibit 17.11** sets out an example of this type of transaction that was entered into by Proctor & Gamble. The transaction unfortunately resulted in large losses as a result of adverse changes in market rates.

Yield curve swaps developed rapidly to become commonly used products, particularly among investors, in the US$ market. Subsequently, it has been applied in a number of other markets (primarily Euro and Yen), allowing investors of liability managers and financial institutions to take advantage of the prevailing shape of the yield curve.

A number of variations on the standard yield curve swap structure have also emerged. Yield curve swaps, as between various term interest rates (for example, five year against ten year, etc) have been undertaken. A major variation has been the emergence of options on yield curve shapes. This type of instrument effectively allows traders, borrowers and investors to buy and sell volatility on the *shape* of the yield curve.

Exhibit 17.11   Proctor & Gamble ("P & G") – Structured CMT Transaction[26]

1.   Overview
In 1993, P & G entered into a structured CMT transaction with Bankers Trust ("BT"). The transaction was entered into to lower the borrowing cost of P & G. The transaction resulted in (pre tax) losses of US$157 million to P & G. P & G instituted legal action against BT.

2.   Transactions
P & G had an alleged history of undertaking complex and structured transactions. The primary objective of the transaction was the reduction in the borrowing cost of P & G.
In autumn, P & G needed to re-finance maturing debt. The maturing debt had a cost of commercial paper ("CP") rates minus 40 bps pa. P & G sought to re-finance at an equivalent or better cost. P & G approached BT seeking proposals.

---

[26] See Brady, Simon "Proctor & Gamble vs Bankers Trust" (December 1994) Corporate Finance 21–25; Gamze, Michael S. and McCann, Karen "A Simplified Approach to Valuing an Option on a Leveraged Spread: The Bankers Trust, Proctor & Gamble Example" (Summer 1995) Derivatives Quarterly 44–53. See also Shireff, David "Can Anybody Fix Bankers Trust?" (April 1995) Euromoney 34–40; Harris, Alton B. and Kramer, Andrea S. "Suitability and Derivatives Transactions: Inconsistencies, Developments, and Lessons for the Future" (Spring 1995) Derivatives Quarterly 18–23; Hanley, William J. and Moser, James T. "The Policy Implications of the Bankers Trust Settlement" (Spring 1995) Derivatives Quarterly 24–46; DiMartino, Dawn, Ward, Linda, Stevens, Janet and Sargisson, Winn "Proctor & Gamble's Derivatives Loss: Isolated Incident or Wake-Up Call?" (Spring 1996) Derivatives Quarterly 10–21.

BT offered two proposals (so called proprietary structures). The structures were based on P & G's interest rate outlook and risk parameters. There are suggestions that the transactions were similar to earlier proposals that P & G had rejected as being outside the company's risk parameters. Eventually, P & G entered into a transaction with BT. The transaction was based on one of the proposals known as the 5/30 linked swap[27].

The transaction entered into was structured as follows:
- The transaction was for US$200 million for 5 years.
- P & G received a fixed rate of 5.30% pa.
- P & G paid a floating rate as follows:
  1. For the first 6 months, CP rate minus 75 bps.
  2. After the first 6 months, CP rate minus 75 bps plus Spread.
- The spread was calculated as follows:
  [98.5 × (5 year CMT/5.78%) − 30 Year Treasury bond price]/100
  Where the 30 year Treasury bond price is the price of the 6.25% coupon August 2023 bond.

3. Transaction Economics/Value Dynamics

The economics of the structured CMT swap undertaken by P & G is dependent on the value of the spread term[28]. The spread term can be simplified as follows: [17.04 × 5 year CMT − 30 year Treasury bond price]/100.

A number of aspects of the spread must be considered:
- The spread can never be less than zero. This means that P & G's most favourable cost of funds was CP rate minus 75 bps.
- The spread is applicable to the notional principal of the transaction.
- The spread term superficially appears to be on the spread between the 5 year CMT and the 30 year Treasury bond. However, this is misleading. The spread is dependent on a yield and a price. It operates in a manner where P & G is effectively long both the 5 year and 30 year Treasury bonds. This is because P & G suffers a loss (from increases in the spread) if rates increase at either point in the yield curve. The use of the CMT term is also misleading. The 5 year rate is constant while the 30 year Treasury bond is subject to time decay (albeit minor over the 6 month life of the spread).
- The structure entails greater exposure to the 5 year CMT rate. The 5 year CMT rate is multiplied by 17.04 (in the simplified version of the formula). In part, this reflects the need to convert the 5 year CMT rate into a price equivalent. After adjustment for this,

---

[27] During the subsequent litigation, it emerged that P & G had also entered into a second structured transaction. The second transaction was an overlay on an existing Deutschemark ("DEM") swap.

[28] For an analysis of the economics of the transaction, see Gamze, Michael S. and McCann, Karen "A Simplified Approach to Valuing an Option on a Leveraged Spread: The Bankers Trust, Proctor & Gamble Example" (Summer 1995) Derivatives Quarterly 44–53.

the 5 year CMT appears to be around 4 times the 30 year position in face value terms and around 2 times in price sensitivity terms[29].

- The structure is significantly leveraged. This is because P & G are effectively short options on both the 5 year CMT and the 30 year bond. Moreover, the position is leveraged in the 5 year CMT rate. This means the structure is very sensitive to changes in interest rates.

The spread is sensitive to two factors:

- **Absolute level of rates** – if rates increase across the yield curve, then the spread increases.
- **Slope of yield curve** – if the yield curve flattens (the yield spread between the 5 year CMT and the 30 year Treasury bond decreases), then the spread increases.

An increase in the spread results in P & G's cost of funding increasing. If the spread increases above 75 bps, then the benefit of the structured swap is eroded and P & G's cost of funds rises above CP rates.

The inherent leverage has the effect of creating a specific exposure for P & G to the slope of the yield curve (in particular to changes in the 5 year CMT rate). For example, if the price of the 30 Treasury bond is 98.5 and the 5 year CMT rate is 5.85% pa, then the spread is 118 bps. If the 5 year CMT rate increases by 5 bps to 5.90% pa, then the spread increases by 85 bps (to 203 bps)[30].

The analysis indicates that the transaction entails the following components:

- Sale of 6 month put options on the 5 year CMT rates and on the 30 year bond Treasury bond price.
- The premium received is used to lower the cost of borrowing[31].
- P & G assumes the risk on the two options. This exposes P & G to increases in Treasury yields and a flattening of the yield curve. P & G also has exposure to the implied volatility of the 5 year CMT option and the 30 year Treasury bond price option.

4. Performance of the Transaction

On the date the transaction was entered into the spread was – 0.1707% pa. After the transaction was entered into, US$ Treasury rates increased. The US$ Treasury yield curve also flattened. The spread became very large and P & G was obligated to pay around 14.10% pa above CP rates. This resulted in a loss on the transaction of US$157 million.

---

[29] The modified duration of the 5 year CMT is around 4.4. This implies a leverage of 4 (17.04/4.4) in terms of face value of bonds. The duration of the 30 year bond is around 7.2. This means that the price leverage is lower. It is around 2.4 (17.07/7.2).

[30] See Gamze, Michael S. and McCann, Karen "A Simplified Approach to Valuing an Option on a Leveraged Spread: The Bankers Trust, Proctor & Gamble Example" (Summer 1995) Derivatives Quarterly 44–53 at 46.

[31] For discussion of the value of the option, see Gamze, Michael S. and McCann, Karen "A Simplified Approach to Valuing an Option on a Leveraged Spread: The Bankers Trust, Proctor & Gamble Example" (Summer 1995) Derivatives Quarterly 44–53.

5. Dispute Between P & G and BT

P & G sued BT in relation to the transaction. It basically alleged misrepresentation on the part of BT. The case was complex[32]. The focus was on several issues, including:

- **Nature of transaction** – this focused on whether the transaction was entered into within P & G's internal guidelines. This focused on the fact that the transaction was outside P & G risk parameters and the leveraged nature of the transaction.

- **P & G's understanding of the transaction** – this focused on P & G's actual understanding of the transaction and the ability to understand the complex transaction undertaken. This also included allegations of misleading and deceptive conduct by BT in relation to the transactions both prior to entry and during the term of the transactions (specifically in relation to mark-to-market values of the transaction).

- **"Lock-in" feature** – there was considerable dispute about whether P & G had entered into the transaction on the basis of a "guaranteed" lock in feature. This feature revolved around whether P & G could limit its risk and also shorten the period at risk to less than 6 months. There were some suggestions that P & G could lock in a cost of funds of CP rate minus 40 bps. This appeared to be based on P & G repurchasing both options from BT after 2 months. This relied on rates and interest rate volatility remaining at the same level at the time of entry into the transaction. The time decay of the options would apparently allow repurchase at a price that would lock in a substantial profit on the options. This would allow P & G to have a borrowing cost of CP rate minus 40 bps with no exposure to US Treasury rates. P & G alleged that BT had guaranteed this lock in. BT argued that it had undertaken to buy back the options at market if requested. The pricing indicated was based on certain interest rate forecasts.

- **Proprietary valuation formula** – this related to the "lock-in" formula. There were allegations that the pricing methodology was not transparent. This meant that P & G could not determine how the structure was being valued. This also related to P & G allegations of misrepresentation and deceptive conduct by BT.

6. Postscript

The BT/P & G dispute had far reaching ramifications beyond the specifics of the litigation. The litigation itself was eventually settled in 1996.

The business consequences for BT were extremely serious. There were investigations by banking and securities legislators. The result of the process was an agreement with the regulators regarding sales practices on leveraged derivatives. It also resulted in the re-assignment of senior personnel. During this time, a number of other structured derivative disputes involving BT emerged. Some of these were settled. BT made provisions of over US$400 million in relation to exposures on its leveraged/structured derivatives transactions. The P & G transaction and similar transactions adversely affected the BT derivative business franchise that had been a cornerstone of the firm's global business. Subsequently, Deutsche Bank AG acquired BT.

---

[32] The litigation was especially acrimonious and damaging. It involved salacious and often unpleasant disclosure of internal BT conversations relating to the P & G trade.

7 CMT Market

The market for CMT based products developed in response to demand for instruments (in derivative or structured note form) that allowed investors to hedge or trade changes in yield curve shape as distinct from absolute rate movements.

Low nominal interest rates and the positive slope of the yield curve that prevailed through the 1990s in a number of currencies created demand for the structures. The investment environment was dominated by the search for returns, and strategies based on capturing value from the forward rates created additional demand for the types of structures. A further source of demand related to the use of CMT based products by fixed income portfolio managers to replicate the performance of benchmark indexes against which their performance was indexed. Additional impetus came from the potential value that could be created from using the forward *term* interest rates embedded in the yield curve.

The advantages of CMT instruments derive from a number of key factors:

- Fixed and certain maturity of the interest rate used.
- Capacity to avoid issues relating to physical bonds/securities including coupon effects, the movement away from par value as yields change relative to coupon and the diminishing term to maturity.

The advantages allowed CMT based products to emerge as the preferred transaction to monetise the yield curve expectations. CMT transactions also have advantages relative to physical transactions that can be used to implement similar strategies. The advantages include lower transaction costs, greater transparency of pricing and the opportunity for off balance sheet structures.

A significant use of CMT based products is in hedging in mortgage backed securities. CMT structures, particularly CMT caps/floors, are increasingly used to hedge prepayment risk on mortgages and mortgage backed security portfolios. This reflects, in part, research that has highlighted the fact that the pattern of prepayment of mortgages is correlated to medium term rates as well as the shape of the yield curve.

The CMT market itself is substantially US$ and US domestic investor focused. CMT based products, usually in the form of structured notes such as the deleveraged note structures, have been successfully marketed to non-US investors (primarily European and Japanese/Asian investors). The transactions have been primarily denominated in US$. The volume of non-US transactions is modest.

In currencies other than US$, the concept of CMT based transactions is substantially replaced by CMS transactions. Transactions involving CMS rates have been completed in Yen, Sterling, A$ and a number of European currencies (since 1999 in Euros). The rationale for the transactions is substantially similar to those applicable in US$.

In recent times, other countries (France and Germany) have introduced their own CMT equivalents. In France, the TEC 10 index (the CMT yield) is the redemption yield on the 10 year notional French OAT (calculated by Le Comite de Normalisation Obligataire daily by a dealer poll mechanism). A TEC 5 index is also available, being linked to the redemption yield on a 5 year notional French OAT. The TEC indexes have become the basis of both issuance (the French government issues a 10 year bond with coupon linked to the TEC index and other issuers have also issued bonds indexed to the TEC index) and derivatives (yield curve swaps and options on the index)[33]. The German equivalent is the REX index. The REX index provides benchmarks for all German government securities with maturities ranging from 6 months to 10 years and 6 months. As with the TEC index, securities issues and derivatives linked to the REX indexes are available[34]. The range of products and typical applications are very similar to those using US$ CMT instruments. The size of the market and the range of products are less developed than in US$[35]. **Exhibit 17.12** sets out an example of a Deutschemark FRN linked to the REX index.

Exhibit 17.12   REX Linked Structured Notes

Issuer	AA Rated Issuer
Amount	DEM 18 million
Issue Price	100
Redemption	100
Maturity	10 Years
Coupon	Year 1: 4.90% pa
	Year 2 to 10: 90% of REX10
	Where REX10 is the closing Deutsche Rentenindex with a maturity
	of 10 years, 2 business days prior to the relevant interest rate period
Payment/Reset	Payable and reset annually
Minimum Coupon	0.00%

---

[33] See "France Introduces Constant Maturity Index" (3 April 1996) IFR Financial Products 20; Saunderson, Emily "Vive Le Tec" (November 1997) Risk 38–40: Priest, Andrew "French Bonds Get TEC Appeal" (May 1996) Risk 13.

[34] See Muller, Jochen and Pedersen, Morten Bjerregaard "REX Floaters" (23 November 1998) Derivatives Week 6.

[35] The longer term prospects for both these indexes following the introduction of the Euro on 1 January 1999 is not clear.

8 Summary

CMT transactions represent an innovative mechanism for capturing returns from interest rate expectations, primarily changes in the shape of the yield curve. Transactions involving forwards, options on the CMT forwards and/or the implied forward spread can be structured to hedge exposures to these rate movements or to position to take advantage of anticipated movements. Transactions structured as pure derivatives or embedded in structured notes are feasible. The greater efficiency of the structures relative to undertaking physical transactions to express these views provides part of the impetus to the development of this market. US$ CMT and, its counterpart in non US$ based markets, CMS based products, are now a feature of the instrument set available in many markets.

18
Index Amortising Products

1 Overview

Index amortising products are structures where the principal amount of the transaction may amortise at a pre-specified rate, depending on the occurrence of specific movements in a nominated market rate. The market rate is usually a specified interest rate such as LIBOR. In this Chapter, index amortising products are examined.

The structure of the Chapter is as follows:
- The concept and structure of index amortisation products is described.
- Applications of index amortising structures are discussed.
- Valuation and pricing issues are considered.
- Product extensions and variations are outlined.
- The market for index amortising products is analysed.

2 Index Amortising Products – Structure

2.1 Concept

Index amortising products entail transactions (structured notes or swaps) where the rate of amortisation of principal is linked to changes in a specific rate index. Index amortising products usually take two forms. The common structures are Index Amortising Notes ("IANs") and pure derivative (off balance sheet) transactions such as Index Amortising Rate ("IAR") swaps. The essential elements of the transaction are identical, irrespective of the format used.

IANs and IAR Swaps are essentially cross market derivative products creating a relationship between changes in a specified market variable and cash flows in another instrument (the rate of amortisation of principal or notional principal).

IANs and IAR Swaps developed in the late 1980s. The structures proved popular with fixed income investors in the 1990s in an environment of low nominal interest rates, steep positively sloped yield curves and narrow spreads. The product was originally developed in US$. It was an important innovation with special importance in the US market. The concept has been adopted in a number of other markets.

2.2 Structure[1]

Exhibit 18.1 sets out an example of the terms and conditions of a typical IAN. **Exhibit 18.2** sets out an example of the terms and conditions of a typical IAR swap.

In the IAN transaction identified, the investor enters into a structured investment where the maximum maturity of the investment is 5 years. The investment may have an actual maturity of between 2 and 5 years, depending on the performance of 3 month LIBOR. The minimum investment period is predicated on the lockout period that dictates that the note cannot be amortised for the first two years. The 5 year maximum maturity is dictated by the absolute final maturity specified, where any principal outstanding not amortised at that date is repaid.

The exact maturity of the note is determined by the behaviour of the reference index (3 month LIBOR) consistent with the amortisation matrix specified. If 3 month LIBOR remains at or falls below its current level of 3.50% pa, then the note will amortise in full after 2 years. If 3 month LIBOR rises by 300 bps (to 6.50% pa), then the note principal does not amortise at all until final maturity. In between the two rate levels, the rate of amortisation is gradual in accordance with the agreed schedule. The transaction structure specifies amortisation as a percentage of the note's outstanding balance.

The structure of the IAR Swap is very similar to the IAN structure. The major difference is that the transaction is structured as a standard fixed for floating swap, with the notional principal of the swap declining in accordance with a structure that is similar to that applicable to the IAN.

In practice, the two structures are often closely inter-related. This requires the IAN to be specifically structured for an investor. The issuer is insulated from the

---

[1]   See Cheung, Kin S. and Koenigsberg, Mark (4 September 1992) Index Amortising Notes; Salomon Brothers United States Derivatives Research, New York; McDermott, Scott and Huie, Marcus (February 1993) Index Amortisation Swaps and Notes; Goldman Sachs Fixed Income Research, New York; Petersen, Bjorn and Raghavan, Vijay R. "Index Amortising Swaps" in Dattreyava, Ravi E. and Hotta, Kensuke (Editors) (1994) "Advanced Interest Rate and Currency Swaps"; Probus Publishing: Chicago, Illinois at Chapter 3; Williams, Christopher J., Twomey, Melinda M., Latif, Hasan, Usher, Bruce M., Hsia, Ming Jiao, and Calabrisotto, Dianne "Fixed Income Hybrid and Synthetic Securities" in Dattreyava, Ravi E. and Hotta, Kensuke (Editors) (1994) "Advanced Interest Rate and Currency Swaps"; Probus Publishing, Chicago at Chapter 6.

index amortising features of the transaction through the entry by the issuer into an IAR Swap with a dealer to hedge the index amortising exposure. **Exhibit 18.3** sets out an example of this type of transaction.

Exhibit 18.1   Index Amortisation Notes

Assume an investor seeks a structured investment that can be met through the following IAN transaction.

General

Issuer	AAA or AA rated institution
Amount	US$100 million
Maturity	5 years (Original)
Interest Coupon	5.50% pa (2 year Treasury Note (4.20%) plus 130 bps)

Index Amortisation Features

Lock Out Period	2 years (8 quarters). No amortisation during this period.
Reference Index	3 month LIBOR set 5 days prior to each quarter or interest rate payment date
Current Index Level	3.50% pa
Amortisation Table	The principal amount of the note will amortise in accordance with the Table set out below.
	If future movements fall between the points indicated on the matrix, then the amortisation rate is determined by linear interpolation between the nearest points on the matrix. Any unamortised principal outstanding is repaid in full at the maturity.

Reference Index (% pa)	Amortisation of Remaining Balance (% pa)	Average Life (years)
3.50 (Unchanged or below current index level)	100%	2
4.50 (current index level plus 100 bps)	12%	3.5
5.50 (current index level plus 200 bps)	3%	4.5
6.50 (current index level plus 300 bps or more)	0%	5

Clean-up provision	The note matures if the outstanding principal amount reaches 10% or less of the original principal amount.

The mechanics of the calculation of the amount of amortisation of principal are as follows. For example, if the rate of interest rises from 3.50% pa to 4.00% pa (a rise of 50 bps), then 56% of principal is amortised [(100% +12%) × 50 bps/100 bps]

Exhibit 18.2   Index Amortisation Rate Swaps

Assume a transaction where a counterparty pays fixed rate and receives floating rate (LIBOR) on a 5 year transaction with the following characteristics:

General
Notional amount	US$100 million
Maturity	Five years (Original)
Fixed Rate	5.50% pa (2 year US treasury (4.35% pa) plus 115bps).
Floating Rate	3 month LIBOR

Index Amortisation Features

Lock Out Period	2 years (8 quarters). No amortisation during this period.
Reference Index	3 month LIBOR set 5 days prior to each quarter or interest rate payment date
Current Index Level	5.25% pa
Amortisation Table	The notional principal amount of the swap will amortise in accordance with the Table set out below. Linear interpolation will be used where interest rates change by an amount in between the levels set out in the Table.

Reference Index (% pa)	Amortisation of Remaining Balance (%)	Average Life (years)
2.25 (300 bps or more below current index level)	100	2
3.25 (200 bps below current index level)	100	2
4.25 (100 bps below current index level)	100	2
5.25 (at current index level)	100	2
6.25 (100 bps above current index level)	80	3
7.25 (200 bps above current index level)	30	4
8.25 (300 bps or more above current index level)	0	5

Clean-up provision	The swap matures if the outstanding notional amount reaches 10% or less of the original notional principal amount.

The mechanics of the calculation of notional principal outstanding under this swap are set out below.

If rates rise 100 bps from the initial base rate of 5.25% on the first reset after the initial lock-up period, then the new principal amount will be $80 million. The new principal is derived as follows:

Initial principal − (initial principal × annual amortisation rate)/number of periods per year (in this case, four) = $100− ($100 million × 80%)/4 = $80 million

Subsequent principal amounts will depend on the next reset rate and will be calculated on the remaining principal amount until the new principal reaches 10% of the original, when the clean-up provision takes effect.

Exhibit 18.3 Index Amortisation Note Combined with Index Amortising Rate Swap

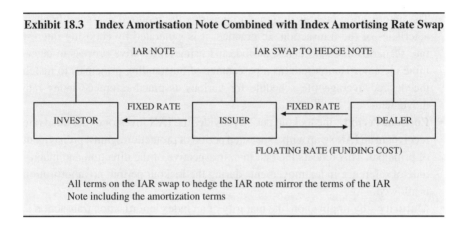

All terms on the IAR swap to hedge the IAR note mirror the terms of the IAR Note including the amortization terms

2.3 Structural Features

The key structural features of index amortising transactions include:

- **Issuer** (only applicable to IAN format) – the issuer of such instruments is generally a borrower with high credit quality. In the US domestic market, issuance has been dominated by the government agencies. In contrast, IAR swap structures have been undertaken by a wide variety of institutions in order to synthesise specific asset liability management positions.
- **Reference Index** – the reference index is central to the structure as it determines the rate of amortisation and the effective life of the security. The reference index is agreed between the issuer and the investor in an IAN and between the counterparties in an IAR swap. The reference index also usually applies throughout the life of the transaction and is not capable of alteration. The typical index used is a short term or money market rate (such as LIBOR). The reference index can be intermediate or longer term interest rates such as 5 or 10 year Constant Maturity Treasury ("CMT") yields. Non interest rate indexes such as currency rates are also feasible. The selection of reference index will be predicated on the investor or counterparty's rate expectations and requirements. For example, the structure may be designed to create exposure to one portion of the yield curve.
- **Amortisation Table** – the amortisation table agreed determines the amortisation amount and the amortisation rate for given movements in the reference index. It embodies the maturity risk of the structure in that the average life of the transaction is determined by the rate of amortisation. The amortisation amount can be expressed in two separate formats:
  1. Percentage of the IAN's remaining balance or the IAR swap's remaining notional principal.
  2. Percentage of the transaction's original balance.

The amortisation table is designed to generate the required average life characteristics of the transaction. In practice, it is generated by choosing interest rate scenarios at each interest period, and using an iterative process to determine the amortisation rate (as a percentage of outstanding principal) to match the desired average life schedule for various assumed reference index rate movements[2].

- **Lockout Period** – the lockout period provides the IAN investor or the fixed rate receiver in an IAR swap with a specified period of protection against prepayment of principal. This reflects the fact that, irrespective of the direction and magnitude of reference index movements during the lockout period, no amortisation is allowed.

- **Maturity** – by implication, the maturity of an index amortisation transaction is the final date by which (unless previously amortised) the IAN principal is repaid. The maturity has a similar significance for an IAR transaction. It signifies the termination of the swap (unless previously terminated) through the amortisation of notional principal.

- **Clean Up Provision** – the clean up provision places an obligation on the issuer in an IAN to call the note where the outstanding balance falls below a nominated de minimus level, typically 10 to 15%. For practical purposes, it is designed to terminate the transaction where the balance outstanding is not meaningful. For an IAR swap, the concept is very similar, with the swap being automatically terminated on any payment date where the notional principal falls below the nominated level.

- **Average Life** – the average life of the transaction (calculated in a manner consistent with standard fixed interest market convention[3]) is indicated to provide a measure of the term and interest rate risk of the structure.

2.4   Transaction Economics

The essential economic rationale of the transaction is driven by the fact that the investor in an IAN or the fixed rate receiver in an IAR swap receives a higher fixed rate compared to a similar (non index amortising) structure. The additional return represents the capture of return designed to compensate for the prepayment

---

[2]   For an example of how the amortisation rate is calculated see Petersen, Bjorn and Raghavan, Vijay R. "Index Amortising Swaps" in Dattreyava, Ravi E. and Hotta, Kensuke (Editors) (1994) "Advanced Interest Rate and Currency Swaps"; Probus Publishing, Chicago, Illinois at 58,59.

[3]   See examples of average life calculation in Chapter 13.

risk assumed. The risk can be effectively modelled as the sale of options on the relevant reference index. The economics are driven by the optionality embedded in the structure.

Transactions using index amortising structures developed in the low nominal rate and steep yield curve environment (primarily in US$) that existed in the early 1990s. This interest rate environment created opportunities for investors to undertake structured investments with maturity uncertainty through the linkage to the movements in the reference index to generate enhanced yields. The primary benefit to investors was higher returns in combination with a relatively short maturity, particularly where short term rates stayed low, maximising the rate of amortisation under the structures.

The economic logic of the IAR swap was more complex. Receipt of the fixed rate under an IAR swap combined with an investment in a LIBOR based FRN allowed the synthetic creation of an IAN investment. In contrast, the rationale of the transactions for liability managers was reduction of borrowing cost. In a steep yield curve environment, borrowers prefer to fund at the short end of the yield curve (that is, floating rate borrowing). The strategy entailed lowering interest costs significantly by issuing debt in longer maturities (five to ten years) and swapping it into a floating rate basis using an IAR swap. The benefit in this case was from the higher fixed rates received relative to conventional swaps.

A significant feature of index amortising structures is the negative convexity of the instrument. Convexity is a measure of the rate of change in the price of an instrument for a given change in interest rates. Generally, a fixed income security has positive convexity where the price of the instrument increases when interest rates fall[4]. This condition holds where the investor in the security does not grant an option through any feature of the instrument.

An index amortising instrument features negative convexity in that the price of the instrument will generally decline as interest rates fall. This reflects the feature that the rate of amortisation of principal or face value under the structure is highest when the reference index (short term interest rates) declines. **Exhibit 18.4** sets out the negative convexity feature of an index amortising structure.

---

[4] Convexity can be defined as the change in duration of a fixed interest security due to a change in interest rates, where duration measures the weighted average term of cash flows of the fixed interest instrument and effectively provides a measure of its interest rate sensitivity (the relationship of change in price to the change in its yield). See discussion in Das, Satyajit (2004) Derivative Products & Pricing; John Wiley & Sons (Asia), Singapore at Chapter 5.

Exhibit 18.4   Index Amortising Structures – Convexity Dynamics

The convexity of an interest rate product describes the rate of change in its price for a movement in interest rates. If the rate of change is linear (it changes price in a constant ratio whether rates move up or down), then the product has no convexity. Fixed rate bonds and swaps (receiving fixed) have positive convexity. When rates rise, the rate of change in their price is slower relative to the interest rate move than when rates fall. Buying options will increase the convexity of an instrument or a portfolio. Certain instruments including callable bonds, mortgage instruments and synthetic equivalents have negative convexity. When rates rise, the price change is faster relative to the interest rate move than when rates fall. Selling options will reduce the convexity of an instrument or portfolio. IANs and IAR Swaps (receiving fixed) have negative convexity since they effectively involve the sale of put options to the fixed rate payer.

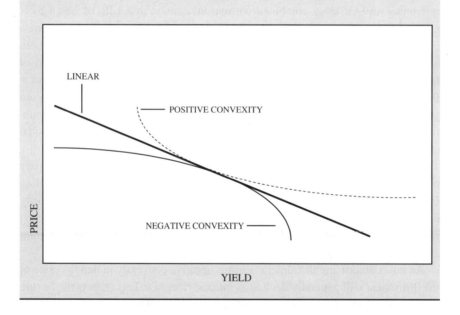

---

3   Index Amortising Products – Applications

3.1   Yield Enhancement

The central feature of IAN and IAR swap (for the fixed rate receiver) structures is the yield enhancement provided by such structured investments. The yield enhancement is obtained in return for assuming maturity risk in terms of the extension or shortening of the life of the instrument.

The yield enhancement effected through the sale of interest rate options is analogous to investments in mortgage backed securities ("MBS")[5]. MBS securities exhibit similar behaviour to index amortising structures. Lower interest rates trigger prepayment on the underlying mortgages with a resultant shortening in the life of the MBS investment. The structures share an exposure to interest rate driven prepayment risk.

However, the two structures also have significant differences. In particular, index amortising structures provide competitive returns under certain market conditions. In addition, index amortising structures have certain superior features to MBS transactions, providing investors with the capacity to diversify and customise credit risk and prepayment risk, have greater control over the average life ranges and greater flexibility. **Exhibit 18.5** summarises the major differences in features between MBS and index amortising structures.

**Exhibit 18.5   Index Amortising Structures and Mortgage Backed Securities –
Comparison of Features**

Feature	MBS/CMO Transactions	IAN/IAR Swaps
Interest Rate Exposure	Exposure to mortgage refinancing rates	Exposure to reference index
Prepayment/ Amortisation Risk	Prepayment is only capable of estimation as it is a function of complex factors including: 1. Yield curve shape 2. Demographics 3. Mortgage financing alternatives	Prepayment is capable of being specifically structured and is certain, being a function of only the movements in the reference index
Option Exposure	Investor sells prepayment options	Investor sells call and put options on reference index

---

[5]   See Fabozzi, Frank J. (Editor) (1992) The Handbook Of Mortgage Backed Securities – Second Edition; Probus Publishing Company, Chicago, Illinois. See also Henderson, John and Scott, Jonothan P. (1988) Securitisation; Woodhead-Faulkner, New York; Rosenthal, James A. and Ocampo, Juan M. (1988) Securitisation Of Credit; John Wiley, New York; Zweig, Philip (Editor) (1989) The Asset Securitisation Handbook; Dow Jones- Irwin, Homewood Illinois; Shaw, Zoe (Editor) (1991) International Securitisation; MacMillans, London.

Feature	MBS/CMO Transactions	IAN/IAR Swaps
Nature of Maturity Exposure	Uncertainty as a result of: 1. Prepayment predictions 2. Absence of Lock-Up and Clean-Up provisions 3. Risk of unusual prepayment scenarios	Greater certainty as a result of: 1. Specific reference index based prepayment model 2. Lockout period and final maturity provides well defined term boundaries 3. Clean up provisions prevents typical MBS "tail"
Customisation - Prepayment Risk	Linkage only to mortgage rates	Capacity to link to specific rate which, because of imperfect correlation with mortgage rates, allows diversification of prepayment risk
Customisation - Credit Risk	Credit risk is linked to mortgage pool and security structure.	Credit risk can be precisely structured to allow greater diversification of credit risk

3.2   Liability Applications

The liability management applications of index amortising structure are more varied. They generally fall into two separate categories:
• Borrowers using the higher fixed rate receivable under an IAR swap to generate cheaper floating rate funding.
• Borrowers using IANs or paying fixed in IAR swaps to create customised risk profiles consistent with interest rate expectations.

The first application developed in the steep yield curve environment primarily in US$ that existed in late 1991 and 1992. The transactions involved IAR swaps. The rationale of the transactions was that in a very steep yield curve environment, borrowers were seeking to price debt at the short end of the yield curve (that is, floating rate borrowers). The strategy was adversely affected by the fact that interest rate swap spreads in US$ fell sharply to historically low levels at this time. The IAR structure allowed borrowers to receive at higher interest rate swap spreads.

For the borrower, the benefit of the strategy included:
• Substantial savings on interest cost.
• Lack of liquidity risk as the underlying debt was medium to long-term.

- The interest rate savings (generated by the shape of the yield curve) gave the borrower protection against a future increase in the absolute interest rate levels or a change in the shape of the yield curve.

In the yield curve environment that prevailed, borrowers could lower interest cost by up to 200–250 bps by issuing debt in longer maturities (5 to 10 years) and swapping it into a floating rate basis using an IAR swap. Under the arrangement, the borrower had the following cash flows:
- The borrower received a fixed rate from the swap counterparty.
- The borrower paid a floating rate payment to the swap counterparty, usually based on US$ LIBOR or US$ CP.

The final maturity of the swap was between 7 and 15 years (typically around 10 to 12 years). At the commencement of the transaction, an agreed amortisation schedule was agreed based on the prevailing level of either short term rates (LIBOR or T-Bills) or CMT Treasury rates and the stated final maturity.

For the first 5 years (the lock-up period), the swap operated as a regular interest rate swap. After the expiry of the lock-up period, the IAR swap amortised in a manner consistent with the pre-agreed amortisation structure. The variable amortisation structure resulted in a quicker (slower) amortisation depending on whether 10 year rates increase (decrease). The major advantage of this type of structure was the increase in the achievable swap spread. For example, in late 1991 it was possible using this structure to increase the swap spread over Treasury for maturities of 10 to 12 years by an additional 25 to 30 bps pa.

The transaction structure appealed to borrowers as it was viewed as being self hedging from an economic perspective. If 10 year interest rates fell, then the borrower benefited from lower interest costs, creating additional cash flows. This coincided with the slower amortisation of debt and the higher effective cost of borrowing.

The fixed rate under the IAR swap was higher than for a conventional interest rate swap of the same maturity. This reflected the fact that the receiver of fixed rates had written a series of options on interest rate swaps. The premium was embedded in the higher swap rate.

The second application entailed issuers and payers of fixed rates under IAR swaps. The rate paid was higher than for a comparable conventional swap. Borrowers used the structure to essentially create interest rate sensitive hedges for underlying liability portfolios to engineer interest rate exposure hedges. If the reference index fell, then the term of the liability or interest rate hedge automatically shortened. If rates rose, then the term of liability or hedge lengthened until it reached the final maturity of the transaction. This afforded protection to the borrower as the reference index increased. In effect, the higher coupon cost of the borrowing or hedge reflected the cost of the options purchased to create this interest rate sensitive hedge structure.

4 Index Amortising Products – Valuation and Hedging Issues

4.1 Performance Characteristics

The central valuation issue of index amortising structures relates to the options on the reference index sold by the investor or fixed rate receiver to enhance yield. The valuation problem is best analysed with reference to the performance characteristics of the instruments.

The index amortising structure provides above market returns where interest rates remain static or decline from current levels. In a typical structure, the amortisation rate is based on the current level of the reference index with rises above the index resulting in an increasing average life. The performance characteristic reflects the fact that only where rates perform in the identified manner does the investor or fixed rate receiver enjoy returns above the market returns prevailing at the time of entry into the transaction.

For example, in the examples set out in **Exhibit 18.1** and **Exhibit 18.2**, the investor and fixed rate receiver enjoy higher fixed rates relative to the underlying 2 year Treasury note or swap rate prevailing at that time for a non index amortising transaction. If the reference index increases, then the average life of the transaction increases, with the result that the investor or fixed rate receiver suffers erosion of value from separate sources, including:

* As the average life of the transaction increases in a positively sloped yield curve environment, the return from the transaction decreases (at least in a spread) as the reference rate level moves up the yield curve.
* As the absolute level of rates rise as the reference index increases, the actual value of the investment and the swap falls, reflecting the higher interest rates[6].

The performance characteristics of index amortising instruments reflect the implicit interest rate outlook embedded in the options sold. The expectation is that interest rates will not rise at the rate implied by the positively sloped yield curve.

---

[6] The fall in value assumes a degree of correlation between rises in the reference index and the rates used to discount the cash flows associated with the transaction.

This expectation has two separate implications. It increases the value capture facilitated by the sale of the options. It also reflects the expectation on the part of the investor or fixed rate receiver regarding the possible exercise of the options to lengthen the average life of the instrument.

There are several separate elements to the relationship between the amortisation rates embodied in an index amortisation structure and the structure of forward rates, including[7]:

- **Absolute level of forward rates of the reference index** – in a positively sloped yield curve environment, implied forward rates lie above the current yield curve. The steeper the slope of the yield curve, the higher the momentum of the forward rate curve, with the implied forward rates being at progressively higher levels above the current yield curve. This was the actual swap curve and implied forward curve that prevailed during the period when index amortising structures were used. Based on historical evidence, implied forward rates are poor predictors of *actual* LIBOR rates. Over the relevant period, forward 3 month LIBOR was consistently different from actual 3 month LIBOR. The forward curve over or underestimated actual spot LIBOR rates. The extent of over or under estimation was also substantial. Index amortising structures allowed the investor or fixed rate receiver to monetise the expectation that actual LIBOR rates will not rise at the rate or to the levels implied by the yield curve. This reflects the fact that the index amortising structure will generally outperform a conventional non amortising instrument with an average life equal to the base case average life of the index amortising structure under this rate scenario.
- **Volatility of the reference index rates** – the index amortising structures entail the sale of options on the underlying reference index. As the investor or fixed rate receiver is the seller of options, a fall in the volatility of the reference index will benefit the value of the instrument. The level of volatility will also impact on the premium received from the sale of the options sold, and will determine in part the incremental return generated from the assumption of maturity risk. Investors in IANs or fixed rate receivers in IAR swaps maximise the value of the structure where implied volatility of the reference index rate is high and subsequently declines.
- **Yield curve shape risk** – the value of an index amortising instrument is a function of the interaction of two separate interest rates. The relevant rates are

---

[7] The analysis of performance characteristics of an index amortising structure is illustrated using a LIBOR reference index based instrument - in practice, the major interest rate index utilised.

the reference index (LIBOR) and the term interest rate that will determine the value of the future cash flows under the structure upon extension or reduction of the average life. The structure creates an exposure to the changes in the shape of the yield curve. While the amortisation and the average life of the transaction is driven by movements in LIBOR, changes in term rates and in the shape of the yield curve can impact upon the investor or fixed rate receiver. For example, if the yield curve flattens (LIBOR rises while term rates fall), then the underlying fixed rate instrument may increase in value. The increase in value may be accentuated by the lengthening in the average life of the transaction triggered by the rise in LIBOR. Conversely, a steepening yield curve will negatively affect the value of the instrument. This is a result of a shortening of the average life and the impact on the value of the cash flows from the higher term interest rates. The change in the yield curve shape will also impact upon the forward rate structure and the corresponding values of the options sold by the investor or fixed rate receiver. In a scenario of curve flattening, the value of these options may change in a manner favourable to the investor or fixed rate receiver.

The exact interaction of the above factors in the value and performance of an index amortising structure will depend on the individual structure. In practice, a key determinant will be the relative level of the base level of the reference index. A higher base rate will usually require a greater amortisation speed and a shorter average life.

The actual performance of an index amortising instrument can be inferred by utilising simulation approaches and modelling the behaviour under certain scenarios. Two researchers[8] examined the performance of a 5 year final maturity/ 2 year lockout and a 5 year final maturity/3 year lock out structure for a 3 month LIBOR index amortising instrument with different base rates. It was assumed that LIBOR rates increased at (1) levels slower than implied by forward rates, (2) a rate consistent with the implied forwards and (3) levels greater than that implied by the forward rates. For each scenario, the average life and the gains or losses were computed. The results are summarised in **Exhibit 18.6**.

The analysis concludes that:

• Increasing base rates decrease average lives because of the increased speed of amortisation.

---

[8]   See Petersen, Bjorn and Raghavan, Vijay R. "Index Amortising Swaps" in Dattreyava, Ravi E. and Hotta, Kensuke (Editors) (1994) "Advanced Interest Rate and Currency Swaps"; Probus Publishing: Chicago, Illinois at 59–63.

Exhibit 18.6   Comparative Performance of Indexed Amortising Structure Under Different Interest Rate Paths

Base rate	Slower than Forward		Forward Curve		Faster than Forward	
	Average Life (Years)	Gain ($ million)	Average Life (Years)	Gain ($ million)	Average Life (Years)	Gain ($ million)
5/2 Structure						
5.375	2.00	3.7	2.54	2.3	3.70	−1.3
4.875	2.00	3.9	3.52	2.1	4.23	−0.4
4.375	2.16	4.3	4.04	2.0	4.67	−0.8
4.125	2.74	5.4	4.31	2.2	4.84	−1.0
3.875	3.35	5.9	4.54	1.7	4.95	−1.2
3.625	3.58	6.1	4.76	1.5	5.00	−1.3
3.375	3.84	6.1	4.91	1.3	5.00	−1.4
5/3 Structure						
5.375	3.00	4.8	4.12	1.5	4.39	−1.1
4.875	3.15	5.2	4.19	1.4	4.39	−1.6
4.375	3.88	6.1	4.51	1.2	4.98	−1.9
4.125	3.88	6.1	4.70	1.1	5.00	−1.9
3.875	4.11	6.1	4.88	0.9	5.00	−1.9
3.625	4.26	6.1	4.98	0.7	5.00	−2.0
3.375	4.42	6.1	5.00	0.7	5.00	−2.0

Source: Petersen, Bjorn and Raghavan, Vijay R. "Index Amortising Swaps" in Dattreyava, Ravi E. and Hotta, Kensuke (Editors) (1994) "Advanced Interest Rate and Currency Swaps"; Probus Publishing: Chicago, Illinois at 61.

• Average lives tend to be higher for higher versus lower rate increases.
• Average lives increase with increases in the lockout period.
• The gains and losses are consistent with the average life behaviour. Gains tend to increase with lower base rates (higher average lives) at least where rates increase slower than implied by the forward curve. Higher than implied rate rises contribute to higher losses, consistent with the extension risk.

The analysis, while specific to the actual market conditions upon which it is based, highlights the complex performance dynamics in index amortisation structures.

The essential element of structuring such an instrument requires a trade-off between the amortisation rate and the selected base rate. For a typical given scenario, accelerating the amortisation speed (either by using higher base rates or quicker amortisation rates) decreases the average life and the break-even fixed rate.

The yield enhancement level can be increased by enhancing the value of embedded options sold. This is achieved by an optimal choice of the base rate level and by increasing the time period from lockout to final maturity. The higher option value captured reflects the increased uncertainty in the duration of the instrument. **Exhibit 18.7** sets out an example of the trade-off between the level of yield enhancement achieved in one specific instance.

Exhibit 18.7 Relationship Between Return and Base Reference Index Rate		
Reference Index - Base Level	Fixed Rate Coupon (bps spread to 2 Year Treasury Note Yield)	Average Life (years)
3.5	167	4.67
4.0	170	4.42
4.5	171	4.12
5.5	160	3.34
6.5	123	2.70

The above relationships between return enhancement levels and base rates on the reference index are based on a 5 year final maturity/2 year lockout index amortisation note. The average life is based on a probability weighted Monte Carlo simulation of future interest rate scenarios.

Source: McDermott, Scott and Huie, Marcus (February 1993) Index Amortisation Swaps and Notes; Goldman Sachs Fixed Income Research, New York at 8.

4.2 Valuation and Hedging

The valuation and hedging of the structures is a function of the decomposition into and pricing of the option elements in an index amortising transaction. The structures can be characterised as effectively callable bonds or swaps where the call feature is triggered by movements in a specific rate movement in the reference index.

The value of the index amortising instrument is driven by the valuation of the embedded interest rate options. **Exhibit 18.7** sets out an example of the trade-off between the level of yield enhancement achieved in one specific instance. The example highlights the fact that the highest level of return enhancement is achieved when the amortisation schedule is centred on the implied forward rate to maximise the premium value captured from the sale of options.

This is evident from the actual increase in return enhancement as the base rate level of the reference index is increased. This reflects the fact that where the base rate is 3.50% pa (6.50% pa), the transaction has a long (short) average life against which call options representing the prepayment risk (put options representing the extension risk) have been sold. The transaction with a base rate level of 4.50% pa represents an intermediate average life security with both prepayment and extension risk. In effect, the IAN investor or fixed rate receiver in an IAR swap has sold an at-the-money straddle capturing a higher premium level that results in the higher level of return enhancement achieved.

The valuation of the identified options is complex, reflecting a number of factors:

- The exercise of the option is determined with reference to the reference index. The value of the amortisation is dependent on the term interest rate to the maturity of the transaction as of the relevant amortisation date. This requires the term structure of interest rates or the yield curve shape to be known at each amortisation date.

- The principal reduction at a given amortisation date is dependent on not only the term structure of interest rates on that date, but on the unamortised principal at that date. This means that the structure requires a history of interest rates (it is path dependent).

The valuation of the options requires a trade-off between computational simplicity and accurate estimation of the values of the optionality involved. The following approaches have evolved:

- **Simple One Factor Models** – these types of models assume all yields along the yield curve are correlated.

- **Term Structure Models** – these models belong to the class of options used to price interest rate options generally. Typically, the models introduce a second factor to allow generation of a more complete yield curve to more accurately model term structure movements. A number of models are available. Each of the models makes specific assumptions regarding the term structure of interest rates[9].

- **Simulation Models** – these approaches typically involve Monte Carlo simulation procedures to generate arbitrage free paths consistent with given yield and volatility structures. The cash flows generated on the paths are then discounted back to determine the value of the structure.

The relative merits of the identified approaches differ. The one factor models, while simple in computational terms, may be inaccurate in practice because of the simplified yield curve structure assumed.

---

[9] See discussion of debt option pricing in Das, Satyajit (2004) Derivative Products & Pricing; John Wiley & Sons (Asia), Singapore at Chapter 8.

The term structure models assume the ability to appropriately calibrate the term structure variables in the model. This assumes the existence of a liquid market and availability of pricing information that allows the correlation between different parts of the yield curve to be tested and adjusted. The difficulty lies in the absence of such markets. The emergence of markets in such yield curve products increasingly enables calibration. The use of historical data to determine the relationships is inherently risky, given the non-stationary nature of correlations.

The identified estimation problems mean that in some instances, the advantage of the introduction of a second factor to determine term structure may introduce distortions. The errors inherent in assuming a more simplified term structure (as in a single factor model) may be less significant for particular structures such as short (2 to 3 years) average life structures. For longer dated structures, the need for a term structure model is more important.

The use of simulation approaches is attractive. The major disadvantage is the computational and data intensity of such approaches that makes them slower and less than ideal from a practical standpoint.

In practice, the pricing of index amortising structures is driven by procedures that have regard for the manner in which dealers will hedge the transactions. Consistency of hedging and pricing dictates the need to adjust the valuation model for index amortisation products to the following traded market rates and volatility:
- The swap yield curve and the implied forward rates.
- Short term interest rate option volatility.
- Swaption volatility.

The calibration of the valuation model (irrespective of the model used) to these variables reflects the use of US\$ Eurodollar futures contracts (FRAs in other currencies), interest rate swaps, caps/floors and swaptions to hedge portfolios of index amortising instruments.

Hedging portfolios of index amortising products is similar to the procedures used for other similarly traded financial instruments. The hedging technique used seeks to find the price or value sensitivity of an index amortising structure to each of the relevant rate and volatility inputs. This is usually done by utilising the valuation model and perturbing each pricing parameter separately to identify the price sensitivity of the structure. The index amortising instrument is then hedged using a dynamic hedging approach. This involves establishing and periodically re-balancing positions in a set of the identified instruments to match the sensitivity of the index amortising structure to that of the hedges.

The hedging costs, consistent with dynamic hedging techniques generally, are derived from the cost of trading in the underlying hedge instruments and hedge re-balancing costs. A major factor in determining hedge costs is the relative stability of the hedge to index amortising product relationships. The relative stability or instability of the relationship, particularly for larger rate movements or jumps (discontinuous) in the rate, is an important determinant of hedge cost and performance.

The hedge structures are based on standard hedge measures such as delta, gamma and vega[10]. In general, the delta or absolute price sensitivity of index amortising structures exhibits the following pattern:

- Delta corresponds to that of a corresponding fixed interest security during the lockout period.
- The delta of an index amortising structure is particularly sensitive to the underlying rate movements after the end of the lockout period.
- The delta of an index amortising structure becomes gradually lower than that for a fixed interest security, reflecting the expected lower principal as a result of the expected amortisation.

Index amortising structures have relatively low gammas. Index amortising structures have vegas significantly different from zero, reflecting the embedded options in the structure. The corresponding fixed interest security has zero vega as its value is not affected by volatility changes as it does not have any option elements. For two factor term structure models, two vegas are relevant, reflecting the sensitivity to both a uniform change in the volatility curve and the change in the shape of the volatility curve[11].

5 Index Amortising Products – Product Extensions and Variations

5.1 Overview

The market for index amortising structures has developed a number of variations and product extensions. The extensions/variations include:

- Various off-balance sheet methods of structuring index amortising cash flow features.
- Variations in each of the key elements including:
  1. Alternative coupon structures.

---

[10] See Das, Satyajit (2004) Derivative Products & Pricing; John Wiley & Sons (Asia), Singapore at Chapter 15.

[11] See discussion in Hull, John and White, Alan "Finding the Keys" (September 1993) Risk 109–112.

2. Use of alternative reference indexes.
3. Shorter maturity index amortising instruments.
4. Alternative amortisation schedules.
5. Use of alternative credit structures.

- Creation of structures featuring embedded exotic options.
- Index amortisation linked to alternative non-interest reference indexes.

5.2   Off-Balance Sheet Index Amortising Instruments

Both on and off balance sheet structures for index amortising instruments have emerged. The major off-balance sheet format is the IAR swap. The IAR swap is clearly the equivalent of an IAN transaction provided that the face value of the transaction is invested in a floating rate investment that yields at least LIBOR flat. The principal amortisation is replicated by the reduction in the notional amount of the IAR swap.

The use of the off-balance sheet variations was motivated by a variety of considerations:

- Absence of impact on balance sheet with the resultant lack of impact on financial ratios. This allowed the investor to improve returns through the higher return available on index amortising structures.
- The different status of IAR swaps from a capital adequacy standpoint for financial institutions, where the swap required lower capital amounts to be held against it than for a corresponding IAN[12].
- The ability to further boost the return on the transaction by investing in floating rate assets that provided a return in excess of LIBOR. This was achieved, in part, by altering the nature of the credit risk on the actual investment. In this regard, the IAR swap structure assisted in extending the range of credit risk available in index amortising instruments.

5.3   Variations in Key Structural Features

5.3.1   Coupon Variations

Index amortising structures entailing a zero coupon format have been undertaken[13]. The zero coupon index amortising structure is identical in all respects with more

---

[12] Similar advantages may apply to insurance companies where a risk adjusted capital framework is applicable.

[13] See for example, Salomon Brothers Variable Maturity Strips ("VMS") Product.

conventional coupon paying transactions featuring the early amortisation provision where the reference index declines, the minimum and maximum maturity and the lockout period during which no amortisation occurs. The investor receives compensation for the prepayment risk assumed through a higher discount in the price of the security.

The major motivation of the coupon adjustment was to replicate the Principal Only ("PO") structures in the US mortgage market. In periods where demand from MBS investors for PO structures is high, reflecting the requirement for either high duration assets or to hedge interest only ("IO") structures, zero coupon indexed amortising structures were created to meet this demand. The other advantages of index amortising structures over MBS transactions are also applicable.

5.3.2 Shorter Maturity Index Amortisation Instruments

Maturity variations in index amortising instruments have also evolved. In late 1994, shorter index amortising transactions emerged. The structure featured a 3 year life with a 1 year lockout and total amortisation after 1 year if rates decreased. **Exhibit 18.8** sets out typical terms for such a transaction (in the IAN format).

The short term index amortising transactions were motivated by market conditions where implied volatility in LIBOR caps and swaptions rose. Cap/swaption volatility (a 1 year option to enter into a 2 year swap and a 2 year LIBOR cap) is a close surrogate for the volatility of the option embedded in the short maturity (3 year/non call 1 year) index amortising transaction identified. For example, in 1995 the implied volatility of a 1 year option into a 2 year swap rose to 19.5% (from 16.5% earlier in the year). 2 year cap volatility rose in the same period by some 2.5% to 21.0%. This rise in volatility allowed investors in short maturity IANs and receivers of fixed rate in IAR swaps to sell volatility at higher levels, allowing generation of increased premium levels that increased the return levels on these structures.

For example, the IAN transaction described in **Exhibit 18.8** would have provided the investor with a return equivalent to around 100 bps over 1 year Treasury Bills. The return was 55–60 bps and 25–30 bps over the 1 and 3 year swap rate respectively. The higher return, combined with an expectation of the impending end to the tightening of US monetary policy, created demand for the structures.

5.3.3 Index Amortisation Linked to Alternative Reference Indexes

The transactions identified have focused to date on amortising schedules linked to LIBOR as the reference index rate. One common variation entails linking the amortisation to an alternative index such as the 5 or 10 year Treasury Bond rate

Exhibit 18.8   Short Maturity Index Amortisation Notes

General

Issuer	AAA or AA rated institution
Amount	US$100 million
Maturity	3 years (Original)
Interest Coupon	7.125% pa (1 year Treasury Note plus 100 bps)

Index Amortisation Features

Lock Out Period	1 Year (4 quarters). No amortisation during this period.
Reference Index	3 month LIBOR set 5 days prior to each quarter or interest rate payment date
Current Index Level	6.25% pa
Amortisation Table	The principal amount of the note will amortise in accordance with the Table set out below.

Reference Index (% pa)	Amortisation of Remaining Balance (%)	Average Life (years)
6.25 (unchanged or below current index level)	100	1
7.50 (current index level plus 125 bps)	100	1
7.75 (current index level plus 150 bps)	15.70	2
8.25 (current index level plus 200 bps or more)	0	3

(the CMT rate is usually used)[14]. The Constant Maturity Swap ("CMS") rate can also be used as the term interest rate alternative to LIBOR as the basis for amortisation.

The use of CMT in preference to LIBOR as the reference index reflects the trade-off between a number of factors:

- The typically lower level of volatility in term rates relative to LIBOR volatility.
- The closer relationship between 5/10 year CMT rates and MBS transactions.
- The desire by the investor to customise the structure to expectations about the future path of LIBOR and CMT rates.

The lower volatility of CMT rates constitutes a disadvantage in the case of an investor or fixed rate receiver. The lower volatility can actually be an advantage

---

[14] For discussion of CMT rates see Chapter 17.

in the case where the relevant investor *pays* fixed rate in an IAR (going short an IAN) to hedge a portfolio of MBS. The lower volatility translates into a lower cost as represented by the fixed rate paid of the hedge. Similarly, the closer correlation of CMT rates to MBS rates may assist in the efficiency of the hedge.

5.3.4 Alternative Amortisation Schedules

An important variation to the structural features of index amortisation transactions is the incorporation of alternative amortisation schedules. The most important of the structures is the reverse index amortisation structure. Under this structure, the principal of the IAN or notional principal in the case of IAR swaps *increases* as the reference rate declines. **Exhibit 18.9** sets out the typical terms for such a transaction (in the IAN format).

Exhibit 18.9   Reverse Index Amortisation Notes

General

Issuer	AAA or AA rated institution
Amount	US$100 million
Maturity	7 years (Original)
Interest Coupon	6.25% pa (3 year Treasury Note minus 30 bps)

Index Amortisation Features

Lock Out Period	3 Year (12 quarters)
Reference Index	3 Year CMT set 5 days prior to each quarter or interest rate payment date
Current Index Level	6.375% pa
Amortisation Table	The principal amount of the note will increase in accordance with the Table set out below.

Reference Index (% pa)	Amortisation of Remaining Balance (%)	Average Life (years)
4.375 (current index level minus 200 bps)	0	7
5.375 (current index level minus 100bps)	17	5
5.875 (current index level minus 50 bps)	33	4
6.375 (current index or current index plus 100 bps or more)	100	3

The change in amortisation creates positive convexity (rather than the negative convexity of traditional index amortising formats). This can be structured in a manner consist with the investor's specific requirements. The investor is effectively buying call options on the reference index. In the example, the call options are on the CMT rate. The lower coupon reflects the cost of the option purchased.

The primary motivation for the reverse index amortisation structures is the positive convexity acquired, reflecting the increasing average life as the reference index falls. This allows the structure to be used to hedge existing MBS investment portfolios that have negative convexity, reflecting the prepayment risk in a falling interest rate environment.

5.3.5 Alternative Credit Issuers

Further enhancement of returns on index amortising products can be achieved by altering the credit risk of the structure. This is achieved by substituting a lower rated issuer in the case of an IAN or altering the nature of the underlying floating rate investment in the case of an IAR swap.

The principal type of return enhancement in IAN transactions was through the introduction of corporate IANs. The basic features of the structure were identical to the generic features of index amortising products.

The corporate issuance fell into two distinct categories:
- **Arbitrage funding by high quality credits** – the issuer was insulated from the prepayment risk with a matching IAR swap. This type of transaction did not offer a great deal of additional return.
- **Issuers willing to assume the prepayment risk** – this group of issuers were prepared to take the prepayment risk as a form of economic interest rate hedge. The additional coupon constituted the effective cost of the hedge. The hedge served to reduce the issuer's average life of fixed rate debt as rates declined. This allowed re-financing where rate declined. The structure extended to the agreed final maturity where rates rose, effectively hedging the issuer from the impact of higher interest rates. This type of issuance tended to use the CMT rates as the reference index in order to reduce the effective cost of the hedge for the issuer.

For the issuer and the investor, index amortising structures issued by corporations were analogous to callable bonds with a number of differences, including:
- When a note is called in the case of a callable bond, the entire issue is redeemed, whereas with a corporate IAN the bond principal is amortised gradually in most cases.

- The issuer has no discretion in relation to the repayment with the IAN.
- The linkage to a reference index may mean that there is imperfect correlation between the rate driving amortisation of the IAN and the issuer's refinancing rates (effectively the credit spread).

An alternative means for enhancing the returns in an index amortising product entails the use of term repurchase agreements or other higher yielding assets such as asset swapped securities in combination with IAR swaps.

In the US, the use of Government Agencies as the issuer in IAN issues dictated that the investor was sacrificing return for the government credit risk of the transaction. Some investors used term repurchase agreements that provide higher returns than government debt to improve the return on the transaction.

5.4 Exotic Option Embedded Index Amortisation Products

Structures incorporating exotic optionality have also evolved. The most common type of transaction is the knock out index amortisation structures that incorporate barrier options on the reference index[15].

In a normal index amortisation product, the principal or notional principal amortises as a function of changes in the pre-specified index. In contrast, in a knockout index amortisation structure, the amortisation is also dependent on the level of the reference index attained on a specific date before the end of the lockout period (in effect, the knockout date). If the index is below an agreed level (in effect the knockout strike level) on or by that date, then the principal will amortise in full after lockout irrespective of future levels of the index. Amortisation will follow the agreed schedule only where the index is at or above the outstrike level (the price which triggers the knock out feature of the transaction) before the knockout date.

The rationale for the knockout feature was demand from investors who had an expectation that rates would remain low or decrease over the near future, but were more uncertain about the path of interest rates beyond that time horizon.

The impact of using a barrier option effectively reduces the premium captured by the investor, as the option sold may become inoperative where interest rates fall to below the knockout strike (the outstrike rate). **Exhibit 18.10** sets out an example of the price dynamics of the knock out index amortising structure. The conventional index amortising structure would have generated a return for the investor over

---

[15] For discussion of barrier options, see Chapter 9.

Exhibit 18.10   Knock Out Index Amortisation Notes

Conventional Index Amortisation Product

General

Issuer	AAA or AA rated institution
Amount	US$100 million
Maturity	5 years (Original)
Interest Coupon	5.50% pa

Index Amortisation Features

Lock Out Period	2 years (8 quarters)
Reference Index	3 Month LIBOR set 5 days prior to each quarter or interest rate payment date
Amortisation Table	The principal amount of the note will increase in accordance with the Table set out below.

Reference Index (Current Index +/− bps)	Average Life (years)
−300	2
−200	2
−100	2
0	2
+100	3
+200	4
+300	5
+400	5

Knock Out Index Amortisation Product

All terms same as above, except coupon that is contingent on level of knock out level selected.

Knock Out Strike Level on 3 Month LIBOR (% pa)	Coupon Level (% pa)
3	5.50
4	5.20
5	4.80
6	4.40

the 2 year Treasury rate. The addition of a knock out feature reduces the coupon received as the strike increases approaching the 2 year swap rate, reflecting the increasing likelihood of the transaction having an average life equal to the lockout period.

6 Market for Index Amortising Products

The market for index amortising products developed in an environment of low nominal interest rates and steep positively sloped yield curves in US$. The driving force behind the development of the instruments was the investor's desire for enhancement of yield. Index amortising products competed with both physical securities (MBS investments and callable bonds[16]) and derivative based structured notes (capped and collared FRNs, reverse FRNs, arrears reset structures[17] and range/accrual notes[18]) to provide investors with the required yields levels commensurate with the risk parameters specified.

The market evolved rapidly. Investors willing to assume prepayment risk through the sale of optionality increasingly viewed index amortising products and MBS products as comparable investments. The dynamics of the market consistent with the premise revolved around the competing features of the two instruments, and the relative value that could be extracted from either structure at any point in time.

The two instruments were broadly comparable. Movements in pricing parameters such as interest rate volatility on LIBOR (that was an important element in the valuation of index amortising structures) allowed investors to create the required investment through direct investment in MBS or indirectly through the index amortisation product to generate the highest possible returns.

The emergence of index amortising structures allowed investors who traditionally have not undertaken MBS investments to synthesise the prepayment risk profile of such transactions without the need to assume the complex credit risks and other features of direct MBS. The investors included both asset managers and financial institutions. The development of the product allowed investors to also hedge prepayment risk in appropriate interest rate environments. It also allowed borrowers to hedge interest rate risk. The later applications, while not insignificant, are major factors in the market for index amortising products.

The initial market for index amortising structures was in US$. The US market continues to be the major component of the global market for these products. The concept has been applied in other currency markets. In these markets, the ability to synthetically create the prepayment risk profile of a MBS investment where a physical market for such securities is not available has been a factor in the use of

---

[16] See Chapter 16.
[17] See Chapter 14.
[18] See Chapter 19.

such structures. The penetration of such products outside the US$ market has been modest.

Increasing applications of the concept of amortisation of principal with its inherent liquidity impact, where the prepayment profile is linked to a different underlying asset, have emerged. Transactions entailing amortisation linked to exchange rates and commodity prices have emerged in the context of highly structured and customised risk management applications for corporations. **Exhibit 18.11** sets out an example of this type of transaction. The cross market hedges, with their rich inter-relationships to underlying economic exposures and their management, represent significant opportunities for the further development of index amortising instruments.

Exhibit 18.11   Index Amortisation Notes Linked to Currency Movements

Assume a US company is a major exporter with strong foreign sales (in Yen). Growth in export sales has created increased working capital requirements that must be financed. The company seeks to borrow on a fixed rate basis in US$ to take advantage of low US$ interest rates. It also seeks protection from a higher US$/Yen exchange rate that could reduce its export competitiveness and its foreign Yen sales, thereby reducing its working capital funding requirement.

The company has the following hedging alternatives:
1. US$ interest rate swap that is callable.
2. Index amortisation swap (IAS) where amortisation is linked to the US$/Yen rate.

Under the first alternative, the position is as follows:

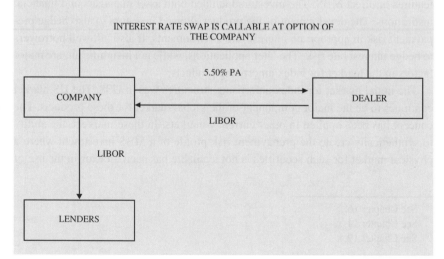

INTERREST RATE SWAP IS CALLABLE AT OPTION OF
THE COMPANY

5.50% PA

COMPANY   DEALER

LIBOR

LIBOR

LENDERS

The swap is for 5 years and can be terminated at any time. The company incurs additional cost (the premium for the swaption) that may not be required.
Under the second alternative, the position is as follows:

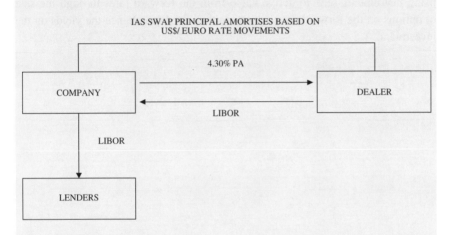

IAS SWAP PRINCIPAL AMORTISES BASED ON
US$/ EURO RATE MOVEMENTS

The IAS swap would link amortisation of the principal amount of the swap to movements in the US$/Yen in accordance with the following schedule:

US$/Yen Spot Rate	Average Life of US$ Interest Rate Swap	Early Repayment Rate (as % of Original Notional Principal)
140.55	2	100
128.33	3	11
118.41	4	5
110.00	5	0

As the US$ appreciates against the Yen, the US$ interest rate swap effectively shortens in life (the notional principal reduces), facilitating early repayment of the underlying loan. The structure provides the required hedging arrangement to offset the reduced need for working capital as a stronger currency reduces foreign sales revenue flows.

7 Summary

Index amortising products entail the design of notes or off-balance sheet equivalents where the investor receives an enhanced return in return for accepting a prepayment risk that is linked to the performance of an interest rate index. In an environment of low and falling interest rates, the structures have provided investors with significantly enhanced returns with the securities being amortised and prepaid.

The economic logic of such transactions seeks to capture value from the forward interest rate curve which, in a steeply positive yield curve environment, is above the spot yield curve, implying an increasing pattern of interest rates. Index amortising instruments seek to derive value from the forward rates through the sale of options on the forward rates which are then used to enhance the yields on the investment.

19
Interest Rate Linked Notes

1 Overview

Interest rate linked notes are bonds with structured exposure to interest rate risk. The exposure to interest rate risk is created by linking the value of the coupon or principal repayments to an identified interest rate or prices of a specific debt security. Interest rate linked notes are a specific type of synthetic asset[1]. The transactions are driven by investor requirements for specific exposure to interest rates. The different types of interest rate linked notes are discussed in this Chapter.

The structure of this Chapter is as follows:

• . The types of interest rate linked notes are outlined.
• Individual interest rate linked note structures are then described and analysed.

The focus is on the analysis of the structure, value dynamics for investors and pricing/hedging of the structures.

2 Interest Rate Linked Notes – Types[2]

Interest rate linked notes are bonds (fixed or floating) where the coupon and/or the principal payments are linked to interest rate movements. The structures entail conventional bond structures combined with embedded interest rate derivatives.

---

[1] See Chapter 4.
[2] For examples of interest rate linked notes, see Koh, Kenny (1986) Option or Forward Swap Related Financing Structures Unpublished research paper presented to course on Swap Financing, Centre for Studies in Money, Banking and Finance, Macquarie University; Cunningham, Michael M (1987) Selected Analysis of Recently Issued Index-Linked and Option Embedded Securities; unpublished research paper presented to course on Swap Financing, Centre for Studies in Money, Banking and Finance, Macquarie University; Das, Satyajit "Option Swaps: Securitising Options Embedded in Securities Issues" (Summer 1988) Journal of International Securities Markets 117–138.

Interest rate linked notes allow investors to assume structured exposure to specified interest rate changes. The investor's objectives include enhancement of return or monetisation of anticipated interest rate movements over the term of the investment. The structures allow investors to create exposures/assume risk that is not available directly from traditional investments. Demand for interest rate linked notes is driven by investor acceptance of the structured note investment format. This is in preference to the underlying derivative format[3].

Interest rate linked notes are combinations of bonds and interest rate derivatives. The derivatives used are generally standard or non generic structures traded in the derivatives market. The interest rate linked note is priced/hedged by decomposing the structure into the individual components. The components are then priced and hedged normally. The ability to decompose interest rate linked notes into liquid available components is critical. This allows the structures to be constructed, traded and hedged.

Issuers of interest rate linked notes include natural issuers (arbitrage funding entities[4]) or special purpose repackaging vehicles[5]. The transaction structure is designed to insulate the issuer from the impact of the embedded derivative by the dealer arranging the transaction. This is achieved by hedging the exposure of the issuer through a hedging structure that leaves it with funding at a known cost.

There are several types of interest rate linked note structures:
- **Interest rate forward embedded structures** – this includes:
  1. Inverse/reverse FRNs.
  2. Bond price/interest linked structures.
  3. Arrears reset/delayed LIBOR set notes[6].
  4. Constant maturity rate linked structures[7].
- **Interest rate option embedded structures** – this includes capped and collared FRNs.
- **Exotic option embedded structures** – this includes notes featuring embedded exotic interest rate options (primarily barrier and digital options).
- **Bond index linked structures** – this includes bond index linked notes.

---

[3] See discussion in Chapter 4.
[4] See Chapter 3.
[5] See Chapter 4.
[6] These structures are covered in Chapter 14.
[7] These structures are covered in Chapter 17.

3 Inverse Floating Rate Notes

3.1 Evolution

Inverse FRNs (also known as reverse or bull FRNs)[8] are fixed income structured notes that were popular amongst investors in the period 1985 to 1986 and again in the 1990s. The major attraction of the instrument is the higher returns generated in an environment of declining interest rates and/or steeply sloped positive yield curves.

In early 1986, during a period of sustained decreases in interest rates, investors were seeking to benefit from expected declines in short-term interest rates. The investors required an instrument where the yield increased as interest rates fell. The inverse FRN was created in response to this demand. The concept of inverse FRNs enjoyed a significant resurgence in the 1990s. This period was characterised in major markets by declining interest rates and sharply upward sloping yield curves.

3.2 Structure[9]

3.2.1 Concept

The inverse FRN is a floating interest rate instrument where the coupon (reset usually 3 or 6 monthly) is calculated as a fixed rate (17.25% pa) less a floating money market interest rate (3 or 6 month US$ LIBOR). If LIBOR decreases, then the return payable under the note increases. The return on the inverse FRN cannot be negative. It is being floored at 0% pa. **Exhibit 19.1** sets out the terms of an inverse FRN.

The inverse FRN can be unbundled into three separate components (see **Exhibit 19.2**):

- A fixed rate bond (yielding 8.50% pa in the example set out in **Exhibit 19.1**).
- An interest swap where the investor receives fixed rate and pays floating rate (receiving 8.75% pa/payment of 6 month LIBOR in the example set out in **Exhibit 19.1**).

---

[8] The term inverse FRN is used throughout this Chapter.
[9] See Fisher, Mark "At Issue the Interest Rate"(February 1993) Corporate Finance 29–33; Powell, Amy "Structured Derivatives Boost Returns" in (1994) Corporate Finance Risk Management & Derivatives Yearbook 61–63; Babbel, David F., Ma, Cindy W. and Ni, Bing J. "The Usefulness of Inverse Floaters" (Winter 2000) Journal of Portfolio Management 71–80.

- An interest rate cap on the floating rate index purchased by the investor from the issuer (with a strike of 17.25% pa in the example set out in **Exhibit 19.1**).

In effect, the inverse FRN is a fixed interest bond combined with an embedded interest rate swap and an interest rate cap.

Exhibit 19.1   Inverse FRNs – Structure

Amount	US$100 million
Term	5 years
Interest	17.25% less 6 month US$ LIBOR
Interest Payment	Interest is payable semi-annually (calculated on bond basis)
Minimum Interest	0% pa
	At no time will there be negative interest for the investor. If US$ 6 month LIBOR reaches 17.25% pa or above, then the investor will not be required to make any payment to the issuer

---

Exhibit 19.2   Inverse FRNs – Decomposition

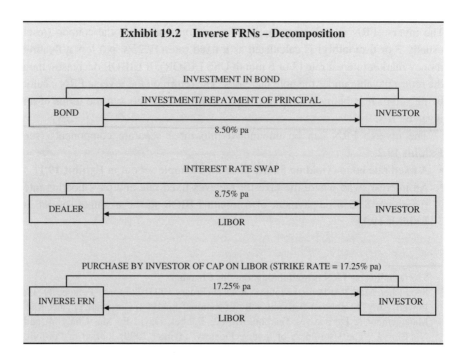

3.2.2   Investor Perspective

The investors in inverse FRN structures were typically money market or traditional FRN investors.

From the perspective of the investor, the inverse FRN provides increased returns where interest rates fall or the yield curve is upward sloping. The return behaviour of the inverse FRN is exactly the opposite of a conventional FRN. This explains, in part, the type of investor in the instrument. In the yield curve environment identified, the traditional mechanisms for capturing value entail in the physical market extension of the term/duration of fixed interest investments in the portfolio. In the derivative market, traditional mechanisms for capturing value entail purchasing forward the securities or receiving fixed/paying floating under an interest rate swap. The transactions would benefit from the continuation of a strongly upward sloping yield curve or falls in interest rates. The inverse FRN provides similar exposure in structured form for the investor. The structure enables investors unable to extend maturity or enter into derivative transactions to capture value from this rate environment.

The investor benefits under the following market conditions:

- **Falling interest rates** – this creates benefits from the appreciation of both the bond and the interest rate swap component of the transaction.
- **Positive yield curve** – this allows the investor to benefit from the positive carry in the interest rate swap where the fixed rate receipts exceed the floating rate outflows.

The inverse FRN effectively entails the investor purchasing forward interest rates on the relevant money market index (LIBOR in the above example). If the current implied forward rate curve *overestimates* the actual rise in interest rates over the term of the security, then the investor will obtain a benefit from the inverse FRN investment.

Exhibit 19.3 sets out an analysis of the financial performance of the inverse FRN described in **Exhibit 19.1**. The return to the investor is analysed under a range of interest rate scenarios entailing progressive increases or decreases in the 6 month LIBOR rate. The analysis indicates that the inverse FRN provides returns above the swap rate at the commencement of the transaction under certain conditions. The investor achieves higher returns where the yield curve does not change, rates decline and/or the yield curve remains positive. If 6 month LIBOR increases at a rate exceeding 30 bps per semi-annual period, then the return on the inverse FRN underperforms the swap rate at the commencement of the transaction.

Exhibit 19.3 Inverse FRNs – Return Analysis

The following Table projects returns on the Inverse FRN (described in **Exhibit 19.1**) where interest rates decrease or increase progressively by 25 or 50 bps per semi-annual period. The rates at commencement are assumed to be as follows:

6 month LIBOR: 7.25% pa
5 year Swap rates: 8.75% pa

Progressive Change in LIBOR (% pa per semi annual period)	−0.50	−0.25	0.00	0.25	0.50
Yield (% pa)	12.01	11.01	10.00	8.97	7.91
Spread to Swap (% pa)	3.26	2.26	1.25	0.22	−0.84
Period (Semi annual)	**LIBOR (% pa)**	**LIBOR (% pa)**	**LIBOR (% pa)**	**LIBOR (% pa)**	**LIBOR (% pa)**
0					
1	7.25	7.25	7.25	7.25	7.25
2	6.75	7.00	7.25	7.50	7.75
3	6.25	6.75	7.25	7.75	8.25
4	5.75	6.50	7.25	8.00	8.75
5	5.25	6.25	7.25	8.25	9.25
6	4.75	6.00	7.25	8.50	9.75
7	4.25	5.75	7.25	8.75	10.25
8	3.75	5.50	7.25	9.00	10.75
9	3.25	5.25	7.25	9.25	11.25
10	2.75	5.00	7.25	9.50	11.75

3.2.3 Issuer Perspective

Inverse FRN issuers are insulated from the embedded interest rate derivatives in the structure. The issuer enters into a hedge with a dealer to eliminate exposure to the embedded derivative components.

Exhibit 19.4 sets out the derivative structure designed to protect the issuer from the embedded derivatives. Under the hedge, the issuer undertakes conventional interest rate swaps for *double* the amount of the FRN issue to create a synthetic floating rate liability. The larger face value of interest rate swaps is required to hedge the embedded interest rate swap and the fixed rate bond (into floating rate funding). In the event that the issuer wanted a fixed rate liability, it would have entered into an interest rate swap for an amount equal to the face value of the inverse FRN. In addition, the issuer would purchase a cap from the dealer to hedge the cap sold to the investor within the inverse FRN structure.

There is an interesting variation on the hedging structure described. The issuer undertakes the issue of a conventional FRN for an amount equal to the face value of the inverse FRN. The conventional FRN is the same maturity as the inverse FRN. The combination of an inverse FRN and a conventional FRN is that the issuer has a fixed rate issue for the combined amount. For example, assume the structure described in **Exhibit 19.1**. If the issuer issued a 5 year US$100 million conventional FRN with a coupon of 6 month LIBOR, then the issuer would have acquired 5 year US$200 million funding at a fixed rate of 8.625% pa[10].

Exhibit 19.4   Inverse FRNs – Hedge Structure

The inverse FRN issue is hedged using a derivative structure whereby the issuer enters into a conventional US$ interest rate swap on the following terms:

Notional principal amount	US$200 million
Term	5 years
Issuer pays dealer	6 month LIBOR
Issuer receives from dealer	8.75% pa payable semi-annually

The total transaction can be depicted as follows:

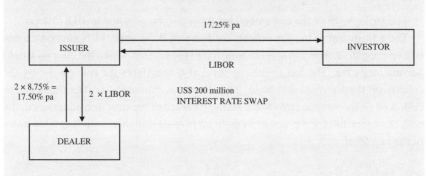

The net effect of the transaction is to generate LIBOR less 25 bps on a principal borrowing of US$100 million for the issuer.

This is achieved where LIBOR is less than 17.25% pa (that is, below the basic fixed interest coupon on the FRN issue). Where LIBOR exceeds 17.25% pa S/A, the sub-LIBOR

---

[10] A transaction such as that described was undertaken by Mass Transit Railway Corporation ("MTRC") in June 1986. The issues were as follows: (i) inverse FRN with coupon 17% – 3 month HIBOR and (ii) conventional FRN with coupon 3 month LIBOR plus 0.125% pa; see (21 June 1986) International Financing Review Issue 627 at 1835.

margin to the issuer would be eroded. This exposure is hedged by the issuer purchasing a cap with a strike price of 17.25% pa on US$ 6 month LIBOR from the dealer.

3.2.4   Leverage

The inverse FRN structure has inherent leverage. This is because the inverse FRN creates an exposure to interest rate movements on *double* the face value of the instrument. This reflects the fact that the structure has two sources of exposure to interest rate – the fixed rate bond and the interest rate swap.

The degree of leverage can be increased if required. This is done by combining the fixed rate bond with an increased face value amount of interest rate swaps. In **Exhibit 19.5** an example of adding leverage is set out. In this case, the example discussed in **Exhibit 19.1** is leveraged by a factor of 4 times.

The leveraged inverse FRN coupon is:

$$\begin{array}{l} \dfrac{\text{Fixed rate}}{\text{bond coupon}} + 4 \left(\dfrac{\text{Fixed rate}}{\text{swap receipts}} - \dfrac{\text{Floating rate}}{\text{swap payments}} \right) \\[2mm] = 8.50 + 4 \times (8.75 - \text{LIBOR}) \\[2mm] = 43.50 - 4 \times \text{LIBOR} \end{array}$$

The strike level of the cap embedded must also be adjusted to 10.875% pa.

The adjustment to the cap reflects the fact that the inverse FRN coupon cannot become negative. The cap level is adjusted to the level at which the coupon would become negative. The fall in the cap level also highlights the role played by the coupon on the fixed interest bond. The coupon is available to offset the negative cash flow on the interest rate swaps. As the leverage of the structure is increased, the cash flow shortfall for a given movement up in rates is higher, requiring a lowering of the cap level[11].

3.3   Pricing/Valuation[12]

The pricing and valuation of the inverse FRN is based on the structural components. The value of the inverse FRN is the combination of the value of the fixed rate bond,

---

[11] For a more recent example of a leveraged structure, see "Reverse Thrust" (5 June 1997) Financial Products Issue 67 8–9.

[12] See Smith, Donald J. "The Pricing of Bull and Bear Floating Rate Notes: An Application of Financial Engineering" (Winter 1988) Financial Management 72–81; Jones, Morven and Perry, Simon "How to Hedge a Reverse Floater" (September 1990) Corporate Finance 47–48.

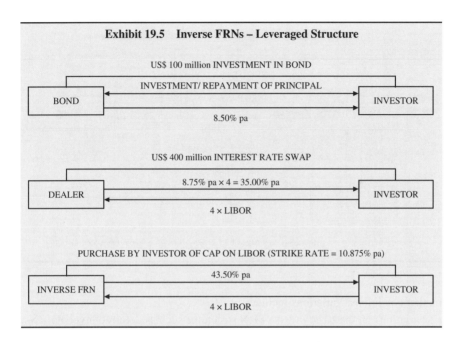

Exhibit 19.5   Inverse FRNs – Leveraged Structure

the interest rate swap and the interest rate cap. The only additional pricing parameter required is the target floating rate cost required by the issuer. The components are priced in accordance with normal pricing approaches for the individual instruments.

The sources of value shifts in an inverse FRN should be noted:

- Changes in *term* interest rates that will create changes in the value of both the bond and the interest rate swap.
- Changes in short term rates will affect value through the changes in the shape of the yield curve. The changes combined with term rate movements will dictate changes in value in both the interest rate swap and the cap.

Secondary market valuations of inverse FRNs entail the reversal of the embedded derivative elements and a repackaging as a fixed or floating rate security. **Exhibit 19.6** sets out an example of such a repackaging.

3.4   Product Variations

There are a number of variations on the basic structure of an inverse FRN[13]. The structural variations reflect attempts to capture value from this format in different

---

[13]   See "Reverse Floaters - Riding High" (17 February 1993) IFR Swaps Weekly Issue 6 6–7.

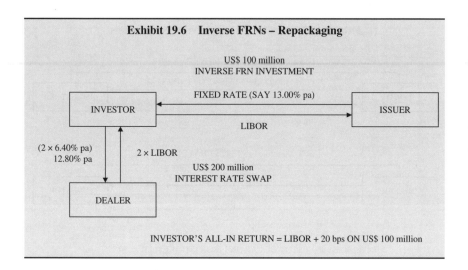

Exhibit 19.6   Inverse FRNs – Repackaging

US$ 100 million
INVERSE FRN INVESTMENT

FIXED RATE (SAY 13.00% pa)

INVESTOR   ISSUER

LIBOR

(2 × 6.40% pa)   2 × LIBOR
12.80% pa
US$ 200 million
INTEREST RATE SWAP

DEALER

INVESTOR'S ALL-IN RETURN = LIBOR + 20 bps ON US$ 100 million

market conditions. Variations include:
• Variations on the basic inverse FRN structures such as deferred inverse FRNs, step-up FRNs and minimum coupon inverse FRNs.
• The superfloater (or bear) FRN.

Exhibit 19.7 details an example of a Deutschemark ("DEM") inverse FRN issue. The issues were undertaken in the early 1990s in Germany. The driving force behind this type of structure was the negative slope of the yield curve and the expectation of falling short term money market rates.

The structure combines a fixed interest bond with a *forward* interest rate swap and a deferred interest rate cap. The major benefits of the structure for the investor include:
• The capacity to enjoy higher interest rates in the early part of the transaction based on the prevailing yield curve.
• Capture the benefit from falling short term interest rates over the life of the transaction after the initial fixed rate period.

The hedging and pricing of this structure was identical in concept to that applicable to the standard inverse FRN.

In recent times, a number of deferred inverse FRN structures have been issued in a number of European currencies. **Exhibit 19.8** sets out some examples of these structures. The minimum coupon on the second structure is created by adjusting the strike level of the embedded cap.

A variation on the inverse FRN is the incorporation of a step up pattern in the coupons. **Exhibit 19.9** sets out the terms of such an issue. **Exhibit 19.10** sets out an example of this structure in Yen. The structure embeds a series of forward swaps and deferred interest rate caps in the issue, designed to maximise the value capture from the yield curve. The second structure in Yen entails several additional structural features, including a variable amount of forward swaps embedded and the call options (effectively sold receiver swaptions) embedded in the structure.

Exhibit 19.11 sets out an example of an inverse FRN with a guaranteed minimum coupon. This transaction was designed to take advantage of expected monetary policy easing in DEM. The issue was a DEM denominated inverse FRN where the coupon is linked to the 6 month DEM LIBOR rate. The typical coupon was 11.50% minus 6 month DEM LIBOR. The only unusual feature of the issues was the guaranteed minimum coupon of 3.50% pa. The minimum coupon was generated by embedding a cap on 6 month DEM LIBOR at 8.00% pa in the issue. The issue return profile is also set out in **Exhibit 19.11**.

The superfloater FRN is designed to provide investors with an enhanced return in an environment of rising interest rates. **Exhibit 19.12** sets out the terms of a typical transaction. **Exhibit 19.13** sets out the hedging structure of such an issue.

The basic concept is a FRN that carries a coupon of 2 times LIBOR minus a fixed rate. It is designed to appeal to investors concerned about future increases in short-term interest rates. The structure effectively combines the purchase of a LIBOR FRN and an interest rate swap (where the investor pays fixed and receives floating rates). To eliminate the possibility of negative interest rates, the investor must also purchase a floor on the floating rate index (in the example in **Exhibit 19.12** a floor on US$ LIBOR at a strike of 8.00% pa).

Under the structure, as in the inverse FRN, the issuer is insulated from any interest rate risk. The issuer achieves floating rate funding related to LIBOR at an all-in cost below its normal floating rate funding cost.

The inverse FRN concept has also been adapted to mortgage backed securities markets. Inverse floating rate collateralised Mortgage Obligations ("CMS") issues have been undertaken in the US market[14].

---

[14] For a discussion of this market segment, see Borg, Bella, Lancaster, Brian and Tang, Jane "Inverse Floating-rate CMOs" in Fabozzi, Frank J. (1992) The Handbook of Mortgage Backed Securities – Third Edition; Probus Publishing, Chicago at Chapter 21; Winchell, Michael L. and Levine, Michael "Understanding Inverse Floater Pricing" in Fabozzi, Frank J. (1992) The Handbook of Mortgage Backed Securities – Third Edition; Probus Publishing, Chicago at Chapter 22.

Inverse FRNs are increasingly combined with currency hedges. This entails a currency protected structure that embeds a quanto option[15] within the standard inverse FRN structure[16]. The structure is generally used in emerging markets (such as Asia) where investors want to monetise their expectations on interest rates in other currencies (such as US$ or Yen) without currency risk. In a typical example, an inverse FRN can be structured in New Taiwanese Dollars (NT$) based on US$ 6 month LIBOR. The note pays a coupon in NT$ based on 7.60% pa minus 6 month *US$ LIBOR*. The payments under the US$ FRN have, in effect, been combined with a US$/NT$ quanto option linked to US$ LIBOR[17]. The structure allows the investor to take a position on US$ short term rates without currency risk.

Exhibit 19.7   Deferred Inverse FRN Issues – Example 1

1. Structure
The issuer undertakes a deferred inverse floater denominated in DEM on the following terms:

Amount	DEM 100 million
Maturity	10 years
Interest	Years 1–3 fixed at 9.00% pa
	Years 4–10 floating calculated as 16.00% minus 6 month DEM LIBOR
Minimum Coupon	0% pa. [The coupon cannot be negative.]

2. Investor Perspective
The investor in the deferred inverse FRN will benefit in years 4 to 10 where DEM LIBOR falls. For example, the return to the investor at varying DEM LIBOR levels is set out below:

DEM LIBOR (% pa)	Investor Return (% pa)
9.00	7.00
8.50	7.50
8.00	8.00
7.50	8.50
7.00	9.00
6.50	9.50
5.50	10.00
5.00	10.50

---

[15] See Chapter 11.

[16] See Semonin, Lionel "Structured Hybrid Investments" (September 2002) Asia Risk – Structured Statement.

[17] The structure is similar to an index differential swap embedded in a note; see Chapter 14.

3. Hedging Structure

The issuer is hedged against the inverse characteristics of the structure through the following swaps:

- A 3 × 10 forward DEM interest swap (swap for 7 years commencing 3 years forward) where the issuer receives fixed DEM at 8.85% pa and pays 6 month DEM LIBOR.
- The issuer also purchases a deferred 7 year cap commencing in 3 years at a strike price at 16.00% pa for a premium of 25 bps.

The cap is designed to protect the issuer from the contingency that DEM LIBOR rises above 16.00% pa as the coupon cannot be negative. If DEM LIBOR rises above 16.00% pa, then the investor receives no interest on the bond, the issuer must pay DEM LIBOR under the terms of the forward interest rate swap. The issuer's payment under the swap is effectively hedged by the cap that generates the shortfall where DEM LIBOR is above 16.00% pa.

The issue and accompanying swap structure are set out below:

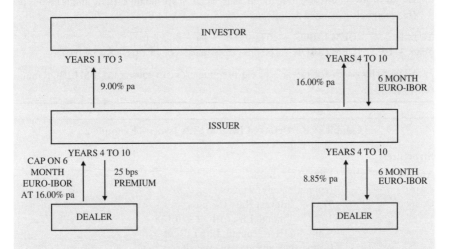

The all-in cost to the issue of the transaction is 7.86% pa (before any issue fees or the cost of the cap). Assuming issue fees of 1.25% and a cap premium of 25 bps, the all-in cost of the transaction to the issuer is approximately 8.09% pa.

In the event that the issuer wishes to generate floating rate funding, the issuer would enter into a 10 year DEM interest rate where it receives DEM fixed at 8.75% pa and pays six month DEM LIBOR.

The issue and swap structure are set out below:

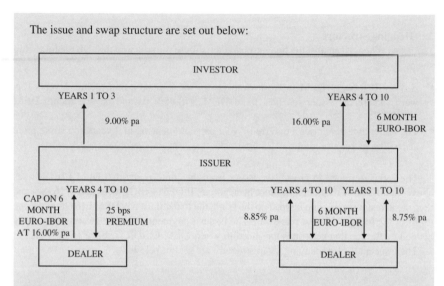

The all-in cost of this structure to the issuer is DEM six month LIBOR minus 66 bps pa. This margin is generated as follows:

Years 1–3   DEM LIBOR + 25 bps (9.00% pa − 8.75% pa)
Years 4–10   DEM LIBOR − 160 bps (16.00% pa − (8.75% pa + 8.85% pa))

Adjusted for issue expenses and the cap premium, A's cost equates to DEM LIBOR minus 66 bps pa.

Exhibit 19.8   Deferred Inverse FRN Issues – Example 2

Structure 1

Amount   Lira 20,000 million
Term   (approximately) 9 years
Coupon   **Year   Interest Rate (% pa)**
                  1–2   3 month Lira LIBOR + 0.125
                  3–9   21% – 6 month Lira LIBOR
                  Coupon calculated semi-annually
Minimum Coupon   0% pa

Structure 2

Amount   Portuguese Escudos 10,000 million
Term   10 years
Coupon   **Year   Interest Rate (% pa)**
                  1–4   6.50
                  4–10   13% – 12 month Lira LIBOR
                  Coupon calculated annually
Minimum Coupon   4.00% pa

Exhibit 19.9   Step Up Inverse FRNs – Example 1

Amount	US$100 million
Term	3 years
Coupon	**Year Interest Rate (% pa)**

Year	Interest Rate (% pa)
1	10% – 3 month LIBOR
2	11% – 3 month LIBOR
3	12% – 3 month LIBOR

Coupon calculated quarterly on bond basis.

Minimum Coupon	0% pa

Exhibit 19.10   Step Up Inverse FRNs – Example 2

Amount	Yen 5,000 million
Term	5 years
Coupon	**Year Interest Rate (% pa)**

Year	Interest Rate (% pa)
1	2.00
2	2.70% – (0.8 × 6 month Yen LIBOR)
3	2.90% – (0.6 × 6 month Yen LIBOR)
4	3.10% – (0.4 × 6 month Yen LIBOR)
5	3.30% – (0.2 × 6 month Yen LIBOR)

Coupon calculated semi-annually

Minimum Coupon	0% pa
Call Option	The note is callable at par after 1 year and every year thereafter

Exhibit 19.11   Inverse FRNs – Minimum Coupon Structure

Amount	DEM 100 million
Issue Price	100%
Maturity	5 year
Coupon	11.50% – 6 month DEM LIBOR
	Payable semi-annually on actual/360 day count basis
Minimum Coupon	3.50%

The return profile of the transaction is set out in the Table below:

Change in 6 month DEM LIBOR (per semi-annual period) (bps)	Final 6 Month DEM LIBOR (%)	Inverse FRN Yield (%)	Approximate Spread to 5 Year DEM Swap Rate (bps)
−40	1.65	7.92	152
−20	3.45	7.09	69
0	5.25	6.25	−15
+20	7.05	5.39	−101
+40	8.85	4.52	−188

Exhibit 19.12 Superfloater FRNs – Terms	
Amount	US$100 million
Term	3 years
Coupon	2 times 3 month LIBOR minus 8.00%
	Coupon calculated quarterly on bond basis.
Minimum Coupon	0% pa

Exhibit 19.13   Superfloater FRN Issue and Hedge

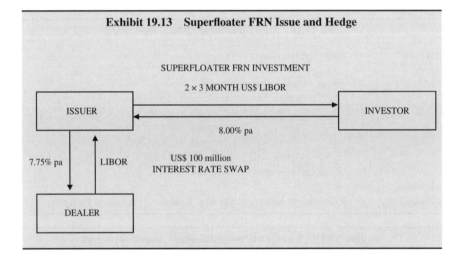

3.5   Inverse FRNs – Investment Risk

The risk of the inverse FRN is where short term rates increase and/or the yield curve flattens/inverts. The coupon on the inverse FRN declines if interest rates change in this manner. The risk of the inverse FRN is analysed as follows:

- **Hold to maturity risk** – where the inverse FRN is held till maturity, the investor is only exposed to loss of coupon. This reflects the fact that the principal of the inverse FRN is not at risk[18]. The risk relates to the reduction of coupon. In the worst case, the investor receives no coupon (if LIBOR exceeds the fixed rate). Under these condition, the investor holds a zero coupon security. The hold to maturity is driven primarily by the short term interest rate (LIBOR). The investor benefits to the extent that LIBOR sets below the fixed rate.

---

[18]   This excludes the impact of credit risk of the issuer.

- **Mark to market risk** – where the inverse FRN is held for trading purposes or the investment is marked to market, the position is different. The mark-to-market is driven by a combination of the following factors:
  1. *Current price of bond* – the price of the bond falls as interest rates increase.
  2. *Mark-to-market value of the interest rate swap* – the position shows losses where the swap fixed rate (for the remaining maturity) increases.
  3. *Mark-to-market value of the cap* – the position shows gains as interest rates increase.

This means that the value of the inverse FRN behaves in a complex manner prior to maturity. The position is significantly affected by term interest rates. Increases in term rates reduce the value of the structure. Conversely, decreases in term rates increase the value of the structure. The exposure is exacerbated by the leverage inherent in the inverse FRN. The value of the cap is affected by changes in term rates, the slope of the yield curve (forward rates) and interest rate volatility. The changes in the value of the cap insulate the investor to a limited extent from the changes in the price of the bond and the gain/loss on the swap. This reflects the fact that the value of the cap tends to move in the opposite direction to changes in the value of the other components. However, as the cap is generally significantly out-of-the-money and time decay reduces the value of the cap, the impact is small relative to the other components. The impact of term interest rates and interest rate volatility diminish over time. At maturity, the bond value reverts to par. The swap/cap have no value.

Exhibit 19.14 sets out a case study of the investment risk of inverse FRNs. The case study focuses on Orange County. The County invested in a significant portfolio of structured investments, primarily inverse FRNs. The portfolio was subsequently liquidated at a loss in excess of US$1.5 billion. The case highlights some of the investment risks and issues in relation to inverse FRNs.

Exhibit 19.14   Orange County – Inverse FRN Investments[19]

1. Overview
In the period leading up to 1994/1995, Orange County invested in structured investments, including inverse FRNs. The portfolio was also leveraged. This was done using

---

[19] This case is considered in the context of interest rate linked note structures in Chapter 54. See Falloon, William "Structure Shock" (December 1994) Risk 18–22; Irving, Richard "County in Crisis" (March 1995) Risk 27–31.

repurchase agreements to borrow against the securities in the portfolio. As a result of interest rate movements, the investment portfolio incurred US$1.5 billion in losses. The portfolio of structured investments was sold and Orange County was forced to seek bankruptcy protection.

2. Structured Investments

In the early 1990s, the US$ interest rate environment was characterised by low nominal rates and steep yield curves. Orange County was a relatively conservative investor. Investment assets were limited to high credit quality issuers and relatively short duration securities. Orange County's investment strategy sought to enhance returns within these constraints.

During this period, Orange County's investment strategy (under the control of Robert Citron, the Treasurer of Orange County) entailed the following:

* **Investment in structured notes** – the major investment was in inverse FRNs, including leveraged FRNs. Other structured investment structures were also used.
* **Leverage** – Orange County used repurchase agreements to leverage the portfolio. This entailed Orange County doing sales/re-purchases of its securities (including structured notes) with investment banks/dealers. The proceeds of the repurchase agreements were invested in additional securities (including further investments in structured notes).

The structured investments were designed to generate higher returns where interest rates continued to remain low or decreased further. The investments were also designed to take advantage of the positive yield curve. Inverse FRNs were the principal investment used to enhance returns in this case. The inverse FRNs provided Orange County with high returns where interest rates remained low/declined and the yield curve was positive.

The structured notes purchased by Orange County were issued mainly by high credit quality US Government agencies (Federal Home Loans Bank ("Freddie Mac"), Federal National Mortgage Association ("Fannie Mae" etc). The issuers had hedged the exposure under the structure through hedges with the dealer arranging the note issue. Issuers achieved attractive cost of funding under the structured notes.

The repurchases enhanced return by introducing leverage into the investment strategy. This leverage was additional to the inherent leverage of inverse FRNs. The leverage strategy enhanced return where investment returns exceeded the cost of borrowing under the repurchase agreements.

The investment strategy used resulted in the Orange County portfolio having the following characteristics:

* The portfolio had around 60% of its investment in structured notes.
* The portfolio was leveraged around 3 times (the portfolio investments were around US$20 billion on funds under management of US$7.5 billion).

The structured investments exposed the Orange County portfolio to the following risks:

* Increases in US$ interest rates.
* Flattening/inversion of the US$ yield curve.

The investment in inverse FRNs and the use of leverage significantly increased the interest rate sensitivity of the portfolio. The portfolio's interest rate sensitivity was comparable to that of a long position in 20 year bonds[20].

3. Investment Performance

The Orange County portfolio provided high returns through the early 1990s. In 1994, US$ interest rates (particularly short term rates) increased rapidly and the yield curve flattened. The changes in interest rates affected the Orange County portfolio in the following ways:

* The value of the structured notes fell.
* The cost of short term borrowing under the repurchase agreements rose.

Both developments reduced Orange County's returns. The mark-to-market (effectively liquidation) value of the portfolio showed losses in the range US$1.5 to US$2.0 billion.

The changes in interest rates created additional problems because of the leveraged structure of the investment portfolio. The structured notes had been used to collateralise short term borrowing under the repurchase agreement. As the structured notes declined in value, the collateral value declined. This meant that the loan to collateral value increased. In some cases, this triggered the need for more collateral. In other cases, dealers sought to terminate the repurchase agreements as the transactions matured. Orange County had limited funds available to meet additional collateral requirements or repay borrowings. This meant that Orange County would have been required to sell investments in order to generate liquidity. This would realise the mark-to-market losses on the portfolio.

4. Portfolio Restructuring

Faced with a financial crisis, Orange County filed for bankruptcy protection. The County also appointed financial advisers (Capital Market Risk Advisers and Salomon Brothers) to help it manage the portfolio. The advisers assisted Orange County in re-defining its investment strategy and developing approaches to restructure its existing portfolio.

In late 1994, Orange County liquidated its structured investment portfolio[21]. The liquidation was undertaken in several ways:

* A series of auctions were used to liquidate the structured note portfolio. This was done primarily by restructuring the inverse FRNs. This involved purchasing the inverse FRNs and entering into interest rate swaps and selling a cap (see **Exhibit 19.6**). The hedges converted the inverse FRN into a conventional fixed rate or floating rate security. The restructured security was then sold to banks and investors. The restructured bonds were

---

[20] See Jereski, Laura "Merrill Lynch Officials Fought Over Curbing Orange County Fund" (6 April 1995) Asian Wall Street Journal.

[21] See "Earthquake in Southern California" (3 December 1994) International Financing Review Issue 1059 102; "Salomon to Clock Orange County's Work" (10 December 1994) International Financing Review Issue 1060 82; "Orange County Begins Sale of Portfolio" (17 December 1994) International Financing Review Issue 1061 86; "Banks Suck Up Orange Juice" (24 December 1994) International Financing Review Issue 1062 60; Irving, Richard "Orange on a Banana Skin" (January 1995) Risk 6–7.

placed at LIBOR plus 5–25 bps pa. Based on the AAA credit rating of many of the issuers, the repackaged securities provided attractive returns. The repackaging transactions were done directly with investors and using repackaging vehicles.
- A number of issuers repurchased the notes from Orange County. The repurchase was undertaken at market prices. Where the note was repurchased, the issuer simultaneously terminated the original hedges.

The restructuring of the Orange County portfolio attracted criticism[22]. The restructuring achieved the objective of placing a cap on further losses and allowing Orange County to move its investment into short dated high credit quality securities. However, the sale of the structured investments realised the mark-to-market losses.

The value of inverse FRNs can be considered on a hold to maturity or mark to market basis. On a hold to maturity basis, the interest rate increases had reduced the coupon on the inverse FRN (in some cases to 0% pa). However, the principal amount of the inverse FRNs was not at risk. Given the high credit quality of the issuers, the principal amount of the investment would be received at maturity. In this case, holding the investments through to maturity would minimise the losses from the term rate movements that were producing the mark-to-market losses on the bond and embedded interest rate swap. Orange County would suffer a sharp decline in income in the period until the structured investments matured. The principal of the investments would be preserved. The mark to market valuation is based on the liquidation of the positions in the market at the relevant time. This would be affected by the losses on the bond and the swap as a result of changes in term interest rates. The decision to liquidate the portfolio realised these losses.

An additional advantage of holding the inverse FRNs to maturity would have been the potential to benefit from favourable changes in interest rates in the period before maturity. In contrast, liquidation realised the mark-to-market losses, with no prospect for recovery from changes in interest rates. Liquidation also ensures that the mark-to-market losses do not increase.

The use of the structured investments as collateral is more complex. The problem related to the decline in value of the collateral. As the value of the structured investments fell, the dealers required the borrowing to be terminated or additional collateral to be posted. The problem could be dealt with by extending the maturity of the borrowing to the maturity of the collateral. As the collateral is of high credit quality, the borrowing would be secured at maturity. The credit exposure to interest rate payments and the market risk to changes in interest rates would remain. In effect, the leverage in the portfolio, resulting from borrowing using repurchase agreements, created restrictions in dealing with the structured investments.

5. Postscript
The Orange County case resulted in the liquidation of the structured investment portfolio and the realisation of the loss of US$1.5 billion. Subsequently, a number of investigations

---

[22] The criticism was from Nobel laureate Merton Miller; see Irving, Richard "Miller Challenges Orange County's Bankruptcy" (June 1996) Risk 11.

and court actions were launched. Orange County sued Merrill Lynch. Merrill Lynch had sold a significant amount of the structured investments to Orange County[23]. The litigation was subsequently settled.

4 Interest Linked Notes

4.1 Overview

The concept of embedding interest rate exposure in bonds extends to transactions where the implicit interest rate derivative is engineered through a variable redemption amount. The movements in the value of the derivative component are reflected in the changes in the value of the principal repayment.

There are a variety of structures available:
- Bull-bear structures.
- Bond price or interest linked notes.
- Swap rate linked notes.

In each of the structures, the issuer does not have any exposure to the embedded interest rate derivative. The issuer is hedged through a derivative transaction with a dealer that offsets the exposure.

For the investor, the link to the nominated interest rate/bond price provides full price exposure to fluctuations in the manner and format required. Importantly, the ability to engineer specific linkages allows the separation of liquidity risk (related to the *maturity*) of the security and the area of the yield curve to which *price* exposure is sought (related to the embedded interest rate derivative). This allows a significant expansion in the range of investment strategies that can be implemented. The ability to create desired levels of leverage is also important.

4.2 Bull-Bear Structures

The concept of embodying interest rate derivatives in securities in the form of bull-bear bonds was originally introduced for Japanese investors in relation to Japanese interest rates. The concept has since been used in a variety of markets.

---

[23] For an interesting insight into the internal discussions within Merrill Lynch regarding the firm's dealing with Orange County, see Jereski, Laura "Merrill Lynch Officials Fought over Curbing Orange County Fund" (6 April 1995) Asian Wall Street Journal.

These types of transactions took the following form:

- Bull-bear structures involving the creation of offsetting tranches designed to appeal to bullish and bearish investors that produced a known maximum cost of funds to the issuer.
- High coupon Yen issues where the redemption formula was calculated with reference to future Japan Government Bond futures prices to engineer an implicit forward interest rate position into the security.

Exhibit 19.15 sets out an example of a Yen bull-bear JGB linked bond. **Exhibit 19.16** sets out an example of a Yen JGB linked bond issue and swap. The structures were specifically designed for particular investors seeking to create synthetic interest rate derivative positions to manage investment portfolios.

Exhibit 19.15   Yen Bull-Bear JGB Linked Notes

In February 1988, Societe Generale issued Yen 10 billion of five year bonds underwritten by Nikko Securities with the redemption value linked to the Tokyo Stock Exchange ("TSE") Japanese Government Bond ("JGB") December 1992 futures price.

The bonds carried a coupon of 7% pa compared to five year JGB yields of approximately 4.40/4.50% pa. The issue consisted of two tranches: a Yen 5 billion bear tranche and a Yen 5 billion bull tranche. The redemption value of the bonds was indexed to the December 1992 JGB futures price as follows:

Bear Tranche: R = 195.45% of principal minus TSE JGB December 1992 futures price
Bull Tranche: R = TSE JGB December 1992 futures price minus 20.55%
where
        R = redemption amount
TSE JGB = Tokyo Stock Exchange Japanese Government Bond

The payouts on the security were subject to certain constraints:

Minimum price = 0.00%
Maximum price = 17.90%

The offsetting nature of the two tranches and the counter balancing changes in the value of the tranches ensures that Societe Generale is immunised from the risk of the JGB linked redemption feature of the bond.

For example, assume the TSE JGB December 1992 price = 125%:

Bear Tranche   R = (195.45% − 125%) of Yen 5 billion = 70.45% of Yen 5 billion
                         = Yen 3,522,500,000
Bull Tranche   R = (125% − 20.55%) of Yen 5 billion = 104.45% of Yen 5 billion
                         = Yen 5,222,500,000
Total redemption payout = Yen 3,522,500,000 + Yen 5,222,500,000 equals Yen
                         8,745,000,000.

Assume TSE JGB December 1992 price = 75%:

Bear Tranche   R = (195.45% − 75%) of Yen 5 billion = 120.45% of Yen 5 billion
= Yen 6,022,500,000
Bull Tranche   R = (75% − 20.55%) of Yen 5 billion = 54.45% of Yen 5 billion
= Yen 2,722,500,000
Total redemption payout = Yen 6,022,500,000 + Yen 2,722,500,000 equals Yen 8,745,000,000.

The structure results in identical payouts for the issuer.

The structure results in the issuer repaying less than par on the bonds. If Societe Generale borrows Yen 10 billion and is only required to repay Yen 8,745,000,000, then it has an effective book profit of Yen 1,255,000,000. At the risk-free 5 year JGB rate of 4.40%, this profit of Yen 1,255,000 equates to an annual annuity of Yen 229,862,335 each year for 5 years.

Incorporating the annuity (Yen 229,862,335) benefit, the net funding cost of the issue equals Yen 470,137,665 or 4.00% pa. This rate is 30 bps above the comparable Yen risk-free rate but well below the coupons offered on conventional Euro-Yen issues raised at this time (4.90–5.00% pa). This allows Societe Generale to swap into attractive floating US$ funding at a substantial margin below LIBOR.

Source: This example draws on Cunningham, Michael M (1987) Selected Analysis of Recently Issued Index-Linked and Option Embedded Securities; unpublished research paper presented to course on Swap Financing, Centre for Studies in Money, Banking and Finance, Macquarie University.

Exhibit 19.16   Yen JGB Linked Notes

In January 1988, Societe Generale undertook an issue through Mitsui Finance International of Yen 7 billion 5 year bonds.

The issue's redemption value was linked to the value of the TSE December 1990 JGB futures price. The issue carried a 7.00% pa coupon that was significantly above the equivalent 5 year JGB rate of 4.40/4.50% pa or equivalent Euro-Yen yields in the range of 4.875/5.00% pa for comparable issues.

The redemption value of the bond was calculated in accordance with the following formula:

R = 193.60% minus opening TSE JGB December 1990 futures price.

The redemption payment is calculated on the JGB futures index 2 years hence, but not payable for a further 3 years. This allows both the issuer and investor to know the payout profile of the debt in advance.

The issue was targeted specifically at Japanese institutional investors as the issue is designed as a hedge for holders of Japanese bonds should rates increase markedly. This is reflected in the structure whereby as the JGB futures price falls (Yen interest rates increase), the redemption payout increases, presumably compensating the investor for losses on its physical JGB portfolio. This redemption structure effectively embeds a forward position in the December 1990 JGB futures contract within the bond.

The issuer (investor) benefits from a general decrease (increase) in Japanese interest rate structures and a commensurate rise in the index price 2 years hence. While the investor had to accept the symmetric nature of the exposure, Societe Generale insulated itself from the risk of the implicit JGB futures position through a derivative transaction with Mitsui.

Mitsui can hedge and securitise the inherent forward position in the following ways:

• Mitsui could take a long forward JGB futures December 1990 position 2 years hence. By arranging this hedge, Mitsui could expect to receive Yen 420 million (6% of Yen 7 billion) as payment for its services. Therefore, a fall in the JGB December 1990 futures price in 2 years time will work against Societe Generale on the redemption repayment. However, this impact will be offset by the short position it has been allocated by Mitsui (who matched out the position by establishing a corresponding long position for a counterparty).

• Mitsui could also strip and securitise the embedded option position. Mitsui could sell at-the-money 2 year call on the JGB December 1990 futures contract. Mitsui could expect to receive Yen 455 million (6.5% of Yen 7 billion) for this position, considering the lack of long-term option hedging tools for Japanese institutions at the time the transaction was undertaken.

The funds received were Yen 875 million (Yen 420 million for the forward position plus Yen 455 million for the option) which equals Yen 1,085,201,902 after 5 years. Using the risk free rate of 4.40% pa, this equates to an annuity of Yen 198,762,584.

This annuity, when offset against Societe Generale's annual interest cost of Yen 490 million, results in an annual effective coupon cost of Yen 291,237,416 equivalent to a nominal borrowing cost of 4.16% pa. This is 24 bps below the risk free rate. Based on Yen swap rates of approximately 4.60/4.80% pa, Societe Generale would have been able to obtain funding at a substantial margin under LIBOR through a Yen/US$ currency swap.

Source: This example draws on Cunningham, Michael M (1987) Selected Analysis of Recently Issued Index-Linked and Option Embedded Securities; unpublished research paper presented to course on Swap Financing, Centre for Studies in Money, Banking and Finance, Macquarie University.

4.3 Bond Price/Interest Linked Notes

The concept was introduced in two issues launched in April 1987 by Nomura International for GMAC and Mitsui and Co (USA)[24]. The basic concept has been extended to other structures, including dividing the issue into two tranches, with one tranche providing the upside potential and the other the downside potential to better attune the structure to the individual investor's interest rate expectations.

---

[24] The GMAC issue was subsequently withdrawn due to problems with tax regulations.

The basic transaction entails the issue of debt securities bearing a higher than market coupon. The redemption amount repaid to the investor at maturity is linked to price fluctuations (and by implication yield movements) on an identified debt instrument.

In a typical transaction, the coupon was set at 10.00% pa (approximately 200 to 250 bps above the market yield) for 3 years. The redemption of the bond was linked to a formula as follows:

- If the benchmark 30 year US Treasury bond at the end of 3 years (the maturity of the debt instrument) is at a break-even yield (say 7.10% pa), then the bonds are redeemed at par (100%).
- If the yield is above (below) the break-even yield, then the amount received by the investor will be less (greater) than par.
- In any case, the redemption amount cannot be less than zero.

Implicit in the variable redemption formula in this particular structure is a long 3 year forward position on the 30 year US Treasury bond. The position can also be restated using put call parity as (European) options with a maturity of three years. The investor grants a put option on the 30 year bond with a strike yield of 7.10% pa and simultaneously purchases a call option with an identical strike yield (effectively a forward purchase of the 30 year Treasury bond in three years).

The forward position is hedged with offsetting derivative transactions, effectively insulating the issuer from the risk of variations in the redemption amount. The swap usually generated funding at an attractive margin relative to a floating rate index such as LIBOR.

The economic logic underlying the transaction is based on the economics of the embedded derivative position. The investor (in the example) would usually be writing a put that was substantially in-the-money (by about 40 bps) and buying an out-of-the-money call (by the same margin). The dealer would sell the put on the 30 year bond at a higher premium than the outlay needed to purchase the call, with the difference being used to subsidise the issuer's cost. An alternative manner of expressing the same point is that the forward contract is entered into at an *off market rate*.

The derivative could be simulated as an equivalent forward position by holding an appropriate amount of 30 year bonds purchased at market price (the yield would be approximately 7.50% pa) for the 3 years and liquidating them at market rates at the end of that period. The variable redemption structure would lock in the 40 bps profit on the bonds that could be used to subsidise the swap. The fact that the structure can be simulated through a long forward position with the underlying securities reflects the fact that the simultaneous purchase of a put option and the granting of a call option is equivalent to a short forward position in the relevant security.

Where the issuer does not wish to alter the currency or interest rate basis of the borrowing, the transaction need *not* technically be a swap, but merely a series of option trades or forward transactions. This is a consequence of the fact that buying put options and selling call options at the same strike price is economically identical to paying fixed rates under a swap.

Exhibit 19.17 sets out the detailed underlying logic for such transactions using the example from Quatrain, a vehicle guaranteed by the South Australian Financing Authority.

Exhibit 19.17   Bond Linked Notes – Example 1

Quatrain Co., through Nomura International, undertook a 3 year 10.00% US$100 million issue of Treasury indexed bonds on 15 May 1986. Redemption value was linked to the 9.25% 2016 US Treasury bonds via the following formula:

$$R = US\$100,000,000 \times (MIP - 26.491782)/100$$

where

R = redemption value in US$

MIP = market index price of the 9.25% 2016 US Treasury bond at maturity of the issue

This exposure to the 30 year Treasury is hedged by Quatrain with Nomura via a series of derivative transactions. Nomura hedged its exposure (equivalent to taking on a short forward Treasury position) as follows:
- Purchase of the 30 year Treasury bond that is then funded and held for 3 years.
- Enter into a simultaneous forward commitment to buy US$100 million 9.25% 2016 bonds in 3 years time.

Assume Nomura purchases the underlying Treasury and funds it for 3 years at a rate not higher than the yield on the 30 year bond. Nomura can buy the 30 year Treasury at the current market yield of 7.65% pa and lock in a corresponding 3 year funding cost at or less than 7.65% pa. The profit dynamics of the hedge are set out below.

Assume:
- 30 year US Treasury bond yield is 7.65% pa
- 3 year US Treasury bond yield is 7.50% pa.

Nomura's net profit position from the purchase that is offset by the short forward position (bond price of 118% equivalent to a yield of 7.65% pa) is:

$$Profits = US\$100,000,000 \times (MIP - 118)/100 + US\$100,000,000$$
$$\times (126.491782 - MIP)/100$$

$$= US\$100,000,000 \times (8.491782)/100$$
$$= US\$8,491,782 \text{ at maturity}$$

where

$MIP = MIP$ at maturity.

Nomura's US\$8,491,782 gain is equivalent to a US\$2,628,526 annuity for 3 years at an interest rate of 7.50% pa. This annuity of US\$2,628,526 can be used to reduce the Treasury indexed bond's interest cost from US\$10 million (that is, 10.00% of US\$100 million) to US\$7,371,474 (US\$10,000,000 − US\$2,628,526). The effective interest cost is 7.37% pa (US\$7,371,474/US\$100,000,000), below the equivalent 3 year Treasury rate. In practice, the annuity stream will only be used to reduce the effective cost to a level at which the issuer's sub-LIBOR target is satisfied, with the surplus representing Nomura's profit from the transaction.

The accompanying US\$ interest rate swap will entail Quatrain receiving the fixed rate equivalent of US\$10 million or 10.00% pa and paying LIBOR minus the agreed margin. An off-market rate swap is required because of the high bond coupon.

The structure described is fairly generic and has been adopted in a large number of transactions in a variety of currencies. It places principal at risk of loss with the derivative being linked to the transaction principal. This is achieved by embedding a (off market) forward on the relevant bond within the structure. Alternatively, this structure entails the investor selling embedded options to enhance return. **Exhibit 19.18** sets out an example of this structure in Yen, where the investor is effectively writing an out-of-the-money put on the bond.

In recent times, the bond price linked structures employed have been more conservative in nature, with the principal of the structure being protected. This is achieved by using some or all of the interest coupon (and in some cases, a part of the principal of the transaction) to purchase an option on the relevant bond. The payoff of the option is then engineered into the structure. **Exhibit 19.19** sets out an example of a bond linked to the 30 year US Treasury bond with principal protection. The structures have been used in a wide variety of markets. Structures where the coupon is linked to the underlying bond have also been used. **Exhibit 19.20** sets out a structure where the note coupon is linked to Yen bond futures.

In the 1990s, German investors bought Deutschemark structured notes linked to US Treasury bond yields[25]. The issues were undertaken by German banks (primarily private banks and Landesbanks) in Schuldscheine format. The issues had a final

---

[25] See "German Investors Lap-Up Structured Diversification" (12 September 1998) International Financing Review Issue 1250 72.

maturity of between 30 and 40 years. The return on the bonds was an initial coupon of 8.00% pa. After this initial period, the note offered returns linked to the yield on 10 year US Treasury bonds. The bond was callable annually at a yield of around 8.00% pa. The notes offered returns of over 6.00% pa. This was significantly in excess of the yield on German bonds of comparable maturity. The structure was popular because it offered German investors the opportunity to create exposure to US Treasury yields with no currency exposure.

The structures were feasible because the relative shapes of the Deutschemark and US yield curves reduced the cost of currency protection (through the embedded quanto option[26]). However, the structures were difficult to hedge for traders. This is because the note represented a complex mixture of currency risk and interest rate risk (to a constant maturity US Treasury bond) [27].

In the 1990s, the increased interest in emerging markets led to adaptation of these structures to emerging markets bonds. **Exhibit 19.21** sets out an example of a structure with an embedded forward on an emerging market bond index. The investor's principal investment is at risk in this structure, with return contingent on the performance of the index. **Exhibit 19.22** sets out an example of a transaction combining a zero coupon bond issue with a call on a basket of emerging market bonds, designed to allow investors to create asymmetric exposure to emerging market debt. **Exhibit 19.23** sets out a second example of this type of structure.

Exhibit 19.18 Bond Linked Notes – Example 2	
Amount	Yen 10 billion
Maturity	1 year
Issue Price	100.00
Coupon	1.00% pa
Redemption Value	Redemption amount is based on the following formula: • If JGB Number 1999 is trading at or above par at the Value Date, then 100.00 • If JGB Number 1999 is trading below par at the Value Date, then redemption is by way of physical delivery of the securities.
Maximum Redemption	100.00
Minimum Redemption	0.00
Value Date	5 business days before maturity

---

[26] See Chapter 11.

[27] The structure effectively combines a constant maturity swaption and a quanto option.

Exhibit 19.19   Bond Linked Notes – Principal Protected Structure Example 1

The following 1 year note entails an embedded exposure to the 30 year US Treasury bond. The note is structured to ensure that the investor's principal investment is fully protected against loss at all times.

The terms of the issue are as follows:

Amount	(up to) US$50 million
Maturity	1 year from commencement
Issue Price	100%
Interest Rate	0% pa
Redemption Value	100% of Amount plus Redemption Payment payable at maturity
Redemption Payment	Amount $\times$ Leverage Factor $\times$ $[Y_0 - Y_m]$
	Where
	Leverage Factor $= 17$ times
	Y_0 = Yield on Reference Bond at commencement of transaction (5.50% pa)
	Y_m = Yield on Reference Bond at maturity
Reference Bond	The on-the-run 30 year US Treasury bond at the time of issue
Minimum Redemption	100% payable at maturity

The note is designed to allow the investor to monetise expectations of a decline in interest rates on the 30 year US Treasury bond over the next 1 year period. The note provides the investor with a capital protected investment where, in return for forgoing the interest coupon, the investor has the ability to generate a highly leveraged exposure (17–18 times)[28] to the actual decline in the 30 year US Treasury bond yield.

The payoff profile of the note is set out in the Table below. The payoff profile is calculated using a 30 year yield of 5.50% pa at commencement of the transaction and a leverage factor of 17.

Yield on 30 Year US Treasury Bond (% pa)	Principal Redemption at Maturity (%)	Redemption Payment (%)	Total Redemption Amount at Maturity (%)	1 Year Yield to Maturity (% pa)
4.50	100	17.00	117.00	17.00
4.60	100	15.30	115.30	15.30
4.70	100	13.60	113.60	13.60

---

[28] Please note the leverage factor substantially relates to the fact that a 1 bps movement in yield results in a large price change in the price of the bond. The leverage factor therefore refers to the modified duration or PVBP of the underlying 30 year Treasury bond. Assuming a 30 year term and a coupon and yield to maturity of 5.50% pa, the modified duration of the bond is around 14.6. This means that a leverage factor of 17 translates into true leverage of around 1.16 $\times$. This means that per US$100 of the bond, approx US$116 of options on the 30 year bond are embedded in the note.

4.80	100	11.90	111.90	11.90
4.90	100	10.20	110.20	10.20
5.00	100	8.50	108.50	8.50
5.10	100	6.80	106.80	6.80
5.20	100	5.10	105.10	5.10
5.30	100	3.40	103.40	3.40
5.40	100	1.70	101.70	1.70
5.50	100	–	100.00	0.00
5.60	100	–	100.00	0.00
5.70	100	–	100.00	0.00
5.80	100	–	100.00	0.00
5.90	100	–	100.00	0.00
6.00	100	–	100.00	0.00

The structure entails using the forgone coupon on a 1 year security to purchase a 1 year call on the 30 year Treasury bond to generate the bond price exposure.

Exhibit 19.20   Bond Linked Notes – Principal Protected Structure Example 2

Amount	Yen 5 billion
Maturity	1 year
Issue Price	100.00
Coupon	Calculated in accordance with the following formula:

$$2.23 \times (1 - (JGB(f) / JGB(i)))$$

Where

JGB is the Japanese Government Bond futures contract
JGB(i) is initially equal to 124.00 and is adjusted on each JGB futures contract maturity by adding the spread between the closing price of the maturing contract and the closing price of the next listed contract
JGB(f) is the official closing price of each contract.

Minimum Redemption	100.00

Exhibit 19.21   Bond Linked Notes – Emerging Market Structure Example 1

Amount	US$10 million
Maturity	3 year
Issue Price	100.00

Coupon	0.00% pa
Redemption Value	Redemption amount is based on the following formula:
	Amount × Index/131.8
	Where
	Index is the JP Morgan Emerging Local Markets Index (in US$) on the Value Date
Minimum Redemption	0.00
Value Date	5 business days before maturity

Exhibit 19.22   Bond Linked Notes – Emerging Market Structure Example 2

In early 1995, following a major sell off in emerging markets, a number of structured notes linked to emerging market securities (usually Brady bonds) were issued. The following note was typical of the type of securities issued:

Maturity	1 year
Coupon	0%
Principal Redemption	The higher of 100 + (Final Basket Price − 48%) or Minimum Redemption
Minimum Redemption	100%
Basket	40% Par Bond of Latin Country A
	30% Par Bond of Latin Country B
	30% Par Bond of Latin Country C
Current Basket Price	48%

The note combines a zero coupon bond with a call option on a basket of 3 Brady bonds. The call option is engineered through the linking of the redemption value to the price of the Brady bonds. The call option is financed through the forgone interest on the note.

The issue was designed to allow investors to increase exposure (on a risk averse basis) to emerging market debt. This followed the Mexican crisis where emerging market Brady bond spreads widened between 100 and 400 bps, bringing the spreads to their highest levels for many years.

The economics of the transaction were as follows:

- The 1 year yield on AAA or AA rated notes at the time of issue was around 7.00 to 7.25% pa. The breakeven price on the note, to equate the return to that on a conventional note, was around 93.25/ 93.50.
- The breakeven price increases on the basket, so that the noteholder would earn the yield on 1 year securities, was around 14.58/15.10% pa, implying a final basket price of 55–55.25% pa.

Exhibit 19.23	Bond Linked Notes – Emerging Market Structure Example 3
Amount	US$25 million
Maturity	3 year
Issue Price	100.00
Coupon	1.00% pa
Redemption Value	Redemption amount is based on the following formula: $100 + [\text{Amount} \times \text{Max}\,(0;\ \text{Index} - 82.25\%)]$ Where Index is the value of the Security Basket calculated on Value Date
Security Basket	The value of the Security Basket is calculated as the product of the price of the Reference Bonds multiplied by their weight. <table><tr><td>Reference Bond</td><td>Weight</td></tr><tr><td>Latin Country A</td><td>30%</td></tr><tr><td>Latin Country B</td><td>20%</td></tr><tr><td>Latin Country C</td><td>10%</td></tr><tr><td>Asian Country D</td><td>20%</td></tr><tr><td>Eastern European Country E</td><td>20%</td></tr></table>
Minimum Redemption	100.00
Value Date	5 business days before maturity

4.4   Swap Rate Linked Notes

The concept of securities with redemption values linked to bond prices has been extended to notes where redemption values are linked to *interest rate swap rates*. The use of swap rates reflects:

- The benchmark function performed by these rates in markets where the underlying government bond market is less liquid and inefficient in pricing.
- The ease of hedging the derivative element embedded in the structure.

The incorporation of swap rates does not alter the underlying logic of the transactions. The basic structure entailing embedded forwards or options remains identical.

The swap rates are usually determined for the purposes of these transactions by either reference to a screen quotation service or a dealer polling mechanism from a group of reference dealers.

Exhibit 19.24 sets out an example of a note linked to Swedish Kroner ("SKR") swap rates. The note effectively embeds a 1 year forward start 3 year SKR interest

---

Exhibit 19.24   Swap Rate Linked Notes – Example 1

Issuer	Swedish Export Credit
Amount	SKR 200 million
Maturity	1 year
Issue Price	100
Coupon	9.50% pa (annual bond basis)
Redemption	100 plus 15 times (7.85% pa less 3 year SKR swap offered yield)
Minimum Redemption	0

---

swap, where the investor receives fixed rate and pays floating rates within the transaction[29]. The investor's payout reflects the movements in the swap rate as follows:

- If the 3 year swap rate goes to 6.85% pa at maturity, then the investor receives a redemption payout equivalent to 115% of par.
- If the 3 year swap rate goes to 7.95% pa at maturity, then the investor receives a redemption payout equivalent to 98.5% of par.

The investor achieves both an exposure to the 3 year sector of the yield curve on a forward basis and an above market yield. The above market yield represents the present value of the difference between the forward swap rate embedded in the note and actual market forward swap rates.

Exhibit 19.25 sets out an example of a note linked to Sterling ("GBP"). **Exhibit 19.26** sets out the hedging structure for the transaction. The return profile of the transaction reflects the embedded option on GBP swap rates (effectively an option on a GBP swap). As GBP rates decline from current levels, the investor's return increases. Increases in swap rates do not translate into losses for the investor because of the minimum redemption feature. The investor finances the purchase of the option on the swap through the forgone coupon on the note itself.

---

[29] Please note the number by which the yield difference at maturity is multiplied is a mechanism for equating the yield movement to price terms together with a leverage factor. The PVBP of a 3 year swap at the relevant yield level is around 3 (that is, a 1 bps movement in yield results in a 3 bps change in the value of the swap). This means that the transaction is effectively leveraged 5 times. In effect, the investor is entering into forward swaps for a notional principal amount equalling 5 times the face value of the note (SKR 1,000 million).

Exhibit 19.25   Swap Rate Linked Notes – Example 2

Amount	US$10 million
Maturity	18 months
Issue Price	100
Coupon	0% pa
Redemption	100 plus 5 times (7.70% pa less 2 year GBP swap yield) paid in US$
Minimum Redemption	100

Source: Lehman Brothers International

Exhibit 19.26   Swap Rate Linked Notes – Hedging Structure

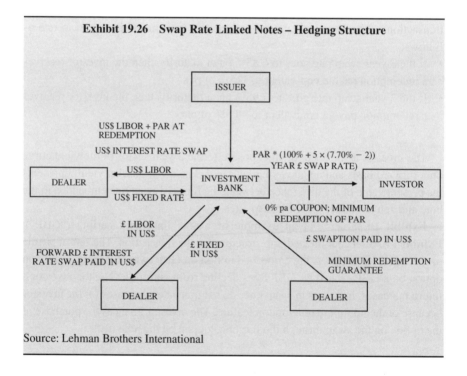

Source: Lehman Brothers International

The transaction, while similar to the SKR note described above, has a number of differences:

- The investor does not risk principal, only the coupon, as the minimum payout is restricted to par.

- The transaction is fully currency protected, with the GBP exposure being fully hedged back into US$.

The coupon at risk structure effectively requires a forward (1 year forward into a 2 year swap) GBP swap, where the investor receives fixed rates combined with a swaption to pay fixed rate (for 2 years, 1 year forward), purchased by the investor to be embedded in the swap. The swaption is designed to provide the guaranteed return of principal. The strike on the swaption relative to the forward swap rate, and the swaption premium in conjunction with the cost of currency protection, will be adjusted to equate to the coupon foregone by the investor to generate the transaction economics.

The currency protected structure is created by incorporating quanto options in the structure. The quanto structure ensures that the GBP values are translated into US$ at a pre-agreed rate[30].

In the mid to late 1990s, swap linked structures were commonly used to seek to monetise expectations of convergence in interest rates between European countries planning to become part of the monetary union and foundation members in the Euro. The expectation was that interest rates in the participating countries should converge. This would basically entail interest rates in Italy, Spain and Portugal declining towards the level of interest rates in Germany.

In order to take advantage of this expectation, a number of note structures linked to the forward rates in these currencies were created. The basic concept was to receive the forward swap rate in the high interest rate currency and pay the forward swap rate in the lower interest rate currency. The swaps were then embedded in the principal redemption of the note. Other structures involved options designed to create asymmetric exposures to expected rate movements. If the structures matured before the planned introduction of the Euro, then the structures required a quanto element to be incorporated. This was to ensure that the values in each currency were translated into the other currency at a pre-agreed exchange rate. If the structures matured after the planned introduction (where the relevant currencies were to be incorporated in the Euro), then in theory, no currency protection was required. However, in practice, there was exposure to the agreed exchange rate to the Euro and the possibility of the Euro not proceeding.

Exhibit 19.27 and **Exhibit 19.28** set out two examples of the structure. The first structure is linked to the spread between 10 year Lira and Deutschemark swap rates. The investor receives a return where the spread is above 2.00% pa and suffers a loss where the spread is below 0.50% pa. The second structure is a

---

[30] See Chapter 11.

Exhibit 19.27 Swap Rate Linked Notes – Example 3	
Amount	DEM 50 million
Maturity	2 years
Issue Price	100
Interest Rate	0% pa
Redemption Value	Redemption value is calculated in accordance with:
	Amount × Factor
Factor	100% − 7 × Max[0; 0.50% pa − Index]
	+ 7 × Max[0; Index − 2.00% pa]
	Where
	Index = Lira 10 year swap rate − Deutschemark 10 year swap rate

Exhibit 19.28 Swap Rate Linked Notes – Example 4	
Amount	DEM 50 million
Maturity	2 years
Issue Price	100
Redemption Value	100.00
Coupon	Interest is calculated in accordance with:
	Amount × Factor
Factor	4.45% pa + (7 × Index)
	Where
	Index = ECU 2 year swap rate − Deutschemark 2 year swap rate
Minimum Coupon	0.00% pa

principal protected note where the interest is linked to the spread between European Currency Unit ("ECU") and Deutschemark rates. The investor receives enhanced coupon where the spread increases. The investor receives a lower return where the spread diminishes. In both cases, the investor created a position that resulted in gains if the planned monetary union did not proceed. The European Economic and Monetary Union ("EMU"), which was implemented in January 1999, was expected to result in converging interest rates between member currencies.

The concept of notes linked to swap rate differences between currencies is generic. It has been extended beyond the special context of the EMU. The basic concept of the transactions has also been extended to spread between two points of the swap curve *in the same currency* as well as the *swap spread itself.*

Exhibit 19.29 sets out a swap spread based structure based in non European currencies. The transaction is linked to the spread between Yen and US$ swap rates.

The investor has created an exposure that will benefit from a decrease in the spread between 10 year US$ and Yen swap rates.

Exhibit 19.30 and **Exhibit 19.31** set out transactions where the return is linked to the shape of the swap curve. In the first example, the investor benefits from an increase in the slope of the Sterling swap curve. The benefit is capped at a spread of around 80 bps. At this level, the investor receives an effective return of around 9.54% pa. If the spread remains at the level prevailing at the time of entry into the transaction (5 bps pa), then the investor receives a below market return of 5.62% pa. The structures were designed to enable investors to position for a steepening in the Sterling yield curve that was exceptionally flat between 3 and 15 years during this period. The second transaction is a derivative structure, where the investor is taking a position that the difference between the swap curve slope in Deutschemark relative to Sterling will decrease. If the difference between the two slopes is above 2.10% pa, then the investor receives no return. The return to the investor increases by around 1.00% pa for each 0.10% pa reduction in the slope difference. The maximum return to the investor is where the slope differential between the currencies is zero.

Exhibit 19.32 sets out the terms of a transaction where the return is linked to changes in US$ swap spread. The investor return improves (deteriorates) as the swap spread decreases below (increases above) 80 bps. The investor has effectively entered into a forward on the swap spread that is embedded in the bond structure.

Exhibit 19.29   Swap Rate Linked Notes – Example 5

Amount	US$25 million
Maturity	1 year
Issue Price	100
Interest Rate	0% pa
Redemption Value	Redemption value is calculated in accordance with:
	Amount × Factor
Factor	11.5 × [4.20% pa − Index]
	Where
	Index = US$ 10 year swap rate − Yen 10 year swap rate
Minimum Redemption	100.00

Exhibit 19.30   Swap Rate Linked Notes – Example 6

Amount	Lira 50 billion
Maturity	2 year

Issue Price	100
Interest Rate	0% pa
Redemption Value	Redemption value is calculated in accordance with:
	Amount × Factor
Factor	12.05 − 10 × Index
	Where
	Index = GBP 10 year swap rate − GBP 5 year swap rate
Minimum Redemption	100.00
Maximum Redemption	120.00

Exhibit 19.31   Swap Rate Linked Notes – Example 7

Amount	Lira 50 billion
Maturity	3 year
Issue Price	100
Interest Rate	0% pa
Redemption Value	100
Coupon	Interest is calculated in accordance with:
	Amount × Factor
Factor	12.00% − 10 × (Index − 0.95%)
	Where
	Index = (DEM 5 Year Swap rate − DEM 3 Month LIBOR)
	− (GBP 5 year swap rate − GBP 5 year swap rate)
Maximum Coupon	21.00% pa
Minimum Coupon	0.00% pa

Exhibit 19.32   Swap Spread Linked Notes – Example 8

Amount	US$25 million
Maturity	2 year
Issue Price	100
Interest Rate	5.00% pa
Redemption Value	Redemption value is calculated in accordance with:
	Amount × Factor
Factor	10 × [0.80% pa − Index]
	Where
	Index = US$ 10 year swap rate − US$ 10 year Treasury bond rate
Minimum Redemption	0.00

5 Capped and Collared Floating Rate Notes

5.1 Evolution

Capped and collared FRNs have been undertaken at various periods commencing in the middle 1980s. Investor interest in the instruments has coincided with positive yield curves and opportunities to extract value from the sale of options on short term interest rates.

5.2 Capped FRNs[31]

Capped FRN and certificate of deposit ("CD") issues are typically structured as 7 to 12 year FRN/2 to 5 year CD issues with ceilings on interest payments. The issues are undertaken by highly rated borrowers, primarily banks or sovereign entities. Investors in the issues, in return for accepting a cap or maximum interest rate, receive a higher than normal current coupon or margin on the FRNs and CDs.

Capped FRN and CD issues were initially undertaken in June 1985 in US$ in the Euromarkets. Since introduction, the capped FRN concept has been extended beyond US$, with transactions in a variety of currencies. Variations include delayed cap FRNs where the maximum interest rates do not operate for the first 3 to 4 years. A variation on the capped FRN structure is the maximum rate notes ("MRNs"). MRNs involved the issue of fixed rate debt combined with a nominated cap rate on a floating rate index (6 month LIBOR). If 6 month LIBOR exceeds the cap rate, then the fixed rate coupon decreases by the same amount. Functionally, MRNs operate in the same way as capped FRNs.

The cap is structurally a put option on the price of a short-term security, priced off the underlying short-term interest rate index. The investor sells the cap to the issuer. The premium for the cap is received by the investor in the form of higher interest rates (higher margin relative to LIBOR). The cap is sold by the issuer to a dealer. The option premium is used to lower the issuer's borrowing cost, usually below market rates. Where the market rates exceed the capped rate, the investor's return is limited to the specified maximum rate, allowing the purchaser of the cap to receive the difference between the cap and market rate from the issuer.

The detailed structure of the transaction is more complex. For example, the Banque Indosuez transaction arranged by Shearson Lehman Brothers (which introduced this structure in the market) was an issue of 12 year US$200 million FRNs

---

[31] See Sowanick, Thomas J. and Tally, John G. (28 August 1985) Floating Rate Notes with Interest Rate Caps; Merrill Lynch Capital Markets Securities Research Division, New York; Grant, Charles "Can Caps Beat Swaps" (July 1985) Euromoney 12–13.

carrying an interest coupon of 0.375% over three month LIMEAN[32]. The FRN coupon was capped at 13.0625%. It should be noted that the cap level on LIMEAN is equivalent to 12.6875% (13.0625% pa minus the 0.375% pa margin).

Shearson arranged for the sale of the cap (with a strike of 12.6875% pa on LIMEAN) to a US corporation. Indosuez pays out LIMEAN plus 0.375% or 13.0625% to the holders of the FRNs unless 3 month LIMEAN exceeds 12.6875% pa. For example, if LIMEAN goes to 14.0625%, then Indosuez pays 13.0625% to the FRN holders and 1.375% to Shearson. Shearson passes the payment on to the purchaser of the cap to compensate it for rates rising above the cap level. Indosuez is compensated for the cap by a payment of 0.375% pa of the principal amount (effectively the option premium). Indosuez receives the premium as a quarterly cash flow rather than an up-front payment. This brought Indosuez's cost of funds down to LIMEAN. To avoid any credit risk, the purchaser of the cap paid Shearson a lump sum that was reinvested in Treasury zero coupon securities which produced the quarterly income stream equivalent to 0.375% pa. **Exhibit 19.33** sets out the structure of the transaction.

The structure of the capped FRN is engineered so that the investors sell out-of-the-money caps. Analytically, the investor sells a series of put options, expiring every 3 or 6 months, until maturity on the underlying index (LIBOR). The premium paid to the investor is the higher spread on the FRN. Studies undertaken conclude that the values implied for the caps are low compared with theoretical values derived from historical levels of volatility. This undervaluation provides a significant arbitrage opportunity where dealers purchased the caps stripped from the FRNs or CDs at low theoretical values.

The capped FRN structure has been used extensively in Yen. **Exhibit 19.34** sets out an example of this structure.

A variation on the capped FRN was the mini-max FRN structure where the investor was subject to both maximum and minimum rates of interest. The first mini-max issue undertaken by Goldman Sachs for the Kingdom of Denmark was a 10 year US$250 million FRN with a coupon subject to a minimum rate of 10.00% and a maximum rate of 11.875% pa. A series of issues for SEK, Commerzbank and Christiana Bank followed before investor interest evaporated. The mini-max FRN concept re-emerged in 1992/93 in the form of collared FRNs discussed in the next Section.

---

[32] LIMEAN is the London Interbank Mean Rate (being the arithmetical average of the LIBOR and London Interbank Bid Rate ("LIBID")). This has traditionally been around 6.25 bps below LIBOR.

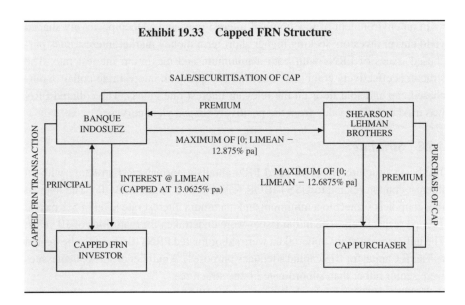

Exhibit 19.33   Capped FRN Structure

Exhibit 19.34   Capped Yen FRNs

Amount	Yen 5 billion	
Maturity	5 years	
Interest	Yen 6 month LIBOR	
Maximum Interest	Year	Maximum Interest (% pa)
	1	1.50
	2	2.00
	3	2.50
	4	3.00
	5	3.50
Interest Coupon	Semi-annually	

5.3   Collared FRNs

5.3.1   Background/Origins

The collared FRN structure has its origins in the capped FRN and Mini-Max FRN transactions completed in the mid 1980s. The collared FRN market emerged around August 1992 when Kidder Peabody (a US investment bank) reintroduced the concept with issues for JP Morgan and Credit Local de France.

In an environment of low nominal interest rates and a steep positively shaped yield curve, investors seeking higher short term money market interest rates purchased issues of FRNs with both a minimum and maximum interest rate. The structures effectively combined a normal FRN with an interest rate collar (a purchased cap and sold floor on the relevant interest rate index). The collared FRN was used to extract value from the positively shaped yield curves.

5.3.2   Structure

The basic structure of the collared FRN entails a normal FRN structure with an interest coupon related to US$ LIBOR (either 3 or 6 month LIBOR). The interest rate coupon is subject to a minimum and maximum interest rate level of 5% pa and 10% pa respectively. The initial issues were undertaken for maturities of 10 years. The initial transactions undertaken were subordinated FRNs (designed to be treated as Tier II Capital for BIS capital adequacy purposes). A number of subsequent issues were senior rather than subordinated issue structures.

Exhibit 19.35 sets out the terms of the JP Morgan issue, one of their first transactions to be undertaken.

Exhibit 19.35 Collared FRN Structure	
Issuer	JP Morgan and Co Inc
Amount	US $200 million of subordinated FRNs
Maturity	10 years (due 19 August 2002)
Interest rate	3 month LIBID[33] flat
Fixed re-offer price	99.85
Minimum interest	5%
Maximum interest	10%
Amortisation	Bullet
Call option	None
Listing	Luxembourg
Governing law	New York
Denominations	US$5,000, US$100,000
Commissions	0.50% (management & underwriting 0.25%; selling 0.25%)
Payment	18 August
Outstanding rating	Aa2 (Moody's), AA + (S&P)
Lead manager	Kidder Peabody Intl (books)

---

[33] LIBID is the London Interbank Bid Rate. This has traditionally been 12.5 bps below LIBOR.

Co-lead managers	JP Morgan Securities, Merrill Lynch Intl, Salomon Brothers Intl, CSFB
Co-managers	Lehman Brother Intl, Goldman Sachs Intl, Morgan Stanley Intl

Source: (1992) (August) International Financing Review Issue 940, 56.

5.3.3 Economics

The economics of the collared FRN is driven by the fact that it combines a standard FRN transaction with a US$ LIBOR interest rate cap and floor. Based on the structure described, the investor purchases a package consisting of the following elements:

- 10 year US$ LIBOR based coupon FRN.
- Sells a cap on US$ LIBOR at the maximum interest rate (10% pa).
- Purchases a US$ interest rate floor at the minimum interest rate level (5% pa).

The sale of the cap and purchase of the floor equates to a sold interest rate collar on US$ LIBOR.

The position of the issuer is the exact opposite of that of the investor. The issuer has borrowed using a US$ LIBOR-based FRN while simultaneously purchasing a US$ LIBOR interest rate cap and selling a US$ LIBOR based floor (a purchased interest rate collar on US$ LIBOR).

Exhibit 19.36 sets out the structure of the collared FRN decomposed into the relevant components.

The issuer hedges this exposure under the collar by onselling the cap and purchasing the floor to generate normal US$ LIBOR-based funding.

The economics of the transaction is driven by the shape of the US$ yield curve. The strongly positive nature of the yield curve means that forward rates in US$ are significantly above the prevailing rates for particular maturities. For example, the rate for US$ LIBOR in 3, 6, 9, 12 etc months is significantly above the current LIBOR.

The steepness of the yield curve, and the fact that the US$ LIBOR forward rates implied from the curve are significantly above current LIBOR, drives the values of the cap and floor. This dictates the economics of the transaction. The fact that forward US$ LIBOR rates are significantly above current yield curve rates means that the US$ LIBOR floors purchased by the investors, while significantly in-the-money in the initial periods, are out-of-the-money for much of the life of the transaction. In contrast, the higher US$ LIBOR forward rates are closer to the

Exhibit 19.36   Collared FRNs – Decomposition

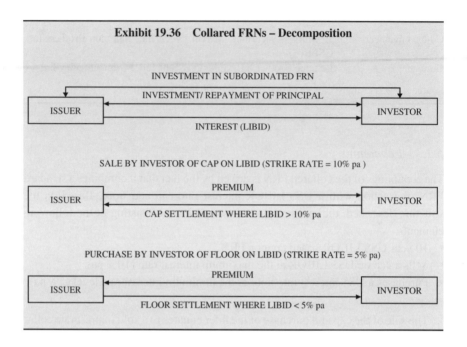

strike rate of the US$ interest rate cap. This relativity of the minimum and maximum rates (effectively the strike rates for the floor and cap respectively) determines their relative value.

At the time the transactions were undertaken, the market value for the cap and floor indicated that the investors were entering into the collar for approximately 25 to 50 bps pa less that the theoretical value. In other words, the collared FRN had an implied yield of approximately LIBOR minus 25 to 50 bps pa. The forgone value effectively allowed the issuer to create attractively priced funding as described in detail below. The return forgone by the investor is required to provide an incentive to the issuer to undertake the issue, providing the customised return profile sought by the investor.

5.3.4   Investor Perspective

The demand for the collared FRNs was from money market investors, primarily money market funds. The investor sought to benefit from the minimum coupon. With US$ short-term interest rates at historically low levels and falling, investors were prepared to trade off the potential interest loss from the cap for the high short term current coupon income generated by the floor (implicit in the minimum interest level). In effect, the investors were willing to sell the cap (at lower than theoretical value) to fund the purchase of the in-the-money floor.

The value of the floor for the investor was driven by a number of factors, including:

- Investors placed great importance on current income.
- Investors expected forward interest rates on US$ LIBOR to be significantly below those implied by the current yield curve.

5.3.5 Issuer Perspective

From the perspective of the issuer, the transactions were fully hedged into normal US$ LIBOR based funding, typically at relatively attractive borrowing rates. The issuer had effectively purchased a US$ interest rate cap at the maximum rate, and sold the investor an interest rate floor at the minimum interest rate. The issuer hedged its exposure by simultaneously onselling the interest rate cap and purchasing a corresponding interest rate floor to immunise itself from the risk of the transaction. The hedging interest rate cap and floor transactions were generally directly undertaken by the issuer with a dealer.

The attractive funding cost for the issuer was generated by the investor's valuation of the collar. Investors were entering into the collar transaction at a premium level that was lower than the economic value of the separate interest rate cap and floor. This allowed issuers to typically on sell the interest rate cap and purchase the interest rate floor for premiums that generated a net cash inflow to the issuer, reducing their borrowing costs.

From the issuer's perspective, the transactions were particularly appealing as they generated attractively priced funding for long terms (typically 10 years) at a time when arbitrage opportunities in traditional bond markets were relatively scarce. An additional advantage for banks was the capacity to structure a number of these transactions as subordinated issues. This allowed the banks to raise cost effective Tier II Capital to enhance their capital adequacy positions.

5.3.6 Market Evolution and Product Variations

The market developed rapidly after its re-emergence in the early 1990s. As the market developed, a number of variations on the basic product concept emerged. The variations focused on a number of elements of the transactions:

- Variations on the interest formula used.
- Transactions in currencies other than US$.
- Securitisation of the option elements of the transaction.

Initially, the collared FRN market operated around the basic formula described above, but with minor variations. The major differences related to credit quality of the issuer and changes in the cap or floor element, reflecting shifts in the US$ yield curve. As the margins in such transactions narrowed, a number of transactions sought to maximise available opportunities with changes in the interest rate formula used.

The variations included:

- **Adjustment of maximum/minimum interest rate** – in order to extract more value from the shape of the forward US$ LIBOR yield curve, the maximum interest rate was "tiered", with the rate increasing over time. For example, in a transaction completed for Abbey National Treasury Services Plc in late August 1992, the maximum interest rate was set at 6.00% pa in years 1 and 2, 7.00% in years 3 and 4 and 8.00% in year 5. A similar structure was used in an issue for Bayerische Hypotheken und Wechsel Bank, with the maximum interest rate rising from 7.00% pa to 9.00% pa and with a lower minimum interest rate of 4% pa. A central feature of the transactions requiring the tiered maximum interest rate was the issuer's desire for shorter maturities. This necessitated adjustments to the maximum interest rate level to generate premiums from the sale of interest rate caps to subsidise the purchases of floors required. The other major change in the interest rate formula of such instruments emerged later in September 1992 when changes in yield curve shape dictated a reduction in the maximum interest rate to levels around 8.00–8.25% pa to extract the required value from the forward rates in the yield curve. The lower band level was repeated in March 1993 as the flatter shape of the US$ yield curve forced a lowering of the maximum interest rate or cap strike level to generate the necessary premiums to allow these transactions to proceed.

- **Use of different index** – this involved undertaking transactions where the underlying interest rate was a term Constant Maturity or swap rate (such as a 10 year swap rate) rather than the traditional short term money market rates. One of the structures is linked to the 10 year Constant Maturity Treasury (CMT) rate (known as deleveraged FRNs)[34]. The products seek to take advantage of the prevailing interest rate environment in a manner similar to collared FRNs. They extract value from the higher forward US$ LIBOR rates implicit in the steep yield curve that is translated into a higher current income level through the purchase of a floor by the investor.

---

[34] See Chapter 17.

- **Securitisation of the floor** – as the market evolved, an interesting product variation focused on securitising the option elements of the structure. Under this arrangement, the issue of FRNs was combined with a maximum interest rate, but was sold in conjunction with the issue (by the borrower) of floor certificates that were detachable. The floor certificates were effectively the minimum interest rate element of the transaction, and allowed the investor to freely trade in the floor certificates quite separate from the capped FRN itself. **Exhibit 19.37** sets out an example of this particular variation, detailing the terms of an issue for the World Bank completed in March 1993. The structure is interesting for a number of other features including:
  1. The deferral of the maximum interest level, which only operates from the beginning of the fifth interest rate period (effectively, 2.5 years into the term of the ten year transaction). This reflected the fact that DEM LIBOR was higher than the maximum rate at the time of issue.
  2. The maximum interest rate is lower than the then prevailing DEM LIBOR rate, reflecting the inverse slope of the DEM yield curve and the different pattern of forward DEM LIBOR rates implied.
  3. The structure of the floor certificates that have a strike rate at a level of 7% (which is unusually close to the maximum interest rate level) and operate for the full life of the transaction, reflecting the particular shape of the DEM yield curve.

  The concept of securitised floors, in conjunction with an issue of FRNs (without the cap), has been used in the GBP market with the issue of FRNs with detachable Additional Detachable Interest Rights ("ADIRs"). The first issue for Britannia Building Society was arranged by Samuel Montagu in June 1993. It entailed a GBP 100 million FRN paying 3 month GBP LIBOR plus 15 bps in combination with ADIRs that entitled holders to receive 5.00% pa less 3 month GBP LIBOR, where GBP LIBOR is less than 5.00% pa. The ADIRs were effectively floors on GBP LIBOR with a strike price equivalent to 5.00% pa. The structure securitised the minimum coupon on the FRN. The ADIR structure was used to create additional value for the issuer to allow a higher price for the minimum coupon element to be realised. In addition, the use of ADIRs avoided potential problems regarding the capacity of the UK Building Society issuer to separately sell a 5.00% floor.

- **Ratchet FRNs** – the one way or ratchet FRN offered investors a yield around 3 or 6 month US$ LIBOR plus 35 bps, with a floor equal to the previous coupon and a cap equal to the previous coupon plus 25 bps. The floor locks in any increase in LIBOR while the cap allows LIBOR to rise moderately. Effectively, the structure creates a "ratcheting" return for the investor. For example, at the time the transactions were undertaken around late November/early December 1992, the first interest payment was set at around 4.2875% pa. This effectively means that given that the interest rate on the issue can rise by 0.25% for 20 semi-annual interest periods, the issue had an increasing cap that peaks at 9.2875% pa for the last interest rate period. **Exhibit 19.38** sets out the terms of a typical ratchet FRN issue. The value in the ratchet structure is driven by the interaction in the premium levels of the tiered cap relative to that of the tiered floor that operates in such transactions. This type of structure yields the most economic value for the issuer under certain yield curve conditions. The value is maximised where the interest rate caps sold by the investor through the ratchet structure are substantially at or in-the-money, and the corresponding floors are out-of-the-money. The structure is very similar to a cliquet option.

Exhibit 19.37   Collared FRNs with Securitised Floor Structure

Capped FRN

Issuer	World Bank
Amount	DEM 200 million of FRNs
Maturity	Ten years (due 28 April 2003)
Coupon	Six month LIBOR plus 0.25% payable semi-annually on 28 April and 28 October
Maximum interest	7.25% as from the beginning of the fifth interest period
First interest determination date	26 April
Issue price	100%
Amortisation	Bullet
Call option	None
Listing	Frankfurt SE
Denominations	DEM 10,000 and DEM 250,000 (global note)
Commissions	0.20% (management and underwriting combined 0.10%, selling 0.10%)
Launch date	11 March 1993
Payment	28 April 1993
Lead manager	Commerzbank (books)

Floor Certificates

Issuer	World Bank
Number	20,000 certificates
Exercise	Each certificate entitles the holder to payment on 28 April and 28 October corresponding to the positive difference between 7% and six month LIBOR. Each certificate relates to DEM 10,000.
Issue price	DEM 695 per certificate

Expiration	28 April 2003
Selling concession	0.25%
Listing	Frankfurt SE
Launch date	11 March 1993
Payment date	28 April 1993
Lead manager	Commerzbank (books)
Pre-market price	DEM 720, 740

Source: (1993) (March) International Financing Review Issue 970, 72.

Exhibit 19.38   Ratchet FRN Structure

Issuer	Credit Local de France
Amount	US$100 million
Maturity	5 years
Coupon	3 month LIBOR plus 0.35%
	The coupon cannot be increased by more than 0.25% per interest rate reset and cannot be decreased.
Issue price	101.625
Fixed re-offer price	100
Amortisation	Bullet
Call option	None
Put option	None
Listing	Luxembourg
Denominations	US$10,000, US$100,000, US$1 million
Commissions	1.875% (Management & Underwriting 0.05%; selling 1.825%)
Payment	23 December
Swap	Into a variety of fixed rate European currencies
Outstanding rating	Aaa (Moody's), AAA (S&P)
Lead managers	Morgan Stanley International (books)

Source (1992) (December) International Financing Review Issue 958, 58.

---

6   Exotic Interest Rate Linked Notes[35]

6.1   Overview

A central element in interest rate linked notes is providing investors with customised risk return profiles. Exotic options are also driven by the need to increasingly refine the risk return profiles *within instrument structures*. The combination of the two

---

[35]   For discussion of exotic options, see Chapters 5, 7, 8, 9, 10 and 11.

formats is therefore inevitable. Exotic options are frequently embedded in interest rate linked notes. The principal types of exotic option used are barrier and digital options.

6.2 Barrier Option Embedded Structures

The economic benefit of the barrier option structure derives from the fact that it usually has lower premiums relative to conventional options. The lower premium amount reflects the possibility that the option will be extinguished or not activated. The lower premium is used in structured interest rate linked notes to reduce the cost of an embedded option. For example, the lower option premium allows a higher degree of participation in the movement in the relevant asset to be created for a given coupon or principal sacrifice. However, the barrier feature may significantly reduce the participation in any market value shift that results in the barrier level being reached. This dictates that the structure is most attractive where the investor expects a modest market move (at least less than the barrier level) to achieve the maximum benefits from the incorporation of this type of exotic optionality.

Exhibit 19.39 sets out the terms of a FRN incorporating embedded interest rate barrier options on a short term interest rate index. The note is attractive to investors seeking to monetise an expectation regarding the *future path* of LIBOR. This is done through the sale of barrier options on the forward rates. This type of structure is used particularly in an environment of a steep yield curve, declining bond yields and narrow credit spreads.

Exhibit 19.39   FRNs Incorporating Interest Rate Barrier Options

1. Structure

Amount	US$100 million
Maturity	3 years
Issue Price	100
Floating Coupon	3 month LIBOR plus 37.5 bps pa payable quarterly
Barrier Coupon	1.50% pa payable quarterly
Commencement Level	40 bps over current 3 month LIBOR
Current 3 Month LIBOR	3.50% pa
Step Up	1.00% pa (effectively 25 bps per quarterly interest period)

2. Analysis

The return to the investor under this structure is predicated on the interaction of the spread, the barrier level and the conversion coupon. In the example, the barrier is set at a level (the commencement level) of 40 bps over LIBOR that increases at a fixed increment rate of 25 bps per period. The structure entails a trade-off between the floating coupon margin and the barrier coupon. Where the desired barrier coupon is set at higher levels, the corresponding enhancement to the margin, relative to LIBOR, is reduced.

Where the barrier level is not reached, the coupon payable is the floating coupon. The barrier coupon is the fixed rate payable where the barrier is reached. If LIBOR plus the spread does not exceed the barrier level on a reset date, then the FRN pays LIBOR plus the spread of 37.5 bps. If the barrier is reached, then the next coupon is the barrier level and the fixed conversion coupon of 1.50% pa is paid for all subsequent periods. In effect, the security behaves like a high margin FRN *unless LIBOR reaches the barrier level*, when it becomes a fixed rate note with a 1.50% pa coupon.

The investor achieves an enhanced return as long as LIBOR does not increase by 100 bps pa over 1 year and 300 bps over 3 years. The barrier levels are set above the implied LIBOR forwards. The investor will benefit from the sale of the barrier options where LIBOR reaches the forwards or exceeds them by a small margin. The additional spread, relative to a normal FRN, ensures that the barrier FRN outperforms the conventional FRN where the barrier level is not breached until well into the term of the note. If the rate of increase rises and the barrier level is breached at earlier dates, then the relative advantage of the barrier floater decreases. The breakeven rate of increase is around 30–40 bps and a barrier breach time of 12 to 18 months. The additional enhanced return on the barrier FRN is preserved as long as LIBOR increases at a rate of less than the breakeven level per quarter. If the increase in LIBOR exceeds this level, the return on the barrier FRN falls sharply, reflecting the lower conversion coupon.

An alternative method of analysis of the break even slope between the barrier FRN and the conventional FRN is to consider the case where LIBOR stays at current levels for (up to) 3 to 4 quarters and subsequently increases at a constant rate. The slope of the break even rate *increases* the greater the number of quarters that the interest rate curve stays static. This signifies that if LIBOR is initially constant, than it will have to increase at a higher constant rate to reach the barrier level. An initial period of static interest rates thus significantly enhances the benefits of the structure to investors.

Traditional barrier options are activated or extinguished by the behaviour of the price of the asset that underlies the actual option contract. Defined exercise options entail option structures where a second variable determines whether the option is knocked in or knocked out[36]. **Exhibit 19.40** sets out an example of a defined callable structured note. The structure of a defined callable note is a bond that is callable if the underlying index is below the strike at the call date. In the example, the note is callable unless US$ 3 month LIBOR increases some 200 bps above the spot rate over 12 months. The note becomes a 1 year note yielding around 90 to 100 bps over the current 1 year Treasury rate if 3 month LIBOR does not increase

---

[36] See Chapter 9.

at the specified rate. Alternatively, it extends into a 3 year note yielding 5–10 bps over the current 3 year Treasury rate if 3 month LIBOR increases by the requisite amount.

Exhibit 19.40   Indexed or Defined Callable Notes

1. Structure

Amount	US$100 million
Maturity	3 years
Issue Price	100%
Coupon	7.375% pa payable quarterly on a bond basis (around 90 bps over the 1 year Treasury and 5–10 bps over the 3 year Treasury)
Call Date	In 1 year if the underlying index is below the strike level
Underlying Index	3 month LIBOR
Strike Level	7.50% pa (200 bps over current 3 month LIBOR of 5.50% pa)

2. Analysis

This structure is driven by the trade-off between the coupon of the defined callable note and the strike level on the underlying index. The higher coupon, designed to compensate the investor for the embedded option risk, demonstrates the following behaviour:

- If the strike level is low, then the note behaves like a 3 year note, reflecting the fact that the probability that the strike level is breached is very high (reflecting the fact that the strike level is below the *implied* 3 month LIBOR forward rate). The transaction is a 3 year note and a sold deep-out-of-the money defined call option.
- If the strike level is high, then the note behaves like a 1 year note, reflecting the low probability of the strike level being attained. The transaction is effectively a 1 year note with a sold deep-out-of-the money defined call option. In these cases, the options have low value resulting in limited yield enhancement, with the note interest approximating that for a conventional transaction for the equivalent maturity.
- The maximum coupon is achieved at a strike level set at around 100 to 150 bps over spot 3 month LIBOR where the value of the embedded option is maximised.

The exercise of the call option follows the following pattern:

- The call is driven by the behaviour of 3 month LIBOR (the underlying index) rather than *the 2 year Treasury rate* at the call date.
- This means the call exercise may be *inefficient* in that the issuer may be forced to prepay the note, even where it is economically disadvantageous to do so. This would occur where the 2 year Treasury rate is at a level that does not allow the note to be re-financed at a lower rate.
- *Efficient* exercise is achieved only where 3 month LIBOR is above the strike level *and* 2 year Treasury rates are below the coupon of the note.

The most efficient rate at which exercise is achieved is dependent on the forward rates for both Treasury rates and 3 month LIBOR, the volatility of the two rates and the correlation between the two rates.

From the viewpoint of the issuer, the call option is transferred through the offsetting sale of a defined purchase call which is designed to generate lower cost funds for the issuer, albeit with uncertainty of final maturity (1 or 3 years).

The investor views this type of security as a short term (corresponding to the call date) security *with extension risk*[37]. The risk of extension is lowered by setting the strike level above the anticipated increase in LIBOR over the relevant period. The extension risk can be quantified by considering the interest scenario and expected volatility. The risk of extension is related to the mean and the standard deviation of the distribution of the underlying index (in the above case, 3 month LIBOR). If the distribution is assumed to be log normal, then the expected interest rate scenario can be used as the mean of the distribution and volatility as the standard deviation of the distribution. The probability of extension increases with the increase in the mean. If the mean future rate is the forward 3 month LIBOR and volatility is around 15% pa, then the probability of extension (an increase in 3 month LIBOR of 200 bps over 1 year) is around 1.75 to 2.00%. If the mean LIBOR rate (the implied forward rate) rises to higher levels, then the probability of extension increases quite rapidly.

The extension risk behaviour is as follows:

- If the mean is lower than the strike, then higher volatility increases the risk of extension. For example, volatility increase where the mean is at current LIBOR will increase the risk of extension. This reflects the fact that the increase in volatility increases the probability of the index finishing above the strike level.
- If the mean is above the strike, then higher volatility may decrease the risk of extension. Where the mean is at the implied forward rate, that will decrease the risk of extension. This reflects the fact the higher mean will dictate that higher volatility increases the probability of the rate finishing below the strike level.

A defined callable note can incorporate European or American exercise. In the case of an American exercise, the note is callable at any time after a non call period if the underlying index is above the strike price *on any interest payment date prior to maturity.*

The behaviour of the coupon on a defined call note of either exercise feature is complex. The coupon on American defined call options appears to *decline* where the strike is set well above the spot 3 month LIBOR level. The lower option premium is reflected in the lower coupon, as the investor effectively sells the option embedded in the bond. The lower option value is the result of the call behaviour in a European and American defined call bond where the strike level is set higher above spot. If 3 month LIBOR is below strike, then both bonds are called. If 3 month LIBOR rises by more than the nominated level, then the notes are not called. In the case of a European defined call note, the investor may have a 2 year bond that is trading below par, depending on the rise of 2 year rates relative to the rise in 3 month LIBOR rates. For the investor in the American defined call bonds, if rates fall below the strike level, then the bond will be called at par, allowing this note to trade at a value above that of the comparable European defined call bond. This protection feature means that the option value is lower, as the continuous exercise feature favours the note holder.

---

[37] This is similar to the approach with various types of other structured notes (IARs and step up callable bonds); see Chapters 16 and 18.

6.3 Digital Option Embedded Structures

6.3.1 Overview

One of the major types of exotic options commonly used in structured notes is digital options[38]. Digital options are options where the pay-off is fixed. The known loss profile makes the options ideal for use in structured note transactions. This is because the digital payout allows quantification of the loss profile. This allows minimum return or maximum loss values in relation to principal risk to be determined.

6.3.2 Range Notes

Concept[39]

Range notes are the principal example of digital option embedded notes. The structures are also referred to as digital notes, binary notes/FRNs, corridor (or "fairway") FRNs and accrual notes.

The range note entails the sale of embedded digital options to enhance yield on either fixed or floating rate notes. The use of digital options because of the defined loss profile allows the customisation of the risk relative to the return enhancement achieved. In particular, the structures are used to monetise investor expectations on the *evolution or path* of future asset prices or value in relation to the values implied by the current forward rates.

The structure evolved in an environment characterised by low nominal levels of interest rates and positive (steep) yield curves. Investors used the range note to monetise expectations that the current structure of interest rates was likely to continue.

Range Notes – Structure

The structure of a range FRN embodies the following features:

- It is a floating rate security paying a return relative to the normal money market index (US$ LIBOR).
- The range FRN typically pays coupons higher than that available on a comparable conventional FRN.
- The coupon payment on the FRN is conditional on a specific financial market variable fixing within a set range at specific points in time.

---

[38] See Chapter 10.

[39] See Smithson, Charles (1995) Managing Financial Risk – 1995 Yearbook; Chase Manhattan Bank at 134–136; Das, Satyajit "Range Floaters" in Konishi, Atsuo and Dattatreya, Ravi (Editors) (1996) The Handbook of Derivative Instruments; Irwin Publishing, Chicago at Chapter 12.

The last two elements require additional explanation. The financial market variables that were initially used in range FRNs were typically interest rates. Under this arrangement, the range FRN would pay an above market coupon relative to LIBOR only for each day that LIBOR fixed within the set range.

The timing and denomination of the range varies between transactions:

- The LIBOR range is typically set at the outset of the issue.
- The actual dates on which LIBOR fixes must be within the set range also vary. There are two general formulae:

1. *Periodic Set* – in this case, the relevant financial market variable (LIBOR) must set within the specified range at the start of each reset period coinciding with the interest period on the FRN (3 or 6 months). In a range FRN structure based on the periodic set approach, the coupon *for the full interest rate period* would be set at either the nominated coupon or zero. The rate depends on whether the relevant benchmark rate sets within or outside the range at a specific date at the start of the interest rate period.

2. *Daily Set* – in this case, the financial market variable fixes are on a daily basis. On each day that the financial market variable sets outside the rate, the coupon on the range FRN is 0% pa. In contrast, when the financial market variable sets within the rate range on the relevant day, the range FRN pays the normal above market coupon relative to LIBOR.

Exhibit 19.41 sets out the terms of a typical transaction.

Where counterparties wish to gain the cash flow and return profile of a range FRN without the necessity of purchasing the underlying security, the return profile can be constructed through an "accrual swap". Under this structure, the dealer pays an investor a floating rate (LIBOR) plus a margin in return for receiving fixed rates or floating rates when a nominated financial market variable sets within a specified range. This would enable an existing investor to swap either a fixed or floating rate asset into a range FRN structure. Alternatively, a liability manager could structure a swap where the LIBOR receipts under a fixed-floating interest rate swap have a pay-off profile matching that of a range FRN. In effect, this lowers the fixed rate under an interest rate swap[40].

Exhibit 19.41 Interest Rate Range Notes	
Amount	US$100 million
Term	2 years

---

[40] For an example of an accrual swap, see **Exhibit 10.7**.

Issue Price	100
Redemption Price	100
Coupon	[3 month US$ LIBOR + Margin % pa] × Accrual Factor/Number of days
Margin	1.00% pa
Number of Days	360
Accrual Factor	The number of days during the relevant interest rate period that US$ 3 month LIBOR is fixed within the range set out below:

Period	Maximum Rate (% pa)	Minimum Rate (% pa)
0–6 months	4.00	3.00
6–12 months	4.75	3.00
12–18 months	5.50	3.00
18–24 months	6.00	3.00

Reverse Engineering

The range note can be reverse engineered into the component parts which are easily discernible. The range FRN consists of the following elements:

- A conventional FRN.
- Sold digital options on the relevant financial market variable (in the above example, US$ 3 month LIBOR rates). In effect, the investor sells a series of digital options. The digital options are sold either on specific dates during the term of the note (the periodic set structure) or daily (the daily set structure). The above market coupon effectively equates to the premium captured for sale of the digital options. The loss of coupon, on the days that the relevant financial market variable is outside the range nominated, represents the fixed or digitised payout under the digital option that is owing from the investor to the purchaser of the digital option.

The objective of the issuer and investor in a range note transaction is clear. Typically, the issuer will be insulated from the exposure under the digital option. The issuer will enter into a transaction with a dealer to sell the embedded digital options. The issuer will receive the premium for the sale of the options. The proceeds received from the sale will lower the cost of the issuer to or below its target borrowing costs.

For the investor, the major attraction of the range FRN is the higher coupon. The higher coupon is designed to increase portfolio earnings through the premium received for the sale of the digital options. The range FRN assumes that rates will continue to move in a relatively narrow range[41]. Investors derive an enhanced return

---

[41] This is equivalent to a state which biologists refer to as "homeostasis", where organisms regulate their activities such that their temperature does not fluctuate wildly; see "Fashion and Homeostasis" (2 March, 1994) IFR Swaps Weekly Issue 58.

by creating digital options that reflect this underlying economic view. The value of the digital options also derives from the forward rates implied in the yield curve. If the implied forward rates are higher than actual LIBOR rates, then the value received from the sale of the digital option will be greater than the realised value of the options. Investors expecting that the implied forward rates are likely to exceed realised rates use range FRNs to enhance returns.

Investors in range FRNs often derive a breakeven point of the strategy. This is calculated in terms of the number of days that the underlying market variable has to stay within the range for the instrument to return at least the prevailing money market interest rate for the relevant period. In the example in **Exhibit 19.41**, assuming US$ 3 month LIBOR is trading at 3.50% pa, the breakeven point would be as follows:

Breakeven number of days = (US$ 3 month LIBOR rate × number of days in interest rate period)/(US$ 3 month LIBOR plus Margin) = (3.50 × 91)/(4.50) = 71 days (or 78% of the period)

Pricing and Hedging

Pricing and hedging of range FRNs is based on the components of the structure. The pricing process requires the following steps:

- Conversion of the FRN component into a fixed rate equivalent (using the swap rate).
- Valuation of the digital option itself.

The conversion of the floating rate payments into a fixed equivalent is needed to create a net uniform series of cash flows (that is, the dollar amount of the FRN payments as implied by the current yield curve are calculated). This is necessary to calculate the digitised payout under the digital option. This is because the digital option payout is the daily accrued interest rate or the accrued interest over the interest rate period.

The digital option is priced normally[42]. The value of the embedded digital options is primarily affected by the strike level (relative to the implied forward rates) and the volatility of the underlying index.

6.3.3 Range Notes – Structural Variations

Range FRNs originally emerged in 1993. The majority of transactions were in US$. In early 1994, increases in US$ short term interest rates made the traditional range FRN linked to US$ LIBOR rates increasingly unattractive. However, investor

---

[42] See Chapter 10.

demand for enhanced return continued to favour investment in structured floating rate investments, prompting a series of product variations.

The variations fall into a number of categories:

- **Adjustments to the traditional range FRN structure** – this included amendments to sampling period, a one-sided exposure to value shifts and refinement of the risk to large changes in the index.
- **Extensions to the concept** – this included incorporating a broader range of underlying indexes and currency hedged structures. The logic of the range notes based on alternative assets is identical to that for the interest rate linked range notes. The major difference is the digital option is based on currency values, commodity prices and equity index values rather than interest rates[43].

Variations in interest rate linked range notes included:

- **Sampling period adjustments** – this reflected concern from investors that they were significantly exposed under the range FRN pricing formula to LIBOR sets on specific days. This concern led to the evolution of the daily accrual formula, with the LIBOR fixes being undertaken on a daily basis to measure relative to the range. This allowed the investor to reduce exposure to specific fixing dates.
- **Risk exposure adjustments** – this focused on adjusting the risk to the seller of the embedded digital options. The refinements to the risk of the structure focus principally on:
  1. Adjusting the risk exposure to isolate the risk of an increase or decrease of the value of the index. This is usually structured as an accrual note or binary FRN.
  2. Limiting the exposure to a large change in the underlying index that would result in the note not paying any coupon at all over the entire life of the note. This is structured as a range or accrual note, where the digital option feature is only applicable for part of the life of the note, or as a constant spread structure where the strike levels can be adjusted during the life of the transaction.
- **Interest rate utilised** – this entails range FRN structures linked to term interest rates (typically 5 or 10 year CMTs). The linkage to long term rates related to an expectation that the yield curve would flatten, with increases in interest rates and volatility being focused at the shorter end of the yield curve.
- **Alternative asset markets** – this includes:
  1. *Alternative asset market range or accrual structures* – where the note is linked to financial assets other than interest rates.
  2. *Quanto range structures* – where the range FRN is hedged through a quanto option into a third currency. An example of a quanto option embedded

---

[43] See Chapter 20 and Das, Satyajit (2004) Structured Products Volume 2; John Wiley & Sons (Asia), Singapore at Chapters 4 and 9.

range note was a transaction undertaken by Creditanstalt for Osterreichische Postsovarksse. The transaction was based on a range on 3 month Italian Lire interest rates with the currency risk hedged through the quanto option into US$. The one year transaction paid a coupon of 4.50% in US$. The range nominated was 7.50–9.00% pa (for the first 6 months) and 6.50–8.50% pa (in the second 6 months).

Other variations include incorporating additional credit risk in the structure by combining the range note with a credit derivative[44].

Exhibit 19.42 sets out an example of an accrual note where enhanced returns are generated for the investor if LIBOR is above a specified level. **Exhibit 19.43** sets out an example of an accrual note where enhanced returns are generated for the investor if LIBOR is below a specified level. The structures are designed to create customised exposure to specific interest rate changes. The investor gives up coupon in circumstances that are considered improbable in return for enhanced returns in situations considered more likely.

The desire to customise interest rate expectations may take the form of limiting exposure to a shorter period than the life of the note. In the examples considered to date, the digital options were sold either periodically or daily throughout the life of the note. If the investor wishes to take a position on the level of rates for the next year, then a semi-accrual note structure can be used.

Exhibit 19.44 sets out an example of a semi-accrual note where the accrual period (the period in which the digital options are sold) covers only 1 year in the life of a 5 year note. The transaction is similar to the range notes except that the time horizon is reduced to 1 year. If the investor's view is realised, then the structure returns an enhanced yield over the term of the note. If the investor's view is not realised, then the returns under the structure are reduced. The 5 year semi-accrual structure returns a coupon of 6.00% pa or 100 bps above the 5 year Treasury rate. Using the same strike levels, a 1 year final maturity accrual note would yield a return equivalent to around 50–60 bps pa over the 1 year Treasury note. The incremental yield in the shorter maturity structure is reduced because the payout is a function of the coupons sacrificed. In the semi-accrual structure, the value of the digital options are a function of the average exercise value of the options that, in the longer maturity version, corresponds to selling an option with a larger fixed payout or a larger number of options with the same fixed payout. The semi-accrual note therefore behaves like a more leveraged version of the conventional accrual note structure.

---

[44] See Das, Satyajit (2004) Structured Products Volume 2; John Wiley & Sons (Asia), Singapore at Chapter 11. See also Semonin, Lionel "Structured Hybrid Investments" (September 2002) Asia Risk – Structured Statement.

Exhibit 19.45 sets out a semi-accrual note structure where the return on a 1 year note is linked to the performance of a specified 5 year Treasury Note over a 3 month period. If the 5 year Treasury Note trades in a range of 5.39% pa to 5.89% pa, then the semi-accrual note pays a coupon of 9.00% pa. The note is structured with a minimum coupon of 3.00% pa if the 5 year Treasury note trades outside the range of 5.14% pa and 6.14% pa during the next 3 months.

The range/accrual note structure exposes the investor to the risk of a sudden increase or decrease in rates. This causes the coupon of the note to set at zero. A constant spread structure evolved to provide additional protection for the investor in a higher volatility environment. The structure is known as choice or ratchet notes. **Exhibit 19.46** sets out an example of this type of structure.

The major feature of the constant spread range structure is that the target range is reset if the original range is broken. The target range is set at a wider range if the initial range is breached. The range FRN coupon is also adjusted to a lower level. The additional returns generated from these transactions are lower than those generated by traditional range FRNs. This reflects the lower value of the digital options which, in turn, reflects the lower risk to the investor of this structure.

Exhibit 19.47 sets out a callable range note structure. **Exhibit 19.48** sets out a collared FRN structure with an embedded digital option.

Exhibit 19.49 sets out an example of a CMT linked accrual note linked to 10 year CMT rates. The structure described can be structured on either a fixed rate or floating rate basis. The structure is largely identical with that of other range or accrual structures, with the major difference being the ability to monetise expectations on *term* interest rates through digital options on these indexes. The major advantage of the CMT based accrual structures is the forward rates and interest rate volatility relate to the CMT curve. The major use of the range or accrual structures based on CMT rates in risk management applications are in the context of mortgage portfolio management[45].

Exhibit 19.50 sets out an example of a range note structure based on interest rate differentials between two currencies.

Exhibit 19.42 Accrual Note FRNs – Example 1	
Amount	US$100 million
Issue Price	100%
Maturity	5 years

---

[45] See Chapter 17.

Coupon (payable semi-annually)	• For first 6 months: 5.50% pa
	• For remaining life:
	  1. If underlying index is above or equal to strike level - LIBOR plus 100 bps
	  2. If underlying index is below strike level - 0%

Underlying Index	6 month US$ LIBOR

Strike Levels	Reset Dates (years)	Strike Level (% pa)	LIBOR Forward Rate (% pa)
	0.5	4.00	4.63
	1.0	4.50	4.98
	1.5	5.00	5.27
	2.0	5.25	5.41
	2.5	5.50	5.57
	3.0	5.75	5.81
	3.5	6.00	6.12
	4.0	6.25	6.45
	4.5	6.25	6.68

Exhibit 19.43   Accrual FRNs – Example 2

Amount	US$100 million
Issue Price	100%
Maturity	3 years
Redemption	100%
Coupon	• If underlying index is below strike level - 3 month LIBOR plus 75 bps • If underlying index is above strike level - 0%
Coupon Payments	Coupon is calculated daily and paid quarterly based on an actual/360 day basis
Underlying Index	3 month LIBOR

Strike Levels	Reset Date (months)	Strike Level (% pa)
	0 to 6	5.00
	6 to 12	5.50
	12 to 18	6.00
	18 to 24	6.50
	24 to 30	6.50
	30 to 36	6.50

Exhibit 19.44   Semi Accrual Notes – Example 1

Amount	US$100 million
Issue Price	100%

Maturity	5 years
Redemption	100%
Coupon	Year 1: 6.00% subject to Accrual Provision
	Year 2: 6.00% × Accrual Percentage
Coupon Payments	Coupon is calculated daily and paid quarterly, based on a bond basis
Accrual Provision	The coupon will accrue for each day that LIBOR is at or below the Strike Level.
Accrual Percentage	The percentage of days within the first year that the underlying index is at or below the strike level.
Underlying Index	3 month LIBOR

Strike Levels	Reset Date (months)	Strike Level (% pa)
	0 to 3	4.50
	3 to 6	4.75
	6 to 9	5.00
	9 to 12	5.25

Exhibit 19.45   Semi Accrual Notes – Example 2

Amount	US$100 million
Issue Price	100
Maturity	1 year
Redemption	100%
Coupon	Coupon will be determined by reference to the yield level of Underlying Index trading over next 3 month period
Coupon Payments	Coupon is paid quarterly based on a bond basis
Underlying Index	Current on the run specified US 5 year Treasury Note
Current level of Underlying Index	5.64% pa

Coupon & Strike Levels	Strike Level (Current level of index +/− bps)	Coupon (% pa)
	25	9.00
	30	8.00
	35	7.00
	40	6.00
	45	5.00
	50	4.00
	Outside Above Ranges	3.00

Exhibit 19.46   Ratchet Accrual Notes

Amount	US$25 million
Maturity	1 year

Issue Price	100%
Redemption Price	100%
Reference Rate	US$ 10 year CMT rate
Coupon	US$ 1 year LIBOR plus Margin payable at maturity. The coupon will accrue for each day that the Reference Rate is within Initial Range or following a Ratchet Event, the Adjusted Range:

	Maximum Rate (% pa)	Minimum Rate (% pa)
Initial Range	5.80	5.20
Adjusted Range	6.20	5.10

Margin	1.50% pa (Initial Margin) or following a Ratchet Event 0.65% pa (Ratchet Margin)
Ratchet Event	If the Reference Rate touches the Initial Range on any day, then:
• The Margin will be adjusted from the Initial Margin to the Ratchet Margin for all subsequent days; and
• The Initial Range will be replaced by the Adjusted Range over the remaining term of the Note.

Exhibit 19.47   Callable Range Notes

The terms of the issue are as follows:

Amount	US$25 million
Term	3 years
Issue Price	100
Redemption Price	100
Coupon	[3 month US$ LIBOR + Margin % pa] × Accrual Factor/ Number of days payable quarterly
Margin	1.10% pa
Number of Days	360
Accrual Factor	The number of days during the relevant interest rate period that US$ 3 month LIBOR is fixed within the range:
Maximum Rate – 7.00% pa
Minimum Rate – 5.00% pa
Minimum Coupon	0.00%
Call Option	The issue is callable at the option of the Issuer after 1 year and at each subsequent coupon payment date

The structure is similar to the structure of a normal range FRN. The additional feature is the ability of the issuer to call the issue after 1 year and quarterly thereafter. The issuer (purchaser of the digital option) will terminate the transaction (sell the digital back to the investor) if the value of the digital option at a call date is lower than the original value. This will be the case where interest rate volatility and implied forward rates change to reduce the implied value of option.

Exhibit 19.48   Digital Collared Notes

The terms of the issue are as follows:

Amount	Euro 12.5 million
Term	6 months
Issue Price	100%
Redemption Price	100%
Coupon	0.10% + (125% × Minimum [3.75%; Maximum {0, (6m Swiss Franc ("CHF") LIBOR − 1.62%)/1.62%}]) payable in accordance with an actual/360 day basis at maturity

Source (30 April 1999) MTN Week

Under the structure, the investor will receive an interest equal to the percentage surplus of 6 month Swiss Franc LIBOR over 1.62% pa geared by a factor of 1.25 plus 10 bps. The formula will yield maximum interest of 4.79% pa and a minimum of 0.10% pa.

The final coupon will outperform the Swiss Franc LIBOR if the latter sets above 1.64% pa. If LIBOR fixes at or below 1.62% pa, then investors will receive the minimum coupon of 0.10% pa. The following graph shows the return structure for different levels of the six-month Swiss Franc LIBOR.

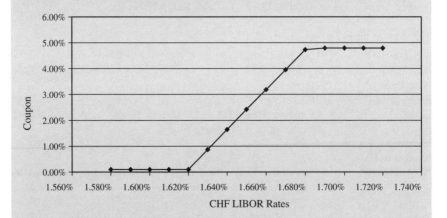

The structure can be decomposed as follows:
- Investor purchases a FRN.
- The investor sells:
    1. A normal cap with a strike of 1.69% pa (on 80% of the face value of the Note (100%/125%)).
    2. A digital floor at a strike of 1.62% pa (on 125% of the face value).

The premium from the digital floor and cap increases the yield on the floater, provided rates stay above 1.62% pa and below 1.69% pa. If rates are below 1.62% pa, then the binary payoff (equivalent to the expected LIBOR as implied by the forward rates and the premium received less 0.10% pa) reduces the return to the minimum coupon. If rates rise above 1.69% pa, then the investor gives up all the upside above 1.69% pa. The issuer hedges by reversing the original elements of the trade with the dealer.

Exhibit 19.49   CMT Accrual Notes

Amount	US$100 million
Maturity	1 year
Issue Price	100%
Redemption	100%
Coupon	10 Year CMT + 30 bps subject to accrual conditions
Coupon Payments	Coupon is calculated daily and paid quarterly based on an actual/actual basis
Accrual Provision	The coupon will accrue for each day that the underlying index is at or below the Strike Level
Underlying Index	10 Year CMT rate

Strike Levels	Reset Date (months)	Strike Level (% pa)
	0 to 3	5.50
	3 to 6	5.70
	6 to 9	5.85
	9 to 12	6.00

Exhibit 19.50   Spread Based Range Notes

The terms of the issue are as follows:

Amount	Italian Lira 20 billion
Maturity	2 Years
Issue Price	100%
Principal Redemption	100%
Underlying Index	The spread between the 5 year DEM swap rate and the 5 year GBP swap rate
Range 1	The number of business days where the Underlying Index is within the range specified below: Maximum – 250 bps pa Minimum – 150 bps pa
Range 2	The number of business days where the Underlying Index is outside the range specified below: Maximum – 250 bps pa Minimum – 150 bps pa
Interest	[7.55% × Range 1/360] × [0.50% × Range 2/360]

Source: (24 October 1997) MTN Week

The issue provides the investor with an enhanced return where the spread between the 5 year DEM swap rates and the 5 year GBP swap rates traded within the range of 150 to 250 bps pa. The structure was designed for investors with the view that interest rates between Euro bloc countries and the UK would diverge after monetary union in 1999. The spread at the time the transaction was undertaken was 154 bps pa. If the spread moves outside the range, then the investor receives a low nominal return. The structure embeds digital call and put options on the spread between the two rates.

6.4 Multi Factor Option Embedded Structures

Multi factor options refer to a special class of exotic options whose primary distinguishing characteristic is that the option payout is based on the relationship between more than one asset[46]. Multi factor option embedded options are not commonly used in interest rate linked structures.

The major examples of multi factor option embedded structures are:

- **Interest rate basket linked notes** – these are structured notes with an embedded basket option. **Exhibit 19.51** sets out an example of a basket linked note structure used to express investors' views on European interest rate markets.
- **Index differential swap/quanto option linked notes** – these include various structures involving bonds with embedded index differential swaps[47].

7 Bond Index Linked Notes[48]

A separate class of interest rate linked notes is bonds where the return (both principal and interest) is linked to the total return on a specified bond price index[49].

The principal building block of a bond index note is a bond index swap[50]. **Exhibit 19.52** sets out the structure of a bond index swap. **Exhibit 19.53** sets out an example of a bond index swap. **Exhibit 19.54** sets out the return computation mechanics. **Exhibit 19.55** sets out the structure of a bond index linked note. The note combines the purchase of a floating rate asset with entry into a bond index swap.

---

[46] See Chapter 11.

[47] See Chapter 14.

[48] See Efraty, Ravit (March 1995) An Introduction to Index Swaps and Notes; Salomon Brothers US Derivatives Research Fixed Income Derivatives, New York.

[49] A variety of bond price indexes are published by a variety of investment banks, including Salomon Brothers, Lehman Brothers, Goldman Sachs, JP Morgan etc. The indexes are available on a variety of underlying bond universes – for example, investment grade, high yield, emerging market, specific currency markets etc.

[50] Bond index swaps are similar to equity swaps, see Das, Satyajit (2004) Structured Products volume 2; John Wiley & Sons (Asia), Singapore at Chapter 1.

Exhibit 19.51   Interest Rate Basket Linked Notes

The transaction structure described emerged in the aftermath of the September 1992 European exchange rate mechanism ("ERM") crisis and the subsequent (in August 1993) widening of the ERM bands. Against a background of expectations of lower or declining rates, albeit with some volatility (particularly in the higher yielding European community currencies), a number of investors sought to purchase structured notes that created a diversified view on declines in European rates. The diversified structure embedded in the basket linked note was designed to lower the risk of market events *in any one market* affecting the investor's strategy.

The terms of the transaction are as follows:

Amount	US$100 million
Maturity	3 years
Issue Price	100%
Coupon	5.25% pa payable annually
Redemption	100% + 15 × (Average of Basket at commencement − Average of Basket at maturity)
Basket	Swedish Kroner ("SEK"), Italian Lira ("LIT"), Spanish Pesetas ("ESP") and French Franc ("FFR") 3 year Constant Maturity Swap Rates

The note pays out the average of SKR, LIT, ESP and FFR 3 year rates. The rates used are the constant maturity swap ("CMS") rates. Each basis point fall of the basket average increases the redemption payment by 15 bps. The structure effectively combines a bond with the forward purchase by the investor of the basket. There is an embedded option to prevent the redemption from becoming negative.

The return to the investor in this transaction is driven by the path of the selected basket rates and reflects the following factors:

- The actual movements in each yield curve relative to the implied forward three year rates in each currency.
- The leverage factor included in this case gears the investor's return to enhance sensitivity to market movements. A more risk averse structure could be engineered to guarantee a minimum redemption amount. The minimum redemption would incorporate the purchase of a put on the price of the basket (call on yield) to offset the risk of rising rates. The purchased put converts the transaction into a synthetic call purchase.
- The currency protection of the structure, whereby all payments are in US$. In effect, the incorporation of a quanto option to eliminate the currency risk of the structure.

The basic structure incorporates no optionality. However, a variation on the structure embeds a call option on the basket. The coupon level is reduced to finance the purchase of a call option that provides asymmetric exposure to a fall in interest rates on a diversified basis. The basket option pricing would reflect the impact of volatility of the individual currency CMS rates and the correlation between the changes. The volatility of the average will be highest for highly correlated rates. A decline in correlations will reduce the volatility. This means that the basket volatility will substantially be a function of the degree of correlation between the basket elements that will influence the option pricing. A basket that incorporates interest rate markets in different currencies is designed to reduce the correlation to effectively lower the cost of the option. This allows a higher level of effective exposure to the basket to be created at a lower cost.

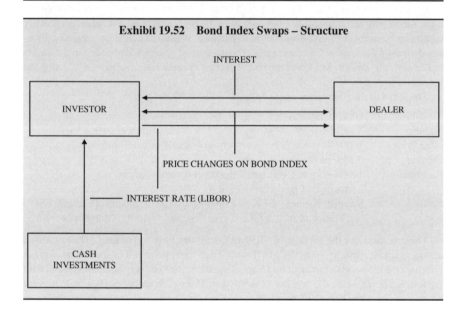

Exhibit 19.52   Bond Index Swaps – Structure

The major advantages of bond index linked notes (as with the bond index swap) include:

- The ability to gain diversified exposure to selected bond markets. This is achieved without the difficulties of physical replication of an index, including tracking errors and re-balancing costs.
- Lower operational costs through avoiding physical purchase of securities including back-office, custody and settlement costs.
- Potential tax benefits for some investors unable to recover withholding tax on bonds in certain markets.
- Ability to short bond markets without the need to liquidate physical holdings.
- Ability to enhance return through:
  1. Receiving index returns combined with purchase of higher yielding floating rate assets to generate above index returns.
  2. Transferring funds management expertise in one bond market into different markets by paying the index on that market and receiving the desired bond index.
- The off-balance sheet nature of the transaction that increases its capital efficiency.

Exhibit 19.53   Bond Index Swaps – Terms

Total Return Swap on Bond Index

Amount	US$100 million
Maturity	1 year
Investor Receives	Total Return of [Nominated Index]
Investor Pays	1 month LIBOR plus [margin]
Payment/Resets	All payments and index resets are monthly

Total Return Swap on Currency (Deutschemark ("DEM")) Sector of Index

Amount	US$100 million
Maturity	1 year
Investor Receives	[(end period US$/DEM)/(beginning period US$/DEM) times (1 + Total Return on DEM sector of [Nominated Index] − 1
Investor Pays	1 month LIBOR plus [margin]
Payment/Resets	All payments and index resets are monthly.

Exhibit 19.54   Bond Index Swaps – Return Computation[51]

Index returns are calculated on several basis local currency terms, base currency terms, unhedged and currency hedged.

The local currency return is calculated as follows:

Total rate of return = [(End Period Value/Beginning Period Value) −1] × 100
Where
Beginning Period Value = (Beginning Price + Beginning Accrued Interest) × Beginning
Par Amount Outstanding
End Period Value = (End Price + End Accrued) × (Beginning Par Amount Outstanding −
Principal Repayments) + Coupon Payments + Principal Payments +
Reinvestment Income

The local currency sector return is the weighted average of individual bond returns using each bond's beginning of month market value as its weight.

The base currency return is calculated by multiplying the local currency return by the end of period exchange rate divided by the beginning of period currency exchange rate.

The calculation of the next total return payment of a currency hedged return is as follows:

Total rate of return = [(End Period Value/Beginning Period Value) −1] × 100

---

[51]   This is based on Efraty, Ravit (March 1995) An Introduction to Index Swaps and Notes; Salomon Brothers US Derivatives Research Fixed Income Derivatives, New York.

Where

Beginning Period Value = ((Beginning Price + Beginning Accrued Interest) × Beginning Par Amount Outstanding × (Beginning of Period Spot Exchange Rate))

End Period Value = [(Yield for Forward Settlement at End of 1 month + Expected Change In Accrued Interest Over 1 Month + Cash Flow and Reinvestment Income) × Beginning of Period 1 Month Forward Exchange Rate] + [Change In Market Value of Principal Amount Due to Yield Change × [End of Period Spot Exchange Rate]

The currency hedged base currency sector return is the weighted average of individual bond returns using each bond's beginning of month market value as its weight.

Exhibit 19.55   Bond Index Linked Notes

1. Terms

Amount	US$100 million
Term	1 year
Coupon	0% pa
Redemption	Par plus or minus Total Return of [Nominated Index] minus [margin]

2. Structural Decomposition

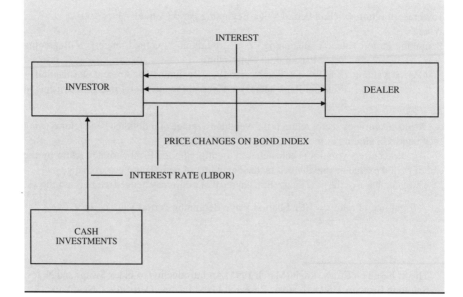

8   Summary

Interest rate linked notes are bonds with structured exposure to interest rate risk. The exposure to interest rate risk is created by linking the value of the coupon or principal repayments to an identified interest rate or prices of a specific debt security. A variety of structures have emerged allowing investors to monetise specific views in relation to the shape of forward interest rates and/or interest rate volatility. The structures are now well accepted and available in a wide variety of currencies. Increasingly, investors combine multiple building blocks to match their requirements and/or market expectations. **Exhibit 19.56** sets out an example of this type of activity.

Exhibit 19.56   Interest Rate Linked Notes – Investor Application

In 2002/2003, the US$ yield curve was characterised by low absolute rates and a steep slope. Assume the investor is a floating rate investor. In the existing environment it would earn around US$ LIBOR flat on a 5 year FRN. The investor is seeking to enhance yields on its investments. The investor's expectation is US$ short term rates will stay low and perhaps decline further. The investor believes that the forward curve is overestimating the rate of increase in US$ LIBOR.

The investor could consider an investment in a 5 year US$ inverse FRN[52] on the following terms:

Coupon:	1st 6 months: 4.00% pa
	Next 4 years 6 months: 5.00% minus 3 month US$ LIBOR
Minimum Rate:	0% pa

Depending upon the investors risk appetite and price/rate expectations, the basic investment structure can be amended as follows:

• If the investor is willing to take re-investment risk, then a callable feature can be embedded in the inverse FRN to further enhance returns. The terms of the callable inverse FRN[53] would be as follows:

Coupon:	1st 6 months: 4.50% pa
	Next 4 years 6 months: 6.25% minus 3 month US$ LIBOR
Minimum Rate:	0% pa
Call Option:	Callable, at the option of the Issuer, on any interest payment date after 6 months

• If the investor is willing to take re-investment and also leverage its position, then leverage can be incorporated in the inverse FRN to further enhance returns. The terms of the

---

[52]   See discussion earlier in Chapter.
[53]   See discussion earlier in Chapter.

callable leveraged inverse FRN[54] would be as follows:

Coupon: 1st 6 months: 4.70% pa
                     Next 4 years 6 months: 7.30% minus 2 time 3 month US$ LIBOR
Minimum Rate: 0% pa
Call Option: Callable, at the option of the Issuer, on any interest payment date after
                     6 months

- If the investor is unwilling to take re-investment or leverage its position, then other features can be embedded in the inverse FRN to enhance returns. For example, if the investor expects US$ 3 month LIBOR to trade within a narrow range then a range accrual[55] feature can be embedded in the inverse FRN. The terms of the range accrual inverse FRN would be as follows:

Coupon: 1st 6 months: 5.00% pa
                     Next 4 years 6 months: (6.50% minus 3 month US$ LIBOR) times
                     Accrual Factor
Minimum Rate: 0% pa
Accrual Factor: Number of days that US$ 3 month LIBOR is fixed within the
                     following range divided by the number of days in the relevant period:
                     Year 1: 0–2.00% pa
                     Year 2: 0–3.00% pa
                     Year 3: 0–4.00% pa
                     Year 4: 0–5.00% pa
                     Year 5: 0–6.00% pa

- If the investor is willing to assume additional credit risk, a credit default swap[56] can be embedded in the range accrual inverse FRN to enhance returns. For example, if the investor is willing to assume credit risk on Daimler Chrysler then a credit linked note with range accrual inverse FRN features can be structured. The terms of the range credit linked accrual inverse FRN would be as follows:

Coupon: 1st 6 months: 5.00% pa
                     Next 4 years 6 months: (8.00% minus 3 month US$ LIBOR) times
                     Accrual Factor
Minimum Rate: 0% pa
Accrual Factor: Number of days that US$ 3 month LIBOR is fixed within the
                     following range divided by the number of days in the relevant period:
                     Year 1: 0–2.00% pa
                     Year 2: 0–3.00% pa
                     Year 3: 0–4.00% pa
                     Year 4: 0–5.00% pa
                     Year 5: 0–6.00% pa

---

[54] See discussion earlier in Chapter.
[55] See discussion earlier in Chapter.
[56] See discussion earlier in Chapter.

Reference Entity:	Daimler Chrysler
Credit Event and Settlement:	If a credit event (defined as bankruptcy, failure to pay and bankruptcy) occurs in respect of the Reference Entity, then the FRN will terminate. In the event of termination, the investor will be delivered defaulted bonds issued by the Reference Entity equal to the face value of the FRN.

The variety of structures illustrates the use of different structure either on a stand alone basis or in combination to design investment alternatives for investors to monetise market expectations.

20
Currency Linked Notes

1 Overview

Currency linked notes are bonds with structured exposure to currency risk. The exposure is created by linking the coupon or principal repayments to changes in an identified currency. Currency linked notes are a specific type of synthetic assets[1]. The transactions are driven by investor requirements for structured exposure to currency movements. The different types of currency linked notes are discussed in this Chapter.

The structure of this Chapter is as follows:

- The types of currency linked notes are outlined.
- Individual currency linked note structures are then described and analysed.

The focus is on the analysis of the structures, value dynamics for investors, and pricing/hedging of the structures.

2 Currency Linked Notes – Types[2]

Currency linked notes are bonds (fixed or floating) where the coupon and/or the principal payments are linked to currency movements. The structures entail conventional bonds with embedded currency derivatives.

Currency linked notes allow investors to assume structured exposure to specified currency changes. The investor's objectives include enhancement of return or

---

[1]   See Chapter 4.

[2]   For examples of currency linked notes, see Koh, Kenny (1986) Option or Forward Swap Related Financing Structures Unpublished research paper presented to course on Swap Financing, Centre for Studies in Money, Banking and Finance, Macquarie University; Cunningham, Michael M (1987) Selected Analysis of Recently Issued Index-Linked and Option Embedded Securities; unpublished research paper presented to course on Swap Financing, Centre for Studies in Money, Banking and Finance, Macquarie University; Das, Satyajit "Option Swaps: Securitising Options Embedded in Securities Issues" (Summer 1988) Journal of International Securities Markets 117–138.

monetisation of anticipated currency movements over the term of the investment. The structures allow investors to create exposures/assume risk that is not available directly. Demand for currency linked notes is driven by investor acceptance of the structured note investment format. This is in preference to the underlying derivative format[3].

Currency linked notes are combinations of bonds and currency derivatives. The derivatives used are generally standard or non generic structures traded in the derivatives market. The currency is priced/hedged by decomposing the structure into the individual components. The components are then priced and hedged normally. The ability to decompose currency linked notes into liquid available components is critical. This allows the structures to be constructed, traded and hedged.

Issuers of currency linked notes include natural issuers (arbitrage funding entities[4]) or special purpose repackaging vehicles[5]. The transaction structure is designed to insulate the issuer from the impact of the embedded currency derivative component through a transaction entered into with the dealer arranging the transaction. This is achieved by hedging the exposure of the issuer through a hedging structure that ensures funding at a known cost.

There are several types of currency linked note structures, including:

- **Dual currency structures** – this entails notes where the coupon is denominated in a currency *different* from the currency of the principal.
- **Currency linked structures** – these include a wide range of note structures entailing structured currency risk. The notes feature a bond combined with a currency derivative (forward or option). The derivative is used to alter the coupon or principal payments of a conventional bond to create specific exposure to currency movements.
- **Exotic option embedded structures** – these are notes featuring embedded exotic currency options such as barrier and digital options.

3 Dual Currency Notes

3.1 Concept[6]

A dual currency bond involves an issue where the interest coupon is denominated in a different currency to the underlying principal of the bond. For example, a dual

---

[3] See discussion in Chapter 4.
[4] See Chapter 3.
[5] See Chapter 4.
[6] See Jones, W.R. (1987) Dual Currency Bonds; unpublished research paper presented to course on Capital Raising, Centre for Studies in Money, Banking and Finance,

currency US$/Swiss franc bond may be structured to have interest payable in Swiss francs and the principal in US$ or vice versa.

There are two basic structures:

- **Dual currency bonds** – this is usually a bond structured with coupons payable in the currency of the investor and the principal payable in a foreign currency. For example, in the case of a Yen based investor, this would entail an initial investment in Yen, interest coupons in Yen and *a principal redemption in a foreign currency (US$)*.
- **Reverse dual currency bonds** – this is usually a bond structured with coupons payable in a foreign currency and the principal payable in the currency of the investor. For example, in the case of a Yen investor, this would entail an initial investment in Yen, principal redemption in Yen and *interest coupons denominated in a foreign currency (A$)*.

The fundamental difference between the structures is the nature and extent of foreign exchange risk assumed. In a dual currency bond, the currency risk is on the full principal value of the investment. In a reverse dual currency bond, the currency risk is on the interest coupons only.

3.2 Economics and Structure

The structure of a dual currency note effectively combines the following elements:
- A fixed interest bond.
- A single or a series of currency forward contracts to convert the principal or coupon flows into the desired currency.

Exhibit 20.1 sets out an example of a dual currency bond. The transaction is a Yen/US$ dual currency bond. The transaction described is one of the earliest dual currency bonds undertaken. These transactions were undertaken in the 1980s. The initial transactions were Swiss Franc ("SFR") bonds where the redemption was in US$. The bonds typically were of long maturity (8 to 10 years) and carried coupons around 100 to 200 bps higher than comparable SFR bonds. The US$ redemption structure was at an implied US$/SFR rate of 1.60 to 1.90 which compared to the

Macquarie University; Rosenberg, M.R. "The Pricing of Dual Currency Bonds" (November 1985) Intermarket 40–52; Crabbe, M. "Are Two Currencies Better Than One?" (October 1985) Euromoney 206–207; Sender, H "The Dual Currency Phenomenon" (April 1986) Institutional Investor 254–257.

Exhibit 20.1 Dual Currency Notes	
Principal Amount	Yen 25,000 million
Term	5 years
Coupon	7.75% pa payable annually in Yen
Redemption Amount	US$115.956 million (payable in US$)

US$1:SFR 2.00 spot rate prevailing at the time of issue. The concept was extended to Yen bonds where the principal redemption was in US$.

In the example, the investor makes a Yen investment and receives Yen coupons. The principal of the bond is redeemed in US$. The coupon on the dual currency bond was around 100 to 150 bps above yields on comparable Yen securities. The implied exchange rate on redemption was US$1:Yen 215.60. This was below the prevailing spot rate which was around US$1:Yen 235.

The instrument was targeted at a Japanese investor and has the following characteristics:

- The investor has *no currency exposure on the coupon payments of the note*. This reflects the fact that the note pays interest in Yen.
- The investor receives a coupon that is *higher* than the Yen interest rate for a comparable investment.
- The investor has a *currency exposure on the principal amount of the investment*. This reflects the fact that the principal redemption is in US$ (a currency other than the home currency of the investor).

Exhibit 20.2 sets out the return profile of the investor under different currency (US$/Yen) scenarios. The analysis illustrates the economic characteristics of the security:

- If the US$/Yen exchange rate at maturity is the same as the embedded redemption exchange rate, then the realised return to the investor is equivalent to the coupon rate of 7.75% pa.
- If the dual currency note US$ principal is hedged back to Yen (through the entry into a forward contract to sell US$/purchase Yen at the prevailing forward rate at the time of entry into the transaction), then the investor return is around 6.28% pa. This is equivalent to the approximate Yen return on a *Yen denominated* conventional security with comparable characteristics. This reflects the fact that where the US$ principal amount is hedged into Yen, the bond is economically a Yen security.

Exhibit 20.2 Economics of Dual Currency Notes

The **Table** below sets out the issue cash flows together with the realised return to the investor under four US$/Yen exchange rate scenarios:

- The US$/Yen rate at maturity coincides with the embedded redemption exchange rate of US$1:Yen 215.60.
- The prevailing US$/Yen forward rates.
- The US$/Yen rate remains at the level at the time of issue of US$1:Yen 236.80.
- A steady depreciation of the US$/Yen exchange rate by 5% pa.

Table – Issue Cash Flows

Period (Years)	Dual Currency Bond Principal & Interest (Yen)	Principal Redemption (US$)	Case 1: Embedded Redemption Exchange Rate Yen/US$ Rate	Bond Cash Flows (Yen)	Case 2: Forward Exchange Rate Yen/US$ Rate	Bond Cash Flows (Yen)
0	-25,000,000,000			-25,000,000,000		-25,000,000,000
1	1,937,500,000			1,937,500,000		1,937,500,000
2	1,937,500,000			1,937,500,000		1,937,500,000
3	1,937,500,000			1,937,500,000		1,937,500,000
4	1,937,500,000			1,937,500,000		1,937,500,000
5	1,937,500,000	115,956,000	215.60	26,937,500,000	197.60	24,850,405,600
			Realised Yen Yield	7.750%	Realised Yen Yield	6.28%

	Dual Currency Bond		Case 3: Spot Exchange Rate at Commencement		Case 4: 5% pa Depreciation in Exchange Rate	
Period (Years)	Principal & Interest (Yen)	Principal Redemption (US$)	Yen/US$ Rate	Bond Cash Flows (Yen)	Yen/US$ Rate	Bond Cash Flows (Yen)
0	−25,000,000,000			−25,000,000,000		−25,000,000,000
1	1,937,500,000			1,937,500,000	236.8000	1,937,500,000
2	1,937,500,000			1,937,500,000	224.9600	1,937,500,000
3	1,937,500,000			1,937,500,000	213.7120	1,937,500,000
4	1,937,500,000			1,937,500,000	203.0264	1,937,500,000
5	1,937,500,000	115,956,000	236.80	29,395,880,800	192.8751	1,937,500,000
					183.2313	23,184,271,638
			Realised Yen Yield	9.38%	Realised Yen Yield	5.03%

- If the US$/Yen exchange rate remains at the level prevailing at the time of entry into the transaction, then the investor return is 9.38% pa.
- If the US$ depreciates over the life of the security against the Yen at a rate of 5% pa, then the return to the investor is around 5.03% pa. This represents a reduction in yield of around 120 bps against a Yen investment.

The analysis of the performance of the security illustrates its economic nature. The additional yield from the dual currency note structure is generated from the combination of the bond with a currency forward. In the above example, the additional return of around 100–150 bps is derived from the fact that the US$ is at a substantial discount relative to Yen in the forward market, reflecting the higher interest rates in US$ relative to Yen. The additional coupon represents the value of this discount that is captured by the investor and then amortised across the coupons of the bond. In addition, the embedded forward is *off market*. This is an additional source of value. In effect, the investor is purchasing a US$ forward at the embedded redemption exchange rate of Yen 215.60. At the time of entry into this transaction, the implied forward (based on interest rate differentials between the currencies) was around US$1:Yen 197.60. This means that the investor is purchasing US$ at an above market rate. The extra payment is used to enhance the coupon of the dual currency bond itself.

The structure entails the investor having a position in the forward US$/Yen exchange rate. The position monetises the expectation that the forward rates *overestimate* the depreciation in the US$ relative to the Yen. Given that the currency forwards are based on the prevailing interest rate differential, the dual currency note entails positions in movements in the US$/Yen spot rate and in the interest rate differential. To the extent that the *actual spot* US$/Yen rates are *above* the implied forward rates, the investor will realise a higher economic return from the investment.

In effect, the dual currency note structure is designed to engineer an exposure to the path of currency rates. This allows the investor to monetise a view that the spot rates at the relevant dates will prove to be different from that implied by the forward currency rate structure.

Exhibit 20.3 sets out an example of a reverse dual currency bond. In this example, the principal of the bond is set in Yen while the coupon of the bond is denominated in A$. The coupon on the bond is calculated as the yield applied to the A$ equivalent of the Yen principal at the spot rate applicable at the start of the transaction.

The instrument is targeted at a Japanese investor. It has the following characteristics:

Exhibit 20.3 Dual Currency Notes	
Term	10 years
Principal Amount	Yen 20,000 million
Coupon	8.00% pa payable annually. The coupon is payable in A$ calculated on A$ equivalent of the Yen principal amount at the A$/Yen rate at the time of issue (assumed to be A$1:Yen 118) equal to A$169,491,525. This equates to an annual cash flow of A$13,559,322.
Redemption Amount	Yen 20,000 million (payable in Yen).

- The investor has *no currency exposure on the principal face value of the note*. This reflects the fact that the note redeems in Yen.
- The investor receives a coupon that is *higher* than the comparable Yen interest rate for a comparable investment.
- The investor has a *currency exposure on the interest coupons*. This reflects the fact that the coupons are payable in A$ (a currency other than the home currency of the investor).

Exhibit 20.4 sets out the return profile of the investor under different currency (A$/Yen) scenarios. The analysis illustrates the economic characteristics of the security:
- If the A$/Yen exchange rate remains at the level prevailing at the start of the transaction, the realised return to the investor is equivalent to the coupon rate of 8.00% pa.
- If the dual currency note A$ coupons are hedged back to Yen through the entry into a series of forward contracts to sell A$/purchase Yen, then the investor return is around 5.79% pa. This is equivalent to the approximate Yen return on a *Yen denominated* conventional security with comparable characteristics. This reflects the fact that where the A$ coupons are hedged into Yen, economically the bond is a Yen security.
- If the A$ depreciates over the life of the bond vis a vis the Yen at a rate of 5% pa, then the return to the investor is around 6.39% pa. This represents an additional yield of around 50–60 bps against a Yen investment.

The analysis of the performance of the security illustrates its economic nature. The additional yield from the dual currency note structure is generated from the combination of the bond with the currency forwards. In the above example, the additional yield of around 221 bps is derived from the fact that the A$ is at a

Exhibit 20.4 Economics of Dual Currency Notes

The **Table** below sets out the issue cash flows together with the realised return to the investor under three A$/Yen exchange rate scenarios:

- The A$/Yen rate remains at the level at the time of issue of A$1:Yen 118.
- The prevailing A$/Yen forward rates.
- A steady depreciation of the A$/Yen exchange rate by 5% pa.

| | Bond Cash Flows | | Realised Return to Investors | | Realised Return to Investors | | Realised Return to Investors | |
| | | | Case 1: Steady Currency | | Case 2: Forward Currency Rates | | Case 3: 5% Depreciation | |
Period (Years)	Principal Yen	Interest A$	Yen/A$ Rate	Bond Cash Flows (in Yen)	Yen/A$ Rate	Bond Cash Flows (in Yen)	Yen/A$ Rate	Bond Cash Flows (in Yen)
0	−20,000,000,000		118.00	−20,000,000,000	118.00	−20,000,000,000	118.0000	−20,000,000,000
1		13,559,322	118.00	1,600,000,000	109.35	1,482,730,506	112.1000	1,520,000,000
2		13,559,322	118.00	1,600,000,000	101.55	1,376,936,365	106.4950	1,444,000,000
3		13,559,322	118.00	1,600,000,000	94.23	1,277,681,719	101.1703	1,371,800,000
4		13,559,322	118.00	1,600,000,000	86.94	1,178,804,337	96.1117	1,303,210,000
5		13,559,322	118.00	1,600,000,000	81.27	1,178,804,337	91.3062	1,303,210,000
6		13,559,322	118.00	1,600,000,000	75.85	1,101,984,082	86.7408	1,238,049,500
7		13,559,322	118.00	1,600,000,000	70.84	1,028,539,295	82.4038	1,176,147,025
8		13,559,322	118.00	1,600,000,000	65.48	960,483,943	78.2836	1,117,339,674
9		13,559,322	118.00	1,600,000,000	60.89	887,826,856	74.3694	1,061,472,690
10	20,000,000,000	13,559,322	118.00	21,600,000,000	56.39	20,764,671,668	70.6510	20,957,979,103
			Realised Yen Yield	8.000%		5.787%		6.392%

substantial discount relative to Yen in the forward market, reflecting the higher interest rates in A$ relative to Yen. The additional coupon represents the value of this discount that is captured by the investor, and then amortised across the coupons of the bond.

The structure entails the investor having a position in the forward A$/Yen exchange rate. The position monetises the expectation that the forward rates *overestimate* the depreciation in the A$ relative to the Yen. The dual currency note entails positions on movements in the A$ spot rate and in the interest rate differential. To the extent that the *actual spot* A$/Yen rates are *above* the implied forward rates, the investor will realise a higher economic return from the investment.

In effect, the dual currency note structure is designed to engineer an exposure to the path of currency rates. The investor is seeking to monetise the view that the spot rates at the relevant dates will prove to be different from that implied by the forward currency rate structure[7]. In the dual currency structure, the investor takes a position on a single forward. In the reverse dual currency structure, the investor takes a position on a series of forwards. The reverse dual currency position is more path dependent.

3.3   Pricing, Trading and Hedging Dual Currency Notes

The creation of a dual currency note structure requires both engineering of the currency exposure for the investor and the immunisation of the issuer from that exposure. The issuer will generally seek to enter into a series of hedges that eliminates the specific currency exposure and provides a guaranteed rate of funding. The hedge of a dual currency issue entails separate transactions involving currency/interest rate swaps and a series of currency forward (LTFX[8]) contracts.

For example, for the Yen/US$ dual currency issue (coupons denominated in Yen and principal in US$), the issuer would enter into a currency forward contract to hedge the US$ to Yen create a synthetic Yen liability. This would then be swapped into floating rate US$ through a currency swap. In the case of a reverse dual currency

---

[7]   This is not substantially different from the positions in respect of the forward interest rate curve embedded in interest rate structured investments and derivatives.

[8]   LTFX equates to Long Term Foreign Exchange and is sometimes used in connection with forward foreign exchange contracts with longer maturities (say, beyond 1 year); see Das, Satyajit (2004) Derivative Products & Pricing; John Wiley & Sons (Asia), Singapore at Chapter 3.

bond issue (A\$ coupon and Yen principal), the hedges would include a series of A\$/Yen currency forward contracts to hedge the A\$ coupons to Yen. This creates a Yen liability. This would then be swapped into floating rate US\$ through a currency swap.

Exhibit 20.5 sets out the mechanics of hedging the Yen/US\$ dual currency bond issue. **Exhibit 20.6** sets out the mechanics of hedging the Yen/A\$ reverse dual currency bond issue.

The dual currency bond swap layers a complex initial transaction with a series of foreign exchange and swap transactions basically designed to generate, at least initially, cost-effective floating rate US\$ funding.

Exhibit 20.5   Hedging Dual Currency
Note Transactions

Assume a dealer is asked to price a Yen/US\$ dual currency swap in connection with the following issue:

Issuer	AA rated Financial Institution
Term	5 years
Principal Amount	Yen 25,000 million
Coupon	7.75% pa payable annually in Yen
Redemption Amount	US\$115.956 million (payable in US\$)

The issuer of the bond wishes to be completely immunised from the dual currency characteristics of the transaction. The issuer wants to use it as a basis for generating LIBOR based US\$ floating rate funding. The dealer enters into a structured currency swap where:
- At closing, the issuer pays the Yen 25 billion proceeds to the dealer in return for receiving the equivalent amount of US\$105,529,759 (based on a spot exchange rate of US\$1:Yen 236.90).
- Over the life of the transaction, the issuer pays US\$ 6 month LIBOR minus a margin semi-annually in return for receiving Yen 1,937,500,000 (the exact Yen coupon due to the bondholders, thereby eliminating any currency exposure).
- At maturity, the initial exchange is reversed, with the issuer paying US\$105,529,759 to the dealer in return for receiving US\$115,956,000 (covering the redemption of the dual currency issue). In practice, there would only be a net settlement on this part of the transaction.

In order to hedge its exposure under the transaction with the issuer, the dealer will enter into two sets of transactions:
- A US\$/Yen currency forward contract selling US\$115,956,000/buying the equivalent Yen for value in Year 5 (matching the maturity of the dual currency bond issue). This transaction is undertaken at the prevailing US\$/Yen forward rate of US\$1:Yen 197.60.

- A conventional Yen fixed US$ floating LIBOR swap under which it receives Yen at the market rate of 7.00% pa and pays US$ 6 month LIBOR minus margin.

The currency forward contract creates a synthetic Yen liability at 6.28% pa as set out in the Table below.

Period (Years)	Principal & Interest (Yen)	Principal Redemption (US$)	Yen/USD Rate	Bond Cash Flows (Yen)
0	−25,000,000,000			−25,000,000,000
1	1,937,500,000			1,937,500,000
2	1,937,500,000			1,937,500,000
3	1,937,500,000			1,937,500,000
4	1,937,500,000			1,937,500,000
5	1,937,500,000	115,956,000	197.60	24,850,405,600

Realised Yen Yield   6.28%

The transaction has the effect of creating funding for the issuer at US$ LIBOR minus 79 bps pa (assuming the full benefit is passed on to the issuer). This is calculated as follows:

Dealer receives   Yen at 7.00% pa annual
Dealer pays   Yen at 6.28% pa annual
Yen Surplus   Yen 72 bps pa

The Yen surplus of 72 bps pa translates into 79 bps pa in US$. This is based on a currency conversion factor where Yen 1 bps is equal to US$ 1.1 bps[9].

Exhibit 20.6   Hedging Reverse Dual Currency Note Transactions

Assume a dealer is asked to price a Yen/A$ dual currency swap in connection with the following issue:

Issuer   AA rated Financial Institution
Term   10 years
Principal Amount   Yen 20,000 million
Coupon   8.00% pa payable annually.
    The coupon is payable in A$ calculated on the A$ equivalent
    of the Yen principal amount at the A$/Yen rate at the time of

---

[9]   For details of the calculation of currency conversion factors (also known as foreign exchange basis points), see Das, Satyajit (2004) Derivative Products & Pricing; John Wiley & Sons (Asia), Singapore at Chapter 11.

	issue (assumed to be A$1:Yen 118) equal to A$169,491,525. This equates to an annual cash flow of A$13,559,322.
Redemption Amount	Yen 20,000 million (payable in Yen).

The issuer of the bond wishes to be completely immunised from the dual currency characteristics of the transaction. The issuer seeks to use it as a basis for LIBOR based US$ floating rate funding. The dealer enters into a structured currency swap where:

- At closing, the issuer pays the Yen 20 billion proceeds to the dealer in return for receiving the equivalent amount of US$129,728,814 (based on a spot exchange rate of US$1:Yen 154.17).
- Over the life of the transaction, the issuer pays US$ 6 month LIBOR minus a margin (say 20bps pa) semi-annually in return for receiving A$13,559,322 (the exact A$ coupon due to the bond holders, thereby eliminating any currency exposure).
- At maturity, the initial exchange is reversed, with the issuer paying US$129,728,814 to the dealer in return for receiving Yen 20 billion (covering the redemption of the dual currency issue).

In order to hedge its exposure under the transaction with the issuer, the dealer will enter into two sets of transactions:
- A conventional Yen fixed US$ floating LIBOR swap under which it receives Yen at the market rate of 5.78% pa and pays US$ 6 month LIBOR minus 20 bps.
- A series of A$/Yen currency forward contracts selling Yen 1,156 million/buying the equivalent A$.

The structure of the hedge and the detailed cash flows from the viewpoint of dealer are summarised below in the Table.

The Yen/US$ currency swap (which matches the US$ floating cash flows) leaves the dealer with net cash flows where it is long Yen (Yen 1,156,000,000) and short A$ (A$13,559,322) on each bond coupon date. The currency forward contracts are designed to cover this exposure. The currency forward contracts result in a distinctive pattern of cash flows. The dealer is short A$ in the early years. This reflects the fact that the Yen surplus does not, at the relevant currency forward rate, cover the A$ outflow. The dealer is long A$ in later years. This reflects the falling A$/Yen currency forward rates which result from the interest rate differential between A$ and Yen. The dealer has to fund this shortfall in the early years and recover the shortfall, together with the funding cost, from the surplus in later years.

Based on the assumed zero coupon interest rates, the dealer generates a profit (on a present value basis) of A$1,912,861 from this transaction. This profit is additional to any earnings generated by the dealer from the Yen/US$ swap on the currency forward contracts (presumably the bid-offer spread) or the dual currency issue itself.

Source: This example draws on Maxwell G W Morley "Swapping An Australian Dollar/Yen Dual Currency Bond Issue" in Satyajit Das (Editor) (1991) The Global Swap Market; IFR Publishing, London.

Table

Yen/US$ Swap

Years	Swap Payments		Swap Receipts	Receive Yen at 5.780% pa	Pay US$ LIBOR	Net Flows Yen	Net Flows A$
0	Yen	20,000,000,000	US$ −129,728,814	−20,000,000,000	129,728,814		−13,559,322
1	A$	−13,559,322	US$ LIBOR − Margin	1,156,000,000	(LIBOR − Margin)	1,156,000,000	−13,559,322
2	A$	−13,559,322	US$ LIBOR − Margin	1,156,000,000	(LIBOR − Margin)	1,156,000,000	−13,559,322
3	A$	−13,559,322	US$ LIBOR − Margin	1,156,000,000	(LIBOR − Margin)	1,156,000,000	−13,559,322
4	A$	−13,559,322	US$ LIBOR − Margin	1,156,000,000	(LIBOR − Margin)	1,156,000,000	−13,559,322
5	A$	−13,559,322	US$ LIBOR − Margin	1,156,000,000	(LIBOR − Margin)	1,156,000,000	−13,559,322
6	A$	−13,559,322	US$ LIBOR − Margin	1,156,000,000	(LIBOR − Margin)	1,156,000,000	−13,559,322
7	A$	−13,559,322	US$ LIBOR − Margin	1,156,000,000	(LIBOR − Margin)	1,156,000,000	−13,559,322
8	A$	−13,559,322	US$ LIBOR − Margin	1,156,000,000	(LIBOR − Margin)	1,156,000,000	−13,559,322
9	A$	−13,559,322	US$ LIBOR − Margin	1,156,000,000	(LIBOR − Margin)	1,156,000,000	−13,559,322
10	Yen	−20,000,000,000	US$ 129,728,814	20,000,000,000	−129,728,814	1,156,000,000	−13,559,322

Years	Net Flows Yen	Net Flows A$	Zero Coupon Interest Rates Yen	Zero Coupon Interest Rates A$	Currency Forward Rates (A$:Yen)	Net Cash Flow A$	Present Value A$
0					118.0000		
1	1,156,000,000	−13,559,322	6.84 %	15.29 %	109.3514	−2,987,896	−2,591,635
2	1,156,000,000	−13,559,322	6.72 %	15.04 %	101.5491	−2,175,661	−1,643,969
3	1,156,000,000	−13,559,322	6.59 %	14.89 %	94.2290	−1,291,340	−851,518
4	1,156,000,000	−13,559,322	6.34 %	14.78 %	86.9968	−262,309	−151,129
5	1,156,000,000	−13,559,322	6.29 %	14.52 %	81.2713	664,637	337,425
6	1,156,000,000	−13,559,322	6.25 %	14.37 %	75.8548	1,680,325	750,794
7	1,156,000,000	−13,559,322	6.18 %	14.21 %	70.8357	2,760,135	1,088,934
8	1,156,000,000	−13,559,322	6.02 %	14.12 %	65.4772	4,095,670	1,423,741
9	1,156,000,000	−13,559,322	5.91 %	13.99 %	60.8855	5,427,134	1,670,205
10	1,156,000,000	−13,559,322	5.84 %	13.95 %	56.3945	6,939,118	1,880,014

Net Cash Flow   1,912,861

3.4   Market for Dual Currency Notes

The market for dual currency notes has evolved significantly over the period since inception. The earliest transactions were undertaken in the 1970s. These transactions were designed to allow (primarily European) investors to take positions in currency markets. A key driver was that it would otherwise have been difficult for the investors to take currency positions directly. The concept has been applied since that time under the appropriate market conditions. The use of dual currency notes has expanded to encompass a broader range of applications, including:

- **Regulatory arbitrage** – this entails the dual currency bond being decomposed into a zero coupon bond and an annuity bond (in different currencies). In this form, it can be used to arbitrage tax rules in certain jurisdictions.
- **Income versus capital distinction** – the structure can also be used to overcome income/capital distinctions. The Japanese investor targeted dual currency transactions are often predicated on specific regulatory issues. Under Japanese insurance laws, Japanese life insurers are only allowed to distribute dividends/bonuses from the income on investments. Realised capital gains or losses, as well as foreign exchange gains or losses, are charged to reserves and capital accounts. These items are excluded from any calculation of income out of which distribution could be made. This dictates that the insurers seek to increase yield or income on the portfolios to allow higher rates of distribution. The dual currency structures are consistent with this objective. Higher income is received over the life of the investment. The expected loss embedded in the structure (for example, in a dual currency structure from the embedded redemption exchange rate) economically offsets this higher early income, but may be classified as a foreign exchange or capital item, and therefore not included in the determination of income available for distribution.
- **Higher yield** – the structure has been used to generate higher yielding securities with limited currency exposure. In the case of a dual currency structure, the exposure is on the redemption face value but not on the coupons. In a reverse dual currency structure, the currency exposure is only in relation to the coupons, with the principal amount being protected.
- **Forward currency rate monetisation** – use of dual currency structures to monetise expectations in relation to the forward currency rate curve.

The major emphasis in relation to dual currency notes is yield enhancement and monetisation of currency expectations, although the other objectives are also relevant. **Exhibit 20.7** sets out examples of dual currency issues undertaken in

Exhibit 20.7   Dual Currency Notes – Examples

DEM/Yen Reverse Dual Currency Note

Amount	Yen 100 billion
Maturity	10 years
Coupon	4.45% pa payable in Deutschemarks
Redemption Amount:	Yen 100 billion

A$/Yen Dual Currency Note

Amount	Yen 10 billion
Maturity	4 years
Coupon	6.20% pa payable in Yen
Redemption Amount	A$108.932 million (fixed redemption exchange rate of A$1: Yen 91.80)

A$/Yen Reverse Dual Currency Note

Amount	Yen 50 Billion
Maturity	2 years
Coupon	5.90% payable in Australian dollars
Redemption Amount	Yen 50 billion

Lira/US$ Reverse Dual Currency Note

Amount	US$100 million
Lira Notional Amount	The equivalent of the US$ Notional Amount at the Lira/US$ exchange rate
Issue Price	100%
Maturity	10 years
Coupon	7.85% pa payable in Italian Lira of the Lira Notional Amount on a annual basis calculated on a bond basis
Redemption Amount	US$100 million
Lira/US$ Exchange Rate	The exchange rate on the date the transaction is undertaken (1678)

the second half of the 1990s. The transactions were aimed primarily at Japanese investors seeking additional yield and prepared to trade off currency risk on the coupons in return for that additional yield[10]. More recently, there has been increasing interest in dual currency structures from European investors[11].

---

[10] "Yen Moves Unsettle Yield Hunters" (June 1997) Risk 35.

[11] See Mahtani, Arun "Dual Currency Bonds Provoke Derivative Headache" (27 June 1998) International Financing Review Issue 1239 114.

Exhibit 20.8 Callable Reverse Dual Currency Notes	
Transaction 1 – European Call	
Amount	Yen 10 billion
Maturity	10 years
Redemption Amount	Yen 10 billion
Coupon	A fixed amount of DEM 5,590,900 (calculated as 3.43% pa based on a DEM principal amount of DEM 163 million)
Call Option	The issuer has the right to call the note with 21 days notice on the coupon date at year 2
Transaction 2 – Bermudan Call	
Amount	Yen 10 billion
Maturity	10 years
Redemption Amount	Yen 10 billion
Coupon	A fixed amount of DEM 5,590,900 (calculated as 3.43% pa based on a DEM principal amount of DEM 163 million)
Call Option	The issuer has the right to call the note with 21 days notice on any coupon date after year 2

As opportunities for yield enhancement from dual currency structures diminished due to changes in market conditions, a number of alternative structures have evolved[12]. These include:

• **Callable reverse dual currency structures** – this structure combines a dual currency bond with embedded interest rate optionality through incorporation of a call option. **Exhibit 20.8** sets out an example of this structure. In the first case, a European option is incorporated. In the second case, a Bermudan call option is embedded. In both cases, the investor has sold an option in exchange for a higher coupon. The coupons on these structures provided between 5 and 10 bps pa additional yield over and above a normal dual currency structure to the investor. The enhanced yield is in exchange for the call risk assumed by the investor. The call risk under these types of structures is a mixture of currency and interest rate risk. The call may be triggered by changes in interest rates and/or currency rates. If early redemption occurs, then the investor forgoes future coupons denominated in foreign currency. From the viewpoint of a Yen based investor, this may represent an acceptable risk. This is because the redemption would provide the investor with Yen proceeds that could then be reinvested in Yen assets.

---

[12] See "Structured Derivatives as an Investment Vehicle" (September 1995) Asiamoney 52–55.

The issuer in these issues is fully hedged through a swap entered into with the arranger. The structure creates significant hedging risks. The hedging of these long dated options is problematic. This is particularly the case with the structures that incorporate a Bermudan option. Typically, the arranger would seek to enter into a long dated Bermudan currency option with a derivative dealer. The market for such options is illiquid. Often, the structures are hedged with shorter dated options, leaving the trader with a volatility spread position. The linkage of currency and interest rate risk creates additional complexity because of the need to incorporate the correlation between the two in pricing and hedging the structure.

- **Variable currency coupon or dual currency bonds with embedded currency options** – this structure entails a dual currency structure with embedded optionality. The issuer in these structures is allowed to select the coupon currency. The applicable rate is set at the time of issue. The selection is usually between two or more currencies. **Exhibit 20.9** sets out examples of this structure. The structure embeds an exchange or best-of option[13] within the note, allowing the issuer to pay the coupon which has the lowest value at the time of payment. The investor, in this case, is selling a series of *options on the currency pair or pairs*, with the premium received being used to enhance the yield on the security. The option sold is contingent both on currency value *and* the embedded interest rate in the relevant currency. The issuer would typically on-sell the option and immunise itself from any exposure to the option pay-offs.
- **Power reverse dual currency structures**[14] – this structure entails a dual currency bond where the coupon is an amount in a foreign currency less an amount in yen. The structure is designed to provide the investor with increased gearing on the coupon or yield on the security. **Exhibit 20.10** sets out an example of the power reverse dual currency structure.

Exhibit 20.9	Dual Currency Notes With Embedded Currency Options
Transaction 1	
Amount	Yen 10 billion
Maturity	10 years
Redemption Amount	Yen 10 billion
Coupon	On each interest payment date, the Issuer has the option of paying:
	1. A fixed amount of Yen 343 million (equivalent to 3.43% pa); or

---

[13] See Chapter 11.
[14] See Sippel, Jason and Ohkosi, Shoichi "All Power to PRDC Notes" (November 2002) Risk – Japan Risk Special Report S31–S33.

2. A fixed amount of DEM 5,590,900 (calculated as 3.43% pa based on a DEM principal amount of DEM 163 million).

Transaction 2

Amount	Yen 10 billion
Maturity	10 years
Issue Price	100.50
Redemption Amount	Yen 10 billion
Coupon:	On each interest payment date, the Issuer has the option of paying:

1. In A$ at a rate of 5.86% pa calculated on a specified A$ principal; or
2. In DEM at a rate of 5.31% pa calculated on a specified DEM principal; or
3. In US$ at a rate of 6.61% pa calculated on a specified US$ principal[15].

Exhibit 20.10   Power Reverse Dual Currency Notes

1. Structure

The structure entails a dual currency bond where the coupon is an amount in a foreign currency less an amount in Yen. The coupon is payable in a nominated currency after being converted into a single currency at the current exchange rate at the time of the payment. The coupon cannot be negative.

The typical terms are as follows:

Amount	Yen 10 billion
Maturity	(up to) 30 years
Redemption Amount	Yen 10 billion
Coupon Currency	Yen
Coupon	Maximum [C(US$) × Notional (US$) × (FX/Strike) − C (Yen) × Notional (Yen); 0]
	Where
	C (US$) = coupon in US$ (10.50% pa)
	Notional (US$) = notional amount in US$ based on the Yen notional principal converted at the spot rate at time of issuance of the note
	FX = US$/Yen exchange rate at the time of payment of the coupon
	Strike = Pre-agreed US$/Yen exchange rate
	C (Yen) = coupon in Yen (6.00% pa)
	Notional (Yen) = notional amount in Yen equivalent to face value of transaction

---

[15] The specified principal in each of the currencies is calculated as the spot value of the relevant currency against Yen based on the spot rate at the date of issue.

The key features of the structure include:
- The investor receives a fixed coupon (usually in US$ or other high yielding currency) and pays a fixed coupon in Yen.
- The coupon is subject to a minimum of 0% pa (that is, it can never be negative).

The economics of the structure are driven by the following factors:
- The investor has no currency exposure on the principal.
- The coupon structure provides the investor with exposure to the spot US$/Yen rate. The investor is effectively long a call on the foreign currency. The investor is also short a call on the Yen. The short call option is structured as an option spread as the coupon on the note cannot become negative.
- The structure has inherent leverage to currency movements. The leverage is driven by the coupon (the higher the foreign currency coupon rate) and the strike (the lower the strike, the higher the leverage embedded within the structure). This means that for a given coupon, leverage increases as the spread between the foreign currency and Yen coupon is reduced and the currency strike is lowered.

The demand for the structure is based on:
- The coupon structure provides a higher yield than a comparable reverse dual currency note.
- Japanese investors used the structure to monetise their view that the Yen would not increase in value against the foreign currency during the term of the note. In this regard, the structure is very similar to standard dual currency and reverse dual currency structures, where the investor monetises expectations about the future spot currency rate relative to the current implied currency forwards.

2. Variations
In practice, a number of variations on the basic structure have evolved:
- **Callable structure** – a variation on the basic structure is the callable power reverse dual currency note. Under this structure, the issuer has the right to call the note. The call option is usually structured as a Bermudan option. This increases the return to the investor. The investor assumes the risk of the call (specifically the US$/Yen currency rate and interest rates (US$ and Yen)). The call is designed to reduce the duration and consequently the currency risk to the investor. In general, investors consider the structure as a short (1 to 2 year) investment (up to the first call date) providing a high coupon (Yen LIBOR plus say, 300 bps). A variation on the callable structure entails the note being redeemed at a premium to enhance the investor's return. A further variation is a callable power dual currency note where, if the note is not called, the note is redeemed in US$ *not yen*.
- **Exotic options** – this structure incorporates a currency barrier option (knock-out)[16] to reduce the call risk. The knock out is designed to ensure that the note is redeemed prior to final maturity. The structures are generally adjusted to investor requirements. An outstrike (knock-out) set out-of-the money will be equivalent to a reverse knock-out (the note will knock-out/redeem in circumstances where the coupon on the note is high).

---

[16] See Chapter 9.

This structure will increase the coupon significantly. However, the risk of early termination is reduced. In contrast, the outstrike (knock-out) can be set closer to in-the-money levels. This will increase the possibility of early termination. This structure will result in a lower coupon but also reduces risk to the investor.

- **Currency option strikes** – the strikes within the structure can be varied to adjust the risk and return on the note. Common variations are step-up or step down strikes designed to adjust the currency risk over the term of the note.
- **Capped structures** – there are a number of variations where the coupon is capped, including:
  1. The coupon may be capped at a fixed level. The cap coupon level may be adjusted in accordance with a step up/step down pattern.
  2. The coupon may be adjusted using an embedded digital/binary option[17]. In this structure, the coupon is payable normally until the currency trades above a pre-agreed level (usually if the Yen strengthens significantly against the foreign currency). If this event occurs, then the coupon is fixed at a pre-agreed level for the remainder of the term of the note.

In practice, a number of the variations are combined within the same structure. The most common structure used is the power reverse dual currency structure incorporating a call option and/or currency barrier option.

4 Currency Linked Notes

4.1 Overview

Currency linked notes are characterised by the linkage between the coupon and/or the principal of the note and changes in a nominated exchange rate. The mechanics of the linkage are the same as those identified previously in connection with interest rate linked notes. There are some distinguishing features of the market for currency linked securities.

The major distinguishing feature is the nature of the underlying debt utilised. Currency linked structures exist in a wide variety of formats, including:

- Conventional fixed and floating securities.
- Bank loans.
- Off balance sheet derivative formats combined with underlying funding.

The currency linked structures using conventional fixed/floating securities and bank loans are similar. In each case, the coupon and/or principal payments are linked to currency rates.

---

[17] See Chapter 10.

Loan transactions with embedded currency positions have been used to lower the cost for the borrower. In general, the structure used is a conventional loan where the lender has the right to switch the currency of the interest and/or principal payments. For example, the loan may be denominated in US\$. The borrower pays US\$ 3 month LIBOR minus 50 bps (compared to its normal borrowing cost of LIBOR plus 100 bps). Under the structure, the lender has the right to ask for payment of interest in either US\$ or Yen (Yen 3 month LIBOR minus 40 bps) at each interest payment date. The borrower has effectively written a series of currency options. The premium received is embedded in the lower borrowing cost.

The transaction can be structured as an off balance format as well as embedded in the loan. This type of transaction typically takes the following form:

- The borrower arranges a fixed rate financing for a term of 5 years.
- Simultaneously, the borrower enters into a swap with a dealer, where the borrower agrees to receive fixed rate in the currency of the financing (US\$) and pay floating rate in its selected currency (Yen) at a rate of say, Yen LIBOR minus a margin per annum.
- Typically, following the first interest period, at every interest rate reset date the dealer has the right to receive interest at *either* Yen LIBOR minus say 50 bps or US\$ LIBOR minus 50 bps.

The dealer has a one time election to switch its interest receipts to US\$ LIBOR. If the dealer elects to exercise the option, then it will receive US\$ LIBOR for the remaining term of the swap. It is unable to switch from Yen to US\$ and reverse the selection during the life of the loan.

This structure effectively embeds a Yen put/US\$ call option into the currency swap. The borrower has written the Yen put/US\$ call. If the Yen declines in value relative to the US\$, then the dealer will make an election under the swap to receive US\$, capturing the foreign exchange gain. The premium due to the borrower for creating this option is embedded in the swap structure in the form of a lower margin under LIBOR.

The off balance sheet structure is almost identical to the loan. The structure described is embedded in the format for interest payments[18].

A number of variations on the structure exist. This includes arrangements where the dealer has an independent and separate choice as to the currency of its receipt *at each interest rate reset date*. This merely means that the borrower is creating a series, as distinct from a single option. In another variation, the borrower may

---

[18] See discussion in Chapter 13.

grant the swap dealer a "one-off"' option to switch at a specified time during the life of the transaction such as the first interest rate reset period (which is analogous to an option on a currency swap).

An interesting aspect of the transactions is the fact that the motivation for this class of transactions was *issuer driven* rather than investor driven (as is the case with structured note formats). The issuer motivations included:

- Lowering borrowing costs through increase in foreign exchange risk.
- Structures used to exploit the natural currency portfolio positions with known cash inflows or outflows in the relevant currencies in order to monetise expectations regarding future currency movements.

In the remainder of this chapter, the focus is on the conventional structured note with engineered linkages of interest coupon or principal to currency movements.

The initial focus is on a series of transaction from the middle to late 1980s that introduced the structure in capital markets. The transactions, while dated, are nevertheless useful examples of the key dynamics of structuring and value applicable in relation to these securities. These transactions created the basic template that all currency linked securities subsequently followed. Subsequently, the focus is on more recent transactions which highlight the modern structure of currency linked notes[19].

4.2 Indexed Currency Option Notes

In 1985, an issue of indexed currency option notes ("ICONs") saw the combination of a conventional fixed rate debt issue with a currency option[20] for the first time. **Exhibit 20.11** sets out the structure of this transaction. The ICON structure is very similar conceptually to, and in fact predated, similarly structured interest rate linked notes[21].

The initial issue was for the Long Term Credit Bank of Japan. The structure entailed the issuer paying the investor a higher than usual coupon in return for

---

[19] For a discussion of transactions during this period, see Das, Satyajit "Option Swaps: Securitising Options Embedded in Securities Issues" (Summer 1988) Journal of International Securities Markets 117–138.

[20] See French, Martin "Bowing Before the ICON" (December 1985) Euromoney 85–87; Rosenberg, M.R. "Dual Currency Yen Redemption Bonds: Combining the Features of "Heaven and Hell" (ICON) Bonds with Traditional Dual Currency Bonds" (24 February 1986) Merrill Lynch Currency & Bond Market Trends vol 2 no 7 1–3.

[21] See Chapter 19.

Exhibit 20.11   Indexed Currency Option Notes ("ICON")

1. Issue Structure

The ICON issue was lead managed by Bankers Trust ("BT") for the Long Term Credit Bank of Japan ("LTCB"). The issue was for US$120 million for 10 years with a coupon of 11.50% pa.

The redemption value was calculated according to the following formula if the Yen strengthened beyond US$1 = Yen 169:

$$R = US\$120,000,000[1 - ((169 - S)/S)]$$

Where

R = Redemption value in US$

S = Yen/US$ spot exchange rate on 21 November 1995

If the US$/Yen exchange rate was weaker than US$1 = Yen 169, then investors would receive the face value of the notes.

2. Currency Hedge

Under the terms of the accompanying US$ interest rate swap, LTCB achieved an all-in cost of approximately LIBOR minus 40–45 bps pa. The swap structure effectively securitised the currency option. BT purchased the US$120 million US$ put/Yen option at a strike price of US$1 = Yen 169.

To securitise the option position:

- BT arranged either directly or indirectly for a Yen issue at 6.65% pa for 10 years for Yen 24,240 million.
- Exchanged the issue proceeds for US$120 million on the spot market.
- Hedged the interest commitments forward, leaving the capital redemption unhedged, and charged the counterparty 10.70% pa for the US$120 million loan.

3. Transaction Economics

The profit dynamics of the transaction are set out below.

Assumptions:

- 10 year United States Treasury bond rate was 10.50% pa.
- Yen risk free rate (the 10 year Japanese government bond) was 6.50% pa.
- US$/Yen spot exchange rate at November 1985 was US$1 = Yen 202.
- Forward exchange rates were (per US$1):

1 year	Yen 194.69
2 year	Yen 187.64
3 year	Yen 180.85
4 year	Yen 174.30
5 year	Yen 167.99
6 year	Yen 161.91
7 year	Yen 156.05
8 year	Yen 150.40
9 year	Yen 144.96
10 year	Yen 139.96

At maturity, the worst case exchange rate BT had to repay its Yen commitment was US$1 = Yen 169. Therefore, the shortfall in Yen amount on that date in the worst case was: Yen 24,240,000,000 − Yen 20,280,000,000 = Yen 3,960,000,000. This shortfall translated into an annual payment of Yen 293,454,573. Therefore BT had to hedge the interest payment of: Yen 1,611,960,000 + Yen 293,454,573 = Yen 1,905,414,573 forward annually.

Cash flows from the Yen 24,240 million debt issue were as follows:

Year	Yen Interest Commitment (Yen)	Annuity For Capital Redemption (Yen)	US$ Amount to Hedge Cash Flows (US$)	Counterparty Interest Payments (US$)	BT's Profits (US$)
0	24,240,000,000 (at US$1:Yen 202)			120,000,000	
1	1,611,960,000	293,454,573	9,787,026	12,840,000	3,052,974
2	1,611,960,000	293,454,573	10,154,629	12,840,000	2,685,371
3	1,611,960,000	293,454,573	10,536,024	12,840,000	2,303,976
4	1,611,960,000	293,454,573	10,931,729	12,840,000	1,908,271
5	1,611,960,000	293,454,573	11,342,307	12,840,000	1,497,693
6	1,611,960,000	293,454,573	11,768,284	12,840,000	1,071,716
7	1,611,960,000	293,454,573	12,210,282	12,840,000	629,718
8	1,611,960,000	293,454,573	12,668,896	12,840,000	171,104
9	1,611,960,000	293,454,573	13,144,779	12,840,000	−304,779
10	1,611,960,000	293,454,573	13,638,443	12,840,000	−798,443
	24,240,000,000	−3,960,000,000 (at US$1:Yen169)		120,000,000	

BT's profits from the above transaction, at a discount rate of 10.50% pa after 10 years, would have been US$25,564,688, equivalent to a US$1,566,024 annuity over ten years.

This annuity was used to reduce LTCB's borrowing cost from US$13,800,000 (11.50% of US$120 million) to US$12,233,976 pa (US$13,800,000 − US$1,566,024). This translated to an effective interest rate of US$12,233,976/US$120,000,000 or 10.20% pa. This is equivalent to a rate under the equivalent United States treasury rate if all the profits are distributed to the issuer (an unlikely scenario).

which the investor created what was effectively a currency option. The investor in that case granted a European 10 year US$ put/Yen call option with a strike price of US$1 = Yen 169.

The redemption structure of the ICON effectively simulated the characteristics of a call on Yen/put on US$. The investor (the seller of the option) suffers a loss as the Yen strengthens against the US$. Conversely, the issuer (the purchaser) gains. The currency option was implicit in the redemption terms of the issue where notes were to be redeemed at par (100) if the Yen/US$ rate was equal to Yen 169 or more at maturity. If the US$ was below Yen 169 at maturity, then the redemption amount received by the investor was reduced in accordance with a formula. Analytically, the investor had granted a currency option in exchange for the higher coupon on the transaction (approximately 55 to 65 bps pa), which represented the option premium.

The net result of the transaction was that the issuer (Long Term Credit Bank of Japan) had purchased a 10 year European Yen call/US$ put option at the strike price of US$1 = Yen 169 from the investor. The issuer sold the option to a dealer (the originator of the transaction) using the premium to reduce its borrowing costs. The dealer compensated the issuer for the option through an annuity payment designed to lower the all-in funding costs of the issuer. This was usually incorporated in the accompanying swap for the transaction.

The dealer purchasing the option has a number of alternatives to securitise this currency option:
- The dealer can, in turn, sell the currency option.
- The market for long-dated currency options was limited at the time the issue was undertaken. Therefore, as an alternative to selling the option on identical terms, the intermediary could write short dated US$ put/Yen call options and roll the positions. The high level of premium for short dated options would have allowed the dealer to recover the price paid for the option in a relatively short time. However, there would be significant cash flow mismatches. This would make it difficult to ensure a profit from the transaction.
- The dealer can use the US$ put/Yen call option position as part of the hedge for a Euro Yen debt issue for a counterparty wanting US$ funding. This structure proved the most attractive means of securitising the option.

A variation on this basic structure was undertaken in an issue for IBM (known as "Heaven and Hell"). Under this structure, in return for taking a risk of loss if the Yen strengthened beyond US$1 = Yen 169, the investor would receive a higher redemption payment if the Yen was weaker than US$1 = Yen 169 at maturity. This contrasted with the ICON structure above where the investor did not receive any benefit over and above the premium, but could potentially suffer a loss equivalent to the *full principal amount of the investment* (which gave rise to the term, the "Hell" bond).

The redemption arrangements analytically constitute a Yen call/US$ put granted by the investor and the simultaneous purchase of a Yen put/US$ call by the investor. Both options have a strike rate of US$1 = Yen 169 and a term of 10 years. The options are equivalent to a long US$/short Yen 10 year forward position.

In the IBM transaction, the issue was structured in two tranches (a fixed rate and a floating rate issue). In the fixed (floating) rate portion, the investor received approximately 70 bps pa (25 bps pa) in extra yield in return for the variable redemption arrangement. In this structure, the currency position created was securitised in a manner very similar to that used for the ICON issue. Both options were capable of being traded separately or combined into a synthetic currency forward position to reduce the overall borrowing cost of issues.

Exhibit 20.12 sets out the detailed structure of the Heaven and Hell issue and accompanying currency linked swap. The structures were rapidly commoditised. They came to be known as Principal Exchange Rate Linked Securities ("PERLS"). **Exhibit 20.13** sets out the generalised structure and related hedges.

The fundamental element of the transactions was the full linkage of *principal* to the currency movement. The value extracted from the forward discount or premium was built into the higher coupon on these notes. Additional yield enhancement was often created by engineering the currency forward at an *off-market rate*, with the intrinsic value of the derivative position *at commencement* being used to further increase the running yield.

Exhibit 20.12   Heaven and Hell Notes

1. Issue Structure
The first issue of Heaven and Hell notes was arranged by Nomura International for IBM Credit Corporation. The IBM issue raised US$50 million for 10 years with a maturity date of 4 December 1995. To entice investors to invest in this bond, IBM paid a high coupon of 10.75% pa in US$. This was equivalent to 84 bps over US Treasuries. In a prior comparable issue, IBM had only paid 14 bps over US Treasuries for a straight Eurodollar issue. The redemption amount for the issue payable in US$ varied according to the following formula:

$$R = US\$50,000,000[1 + ((S - 169)/S)]$$

Where

R = Redemption value in US$
S = Yen/US$ spot exchange rate on 21 November 1995

If the Yen/US$ exchange rate at maturity was stronger than Yen 84.5/US$1, investors would get no principal return.

2. Derivatives Hedge
IBM securitised the currency position implicit in the transaction to Nomura in return for payments that effectively lowered its cost of funds.

From the IBM Heaven and Hell debt issue, Nomura had a short US$ position in 10 years time at a forward price of US$1 = Yen 169 for US$50 million. To use this forward position effectively, Nomura issued Yen 10,212,500,000 at 6.70% pa for a counterparty who wanted 10 year US$ funds. Nomura exchanged the Yen proceeds on the spot market, hedged the interest commitments forward and left the final capital redemption amount unhedged. Nomura charged the counterparty approximately 10.25% pa for the US$ funds.

3. Transaction Economics

The profit dynamics of the issue are set out below:

Assumption

- Yen 10 year risk free interest rate was 6.50% pa.
- 10 year United States treasury interest rate was 10.00% pa.
- US$/Yen spot exchange rate was US$1 = Yen 204.25.
- Forward exchange rates were (per US$1):

1 year	Yen 197.75
2 year	Yen 191.46
3 year	Yen 185.37
4 year	Yen 179.47
5 year	Yen 173.76
6 year	Yen 168.23
7 year	Yen 162.88
8 year	Yen 157.70
9 year	Yen 152.68
10 year	Yen 147.82

At maturity, Nomura exchanged the US$ into Yen at the rate of US$1 = Yen 169. This gave Nomura Yen 8,450,000,000 to repay the Yen 10,212,500,000 loan, leaving a shortfall of Yen 1,762,500,000. This shortfall translated into an annual payment of Yen 130,609,517 at the risk free rate of 6.50% pa. Nomura therefore had to enter into an annual forward agreement to hedge Yen 814,847,017 annually (Yen 684,237,500 plus Yen 130,609,517).

The cash flows involved were as follows:

Year	Yen Interest Commitment (Yen)	Annuity For Capital Redemption (Yen)	US$ Amount to Hedge Cash Flows (US$)	Counterparty Interest Payments (US$)	Nomura's Profits (US$)
0	10,212,500,000	(at US$1:Yen 204.25)		50,000,000	
1	684,237,500	130,609,517	4,120,571	5,125,000	1,004,429
2	684,237,500	130,609,517	4,255,987	5,125,000	869,013
3	684,237,500	130,609,517	4,395,858	5,125,000	729,142
4	684,237,500	130,609,517	4,540,322	5,125,000	584,678
5	684,237,500	130,609,517	4,689,524	5,125,000	435,476
6	684,237,500	130,609,517	4,843,649	5,125,000	281,351
7	684,237,500	130,609,517	5,002,837	5,125,000	122,168
8	684,237,500	130,609,517	5,167,234	5,125,000	−42,234
9	684,237,500	130,609,517	5,337,065	5,125,000	−212,065
10	684,237,500	130,609,517	5,512,465	5,125,000	−387,465
	10,212,500,000	−1,762,500,000 (at US$1:Yen169)		50,000,000	

Nomura's profits from the above transaction at the end of 10 years (using a discount rate of 10.00% pa) would be US$7,291,912, equivalent to a US$457,534 annuity over 10 years. The annuity was used to reduce IBM's annual interest cost of US$5,375,000 (10.75% of

US$50 million) to US$4,917,467 (US$5,375,000 − US$457,533). This would reduce IBM's interest cost down to US$4,917,467/US$50,000,000 or 9.835% (a rate below United States treasuries). However, because investors of the IBM Heaven and Hell issue also purchased a US$ put option with a strike price of Yen 84.5/US$1, Nomura was left with a residual foreign currency risk should the Yen/US$ exchange rate strengthen beyond Yen 84.5/US$1. Nomura could leave this position unhedged or hedge this residual exposure by buying a US$ put option with a strike price of Yen 84.5/US$1, or it could delta hedge the position to create a synthetic option.

Exhibit 20.13   Principal Exchange Rate Linked Securities ("PERLS")

1. Issue Structure
The PERLS structure is a generalisation of the ICON concept. The typical components include:
- A US$ denominated bond, typically 5 years in maturity.
- A coupon which is significantly higher than the coupon payable on an equivalent conventional bond at the time of issue. The coupon increment was initially around 250 bps. Subsequently, the coupon increment declined to around 50–100 bps.
- Principal redemption is linked to a nominated exchange rate (US$/Yen) at the maturity date.

The normal redemption formula for a PERLS would be:

$$\text{Principal Redemption} = \text{Face Value} \times [1 - ((S - F)/S)]$$

Where

S = Specified US$/Yen rate at issue date
F = Spot US$/Yen rate at the bond maturity date

The principal redemption structure effectively embeds a currency forward into the note. Any desired exposure can be generated. In the above example, an investor requirement to increase exposure to an appreciation of the US$ is achieved through incorporation of a currency forward to purchase US$/sell Yen. The coupon increment is generated by structuring the forward at an off market rate. The value of the forward (resulting from this adjustment in the rate) is used to create the annuity to enhance the return on the bond.

The effect of the redemption linkage is to create the following return payoff for the investor. The investor receives a boosted running yield. At maturity, using the above example, the investor will receive further enhancement of return (potentially unlimited) where the US$ appreciates against the Yen *above the embedded rate*. However, if the US$ decreases in value, then the investor suffers a potential loss of principal. The investor could suffer a loss equal to the face value of the transaction (typically, in the absence of any leverage, where the spot rate at maturity is equal to or below the spot rate at the commencement of the transaction).

The structure combines:
* A fixed interest bond.
* An off market currency forward.
* An out-of-the money Yen call/US$ put.

The option is necessary to limit the losses on the forward (in the event of a fall in the value of the US$ below the spot rate at commencement) to the *face value of the bond*.

2. Derivatives Hedge

The issuer of a PERLS would be immunised from the impact of the embedded currency forward through the entry into the following transactions:

* A currency forward to buy US$/sell Yen for value at the maturity of the note. The currency forward would generate a gain (loss) where the Yen depreciated (appreciated), offsetting the loss (gain) resulting from the increase (decrease) in the redemption amount. The principal amount of the forward should be the US$ (reflecting the currency of the bond) principal amount adjusted by the ratio of the spot rate to the 5 year outright forward rate. In effect, the issuer is required to sell forward the *current* Yen equivalent of the US$ principal amount rather than the forward Yen equivalent of this US$ amount.
* Purchase of the Yen call/US$ put and an expiry coinciding with the maturity of the Note. The call would show gains where the Yen appreciated beyond the strike, offsetting losses on the currency forward which would exceed the gain resulting from the decrease in the redemption amount (which is constrained to 100% of the face value of the bond). The principal amount of the option generally must be set at an amount larger than the face value of the transaction.

The entry into the hedges would insulate the issuer from the embedded currency derivative elements creating a fixed rate bond. This fixed rate liability could be converted into a floating rate borrowing in US$, or a fixed or floating rate liability in other currencies through interest rate or currency swap transactions as required.

4.3   Indexed Currency Option Notes – Variations

The ICON/PERLS type structure which yielded currency positions that were securitised and on-sold was extended in a number of directions:

* Variability linked to currency rates has been extended to coupon amounts, thereby creating a stream of currency options.
* Mini-max notes where the variable redemption amount operates *only* if the currency rates are outside a stated band.
* Inclusion of ICON features in dual currency issues.
* Variable redemption structures linked to both currency and interest rates.

The ingenuity of the currency linked variable redemption bonds and also their creators (primarily Japanese securities houses) is best illustrated by two examples. **Exhibit 20.14** sets out the intricate and elegant combination of an issue by OKB and BFCE that allowed simultaneous foreign currency options to be securitised. **Exhibit 20.15** sets out the structure of "Duet" bonds where the linkage to currency rates has been extended to coupon amounts[22].

Exhibit 20.14   Yen/US$ Variable Redemption Reverse Dual Currency Notes

1. Issue Structure

On 15 April 1986, Oesterreichische Kontrollbank ("OKB") issued a Yen 20 billion 10 year variable redemption bond. The coupon was 8.00% pa payable in Yen. Redemption was in US$ based on the following formula:

$$R = US\$114,155,252 \times [1 + (S - 169)/S]$$

Where

R = Redemption amount in US$
S = US$/Yen spot exchange rate at maturity of the bonds

If Yen strengthens beyond US$1/Yen 84.50, then investors will not receive their principal back.

On the same date, Nomura also lead managed a reverse dual currency bond issue worth Yen 20 billion with a maturity of 10 years for Banque Francaise du Commerce Exterieur ("BFCE"). This issue involved BFCE paying a 7.50% pa coupon, payable in US$ at a fixed exchange rate of US$1 = Yen 179. The redemption amount payable in Yen was at par as long as exchange rates were above US$1 = Yen 84.5, and declined below par if the Yen strengthened beyond US$1:Yen 84.50. The foreign currency positions implicit in the two issues were securitised by Nomura.

2. Derivatives Hedge

The OKB and BFCE issues complemented one another as the redemption amount in the OKB issue was in US$, while the redemption amount of the BFCE issue was payable in Yen. The redemption formula of both issues *jointly* gave a short US$ position at a forward price of US$1 = Yen 169.

Interest payment of the OKB issue was in US$ but that of the BFCE issue was in Yen. Therefore, if BFCE wanted US$ funding, Nomura had to hedge the Yen interest commitments of the BFCE issue forward. To capitalise on the short US$ position obtained from both issues,

---

[22] For more detailed discussion of these transactions, see Das, Satyajit "Option Swaps: Securitising Options Embedded in Securities Issues" Journal of International Securities Markets (Summer 1988) 117–138.

Nomura would not have hedged the capital redemption of OKB's Yen redemption amount
forward.

3. Transaction Economics

The profit dynamics of the transaction are set out below.
Assumptions:
* Yen 10 year risk-free interest rate was 6.50% pa.
* United States 10 year Treasury interest rate was 8.50% pa.
* US$/Yen spot exchange rate was US$1 = Yen 175.20.
* Forward exchange rates were:

1 year	Yen 171.97
2 year	Yen 168.80
3 year	Yen 165.65
4 year	Yen 162.63
5 year	Yen 159.64
6 year	Yen 156.69
7 year	Yen 153.81
8 year	Yen 150.97
9 year	Yen 148.19
10 year	Yen 145.46

Interest flows for BFCE were as follows: assuming OKB paid Nomura the equivalent
of 8.30% pa (a rate under United States Treasuries), BFCE paid an interest flow to Nomura
of US$9,474,886 [(Yen 20 billion/175.2) × 8.30%]. Nomura paid investors US$8,379,888
[(Yen 20 billion × 7.50%)/US$1 = Yen 179]. Therefore, Nomura obtained an annual profit
of US$1,094,998 from this part of the transaction.

Interest flows for OKB were as follows: assuming it paid Nomura the equivalent of US$
8.30% pa, BFCE paid Nomura US$9,474,886 [(Yen 20 billion/175.2) × 8.30%] and Nomura
paid investors Yen 1,600,000,000 [Yen 20 billion × 8.00%]. Nomura would have to hedge
this obligation forward to limit any losses.

The interest flows under the OKB transaction are set out below.

Year	OKB Yen Interest Commitment (Yen)	US$ Amount to Hedge Cash Flows (US$)	OKB's Interest Payments (US$)	Nomura's Profits (US$)
1	1,600,000,000	9,303,949	9,474,886	170,937
2	1,600,000,000	9,478,673	9,474,886	−3,787
3	1,600,000,000	9,656,588	9,474,886	−181,722
4	1,600,000,000	9,838,283	9,474,886	−363,417
5	1,600,000,000	10,022,551	9,474,886	−547,685
6	1,600,000,000	10,211,245	9,474,886	−736,379
7	1,600,000,000	10,402,445	9,474,886	−927,579
8	1,600,000,000	10,598,132	9,474,886	−1,123,266
9	1,600,000,000	10,796,950	9,474,886	−1,322,084
10	1,600,000,000	10,999,588	9,474,886	−1,524,722

Nomura's net profit position from the two transactions was:

Year	Profit From BFCE (US\$)	Profit From OKB (US\$)	Net Profit (US\$)
1	1,094,998	170,937	1,265,935
2	1,094,998	−3,787	1,091,211
3	1,094,998	−181,722	913,276
4	1,094,998	−363,417	731,581
5	1,094,998	−547,685	547,313
6	1,094,998	−736,379	358,619
7	1,094,998	−927,579	167,419
8	1,094,998	−1,123,266	−28,268
9	1,094,998	−1,322,084	−227,086
10	1,094,998	−1,524,722	−429,724

At the US\$ risk-free interest rate of 8.50% pa, the value of this net profit cash flow at year 10 was US\$8,368,408.

The redemption amount, which OKB and BFCE paid Nomura at maturity, was equal to US\$228,310,504 (US\$114,155,252 × 2). Premium from the OKB issue was Yen 300,000,000 and for BFCE it was Yen 350,000,000. This totals US\$3,710,045 at US\$1 = Yen 175 (both issues were made at a premium to par).

Total amount of cash available to Nomura to repay investors was US\$240,388,957 [US\$8,368,408 (Nomura's profit) + US\$228,310,504 (principal repayments in US\$ by OKB and BFC) + US\$3,710,045 (issue premium)].

Amount owed by Nomura to investors of both issues at maturity if the spot exchange rate is weaker than Yen 84.5/US\$1 depended on the following formula:

$$R = \text{Yen } 20 \text{ billion}/179[1 + ((S - 169)/S)] + \text{Yen } 20 \text{ billion}/S$$

Where

R = Redemption amount in US\$
S = Yen/US\$ spot exchange rate at maturity

Therefore, Nomura's profit was as follows:

Spot Rate (S)	Cash Available to Nomura (US\$)	Redemption Amount (US\$)	Gain (US\$)
300	240,388,957	227,188,083	13,200,874
200	240,388,957	229,050,280	11,338,677
150	240,388,957	230,912,477	9,476,480
100	240,388,957	234,636,872	5,752,085
90	240,388,957	235,878,337	4,510,620
85	240,388,957	236,608,610	3,780,347
84.5	240,388,957	236,686,391	3,702,566
80	240,388,957	235,937,500	4,451,457
60	240,388,957	197,222,222	43,166,735

From the above profit table, it is evident that it was possible for Nomura to reduce the cost of borrowing of both entities to below United States treasuries and still not incur a loss on the capital redemption amount at maturity.

Exhibit 20.15   Duet Bonds

1. Issue Structure

The first duet bond was issued for the Kingdom of Denmark and managed by Dai-Ichi Kangyo Bank ("DKB"). It was a five year debt issue worth US$100 million issued on 8 August 1986.

The coupon, payable in US$, was based on the following formula:

$$C = \$100,000,000 \times 0.165 - [(\text{Yen } 16,300,000,000 \times .065)/S]$$

Where

C = Coupon payable in US$
S = Yen/US$ exchange rate at coupon date

The capital redemption amount, also payable in US$, was calculated using the following formula:

$$R = \$100,000,000 \times 2 - [(\text{Yen } 16,300,000,000/S]$$

Where

R = Redemption amount in US$
S = Yen/US$ exchange rate at maturity of the bonds

From the formula, it is clear that Denmark had an exposure to the US$/Yen exchange rate on each coupon date and at maturity of the bonds. The currency positions were securitised by DKB.

2. Derivatives Hedge

Under the swap structure, Denmark effectively sold the currency positions implicit in the structure to DKB. DKB assumed an annual exposure to Yen coupon payments as a result of the duet bond's coupon payment formula. In addition, DKB had a short US$ forward exposure for US$100 million in 5 years time at a forward rate of US$1 = Yen 163.

To monetise this position, DKB arranged a Yen issue for a counterparty wanting US$ funding with an annual coupon payment equivalent to Yen 1,059,500,000. If the Yen interest rate on the issue was 5.20% pa, then DKB would have issued a Yen 20,375 million principal amount of bonds.

The duet bond, because of the amount issued, would only support US$100 million or Yen 16,300 million of the Yen issue to be perfectly hedged. Therefore, Yen 4,075 million from the Yen issue will be unhedged. DKB had to undertake a five year forward agreement to purchase Yen to hedge this exposure.

3. Transaction Economics

The profit dynamics of this transaction are set out below.
Assumptions:
• 5 year Yen interest rate was 5.00% pa.
• 5 year US$ interest rate was 7.50% pa.
• Spot exchange rate was US$1:Yen 163.
• 5 year forward rate was US$1:Yen 144.91.

Therefore, DKB required US$28,121,329 (Yen 4,075,000,000/Yen 144.9078) to hedge the Yen 4,075,000,000 forward exposure.

If DKB charged the counterparty 7.70% pa for US$ funding, then the borrower paid DKB US$9,625,000 (7.70% of US$125,000,000) and DKB was committed to pay Yen 1,059,500,000 (5.20% of Yen 20,375,000,000 at US$1 = Yen 163) for the straight Yen debt. The duet bond coupon formula covered this, leaving DKB with US$3,125,000 (US$9,625,000 − US$6,500,000) annually for the next 5 years. This accumulated to US$18,151,222 at the end of 5 years at the interest rate of 7.50% pa.

At maturity, DKB had US$125 million to pay off the Yen 20,375 million straight Yen debt. The duet bond hedged Yen 16,300 million (equivalent to US$100 million) and the forward agreement hedged the remaining Yen 4,075 million. This amount was covered by the US$18,151,222 from the coupon receipts and US$25 million from the capital redemption amount. This left DKB with US$15,029,893 (US$25,000,000 + US$18,151,222 − US$28,121,329) profits at maturity.

This profit at maturity (US$15,029,893) would be used to reduce the duet bond's interest cost. The US$15,029,893 plus the US$1,625,000 premium from the issue of duet bonds would give an annuity of US$2,989,260 over 5 years at 7.50% pa. Interest cost of the duet bond was US$10,000,000 (10.00% of US$100,000,000). Effective interest cost of the bond after deducting the annuity was 7.02% pa [(US$10,000,000 − US$2,989,260)/US$100,000,000]. This was a rate under the equivalent United States Treasury bond rate if the full benefit is passed on to the borrower.

4.4   Currency Linked Bonds – Evolution

Currency linked notes continue to be structured and issued. The structures incorporate embedded currency forward or option positions. The implicit currency forward or option positions embedded in security issues are hedged in the market to insulate the issuer from exposure to the currency elements of the transaction.

The basic structures used are the types of transaction already outlined. Some more recent examples of these types of transactions are set out in this Section. **Exhibit 20.16** sets out an example of a currency linked transaction where the underlying debt is short dated commercial paper that is packaged with a participating currency forward[23]. **Exhibits 20.17**, **20.18**, and **20.19** set out examples of bonds with engineered linkages to exchange rates. **Exhibit 20.20** sets out examples of bonds designed to create exposure to emerging market currencies.

The distinguishing features of these transactions include:
- Shorter maturity.
- Structures that protect principal and place only the coupon at risk.
- Guaranteed minimum coupon.

---

[23]   See Kimelman, Nancy, Callahan, James, and Demafeliz, Salvador (23 September 1986) Performance Indexed Paper-A Foreign Currency-Indexed Money Market Instrument; Salomon Brothers Inc., New York

Exhibit 20.16   Currency Linked Commercial Paper

A typical currency linked commercial paper (either domestic US or euro) issue may be structured as follows:

Issuer	A1+/ P1 Rated Issuer
Amount	(multiples of) US$1 million
Maturity	90 days
Coupon	Indexed to the currency (calculated 2 days prior to maturity) subject to the Minimum and Maximum Coupon.
Minimum Coupon	2.50% pa
Maximum Coupon	6.00% pa

The investor selects the minimum return and the Issuer (the dealer acting on behalf of the issuer) establishes the maximum rate. In this example, the rates were based on a US$/Yen range of US$1 equals Yen 1.46/1.60.

If the Yen appreciates against the US$, then the investor receives a return in excess of that available on conventional commercial paper of the relevant maturity. If the Yen depreciates, then the return to the investor will be below that on equivalent commercial paper, subject to the minimum return of 2.50%.

The diagram below sets out the investor's return profile from this transaction:

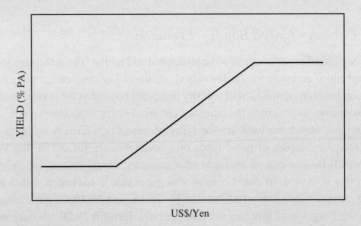

The pay-off profile illustrates the nature of the currency exposure created. The structure effectively combines the following elements:

- Investment in 90 day commercial paper.
- Selling the US$ principal and interest forward to the maturity of the commercial paper.
- Repurchasing US$ back via a Range Forward contract or collar[24].

---

[24] A Range Forward contract is basically a zero cost currency option collar entailing the simultaneous sale and purchase of two currency options with different strikes but the same maturity; see Chapter 6.

The issuer of the currency indexed commercial paper hedges its currency exposure by offsetting its position with the dealer/investment bank through the entry into a contract to sell US$/buy Yen forward for value at the maturity date of the commercial paper, and entry into a Range Forward contract to sell Yen/buy US$ (the currency range in the Range Forward is set to that embedded in the issue).

At maturity, if the Yen appreciates (depreciates), then the Range Forward will provide additional US$ gains that are passed through to the investor (losses which lower the return to the investor). The investor's loss is limited as the floor on the Range Forward guarantees the agreed Minimum Coupon.

Exhibit 20.17   DEM/US$ Currency Linked Notes

The following example is based on an actual transaction undertaken in DEM before the introduction of the Euro.

Amount	US$100 million
Maturity	1 year
Issue Price	100% of Face Value
Redemption Value	100% of Face Value
Coupon (annual)	Calculated in accordance with the following formula:
	$2.00\% + [100 \times ((\text{Index} - 1.46)/\text{Index})]$
	Where
	Index = DEM/US$ rate on the Index Set Date
Index Set Date	2 days before maturity
Minimum Coupon	2.00% pa
Maximum Coupon	10.75% pa

The Note can be decomposed into the following components:
- A 1 year fixed interest bond.
- A 1 year put spread (denominated in US$) on DEM as follows:
  Purchased DEM put at US$/DEM 1.4600
  Sold DEM put at US$/DEM 1.6000

The investor's return profile is as follows:
- US$/DEM above 1.60, return equivalent to 10.75% pa.
- US$/DEM below 1.46, return equivalent to 2.00% pa.
- US$/DEM between 1.46 and 1.60, return as per the following Table:

US$/DEM Exchange Rate at Maturity	Coupon (% pa)
1.46	2.00
1.48	3.37
1.50	4.74
1.52	6.11

US$/DEM Exchange Rate at Maturity	Coupon (% pa)
1.54	7.48
1.56	8.85
1.58	10.22
1.60	10.75

Based on a 1 year Treasury rate of 5.75% pa, the Investor requires the US$ to strengthen to around US$/DEM 1.52 to generate returns above this benchmark.

Exhibit 20.18   US$/Yen Currency Linked Notes

Amount	US$100 million
Maturity	1 year
Issue Price	100% of Face Value
Redemption Value	100% of Face Value
Coupon	Calculated in accordance with the following formula:
	2.50% + (Index − 102.00)
	Where
	Index = US$/Yen rate on the Index Set Date
Index Set Date	2 days before maturity
Minimum Coupon	2.50% pa
Maximum Coupon	12.50% pa
Interest Basis	30/360 annual payment

The Note can be decomposed into the following components:
- A 1 year fixed interest bond.
- A 1 year put spread (denominated in US$) on Yen as follows:
  Purchased Yen put at US$/Yen 102.00
  Sold Yen put at US$/Yen 112.00

The investor's return profile is as follows:
- US$/Yen above 112, return equivalent to 12.50% pa.
- US$/Yen below 102, return equivalent to 2.50% pa.
- US$/Yen between 102 and 112, return as per the formula. For example, if US$/Yen is equal to 107, then the Investor receives 7.50% pa (2.50 + (107 − 102)).

Based on a 1 year Treasury rate of 5.75% pa, the Investor requires the US$ to strengthen above US$/Yen 105.25 to generate returns above this benchmark.

Exhibit 20.19 US$/Yen Currency Linked Notes

1. US$/Yen Linked Note

The period of persistent low interest rates in Yen that has prevailed since the middle 1990s has encouraged the design of a number of currency linked structure for Yen based investors. The structures are designed to provide investors with a higher yield than would be available directly in return for assuming currency risk (generally monetising the expectation of a weaker or steady Yen). A typical structure is described below:

Amount	Yen 5 billion
Maturity	10 years
Issue Price	100% of Face Value
Redemption Value	100% of Face Value
Interest Coupon	Payable annually calculated in accordance with the following formula: $8.40\% \times (\text{Index}/120) - 4.90\%$ Where Index = US$/Yen rate on the Index Set Date
Index Set Date	2 days before each interest rate payment date
Minimum Coupon	0.00% pa
Interest Basis	30/360 day count basis payable in Yen

Under the structure, the investor receives an annual coupon linked to movements in the Yen/US$ exchange rate. If the US$/Yen rate is above 120 (weaker Yen), then the investor receives a coupon in excess of 3.50% pa (well above available returns in Yen at the relevant time). If the US$/Yen rate is below 120, then the investor receives a coupon below 3.50% pa. If the US$/Yen exchange rate is at or below 70, then the investor receives no interest. The investor's principal investment denominated in Yen is not at risk and is returned at maturity.

The structure entails the investor entering into the following transactions:
- Purchase of a Yen note.
- A series of Yen/US$ forwards where the investor purchases US$/sells Yen for value at each of the interest coupon dates. This component creates the linkage to currency fluctuations.
- A series of US$ put/Yen call options at a strike of Yen 70 with expiry dates corresponding to each of the interest rate payment dates. The options are designed to ensure that the coupon on the bond does not become negative.

The value dynamics of the structure are driven by the fact that the currency forwards are at off market rates.

2. US$/Yen Linked Bermudan Callable Notes

The following structure is a variation on the structure outlined above. The basic terms are as follows:

Issue Size:	¥1 billion
Maturity:	30 years (callable at par from Year 2 and thereafter on each interest payment date)

Coupon:	The following coupons are payable annually on a 30/360 day basis:	
	Year 1–2:	2.90% pa
	Year 3–10:	$13.90\% \times FX/120 - 11.00\% \leq 3.00\%$ pa
	Years 11–20:	$13.90\% \times FX/120 - 11.00\% \leq 3.50\%$ pa
	Years 21–30:	$13.90\% \times FX/120 - 11.00\% \leq 4.00\%$ pa
	The minimum coupon shall not be below 0.00% pa.	
FX:	The rate for USD/JPY 2 Business days prior to the relevant Payment Date.	
Call Option:	The Issuer has the right to redeem the notes, in whole but not in part, giving not less than 10 business days notice to the note holders at Year 2 and thereafter on each interest payment date.	

Under the structure, the investor receives an annual coupon linked to movements in the Yen/US$ exchange rate. If the US$/Yen rate is above 120 (weaker Yen), then the investor receives a coupon of 3.00 to 4.00% pa (well above available returns in Yen at the relevant time). The coupon is capped at the level of 3.00 to 4.00% pa. If the US$/Yen rate is below 120 (stronger Yen), then the investor receives a coupon below the maximum coupon. The return to the investor declines as the Yen strengthens. For example, in Years 3 to 10, if the US$/Yen exchange rate is at or below Yen 94.96 (79% of Yen 120), then the investor receives no interest. The investor's principal investment denominated in Yen is not at risk and is returned at maturity.

The structure entails the investor entering into the following transactions:

* Purchase of a Yen note.
* A series of Yen/US$ options to create the linkage to currency fluctuations. The option transactions can be illustrated by reverse engineering the options used in Years 3 to 10. Similar transactions are used in the remainder of the transaction. In Years 3 to 10, the investor enters into the following options as at each coupon payment date:
  1. Investor buys Yen put/US$ call with strike of Yen 120 and also sells Yen put/US$ call with strike of Yen 120.86. This option spread allows the investor to participate in any weakness in the Yen up to the maximum coupon rate. [The spread between the strike is greater in future years reflecting the higher maximum coupons.]
  2. Investor sells Yen call/US$ put with strike of Yen 120 and also buys Yen call/US$ put with strike of Yen 94.96. This option spread reduces the investor's coupon where the Yen appreciates. The loss to the investor is capped at the amount of the coupon by the purchased option.

The value dynamics of the structure are driven by the net premiums generated by the options. The currency options sold and bought are structured to generate a net premium receipt for the investor. The premium amount is used to enhance the yield to the investor.

The inclusion of the call option adds value to the structure. The issuer hedges the currency position and call option with the dealer arranging the issue. The dealer hedges the issuer into its desired form of funding (currency and interest rate basis). The dealer in turn hedges the embedded currency positions in the market. The dealer has the right to terminate the hedge as at Year 2 and each interest payment date. In the event that the dealer terminates the hedge, the issuer would need to call the note to insulate itself from any exposure under the note to the investor.

The call option adds interest rate optionality to the currency optionality embedded within the structure. As the dealer is paying fixed rate Yen under the hedge with the issuer unless Yen rates rise above the coupon level as at Year 2 or thereafter, the dealer is likely to terminate the hedge and effectively trigger the call of the issue. This will be the case unless the currency positions have significant embedded value for the dealer. This means that the interaction between the US$/Yen currency rate and Yen rates affects the performance of the note.

Exhibit 20.20   Emerging Market Currency Linked Notes

The increased investment and trading interest in emerging markets through the 1990s created demand for currency linked notes where interest and/or principal was indexed to the local currency unit. The transactions were driven by a variety of factors in addition to the traditional considerations motivating structured note transactions. The factors included:

- Regulatory environment, including the existence of currency controls which restricted trading in some of the currencies.
- Low credit quality of issuers and counterparties in some of the jurisdictions.
- Presence of convertibility risk, including the risk of imposition of restrictions on funds transfers.
- Lack of liquidity in the domestic markets and uncertainty regarding the efficacy of the trading and settlement mechanisms in these jurisdictions.

The factors made it attractive for traders and investors to use structured notes to access these markets and create exposure to the local currency and local currency interest rates. Transactions were undertaken in a wide variety of currencies including Asian currencies (Korean Won, Thai Baht, Indonesian Rupiah, Indian Rupee etc), Central/Latin American currencies (Mexican Pesos, Brazilian Reals etc) and Eastern European currencies (Polish Zlotys, Czech Korunas etc). Such transactions were also undertaken in some Southern European currencies (Spanish Pesetas, Portuguese Escudos, Greek Drachmas etc) prior to the introduction of the Euro.

The basic structures entail embedded forwards to create the relevant underlying currency exposure or embedding options to create asymmetric risk exposures to the local currencies. A number of examples of these types of transactions are set out below.

Example 1 – Indian Rupee Linked Note

Amount	US$25 million
Maturity	6 months
Issue Price	100% of Face Value
Interest Coupon	Payable at maturity calculated in accordance with the following formula:
	Amount $\times$ 22.00% $\times$ (40.00/Index) $\times$ 182/365
Redemption Value	Amount $\times$ (40.00/Index)

Index	US$/Rupee rate on the Index Set Date
Index Set Date	2 days before maturity
Minimum Coupon	0.00% pa
Minimum Redemption	0.00
Interest Basis	Actual/365 day count basis payable in US$

The structure creates a linkage between the coupon and principal received and the US$/Rupee exchange rate. The structure entails the purchase of a US$ note and simultaneous entry into a currency forward where the investor sell US$/buys Rupees at US$1 = Rupee 40.00.

The effect of the transaction is to replicate a local currency (Indian Rupee) investment with full currency exposure. The investor gains where the Rupee appreciates but suffers losses where the Rupee devalues.

Example 2 – DEM/Portuguese Escudo ("PTE") Linked Note

Amount	DEM 20 million
Maturity	6 months
Issue Price	100% of Face Value
Interest Coupon	Payable at maturity calculated in accordance with the following formula: Amount × [0.50% + 50 × Max (0, Index − 110)] × 182/365
Redemption Value	100%
Index	DEM/PTE exchange rate on the Index Set Date
Index Set Date	2 days before maturity
Minimum Coupon	0.50% pa
Interest Basis	Actual/365 day count basis payable in DEM

The structure entails a principal protected DEM investment where the coupon is linked to the DEM/PTE exchange rates. The investor is guaranteed a minimum coupon of 0.50% pa with participation in any appreciation in the DEM against the PTE. The structure entails the investor purchasing a DEM bond and forgoing all but 0.50% of the coupon, with the forgone coupon being used to purchase a DEM call/PTE put to create the desired currency linkage.

Example 3 – Japanese Yen/Thai Baht ("THB") Linked Note

Amount	US$20 million
Maturity	1 year
Issue Price	95% of Face Value
Interest Coupon	0%
Redemption Value	100% + Adjustment Factor
Adjustment Factor	160% × Amount × [(Yen Payout) + (5 × THB Payout)]
Yen Payout	(Yen/US$ on Index Set Date − 120)/Yen/US$ on Index Set Date. The Yen Payout cannot be less than 0.
THB payout	(25 − THB/US$ on Index Set Date)/THB/US$ on Index Set Date
Index Set Date	2 days before maturity
Interest Basis	Actual/365 day count basis

The structure creates a simultaneous exposure to Yen and THB. The investor benefits where the Yen weakens against the US$ and the THB strengthens against the US$. The exposure in respect of the Yen is asymmetric with the investor having limited exposure to a decline in the US$ because of the minimum constraint condition. The investor has an outright forward position on the THB/US$ exchange rate. If the THB falls below 28.57 (a decline in value of 12.5%), then the investor suffers a loss of its principal investment. In fact, the Asian monetary crisis that commenced in July 1997 resulted in investors suffering significant losses under many of these structures.

In part, the changes reflect broader changes in the structured note market generally.

Individual structures have evolved in specific ways. For example, the structures depicted in **Exhibit 20.19** involving Yen are designed to create asymmetric currency exposures through the embedded options. The structures also include embedded Bermudan call options. **Exhibit 20.20** sets out examples of bonds where the payoffs are linked to the price performance of emerging market currencies, primarily to give the investor exposure to the relevant currency (often also the higher yields available in the local currency) without the necessity to purchase local currency securities.

5 Exotic Currency Linked Notes[25]

5.1 Overview

A central element in currency linked notes is the need to provide investors with customised risk return profiles. Exotic options are also driven by the need to increasingly refine the risk return profiles *within instrument structures*. The combination of the two formats is frequently used to create currency linked structures for investors.

5.2 Barrier Option Embedded Structures

The economic benefit of the barrier option structure derives from lower premiums relative to conventional options. This lower premium amount reflects the possibility that the option will be extinguished or not activated[26]. The lower premium is critical in lowering the cost of any embedded option. **Exhibit 20.21** sets out an example of a structured note entailing a sold barrier option on currency values.

---

[25] See Chapters 5, 7, 8, 9, 10 and 11.
[26] See Chapter 9.

Exhibit 20.21   FRN Incorporating Currency Barrier Option

The terms of the issue are as follows:

Amount	(up to) US$25 million
Maturity	1 year
Issue Price	100%
Coupon Rate	10.50% pa
Redemption Value	Redemption (per US$1 million) will be:
	1. If the Exchange Rate does not trade above Yen 130 at any time over the term of the note and the Exchange Rate at maturity is below Yen 110, then US$1 million.
	2. If the Exchange rate trades above Yen 130 at any time over the term of the note and the Exchange Rate at maturity is above Yen 110, then Yen 110 million per US$1 million.
Exchange Rate	US$/Yen spot exchange rate

The basic dynamics of the structure is that the investor receives a higher coupon in relation to available market rates through the sale of a knock-in put option on the US$/Yen exchange rate. The knock-in put option has a strike of US$1 = Yen 110 and an instrike (or trigger) of US$1 = Yen 130. If the Yen trades above Yen 130, then the put is activated. However, as with any option, the put does not provide a pay-off for the investor unless the Yen value *at maturity (not the knock in date)* is below the strike level of Yen 110. If the option is triggered and the Yen is trading below Yen 110, then the investor receives *less valuable Yen (in US$ terms)* through the redemption. The higher coupon incorporates the premium received for the sale of the barrier option. From the investor's point of view, the structure creates a specific risk to the US$/Yen exchange rate. The specific risk is that the Yen weakens beyond Yen 130 and remains at that level at the maturity of the note.

5.3   Digital Option Embedded Structures

Digital options are commonly used in structured notes[27]. The structure is attractive to option grantors or writers because the digital structure means a known and limited loss in the event the option is exercised. The known loss profile makes these options ideal for use in structured note transactions, allowing minimum return or maximum loss values to be determined in relation to principal risked.

A common structure is the range note where the pay-off is linked to currency trading. The structure of currency linked range notes is similar to that for the interest rate linked range notes[28]. **Exhibit 20.22, Exhibit 20.23, Exhibit 20.24** and **Exhibit 20.25** set out examples of range note structures linked to currency values.

---

[27]   See Chapter 10.
[28]   See Chapter 19.

Exhibit 20.22   Currency Range Notes – Example 1

The terms of the issue are as follows:

Amount	Yen 1 billion
Maturity	1 year
Issue Price	100%
Redemption Price	100%
Underlying Index	US$/Yen
Spot Reference Rate of Underlying index	US$1:Yen 120.50
Range	Maximum: Yen 125
	Minimum: Yen 116
Reference Interest Rate	1 year Yen deposit rates were 0.75% pa
Interest	Payable in Yen at maturity in accordance with the following formula:

1. If the underlying index never trades outside the selected Range during the period to maturity, then the interest rate is 2.50% pa.
2. If the underlying index trades at or outside the upper or lower boundary of the Range at any time during the period to maturity, then the interest rate is 0.25% pa.

The structure of the issue is identical to interest rate based range notes. In this case, the note pays a higher than market return if the US$/Yen rate stays in a narrow range around the current spot price. Unlike the interest rate range notes, the currency range note entails the investor selling *a single* digital option on the currency. The option is typically structured as a one touch payment at maturity digital option with a maturity identical to that of the note.

Exhibit 20.23   Currency Range Notes – Example 2

The terms of the issue are as follows:

Amount	US$25 million
Maturity	1 year
Issue Price	100%
Principal Redemption	100%
Underlying Index	GBP/US$
Spot Reference Rate of Underlying Index	GBP 1:US$1.5950
Range	Maximum: 1.6458
	Minimum: 1.5250
Reference Interest Rate	1 year US$ deposit rates were 5.50% pa

Interest	Payable in US$ maturity in accordance with the following formula:
	1. If the underlying index never trades outside the selected Range during the period to maturity, then the interest rate is 14.00% pa.
	2. If the underlying index trades at or outside the upper or lower boundary of the Range at any time during the period to maturity, then the interest rate is 1.00% pa.

The structure is similar to that depicted in **Exhibit 20.22**.

Exhibit 20.24   Currency Range Notes – Example 3

The terms of the issue are as follows:

Amount	US$10 million
Maturity	1 year
Issue Price	100%
Principal Redemption	100%
Underlying Index	US$/Thai Baht
Spot Reference Rate of Underlying Index	US$1:Thai Baht 24.65
Limit	25.50
Interest	Payable in US$ or Thai Baht at maturity in accordance with the following formula:
	1. If the underlying index remains below the limit at all times during the period to maturity, then the interest rate is 13.0% pa.
	2. If the underlying index is at or above the limit at any time during the period to maturity, then the interest rate is 0% pa.

The structure is similar to that depicted in **Exhibit 20.22**. The major difference is that the linkage is to an emerging market currency. In addition, the structure is based on a single digital option rather than multiple digital options. The structure described is typical of those issued in Asia in the period preceding the Asian monetary crisis that commenced in 1997.

Exhibit 20.25   Currency Double Range Notes

1.   Structure

The terms of the issues are structured as follows:

Issue 1

Amount	Italian Lira 10,000 million
Maturity	18 months

Issue Price	100%
Coupon	3.75% pa
Underlying Index	US$/Italian Lira
Redemption Price	• If the Underlying Index is within range 975 and 1,035 during the term of the transaction at all times, then 112.38%. • If the Underlying Index is within range 955 and 1,055 during the term of the transaction at any time then 102.84%.

Source: (6 December 1996) MTN Week

Issue 2

Amount	US$10 million
Maturity	6 months
Issue Price	100%
Principal Redemption	100%
Underlying Index	US$/Swiss Franc
Narrow Range	The number of business days where the Underlying Index is between the range specified below divided by the business days in the relevant period: Maximum −1.48 Minimum −1.42
Wide Range	The number of business days where the Underlying Index is between the range specified below divided by the business days in the relevant period: Maximum −1.52 Minimum −1.35
Interest	[11.40% × Narrow Range] + [3.80% × Wide Range]

Source: (12 December 1997) MTN Week

2. Economics

The double range notes structure generates higher returns for the investor where the underlying asset price (currency values) remains within a narrow range. In the event that the asset price moves outside the narrow range, the investor receives a lower return as long as the asset price stays within a second range *that is wider*. It is only if the asset price moves outside the second wider range that the investor receives a nominal or no return on the structure. The structure is similar to ratchet structures used with interest rates[29]. The structure is created using a package of digital options. The investor sells digital calls and puts at the narrower and wider ranges. The investor also simultaneously repurchases the digital calls and puts at the narrower range with a different digital payout. The combination of digital options creates the pay-off profile.

---

[29] See Chapter 19.

6 Summary

Currency linked notes are structured investments that embody links to foreign exchange or currency values. The structure entails linking the value of coupon payments or principal repayments to an identified exchange rate.

A variety of structures have emerged allowing investors to monetise specific views in relation to the shape of forward currency rates and/or currency volatility. The structures are now well accepted and available in a wide variety of currencies.

Index

R

S

The Swaps & Financial Derivatives Library

The Swap & Financial Derivatives Library is a unique, authoritative and comprehensive 4 volume reference work for practitioners on derivatives. It brings together all aspects of derivative instruments within a cohesive and integrated framework covering:

- **Derivative Instruments and Pricing** – including derivative instruments (exchange-traded markets and over-the-counter markets), pricing, valuation and trading/hedging of derivatives.
- **Risk Management** – including market risk, credit risk, liquidity risk, model risk, operational risk as well as documentation, accounting, taxation and regulatory aspects of derivatives.
- **Structured products** – including synthetic asset structures (asset swaps), exotic options, interest rate/ currency products, equity products, commodity (energy, metals and agricultural) products, credit derivatives and new derivative markets (insurance, weather, inflation/ macro-economic indicators, property and emissions).

The *Library* is organised into individual volumes:

Derivative Products & Pricing
Risk Management
Structured Products Volume 1: Exotic Options, Interest Rates; Currency
Structured Products Volume 2: Equity, Commodity, Credit; New Markets

Each volume is a standalone work. The reader can acquire and use an individual volume or any combination of the 4 separate volumes based on their requirements.

The organisation of each volume is as follows:

Derivative Products & Pricing

Role and Function of Derivatives
1. Financial Derivatives Building Blocks - Forward & Option Contracts
   Derivative Instruments
2. Exchange-Traded Products - Futures & Options On Futures Contracts
3. Over-The-Counter Products - FRAs, Interest
   Rate Swaps, Caps/ Floors, Currency Forwards, Currency Swaps, Currency Options
   Pricing & Valuing Derivative Instruments
4. Derivatives Pricing Framework
5. Interest Rates & Yield Curves
6. Pricing Forward & Futures Contracts
7. Option Pricing
8. Interest Rate Options Pricing
9. Estimating Volatility & Correlation
10. Pricing Interest Rate & Currency Swaps
11. Swap Spreads
    Derivative Trading & Portfolio Management
12. Derivatives Trading & Portfolio Management
13. Hedging Interest Rate Risk - Individual Instruments
14. Hedging Interest Rate Risk - Portfolios
15. Measuring Option Price Sensitivities - The Greek Alphabet Of Risk
16. Delta Hedging/Management Of Option Portfolios

Risk Management

Risk Management Principles
1. Framework For Risk Management
   Market Risk
2. Market Risk Measurement - Value At Risk Models
3. Stress Testing
4. Portfolio Valuation/Mark-To-Market
   Credit Risk
5. Derivative Credit Risk: Measurement
6. Derivative Credit Exposure: Management & Credit Enhancement
7. Derivative Product Companies
   Other Risks
8. Liquidity Risk
9. Model Risk
10. Operational Risks
    Organisation of Risk Management
11. Risk Management Function
12. Risk Adjusted Performance Management

Operational Aspects
13. Operational, Systems &Technology Issues
Legal/ Documentary, Accounting & Tax Aspects of Derivatives
14. Legal Issues & Documentation
15. Accounting Issues
16. Taxation Aspects of Swaps and Financial Derivatives
Regulatory Aspects of Derivatives
17. Credit Risk: Regulatory Framework Appendix: Basle II
18. Market Risk: Regulatory Framework Appendix: Basle 1996

Structured Products Volume 1
Applications of Derivatives
1. Applications of Derivative Instruments
2. Applications Of Forwards/Futures, Swaps & Options
3. New Issue Arbitrage
Synthetic Assets
4. Synthetic Assets - Asset Swaps, Structured Notes, Repackaging And Structured Investment Vehicles
Exotic Options
5. Exotic Options
6. Packaged Forwards & Options
7. Path Dependent Options
8. Time Dependent Options
9. Limit Dependent Options
10. Pay-off Modified Options
11. MultiFactor Options
12. Volatility Products
Interest Rate & FX Structures
13. Non Generic Swap Structures
14. Basis Swaps
15. Options On Swaps/ Swaptions
16. Callable Bonds
17. Constant Maturity Products
18. Index Amortising Products
19. Interest Rate Linked Notes
20. Currency Linked Notes

Structured Products Volume 2
Equity Linked Structures
1. Equity Derivatives - Equity Futures, Equity Options/ Warrants & Equity Swaps
2. Convertible Securities
3. Structured Convertible Securities
4. Equity Linked Notes
5. Equity Derivatives - Investor Applications
6. Equity Capital Management - Corporate Finance Applications Of Equity Derivatives
Commodity Linked Structures
7. Commodity Derivatives - Commodity Futures/Options, Commodity Swaps And Commodity Linked Notes
8. Commodity Derivatives - Energy (Oil, Natural Gas And Electricity) Markets
9. Commodity Derivatives - Metal Markets
10. Commodity Derivatives - Agricultural And Other Markets
Credit Derivatives
11. Credit Derivative Products
12. Credit Linked Notes/ Collateralised Debt Obligations
13. Credit Derivatives/ Default Risk - Pricing And Modelling
14. Credit Derivatives - Applications/ Markets
New Markets
15. Inflation Indexed Notes And Derivatives
16. Alternative Risk Transfer/ Insurance Derivatives
17. Weather Derivatives
18. New Markets - Property; Bandwidth; Macro-Economic & Environmental Derivatives
19. Tax And Structured Derivatives Transactions
Evolution Of Derivatives Markets
20. Electronic Markets And Derivatives Trading
21. Financial Derivatives - Evolution And Prospects

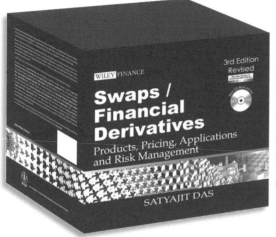